"Best-selling psychology writer Maggie Scarf is on to a new paradigm: getting at the mind's deep wounds through physical therapies. . . . [Scarf is] one of the few journalists around who's gifted enough to influence the field she writes about."

—*Elle*

"Any reader would have a hard time reading *Secrets, Lies, Betrayals* without an 'aha!' moment or two."

—*San Jose Mercury News*

"Admirers of [Scarf's] work will enjoy her ability to evoke relationship dynamics . . . her seductively flowing style and her emphasis on perceptive readings of life histories."

—*Publishers Weekly*

"This is truly a remarkable tour de force, a book that one cannot put down."

—CAROL NADELSON,
past president of the American Psychiatric Association

"Here is mind connected to body—and done so with the help of a documentary effort: the author herself, and others she has come to know, enable us, through their personal narratives, to understand human psychology, its pleasures and its darker side, as an aspect of the physical existence each of us has, experiences."

—ROBERT COLES, M.D.,
professor of psychiatry and medical humanities,
Harvard Medical School

"Maggie Scarf is brilliant, a writer with foresight who has always been ahead of the pack, and she writes in language people can relate to. Her humanistic way of looking at life shines through in this astonishing book about how the past resides in our bodies—and what we can to do about it."

—NANCY FRIDAY,
author of *My Secret Garden* and *Women on Top*

"The mix of theory and story is one of the things Maggie Scarf does so well. I found the book compelling, convincing, and, in a good way, shocking."

—
, *You Cry* and *Last Wish*

Also by Maggie Scarf

INTIMATE WORLDS

BODY, MIND, BEHAVIOR

INTIMATE PARTNERS

UNFINISHED BUSINESS

SECRETS, LIES, BETRAYALS

SECRETS, LIES,

BALLANTINE BOOKS

NEW YORK

Maggie Scarf

BETRAYALS

HOW THE BODY HOLDS THE

SECRETS OF A LIFE, AND

HOW TO UNLOCK THEM

For my beloved husband, Herb,
and for the dear family we created together

Ph.D., Distiguished Faculty, Santa Barbara Graduate Institute and President, Foundation for Human Enrichment; Babette Rothschild, M.S.W., psychotherapist and body-psychotherapist; Susan Gombos, M.S.W., Steven Lazrove, M.D., Leslie Weiss, Ph.D., Carol Nadelson, M.D., Professor of Psychiatry at Harvard and Director of the Partners Office for Women's Careers at Brigham and Women's Hospital in Boston; and Gary Tucker, M.D., Professor Emeritus in the Department of Psychiatry and Behavioral Sciences, University of Washington, and editor of *Psychiatry Journal Watch*. I should add that Gary Tucker is a friend and mentor of long standing and that he served in a particularly valuable capacity as the expert commentator on and reviewer of my discussion of recent work in the area of brain research.

My very special thanks go to Francine Shapiro, Ph.D., the founder and guiding spirit of the reprocessing (Eye Movement Desensitization and Reprocessing or EMDR) movement, who offered me access to her Level I and Level II training sessions and generous amounts of her private time as well. I am also grateful to William Zangwill, Ph.D., therapist and EMDR instructor, and to Patti Levin, Ph.D., who has been my steadfast adviser, sometime therapist, and who became a dear friend of mine along the way. I am indebted, too, to Katherine Davis, M.S.W., C.S.W., for many intriguing, wide-ranging conversations filled with clinical wisdom and insight.

For those parts of the book that have to do with the recent scientific findings on human memory, my thanks go to the eminent memory researcher Larry Squire, Ph.D., whose own highly original work is discussed here, and who was an ever-obliging reader and reviewer. For those parts of the book that are concerned with infidelity, my debt to the late, incomparable psychologist Shirley Glass, Ph.D., is enormous. Shirley and I talked long, both in person and on the telephone, about the impact of sexual betrayal in general and in particular about the story of marital infidelity described in this book. I also benefited greatly from interviews with other experts in the field of extramarital sex—most particularly from conversations with psychologist Don Lusterman, Ph.D., and Janis Abrahms-Spring, Ph.D.

I am also deeply indebted to Al Pesso and Diane Boyden for welcoming me into their psychomotor (Pesso Boyden System Psychomotor or

Acknowledgments
—

"THE LONGEST JOURNEY BEGINS WITH A SINGLE STEP," AC-
cording to the ancient Chinese proverb. But although taking that first step
into the unknown is clearly a pivotal act, it's also vitally important that one
move off in the correct direction. I feel fortunate to have had the road map
pointed out to me, early on in this project, by Dr. Bessel van der Kolk,
M.D., who is Medical Director of the Trauma Center in Boston and a
Professor of Psychiatry at Boston University School of Medicine. Bessel
van der Kolk is an internationally renowned trauma expert—many people
consider him to be the father of present-day research in the field—and he
has pioneered the use of the body-oriented forms of therapy described in
this book. My series of important conversations with him has served to
guide and orient me throughout the course of this work; indeed, Bessel
van der Kolk's knowledgeable, supportive presence is to be found everywhere in these pages, and for this I wish to express my heartfelt thanks and
deep gratitude.

During my years of research and writing, I have also been assisted
greatly by a number of other researchers and therapists. Those with whom
I have had one, several, or a great many enlightening and helpful conversations include: Jim Hopper, Ph.D., Research Fellow in Psychology at
McLean Hospital and Harvard Medical School; Dr. J. Douglas Bremner,
M.D., Director of Emory University's Center for Positron Emission To-
mography and Associate Professor of Psychiatry and Radiology at Emory's
school of medicine; Steven M. Southwick, M.D., Professor of Psychiatry
at Yale University School of Medicine; Julian Ford, Ph.D., Director, Center for Trauma Response, Recovery and Preparedness (CTRP) and Associate Professor, University of Connecticut Health Center; Peter A. Levine,

PBSP) training programs with such enthusiasm. The Pessos generously facilitated my learning of a body-oriented theory and therapy that they had developed over years of work and experience but which I was trying to absorb at high speed. My grateful thanks go, too, to Lowijs N. M. Perquin, M.D., psychiatrist and co-director of the Institute for Psychiatric Training, Free University, Amsterdam, and Trainer in Pesso Boyden System Psychomotor (PBSP).

I would also like to express my gratitude to Dr. Janet Geller, who invited me to sit in on her course on partner abuse—a series of lectures designed primarily for therapists dealing with people in emotionally and/or physically violent relationships—which I found remarkably edifying. And thanks go to Charles V. Ford, M.D., Professor of Psychiatry and Neurobiology at the University of Alabama's School of Medicine, and to Evan Imber-Black, Ph.D., Professor of Psychiatry at the Albert Einstein College of Medicine, in New York. Both Ford and Imber-Black have made "secrets, lies, and betrayals" the subject of intensive, rigorous study, and my conversations with each of them proved extremely productive and illuminating.

So, too, did my periodic consultations with family therapist W. Leonard Hill, Jr., L.C.S.W., Assistant Professor of Clinical Psychiatry at Yale University and Director of the Adult Day Program at Yale–New Haven Hospital, with Hannah Fox, M.S.W., and with psychologist Jesse D. Geller, Ph.D., who is an Assistant Professor of Psychiatry at Yale and Columbia Universities. These clinicians were not only wonderful sounding boards for my own thoughts and ideas; they were also nothing short of *ingenious* at helping to tease out the underlying dynamics of the many secrets I was hearing.

As always, a fond word of appreciation is due to my assistant, Felicia Dickinson, who came to work with me when she was a graduate student— I have a vivid picture of a pretty dark-haired young woman flouncing up my front walk—and who has remained with me throughout my entire researching and writing career. Thanks are also due to my library assistant, the dauntless, determined Jean Emmons, who has never entertained the thought that there could be an out-of-print book or obscure scientific paper that she was unable to locate.

Lastly, I cannot fail to say a word of thanks to Susan Cheever, who invited me to sit in on her wonderfully enjoyable writing class at Yale—a class that, at the outset of my work on the manuscript, helped me to get my starter motor running. And I am grateful to my agent, Amanda Urban, for her enthusiastic readings of the book, in its several incarnations, and for the advice and encouragement she offered as the manuscript moved from its initial seedling state to its ultimate maturation.

As for my longtime editor and friend, Kate Medina, no paean of praise seems sufficient to describe her patience, tact, intelligence, and skill. Kate is simply one of the most creative and gifted practitioners of her craft that an author could ever imagine. I have collaborated with her on all of my books, and have been impressed by her careful attention to every detail. However, *this time* she has worked like a sculptor, scrutinizing every aspect of the raw first draft and indicating innovative ways of fashioning the material and shaping it into its present form. Kate is always tactful, always aware of a writer's sensitivities; and while I have found that our interaction is invariably an educational and deeply gratifying experience, it's only lately that I've come to realize that she is nothing other than a genius at what she does.

Finally, when it comes to expressing my thanks to the many, many individuals who volunteered to be interviewed on the subject of "secrets and lies," I hardly know where or how to begin. All that I can put into words is that I am profoundly grateful to you for your courage, your forthrightness, your willingness to open the most secret, often shameful parts of your lives to my gaze. I have thought about my conversations with you incessantly, wondered about you, worried about you, admired you; above all, *learned* from you—and in the course of the process have found myself becoming someone different, someone far more open to the world around me and more willing to be open with myself.

Maggie Scarf
Jonathan Edwards College, Yale

Author's Note

—

THE INDIVIDUALS WHOSE INTERVIEWS HAVE BEEN USED IN these pages have agreed to let their stories be told, with minor changes as far as identifying details are concerned (name, names of family members, profession, geographical location in some cases, etc.). The secret stories described here are therefore factual, aside from the omission or change of such unnecessarily specific and revealing information.

Contents

—

WHAT THE BODY KNOWS

*T*HE BASIC THEME OF THIS BOOK IS, IN A PHRASE, THAT the body knows more about our experiences—about the things that have happened to us in our lives—than words can possibly express. For example, if I were to introduce myself to you by saying, "Hello, my name is Maggie Scarf," what I'm really saying is: "Hello, the name of the frontal area of my brain [the prefrontal cortex] is Maggie Scarf"—because the rest of my being has no name, no language, no consciousness. And yet that rest of me is really the engine of my being.

So an important question—and one that all the recent work on brain imaging and the study of memory is currently raising—is to what degree processes that are initiated in the prefrontal cortex (that is, the usual kinds of "talking" therapy) actually access the deeper levels of the brain, where the engines of emotion and arousal are percolating? While the traditional forms of verbal therapy can be extremely important, there are, in practice, a great many situations in which they do not really prove effective.

My point of entry into this subject is, of course, secrets, lies, betrayals, and the long-lasting effects that they can leave not only upon our mental lives but upon our physical beings. These may be secrets that are too shameful to talk about, to think about, or in some instances even to *know* about; for the distressing, painful, traumatic events that we experience are often so untenable that they've become lodged in the deeper, inarticulate parts of the brain. But even in cases where we aren't consciously aware of them, our bodies always *do* know, and in many cases, they are signaling us in their own wordless way—which may be by means of symptoms.

What types of symptoms? The answer is that our bodies may be "speaking" to us by means of sleep disorders, persistent headaches, stomach problems, anxiety, hyperarousal, irritability, angry outbursts, feelings of isolation, and depression. Or they may be contacting us by means of a profound numbness, of our not feeling really present in our lives or of our repetitively getting into abusive or otherwise distressing emotional relationships. These may result in alcohol or drug abuse or in eating disorders—which may best be understood as attempts to self-medicate feelings of being profoundly unsafe in one's body. These are feelings that a person often is, at a conscious level, utterly unable to explain.

As we now know, being in a situation where you feel endangered and helpless turns on an alarm system in the brain. This alarm system is set off in situations where people feel at a loss, frightened, unable to cope, dissociated—especially if they've been involved in situations that feel overwhelming, or, for that matter, if they've merely witnessed them. This was true of Claudia Martinelli, whom I write of in this book, for she had witnessed abuse in her early childhood and kept getting into abusive relationships in her adult life.

In any case, as adults, people who are holding on to secret or compartmentalized knowledge of what's happened in the past—whether in early childhood or as a result of later catastrophes, such as proximity to the World Trade Center or wartime experiences on a battlefield—often feel misunderstood and isolated, and are unable to trust anyone. They are likely *not* to know how to feel safe, and to feel helpless and out of control of their emotions. Some of them feel permanently damaged and worthless. And inevitably this will affect their ability to use good judgment, think clearly, maintain their intimate relationships. But they themselves won't know what's happening—that the brain's survival alarm system has been triggered and hasn't integrated the realization that the dangers of the past are long over.

This book is not only about secrets and lies; it is about what I call small-*t* trauma. In other words, my main focus is not on disasters or earthquakes but on the kinds of pain that we may have experienced at the hands of those upon whom we most depend—the parental caretakers who are programmed to shower their care upon their offspring and whom we are, in infancy, genetically *programmed to adore*. Those individuals who have *not* received the love that was expected and needed early in life are, in fact, the kinds of patients that most trauma therapists actually do see.

The age of trauma is upon us. Early reports are that the amazing fire-fighters who showed such bravery on 9/11 are now requesting marital or family counseling at vastly increased rates—more than triple the number of requests that were received before that horrific event. And recent estimates of servicemen returning from the Iraqi front indicate that a high percentage—one in six—are suffering either from some outright post-traumatic stress disorder or from "emotional difficulties" of some kind. Although my focus in this book is on the kinds of trauma that do not (like PTSD) involve staring death in the face, I do discuss the painful kinds of matters that have had a huge and powerful impact upon my interviewees' lives for many years after those distressing events occurred.

Let me add that shortly before this book's hardcover publication, an enormous revolution in psychotherapy began to occur. It made its first appearance in the January/February 2004 issue of *The Psychotherapy Networker*, which has the largest clinical audience in the nation, some 125,000 readers. The lead article, "In the Eye of the Storm," posed the then-heretical question What are the "limits of talk"? It was the first public indication that the practice of traditional "talking" therapy, as it has existed for the past hundred years or so, was in the process of undergoing seismic change.

Many therapists had begun to acknowledge that while talk is a valuable therapeutic instrument, the undeniable truth is that many of our lives' most distressing experiences cannot be talked away. No matter how brilliant the clinician may be, and how many insights and new meanings he might have introduced into the client's life narrative, nothing much seemed to change. The patient kept reciting the story of this pain but often stayed stuck with it in some fashion. This situation, familiar to most psychotherapists, has led to the development of the body-centered therapies that are described in this book.

The conventional "talking" therapies have always relied upon brain processing that starts out in the prefrontal cortex, which would hopefully initiate change. This is called "top-down" processing. But the question now being explored is: How, when this strategy fails, do both patient and clinician break out of the old script in order to make something different happen?

The answer, many experts believe, lies in the promise offered by "bottom-up" processing, working from the body to the brain—that is, *making use of the body's memory*. As has oft been repeated, "The body keeps the score." And a newly evolving definition of what is meant by a "self"—one that isn't solely psychological in nature but includes the deeper, wordless levels of the brain and the body's nervous circuitry—is in the process of emerging. Body memories, like psychological memories, are becoming increasingly important and have led to increasingly useful, well-accepted methods and techniques in the therapist's ever-growing armentarium. I have focused upon two of the body-oriented therapies that most intrigued me in the pages that follow.

January 2005

If you were going to tell or write the story of your life—which would, of course, begin when you were a small infant in your own family—what would the first sentence of your autobiography sound like? Some years ago, while I was doing research for a book about families (*Intimate Worlds*), I routinely posed this question to every member of a family I was interviewing—anyone who seemed old enough and willing to try to answer it.

I would watch as people struggled to formulate their replies—many of which were weird, extraordinary, completely surprising. But nobody ever challenged me to respond in kind, to reveal what my *own* answer to that question might be. Nevertheless, it always popped into awareness, stood out so clearly against the background of my mind's horizon: "I was born, and nobody noticed."

But how could this possibly be an elemental truth of my life, the actual starting point of my own autobiography, when I remembered my mother as the most caring, gentle, generous of persons? This was a question I always seemed to sidestep, never confront head-on. It was so much at variance with my vivid memories of my mother, with that sense of loving and being loved, that—whatever else was happening in the desperate household in which I grew up—I'd always believed had filled up my psychic fuel tank for a lifetime.

Even in the middle of my life, when I was married, a mother, and long gone from my original family, I kept encountering "hard evidence" of my mother's caring and her love for me. For instance, once, while gathering material for a *New York Times* article on sleep disorders, I learned how to self-induce body muscle relaxation with the aid of a biofeedback device. What this device was used for was "feeding back" to the sleep patient ongoing information about the state of his or her own muscular tension.

Beforehand, I'd been ushered into a soundproof room, asked to lie down upon a comfortable sofa with a set of earphones over my ears and electrodes pasted on the mobile, reactive muscles of my forehead; this enabled me to "hear" my facial musculature clenching each time I thought about something that made me feel taut and anxious. The biofeedback mechanism translated the electrical charge of the muscles into sounds: What I heard first was a rapid barrage of *click-click-click*s. Nothing, I soon found, could slow the sounds so effectively as imagining myself as a small infant, lying on a table, kicking my legs, "talking" to my mother, and laughing.

It didn't take me long to discover that certain kinds of thoughts evoked an avalanche of sounds. Thinking about how to write the sleep article for the *Times,* for instance, evoked an auditory bombardment. But other thoughts tended to slow down the barrage of noises. When I set myself to focusing upon *those* thoughts, I was rewarded by hearing a widely spaced *click . . . click . . . click . . . click.* The image of my mother, whenever I brought it into sharp focus—complete with the image of her smiling and leaning over me—actually brought about extended periods of time during which I heard no clicks at all. How could this powerful, revealing experience compute with that recurring first sentence of my life's narrative: "I was born, and nobody noticed"? If this message, so discordant with anything I consciously believed about my past, was coming to me from within my body, a part of me didn't really want to decode it.

This book is about the ways in which the body remembers, and may be expressing symptomatically, not only those secrets we may be keeping from others, but those we are keeping from ourselves. For in the course of my studies I was to confront the shocking realization that my deep love for my mother was the motivation for my "stuffing down" certain hurtful thoughts and memories of her that I couldn't bear to acknowledge consciously. Nevertheless, what *my body knew* was being expressed via a bodily symptom—that of tension in my jaw, which would tingle painfully at times or grow rigid, even frozen.

One morning—had I had a nightmare?—I'd even woken up and found my jaw so locked that I had trouble opening my mouth to brush my teeth. But until I became involved in the research for this book, it hadn't ever occurred to me that there might be some link between this occasional mysterious symptom—tension in the jaw—and lingering memories, stored in my body, of certain distressing life experiences.

Ultimately, this book is about the secrets and lies we may tell to others, or to ourselves, about the actual truths of our lives—about those painful or shameful or wounding experiences of the past or the present that we may strive to ignore or may simply forget, but which *our bodies hold and remember*. Our bodies not only remember, but frequently "speak up" about these truths in the form of isolated symptoms (back or jaw tension), or of certain disorders (depression, alcoholism), or of repetitively problematic patterns of positioning ourselves in our most intimate relationships. However, it is only recently—due to astonishing advances in brain research and the study of human memory systems—that we have been learning how to listen to what the body has to tell us and to *use* what we are learning therapeutically.

It is now widely recognized that the body stores memories of intensely stressful experiences, particularly in certain regions at the core of the brain (the limbic system, which is the seat of our emotions). We may not care to speak of these events to anyone, but memories of them—whether vividly recalled or lost to awareness—color many aspects of our daily existence, often without our conscious realization.

The Body's Reactions to High Stress:
Hyperarousal and Numbing Out

As the daughter of a messianic, irrational father—a man who was prone to unpredictable, inexplicable rages—I grew up with a sense that anything could happen at any moment. Everyone in the household, including my docile mother, was afraid of my father—and we children knew that she was powerless to protect us from him. Growing up, as I did, in an atmosphere of unknown but palpable dangers had instilled in me an ingrained sense of readiness to meet a threat—a threat that could come from anywhere, at any time, without explanation.

However, it was only in the course of working on this book that I came to learn that this state of bodily hyperarousal and hypervigilance is one of the two major reactions to events that are experienced as overwhelming.

The body's other mode of responding is the diametrically opposite one—it is shutting down, distancing emotionally, feeling numb, "spacing out."

These two bodily reactions have a very different outward appearance, but internally, similar things are happening. In both instances, the body's "emergency alarm system" has been switched on and an instantaneous physiological readiness to meet the threat has come into play: the well-known "fight or flight" (or "freeze" if there's no way out) response.

This lightning-swift neurobiological reaction to situations of danger, which involves an elaborate, integrated set of bodily and psychological changes, is actually a survival mechanism—one that has served our species well over time and which we share with all other mammals. The downside, however, is that a complex, highly developed memory network enables us to keep certain experiences alive within us. A person's body may, therefore, remain in a state of high arousal and preparedness to meet a threat long after the danger itself is in the past. The body "remembers" what once happened—and at times neutral, even benign, occurrences can trigger similar kinds of biologically based, internal alarms.

In any case, as my intensive reading and my interviews with secret holders and with a host of varying experts proceeded, I came to the realization that I was not only *discerning* a picture emerging from the research for this book; I myself was a part of the picture that was emerging. Before this time, I'd never taken special note of the pervasive feelings of wariness, of worried expectation, that were held by me *within my body*—never thought these might be an expression of unresolved, unintegrated memories that were held within my nervous circuitry but not within my conscious thought processes.

Quite the contrary: I'd always viewed my sense of physical high alert, of vigilance, as something that was simply "me"—simply who I was, a part of the way I was constructed. I'd never even considered the odd notion that how a person's body felt *inside* at the present moment might be integrally linked to the things that had happened in his or her life, even long ago—linked, that is, to events that had once felt overwhelming and to their often disturbing, long-abiding aftereffects.

Secrets, Lies, Betrayals

At a more superficial level, the question of what first kindled my interest in the powerful, often subterranean effects of secrets, lies, and betrayals is an easy one to answer. At the twenty-ninth annual conference of the New York Society for Clinical Social Work, where I was the designated honoree, I attended a series of talks on the topic *Secrets and Lies: Intrapsychic and Interpersonal Dimensions*, and the repercussions of this conference were to remain with me for months and then for years to come. For that day's events seemed to affect me like a tuning fork, whose vibrations began resonating with a hitherto silent part of my internal world.

During the afternoon sessions, I heard presentations with such titles as "Living Everyday Lies," "Sex, Lies, and Infidelity," "Seeing Is Not Believing," and "Transgenerational Family Secrets"—and the sessions didn't disappoint. The more I listened to these narratives of marital affairs, wife battering, traumatic bonding, unspoken family shame, hidden food-related maladies, verbal/emotional abuse, and alcohol and drug disorders, the more fascinated I became; and I decided to undertake some further study of the subject of secrets and lies on my own. And, as the work progressed, I came to appreciate how closely related to bodily symptoms and repetitive problems with relationships (to spouses, lovers, colleagues, friends) these subjects actually were.

I had thought that the idea of talking about secrets and lies would make it hard to find a list of people who would be willing to be interviewed for the project, but I could not have been more mistaken: Volunteers came to me from a number of sources, including audiences at lectures I was giving at the time. It didn't take long—a mere matter of months—before I'd amassed a freightload of highly privileged secrets and confidential, personal data. And at the same time, quite unexpectedly, I'd found that a strong, even inexorable current was carrying me toward fascinating research on traumatic experience and the lingering effects that certain long-past events could exert upon the body, the brain, and ongoing behavior in the present.

In retrospect, the reason I became so captivated by this work seems to me both logical and obvious. For what could be more secret, more mortifying and shame-ridden, than those painful, sometimes overwhelming remembrances of the past that most of us don't want to examine candidly, even think about, much less reveal to other people? In any event, what the trauma literature—and the research on the brain and on human memory systems as well—was telling me was that the body has a way of remembering those things that we may most wish to forget.

Shame-Related Secrets

Not surprisingly, in the course of the interviews, I found myself encountering a dizzying *variety* of secrets; I also discerned in people a broad range of motivations for keeping the information under lock and seal. But some motivations for secret keeping did, I noticed, recur with great frequency, and for that reason they stood out from all the rest.

One virtually omnipresent reason was *shame*—about those aspects of a person's early or present-day life that had to be disclaimed and disavowed. A parent's mental illness or alcoholism, or the fact that a family member had gone to prison, or the existence of emotional maltreatment or physical violence in the family of origin, might be the matter that had to be hidden. In other cases, the confidential narrative I was hearing had to do with neglect or the terrible invalidation that a person had experienced as a child—people are often deeply *ashamed* of having been victimized. On yet other occasions the secret had to do with worse cruelties, such as interpersonal abuse that was ongoing at the time of the interviews but being kept under wraps in order to keep up a presentable social facade. These abusive relationships often bore an uncanny resemblance to "familiar" situations—situations that one or both partners had encountered in their family of origin.

Another conspicuous motivation for keeping secrets was *fear*—and the most frequently encountered fears were those revolving around the threat of rejection and abandonment. Here, the individual's deepest certainty was that if the real truth about him or her were known—about an abortion, a period of promiscuity, a drug habit, the kind of family he or she came from—the secret holder would be revealed as unworthy or contemptible, someone whose past history or behavior was so unsavory that he or she deserved to be cast off, deserted.

For example, a deep-seated fear that her new bridegroom would *leave* the relationship precipitously if he ever learned the full truth about her past was the rationale for Claudia Martinelli's ongoing lies and deceptions about her past. So, too, were a poisonous admixture of shame, guilt, and a deep belief in her own *badness* that had been with her since earliest childhood. Such ingrained beliefs were reflected in her body, which was in a state of constant, tense hyperarousal.

Claudia Martinelli, whose story is woven throughout Part One, seemed to be responding to a blaring internal alarm that was sounding off within her, one that made a state of calm and relaxation impossible. This clamorous alarm—a "fight or flight" response that kept her body on continual high alert—was actually drowning out the more subtle communiqués that our bodies send to us on a routine basis. For this reason, Claudia couldn't hear the less strident warning signals from within that our bodies routinely dispatch to us and that might have guided her behavior—messages such as "Something doesn't feel quite right here," or "There's a problem," or "Can I trust this person to be on my side?"

Claudia's story is at once her own—unique—and also illustrative of many of the other life narratives that I heard in the course of my interviews for this book. Her state of high arousal and mistrustful vigilance, which kept her anxiously patrolling the outer walls of her world—fully expecting an attack from without—led to an incapacity to be *fully present inside her body* and therefore able to be responsive to the important messages being beamed to her from within. This deafness to the body's internal stream of informational signals is a well-recognized, often long-lived aftereffect of disturbing events that were once experienced as overwhelming.

At the level of conscious awareness, Claudia Martinelli was out of touch with her body. And because she had never been able to integrate what was happening inside her body with what was going on in her mind, she had no understanding of *why* she was doing the things she was doing. Instead, she seemed to be drawn toward continually reenacting and reexperiencing, *in her life*, the familiar distressing feelings. These bodily feelings and sensations were her baseline, her accustomed way of being.

People with a history like Claudia's—which is to say, those who have been witness to, or the target of, early trauma such as emotional neglect or abuse or physical violence—have a tendency to become involved in restaging strangely similar events in later adulthood. By getting into the same or a very similar situation, they return to a world with which they are familiar, one that *feels consonant with what is happening inside their bodies*—with the high arousal, shame, and fear they're experiencing. So Claudia's love choices kept re-creating, in the present, the secrecy, lying, hypocrisy, and abuse that she'd witnessed in her own original family. (See chapter 5, "Behavioral Reenactments: Was Claudia Martinelli in an Emotionally Abusive Relationship? What *Is* an Emotionally Abusive Relationship?")

Secrets Motivated by Love and Loyalty

Yet another oft encountered rationale for secret holding was *loyalty—the need, engendered by loving feelings, to keep someone else's secret or, alternatively, to protect that someone from learning information that would cause terrible pain.* Most commonplace among those secrets motivated by love and loyalty were, in my experience, secrets of a sexual nature—for example, a situation in which a person has grown up knowing of one parent's infidelity and yet has felt impelled to keep the secret from the other.

"My father was a serial adulterer, and he made *me* his confidante," an elegant woman in her late thirties told me. "I don't know why he did that—I think we'd call it sexual abuse nowadays—but I was only about thirteen or fourteen years old at the time. So his bringing all that stuff to me was terribly confusing. . . . The message I was getting was that *I* was his real intimate, and my mom was just the workhorse, there to run the house."

Worst of all, she said, was her dad's putting her into a painful triangle that involved keeping secrets from her mother—she'd felt so consumed with guilt, so helpless, so caught in the middle of that unhappy situation. "Somewhere around that time, I got something that was diagnosed as migraine syndrome—I would get these dizzy feelings, see bouncing lights, feel sick to my stomach. My mouth would go numb, too." Metaphorically speaking, her lips had frozen; it was as if her body were telling her to keep her mouth shut.

Secrets Being Kept from the Self

All in all, the most curious kinds of secrets that emerged in these interviews were those that could be called "secrets being kept from the self." In these instances, it often seemed as though one part of the individual's brain were resisting knowledge of an event or experience that was so startling, so overwhelming, so unthinkable, that it couldn't be integrated into the person's conscious awareness. The memory of the event had simply fragmented, dropped out of the individual's mind, even though his or her *body* or behavior often bore witness to the episode's existence.

There are many situations, which frequently go unseen for what they are, in which our bodies "talk" about hurtful, frightening, but seemingly forgotten events that we're loath to "know about" and acknowledge. They may do so in the guise of feelings of numbness and deadness, including sexual apathy, *or* in the form of high arousal, irritability, and unending tension. Yet again, they may "speak" about a person's pain and grief in the form of somatic reactions, appearing as "physical" problems—for example, severe headaches, perpetual stomach distress, irritable bowel syndrome, eating or sleep problems, painful muscular tension of the back, neck, or jaw.

The body's "memories" may, on the other hand, make their appearance in the form of some apparently inexplicable kind of behavior, such as Beverly Scanlon's panicky reaction when she'd been given the mundane task of overseeing the changing of the locks in the academic department that she usually ran with such admirable efficiency. (See chapter 12, "Secrets from the Self: Beverly Changes the Locks.")

Secrets of this sort are usually connected to experiences of painful, even traumatic significance to the individual involved. And as the interviews continued, I was coming to realize that a great many—though not *all*—of the secrets being told to me bore some connection to traumas, past and present, large and small.

Daddy

Although my father had had four wives by the time he died in his nineties, he didn't much like women, and he liked children even less. I can't remember ever having an actual conversation with my father, but I do remember those angry-sounding conversations—they sometimes rose to a shout—that he used to have with himself. He was talking to an unseen being—was it God?—but he wasn't to be interrupted. I would watch him apprehensively as he marched up and down the dining room, presumably at his morning prayers but sounding as if he were infuriated.

What were those angry colloquies about? It was impossible to decipher what he was carrying on about, why he sometimes sounded so enraged. You could never know what my father was thinking, surely not what might make him happy or please him—I try hard to remember him smiling—but most dangerously of all, you never knew what would set him off.

I can remember an incident that I tried hard to make sense of, something that happened when I was about twelve or thirteen years old. I was staying home from school with some symptoms of a flu, running a low fever, and feeling thoroughly contented with a book I was reading and with our new kitty—an endearing, furry little ball of excitement who was bounding back and forth across the bedspread.

I did hear my father's heavy tread on the staircase but felt no alarm until I saw him standing in the doorway as if dumbstruck by the scene before him—myself, under the covers, the book, the little gray-and-white kitten. He was scowling at me, horrified, his entire body puffing up with outrage until it seemed to fill the entire door frame. I felt my heart pounding in my chest, looked around me swiftly. What was happening—what had I *done* that was wrong?

He didn't say a word, simply stalked into the room and grabbed me by one skinny shoulder. Then he brought his face down close to mine, his eyes glittering with outrage. "What are you *doing*?" he demanded, giving my shoulder a rough shake.

"I'm sick, I have a fever, Daddy," I blurted quickly. "Mommy said I should stay in bed." But his accusatory gaze remained fixed upon me, and he shook my shoulder again. I was staring up at him, and I can still recall the sensation, the feeling that the whole world had narrowed down so that it consisted of this one threatening being looming over me. I waited, frozen.

It took a long time for him to find the words, but at last he said furiously, saliva forming around the edges of his lips, "*You* say you're sick! And you're lying here playing with the *cat*! What kind of *sick* is this, playing with the *cat*!" With that, he gave the kitty a rough swipe with his large hand, so that she mewed loudly as she careened off the bed and onto the floor.

"Well, you're not getting away with *this*." He let go of my shoulder with a last, abrupt shove backward against the bed pillows, then turned on his heel. "I'm going down, and I'm going to call the school, the principal! And I'm going to tell him! She's lying in bed *pretending* to be sick, but she's playing with the cat in her bed!"

I lay there rigidly, too petrified to move, hearing the door bang at the bottom of the stair hallway. My heart was slamming hard, yet I was confused: What was so wrong with being sick and having a cat playing on your bedspread? I didn't understand, it made no sense. Would it make sense to the principal or the teachers? What would they think when they got that call? Would they believe I was *bad*—that I'd been pretending, not sick at all, not running any fever—and that having the kitty on the bed proved this to be so?

It didn't seem rational to me, but then my father was hard to fathom—and I was only about twelve-plus years old. Perhaps the people in the school office would think I was faking, as my father said—or maybe they would think *he* was crazy. Then again, if they thought the latter, what did that make me . . . the daughter of a crazy parent? I wouldn't want my classmates to think so, to have that kind of word get around.

At the age of twelve, a young person wants nothing other than to be a clone of everyone else; being singled out for negative attention is humiliating. So, when I returned to school, I felt terrified of being "outed"—known as someone who must be *weird* because she came from a family that was so strange and so bizarre. I remember waiting breathlessly to be summoned to the principal's office—knots in my stomach, tightness in my chest—but I spoke to no one else about my awful fear that I was going to be pulled out of class summarily. It was one of the most interminable days of my life, but although I expected to be called to the gallows momentarily, nothing further ever happened.

Later, I wondered if my father had ever called. And if so, had the principal simply recognized the strangeness of the situation and decided not to pursue it any further? Whatever the reasons, the incident was dropped, and I was able to go on with my daily struggle to look like a normal girl from a normal family. But of course, *I* knew the truth to be otherwise.

Being Familiarly Uncomfortable: What Is Written in the Body's Physiology

This episode was, however, paradigmatic of the many damaging experiences of childhood that my interviewees spoke about with me— experiences that often are taken inside and interwoven with a person's identity and personality. Certainly my own sense that "anything can happen at any moment"—that I had to be in a bodily state of readiness to meet a threat—had been reinforced by the fact that I'd been lying peacefully in bed, reading a book and playing with my kitten, when suddenly the walls of my world—in the person of my father—had come crashing in upon me.

Events of this sort are, of course, not the kind we usually think of as traumatic, in the sense of a highly dramatic, catastrophic occurrence—for instance, the murder of a sibling (see chapter 15, "Reenactments of the Past: The Barrys and the Freeds"), being sexually assaulted, getting caught in a fire, or losing a loved one in a terrorist attack. Still, frightening, stressful experiences, such as that mystifying encounter with my father, have a way of becoming situated in a person's body in such a way that they feel completely familiar.

I don't mean to say that they feel comfortable, only that they feel *familiar*—that is, *familiarly uncomfortable*—for they have become written into the body's physiology. And, as a result, it becomes difficult for a person to conceive of an interior world that feels profoundly *different*—that is, a body that is not hyperaroused, that feels relaxed and safe inside.

Big-T and Little-t Trauma

Let me hasten to say that the incident with my father and the kitty, searing though it had been to me, would never rise to the level of major trauma as defined in the standard psychiatric reference book, *The Diagnostic and Statistical Manual of Mental Disorders*. According to the manual, only certain *kinds* of experiences can surmount the bar when it comes to diagnosing post-traumatic stress disorder, and they are those that involve staring death in the face. These would be along the lines of military combat, violent personal assault, natural or man-made disasters, severe automobile accidents, learning of a potentially fatal illness, and events of this life-threatening dimension. Moreover, the diagnosis requires that the person experiencing the trauma must have responded with "intense fear, helplessness or horror. . . ."

There is ongoing controversy about this strict definition of what is meant by "trauma," for in clinical practice, many people respond to much less apocalyptic stressors with clear-cut post-traumatic reactions. To take an example, when Karen Barry-Freed's husband announced abruptly that their marriage was over, that he had another woman, and that she should get herself a lawyer (see chapter 13, "The World Turned Upside Down: Extramarital Affairs"), this elicited a classic traumatic response. Karen reacted with shock and dissociation—she "numbed out," which is the body's other major behavioral reaction to events that are experienced as overwhelming.

For many months after this occurrence, Karen had felt spacey, disconnected, as if injected with an emotional anesthetic—although clearly, no confrontation with mortality was involved. This kind of frozen immobility (the rabbit in the headlights) is a *classic bodily response to situations of extreme danger* and is often seen in the aftermath of traumatic experiences—those that leave a person feeling devastated, damaged, unable to function normally, due to her or his "intense fear, helplessness or horror."

A person in Karen's situation may not have undergone the kind of horrific event or series of events that clearly merit a diagnosis of post-traumatic stress disorder, but may nevertheless be exhibiting some or all of the bodily signs and symptoms of a severe stress response syndrome—in this instance, a sense of emotional deadness and a host of physical symptoms, such as migraines, stomach distress, nausea, and other somatic complaints. Karen Barry-Freed's story, which is told throughout part 3 of this book, is illustrative not only of the second mode of responding to terrible events—that is, "zoning out," turning off the feelings spigot entirely; her story also illustrates how devastating experiences can remain *in the body*—and then suddenly jump out like a bogeyman, long after a person's difficulties appear to be completely resolved and in the past.

I should add that in some situations a person will seem to alternate between states of numbness and deadness and states of high emotional reactivity. But in any case, the overriding point to be made here is that the fine line differentiating "big-T trauma" (post-traumatic stress disorder) and "little-t trauma" (post-traumatic stress) remains somewhat blurry, indeterminate. Therefore, let me be clear about the fact that the word *trauma*, as I use it in this book, will *not* for the most part refer to big-T trauma—catastrophic happenings such as hurricanes, floods, fires, rape, and other events of a potentially fatal nature. My book's focus will be upon little-t trauma—those less obviously cataclysmic but nevertheless damaging experiences that are widespread and are at present widely underdiagnosed.

Perhaps this happens because exposures to trauma are considered to be rare, even though the statistics indicate otherwise. For example, a recent government study involving some fifty-nine thousand respondents found that "events and experiences that qualified as traumas" had been experienced by *60 percent of the adult men* and *51 percent of the adult women* interviewed.

Interestingly enough, the social scientists running this study never used the word *trauma* in the course of their interviews; each person in the sample was simply asked, "Has such-and-such an event ever happened to you?" When it was concluded, the results of this large-scale investigation surprised even the researchers themselves, for their findings demonstrated that exposures to traumatic stress are actually astonishingly commonplace.

Nevertheless, there does exist a widespread reluctance to think in terms of trauma—the word itself sounds so ominous—absent an out-and-out calamity. This, in turn, has created a situation in which the symptomatic aftereffects of profoundly disturbing experiences often go unrecognized as what they are—which is to say, the body's reactions to overwhelming stress.

New Findings, Powerful Therapies

For most of medical history, it has been taken for granted that the human brain, sequestered behind the hard, bony structure of the skull, was an inviolate "black box"—a marvelously complex yet totally sealed-off organ that could never be looked at directly, much less studied, while it was in action. Then, starting in the mid-1980s, an increasingly sophisticated battery of brain-imaging techniques made it possible to observe the functioning—that is, *thinking, feeling, remembering*—brain of a living, communicating person. Scientists could, for example, *look at* what changes in cerebral blood flow took place deep within the "old," emotional regions of the brain while a person was recollecting and describing an intensely anxiety-producing, stressful experience.

This fascinating work (which is described in chapter 4, "The Body Remembers") is part of an ever growing body of work that has served to highlight the neurobiological—that is, fleshly—roots of our mental existence. So, too, has the explosively expanding literature on human memory systems. The current understanding is not only that our memories exist at an impalpable, psychological level, but that they also have a *physical, corporeal* existence within the body's nervous circuitry. We now know that there are many situations in which we are having powerful somatic reactions to experiences that may have long since slipped beneath the surface of awareness.

Why and how does it happen that our brains and bodies can hold the knowledge of situations and events that we ourselves may have put aside or forgotten completely? Again, the answer, supported by the most recent scientific work on memory, is that while we usually think of our emotional lives as being immaterial in nature, they are in fact *deeply rooted in our bodily experiences* of emotionally charged events that are currently happening or that have happened in the past. (See chapter 3, "Physioneurosis: The Body Keeps the Score.")

What, then, can be done about disturbing memories—most especially strongly encoded *early* memories—that we are out of touch with, but which may be affecting areas of our work lives and close relationships? Are there ways to "cure" a difficult experience in the past that lives on, in the most literal, *physical sense*, within our body's nervous circuitry? Can words alone—that is, the more conventional, "talking alone" forms of psychotherapy—ever suffice, given our growing understanding of traumatic stressors, of the complexities of memory and the neurophysiology of the brain? And how, practically speaking, can one take advantage of the great smorgasbord of recent scientific findings in ways that might improve one's physical and emotional well-being?

One interesting development—and thus far the best answer to this question—has been the emergence of a group of relatively new therapeutic methods and procedures that rely heavily upon "somatic memory"— that is, upon what the body knows. These body-oriented approaches to the treatment of intense suffering vary widely and can *look* very different; still, they do have a crucial feature in common. That is, they are all geared toward targeting and then integrating scattered bits of data stored within the patient's *physical* as well as psychological self.

Moreover, all of them seek to promote a state of heightened bodily awareness by actively summoning up the person's feelings, emotions, and sensations—for example, what was seen, touched, smelled, heard, during certain critical events or time periods. The body's "memory" is thus put into play as a way of gaining access to regions deep within the brain where hugely oversensitized networks of reaction have been established. I should mention that in the course of researching this book, I myself sampled several of these "power therapies," so named because they often prove effective with such rapidity, especially when compared with the far slower-paced, traditional, verbal methods of treatment. And, to my own amazement, in the course of this "research," I came to understand why I'd answered that question—"What would the first sentence of your autobiography be?"—in such a seemingly incomprehensible fashion. Around that same time, the tension in my jaw vanished completely, and it has never returned.

What follows, then, is an exploration not only of the ways in which the body holds the secrets of a life, but of the ways in which one might go about unlocking them and freeing the self from their power. This book is, too, a meditation upon memory, upon matters such as why certain memories are particularly long-lasting while others fade very quickly. I have also written about trust, sexuality, the recognition of emotional abuse, the reenactment of the past in the present, the latest scientific findings on severe stress and the brain, and a variety of kindred topics. My research has taken me to places that I could not previously have imagined and has actually transformed my thinking about the body, the mind, and the nonexistent division between them.

—

Part One

KEEPING SECRETS

THE HYPERAROUSED BODY,
BEHAVIORAL REENACTMENTS,
CLAUDIA MARTINELLI'S DILEMMA

Chapter One

IS IT FAIR TO GO AHEAD
WITH THIS WEDDING?

*I*T'S STILL NOT CLEAR HOW OR WHY THAT STRANGE MISUN-
derstanding occurred. The plan we'd made was pretty straightforward:
Claudia Martinelli and I were to meet each other in the lobby of the Yale
Club, which is just across the street from Grand Central Terminal. That
waiting area isn't large, so it never occurred to me that we needed to describe ourselves, put carnations in our lapels, do anything of that sort.

When I arrived, ten minutes late, out of breath, the lobby was unusually crowded and noisy. Clusters of people stood around talking, laughing;
their high-pitched voices echoed off the marble walls, muffling phrases of
the familiar carols being piped in from unseen speakers. The whole lobby
was dressed up for the Christmas holiday: Huge red velvet bows festooned
the high archways leading to the elevators on the right side of the lobby;
and on the opposite side, the same red velvet bows graced the handrails of
the wide stairway leading up to the cocktail lounge on the mezzanine.
The sounds of a loud party floated down from up there. I looked around
but didn't see the woman I was expecting.

Very few people were actually sitting in the club's waiting section,
which consists of several dark blue sofas and blue, comfortable-looking
chairs arranged in an elongated oval. There *was* one person, actually, a
strikingly attractive woman sitting by herself; but she surely didn't correspond to my image of the person I was meeting. Anyhow, this woman
didn't seem to be on the lookout for *me*; her gaze slid right past without a

flicker of interest and remained fixed upon the revolving door at the entrance.

She's waiting for a date, I thought. Someone important to her, for she was sitting forward on her seat intently. At her feet was a striped pale green shopping bag that bore the label Emporio Armani.

Behind me the front door went on swishing steadily, letting in blasts of cold air and new arrivals. I stood there, uncertain, feeling guilty about my perennial tardiness. The tall grandfather clock, which had been decorated with fragrant Christmas greens, suddenly emitted a loud, single chime. For a moment all the cheerful hubbub halted. It was actually six-fifteen, not ten after, so I'd arrived even later than I'd thought.

Was it possible that my interviewee had gotten here on the dot of six, waited briefly, and then left because I was nowhere to be seen? Or was this a plain and simple no-show? Claudia Martinelli had sounded pretty agitated during our several preliminary phone calls; she might have gotten confused about the plans, which had been changed a couple of times, or even decided against participating in this project—an exploration of secrets and lies and how they affect us mentally and physically. Had *I* said anything that might have sounded overly intrusive or alarming?

I sank into one of the deep armchairs with my back to the revolving door and soon found myself gazing covertly at the handsome woman sitting across from me. She had wide, pale blue eyes, fringed with black, unblinking as a bird's and focused on the entryway in back of me. Her hair was light colored—masses of curls, which looked carefully disarranged—and she wore a very short dark wool dress, clockworked stockings, and polished boots with heels so tall and narrow that the whole effect was faintly pornographic. She wasn't merely good-looking, as I'd first thought; she was *beautiful*—the kind of woman whose mere existence eclipses every female around her.

It was six twenty-five, and whoever she was meeting still hadn't arrived. In the meantime, a smattering of other people sitting in the area had linked up with their friends, and some new personnel had come to take up places on the dark blue patterned sofas. I was growing ever more certain that Claudia Martinelli wasn't going to show up and feeling responsible for whatever might have gone wrong. I had been too casual in making arrangements for this meeting. I had come too late, and she'd gone before

I got here. I'd made some ill-advised remark that had disturbed her, and she'd decided not to be interviewed.

I began to console myself with the fact that I had a goodly number of *other* volunteers for the research I was engaged in—a project that had begun as a straightforward study of secrets and lies, but then expanded as I'd reflected upon the narratives I was gathering. For as I'd moved from interview to interview, it had become ever clearer to me that there was so often a mysterious link between the secrets a person holds and painful events of the past—including painful events that he or she believes to have been fully dealt with and resolved. There was, too, a link between things that were happening in the person's current-day life and those same toxic experiences—which may have happened recently or so long ago that they'd become lost to everyday, conscious awareness.

But whether they're "forgotten" or present in the here and now, highly stressful events—by which I mean experiences that felt and still *feel* harsh, overwhelming, traumatic—can leave in their wake a sense of inner chaos, of being helpless, disorganized, unable to cope or self-soothe and calm oneself down. Traumatic situations leave their symptomatic calling cards, and while the story of what originally happened may go underground in the form of a closely held secret, the body "remembers" what occurred, for it remains stored within the neural circuitry. Not only does the body remember, but the original story goes on being told and retold in disguised form—often as incomprehensibly powerful emotional and physical reactions or as inexplicable, self-damaging, repetitive patterns of behavior.

Those symptoms that are carried in the body may emerge in subtle or in strikingly clear-cut ways. For example, they can show up as muscle tension, hyperarousal, stomachaches, headaches, anxiety, changes in sleep patterns, depressed mood, fatigue, colitis, irritable bowel syndrome, or an enhanced vulnerability to colds and other illnesses. The aftereffects of such experiences may also be expressed in the form of behavior, such as becoming involved in relationships that are hurtful and demeaning or in dangerous kinds of acting out, including wild sexual escapades, compulsive gambling, or addictions to drugs, alcohol, or food.

Less obviously, a trauma of some kind may leave a permanent mark upon a person's view of the self and of his or her world. Some fall into a way of being best described as a kind of "learned voicelessness," a peculiar talent for getting into depriving relationships. Such relationships foster a state of emotional numbness, a pervading silence about the individual's own desires and preferences; and in such situations, the voiceless partner's needs and wishes go unheard; they almost seem to have no existence.

This is by no means disconnected from the common observation that severely stressful events can leave an individual with a sense of not being fully present in his or her life, of being "out of it" somehow. The person is eminently capable of going through all the right motions yet lacks a real sense of being fully embodied in the here and now of the present moment.

It's now well recognized that traumatic events leave their neural imprint upon what is called the "old," emotional brain, and that even small reminders of the trauma can immediately activate the body's survival alarm system. This is the renowned "fight-or-flight response"—an instantaneous, physiological reaction to danger that has served our species well over aeons of evolutionary time. The only drawback to this wonderfully automatic, self-defensive reaction is that after the challenge, when all threat is long past, some people cannot calm their minds and their bodies down again. They remain battle-ready, sometimes for years—on the alert for fresh danger, mistrustful of others, prone to feelings of shame, anger, and apprehension.

Just recently, in the course of several long telephone conversations with Claudia Martinelli, it had seemed to me that I was hearing this kind of gut-level agitation and alarm in her fearful, pressured tone of voice.

To be sure, when it came to secrets and lies, Claudia was dealing with some very big ones; her current situation was distressing enough to get anyone upset. Still, as I sat there waiting, I found myself speculating about whether or not there had been earlier events in her life, some profoundly disturbing experiences, that had set the stage for her becoming embroiled in her current situation. For as I'd already come to realize in the course of my interviews, the secrets people keep, and the lies they tell, frequently stem from odd acts of loyalty and protection.

Those matters that we choose to censor or completely conceal from the world (and, in some instances, even from ourselves) often have to do with painful memories involving those we have loved, and may remain deeply loyal to, even though their behavior toward us or their heedless neglect of our needs once caused us great harm. So you had to wonder: Was something from the past driving Claudia's wildly mistrustful behavior, making her feel that the very notion of confiding in the person closest to her, her new husband, was completely out of the question—that simply being herself would drive him away? Moreover, what (if any) signals was her body sending her whenever she contemplated opening up and telling him the truth?

As Claudia was to tell me later on, the mere thought of doing so always set off some frantic reactions in her body—most prominently, feelings of constriction in her throat, as if she couldn't catch her breath, and a wildly thumping heartbeat. She took these to be urgent communiqués of alarm that translated into "Don't even think of it!"

Claudia Martinelli was behaving as if her life's experience had taught her, and taught her well, that trust and openness were simply *not* among the options to be considered in an intimate situation. Deeply ingrained within her physical being, as well as her belief system, seemed to be the basic assumption that lies and falsifications about who she really was, and what had actually happened in her past, were her only means of staying safe, if not to say surviving.

He Doesn't Know Who I Really Am

Before making plans to meet her in person, I'd gained some preliminary understanding of the difficult and potentially disastrous circumstances in which Claudia Martinelli had recently found herself. As she'd described recent events in her life, she had gone to see a psychotherapist two weeks in advance of her second marriage, which had taken place some eight months earlier. At that point in time, elaborate arrangements for her wedding ceremony and reception—flowers, music, caterers—had been made and were all set to go, but she'd had an agonizing problem on her mind.

The dilemma that had suddenly sprung to front and center at that time had to do with everything about herself that she *hadn't* told the man she was on the verge of marrying. For insofar as outward appearances were concerned, Claudia Martinelli was an attractive, stable, and reputable woman in her mid-thirties, who was on the fast track upward in the management hierarchy of an elegant Manhattan department store. However, unknown to Paul Novak, her bridegroom-to-be, there had been a period in her life—it was after the breakup of her first marriage—when she'd been partying uproariously, drinking too much, snorting cocaine, on the loose, living a wanton, promiscuous existence.

She'd said not a word about this to her future husband, even though she knew that Paul had been through a similar "crazy time" himself, after the bitter ending of his own first marriage. He'd gone through a period of living the same frenetic, drinking and drugging, dissolute life on the edge. He'd been a high-risk gambler for a while, too. The cardinal difference between them was that he had told her all about his past, while she'd held back about her own history and her reckless, extravagant experiences.

Why, I wondered, hadn't she told him her story early on, during the highly romantic and potentially more forgiving period when they were just becoming involved? It would have been far easier at that point, but she had been afraid to take the risk. She'd probably been frightened that he would look down upon her as a wanton woman and lose respect for her, perhaps end the relationship on the spot. That would have been *hard,* for he'd been so kind and caring then; she hadn't wanted to take the chance of spoiling things.

The truth was that this relationship had felt so *right* to her, and Claudia had been very tired of living on her own; she'd wanted to settle down, have a child or children, a real home. Moreover, as I was to learn, keeping secrets had been a way of life in the household in which she'd grown up. So she'd postponed making any revelations while events kept moving along, from courtship to an engagement to the plans for the wedding; and it wasn't until just before her marriage that she began to panic about the secrets she was holding.

At that penultimate moment, she'd needed to consult someone outside the situation (not a close friend, not a relative, not anyone who knew her) about the pressing question she was asking herself over and over: Is it fair to go ahead with this wedding when the man I'm marrying doesn't actually know who I am or the truth about my past? She was feeling beset by strong urges to unburden herself and just *tell* Paul about that period of her life; but each time she came close to doing so, those frantic warnings from within began prompting her to consider the probable consequences.

She seemed to know enough about her future spouse to realize that forgiveness wouldn't come to him easily. In truth, her fears about the potential magnitude of his reaction always drew her up short, horrified. With the wedding arrangements all in place, and so many acceptances in, how could she spring this information on him from out of nowhere? Besides, wasn't there a realistic danger that Paul would be so infuriated that he'd decide to call the whole thing off? If something like that did happen, she would be shamed and humiliated in front of all her and his family members and their entire circle of friends. Yet if she *didn't* talk to him until after the wedding, there was the very real threat that her new husband would feel cheated and manipulated—as if he'd been hoodwinked into marrying a woman who wasn't what she had appeared to be and who was, in fact, damaged goods.

Eleventh-Hour Wedding Jitters

I wondered what had really sparked those eleventh-hour wedding jitters and sent Claudia scurrying to seek a therapist's advice with virtually no time in which to consider her options and make a well-examined choice. Was it possible that her upsurge of anxiety had less to do with "being fair to Paul" than it did with her own doubts about the viability of the relationship— about how she really *felt* when she was with him? Did she go to that clinician because she herself, at some level, wanted to call the marriage off? It seemed quite plausible that she'd never been forthright with him about her own past because she knew, *in her gut*, that she couldn't trust him to hear her in a spirit of compassionate acceptance.

Indeed, she could have had her doubts about whether she really loved Paul—at least not for himself. But then, why had she chosen him? Maybe the underlying agenda that had pushed things this far had to do with her being a woman who was moving into her upper thirties and was eager to start a family before her biological clock ran out of time. Consulting a therapist might have represented the other side of a deep ambivalence (marrying a man she was coming to know as critical and judgmental versus giving up on ever having a child).

As I saw it, getting married with a secret of this sort on your conscience would be like getting married with a time bomb in your pocket; honest and open communication between the members of the couple would be impossible. However, the psychologist Claudia met with in that eleventh-hour consultation suggested a different, and in its own way reasonable-sounding, way to look at the situation on the ground.

That therapist had taken the position that the details of Claudia's past were her own "private information"—information that she could share or *not* share with her husband-to-be, just as she chose. Her biographical data belonged to *her* and to her alone. She could choose to hold on to it her-self or not, but it existed on a completely different moral plane from any current-day secrets affecting their own relationship that she might be keeping from her prospective bridegroom.

This rational (you could say rationalized) perspective on the dilemma had sounded levelheaded enough to Claudia and enabled her to feel suf-ficiently comfortable to go ahead with the ceremony. But in my own view, she'd been withholding information that she knew to be highly pertinent to her partner and to the relationship. Did this fall into the domain of "maintaining privacy," or was it more on the order of "keeping secrets"—entering the marriage feeling that she'd offered only an airbrushed version of herself? In any case, in the months following the marriage—not too surprisingly—the time bomb had gone off. Paul began questioning her about her past.

Why in the world hadn't he done so earlier? They'd been engaged for over a year, and during that time her bridegroom-to-be had asked Claudia relatively little about what her life had been like after the ending of her first marriage or about the nature of her more recent relationships. You had to wonder why he hadn't discussed these matters with her during that prolonged, rose-tinted period of their courtship, when he had talked so much about his own past.

Was it possible that Claudia had been responding to *Paul's* signals by not telling him outright what he clearly hadn't wanted to hear (otherwise, he could have asked)? Perhaps he did suspect her, in a sub-rosa fashion; but there was a sense in which the two of them had been honoring a silent pact. Her past was to be a taboo subject, at least for the time being.

It wasn't until after they were man and wife that those concealed parts of her history began to emerge and affect the couple's relationship in pro-foundly damaging, destructive ways. For only then did Paul's curiosity about the details of her recent past—most particularly, the saga of her sex-ual adventures—begin to make its appearance and thereafter continue to escalate steadily. By the time of our interviews—which got under way about eight months after the marriage—Claudia was sounding as if she'd been taken hostage. Her husband was now interrogating her, demanding that she fill in the blank spaces, complete with all the distressing, upsetting details—things he'd never asked about before.

Who were the men she had gone out with, and which ones had she been to bed with? he wanted to know. What kinds of sexual activities had she engaged in? Had she ever been involved with a certain mutual acquaintance (a high executive in the firm for which she now worked) whose erotic exploits were legendary? Perhaps most heinous of all, had she, a religious Catholic woman, ever had an abortion? Paul was badgering her continually, trying to get her to say that she *had* done so.

She felt isolated, full of self-blame, so worthless and unsafe. Such feelings, it should be said, are fairly commonplace among people who have experienced acute stress at some period of their lives, particularly during early childhood; and this did prove to be relevant in Claudia's case. But for now she insisted that no matter what else happened, or how scared or bad she felt, being open with her husband was an option that was off the table, totally out of the question. He would "torture" her; she would never hear the end of it.

Actually, he was "torturing" her at this moment. The pair seemed to be locked in a marriage of mutual projections: She carried all the "badness" in the relationship, while Paul had assumed the robes of righteousness and represented morality, truth, and "goodness." Did this domestic scenario—a flagrant distortion of reality, in which she was the base, humiliated, powerless one and he was the fierce, upright, and judgmental one—have an air of familiarity to both of them? In the course of our conversations, I'd begun to wonder whether Claudia Martinelli had placed herself in a relational position that she knew well and that felt deeply *fitting* to her, even though it kept her in a state of distress and high bodily arousal.

Keeping Secrets

I suppose I'd fallen into a kind of reverie, for when the chimes of the grandfather clock pealed for a second time, they caught me by surprise. My thoughts had wandered afield, and I'd begun musing about the high costs of keeping secrets, especially secrets from a person with whom you share an intimate relationship. Holding out on undesirable, embarrassing information can turn you into a kind of undercover agent, someone who must be on guard constantly lest the dangerous truths about your character and history emerge. You can't be open about certain important matters that are really on your mind, and the upshot is that you move into a position of isolation—the secret is your closest companion.

This state of affairs generates great tension within a person and in a relationship, not only in yourself as secret holder, but in those close to you, who become confused, uneasy, mystified. The partner (or close friend or family member) has a sense of being shut out—unable to connect with you and understand what is happening in your life. And while, at the outset, maintaining silence may have presented itself as the simplest, easiest, most sensible way of preserving an appealing exterior or persona, in reality this kind of "solution" exists only at the problem's surface: The secret itself doesn't go away.

Instead, what is untold and feels as if it *cannot* be spoken of (in part because one *hasn't* ever spoken about it) seems to inflate in the dark, as if its forbidden nature has endowed it with a yeastlike quality. The hidden truth takes on more and more power and dimension, silently increasing the emotional space between the secret keeper and the unaware other, thus rendering trustworthiness and clear communication between the self and the partner impossible. And inevitably, that sequestered material assumes a menacing importance that it might never have had if it hadn't been thrust out of sight. For not only the secret itself, but the series of lies, omissions, and/or cover-ups that have been utilized to maintain it have a poisonous effect upon the secret holder's most needed, valued relationships —upon friendships and family ties as well as the emotional attachment to a mate.

Why, then, does keeping secrets strike so many people as the most efficient way of dealing with those awkward, uncomfortable facts about ourselves or our family members that we wish would go away? Many secrets are created because it seems much simpler to suppress certain less than flattering data—to "stuff it," whisk it out of awareness, never speak about matters that might place us in a vulnerable or embarrassing light. Who needs to know about your parent's alcoholism; a brother's mental illness;

an illegitimate half-sibling; your level of income; the true nature of your inner feelings; the pornographic films you sent away for; the psychoactive medications you're taking or once took; an extramarital affair; or the relationship struggles you and your partner were involved in or are involved in at the moment?

According to most marital and family experts, the primary underlying motive for secret keeping has to do with shame. Secrets are founded upon the belief that if certain aspects of your life and history were to see daylight, you would not be regarded as an acceptable human being; you would be seen, and see yourself, as outside the pale of decency, the shameful violator of some kind of taboo. When it comes to holding back or opening up, fears of spoiling other people's images of you or of disrupting important relationships are always being weighed in the balance against the heavy psychological and interpersonal burdens of living alone with the information.

Also, it hardly needs saying that there are many situations in which, practically speaking, it seems wiser and more judicious to remain silent. For even though the suppressed information may weigh heavily on the secret keeper's spirit, daring to reveal it can generate brutal counterattacks.

One woman I interviewed in the course of this work had had an incestuous relationship with her father during her late adolescence. Much later on, when she wrote about her experiences in an exquisitely poetic and painful book, many people were scandalized. A number of reviewers attacked her for not having kept quiet about what had occurred. As she later said wryly, no one appeared to be bothered by the fact that these things *had* happened to her; they were far more outraged by her daring to discuss them openly! Societal pressures had been brought to bear to keep a secret out of sight—to suppress the ugly truth that such episodes do occur, to simply live with it, never speak of it aloud, move on, and pretend it never happened.

The reasons for maintaining silence are not only shame and self-protection, but family loyalty as well—an entire kinship network often depends upon the secret keeper's silence. When I asked this woman how she had managed to endure the consequences attendant upon her public truth telling, she responded by saying that difficult as it had been—and it had been *hard*—she had no regrets about having done it.

"I was living a life that felt completely fraudulent, because no one knew who I really was. Now I don't have to pretend to be anyone but who I am. I am *myself*, the person who underwent those experiences," she told me. Her strong motivation, which had been more powerful than the need for self-protection, the feelings of shame, or the pull of family loyalty, had been to get to a place where she could live a life that *felt real* to her; a life in which she felt like a real person. My own thought was that it takes tremendous courage to open up a raw and explosive family secret of this sort—to face the barrage of flak that's sure to follow and get to a place where moving on becomes possible.

Just recently, a friend's loyalty to her family of origin had been the major underlying factor in a secret that was being kept from me. The truth had tumbled out in the midst of a seemingly desultory conversation I was having with this friend, with whom I've shared a close, confiding relationship for many years. I knew that her older sister had died some six months earlier, but suddenly, with no preamble, she told me that her sister's death had come about largely as the result of years of domestic violence: Her husband had been a wife beater.

I'd found this revelation startling. Why hadn't my friend ever talked with me about this while her sister was still alive? Given that this sibling lived across the country in San Francisco, there wasn't the remotest chance of any untoward consequences. Nevertheless, despite our long-time attachment, my friend hadn't even mentioned what had been happening until many months after her sister's death. It was as if she'd been loyally guarding this secret all the while, protecting her sister's ugly story from an outside world, which included me, a close friend.

At one level, I could understand why my friend had done so; it is *hard* to speak of sorely painful, hidden matters that place members of our families (and, by extension, ourselves) in an ignoble light. Also, I was well aware that almost everybody keeps secrets and tells lies on occasion: I knew that when a nationwide poll on truth telling was carried out in the 1990s, a full 90 *percent* of the respondents had acknowledged having been deceitful (and who can say whether or not the other 10 percent were being perfectly aboveboard?). Keeping secrets appears to be fairly normative in the general population.

Nevertheless, on another level, my friend's revelation about her sister left me feeling cut off and frustrated: If my friend had ever talked with me about this situation while it was occurring, I might have offered her my comfort and support, perhaps even suggested options that hadn't been thought of or considered before. Secrets do erect barriers that shut other people out, closing off possible sources of emotional supply and help— this was something I surely knew from my own life.

A Loyal Liar

Shame, loyalty, protection: All of these had motivated my steadfast keeping of the big family secret that had preoccupied much of my adolescence. "Don't ever tell people your parents are divorced, or they won't respect you," my mother had counseled me in the most ominous, fiercely cautionary tone of voice.

How young and how credulous I'd been—it was almost endearing— but I'd believed her, oh, I'd believed her. It all seemed so screwy now, this so-called momentous family secret with which my own adolescent years had been burdened. She and my father had parted for good when I was fourteen.

My mother. Her warnings came from a world she knew, but it was the old world, another world; she was walking around with a tiny nineteenth-century village inside her head. I embraced the truth of everything she'd told me, but how does a fourteen-year-old girl keep a secret like *that* one?

I did it, somehow. I did it for her, and for me. I did it to fend off the never specified but clearly terrible consequences that would surely follow upon any foolishly candid revelation. It meant that I couldn't let anyone get too close to my real life, not so close that they were in danger of knowing who was in my family and how we actually lived. Even years later, when one of my college suite-mates complained continually about her *own* parents' divorce, I followed my mother's stricture and kept the monstrous secret of my family's breakup.

But simply saying nothing in that kind of situation can make you feel like a fraud and a liar. You feel disconnected, watchful, haunted by the thought: He or she wouldn't like or respect me if the shameful truth were to come out. Inevitably, I developed well-defended, sealed-off compartments within my head. In one such compartment my suite-mate was perfectly entitled to talk about her parents' "disgusting" split-up, and in another compartment was the forbidden knowledge of my own parents' divorce. *That* could never be divulged lest I be sunk in degradation, become the object of everyone's scorn. Worst of all would be the sin of disloyalty—betraying my mother's edict and her confidence, the shameful knowledge that had been left in my keeping.

The imposing clock nearby emitted a sonorous single *bong!*, snapping me back again into the present. Another fifteen minutes had gone by: Strange how the memory of that onerous secret could still affect me, so many years later. My cheeks were feeling hot and flushed, and I could hear the tom-tom of my speeded-up heartbeat reverberating within my chest. I'd been reflecting upon matters that belonged in the long-ago past, yet my body was reacting as if this whole dilemma existed in the "real time" of the present moment.

A quick glance at my watch told me that it was now six forty-five—time to give up on this appointment. The glamorous woman (was she a model?) sitting across from me seemed to be coming to the same conclusion; I noticed that she'd gotten up and was standing there, frowning, looking uncertain. Then she strode across the lobby to talk to the bedazzled young Hispanic clerk at the front desk.

I stood up, too, crossed to the other side of the seating area, and plumped myself on a sofa near where she'd been sitting. I wanted to spend a last few minutes keeping my eye on the front door. But there was a lull, nobody seemed to be arriving or leaving; this interview wasn't going to happen.

I'd begun gathering my things together and was just buttoning up my coat when the woman who'd been sitting across the way came back, approached me, and said hesitantly, "You aren't . . . by any chance . . . Maggie?" I must have looked startled—and I think I startled her, too—for she took a small step backward.

I stood up immediately and then just stared at her, as dumbfounded as if a statue had suddenly sprung to life and spoken to me. "Are you *Claudia*?" I asked incredulously. The two of us gazed at each other, openmouthed, and then just burst out laughing; the ridiculousness of the situation had struck us both immediately. Here we were, the only two women sitting alone in the lobby—and we'd sat there without either one making a move to identify herself! It was as though we'd each decided, on the spot, that the other *couldn't* be the right person!

Even now, as I think back upon that curious episode, I'm hard put to come up with some explanation about why neither one of us stepped forward. As far as my own part in that strange scenario is concerned, however, I have several alternative theories. My best guess is that I saw the woman in the Yale Club lobby area as too flawless, too well organized, too in charge and in control, to be the distraught person I'd spoken to on the telephone. I'd been completely misled by an outward presentation of self that was so utterly at odds with everything about this woman that I believed I'd already learned—a potent reminder that many people are marvelously skilled in showing to the outside world those parts of themselves that they want the outside world to see.

The Filtering Lens of the Past

Claudia and I went up to the fourth-floor library, but we couldn't find a completely private place to talk. The best we could do was to settle in a small, book-lined room just off the main reading room; but we had to talk to each other in quiet voices. Someone else was present, a woman curled up in a leather chair, riffling through a stack of magazines. She was sitting on the far side of this cozily shabby, enclosed little area.

The two of us pulled a couple of library chairs up to an old, round lamp table, and I put my tape recorder upon it, midway between the two of us. Then I opened my large drawing pad, leafing through it till I came to an empty page. I began the interview in my customary fashion, which is by quickly sketching in the most significant facts of Claudia Martinelli's life history, as it had commenced in her family of origin and as she'd lived it out thus far.

In so doing, I made use of a favorite clinical device known as a "family genogram." The genogram is the shortest, safest, most efficient way of gathering an overview of a person's emotional and relational biography— his or her family's narrative and its major themes. The method is so simple that it almost borders on the silly, for it consists of nothing more than a se- ries of straightforward, mundane questions—questions such as: What is your mother's first name? Is she living? Did she work while you were growing up? Is she retired now, or is she still working? Can you give me a few adjectives that would describe her, generally speaking, such as "warm" or "stern" or "tender" or "reserved"?

Dry and factual as these questions may sound, they are always strongly evocative, for the answers to them are inevitably laden with rich associations—associations that begin spilling out in the course of the discussion. As the person being interviewed talks about each individual parent and about what their marriage was like; as she gives the names of her siblings and perhaps talks about other relatives (such as grandparents) who were important in the family's life; as she describes her present partner, her ex-partner (or partners), and her children (if there are any)—something both remarkable and totally predictable occurs. Even as she focuses intently upon the past, and the tenor of life in her family of origin, the particular words she chooses and the associations she makes create an uncannily accurate overview of the structure of her present-day consciousness.

Why and how does this happen? Because there are reliable continuities between *what is now* and our stored remembrances of *what has gone before*; the past becomes incorporated in our psyches and our bodies. The basic components of consciousness itself—our ways of perceiving ourselves, others, and the world around us; our emotional reactions to those perceptions; and the ways of thinking that accompany those perceptions—are powerfully defined by the framework for living with which our embedded memories have provided us. We are always experiencing the present moment stereoscopically, seeing it through the filtering lens of what has happened to us earlier.

Thus, the very act of *seeing*, in the immediacy of the here and now, is to some considerable degree an act of remembering—remembering from a certain perspective. "While sifting through the sensory present, the brain triggers prior knowledge patterns, whose suddenly reanimated vigor ricochets throughout the [neural] network. Old information comes alive, and a person then *knows* what he used to know," as memory researchers Thomas Lewis, Fari Amini, and Richard Lannon have written. In brief, the brain is constantly responding to experiences in the present by linking them to associated experiences in the past.

And in some instances the past is exerting such spellbinding power that an individual behaves, all unwittingly, as if compelled to continually play out a familiar role in a well-known script or family libretto. It is almost as if this role has become the individual's single option for being, the behavior software of the self; it's deeply lodged within his or her body and psyche. Typically, however, when the connection between *what used to be* and *what is right now* is recognized, it is experienced as a shocking revelation. It is the hardest thing in the world to *know* this about the self.

The realization that a forgotten but eerily familiar family theme is being re-created in one's present-day existence usually comes as a sobering, eye-opening experience—yet it can be a liberating and life-enriching experience as well. This is especially true in those frequent instances in which there's been a disconnect between certain body-based emotional states—for instance, pervasive feelings of anxiety, anger, or grief—and the network of subliminal thoughts and associations that have given rise to them.

What the body remembers has been encoded and stored within the central nervous system's vast internal filing system. And often it is only when these bodily data have been summoned forth and integrated with an understanding of the milieu in which certain destructive patterns of being have emerged that *something new can happen*. Later on in this book, I will be describing some of the ingenious, relatively new therapies that are oriented toward freeing the body from the hurtful memories it may hold and achieving a kind of body/mind integration—that is, toward accessing and resolving the past as it exists within our mental and physical beings, simultaneously.

Core Schemas and Dynamic Themes

Not only is it true that there are strong continuities between our past histories in our families of origin and the basic organization of our present-day consciousness; there are also continuities between what *used to* be, what is now, and what *will be* in the future. For our expectations of what *is likely* to happen to us are strongly predicated upon what *did* happen: The fundamental truths that our life's experiences have already taught us seem to move us in the direction of making those familiar things occur once again—though frequently, at a conscious level, we really don't want that to be so.

In brief, we often operate in ways that will result in our inner expectations—good and bad—being fulfilled. Our most basic perceptions of the world around us are always being selected and shaped by an internalized blueprint for living that we've developed over time. This "framework for living" contains the core schemas and dynamic themes—the images of who we are and what we will be—that shape our perceptions of the past and understanding of what lies in the future. At an unconscious level, our personal blueprint underlies the well-known "self-fulfilling prophecy," which is to say that what we believe in our hearts—that is, our bodies as well as our minds—about "the way things are" tends to become true in reality. In some subtle fashion, one that's usually not within reach of conscious awareness, we shape the way the narrative of our life develops.

A Carousel of Slides

As Yale psychologists Jefferson Singer and Peter Salovey observe in *The Remembered Self*, "Imagine that each individual carries inside his or her head a carousel of slides of life's most important memories. These slides have been carefully selected to represent the major emotionally evocative experiences that the person has ever had. . . . Although memory is perpetually taking snapshots of each and every experience that we encounter, there always emerges a core of slides to which we return repeatedly. This dog-eared bunch of slightly obscured or distorted images comes to form the central concerns of our personality."

These are the very images that come to dominate our interactions with the world around us. They are the things we "know" and become—and because we know them so well, it's often difficult to see ourselves or our lives in other ways, to consider fresher, less familiar, perhaps healthier and more effective options for how to be and how to interact with those around us. Thus, reflecting again upon Claudia Martinelli's current marital situation, I couldn't help but wonder: Had she found herself hopelessly entangled in such no-win secrets before, a life where lies and subterfuges—and feelings of inner turbulence and hyperarousal—had become a deep-rooted part of her existence? And if so, what had her secrets been about?

Chapter Two

LAYER UPON LAYER
OF SECRETS

O N THAT EVENING OF OUR FIRST INTERVIEW, CLAUDIA Martinelli and I spent most of our time working on her family genogram. When I asked her for some adjectives that would describe her mother, Claudia responded with the following words and phrases: "blunt; smart; a good person; energetic; self-reliant; independent; she sometimes settles too easily." I wasn't sure what she meant by the last-named quality but later realized that she was referring to her mother's habit of backing down in any real confrontation, of constantly giving way to Claudia's dad.

At this point, however, I simply jotted down these mainly positive-sounding terms on the chart, just beneath the round circle designating "Sylvia, age 69." As I did so, I couldn't help but notice how nonmaternal her depiction of her mother sounded. I could probably be accused of gender stereotyping, but when I heard "blunt, smart, good, self-reliant," I couldn't help thinking of a guy. I didn't hear anything warm or womanly in that characterization, especially when it came to a daughter's description of her mom.

Still, Claudia's feelings about her mother were far more favorable than were her feelings about her father, Nick, who was just turning seventy. The words she used to describe Nick were "a hypocrite; inconsistent; moody; depressive; critical; judgmental; a tightwad." Her father was going to be a *priest* before he met her mother, she added, an expression of derision flickering across her features. "Which is so ironic, because he's a real holy roller—he goes to church every morning—but he doesn't practice, he can be a *mean* person."

She paused, then added in a clipped tone of voice, "That's a good adjective for him, hypocrite. My father *is* a hypocrite." My gaze slid downward to a section of the genogram I'd sketched in earlier. I was struck by the fact that when I'd asked Claudia for adjectives that would describe her new husband, Paul Novak, the responses she'd given without hesitating were "judgmental; controlling; inconsistent; generous to a fault." Clearly, there was some intergenerational continuity here.

Aside from the single discrepancy—her dad was a "tightwad" and Paul was "generous to a fault"—there was an overlap between many of her husband's and her father's outstanding qualities, at least in her own mind. I asked her then if the word *hypocrite* could apply to Paul as well.

Claudia shook her head and said it didn't; but then she paused. She drew in a deep breath, exhaled with a kind of sigh, and recanted: "Paul *is* Mr. Nice-Guy, too—on the outside, to everyone *else*, I mean. He'll help *anyone* with any kind of problem, but at home he's different, very critical. Which is just the way my dad was when we were growing up." Both men were given to presenting a hypocritically genial face to the world outside the family but were demeaning and judgmental within the household.

She folded her hands in her lap, stared down at them like a sullen schoolgirl, murmured almost inaudibly, "The way he *talks* to me . . ." Then she looked up, stared at me fixedly for a few moments, and said, "My husband is a very smart, quick-witted man. He's really *funny*, but he can cut you down in two seconds. And he's very sarcastic." I nodded, acknowledging how that could make a person feel: Sarcastic people can often misread the line between what is funny and what is cruel.

Claudia looked grim. Once again I had the thought that she and Paul had fallen into a pattern that involved his playing the part of the condemning, judgmental father/parent and her taking on the role of his blameworthy (secretive, sexual) adolescent daughter. But when I asked her directly if her husband tended to take on a faultfinding, "parental" role in his relationship to her, Claudia merely shrugged and said she couldn't answer that question—she thought he would have been equally controlling and critical with any other partner in any kind of circumstance.

She thought it was "the way he was," and to some extent this was obviously so. For while it might seem that all the anguish in the relationship was being created by her secrets—that the relationship itself was *defined* by her secrets—Paul was surely reacting to a script of his own. Indeed, like many troubled couples, both partners seemed to be involved in reenacting a highly patterned minidrama over and over again. *His* script had to do with projecting all the blaming and the badness outward, away from himself, and seeing it as existing in the "immoral" Claudia. *She* was reacting to a guilt-ridden, shame-filled script of her own—a script that interfaced with her husband's all too well and left her in a continual state of fear, wariness, and high arousal.

At this moment the major area of discord between the partners had to do with Paul's stance in the relationship, which was that of the prosecutor, the paramount authority, the one who is always in the right and has all the forces of moral law and rectitude behind him. He was constantly hounding Claudia for information, pummeling her with questions that she felt far too intimidated to answer in an honest way. There were so many things about her past that made her feel tarnished and stigmatized, secrets she couldn't even dream of telling him.

Abortion was one such taboo topic—the real truth was that she'd had not one but two of them and had never said a word about them to anyone (though she believed an older sibling had her suspicions). I paused momentarily on hearing this, for it signaled the fact that holding on to secret information was nothing new in Claudia's life. Her way of dealing with the less palatable aspects of her reality seemed to be to maintain sole control of all potentially damaging information and to trust nobody—even those closest to her, who might otherwise have been sources of comfort and support. Clearly she had adopted this lonely, emotionally distant strategy in that "basic training camp for later living" that is the family of origin.

In any event, information that's suppressed and "disappeared" doesn't truly vanish or diminish in intensity: Even in situations where a person dissociates and puts the matter out of mind entirely, the body holds the knowledge of what has happened. In this instance, Claudia's feelings about those abortions *seemed* to have been resolved and faded; but suddenly, perhaps due to the harsh questioning she was undergoing, she'd found herself filled with grief and ruminating about them all the time.

Thought of those abortions preyed on her, she said, making her feel ashamed, guilty, and sick at heart. Claudia placed one hand on her abdomen, the other on her breast, and said that these thoughts often gave rise to woozy, lurching sensations in her stomach and feelings of tightness in her chest. Then she stopped speaking; tears were brimming in her eyes, and she paused to take a tissue from her purse. But she merely began wringing it in her hand without wiping away the plump, glistening tear that was sliding down her cheek.

"I'm sorry, it gets me so upset to think about it," she said in a low, muffled tone of voice. Then she added with a small, hopeless shrug that talking with Paul about these matters that so weighed upon her was completely out of the question. "He would feel *totally betrayed*, because he's asked me any number of times, 'Have you ever had an abortion?' and I've always said that I haven't." She knew he didn't believe her; and in fact he was pressing her harder and harder on this subject.

Why had this issue suddenly taken on such importance to him? Had the question of abortion played a role in some episode earlier in Paul's own life? Or had Claudia's reactions been such that he'd realized "abortion" was an agonizing issue for her and therefore a winning card in the fierce win-all or lose-all marital game the pair seemed to be playing? Was there a level at which this sense of embattlement felt uncomfortable, but *familiarly uncomfortable*, to both of them—the way a marital relationship ought to be? One couldn't know, but just recently Paul had begun upping the ante on this inquisition and subjecting her to ever fiercer cross-examinations.

"He will hammer at me, 'You *did* have an abortion, right? Tell me the truth! You *did*.'" She would try to deny it, but Paul would come back at her immediately, "You did; come on, you *did*. I think you did, right? *Tell me!*" Even as she said these words, Claudia and I were both startled by a sudden *thump!* It was the sound of a book dropping on the floor. The woman at the other end of the room, whose existence had disappeared from our mutual consciousness, had gotten up and was shrugging into her overcoat. She stooped over to pick up the book, then stood again and couldn't resist a curious look in our direction.

We turned back to our conversation, for she was clearly at too great a distance to have heard what we'd been saying. The next time I looked around, she was gone. We were alone, and the two of us had fallen silent. Claudia's eyes were fixed upon me, her expression taut, the portrait of vulnerability and fear. I met her gaze with compassion but was wondering how and why she'd managed to box herself into so untenable a position . . . and why she was allowing this state of affairs, with its obvious impact upon her highly aroused physical and mental state, to continue.

How Can I Trust Him?

Claudia was acting as if she lived in a one-option world, one in which there was no method of responding other than to stick adamantly to the original version of her story. And even though this basically unworkable strategy was requiring that she pile lie upon lie—to the point where the relationship threatened to buckle under the strain—she was behaving like the proverbial horse who *knows* his way back to the barn and cannot deviate one step or conceive of any other means of getting there. Why was it so hard for her to envisage any of the possible alternatives when it came to coping with this impasse—ways of proceeding that might serve to lower the tension level without setting off an explosion?

One such strategy might be for her to go to Paul and say directly, "You know, by putting me through these constant inquisitions, you're destroying our relationship. These grilling sessions make me feel as if you're searching for some terrible wrongs that I committed earlier in my life, and I'm not sure why you're doing this. Where is all of this heading? Are you looking for a full confession, so you can give me absolution and we can go on? Or are you just looking for reasons to be upset and angry, so that we have to dredge up things that happened in the past—things that can't be changed at this point in time? If so, I don't want to continue doing this."

A statement such as the above would serve to let him know that she had her limits, and he had reached them: that she would no longer enact the role of the bad, immoral victim as his counterpart, so that he could play the role of her indignant, righteous denouncer. And if she were able to maintain this posture, it would also stop the cycle of aggressive accusations and disbelieved, discounted denials.

Yet another, fairly similar approach to the situation might be for her to say to Paul, "I know I haven't lived a perfect life—you haven't, either—but do you think it's going to be helpful to continue going back there, when neither one of us can undo our own history? Can't you accept me as I am, at this moment in time, so that the two of us can go on from here? You yourself must realize that these inquisitions are making us both miserable and destroying the good things we had together. So for the meanwhile, for both our sakes, *I'm not going to respond to any of these questions anymore.*"

Of course, availing herself of an option of this sort would require a level of inner fortitude, entitlement, and healthy self-regard on Claudia's part—and Paul's interrogations put her on the defensive so quickly, made her feel so demeaned, guilty, and frightened. As I contemplated her situation, it seemed to me that in the process of withholding information in order to keep the relationship going, she had backed herself into an existential corner. As matters now stood, Claudia felt she had no choice but to go on lying to her husband about her past—her personal history might once have been her "private information," to be revealed at her own discretion, but in this relationship it had assumed a fissile potential that was akin to TNT.

In a strictly operational sense, that psychotherapist's carefully reasoned statement *hadn't* proven true: Claudia's past didn't seem to belong to her, despite the fact that it predated that period of her life when she and her husband had become involved. And at present Paul wasn't behaving only like a prosecutor, he was also like a hanging judge, harassing her for the very information that would condemn her in his eyes. It was as if he had *chosen* her so that she could play out this role in his internal drama. And she herself was in a no-win situation, for the very things she needed desperately to talk over with a loving, supportive partner were the things she couldn't dream of telling him—despite his own flamboyant past, he was fiercely critical and judgmental of other people, especially his wife.

"He would *use* this stuff against me, as my first husband and my father always did," Claudia said, looking terrified.

I paused, thinking about this statement: It was clear that this situation was deeply familiar to Claudia in many respects, a situation she'd found herself in before. This suggested that she might be involved in an unconsciously staged reenactment of a long past relationship, one involving a man who is critical, judgmental, and in a state of chronic anger and a woman who is subservient, "settles" (gives way, as her mother did) all the time, and feels culpable and frightened. Was Claudia reliving, as many people do, charged aspects of an unintegrated, unresolved past—one deriving from an old family pattern—in the context of this present-day relationship?

One could only speculate about that possibility at this point: Far more pressing and starkly obvious was that the existence of so much secret information was making it impossible for this couple to get on with their lives, to bond with each other and create any sense of mutual closeness.

"If I can't feel comfortable talking about these things with Paul, how can I *trust* him?" she now demanded, then didn't pause to hear an answer. "And why should he trust *me*, if I'm holding back on him?" Prior experience seemed to have taught Claudia Martinelli that being open and honest with the men in her life was neither safe nor advisable; and her current-day experience was confirming—underlining—what she'd already known beforehand.

She leaned toward me expectantly, looking hopeful, as if she thought I might come up with her answers in some magical fashion. I looked at her sympathetically but said nothing—given her agitated, hyperaroused state, there didn't seem to be any calmly reasoned, carefully worked-out solutions to the dilemma in which she'd found herself. But as we sat there, I found myself speculating about those wedding jitters and that desperate, last-minute trip to the therapist. Had that eleventh-hour request for help actually represented her wish and her hope that *this* relationship might be better, more open, and more honest than any of the ones she'd been involved in earlier?

One couldn't know, for by now it wasn't only her past that was causing their fierce, ongoing arguments. They were fighting about all sorts of *other* issues, too, most especially about the handling of money and her style of interacting with Paul's adolescent children by his first marriage. These items were both hot topics, which frequently led to ugly, unresolvable conflicts, fights that always ended in his triumphant rightness and her being in the wrong—and wanting to leap out of her own skin, unable to soothe herself or to calm down. Claudia was feeling desperately afraid that this new marriage—her "second chance at happiness"—was doomed and might not even make it through the coming year to the time of their first anniversary.

I glanced down at her partially completed family genogram. She was essentially giving this marriage no more than a year, and I noticed that her first marriage had actually lasted much longer—she'd been married for five years, having wed at twenty-six and divorced at thirty-one. Gazing down at that five-year time span—designated by a slashed line on her chart, indicating the marriage and the breakup—I couldn't help but speculate about how and why *that* relationship had ended. Had her first husband been as angrily "critical" and "judgmental" as the other males in Claudia Martinelli's life always seemed to be or to become? And had she been in the one-down position in that relationship as well?

I paused, inhaled, and exhaled deeply before resuming; the magnitude of her emotion was such that it seemed to have leapt the arc between her body and my own. As if by means of some communicative miracle, I'd started feeling that I wasn't merely listening to her talk about her fears, I was feeling her tension and anxiety *inside* my body as well.

—

Chapter Three

PHYSIONEUROSIS:
THE BODY KEEPS THE SCORE

INEVITABLY, IN THE COURSE OF THE RESEARCH, I BEGAN looking backward in time and wondering whether something in my own life had kindled this interest in secrets, lies, and traumatic experience. Had I myself ever felt overwhelmed by severe early stresses? In terms of life's potential catastrophes—earthquakes, floods, rapes, childhood sexual exploitation, being threatened with death, or witnessing a homicide—I was surely not a "trauma survivor." There had been no alcoholism, incest, drug abuse, or wife battering in the household in which I grew up.

Nevertheless, as I talked with various women, including Claudia Martinelli, about their relationships with their fathers, I found myself thinking hard about my relationship with my own—or, more accurately, about the void that had always been "Daddy." Our household had always been filled with his silences, with closed doors and unfathomable events. Daddy almost never spoke, either to me or to anyone else in the family; he was a cold, simmeringly angry, unapproachable human being, and everyone in the household, including my beloved mother, was afraid of him.

I have such graphic memories of his staring, expressionless gray eyes, not meeting anyone's gaze but forever looking beyond, as if searching out new grounds for his ever seething indignation. But does spending your young years in a domestic police state constitute "developmental trauma"? The question of what actually *constitutes* a traumatic experience remains unsettled, a subject of ongoing controversy, while newer definitions continue to be proffered. For example, a task force of the American Psychological Association has recently defined a traumatic stressor as "an event or process that leads to the disorganization of a core sense of self and safety in the world and leaves an indelible mark on one's world view."

What is meant by a "traumatic stressor" would obviously never be in doubt in certain instances—for example, a serious car accident that proves fatal to a family member riding in the car or, more globally, the cataclysmic attacks upon the World Trade Center. Those brutal attacks involved civilian losses never seen before; and for those who made their terrified way out of the collapsing towers as well as those who lost fathers, mothers, sons, daughters, sisters, brothers, and/or friends in that morning of catastrophe, the world will never look the same again. Altogether shattered were their basic assumptions about their own personal safety, and they were left with a haunting sense of personal vulnerability with which most Americans had been unacquainted before.

Could growing up in an atmosphere of chronically oppressive threat be compared in any way to such hugely calamitous sorts of events? I couldn't point to any clear-cut trauma that was making me feel vulnerable and scared; still, as I reflected on that long-ago time, I stumbled upon so many shut doors, so many unknowns in my family of origin—mysterious fragments of distant events that could emerge at the surface and then vanish again, unexplained. There was the visit of an "uncle"—his name was Albert—who came to see my father on one occasion. He never returned, and in the prevailing silence of my childhood home, he seemed to have disappeared as abruptly as he had materialized. He was a jack-in-the box uncle, who'd bobbed up and then disappeared without anyone's ever alluding to him again. It wasn't until many years later that I learned that "Uncle Albert" was actually my half-sibling. He was my father's grown son by a second marriage (my mother was his third wife, and another wife was to follow).

An Economic Slave

When I think about my childhood, my most vivid memories are always of my mother. I worshipped her, yet even so, the immediacy with which that little-girl ardor sprang into being during that sleep clinic biofeedback session amazed me. It was as if my feelings about my mother were as present as ever, fully intact within my very brain cells; and those feelings had the capacity, at the deepest levels of my being, to relax me and make me happy. Beneath all later misadventures and setbacks there still existed that central and fundamental image, described in the preface, myself as the baby of my mommy. When it came to self-inducing a state of calm and contentment, no other imagined scene had the same ability to cut off those clicking sounds of tension so completely.

An early, very strong aspiration—the fiercest goal of my girlhood and what I wanted more than anything else—was for my mother to be happy. "You *will* be happy someday, Mommy," I, her impassioned confidante, would assure her. I willed it to be so and believed that it *would* be so, in the brighter, more fulfilling future that awaited her. But unless there are aspects of my mother's life of which I know nothing, that brighter day never did come.

These days, an early photograph of my parents sits on an antique cherrywood bureau in the bedroom. It must have been taken around the time of their marriage. She looks so limpid, so wide-eyed, tentative; she can't be more than eighteen or nineteen. He was almost fifty, twice married when they wed, and his jaw juts out sternly, as though he's her irritated parent. His image is sharp edged, hers hazier, as though each stood in a separate light. She is all softness, soft dark hair, a dark V-necked blouse. Lining the V is a long strand of pearls, and even they are not well defined, but glimmering vaguely. She tried to leave my father, she told me, when my oldest sister, Norma, was still a tiny baby.

"What could I do, though? Where could I go?" She always sighed when she got to that point in the story. She couldn't have survived with a small child, in a strange land whose language was not her own. Why had she ever agreed to come here, to marry him? I wanted to know. She explained that her own father, whom she'd loved dearly, had died young; he'd left a widow, five children, and a Warsaw dry goods store that soon began failing miserably. My grandmother, a less sympathetic-seeming character—she sounded to my childish ears like the Old Woman Who Lived in a Shoe—had ultimately told my eighteen-year-old mother that she was literally unable to keep her.

The upshot was that my mother had been contracted to go to America as the bride of the aging ogre who was to become my father. The brutal, economic truth of the matter was that she'd been condemned to a form of domestic slavery, and over time she'd been forced to bend to the yoke of that marriage.

I think, every once in a while, of a certain contest that I, as a young schoolgirl, entered and reentered time and again. The contestant completed an endorsement of a certain product "in twenty-five words or less," and the winner's prize was a genuine diamond ring. I can bring to mind so readily the fantasies with which I indulged myself: joyful scenarios in which I sprang that genuine diamond ring upon my astonished and ecstatic mother. I would have done anything to make her life better.

There are other scenes, real-life scenes, remembrances of sitting alone with my mother. I was a little older then, and I watched her as she shoveled coal into our basement furnace. Her face was beautiful in the flickers of light as she talked about her girlhood, her own mother, and the good-looking captain of the boat that had brought her to America. He had really *admired* her, she recalled; but she was already promised—on her way to be married. I was so filled with sorrow and regret about that lost possibility, that romance that had never come into being.

"You'll be happy someday, Mommy, you'll see," I assured her passionately. If only I could have changed her history, willed her elopement with that unknown captain! She must have believed it, too, because she often sang or hummed her favorite song, "Bluebird of Happiness" ("Be like I, Hold your head up high / . . . Somewhere there's a bluebird of happiness . . ."). Besides, there was the Gypsy's prophecy. On the eve of her departure from Warsaw, my mother had consulted an ancient Gypsy woman, who'd read her palm and foretold her future.

The Gypsy had predicted that my mother's forthcoming marriage would produce four children (it did; I was the third) and that it would be an unhappy union. The fortune-teller also said that the marriage would end in the middle of my mother's life (this proved true as well; my parents divorced when I was fourteen years old). On a more positive note, the Gypsy had told my mother that she would eventually marry again and that this second marriage would prove a very different one—one in which she'd find the peace and happiness she had been seeking throughout many long years. In the wake of my parents' separation and divorce, when so much family ugliness of all kinds erupted, I know I hung on to that bright prophecy like a lifeline.

Another Kind of News Flash

Obviously, that consistently repeating first sentence of my life's narrative, discussed in the preface—"I was born, and nobody noticed"—was at variance with such passionate, loving memories as those just described. I was my mother's adorer, her oh-so-willing vassal, and I'd listened to her, empathized with her, and worshipped her as long as I could remember. My very consciousness—who I was, and the person I became—took shape within the cradle of this initial, magical attachment. Yet from somewhere deep within my being came this other kind of news flash, this piece of information I didn't want to contemplate or even register.

For the statement's obviously painful translation was this: While I'd always listened to my mother well and willingly, my own normal child needs for attention and affirmation had gone unheard. The first sentence of my story was about a little girl who had emerged into consciousness in an environment that contained barely enough emotional nutrients for any family member's survival. It was about a young child who'd found her own special niche in a depriving world by listening scrupulously and barely realizing that no one was listening to her in return.

I know that I felt sorrier for my mother than I ever felt for myself. I loved her so unreservedly, so indebtedly, that it took me more than half a lifetime to recognize how profoundly neglected a child I'd been. Of course, denial and excuses on her behalf were always readily available. She had lost her adored father as a young girl and then been delivered into economic slavery in her adolescent years. If these terrible blows had left her with what E. M. Forster called "the undeveloped heart"—by which he meant the ability to *care enough* about another human being—the reasons why were all too apparent.

I knew that I'd been a shabby, ill-kempt child—there were never any clean clothes in my bureau drawer. At times I'd even arrived at school with my hair uncombed, and I recall one humiliating occasion when the teacher chewed me out in front of the entire class, then sent me to the girls' bathroom to make myself presentable. The trouble was that I didn't have a comb with me. I remember being unable to admit this when I was exiled from the classroom, and I remember trying to comb my curly hair with my fingers in front of the bathroom mirror.

Why was it, then, that the opening sentence of my autobiography—"I was born, and nobody noticed"—ultimately burst upon me as a shocking realization, one that turned all prior understandings upside down? I suppose that this disconcerting knowledge had been contained within me for a lifetime, for that first sentence of my life's narrative had popped up so briskly and so immediately. From the point of view of empathy, validation, and affirmation, it was clear that I had been my mother's mother. In this magical first love attachment of human existence, the normal caring-parent/dependent-child roles had been reversed.

How did that scene at the school bathroom mirror end? I have a shadowy notion that an older girl came in, took pity on my situation, and let me use her comb; but I don't really know whether such a thing actually happened. The still vivid, emotion-packed parts of the episode are like a reel of film that ends abruptly at that moment of panic: I am standing there trying to comb through the tangles in my hair with my fingers.

And even many years later, the evocation of that scene could pack a wallop, one I felt in my rigid jaw, and the cavity in the pit of my stomach. Its message was that even if my own legitimate growing needs had gone unnoticed at an explicit, conscious level (by myself as well as anyone else), those unmet needs had, at another, more subterranean level, been silently encoded. At the silent, wordless level of the brain and the peripheral nervous system, my body had always kept the score.

Highly Arousing Events

There is now a large body of preclinical (which is to say, animal) literature—and some fascinating evidence from clinical research involving human subjects as well—indicating that the brain has a way of specially bookmarking highly arousing events. What we remember with the greatest clarity are the things that happened when we were very happy, very sad, very angry, or very frightened. We remember these happenings well, and for extensive periods of time, because of the intense, immediate, body-wide reactions they evoked—and often *continue* to evoke, despite the passage of years and what may be the vastly changed circumstances of a person's life.

Seen from a purely biological vantage point, it is well known that bodily states of emotional stress—for example, those associated with feelings of intense fear—trigger a panoply of psychophysiological responses. In a situation of threat, activating biochemicals, such as the hormone cortisol (which is manufactured in the tiny adrenal glands, above the kidneys), are immediately pressed into states of high activity. So, too, is the neurotransmitter norepinephrine, a chemical substance that ferries electrical impulses across the tiny gaps, or synapses, that separate neighboring nerve cells in the brain.

These rapidly circulating neural "messengers" serve to augment vigilance and sharpen the focus of the individual's attention upon the danger at hand. They promote a sense of being fully in the moment, and of perfect clarity, as if all of one's perceptions had been fine-tuned instantaneously. Such reactions are, of course, a part of the immediate, bodywide reaction that many experts view as evolution's gift to us—the instantaneous "fight or flight" response—which prepares us to stand and do battle or to flee the alarming situation as quickly as possible.

What is most arresting, however, is that this cascade of brain chemicals not only prepares us for emergencies, it enhances the retention of memories as well. In other words, what becomes quintessentially *memorable* appears to have its all-too-fleshly roots in the underlying neurochemistry of the body during states of emotional arousal.

Emotion and Remembering

One of the most ingenious demonstrations of this biological reality is a study carried out by neuroscientist Larry Cahill and his colleagues at the University of California at Irvine. In the first phase of this remarkable research, two groups of college students were asked to view a set of slides. One group heard a dramatic and upsetting voice-over narrative during the viewing—a story that commences with a mother and son leaving home, after which the boy gets caught in a terrible accident while crossing the road, receives critical injuries during the fray, and then is rushed to the hospital. The other group of subjects was told a completely different story about what was happening during their separate viewing of the same slides—a rather bland version in which a mother and her son are leaving home; they cross the road, and along the way, the boy sees some wrecked cars in a junkyard. Then they go to visit the boy's father, who works at a hospital. In this more benign version of the tale, nothing much happens.

One week later the students returned and were given a surprise memory test. Those who'd heard the traumatic version of the narrative recalled the story far better and in much greater detail. The Cahill researchers then hypothesized that a surge in the brain hormone norepinephrine had enhanced and sharpened those subjects' ability to remember. So in the second phase of the study, they recruited two different groups of students and had them look at the same slides with their differing accompanying stories.

In this second go-round, however, the scientists had previously injected a beta-blocker (propranolol, which would block the upsurge of the neurotransmitter norepinephrine) into half their subjects about an hour before the viewing. The remaining volunteers were also given an injection at that time, but theirs was an inert substance, a placebo. The two groups were then mixed together into one larger group, and then the original experiment was repeated. That is, the students were once again divided into two sections and asked to view the same set of slides while the varying versions of the narrative were told to them.

Then, as in the previous go-round, the students were summoned back for surprise memory testing one week later. In this case, the participants who'd heard the upsetting narrative and received propranolol—which of course blocked the actions of the brain hormone norepinephrine—could not recall the slides any better than those who'd listened to the neutral voice-over. But those who'd received the placebo *and* heard the upsetting story were well able to recall the slides; they remembered them much more clearly than did those who'd listened to the mundane narrative. The highly galvanizing neural hormone norepinephrine clearly played a critical role in human memory retention.

Physioneurosis

As recent experimental work with a variety of mammals—cats, rats, monkeys, and human beings—has compellingly shown, memory preservation occurs in what might best be described as the shape of an upside-down or inverted U. If you're in a situation in which the levels of your stress-related brain biochemicals happen to be low—say, out to lunch with a friend—you're likely to focus less intently on the experience and to forget the details of the lunch conversation later on. You can think of low levels of these "fight or flight" hormones (such as norepinephrine, also called adrenaline) as existing at one end of our envisaged upside-down U. At this peaceful, nonthreatening side of the U, the details of the luncheon, perhaps even the memory of the event itself, are likely to fade fairly soon.

But if on that occasion you should hear some personally threatening news—your friend thinks you should know that your son's been getting plastered at recent high school parties; or your job promotion is being challenged by a recently hired competitor; or your husband has been spotted in some highly questionable circumstances—the levels of your stress-induced, circulating neurotransmitters will surely rise abruptly. As they do, the memory of this occasion will be highlighted internally: That remembrance will be highly likely to become preserved within your body's neural circuitry, as will the strong emotions that attended it.

The basic principle here is that higher levels of fight-or-flight-related brain biochemicals equal better memory—*but only until the summit of that inverted U has been reached.* Then the opposite effect begins to emerge, and as the outpouring of fight-or-flight substances continues, the quality of remembering declines. At dramatically heightened levels of stress, memory becomes disrupted and fragmented, and in some cases an experience may be so shocking that all (or parts) of it is deleted from conscious awareness. This occurs, of course, in cases of amnesia.

There are countless examples of this phenomenon cited in the animal literature. To take a very simple one: A rat that's learned a maze, and immediately upon completing the learning task has been given an arousal-inducing norepinephrine injection, will typically traverse that maze more efficiently the next time around. The injected rat will perform this task much *better* than will a noninjected peer, who has forgotten the "neutral," unexciting experience shortly afterward.

But—and this is an important "but"—if the injected rat's norepinephrine levels are then augmented by further doses of this potent neurochemical, there will come a point at which there's a conspicuous *decline* in the animal's performance. The rat will run the maze far more haphazardly, because too much of the stress-related norepinephrine affects memory as adversely as does too little.

Actually, when you think of this from the point of view of species survival, it does make overall good sense. It makes *sense* to mark well those situations that have ignited feelings of alarm and anxiety, so that they're held firmly in mind and avoided in the future. Such memories, with their strong component of powerful emotion, would clearly be of crucial importance in terms of living long enough to mate, reproduce, and pass on one's genes—which is always the bottom line, biologically speaking.

During the human species's extended prehistory in the natural habitat, this highly italicized kind of remembering was probably programmed into the human genome. For chances were that if an individual didn't remember *keenly* those situations that felt threatening, he or she might not live long enough to be threatened again. It goes without saying that things have changed over the aeons of intervening evolutionary time, so that the nature of "what is dangerous" looks very different—the psychological and physical threats that we face in a modern-day industrial environment are vastly different, and infused with far more complexity, than simply managing to not get eaten by a hungry saber-toothed tiger or lion!

Still, when it comes to human coping mechanisms, our brains and our nervous systems haven't changed significantly since the relatively recent (in terms of evolutionary time) period when large predators roamed and ruled the earth. Nowadays it may be your explosive, abusive, short-tempered parent or stepparent who threatens you, rather than a charging animal; but memories of situations that *have once been experienced as highly dangerous* still tend to be what experts call "overencoded" or "overlearned"— that is, etched deeply into our cerebral wiring.

Aversive, distressing memories of this sort appear to be concentrated, and perhaps stored as well, in a tiny brain structure, the "amygdala." Within this diminutive, nut-shaped structure, potent memories of danger and threat can abide for days, months, or even years after the crisis situation itself has ended. Even in instances where a person realizes, at a rational and intellectual level, that a position of safety has long since been attained, his or her nervous circuitry can nevertheless remain fixed in a state of high tension, supervigilance, and hyperarousal.

This state of internal affairs makes it impossible to relax completely, to feel calm within, to trust, to truly let down one's guard; there is always that pervasive sense of the danger hovering around the corner. One of the pioneer trauma theorists, Abram Kardiner, called this sort of human plight a "physioneurosis"—an affliction that is neither purely physical nor purely psychological in nature, but a combination of both.

Chapter Four

THE BODY REMEMBERS

*W*HY AND HOW DOES IT HAPPEN THAT OUR BODIES CAN hold the knowledge of situations and events that we ourselves have forgotten? The answer is that while we usually think of our emotional lives as being psychological in nature, they are in fact *deeply rooted in our bodily experiences* of charged events that are occurring or have occurred in the past.

The human brain, with its hundred billion nerve cells and its million billion connections, holds boundless numbers of impressions, some briefly and for a passing moment, some throughout an entire lifetime. These are our memories, which not only exist at an impalpable, psychological or "mental" level, but also have a corporeal existence within the body's nervous system.

To be sure, we are far from being able to point to a particular location within the dynamically active brain where a distinctive memory resides. However, we do know that thoughts pertaining to that memory can give rise to *body-based emotions* and that there are many situations in which we are having powerful somatic reactions to experiences that may have long since slipped beneath the surface of awareness.

To take an example: Suppose it was late at night and you were driving through a dangerous-looking area. Having found yourself feeling thoroughly disoriented and in need of directions, you might be thinking, I'm afraid of this strange neighborhood, and I think I'm lost. You might even be on the verge of panic but still feel too frightened to roll down your window and ask a questionable-looking passerby for directions. The main thing to realize about this experience of fear is that although it *feels* as if it's happening at a cognitive, "thinking" level, it is actually being accompanied by an instantaneous cascade of internal, neurobiologically driven bodily reactions and responses.

You might experience these internal responses as a speeded-up heartbeat, a shallowness of your breathing, gooseflesh on your skin, a trembling of your lips and hands, or a tight feeling in the pit of your stomach; but the important point to be made is that this fear experience is occurring *in your body and your mind simultaneously.* And even if no outright harm actually arises in the course of this episode—aside from a storefront gang screaming sexually loaded comments at you and banging on the car's window— it might well happen that long after the memory of this incident has become hazy or faded from your thoughts entirely, the mere suggestion of a night drive in an unfamiliar neighborhood makes you (that is, *your body*) feel agitated and queasy.

The body remembers. Curiously enough, however, this widely acknowledged biological truth—that our memories are *physically* as well as mentally present within us—is one that's often overlooked by practitioners of the more traditional forms of verbal ("talking") psychotherapy. This is regrettable, because there do exist many situations in which all the discussion, understanding, and insight in the world never succeeds in dispelling the painful images, reactions, and somatic aftereffects (such as hypervigilance, jumpiness, or a depressed mood state) of events that were once experienced as horribly out of control or overwhelming.

According to world-renowned trauma expert Bessel van der Kolk, M.D., numerous treatment impasses occur because "top down" brain processing—cerebral processing that proceeds downward from the neocortical, "thinking" areas of the brain, where language and higher reasoning processes are represented—cannot fully access and effect changes in the deeper, wordless regions of the midbrain, where the engines of anxiety and hyperarousal are churning.

An afflicted person may, therefore, reach an exquisite intellectual and emotional understanding in regard to some of the painful events she or he has been through yet remain in a *bodily* state of apprehension— perennially jammed on high alert, internally mobilized for a danger that has long ceased to exist in reality. In these not uncommon cases, the reasons for the fear are past—and may have been thoroughly analyzed and interpreted—but the sense of dread and foreboding persists at a visceral, bodily level.

This happens because our conventional therapies tend to rely upon what psychiatrist van der Kolk calls "the tyranny of language." In clinical practice, he asserts, it often proves difficult, if not downright impossible, to alter an individual's underlying *physiological* state even when the person is making giant strides in terms of his or her psychological understanding and self-awareness.

Achieving insight about a chronically neglectful or emotionally abusive history, or a loss or fearful incident of some other kind, doesn't necessarily succeed in changing certain *bioemotional* reactions and responses. Very often the body is still reacting to the past as though it were the present; and even though the person may have made sense of and seemingly resolved painful bygone problems, the relief is only partial—the body holds the memory of what has happened, even at a cellular level.

Inside the "Black Box" of the Brain: Trauma

Until relatively recently, most neurological researchers took it as a given that the functioning—thinking, feeling, remembering—brain of a living human being would never be accessible to scientific observation. For the brain, solidly sequestered behind the hard, bony structure of the skull, seemed to be an inviolate "black box"—a marvelously intricate, yet totally sealed-off organ that could never be looked at directly, much less studied while it was in action.

Then, starting in the mid-1980s, an increasingly sophisticated array of computerized brain-imaging techniques—among them functional magnetic resonance imaging (fMRI) and positive emission topography (PET) —came into being. These new technologies enabled researchers to look directly at the brain's interior regions and *observe what things happened* when a person was responding to memories of an emotional nature—for instance, recollecting an intensely stressful, fearful experience.

At the present time this neuroimaging research is, relatively speaking, still in its infancy, but it has already yielded some remarkable results. One fascinating study, undertaken in the mid-1990s by Bessel van der Kolk and a group of Harvard colleagues, involved carrying out PET scans of the brains of trauma survivors at the same time as they were reminiscing about the terrifying experiences they had undergone. In other words, these scientists *took a series of photographs of the brain's interior* while memories of the trauma were on the individuals' minds.

To their surprise, the researchers found that in terms of oxygen flow, there was clear-cut *increased* activity in the right hemisphere of the brain, which appears to be more associated with states of emotion and bodily arousal. At the same time, there was a marked *decrease* in oxygen utilization in a brain region in the left hemisphere known as "Broca's area," which is known to be responsible for putting words to internal experience.

These results raised an intriguing question: Could this shutdown of the language-related Broca's area, in conjunction with a surge of activity in the "emotional" right hemisphere of the brain, be the cerebral model for a state of speechless terror? If such a link existed, it could explain why some people find it impossible to put their feelings into words and instead express those feelings in the guise of symptoms or as repetitions of self-defeating behaviors.

A Difference in the Brain: The Hippocampus

We now know, due to our newfound technological capacities, that the brains of adults who underwent chronic physical or sexual abuse during childhood tend to look somewhat *different* from the brains of people who experienced no such early mistreatment. The particular region of the brain in which this difference shows up is called the "hippocampus"—a name that derives from the Greek and means "horse-shaped sea monster," for this small, lobelike structure does resemble a sea horse when viewed in cross section. To be more precise, the hippocampus actually consists of *two* small lobes, one on each side of the brain, but it is generally referred to in the singular.

The hippocampus is situated deep within the brain's unconscious core, the midbrain—also known as the "old" or "mammalian" brain because in evolutionary terms it is believed to have first emerged in mammals. While much about this structure remains unknown, it is now widely recognized that it is crucial to the processing and retention of short-term memory—it can, indeed, be thought of as "short-term memory central."

The hippocampus is responsible for the ongoing sorting and organizing of the steadily arriving streams of sensory data that we are constantly receiving; in other words, it functions as a kind of high-speed, superefficient reception center where newly incoming information (for instance, sensory data, such as what is being seen, felt, heard, and so forth) is instantaneously sorted, cataloged, and held in short-term memory for an unspecified period of time. Short-term memory is also known as "working memory," for its primary focus is upon recognition and processing of what's happening in the present.

Some of this incoming data may fall into the realm of the familiar—information that's been encountered earlier—and therefore be speedily identified, categorized, and preserved provisionally for possible long-term retention. Or the arriving information may be surprising, novel, unfamiliar—and therefore be responded to with an enhanced degree of emotionality before being passed upward to the topmost, outer "thinking" areas of the human brain (the "neocortex") for further assessment. What is unknown and unfamiliar requires *attention* and may possibly demand some kind of defensive response on the part of the individual.

Brain Cells and High Stress

In the late 1990s, three different brain-imaging studies, all focusing on the hippocampus, produced the same remarkable findings. Two of these research investigations demonstrated that people who'd undergone traumatic stress during childhood—chronic physical or sexual abuse—tended to have *smaller* hippocampi than did a group of "controls" (non–severely stressed individuals). The third research study involved war veterans who were suffering from lingering symptoms of trauma; and in this case, too, that same strange hippocampal shrinkage was prominent among the volunteers.

Why should severe stress lead to shrinkage of the hippocampus, and what might be the meaning of these findings? Well, one clear inference flowing from the results was that individuals who had been subjected to chronic, bruising stress tended to experience cell loss in this vital brain area that is so critically important when it comes to the temporary storage of short-term memories. Could this be a *physically* based reflection of the common clinical observation that people who have been exposed to traumatic experiences often have great difficulty integrating certain fragments of memory into a coherent autobiographical past that makes sense?

Moreover, could this reduction in hippocampal volume explain why such individuals often find it difficult to experience the past as something *that is over* and often feel that what happened *then* is continuing to happen in the here and now? It is known that the hippocampus is where aspects of personal history (so-called episodic memories) are put into their proper context of space and time. These memories are organized along the lines of what happened, and where it happened, and when (for example, "I went to the park; met my friend; stopped and had a coffee with her; left her at the corner; promised to call tomorrow").

The experience I've just described has a neutral, benign quality and is therefore likely to be retained for a while and then eventually fade. However, if that coffee shop were robbed during this outing, and my friend and I were in fear for our lives, that memory would be extremely emotionally charged. Furthermore, if I were someone whose short-term memory had been impaired by awful stresses earlier in my life, I might have extraordinary difficulties when it came to sorting, processing, metabolizing, and digesting this traumatic experience. Then, instead of moving along into long-term memory retention and becoming part of my past, this terrifying episode might exist only in splintered form, and remain stuck in short-term memory—that is, in the here and now of an unending present, neither fading away nor undergoing further processing.

Response Readiness: The Amygdala

Close by the hippocampus and located just above it is another important brain structure, the amygdala. The word *amygdala* means "almond" in Greek, and this part of the brain has been so named because of its small size and nutlike shape; again, though it's referred to in the singular, there are duplicate amygdalae, one in each cerebral hemisphere. Both the hippocampus and the amygdala are part of an intricate, varied group of modules that make up the brain's *limbic system*, that cerebral area where our emotions and emotional responses are thought to be generated.

The limbic system is responsible for a host of functions related to survival, including monitoring of the organism's internal state (body temperature, rest/activity cycles) and its instantaneous physiological reactions to situations of fear and danger. The latter, of course, is the fight-or-flight response, to which must be added the "freezing" or "numbing out" response in situations where battle or escape is completely impossible. This body-wide crisis response is mediated by the amygdala—often called the brain's "emergency alarm system"—for it is within this tiny knob of nervous tissue that information about a potential threat is received and powerful emotions such as anger, fear, and rage are generated.

Due to the work of neuroscientist Joseph LeDoux, whose careful studies have traced the neural pathways of fear in an animal model (the rat), we now know that the amygdala can rapidly traverse what LeDoux terms a "quick and dirty" shortcut to another limbic system structure called the hypothalamus. On receiving the amygdala's signal, the hypothalamus initiates a series of bodily reactions that puts the threatened organism into a state of immediate readiness to meet the stressful challenge—sometimes even before the conscious mind has fully grasped the presence of any menace or peril. In other words, via this newly detected cerebral pathway, our "emotional brains" can be recognizing and responding to an imminent threat before we ourselves—our thinking, evaluating selves—have even appreciated the fact that it's present.

In any event, whether we are or are not consciously aware of a looming danger (which may indeed have arisen from within, in the form of a terrifying memory), our innate fight-or-flight emergency reaction will automatically switch to "on." This body-rooted emotional response, which has evolved to aid survival under conditions of peril, involves a vast array of physiological changes throughout our bodies and our brains.

These include an elevation in heart rate and blood pressure as more blood flows to the muscles of the arms and legs (to promote running or fighting) and a rise in oxygen consumption as bodily metabolism moves into high gear to meet the emergency. Also evident is the stepped-up secretion of neurohormones such as norepinephrine (aka adrenaline) to help mobilize a host of other "crisis" resources. For example, the spurt of norepinephrine entering the bloodstream causes the pupils of the eyes to dilate; an individual can literally see better when under stress. In short, this resultant surge in physical energy and mental acuity, brought about by means of sympathetic nervous system arousal, is elicited with lightning speed by situations that are seen as menacing to the organism's integrity.

The good news is that the body's resources are rapidly mobilized to meet the danger or to contain and control it as much as possible. However, the bad news is that there are many instances in which the emergency itself is over—and perhaps has been for many years—but the brain's survival alarm system hasn't been fully turned off. The threatening situation may be part of the long-ago past, but it feels as if it's free-floating in time, with you at every moment.

In the wake of overwhelming stress, which has never been fully metabolized and integrated, a person is likely to feel profoundly unsafe and to see dangers and difficulties lurking everywhere. Curiously enough, though, that same person is often credulous and unseeing when it comes to recognizing and identifying the realistic threats that do exist in his or her life. It's as if the noise level generated by the predominant warning system is so compelling and attention demanding that myriad smaller, yet utterly essential warnings are being drowned out.

Chapter Five

BEHAVIORAL REENACTMENTS: WAS CLAUDIA MARTINELLI IN AN EMOTIONALLY ABUSIVE RELATIONSHIP? WHAT _IS_ AN EMOTIONALLY ABUSIVE RELATIONSHIP?

So MANY TERMS IN DAILY USE ARE BANDIED ABOUT WITHout anyone being certain of their exact meaning, and the phrase _emotional abuse_ is surely prominent among them. For even though many people think they're quite clear about what is meant by this expression, if asked to define it precisely, they'll hesitate and their faces will turn blank.

Then, after a long pause, one person may characterize emotional abuse as verbal bullying: one partner constantly storming and shouting at the other, who then exists in a cowering state of fear. Someone else may define it as having to do with expressing dislike and icily ignoring or neglecting the other's needs and requests—an example that comes to mind is that of an interviewee of mine who had developed a breast lump, but whose husband never talked with her about what was happening or showed any interest or concern as she underwent the frightening process of diagnosis. Still another person may conceive of emotional abuse as an ongoing series of put-downs—one mate's continual undermining and devaluing of the other's intelligence, competence, and basic worth as a human being.

Actually, all of the above contain a piece of the truth, for "emotional abuse" covers a vast expanse of ambiguous and often elusive territory. A very broad definition of the term, suggested by expert Marti Tamm Loring, is that it is "an ongoing process in which one individual systematically diminishes and destroys the inner self of another. The essential ideas, feelings, perceptions, and personality characteristics of the victim are constantly belittled."

A core element of both emotionally and physically abusive relationships is that there is a power imbalance between a controlling tyrant and his or her oppressed partner; this was surely the case in Claudia Martinelli's marital relationship. In such instances, where the aggression is only on a psychological level, the partner under attack—typically, though not invariably, the female member of the pair—is often completely unaware that she's involved in an emotionally abusive relationship. This is because nonphysical violence leaves no black eyes, bruises, or broken arms and is often occurring at a subtle level in some quite innocent-appearing situations. An additional reason why the victim of abuse fails to recognize what's actually happening is that she is often someone who feels that whatever is going wrong is her own fault: Again, this was true of Claudia, who felt deeply responsible for her mate's behavior and as if she actually deserved it.

This assumption of blame feels natural to the abused partner, who has typically grown up in a situation where—owing to a child's magical sense of being at the center of the universe—she has taken on all the responsibility and blame for everything that is going wrong in her world. For such feelings of omnipotence, a normal aspect of early childhood, lead many a youngster to feel personally at fault for a parent's bad or frankly outrageous behavior, or even the adult couple's decision to divorce. Here, the child's thinking is, If only *I* were better, the *right* kind of person, my mother or father would be different, and this sweeping sense of guilt and failed responsibility has often been carried into adulthood.

The target of emotional abuse, therefore, is often someone who (despite the fact that she's being undermined, scorned, trivialized, and misunderstood in her most intimate relationship) has found herself living in a tense domestic atmosphere with which she is deeply *familiar*. For as author Loring and other workers in the field have noted, *there is a recurrent relationship between early trauma and psychologically abusive attachments later on in adulthood*.

This is because, in Loring's view, emotionally victimized women often remain oblivious to the fact of their abuse. "For them, emotional violence has become a way of life. As the experience of being emotionally mistreated often begins early in childhood, the victim cannot conceive that another, entirely different kind of relationship is possible. Yet although they have become accustomed to emotional violence, they never cease to feel its pain. Each new wound is as devastating as the preceding demeaning assault."

Clearly, the defining difference between physical and nonphysical abuse is that the victim of wife battering *knows* that someone is periodically attacking and hurting her—she has the bruises to prove it. The victim of psychological aggression, on the other hand, is often in a state of internal chaos, confusion, and uncertainty about what is, or is not, taking place. This is why it is so important for individuals of *both* sexes, who want to maintain healthy partnerships, to identify and familiarize themselves with the multiple forms in which this type of emotional violation can occur.

An extremely illuminating list of behaviors that fall under the rubric of emotional abuse—you might call it an early warning list, setting forth the most significant features of this form of interpersonal aggression—will be presented further along in this chapter. But first I'd like to talk about abusive attachments more generally—about why some people are drawn into these relationships and why they so frequently remain in them while their confidence and sense of security are slowly drained away.

Overt and Covert Abuse

As the poet Yehuda Amichai has written, "The past throws stones at the future / And all of them fall on the present." In the course of our second interview, Claudia Martinelli described a recent quarrel with her husband that had erupted like a geyser the previous Saturday night. It had gotten so out of hand that, as she put it, "I was ready to put on my sneakers and *run* for it. My gut feeling was just *that*—I'm out of here! I'm out! I don't have to be treated like this! It isn't *right*; I'm being abused!"

Still, by the time of our meeting, that particular argument had been settled and Claudia didn't appear to be taking the idea that she was "being abused" too seriously. Hers was, of course, a characteristic kind of reaction; the last thing that she or any other successful, seemingly independent woman ever wants to fully confront is the fact that she's become marooned in a devaluing, emotionally injurious relationship.

But although such situations can't be easily identified and tallied up in terms of incidence within the general population, most clinicians believe emotionally abusive attachments to be extremely pervasive. As psychologist Joan Lachkar points out in *The Many Faces of Abuse: Treating the Emotional Abuse of High-Functioning Women*, a surprisingly large number of individuals who (like Claudia) are competent, attractive, and successful players in the career marketplace—lawyers, executives, physicians, and the like—come home in the evenings to endlessly belittling, frustrating, ego-draining relationships with their intimate partners. And only slowly, if ever, do they come to recognize their close attachments as being "abusive" in any way, shape, or form.

There is simply huge inner resistance to doing so. For among the many other reasons for "not knowing" what is happening, there is the victim's effort to maintain some inner sense and outward image of her personal dignity. This is why it is only with the greatest of reluctant foot-dragging that a woman who has earned the respect of the world around her becomes willing to recognize that an unsavory word like "abuse" has anything to do with a process happening in her own life.

Moreover, there are many kinds of emotional aggression that are difficult to detect. *Overt* abuses (derisive put-downs, constant criticisms) are obviously easier to recognize, but there are a great number of *covert* forms of attack that are insidious, confusing, and extremely hard to discern clearly. For example, a seemingly loving, well-disposed partner may always be in "objective" agreement with anyone who states an opinion or position that is at variance with that of his mate: It is as if the game that he's playing is always on the side of the net that is opposite to his partner's, and she is being consistently invalidated and belittled.

Behavioral Reenactments

Claudia Martinelli was an adult, experienced woman at the time of her second marriage, not a starry-eyed, unformed teenager. So I couldn't help but speculate about whether the "stones of the past" had fallen into her present-day existence. Had she walked into—even helped to construct—an intimate relationship in which she would be periodically attacked and castigated; and had she done so because such experiences had become (in Loring's phrase) "a way of life" much earlier in her own personal history?

Claudia's track record through adulthood (at least what I knew of it thus far) surely did bespeak an individual who feels profoundly *bad* about herself; she'd been involved in so many self-damaging behaviors—drinking, drugging, emotionally uninvolved sex—that had left her feeling empty, degraded, and worthless. People who are filled with negative feelings about themselves will frequently "act out" in this way, do things that will make them feel ashamed and guilty, thereby confirming their ingrained views about their basic worthlessness and unacceptability.

As many trauma experts have observed, such people seem to be under the sway of strong internal forces to re-create, in their present-day relationships, certain core experiences of early life that once terrified and overwhelmed them. This reliving of certain problematic or downright menacing aspects of the past is known as a "behavioral reenactment"—which is to say, an unconscious drive to replay the devastating experience(s), either just as it, or they, occurred or in some slightly disguised version.

It was Sigmund Freud who first drew attention to this curious tendency and called it the "repetition compulsion." Freud was struck, as have been many subsequent clinicians, by the frequency with which people behaved as if they were under some curious pressure to stage reenactments of painful early dilemmas. It was, observed Freud, as if the individual's "way of remembering" the past was to restage the problem in the present—to keep getting into strangely repetitive revivals of traumas that had never become integrated, resolved, and part of a time that was *over*.

There are, not surprisingly, important sex differences when it comes to reenacting, in adult life, overwhelming stresses that were experienced during childhood. As psychiatrist Bessel van der Kolk observes, in an important article entitled "The Compulsion to Repeat the Trauma," a number of research studies indicate that "abused men and boys tend to identify with the aggressor and later victimize others whereas abused women are prone to become attached to abusive men and allow themselves and their offspring to be victimized further."

Efforts to Master and Resolve Unfinished Business

Most modern-day therapists view the tendency to stage reenactments of painful aspects of the past as driven by unconscious efforts at mastery—that is, the deeply cherished hope that by resurrecting the traumatic experience(s), one can try again to work it through and resolve it. This "unfinished business" kind of explanation certainly did strike me as one of the more plausible reasons why a woman like Claudia Martinelli—highly attractive, successful—would have walked into a marriage with so critical and ferociously blaming a partner, someone whom she dared not be honest with because she was sure any efforts at openness on her part would be greeted with contempt and rejection on his.

In any case, it was reflections such as these that made me wonder whether Claudia's parents—whom she'd dryly dubbed "the Bickersons" because they quarreled all the time—had done more than merely bicker. Had there been more serious physical or emotional aggression in her home, aggression that was currently being resurrected and relived in her relationship to Paul? If Claudia was in fact involved in a behavioral reenactment—one that might have to do with a hypocritical, hostile, tyrannical man and a devalued, invalidated woman—then it was clear that her irate, verbally abusive mate was in some ways the perfect partner in a script that felt all too familiar.

Traumatic Bonding: Why She Stays

Why would anyone stay in an intimate relationship where one partner—the powerful one—is periodically trivializing, deriding, harassing, threatening, intimidating, or even physically attacking his disempowered mate? One important factor in such situations is a phenomenon psychologists have termed "traumatic bonding." Traumatically bonded relationships are characterized by what is known as "intermittent reinforcement"—in plain words, alternating intervals of reward (lovingness and warmth) and punishment (psychological or physical abuse).

It has been well established that relationships of this kind—that is, those that fluctuate between outbursts of aggression and times of loving tenderness—create emotional attachments that are far *stronger* than attachments that proceed on a steadier, more even keel. The paradoxical truth is that this mode of inconsistent, unpredictable relating creates a gluelike connection between the oppressor and his oppressed, always apprehensive partner. This is why, as painful and damaging as these fear-ridden relationships may be, they are extremely hard to sever.

Why should this be so? According to Dr. Janet Geller, who works with couples in emotionally and physically abusive relationships, most individuals living with an assaultive partner can recall an earlier time when the relationship felt safe and secure and the mate's behavior was far more caring and affectionate. "Things were *good* at one time," Geller told me, "and maybe they still *are* good from time to time, especially in the wake of an outburst, when the partners are in the making-up phase. So the abused person in this situation hangs in, waiting for the rewarding part; she's always trying to get the relationship back to the way it was in the beginning. This makes it very hard for her to extricate herself."

In addition, the fact that the submissive partner's efforts *are* thus rewarded from time to time provides her with even more of an incentive to stay. For what learning theorists call an "intermittent reinforcement schedule" of this kind serves to keep the victim in a state of anxious anticipation. She is always holding fast to the hope that she will get it *right* eventually—that whatever she does that keeps making him turn surly and aggressive will be clarified and worked out, and the relationship will proceed much more smoothly in the future.

Her dilemma is that, being human, her natural impulse is to run for comfort to the person closest to her—her partner—when she is feeling endangered. But this dilemma is complicated by the fact that she is in need of comfort and soothing from the very person who is *causing* the fear and trepidation that she's feeling. Furthermore, in the course of the couple's ongoing interaction, he is becoming ever more empowered as she becomes more and more unsure about who she is as a person. Over time, the abuse she's been absorbing has inevitably begun to affect her sense of her adequacy, self-worth, and basic lovability, while her psychological dependence upon her domineering, controlling mate's acceptance and approval has continued to increase.

This unstable, confusing state of affairs is rendered ever more bewildering by those periodic glimpses of the *good* parts of the relationship—the way things were at the beginning and the way she thought they would always remain. This periodic positive reinforcement serves to keep her hopes alive, and during those times when things are going well, she will often indulge in the fantasy that their problems have been settled and the rewarding parts of the attachment are here to stay. This fond belief is especially bolstered by his changed behavior during the couple's making-up phases, for at these times he may show some remorse and be far more understanding, friendly, and affectionate. He is on his best behavior, and this calms her down; she experiences a huge, if temporary, sense of relief.

This sense of relief is not only mental; it exists at a *physical* level as well, for her bodily reaction to the partner's attack has been to switch into an instantaneous readiness (fight, flight, or freeze) to meet the threat that confronts her. Thus, whether or not she recognizes the mate's aggression for what it is—that is, whether it is overt and blatant, or covert and subtly demeaning—the victim's *internal being* is in a highly agitated state of heightened arousal. Indeed, some experts believe that the reason traumatic bonds are far stronger and more difficult to sever than are healthier bonds is that they are forged in an atmosphere of such high intensity—an atmosphere in which deep-seated bodily fears and alarms alternate with the release of disagreeable mental and physical tension during times of relative tranquillity.

The traumatic bonds that are formed in emotionally and physically abusive relationships are, it should be said, not dissimilar from other strong emotional attachments formed between a periodically attacking, dominant person and someone who perceives him- or herself to be hopelessly subjugated. The famous Stockholm syndrome was one such instance, in which, during the course of their captivity, some female flight personnel fell in love with the terrorists who had taken them hostage. Other such intermittently terrifying/loving relationships that one might think of are those that can spring up between master and slave or between the maltreated child and his or her tyrannizing parent. In this regard, it is well known that children who have been abused by hostile or severely neglectful caretakers still love their parents passionately and resist being made to leave their homes.

Recognizing Psychological Abuse

What are the specific behaviors that *constitute* emotional abuse? One of the most illuminating answers to this question, at least in my opinion, is that provided by a Boston-based human rights organization called Peace at Home, Inc. In the comprehensive Warning List that this group has drawn up, a particular cluster of behaviors is identified as abusive—behaviors seen in situations where ongoing psychological assaults on the mate, but not necessarily any physical attacks, are taking place.

Again, it should be emphasized that in the majority of cases the victim has no conscious knowledge that anything "abusive" is actually happening; far more often she is blaming herself and her own failings for the fact that the relationship feels so flawed and ungratifying. For, over time, the abuser's sense of his own legitimate power, control, and essential "rightness" has continued to expand, while his partner's sense of her self-esteem and competence has undergone a process of attrition. She may be feeling bad, lost, guilty, isolated, and despairing; she may be suffering from fierce headaches, painful stomach troubles, a sense of constant tension, heart palpitations, fatigue, or back or neck problems; but all too rarely will she make the connection between her mental and bodily state of being and anything so alien sounding as "emotional maltreatment."

The Peace at Home, Inc., Warning List*

1. *Destructive Criticism/Verbal Abuse:* Name-calling; mocking; accusing; blaming; swearing; making humiliating remarks or gestures.

---

* The list may be subject to future fine-tuning, but I consider it an excellent overview of what is meant when we talk about emotionally abusive behavior.

2. *Abusing Authority:* Always claiming to be right (insisting statements are "the truth"); telling you what to do; making big decisions without consultation; using "logic."

3. *Disrespect:* Interrupting; changing topics; not listening or responding; twisting your words; putting you down in front of other people; saying bad things about your friends and family.

4. *Abusing Trust:* Lying; withholding information; cheating on you; being overly jealous.

5. *Emotional Withholding:* Not expressing feelings; not giving support, attention, or compliments; not respecting feelings, rights, or opinions.

6. *Breaking Promises:* Not following through on agreements; not taking a fair share of responsibility; refusing to help with child care and housework.

7. *Minimizing, Denying, and Blaming:* Making light of disturbing behavior and not taking your concerns about it seriously; saying the abuse didn't happen; shifting responsibility for abusive behavior; saying you caused it.

8. *Pressure Tactics:* Rushing you to make decisions through "guilt tripping"; sulking; threatening to withhold money; manipulating the children; telling you what you must do.

9. *Intimidation:* Making angry or threatening gestures; use of physical size to intimidate; standing in doorway during arguments (as if to block the way out); outshouting you; driving recklessly (to scare the partner, even put her in fear for her life).

10. *Destruction:* Destroying your possessions (such as furniture); throwing and/or breaking things.

11. *Threats:* Making threats to hurt you or others.

Friendly Advice and Constructive Criticisms

The most clear-cut distinction between emotional violence and abuse of a physical nature is that an attack on someone's body is a tangible *event*—one that's likely to leave evidence, in the form of bruises and scars. Psychological mistreatment, on the other hand, usually involves an indirect, far more bewildering kind of process: Disgusted looks, muttered insults, and mocking jokes about a person's adequacy, intelligence, appearance, integrity, or moral value leave no injuries that can be seen or photographed, and to my knowledge no one has ever called 911 because a partner was assaulting her sense of self-worth.

Furthermore, hurtful and invidious comments are frequently couched in the wrappings of "friendly advice" offered by a concerned and well-meaning partner. As one female attorney, now separated from her husband, said to me, "Nothing I did was ever *right*; I was always off the mark, somehow. I can't tell you how many times, after we'd been out for an evening, my husband had some 'constructive criticisms' to offer.

"Maybe it was about something I'd worn that night, or about some 'ridiculously naive' remark that I'd made. Maybe I'd just been talking too much, or too loudly, or on the other hand looking spacey, seeming zoned out. . . . *Or* my laughter was so shrill, and you could hear me all the way across the room! God, that man could just slice me right down the middle! And I'll have to admit it, he was *good*, it was like radar! He had a way of being 'helpful' that could lock right on to my worst insecurities."

If, in this instance, the partner tries to defend herself and resists the emotional abuser's condescending judgments, an epic confrontation may ensue. Or if she is silent and just "takes it"—even accepts his denigrating comments as the impartial truth—her sense of selfhood will undergo a process of steady erosion. She will feel more and more defined by his negative appraisals and confused about who she really is, while he will emerge as the ever stronger, more powerful member of the pair. The abusive partner sups grandly on his mate's feelings of self-esteem, competence, and dignity in order to augment his own uncertain sense of efficacy, mastery, and control.

Shocks and Ambushes

While some interpersonal attacks are relatively explicit—that is, above the waterline of the victim's awareness—there are, as mentioned earlier, a variety of subtler forms of psychological aggression. One such tactic is that of habitually disparaging the partner's views, beliefs, ideas, and opinions.

A fine example of this undermining ploy was told to me by an editorial assistant in her late twenties, Carole, who said that almost *any* expression of her own independent point of view was likely to elicit dryly invalidating statements from her lover, such as "You can't possibly *think* that," or "You know nothing about the subject," or simply "That's completely *mistaken*."

If her partner spoke to her in this way when the two were in a social situation, which *did* happen from time to time, everyone present seemed to stop listening to anything else that she had to say. It was as if they'd taken their cue from him—she was a birdbrain, who had no idea what she was talking about—and after that, they ignored her. But instead of blaming her lover, who was a divorced senior executive within her firm, Carole absorbed the blame herself. She internalized his derogatory estimates of her; and came to believe that she was ill informed, not sufficiently quick-witted, and by no means up to his high intellectual standards. She often came home from such evenings out feeling thoroughly discredited, humbled, and in a numbed state of disbelief.

What seemed most peculiar to her, in retrospect, was the fact that each time her partner demeaned her publicly in this way, she'd felt as shocked and ambushed as if it hadn't ever happened earlier. This kind of bewildered, incredulous reaction to an abuser's sudden onslaughts isn't at all unusual. For as author Joan Lachkar has written, "The intimate partner who is abusive is the same one who provides hope, love, caring, validation, and intimacy." What could be more impossible, more unreal and confusing, than this sort of open derision and disrespect emerging in what is supposedly a trusting, nurturing relationship?

It is quite understandable that in such cases the wish to preserve the loving parts of the bond (and, often, to gain a sense of mastery over a depriving past) renders the victim resistant to recognizing the mate's cruelty for what it is in the here and now. And as a result, she often begins to inhabit a dual reality. In one small corner of her mind she *does* know what is really going on; but on a more global level, she remains unaware. She cannot confront the painful knowledge face-on and develops a kind of self-protective obliviousness. This involves making light of each hurtful incident, viewing it as an aberrant, exceptional occurrence in an otherwise caring, committed relationship.

Still, this sort of personal betrayal often *feels* nothing short of cata-strophic, and over time, it can lead to those omnipresent feelings of terror, insecurity, and dread (When will the next assault come?) that are ordinar-ily associated with post-traumatic stress. The emotionally abused individ-ual's reactions may then materialize in the form of extreme hyperarousal, bodily tension, hypervigilance, and generalized anxiety. Alternatively, the person may respond by shutting down emotionally, which is the body's other typical reaction to shocking, dismaying experiences. This kind of response involves numbing and constriction, inactivity, self-blame, an aching self, and a stark, boundless sense of deadness and helplessness.

Nevertheless, despite the fact that both her body and mind are being profoundly affected, the clear link between the state of the victim's rela-tionship and the state of her mental and physical being is likely to remain unnoticed. There are so many ways in which she depends upon her mate and values the *good* parts of the attachment—those times of warmth and closeness—that she simply cannot allow her thoughts to go to certain places. Over time, her judgment becomes more clouded, and she is less and less sure that she is thinking correctly.

Her body may be sending her messages about her misery—in the form of ongoing agitation and hyperarousal or in the guise of a "numbed out" sense of paralysis—but at the level of awareness, she is deeply committed to *not* comprehending them.

Intimate Sabotage

The myriad ways in which a psychologically abusive mate can sabotage his partner's confidence and self-respect can't be definitively cataloged, but I'll describe a few more of the well-documented maneuvers here. He can, for starters, simply ignore or override the majority of her requests, needs, and wishes by behaving as if her input is irrelevant and, in any event, not nearly as important as his. He can behave as if she's the last per-son on his mind, and certainly no one with any power or rights that need to be respected.

Or he can make slyly invidious, undermining comments, then resist taking responsibility for them by either denying or contradicting what he just said; he can at times "not remember" having made any such comments, even if he made them thirty seconds earlier! Then again, he can deftly switch the topic of a discussion that's not going his way and do it so adroitly that she hardly realizes what's happening at the time. She may not even realize it afterward—all she knows is that she's feeling disoriented, stranded, and bewildered. This tactic is somewhat similar to a basketball play, for the attachment abuser has suddenly grabbed the conversational ball and dribbled it swiftly to the other end of the court.

On the other hand—staying with the basketball metaphor—the abusive partner can simply *drop* the conversational ball unceremoniously by not even troubling himself to answer when she addresses him. This is a passively aggressive way of saying, "I don't think what you said merits any feedback, so I'll just make that remark go away." If, then, she tries to confront him about his subversive nonresponsiveness, the partner may fob her off with further double-talk, such as "Oh, I didn't quite hear what you were was saying" or "I didn't understand what you were talking about." She is then left to wonder what happened, why he'd simply dismissed the matter so unceremoniously. Why didn't he question her further if he didn't hear or understand what she'd been trying to tell him?

Still another disconcerting conversational gambit that crops up in emotionally abusive relationships is a highly confusing kind of patter that might justly be called "fuddle speak." This is basically a meaning-mashing kind of blather that decimates all coherence and scuttles any chance the pair might have of focusing upon a real issue or misunderstanding. Fuddle speak is just plain goofy talk, a mode of interacting with the partner in ways that are intended to mislead and disorient her.

For example, an interviewee of mine, Carla, told me that she and her husband had attended a revival of a Broadway musical being staged at a country playhouse. During the intermission, the pair turned to each other and agreed that they were disappointed; it was a poor performance, which neither one of them was enjoying at all. Carla then went to the women's room and stood in line for so long that when she came out her husband was already reseated. He then turned to her and said enthusiastically, "Isn't this a *wonderful* treat?"

She was startled and asked him what had happened during the intermission that could possibly have changed his mind. He insisted that he hadn't changed his mind at all; he'd been enjoying the show all along.

"Then why did you say otherwise?" she demanded. He in turn reacted indignantly and asked her what *her* problem was and why she was trying to start a quarrel. She could not calm down throughout the rest of the show, and the couple got into a furious, thoroughly incoherent argument as they drove home.

What had caused his strange turnabout? When I asked her, Carla said she could think of no explanation. She did recall that during the intermission he had chatted with two senior partners from his architectural firm; they and their wives were enjoying the presentation enormously. One hypothesis she had was that *their* judgment had overridden his own, and he hadn't wanted to admit it, even to himself—it would make him seem too much like a wimp, someone without a mind of his own. So he'd insisted on pretending that he'd been pleased with the performance from the outset, then been provoked when she hadn't been pliantly accepting and simply gone along.

This was, Carla hastened to add, her guess, but not a certainty. In any event, this kind of incident, which occurred from time to time, left her feeling as if the very earth were moving beneath her. Fuddle speak does do that: It serves to shift the solid ground of rational thought right out from under its hapless victim, leaving her in a tension-filled state of uncertainty and hyperarousal. She is trying to maintain a relationship in an interpersonal realm permeated by absurdity and shifting understandings—one in which real engagement and rapport are being avoided as the oppressing partner maintains his strict control over "what is real" and what has actually occurred.

Anxious and agitated, his bewildered victim flip-flops from one possible "reasonable explanation" of what's really going on to the next one. *Her* struggle is not only with the emotional abuse she is absorbing—which she's typically highly reluctant to recognize for what it is—but with a lack of any outside validation that her own perceptions, thoughts, and feelings are actually the result of genuine provocations. It is only her internal, physiological state—what is happening inside her body—that accurately reflects the true nature of her situation, for so often the body knows what the person herself, intent upon preserving the intimate relationship, is steadfastly refusing to realize.

And in Carla's case, an important piece of personal history had sent her body's emergency alarm system into a state of high alert, for she happened to be the daughter of a binge-drinking father, whose occasionally irrational behavior had terrified her as a child. "As we were driving home from that night, the weather was stifling, and my chest felt so tight; I was even having trouble breathing," she told me. "I was holding a flashlight on the map, and my hand was shaking so hard that I couldn't read it."

As trauma expert Bessel van der Kolk has observed, both *internal* experiences, such as particular states of feeling, and *external* events that are reminiscent of earlier trauma can trigger a return to a sense of being in the original overwhelming situation. For Carla, a fear-ridden past and an alarming present had converged; she'd found herself striving desperately to make sense of a loved and needed male's inexplicable, illogical behavior. And while she herself, at a conscious level, was unaware of the scope of what had happened, she'd been unable to calm herself down for some days afterward, for her body *was* remembering and was keeping the score.

Cutting Off

Perhaps the most wrenching of all abusive tactics is the dominant mate's steely withdrawal and communicational shutdown when he is registering his disapproval or simply in a bad mood about matters in his own life that have nothing at all to do with her. So much of the subjugated partner's selfhood is being abraded over time that this sudden cutoff is terrifying and leaves her feeling beached, forsaken, unsure about whether or not she'll be able to survive on her own emotional supplies. So frightening does she find this minidesertion that it invariably serves to bolster *his* sense of ascendancy and leaves her in a state of fear and abject confusion.

Because she has become so psychologically dependent upon him for whatever degree of approval and validation she receives, she cannot gain enough distance from the relationship to think independently and validate herself. Thus she finds the threat of emotional abandonment so upsetting that she cannot focus on the real truth, in terms of what's going on in their lives together. What was it that *did* trigger that most recent, intense two-day argument? She's unable to piece together who said what to whom, and when and how the whole thing got started. Is her partner arrogantly deriding and discounting her feelings and perceptions, or is she herself overresponding?

Inevitably, as time passes, the subordinate partner surrenders more and more of her unique personhood—*who she was before becoming involved in this relationship*. And as she does so, the intimacy abuser encroaches ever further as the owner and interpreter of her subjective experience. It is he who, in the role of the superior, knowledgeable partner, lets her know *what is real and what actually matter*s. His interpretations, however, are always framed (whether consciously or unconsciously) in ways that will fortify his own sense of superiority and advantage. Her internal world has become occupied territory—occupied by him and by his self-promoting views about the sort of person each of them is.

The Knower of Truth

One striking instance of the kind of situation in which the dominant partner makes himself the infallible "knower of the truth"—the supreme judge of what is true and real—was recounted to me by Anna Jellinek, a graphic arts designer in her early forties. Some five years earlier, the Jellineks had hired a Norwegian exchange student to come in every afternoon and help out with the family chores.

"At first, we thought the whole arrangement was delightful," Anna told me in the course of an interview. "This young woman, whose name was Karin, was in the grad school at Columbia, where my husband, David, teaches. She watched the kids two days a week while I went to the office, and she also cooked the family dinner on those evenings. As it happened, she was an exceptional cook; and the twins, who were three years old at the time, just *loved* her. It was great, it couldn't have been more perfect!"

After a while, though, certain small items started disappearing. They were inconsequential things, most of which belonged to Anna—a special hairbrush, a blue silk blouse, a pair of brown suede boots she hadn't worn for a while. It was certainly possible that the brush and the boots had been misplaced and that the shirt had disappeared at the cleaners. Nevertheless she began feeling mildly alarmed—"You could say my yellow light was on," she told me—and she talked with David about what was happening.

In *his* view, Anna was imagining things, and he dismissed his wife's suspicions out of hand. David even seemed to view her misgivings as personally offensive; he couldn't understand how she could *entertain* such ugly, unfounded ideas! As he saw it, Anna's apprehensions had an overly suspicious flavor, for she'd probably misplaced those unimportant items herself. Moreover, he thought his wife was curiously ready to pick on the au pair for reasons that weren't completely clear to him—in any case, what did a hairbrush, a blouse, and some worn boots *matter*? These comments were not made to Anna as if they were merely her husband's opinions; they were made to her as declarations about reality itself.

He was sure that the friendly, capable, good-natured Karin couldn't possibly be a thief, and he surely hoped Anna wasn't going to make unfounded accusations and upset what was obviously a splendid arrangement. "David managed, somehow, to enforce a code of silence around the whole issue," she told me, her eyes widening like an animal's caught in the headlights.

Throughout the following months this series of petty thefts had continued, but her husband continued to make light of this as a real problem. "It got to the point where I could feel my stomach lurch every time I opened a bureau drawer. Sometimes I'd know that something was different—*gone*—but I couldn't figure out what it was. . . . One of my silk scarves? It could even be my underwear! The pile would look a little lower, but of course I didn't have the whole inventory in my head."

She inhaled deeply, let the breath out, then said, "It was never anything *valuable*. No jewelry—nothing that wouldn't have sounded ridiculous if I'd ever gotten up the nerve to confront her! It started making me feel like a—I don't know—a nutcase. And the worst of it was the way David would roll his eyes and look pissed off every time I tried to talk about what was happening. He was acting as if *I* were the crazy one, as if *I* were the one making trouble!"

It was his certainty that had made her doubt herself. An expression of chagrin crossed Anna's face, and she said in a voice of apology, "I know this all sounds absurd, but I was really suffering. It was *painful*."

I nodded my understanding, for this sounded like a prime example of "gaslighting"—a term now in clinical use but derived from the classic film *Gaslight*. The film is about a woman whose perceptions of reality are being systematically invalidated by her seemingly devoted mate. For example, the husband hides his wife's possessions and then convinces her that she's misplaced them herself. He takes a cherished painting off the wall and then insists that it was *she* who removed it. His efforts are methodically destroying the heroine's trust in her experience of reality, and at the climax of the drama there's a moment when she's certain that she's going insane.

In the movie, in the service of her love for her new spouse, this wife is losing faith in herself, her own thoughts, senses, memory, and judgment —slowly coming to agree with him and their housekeeper, who is colluding with him, when they keep insisting, "You didn't *have* that experience. You don't really know what you believe you know. Nothing ever did happen, or *is* happening, in the ways that you think." This nullification of a person's basic experiences constitutes a major assault upon the self, an undermining of her very sense of inhabiting a world that is safe and predictable.

I suppose it was these reflections on "gaslighting" that made me wonder why, in this instance, Anna's husband had taken such a decisive stance against her. Why had he landed on the side of the issue that was so antithetical to *her* interests and her fundamental sense of security and comfort in their own home? Had it been because he couldn't bear to think that the young and cheerful Karin was robbing them, which would have been a betrayal not only of his wife, but of him and the entire family?

When I questioned Anna about this—not directly, but in a roundabout manner—her only reply was a brief shrug. Then, after a prolonged silence, she gave me an approximation of an answer. In a hushed, almost guilty-sounding tone of voice, she admitted that even now—years after Karin's ultimate dismissal—she found it hard to focus upon the question of David's unfeeling behavior.

Why had he downplayed and even derided her legitimate anxieties over such an extended period of time? Had he simply not wanted to be hassled by any issues that might lead to an outright confrontation? David was not an assertive person and would typically do anything to avoid a conflict, even in situations where conflict could legitimately have been called for. Also, when she'd first come to them, the au pair's enthusiastic employment reference had been from a departmental colleague at Columbia whom David valued greatly and with whom he was on close and friendly terms.

All in all, Karin had been with the Jellineks over two years, during which Anna's husband had insisted that he *knew what was true*; it was Anna herself who was confused and mistaken. He'd been so sure there was no real problem—that amid the hurly-burly of their hectic work and family lives, Anna was routinely misplacing things, then entertaining suspicions about poor Karin.

Eventually, however, their young helper's petty thieveries began to escalate—she almost seemed to want to be caught. It slowly became clear to *both* members of the couple that she was in fact stealing things and had been doing so all along. But for the sake of the kids, the parents decided not to confront Karin openly; instead, they let go of her quietly, and the entire sorry episode had ended there, with very little discussion of what had happened.

Nevertheless, even now—it was some five years later that Anna recounted these events to me—there was a look of alarm on her face as she talked about this phase of her life. She was still unable to think back upon that time without being assailed by memories of her utter helplessness and a sense of mortification about the way she'd let herself be victimized by this form of intimate treason.

These days, she and David never referred to the matter—it had migrated into the area of the taboo—but the whole experience was one that had never been resolved in her own mind. Why had he, her life's partner, summarily rejected—even refused to consider—her own version of what was happening? Why had he opted so confidently for the model of reality that left *him* feeling most at ease and untroubled—even though it meant leaving *her* hanging out to dry?

By completely denying (to himself as well as to her) that anything untoward was actually occurring in their home, he'd managed to avoid the kind of open hostility that she knew he feared and deplored. But in so doing, he'd made himself remarkably impervious to *her* suffering, *her* mystification, the constant state of agitation—both psychological and in her body—that she'd experienced throughout. She still couldn't comprehend that, at least not completely. Why had he taken her well-being so lightly?

And why, I wondered, had she been so excessively dependent on her husband's approval that she hadn't defended herself and simply given the au pair her walking papers early on? Anna had behaved as if remaining in lockstep agreement with her unempathetic, unconcerned spouse—which meant accepting *his* version of the truth—was far more important to her than was her own sense of herself as a rational, sane human being.

Symptoms as Witnesses

In retrospect, would Anna Jellinek have labeled her husband's behavior as "emotionally abusive"? I didn't think so. Would she view the long, painful episode with Karin, and her own frozen, paralyzed reaction to it, as having anything to do with trauma, past or present? I doubted it. For even though abuse of this kind can produce a variety of post-traumatic stress symptoms, it is, as mentioned earlier, both difficult to identify and something that the victim is usually loath to recognize clearly.

Many individuals would rather endure real psychic suffering—feel "crazy" and suffused with tension as Anna had, over such a long period of time—than recognize the source of their suffering as problems emanating from a vitally important and needed other, in an intimate relationship. This is why the psychological assaults a person may be experiencing will often find expression in one or more of an array of seemingly unrelated bodily and/or psychological symptoms.

The Body Speaks: Physical and Psychological Symptoms of Abusive Situations

What sorts of symptoms are prone to emerge in these abusive situations? The list of unpleasant possibilities is a long one. At a predominantly mental and behavioral level, the problems may include chronic anxiety, agitation, social withdrawal, feelings of emptiness, persistent melancholy, reveries about suicide, emotional numbness, persistent nightmares, and a sense that the world and the self are not actually real (in technical language, "derealization").

At a purely *physical* level, the target of abuse may manifest such symptoms as chronic headaches, stomach distress, life-draining fatigue, nausea, insomnia, dizziness, chest pain, muscular aches and joint pains, heartburn, and palpitations. Problems of this sort are often perceived and treated as strictly *medical* difficulties, and in some instances that may be what they are. But there are also many situations in which a person's bodily symptoms are actually a garbled SOS in need of translation. The body is bearing physical witness—in disguised form, but still the only witness that exists—to the battering of soul and spirit that's going on in an intimate relationship.

Nasty Quarrels Versus Emotional Abuse

Let me call a "time-out" at this juncture, for a vitally important caveat is in order here. We all know it to be true that many loving, caring, ordinarily supportive partners will sometimes treat each other in ways that are invalidating, unfeeling, unfairly critical, or otherwise "emotionally abusive." It's also true that most couples will become involved in an occasional nasty confrontation, during which regrettable, below-the-belt insults may be flung about.

Still, in the main, these partners feel reliably connected to and nourished, truly seen, and intimately known by the trusted and trustworthy other. They can be open about their most personal (even shameful and embarrassing) thoughts and feelings without fear of rejection, mockery, or misunderstanding. They are able to grasp and to respect the real differences that exist between them—to understand, accept, and even *cherish* the fact that their individual beliefs, preferences, and ways of looking at life are not always going to be in sync and may at times diverge radically.

Ultimately, however, these mates care about who the partner really *is* and how he or she really thinks and feels. They're not trying to impose upon each other their unique agendas about how the other *should think* or *should feel*. Moreover, the members of these couples are far less interested in vying with each other for power and control than they are in achieving a sense of "what's right," of fairness and mutual gratification.

Clearly, relationships of this sort are fundamentally different from those of mates who are involved in ongoing virulent struggles. In abusive kinds of attachments, the dominant mate is engaged in grinding down his partner's sense of selfhood, in order to maintain the illusion that he himself is independent, strong, and self-sufficient. In actuality, though, it's been well established that abusive males are anything *but* the above. A good deal of research with men who mistreat their partners has demonstrated very consistently that abusers are narcissistically vulnerable individuals who are struggling with acute feelings of weakness and dependency.

The term *narcissistic vulnerability*, clinically speaking, is a shorthand way of referring to people who have fundamental problems when it comes to maintaining a good internal image of themselves. Men who abuse harbor profoundly negative images of themselves—as inept, uncertain, unmasculine—and are operating not from a source of inner strength, but from a fear of further harm to their already damaged, brittle egos.

This kind of domineering, controlling partner relies very strongly on the primitive psychological defense mechanisms of *denial* and *projection*. That is, he has an unconscious but overriding need to *deny* all the weakness, ineptness, insecurity, and vulnerability that exist within himself, and he *projects* these intolerable aspects of his inner world onto someone close to him. That "close other" may be a child, or a boss, or some other person with whom he shares an intense relationship; but most frequently, the recipient of his projections will be she who is closest to him of all—that is, the intimate partner. He projects onto her, then perceives as *existing within her* all of the unacceptable attributes that he has so stoutly disowned as anything that is part of his own inner being.

Partner Abusers: Getting Rid of the Bad Stuff

By thus emptying himself of his own pervasive feelings of powerlessness and deficiency, the partner abuser can locate all of the shortcomings, faults, and failings as existing within the hopelessly defective mate. In other words, his way of dealing with his suppressed self-loathing is to project his intolerable feelings and thoughts about himself onto his unwitting partner, who is then disdained and criticized. He shields himself from his own ongoing stream of self-directed invective by externalizing the bad stuff; and he sees in her, and mercilessly attacks in her, those flaws and inadequacies that he cannot "own" and take responsibility for as existing inside himself.

Then he either denounces her for her failings or behaves in taunting ways that will inflame her into striking out at him. Whichever way the particular scenario plays itself out, though, she has been co-opted into holding *for him*, and is carrying *for him*, those aspects of his own inner world that he finds to be unbearable. The emotional abuser's partner thus serves as the psychic "container" for his most disavowed, unacceptable, self-hating thoughts and feelings.

For example, Paul's own "bad sexuality" was being denounced *in Claudia*, who was carrying all the guilt and blame in the relationship; by mutual, if unconscious, consent, *she* was being seen as the wanton, immoral member of the pair. Nevertheless, Paul's fulminating rage on the subject of abortion did make me wonder if someone in his own wild, boisterous past had actually *had* an abortion—one that was carried out at his behest.

According to psychologist David Curran, pathologically dominant, abusive, and controlling men are those who feel deeply unsure about whether they're good enough, strong enough, forceful enough, self-sufficient enough, independent enough—whether they are *real men*, in other words. These individuals are profoundly rejecting of their own gentler, more "feminine" feelings; they cannot, therefore, provide compassion, support, or empathy to their female partners.

The domineering male, writes Curran, "is unlikely to possess a capacity for honest introspection, self-appraisal or objectivity. His internal emotional life is incomprehensible to him. He will have minimal capacity for insight into and understanding of the internal feelings and thoughts of his female mate. He is uncomfortable with emotions and cannot identify any of them except anger."

While the external trappings of this person's existence may make him *appear* to be confident, self-assured, and in charge of his life, the abuser lives with a gnawing sense of his own inferiority and a fluctuating, sometimes wildly rocking, estimate of his own significance and status. Furthermore, because he feels so incomplete and basically unlovable, this kind of person fears that a highly confident mate, whose own sense of self-affirmation was intact, would be unlikely to hang around him for very long.

It is, therefore, in the interests of his own security that he needs to weaken her and to assume a watchful control over his partner—to intimidate her, chip away at her sense of self-worth, and curtail her capacity for independent thinking, living, being. In order for him to feel completely safe—and certain that she will stay—he must make sure that she is somewhat debilitated and helpless; and in fact, his episodic emotional assaults do keep her feeling fragmented, devitalized, dependent, unsure about what is really happening, and deeply unsure of herself.

The Three-Stage Cycle of Physical Violence

We all know that the physically bruising "sticks and stones" of partner violence do break real bones and sometimes cause serious injuries; nobody is disputing the fact that the batterer's blows can have a devastating impact upon his victim's entire existence. Still, many experts in the field of partner abuse have told me that assaults of a strictly verbal and emotional nature can have even more damaging, long-lasting effects.

Why should this be so? One hypothesis is that verbal assaults are much more unpredictable—they can blow up at any moment—while physical abuse usually follows a clearly recognizable, patterned course: This is the three-stage "cycle of violence" first outlined by researcher Lenore Walker in her celebrated book *The Battered Woman*.

According to Walker, stage 1 of a physically violent episode is characterized by a slow accretion of tension and resentment in the dominant member of the couple (statistically, the likelihood that this will be the male is about 95 percent). The attachment abuser's simmering bad feelings amplify until there comes a moment at which they can no longer be contained. Then there is a precipitant of some sort, one that may appear to be remarkably trivial—the mate delivers a snappy comeback or serves an overcooked steak, and he feels she is deliberately provoking him, willfully refusing to meet his needs (which may include reading his mind). This minor incident lights a fuse in the already tense domestic atmosphere, which then explodes into a chaotic, out-of-control, enraged attack upon the insufficiently "respectful," subservient mate.

This is stage 2 of the cycle of violence, and it can involve the indiscriminate punching, shoving, beating, choking, or sexual overpowering of a person who is typically much smaller in stature than is the batterer himself. Finally, when the abuser's fury is spent and he himself is exhausted (stage 3), he "comes to his senses." At this point, the cycle of violence has run its course and a period known as "the honeymoon" ensues.

Now, the intimacy abuser is filled with remorse, regret, and repentance. During this phase, he courts his injured partner, often bombards her with gifts, flowers, profuse apologies, and heartfelt promises that it will never, never happen again—and indeed, in the aftermath of the explosion, the domestic atmosphere may remain calm for a period of time.

Blaming the Mirror for What It Reflects

How long does it take to go through one full sequence of the cycle of violence, and how long does the ensuing "honeymoon" phase of relative peace and tranquillity persist? The answer is that it can be very different for different couples. Each pair seems to have their own time frame, and a single progression can take place over a period of days, weeks, months, or even years. Where partner battering is concerned, however, it's been well documented that over time, as the relationship continues, the severity of the abuse escalates and the honeymooning, "makeup" phase diminishes or disappears completely.

Much less is known about the typical course of events in abusive situations where *no* physical attacks occur, for emotional abuse is not a well-studied area. But experts in the field have told me that women who've experienced *both* kinds of assault will often state unequivocally that it's the incidents of emotional abuse that hurt the most and take the longest to heal.

Why should this be so? Some people believe it is because nonphysical abuse occurs so much more erratically than physical violence and doesn't follow the same fairly predictable "one, two, three, and it's over" sequence. On the basis of my own interviews, however, I'm not sure I'd agree: A number of my interviewees *have* in fact described an emotionally abusive sequence that closely resembles Walker's three-stage cycle of physical violence.

There is the same initial episode of pressure building, during which the dominant partner becomes ever more controlling, thin-skinned, and oppressive. For any of a variety of reasons, he is experiencing great tension.

His state of agitation could be due to some external rebuff, perhaps something that happened at the office; he could, on the other hand, be experiencing an upsurge of self-directed criticisms, about which she knows nothing whatsoever—and of which he himself may be oblivious, at the level of conscious awareness.

In any case, though, he is building up a head of steam, and the partners are heading for an emotional explosion—which again, when it erupts, will often be triggered by something remarkably unimportant. When it does erupt, the angry clash will not be initiated by real conflicts within the couple's relationship; the drama being enacted with the mate will have far more to do with the abusive spouse's own internal state. *His* basic predicament is that while he is filled with self-directed negativity and noxious sensations, no intelligible, coherent thoughts are attached to them. He is full of subliminal self-condemnation, which he's not only out of contact with but is unequipped to handle.

For he is a person who hasn't ever developed the capacity for focusing upon his own issues, getting them out on the table, and—with the help of his partner—perhaps succeeding in putting them to rest. In emotionally abusive situations, this healthier, more efficient way of being in a relationship simply doesn't exist. Instead, the dominant spouse's ever amplifying internal pressures build up until they eventually burst forth in an emotional onslaught against the mate—who hasn't got a clue about what's happening, because so often it has nothing to do with her.

The basic problem is that the attachment abuser has fallen prey to the total fallacy that he can hold the partner to account for his own mortifying feelings of deficiency, failure, and deep-dyed unlovability—in other words, as therapist Steven Stosny has observed, he is someone who "blame[s] the mirror for the reflection."

The Familiar Script

"What makes me angriest is the *instability* of the relationship, the inability to keep things on an even keel," Claudia said irately at some point midway through our interviews. She found herself vacillating continually between two varying images of herself—that of the attractive, highly competent career woman and that of the insecure, periodically subverted wife. She seemed unaware of the pattern of their marital imbroglios, which always moved through a familiar sequence. These episodes began with a period of nervous, edgy buildup on Paul's part, followed by an inevitable outburst, which eventually subsided into an apologetic, anxious-to-please, positively toned ending.

But Claudia never could tell, in the heat of the moment, what got the whole, draining process into motion; and she thought that Paul didn't know himself. He was always quick to anger at her (though he was a perennial "nice guy" with others), but he never seemed to have any insight into what, exactly, was ticking him off. At one point, at his wife's urging, the couple had consulted a clinician together, but Paul had failed to show up for any appointments after the initial one—as far as he was concerned, seeing a "shrink" was an unnecessary waste of his time and resources. So during those intervals when he was growing ever more tense and irritable, neither one of them could put a finger on exactly what was happening.

It was only later on, in the aftermath of a furious encounter, that Paul might talk about the fact that he was having trouble with a colleague at the large merchandising company he worked for, which was then undergoing a period of restructuring. Or it might be that he was having some financial difficulties with his ex-wife, Barbara, or problems with the children of that marriage, who made him feel so guilty because he was the parent who had walked out.

But early on in the cycle, instead of talking with Claudia about whatever might be the issue, he would withdraw from her abruptly—"shut down" and shut her out completely. She knew she should be used to this, but the suddenness and unexplained quality of the cutoff always left her feeling abandoned, frightened, in a state of what she called "agita," the Italian word for bodywide agitation and hyperarousal—a state of internal distress and discomfort with which, I believed, she was uncomfortably familiar.

To be sure, there were *other* times when this early, tension-building phase got under way differently. In these instances, when Paul was getting uptight he didn't walk away emotionally; instead, he turned increasingly sour, rigid, and authoritarian. If Claudia then asked what was bothering him, he became edgy and defensive. He heard her solicitous questions as criticisms and began insisting that she was attacking *him*; frequently she ended up losing patience and started acting as irritated as he'd accused her of being. In this kind of projective interaction, she was being subtly cued, goaded, and pressured into feeling and behaving in ways that were congruent with his fantasies about her as the "all bad," withholding, nagging, untrustworthy partner and himself as the highly moral, dependable, honorable, "all good" one whom she was always letting down.

Then, as the smoldering resentments in the atmosphere continued to escalate, Paul found more and more reasons for feeling furious. At this point, anything at all could set him off: Claudia's working hours, the clothes she wore, her lecherous colleagues, her independent ways, the dishes she'd left in the sink that morning. Once, he had even gone into a major burn because she'd packed away some old, cracked plastic tumblers that he'd kept from his college days, even though nobody ever used them; it was as if she'd invaded some territory that was supposed to be under *his* sole control.

This had occurred at a time when the emotionally abusive cycle was heading toward its crest—its middle "fighting phase"—and the inane, frenzied, and insoluble argument that would predictably erupt. This quarreling went on and on, until both of them were wrung out, after which Paul always did become calmer; the frantic exchange of insults had served to siphon off some of his inner turmoil. The argument had now served its unconscious purpose, which was to divert his own attention from the barrage of harsh, self-directed negativity he'd been experiencing.

In this third and final stage of the psychologically abusive cycle, Paul's agitation was subsiding. At this stage of the game, he usually became aware that he'd let things get out of hand; he was full of apologies and did try to set things right. Perhaps he felt pacified because Claudia and he were now in the same place emotionally—that is, because she now felt as upset and flooded with anxiety as he did. Now, however, it was she who wanted more distance in the relationship. She had withdrawn emotionally in order to protect herself, and it was Paul who became the ardent pursuer.

He could be so conciliatory and complimentary now, so much the giving, attentive person he'd seemed to be when they'd first begun going out. He behaved as if he were truly sorry about some of the harsh things he'd said to her and wanted to set things right. He knew he shouldn't talk to her in the ways that he did, but he maintained that *she* shouldn't provoke him so much, either. Nothing had actually been resolved when the depleting quarrel ended, but in its wake the couple did move into a honeymoon "riff" of smoother, calmer weather. The pair of them would feel relatively contented and relaxed for a while, for in situations of intermittent abuse, the sweeping sense of bodily and psychological relief that succeeds the periods of turbulence is rewarding in itself. The *good* parts of the relationship have returned, at least for the meanwhile.

—

Chapter Six

A WITNESS TO VIOLENCE

HY HAD CLAUDIA MARTINELLI CHOSEN TO LINK UP WITH a partner like Paul? As a mature, polished, experienced adult woman, she'd certainly been sufficiently capable of assessing her future husband's character and attitudes to have known that she was walking into a potentially incendiary situation. So I couldn't help but wonder if her willingness to enter so punishing an attachment—one in which she had to keep secret the most basic aspects of who she really was—had been predicated on much earlier experiences of shame and guilt.

Was she in a situation that *felt* strangely right, because secret keeping and the uncomfortable bodily sensations that accompany shame and guilt were what she'd always been accustomed to feeling? Claudia had the air of someone whose feelings of deep unworthiness have never been resolved and are being recycled continually.

She and her husband remained deadlocked in a struggle, one that seemed to me to revolve around the basic issue of authenticity. At issue was the question of how she could ever be a whole, genuine person in this relationship, given the energy it took to keep on editing out important segments of her life's actual experiences and her husband's tendency to construe matters so that he was always the superior, "right" member of the pair.

Land Mines of Memory: The Scapegoat

In the course of our conversations, I asked Claudia whether or not the behaviors cited on the Peace at Home, Inc., Warning List ever occurred in her relationship with Paul or in relationships she'd been involved in earlier. As I read out each of the definitions, she paused, considered it briefly, and then nodded her recognition and assent. When I finished reading, she acknowledged that probably all of these things had happened at one time or another in her marriage to Paul, and some of them happened fairly often.

I looked at her reflectively, wondering if—as I suspected—keeping secrets about the self, telling the lies that were necessary to maintain them, and feeling shame and guilt about who she truly was were part of a pattern of being that stretched far backward in Claudia Martinelli's lifetime.

"This may be slightly off the track, Claudia," I said, "but there's something I'd like to ask you." I glanced down at the family genogram briefly, and when I raised my eyes, she met my gaze expectantly. I said, choosing my words carefully, "You know, of course, that in lots of families there are certain roles or 'parts' that people tend to fall into. For instance, there may be someone who's 'the optimist' and someone who's 'the pessimist,' someone who's 'the pretty one' and someone who's 'the clown.' If you had such a role or nickname, what would it be?"

She paused, then said with a bleak certitude in her voice, "I guess . . . I was 'the scapegoat.' . . ."

We sat there, saying nothing, until I asked Claudia if she could bring to mind some incident—an example of a time when she remembered being put in the role of the scapegoat. The question seemed to stump her.

There was another extended pause, after which she shook her head and said that even though she was searching through her memory, she actually couldn't come up with a single concrete instance. All she could produce was a vague comment to the effect that she'd been the one who was always being blamed for everything, including many things she hadn't done.

I prompted her a third time, but she still couldn't remember any scapegoating incident in particular. This was highly atypical: Most people who recall playing a role in the family have the "evidence" ready at hand. But here was Claudia, usually so articulate and forthcoming, acting as if she'd taken an eraser and run it over certain regions of her brain—those areas where you'd suppose the relevant memories and associations would be stored. And I couldn't help but wonder if she was "zoning out" in order to steer clear of certain experiences too distressing or overwhelming to think about or even remember.

Mind/body disconnections of this sort are often linked to severe early stress, as are the ongoing internal states of hypervigilance and hyper-arousal that Claudia appeared to be experiencing. So, too, is the inability to tune in to the body's internal warning cues and signals—those gut-based kinds of intuitions ("Uh-oh, there's something wrong here!") that help to steer a person through the highly nuanced, convoluted shoals of adult life. This situation, in turn, feeds into an unfortunate propensity to make gross errors in judgment when getting into close relationships, for when it comes to making practical use of the body-based information nor-mally flowing into conscious awareness, the hyperstressed individual's data receivers are jammed.

Then, added to these suggestions of unresolved injury and pain some-where in her past, Claudia's period of wild drinking, wanton sexuality, and cocaine involvement was a further indication that she might have been self-medicating and acting out around an unprocessed history of trauma. Thus, I found myself puzzling over whether there were other, unknown matters in her earlier life—the life she'd lived in her original family—quite aside from the present-day secrets she was keeping from Paul. Were there land mines of memory buried in her neural circuitry—events long forgotten and never talked about or even *thought* about these days—which were nevertheless having a profound effect upon her and subtly act-ing to keep her stuck in her one-down, scapegoated position?

Seeing What Is Not Supposed to Be Seen

When we met again several weeks later, Claudia told me that she'd been giving a lot of thought to the issue of "scapegoating" that had arisen during our previous interview. She'd been thinking most of all about the fact that her parents were always at each other's throats, perpetually fighting about one unimportant issue or another. They'd been fighting like that—over everything and nothing—ever since she could remember. "That's why I nicknamed them 'the Bickersons,'" she reminded me with a sardonic smile.

That afternoon it was raining hard, and gusts of water were crashing against the glass windows of the living room in which we sat. We were in a small apartment/office that I'd sublet from a friend, but it felt as if we were inside a diving bell. Claudia's family genogram was on the table between us, and we both gazed down at it for a short while. She kicked off her high-heeled shoes, which were wet around the edges. Then she said, "So I've been wondering if maybe that's what the scapegoat feeling comes from. I mean, trying to help them settle their differences and taking the heat myself." Her intuition, a highly astute one, was that she might have been part of an emotional triangle—one consisting of her mother, her father, and herself as the "lightning rod," or third party who had absorbed all the excess heat of the couple's conflict-ridden, ungratifying relationship.

I shook my head and shrugged as if acknowledging that it was a good question but one to which there was no reply; its answer was lost in time. Claudia nodded. "I don't know, myself. I can't say for sure—I don't remember a lot from my childhood—I remember it in bits and pieces." She turned away, began staring fretfully out at the rain.

I looked at the marital line connecting Claudia's father, Nick, and her mother, Sylvia, on the genogram. Just above it I'd inscribed the notation "constant fighting," so I said, my voice carefully neutral, "It sounds as if there's been a continuing power struggle between your folks." Claudia turned back to me, fixed me with a look I found hard to read.

"I don't know if you could call it a *struggle*, not in the real sense of that word, because my mother never won," she said. "She lets things *go* a little too easily . . . she gives in . . . she *settles*." There was irritation, even a note of contempt, in her voice.

"You're saying that your mom doesn't have a real voice in the marriage?" I asked, and Claudia didn't miss a beat before responding tartly, "Oh, my mother has a voice! She definitely has a voice. But she doesn't get her way, ever . . . not really." I wondered whether Claudia herself, as the senior female in a row of five siblings, had taken on the job of referee or "therapist" in those ongoing parental quarrels. If so, such efforts were highly likely to have left her feeling both impotent and responsible.

In any case, it sounded as if her family's "rules," in terms of adult male and female relationships, had allowed for a woman to battle noisily for her rights and to voice her own point of view but never to gain access to real power, which is the power to be heard and to participate in making important decisions. But this could only be part of a longer story, or so I believed.

Claudia then said, out of nowhere, that she was "trying hard to accept responsibility" for some of the unhappiness and negativity that were going on in her marriage at this moment. I paused, stared at her. Was this an example of "the scapegoat" in action? I told Claudia that I wasn't completely sure what she meant.

She responded with nothing other than an enigmatic smile. Then she murmured something to the effect that she knew she had trouble "seeing things." This statement left me even more at sea.

"You have trouble seeing things?" I repeated.

She nodded, and then the two of us sat there for a few moments, simply looking at each other. I picked up my teacup, took a sip, put it back down. Then I took a flyer and said, "Claudia, you tell me you have trouble 'seeing things,' and it makes me wonder if there were things happening in your family that you weren't supposed to see."

She shot me a quick "aha!" look, that look of someone who feels well understood; but she didn't say anything aloud. So I went on and said in an even tone of voice that *lots* of families have secrets, of the small and large variety. Did she believe she knew the secrets that had existed in her own?

Claudia jumped slightly, as if suddenly recalling something. Then she looked down at the narrow gold watch on her wrist, and I thought she'd suddenly remembered that she had another appointment at this time and that this interview would be ending. I started to get up, expecting her to do so, too; but she didn't. Instead she leaned back in her chair and exhaled deeply. I did so as well.

"It wasn't so *much* of a secret, because my parents didn't try to keep it a secret. But one of my brothers, Nicky, was brain-damaged. The doctors called it a 'pervasive developmental disorder.'" I nodded; she had mentioned this impaired sibling, four years older than herself, early on in our work on her family genogram.

"He had seizures, too, and he definitely was a problem," she continued. "Nicky and my father never got along; they still don't. And the funny thing is that he's very *like* my father. They have similar attitudes, similar ways of dealing with things—like they'll both hold on to grudges. They're just *alike*, and there's always been a lot of fighting between the two of them—*physical* fighting—sometimes to the point where there'd be blood."

She paused, took a sip of tea, and the cup clattered against the saucer. "So you didn't want to bring your friends home," she said in a flat, tonelessly reportorial voice, "because you never knew what Nicky was going to do. You didn't know if he was even going to be *around,* because he started running away when he was in his teens. He finally went out to the Northwest— to Seattle—when he was seventeen. And upsetting as it was when he ran away like that, the house was really peaceful."

I noticed that red patches were appearing on Claudia's face and neck; they were like red flags of embarrassment and culpability being waved from within. "So then," I asked, "everyone must have been feeling relieved and a bit guilty at the same time?"

She nodded. "Right. But while it was happening we never spoke about it much. Outside the house, we kids *never* spoke about it; but inside, things were very chaotic and scary. Nicky was on major drugs for his seizures and for his retardation. He was on lots of barbiturates, too, like massive doses of phenobarbital to keep him calmed down.

"He eventually got into other drugs, too—a *bad* cocaine habit— though none of us realized it for a long time. He was stealing from my parents; he stole anything he could lay his hands on. So it wasn't safe. You had to keep all your stuff locked up." Her voice had taken on a throbbing undercurrent of alarm, and her arms were folded tightly across her chest once again.

I asked her if she could recall just when these pitched family brawls— especially the physical, sometimes bloody clashes between her brother and her dad—had gotten under way. "Oh, this stuff went on throughout my whole life," she answered tautly. "At least, until Nicky moved out of the house."

Chapter Seven

ATTACHMENT TRAUMA

ERELY WITNESSING, AS CLAUDIA HAD, THE CHRONIC violence being visited by your dad—an out-of-control adult—upon your sibling contained the elements of what Freud viewed as the essence of a traumatic experience, which is to say *a situation in which a person feels completely helpless and ineffective in the face of what is perceived to be overwhelming danger.* For what could this younger sister, or any of the other children, do without taking the chance of being drawn into the ongoing familial violence? If the children's mother wasn't able to stop the wild physical clashes between father and son, who else in the family could?

A Discontinuity in the Thread of the Self

Any startling, frightening, and inescapable situation has the potential to overwhelm a person, whether that person is a mature adult or a young child. However, as trauma experts Steven Marans and Anne Adelman have pointed out, a traumatic event will be experienced very differently depending upon the individual's age and stage of development. And obviously, a child's coping skills and self-protective capacities will be far more limited than the skills and capacities available to a grown-up.

"In the throes of the maturational process, children have fewer and more uneven psychological resources at their disposal; their developing defensive organization is acutely vulnerable to traumatic disruptions . . . from the environment," these clinicians write. As a consequence, the child's strategies for dealing with threatening experiences will be relatively weak and his defenses easily breached; he is, moreover, in a dependent situation, usually without any recourse in terms of finding shelter elsewhere.

In situations where neither of the well-known instinctive human reactions to danger (fighting or fleeing) is a viable option, that third, less familiar but similarly automatic reaction (freezing helplessly in place) is the usual outcome. In the instance of the young child, this is frequently the most adaptive response available, for in the midst of the traumatic event itself, many of his immature coping capacities will be effectively knocked out of commission.

What "coping capacities" am I referring to? Among others, the ability to differentiate what is real from what is fantasy; the ability to think clearly; and the ability to self-regulate bodily sensations. Given that dealing with the fearful situation *actively* is usually out of the question, the child's best (if not to say sole) response option is often that of spacing out—shutting down emotionally. This results in a feeling of being "not really here" despite the fact that one is physically present.

The resulting state of self-induced mental anesthesia—which is, of course, accompanied by a souped-up internal bodily state—is the human organism's way of distancing itself from the intolerable experience of feeling utterly helpless in an unavoidable predicament. It is like disengaging an inner steering wheel, even though the machine itself is in high gear. The upshot is that the whole body "knows," and expresses in its state of hyperexcitation, what the individual cannot bear to comprehend clearly at the level of conscious awareness.

This in turn creates what the great theorist D. W. Winnicott called a "discontinuity in the thread of the self." For while this zoning-out reaction does serve to mitigate the immediate impact of the overwhelming experience in the short run, in the longer run it produces its own set of consequences: As long as areas of the individual's internal being remain a vast terra incognita, the traumatizing experiences can never become processed, resolved, and integrated into an understanding of his own personal history.

Then, instead of dealing with what did happen once upon a time, the individual will be apt to avoid, minimize, or perhaps forget entirely the frightening events that actually did occur. Nevertheless, a bodywide physiological alarm reaction has been set off; and because the danger has never been recognized as belonging to the past, the body remains on chronic high alert to meet an unnamed threat that exists in an eternal time present.

A Boundary of Silence

Trauma exposes a child to his own absolute helplessness and lack of control of his world at the very time when he is struggling with the crucial developmental issues of competence and mastery. At the same time, traumatic experiences strike at the heart of a youngster's sense of self for a very different, somewhat paradoxical reason: Early in life, children are wonderfully grandiose and experience themselves as *central to* and the *cause of* anything and everything that occurs around them.

Therefore, when bad things happen in their worlds, they are prone to experience an exaggerated sense of responsibility for whatever is occurring—for example, many a youngster believes that his parents would not have divorced if he'd just been better behaved and brought home a perfect report card. Similarly a child who, like Claudia, has seen her brother being punched and pummeled to the point of bloodiness may have felt responsible in a variety of different ways. She may have thought she was bad because she *should* have spoken up and yet felt utterly without power because she was too frightened to do so. She may have believed she *could* have helped her brother if she herself had taken some of the heat, instead of trying to melt into the background when the fighting got ugly. She may have had such shame-inducing thoughts as "I'm glad he's the one who's getting it, and that it isn't me!"—and then felt guilty about seeing Nicky getting beaten up without anyone stepping in to stop what was happening. Or if she'd actually said or done something that had gotten her brother into trouble, she might have experienced herself as a vile, nasty human being who'd actually deserved that beating herself.

Shrouded as it was in family secrecy, this domestic situation had clearly created a boundary of silence around the household—one that could only amplify the sense of guilty secrecy, of stigma, shame, and embarrassment of everyone within it.

What had those bloody battles been about? As an adult, Claudia had little or no understanding. All that she could say about her father's periodic attacks upon the troubled, troublesome Nicky was that "while it was happening we never spoke about it much. Outside the house, we kids *never* spoke about it." I wondered if it had been talked about *within* the home, among the members of the family; I suspected that it had been talked about very little, if ever.

But now it seemed to me that Claudia's cryptic remark—"I have trouble seeing things"—had become more comprehensible. It made sense in the context of what had been going on during her childhood. She had, I thought, received intensive training in "not seeing" and "not knowing" too much in a household where violent, bloody outbursts were occurring.

To be sure, not knowing too much about what was happening had been highly adaptive *at that time*—for a dependent child, dissociating, spacing out, and not feeling too much would be the most natural ways of protecting the self from unbearable pain in situations where no action is possible. But in adulthood, "not seeing" and "not knowing" are extremely *maladaptive* ways of responding. Life is far too complex, and the choices to be made are too nuanced, for a grown-up person to be zoned out and functioning on autopilot.

Moreover, this kind of stark disconnection between *what the body knows* and what thoughts, feelings, and memories are available at the level of conscious awareness is probably what motivates the powerful urge to resurrect the unfinished business of the past in the real time of present-day existence. This did appear to be happening in Claudia's troubled relationship to Paul, for she was engaged in the re-creation of a theme that harked back to her earliest history: She had somehow "found herself" in a cowering, subordinate position in relation to a periodically eruptive, dominant male. Her husband (like her father) always presented himself to everyone outside the home as an affable nice guy, but in the privacy of their intimate relationship, Paul was projecting his simmering anger and his frustrations outward.

He was perceiving as existing *in Claudia*—the unforgivably defective, morally flawed member of the couple—everything that was bad and wrong about his own life, just as her father must have seen in his unforgivably imperfect son everything that was damaged and defective about himself.

Who Was the Scapegoat?

What I found surprising was the fact that Claudia had described her role as that of "scapegoat," when it surely could be said that her brother Nicky had been the chief contender for that hapless position. But when I asked her about this directly, she shot me a strange look. "Yes, I guess you're right there," she conceded after pondering the thought for a few moments.

Then she went on to say, in a glum, depressed tone of voice, that her brother now lived in the Northwest with his girlfriend and was not included in any of the family functions. He hadn't even been invited to her wedding to Paul, because her parents didn't want him there. "My mother *does* send him money that my father doesn't know about. And she says it's 'guilt money.'" Evidently her mother still had lingering qualms about her inability to protect her son and was secretly trying to make whatever small amends were possible.

Aside from that fragile and secretive connection, though, her brother had been dismissed from the family. He was among "the departed," though clandestinely alive, and as she explained this situation to me, Claudia's face took on a withdrawn, frozen expression. It occurred to me that not only her mother, but she herself was probably still carrying a burden of guilt and responsibility for Nicky's having been eliminated from the family portrait in this way. But she said nothing further, as if the family injunction to maintain silence on the subject of this brother had not been lifted to this day.

Claudia had speculated that her sense of herself as "the scapegoat" might have been caused by her trying to intervene in her parents' constant quarreling and ending up by taking the blame for things she hadn't actually done. Now, I reflected upon the meaning of the word *scapegoat* itself. And my thought was, Who *is* a scapegoat if not someone who's being held responsible—and perhaps *feeling* deeply at fault for—problems that she never caused and couldn't cure no matter how much of the family "heat" she tried to take upon herself?

Trauma: A Wound to the Self

In *The Random House Dictionary of the English Language,* the psychiatric meaning of "trauma" is given as *"a startling experience which has a lasting effect on mental life; a shock."* The word itself derives from the Greek and means "wound." Some traumatic events, such as seeing your brother beaten bloody, may not be life threatening in the sense of your own physical survival; however, they can be nothing short of self-defining in terms of telling you who you are in the very dawn of your lifetime (helpless, powerless, scared, cowardly, bad, overwhelmed, out of control).

Such events are highly likely to leave you in a state of chronic bodily arousal, with a highly uncomfortable overreactivity to life's minor insults, threats, and dilemmas. This physiologically based state, a bodily condition of dysregulation, makes it very hard for a person to soothe herself, calm down, and regain stability in the wake of *any* negative event, even one that has nothing to do with the painful experiences of the past.

Perhaps most troublesome of all, however, is the subtle, devilish way in which shocking early experiences can lead a person into endless repetitions of the same unhappy situations she saw earlier in her life. The famed theorist Harry Guntrip once suggested that all of human pathology is in reality just "failed metabolism"—which is to say, the inability of the overwhelmed self to process and absorb indigestible hunks of intolerable experiences. In short, symptoms develop when aspects of a person's past history are so "stuck" in her body and her psyche that they become regurgitated endlessly into her current-day existence.

Attachment Trauma

It has now been over two decades since the American Psychiatric Association added a new classification to its official *Diagnostic and Statistical Manual of Mental Disorders* and called it "post-traumatic stress disorder" (PTSD for short). The *Diagnostic and Statistical Manual* then listed the particular symptoms that individuals are prone to develop in the aftermath of traumatic experiences—such as persistent agitation, intrusive thoughts, nightmares, flashbacks, and the compulsion to replay the traumatic event in some disguised form. It was also noted that such symptoms might emerge immediately or, in some cases, weeks, months, or even years afterward.

A widespread belief at that time, and indeed one that persists to this day, is that traumatic experiences are relatively rare happenings in the population at large—that they're limited to such things as having been in military combat or involved in a natural disaster, such as a flood, fire, or earthquake, and similar high-profile events. But as mentioned in the preface, a huge, government-sponsored study, led by sociologist Ronald C. Kessler, involved actually asking some fifty-nine thousand people about which "events and experiences that qualified as traumas" they had gone through. And to everyone's surprise, the researchers found that exposures to traumatic stress are not at all uncommon.

In fact, the Kessler team's findings indicated that *60 percent of the adult men* and *51 percent of the adult women* interviewed reported having experienced at least one—and sometimes more than one—of the adversities about which they were being systematically interviewed. All in all, the most frequently encountered traumas were found to be 1) witnessing someone being injured or killed; 2) being involved in a fire, flood, or natural disaster; and 3) being involved in a life-threatening accident.

A higher proportion of males in the study reported having been through one of these three experiences; also, many more males had been exposed to such events as physical attacks, involvement in military combat, being threatened with a weapon, and being held captive or kidnapped. By way of contrast, a significantly higher proportion of females reported having been raped, sexually molested, or subjected to parental neglect and physical abuse during their childhoods.

There were also clear-cut male/female differences when it came to what happened *in the wake* of a traumatic event. Here, it is important to realize that an event that clearly qualifies as traumatic does not necessarily produce a post-traumatic stress disorder in everyone exposed to it. Despite the widely held belief that dramatic symptoms are sure to follow in the wake of terrible experiences, the statistics tell us otherwise. Only a subset of trauma survivors actually go on to develop full-blown PTSD.

However, arrestingly enough, the results of the Kessler research indicated that in the aftermath of trauma, women were more likely—*more than twice as likely*—to develop post-traumatic stress disorders than were men. The figures themselves told an extraordinary story: In the wake of trauma, 20.4 percent of the women (some fifteen to twenty million) tended to become symptomatic, as contrasted with 8.2 percent of the men (roughly six to nine million). In discussing these findings, the researchers acknowledged that they could spin theories about—but not fully account for—the striking gender differences that had emerged from their results.

What this nationwide study did make very evident, however, was that exposure to trauma is omnipresent in the population—far more so than anyone had previously imagined. Still, because traumatic events are considered to be highly exceptional experiences, their profoundly distressing aftereffects—which can persist for years—all too often go unrecognized, undiagnosed, and untreated.

Big-T and Little-t Traumas

In the years since 1980, when PTSD first made its debut upon the psychiatric stage, the effort to hammer out a universally acceptable definition of what trauma actually *is* has proven extremely elusive. But in the most recent update of the *Diagnostic and Statistical Manual* (known as *DSM-IV*), trauma is defined not only as an event involving direct personal injury or the threat of injury to the self, but as the *"witnessing [of] an event that involves death, injury, or a threat to the physical integrity of another person. . . ."*

The italics are mine and are meant to emphasize the notion that you don't need to be the direct victim of an assault in order to be traumatized by it; you can be profoundly damaged simply by *being present when it's happening*. The phenomenon of witnessing, and later becoming symptomatic in some way, is known as "vicarious traumatization."

I should, however, underscore the fact that the word *trauma*, as I am using it here, doesn't for the most part refer to those hugely dramatic events such as hurricanes, floods, fires, serious auto accidents, incest, rape, and witnessing a homicide or other catastrophic occurrences that basically involve looking death in the face. My focus, in these pages, is upon those far less cataclysmic, but nevertheless damaging—sometimes life-changing— experiences that are often referred to as "traumas with a little 't.'"

Of course, the fine line differentiating little-t and big-T traumas will often be indistinct. For example, it's obvious that a sensational headline appearing in the morning's newspaper—GIRL, 10, WATCHES AS SISTER IS STABBED TO DEATH—falls into the big-T category. But where does a life-time of watching sudden, unanticipated, sometimes bloody battles be-tween your father and a sibling belong?

Seeing People You Love Hurt Each Other

You may well ask, Was Claudia Martinelli actually suffering from post-traumatic stress disorder—that is, big-T trauma—as formally defined in the psychiatric reference bible, the *DSM-IV*? She had surely not experi-enced a big-T event on the order of "military combat, violent personal as-sault (sexual assault, physical attack, robbery, mugging), being kidnapped, being taken hostage, terrorist attack, torture, incarceration as a prisoner of war or in a concentration camp, natural or man-made disasters, severe automobile accidents, or being diagnosed with a life-threatening illness."

Nor had she witnessed horrifying events such as "observing the serious injury or unnatural death of another person due to violent assault, accident, war, or disaster or unexpectedly witnessing a dead body or body parts," as described in *DSM-IV*. She wasn't having the emblematic "flashbacks"— those terrifying episodes of reexperiencing the trauma as if it weren't long over but were happening right here and right now. She didn't complain about intrusive, crazy, out-of-context thoughts that would pop into her mind as if from nowhere. Nor did she speak of difficulties in falling or stay-ing asleep owing to persistent, terrifying nightmares.

Still, many clinicians who work with trauma patients believe that the current version of the *Diagnostic Manual* places too much emphasis on extraordinary and rare occurrences, such as earthquakes, floods, terrorist attacks, and other high-profile disasters. These trauma workers also main-tain that far too *little* attention is paid to the lasting effects of chronic in-terpersonal abuse of the kind that Claudia had witnessed as a child.

As therapist Babette Rothschild has observed, no statistics have been gathered on the number of people who are suffering from PTS (post-traumatic stress, or little-t) as compared with those suffering from the highly dramatic symptoms seen in full-blown PTSD (post-traumatic stress disorder, or big-T). "One can guess," writes Rothschild, "that there are a significant number of trauma survivors with PTS, those who fall between the cracks—not recovered from their traumas, but somehow without the debilitation of PTSD."

As Rothschild notes, situations of unremitting tension generated by "an environment, life style or chronic situation that is constantly and extremely emotionally stressful . . . [and/or] . . . certain kinds of strict or neglectful childhood environments, dysfunctional relationships," and the like can at times be so overwhelming that they will in fact produce psychological and physical conditions that resemble the more disabling PTSD. A child's early experience of severe early stress is very like an adult's experience of a cataclysmic event in that it can shatter the individual's sense of basic safety in the world, of her or his invulnerability to harm.

Certainly, in the view of trauma researcher Bessel van der Kolk, witnessing terrible things going on inside your family is in many ways far *worse* than experiencing huge natural or man-made catastrophes. "The real trauma, and the actual cause of most post-traumatic suffering, is 'attachment trauma.' It's seeing people whom you love hurt each other in physical, horrifying ways," van der Kolk told me in the course of one of our many discussions.

We humans are, after all, social creatures, who grow up in the protective environments provided by our caretaking families. Thus, when bad things happen at the hands of the very people who are supposed to love and nurture us, our basic conception of ourselves and of the world we inhabit is inevitably impacted in enormous ways. Physical or emotional battering—or cold indifference and neglect—*within* the family group is at some basic level the most traumatic occurrence of all.

For this early exposure to domestic cruelty—or to callous disregard—transforms some of the crucially important figures within the child's world into creatures who cannot be trusted and who are fundamentally undependable. And in van der Kolk's view, it is this homegrown form of emotional injury that is the root cause of the vast majority of post-traumatic stress disorders that he and other physicians encounter.

Chapter Eight

FAMILIAR
FEELING-STATES:
THE BODY REENACTS

HEN NEXT WE MET, CLAUDIA WAS IN MUCH BETTER spirits than the last time I'd seen her. The marriage seemed to be on an uptick, and she said, "Right now, I'm feeling hopeful," as she shrugged out of her brown suede overcoat and hung it over the back of a chair. She had arrived at the end of her workday, bringing with her a rosy-cheeked sense of nippy early spring and a strong whiff of pleasant-smelling perfume. As her quasi hostess, I'd put cheese, crackers, and two glasses of white wine on the low table between us; and Claudia's good mood served to augment the festive feeling with which the interview began.

As always, we started out by spending some time on her family genogram. This time I found myself focusing on the crosshatched line denoting both the marriage and later divorce of Claudia and her first husband, Steven. Looking at the scribbled notation just above that line— "5 years"—I thought once again that five years is not an insignificant length of time. I asked her what her first husband had done for a living.

She responded with a dismissive hand gesture and said, "Basically, nothing. And that was probably the major reason why the marriage didn't work out." She explained that when they'd first gotten to know each other, Steven had talked a lot about the thriving baked goods–distributing business that he owned. At the time, he'd told her that he was plowing all his earnings back into the company; but he had assured her that eventually—

at some point in the future—it was going to make them a very wealthy couple. "We'd often drive past a certain building in which his company was supposedly housed, and I'd say, 'Let's go in.' But he'd always say that we couldn't, because he and his partner had agreed that they weren't going to get the wives involved."

The whole thing had been an elaborate setup. Throughout most of the five years of that marriage, Claudia had been made to believe that her husband was working at "the business" in the mornings and showing real estate in the late afternoons and early evenings—"Not very successfully, either," she remarked dryly. And while he was supposedly putting all his profits back into the concern, it was *she* who was paying the mortgage, the maintenance charges, the upkeep of the cars, and the electric and telephone bills.

"Steven wouldn't ever give me the phone number of his company; he always had a beeper. I would keep *asking* him for his business number, but he'd get mad and he would get in my face. Next thing you know he'd turn it around, and so now I was wrong; I was the one who was pushing. We'd get into a fight, and then what do you know, *I'd* end up backing off."

I said nothing for a moment but took note of the fact that once again she'd been maneuvered into the position of the bad guy. At the same time, many reactions to this strange story—and questions about it—began popping into my mind. How could she *not* have suspected that something was seriously amiss here; she had, after all, been the one who was shouldering all of the bills! And what, for that matter, had her ex-spouse done with so much empty time on his hands and nothing productive to occupy him?

When I asked Claudia if she had any idea just *how* Steven had spent all that blank time, her expression turned bitter. "What did he *do* with his time?" she said. "Slept and lied. He was a compulsive liar. Maybe he did real estate from about three to eight P.M., but he slept throughout the morning."

This lying, hypocritical state of affairs had gone on for five years. Ultimately, it was the issue of the company telephone number that had given her husband's bogus undercover life away. "I'd kept hounding Steven until he finally did give me what was supposedly the number of his business. But it was a scam; and the way he'd arranged it was that he'd had an extra telephone jack installed," she said. This secret jack had, in turn, been connected to a telephone answering machine, and the entire apparatus was then hidden in back of some stacked-up shoeboxes on *her own side* of the clothes closet. "The way it worked was that when I called I'd reach a recording of this so-called wholesale baked goods concern that he owned."

I stared at her. "So he was a total impostor," I said flatly.

She nodded, then went on to say that a steady buildup of odd incidents had finally caused her to do some active investigating; and that it had been this effort that finally culminated in her discovery of the concealed telephone jack.

I wrote the word *impostor* above Steven's name on the genogram.

Then I looked up at Claudia, as if prompting her to continue, and she picked up the tale with her discovery of the elaborate setup in the back of her closet. "I knew then that I was going to be leaving him, and I told him so," she said. "*His* reaction was that he came right up close to my face with this big, broad smile. And he asked me, 'How did you ever figure it out?'"

I noticed that her hands, which had been resting lightly on her lap, had become fists as she spoke and that her normally rosy skin had turned a grayish color, as if the life had suddenly drained out of her. "What a story," I said quietly.

Five whole years, I was thinking. Five years of cohabiting with—and being in a supposedly intimate relationship with—someone who was living a completely fraudulent existence, just plain *lying* to you about everything in his life. I paused, struck by the fact Claudia Martinelli had gone directly from a dad whom she described as a "holy roller and a total hypocrite" to a husband whose *exterior* life and whose *real* life bore no connection whatsoever. There was, it seemed to me, a somewhat poignant, daughterly sense of generational loyalty and continuity here—for what is a false life if not the very embodiment of hypocrisy?

Narratives and Myths About the Self

An arresting thesis, put forth by psychiatrist Charles Ford, is that it's not just the impostor but *all of us* who to some extent devise a "personal myth" about who we really are. This ongoing, self-told tale is basically the story of the self—a narrative we not only believe in, but organize our lives around.

This personal mythmaking is aided and abetted by a selective memory process that helps us to "remember" most clearly whatever fits into our schema and buttresses our images of ourselves. "We also present ourselves to others duplicitously, playing certain roles and providing selective information about ourselves. Responses from others confirm and help mold the resultant myth," writes Ford in his book *Lies! Lies! Lies!*

It is in the course of creating and elaborating upon such personal myths—a process that gets under way early in life, in our families of origin —that a particularly core, salient theme tends to come to occupy front and center of our awareness. For example, we may see ourselves in the central role of "the victim" or "the hero"; the "outcast" or "the entitled one"; the "nice guy" who is miraculously free of aggression or "the angry, injured guy," the person with a perennial chip on his shoulder. In this sense, we are all impostors to some greater or lesser extent—enacting for ourselves and those around us a life role that we've come to believe in.

Of course, there will be times when we're confronted with information that *doesn't* quite fit into the dominant story line: when the always unflappable "good guy" is feeling consumed by rage or the "tough, unemotional guy" feels weak, needy, and vulnerable. When this happens, our impulse is to quickly "stuff" these forbidden emotions, banish them from sight. The nice guy deceives *himself* as well as those around him by completely denying his own taboo feelings of aggression, just as the tough guy suppresses his intolerable sense of powerlessness and fragility. They are the secrets we keep from everyone, including from ourselves.

Needless to say, there is a close connection between the development of a personal myth and a person's development of his or her own individual self—by which is meant that subjective sense of "This is me, this is who I am" and "This is the body I inhabit." It is in this precise area that the impostor clearly differs from the rest of us. His inner sense of "who I am" and what manner of "self" his body contains is rudimentary, while his skill at being who and what *someone else wishes him to be* is often wonderfully well developed.

He is perfectly able to present himself as successful and competent to those around him—Claudia's husband had passed himself off as the co-owner of an up-and-coming baked goods–distributing company—while inside he is all emptiness, a vacuum, doing nothing. He is someone who lacks a secure identity and place in the real world and has therefore invented a fictional one.

Why should the impostor, who tends to be a highly intelligent person, want to renounce his individual personhood and playact at being someone he is not? You might say it's in order to get a free ride in life, with someone else paying all the fare; but most psychiatric experts working in this area believe there are other, far deeper reasons for his behavior. The most favored working hypothesis is that the very act of imposturing represents a person's attempt to fill up the painful existential void that yawns inside him.

For the impostor's playacting gives him an organizing, energizing "role" to play, which in turn fills him up with a jerry-built sense of identity—and a false identity is probably better than no identity at all. And perhaps more important, the act of imposturing transforms that individual's sense of himself as a weak and insignificant nobody—someone who has nothing inside himself and nothing worthwhile to show for his life—into a secretly significant, powerful somebody who is obviously superior to everyone around him. After all, hasn't he succeeded in manipulating and deceiving them all?

The Impostor's Dilemma

A surprising yet oft noted finding is that when the impostor's "cover" is blown, it's often *not* completely due to bungling or error. For the paradox of this individual's entire existence is that his major skills and achievements are in the area of manipulating and deceiving other people. So if those around him never *do* find out how brilliantly they've been taken in, they never will learn about his cleverness and superiority! They'll never realize what hopeless dimwits they've been or how masterfully he's led them along. Claudia's husband's slow smile of amusement and his disdainful question to his wife—"How did you ever figure it out?"—bespoke a certain pleasure in her mortifying discovery of how obtuse and gullible she'd been.

Indeed, her prolonged inability to "get it" does raise a question: Is there anything special or different about the kind of person who *can* be duped so thoroughly by an impostor—someone whose entire presentation of self is one gigantic lie? Is she a person who's simply been unlucky, someone whose too trusting nature has led her to ignore the manifold warning signals of which wiser, more wary heads would have taken notice? The current thinking about impostors and their chosen victims suggests that no single, clear-cut explanation for the vulnerability of the "target" is sufficient.

At a surface level, she can be seen as someone with an agenda of her own—an agenda that renders her all too ready to believe what she wants to believe. For example, if a woman's agenda is to find a mate and get married, she's prone to see whatever fits into her schema and to fail to take into account any information that doesn't fit into her self-constructed, highly optimistic picture. She may therefore view her potential partner as generous, competent, straightforward, loving, affectionate, and trustworthy, owing to the fact that she *needs* to see him in that light. In her own eyes, that person has all the attributes that she *wants* him to have, and if he seems to lack some of them, she goes ahead and fills in the blanks.

The individual she believes she knows is, in truth, a figment of her own fantasies, and the relationship they share is the one that exists primarily in the world of her imagination. It is as if she is committed to "not know" anything negative about him—to banish from her conscious awareness any potential doubts, fears, or painfully discordant feelings.

Errors in Judgment

As mentioned earlier, it has been well established that people who've been exposed to early trauma have a tendency to make gross errors in judgment when it comes to getting into intimate relationships. And in Claudia Martinelli's case, it could be said that both her current and her previous marital choices indicated that her "partner selection mechanism" was clearly out of kilter. Certainly her track record through life (which included several other ego-busting love affairs not described here) did indicate a penchant for getting into passionate involvements without any real sense of the other person's basic qualities—including his faults, his human failings, and the kinds of problems that might arise between them.

It was true that Claudia did, at one level, want to move ahead in her life and do all the normal womanly things that everyone around her expected of her—to marry, remain married, and have a family of her own eventually. At another level, though, her *behavior*—in terms of the partners she chose and the degree of emotional distance that always resulted—bespoke an equally powerful urge to *avoid* becoming intimate with anyone. For while she appeared to want a warm, trusting, gratifying relationship, her feet always seemed to walk her in a direction that would make achieving that relationship impossible.

A problem she was struggling with repetitively revolved, it seemed to me, around the issue of intimacy—specifically, the basic truth that it's impossible to become truly intimate without opening up and making yourself vulnerable. For many people, this feels dangerous—you could lower all your defenses and then meet with hurt, rejection, or abandonment—but it's *sure* to feel dangerous if you've experienced emotional injuries earlier in your lifetime. So Claudia, like many others, was full of warring wishes and contradictory-seeming motivations.

"The Body, Like the Mind, Is Subject to the Repetition Compulsion"

As I saw it, there were still some missing puzzle pieces here, some *other* leads to the mystery of why this lovely, intelligent woman had come to believe that the only relationship she was entitled to was a painful and humiliating one. And as I sat opposite her, what sprang to my mind was an extraordinary observation made by the analyst and author Joyce McDougall: "The body, like the mind, is subject to the repetition compulsion."

It is surely true that emotional experiences—fear, pain, and humiliation among them—are experiences *of the body*. These experiences do not, as we know, exist solely in an airy, abstract mental sphere; in reality, they involve a host of neurobiological reactions and many *physical feelings and sensations*. And it might well be the case, as McDougall contends, that a person's internal feeling-state—that is, *what is happening inside the person's body*—may, in certain instances, provide the unseen, underlying motivation for reviving and reenacting charged aspects of the past. The suggestion is that by recapitulating not only "the way it was," but "the way it *felt inside*," a person can reconnect with the inner state of being he knows best and the bodily feelings and sensations with which he is most familiar.

Seen from this novel vantage point, it could be said that Claudia had, all unknowingly, sought out those kinds of relationships that would lead her to reexperience certain ways of being in her body—those internal feeling-states associated with feeling like a victim and living in an atmosphere rife with fear, abuse, and humiliation. For these were the familiar feelings and sensations she had known since time immemorial. Moreover, it occurred to me that she probably hadn't the remotest idea of what it would be like to live inside a *different* kind of body—a body that felt relaxed, full of trust, and gratified.

"Zoned Out," Yet Hyperaroused

Perhaps most central of all to an understanding of Claudia's current-day situation was an appreciation of the impact of traumatic stress—in this case, the witnessing of intermittent, unpredictable violence in her family of origin. For, as noted earlier, "zoning out," or dissociating from one's own emotional responses, is a frequent response in those instances where the caretaking parent is at the source of a child's suffering and pain. Young children have a powerful, *biologically based* need to form and maintain strong emotional attachments to the adult nurturers upon whom they're so utterly dependent. The human imperative is to maintain faith and belief in the instinctively adored, utterly irreplaceable parent—no matter what the psychological cost to the growing youngster and no matter how badly that parent may be behaving.

Again, in those unhappy circumstances involving an abusive, chronically neglectful, or emotionally exploitative caretaker, the child's best defensive action is often that of shutting down, not feeling too many things too deeply. Closing off access to her own internal experiences makes it possible to retain an all-unmerited faith and belief in the irreplaceable parent. It is for this reason that children who've been severely stressed during their earliest years will so often grow up to become adults who are deaf to their own bodily cues and warning signals.

Experience has taught them to believe it's safer to stay disconnected from this part of their internal wiring. Nevertheless, while someone in this situation may have managed well enough by shutting down many of her body's emotional warning signs and signals, her body's overall emergency warning system is on high alert and liable to be sounding off continually. For in the aftermath of traumatic experiences that have never been dealt with, a person's body is girded to confront the menace that is felt to be everywhere.

Her inner state is one of high arousal, and she is highly likely to respond in exaggerated ways to all sorts of minor challenges. Thus, a passing criticism from a boss, friend, or lover can precipitate the classic bodily reactions to a situation of crisis: a speeded-up heartbeat; clenched chest muscles; shallow, rapid breathing; and an outpouring of crisis situation neurohormones. Although outwardly the person may appear to be responding calmly, her body is in a state of perennial readiness to meet with threat, and perfectly ordinary, neutral kinds of events can be experienced as catastrophic ordeals.

In brief, the long-term consequences of growing up in severely stressful circumstances are twofold: First, the developing child tends to become disconnected from her own physiologically based sources of information —those subtle, body-based warning cues and signals—and second, she inhabits a body that feels tremendously tense and uncomfortable, for her central nervous system is in a state of perpetual defense readiness. She is so highly reactive to small occurrences, so braced to meet the next expected danger, that she never quite experiences her interior world, never knows it to be safe and under her control.

And because a person in this situation doesn't have a sense of owning the body inside which she lives—and is deaf to so many of the signals coming from inside it—she experiences her unruly feelings, urges, and impulses as if they're somehow attacking from outside. As a result, and as part of an effort to self-soothe and calm herself down, she will often become involved in addictive behaviors of some sort: drinking, drugs, gambling, promiscuous sex, or disorders involving food—which, of course, is the universal symbol of nurturance.

Actually, all of these addictive disorders can be viewed as attempted distractions from the roiling world within—a world that feels barren and fraught with dangers simultaneously. For even though people in this situation may be feeling "spaced out," in the most fundamental sense, they are nevertheless acutely sensitized to the plethora of dangers, possible betrayals, losses, and rejections that threaten them on every side. They are therefore drawn to any form of relief from their inner pain, no matter how self-destructive that behavior may prove to be in the long run—and not surprisingly, their lives take on a tormented flavor.

Unheard Dispatches from Within

Claudia came to our next meeting, the last of these interviews, looking as rattled as I'd ever seen her. She told me at once that she and Paul had had a bad quarrel this past weekend, then added quickly, in a defensive tone of voice, that she wasn't giving up on this marriage anyway.

This was because they'd eventually settled their differences amicably, and she'd felt *heartened* by that. It seemed to bespeak her growing capacity for hanging on to herself when the gale winds of one of their stormy, irrational arguments were blowing. In this instance, instead of "losing it," she had been able simply to walk away—something she'd been unable to do before getting into her therapy, which had begun two weeks before she'd gotten married and had been continuing in tandem with our conversations.

The fight with Paul had erupted the previous Saturday night, Claudia told me, flopping down on the sofa as if exhausted. Then she stopped speaking, looked dejected and lost in thought. I waited to see if she would continue on her own, but when she didn't I asked her how this past weekend's argument had gotten started.

Instead of responding to the question, she leaned forward, then put a chunk of cheese on a cracker and lifted it to her mouth with a slightly trembling hand. As she did so, I noticed that her skin had begun to look patchy, mottled with red blotches, as if her remembered anger had brought on a sudden outbreak of chickenpox.

The sense of her profound misery was such that I looked away, as if intruding on a moment that felt too intense and personal. I found myself staring at the wall behind her, which was lined with mahogany bookshelves and fully stocked with beautifully bound first editions—the kinds of books that appear designated for looking at rather than for reading. This valuable collection had once belonged to the grandfather of the apartment's owner, who was my friend and landlord.

"It's *Paul*—he has absolutely no patience, no tolerance," Claudia said, breaking the silence. "He just flies off the *handle*. For instance, we started going at each other because he pushed me out of the bathroom—*he* wanted to brush his teeth first!" I couldn't help but smile at the slightly comic quality of the complaint, and Claudia answered with a rueful smile of her own.

"I know, it's *so* ridiculous," she said.

The dispute had actually gotten under way earlier, when the two of them came home late on Saturday evening and found her husband's fourteen-year-old son, Christopher, entertaining a bunch of his pals in the living room. Although this teenage party had been prearranged and agreed to, Paul was ill at ease when he arrived and found those kids sprawled all over their brand-new, still pristine furniture. In Claudia's opinion, her husband had seemed self-conscious, stilted, "not himself," and not at all certain how to behave with his son's friends.

But as she saw it, it wasn't her problem, so she'd simply said a brief hello, then made a beeline into the bedroom area. Then she'd gone into the bathroom in order to remove her makeup and the contacts she was wearing. "I didn't think it was my place to start socializing with these boys; *I'm* not the parent," she explained to me crisply. But Paul had come dashing in after her and begun urging her to go out into the living room and talk with Christopher and his guests for a while.

"He wanted me to check the kids out, to see if any of them had beer or 'anything weird' on their breath," Claudia said. "But I told him, '*I'm* not going. Why should *I* go? *You* go!'" Her voice was rising indignantly.

"That's when he told me—I mean *ordered* me—'Move over, I want to brush my teeth.' And I said, 'When I get out of the bathroom, you will!' So he just *shoved* me out of the way so he could brush *his* teeth!" she said, looking completely furious.

A moment later, though, she seemed to have a change of heart, for to my surprise she said pacifically, "I think that Paul was probably dealing with a couple of different, and pretty complicated, issues on that occasion. First of all, I think he felt inadequate about going out there in front of his son and his son's friends—he didn't know what to say or how to be with them."

She was sounding as if she'd stepped into the role of her husband's counsel and was pleading his case before me, the stern, disapproving judge. I said nothing but felt somewhat confused about where this conversation might be going. Claudia had a way of stating her legitimate complaints and then backing off in an eyeblink. It was as if she were taking herself out of the equation somehow and nullifying what seemed to be her own appropriate reactions.

"Secondly, he *did* have a serious drinking problem earlier in his life, and although he's not touched liquor for the past seven years, I think he's still a 'dry drunk' right now," she said. In other words, his behavior was still *like* that of an active alcoholic in terms of his being provocative, controlling, and short-tempered. She was sounding more concerned, empathetic, and understanding about her husband's state of being than she was about any of the mental or physical distress she might be experiencing herself.

Claudia fell silent then, sat there staring out at the Manhattan skyline, which had lit up while we'd been talking. In the ensuing space of quiet, the distant sounds of honking horns could be heard, and a far-off ambulance siren blared the news of a distant crisis. But we were high up on the twenty-sixth floor of the apartment building, so the babble from the busy street below was not at all invasive. It was more like a humming backdrop to our conversation, one that gave the room an enclosed, safe, cocoonlike quality.

I looked at her thoughtfully, bemused again by the fact that this handsome woman, who had so much going for her, had hooked up with a husband who sounded so irascible, punishing, and blaming. Why hadn't she been able to recognize and react to those small, internal warning signs and signals—the knotted gut, the tension headache, the feelings of anxiety—that we all experience within our body/selves when we sense that something in our lives is going awry? It seemed evident that none of these small somatic alarms—which must have been sounding from time to time *before* the marriage—had been recognized and reacted to by her at the level of conscious awareness. Yet it was these very dispatches from the body's interior—a crucially important aspect of our everyday decision making—

that could have signaled her fair warning about what living with this partner was going to be like.

Deciphering the Data

There are innumerable life situations in which our bodies are sending out
somatic cues, signals, and announcements—"Something's feeling 'off'
here" or "I'm not sure this person can be trusted"—but transmitting this
information in the form of vague physical discomforts or minor symptoms
rather than through the more precise medium of thoughts and language.
These body-based data contain vital information and need to be attended
to on a routine basis—translated from what are crude physiological signals
("My stomach is in knots") into important bulletins that can at times be
crucial to the whole person's well-being.

Of course, these messages *do* need to be decoded on a case-by-case
basis: For example, a stomach pain may be symptomatic of a problem in
your life, but it can also have to do with a medical issue or, for that matter,
be traced to something that you ate earlier in the day. But in those cases
where there is an unprocessed, unresolved history of trauma, one of the
most typical reactions is that of going away internally—tuning out, becoming spacey, not fully present in one's mental or bodily self. The upside
of this "solution" is that feeling distanced and not quite registering the disturbing experiences internally helps to keep the pain at a greater remove.
You won't feel the "pain in your life" so keenly.

The serious downside, however, is that losing touch with this body-
based feedback is highly maladaptive in the long run. For in the process,
those gut feelings and responses—which so often bring us important, up-
to-the-millisecond data about our true emotional state of being—become
deactivated, blocked off. And as a consequence, a person may go charging
forward in circumstances that might give someone more in touch with
herself clear grounds for proceeding with caution.

—

Chapter Nine

WHAT LESSON
AM I NOT LEARNING?

SOME THREE MONTHS AFTER OUR INTERVIEWS HAD CON-
cluded, I phoned Claudia at her office. This was meant to be a brief, routine follow-up call, but she sounded distraught and said she was very glad
to hear from me. Her office was busy at this moment, but she told me that
she'd call back that evening shortly after eight o'clock.

When she phoned it was with news, and it was bad news. She and Paul
had just come back from a luxurious resort in the Bahamas, where they'd
gone to celebrate their one-year anniversary. The "celebration" had
turned out to be a hellish experience, and the two of them were now living
apart—at this point, it was a trial separation.

As we talked, I realized that Claudia's voice sounded muffled, lower,
almost an octave lower than I remembered. It was as if her voice were
weighted down by strain and embarrassment, and I kept having trouble
hearing what she was saying. She was clearly so depressed, so shaken to
the roots of her being, that I hated having to ask her to repeat herself; but
at times, during our long conversation, I simply had to do so.

As she described it, that anniversary trip had gone sour almost immediately on their arrival. They'd been unable to check in at the hotel because
their room wasn't ready, so they'd been offered the use of a hospitality
suite in order to change their clothes. "We had to get our bathing suits and
stuff out of our bags, and I guess I took ninety seconds more than Paul
thought I should have taken, and he blew up at me. I couldn't *believe* he

was acting that way over something so ridiculous, but I heard him mumble a name at me under his breath. . . ."

What kind of name? I asked her.

She hesitated, then said, "Fucking birdbrain." She found it humiliating even to talk about, she said, but that incident had set her off, and after that she'd found it hard to shake the agitated feelings. Her *own* part in all of this was that once Paul got her going, she just couldn't calm herself down and let go of the issue. This was *her* problem—letting go of things—and it was something she'd been continuing to work on with her therapist. As always, she was eager to step forward and take her share, or more than her share, of the blame.

I did remember her saying that when Paul was acting moody, tense, or short with her, she could get pretty nasty herself. "I'm not too pleasant to be around. I obsess on things and pick them apart," Claudia had said at that time. Still, my own reaction was that if *my* partner had called me something like that, for a reason like that, I'd have had some trouble letting go of the issue myself!

It had been a *hard* vacation, Claudia repeated in that same heavy, teary tone of voice. At one point, the pair of them had strolled around for a while, and then Paul had decided he was hungry. They'd sat down, and he'd ordered a ham and cheese sandwich and a soda, and the bill had come to around $20. Claudia had thought that sum was really off the wall.

"What I said was, 'Gee, this place is expensive; God forbid that you come here with a family because you could really go broke.'" That remark had caused another eruption, for her husband took the statement to mean that she wanted him to spend all of his money on *her* and none of it on his kids.

Just recently, I recalled, there had been some sudden financial demands coming from his children, which had both infuriated Paul and made him feel guilty toward them. The largest of these demands had been his seventeen-year-old daughter's request for a new car, which she "needed" to get to school and to her part-time job. "There was just a whole lot of stuff flying between the two of us, and it wasn't good," Claudia said, her voice taut. They had come home that Monday night and separated shortly afterward.

"So, where is this marriage now?" I asked her.

"I definitely have one foot out the door," she responded, and I heard her begin crying softly, a low, throbbing sound. "I've been having a tough time these past weeks. It's been very, very difficult. And you know, I'm totally *ashamed* at this second marriage failing. I just feel so humiliated, in every way. . . . But as I told Paul, I just don't know if I'm *strong* enough to handle this relationship."

"Strong enough?" I asked. This seemed to me an odd way to characterize the situation. She was putting herself down, describing herself in negative terms—her "weakness" in contrast with her partner's "strength" —when there were many other words that could have been used to portray what was happening between them. At one point during our interviews, I'd actually met with the couple together and found Claudia's husband engaging, good-looking, fastidiously dressed, and very, very tense. During the course of that conversation, he'd acknowledged that he had a lot of anger inside him and had been angry as long as he could remember—he didn't know why. Now I said to her, "You do realize that Paul is very tightly strung? He's really on a short fuse; you can feel it."

"Oh yes," said Claudia, sounding relieved by that remark. Then she said, "You know, I told his mother recently that God forbid the pair of us ever get caught in bad traffic; I just can't believe the way he acts! And then he turns around and says he acts that way because *I'm* bugging *him*! That *I'm* the one who doesn't know when to back off! But you know, the last time we were out driving together, he told me that if I didn't shut the 'f' up, he was going to punch me in the mouth, and all my teeth would fall out! Or better yet, he was going to throw me out of the car and run me over! And he will say, 'Claudia, I'm not saying that this kind of talk is right—it's *so wrong*—but it's *you*. You just push me to the limit!'"

I was startled. This was a degree of verbal violence that she'd never reported earlier. "There is simply no excuse for that kind of abusive talk," I said flatly.

"Well, that's where I am," she said wearily, and then began to sob again. "Maggie, I'm not *good* with this kind of stuff. And the truth is, with the exception of my first husband, I've always had every man break up with me. This goes all the way back to high school—everyone's always broken up with me. I did leave my ex-husband after five years, but I think any normal woman would have left that scam artist four years before I did.

So to make this final decision and walk out on Paul is really *hard*—I almost wish he'd do it to me."

She wished that *he* would be the one to break up the marriage, so that she wouldn't have to bear the guilt and be the "bad guy"—she felt so profoundly *bad* about herself already.

Claudia then told me there had been an entire year when she'd simply stopped dating any men at all, gone to see a therapist several times a week, and really tried to get to know herself. She'd tried to *be* herself; to live alone and *like* herself; and she'd really believed she'd gotten her act together during this period. "Eventually I started seeing different people, and then I started dating Paul, who was so kind and caring then; and we were together from that time onward. So I'm just sitting here, completely flabbergasted, and I'm saying, 'Here I am again, in this same position.' And I'm wondering, What lesson am I not learning, that I keep getting knocked over the head with the same thing?"

"I don't know, Claudia," I responded honestly. Then she began to cry again, and I simply sat there, listening, saying a soothing word from time to time. At the same time, I was thinking of how many similar situations I'd seen—instances in which a person had worked *hard* in psychotherapy, gained a new understanding of her or his ongoing problems and their origin in the painful experiences of the past, but then been unable to resist the magnetic pull toward repeating some version of the same history again. It was as if there were a deep stratum of the person's being that all this newfound intellectual and emotional knowledge had been unable to penetrate.

It may well be, as Bessel van der Kolk and other trauma experts have suggested, that this less accessible stratum of the self corresponds to that mysterious, wordless region of the "old, emotional" brain where our body-based feelings, sensations, and memories are believed to reside. But in any case, while the "talking cure" has surely been effective in helping people to make sense of, and give meaning to, a troubled past, it frequently *hasn't* helped them to change their repetitive ways of behaving and improve upon their present lives.

For example, Claudia, by maintaining her family's pattern of silence about matters that were *not* to be discussed (for instance, "bad behavior"), and therefore lying to Paul from the very outset, had almost scripted him to play a role in the secretive, abusive drama that was the story of her life. She was operating as if a certain internal "blueprint for being"—as forceful as it was invisible—had been incorporated by her, body and mind.

As it happened, it was during this selfsame period that I was starting to look seriously at some of the more offbeat, nontraditional, body-oriented approaches to treatment—therapies such as EMDR (eye movement desensitization and reprocessing) and PBSP (Pesso Boyden System Psychomotor)—which I shall be discussing at greater length further along in this book. These forms of treatment do much more than offer insight on an intellectual and emotional level; as shall be seen, they also *engage the body* at a somatosensory level, which is to say at the level of body-based feelings, sensations, and remembrances. And I believe it was my own sense of helpless, frustrated sympathy during this conversation with Claudia that galvanized me into accelerated action at that time.

For in the wake of this exchange, I began to look, with a new urgency and focus, for answers to a question I now viewed as the crux of the matter: Were there effective forms of therapy that were targeted specifically upon releasing, from the body, those painful secrets that could lead to repetitive, self-destructive behaviors and "familiarly uncomfortable" bodily states? I was to find, in the course of my work, that the answer to this question is yes.

Part Two

—

REPROCESSING

Chapter Ten

—

DETOXIFYING THE
BODY'S MEMORIES:
REPROCESSING

HAT LESSON AM I *NOT* LEARNING?" MANY OF THE PEOPLE I was interviewing at this time had, like Claudia Martinelli, raised this bewildered question in one form or another. And as a result, I'd begun to look outside the boundaries of the more standard forms of psychotherapy and to explore a variety of newer, very different modes of treatment. It was in the course of this odyssey that I became an invited guest at a packed training workshop where a therapeutic treatment called reprocessing (short for eye movement desensitization and reprocessing, or EMDR) was being taught to an auditorium filled with clinicians.

As a guest, I was able to attend daily lectures on the reprocessing method and observe—but not take part in—the experiential, hands-on part of the training. But as the three-day workshop progressed, the obvious and unmistakable power of the process made me wish I could experience it from the inside rather than being fixed, as I was, in the position of onlooker and outsider. I had absorbed all that I could by sitting in on lectures and observing the hands-on part of the training. Now I wanted to acquaint myself with the experiential part of the therapy—to dive right in by putting myself in the role of "the client."

I did so more in the spirit of learning the procedure than of personal problem solving, but in fact the sessions turned out to be a serious eye-opener for me. For as it developed, there were secrets I'd been keeping from myself—matters that I'd been carefully avoiding "knowing" but which I *did* know—experiences long "forgotten" that I was holding in my body and mind and that were affecting me at the very core of my being.

Targeting a Memory

Like most other psychotherapeutic encounters, EMDR commences with an initial assessment phase that is a schematic overview of the client's lifetime. This synopsis consists of biographical information, such as where the person grew up, the major events of her or his life, and an account of the person's medical, psychological, relational, educational, and career history.

Such an assessment will often include information about previous therapies—their success or failure; what was helpful, what was not—and a rundown of the medications or nonprescription drugs that the patient has taken or is currently taking. In the usual kind of situation, the client has come in with an unresolvable problem or is in the midst of a life crisis. However, my own goal, when I went to see EMDR facilitator Dr. Patti Levin in her New Haven office, was a distinctively oddball one: I just wanted to see what reprocessing therapy *felt* like. What then happened was much more than I'd bargained for.

Reprocessing the Past

I'd heard a lot about EMDR before ever seeing it in action. I was aware that it relied far less heavily on the spoken word and the clinician's abilities and sophistication than it did upon a carefully designed eight-stage protocol—a therapeutic recipe of sorts. I'd also heard a lot about reprocessing therapy from a clinician friend who used it often in her office and had found it to be remarkably effective. But when she'd first described EMDR to me, it sounded like some sort of therapeutic hokum.

At that time (the early 1990s), I'd tried to listen to my friend Katherine Davis, whom I knew to have an impressive amount of experience under her belt. She'd been clinical director of the Hamden Mental Health Service in Connecticut for many years before opening a private office of her own. Still, I listened dubiously as she described therapeutic outcomes that smacked of hallelujah cures—sudden resolutions of patients' long-

standing problems that had come about when she made use of this reprocessing technique (still relatively unknown at the time).

One such case had to do with a trauma patient in her late twenties,
someone whom Katherine had treated with conventional, insight-oriented
psychotherapy for over a year. This client had suffered a harrowing loss:
She'd seen her three-year-old daughter run down and killed by a speeding
teenager who'd suddenly lost control of his car and careened into the child
while she was riding her tricycle up and down along the sidewalk.

The mother had been standing nearby, watching over her daughter,
and thus she was the helpless witness as the whole incident unrolled before her eyes. In the aftermath, the child's parent was so distraught that she
could barely function in her day-to-day life; she'd simply remained trans-
fixed in that terrible moment of the accident's occurrence. In session after
session, this tormented client had dwelled upon the visual image of that
horrifying scene, which preoccupied her thoughts and continued to flood
her with a grief that was seemingly unresolvable. She was also experiencing many of the classical symptoms that follow upon traumatic events: intrusive thoughts, bursts of irrational anger, feelings of ongoing agitation,
and horrible nightmares that sent her hurtling into wakefulness.

According to Katherine, this state of affairs had persisted for weeks,
months, and then a year of traditional insight-oriented therapy, bolstered
by antidepressant medication; still, nothing seemed to change things. The
treatment was clearly going nowhere, and in fact, as Katherine later described it to me, it was in the nature of a frustrated, last-ditch effort to get
the treatment moving that she'd first tried using reprocessing therapy. She
herself was a novice, having just received training in the use of EMDR,
and she hadn't actually tried putting her new knowledge to the test. What
happened then amazed both therapist and client.

For in the wake of that single ninety-minute reprocessing session, the
deadlock in the treatment came to a sudden, dramatic ending. Something
remarkable had taken place—it was hard to understand just *how* or *why* it
had taken place, but at the close of this meeting, the patient focused her
gaze upon the therapist and said, "Okay, that's *it*. It's *over*. It happened,
and there's nothing anyone in the world can do to make it *un*happen. It
was and *is* horrible, but it's in the past. I have to get on with my life, but I
feel that I can deal with it now."

"And that," Katherine told me, "was that." The therapy was essentially over, and in a few subsequent sessions, the young mother moved through a process of normal mourning.

Her tragic loss was no longer being experienced in the here and now—undigested and indigestible, stuck in her throat. Somehow, that single reprocessing session had enabled her to integrate a welter of thoughts, feelings, and images that had kept her locked in the moment of the trauma—the process had enabled her to swallow down and assimilate what her mind and body had been rejecting ever since her little daughter's death. The loss had been transformed into an awful memory, but it was now a part of the past—no longer something that was continually happening in an eternal, breathless, terrifying present tense.

Therapeutic Turnarounds

In the course of my work, I soon began encountering other clinicians who had the same kinds of amazing turnarounds to report. One New York analyst told me about a patient of his, a young college student whom he'd treated in psychotherapy over an extended period of time.

This young client had come in twice a week, every week, always complaining about the same problem—a painful relationship with an older, married professor. It was an affair she hated being involved in and wanted to break off, but somehow she couldn't bring herself to do it. She felt that the relationship was not only bad morally, but bad *for her* as a person; there were many ways in which her lover was being cruel to her, even sadistic, and she was well aware that this was so. Nevertheless, after months of psychotherapy, she'd been unable to bring this degrading attachment to a halt.

As had been true in my friend Katherine's case, this clinician had turned to the reprocessing method as a last resort, for he himself was in a state of "therapeutic despair." He was playing EMDR as a last clinical card, but in this instance, the patient hadn't appeared to respond—at least not in any way that was apparent.

During the rapid eye movement sets, she'd merely placed her hand upon her own body in different, innocuous-seeming places—at one point, her shoulder; at another, her arm; and then her forehead. But she'd had very little to *say* during the reprocessing procedure, and it didn't seem to her therapist that EMDR was going to have any effect. However, between that clinical session and the client's next appointment, her life took a startling 180-degree turnaround. Upon her arrival at his office, she informed her therapist that she'd finally ended the demeaning affair that had been causing her so much pain for so long.

She wasn't sure *why* she'd suddenly felt so capable of bringing that ugly situation to a close, but she *had*—and she felt really good about having done so. That was it. This young woman's presenting problem had been resolved with mysterious ease—and with few words having been said—in the aftermath of that single reprocessing session.

In this case, and in the many other clinical anecdotes I was hearing, reprocessing therapy had made a real difference in terms of bringing about clear and palpable change—not always with the same remarkable rapidity seen in the cases just described, to be sure. (Of course, in both these instances, the EMDR sessions had been preceded by extensive verbal psychotherapy.) Still, I will confess that such glowing reports had left me feeling skeptical, uneasy. For from a scientific point of view, how could miraculous resolutions of this sort possibly be explained? They sounded too sudden and dramatic, too good to be completely true.

Detoxifying Painful Memories

It was by serendipitous accident that Francine Shapiro, Ph.D., the originator and pioneer of EMDR, first stumbled across the peculiar notion that rapid eye movements might affect mental functioning in some unaccountable but distress-relieving fashion. She had been walking in a California park, thinking unhappily about some matter that was troubling her—she can no longer remember exactly what it was. Perhaps her mind was on the cancer, discovered and treated successfully a decade earlier (in the late 1970s). She was certainly in good health at the moment, but her physician had told her at the time of discharge that her disease might reappear, without warning, at some later point in time. This did happen to some cancer survivors, for reasons that were not at all predictable.

On that afternoon, Shapiro happened to be following a footpath lined by trees whose branches were swaying in the soft breezes. Strolling along, she eventually noticed something that was peculiar. As she walked, she'd begun feeling better. Much better. And by the time she reached the end of that pathway, the disturbing thoughts that had been preoccupying her seemed to have vanished from her mind. When and how had this happened?

She was puzzled, but grateful for this lifting of her spirits. At the same time, since she was a graduate student in clinical psychology, Shapiro's professional curiosity had been aroused. Not only her professional but her very personal curiosity, for she believed that mood-state, and its relation to the body, had some still undiscovered connection to the growth or regression of illnesses such as her own. What had brought about this sense of psychic relief? She called up other negative thoughts, in a purposeful fashion, and as they also vanished, discovered that her eyes had been moving diagonally, from side to side, very quickly, with the steady regularity of a metronome.

The year was 1987, and that trek through the park has since attained legendary status. Indeed, it has evolved over the subsequent years into the creation myth of a new form of therapy, one that has affected the lives of thousands and thousands of people. For having taken note of what had just occurred, and her own changed state of mind, Shapiro wondered whether emotional distress might be affected by the kind of rapid back-and-forth eye movements she had been making as she'd been walking down the pathway. Was it possible that rhythmical eye-tracking in this fashion had some effect upon the nervous system which no-one had noticed before?

In order to test out this strange notion, she summoned up another mildly anxiety-provoking concern that had been preoccupying her at that time. And as she did so, Shapiro moved her eyes back and forth at the same rapid pace and in the same arclike motion as before—following the motion of the branches from left to right and back again, in a continuously moving fashion. Once again, the anxious thoughts seemed to lose their emotional intensity. This was bizarre!

Had thinking those disturbing thoughts, in tandem with the rapid back-and-forth eye movements, tapped into some obscure neurophysiological mechanism that brought about the relief of psychological pain? It was an odd-sounding but nevertheless fascinating idea; and Shapiro, intrigued, began testing out the hypothesis informally with friends, acquaintances, and students—some seventy "volunteers" all told.

However, it didn't take her long to realize that a lot of people had difficulty making the desired swift left-to-right-and-back eye movements spontaneously. So she devised a method that involved asking the subject to bring up a distressing incident and then keep it in mind while eye tracking the movement of her index fingers, which she held up and waved back and forth rhythmically at a comfortable distance from the person's face. This simple procedure—bringing a source of distress to mind while visually tracking the rapid back-and-forth motion of a moving stimulus—appeared to have the curious effect of detoxifying painful, worrying thoughts and putting hurtful memories at a distance and in the past, where they rightfully belonged.

Next, Shapiro began to study this phenomenon within the framework of a formal research project, which was eventually to become the core of her doctoral thesis. The twenty-two subjects taking part in her study were all suffering from clear-cut cases of post-traumatic stress disorder that had developed in the wake of big-T events—such as rape, battlefield experiences, and childhood sexual abuse—and on average, their symptoms had persisted for some twenty-three years. All of them held low opinions of themselves (self-blame is commonplace in these situations), and all had significant problems in relating to others despite having undergone years of therapy.

After one sixty-minute session of EMD (eye movement desensitization, as Francine Shapiro first called her new technique), targeted upon a particular memory *that was troubling the person at the present time*, every one of the participants in this research reported feeling significantly better. The painful memory that had been focused upon had mysteriously lost its biting quality; moreover, all of the subjects felt more positive about themselves and more hopeful about the future. And at a three-month follow-up, many of the concrete gains made by Shapiro's research subjects seemed to have persisted with a surprising robustness.

A control group for this study consisted of PTSD subjects who'd been instructed to call up a troubling memory, which was then discussed at length. However, there was no periodic use of rapid eye movements during these individuals' sessions. It was talking therapy only, and these trauma survivors showed no improvement whatsoever. Shapiro, as astonished by her results as anyone, felt like an explorer who has suddenly emerged upon a wondrous terrain where no one has ever set foot before. True, there was solid earth beneath her feet, in terms of real research results, but where could they possibly lead her?

Desensitizing the Pain

At first it was Shapiro's belief that her new rapid eye movement technique belonged under the umbrella of behavioral therapy, for it involved the slow, systematic desensitization of unbearably hurtful memories—a treatment approach that had long been in use. This behavioral method entails carefully exposing the patient to the original traumatizing situation (often by asking the person to summon up the event or scene in his or her imagination), but at the same time managing to keep the level of emotional intensity lower, under control. The purpose is to enable the patient to feel comfortable enough to begin to *think* about, integrate, and process what did happen, while feeling anchored by the sense of safety provided by the therapeutic situation.

Then, if the treatment moves along according to expectation, the trauma survivor will become increasingly capable of tolerating feelings, thoughts, memories, and images—which come into ever sharpening, more vivid focus—*without* becoming overwhelmed by his or her own fear and terror. The basic theory here is that over time, repeated exposure to the alarming event or events makes what happened feel less horrifying (one becomes habituated to it, "desensitized") and that ultimately this proves far more curative than efforts to deny or avoid what actually occurred. Clinically speaking, denial and avoidance are strategies that may be helpful in the short run but don't work well over time. Painful though it may be, systematically confronting *what really happened* and slowly processing it is far more effective than trying to run away inside—which typically proves impossible anyway.

For when the traumatized person's truth takes the alternative low and secret road, it tends to erupt in the form of symptoms—memories that are split off from consciousness, obsessional ruminations, exaggerated startle responses (an unexpected touch on the shoulder may spark real terror), hyperagitation, and behavioral reenactments of the harmful things that happened earlier. But there is a problem inherent in the use of exposure therapy, which is that many traumatized people find it thoroughly intolerable. Returning to the scene of the trauma, even in imagination, is so agonizing that many patients freak out early in the process; they retreat from the process rapidly and then live out lives that are controlled by their post-traumatic symptoms.

Thus it was that Francine Shapiro—at least initially—viewed her new eye movement desensitization technique as a simple but wonderful tool to be used for making the process of desensitization more bearable. The rapid eye movement procedure appeared to make it possible for the client to bring up a racking, horrible memory and then use the swiftly alternating stimulation (left to right and back again) to draw the poisons from it rapidly and without the same degree of mental pain.

A Psychic Splinter

With the passage of time, however, and the appearance of a raft of psychological studies of the rapid eye movement phenomenon (many pro, a few con), Shapiro eventually decided to add the "R"—which stands for "Reprocessing"—to EMD, her strange-sounding but remarkably effective new approach. For by now she had come to believe that the rapid eye movements were actually initiating some kind of accelerated information processing within the central nervous system itself—one whose mechanism of action was very probably similar to what happens during REM (rapid eye movement) sleep.

This is the phase of sleep during which the raw data of the day's events are reawakened in the form of dreams—and the dreamer's eyes shift back and forth very swiftly, although she or he remains deep in slumber. A way of thinking about what happens during REM sleep is that these reactivated events are like pieces of a jigsaw puzzle that are being quickly scanned, assessed, then fitted together in some way that provides an integrated whole—a "portrait" or summation of the experiences that is meaningful and makes sense. When, like a picture puzzle that has been finished, it feels complete, it can be left behind: The events have been integrated into the person's wider understanding and become part of her or his history.

In Shapiro's view, and the view of other researchers as well, it had come to seem highly likely that there was some neurological analogue between REM sleep and EMDR. For in some mysterious fashion, EMDR seemed to enhance the brain's capacity to deal with those unassimilated bits of experience that had never been properly integrated and processed—which had, metaphorically speaking, become stuck in the patient's throat.

Simply by following the alternating, visual stimulus of the therapist's moving fingers—while keeping the mind focused directly upon those thoughts and memories that gave rise to distress—it often became possible for the person to process painful information that had hitherto existed within the brain as disassembled pieces of coarse, disorganized data. In some ill-understood fashion, the rapid eye movements helped the person to gather together the scrambled chunks and bits of stored material pertaining to the trauma so that it could be confronted and processed. Shapiro herself, along with a number of her colleagues, had come to believe that the rapid eye movements (rhythmic, alternating hand taps and ear tones have proven effective, too) were accessing some unknown, natural healing and integrating process in the brain.

At the present time, almost two decades since that famous walk in the park, many clinicians and researchers will attest that rapid eye movements *do* affect the brain in some mysterious fashion, but nobody is clear about *how* or *why* this happens (of course, still relatively unexplained are the bases of many drug actions, including the actions of most antidepressants). And in the meantime, psychologist Shapiro's reprocessing therapy has changed and evolved into a methodically ordered, full-fledged method of treatment that occupies its own clinical ground. However, as is always the case when a new kind of therapy makes its debut upon the clinical stage, a chorus of objections and criticisms has accompanied its emergence. One of the major critiques has been that EMDR works far too rapidly, a grievance that Francine Shapiro views as humorous.

She likes to compare her way of dealing with the aftermath of trauma to what happens when you remove a splinter from the flesh. A splinter can develop into a horrible infection if it's left to fester, but healing happens quickly once it is removed. So it is, she says, with toxic thoughts and memories. While nobody has been able to state definitively why reprocessing therapy works so frequently and with such rapidity—and while it is only grudgingly being accepted within mainstream clinical psychology despite a good deal of positive outcome research—it can be seen as taking out an emotional splinter. Once the splinter has been removed, healing can take place with surprising swiftness.

Similarly, maintains Francine Shapiro, once the raw, fragmented information—fractured thoughts, torn memories, partially obscured visual images, weird, inexplicable body sensations—has been integrated into the person's autobiographical history, it loses its dangerous intensity. The bad memory or memories don't go away, but they are now incorporated into the body and self in a different manner, and they hold different meanings. Thus, a sexually molested child who has grown up feeling that she's polluted in her very being can be helped to the realization that "I did the best I could, under the circumstances in which it happened." She can put the disturbing past *into the past* where it belongs and stop viewing herself as the soiled creature whom events that were in reality uncontrollable have caused her to believe that she is. Such views and beliefs are no longer part of an ingrained, negatively charged, often paralyzing sense of the self and the self in the world—which makes room for new learning and for the therapy client's interrupted life and development to move in a far healthier, more forward direction.

The Onlooker and the Outsider

I had been introduced to Dr. Patti Levin at one of the EMDR workshops and been impressed by her sensitivity; her tall, ramrod-straight dark-haired beauty; her quick intelligence and readiness to become engaged. When I went to see her in her office, we began with the initial assessment interview, which is the first stage of reprocessing therapy.

This information-gathering session is, it seems to me, in the nature of a fishing trip. The clinician is casting out a wide net in which she hopes to bring to the surface those toxic memories that existed within the client's brain and body—to bring them up and then "neutralize" them one by one. For the basic assumption here, as in so many other forms of therapy, is that the experiences of the past are often a hidden, driving force when it comes to what's happening in the present.

This happened to be true in my own case, for during the assessment process an unresolved concern I was struggling with did come tumbling out. It had to do with a recent bout of back pain that had kept me immobilized for several months. During this period, many friends and acquaintances had checked in with me frequently and been solicitous in numerous ways. But the two women whom I'd most depended upon to *be there* for me—one of whom I'd cared for daily after a bad accident—simply vanished from my life completely. They'd neither e-mailed nor telephoned—a radical behavior change in both instances—nor had they come to visit, although I'd asked them both to "please come and make a sick call." What had followed was nothing, silence.

Later on, when I was well and fully on my feet again, there were many proffered apologies, but the message that had come through was clear. These close, trusted confidantes were able to receive, but giving out was not on their agenda: If you were creating claims on their time or emotional resources, they'd move off until the demand was gone. I was shaken by such callous indifference and yet in some way not startled at all, for this was a familiar theme in my life—being ignored. After all, the first sentence of my autobiography, the one that always popped into my mind, was "I was born, and nobody noticed."

To be sure, I'd long known, at least at a certain level, that my most intense relationships were with female friends who hooked on to me when in situations of emotional need. It was as if I were giving off some sonar signal: "I will help you." They found me, and at a gut level, I found myself drawn in. As the daughter of my mother, I was the perfect partner of someone who needed nurturing; but in that situation I'd needed it myself.

"That must have been *hard* for you," Patti Levin said sympathetically, "when these women, on whom you were depending, didn't validate your own needs and act like friends. When they didn't even phone and say, 'How are you doing?'"

I smiled wryly, said that this lack of reciprocity was an old story, a pattern of unbalanced friendship I'd fallen into before. Patti nodded and asked me if I could pinpoint a time in my life when this prototypical relationship had first come into being.

I shook my head; I really couldn't. But my thoughts hurtled backward in time to long-ago memories of my two older sisters, who'd been locked in a poisonous, bitter rivalry as long as I could remember. They'd shared a bedroom, but like many children of a cruel parent, they'd turned on each other and begrudged each other any morsel of affection or attention, any good thing in life. I was out of the loop until much later on, when each of them wanted only one thing from me: to join in an angry coalition against the other.

My sisters scared me. The intensity of their mutual rage, which persisted long into adulthood, had the power to suck me into the vortex of a surging wave that could tumble me over and over and eventually deposit me back in a place to which I didn't want to return. In time, moreover, certain hurtful interactions began occurring—some around my budding writing career—and I came to realize that they bore ill will not only to each other, but to me. I had the notion that if a pennant bearing our family coat of arms had been fluttering over what remained of that household, the motto it bore would have been "You can't have anything that *I* don't have. . . . And if you do, it will make me want to kill you."

I met Patti Levin's gaze directly and said that in terms of internal supports, my mother's love for me was the sole bulwark I'd always clung to. She gazed at me briefly, then murmured quietly that nevertheless she believed that my older sisters' competitiveness and their wish to *use* me were issues that were being played out constantly in my current-day life.

I nodded; she was right. But at that moment, the recollection of a profoundly shocking incident—one that had nothing to do with my sisters—ballooned up from the subsurface of my being. It made me feel a little dizzy, and my heart began to pound; I found myself half rising from the chair. The vivid recollection of my mother's last visit to my home in Connecticut had suddenly assailed me, and it was a narrative that ran directly counter to all of the loving things I'd just been saying—something like a secret I'd been keeping from myself. As I sank back into my seat and began describing what had happened, Patti and I decided to target and "detoxify" this memory during the EMDR session that followed.

—

Chapter Eleven

FOLLOWING THE LIGHTS

$\mathcal{M}$Y MOTHER LOOKED SURPRISINGLY SHORTER—HER spinal disks had compressed with the passage of time—and she'd been like a taut bundle of rage from the moment she'd arrived. It was the early seventies, and she had been living in Israel, where she'd remarried. She was now convinced that her second husband was trying to defraud her of her small savings and income. Was it true? We couldn't ever confirm or deny it, not with certainty. When we'd met her new husband, he had seemed like such a sweet, scholarly man, and there was an overwrought, frantic air about my mother's anger and her accusations.

At the very outset of the visit, she'd marched upstairs to inspect the second floor (she hadn't seen this house before) and come right down with her chin jutting out triumphantly. "I notice that the two of you don't sleep in the same bed," she told me, her face alight with approval, "and I don't blame you. *I* don't need a man in *my* bed, either!" I was startled by this off-the-wall comment and stood there looking at her, speechless. Then I realized that she had mistaken one of our daughters' rooms, which had twin beds in it, for the bedroom my husband and I occupied ourselves.

"No, Mom, we do sleep together—in that big front bedroom, where there's a big double bed. Didn't you happen to look in *that* room?" I asked. Judging from her facial expression, the news was anything but welcome. She turned away from me coldly and went prowling through other parts of the house as if on a search for clues to a truth I was withholding.

I'd felt strangely at fault, as if I were letting her down. If I wasn't a disgruntled, male-abhorring wife who didn't need a man in her bed, then we two hadn't remained merged and "as one," in perfect synchrony, as we had been throughout my childhood. "You can't have anything that *I* don't have," Patti Levin murmured on hearing this part of the story.

She was parroting back to me what I'd said about "the family pennant" earlier. I stopped, gave her a blank look, then asked what that meant in this context.

She gave me a quizzical look, raised an eyebrow. "If I don't have a man in my bed, *you* can't have a man in your bed. And if you *do*, it will make me feel bitter and vengeful." Those weren't the exact words I'd spoken, but they did echo their spirit, and I was taken aback. I'd surely never connected the competitiveness and ill wishing of my sisters with anything that had transpired between my mother and myself; the idea was simply unthinkable. It had no place in the cherished narrative of the loving, grateful bond I'd always shared with this deeply loved parent.

And yet the memory of that moment did reawaken another long-forgotten memory—something else that had occurred during that same, difficult visit. It had to do with my career as a science journalist, which was then just getting under way. Throughout the decade that was to follow, the 1970s, I did in fact turn out one *New York Times Magazine* cover story after another (and eventually see them brought together in a book of essays called *Body, Mind, Behavior*). But at the time my mother came to stay with us, I had only a small sheaf of published articles to show her. I remember presenting them to her proudly and then leaving her on the back porch to read them.

It was a pleasantly hot day in June, and the back porch on which she sat is at the base of a hill that rises in back of our home. The land our house is built upon was once part of inventor Eli Whitney's sprawling farm, and part of our view is an old drystone wall dating from the time the Whitney family lived here. The shape of the terrain we face is rounded and rising, like one side of a great bowl; and it's thick with old trees—tall oaks, some pines, some beech trees, and an ash or two. At midday, when the sunlight comes streaming down through the leafy foliage, the setting takes on a hushed, holy quality.

I waited, time passed; but there was silence aside from the occasional cawing of a crow. I remember going about a few kitchen tasks, feeling charged up, excited. My thoughts were filled with imaginings of my mother's pleasure and my own reactions to her pleasure—does anything ever equal the magical joy of a parent's admiration? But a half hour and then almost forty-five minutes passed by, and I'd reached that outer limit where anticipation begins to merge into worry. All this time I'd been expecting her to come inside and say something, but she hadn't. So at last I went out to the porch and asked, "What do you think of them, Mom?"

She was sitting there, motionless. The articles were beside her on our wicker sofa, and her horn-rimmed glasses had been placed on top of them. Her hands were folded calmly in her lap, and she said, "I have better things to read."

A Safe Place and Two Metaphors

Patti Levin now asked me, "When your mother said, 'I have better things to read,' how did that make you feel?"

I reflected briefly, could summon up nothing more than a hazy, out-of-focus recollection of having picked up the stack of articles and gone back into the house once again. "Stunned. *Not* angry, strangely enough. Confused . . . disoriented." I was experiencing an upsurge of the same feelings now, for the recollection of that incident was swamping me with the sense I'd had then—a desolate sense of being orphaned. This part of my life's story didn't really fit in with so many other loving, soothing, earlier memories of my relationship with my mother. In fact, it was a kind of counternarrative, one in which all the affection and gratitude that existed at the surface threatened to give way to an underlying sense of disappointment and betrayal.

But this way of thinking felt aberrant. As far as I was concerned, the basic plot line of my childhood featured a brutally repressive father and a victimized, exploited mother who had nevertheless protected and saved me. And if certain events (such as the scene just described) had no place in the historical chronicle, I'd tended to discount and ignore them. I can't say I'd forgotten such discordances completely—only that they resided within my internal world as isolated, unintegrated islands of information, disconnected from the mainland of conscious awareness.

At this point in the preparation process, the EMDR protocol called for

the establishment of what is called a "safe place." So Patti Levin asked me
if I could summon up a kind of sanctuary inside my head—a spot I could
go to (real or imaginary) that felt perfectly calm, secure, and comfortable.
It might be a beach, a park, or some other mellow, relaxing spot that I recalled or could envision. "Do you have something of the sort that comes
to your mind?" she asked.

I nodded; I had several. The beach at Cape Cod was certainly one, I
mused aloud, as was the quiet dock in front of a lake cottage that we rent
in the summers. But come to think of it, the safest place was probably a
small upstairs sitting room in our house. My husband and I like to spend
time there, reading, watching the evening news, listening to music on the
stereo. "That little den," I said. "I can picture being there, with my husband, and we're both reading and I'm feeling peaceful and dozy. . . ."

"Okay, then," said Patti, "I'd like you to bring up the memory of feeling
safe and protected in that room, with your husband nearby, and really feel
it all through your body. And let's give it a word . . . a single cue word. . . ."

"I guess it would be 'home,'" I said, then amended quickly, "No, it
would be 'the den.'"

She nodded and said, "'The den.' So I want you to bring up 'the den'
and just follow the lights." Then she flicked the control switch on a device
(it's called the Neuro*Tek* light scan) that she uses instead of recurring
hand waves to guide the client's rapid eye movements. This ruler-shaped
apparatus consists of a flashing row of minilights that keep shifting swiftly
from left to right and back again. I tracked the rhythmically alternating
visual stimulus, hearing Patti's soothing voice in the background: "I want
you to *feel* that safe place inside you. How it feels in your skin. The sounds,
the smells, the serenity, whatever makes you feel safe and makes you *know*
that it's yours."

As my gaze followed the rapidly oscillating left-right-left lights on the
bar, I could bring to mind the two of us sitting there, reading, and almost
hear soft music playing—a Mozart quartet? I could smell the wool of my
favorite rose-and-magenta shawl, which was tucked around my knees; I
felt comfortable, relaxed. "Have you got it?" Patti asked me.

I said I thought so. "I'm getting sleepy," I murmured with a smile.

I felt a sense of relief throughout my body. I hadn't realized I was nervous about what would happen next, but at the training conferences I'd cer-

tainly seen some dramatic responses to the rapid eye movement sets. This brief, calming preliminary step served to give me the sense of a safe port to which I could quickly retreat if a storm of unexpected feelings blew up. Patti then offered me a set of headphones that come with the Neuro*Tek* light bar and can be used to augment the eye tracking. I tried them on and liked the *tick-tock* of the continually shifting sounds—a brief tone in the left ear, then a brief tone in the right, and then back to the left ear—that seemed to be in synchrony with movements of the lights. The sounds were bringing into play another of the body's sensory modes, making it possible for me to *hear* as well as observe visually the cyclic, continuous alternation from one side of the brain to the other.

The next order of business (familiar to me in my role as observer, but completely strange as a participant) was that of fixing upon the distance from the light bar that felt most comfortable to me. After this matter had been settled, Patti described the two major metaphors that EMDR clinicians often present to their clients before the actual reprocessing begins.

One is to imagine that you are getting on a train at point A and that your eventual destination is point B. At point A you are carrying with you all the troublesome junk that you want to unload, so that on arrival at point B, you won't be burdened with it any longer. "Along the way, you'll be looking out the window and seeing some of the stuff you're leaving behind—it's just scenery, and you're passing beyond it. At times you may want to avert your eyes, bring your gaze back on the train. That's okay; if it gets too uncomfortable, you don't have to watch it. At every stop along the way, when we pause and I ask, 'What are you noticing?' you can think of that as a station where dysfunctional information is being discarded and more functional information may be being taken on," she said, then paused and looked at me questioningly, as if to ask whether or not I understood her fully.

I nodded. Then she reviewed the other favored EMDR metaphor, which was to imagine that I held in my hand the remote control to a video that was playing on the screen of a large TV. The dysfunctional material I was processing was unfolding on that screen, and I was watching it as if I were watching a film. If the scenes I was seeing (such as that scene on the porch) were getting me upset, I could use the remote control to slow the film down. Or I could use it to mute the sound; I could speed up the film if I wanted to, or pause it, or just turn it off completely. What happened was entirely in my hands.

"Does one or the other metaphor appeal to you?" asked Patti.

"The train," I replied without hesitating. I realized that the image of embarking on a sea voyage into the past had been floating through my mind, but now my thought was that a train journey would do very nicely instead.

That Mother Was Not a Crazy Lady

During the preparation phase of the process, Patti had been typing occasional brief notes into the slender, envelope-shaped computer that she held upon her lap. Throughout this phase (not one but two prior sessions), I'd been trying to convey to her a sense of the deep fear that had pervaded my early family household. We children were like prisoners taken in a war we couldn't begin to understand. My father, the silent, steely-eyed commandant of the compound, was the source of a perennially threatened, unpredictable eruption about some issue that made no rational sense. My mother was the sane, reachable parent, but she was as much at my father's mercy as we siblings were. Nevertheless, I always saw her as doing her brave best to stand between his craziness and our vulnerability.

By the time she visited us in the early seventies, though, she was changed—a classic example of what Freud called "identification with the lost object" or, more simply, *becoming just like the person who is gone.* This process had begun shortly after my parents' divorce, when my mother had begun her strange transformation into someone remarkably similar to the husband she'd defied, resisted for years, then ultimately left—that is, fanatically religious, frowning angrily much of the time, praying constantly, unreachable.

One Friday evening during my mother's visit, my husband and I went out to dinner with one of his colleagues, a visitor from California. When we returned I went up to our third-floor guest quarters to kiss my mother good night, calling out, "Mom, Mom, I'm coming up for a moment!" as I'd run up the stairway. Perhaps she hadn't heard me—I'm not certain—

but in any case her false teeth were out, and my sudden arrival caught her by surprise.

I remember her leaning over the bed, about to slip in under the covers, then straightening up like a steely ramrod, looking at me with an expression of the purest, utmost rage and hatred. I stopped short. What had I done? Had I humiliated her because her teeth were out, which made her mouth look strange and sunken? Was she infuriated because we'd been out on a Friday night instead of welcoming the Sabbath with her? We didn't observe this ritual customarily, and she knew it, but the expression on her face was terrifying. I don't think anyone had ever looked at me with such murder in her eyes before; this had no place in my self-told narrative of our deeply loving, caring relationship.

Yet parts of that caring narrative *were true*. I thought of my mother as having saved me, in so many figurative and literal ways. She'd even given me the tuition for my third year of college—practically her last cent, as I understood it, and she hadn't been young at the time. So there were different parts of the story, parts of a larger puzzle whose pieces didn't fit. "Her own fate was so *hard*," I told Patti Levin, as if trying to explain how unentitled I felt to any feelings of indignation.

But then the full-blown memory of that expression on my mother's face burst back into my mind with a sudden force that felt assaultive. "I guess it's pretty obvious that she did *not* want me to live happily with a man, or sleep in the same bed with a man. And she did not want me to shine in the world," I said, thinking of her acid reaction to the articles I'd shown her.

Patti nodded. "You can't have anything that I don't have," she said, and her reiteration of that theme felt like the small but painful dislodging of an ax that had settled deep within me much earlier in my life. "Which is basically what was going on between your sisters. Nobody could have one tiny scrap of something that someone else didn't have, or the jealousy and rage would go wild . . . ?"

Her statement had ended as a question, and I could only nod and say that, yes, it had been a kind of primeval warfare. Then a feeling of colossal desolation descended upon me. I felt lost, obscured in a sandstorm of prickling, hurtful little thoughts about my mother, my sisters, and the two friends who had been "like sisters" to me and who'd vanished at a time

when I'd most needed them—that is, during the months I'd been inca-
pacitated by a painfully injured back.

Patti leaned forward, looked at my face intently, and asked me if I
would like, now, to review the narrative of my mother—perhaps one that
contained those seeming "inconsistencies" I'd been systematically delet-
ing from my own idealizing account. I agreed with a silent nod of my
head, for I could perceive the existence of a pattern here—some underlying game plan I was following whose end point, disappointment, a part of
me was always expecting to emerge.

"I think that for a long, long time I've been telling myself just *half* the
story," I said, hearing the incredulity in my own voice. "And what's been
left out is the stuff about the kid whose hair wasn't combed when she went
to school. The kid who never had clean clothes ready, who was not protected in any way, who wasn't even called in when it was time for dinner,
as the other children were—the kid who was fending for herself from
pretty early on, in many, many ways. Okay, my mom's life was hard, but
she *could* have kept the house clean; it was always dirty, disorganized. She
could have made sure her child had clean school clothes—a lot of people
in tough circumstances *do*."

"Right," said Patti, and that single word made me feel validated, *heard*.

"Being a parent myself, I really don't understand it," I said unhappily.
Patti shook her head from side to side, very slowly, as if to say she didn't understand it, either.

Then she returned to the target scene that we'd agreed we were going
to focus upon today, saying, "Do you remember how you felt, *in your
body*, when you showed her your articles and she said, 'I have better things
to read'?"

Remember? I smiled wryly, for those feelings were coursing through
me right now. "Stunned. Confused," I said. "As if I'm watching that scene
at this moment and yet still can't decipher its meaning. Was it something
to do with her ever growing religiosity—that she saw my writing as a bad,
unwomanly thing to do? Did she mean that the Bible was better
reading—or *what*?" I hesitated, then added with a shrug that I'd thought
she might just be getting kooky.

Patti looked at me thoughtfully, then said, "Thinking back to your relationship with your mother, and keeping in mind the themes of compet-

itiveness, jealousy, no protection, no validation—all of the suppressed parts of the narrative—can you bring to mind a memory or experience, a point in time, when you first realized that your mother wasn't perfect?"

I nodded; yes, I could. Our relationship had begun to deteriorate soon after my parents' separation, for it was then that my mom had started to take on religion with a thoroughly unexpected force and fanaticism. "She started behaving in ways that she'd always pooh-poohed in my father. And I remember her going wild and slapping me around because I'd brushed my teeth on one of the High Holidays; she was having all kinds of irrational outbursts at the time. I felt lost. We'd moved away from the neighborhood we'd lived in, and I'd had to change the high school I went to. But worst of all, I'd lost the mother I knew. *That* mother was not a crazy lady."

"So you realized then that your mother had become a crazy lady, and you'd never realized that before?"

I paused, looked at her in puzzlement, unsure what she meant. "No. . . . Why?"

"Wasn't it a little crazy to send a kid to school without her hair combed, and not to have her school clothes ready, and to keep a chaotically disorganized, disheveled house?"

I said nothing; I simply stared at Patti in amazement. I'd worshipped my mother so, and felt such sorrow on her behalf that I'd never entertained so perfidious a notion before.

The Worst Moment

The next order of EMDR business was to focus down sharply, as if with a high-powered microscope, upon the remembered point of maximal distress that I would target in this session. So Patti asked, "When your mother visited, and you showed her your articles, and she said, 'I have better things to read,' what was the *worst* moment of that experience? What is the image that springs to your mind?"

It didn't seem to me that I had one particular moment; it was more like a short reel of memory that began playing through my head immediately. It started with her sitting on the back porch, then moved to my coming out from the kitchen and asking, "What do you think of them, Mom?" Then, her saying coldly, "I have better things to read."

This was good enough for Patti, who said, "Okay, so when you think of that memory of your mother sitting on the back porch—and she's looking at your articles, and you come out and say, 'What do you think of them, Mom?' and she says, 'I have better things to read'—what is your current negative or irrational belief about yourself?"

"About myself?" I stared at her blankly, familiar though I was with the reprocessing protocol.

"About yourself," said Patti firmly, with a nod.

I couldn't imagine. I began casting about inside for some sort of answer but managed to come up with only a deep sigh, almost a groan. Finally I said, "I guess it would be . . . 'I'll never get what I need,'" though I myself wasn't sure just what that statement meant.

"And going back to that scene once again, your mother sitting on the back porch, looking at the articles, and you come out and say, 'What do you think of them, Mom?' and she says, 'I have better things to read.' Rather than believing 'I'll never get what I need,' what would you *rather believe now* as you think back to that moment?"

I laughed, embarrassed; it was not an easy question to answer. But Patti's expression remained serious, so I tried to think of a possible answer to the question. I couldn't. All that I was able to come up with was an answer in the subjunctive: "I'd rather believe that I *could* know how to get what I need," I said uncertainly.

She then asked me to bring to mind once again that memory of my mother saying, "I have better things to read," accompanied by the words "I *could* know how to get what I need." On a gut level, how true did that latter phrase *feel* to me?

I considered it momentarily. "Not very true, I'd say." I could hear the discouragement in my voice. Patti then asked me to represent my answer by a number on a scale that ranged from one to seven; the high figure, seven, stood for "completely true," and the low figure, one, stood for "not true at all." I assessed my degree of belief at about a one or a two; and she paused briefly to inscribe that figure on her laptop.

She looked up. "And when you go back to seeing your mother on the back porch, and she's looking at your articles, and you come out and say, 'What do you think of them, Mom?' and she says, 'I have better things to read,' and your thought or belief is, 'I'll never get what I need,' what emotions come up for you right now?"

"Stunned. *Not* angry," I repeated. There were no angry feelings connected with that scene, just an awful feeling of being lost, of being the daughter of a crazy mother. "It was over, hopeless . . . the relationship was gone." I shrugged, as if to say that the past was the past and I'd packed it all away years earlier.

But Patti looked at me searchingly and asked, "How upsetting does that scene feel to you at this moment—say, if you think of it on another, different scale, one where ten is the worst you can imagine and zero is no disturbance at all?"

I realized that the degree of distress I was feeling was pretty high and rated it at about an eight or a nine. She then asked me where, in my body, I noticed the disturbance. I pointed to my jaw, saying, "I feel it here. Actually, I never get headaches or stomachaches—any stress symptoms of that sort. But when I feel upset, my jaw clenches; and I feel it clenching *hard* right now." In fact, my jaw felt so tight that it was actually hurting. Patti typed a comment in her file, then nodded. The rapid eye tracking was about to get under way.

I'll Never Get What I Need

Patti said, "I want you to go back to that memory of your mother sitting on the back porch, looking at your articles. And you come out and say, 'What did you think of them, Mom?' and she says, 'I have better things to read.' *Hold that together with the words* 'I'll never get what I need.' Notice the feelings of being stunned, lost; of feeling hopeless, like the daughter of a crazy mother; notice, too, where you feel it in your body. And then let whatever happens happen." These brief instructions were followed by her switching on the bar of rapidly moving, fluctuating, left-to-right-to-left lights.

At first I couldn't focus upon anything but the light bar itself. The lights were flashing back and forth so swiftly that I couldn't quite keep up with them. Was I doing this correctly, or should I call a halt and ask Patti to slow down the scanning device—she'd already explained that the Neuro*Tek* could do that. But I said nothing and before long found myself keeping up more easily. I noticed a strange tingling in my jaw, but not much else.

Then the words "I'll never get what I need" began floating through my head in the bannerlike shape of some skywriting following in the wake of a plane. I thought of bits and pieces of my history as a daughter and as a mother, and of the good and not so good reenactments of the past that had occurred. I recalled occasional outbursts I'd had with my own kids—so reminiscent of my mother's flare-ups—and those unwelcome recollections filled me with self-reproach. But I'd never been involved in anything remotely like her hair-pulling fights with my oldest sister, and it occurred to me that my track record through life was actually far stronger on the plus side than it was on debits and failings. Then, like the sudden sprouting of a spring crocus, a new thought popped up in my mind: "Maybe it's not so hopeless after all."

It remained only briefly, and then the phrase "I'll never get what I need" appeared in my mental sky again. It was succeeded by a vivid image of Sisyphus pushing the same heavy rock up the same familiar hill. At that point, Patti stopped the flashing lights, told me to take a deep inhale and exhale, and then asked me what I had been noticing. I mentioned the tingling in my jaw, my guilt about not being the perfectly unflappable parent, and the sudden realization that nevertheless there were many good things in my life. Almost as an afterthought, I told her about the image of Sisyphus pushing a rock up a hill—the same rock that cascaded down eternally.

Patti made no interpretations of these remarks; she simply said, "Go with that," and started the reprocessing again.

I found myself keeping pace with the moving lights more easily, and I was pleasantly aware of the alternating ear tones; but no particular thoughts or images came to mind. Instead, I found myself diverted by the loud voice-overs of outside traffic, the screeching truck gears and howling of some passing sirens, for Patti's office is near a busy feeder to the freeway. Then my thoughts turned to my older sisters, and how, when I was a little girl, they'd seemed like such goddesses to me. They'd seemed so lovely, but out of reach, as if they existed in a rarefied realm that was utterly different from the one I inhabited.

For one thing, they'd had a room of their own, one the two of them shared. I was in a large front bedroom, where not only I but my parents and my baby brother slept. My brother was six years younger than I; and for reasons that were forever unclear to me, he hadn't remained in our household very long but instead had been sent off to a religious boarding school in another city. In his adult years, he'd moved to California and cut off all contact with the family.

Patti halted the movement of the lights, then, and told me to take a deep breath.

I inhaled, and when I exhaled I said, "My family dismantled itself. There's no 'there' there, in terms of a family. My younger brother speaks to no one, and I've had to pull away, too. . . ."

"Mmm," was all she said, a contentless, sympathetic noise.

"A friend of mine was telling me how close she was to her sister, and I thought of something one of my kids once said to me. She said, 'Your sister wants to harm you,' and I do have this scary feeling that it's true, it's really *true*. My daughter made that remark after our family had had a big celebration and my sister had been acting like Hedda Gabler, sowing ill will and conflicts everywhere she went." I paused, for not surprisingly, the statement "You can't have anything that I don't have" had popped into my head.

"Maybe she felt that I had some things that she didn't have—a flourishing career, whatever . . . ?" This was, of course, a rhetorical question, and Patti shook her head as if to say she could not possibly have the answer. Or had it been my intact marriage and family? I wondered. My sister had been divorced for years and living abroad. Her relationships with the children she'd left behind, in the care of her ex-husband and their stepmother, were understandably dicey. Another fact of her history, a tragic one, was that her second-born son had vanished under mysterious circumstances at the age of nineteen.

My nephew Richie had simply disappeared from the world and never been heard from again. There were differing accounts of the circumstances surrounding this event that we'd heard from my sister at various points in time. Still other versions had been told to us by her children, and we'd heard yet another story from one of her European friends, a psychoanalyst. Finally, we'd settled upon the only answer possible, which was that there was *no* definitive answer, at least none that we would ever learn.

Still, my sister's choices had been none of my making, and the notion that she could wish me actual harm was awful, a cause of harm in itself. Even at this moment, the idea filled me with an atavistic kind of fear, and my brain seemed to go blank; it was as if my thoughts had come to an inner barrier, someplace beyond which thinking was no longer possible. I felt as if there were nothing but empty space inside my skull, and I wanted to stop now; there was nothing further to be said. "I don't know what I'm— I'm not sure where all of this is leading," I said, feeling as if my internal compass had gone hopelessly askew and I'd lost all sense of direction.

"It's fine," Patti said calmly. "Go with it. . . . Keep going." She flicked the moving lights into motion once again.

Past and Present

The image of the moving train that periodically slows to a halt, unloads dysfunctional information, and then takes on other, more wholesome kinds of material proved consistent with my own unfolding experience. For once I'd resumed the rapid eye tracking, I felt as if I'd moved forward in the journey and entered a surprisingly different bodily and mental state. My breathing was deep and even, and I found myself yawning widely. As I followed the swiftly moving lights from one end of the bar to the other, I felt calmer, forgiving, even philosophical and ready to look at the wider context in which such things had occurred.

I held up my right hand, which is the EMDR signal that it's time to call the reprocessing to a halt. (The word *stop* in itself is not sufficient, for the client may be saying "Stop!" to an imaginary someone who's part of a disturbing event that's being reexperienced inside his or her head.) Then I said, "Part of this has to do with the immigrant experience, with being lost between two cultures. My mom once told me that when he was a baby she'd put my brother down in the basement at night so he could 'cry it out' and not wake the family up at night—something that I, as an American mother, would have considered unimaginable. So God knows what else she did with her babies—things that, given her own upbringing, she felt were perfectly acceptable." I sighed.

Then I said that no matter what, in my eyes my mom had been a magical being. I could remember a time when she'd taken me and my kid brother downtown on New Year's Eve. "There was so much confetti, and there were horns and so much excitement. And coming home at midnight on the trolley car—it was *thrilling!*" I smiled and said that whatever was good in my life had come from my mother, but that her own life had been a tough one.

In retrospect, I realize that my thoughts had migrated back to square one, my emotional default position: I was the all-forgiving, totally empathetic daughter of a loving mom who was a victim. But Patti let this pass without comment and merely said, "Go back to that memory that we started with. What do you notice about it?"

I hesitated. For some reason, I couldn't seem to call up the memory very clearly. I retrieved some hazy scraps—the porch, my mom, her comment—but it all seemed blurred and out of focus. What I *did* become aware of was an increased tightness, a rigid feeling in my jaw.

"All right, go with that," said Patti. "Notice your jaw." And she set the light bar in motion once again.

A Kind of "Sophie's Choice"

I followed Patti's instructions, but focusing upon my jaw seemed to make the rigidity and strange tingling sensations intensify. It felt as if tiny electric currents were coursing through those chin muscles, and instinctively, I brought both hands up to my jaw and held them there. Then I tried to divert myself by the fantasy that I was looking out the window of the imaginary train upon which I was traveling.

There, the scene that greeted me was one of being with my mother, the last time I'd seen her alive. That had been in Israel, just after she'd had a serious stroke; one side of her body was paralyzed. Alas, by then our relationship was so attenuated that it existed only at the most superficial level. My mother's rage at her second husband was the dominant theme of her existence; she made no pretense at being interested in me, my spouse, my children, anything about my life. Throughout our stay, her main concern had been making sure that any assets she left behind would go *not* to her husband and his grasping (according to her) family, but to a cultlike, Orthodox religious charity that had become dear to her heart. We were enlisted to arrange a secret transfer of her funds; and if we did have any importance in her eyes, rendering this important service was the source of it.

Two watershed events in my own life were in the offing at that time. My middle daughter, Betsy, was to be married in the early summer; she and her new husband would be moving to Dallas in the following September. That same fall, my book on women and depression, *Unfinished Business*, was slated for publication; but due to its then relatively taboo theme, few people expected it to garner much attention. To everyone's surprise, however, the moment was ripe for a frank discussion of depression, and the book was greeted by a blitz of newspaper, television, radio, and magazine publicity. I became caught up, rolled over and over, tossed hither and yon in my own personal tsunami.

As a result, my typically flexible personal schedule was being trumped almost as soon as any arrangements were put in place. My plan had been to visit my daughter's new home in Texas in October, but that intention was subverted by a highly pressured book tour that was whisking me all over the country; I was moving from city to city on a daily basis. What had begun as an exciting, novel experience soon evolved into a sense of constant strain and loss of control—a sense of trying to stay the course on a wild ride that was sapping my energy and keeping me balanced precariously between health and exhaustion.

My plans to visit Dallas kept changing, for I was flying off in other directions, coming home, recovering, and working out fresh plans for a Texas visit that then had to be altered. "I think Betsy's getting upset," I told my husband, worried.

"No, she understands," he assured me.

But he couldn't have been more mistaken. By the time the blizzard of demands upon me had begun to lessen, Betsy was feeling hurt and absolutely furious. No matter *what* might happen next, I decided, the conflict between "mom time" and "me time" would be decided in Betsy's favor.

But on the eve of my departure for Dallas, my mother suffered a second stroke, one that left her in a deep coma. So I was presented with a kind of "Sophie's Choice" between a parent who I'd been warned would not be alive by the time I got to her bedside—she couldn't even know I was with her—and a daughter who was feeling aggrieved, ignored, and abandoned.

"I went to Dallas," I said to Patti Levin bleakly. "And so when my mother died I wasn't there. Neither were my sisters or my brother; she'd been so far distant from every one of her kids for so many years, in every sense of the word. And realistically, trying to make it there in time would have been a pointless maneuver. . . . But I never got to say good-bye."

Then a surge of loneliness and grief swept over me, as did the realization that all my efforts to evade or bypass such feelings had not been notably successful. My mother's death had not been truly mourned, and in some way I hadn't really parted from her. "I never got to say good-bye externally *or* internally"—the words emerged slowly—"and it's probably time to connect with all the sadness." I sighed, almost a groan, for a weary feeling had swept over me, as had the thought that I'd run and run throughout a lifetime without achieving much real distance from home base.

"Go with that, Maggie," instructed Patti, directing my attention to the light bar once again.

Nurturer/Nurturee

When I recommenced the rapid eye tracking, the imaginary "train" that was carrying me began to wind its way through a different, though neighboring, kind of terrain. The metaphor of the railway journey was proving marvelously apt, for it was congruent with the experience I was having. As I moved along from one reprocessing episode or "set" to the next one (each consisted of some twenty-four back-and-forth eye movements), with brief halts along the way, I found myself gazing out at a landscape thick with images and memories of various relationships I'd had with women friends over the years.

Most of these girl relationships had been structured in strikingly similar ways; they'd tended to be or become asymmetric and short on mutuality. Routinely, they'd been pervaded by a soothing, comforting parent–needful child flavor, for which my bond with my mother had surely been the prototype. Not surprisingly, the role I'd typically assumed was the role I had been playing since the dawn of memory: I was forever struggling to help and comfort a female friend who needed caretaking, and feeling profoundly, very personally involved in and responsible for her fate.

This was, of course, an all-too-familiar scenario, a replication of my earliest bond with my mom: "I'm going to fix things for you; I'm going to make you happy; I feel so guilty about the troubles and misery in your life." Always the wise giver, without needs of her own, I existed as the dedicated helper of a dependent, appreciative receiver; and the friendship always felt cozily familiar and completely appropriate. The underground "deal" here was that I never had to expose my suppressed dependencies or even face any sense of my own vulnerability, for the spotlight of the friendship's attention was always on the beleaguered other person.

I needed to focus more on finding *peers*, I thought, though without any sense of self-condemnation or alarm. On the contrary, I heard the sound of my own regular breathing in my ears, and each breath was deep, long, as peaceful as if I were meditating. Then the memory of a friendship in which the basic structure had been similar but the roles reversed—I myself had been the nurtured one—sprang into my mind's view. I was revisiting some vivid images of being with my friend Valerie (a pseudonym), now deceased, with whom I'd initially had a long, wonderful "friendship honeymoon."

Val, warm, funny, smart, and eleven years older than me, had taken me and our young family under her capaciously nurturing wing when we'd first arrived in New Haven. Given her seniority in terms of age, the fact that she knew her way around the new community, and her generous but imperious nature, she and I slipped right into the roles of all-knowing mentor and compliant disciple. I had never had so unstintingly nourishing a friend before, and not only our own lives, but the lives of our families became intertwined.

This gratifying state of affairs lasted until my aspirations as a writer began to be realized; then, however, I found that I was violating boundaries I hadn't even known existed. The difficulties had probably begun surfacing even earlier, when I'd spoken to Val about an article I was contemplating writing. The subject was to be a new method of inpatient psychiatric care called milieu therapy, which was then being pioneered at Yale–New Haven Hospital. Val was appalled by the idea.

On behalf of our friendship, she told me firmly, I shouldn't think of involving myself in such a project. Since she herself was a practicing clinician (a psychiatric social worker), there was a real danger that if I, her closest friend, were to get it all wrong and write something foolish, she would find it hugely embarrassing. What a pliant, perfectly obliging creature I had been! I'd actually pulled back and not begun researching the article until Val and her family left New Haven for a European sabbatical.

I found myself smiling at the recollection, bemused by the memory of that request. "What's coming up for you?" Patti questioned me after bringing the reprocessing to another temporary halt.

I answered by telling her the story of this friendship and about the way it had started foundering badly when my first *New York Times Magazine* piece was published. That article had marked both the beginning of my career as a science journalist and the initiation of what became a hurtful, confusing, unresolvable struggle between Val and myself. As I told Patti, with a brief, helpless little shrug of my shoulders, "It was the very article about the mental ward that she'd asked me—no, commanded me—*not* to write."

"Because she had better things to read," said Patti dryly—a remark that struck me as a blow of revelation. I'd always believed that I had oriented toward Val as a benign older sister, but perhaps the relationship had actually been more in line with my mother's dicta and her behavior.

The message in both instances was that I could be loved and cherished if I operated within the prescribed limits that existed in the other person's mind. But all affection and nurturance were up for grabs if I set my own goals (which weren't, as it happened, approved goals) and pursued them. In short, loving meant always following the stated and unstated orders about who I should be and become, while moves toward independence and autonomy were accompanied by threats—not idle ones—of rejection, loss, and abandonment.

I Can Get What I Need

As we recommenced the rapid eye movements, an unbidden, novel, hitherto unthinkable thought appeared front and center in my mind. It was, "Mom, you just don't care about me, not *for me*. You just care about me in terms of *you*." When I reported this to Patti at our subsequent rest stop, she nodded in silent, sympathetic agreement.

Then I said, "My feeling is—and I don't mean to sound trite—that I have to get hold of a self that's really *me*. In so many of my relationships, I tend to come on at one end of a tilted seesaw—either 'Take care of me' or, far more commonly, 'I'll take care of *you*.'"

Patti nodded, said that, yes, many of those old caretaking issues were being recycled in my present-day relationships—namely, the two sister surrogates I had supported through some hard times but who'd vanished when *I* was the person in need. I had to learn an important lesson, one I'd never fully internalized, which was how to find equality in my close attachments when it came to giving out and getting.

We fell silent for several moments. I was thinking about how often I'd been amazed by the ways in which so many people I was interviewing were engaged in reenacting the unresolved issues of the past. I'd wondered how this came to be without anyone's realization that what was happening now bore an uncanny resemblance to what had happened earlier—but here I was, heavily involved in much the same thing and at best dimly aware of what was occurring. I had some major reassessments to make.

"Now," said Patti, "when you go back to that original memory, what do you notice?"

The question seemed to me to come out of nowhere, and I found myself staring at her blankly—I found myself unable to recollect what that memory had been! But I did recall that Patti had recorded it in her computer, so I asked her if she would read it back to me now.

She shook her head in the negative, saying that she wanted to see what was left of it, or if there *was* anything left of it, and to hear about it in my own words.

I searched inside my head, located some wispy scraps of that scenario with my mom on the back porch of our house. "It's there, but it's more distant, less vivid," I said in a confused tone of voice. "But I do have some feeling in my jaw."

"How disturbing is that feeling on a zero-to-ten scale?" Patti asked.

I thought for a moment. "Not very disturbing."

"Give it a number," she said.

"I'd give it a one or a two."

"Okay, let's focus on that," she said, and we began the eye tracking again.

This time, however, something strange happened as soon as I began following the lights. I had the impression or vision that my mother was sitting out there on the patio and my body was feeling light, weightless. I was feeling so light that I was floating up the hill that overlooked the porch, and I was calling out, "Good-bye, Mom, good-bye, Mom, good-bye! . . . I wish I could feel real anger at you, because you were a neglectful parent, but I guess I just don't feel it. I appreciate the good things you did!" Then I seemed to see myself drifting up and away into the nimbus of sunlight at the top of the hill, and a vast sense of peace and resolution descended upon me. I did feel tears springing to my eyes, but at the same time I felt absolutely wonderful. "I can get what I need," I decided.

Part Three

BEVERLY, KAREN, JOANNA

THE BODY'S MEMORY "NUMBING OUT,"

EXTRAMARITAL AFFAIRS

Chapter Twelve

SECRETS FROM THE SELF:
BEVERLY CHANGES
THE LOCKS

S I MYSELF HAD COME TO REALIZE, A PERSON WHO HAS grown up in severely stressful, often secretive or semisecretive situations can be seriously compromised when it comes to recalling just what *did* take place on certain highly charged occasions. Nevertheless, there are times when "what the body knows" pops into awareness without warning and presents a person with unwelcome but unavoidable information. In Beverly Scanlon's case, a shocking, long-suppressed memory had suddenly risen to the surface of consciousness, owing to the particular context in which the remembering was taking place.

Beverly was in her mid-thirties at the time of our interviews, but almost a decade earlier, when she'd been in her twenties, she'd held a very responsible position as assistant to the dean of the Department of Human Genetics at a major teaching hospital in Boston. Although she'd subsequently left this job to go on to graduate school, where she'd earned a master's degree in computer science, Bev had taken that administrative position very seriously and felt proud of the harmonious way she'd managed to keep the department running.

But there came a time when she was given a routine project that involved changing every lock on every door in the entire human genetics unit—and this simple task soon developed into a uniquely personal calamity. Her mandate had been to secure, and if necessary rekey, all the offices and laboratories, which involved much lock checking, jiggling of doorknobs, and opening and shutting of the doors to see if they closed securely.

"I would start out each morning to work on this project," Bev told me, a scared frown settling upon her face. "But it always happened that after about fifteen minutes or so, I'd start feeling really uncomfortable—*physically* uncomfortable. Short of breath, heart pounding, completely unable to *focus*—and I'd end up running back to my office. I know this is going to sound crazy, but I was completely panicked. I couldn't figure out why this was happening, and I kept thinking, This is nuts! I felt guilty, too; it was so *unlike* me not to act responsibly, to do the best job I could."

As the days and weeks passed, this strange dilemma didn't seem to resolve itself; on the contrary, matters worsened, and Beverly found herself feeling ever more shaken, driven by impulses that were utterly out of her control. She decided to consult a therapist, but even that got her nowhere, for after weeks of treatment she'd made no headway with the precipitating concern. "The only conclusion I could come to was that, for whatever reasons, I *could not go on with this project.*" It had simply been impossible—*physically* impossible—for her to carry out the seemingly mundane duty assigned to her.

Bev broke off this narrative momentarily to hold up her hand and show me how much it was trembling merely by virtue of remembering that time. "See what I mean?" she asked me, or perhaps the better word is "demanded." Then, in a more subdued tone of voice, she said, "What was the worst, the absolute *worst*, for me was the actual sound of the door opening—you know, the clicking sound that the latch makes when the door opens and closes? That would really *get* to me, and after a while I'd run back to my office and slam the door behind me. I just couldn't go on with it!"

She and her psychotherapist had reached an impasse; the treatment wasn't going anywhere. Then, said Bev, in the midst of one of the sessions, a vivid image suddenly popped into her head. "This happened—literally—in the middle of a sentence, when I was going on and on, feeling very *agitated* about the problem with the locks!" Even as she described this incident her body stiffened; she sat up rigidly in her chair as if an iron spike had hit her between the shoulder blades.

I gave her a quizzical look, but she shook her head as if asking me not to disturb her train of thought. "This image—it was like a photo that you look at. . . . But I wasn't just observing it, I could *feel* it, too. And I felt terrified! The picture was of a little girl in a white nightgown sitting on a bed, with her legs tucked underneath her, waiting for the sound of a door opening." Beverly looked and sounded young and frightened at this moment.

I said nothing, and she sat there staring at my face without seeming to recognize my presence. So I asked her if, when that picture came into her mind, she'd felt as if she *were* the little girl or she were *watching* the little girl. She didn't reply; she merely held up her shaking hand once again to show me how this memory was affecting her. I nodded, murmuring, "Yes, I see that."

Then she repeated her statement to the effect that while she was looking *at* the little girl, she was feeling the terror simultaneously. "Do you know where *you* are in the room?" I asked her. Was she on the ceiling, in a half-opened closet, in a corner? Or where else in the room might she have been?

Bev squinted thoughtfully, as if to summon up all the details of the scene that were available. She was watching, she said slowly, but she wasn't sure where she was watching *from*. "And it's not a dispassionate kind of looking," she repeated. "I'm looking, but I'm also *feeling*. I'm feeling *afraid*. There's also a tremendous tightness in my back, and the tightness is in my legs—*both* my legs—too."

A natural suspicion sprang into my mind, one that was intrinsic to the scenario she was describing. Had the frightened little girl in this picture been trying hard to hold her legs together? I asked Bev if, when she reflected back about that scene—the scared child and the door that was about to open—the door ever *had* opened, eventually?

Oh yes, the door did open, she answered dryly. Then she shrugged her shoulders briefly, as if to indicate her utter helplessness in the face of the events she visualized unfolding. "The door opens," she said. "I don't see a face, but a male figure comes in. Then I get this very smothered feeling, this sense that I can't breathe, and I'm fixed there, absolutely paralyzed. . . . I can feel that paralysis right *now*, but I've never been able to put a face on that person." Her own face was a dark storm cloud of distress at this moment.

We were both silent for a period of time. Then Bev said, "To this day, I'm not exactly sure what did go on. The best way that my therapist and I could put it together . . . because I still do have these huge memory gaps . . . is that whatever happened probably didn't involve intercourse, just some sort of fondling or rubbing."

What impulse was it that led me, then, to ask what *time* of day or night she thought it had been when that bedroom door began to open? "I don't know," she said quickly. Did she think it might have been around bedtime or sometime during the middle of the night? I asked her. Bev then said, "It's ten o'clock; I know that," now with no uncertainty in her voice.

I noticed that she'd switched into the present tense, and this was no surprise. For Bev, like so many people who've been through traumatic experiences, wasn't so much remembering a painful past as she was *reliving* in this moment what had happened. "You're sure of the time?" I asked her, and she nodded.

"It's ten o'clock," she said flatly. I asked her how she knew that. "I *do*, I just *do*," she replied, speaking in a clipped, tight-lipped tone of voice, like a reporter announcing news of a catastrophe. On the spot I decided to bring this interview to a gentle ending as soon as possible, so I told her that I had one last, general kind of question—one that she could respond to or not as it suited her. "When you think back to that time, does anything else spring to mind, in terms of *other* things that were happening then?"

"What I remember most is wanting my *mom* to come home," Bev said resentfully. The expression on her face was that of a sullen, angry child. I waited for her to say more.

"My mom had taken a job around that time—I can't remember what it was, exactly—but she was away from seven P.M. to eleven. So the way it worked, she was there to give us dinner, and then my dad would pick her up later on; but *he* was the one who was in charge of putting us kids to bed. And so I suppose, thinking back—and thinking about the bizarre nature of my relationship with my father, who always treated me like his little wife—there's very little doubt about what did happen." Still, said Bev, she had no conscious memories of any seductive goings-on and had never been able to put her father's face—or *any* face—on the male figure who came through the door.

Disconnected, Disjointed Images

This was, it seemed to me, a classic demonstration of the effects of that "upside-down U curve of remembering"—which is that rising levels of fight-or-flight-related brain biochemicals act to enhance memory retention, *but only until the summit of that upside-down U has been attained.* Then the *opposite* effect begins to emerge, and as the surge of fight-or-flight substances continues, the quality of remembering declines. Eventually, the individual's overwhelmed central nervous system reaches a critical juncture (the top of the upside-down U), beyond which memories become splintered and disorganized or vanish from consciousness completely.

Then, instead of being able to bring to mind the sequence of events in the order in which they happened, the individual may recall only fragments of what occurred—or summon them up in disconnected images—or simply forget that they ever took place. In other words, he or she may suffer either partial or total amnesia for aspects of his or her own life's history. Even so, while the memories seem completely gone, the branching, forking, interconnected neurons of the brain and body cells *do* remember. In their own mysterious fashion, they retain the encoded documentation of long-ago events that have seemingly vanished from the narrative—or at best lingered on as isolated thoughts, random remnants of a lost puzzle, or disjointed, disconnected mental images that seem to make no sense.

Amnesias

"It's true that my dad had a thing for me," Beverly now said. "He liked to take me everywhere he went and surely never made a secret of his preference for me; but I have no recollection of there being any *sexual* component to that. And I have to say that even *after* that picture flipped into my mind, I spent weeks of backtracking in the therapy—weeks and weeks of trying to convince the shrink that I'd probably made the whole thing up."

Her clinician had not bought into this revised, more benign version of events. The very way in which the picture had suddenly materialized in

Bev's mind—like an undeveloped negative that's been plunged into a chemical solution—seemed to argue otherwise. "That image actually came to me in the midst of a session when I was going on and on, just *obsessing* about that rekeying project. I remember telling the therapist that I just couldn't do it—and then *bam*, that picture flashed into my head. It was so *vivid*—I *saw* it and I *felt* it; and in some way I *became* that little kid, sitting there, waiting for the door to open!"

She stopped, scrutinized my face, as if wondering whether I doubted her or believed what she was saying. Then a confused look crossed her features, as if she weren't sure she believed in this remembered image herself. I said nothing, merely nodded, as if to say "I'm with you." I did believe her, for regardless of what anyone might have to say about the fundamental untrustworthiness of "recovered memories," Bev's story didn't have the ring of anything that had surfaced from the sludge of a favored daughter's long-ago erotic fantasies.

Besides, as experts in the field of trauma will attest, amnesias are common in the wake of cataclysmic experiences. As Jonathan Shay, M.D., has observed, a traumatized person's memories cannot be summoned up at will as ordinary memories can be. "Traumatic memory is not narrative," Shay writes. "Rather, it is experience that *reoccurs* [my italics], either as full sensory replay of traumatic events in dreams or flashbacks, with all things seen, heard, smelled, and felt intact, or as disconnected fragments." This is a particularly apt paraphrase of what happens at the "overwhelming challenge" side of that upside-down U-shaped curve of remembering. On one side of that inverted U-shaped curve, the individual isn't concerned enough to remember—the events aren't sufficiently significant—and on the opposite side, remembering is intolerable.

Pathways to Remembrance

What rouses dormant memories and stirs them into wakefulness? When Marcel Proust, our foremost poet of memory, dipped his famous madeleine into a cup of tea, the purely physical sensations—the taste of the little cake, the smell of the brew—opened wide a gateway that propelled him into the magical, almost forgotten world of his childhood.

One of the two overarching themes of Proust's masterpiece, translated as *Remembrance of Things Past,* is the way in which some random sensory event—a bite of a familiar pastry, a sip of steamy tea—can trigger a semi-automatic summoning up of the memories archived within our densely interconnected neural circuitry. The other central theme has to do with the way in which significant memories, *once accessed via physical sensations* (such as taste and smell), can be reexperienced with as much immediacy and emotional intensity as they had when the original experiences occurred.

Truly, this exquisite ability to retain within and revisit the past is one of the great glories of our humanity; but in terms of trauma it can be the cause of great suffering as well. This is especially true in those undramatic and yet chronically damaging situations where an individual's coping capacities are under chronic assault and eventually become overwhelmed. In those situations where neither fighting back nor escaping is a realistic, viable choice, the person's only option is to freeze in place, zone out, and surrender to the inevitable. In the process, his or her basic assumptions about personal safety are shattered.

Many examples of this kind spring readily to mind—an obvious one would be Claudia Martinelli's witnessing of her brother's savage beatings. Another would be that of a young child hearing his alcoholic mother shouting insults at his father, knowing that ultimately the pair would get into a loud physical brawl. The petrified youngster can neither stop his parents' hysterical battling nor escape the situation—where would he go, and who would take care of him?

Still another instance of this kind of unremitting, frightened helplessness would be that of a soldier, hunched in a foxhole night after endless night, with deadly mortar shells flying overhead—any one of those shells could land upon him and kill him. In all of these cases, there's obviously nothing that a person can possibly *do* in terms of taking clear-cut, self-protective action. The individual is immobilized, a rabbit frozen in the headlights, waiting for whatever-will-occur to overtake him.

Internally, though, he is experiencing the huge burst of energy that's been summoned up to sharpen and focus his physical and mental resources upon effectively fighting or fleeing the situation. Concurrently, however—since he can do neither—he's consumed by a terrible sense of his own vulnerability and powerlessness. He is paralyzed in place, and the physiological forces that have come into play *remain* in play, for there's no effective way to utilize and ultimately discharge them.

This state of perpetual mobilization-to-meet-the-danger can affect the human organism profoundly. Traumatic experiences can and often do provoke changes in brain and body functioning that can take years to dissipate and sometimes never fully disappear. Then, much as any of us might want to move forward in our lives and put behind us painful aspects of our personal histories—those times when we felt helpless, inadequate, unworthy, unable to take action—our vast dossiers of encoded memories are what accompany us in the effort. We carry them along with us not only in the evanescent "mental" sense, but in a patently material, bodily sense.

The reality is that memory itself is, ultimately, a series of bodily—neurophysiological—occurrences.

Selective Highlighting

For one person, it can be the powerful aroma of pine needles as she walks through a forest that suddenly floods her with feeling. She may not quite recall the incident itself—one summer at camp, when a boy she was in love with took her in his arms and kissed her—but the pungent smell, the way the sunlight is filtering through the tree branches, and the sweet languor of the afternoon air fill her with a sense of gladness, the goodness of just being alive upon this earth.

For someone else, however, that same smell—the pungent smell of pine needles warming in the sun—may evoke feelings of a radically different kind. She feels herself tensing up and looks around to see if any strangers are hovering nearby. While she may, or may not, bring to mind the leering tramp who suddenly exposed himself one peaceful afternoon when she was reading in the park, the sensory data that she's receiving—plus the woodsy context in which she's receiving it—light up her internal warning board, connecting instantaneously with the part of her cerebral wiring that was laid down in relation to that "forgotten" incident that occurred so many years earlier.

As we all know, there are many such situations, ones in which certain sensory cues evoke a host of seemingly inexplicable, even downright irrational feelings. There are actually times when it can take nothing more than a change in weather to trigger a significant emotional reaction. For example, a period of humid, rainy drizzle—weather reminiscent of long, frightening days in the danger-filled jungles of Vietnam—can make a veteran of that war feel edgy, hypervigilant, tense, unable to sleep and to concentrate at work. "This situation can repeat itself for years—literally—without that individual ever associating his unease and fearfulness to those long-ago wartime experiences," as trauma expert Steven Southwick told me.

The link between the terrifying past and a present-day trigger of memory—in the case just mentioned, the "feel" of the persistent light rain—creates a sense of imminent danger that, at a superficial level, feels completely out of whack. The returned vet is at one level perfectly aware that he's now safely home in America and that the war in Vietnam ended many years earlier. Still, the self-preservation lessons that he learned at that time (You must be ever vigilant! Watch out! Be ready to fight for your life!) linger on within him; and an environmental cue such as a soft, steady rainfall can raise them to the murky surface of awareness. Well though that person may realize that there *is* no realistic threat, his body and brain cells are reacting to sensory cues that connote danger and responding with messages of emergency.

What can explain the persistence of such strong emotional responses, which can occur so far in time from the long-ago lover's first embrace (that kiss in the woods) or the long "forgotten" original fear situation? Once again, the explanation is that these powerfully encoded responses *do* make good biological sense from the point of view of species survival. For we humans are well served by selectively bookmarking those situations that excited and attracted us, in the interests of courting and mating. But *above all else*, we need to keep vividly in mind those situations that have threatened our safety and integrity, for the evolutionary bottom line is always that of staying alive long enough to reproduce and create a new generation.

Nature has, in short, equipped us to learn, and learn well, those lessons that have been invested with survival significance.

The Loss of Mittens the Cat

I have written elsewhere (*Intimate Partners*) about a story originating in my own early life, but I will retell it here, for it is so apt an example of the way in which vital lessons are highlighted within our nervous circuitry: In the 1960s, when our three daughters were very young and my husband, an economist, was teaching at Stanford, we lived on the university campus and had a tiger-striped kitten with pure white paws that looked liked mittens. "Mittens," in fact, was the name we had given him.

Our closest friends, during this era of our lives, were the Ds. They were roughly the same age as we, just moving past the twenties and into their early thirties. I customarily spent a good deal of time with the wife, Anne, and had opened myself up to the relationship completely. She was a part-time social worker, who taught at a school for autistic children. On Wednesday afternoons, I took care of her seven-year-old daughter. So aside from other visits, there was always that predictable time together, when Anne came either to pick up her child or to drop her off.

Our two husbands, who were colleagues on the Stanford faculty, were as close to each other as Anne and I were. The friendship had, in fact, originated with the two men. Although the two of them related to each other differently than we—they enjoyed getting into long, heated, abstract discussions—they were also, especially for males, unusually disclosing and personal with each other.

In short, the relationship between our two families seemed to work at every level and in every permutation—between the varying adult twosomes, between the four girls of the junior generation, and between each child and any of the respective parents. We had misunderstandings and tensions from time to time, to be sure, but we functioned as a quasi–extended family; problems could and did arise, but our attachment to the Ds was never in question. Going out in the evening meant going out somewhere with Anne and Larry, and we did so as often as we could manage it. We went to small restaurants in San Francisco, to the movies, to occasional nightclubs, and to afternoon baseball games. As families, we went on hikes, picnics, excursions to the beach at Santa Cruz, and sometimes camping in the Sierra Nevada mountains.

symbol of the intact family. The loss of the cat was connected, in my own mind, with the family life that was being taken away.

At the age of twelve, one is in part an adult but also to some large degree a child—still able to give credence to magical ideas and notions. I suppose, looking back, that I probably maintained the belief that if our pet were to return, so would my world's stability. Or perhaps my preoccupation with the loss of the cat—so intense that the breakup of my parents' relationship seemed almost incidental—was due to my finding it easier to confront and mourn the loss of the family pet than to mourn the *intolerable* loss, which was the ending of my parents' marriage.

In the case of the Ds, history proceeded to repeat itself. For a few days after our return from that camping trip on which I'd experienced the Ds as "different," my husband appeared at home—unexpectedly, in the middle of the afternoon—with the warning that he had some bad news to tell me. The children were, at that moment, listening to records on their toy phonograph. He and I went outside, to the far end of the garden, and sat across from each other at a picnic table under a blooming wisteria vine. Anne had, he said without preamble, told Larry that she wanted a divorce.

She had, it appeared, been having an affair for most of this past year; now she was leaving her husband for her lover. He—the other man—wanted to marry her and had already left his spouse. I sat there, openmouthed. I was doing my utmost to assimilate this barrage of new information but found it enormously hard to concentrate.

Other matters commanded my attention, such as the perfumed smell of wisteria blossom and the sight of a lazily droning bee scouting for a likely source of nectar. Also, there were the distant voices coming from the record player; the children were listening to a fairy tale. The only thought that crossed my mind, which felt emptied of ideas, was of the cat who was still missing. Will he ever come back again? I wondered . . . and then realized, at once, that it was not the cat that really concerned me.

There is actually a horrible addendum to that Mittens story—one of those incidents in life that are hard to recall without flinching. It concerned the original memory of my parents' separation—and most particularly, the memory of the *way* in which the SPCA workers had carried the cat away that day. Our family pet's neck had been secured in a halter so that the rest of his body hung down stiffly. He was dead, but why did they take him out in that cruelly indifferent way—not cradled gently in their arms, but with his head lolling and his limbs dangling down disrespectfully? "Now I know that life is terrible," was the anguished thought I so clearly remember.

And it was that image that surfaced in my mind, these many years later, when the unthinkable thing, the impossible thing, proceeded to happen. For even as I listened to my husband describing the details of the Ds' separation, and Anne's long-standing affair—and realized that *I* had been the lovers' babysitter on the Wednesday afternoons when they met!—I looked upward and caught sight of Mittens's body, high in the trellis above the picnic table on which we sat. He looked as if he were suspended in mid-flight, his body caught in the thickly tangling vines but elongated tautly—for a mad instant, I thought he was alive and we'd found him. But what had happened became clear at once: The cat had been leaping upward at a bird and had hit a live electric wire. Mittens was dead; in rigor mortis; arrested in the performance of that final act.

I stared at this scene in disbelief, and although I was, at this point in my life, miles away in time, place, and circumstance from the world of my original family, the grief and fear I'd experienced on the day of my parents' breakup assailed me with all the intensity of the original experience. This sorrow and terror-driven memory—the shattering of a marriage and the brutal fate of a beloved pet—had been forgotten, stashed away for years in my mental out-of-circulation files. At that moment, however, my body "remembered" everything that had occurred and presented it to me in a cascade of vivid feelings, sensations, and imagery—evoking an anxiety that hit me like a punch in the stomach. It felt as though it were all happening *right now*, for experiences of this kind seem to have a timeless quality, a way of remaining alive and fresh in an unending present.

Triggers of Memory

As world-renowned researchers Larry R. Squire and Eric R. Kandel (a recent Nobel laureate) have observed, there are three major avenues or cues to memory's awakening. These are 1) *sensory experiences*, such as Proust's tasting of the special cookie and my visual image of the elongated body of the cat; 2) *context*, being in a place or a situation that is very *like* the one in which the original memory was laid down; and 3) the *internal, bodily state* of the individual doing the remembering.

I have already talked about the first important spur to retrieval on Squire and Kandel's list—sensory experience, the way in which certain sights, sounds, smells, and so forth can jostle slumbering memories into the spotlight of conscious awareness—so now let me address the other major triggers of memory they cite. In regard to the second one—context—there is now a large scientific literature supporting the view that being in a setting that is *very like the setting in which the original experience took place* makes remembering that experience much easier and more efficient. There are a number of demonstrations of this phenomenon in the scientific literature, but one I found particularly intriguing was an experiment in which the subjects who took part were all deep-sea divers.

In this study, every one of the participants was asked just to listen to forty unrelated words. However, some of the divers were standing on the beach when doing the listening, while others were standing under some ten feet of water. "Subsequently, they were tested in one or the other of the two contexts, and were asked to recall as many words as possible," report Squire and Kandel in their book *Memory: From Mind to Molecules*. The results of this research showed that *the words learned underwater were best recalled underwater* and *the words learned on the beach were best recalled on the beach*. Simply being in the same situation served to render memory more accurate. Context matters.

So does the third trigger of memory, the individual's *internal state of being*. The impact of a person's neurophysiological status upon his or her capacity to remember was vividly demonstrated by Dr. Steven Southwick and his colleagues at the West Haven Veterans Administration in Connecticut. Their remarkable research showed how effectively and rapidly an altered interior state can summon up a legion of emotional memories and reactions.

The design of the Southwick et al. experiment was wonderfully simple: The researchers asked a group of twenty Vietnam War veterans, all of them identified as suffering from post-traumatic stress disorder, if they would volunteer to receive intravenous injections of a drug called yohimbine. Yohimbine, which is often used as a research tool, is a psychoactive substance derived from the bark of a South American tree; it has the effect of stimulating a rise in levels of the activating fight-or-flight brain hormone norepinephrine.

Yohimbine (which was often used to treat male impotence before Viagra appeared upon the scene) acts to rev up the nervous system by causing a brief increase in the body's norepinephrine. For most people, yohimbine has insignificant or no side effects, but in *this* situation—which involved men who were already experiencing the symptoms of PTSD in their daily lives—the drug elicited immediate and striking reactions. As the investigators reported, nine of the research participants had panic attacks, and six of them experienced frightening flashbacks. That is, they felt transported backward in time, as if they were in the midst of the terrifying battle experiences they'd undergone in the jungles of Vietnam many, many years earlier. These reactions occurred in the absence of any external *sensory* cues or of a *context* that was reminiscent of the traumatic situation. In other words, a *changed internal, bodily state* had propelled these harrowing memories directly to the center of the veterans' conscious attention.

Flashbacks

A word about flashbacks is in order here. A flashback is like a trip through a psychological time machine, inasmuch as what occurred "then and there" is suddenly being experienced as if it's occurring in present time, right here and right now. To cite just one example of this eerie phenomenon, one of the volunteers in the Southwick research was a forty-seven-year-old helicopter gunner who'd flown dozens of missions in Vietnam and witnessed many scenes of death; he'd suffered from PTSD for many years afterward. In the course of the study, this man reacted to the active yohimbine treatment by experiencing a panic attack and a flashback.

"During the flashback," wrote the researchers, "the patient was highly agitated and described a helicopter crashing into flames. He could see the flames, hear the crash, and smell the smoke. He appeared to be in a dissociated state, responding as if the traumatic episode was occurring in the present." This man wasn't merely *remembering*; rather, he was *living through* a full-blown, fully elaborated scenario in the moment—and it had been evoked by nothing other than the rising levels of norepinephrine in his nervous circuitry.

Because his brain and body cells were being exposed to a heightened state of arousal, generated by the drug yohimbine, he'd begun to feel the same way he felt *at the time of the original trauma*; in consequence, his memories of that event erupted onto wide-screen consciousness again. This well-recognized kind of reaction goes by the technical name of "state-dependent remembering"—a term that is basically a synonym for *internal state*, the third of the three important cues to memory retrieval cited by Squire and Kandel.

Basically, the message here is that when a person's internal bodily climate feels *just the way it did* when a traumatic memory was laid down, a vivid reexperiencing of the overwhelming episode becomes far likelier to occur. But actually, when I think back upon that Mittens story, I recognize that *all three* prompts to memory retrieval were present. First of all, there was the powerful visual stimulus of the cat's body, stretched out so unnaturally in the wisteria vines above me. Second, there was the situational context, which is to say the Ds—a couple who felt so much like "family" —were breaking apart and, in the process, revealing themselves as people whose real lives had been shared with us far less than we'd ever imagined. Third, there was the factor of "state-dependent remembering": my internal state of rapidly fermenting agitation and fear about what would happen next. Then, an added fillip to all of the above was the fact that Anne, my trusted "replacement sister," had betrayed me; she'd been lying to me for a long period of time. This too had its precedent in my history with a real sister, so it's no wonder that this incident hit me as hard as it did.

Implicit and Explicit Memories

It must be acknowledged that this discussion of memory research has been excerpted from a vastly more extensive, extremely complex scientific library now dedicated to the subject—a library, I should say, that has sprung up recently in stunning "Jack and the Beanstalk" style and shows no signs of having reached its full growth as yet. The entire field can't be reported upon here—no chance of it!—but I do think it important to make one more point before moving on, which is that modern scientists make a clear distinction between the two ways in which long-term memories are stored.

One of these storage systems is called "declarative memory" (also known by other names, such as "explicit memory" and "semantic memory"). It's this kind of memory that we're generally referring to when we use the word *memory* itself; it refers to our conscious knowledge of facts, ideas, and events that have occurred.

Declarative or explicit memory consists of information that can be summoned up verbally—"London is the capital of England"; "My vacation was great, but too short"—or in the form of mental imagery, such as the annoyed look on the boss's face yesterday or the memory of how much smelly garbage was floating in the Venetian canals the last time you visited that city. It is basically the vast storehouse of information that *you know that you know.*

The other major system of memory storage is called "nondeclarative memory" (also known as "implicit memory" and "procedural memory"). This form of remembering exists at a nonverbal, semiautomatic, partially or completely unconscious level. Nondeclarative or implicit remembering is, for one thing, about the "how to" aspect of memory; it includes skills and habits such as riding a bike, driving an auto, and brushing your teeth on a daily basis. We don't have to summon up an entire set of memorized instructions each time we hop into the driver's seat of the car; we simply put in the key and perform a series of actions without thinking or reflecting. Also, very important, implicit memory encompasses emotional responding, reflex actions, and classically conditioned behaviors—to wit, that Vietnam War veteran's experience of feeling agitated and out of control during a period of humid, drizzly weather, even though the war had been over for more than twenty-some years. Another example, of course, would be my feelings of anxiety about our family cat (even though I'd lost track of the original memory until my husband reminded me about it) and the subliminal connection made somewhere deep in my nervous system between "lost pet" and "something deeply amiss in a relationship that had great meaning to me."

As we all know, psychoanalysts have long maintained that our lives are always being strongly affected by powerful implicit memories with which we have no conscious contact—and the recent hard evidence emerging from a good deal of highly sophisticated memory research appears to bear this suggestion out. We do indeed retain many implicit, nonverbal memories within our cerebral circuitry, where they are thought to exist in patterns of neural associations—you might think of them as a person's "basic wiring," a kind of wiring that is admittedly difficult but by no means impossible to access and to change. For there are now fruitful strategies for bringing such changes about—reprocessing is an important one of them—and these will be further examined and illustrated in the stories of Karen, Joanna, and Deirdre that follow.

—

Chapter Thirteen

THE WORLD TURNED
UPSIDE DOWN:
EXTRAMARITAL AFFAIRS

S KAREN BARRY-FREED RECALLED IT, THAT SUMMER
had been a smoldering one, and she herself had been feeling perplexed
and disoriented. It was as if she'd been aware of certain subsurface tremors
that were still too negligible to suggest the scope of the impending earthquake. True, her husband, Jon, had been strangely unavailable to her and
the children during the long, stifling August afternoons: He'd had a series
of minor illnesses and had spent much of his time sleeping in the garden
hammock. Eventually, though, she'd felt her patience giving way. "When
you're not here you're not here; and when you're *here* you're not here,"
she'd complained, but the conversation hadn't led anywhere.

"I was clueless, totally clueless," Karen recounted. "I had no idea;
never discovered lipstick on his shirt; none of *that* sort of stuff. I never
found out until he *told* me." Her brown-fringed hazel eyes were staring
and enlarged, and her open, friendly face seemed drained of life and
color. It was as though the memory of that domestic catastrophe weren't
five years in the past, but as current as the headlines in this morning's
newspaper.

Throughout that summer's end and the beginning of fall, the Barry-
Freeds' lives went on as usual. "In many respects, the marriage we had
was like a business," said Karen. "We had a partnership; we ran a home;

we were raising children; and that was it. Sex was not great, and to the extent that I thought about that, I thought, Maybe I'm just not a sexy person."

Sex was to her something on the order of an obligation—you had to do it once a week, but it wasn't particularly interesting. She'd never given much thought to how this might be affecting Jon, never wondered about how *he* might be reacting. Having grown up in a family where flawless conduct and keeping up appearances were of paramount importance, Karen was relatively oblivious when it came to the world of feelings. Therefore, she was thoroughly unsuspecting and unprepared—"hurt, insulted, *devastated*"—when her husband's feelings erupted with cataclysmic suddenness and he let her know how barren the marriage felt to him.

That upheaval happened in October, somewhere around the time of his fortieth birthday. Karen's gift to Jon had been a three-day vacation for the pair of them at Canyon Ranch in the Berkshires; but when he'd opened the gift envelope, he was clearly taken aback.

"I was surprised—hurt—by his reaction. I thought, How can you *not* be happy? We're always overwhelmed by these children, and won't this be a great chance for the two of us to get away? But he started making all kinds of excuses, saying he wasn't sure he could spare the time—business reasons, something like that." Jon had seemed downright shaken by her present, as if no prospect could be more threatening than an intimate getaway for the pair of them.

"I pointed out that it was an open reservation; we could go whenever we pleased," Karen said evenly, "but of course it was the last thing he wanted to do with *me*."

The following week had been characterized by appreciable silence and a sense of polite constraint until she'd felt the need to probe again, "I don't know where you *are* anymore, Jon. Where *are* you?" He hadn't offered up any explanations or answers, for he *did* know where he was, and it wasn't with her and with their family. Another week went by, and eventually she made some puzzled comment about the fact that they hadn't made love on his birthday, and they hadn't made love on their anniversary, two significant events that were just a few days apart.

"Not that I was an overly sexual kind of person at that point in time; I really wasn't," Karen hastened to add. "But again, these were *occasions*. . . ." Her voice trailed off momentarily, and then she said, "It just seemed odd. So I brought it up, and he said, 'I have to talk to you. I'm just not—I'm not real happy.' And I said, 'Oh, okay.' But we didn't talk about it that night. I did find myself wondering what was going on with Jon, but strange as it sounds, the thought of another person in the picture didn't even occur to me."

That evening, the Barry-Freeds finally sat down together to talk. "The children were in bed, the house was quiet, and the two of us went into the living room to have this conversation. I can't remember everything he said, exactly, but there's a kind of image of that scene that's just burned into my brain," said Karen, touching both temples with the tips of her fingers. Jon had been sitting in the rocker (she pointed to it at this moment), and she had sat on the sofa, facing him. Then, without any preamble, he'd told her that what he wanted to talk about was the fact that he wanted a divorce.

"It was just like that—that direct—and I couldn't *believe* what I was hearing. I felt as if—as if I'd taken this massive punch to the stomach, and all the wind had been knocked out of me! . . . I mean, this couldn't be happening. . . . This was so surreal. How did I not see this? I just sat there, looking at him, and what he said was, basically, 'You're a wonderful woman; you're the most wonderful mother, the most moral, ethical person I've ever met. I feel just terrible, but I'm very unhappy and I want a divorce. I think you should get an attorney.' It came out just like that, pretty much all in one sentence.

"I was in shock. I really was in *shock*. But I think when there's been as much creeping distance in a marriage as there was in ours, you have no clue whatsoever . . . and I really wasn't clued in." In the course of this short, astounding conversation, her whole world had lurched crazily, rocked back and forth for a few breathless moments, and then came crashing down around her. "At some point, I looked at him, and finally the light is dawning," Karen continued. "It's dawning slowly, and I said, 'Is there another woman?' He couldn't answer me; he just nodded his head up and down—there was. Even so, it didn't seem possible. I mean, I did know this conversation was happening, but at the same time I couldn't take it in, couldn't *believe* it."

In retrospect, the most wounding words she'd heard that evening were not actually about herself; they were what Jon had to say about his responsibilities toward the children. He had always been the most caring and devoted of fathers, but when she asked him, "What about the kids?" he'd bristled and said coldly, "I've got only one life to live, and they'll be fine."

Nevertheless, Karen hadn't responded angrily or even *felt* angry; she'd felt dazed—numbed. Despite everything, her first thoughts had been focused solely upon saving what could be salvaged from the wreckage. Her proposal had been that the two of them go into marital counseling—work on repairing the relationship and forgiving whatever needed to be forgiven—but above all, try to keep the family intact.

Jon was willing, and agreed to participate in twice-weekly therapy with Karen; but at the same time, he had an underlying agenda. He was unhappy in the marriage, in love with someone else, and he wanted out. "He kept talking a lot about 'adventure,' about his craving for more excitement in his life. About his wanting to go white-water rafting, stuff like that. Let's face it, he was just turning forty, and the message was that he didn't want to be living in this house in Lincoln, Massachusetts, with this wife and these three children."

Betrayal Trauma

According to psychologist Ronnie Janoff-Bulman, the essence of trauma is the abrupt disintegration of the victim's inner world. Unbearable, unthinkable experiences have a way of demolishing the basic structure of the self, shattering those fundamental assumptions that have served to make life feel livable and safe. In Janoff-Bulman's view, such assumptions or core beliefs can be subsumed under the following propositions: 1) that the world is benevolent; 2) that the world is meaningful; and 3) that the self is worthy.

Most of us take these reassuring assumptions as facts of our existence —givens—and they usually exist outside our conscious awareness. But when overwhelming, inconceivable events—in the case just cited, the treachery of a trusted partner—demolish and scramble these bedrock beliefs, the injured person's inner world becomes an alien landscape, littered with the debris of destroyed convictions.

"Victims of trauma have come face-to-face with a highly unstable, dangerous universe, which has been made all the more frightening by their total lack of psychological preparation," writes Janoff-Bulman. It is as if a harsh, glaring light has suddenly illuminated the full panorama of the individual's existence, and the terrible fragility of the self has become painfully apparent. Not only is the self vulnerable in ways not hitherto realized, but the person experiences him- or herself as besieged by lies, malice, and meaninglessness in a world that offers no real stability or protection.

At the same time, a loud internal emergency alarm has been set off— one that can't readily be modulated or extinguished. The revelation of the betrayal has put the shocked partner's body into a state of high alert— one that can precipitate a wide range of the familiar physical and mental symptoms that follow upon traumatic experience, such as chronic anxiety, confusion, "flashbulb" memories of certain painful scenes, mood swings, irritability, sleep disturbances, depression, feelings of estrangement, shortness of temper, deep-rooted, ceaseless anger, digestive problems, substance abuse, chronic fatigue, and a host of other greater and lesser difficulties.

However, when it comes to making a formal diagnosis of post-traumatic stress disorder—in the big-T sense—the revelation of a partner's infidelity doesn't qualify. Although such an event is clearly shattering to a person's view of the self and of the world, it doesn't meet the current criteria of the *Diagnostic and Statistical Manual of Mental Disorders*, which stipulates that a PTSD finding must be reserved for traumatic occurrences that involve actual or threatened death or serious harm to the self or nearby others—in other words, horrifying occurrences that put at risk the victim's physical survival.

This is obviously not the case in extramarital situations, for most people don't die as a result of learning about a trusted partner's lies and deceptions. Nevertheless, a number of researchers and clinicians working in the field of EMS (extramarital sex) *have* come to recognize that betrayed partners often respond in ways that are characteristically present in other traumatic situations.

Interpersonal Trauma

Prominent among these EMS experts is the late Dr. Shirley Glass, who has posited the existence of a phenomenon that she has termed "interpersonal trauma." As Glass told me in the course of a series of conversations, she believes the word *trauma* to be apt because it captures the true extent of the stupefying emotional wound inflicted by a disloyal mate upon his or her trusting and believing partner. For the betraying spouse's behavior has in fact been an assault on her fundamental sense of who she is and on many of her most cherished assumptions.

Until the time of the affair's exposure, she's seen herself as someone unique and special in the eyes of another special person—the intimate partner who has bonded with her and promised to prize her above all others. Thus, when faced with the indisputable evidence of his horrifying dishonesty, her self-respect suffers a monumental reversal. In the wake of the revelation, she experiences herself as anything *but* special; she feels inconsequential and discardable, as if she'd been relegated to a kind of human waste dump.

Many of her most basic beliefs about her own personal qualities—her looks, her lovability, even her good judgment—disintegrate precipitously. She may have viewed herself as sophisticated and mature when it came to *other* people's dalliances, but nothing in her experience has actually prepared her for the jolt of coming face-to-face with her own trusted partner's incredible duplicity.

It is so dizzying, so destructive an experience that everything she thought she knew comes suddenly into question. Her world has been shaken from its assumptive foundations—hit by malevolently powerful forces—turned completely upside down. And while the exposure of the partner's sexual betrayal is not *mortally* threatening, it often is experienced as a death—the death of faith in a critically important attachment and the loss of a secure base in a world that makes sense and is meaningful.

A Self-Willed Obliviousness

Later, Karen was to wonder why she had remained so hopelessly ignorant of what was happening during the months leading up to the revelation of her husband's affair. Perhaps it had been what she called the "creeping distance" in her sixteen-year marriage that explained her total lack of awareness, but in retrospect she did recognize that there had been *numerous* indications that something out of the ordinary was taking place.

Among them had been Jon's nervous primping before the mirror on certain mornings just before going into work. He would keep changing his shirt and his ties, keep asking her advice about which tie looked best with the suit he was wearing. Recollections such as these were particularly galling once she realized that this had occurred on the days when his lover—a woman who worked for an affiliate of Jon's family-owned shoe-manufacturing business—was flying into Boston "on business." Although he'd always arrived home in the wee hours on these occasions, her suspicions had never been awakened.

In hindsight, she found her naiveté stupefying; indeed, she felt moronic about the whole thing and looked upon the blindness of that time as her own very personal failing. But in fact this reluctance to register the knowledge of a trusted partner's betrayal is much more the commonality than the exception. So is the sense of perplexity and disorientation that Karen remembered experiencing throughout the period leading up to the extramarital affair's revelation. For even though the sense that something wasn't quite right had been palpable—in the conjugal air, somehow—she'd managed to keep the unthinkable information from her conscious awareness. Karen Barry-Freed, like so many other bright, intelligent people, was ready and eager to deny what was happening before her very eyes, and to do so right down to the wire.

What motivates this kind of self-willed obliviousness? You might explain it on the basis of the old "love is blind" cliché; but many deceived partners are in long-lasting, committed relationships rather than the early throes of romantic passion. What makes them cling so steadfastly to the irrational belief that nothing's amiss, even in the face of accumulating signs and signals to the contrary? Or if they should raise bewildered questions, what makes them so strangely prepared to accept the betraying mate's lies and misrepresentations? The superficial answers to such questions may vary widely, and they do; but they all boil down to the ordinary truth that the thought of a beloved, trusted partner's defection is often too intolerable to penetrate the mind's defenses against experiencing pain.

"Refusing to Know"

Another example of a person "refusing to know" was that of Anne Bailey, who was in her late twenties at the time of our interviews. Anne told me that she had been strangely aware and yet unaware of her husband Mark's extramarital affair for a period of many months but had refused to acknowledge on an overt, conscious level what she *did* know. As she put it, "I just couldn't let my thoughts go down that track." It was as though she'd had the intuition that certain associative tracks could lead directly to a marital train wreck.

In Anne's case, as in that of Karen (and those of so many other deceived spouses), the affair had become known only when knowledge of it became completely unavoidable. This happened to Anne Bailey when she, her husband, Mark, and their six-month-old son, Timmy, were vacationing on Nantucket island. The whole matter came to light by the merest chance—when Anne picked up the downstairs phone to make a call and overheard a scrap of whispered, excited-sounding conversation. It was Mark, talking to a woman, someone whose voice was faintly familiar.

Startled and confused, Anne had replaced the receiver immediately. Then she stood where she was for a heart-pounding few moments. She knew she recognized that person's voice, and yet she couldn't quite place it. After a short interval she tiptoed halfway up the stairs to see if that strangely overheated conversation had ended.

It was quiet on the second floor, so she hurried downstairs again. Come to think of it, she *had* heard the phone ring sometime earlier, so she quickly dialed *69 and found herself connected to the sender of the last call that had come in. "Hi," said the woman at the other end of the line in a bright, friendly tone of voice.

Anne did recognize the voice this time. She knew the person to be one of the young postdocs who'd been working in Mark's laboratory since the previous winter; she replaced the phone on its cradle without speaking. But in that moment, she *knew* with complete certainty everything she'd fought so hard against knowing before.

"It was like having a rug pulled out from under me—not the rug of a room, but the rug of the whole world—and I felt as if I were spinning. It was like whirling through space, breaking apart into pieces—I was *demolished*. And the thought that came into my head was, My life is just *over*."

At the same time, said Anne, those terrible feelings had been accompanied by a strange sense of relief. For so many crazy, confusing things had been going on for such a long period of time, and now she understood why those things made sense. "All of a sudden, things clicked into place, and I could *understand* why I'd been feeling so strange—so unlike myself, so weepy, so mad at the world, rejectable, and quick to take offense."

Scanning backward in time, she realized how long and how elaborately Mark had been lying to her. What a stupid idiot she had been! There had been so *many* clues that he was involved elsewhere—blatant symptoms of an underlying malady for which she now had the firm diagnosis. How *had* she managed to dismiss a whole series of seemingly insignificant incidents from her awareness? The telephone calls he'd been getting at odd hours—from an annoying, klutzy new colleague, he'd said. The unusually long hours he'd been spending at the lab—leaving so early in the morning and coming home so late almost every night. He'd had to work harder than ever on his government grant, he'd told her, for the money was getting much tighter.

It had all been an ingenious stew, a mixture of half-truths and blatant deceptions. She did recall questioning him about one incident along the way and remembered being puzzled by the guilty expression on his face. "I wasn't clear on what *that* could be about. But let's face it, a part of me didn't *want* to push matters. Maybe it was because Mark was so miserable at the time, worried about his laboratory's funding. Maybe it was because my own job was so demanding, and we had a young baby, and I was so involved *there*."

She had done her best *not to know*, but on the morning of that overheard phone call she *had* known with a sense of furious certainty. So she'd marched directly upstairs to confront her husband, said directly, "Look, I have to talk to you. . . . I know you're having an affair."

Mark was working at a small computer in their bedroom, but he'd stiff-ened, then jumped up, almost knocking over his chair. The two of them had just stood there, staring. Anne remembered the scene vividly: the ragged sound of her own breathing, the way she'd crossed her arms over her chest as if to shield herself from him. Mark, looking hangdog, had let out a long sigh, then admitted that it was the truth.

The effect upon his wife was volcanic. It was as if a stockpile of rage that had been silently building up inside her had erupted on the instant. "I felt like I was exploding, literally blowing apart—as if I wanted to *kill* him—him or *myself*, I wasn't sure!" The worst part was having to keep it under wraps for a while, because at that moment the baby woke up from his morning nap and started crying for someone to get him from the crib. It was already close to eleven A.M., and the Baileys had houseguests who were due to arrive somewhere around lunchtime.

"Even now, that whole weekend is a big blur in my mind," Anne re-counted. "But what *is* vivid is the memory of being alone with Mark at bedtime. . . . How *embarrassed* I felt getting undressed in his presence, be-cause now he was someone *strange* to me. I didn't want to be seen by him. I felt so soiled, so humiliated, so utterly *betrayed*."

The Body Reacts

It will come as no surprise that in the aftermath of an affair's exposure, the betrayed and bereaved partner is likely to develop post-traumatic stress symptoms and reactions. Acute hyperarousal was surely one of Anne's most evident reactions, for the exposure of Mark's infidelity had quickly shunted her into an amphetamine-like "high"; she'd felt pressured, super-charged with seething energy, chronically agitated, and unable to calm herself down. Plagued with intrusive thoughts and disturbing images of the lovers' embraces, she'd been preoccupied by fantasies of murdering her deceiving mate or of committing suicide. It was impossible to get to sleep, and when she did manage to do so, she was often wakened by vio-lent nightmares. She simply couldn't soothe herself, calm herself down.

From the point of view of outward behavior, Anne's reactions were completely different from those of Karen Barry-Freed, whose responses looked completely opposite. Instead of speeding up, Karen had slowed down, almost to the point of complete immobilization. Hers had been the second kind of bodily reaction—"freezing" or numbing out.

Karen didn't rage or feel vengeful; she felt "as if I couldn't move, as if I were weighted down with stones." It was as though she were some confused survivor staggering around in the wake of a devastating catastrophe, seeking foggily for some points of orientation in a bizarre world that was no longer safe or familiar.

"In one sense, I knew everything that was happening, but in another sense it all seemed like it was happening to someone else—I was so *out* of it," Karen said. "When I drove my kids to school I didn't even *hear* them when they spoke to me. They kept saying, 'Earth to Mom! Earth to Mom!' because my thoughts were just elsewhere—no, not elsewhere, but *nowhere*. It was like the inside of my head was . . . blank. And I was so disoriented, I could get lost just driving to the grocery store."

At times, for no specific reason, tears would start running down her cheeks; yet those tears felt strangely unconnected to any emotions such as sadness or grief. By and large, she felt *numb*—a leaden feeling that would be pierced now and then by sudden visitations of horror. It was usually an impromptu visualization of that scene in the living room when Jon had sprung the news that the marriage was over and she should get herself an attorney.

That image, when it popped into her mind, had the power to make Karen double over, her entire body gripped by anguish and fear. Sometimes she even imagined she was *hearing* the words that had been spoken—hearing them aloud, in the moment. This made her fear she might be going crazy, for wasn't "hearing voices" a sign that something deadly might be happening?

Fight, Flee, or Freeze

Clearly, here were two women who had reacted to the same traumatic revelation in polar opposite ways. Karen had closed down and become almost paralyzed, while Anne (like Claudia Martinelli) had become visibly "hyper." Anne had been filled with bubbling anger that continually threatened to boil over in some rage-driven destructive act. Despite all outward appearances, however, *inside* Anne's and Karen's bodies a similar physiological situation prevailed.

For the biological bottom line is that when we humans are faced with threats of a potentially overwhelming nature, an inner siren is triggered and we switch into an altered state of high readiness to meet the challenge at hand. Even as we make an instinctive, instantaneous assessment of the danger, an upsurge of neurohormones and neurotransmitters is activated. These substances inundate our brains and bodies: Our hearts start pumping faster; our muscles contract; and our blood vessels constrict in order to reroute blood flow away from those organs most vulnerable to serious damage. On the instant, we are primed, psychologically and biologically, to face up to the threat, to attempt to escape it, or to freeze and "play dead."

This swift bodily reaction to stressful circumstances is, as we know, highly adaptive; it promotes survival. But again, what is generally a vital asset can become a burdensome debit in those life circumstances where neither fight nor flight is a remotely plausible option. We are then simply faced with our terrible inability to do anything about the threatening situation, which therefore remains unresolved; and this in turn leaves our bodies in a state of unremitting preparedness—that is, chronic hypervigilance and readiness to meet with danger. From a physiological point of view, traumatic stress leaves the body's engine running in overdrive.

Thus, despite the fact that Karen looked immobilized and Anne looked intensely souped-up, the two women were in very similar internal, bodily states. This is also true of the many individuals who respond to a faithless partner's deception by ricocheting back and forth from "lows" of frozen, dissociated numbness to "high" bouts of explosive, uncontainable fury. In other words, however disparate various individuals' outward responses to the insult of infidelity may appear to be, the same sorts of reactions to this intense stressor exist within the body itself.

Chapter Fourteen

PARADOXES OF INFIDELITY

EGINNING WORK ON A FAMILY GENOGRAM IS ALWAYS A slightly odd experience. When you start out, you're sitting opposite some-one who is a relative stranger; yet you're aware, from a vast amount of for-mer experiences, that you will soon know that person much better than many of the people numbered among his or her closest friends and ac-quaintances.

Since Karen Barry-Freed had already told me that her first marriage—the marriage to Jon—had ended in divorce, I drew a horizontal line on the sketch pad. This is the "matrimonial" line, connecting the symbols that read "female" (a circle) and "male" (a square). Then I drew the double-slashed, vertical line through it, which symbolizes "divorce," and asked quietly how long that union had lasted.

They had been married for sixteen years, she said in the hushed voice of someone making a confession; and at the time of their separation, Jon had moved to an apartment house nearby. Afterward, despite that chilling remark he'd made about the children on the night of the revelation—"they'll be fine"—he'd remained a highly involved and caring father. Karen, who'd enjoyed her role as a mother from the outset, continued par-enting their three daughters as devotedly as she could. But at the same time, she realized she would have to figure out how to create a profes-sional and social life of her own, one that was different from her former self-definition as "contented suburban housewife."

And she *had* been contented beforehand, she told me quickly—

perhaps subliminally aware, but never really threatened by the "creeping distance" that existed between herself and Jon. "The relationship was really spiraling down, but I didn't know it. At that time I probably didn't know what a good relationship *was*." I tilted my head to one side, raised a questioning eyebrow.

She paused, then said thoughtfully that her parents, both still alive, were basically good, kindhearted people, but there had been "no vocabulary for the emotions" in her own original family. "So I was *dumbfounded* on that October evening when he told me he wanted out. Because, to be truthful, I was actually pretty satisfied, myself. I had my kids, I had my house, I had wonderful friends, and my life seemed good. Also, I was pretty much used to the fact that Jon's business necessitated his traveling abroad for long periods—to Europe, South America, often for two to three weeks at a time. So we'd sort of grown apart, and I think, in retrospect, that he must have been feeling that loneliness acutely—particularly so after his father died."

Shortly after that shattering conversation during which Karen had learned that the marriage was over and she should get herself an attorney, the Barry-Freeds had begun to see a therapist together. But while Karen was struggling to keep the marriage together, Jon was far more invested in his relationship with his mistress. He was in that state of rapturous enchantment where two are as one, perfect company; and as a consequence, he was busily rewriting the history of his marriage so as to view it in its most negative light. This is something that tends to happen in these particular circumstances, when the deceiver is trying to assuage his own guilty feelings and justify his behavior.

Currently, from the vantage point of hindsight, Karen saw that entire affair—which hadn't lasted even a year—as a "fantasy relationship," a midlife re-creation of an exciting, far-off time when Jon had been young, single, and unencumbered. The lovers had been eating out at fine restaurants and staying at first-class hotels, and Jon's mistress had been giving him all of the full-beam, wonderful attention he'd been craving. "There were no screaming kids, no 'Who's taking out the garbage tonight?' kinds of situations," said Karen dryly.

By the following spring, however, the other woman had given Jon his walking papers. For he'd moved out of the family home, which from his lover's point of view made the romance increasingly untenable. She herself was a divorced parent; and while she'd been enthused about those dreamy, periodic trysts, she wasn't interested in taking on the added burdens of domesticity that a serious commitment to Jon would have involved.

So he was on his own. And although by then he and Karen were living apart, they were consulting a marital therapist together—a slow and painful process that didn't seem to be going anywhere. For even though, technically speaking, it was she who was the wronged party, Karen was the only one putting in any real effort. Jon was licking his own emotional wounds and remaining distant, disengaged, and coolly critical.

He was insisting that *Karen* was the one who needed to do some serious changing—she needed to lose ten pounds; to make some improvements on the cooking front; to give him a big hello when he came home in the evenings—he'd even complained that one of the major problems in the marriage was that he was no longer "the apple of her eye." And while Karen had recognized the childishness of this statement, her self-esteem was taking a beating.

"There's no way I can describe the *pain* of hearing 'You're just not sexual, you're not desirable; this other person was so different, so exciting' . . . and buying into all of that when I heard it, which I did. I felt—it's hard to even describe it—so totally *invalidated* as a woman," she said. Any hope of reviving the relationship soon faded, and Karen continued to experience waves of nausea, migraines, intense stomach pain, and insomnia. Moreover, having been out of the workplace for many years, she was feeling directionless and more frightened than she could ever remember.

A Trite and Ordinary Story

Karen and Jon had arrived at the bleak consummation of what she knew to be a trite and ordinary story—but one that *felt* like the dead-ending of her entire lifetime. However, as time passed, matters moved in a more positive direction. Realizing that she would have to go to work in the near future, Karen enrolled in a nearby college and earned the credits necessary for teaching physical education on a part-time basis. She also began to join some singles groups and form strong new friendships, some with women who were in positions similar to her own. And although she didn't begin dating until after her divorce, she eventually became involved in two important relationships.

The first was with a divorced man, someone she had known for many years, whom she described as a caring and wonderful person. But early on, the pair of them had recognized that the relationship wouldn't go anywhere in terms of marriage, because they were very different people with divergent points of view on every topic—religion, politics—imaginable. Eventually they had parted, on the best of terms, Karen said. Then she paused, gave me an assessing look, and took a deep breath before continuing.

"The other big experience that I had was with a young teacher, a colleague, who was twenty-something years old and so *handsome* that he could have been a male model. I couldn't *believe* it when he let me know he was attracted to me, but he was, very much so . . . and that was good." He had made her feel like the sexiest dish alive, she said, and that had done a lot for her still-damaged ego.

"My divorce was actually the beginning of my birth as a person, in many ways." Karen's eyes widened and her expression brightened as she spoke. It was certainly, she said, the time when she'd given up on being an intimidated little girl and begun getting to know herself as a grown-up, sexual, desirable woman. So in that respect, the traumatic crisis hadn't been the end; it had been a beginning.

A Matter of Timing: Trigger Points of Infidelity

As Hamlet reflects in Shakespeare's famous play, "There's a certain providence in the fall of a sparrow. If it be now, it will not be later; if it be later, it will not be now. . . ." When a sparrow *does* fall, however, we humans usually hunger for some understanding of the meaning and context of the event. *Why* did it happen? What caused it to happen *now*?

In cases of marital infidelity, the reasons given vary widely, but the most commonplace explanations tend to cluster under the headings of "falling in love," "desperate emotional neediness," "irresistible lust," "tantalizing opportunity," or some heady combination of all four. Typically, the explanations given are ones that anyone can understand, and as such, they seem to be complete in themselves.

There are, however, often other, more subtle questions to be probed—questions that fall into the "why *at this time?*" domain. These often have to do with a fateful but unnoticed confluence of forces, involving not only the pressures of the present moment, but far more distant issues rooted in the partners' families of origin. These issues and concerns, which may have lain dormant for many years, tend to waken at certain trigger points in the life cycle, such as the birth of a first baby (the trigger in Anne Bailey's case), the graduation or wedding of a grown child, a break with a valued career mentor, or the looming retirement or death of a parent. Clearly, these times of transition involve additions to, or losses from, the family system as an emotional entity.

The Loss of a Dad

In the course of my conversations with Karen Barry-Freed, which ranged over various periods of her life, I became aware that her husband's affair seemed strongly linked in her own mind to Jon's father's final—fatal—heart attack. It had been only a matter of months after Jon's dad's massive coronary—which had been the culmination of many attacks over the preceding years—that Jon had embarked upon the affair.

Karen knew that her husband had been feeling profoundly lost and abandoned at that time, for father and son had been extremely close—*so* close that she'd been somewhat jealous of their relationship. The two had always talked on the telephone almost daily, and she'd sometimes had the sense that after her father-in-law's death, there was nobody else in the entire world—"and I include myself," admitted Karen—who could make Jon feel adequately validated and self-sufficient. Her father-in-law had heaped approval on Jon all the time, told his son how special and wonderful a person he was—so much so that Karen sometimes wondered if the upshot was that Jon never felt good enough all on his own.

I paused, then asked her directly if she saw some connection between his dad's death and her husband's affair. I'd begun to wonder if Jon was one of those seeming adults who've managed to leave home, in the geographic sense, without having fully individuated—grown up, achieved a sense of being a fully autonomous person who's no longer dependent on a parent (or both parents) for ongoing support and guidance.

She paused to draw in a breath, then said on the outbreath, "To answer your question—*yes*. The loss of the person Jon loved most in the world—the only person who, he felt, really understood him and loved him unconditionally—was very *much* connected, in ways I still don't fully understand, to everything that followed."

Isn't Everybody Doing It?

Pragmatically speaking, doesn't marital infidelity involve the breaking of a promise that nobody's really expected to keep? Isn't extracurricular sex a commonplace—no calamity, but simply part of normal everyday life? *The Random House Dictionary of the English Language* describes normalcy as "conforming to the standard or common type . . . usual; not abnormal; regular; approximately average in any psychological trait. . . ." In other words, what is common to most people, that which occurs in most cases, is what is "normal."

In the late 1940s and early 1950s, pioneer sex researcher Alfred Kinsey and coworkers surveyed sexual behavior in the United States and came up with findings that astonished many Americans. His results indicated that a full *half* of all married males had been unfaithful before the age of forty, and so had more than a quarter (26 percent) of their wives. In other words, *one in every four married women* had been unfaithful before the middle of her life.

Were Kinsey's statistics reliable? They were certainly greeted with disbelief and controversy, but later surveys seemed to bear them out. A study conducted in the early 1980s by psychologist Anthony P. Thompson indicated that the rates of infidelity among committed couples were not only high but rising in the female population. Thompson's best estimate was that "at least 50% of married men" engaged in extramarital sex and that the rates of infidelity among married women were swiftly ascending toward the same level. And in 1981, sex researchers G. D. Nass, R. W. Libby, and M. P. Fisher published their "educated guess" to the effect that 50 to 65 percent of husbands and 45 to 55 percent of wives had been unfaithful before reaching that magic forty-year-old age mark.

These studies appeared to confirm the now widespread impression that infidelity rates were not only high but continually rising. However, more recent sex surveys tell a mixed and somewhat ambiguous story. In their 1992 study of extramarital sexual activity, researchers Shirley Glass and Thomas Wright found that less than half of the husbands and one-quarter of the wives in their sample had had at least one sexual experience with someone other than the mate. These figures were slightly lower than—but generally in line with—the Kinsey data, but they were very *different* from the findings of the National Opinion Research Center (NORC) at the University of Chicago.

The NORC figures are derived from random annual surveys of the population carried out in the decade of the 1990s, and these surveys involved more respondents than had ever before been polled about their sexual behavior. When presented with the question "Have you ever had sexual intercourse with someone other than your spouse when you were married?" only 21.5 percent of ever married men and 12 percent of ever-married women acknowledged having strayed from the connubial fold. These surprising figures suggested that the rates of extramarital sex might in reality be *lower* than anyone has thought since the Kinsey findings erupted upon the cultural scene. Had the incidence of infidelity changed owing to the fear of AIDS and other sexually transmitted diseases? Or had Kinsey's figures been erroneous in the first place?

After the publication of the NORC results, some critics suggested that the manner in which the surveys were conducted—which involved interviewing people in their homes and therefore in the bosoms of their families—affected the accuracy of the answers that the researchers received. However, the NORC interviewees weren't actually asked to talk about their sexual behavior *during* the face-to-face part of the interchange; they were simply asked to fill out a self-completion form in private, then place it, unsigned, in a sealed envelope and mail it off later on.

Nevertheless, it's difficult to be absolutely confident that the NORC's much lower figures *do* reflect the actual rates of infidelity in America; it's just as likely that many individuals decided that answering a sexual questionnaire truthfully was *not* the better part of discretion. So the question itself is still out there: *Is* infidelity the norm, and *is* everybody doing it? The definitive, incontrovertible answers aren't in, and they probably never will be, for we'll never know how many people are willing to talk frankly about their sexual behavior.

What's more, many other issues are worth bearing in mind when it comes to assessing rates of infidelity—for example, what constitutes an act of partner betrayal? When we're talking about extramarital sex, is oral sex or only genital sex to be counted? Is a highly sexualized relationship that takes place only on the Internet to be considered merely a game, or is it a form of real marital deception? Are we distinguishing among a one-night stand, a brief fling, an affair involving sex but no real emotional relationship, and an affair involving an intensely sexual *and* emotional connection? Many of the extant surveys lump together some or all of these behaviors in ways that reflect none of the serious differences among them.

Moreover, the current EMS data doesn't take into account the fact that many *unmarried* couples are in seemingly sexually exclusive, committed relationships. In these instances, despite the absence of a marriage license, learning of a partner's betrayal can be just as horrible an experience but never be reflected in the overall sexual treachery statistics.

The Trust Issue

During a preliminary telephone conversation, Karen had told me that she was in a second marriage. So in the course of this first interview, I drew a fresh marital line and asked her how long she and her current husband had been together. It seemed like a simple question, but she hesitated and looked at me strangely, then asked me which marriage I was referring to.

My pencil remained aloft in the air. "This marriage," I said, pointing to the line I'd just drawn on the sketch pad.

She looked at it, nodded, then warned me that in terms of time frames, the discussion might get confusing: Her first and second marriages were to the same man.

She smiled broadly, obviously amused by the startled look on my face. Then she told me that although she had gotten married to the same husband on two different occasions, her first and second marriages were very *different* in her own mind and in their day-to-day reality as well.

Karen explained that after a year of heavy-duty marital counseling, the marriage—their *first* marriage—had taken on a Humpty-Dumpty quality.

Despite Jon's breakup with his lover, and her own desperate efforts to save the relationship, they couldn't put it back together again. And at last, the Barry-Freeds had given up trying to do so; their long separation ended, and the divorce was finalized. This seemed to mark the definitive ending of their conjugal story, for both ex-partners were by now firmly set on their different and disparate life paths.

Then, one blustery winter afternoon a few years later, Jon called and asked his ex-wife if she would do him a favor. He had the flu and was running a temperature; there was a prescription waiting for him at the local pharmacy, but he was feeling too sick to go out and get it himself.

Karen agreed to drive down to the drugstore and pick up the prescription. But when she brought it up to his apartment, Jon met her at the door and said that there was something he wanted to talk to her about. She stepped just inside the doorway, and he asked her, in a muffled, humble tone of voice, if she would give some consideration to going out for a friendly dinner with him some evening, with absolutely no strings attached. Surprised, Karen hesitated, then agreed in principle that at some undetermined time in the future she would do so—right now it was impossible, for the Christmas holidays were almost upon them.

A couple of months later, the ex-partners *had* met for dinner, and this in turn had led to more meetings—all enjoyable, if permeated by an undertone of strain and wariness. On one such evening, a few months after these casual "dates" had begun, they sat in Jon's car for a while, discussing the plot of a film they'd seen—in an uncanny way, the plot resembled some of the things that had happened in their own lives. And suddenly Karen realized that Jon was weeping.

Then he began talking, in a choked and muffled voice, about what a damned fool he had been. He accused himself of having sabotaged everything in his life that had any real meaning and done so much damage to the people he loved in the process. He told Karen that there was no *way* he could apologize enough—he realized that it wasn't possible—but that he would, if given a chance, do anything, *anything*, to put their marriage back together again. He did understand that if this should ever come to pass, the relationship would have to exist on a different footing entirely.

Now, the balance of power between the members of the pair had shifted dramatically. It was Jon who was pressing to restore the marriage, while Karen remained dubious about getting reinvolved. "I'd arrived at a place in my life where things felt pretty stable, and I was skeptical about making myself vulnerable again," she said, two fingers flying to the base of her throat, as if a body sliver of pain had lodged itself there.

Still, she'd agreed to Jon's request to join him in a fresh round of couples' counseling, even if only with the modest goal of better understanding what had gone wrong between them. "We started back into therapy, and that's when it really got heavy—*that's* when we got into the difficult stuff. . . ."

"The difficult stuff?" I asked.

"Well, the *trust* issue," she said tensely. "I said to Jon, 'I've been lied to and I've been betrayed; and I don't know that I will *ever* trust you again!' I told him, 'You can apologize to me until forever'—and he *has* apologized to me, just endlessly—'but still, I can look at that scar, and it's *there*—and a part of it still hurts—and I think it always will. . . .'" Her hand had drifted downward, and she held it palm inward, fingers splayed wide, against the middle of her chest.

I said nothing; I simply met her gaze and nodded sympathetically to let her know that I'd heard what she was saying: The loss of a certain wholehearted, innocent faith in the safety and security of her partner's love was gone and wasn't ever going to be replaceable.

"Usually it doesn't hurt; it's pretty much healed by now," Karen said slowly, reflectively. "But you know, I don't know that I'll *ever* be free of that little nagging sense. . . ."

Nevertheless, said Karen, she'd be the first to acknowledge that all the suffering they'd been through had actually had a colossal upside. For during this second course of couples' therapy they'd *both* become deeply engaged in the process; and their relationship had opened up and deepened in ways they hadn't ever thought possible. They had come to know and accept each other as the very different individuals they really were, and this had helped them feel less threatened by their differences, much more willing to come closer. In the course of time, this second courtship had resulted in the partners' decision to marry each other again. And by the time our interviews got under way, Karen had been in her "second marriage" for a little over two years. She did seem to have a buoyant air about her, and she told me that this marriage was infinitely happier and more intimate than her "first marriage" ever had been.

The Paradoxical Aftermath

The marked improvement of the Barry-Freeds' relationship in the aftermath of the affair was actually a development that's not at all uncommon. At the outset, the impact of the revelation had shattered many of the couple's long-held assumptions, jarring violently and then demolishing the framework of the marriage that had existed earlier. The damage wreaked by this psychological tornado had left in its wake a sense of desolation and emptiness—a bleak nothingness where all of the comfortable beliefs and soothing predictabilities of their long relationship had once existed.

It was in this atmosphere of disillusionment that the couple had begun confronting the scary truth that making sense of the relationship would require a degree of honesty and disclosure that hadn't existed between them before. If they were to face up to the "creeping distance" that separated them, they would have to be dangerously forthcoming—speak to each other openly about all of the frustrations, disappointments, and polite evasions that had been there *before* the marriage's eruption.

It was a slow, agonizing enterprise, yet after the fact, Karen was very clear about one thing: In the wake of the affair, her marriage to Jon was much happier and stronger. This sort of outcome is not at all uncommon, for one great paradox of infidelity is that while it has all the high-octane potential to decimate a relationship, there are many situations in which the couple's life together improves dramatically in the wake of an intimate betrayal.

Indeed, the truly *atypical* aspect of the Barry-Freeds' story was not the radical turnaround and marked improvement of their relationship. The most unusual part of their tale was the fact that they'd gone through all the wrenching agony of a divorce, and the turmoil around a family breakup, then reversed course after all the hell they'd been through. It was as if these partners had had to completely obliterate the old marriage before rolling up their sleeves and undertaking the labor of restructuring their lives together anew.

A Garbled Plea for Change

After the initial havoc of an extramarital crisis has been weathered—if it *is* weathered, and that's always a big "if"—a significant number of couples will do what the Barry-Freeds eventually did. They will construct a marriage that's much closer, more honest and mutually satisfying than it ever was beforehand (but very rarely will they have divorced in between). It's not at all exceptional for an affair's exposure to serve as a catalyst for change in a relationship that feels lifeless, stunted, and shut down.

Why should this be so? One possible explanation is that adultery often serves as a compelling form of communication—a harshly strident, attention-grabbing announcement, delivered in the language of behavior, whose content boils down to one very essential statement: "For me, this marriage isn't working."

In this "communicative" sense, the affair can be viewed as a *challenge* to the marital relationship, a garbled plea for change that has not been otherwise articulated. The Barry-Freeds' narrative can serve as a fitting example, for prior to the extramarital crisis, their way of relating to each other had been structured along the lines of a "businesslike arrangement"—one that both of them experienced as emotionally disengaged and sexually dormant.

At the Level of the Body: Keeping Score

Since denial and avoidance were the couple's main ways of managing their differences and difficulties, their sense of profound disconnection was not being acknowledged at the level of conscious awareness.

At the *level of the body*, however, defensive strategies such as denial and avoidance are not available; the body's nervous circuitry is always keeping score in terms of what is actually occurring. This is why many people experience only *in their viscera* the unthinkable messages they can't bear to receive—messages that may come to them as feelings of inner emptiness, physical deflation, isolation, abandonment, or the like. But when an individual has lapsed into a state of emotional shutdown, body-based communiqués of this sort are *not* consciously linked to the hurtful thoughts to which they might give rise. For, like Sleeping Beauty in the well-known fairy tale, the person has fallen into a form of pseudo-death; and though "alive," she remains numbed and frozen, walled off in an emotional slumber that serves to shield her from painful knowledge in a menacing environment.

It was not a kiss, but Jon's abrupt confession that had shocked the Barry-Freeds into full wakefulness. It had presented them both with an in-your-face confrontation about what had been happening—and *failing to* happen—between them. His admission had exposed the underlying truth of their marriage, which was that their intimate connection had become so tenuous over time that they were living together in an atmosphere of in-sincerity and estrangement.

This underscores another paradox of infidelity, which is that there's a real sense in which many extramarital affairs can be understood as a dis-couraged, unhappy partner's way of being *truthful* about a relationship that has actually stopped functioning beforehand. As one marital therapist told me in the course of an interview, "I've always found it curious that a partner who doesn't want to hurt his partner's feelings by telling her how disappointed and miserable he's feeling will turn around and get into an affair instead. It's a peculiar form of politeness: In the effort to avoid wounding the mate by talking with her openly, the betrayer becomes in-volved in something that will, when the truth emerges, strike at the very heart of her being."

The huge upheaval created by an affair's revelation, and the chaos and despair attending its painful aftershocks (finding out the identity of the other person; the length of the affair; mutual friends who've been in on the secret all along; and so forth), does pose a mortal threat to the re-lationship's survival. And even if the marriage endures, its innocence is gone and will not return. According to a recent survey, most psychothera-pists consider extramarital affairs to be second only to physical violence in terms of the emotional damage they inflict.

Still, you can't ignore the *other* reality, which is that an extramarital crisis can and frequently does have exactly the *opposite* effect. If the initial blowup doesn't spin so completely out of control that the marriage deteriorates beyond repair, that selfsame crisis may create the conditions for mutual soul-searching, enhanced openness, and the growth of a new, deeply satisfying mutual understanding. The admittedly ambiguous truth of the matter is that while infidelity can sometimes kill a relationship, it can sometimes bring a dying relationship back to life.

Chapter Fifteen

REENACTMENTS OF
THE PAST: THE BARRYS
AND THE FREEDS

HEN IT COMES TO A DILEMMA IN THE PRESENT SUCH as an extramarital affair, why bother looking backward at the partners' earlier lives in their separate families of origin? If you were to ask each member of the couple what *caused* the affair, you'd be likely to get two diametrically different answers, yet *both* partners' explanations would be fixated on whatever was going on in the here and now of the current moment.

Typically the betrayed mate would, like Karen, view the partner's lying, sexual cheating, and the other person in the triangle as the main *reasons* for the turmoil in the marriage, while the deceiving partner, like Jon, would be more likely to see the affair as the *effect* of all the disappointments and deficits in the marital relationship. Overall, the focus of attention would be upon who bore the major responsibility and on whose shoulders the burdens of shame and guilt most rightfully belonged.

Did the misery in the relationship precipitate the affair, or was the affair a consequence of the slow-burning anger and alienation someone was experiencing beforehand? In general, the partners are so caught up in the chaotic emotionality of the moment that the importance of the baggage each of them has brought to the relationship often goes unnoticed. And although in fact the affair has often been motivated by unresolved struggles rooted in one or both mates' earlier family histories, the crucial, underlying connection between the "here and now" and the "then and there" is never really explored or addressed. As a result, the couple suffers without ever making sense of what happened; and even if they do manage to stay together, nothing is learned, and nothing changes. What this amounts to is an opportunity lost, for a crisis without real learning, and ensuing change and growth, is a crisis that has been wasted.

Karen's Family: Keeping Up Appearances

As I learned in the course of sketching out the couple's multigenerational genogram, Karen Barry had grown up in Minnetonka, Minnesota, a suburb of Minneapolis. Her family had lived on a quiet cul-de-sac where all of the neighbors were good friends. And as she described it, the communal life they'd lived there was in many ways idyllic.

There were skating parties when a nearby river froze; there were wonderful, progressive New Year's Eve parties, which involved all the parents and the kids moving from house to house for each course of a long night's dinner, then ending up sleepy and ecstatic as they all counted down to midnight. There were hunting parties for the men and boys—her dad usually took her older brother, Scott—and family camping trips and cookouts in the summer. "I really felt there was this magic bubble. . . . Bad things did *not* happen to the Barry family from Minnetonka, Minnesota," Karen said.

Growing up in that world had been harmonious and pleasant—it had been nothing *but* harmonious and pleasant—yet as she now recognized, it had also been emotionally flat and highly conformist. An unstated but strictly enforced rule of the household was that keeping up appearances was of paramount importance: It didn't matter how you actually felt as long as you *looked* as though you felt all right. Thus, while the family she'd grown up in had felt secure and very sheltered, it had also felt inhibited and devitalized. "There was a low-energy, 'flat tire' kind of a feeling. At the dinner table, people passed the plates around, but no one had very much to say."

As Karen saw it, what had been missing in her family was some way to connect at an emotional level; and if she complained about something—perhaps an incident at school that had hurt her feelings or made her angry—her mother's response was always "You shouldn't feel that way."

"I wasn't *supposed* to feel that way," she said emphatically, "but I *did*. So as a little kid there was always the sense that I shouldn't be feeling what I was feeling, but I *was*. And this kept me wondering, What's wrong with *me*?" I nodded in sympathy, for this sort of emotional invalidation can make a person feel that her normal emotions are really *bad*. Then she observed that the main unwritten rule of her family had been "Don't stick out; don't be different from anyone else." "It was never anything like 'You're great' or 'You're special.'"

It wasn't that she'd felt unloved as a child, Karen hastened to say, but there had been no interest whatsoever in what was going on *inside* her—in her feelings, her thoughts, on who she *was* as a growing human being. She had simply been expected to go along with the family program—follow the rules, do well, get good grades—but never behave in ways that would make her stand out too much or command an excess of attention. And she *had* done what was expected of her, always, as long as she could remember.

Jon's Family: A Novel, More Vivid World

Meeting Jon's family, shortly after they'd begun going out with each other, had come as a revelation to Karen; she'd found herself entranced by all of them. Like Dorothy leaving Kansas and finding herself in Oz, she'd had the sense of a black-and-white existence suddenly becoming radiant with color and emotionality. For life among the Freeds was so different from the family life she had known: Everyone was lively and challenging; people leapt into the ongoing conversations, bantered with one another, talked easily and openly about their feelings.

It was wonderful, but it made Karen edgy, too, for she'd felt disconnected from so many of her own feelings and emotions at the time. She told me this with a bemused smile, as if recalling what a prim, constrained, wide-eyed girl from the Midwest she had been.

Since Jon's background was Jewish and his parents were observant, I asked Karen whether there had been any objections to their interfaith romance from either hers, his, or from both sets of parents. She shook her head and said there had been none from her side and none from Jon's father, either. "His dad was—well—such a genuinely *loving* human being." Her father-in-law, now deceased, had been a man with a truly generous heart, someone who was always building everyone up in the most affectionate way, making people feel good about themselves.

"With Jon's mother, it was different—her love was more conditional." Karen's expression clouded over. She said she now knew—but hadn't suspected at the time—that her mother-in-law, Anita, had been vehemently opposed to her son's choice and had been doing everything she could to prevent the relationship from getting too serious. "I myself, with my innocent, fresh little Minnetonka Girl Scout persona, had no idea that these monumental tidal waves were being churned up. . . ." True to her own family's tradition, she had been "clueless" when it came to being aware of anything distressing or unpleasant going on beneath the surface.

The Freed Legend: "We're the Greatest"

In terms of family style, Karen Barry's family had been benign but bland and disengaged, while Jon Freed's family was warm, demonstrative, lots of fun to be with, and highly overinvolved. I had the notion that a significant part of the couple's initial attraction had stemmed from Jon's capacity to offer Karen a taste of intense emotionality and her capacity to offer him some degree of autonomy and space.

But Jon's doting, overinvested parents hadn't found it easy to see him marry and move off into a life of his own. Even after the pair were married and living in a place of their own, Jon's parents would arrive for dinner bringing his favorite meat from the kosher butcher. His energetic, overzealous mother would then make her son hamburgers in special little presses, carefully explaining to the young bride that this was the way her new husband liked them best.

"Jon was their golden child, their only son; he could do no wrong." His older sister, Sandy, now complained that as the older child in the family, she'd had all the rules and the "No, you can't!" responses, while her brother got away with everything. "Jon just charmed everyone around him," Karen said.

"So he was Prince Jon?" I asked with a smile.

She laughed. "He was Prince Jon, he was *definitely* Prince Jon! And if we came to his folks' house for dinner, and he didn't like what they were serving, his mother would make him a special meal of his own."

I laughed, too, then asked Karen, "If you were going to call your husband 'Prince Jon,' what would you call his sister, Sandy?"

"His sister was definitely not a princess, so I don't know. . . . I might call her 'Cinderella,'" Karen replied. I asked her how well Sandy and their dynamo of a mother had gotten along.

Karen hesitated for a moment, then explained that in the Freed family there was never any question of *not* getting along. There were rules or ways of being, and everyone was supposed to abide by them. The most important rule was that you weren't to go against Mommy and Daddy. "The basic idea was that 'This is how we raise kids, and this is how we're expecting you to behave.'"

Unlike her own original family, for whom a major concern had been appearances—what the neighbors might think of them—Jon's family had required only *internal* loyalty, and the youngsters could deal with the outside world as they chose. "I think Jon got a very different message from the one I got. His was 'Push the envelope'; 'Bend the rules'; 'You're a Freed'; 'the Freed legend'; 'You do what you want.'"

I raised an eyebrow, smiled, and asked, "And what exactly is the Freed legend?"

"It's 'We're the greatest'; 'We don't need anybody but us'; 'We're terrific people'; and 'If you're in my family, I want you, and if you're not in my family, I don't really want to deal with you. I may not even want to sit *next* to you, because I like my family as it is!'" She was smiling, too, but at the same time rolling her eyes and shaking her head ruefully.

"So I should think it's a hard family to get into?" I asked, thinking of a young midwestern Protestant trying to find her place in this tight-knit Jewish family who lived in the affluent Boston suburb of Newton, Massachusetts.

"No kidding!" said Karen, and we both started laughing. But I was thinking that while the Freed family was probably not only hard to get into, it sounded equally difficult to leave.

Karen, Jon, and Echoes of the Past:
The Good Girl and the Renegade

The curious reemergence of old family scripts in a new generation is a somewhat mystical, if thoroughly commonplace, occurrence. As my interviews with Karen Barry-Freed proceeded, I continued filling in more of the informational dots and connecting lines in an effort to look at the Barry-Freeds' marital crisis in its more extended, familial context.

Karen was, like Jon, the younger of the two children in her family. She was also the favored child, the one who made her parents feel good about themselves: She could be relied on to do everything that was expected of a nice, *nice* girl and not behave in ways that would make her stand out unduly or command an excess amount of attention. But if she was the family's good girl, her older brother, Scott, was the renegade, the outsider.

There had been a six-year difference between herself and Scott, so Karen felt that she'd never really known him well. He'd been married by the time she went away to college, and she'd gone *far* away—to a university on the East Coast. "Anyhow, Scott was always kind of a loner, a different kind of kid. A *very* different kind of kid. He really *did* push the envelope, in all sorts of ways," said Karen in a flat, unemotional voice, as if she were chatting about a stranger.

I had an odd sense that she was tiptoeing around a subject she didn't want to talk about. But eventually she said, as if in defense of Scott, that her brother hadn't been involved in anything that was outright *illegal*; he'd just loved cars and motorcycles. He could fix anything on wheels, and as a teenager, he'd always had some hot rods that he was upgrading. "He could transform old roadsters, and they were *beautiful*," said Karen. Her words were upbeat, but there was a growing edge in her voice, and her facial muscles had stiffened.

I wasn't sure what was happening, so I glanced down at the sketch pad on my lap, eyes seeking the square box in her family's genogram inside which I'd written the name "Scott." Then I looked up again and asked Karen where her brother was now. Was he married, and did he have children? What did he do for a living?

But she'd begun to shake her head in the negative as soon as I began asking these questions, and finally she raised her right arm, palm facing outward, in the universal gesture that signifies "Halt there." "My brother is dead," she said flatly.

"Dead?" I stared at her. "How old was he?"

He had died at thirty-four, she answered, eyes wide and unblinking. My gaze fixed upon her face, I asked her what he'd died of, expecting to hear the word *cancer* or to hear about some other illness. But Karen told me that he had been murdered. "*Murdered?*" I repeated disbelievingly.

She nodded, said, "Yes," in the same dispassionate, almost reportorial tone of voice. Then she went on to say that her brother had dropped out of college after one year because of a shotgun-type marriage; he had definitely *not* wanted to marry the girl he'd gotten pregnant, but intense pressure from both sets of parents had forced him to do so. This teenage marriage had produced one child, a son, but had ended in divorce five miserable years later. After that, Scott had drifted from one unsuccessful job to another and finally gotten into some sort of trouble—she wasn't sure *what* kind of trouble—in the drug scene. He'd begun using various drugs himself, mostly cocaine, she believed, but the whole story was still murky in her own mind.

She still didn't know whether Scott had actually been *selling* drugs or whether he'd had a lot of cocaine in his possession, Karen told me. All she knew for sure was that her brother had been arrested at one point, then agreed to cooperate with the police in lieu of serving jail time. Had he been killed because he was slated to testify in an upcoming drug trial, which was going to court a few weeks hence? Or had it happened because he'd owed a lot of money to someone?

Karen shook her head, said with a small, helpless shrug of her shoulders that all her speculations had remained just that—speculations. By that time, she herself had been long gone from Minnetonka. She was married, the mother of her first child, and living in the Greater Boston area; and everything in her brother's life had been happening at a great distance. The family *did* know that Scott had been beaten and tortured before being shot in the head three times, execution style, she added, her tone of voice remaining even and controlled. But her brother's killers hadn't ever been found, and the case remained unresolved.

I must have looked puzzled by the dispassionate way in which she was relating this awful story, for Karen leaned forward, as if to meet my gaze more fully. "Most of the pain I felt at the time was for my poor, mild, inoffensive, good-hearted parents," she said. "The police called my dad at three in the morning to come down and identify the body. . . . I can't even *imagine*, as a parent, having to do anything like that." She shuddered.

I couldn't imagine it, either. And what seemed especially incongruous was how little this startling tale of torture and murder seemed to tally with that "magic bubble" she'd described—life on the pleasant, family-oriented cul-de-sac in Minnetonka, Minnesota. What malevolent trajectory had carried her brother from his close-knit, suburban upbringing to a "loner and outsider" sense of self, and then to a shotgun marriage, an interrupted education, a divorce, and a series of failed efforts to find some sort of suitable occupation? How had a boy from this quintessentially "nice" midwestern family fallen into the life of a drifter, a druggie, and ultimately a victim of murder?

I asked Karen what she could remember about her own reactions on first hearing this catastrophic news, and she grew silent, stared at me without replying for a few moments. Then she said, in the hushed voice of someone telling a ghost story, that she'd felt "eerie," "surreal"—as if everything around her, and she herself, were both real and unreal simultaneously. She'd had the weird sense that the news she was hearing couldn't *possibly* be true—yet knowing that it *was* true—even though it felt as if it were happening to someone who was living on an alternative planet.

"Also, what I remember *vividly* was the feeling of time having slowed down. . . . Then, on my way to the airport, I had the strange feeling that the people passing me on the street were receding, floating, like figures seen in a film in slow motion," she said. She'd felt at a remove from everything that was happening around her, like an actress playing in a scene of daily life that she herself was watching.

This kind of reaction is associated with the "numbing" response to traumatic threat, which is one of those three instantaneous bodily reactions—fighting, fleeing, or freezing—to situations of immediate danger. Of course, we don't *choose* among these response options after weighing each of them carefully. Our brains and bodies simply assess the circumstances in an instantaneous, decision-making flash, and they react. Karen's response had been to freeze—to shut down, zone out, and feel emotionally distanced from what was happening. This was her means of protecting herself from experiencing the full shock and pain of the family's loss—its sense of shame as well, for "bad things did not happen to the Barry family of Minnetonka, Minnesota."

"You know, my parents weren't strict, but they did put great stock in *obeying the rules*. That was their mantra," Karen said. "The most horrible thing we kids could ever do was somehow bring embarrassment to the family, through some kind of bad behavior. And I really *heard* their message and I said, 'Okay'; but my brother heard it and he said, 'Forget it.'"

"So Scott's position was that if there was a rule around, he'd bend it or break it?" I asked, and she nodded.

"Exactly," she said disapprovingly, "and it's interesting, because my husband's exactly the same way. And Jon has a low trigger point for anger, as Scott did, too."

I hesitated, my attention caught by this comment. For when Karen mentioned those basic similarities between Scott and the man she'd chosen as her life partner, I couldn't help but notice that an old family theme—one involving the polarized roles of "the good, well-behaved female" and "the difficult, unruly male"—had suddenly materialized in her current-day existence. And it occurred to me that there might have been a bit of a replay going on here—a newly updated, modernized version of an old family scenario involving a conscientious, rule-abiding girl and a restless, rule-bending renegade.

At a surface level, Scott Barry and Jon Freed would seem to have had very little in common. And yet Karen spoke of them both (not only in this, but in subsequent interviews) in similar terms as individuals who had "certain issues with authority," a tendency to "bend the rules" and to "operate outside the box." Had it been a certain recognition that her husband, like Scott, would always live by his *own* rules, that had been a subliminal part of the attraction when she'd first met him?

Repetitive Patterns of Relationship: The Way It Felt Inside

As therapists and theorists Christopher and Lily Pincus have written in *Secrets in the Family*, "We all have a tendency to get into repetitive patterns of relationship that are motivated by wishes in unconscious fantasy form and derived from the way earlier needs were satisfied." In simpler terms, we are drawn toward certain kinds of interactions because they conform to the internal blueprint for being in relationships that each of us begins to develop early in our lives. These are the relationships that feel *right*, because they are the ones with which we are deeply familiar. They have about them a sense of deep recognition, of coming home; it's as if our minds and bodies *know* that we've arrived in a place where we belong and where we're clear about how we're supposed to behave. Just as a woman who's been raised in a violent household *knows* what life is like in a violence-prone relationship, Karen Barry *knew* some things about what life would be like in a relationship with a partner who operated "outside the box" and who had "certain issues with authority."

This brings me to a point well worth noting, which is that there are many instances in which an attachment will feel *right* to us—because it is so *familiar*—but it will not necessarily feel *comfortable*. In many instances, the attachment will feel anything *but* comfortable; but even so, it's a *familiar discomfort*, one that reconnects us not only to "the way it was" but to "the way it felt inside," in terms of our body's well-remembered feelings and sensations. For the old, familiar relationship patterns—the ones that hark back to our earliest experiences in the world—are accompanied by familiar internal states of being.

And in this way they serve to bring us "home," to link us to aspects of the past in subterranean ways of which we're often not consciously aware. Thus, while Karen might have had her issues and grievances about a relational scenario involving an even-tempered, rule-abiding Girl Scout and an overentitled, restless, quick-to-anger, rule-bending male, there was a certain sense in which she'd resurrected in her current life a female-male relationship that she already knew a great deal about, one with which she was deeply familiar.

Jon's Parents: A Royal Match

As Karen saw them, both her in-laws were fundamentally good, caring, affectionate people. However, it was true that in terms of guiding and disciplining their children, they'd divided their parental roles into that of the

bad cop and the good cop. Jon's mother, Anita, was seen as the more difficult one; she could be demanding, controlling, at times impossible to
please. His father, Stan, had always been the softy—the far more nonjudgmental, generous, gregarious member of the pair.

"My father-in-law was a man who was just *bigger than life*," Karen said
warmly, earnestly. "He was universally loved by everyone who knew him,
and *his* love was unconditional. He would always know how to smooth out
his wife's ruffled feathers—settle any difficulties between her and the kids.
And as far as his one and only son was concerned—well, Jon could do no
wrong." But then she frowned and, almost as an afterthought, said dryly
that Jon's father could at times be "inappropriate," too.

"How so?" I asked.

She paused, then told me that even to this day—so many years after
the event—the peculiar way in which she and Jon had become engaged
was something she didn't understand. Why had Jon's father, rather than
Jon himself, been the man who'd actually proposed to her?

That proposal had come simply out of the blue, one afternoon when
she'd been asked to go out for a friendly lunch with her steady boyfriend's
dad. It was during this repast that Stan Freed had suddenly put his silver-
ware down upon the table with the air of someone who's made a decision.
Then he'd looked directly into Karen's eyes and asked her if she really
loved his son.

"Can you *imagine*, coming from Minnetonka, where we don't talk
about feelings at *all*? To have this person ask you straight out, 'Do you
really love my son?'" Karen's eyes widened, and she giggled uneasily, as if
the memory made her squirm even now.

"I didn't know what to say, so I just blurted out, 'Well, yes, I think I do.'
And then his dad said very enthusiastically that he thought Jon loved me,
too, and that our feelings for each other were pretty strong, and *he* believed the two of us would be great for each other! 'So you have to join the
family,' he told me. That's how he put it—'You have to join us.'"

"That's odd," I said, thinking that it sounded more like a proposed
adoption than it did a proposal of marriage.

"It *is* odd." Karen nodded and, as if anticipating my next comment, responded by saying, "Yes, of *course* it was Jon's job to do the proposing, not
his dad's."

Emotional Triangles

Most adult sons would have been *furious* in a similar sort of situation, I reflected. "Talk about being overinvolved," I said aloud. And it occurred to me that Jon and his father might have been in some sort of political collusion to override the heated objections of his "demanding, controlling" mother, who didn't want him marrying out of the faith. If this were so, then Stan's proposal, made "on behalf of the family," would have halted all dissent immediately. It would also serve as a prime example of what family therapists call a "perverse triangle"—that is, a hidden alliance between two members of different generations (in this case, father and son) against a third party (here, the mother, who'd had no prior knowledge of the plan).

Emotional triangles—that is, two-against-one coalitions—are an inherent aspect of family life. Generally speaking, these alliances emerge and then fade away as the problematic issues that spawned them are resolved. As new concerns arise, the involved players may then occupy radically differing positions—someone who was an insider in the last triangle may be temporarily out in the cold. Transient triangles are an aspect of many family and other close relationships—for example, two siblings who are gossiping unkindly about a third sibling are teaming up as the "insiders" in a triangle, while the object of their discussion occupies the triangle's outside leg.

Thus, triangles come, and triangles go, and they usually present no enduring family problems—*except* in those situations where they take on a fixed, enduring quality. Unchanging, rigid triangles have a way of keeping everyone in the group "stuck" on old dilemmas that are no longer relevant in the present, and the triangle involving a parent and child against the other parent is a truly classic one. In the Freed family, Anita was often in the bad cop, outsider position.

As for Stan, it seemed to me that there were many ways in which this loving, gregarious, benevolent father could be pretty controlling, too. Although his way of handling matters was much more genial and velvety than his wife's, Jon's dad was very much the social engineer: He'd put it to his son's prospective bride that in order to marry Jon, she had to "join the family." In his amiable, affectionate way, Stan had taken charge and was shaping the course of events.

Come to think of it, Karen had characterized her husband's role in his family as that of a golden prince—"Prince Jon." And who is a prince but the offspring of a king and a queen? Traditionally, in royal households, the matches were always made by the parents, not the children; it was they who would carefully select a mate deemed suitable for inclusion in the royal family. In this instance, Karen Barry was not the ideal consort Jon's mother had in mind. Yet—despite the evident differences between the lovers—her prospective father-in-law was informing her that he was championing this match and graciously permitting it to go forward. As reigning monarch of the family, Jon's father was also letting her know that she would have to join the ranks of the younger generation of this family—in some symbolic but very important sense become one of the Freed family offspring.

A *Time of High Anxiety: The King's Mistress*

A mere six weeks before what Karen always referred to as her "first marriage," a sudden catastrophe had sent her husband-to-be's entire family spinning. Jon's father, who'd seemed so healthy, vital, and fit, suffered a first but very serious heart attack—one so severe that it compelled Stan Freed's retirement at the impossibly young age of fifty-five. "Obviously it was traumatic for everyone," Karen said quietly. And naturally there had been much discussion about whether or not the wedding should be called off; and if so, for how long?

The ultimate decision had been that the ceremony itself would go forward, but that all the surrounding festivities, including the reception afterward, would be canceled. Stan's doctors thought that even a small party might create too much emotional strain for their patient. And then there were other, more sub-rosa reasons for the anxiety and apprehension coursing through the Freed family system. The story being circulated was that Jon's dad had been on the golf course at the time he was stricken, but in actuality he'd been with another woman when it happened.

Here, I think it worth mentioning that research has shown that men are more prone to suffer heart attacks during sex if they're having sex with someone *other* than the customary partner; they very *rarely* have heart attacks if they're having sex at home. This sort of statistic leaves you wondering if this has to do with much higher levels of sexual excitement or with the tremendous intensity fueled by secrecy and the thrill of the forbidden. It may just have to do with performance anxiety or with plain old-fashioned guilt—guilt that could be related either to the fear of discovery or to strong feelings about violating one's own strongly held code of ethics.

In Stan Freed's situation, any of these explanations could have been on target; but it did seem to me that the looming marriage of his beloved son was probably as relevant as any of them. For Jon and his parents—and most particularly his father—were extremely close, and it sounded as if this "princely" offspring was serving as the repository and container of his family's dearest hopes, dreams, and expectations. He, in turn, was receiving daily supplies of support and affirmation from the older generation—an image of himself as a superior being, heir to the family legend.

Key Family Transitions, and Affairs

As mentioned earlier, many extramarital involvements get under way around key family passages, even joyous ones such as a wedding or the birth of a child. These are times when the emotional system must undergo a profound, earth-moving shift, and certain individuals are likely to be experiencing not only happy feelings but painful feelings, of loss and abandonment. In Jon's father's case, that extramarital affair—seemingly disconnected from the young couple's imminent marriage—might have been the older man's way of seeking solace for the pending departure of his son.

For this was a defining moment in the life of the family: The Freeds' "golden" son and last unmarried offspring (their daughter, Sandy, was already married and living in upstate New York) was moving off into his own adult existence. The family baton was being handed along, and somehow I had the idea that this benignly controlling and directing father—who was such a *presence* in the life of everyone around him—might have been feeling as if part of his own inner self were being wrenched away in the process.

Wall-to-Wall Avoidance and Denial: A Bargain with the Devil

How had the facts of Stan's whereabouts at the time of his collapse become known? Karen herself wasn't sure. Her understanding was that the few facts that were known about Jon's dad's extramarital relationship had come through his sister, Sandy. "I'm not clear on many of the particulars, but somehow Sandy *knew*. . . . Also, when Jon's father came home from the hospital, the woman he'd been involved with—she was a legal consultant working with the company—kept calling the house frantically for news of his condition."

As his colleague, the woman *did* have a pretext to call, because they had a professional relationship. But she would often phone around dinnertime and ask frantically, "How is Stan? How is Stan?" "I think it freaked Jon's mother," Karen said. "She'd ask, 'Why is that woman *calling* here all the time?' And of course nobody answered. We'd all just look down at our plates and then the subject would get changed."

Had Anita Freed ever learned the truth, or hadn't she? According to Karen, this was a question that nobody in the family could answer to this day. All of the specific details surrounding the event—how had Stan gotten to the hospital? who had called his wife?—were hazy in everyone's mind, and the subject of the other woman had been whisked out of sight almost immediately. There had been an initial flurry of discussions between Jon and Sandy, but then this hot-potato topic was dropped, and their mother never, ever broached the subject with either one of her children.

In the wake of Stan's dangerous heart attack, it felt natural for the family to focus their attention upon his symptoms and state of health, while avoiding all allusions to the circumstances in which the emergency had occurred. And within a period of weeks, the phone calls from the other woman had ceased, so the family circle's cardinal mythology—"We're the greatest: We're the most loving, mutually cherishing couple with the brightest, most devoted offspring"—was never openly questioned or challenged. There were never any fierce quarrels, agonizingly candid discussions, expressions of remorse or conflict resolution endeavors of any kind—at least none that Karen knew about. On the surface, the Freeds' family relations seemed to be as unruffled and harmonious as ever.

The crisis had been "settled" by being met with wall-to-wall avoidance and denial. But alas, one of the side effects of a shutdown of this sort is that while it protects the people in the family from experiencing their bad, painful feelings, it also shuts off many of their good, spontaneously happy feelings. The Freeds had, in effect, made a bargain with the Devil, for the need to censor certain topics made it impossible for them to be fully *present*, in touch with what was happening inside themselves in terms of their true thoughts and emotional reactions.

And all the while, the unresolved dilemma remained, for when major issues of this sort are buried in this fashion, they inevitably begin to release pernicious toxins. The sharp disjunction between the family's newly revealed reality and the treasured Freed legend had in fact turned the system on its axis. And no matter how strenuously the truth of the situation was being disavowed, their central vision of themselves—"We're the best, we're the greatest"—had been seriously undermined.

Family "Solutions": Extramarital Affairs

As Bessel van der Kolk has written, severely stressful experiences "can alter people's psychological, biological and social equilibrium to such a degree that the memory of one particular event comes to taint all other experiences, spoiling appreciation of the present." In such instances, the awful memory remains front and center and doesn't permit normal life to continue. In other instances, though, old, heart-stopping experiences can *appear* to be completely forgotten, then be revived and acted out in "real time" without being recognized as thinly disguised repeat performances of actual past events.

Such resurrections of old scenarios, which are not knowingly linked to things that *did* happen, are like strange artifacts or fossil remains of familial history that have suddenly emerged at the surface. When this kind of reenactment takes place, the painful memory is not only being revived in terms of the traumatized person's *behavior*, it is also being reexperienced at an emotional, physiological, and neurohormonal level. All of the suppressed feelings and sensations associated with the original event spring into being, and they *feel* as potent and present tense as ever. For our bodies hold the archival history of everything that has happened to us, including experiences that may seem to be lost in the past and long forgotten.

In the period following Stan Freed's almost fatal heart attack, his health began to improve and his strength to return more rapidly than anyone had expected. And within a few short years, the family's life appeared to be as warm, close, and enjoyable as it had ever been. Jon and Karen had two children, and Jon's sister, Sandy, married to a pediatric surgeon, was the mother of two sons.

But all was not as benign as it appeared to be, for themes of the family's past were beginning to spill into the present. Sandy had become immensely attracted to a fellow member of the choral group with which she frequently rehearsed and sang. The man in question (Dennis) was divorced and was certainly *not* the sort of person who could be guaranteed to meet with her parents' approval: He was a high school sports coach, easygoing, Protestant, comfortable with himself, and unambitious. Over time, Sandy and Dennis had gotten into a deep, confiding friendship, and although they hadn't become involved in a sexual affair, she knew she was in love with him and that her feelings were returned.

Sandy felt blessed, for Dennis was attentive, friendly, warm, appreciative, loving—everything her husband was not, for her marriage (like her brother's) had grown increasingly distant over the years. Still, despite the fact that she was being loyal to her vows, in the technical sense, she felt guilty and conscience-stricken; she knew that she *was* being unfaithful emotionally.

At last, feeling suffocated in a situation that was filled with lies and evasions, she'd decided to bring the matter into the open. But she'd been astonished by her husband's reaction, for he'd greeted this confession with a chilling air of calmness. In his most composed, medical fashion, he heard her anguished story out and then, seemingly untouched, told her that given the circumstances, it was his belief that an amicable divorce would be their best option. (Much later, she discovered that he'd been involved in an affair of his own at the time.) So despite the outraged, scandalized protests of her parents—for divorce had no place in the Freed legend— Sandy's marriage to the archetypical successful, professional Jewish husband ended right there. Within months, the elder Freeds had a new son-in-law—Dennis—a son-in-law who had no place in the legend and would never meet with their unequivocal acceptance.

Do You Feel You Can Trust Him?

Thinking in terms of romantic triangles, past and present, this forbidden love of Sandy's did bear some resemblance to that love affair of her dad's that had ended with such abruptness some four years earlier. For as Sandy had once confided to Karen, she believed her father's extramarital relationship had been deeply significant to him—by no means a casual fling but, rather, a true affair of the heart. Thus, there was a sense in which she might have been acting as his unconscious delegate, on a mission to bring that interrupted, extramarital romance to its ultimate, satisfying conclusion.

In any event, Sandy's recapitulation of her adored father's "secret" narrative was already part of the family's never discussed story, one that had been assimilated into their basic script. For this event had not only stated a theme—specifically, the problem of how you deal with "creeping distance" and disillusionment in an intimate relationship—but provided a model for the way in which the problem could be resolved. If you're feeling discouraged and alienated from your disappointing partner, you don't confront the difficulties directly; you slip quietly off to a place where he or she can no longer affect you—that is, you become involved in an emotional triangle.

Stan could humor his wife when she was being a difficult, controlling bad cop, but he never did defy her directly. Instead, he kept the myth of the perfectly harmonious family intact and moved off to engage his true self elsewhere. Clearly, this was a pattern of managing the inevitable tensions and disaffections of married life that was to have an impact on the lives of *both* his adult children eventually. And who could say whether or not it had existed in previous generations? Perhaps the real origins of this "solution" stretched further back than anyone knew, and there had been secret or semisecret extramarital liaisons in the family in which Stan himself had grown up. As anyone who works with genograms will tell you, when a problematic issue—be it infidelity, depression, alcohol addiction, eating disorders, or illegitimacy—appears on one branch of the family tree, it is more than likely to pop up in other places as well.

Thus, I couldn't help but wonder whether Karen felt that this, her second marriage, was now truly betrayal-proof or whether she had some lingering concern that this pattern of dealing with marital tensions—emotional distancing that could at any moment metamorphose into sexual disloyalty—might recur at some later point in time. "Do you feel you can trust Jon?" I asked her directly as our last interview was drawing to a close.

"Oh yes," she said swiftly, automatically, "I *do*. I—" But she stopped herself in midsentence, began tracing two fingers along the hairs of her right eyebrow, as if to smooth out her own honest thinking on this topic. Then she shifted in her chair and leaned toward me with a mischievous expression, as if to share a particularly juicy bit of confidential information.

Premarital Negotiations

Karen smiled broadly and explained that when Jon had been pressing her to marry him again, she'd come up with the idea of a prenuptial agreement. He had been unhappy about this idea and said that it was painful to him, like having a separation agreement written in advance—a routine they'd been through already. Karen viewed the process differently, said that in her opinion it had been "very collaborative" and they'd been able to compromise.

Then she laughed. "Of course, if Jon were here, he'd say, 'Are you *kidding*? She got everything!' And it's true. Should we ever separate, I get practically everything we own." Karen said that she had made that happen—that every time her lawyer had come up with yet another proposal, Jon would groan and say, "I can't believe I have to look at this again! I can't *believe* I have to fork out all this money to these two attorneys to work out a separation agreement from a woman I love and want to marry in a few months!"

Ultimately, though, he'd agreed to everything; and later on his attorney had said to Karen, "He really wanted to marry you, because you got just everything; it's ironclad."

"What that entire process really did was to empower me, to let me know that I would always have a voice in this marriage," said Karen, sitting up erectly in her seat. She took in a deep breath, and as her chest expanded she seemed to grow in authority. But then she halted suddenly and looked at me questioningly. "I suppose this might sound very negative to you?"

"No, quite the contrary," I replied.

In this second marriage, an altered power situation had been established. At the time of the remarriage, Jon had been the one pressing to remarry and Karen had been the one resisting, so the reins were in her hand. This prenuptial agreement was her insurance against ever finding herself in the same one-down position she'd found herself in before. It was wise, and it was also clear that she herself had grown and changed greatly over the course of this long crisis. She was no longer living in the fictional "bubble" of her girlhood; she was a grown woman who was aware that life was complex and that bad, unexpected things could happen.

I did, however, notice that the question of whether she now trusted her husband—trusted him instinctively, *in her gut*—hadn't actually been answered. She sounded as if her reasons for trusting him were along the lines of the logical and rational—as if they were coming more from her head than from her innards. Karen must have recognized this, too, for she drew in a deep breath, then let it out with a sigh. "I will give you my very abbreviated take on this," she said. "I think we started with two people who were confused about what a real relationship was. I was frightened. Jon was asking himself, Who am I? Is this all there is to my life? Now we've been divorced and had other experiences. I found myself as a sexual, desirable person, which I wasn't in my marriage—there was too much suppressed anger on my part, because Jon was too intimidating, too demanding, too quick to anger. . . . I think I simply went into a shutdown."

She paused momentarily, then went on to say that these days she viewed her first marriage to Jon as a disaster and this second marriage to the same man to be pretty wonderful in many unexpected ways. A faint blush appeared on her face, turning her complexion pink, as she explained earnestly that of course they'd both done a lot of changing and were now very different people. I couldn't help but smile, for her skin had turned rosy and she looked like a bride at that moment.

It seemed to me that she'd put the whole traumatic episode behind her and that her outlook for the future was optimistic—especially since this time around it had been her husband, not his father, who'd done the proposing himself. However, as a trigger of memory was to reveal much later on in time, she was still *holding the experience in her body* without any conscious realization that this was the case.

Chapter Sixteen

A TRUSTING MIND,
A WARY BODY: KAREN

*T*HAT POWERFUL FIRST EXPERIENCE WITH EMDR HAD LEFT me feeling strangely light-headed, as though I'd been free-associating on fast forward. Not only had I accessed a "forgotten" event that was subtly omnipresent in my ways of being, thinking, and behaving, I'd also managed to evoke the thoughts, emotions, and physical sensations associated with that event in the immediacy of the present tense. Then somehow, in the course of that single ninety-minute session, a marked inner shift—one that left me feeling much more positive and entitled—had taken place. Still, I was far from clear about what had happened. The process had moved along with baffling swiftness, almost *too* swiftly, as if some sleight of hand were involved.

Did this tally with ordinary common sense? We know that the reverse often happens: Traumatic experiences can produce profound effects upon the brain's synaptic pathways in the space of an eyeblink—effects that may persist for years as isolated stress symptoms or emerge as full-blown post-traumatic stress disorder. But could the neural consequences that so often emerge in the wake of malignant events be ameliorated or undone by so simple, if not to say simplistic, a process? How did reprocessing work? What was its underlying mechanism of action?

Despite a large and steadily growing research literature on EMDR—which has been studied more extensively than any other psychological approach to the treatment of traumatic experience—therapists worldwide make liberal use of the method without knowing how its effects are brought about. EMDR has, for example, been recommended by Israel's National Council for Mental Health as one of the three best methods of treating the aftermath of trauma. EMDR has also been cited by Northern Ireland's Clinical Resource Efficiency Support Team as one of the two most effective trauma treatments—and, lamentably, in both Israel and Northern Ireland, there have been ample opportunities to test the various therapies.

Of course, using a treatment method before understanding it completely is not particularly unheard of: Many kinds of *biological* medications have become widely utilized before their mode of operation was deciphered. For instance, penicillin was made available for four decades before scientists could figure out how it worked; and researchers still can't explain, in a definitive fashion, the healing effects of most antidepressants.

So not surprisingly, many clinicians find it acceptable to live with the lack of certainty about just why reprocessing often yields such rapid and dramatic results . . . and the movement continues to gain adherents. Currently there are some forty thousand therapists, working in seventy countries around the world, who have received training in the use of the EMDR protocol. And while they don't truly comprehend the strange alchemy that can transform a malignant memory into one that is bad but *integrated into the self and part of the past,* it seems clear that the so-called neutralizing of highly disturbing memories lies at the heart of the curative process.

This brings me back to an earlier discussion, one having to do with the subject of memory retention at its most basic, which is to say molecular, level (see chapter 3). Due to the tremendous advances in our understanding of human memory functioning, we now know that each and every memory consists of a circuit of nerve cells that are related in such a way that when one member cell fires, the others will fire in synchrony. All of our thoughts, sensory perceptions, ideas, preoccupations, reveries, and so forth consist of such *specific* patterns of neuronal associations. Thus, one nerve cell network may correspond to the experience of a note of music, while another relates to the taste of chocolate, while still other patterns of neural wiring correspond to feelings of anger or of fear.

By and large, memories form when a certain stimulus pattern is repeated frequently. For we don't have to be gazing at a cup of coffee to summon up a sense of "coffee cup–ness"—an image of a cup's shape, and perhaps the steam rising from it, springs readily to mind, as does perhaps a sense of anticipation and pleasure. We hold the patterned information corresponding to "coffee cup" inside our heads, and any cell within its corresponding network of near and distant neuronal associations can light up the entire circuit—a momentary whiff of the fresh brew or merely driving past a Starbucks café are among the profuse number of possibilities.

"Neurons fire in synchrony by setting each other off like particles in a trail of gunpowder," writes British author Rita Carter. ". . . The faster a neuron fires, the greater the electrical charge it punches out and the more likely it is to set off its neighbor. Once the neighbor has been triggered to fire, a chemical change takes place on its surface which leaves it more sensitive to stimulation from that neighbor. . . . Eventually, repeated synchronous firing binds neurons together so that the slightest activity in one will trigger all those that have become associated with it to fire, too."

Thus, it is by means of rote and repetition that many of the memories we've retained within our highly convoluted brains have been created. Yet, as noted earlier, there do exist certain circumstances—those fraught with fierce emotionality—under which *no* such reruns of an initial stimulus are required. Abiding memories form rapidly and at times indelibly in situations that are charged with significance in terms of a person's present or future well-being or survival. A sexual assault while out jogging; the news of a terrifying diagnosis; the sudden impact of a nearby explosion; a natural catastrophe such as an earthquake or flood: All are events that need not happen twice for someone to be deeply affected for years or in some cases for a lifetime.

An important caveat here is that an event clearly qualifying as traumatic—one that involves looking death in the face—will by no means necessarily produce a post-traumatic stress disorder in everyone. As mentioned previously, there is a widely held belief that severe symptoms such as persistent agitation, intrusive thoughts, nightmares, flashbacks, and/or the compulsion to replay the overwhelming experience in some disguised form will be sure to emerge in the wake of such an experience. But the research on trauma tells us otherwise: Only a subset of those exposed to overwhelming experiences (somewhere between 15 and 20 percent) will go on to develop full-blown PTSD.

This is but one among the many confusing qualifiers that make diagnosing trauma, and recognizing its aftereffects, so slippery a proposition. For as EMDR originator Francine Shapiro has pointed out, many experiences that don't seem to rise to the level of "traumatic" in the formal objective sense can hit a person *hard*, subjectively speaking. For instance, a mate's ability to function in her job and in her life may become profoundly disrupted on learning of the partner's betrayal, even though she doesn't perceive herself to be in physical danger. Moreover, the person may be not only responding to experiences happening in real time, but plugging into more distant associations having to do with old, unresolved losses and fears relating to emotional abandonment.

"The truth is that most things that bring someone into a clinician's office are not at the level of major trauma," psychologist Shapiro told me, echoing the observations of Bessel van der Kolk and other specialists in the field. "What motivates most people to seek treatment is typically rooted in *memories* based on earlier life experiences."

As Shapiro sees it, little-t trauma emanates from some of the less dramatic but nevertheless profoundly disturbing occurrences that daily existence sends our way. Nevertheless, she observes, such upsetting, often thoroughly unintegrated experiences can result in some of the same feelings as big-T trauma and have similarly far-reaching consequences in terms of symptomatic aftereffects—most particularly, harshly negative attitudes about the self.

Those life situations that have left a person feeling powerless, humiliated, mocked, abandoned, unable to cope, and so forth frequently leave a residue of self-denigrating beliefs, such as "I'm not good enough," "I'm not lovable," "I'm unattractive," "I'm stupid," "I'm out of control," "I'm a loser," "I'm incompetent," "I can't handle things," and the like. Shapiro maintains that it is these kinds of self-attacking, sometimes crippling belief systems—and the cruel memories that spawned them—that can be readdressed and "detoxified" effectively with the judicious use of her carefully honed and continually updated reprocessing technique.

Follow-up

When next I saw Karen Barry-Freed, she and her husband were in a state of turmoil. I was taken aback, because when I'd called to set up this interview three weeks earlier, she had sounded upbeat and not at all upset.

As soon as we'd sat down, however, she said without preamble, "I have to tell you, Maggie, that I think what people say—you know, that there are no accidents in life?—is right on the mark. I had been wondering when I would hear from you again. . . . It's been so long, and I'd wondered if you were going on with your project."

I felt chastened, for I'd fallen far behind in my usual follow-up schedule. Before I could offer a word of apology, though, Karen continued. "And then, just shortly after you called to make this appointment, I had a really big jolt in my marriage." Her voice was clipped, stark, as if she were reporting details from the scene of an accident.

I stared at her in surprise. There was a clock-stopping silence, and at last I said, "What's going on?"

Karen didn't respond, merely shrugged and raised both arms, palms outward, as if asking "How and where am I to start?" Then she took in a deep breath, let it out, and said, "I was in Santa Fe visiting my parents, and I knew that Jon was having dinner with a certain woman—she works for one of the company's affiliates—and she's someone he's been mentioning off and on for about a year." Jon had told her that he didn't like going out with this person alone, Karen said. In fact, he'd made a point of assuring her that he was arranging things so that there were always other people with them. "I'd say to him, 'That's okay, honey . . . whatever,'" Karen said straightaway, as if to let me know she'd not been harboring groundless suspicions.

But then she amended this account by explaining that there *had* been one occasion—a time when she'd come in after a book club meeting on a night when she knew Jon was having a business dinner with "this person." "I remember driving home and feeling really upset because he'd admitted to me that this woman kind of has fantasies about him. . . . And when I came home I marched right into the bathroom and said to him, 'I just want you to know right now that if this ever happens again, it's *over*. I cannot go through this again, no way! Just tell me, and I'm out of here!' And he was just stunned.

"He said, 'Karen, if this ever, *ever* happened again, *I'm* the one who would be out of here—*my* life would be over! You *are* my whole life, you know that!'" Karen nodded, flushing slightly, as if embarrassed to be repeating this conversation to an outsider. Still, in the wake of that episode, she *had* remained aware that in the course of his regular business activities, Jon was having dinner with the woman at least once a month when she came into town.

I paused, wondering. Had this mention of his female associate's "fantasies" been her husband's way of getting Karen to worry and therefore to focus intently upon him? Jon Freed was someone whose father had supplied him with a daily "fix" of attention throughout much of his adult lifetime. Maybe he was needing to be the center of someone's fixed and dedicated interest at this moment. Given this couple's history, my own perception was that Jon's behavior did sound a somewhat provocative note. However, never having interviewed him directly on a one-to-one basis, I felt that I could discern his silhouette clearly but was missing some of the finely etched details that would have emerged in a fuller, more elaborated portrait.

"Let's give 'this woman' a name, so we won't have to keep calling her 'this woman,'" I suggested gently.

Karen glanced at me, hesitated briefly, and said, "Her name is Margo," in a weary, downbeat tone of voice. Then she went on: Another questionable incident had occurred this past January, which was that Jon had mentioned, in a casual way, that he'd driven his female colleague back to her hotel on his way home from their most recent dinner meeting.

This seemingly innocuous remark had taken Karen by surprise. It had felt like a blow to the belly, making her feel wobbly, as if she were losing her balance. "I asked him why he hadn't simply put her in a taxi after the dinner." Her voice had grown nervous and higher pitched. "*He* said that since he was driving right past her hotel in order to get on the pike, it had just seemed like the 'kind' thing to do. To me it seemed too, I don't know, *intimate*."

She gazed at me searchingly, then said, "*I* felt that certain boundaries were being crossed, but I said nothing. I wasn't going to start some big inquisition . . . but I did think, Am I turning into someone naggy, being overly suspicious and sort of edgy when absolutely *nothing's* really going on?" She looked at me but said nothing further, and in the ensuing silence the question hung in the air.

When Something Bad Is Something Good

Karen seemed far away. "You know," she said at last, "a close friend of mine said that Jon always measures himself by whatever's coming to him from outside, especially from women. She said she thinks *my* greatest challenge will always be to be myself, while Jon will always be checking himself out with other people . . . and most particularly with women."

"As in 'Am I still attractive?'" I asked her with a smile. "And as in 'Am I still young?'" She nodded yes to both questions, her expression grave.

"And as in 'Am I an old man or am I a young stud?'" I continued, and this time she smiled back.

"Really, I don't get it," she said, "taking someone out to dinner who you know has a big thing for you—"

"And then coming home and discussing it with your spouse," I completed her remark, and we both laughed at the silliness of the notion. Then I paused momentarily before saying, in a more serious tone of voice, that I saw it slightly differently from her friend—I could see the whole sequence of events as a phenomenal bid for her attention. For what could alert her more, what could rivet her attention more, what could come to dominate her world more, than those dings of alarm that were going off periodically?

"Well, I will tell you it *has* gotten my attention," Karen said with the lift of an eyebrow.

I smiled, said that I had a private, wholly unsubstantiated theory of my own, which was that neither sex, aggression, nor the so-called will to power was the truly central motivation of human behavior. My theory, based on personal observation, was that a fundamental, driving human force is the compelling need for just plain attention. I was half joking, but

Karen looked at me thoughtfully. However, she made no response, so I went on, "It's clearly true that your husband needs *a lot* of attention, and so in this sense to do something bad is to do something good."

Karen nodded her agreement. "Whatever else, it's *still* attention."

"Yes, and we're talking about someone who was raised on whipped cream in terms of how much attention he got from his parents, particularly his dad, and—" I looked up, noticed that she'd changed color in a moment, turned a delicate, faintly flustered shade of rose. I halted in midsentence and looked at her questioningly.

"I hate to say it, but since all this happened we've come together as a couple—sexually, I mean—more intensely and frequently than we had been. . . . And we're just being *nicer* to each other, too. You know?"

I nodded. I did understand, but what she was telling me did make me wonder. Had Jon perhaps been sensing or feeling that some "creeping distance" was reentering the relationship, and had this been his way, his hugely clumsy, ill-considered, and downright dangerous way, of trying to bridge the distance between them?

This Sick, Sick Feeling

The couple's crisis, which was ongoing, had been triggered by an occurrence as ambiguous as the others—but this time, it had been something that Karen found impossible to shake.

She and her youngest daughter, Laurie, had been out in Santa Fe, visiting with Karen's elderly, retired parents. "I knew that while we were away, Jon would be taking this woman out to dinner. . . . Of course he'd *told* me; this was no secret, unknown thing," she said. I noticed that she was still avoiding the use of Margo's name.

Then she explained that on their return, she and her daughter had had a very long, frustrating day. Their connecting flight had gotten canceled, and eventually they'd had to fly into the Providence airport instead. Jon had met them there, even though he'd had an unusually grueling day himself. There had been a death in his family—his grandmother, who'd been in her late nineties—and he'd been in charge of ferrying members of the family from Boston's Logan Airport to the funeral, to the cemetery, to a luncheon gathering of friends and relatives, and eventually back to

Logan again. After that, he'd had to turn around and come to Providence to pick up his wife and daughter. So on the drive back to Boston, said Karen, everyone in the car had been feeling fairly wrung out.

It was at some point during this journey homeward, though, that Jon had suggested they call the house to let their oldest daughter, Pam, know that they were running very late. Then he'd handed the phone to Laurie, who was in the backseat, saying, "I've got all my numbers stored."

"So she goes flipping through them," said Karen, veering into the present tense, "and she looks at one of the numbers and says, 'Margo? Who's Margo?' And I have to say I—it's hard to find the words—it was like an *explosion* went off—I thought I was going to *burst*." Karen, her face wearing a look of horror, was pressing both hands hard against her chest as if manually holding her body together.

She had not said another word after the cell phone incident, but due to the general sense of fatigue, no one in the car had taken notice of her silence. It wasn't until they'd gotten home, and she and Jon were at last alone and in their bedroom, that she'd brought the matter up and found herself becoming frantic, completely distraught. "I said to him, 'I cannot *believe*, given what the two of us have been through, that here we are in *this* place again!' I was just hysterical, no two ways about it! And I told him, 'You cannot imagine what this is bringing up for me—how *painful*—how hurt I feel!'"

An emergency alarm within her body had been triggered, but Jon was shocked and said, "My God, Karen, I *need* to call her from work!" Her reaction made no sense to him: How could having Margo's number punched into his cell phone be the betrayal his wife perceived it to be? "I said I felt *in my gut* that it was! Then he got mad and asked me if I trusted my feelings more than I trusted *him*."

That remark made me laugh. "He really asked you that?" I said.

She nodded and laughed, too. "Yes, he seriously asked me that." Then her expression grew clouded, and she said that many ugly memories had come surging to the surface—*awful* times in their couples' therapy sessions when Jon would say that it wasn't the sex with his lover that mattered to him. The real connection between them was in the *talking*, in feeling close and understood.

"I told him, 'You cannot imagine what this is bringing up for me,'"

Karen repeated bleakly. Then they'd talked and talked, eventually cried together and hugged. "Jon told me that I was the one, the *only* one; he said he'd just have to call off those dinners somehow." She looked at me searchingly, hesitated, and then said, "The real point here is that as secure as I felt in this marriage—and given everything that we'd worked through in the therapy and that I thought was resolved—the mere fact that I saw this woman's number on his cell phone, and that I knew he'd had dinner with her the night before, had undone me in a way that I found astounding. . . . That it was so *painful*—as if none of it had ever been put down, not really."

I nodded in agreement, for a traumatic experience can be like a forest fire that gives every indication of being completely extinguished but has often left behind a residue of kindling that any spark of alarm can set ablaze. Thus, while Karen could reassure herself that there was nothing rational about her response, a presentiment of terrible danger had invaded her.

"I felt *betrayed*—I can't even say at what level. Did I really think that he'd had sex with this woman?" She shook her head in the negative, said the idea was inconceivable. "But I have, since the breakup of our first marriage, learned to be more trusting of my gut responses—and there was something here that didn't feel *right* to me."

"So basically you felt you trusted him in your head, but not in your body?" I asked, as I'd asked her once before.

She nodded. "Yes, that's where these messages, these *powerful* messages, were coming from."

Although she and Jon were about to leave for Europe at that time with three other couples on a long-planned business/pleasure trip, Karen canceled out. She told her husband that she needed that time by herself, and he'd been devastated, beside himself. "But I simply said, 'I'm sorry, I can't do it.' And I couldn't, I *couldn't* go—I felt physically ill. I was going to the bathroom three, four times a day, as I did the first time this happened. . . . I just had this sick, sick feeling."

In truth, said Karen, the intensity and tenacity of her reaction had shocked her just as much as it had shocked Jon. It was as though in the space of that single brief episode—her daughter, sitting in the back of the car and asking, "Margo? Who's Margo?"—she'd been thrust into living contact with a horde of demon memories, terrifying specters of the past that she'd believed had been laid to rest in the rubble of that "first marriage." Yet here she was, feeling *assaulted* by those images of a time when everything about her life had suddenly become unreal, invalid.

The thought that bad things could be happening in *this* marriage did not seem quite believable. Nevertheless, the notion *did* exist side by side with the alarming knowledge that an event that's happened earlier can certainly happen again. "I felt as if this huge rug had been yanked out from under me—no, the very *ground* that I was standing on was giving way. My *trust* had been threatened, and I couldn't get it back . . . so where was I to go with that? How could I ever feel secure? Were we heading for more of the same—the same lying, the same distancing—after all the misery, the breakup, the slow, slow reconciliation, after everything else we'd been through?"

Although Jon had done everything he could to reassure her, and had begged her to reconsider going with him to Europe, Karen remained adamant. "It would have been plain *agony*, putting on a face for those other people," she said without a tinge of regret in her voice. Instead, during the twelve days Jon was away, she'd gone on a personal retreat—used the time to relax, read, do some exercising, and begin regaining some semblance of her former composure and balance.

That had been helpful, at least to some extent, but still, said Karen, about a week after Jon's return from his trip abroad, "an overwhelming sense of sadness" had set in. "Jon picked up on this, and he asked me what was wrong. And I said that I was just feeling very sad—feeling sad for *us*. I told him that it was *inconceivable* that he would lie to me; it was *inconceivable* that he would betray me; but that I felt that his walk was not matching his talk. . . . That something wasn't squaring for me, and that's what I was feeling *in my body*."

"And is that where you are now?" I asked her quietly.

She nodded. "That's where things stand now, though it's healing and sealing over a bit. But basically, we can't just let this drift, ignore it . . . because it's inside me, someplace." Karen's eyes looked watery, and she then said, with a helpless little shrug of her shoulders, that she and Jon were going to see a couples' therapist the following evening—"much as we both dread trotting out all of these old issues, these *hurtful* issues, that we've been through so many times before.

"So this is how things stand at the moment," Karen concluded, "pretty much up in the air."

A Thread on the Rug?

That afternoon, when we parted, Karen promised to get in touch with me in several weeks and let me know how the couples' therapy was progressing. For my own part, driving homeward, I found myself puzzling over the question of what was actually going on (if anything was going on at all). It was impossible to know how much reality did or did not underlie Karen's fears.

But what did come into my thoughts at that moment was a discussion I'd once had with infidelity expert Shirley Glass. In the course of that conversation, Glass had mentioned her irrational but deep-seated fear of snakes, even harmless snakes, and the fact that she lived in a state (Maryland) where these reptiles are not at all uncommon. Once she *had* actually come face-to-face with a large, live, and very long snake, which was slithering across her living room rug and heading straight toward her. She'd gone into an atavistic panic, and even though the situation was handled quickly by a member of her family, the memory of that incident had never lost its power to terrify her. From that day onward, the brisk, very professional Dr. Glass had told me, the sight of a thread on the rug had held the power to send her into a state of immobilizing fear.

It was clearly by no means accidental that this particular story had popped into my mind. For now, thinking about Karen Barry-Freed, I couldn't help but wonder: Was Karen's "gut" reacting to an actual danger or to a mere thread on the living room rug? It was anybody's guess whether her disorienting dread and sense of overwhelming sadness were linked to something real and in the present or something stored in her body but belonging to the past, phantasmagoric.

Chapter Seventeen

REPROCESSING AND
INFIDELITY:
KAREN

HEN KAREN BARRY-FREED CALLED TO TELL ME THAT she and Jon were dropping out of couples' treatment—although their relationship was still nowhere, in limbo—I decided to talk to her about reprocessing and suggest that she might be interested in giving it a try. Without going into elaborate explanations, I'd mentioned that my own experience with EMDR had proven surprisingly successful.

Actually, in the few months following that initial meeting, I'd decided to target and "detoxify" several other oppressive memories in EMDR sessions with Patti Levin (for instance, the death of the family cat on the day my parents separated). I'd done so periodically, and in the course of this venture, something strange had occurred. I've never been sure *when*, but at some point along the way I realized that the stiff tensing up of my jaw— a lifelong signal of emotional bad weather—had mysteriously ceased to occur. It wasn't that my own allotment of daily pressures had vanished; it was just that this bodily reaction to stress, an old familiar companion, had "gotten off the train" in the course of the reprocessing sessions.

On first hearing about EMDR, Karen was doubtful. She said that she hadn't ever heard anything about this new therapy. Still, she did go on to say that she was currently feeling as "demolished" as she had at the time of Jon's initial treachery so many years earlier. The treatment sounded odd to her, but on the other hand, they'd already *had* so much regular talking therapy—they'd said everything there was to say, and she was still feeling terrible. So the idea of exploring some new approach held some appeal for her.

What follows, then, is part of the story of what happened—or, more precisely, the story of what happened in the course of one particular reprocessing session.

The Ten Worst Memories You Can Think Of

Karen Barry-Freed's assessment interview had taken place two weeks before the meeting to be described. At the close of that first, very lengthy meeting, Patti Levin had asked her to jot down what she thought of as her ten worst memories and then bring this list to the subsequent appointment. These sessions were taking place in Patti's second office in Cambridge, Massachusetts, which has three high, large windows and feels airier and more capacious than her office in New Haven.

Today, Karen had come in with that list of "ten worst memories" in hand. She took a chair directly opposite Patti's, and I placed myself slightly off to one side; I had been invited to attend as a participant-observer. This was to be Karen's first EMDR experience, and I thought she looked nervous, for as she briskly removed a single sheet of printer paper from her handbag, it fluttered in her shaky hand.

Was she apprehensive about how this curious process would affect her? I wondered. I couldn't have known, then, that in the short interval between the previous session and this one she'd encountered another so-called thread in the rug. Something else had happened that had set her highly sensitized alarm bells ringing.

She was gazing fixedly at the sheet of paper on her lap, and as she did so, I felt pretty certain *which* memories would be at the top of her list. An obvious one would be Jon's sudden, crushing announcement that there was another woman in his life and he was leaving the marriage; that would have been an 8 or a 9 on the Richter scale of any unsuspecting spouse's life. Another, more recent "bad memory" would be the unnerving incident with the cell phone, which had exposed her just-below-the-surface sense of mistrust, danger, and vulnerability. Somewhere else on that list, without doubt, would be the memory of hearing about her older brother Scott's sudden death.

Patti had questioned her at length about her reactions at the moment of receiving the news, and she'd described the way her parents called her at her work and reported what had happened in a shockingly abrupt three-word announcement: "Scott's been murdered." These tidings, coming from her former life in the Midwest, had been experienced as unreal, fantastic, almost dreamlike. "I do remember being on the flight back home—things around me seemed to be wavering, somehow. I remember seeing colors, and seeing people, but it was all *different*—nothing looked like it did in real time," Karen said, her voice taut with apprehension.

It was clear that she had displayed traumatic stress responses in the aftermath of every one of these staggering events—symptoms such as emotional numbness, a sense that the world around her was tenuous and unstable, unremitting anxiety, and a range of physical disturbances, including headaches, nausea, and diarrhea. All were episodes that had left her feeling debilitated in their wake, literally *ill* in body and in spirit.

Getting Prepped

"So. Any questions or concerns before we begin?" Patti smiled, flipped back a long strand of dark hair that had fallen forward over her shoulder, and leaned her body in her client's direction.

"No, I think we covered it last time," Karen replied. But she looked uncertainly at the NeuroTek light bar, which had been placed in such a way that both Patti and I would be out of her focal view when the actual eye tracking began.

"Okay, then, let me just show you how this works." Patti pressed a handheld switch, and set the back-and-forth movement of the lights in motion. "It can go faster"—she speeded it up—"or it can go slower. Or if you like, we can move it closer to you. You can put the earphones on; they're just an additional form of bilateral stimulation. Now, just watch the lights. Get comfortable. Basically, the point is to keep your eyes moving at whatever speed is most comfortable. . . . In terms of speed, do you have a preference yet?"

Karen shook her head, seemed wary, said she didn't.

Patti adjusted the speed to a moderate level, then asked, "Can we go like this?"

Karen stared at the moving lights for a few moments, then laughed nervously. "I'm *trying* to follow, but I start seeing all the flashing dots as a line." Patti assured her that the dots would blur out and she wouldn't even notice them after a while.

"Okay," said Karen, "because it's almost like I'm getting a little cross-eyed." She giggled, sounding nervous. Uh-oh, I thought, looking at her flushed cheek in profile, for I'd had an intimation that this might not work for her. I knew that some people had huge reactions to EMDR and some reacted little or not at all.

Patti smiled calmly, then asked Karen if she had a "safe place," real or imaginary, that she could go to and feel comforted and serene. Karen nodded, said she had a real one and an imaginary one.

The therapist looked pleased. She shifted and leaned farther in her client's direction. "Great, then I would like you to just bring it up and let yourself really *feel* it, feel it all through your body. All right? And give it a name or a cue word."

"I guess it would be 'the pond,'" said Karen, her voice subdued. Patti switched the light bar into motion, telling Karen that she wanted her to bring up the image of "the pond" and follow the lights. "I want you to *feel* what it's like to be there, to feel it in your skin, to smell the smells and hear the sounds and *experience* that sense of serenity," she instructed her patient in a low, warm voice.

As Karen's eyes tracked the swiftly moving flashes of light, Patti explained that she was using the bilateral stimulation to "install" this safe place as an internal haven—a place to retreat to in the event that the EMDR became too disturbing. "Does it feel like you've got it securely inside you?" she asked after an interval.

Karen said she thought so, but her voice was uncertain, so Patti offered her a few more back-and-forth passes on the light bar.

"Okay," said Karen after a few moments of eye tracking, sounding more relaxed. She leaned back in her chair.

Patti then instructed her about the two principal metaphors that

EMDR clinicians tend to use, as she had done for me. One, you will recall, was that of getting on a train and traveling from point A to point B, while looking out the window at "the scenery"—which is basically the fragmented, painful material being processed. The second is the image of holding the remote control to a video in one's hand, so that the information being processed is being watched as if on a screen. Also, since the client is holding the imaginary remote, she or he can slow the action down or speed it up, pause it or flick it off.

"If what you're seeing through the train window makes you too uncomfortable, you can avert your gaze and bring it back onto the train," Patti explained. "If you're watching it like a movie, you can blank it out, turn the video off. Right? So *you* have control. Does one or the other of those metaphors appeal to you?"

Karen hesitated for several moments, and as she considered the choices I reflected upon the fact that both these metaphors created a sense of *observing* rather than *experiencing from inside* the memory that still lingered, unresolved. "I think . . . the train," she said at last.

Then, after one final small instruction (to signal a "stop" by raising her hand upright in the "Halt!" position rather than by saying the word aloud), Karen had been fully readied for the journey. What needed to be determined now was the destination toward which she would be heading.

What Would You Rather Believe?

"Okay, then, I think this is where we should start." Patti's voice held a bright, faintly official note, like that of a teacher who's announcing to the class that she's now changing subjects and moving on from English to geography. The therapist shifted in her seat and straightened her long slim skirt beneath her.

"So, the next thing we need to do is decide on what we're going to target. My own gut feeling is that we ought to start with—" She caught herself in midsentence. "What is *your* gut feeling?" she asked Karen.

There was a brief silence. Patti prompted gently, "Well, if you think about the original betrayal, and then about the way your body reacted to this most recent experience, which memory feels the most upsetting or disturbing to you?" In other words, did Karen want to look backward to lingering injuries rooted in the past, or did she want to focus upon things that were happening in the here and now?

Karen said in a small voice, "I think the most recent one."

"Good," said Patti, nodding and giving the impression that this was her opinion, too. "So that's where we will start. *Now*, you may find yourself going back to the old experience anyway; you may find yourself going places you can't even imagine. That doesn't matter. Basically, your brain and your body know the way they need to heal. All right?" She gazed directly at Karen, who returned her gaze dubiously.

"Okay, then, when you think of that most recent experience, is there one particular moment—a kind of snapshot, perhaps—that symbolizes that whole experience for you? Perhaps a single sentence that captures the *worst* moment?"

Karen nodded and said, "I think the worst snapshot in my mind is just seeing this woman's name on his cell phone. *Two* of her names! Her regular number and her cell phone number. It was just that, and a bunch of other things, too, that were the culmination of everything else that was happening. Because in that first betrayal, he'd said that it was as much of an emotional need to *talk* with the woman as it was anything else! So that just brought up the whole thing. There was a lot of other stuff that was happening, *little* things, as I've told Maggie—" She glanced over at me as if for corroboration. "But that was the most significant, definitely."

"So then seeing this woman's name on the cell phone," summarized Patti, and Karen nodded her assent. "Okay, when you think of that moment of seeing this woman's name on his cell phone, what is your current negative or irrational belief about yourself?"

"Hmmm," said Karen. "I guess it would be either 'I am being fooled' or 'I am being duped' or 'Am I being taken advantage of in my life?' In other words, 'Am I being totally naive about this?'" Her statements had evolved into questions.

Patti nodded but didn't respond to them directly. She was looking for an "I" statement, a belief about the self that the incident had elicited and fostered. "So when you talk about being totally naive or being duped, what I want to know is what it says about *you*. Does the statement 'I am being totally naive' cover it?"

"Yes, I think so," said Karen.

Patti double-checked by asking, "So 'I am being totally naive' feels like your belief?"

"Yes," repeated Karen in a stronger voice, this time with no hesitation.

The therapist then asked her to cast her thoughts backward to the exact moment of seeing the woman's name on the cell phone. "Picturing that in your mind's eye, rather than believe 'I am totally naive,' what would you rather believe about yourself *now*?"

"Hmmm," said Karen, and a long silence followed. I gazed over at her, waited. She'd come in looking tanned, trim, even taller somehow—she said she was working out with weights and doing a lot of daily walking. Now, however, she seemed to hunch in upon herself, grow more diminutive in size. Her voice sounded tremulous as she replied that she would *rather* believe that it was just a colleague's name, any colleague's name—no different from the fifty or sixty other names, both male and female, listed on her husband's cell phone. She would like to believe that it had no more meaning or consequence than the name of anyone else he needed to talk to for business.

"And what would that say about you?" Patti asked. "I am . . . ?"

"I guess . . . 'I feel secure in myself,'" Karen answered after the briefest pause.

Then the clinician asked her to think back once again to seeing the woman's name on the cell phone and put *that* mental picture together with the words "I feel secure in myself." "How true does that belief feel to you at a gut level? Say, if you put it on a scale where seven equals 'completely true' and one is equal to 'completely false'? And you think of it as it relates to that moment of seeing the name on the cell phone, *not* in your intellect but in your gut?" Here, Patti was making use of the validity of cognition scale (VOSC), a research instrument used to measure the patient's *felt confidence* in his or her positive belief or cognition.

"Thinking back to that moment? I would say, 'Not at all secure in myself,'" said Karen. "I would give it a one or a two," she added with the smallest, infinitely hopeless-looking shrug of her shoulders.

In this exchange, it should be duly noted, Patti had been focusing on her patient's *beliefs* about her own self as they related to that upsetting incident. Next, the therapist would turn the beam of her attention upon the *feelings* that the experience had aroused, feelings that Karen had found intolerable but was unable to shake or put behind her.

Where Do You Feel It in Your Body?

Patti paused to type a few notes into the computer sitting on her lap, then looked up at Karen in a friendly, thoughtful manner. "So. When you think back to seeing this woman's name in his cell phone, and you think of the words 'I am totally naive,' what feelings come up for you now?"

"A whole lot of confusion." Karen's voice was low, strained, hard to hear. "Anger, and just total disbelief. I guess the feeling that the bottom was dropping out from under me. . . . I was flailing, I was in free fall."

"And is that how you're feeling now?" Patti asked.

Karen didn't answer directly. Instead she said while she certainly hadn't made her peace with that scene in the car, she'd been able to make a certain amount of distance between herself and that event by the time of her assessment interview a couple of weeks earlier. "It still hurt, but not with that agonizing kind of sharpness that it had in March, April, and May. Although it's true that the most insignificant thing could set me off."

However, in the interim between the last meeting and this one, she'd gone into a state of true panic, without even understanding what had triggered it. Not until recently, when she'd gotten into a long, confiding conversation with her closest friend, had she become aware of what, precisely, had set it off. "Jon was leaving for work early. We have different wings in the house where we sleep and the girls sleep, and he usually goes in to kiss them good-bye in the morning. So, he went into our oldest daughter Pam's room, which has a full-length mirror; and she, when she came down later on, said, 'Oh, you should've seen Dad, checking himself out in the full-length mirror, turning every which way.' She thought it was so funny, but I felt *blindsided*. Like—'Why is he doing this?'"

Subsequently Karen had mentioned this comment to her husband "jokingly," saying that Pam was amused by the way he'd been checking himself out in her bedroom mirror. And Jon had answered, "I swear to God that was the most expensive suit, and I still don't think the tailor got the pants right. They always look saggy to me."

"Of course, my thought was, Silly me," said Karen, sounding abashed, "but my mind had just skittered off instantly on this. *Why* does he care so much what he's looking like today? Who is he going to see?"

"So there's still a scab there, that gets torn off?" Patti asked sympathetically. Karen nodded, her eyes filling up. I said nothing but was astonished to realize that she hadn't noticed that her danger sirens had been activated by a particularly galling historical precedent—her husband's soliciting her advice about which tie to select to go with which jacket on certain days when he was planning to meet up with his mistress. She felt "silly" because she hadn't remembered or made the connection.

Patti called a short break in the discussion in order to get up and make some small shifts and adjustments in the NeuroTek light bar's position, maneuvering it this way and that until it felt maximally comfortable to her client. "Is that just about right?" she asked at last. Karen, who'd put on the earphones, answered with a nod.

"All right. So, when you think back to seeing this woman's name on the cell phone and thinking the words 'I am totally naive,' and feelings of confusion, anger, and disbelief rise up in you, how disturbing does that feel to you? Let's say if you were to put it on a scale where ten equals 'the most disturbing and upsetting anything could feel' and zero is just 'neutral, no disturbance at all'?"

Karen said that when it happened it had felt like a ten.

"And how does it feel now?" asked Patti. It felt more like a seven, Karen replied. Then the therapist asked her where, in her body, she noticed the disturbance.

"In my stomach and in my chest," said Karen, pointing to those places briefly and then placing both hands upon her abdomen as if to offer herself some support, soothing, and comfort. Here, it should be said, Patti was making use of another well-validated psychological scale—the SUDS, or subjective units of distress scale—which was pioneered by the famed behavioral therapist Joseph Wolpe and has now become a standard component of the reprocessing procedure.

Roadblocks

"*Now*, I am going to lead you along by asking you to hold this information together and follow the lights," said Patti. "I will do that for a little while, and then check in with you and see what you are noticing. If I keep the eye tracking going too long, and you have something you want to say, just say it. Or if I stop too soon and you're in the middle of processing something and you want to keep it in your head, just say, 'Keep going.' . . . Okay? The reins are in your hands."

Karen nodded, and Patti continued: "So, then, I want you to bring up the memory of seeing this woman's name on the cell phone. Hold it together with the words 'I am totally naive.' Notice the feelings of confusion, anger, and disbelief and where they are in your body. And follow the light, letting whatever happens happen." She flicked on the light bar, and the flashes of illumination began moving back and forth.

I shifted my chair slightly, being careful to make no noise, because I wanted to focus on the moving lights even as Karen did. This first pass lasted for about two minutes, after which the therapist halted the movement of the lights. "Take a deep breath," she said to her patient. Then, after Karen had inhaled and exhaled deeply, Patti asked her what she was noticing.

Karen, sounding confused, asked, "I'm just supposed to be holding on to that image—?" She laughed briefly, a high-pitched, nervous sound.

"Yes, but don't worry if it drifts. Whatever happens is what should be happening," said Patti, and switched on the light bar once again. This time she let the reprocessing continue for an even longer time, and when she switched it off, she told Karen to take a deep breath once again. "What are you noticing?" she asked.

"You know, I was thinking mostly about the light," Karen admitted, laughing again and sounding embarrassed. "I mean, I was holding the image of being in the car coming home from the airport when Laurie was scrolling through the cell phone, but then . . . I just started focusing on the lights."

"Okay, go back to that image," Patti said softly. She set the lights into motion, and silence fell as her client began tracking their steady back-and-forth movement. I, too, was doing some eye tracking in the background, but my own sense that the reprocessing wasn't going to be particularly helpful to Karen was growing ever stronger. Sure enough, after the next pause and deep breath, she giggled apologetically and said, "Wow, I'm beginning to realize that it's hard for me to focus on two things at once. I find that when I look at the moving light it's hard for me to keep the image of being in the car with the cell phone. My mind *did* wander to other things, but when I came back to the light, it was all I could focus on. So not a whole lot is really coming up."

Patti suggested that she keep her eyes closed and go back to the image they'd started out with—the scene in the car with the cell phone. Karen would then not be distracted by the lights and could focus on the bilateral stimulation offered by the oscillating ear tones. But this alternative proved equally unsuccessful.

For this time when Patti asked, "What are you getting?" Karen answered in the frustrated voice of a schoolgirl who simply can't make any sense of the problem she's supposed to be solving: "I *did* start off by putting myself in the situation, but then I started listening to the beeps. You know, this beep is louder than this one. . . . Is this one a little higher than the last one? And that's all I was able to focus on." There was that slightly discordant, embarrassed laugh once again.

Patti smiled. "So, what do you think is happening?"

Karen stopped laughing and said that she thought she was blocking somehow. "It's just *hard* to keep that image. It's as if I can't focus on two things at one time."

Patti explained that holding on tightly to that initial image wasn't necessary. It was perfectly fine to let go, to let it drift, to let it change. . . . "No matter what happens, let it happen. Whatever happens is fine," she assured her patient. Then she suggested that Karen go back to whatever the last image had been, to use that image as a starting point and then go anywhere.

"It's kind of funny," Karen said, "but I can't *remember* the last image I was seeing."

Patti suggested that in that case they should go back to the original image and start from there. "Notice where it is in your body and just *go* with it. Don't judge what comes out; don't judge where it goes or what you think or feel . . . just let it go wherever it wants to go, okay?" Karen nodded, and the therapist turned on the earphones once again. By now, however, my own hopes for a "minor miracle" or even a favorable outcome of this session were fading.

Sure enough, when this next interval of sound tracking had ended,

Karen reported that while she *had* found herself able to visualize sitting in the car, she'd gotten no further than that. "We are sitting in the car," said Karen, "but I can't maintain a dialogue and listen to the beeps."

"Does your mind go anywhere else?" asked Patti.

"No, I find I'm really following the beeps," the client replied. She shrugged. "Maybe it's because I meditate, and I focus on the breath. So I'm used to shutting down and staying focused on one thing. And in *this* instance, it's the beeps." There was that off-putting laugh once again. As far as I was concerned, the fact that this was going nowhere seemed glaringly apparent.

Perhaps Karen was erecting internal roadblocks—automatically walling herself off from the painful reexperiencing of a shock that had left her feeling physically and emotionally sick. Surely her reactions to former traumatic events had always been similar—freezing and emotional numbing, resulting in avoidance and a state of nonfeeling. On the other hand, reprocessing simply might not work for her, for any of a variety of other reasons.

Now the therapist said, with no hint of impatience and a friendly smile, "You *don't* need to focus on the beeps. Or the light. I want you to let them just be there, in the background. The only reason for their being there is to keep the bilateral stimulation going, and they will do that whether you listen to them, or watch the light, or you don't. What I want is for you to let go, so that your mind and body can make whatever associations they need to make, so they can find whatever route they need to take." She looked at Karen intently and said with a small shrug, "And who knows what path that might be—your brain and body will find the way they need to go."

Karen met her gaze but made no reply. "So we'll just keep trying," said the clinician, "and you can listen to the beeps, watch the lights, it doesn't matter." She switched on the light bar as she spoke. "So let's begin again with that image we started with, and once again, notice how it feels in your body."

"Okay," said Karen, and a long interlude of EMDR followed.

"What's going on now?" Patti asked when it had ended.

Karen shook her head, said that she still saw them all sitting in the car, and nothing felt very different. "But it's true, I don't feel quite as tense, and maybe I'm feeling slightly warmer . . . ? My hands felt cold when I came in." She sounded as if this puzzled her.

"Okay, go with that," said the therapist, "you're doing fine."

She switched the slowly alternating light into motion once again. But at the close of this pass, once again, Karen shook her head. "I was just sitting in the car. Not talking. I'm finding that I have this whole dialogue in my head—that I'm telling myself not to keep analyzing so much. Because I do that too much—analyze and pass judgments. And I'm conscious of making an effort *not* to do that, but . . ."

She shook her head again, as if to say that the effort to be nonjudgmental was proving unsuccessful. This particular approach wasn't working for her, and she was sounding as if she blamed herself. At this point I was feeling pretty blameworthy, too, for I had been the enthusiastic sponsor of what was turning out to be an obvious and decisive failure. But now Patti said to Karen, "Okay, go ahead with that. Try not to judge whatever happens." Then she turned on the light bar (and also, I assumed, the earphones) yet again.

This time Karen's report was different. "I was thinking"—she began laughing—"that this is sort of funny. I'm sitting in the car, and Laurie is going, 'Margo? Margo? Who's Margo?' And for some reason I'm thinking it's *funny*!" She stopped laughing and said seriously, "I don't know if I'm thinking it's funny because that situation was funny, or because I'm judging that I'm not doing so well with this? . . ." She looked at Patti questioningly, but her voice was trusting.

Instead of responding directly, the therapist instructed her to go back to the target memory—the scene that had unfolded on the way home from the airport—and describe what she noticed about it now. Karen paused, then said, "Well, we are driving in the car and I'm looking at that number on the cell phone, and I just think it's *funny* that Laurie's going, 'Margo? Margo? Who's Margo?'" I stared at her, astonished. Whatever did she mean by the word *funny*? I wondered. Funny as in "strange" or funny as in "ridiculous"?

Patti, looking pleased, said, "So on that scale of zero to ten, where ten is 'the most disturbing something can be' and zero is 'neutral or no disturbance,' how does it feel to you now?"

"It doesn't feel that disturbing." Karen sounded baffled. "I don't know if that's because . . . I just *don't know*. It just doesn't; it feels *funny*. Which is—" She stopped, shrugged as if to say that she wasn't sure exactly where this last remark had been heading. Then, after a brief pause, Patti asked once again if she could rate how she felt on that imaginary scale where zero was no disturbance and ten was the worst disturbance possible.

"I don't know, maybe a three or a four," Karen answered uncertainly.

"What do you think keeps it from going lower?" asked the therapist. "What's still disturbing about it that keeps it at a three or a four?"

"I think I'm telling myself it *should* be disturbing," Karen admitted with a smile.

Patti returned the smile, said, "Okay, go with that," and set the light bar back into motion. After a briefer period of reprocessing, she stopped it, waited while her client took a deep breath, then asked, "Where are you now?"

"Well, I once more have to say it's really not disturbing. I just think it *should* be!" Karen reiterated, sounded pleased, if somewhat taken aback. "But it seems like . . . it doesn't *feel* disturbing. It feels fine. That's how it feels." She turned and looked at me as if hoping I had the explanation of what had just happened. I just smiled and raised both hands outward in a gesture that said, "I don't have any idea."

Patti then asked her to bring up the original image and whatever was left of the memory, then follow the moving flashes of light one more time. "What are you getting?" she asked when this last pass had been completed.

Karen said, "Well, I still think the whole thing is funny." She laughed, and this time it was a lighthearted sound.

For my own part, I was having trouble making rational sense of what had just happened. What nodal moment had I missed seeing that might explain the sudden turnaround that had just occurred? But Patti didn't leave me much time for reflection.

"Now remember," she was saying to her client, "what you said you would *rather* believe when you think back to that memory, which was, 'I feel secure in myself.' Do those words still fit the situation? Is that what you would prefer to believe when you think back to what is left of that old memory? Or is there a better way to put it, perhaps some other words that would describe the way you would *rather* think about yourself?"

"I guess those words are about the right ones," said Karen, sounding much less strung out and more self-possessed. "Somehow, I just don't feel as threatened as I did."

Point A to Point B

If I myself felt nonplussed by this abrupt shift in the dynamics of the session, Patti Levin didn't appear fazed in the slightest. She tossed back the long strands of hair that had now fallen forward on both sides, typed a few notes into her laptop, then looked up at her client brightly. "So. On a scale of one to seven, where seven is 'completely true' and one is 'completely false,' how true do the words 'I feel secure in myself' feel when you bring up that old memory? How true do those words feel *in your gut?*"

Karen answered without hesitation, "I'd say I feel secure in myself as it relates to that old memory," then added that she would rate this feeling at about a five or a six on the scale.

Patti asked her, in a curious but friendly tone of voice, What stopped it from going higher? What prevented it from being completely true? Her patient thought about that for a moment, then said that it just seemed *too easy*. "Maybe it's my cynical self, but I just think, How easy can this be? That I'd just look at this light and picture the scene in the car and start thinking the whole situation is *funny!*" She smiled and said, "I guess I'm making judgments again." She was blushing.

Without responding to these remarks directly, Patti smiled and said softly, "What I want you to do now is bring up whatever is left of that old memory and your feelings about it. Hold it together with the words 'I feel secure in myself,' and just follow the light." A long interval of eye tracking followed, after which the therapist asked, "How true do those words feel?"

"Well, it's true, when I thought about it, I *do* feel secure in myself," said Karen, sounding pleased and even lighthearted, if perplexed. "It's just that I think I *should* still have some residual . . . I don't know . . ." It made no sense to her that this sense of foreboding and all of the suffering of the past few months should simply dissipate in this way. "It's just too easy. I mean, looking at these lights and then feeling like this whole thing is *funny!*"

"It took on a different meaning for you," Patti said.

"I guess so, because the only feeling I got was that it was funny. *Silly* funny!" She laughed.

The therapist smiled and said, "As opposed to serious, meaningful, tragic?" Then, after leading Karen through a last interim of reprocessing —this one a body scan, a surveillance of her internal world to check for any lingering areas of discomfort—the session seemed to be drawing to a close. "Do you have any questions?" she asked her patient.

"*Yes!* How does it work?" It was less a question than a bewildered demand.

Patti only shrugged and held her arms outward in a "Who knows?" kind of gesture. "Nobody's really explained it, though there's been a huge amount of research," she said. Nevertheless, she herself had the delighted but surprised look of a magician who's just pulled a rabbit out of a hat without any clear idea of how it got there. She turned to me and asked, "Anything you want to say here, Maggie?"

I simply held up a hand, signaling her to wait a moment, for the reversal that had just taken place was so startling that I was having trouble absorbing and comprehending it. Then I said, in a low voice, that because I knew what Karen had been through, the sudden denouement of this session had left me feeling ready to cry.

"Using that metaphor of leaving the train journey, I never *did* experience the train as leaving the station," I told her, then turned to Karen directly. "At each standstill I kept thinking, It's not happening, so I believed it wasn't going to work for you. I thought it was a shame. I thought, I guess there are some people it doesn't work for. . . . And suddenly there you were, you'd arrived! It was as if you'd taken the express train from point A to point B with no station breaks in between!" I laughed, feeling elated, turned back to Patti. "The way it happened was a big shock for me," I admitted. "But I found it very moving, and I'm so *glad* it worked for her."

"Me *too*," piped up Karen, exhaling deeply and sounding profoundly relieved, as if a malevolent spirit were leaving her body.

Chapter Eighteen

THE AFFAIR AS
GUERRILLA WARFARE:
JOANNA GRAVES

*D*URING THIS SAME PERIOD I WAS ALSO TALKING WITH A number of women who were, or had been recently, involved in extramarital affairs—no surprise, given that any series of interviews on the subject of secrets, betrayals, and their often traumatic aftereffects is sure to touch frequently upon the subject of infidelity. I soon noticed that a particular motif seemed to pop up time and again in the course of these conversations. This motif or theme had to do with the *justification* for the affair, which the person often portrayed as having to do with her survival—as one participant put it, "the survival of my self as a valid human being."

Confirmation of One's Worth and Dignity

There are, of course, countless motivations and rationales that an individual will cite for having gotten into an extramarital involvement, ranging from plain and simple sexual curiosity to a need for affirmation of one's physical attractiveness to being swept away by a sudden, overwhelming passion. But what I seemed to hear with surprising frequency were accounts in which the underlying but decisive reasons for the affair had to do with someone's desperate search for confirmation of her worth and dignity as a person. Many of the women I talked with were people who'd been dominated and bullied over time—made to feel inadequate, unbecoming, dim-witted, clumsy, or basically *all wrong* by their contemptuous, critical partners.

This kind of situation was typified by the plight of thirty-nine-year-old Joanna Graves, who at the time of our series of interviews was mourning the breakup of a passionate, yearlong affair. When she spoke with me about her lover (who I thought sounded like a bit of a scoundrel), Joanna's face came alive. She described this man as warm, affectionate, deeply interested in her as a person, and truly caring about everything happening in her life. He could enjoy a joke, and he was *fun* to be around.

Admittedly, the affair had had its destructive side, for she'd begun drinking heavily while it was in progress. In defense of her ex-lover, however, Joanna acknowledged that she'd never expected the involvement to be a lasting one. He had been honest with her from the outset, told her that his executive career involved extensive travel, and warned her straight out that he was "something of a philanderer." But at the same time he'd been so attentive, understanding, and *there for her* that any thoughts of "endings" had seemed remote and been banished from her mind.

Joanna's husband, Roger, whom she described as withdrawn and over-controlling, was now fully aware of that yearlong relationship. In fact, it was Roger who, when he'd learned of it, had confronted the lover and threatened to cause serious damage in both the man's own marriage and his professional life. This male-to-male encounter had brought the affair to its precipitous close, and in its stormy aftermath, the couple had ultimately reconciled. Roger had graciously "forgiven" his wife. But life within Joanna's marriage, and life within her family, too, was "bleak" these days, for she'd returned to a situation that felt as empty and unrewarding as it had been when she'd first made her attempted escape.

She explained that her husband, a person who hadn't ever liked to touch or be touched in the best of times, had been sexually passionate for a short period of time after the affair ("He was marking his territory," she said wryly) but had then become angry and withdrawn. Moreover, a cloud of family blame had descended upon her, so that whatever school or behavior problems arose in regard to any of their three children were always ascribed to "*bad*, no-good Joanna's behavior"—her period of drinking and going AWOL emotionally.

"I do accept the guilt and the blame for that," she told me, her expression taut, "but I can see that Roger's never going to let go, never put it down." There was never a question of getting him to look at the difficulties within the marriage that had led to her going outside it. As her husband saw it, the glaring defects in her own sorry character were all the explanation needed. This marriage, as had already become clear in the course of the interviews, was one of those top dog/bottom dog pairings in which the wife had been the thoroughly subjugated partner almost from the outset.

Historically speaking, so had Joanna's own mother, and Roger's mother, too. This was the fundamental system for being in a male-female relationship that both members of the couple had witnessed in their own families of origin. Thus, both had come by their internal model for how a man and a woman will predictably interact in the most clear-cut manner possible— by growing up in an emotional world in which no other option or way of being had ever been presented to them.

The truth, however, is that *no one* is ever really victorious in the marriage of the tyrannizing partner and the disadvantaged spouse. For the intractable problem in these kinds of oppressive relationships is that while maintaining dominion and control over someone else's thoughts, feelings, wishes, and behavior may appear to be effective in the short run, it is always doomed in the longer one. As I have written elsewhere (see *Intimate Worlds: Life Inside the Family*), ". . . like murder, human complexity will out—and inevitably, as in other totalitarian systems, a rebellious fifth column develops." And for obvious reasons, in this era of enhanced sexual possibilities and relaxed social mores, this rebellion often takes the form of an affair.

In Joanna's case, the extramarital love affair had been brought to a precipitous ending; but the couple's sex life was now distant and perfunctory, almost nonexistent. When she told me this, Joanna hastened to add that it wasn't just *sex* that was missing from her marriage, "though I think I would like to have sex," she said, sounding doubtful. "No, it's really more that— oh, I would just like to hold hands, or have Roger put his arm around me sometime. . . . But if I bring it up, he'll say it's just that he's tired, or feeling a cold coming on, or things are so stressful at the office."

She shrugged, gave me a long, assessing look, then said forthrightly that she was "coming to the realization that at least she'd had something *good*" with her lover. "Something *very* good," she underscored, a defiant note sounding in her voice. True, she was currently in despair over the loss of that relationship, but she would never, ever regret it. "It taught me that I could laugh and enjoy myself, that I could be spontaneous . . . that I was intelligent and worth listening to . . . I could be sensual and give affection and receive it, too." She sighed deeply, then said she'd learned a lot about who she really was as a person.

"And if, for example, you take your husband's hand or put your arm around *him*, what happens then?" I asked, meeting her gaze directly.

Joanna shrugged and said dryly, "Roger was going away on a business trip this very morning, and he came down the stairs first, and I *did* put my arms around him. But he backed off and he said, 'No, no, no.' Then he wrote out a list of things I was supposed to do that day—he's great on lists, there's always a list of things for me to do! I didn't raise any objections, but he said, 'Well, walk out to the car with me.'

"I did walk out, and he sort of apologized, said he was sorry, but he had to make the list. And I said he could have made the list another time." She shrugged hopelessly, like a prisoner who's been thrown back into a small dark cell after the briefest taste of joy, light, and freedom. I felt sorry for her, in terms not only of her present pain, but of her past experiences and the future that loomed ahead. She murmured something about Roger needing her as a "presence," not a person—someone in the background of his life who was a helpmate and a mom but not a real woman with whom he could ever become close and intimate.

I already knew, from earlier interviews with Joanna, that there had been a lot of barely suppressed rage in her family of origin. One of the constant refrains of her childhood had been her distant, easily irritated dad telling her more outgoing, high-spirited mother to "hush *up*, Priscilla, for heaven's sake!" As a young girl, Joanna had also witnessed intermittent physical violence visited against an adopted younger brother by her dogmatic, short-tempered father (in this regard, her early history was reminiscent of that of Claudia Martinelli).

Joanna's mother had died when Joanna herself was in her late teens, "just as I was getting to really know her," she'd told me wistfully. Now she seemed stuck in a time warp, one in which a tense, oppressive early history had reemerged in her tense and troubled present-day life. I knew that traditional therapy, which she'd tried, hadn't changed the situation; and that

Roger wouldn't go for joint counseling. So on a compassionate impulse, I suggested throwing a wild card into this seemingly unresolvable marital stalemate—a few sessions of EMDR with Patti Levin or some other reprocessing facilitator.

One of Life's Small Miracles

Once under way, Joanna Graves's course of EMDR proceeded at a surprising pace. I'd been invited to sit in while she targeted certain memories for neutralizing and detoxifying and had placed myself off to one side while she faced Patti Levin directly. The subject of the first and most dramatic of these reprocessing sessions involved a memory she hadn't really given much thought to in a long, long time: witnessing her dad's savage beatings of her kid brother.

Subsequently, over the course of some five or six therapeutic meetings —alternating sessions of EMDR and straight talk therapy—the treatment began to have a clear-cut, in fact transforming, effect upon Joanna's sense of herself as a valid human being. For the first time in her married life, she was finding herself able to marshal the inner resources to confront her husband's abusive put-downs, disapproval, and blaming and to do so from a position of dignity and self-respect.

Moreover, when she held her ground in this way, calmly yet firmly, there were many instances in which she could get him to back off—often in ways that surprised her. She had never thought this to be possible before. And certainly I, in my role as participant-observer, felt that I was watching one of life's small miracles occurring.

Part Four

DEIRDRE

THE POWER THERAPIES,

CREATING "NEW" MEMORIES

Chapter Nineteen

POWER THERAPIES:
ACCESSING WHAT
THE BODY KNOWS

REPROCESSING IS BUT ONE AMONG A SMALL GROUP OF what are called "power therapies," so named because they often prove effective with astonishing rapidity—especially when compared to the far slower-paced, traditional "talking" methods of treatment. These comparatively new techniques and procedures rely heavily upon what the body knows, or "somatic memory." Other than the meticulously researched EMDR, the most well known power therapies are thought field therapy and Hakomi.

These body-centered approaches vary widely and can *look* very different. Still, they do have a crucial feature in common: All are focused upon retrieving and integrating scattered bits of data stored within the patient's *physical* as well as mental being. All of them seek to promote a state of heightened bodily awareness by *actively summoning up a person's feelings, emotions, and sensations*—for instance, what was felt, seen, touched, smelled, and heard during certain critical events or time periods of the individual's life.

The body's "memory" is thus put into play as a way of gaining access to regions deep within the "old," emotional brain where hugely oversensitized networks of reacting have been established.

The Psychomotor Approach

According to trauma expert Bessel van der Kolk, one of the less widely known but remarkably compelling of the alternative therapies is Pesso Boyden System Psychomotor. This innovative form of treatment (often referred to as "psychomotor" or by the acronym PBSP) unites a conventional "talking therapy" approach with a variety of bodily experiences—touching, holding, and the like. Psychomotor techniques have a special way of gently coaxing extremely accessible and vulnerable feeling-states into being. These feeling-states, in turn, become the impressionable medium in which freshly manufactured "memories" can be created. These new "memories" are, basically, imaginary scenes that are dramatized and enacted. The ultimate goal is to introduce into the patient's internal being *a taste of what it would be like* to have had a different, more benign past and thus to engender more hope-filled expectations about the future—expectations that are rooted in the body and yet not grounded in the negativity and pain of the past.

Frozen Emotions

PBSP's originators, Al Pesso and Diane Boyden-Pesso, entered the world of therapy by an improbable route. When they first met, these long-married partners were highly trained creative dancers; later on, when they were no longer primarily performers, they opened a studio in the Boston area and became teachers of dance.

It was in their role as teachers that the Pessos became increasingly aware that certain technically experienced students could at times become virtually immobilized when it came to performing particular movements. It was as though some wordless but profoundly felt emotion had frozen a certain body part in place; and the couple soon recognized that such happenings were often deeply connected to the dancers' earlier life experiences.

Intrigued, the Pessos began to develop a series of exercises and procedures designed to foster exploration of the relationship among inner mental states and the ways in which inner states became manifest in outward, bodily expressions. It was in the course of this process that the couple began to realize that their "emotional movement" sessions were actually bringing about enduring changes in their students' personal lives.

Soon the couple began focusing less upon the teaching of dance *per se* and more upon physical expression as an alternative route into the world of the unconscious.

It was indeed from this curious, almost accidental beginning that the Pesso/Boyden system began its slow development into the highly elaborated method of treatment that exists today. What had started out as a series of therapeutic body movement exercises (and, along the way, become well recognized for its effectiveness by an ever growing number of colleagues) had kept on broadening and taken on a pronounced psychodynamic flavor.

Currently, the psychomotor movement claims groups of adherents in a loose connection of cities throughout the nation. Bands of followers have also sprung up all over the globe; there are Pesso/Boyden outposts in Belgium, Holland, Denmark, Switzerland, Germany, and Brazil. However, the central hub of the worldwide association is a sprawling establishment in northern New England. The place is called Strolling Woods and is located on Webster Lake, near the small town of Franklin, New Hampshire.

At Strolling Woods, the Pessos preside over a spread of some 215 acres, which encompasses hills, densely wooded areas, a large main house, and various outbuildings. Owing to a fire that swept through the property several years after I attended a first, weeklong training workshop there, some of the original structures have been rebuilt. But at the time of that initial visit, which was in the late 1990s, a charmingly rickety white Victorian-style farmhouse stood atop a high promontory, and we participants in the workshop bunked in this rambling central building. For our working sessions, however, we gathered in a smaller place called "the shed," which was at the base of a long, grassy slope and had once served as a guesthouse.

Structures

We met for three sessions daily: morning, afternoon, and evening. Our agenda consisted of 1) lectures on psychomotor theory; 2) demonstrations of the emotional information embedded in various bodily postures and movements; and 3) participation in the intense fifty-minute therapy sessions called "structures."

A structure is best characterized as a carefully constructed mini–theatrical event, presided over by a therapist who functions as a kind of "coach" or stage manager. That is, the therapist guides the choice of certain of the speaking parts, props, and placements-in-space of the various participants in the story, while overseeing the unfolding *and revision* of critical elements of the principal actor's life drama.

These "healing" dramatizations were all presided over by Al Pesso, and I soon noticed their tendency to take on a certain recognizable pattern or rhythm. The therapeutic structure would begin slowly, haltingly, as full of conversational stops and starts as a jet plane inching slowly toward its designated runway before accelerating its engines for takeoff. Then, often with a suddenness that could be breathtaking, the session would lift off and zoom upward into heights of emotionality, sometimes so intense that they teetered on the edge of the unbearable.

At first I found this disorienting, even frightening; but soon I realized that as each individual's structure began drawing to a close, so too would the tension level begin its descent. And eventually, the "protagonist" of the drama would gently bump down to earth once again—having come to rest in a drastically different place than she or he had been in at the session's beginning.

Antidotes

Before describing a prototypical PBSP structure, let me say a bit about the psychomotor method in more general terms. A basic tenet of this theory is that internalized, often very early memories of experiences that *felt* catastrophic foster ways of looking at the world that are filled with negative expectations. Rather than active maltreatment, such memories may involve woeful parental neglect.

In any case, such deeply pessimistic belief systems—often buttressed by feelings of profound hopelessness—may be grounded in the individual's long-ago history, but they bias his or her ways of seeing and comprehending the ongoing events of everyday life in the present. Like chaotic, scrambled bits of raw data that haven't ever been processed and organized into a meaningful whole, these scattered images and memories—of feeling alone, unprotected, overwhelmed in an uncaring universe—create an underlying but all-pervasive outlook on life. It is with the goal of creating alternative, symbolic experiences that can act as mental "antidotes" to this negative worldview that the Pessos' therapy has been created.

But can there be antidotes in the present for injuries that occurred long ago? Common sense would suggest that what once happened *did* happen and that the past cannot be altered retrospectively. For instance, if someone has grown up as the daughter in an alcoholic, occasionally violent household, there is no way to alter her recall of the awful events to which she has been the involuntary, frightened witness. Given that certain menacing, disturbing events *did* take place, they've inevitably become part of the developing person's inner reality, then part of the basic structure of her later, adult existence.

Here, it's important to emphasize that the psychomotor clinician's efforts are *not* directed at making bad memories disappear. Rather than trying to erase the recollection of parental indifference or emotionally or physically abusive events that *did* occur, this therapy is geared toward creating "symbolic, supplemental" memories—an internalization of the simulated experience of growing up in a loving, caring environment where such wounding things could never have happened. Creating a structure, in the psychomotor sense of that word, involves developing a completely novel option for being in the world—one that's hitherto been beyond the individual's imagining, given the psychologically injurious experiences that the client actually did suffer.

Basically, a therapeutic structure involves the creation of an alternative or countermemory, a memory replete with "virtual" images of basic human needs that *were* met and profound hopes that *were* satisfied—*at the right time* (early in life, when the developing person's map of the world was slowly forming) and *by the right people* (the beloved parental caretakers). This "synthetic, supplemental memory" comes into being slowly, and with surprising naturalness, in the course of an intensely moving dramatization. In what follows, I shall try to explain how this comes about and is made to feel surprisingly believable and authentic during the slow construction and acting out of a therapeutic scenario.

Finding a Place

On the first day of the workshop, each member of the group seemed to gravitate toward a preferred place to sit, and most of us returned to that place throughout the course of the weeklong conference. It was a kind of territoriality that I didn't take much note of until one afternoon when I found someone else sitting in my designated spot on one of the couches.

That incident rattled me, partly because the passionate self-reflection generated by the workshop had created an all-around heightened level of intensity. More to the point, however, Al Pesso had been lecturing about the metaphoric aspects of "place"—in this instance, meaning "place in the world." The questions we were being prompted to ponder had to do with the very beginnings of our lives: Had we been born into an environment where a "nest" had already been prepared for us in our parents' dreams, fantasies, hearts, and thoughts? Had we been welcomed joyously into the family's preexisting world, so that we'd felt protected and nurtured—or, alternatively, had we experienced ourselves as unbidden, accidental visitors whose presence had strained our caretakers' thinly stretched emotional, financial, or other resources?

This discourse on "place" had in fact triggered a disturbing recollection, one having to do with a Thanksgiving visit from my oldest sister. On that occasion, my young family and I had just returned to the East Coast after a long sojourn in California. That holiday was the first time in a long time that we adult siblings had been able to bring our growing families together, and naturally, reminiscences were in order. After a big turkey dinner, when we were all sitting in the living room having coffee, my sister said that she recalled very vividly my arrival from the hospital as a newborn.

She herself had been close to six years old at the time, she said. But then she added, with a surprising bite in her voice, that my entrance into the family had created a certain space problem in the household. It had in fact caused my father to tell his grown daughter by a former marriage—her name was Mary, and she was the child of his deceased third wife—that she would have to move out and find a place of her own. This piece of in-

formation shocked me. I stared at my older sister, for I hadn't heard anything about this until that very moment.

In truth, there had been so much family silence about the very existence of these half-siblings that I couldn't recall ever having heard the
name "Mary" before. Nevertheless, elaborating upon this event, my sister
told the gathering at large how close she herself had felt to this kind, moth-
ering older girl and how upsetting it had been to see her tossed out of the
household. The message wasn't hard to miss: My coming into the world
had been the cause of this deprivation. In any case, my sister concluded
this story by saying dryly with a short bark of a laugh, "As far as *I* was concerned, it was a bad bargain."

Could she possibly have thought this to be a lighthearted tale about
the good old days when we were children? I've no idea, but given the circumstances of that moment, I chose not to respond. What I remember
most about what followed is that one of my little daughters slid down
along the sofa, flung an arm around my neck, and nestled her head
sweetly against my shoulder.

Speed-Dialing to the Unconscious

The obvious link between discussions of "place," that recollection, and
the discovery that my usual place on the couch had been usurped wasn't
particularly obscure; what surprised me was the robustness of the memory
of that incident, once that network of associations had been set off. It was
such a vivid illustration of the ways in which we view the small events of
our present-day lives—such as hearing a lecture and finding your usual
seat occupied—through the lens of everything that happened earlier and
how those experiences were interpreted at that time.

Generally speaking, we workshop participants sat in rows on one side
or the other of the two long, wide sofas that lined both sides of the rectangular room. These sofas were strewn with an exorbitant number of throw
pillows of differing sizes and colors; there was also a lavish assortment of
floor cushions scattered throughout the room. This abundance of pillows
and cushions was not, as I soon came to realize, merely decorative in nature. For as soon as the intense work on structures got under way, these ob-

jects began being pressed into service as props. For example, a large green pillow could serve to symbolize aspects of a certain figure—say, the remembered good side of a bullying older brother. A well-worn coral cushion might stand in for a certain locale or setting—perhaps the neighbor's house, where you felt safer and more welcome than in your own home.

More important, we members of the group were expected to role-play important figures in one another's lives, and we did so on a regular basis. On one occasion, you might be enrolled as someone's angry mother; on another, a rejecting father or the ideal parent that the enactor of the structure had longed for but never had. The request to play such a role always came from the client, who chose someone in the group who seemed to fit the part well enough. If the person asked to role-play felt uncomfortable about enacting a certain figure, he or she had the right to refuse—and on rare occasions, someone did.

Al Pesso, in his dual role as lecturer and supervising coach of the therapeutic structures, always sat in his own particular spot. It was a low, cushion-covered bench that stood just to the right of the large fieldstone fireplace that occupied most of the wall at the far end of the conference room. At the opposite end, close to the narrow entry door, was an eclectic assortment of freestanding chairs. These were always occupied by those members of the group who preferred to sit at some distance from Pesso and closer to the exit.

As for the attendees, there were some sixteen of us, and we were as polyglot a gathering as could be imagined. Some of those present were psychotherapists who'd come either for basic grounding in psychomotor techniques or for further technical know-how in terms of creating therapeutic structures. Then there was a small European contingent, all executives with a state-owned Belgian utility. These were people who'd attended psychomotor meetings abroad and had flown in expressly to attend this weeklong workshop.

There was also a woman who was working on her Ph.D. at Harvard and a young, haunted-looking housewife with long, shiny dark hair who was a trauma patient of Bessel van der Kolk's. She had come here at Dr. van der Kolk's suggestion. Other people at the conference were therapy clients, too—people who had heard of Pesso's work through the grapevine, had seen him at one of his frequent lectures or symposia, or were among a group of longtime devotees. One of the latter was a tall, mild-mannered pastor of a church in the Greater Hartford area.

Another was a slim, elegant, fiftyish Chilean-born lawyer. This man told me that he'd suffered from an ongoing, debilitating asthma condition before getting into psychomotor treatment. He said that as long as he could remember, he'd been dogged by nameless anxieties and feelings of imminent danger—an irrational, ever-present sense of threat that had no basis in his real-life circumstances. These symptoms had dissipated slowly in the course of a series of psychomotor therapeutic structures.

Still another frequent returnee, a middle-aged manager in an international banking concern, told me that he appreciated this form of therapy because it had "a focused way of getting to the heart of the matter, and doing so rapidly." Clearly, this was a person who placed a high value on his time. He told me that in his opinion, the Pesso/Boyden approach was "less burdened with abstractions and closer to reality" than other forms of therapy he'd tried, including a long Freudian psychoanalysis that he'd undergone in his early thirties. He said he didn't know whether Al Pesso was an unusually gifted therapist, or some kind of magician, or whether he'd developed a method of speed-dialing to the unconscious.

A Witness for Deirdre

It was Wednesday in a week of training that had begun the previous Sunday afternoon, and the weather was brutally hot. The psychomotor workshop was taking place during that most unusual of northern New England happenings, a heat wave during the first days of July. The conference room in which we were meeting, which was lined with wooden paneling, would have been comfortable and cool in more typical New Hampshire weather. But in these searing temperatures we were roasting, despite the best efforts of an old standing fan and a rumbling, cranky air conditioner.

It was early evening, and the first person scheduled to do a structure was Deirdre Carmody, a woman in her early thirties who was a doctoral candidate in the School of Public Health at Harvard. At the moment Deirdre sat stone-faced and silent, cross-legged on the floor in the center of the room, her gaze fixed upon Al Pesso.

A few members of the group were still chatting with one another quietly, and their low voices were punctuated by the drone of the air conditioner and the labored turning of the fan in the background. The blinds had been pulled down over every single window, but the pitiless rays of a slowly setting sun were poking through the bamboo slats.

I knew very little about Deirdre Carmody, who was one of the more diffident members of the group. She was an attractive person, with hazel eyes, dark wavy hair, and a slim, softly rounded figure; but when she spoke it was in a muted voice, almost a whisper, as if the conversation were taking place in a library. Given her air of extreme reserve, I thought that Deirdre's structure would get off to a very slow start, if it ever got moving at all.

Al Pesso, sitting on his customary bench, was looking from person to person as if waiting for the group to grow still. Pesso is a short, stocky man who exudes an air of zest and high energy, as well as a fund of benevolence and respect. He has strong features and a bald crown, rimmed with a halo of curly gray hair. During the development of a structure, when every word that's spoken *matters*, he always dons a set of earphones to enhance his partially compromised hearing. This gives him the air of an exuberant aviator, about to take the protagonist aloft on the trip of a lifetime.

Slowly, the room was becoming silent. Pesso fixed his gaze upon Deirdre and lifted his shaggy eyebrows as if to say "The next move is yours to make." It was up to her to raise a personal issue, a concern that was troubling her, to talk about anything that came into her mind at that moment. But she said nothing, and my thought was that it must be hard for someone like Deirdre to find herself at the center of so much focused attention. She did look dumbstruck, as if she were sorting desperately through her mental files for some topic, any topic, that she felt able to talk about in so public a setting as this one.

I wasn't optimistic about her finding anything and so almost jumped in my seat when she blurted out in a loud, hoarse voice, "My emotions are running really *high* this evening! I think it's because I've been watching people changing here—taking risks—" She stopped as if unable to continue speaking, as if she'd choked up on her words. Looking around, I could see that I wasn't alone in my surprise. Deirdre's structure seemed to be taking on altitude without even pausing at the runway.

Pesso nodded at her, then observed kindly, "*Moved* by that."

She nodded back, assenting. "Yes, very. But maybe I'm being emotional about something that isn't actually the thing I'm struggling to get to. Because I'm only halfway there, if you know what I mean?" She paused and looked at Pesso, whose expression was puzzled. He shook his head as if to say he didn't understand.

"Well, there's something that's been blocking me for about two years now," she said. "It happens when I start writing—not just the routine stuff that I turn out for my part-time job—but when it's for *me*. When it's *my own stuff*, work on my papers or my thesis, that's when I get into the problem." She paused, as if she were having trouble continuing. "I just feel . . ." She was choking up again, and her eyes were glistening. "I feel this kind of . . . echoing loneliness," she said, then wiped her eyes on her sleeve.

Al Pesso met her gaze fully, his large brown eyes full of compassion. He said nothing for a few moments, then gestured upward toward the ceiling. "Let's put a witness figure in the air. A witness would see how devastated you feel when you think of that echoing loneliness. Is that right?"

"Yes!" She sounded relieved. Pesso had begun the process of "microtracking"—that is, carefully noting each momentary expression of emotion as it appeared on Deirdre's features, then stating aloud what he was seeing. "Devastated and frightened," continued the therapist.

Deirdre, with an eager nod, assented. "And I'm *not* one of those people who always has to be with somebody to feel complete! I mean, I mostly do enjoy my own company. But when I'm working on my own project, something that I need to do for school—" She halted, fighting back tears again. Emile, a member of the Belgian contingent, got up and brought her a box of tissues. Deirdre wiped her eyes and said, "It just feels like . . . like there aren't enough people around."

"Saddened and full of grief that there aren't enough people around," Pesso said softly. He himself was taking on the role of the "witness," a role that on many occasions he would assign to someone else in the group. The "witness figure" makes an appearance very early in the development of a therapeutic structure and serves as an accepting, tolerant observer of the states of feeling that the client's facial expressions are communicating.

The witness not only *names* the protagonist's visible emotion (thereby validating its existence and reality), but *locates* it in the context in which it arose. Here, repeating Deirdre's own spoken words, Pesso had said that "there weren't enough people around" when she tried to work on her own projects. Clearly, this lack of people around her was having a devastating impact upon her ability to function and produce, for she nodded, looking stunned by grief. "Yes, it's like there's someone missing . . . ," she whispered, then began sobbing with abandonment as she pulled a fresh tissue from the box. She patted her eyes, blew her nose, then looked up at Pesso again.

"*Longing* for someone." His voice was gentle, probing.

Deirdre nodded and said almost inaudibly, "Yes."

"Who is it that you'd long for at those moments?" asked the therapist; and for some reason, Deirdre's expression brightened.

"When I was growing up, I did all my studying and writing right in the middle of the house," she said. The memory seemed to cheer her; it even brought a hint of gaiety in her voice. "I'd sit on the sofa and do my work, and there'd be all this *life* going on around me!" She threw her arms wide in a gesture meant to imply the buzz of family activity with which she'd been surrounded. A moment later, though, she grew teary again and used her fingers to wipe below her eyes as if she thought that some eye makeup might be dripping down. Then, surprisingly, she giggled.

Pesso tilted his head to one side, looked interested. "You laugh at that. Why?" he asked.

Deirdre said that most people would have found it impossible to concentrate under such circumstances, but for her it had felt exactly right.

"So that was a lovely remembrance?" Pesso asked, and when she nodded, he said, "A witness would see how *fond* you feel when you remember all that life around you in the house."

"Yes," Deirdre breathed, fresh tears springing to her eyes. "I'm just— missing them. . . . And part of it is that . . . my mother being dead . . . that piece of my life will never come back."

Pesso met her gaze, said quietly, "A witness would say, 'I see how much grief you feel that that piece of your life, when your mother was alive, will never come back.' So your mother is in your mind now?"

Deirdre, weeping, nodded. But then she said that this was part, but by no means *all*, of what weighed on her mind at this moment. Another piece had to do with her father and the fact that his professional life—he'd been a water resource specialist—had always involved frequent travel to developing countries everywhere across the globe. During those periods when her dad had been at home, the climate of the family had become thick with tension, fear, and pressure.

"So now, thinking about your father, you *feel* that anger and that stress coming from him?" inquired Pesso.

A frightened look crossed Deirdre's features, and she nodded; but then she added quickly that there had been long periods of time when he'd been away from home on his trips. "I guess it's good times like that I'm remembering, really. When he was gone, the household was . . . well, it was *happy*." The rough sketch of a scenario, the domestic tableau in Deirdre's mind, was slowly emerging.

This basic tableau involved a lively, friendly family atmosphere that had encompassed and supported her in her strivings and had felt joyful during her father's frequent absences. Deirdre Carmody seemed to be not only mourning the passage of an era when her mother was alive and her siblings had surrounded her, but also grieving about the angry, disgruntled parent who'd never been a caring, loving presence in the first place.

A Voice of Warning

For reasons that she'd never really understood, Deirdre's father had responded to her with less rage and irritability than he had to her four siblings. "I remember him hitting me just once—maybe it happened more times, but I can only remember that once—but I have vivid memories of the many, many times he hit the others. Watching that was very painful."

"You remember how painful it was to watch him hitting the others." Pesso was, once again, adhering closely to her own language as he confirmed and validated Deirdre's experience.

She nodded, her gaze fixed upon his. Then she said that in a way it had been like a wartime setting, one in which the victors make an example of some of the villagers. "You know, they pick some out and shoot them just to let the others know they'd better behave."

"So, he was like a tyrant or a Nazi," said Pesso.

"*Yes!*" The word seemed to burst out of her, as if she were excited by hearing that ugly truth said aloud. Yet at the same time she was clearly taken aback by hearing it stated in such stark, unvarnished terms, for she quickly backtracked and leapt to her father's defense. "He didn't *mean* to be, but that's the way it happened," she countered.

"A witness would see how protective you feel toward him. Because you said, 'He didn't mean to be,'" the therapist clarified her statement sympathetically.

She nodded. "I see now that my father got thrown into parenting and family life when he was way too young a man." She shrugged. "Still, I was left with the memories. . . . And now that I'm married myself, I thought it would be a different kind of life. But in many ways, it isn't. Because I've come to realize that even though my father didn't actively go *after* me as much, there was an awful lot of neglect!" Her expression was stricken.

"*Struck* by how much neglect there was," Pesso, in his role as witness, responded.

Deirdre nodded. "And at the same time, having to pretend that everything is fine!"

"That's a voice," said Pesso, raising his arm, the palm of his hand flattened upward, toward a different area of the ceiling. "And the voice is saying, '*Pretend that everything is fine!*'" He was placing that disembodied voice in the air, as he'd placed the witnessing figure earlier in the sequence.

"Yes, because if I didn't pretend that everything was fine, then *I* would get hurt, too," Deirdre elaborated.

Pesso gestured upward toward the ceiling once again, saying, "So, that's another voice—a voice of warning." Then he said, in a low, foreboding tone, "*If you don't pretend that everything is fine, you'll get hurt, too!*'" Deirdre stared at him, seeming almost mesmerized by what he'd said. Then she blushed deeply and nodded, as if to say she fully accepted the validity of that statement.

Fragment Figures

In psychomotor theory, the witness figure and the various voices (of which there are many, including the voice of truth, the voice of warning, the voice of caution, the voice of doom, and the voice of negative prediction) are known as "fragment figures." That is to say, they are not full role players in the dramatic scenario that slowly emerges as the therapeutic structure develops.

The function of the witnessing figure is simply that of *seeing and naming* ongoing states of feeling, as expressed in micromovements of the facial muscles of the protagonist. This provides constant feedback about whatever emotion the person appears to be experiencing in the here and now of the current moment. (Let me interject here that when I myself did a structure, I found that this steady feedback process made me feel ever safer, more clearly heard and understood.)

The work of the voices is to state openly the thoughts that gave rise to whatever emotion is being observed. In other words, the voices serve as explicit, outward expressions of internalized beliefs, values, and rules for living that have been established early on and considered to be beyond question. In Deirdre Carmody's case, the directive "Pretend everything is fine!" was a clear example of a voice of caution or a voice of warning. In that instance, it was even more—a rule of behavior, a belief, and a pattern of being all rolled up in one internalized injunction.

I should add that there are many instances in which an enactor's statement calls forth *both* a witnessing figure and a voice. For example, in one of the structures that took place during the workshop, the pastor had said in a forgiving tone of voice, "I can't blame my father for being unable to protect me from my mother's crazy rages." At the same time, the expression on his features was one of stark fear. Immediately Pesso had gestured upward, placing a voice of caution in the air: "*Don't blame your father for being unable to protect you from your mother's crazy rages!*" But this was followed by a soft word from the witnessing figure, who'd said empathically, "I see how *terrified* you feel as you remember that situation."

Dependably, as a therapeutic structure develops and is elaborated upon, the enactor's internal map, or "blueprint for being," becomes externalized, visible, and surprisingly tangible. This blueprint consists of a relatively coherent set of perceptions, thoughts, and feelings, patterns of behaving, and ways of looking at the world. It can be thought of as the precipitate of an individual's accumulated experiences of living in his or her body and interacting with the human environment by which he or she has been surrounded.

Deirdre Carmody had commenced her structure by talking about a here-and-now concern: She was finding herself paralyzed by a sense of desolation and echoing loneliness whenever she tried to move forward on her own personal work—primarily, work on a research paper or on her doctoral thesis.

But this manifestly current-day issue, cruelly self-punitive in its effects, was obviously connected to memories that went far back into her personal history. For one thing, she was clearly in a state of desperate mourning for the loss of the family camaraderie that had existed when her mother was alive and her father was away on one of his journeys. For another, she was preoccupied by ambivalent feelings about a household tyrant who'd behaved abusively and uncaringly toward the family and had ignored and neglected her in ways she was just beginning to recognize. Her father had made her feel that "pretending that everything was fine" was a condition of her psychological survival. Moreover, at the present time—so Deirdre had hinted—this rejecting male figure from her past had reemerged in the present, in the figure of a neglectful, invalidating spouse.

A Theater of the Imagination: Role-Playing Figures from the Past

Slowly a symbolic arena was coming into existence—an imaginary theater stage upon which we fellow members of the group would enact the major figures of Deirdre's past and present life in a dramatic presentation fashioned and produced (under Pesso's supervision) by the protagonist herself. In the course of this work, we would be following Deirdre's cues and suggestions meticulously, as we role-played figures and scenes from her remembrances of the world-that-was. Then, importantly, we would begin to enact hypothetical figures in a far more affirmative kind of family world and create a "virtual reality"—one that placed her securely in the world-that-could-have-been, a world that was completely different from the one remembered with such pain.

Chapter Twenty

—

CHOREOGRAPHING
THE SCENE

*P*RETEND EVERYTHING IS FINE!" THIS WAS THE INNER DI-
rective to which Deirdre Carmody had always conformed, as if fending off
some nameless but formidable danger. Now, however, hearing this internalized decree stated explicitly and in the form of a command—a voice of
warning—she'd hesitated, her forehead narrowed in a thoughtful frown.

This particular internal rule, never before questioned, had guided
Deirdre in steering her way through life, and it had governed many of her
patterns of relating. But as she sat there, staring straight ahead, she looked
disconcerted and—was I mistaken?—somewhat defiant.

This kind of reaction to the statement of a "voice" isn't unusual. The
paradoxical effect of hearing an inner rule stated aloud—sounding as if it
emanates from a control center outside the self—is that there's an automatic tendency to muster some resistance to it. Simply hearing the order
"Pretend everything is fine!" has a way of making a person stop and say to
him- or herself, "Wait a minute, everything is *not* fine. Why should I act as
if it is?"

Thus, it wasn't surprising that the link between the voice's injunction
—"Pretend everything is fine!"—and things that were happening in
Deirdre's marriage sprang to the front and center of her thoughts. She and
her husband were about to celebrate their third anniversary, she said, adding that she had waited a long time before marrying because she wanted to

choose very carefully. "Also, I wanted to have a strong enough core so I wouldn't get—you know, *lost*."

"A witness would see how *resolved*, how resolute, you feel when you remember that you waited, and you wanted to have a strong enough core," Pesso said.

She sat up straighter, then nodded. (This confirming nod is a response that the psychomotor therapist always waits for before continuing; it is the signal that the witness's observation was an accurate one.)

"And I really feel like I *do* have a good, solid core," Deirdre said. "And yet I'm noticing"—she inhaled deeply—"neglect happening." It sounded odd, the way she had stated it: not "I am being neglected," but vaguer, as though neglect were occurring somewhere out there in the world.

"A witness would see how pained, and regretful, you feel . . . that neglect is happening," the therapist said.

"Yes!" Her face seemed to brighten in the way that it does when someone feels accurately heard. She waited, gazing at him expectantly.

"So, then, the neglect of your father is being repeated in some way by the neglect of your husband?" Pesso asked.

"Yes." Deirdre sounded energized, as if they were two hunters who were finding their way along the right trail. "And it's the same thing. My husband means well—but *not* well enough!"

There was a brief silence, during which that flurry of excitement dissipated; Deirdre's spirits seemed to droop, and she looked disconcerted. The therapist, sitting there and meeting her gaze while this transformation occurred, said, "A witness would see how discontented you are, that it's *not* well enough."

She nodded, and then Pesso asked her if she would like to choose two members of the group, or even two objects—perhaps a couple of pillows?—one to represent the neglectful part of her real father and the other the neglectful part of her husband. Deirdre nodded, then looked around, scanning those present one by one.

She chose Ernesto, the elegant, lanky Chilean lawyer, to be the neglectful part of her real father. Then she chose Jean-Michel, one of the Belgians, to play the role of the neglectful part of her husband. Each of them enrolled in his part formally, and then Pesso asked Deirdre to place them in the room as she saw them in relation to herself.

She directed Ernesto, as the neglectful part of her real father, to sit up tall and straight, at the maximum possible distance—the far end of a long sofa on the opposite side of the room.

Jean-Michel, as the neglectful part of her husband, was situated on the nearer sofa, somewhere in the middle, and just a few feet away from her.

Pesso, glancing at her choice and placement of the parent figure, said, "So your father is tall?"

Deirdre nodded. "Also, he lives a long way away." She looked comfortable, as if it felt right to have him at that distance.

"And what is your husband's name?" asked Pesso.

His name was Nikos, and he was Greek. He had been born in Alexandria, she replied, then sat there looking from one male role player to the other. After a few moments, Pesso inquired thoughtfully, "What happens as you feel the presence of these two figures?"

Deirdre's Adam's apple bobbed up and down before she said in the muted tone of voice in which she usually spoke, "They're fun, they're good people."

"A witness would see how content a part of you feels—" began the therapist, but then he stopped in midsentence. "But you don't *look* content," he stated.

Deirdre nodded, shrugged, said the fact that they were good company was merely something superficial. Pesso gestured airily toward the ceiling. "That sounds to me like a voice, the voice of reasonableness. It's saying, 'They're good company.'" He then observed that her two role players had been placed in the structure as neglecting figures, and it was interesting that she'd begun by describing them as good company.

"Well, neglect is not very easy to lay your hands on," explained Deirdre. "It's done in ways"—she'd begun to choke up again—"that not many people can see."

Pesso nodded understandingly and suggested that just for now, it should be made clear that Ernesto's role was that of the *neglecting* part of her father, and Jean-Michel's was that of the *neglecting* part of her husband. "We want them out here, in this space, as aspects of your father and your husband that can be *seen* by everyone present. There may be other, 'good company' parts of Nikos and your real father, but right now these two are the neglecting parts only. Is that okay?"

"Yes." Deirdre was looking intently from one man to the other, then back and forth again, as if these two role players were truly those neglectful persons incarnate. And when she spoke again, it was in that same hushed voice. "It was very hard on me to have to—well, to *lie* all the time, growing up," she said.

"A witness would see how pained you are, knowing you had to lie all the time, growing up. And that would be a voice, too." Pesso paused.

Deirdre nodded, offered the voice's statement spontaneously: "'*Say things were one way when they were really another way!'*"

He smiled and said, "Yes, that's a voice of warning: '*Say things were one way when they were really another way!'*"

"'Because if you don't, things will be worse,'" she added immediately. The therapist nodded and repeated her statement. Then he suggested that somewhere along the way they might invent a different family setting where she would be able to tell the truth and wouldn't have to lie. He looked at her questioningly, as if asking if he were still on track, but she shook her head in the negative, saying something here didn't feel completely right.

"Actually, I *could* tell the truth, but the thing was that I couldn't act on it. . . . I was trapped," Deirdre said. It wasn't clear what she meant.

The therapist didn't probe further. "A witness would see how helpless you feel, knowing you were trapped," he said.

"Yes, I was trapped," she agreed, looking miserable.

"Maybe, when we create the antidote, we'll invent the ideal family where you could both tell the truth *and* act on the truth. So then you wouldn't be trapped," suggested Pesso.

At this, Deirdre's expression brightened, as if an inner dimmer switch had suddenly been turned up to full capacity. "Yes, oh! I'd *like* that," she said.

The Voice of "Lower Your Expectations"

Speaking in terms of real time, or "here and now" time, Deirdre Carmody was in this room, in the presence of the workshop leader and the other members of this group. But as she sat there, gazing in turn at each of the two role players representing the neglectful aspects of the most significant males in her life, she was clearly somewhere else as well. In her mind's eye, she was also in historical time, the "then and there" time of experiences that were in the past.

And when she spoke again, she seemed to be musing aloud. "People say that if a husband is a good husband, you can tell it's so, because he doesn't get addicted to things, and he doesn't run around with other women, and he doesn't hit you."

Pesso repeated these words back to her in the oracular tones of a voice: "People say he's a good husband if he doesn't get addicted to things, he doesn't run around with other women, he doesn't hit you."

Deirdre nodded. "And to me that implies another, different voice—a powerful one—a voice that's saying, 'You'd better lower your expectations.'"

"You'd better lower your expectations, that's the best you can get," the therapist intoned, and Deirdre's eyes began filling.

"Yes," she half whispered, head hanging down.

"A witness can see how heartbroken that makes you feel, is that right?" Pesso asked, and she nodded, repeating that she'd waited a long time because she'd wanted more than that.

"So there's a longing for more than that." He was sticking to her own language as closely as possible. "And we can invent that. . . . Why don't we pick someone else to be the kind of husband you longed for?"

"Hmm." Deirdre raised her teary face and looked around the group thoughtfully. Then she asked Jim, the Hartford pastor, if he would take that role.

"I'm Jim, and I will enroll as your longed-for husband," he agreed, using the formulaic words of assent. Deirdre smiled at him, and Pesso intervened to ask her if this choice worked for her, if it felt like a good fit.

Eyes fixed steadily and even yearningly upon Jim, she nodded, and the therapist said quizzically, "You're looking at him with a kind of hope . . . and an expectation . . . ?"

"Yes," she said as the tears began rolling down her cheeks.

"And I can see how much pain you feel as you remember not having that—that hope, that expectation," Pesso said, stepping into his function as witness.

She nodded, unable to speak momentarily, her shoulders shaking with gusts of grief. Then she took out a fresh tissue, wiped her eyes, blew her nose gustily, and grew more composed. "To give an example, I live in this big old house, and the windows fall down really fast, because they don't have ropes or chains. And in many cases, the sashes are broken. So they're heavy, and they come down *hard*. And it's hard to get the storm windows in and out, because they're old and warped. It's hard, grueling work, and it's *hard* to do it alone!"

"A witness would see how pained and lonely you are, knowing that you have to do that alone," said Pesso. He was validating her experience.

Deirdre nodded, looking relieved to have voiced this complaint aloud and been heard. Still, when she spoke, she sounded angry and upset. "As it is, I end up covered with bruises. So okay, I don't have a husband that beats me, but still I'm covered with bruises! You might ask, 'What's going on here?'" she demanded.

"A witness would see how unjust that feels—" Pesso began, but Deirdre interrupted to say heatedly:

"There's something very wrong here!"

"It feels like there's something wrong," echoed the therapist, who then turned to Jim, in his role of the longed-for husband. "Maybe *this* husband would lift the windows," he said speculatively, raising his bushy eyebrows.

Deirdre turned to Jim, too, smiling through her outrage and her tears. "He might even help me *fix* the windows!" she said.

Then the pastor, in his role as the ideal husband she had longed for, was instructed to say, "If I had been your husband, and we lived in that big old house, I would have helped you fix those windows."

"Yes," said Deirdre, staring at him. She was growing calmer, looking mollified.

Pesso then suggested that the ideal husband go on to say, "And you wouldn't be covered with bruises." Jim did so, but this statement brought forth a fresh outburst of grief. Deirdre reiterated, in a despairing tone of voice, that her marriage felt "like a repeat, somehow."

"A witness would see how helpless you feel that you're in a repeat," said Pesso, and she nodded. "A repeat from your father to Nikos."

She looked appalled and said once again that she'd promised herself this would never happen—she would give herself a better fate than that.

"Shocked," said Pesso, "by your disappointment. Because you'd promised yourself more than that." Then he observed that because an older pattern seemed to have made this present-day pattern possible, it might be useful for them to travel backward in time. "Maybe, instead of an ideal husband, we should go back and get an ideal father. Do you want to see what that would feel like?"

"Well . . . I'm willing to try it" was Deirdre's somewhat dubious reply.

Autobiographical Memory and Evolutionary Memory

A basic tenet of psychomotor theory is that human memory falls into two broad general categories. One is "autobiographical memory," a blank tablet at birth, upon which our unfolding experiences in the environment will be inscribed. The other class of memory is "human evolutionary memory," by which is meant a prepackaged set of innate, genetically based programs that are geared toward survival of the self and of the species.

The latter—human evolutionary memory—is conceived of as part of our hereditary endowment and can best be understood in terms of certain fundamental needs that *must be met* in order to promote the growing child's optimal development. These basic requirements fall into five different headings: 1) the need for nurturance; 2) the need for protection; 3) the need for limits; 4) the need for support and 5) the need for "place"— which is, of course, that wonderful sense of belonging in a world that has been primed for and welcomes our arrival.

An apt example of the first of these genetically based programs—the need for nurturance—would be early attachment behavior. As a huge accretion of infant research has now demonstrated, newborns of our species come into existence ingeniously "prewired" for falling in love with *and inspiring the love of* their all-important caretakers, the parents. And, as a raft of important studies has made evident, these earliest, hugely powerful love bonds will have vast consequences in terms of the developing youngster's mental and physical well-being.

As Albert Pesso has written, "Our genes are the source for the information that guides our cells to construct the very systems and neural processes that give rise to perception and action in the first place. We naturally and without thinking access that gene-inspired information—

perfectly suited to provide avenues, strategies, perceptions and actions that can lead to successful outcomes. . . . It is as if our genes 'anticipate' our individual demise and have built into us a craving for sexual and social interactions that can result in the continuity of our species. From that genetic source we yearn to find our mates, find our calling and make our contributions to the world."

To put it plainly, we come into life just raring to form those kinds of passionate attachments that will result in individual survival and the perpetuation of our species. It follows, therefore, that first and foremost on every human being's inborn agenda is the intensely felt hunger for the stable, tender, responsive kinds of experiences with the first nurturers that will foster healthy maturation. And, according to Pesso, those of us who have been fortunate enough to have had the *right* relationships with the *right* kinship figures (the parental caretakers), at the *right* times, will naturally form the expectation that our lives will contain a fair portion of meaning, pleasure, satisfaction, and emotional connectedness. On the other hand, when fortune has dealt us a less favorable hand of cards, we come to anticipate pain rather than pleasure, incoherence rather than meaning, and isolation and alienation instead of a satisfying sense of connection and involvement.

Of course, this kind of theorizing about the fateful importance of early life experience does not represent a radical departure from traditional clinical thinking. What *is* different about the psychomotor approach is the hands-on way in which early deprivations are handled therapeutically. For a basic premise of this work is that there are reliable continuities between what is happening in the current moment and the things that happened earlier; and that our stored memories, *embedded not only in the mind, but in the "body's mind,"* provide the all-important bridge between a person's current state of being and the way in which those four genetically based human needs (for nurturance, protection, limits, and place) were well met or went miserably unsatisfied.

Thus, human memory is seen not only as crucially important in the organization and composition of an individual's present-day consciousness, but as *the* crucially important determinant when it comes to the patterning of his or her future. Again, the notion that our inner expectations, based upon past experiences, mold and shape the lives that are to follow is by no means a completely novel idea. On the contrary, it's so old that it's reflected in the writings of the Buddhist sages and appears in an ancient text called the Dhammapada. There it is written, "What you are now is the result of what you were. What you will be tomorrow is the result of what you are now."

Constructing an Internal Neural Network

In terms of therapeutic action, however, the question remains: Can what an individual will be tomorrow, based on what he or she is now, actually ever be changed or even modified? Psychomotor clinicians do believe it can be done. Their endeavor is to change the client's future (that is, avoid what Deirdre had called "a repeat") by creating a virtual stage upon which comforting "synthetic, supplemental memories" of a far less painful or depriving past can be devised and constructed. These healing scenarios are meant to provide the client with something often completely unknown— an internal action pattern, or neural network, for something that he or she has typically never even had a taste of earlier. That is the *felt sense* of a world in which the earliest caretakers hailed your arrival, held you devotedly, protected you solicitously, and met your normal developmental needs in the most satisfying, fulfilling ways imaginable.

. . . But the Heart Was Wrong

Deirdre's choice of the person to play her ideal father surprised me. She selected David Lucas, a large-framed, bulky therapist in his early forties. Dave, who'd come here accompanied by his wife—she was also a therapist—wore a perpetually aggrieved expression upon his face, as though his life had proven disappointing.

"I will enroll as your ideal father," he said to Deirdre immediately, looking flattered.

Then Pesso asked her where, in this room, she wanted him to be placed. "Let's see," she said thoughtfully, looking around, "somewhere within reaching distance . . ."

The therapist gazed at her, then said, "So maybe he says, 'If I had been your ideal father, I would have been within reaching distance.' Is that all right?"

Deirdre nodded, indicated a small vacancy on the sofa nearest her, and asked two of the women in the group if they'd mind if Dave sat between them. They shifted over, made a space available. There was a long silence as she stared at Dave in his ideal parent role.

"What happens when you see him beginning to take on that function?" Pesso asked softly. When Deirdre made no reply, he asked her if she wanted this ideal father sitting even closer to her.

She didn't hesitate: "Yes." She looked at the person sitting closest by on the sofa, and he, without a word, rose and moved to a floor cushion on the opposite side of the room. Deirdre, still cross-legged on the floor, shifted on her haunches until she was seated no more than a foot away from Dave. Then she sat there staring at her "ideal father," saying nothing but looking somehow absent, as if her thoughts were wandering elsewhere.

"What happens now?" Pesso asked, his voice low.

"Oh . . . uhm," was Deirdre's vague reply, as if speaking out of a reverie or daydream.

"What's coming into your mind?" inquired the therapist, and Deirdre turned to face him as she answered slowly.

"I was thinking . . . about a time when I was sick. . . . I must have been about nineish or tenish, something like that, and we were living in Egypt. It was some sort of tropical disease, one of these things that goes up and down. . . ."

"An undulate fever?" asked the therapist, and she nodded eagerly.

"Yes, that was it! So anyway, my parents kept sending me to school because my temperature was always down in the morning. But after a while it started going up in the early afternoon, and the teachers noticed, and they sent me home."

Pesso, gesturing with his head in Dave's direction, advised Deirdre to keep checking in with him, then asked what she would have wanted her ideal father to do in this situation and what her real father had actually done.

She had wanted her father to *believe* her when she said she wasn't feeling well, she cried out, sounding very young and scared. Dave needed no prompting: "If I had been your ideal father, I would have *believed* you when you said you weren't feeling well," he assured her. She gazed at him irresolutely, as if she yearned to take this statement in and find it credible.

"Anyway, when the teacher sent me home, there was no way to *get* home. There was only one car, and my father had it, and it was many miles across the desert to where we lived. So even if I'd been well, I couldn't have walked it! And he was out drinking at a club."

"So they called him?" asked Pesso, and she shook her head, said that, no, there was no way to reach him. "So then, how—" the therapist began, but Deirdre interrupted to say that her brother had walked her over to her father's club, which wasn't that far away.

"He was in a certain room where kids weren't permitted to go. So we got . . ." She halted, put her right hand over her chest as if to hold her heart in place, and began weeping again. "We got the waitress to go and tell him I was there, and I was sick. . . ." She drew in a breath that became transformed into the despairing sob of a forsaken child. "But he stopped to have another drink first, and in the meanwhile I threw up on the floor."

Pesso said, "So he stayed away, saying"—here, he switched into the pontificating tone of a voice—"*'I'm having another drink!'*" He was highlighting the facts of her real father's actual behavior.

Deirdre nodded, saying that the waitress had been the one to clean up the mess. "But it should have been my father who was doing that!"

The therapist looked at her thoughtfully, glanced briefly at Dave and then back at Deirdre. "So what would *he* say?" he asked her, sounding tentative. "If I'd been your ideal father, and I was at the club—"

"I would have come out right away!" Deirdre completed the sentence indignantly.

Dave then told her that if he had been her ideal father, and had been at his club, and she was sick, he would have come out right away. "And I wouldn't have stopped to have another drink," Pesso instructed him to add.

"And I wouldn't have stopped to have another drink," Dave repeated, gazing at Deirdre compassionately. But her own expression was unreadable.

"What happens when he says that?" the clinician asked.

Deirdre shrugged, said it was helping, but she felt as if they were still in the outer layers of the onion. "The thing is that this incident is just one of many, but it's a picture that gives the whole—" She halted, made a wide, sweeping gesture with both arms as if to say this episode was merely a small, representative piece of a much larger, more highly stratified and complex reality.

"Like a hologram," Pesso suggested.

"Exactly," she said. "So everything *looked* okay on the outside. After all, he did come out eventually."

"That's a voice of truth: 'After all, I did come out eventually.'"

"Yes, and brought me home," she agreed.

"'And I brought you home,'" echoed Pesso, still speaking in the oracular tone of the voice of truth.

"'And I made sure you had a good doctor,'" she said.

"'And I made sure you had a good doctor,'" intoned the therapist.

"But the heart was wrong!" Deirdre burst out, stretching her arm outward in Dave's direction, palm upward, fingers bent around it as if she were literally holding a heart in her hand.

"A witness would see how pained you are to know that the heart was wrong," said Pesso, and Deirdre nodded as tears began rolling down her cheeks. Then, slipping into his role as choreographer of the scene, he addressed Dave: "Talk about his heart. . . . And could you hold your hand the way she held hers when she said the word *heart*?"

Dave nodded and extended his own arm in Deirdre's direction, holding his own "heart in his hand" in the same way she had done. "What happens when you see him make that gesture?" Pesso asked her in a tone between an embrace and a whisper.

She looked affected, even shaken. "An ideal father would have . . . a connection," she said, placing both hands over her own heart. There was a silence.

Pesso turned to Dave, telling him to place his hands over his own heart, then feeding him his lines. "Say: 'I would have had that connection.'"

Dave, placing both hands over his heart, said feelingly, "If I had been your ideal father, I would have had that connection."

Deirdre nodded, looking spellbound. "And it would have told you how to act."

"And my heart would have told me how to act," Dave agreed. Again, Deirdre stretched her arm toward him, her hand cupped as if holding her heart inside it; and Dave, as ideal parent, mirrored the gesture, as if offering his own heart in return.

"Yes" was all she said. "Exactly."

There was a long, long pause, during which everyone present seemed to be holding his or her breath. "What's happening? What are you feeling?" Pesso asked at last.

Deirdre told him that there had been a lot of knots in her chest at the outset of the structure, but now she could feel them beginning to open up. "This one's opened, this one's going," she said, pointing to various places on the left side of her chest.

"Make a sound from the part that hasn't opened up yet," said Pesso, but Deirdre only exhaled deeply. "As you exhale, make a *sound*," he then prompted her. I expected to hear a loud expulsion of air, a profound sigh or even a groan. But shockingly, what emerged was a loud, wrenching, atavistic kind of sound, the kind of groan you'd expect to hear from someone under torture.

When it was over, though, it seemed to leave her feeling better, not worse. She looked relieved.

"And what about your hand?" the therapist asked her in a kindly, curious tone of voice. It had remained extended toward Dave, her ideal parent, still cupped upward as if she were offering her beating heart to him. Deirdre stared at that hand for a moment, almost as though it belonged to someone else. But her only comment was that it felt very steady.

"And the meaning of it?" Pesso asked.

"The meaning is that when people care about each other in a certain way, there's a connection across distance," she replied.

Pesso turned to Dave and asked him to send this statement back to her; and he, in his role as ideal parent, obliged by saying feelingly: "When people care about each other in a certain way, there's a connection across distance."

Deirdre looked moved, deeply gratified.

"A witness would see how convinced you feel about that," said Pesso.

"That *is* the way I feel," she replied unhesitatingly.

We had reached a moment of calm and serenity, and a feeling of peace descended upon all of us—one that seemed sanctified by a sudden chorus of evening birdsong. Dusk was gathering, and those sitting nearest the table lamps began to turn them on. It seemed to me that Deirdre's structure was winding down to its natural conclusion; but in this I was mistaken. For it soon became evident that there yet remained some deeper, more sensitive and painful "onion peeling" to be accomplished.

Chapter Twenty-One

ANTIDOTE: CREATING
"VIRTUAL, SUPPLEMENTAL"
MEMORIES

I N HIS ROLE AS CHOREOGRAPHER OF THIS EMERGING SCE-
nario, Pesso now turned to Dave Lucas and asked if he could make a suggestion. Could Dave, as Deirdre's ideal parent, move himself a little closer
to her, near enough so that their two cupped hands could connect physically?

Dave nodded and shifted his body to the edge of the sofa on which he
sat; and Deirdre, cross-legged on the floor, shimmied closer to him on her
haunches. They reached a position in which they were leaning toward
each other and stretching their arms forward until their concave hands
touched lightly at the backs of the knuckles.

After a long pause, Deirdre murmured, "It feels very warm."

Pesso, leaning forward on his low bench, said to her, "He might say:
'You could *feel* my warmth.'" She nodded her acceptance of this statement, then looked up at Dave with a childlike expression on her face; and
he, with genuine sympathy in his voice, said that if he'd been her ideal
father, she could have felt his warmth. She looked at him gratefully, let
out a sigh of contentment.

"Imagine getting father warmth that way," said Pesso. "What does it
feel like?"

"It feels like I can breathe more easily," she replied, the ring of relief in
her voice.

The therapist then forwarded this new line of ideal father script directly to Dave, who duly repeated it. "If I had been back there then, you would have been able to breathe more easily," he said.

"Yes, and not just me, but my brothers and sisters, too!" said Deirdre, who, while still with us, had in some sense left this setting and everyone present. She had gone into an alternative space, the imaginary world of the-way-it-could-have-been.

Pesso glanced meaningfully at Dave, who repeated her words: "Not just you, but your brothers and sisters, too!"

"Yes," said Deirdre, looking deeply affected.

"A witness could see how convinced you are of that possibility," said Pesso.

Yes, she replied, adding that in reality her brothers and sisters had all suffered from asthma. Then tears began welling up in her eyes once again, and she looked searchingly at Dave, her ideal parent. "We wanted so to miss you when you were away," she said to him mournfully.

Here, the structure leader intervened to tell her that she had left the healing scenario momentarily. "Now you're talking about your *real* father," he said, then turned to Dave and asked him to say that if he had been her ideal father back then, she would have missed him when he was away.

"Yes." Deirdre's voice was girlish but hopeful sounding. "Yes, I would have missed you."

"A witness would see how touched you are by that realization," Pesso observed quietly.

She nodded and said, "Yes, that's what we all wanted." This line became quickly incorporated into the "virtual" memory they were developing; and Dave, as ideal parent, repeated her words as she had said them.

"It would have been the way all of you wanted it," he told her firmly. His cupped hand and Deirdre's cupped hand, both holding their symbolic hearts, were still touching. Her eyes were shining.

"Yes," she said, "yes."

There was a silence. Then Pesso said to Deirdre in a low, inviting voice, "Take that inside yourself, at that age—maybe around nine or ten years old. . . . That kind of heart connection with a father."

She didn't answer, merely emitted a long, peaceful breath. She looked deep into Dave's eyes, then said, "If you were my ideal father, you would *know* what you were doing!" But this seeming criticism was muted by a small, forgiving little giggle.

Dave, smiling, said, "If I were your ideal father, I would *know* what I was doing."

She nodded, still smiling. Here, the therapist intervened to remind her that earlier on she had spoken about her father's having married too young. "Yes," she said, and Pesso turned to Dave with the suggestion that he say, "I would have raised a family *knowing* what I was doing."

This brought a broad grin to Deirdre's face, and she laughed aloud again, saying that this last comment had caused a voice of reason to pop into her head. "And, you know, that voice of reason was saying, 'Hey, he was only twenty years old!'"

In that case, responded Pesso, the ideal father might say, "I would have started a family at—" He halted in midsentence. "At what age, do you think?" he asked Deirdre.

"*Much* later!" she answered merrily.

Then Dave said, "I would have gotten married *much* later."

"Yes," she breathed, gazing at him, looking contented.

"A witness would see how relieved you are by that reassurance," the therapist said. Deirdre nodded, sighed deeply, kept looking fixedly into her ideal parent's eyes. She seemed transported, but she said nothing aloud.

Addressing the "Glut"

As Deirdre and Dave sat facing each other, arms outstretched, cupped hands touching lightly at the knuckles, Pesso urged her once again to *feel* that relief at whatever age she had missed it. "Because you're feeling real relief right now, is that right?" he asked.

Deirdre said that she was indeed feeling relief, but that leaning toward Dave and holding her arm in this outstretched position was beginning to make her shoulder muscles ache. This led Pesso to suggest that the pair move even closer to each other in order to diminish the physical strain upon their arms and still retain their linked "heart in their hands" position. The two then shifted and rearranged their positions until both were comfortable, and Deirdre said, "This feels much better, this feels fine to me."

From this nearer vantage point, she fixed her gaze upon her ideal father, and Dave Lucas met that gaze unflinchingly. "What's happening?" Pesso asked her softly. "What do you see when you look at him now?"

"I see a lot of . . . soul," said Deirdre, her eyes beginning to fill.

"Maybe he says, 'If I had been your ideal father, I would have had a lot of soul.' Does that sound right?"

Pesso was checking in with her about every aspect of this synthetic memory in the making, and now he looked at Deirdre questioningly. Eyes glued upon Dave, she didn't speak; she merely nodded her assent. But when Dave, in his role as ideal parent, said he would have had a lot of soul, she answered energetically, "You wouldn't have been *afraid* of it, either!"

"I wouldn't have been afraid of it, either," Dave agreed.

"*Yes*," she said with a profound sigh, as if she'd unloaded a painful burden. A moment later, though, she inhaled, and her expression turned to one of grief; she exhaled, a sound that was somewhere between another deep sigh and a groan.

"What's happening?" Pesso asked.

Deirdre turned from Dave to him and said, "I feel as if most of the knots are gone." She gestured toward her upper chest. "There's still one here"—she pointed to a place just below her left clavicle—"but it's like this—this *glut*." She looked embarrassed and laughed lightly, as if trying to downplay something shameful.

Pesso looked at her thoughtfully. "I can give you a good way to deal with that," he said. "If you take a deep, deep breath, and tighten hard at 'the glut'—then tighten even harder, harder, harder—and make a *sound* with that tightness . . ." Deirdre, who'd been following these instructions even as he spoke, suddenly emitted a loud racking cough so intense and full of spluttering choking sounds that her body doubled over in pain. It seemed to come out of nowhere and was awful to see, frightening to listen to—like watching someone trying to exorcise a demon or cough up the phlegm of a lifetime.

What had Deirdre said earlier? Hadn't she described herself as the one child in her family of origin who'd been asthma free? This terrible, grinding, hacking episode made you wonder. The coughing fit receded slowly, ending with an extended, long, sobbing, indrawn breath.

"That's the remains of the grief. Do you hear the cry, the desolation, in there?" Pesso asked her softly. She nodded but seemed chagrined and did not look up to meet his eyes. Then he told her that he had another suggestion to make, one that would help her to feel safe and supported as the process of addressing "the glut" continued.

Let the Cry Come

According to Albert Pesso, there are many clients who cannot possibly be helped if approached by means of verbal psychotherapy alone. These are people who have dealt with their unbearable thoughts and feelings by walling them off and who experience their suppressed emotionality in the form of bodily symptoms and sensations—for instance, Deirdre Carmody's "glut." As the therapist now explained to Deirdre, she was going to need the reassurance of what, in psychomotor parlance, is known as a "contact figure."

A contact figure is simply someone in the group whose reassuring physical touch serves to communicate the message that he or she will *be there* to help the protagonist handle whatever painful feelings emerge as work on the structure continues. "I say this because when you cry in that way, it sounds to me like you need someone to hold you," Pesso said. "So, do you want to pick a contact figure? . . . Because I think you have a lot of grief in there, and if we touch it once again, I'm certain it's going to come out."

Even as he spoke, Deirdre was looking around the room for a member of the group who felt right to her when it came to taking this particular role, but she couldn't seem to settle on anyone. "This is so hard for me, I can't seem to choose," she said at last, sounding flustered, even scared, as if no one in this room felt strong or safe enough to be given this particular assignment.

Pesso waited quietly as she scanned the group again, but once more she shrugged, shook her head, looking confounded. Then Pesso, glancing at Dave Lucas, said to Deirdre, "Perhaps he could hold you?"

She nodded. "I'll just move over," she said, and then placed herself, like a child seated on the floor at her parent's foot, next to Dave's right shin.

"I will enroll as your contact figure as well as your ideal father," he said formally.

Then she curled up next to his leg, her head facing downward, her arms entwined around her own torso. She was facing outward to the room, and Dave, seated on the low sofa, was instructed to place a caring, protective arm around the backs of her shoulders.

For a brief while they sat there, the picture of parent/child tranquillity. At last the therapist said, "Tighten that spot in your chest again," and Deirdre did so, then released the breath. This was followed immediately by a long bout of that same racking cough, a cough so hard and wrenching that she doubled over again. Given the peaceful interlude that had preceded this eruption, I felt shaken by the raw pain of this scene. So did others in the group, I thought, for when I looked around all heads were lowered, as if in prayer, and nobody met my eyes.

I glanced at Pesso, who seemed unfazed. He now suggested that Dave put one arm all the way around Deirdre's shoulder, and then hold her forehead with his open palm. The coughing fit petered out slowly, and the pair of them remained in this position for a while. Then the clinician said to Deirdre gently, "Let the cry come. . . ." She drew in a long, shuddering breath that sounded like a sob.

"Hear that?" Pesso asked her encouragingly, and those words seemed to penetrate some kind of internal dike or seawall. The resultant flood of grief and sorrow that came pouring forth was alarming, even given the long bouts of hacking and choking that had gone before. Once again, there were those deep, rasping fits of coughing, but this episode sounded far more desperate. Deirdre was struggling to catch her breath, then getting some air in, then sobbing wildly, coughing hard again. It was hard to sit there simply watching because you wanted to jump up and help. She seemed so much like someone drowning—going under, coming up, gasping and flailing, going down again, and then surfacing anew as if in a mad struggle to take in some swallows of scarce, life-giving oxygen.

At last, as abruptly as it had begun, the horrible episode ended. Deirdre's coughing receded, and she sat up, reached for the tissues box, and began to wipe her eyes and blow her nose. "Wait," said Pesso, as if to say that this episode had not yet reached completion. He asked her to take Dave's hand and place it on her chest just where she felt "the glut," then tighten that spot once again.

"Hold on a moment," she said, "I can't breathe."

"Yes, that's the emotion," Pesso responded.

After a brief time-out, during which she inhaled and exhaled deeply several times, Deirdre placed Dave's hand above her left breast in the spot where she'd have put it if she were saluting the flag. "Now, take another deep breath, and tighten hard, and *sound!*" the structure leader coached her.

Deirdre inhaled deeply, and as she exhaled the breath it became that same deep, racking cough, interspersed with sobs and asthmatic-sounding, indrawn gulping for air.

"It is terrible, terrible sorrow," Pesso commented sympathetically.

Deirdre nodded, head down, still struggling for breath, though the rasping, choking sounds, interspersed with cries of sorrow, were slowly diminishing in intensity. Now the therapist asked Dave, in his combined role of contact figure/ideal parent, to wrap both arms around Deirdre's shoulders even more tightly and hold her forehead firmly in his grasp. As he did this, she let out a sudden anguished cry, a deep, howling "Aaaaah!" that sounded as if it had bubbled up from the inmost recesses of her being.

"It's deep grief you're feeling," Pesso said again. "Did you hear it, those sounds? What did they sound like to you?"

Deirdre sat up, pulled away from Dave, and ran a distracted hand through her wavy dark hair. Then she pulled some more tissues from the box, wiped her eyes, blew her nose, and looked at the therapist directly. "Whatever I might have said, or *not* said earlier, I guess I didn't say how much pain I was in," she said in a wondering tone of voice, sounding amazed to realize it herself.

It Really Got into Your Body

Now Pesso suggested that Dave say to Deirdre, "If I had been back there then, you could have said how much pain you felt."

She nodded, eyes wide and trusting. "Yes, I could," she breathed.

The structure leader smiled and observed that she was gazing at Dave with such a young look on her face. "You look about seven or eight years old . . . you must have felt that way at seven," he said. Then he pointed out the way she was now hanging on to Dave's hand by his little finger, the way that a little girl might have hung on to her daddy's hand.

"Maybe he could say, 'You could have held my hand like this when you were seven,'" Pesso suggested.

Deirdre nodded and laughed with pleasure at the notion; but before Dave could say another word, that laugh had become a sob. She was weeping openly as her ideal parent said, "You could have held my hand like this when you were seven."

She looked up at him through her tears and said, "If you were my ideal father, you would not have let life get so on top of you that you couldn't . . ." She left the sentence incomplete.

"Be there for you?" suggested Pesso.

Deirdre shook her head. "Treat us kindly," she said.

"If I were your ideal father, I wouldn't have let life get so on top of me that I couldn't treat you kindly," Dave said, and she nodded.

"Because we would have been more *important* to you than all those other things that were going on!" She said, her voice charged with reproach.

Dave, as ideal father, said understandingly, "Because you would have been more important to me than all those other things going on."

"Yes," she said, "yes." She sighed again, mollified.

"When you let the air out, let a sound come, too. See what comes of it," the therapist advised her. Deirdre inhaled, exhaled peacefully. "Feeling relief now," Pesso commented.

Deirdre nodded, breathing in and out calmly for a few moments. Then, suddenly, she turned to Dave with a fresh accusation. "There's another thing—if you had been my ideal father, it would have been safe to make noise around you!"

"If I had been your ideal father, it would have been safe to make noise around me," he assured her.

Deirdre breathed in and out deeply, crisscrossed her hands across her chest. "I'm feeling my back letting go as well, this is good," she announced to no one in particular.

"A witness can see how relieved you are—how *pleased* you are—to feel your back letting go," Pesso said. Then, in his capacity as impresario, he turned to Dave and suggested that he repeat that remark in his ideal parent role.

"If I were your ideal father, you could have let your back go like that, when you were young," Dave told her, and Deirdre nodded, began to cry.

"A witness can see how touched you are, to experience that possibility," Pesso said gently.

She nodded, said through tears, "I wouldn't need the armor."

"If I had been your ideal father, you wouldn't have needed the armor," Dave said.

Deirdre nodded, met his gaze, and said in a childish, somewhat truculent voice, "I *like* making noise!"

Pesso quickly interposed himself and instructed Dave to say, "I like *hearing* your noise," and this elicited an excited laugh from Deirdre—a laugh that turned into a sob, then into racking cries of grief. She began rocking back and forth, like a soul in deep mourning, mourning for the way things had really been, so far from the deeply satisfying tableau being created.

Then, as unexpectedly as it had begun, the episode passed. She straightened up, blew her nose, and said with a self-mocking laugh, "This is beginning to look like a video ad for Kleenex tissues!" Her social self was reasserting itself, but her complexion was plaster white and her eyes so rounded and bulging that she looked like a frightened ghost. She jumped when the *beep-beep* of Pesso's timer sounded.

This meant that forty minutes had passed, and the structure had a mere ten minutes left to run. "Okay, I think I'm almost done," Deirdre said quickly, half rising from her seat on the floor. But Pesso, waving her back into place, told her that the beeping signal didn't mean she had to rush, only that the time left to them was limited now.

Sinking back against the side of her ideal father's legs, she sighed peaceably, as if it felt good being back there again. "Let a sound come every time you exhale," the structure leader suggested. Deirdre sighed again, more loudly this time, and Pesso said, "That sounds like relief."

"Yes," Deirdre said quietly, then inhaled and exhaled deeply several more times. "Yes, that feels really *good*," she said, snuggling even closer and resting her head against Dave's thigh trustingly.

"At what age would you have wanted this kind of contact?" the therapist asked her, and Deirdre paused thoughtfully. Then she said that her father had in fact given all his children some measure of contact, but it hadn't been consistent with his other behavior.

"So maybe he'll say, 'If I had been your ideal father, my behavior would have been consistent,'" said Pesso. Deirdre nodded and twisted her position slightly so that she could look directly up at Dave's face as he echoed this statement.

"Yes." She sighed deeply, sounding consoled. "The picture would have matched the inside."

"The picture would have matched the inside," Dave said, needing no prompting.

"Yes," she said, and Dave said, "Yes," right back to her.

Deirdre seemed to sink into a reverie and said nothing for a period of time. "What are you thinking?" Pesso broke the silence to ask her.

"I was thinking that I would have felt safe at night," she said.

"You would have felt safe at night," Dave, as her ideal parent, assured her. A beatific expression settled over her features.

"Go back, now, to some of those nights when you didn't feel safe," Pesso suggested, "and bring this experience back there. See what happens when you do that."

Deirdre closed her eyes, was silent for several moments, then began to cry brokenheartedly. "A witness could see how much you suffered when you were younger," the therapist told her. She nodded, reached for more tissues, and dabbed at the tears rolling down her cheeks.

Pesso, glancing at Dave, said to her, "So maybe he says, 'I would have brought you this safety back then'?"

She nodded and turned to Dave, who repeated this statement with genuine compassion in his voice. Clearly, he had become swept up in the role he was playing. "I would have brought you this safety back then," he said, and she nodded, sighed with relief, then began to cry again.

"I didn't think that it got to me as much as it did," she said, tears streaming down her face.

"A witness would say, 'I can see how surprised you are to realize it got to you as much as it did,'" said Pesso. Then, stepping out of the witness role, he added, "It really got into your body, though you kept it from reaching your mind."

Deirdre nodded and said that all the other kids had gotten asthma, but somehow she hadn't.

"You just got those knots in your chest," the therapist observed, and this remark elicited a huge sigh.

"Yes, I think we would have all been more well—"

Interrupting, Pesso turned to Dave and said, "Say that: 'If I had been—'"

Dave stepped in smoothly and said, "If I had been your ideal father, you would all have been more well."

Deirdre, gazing up into his eyes, said, "Yes," and once again, Dave said, "Yes," back to her immediately. She sighed contentedly, took out a fresh tissue, and blew her nose again. "It's important to me to be able to breathe," she said.

"It would have been important to me that you would have been able to breathe," Dave, as her ideal parent, repeated her words.

"Yes, it would have mattered a lot to me," Deirdre said wistfully.

"It would have mattered a lot to me that you would have been able to breathe," Dave echoed with real caring in his voice.

"So . . . he would have been interested in your breathing. He would have been *present*," Pesso prompted softly.

"I would have been interested in your breathing; I would have been present," her ideal father assured her.

Deirdre sighed deeply, said in a little girl's voice, "And you wouldn't have given up on me."

"I wouldn't have given up on you," Dave said firmly.

She nodded, sighed again, looked at the therapist, and said she was ready to derole and "chew on what had happened." But he merely smiled, pointed out the childlike way in which she'd taken hold of Dave's little finger once again. "So then, *remember* the grip, and remember the touch, and remember the relief in your breathing." Pesso's voice was low, hypnotic. "And put all of that back in time, into a context that has to do with your ideal father being *there for you* at that age. So that all of these sensations, with their life-altering possibilities, get linked in your mind. And they're there *inside you*, at that age level."

Deirdre, listening with her eyes closed, looked as if she were feeling serene, at ease. "I am trying to bring all of this back into that house, into those rooms," she said, as if reporting from a location that she saw in her mind's eye.

"Good," Pesso said encouragingly, for the ultimate goal was to insert something new into Deirdre's internal narrative—not a replacement of her real personal history, but something in the nature of a "supplemental" memory. This satisfying, reassuring "virtual" memory had been developed and designed in such a way as to instill in her a reassuring, vivid sense of having been loved unconditionally by the first important male she had ever known, for it was the memory of having been loved by the *right* person in the *right* kinship relationship at the *right* time of her life.

"Those rooms, where we felt so unsafe. Yes . . . it was very dramatic, but it could have been so different if we'd known we were safe. We could have laughed so much off." Deirdre's reflections were drifting ones; she was musing aloud.

"You would have had another perspective," the therapist agreed.

She nodded, sighed deeply, peacefully. The session ended there, with the process of "deroling." The voices in the air—the voice of truth, the voice of warning, the voice of "lower your expectations," the voice of reasonableness—were all dissolved by successive waves of Pesso's hand. The neglecting parts of Deirdre's father and her husband, Nikos, stepped out of their roles formally and told her that they were resuming their true identities now; they were Ernesto and Jean-Michel once again.

Jim, the pastor, resigned from his part as ideal husband, and then Pesso waved his hand, erased the witness figure from the airy space above him. Last of all, Dave Lucas said, "I derole and am no longer your ideal father. I am Dave." But Deirdre, with a child's stars in her eyes, looked at him and said worshipfully, "I'm grateful . . . thank you." She seemed a bit dazed, as if a part of her yet remained in the world of "then and there" and hadn't yet returned to this time, these people, this wood-paneled shed in the hills of northern New Hampshire.

A Life Worth Living

At the outset of the workshop, Al Pesso had told me that in my role as invited observer I should by no means feel pressured to do a structure of my own unless I so desired. But in the meantime I'd observed the other conference participants "taking a risk" (as Deirdre had phrased it) and profiting mightily from having done so.

I knew that if I did volunteer to do a structure, I would want to work on the subject of "place," for the jarring vision that had surfaced—of having come home from the hospital, as a newborn, to a household that was overfilled and unready to receive me—had raised certain basic, fairly daunting questions in my mind. These questions had to do with things that had been said during Pesso's lectures. People whose "place" in the world has not been prepared for them, the therapist had observed, often struggle with a sense of "Where do I belong?" and sometimes even question their fundamental right to existence.

At week's end, as the psychomotor workshop was drawing to a close, I took a brief hike around a nearby lake along with Deirdre and Bea Ellis, another member of the group. Bea, a tall, elegant African American academic in her mid-fifties, had come to this conference with a specific, well-defined goal in mind. She had been widowed a year earlier, and though she was mourning her husband's loss and missing him desperately, she'd found herself unable to weep. She said she felt "waterlogged with grief," but her tears seemed locked inside her, and crying had proven impossible.

Bea Ellis had done two extraordinary structures during this week, and neither of them had left her (or most of the rest of us) dry-eyed. Both structures had involved large casts of characters and long interchanges with role-playing figures; and I myself had taken part in one of them, enrolling as her "ideal maternal aunt" at her request. Actually, Bea's two healing scenarios could not have been more different from Deirdre Carmody's structure, which had involved far fewer speaking roles and just a handful of people— Dave Lucas more than anyone. In Deirdre's case, the work had focused pretty exclusively on one particular life course–setting relationship—her relationship with her dictatorial, neglectful father, which had erupted into the present and was being reenacted with Nikos, her spouse.

"The past falls open anywhere," the Irish writer Michael Donaghy has written. But as I strolled along with these two women, I wondered if the creation of virtual, supplemental early memories could really intervene and prevent that from happening. Certainly Bea Ellis had become able to cry openly about her husband's death and to connect her long emotional shutdown with certain earlier experiences that had taught her *not to feel* things that seemed too painful to handle. But did her newly minted, happier early "memories" have the real stamp of authenticity?

I had so many questions that I wanted to put to Bea, and to Deirdre, too, about how they'd been affected during and after their structures. I couldn't do this, though, because we participants had been enjoined to respect one another's internal processes and basic privacy by not getting into discussions about the highly personal sessions we'd witnessed. So as we walked along, the three of us chatted lightly, enjoying the beauty of the scene and the fact that the weather was finally cooling down. I was preoccupied by, but didn't even mention, my own most pressing concern—the decision I was struggling with about whether or not to do a structure before the workshop ended. But along the way, I was checking out my companions carefully—Deirdre especially, since we'd both had explosive, neglectful fathers—and trying to take my cues from their behavior, how well they appeared to be doing.

Deirdre *did* seem different in the wake of the session that I've described, most especially in terms of her voice: It was firmer and had lost the hushed quality that so often made it difficult to hear her. Now, as we women strolled down a wide woodland road alive with the humming sounds of summer, she paused and raised her hands in front of her in prayer position, then spread them wide in a huge circle as she inhaled deeply. Bea and I stopped, waited. Deirdre held her breath a moment, then exhaled with a deep "Ahhhh," the sound of satisfaction. Without preamble, then, and apropos of nothing we'd been talking about before, she said, "When I go home I'm letting my husband know something: Either the marriage will change or the marriage will end. . . . And if it *does* end, that's okay, because what's become clear to me now is that I need to get a life worth living."

Once again she spread her arms wide, as if to encompass the whole world, then inhaled and exhaled deeply. And at that moment I decided I would volunteer to do a structure of my own.

HEN CLAUDIA MARTINELLI CALLED TO TELL ME THAT she and Paul had reconciled, I can't say that I was completely surprised. It seemed to me that she'd answered her own anguished question—What lesson am I not learning?—by surrendering to the belief that, at least in her own case, any new relationship would prove to be as damaging as all the past ones. The lesson was one that would never be learned, so she had "settled," as her mother had done.

She was quick to tell me that the marital climate had improved—a change in the weather that she ascribed to the fact that she was now taking Prozac. I received this news somewhat dubiously. I knew that Prozac could be helpful, in terms of blunting the uncomfortable messages her body was sending her, but Claudia still seemed to be making use of massive repression and denial. It was as if she were discounting the effects of her husband's emotionally abusive behavior and suggesting that all their problems had been resolved by a magic bullet into her own brain, Prozac; Paul's periodic aggressions seemed to have vanished from her thoughts. Claudia seemed *not* to want to "know" about (much less confront) his episodic attacks any more than she'd wanted to "know" about her father's physically abusive behavior in the first place.

Of course, Claudia had grown up in a family where violence was occurring (her father was beating her brother "to the point of blood"), one in which everyone knew that there are things *you're not supposed to talk about*. And so not telling other people—or your prospective mate—the truth about yourself was a familiar re-creation of the world she had lived in as a child.

The last time that we met for a face-to-face interview was late in her pregnancy with her daughter Jessica. In the intervening time, Claudia and Paul had bought a new house in a pleasant Connecticut town. They were moving soon and would be living close to one of her sisters, she told me enthusiastically. But then, without warning—and apropos of nothing to do with the conversation we were having—Claudia burst into tears and buried her face in her hands. I was startled, shaken.

I leaned forward, put a light hand on one of her trembling shoulders. "What's happening, Claudia?" I asked her.

She looked up at me and said, "I'm so *ashamed* . . . so *ashamed* . . ." At the same time, she was shaking her head from side to side in the negative, as if to ward off any further questions I might ask her. So I sat there silently, and eventually she murmured something to the effect that Paul was throwing ugly tantrums now and then, episodes that ended with his stomping off and sleeping in another room.

I didn't press the matter further—she was too upset—but I did wonder whether her husband was slapping her around as well; men who are abusive often become even more so during a partner's pregnancy. After a while, Claudia's sobs lessened. She wiped her cheeks with her hands and shuddered briefly, a signal that the crying spell was over. But she said nothing further about what was troubling her so deeply.

It wasn't until months later, during one of our occasional telephone conversations, that I returned to the subject of Paul's stalking out of the bedroom and asked her if this had continued to happen. Claudia said that this *did* go on from time to time, but she didn't feel as startled or shaken up about it anymore. "We'll go through periods where we're very sexual, and we're very close, and then he turns it off; he'll just be really *nasty*. And nowadays, I don't say anything when he sleeps in the other bedroom." She laughed dryly. "I'm almost seeing the positive side, because I can get a good night's sleep and I don't have to listen to anyone's snoring. . . ."

At a surface level, Claudia's life seemed much less stormy. For now that the pregnancy was over, she was back on Prozac, and this served as a palliative to her body's uncomfortable inner state; this medication decreases bodily hyperarousal. She was also attending Al-Anon meetings as the spouse of a "dry drunk" and getting a lot of support from those she'd come to know in that setting. She was back in therapy, too, with someone who was a specialist in alcohol and drug addiction. All of the above, plus the fact that her energies were now focused upon her baby daughter, was serving to take the pressure off the marriage.

On the other hand, these same things were helping Claudia to remain in denial about her inability to build a healthy relationship—and, by doing so, break the intergenerational cycle and build a healthy role model for her daughter. For basically what I was hearing was that nothing in the marriage had changed. In the midst of a subsequent telephone conversation, during which she was describing the way in which Paul could be harsh with their daughter on some occasions but "melt" at other times, Claudia stopped suddenly, in midsentence, and said, "Let's face it, I married my father."

To which I responded, "So the great question on my mind is this: Will Jessica grow up with 'the Bickersons' as the model in her mind?" This question was met with a stunned silence. I asked her then whether Paul ever carried on the way her father had done. "I mean, does he ever lose it and hit people?"

"My father never hit anybody," she replied immediately.

"I mean . . . he hit your brother," I said, confused.

She paused a long moment, then said haltingly, "Ummm . . . they *are* similar in that they both suffer, I believe, from depression. They're both introverts. They're both uncomfortable in social situations." Claudia was still adept at finding rationales and excuses for her father's and her husband's behavior. It was as if she were always erecting walls inside her head so that she wouldn't have to face the full extent of what was really happening; and it occurred to me that the safest way of not telling a secret—in this case, one that had to do with the existence of intermittent emotional abuse—is not even "knowing" what the secret is in the first place. She seemed to be pedaling away furiously without realizing that she was on a stationary bicycle.

Did It Last?

My conversations with Claudia raised an inevitable question in my own mind: Would one of the body-oriented therapies have proven more effective—made a real difference—if she had ever moved in that direction? It was highly likely that some reprocessing would have helped her to contain her emotions, as the Prozac was now doing, and have done so without any of that medication's potential side effects—for example, loss of libido. Also, and very significant, a course of reprocessing might have enabled Claudia to *reassociate what had happened to her as a child with what was happening to her in her current life.* This would have freed her to live more fully in the present and to stop reenacting the events she had witnessed in the past.

Of course, where Karen Barry-Freed was concerned, the foremost question was: Had the effects of reprocessing lasted? For this reason, I called her periodically to ask if the EMDR treatment's effects had held up over the long term. Karen's response, on all these occasions, was similar: "It held, it definitely held. . . . I don't understand why it worked, but it did. And really—I'm a bit of a skeptic; I thought the whole idea seemed kind of"—she paused—"out there." Initially, she told me, she'd been unsure about whether or not she'd had a simple placebo reaction. "When I left that day, I thought that maybe it had worked because I'd *wanted* so much for it to work. . . . I did feel much better, but I had my doubts. And so my thought was, Well, we'll see what happens. . . ."

It will be recalled that when she'd first come in for therapy, Karen Barry-Freed was experiencing body symptoms (severe headaches, nausea) that had been activated by symbolic reminders of the original traumatic shock—one such trigger was the realization that "this woman's" numbers were inscribed on her husband's cell phone, and the other trigger was hearing that Jon had been primping in front of the mirror before going to the office on a particular morning.

Karen was also being plagued by what are called "intrusive thoughts" —ugly thoughts and images of Jon and "this woman" sharing an intimate, romantic dinner—and the notion that she herself was being gulled and betrayed once again. "In the time leading up to my work with Patti Levin, I'd had a lot of sleeplessness, too," Karen said. "As soon as I'd shut my eyes, it would all start flashing up at me; and I'd have to get out of bed and wander. I was so confused, so dazed. It was as if I'd been punched in the stomach and had the wind knocked out of me."

This state of affairs had persisted for months, while the Barry-Freeds' "second marriage" hung in the balance. "Jon was frightened, really *scared*, he was sure he was losing me. And I myself don't know where we would have been without the EMDR. . . . The funny thing is that I couldn't understand why staring at this moving light would have any effect at all. I *still* don't understand how it works, but for me it was like a 'snap!' moment. It was right away, in that first session that something happened—it was like I'd been zapped back into my normal life. You know, I was in one place, and all of a sudden, wow! It wasn't a subtle thing. It was just—boom!"

It was so immediate, so sudden, that in the aftermath of that first EMDR session (she'd had four sessions in toto), Karen had deliberately tested out the treatment's effectiveness by intentionally bringing those tormenting mental scenes to the center of her awareness. "I would think of these horrible, painful images *on purpose*. I'd picture the incident with the cell phone—I'd picture Jon with that woman—images that had been tearing at my gut for months and filling me up with all those sick, angry, hurt feelings." But these internal tableaux had lost their cruel power. "The whole thing just stopped being an issue. And there hasn't really been an issue like it since that time. Basically, I'm feeling grounded these days—I feel as if I know who I am as a person, and who I am in relationship to Jon."

I wondered—and couldn't resist asking Karen—where she thought she would have been right now if she had never had that reprocessing experience. "I don't know what I'd have done or where I would have been without the EMDR," she replied slowly, thoughtfully. "I think that even *if* I had stayed in the marriage, I would have become a chronic worrier. You know, one of those people who worry and worry and worry, and who imagine that if they just *worry* enough, it's going to have some impact on their world and on whatever happens. And of course, it doesn't." Karen laughed ruefully.

Then she added quietly, "I honestly think I was heading that way, continually revisiting that scene in the car with the cell phone, continually filling myself up with all of these horrible, sick feelings. I was just playing that scene over and over in my mind—as if by playing it over, I'd arrive at a different outcome. . . ." After that initial EMDR session, though, the scene's virulent impact was gone; its noxious force had dissipated entirely, and the awful feelings associated with it had not ever returned.

I Can Breathe

Deirdre Carmody told me that she and her husband were now separated. It was only after their separation that she had truly realized the degree of stress and tension she'd been living with; her hair, which had been graying rapidly, had actually stopped losing color in the aftermath.

"It's sad. There are so many things I liked about Nikos, and still *do*—his intelligence, his wit," said Deirdre. "But he's always had this under-handed way of scuttling things that promised to be fun. Say, if I was looking forward to a family event, he would often pick a huge fight just before starting out. It so happens that there are some really terrific people in my extended family, but I'd arrive feeling all shaken up because of his having picked a fight, and the evening was ruined already." Her husband was, she added, a person who was just *filled* with boiling resentment and hatred, especially toward his mother; but as his wife, it had been Deirdre herself who was bearing the brunt of it. Finally, she'd reached a point at which she felt she couldn't handle all that anger and vitriol anymore.

"By the way, this may be off the subject, but something really *strange* happened to me after doing that structure," said Deirdre, shifting the thrust of our conversation on the spot. Her voice took on a buoyant tone as she explained that throughout her life she'd loved to sing. Even now, though she was a full-time graduate student, singing was a serious avocation; currently, she was part of a group of professional performers.

"We've cut CDs, and things like that," explained Deirdre, "but my problem has always been with my breathing—I wasn't always able to sing to the end of a line. I'd have to take a quick breath halfway through, and it didn't sound as professional as I would have liked." She had, she reminded me, been the only one of her siblings who hadn't developed asthma; and she had always thought she'd gotten off lightly. Nevertheless, she said, "in the house in which I grew up you had to be really careful about what you said, and you couldn't make noise. And I suppose I'd always assumed that this was what was keeping me from breathing freely in my singing."

In the course of creating the structure, however, the central focus had been upon "father issues"; and Al Pesso had suggested that there was often a connection between a lack of father-energy and problems in breathing. "That idea came to me as a revelation," Deirdre told me. "I mean, that the problem was *really* about father absence—about a father who was emotionally absent, even when he was at home. And actually, while I was doing the structure—most specifically, during the times when I was connecting to the fellow who played my ideal father—there were moments when I felt very, very safe, as if I could truly 'breathe easy.' . . . As if I could breathe easier, and breathe more deeply, than I ever had before."

Over time, said Deirdre, the effects of this experience had proven to be surprisingly wide-reaching. "One of the first things I noticed after doing that structure—and this is something that's only gotten better over time—is that the breathing aspect of my singing wasn't troubling me, and I was singing much better. Not only was my breathing improved, but all of a sudden, band members were asking *me* for tips on how to improve their singing!" Deirdre laughed. "Also, people who came in as guest singers began inquiring, 'Do you give singing lessons?'"

She laughed again. Gone, I realized, was the whispery voice that was the first thing I'd remarked upon in regard to Deirdre Carmody. "So it wasn't just *me*, noticing a difference; it's clear that other people were noticing, too, that I was changed. . . . Which proved to me that these kinds of traumatic experiences really do lodge in your body in some way." Deirdre paused, then went on to say that during this selfsame time period, she'd had ample opportunities to be exposed to her father's "toxic interaction style."

Then she giggled and said, "Excuse the jargon, but 'toxic' is what my father *is*." To take an example, there had been a recent family reunion during which her father had invited—"by name"—an aunt, an uncle, one of her siblings, and her sibling's husband, to join him at a vacation villa that he'd rented in Italy for the following July. "He'd invited everyone *by name,* except for me. At first I thought that maybe I was being oversensitive. . . . So, after everyone left that evening, I asked him about the dates he was going to be there, so that I could see if I was free. And he frowned, his face darkened—he was really, really *angry*. . . . It was very *obvious* that he hadn't meant to invite me."

And equally obvious, she pointed out, was the fact that her father had wanted her to know she wasn't being invited; otherwise, he could have called the others on the telephone and not invited them right in front of her. So, as a way of defending herself, Deirdre had done her best to sum-mon up the "happier" father memories that had been created during her structure.

"When my real father was targeting me in that way, I tried to imagine the things my 'ideal father' would have been saying. . . . I tried to place that figure in the room and have him say, 'Well, of course I meant to in-clude you! Why else would I have talked about it with you there?' And that helped some. . . . But what helped much *more* was trying to send my body memory back to the structure—to the way my body had felt during the session." In other words, explained Deirdre, "when I felt my body going into the embattled, unloved state—which was what my father wanted—I would send my thoughts back to the structure. . . . I would go back to that moment when Al Pesso was saying to me, 'Now let this feeling of safety, of being loved, of being accepted, extend back into your past and forward into your future. Imagine that *this* is the way that you grew up.' And I would try to recapture that good feeling, hook it into my body again."

And had she been successful? I asked her.

Deirdre paused, then said that to some degree she really had been. "For example, about a week after that incident happened with my father, I was driving along and thinking, Oh, what a mean thing he did. But I didn't take my whole body into it. I could see the clear reality of the situation—he was behaving like a fool—and yet I could remember it without my body getting sucked up in the experience." Then, almost as an afterthought, she added that—at least in her view—that was the basic thing about traumatic mem-ories. These were the memories your body got sucked into, the ones that could take you over completely.

Am I Different?

Although Deirdre's father and my own father bore a distinct resemblance to each other—both had been negative, emotionally absent figures in our early lives—the notion that this lack of "father-energy" might be connected to breathing or vocal problems resonated with nothing in my own experience. My reaction to this situation had been to develop a smoothly competent, self-sufficient exterior, through which no glimmers of neediness might ever become visible.

This required a good deal of vigilance on my part, for even though I thought of my life as divided into two separate segments—one that had to do with an uncared-for little ragamuffin, the other involving a successful wife, mother, and career woman—there was always the danger of leakage from the first narrative to the second one.

Without quite realizing it, I was living on high alert, always scanning for danger, and at the same time always finding some other person—a friend in trouble—to shower with compassion. This was, of course, a reenactment, in my current life, of a familiar scenario: one involving the wary, fearful child of an affectively absent, unpredictable father and a lonely, powerless mother who was in need of comforting.

In brief, while on the outside I looked as if I were unflaggingly secure and in charge, on the inside I was working *hard*, in a state of constant, watchful tension. And this state of hypervigilance, which was reflected in a taut body musculature, often left me feeling one cup short of physical energy; I tended to run out of juice far too easily. These themes and issues tumbled out very rapidly in the course of my first psychomotor structure: It was as if the therapeutic process simply lifted me up, transported me backward in time, and then put me down in the heart of the seemingly discarded part one of my life's story. That portion of my life had to do with a child who'd had hurts and needs of her own, which she'd learned how to ignore and which had gone unattended.

What I remember most clearly from that first structure—I have done others since that time—was the sense of terrible homesickness that assailed me. As Milan Kundera has written, the "Greek word for 'return' is *nostos. Algos* means 'suffering.' So nostalgia is the suffering caused by an unappeased yearning to return." In my case, it was a piercing, unappeased yearning to return to a home that had never even existed—the home in which my ideal father had loved my ideal mother and held her firmly in his embrace while she nurtured and cared for her children. What a chasm had existed between my "real" parents and the ideal ones that Pesso helped me to create during that structure! At some point during the session, I felt an almost physical sensation of something moving inside my body. It was like a boulder rolling away from the mouth of a cave, where so much hurt and grief had been hidden—from my own view as well as the view of those around me.

That particular structure, like all others, had ended with a long, peaceful coda. In this instance, the man who played my ideal father and the woman who played my ideal mother sat just in back of me, their arms entwined around each other affectionately. I, their little child, was snuggled down against and between them, and their free arms were holding me closely and enfolding me securely. It was, for me, an experience of complete relaxation, of being well and unstintingly nurtured by parents who—because of their love for each other—were freely able to love, support, and care for me, their adoring, dependent child. It was a deeply satisfying tableau—a tableau of the family life that I had never known—and I was instructed to linger there awhile, to take it inside me as a "supplemental memory," to *feel* as if I now lived inside a body whose earliest experiences of the world had been different.

Had this experience actually changed me? The best answer I can give is that in the course of researching the various body-oriented methods of therapy—and focusing most intently upon reprocessing and psychomotor structures—I have found that it isn't only the muscles in my jaw that are more relaxed; I feel far more relaxed all over, simply easier in my skin. I have more energy as well.

While I continue to hold the view that there is much that is very valid about the conventional talking therapies, I now believe it to be true that unprocessed, painful memories are often lodged within the nervous circuitry in *physical* locations and are not addressable by means of traditional forms of treatment. These body-based memories, which are very primitive, are not connected to speech or understanding; and they have a way of reasserting their enormous power over a person when they're triggered by a stimulus—being in a similar context, or getting into the same internal state, or experiencing a similar sensation, such as a smell or a taste—that is reminiscent of the original insult. When this happens, the emotions connected to them can surge through the body like a tidal wave and overwhelm the executive functions—the thinking, reasoning powers of the brain.

For my own part, having held so many interviews with secret holders of all kinds and consulted with a variety of researchers in associated fields (as well as having experienced two kinds of body/mind therapy myself), I come away impressed by the ways in which these body-oriented treatments can access not only a person's frontal lobes, but his or her limbic system—the seat of our emotions.

"Have you found me different, in any way, since I've been working on this project?" I asked my husband recently.

"Enormously so, and in important ways," he answered without hesitation.

The research work I'd been doing had, he said, not eliminated any painful childhood memories—it couldn't, obviously—but it had made the hidden places of the past more available to me. "You're just more able to see those things in perspective, as what they are, more finite in size." And as a result, he said, I no longer seemed to hold on to injuries.

Thus, when something from my earlier, familial life was triggered by an event happening in the present—when somebody had hurt my feelings, or I was feeling excluded, or one of our kids was behaving in an uncaring way, or a friend was neglecting me—I was able to separate the current incident from the past. Life's everyday needles and insults didn't linger with me: They were comprehensible, assimilable, not overwhelming. "And that's a matter of *extreme* importance," he repeated, "because the hurt is so diminished, so seen in perspective." That, he said once again, was the most important change he'd seen.

But then he added, "I *love* the person you've become. . . . I've always loved you, loved lots of things about you, but I've felt the shadow of your father. But now I love your ability to love *me*—to look at me through your *own* eyes, not through the eyes of *his* daughter. And that's a matter of extraordinary importance in our relationship, because it means you can trust me and see me as who I am, the *real* me, with all the bad and the good."

SEEKING TREATMENT

1. Reprocessing, or EMDR

For those readers who want to know where to go for further information about the evolving research on EMDR (reprocessing) therapy, or who are interested in a treatment referral, the following suggestions are provided:

Choosing a Clinician

EMDR (or reprocessing) should be administered only by a licensed clinician specifically trained in EMDR. Take time to interview your prospective clinician. Make sure that he or she has the appropriate training in EMDR (basic training is a two-part course) and has kept up with the latest developments. While training is mandatory, it is not sufficient. Choose a clinician who is experienced with EMDR and has a good success rate. Make sure that the clinician is comfortable in treating your particular problem. In addition, it is important that you feel a sense of trust and rapport with the clinician. Every treatment success is an interaction among clinician, client, and method.

Ask:

1. Have they received both levels of training?
2. Was the training approved by the EMDR Institute?

3. Have they kept informed of the latest protocols and developments?
4. How many people with your particular problems or disorder have they treated?
5. What is their success rate?

Background Information: The EMDR Institute

The EMDR Institute has trained over 50,000 clinicians in the EMDR methodology since it was founded in 1990. It maintains an international directory of Institute-trained clinicians for client referrals and trains only qualified mental health professionals according to the strictest professional standards. Trainings authorized by the Institute display the EMDR Institute logo.

For further information on training or referral, the Institute can be reached at:

PO Box 750
Watsonville, CA 95077
(831) 372-3900
fax (831) 647-9881
e-mail: inst@emdr.com
website at http://www.EMDR.com

2. *Psychomotor Therapy (PBSP)*

For those readers who want to know where to go for further information about the evolving research on PBSP (psychomotor) therapy, or who are interested in a treatment referral, the way to make contact is as follows:

To reach the Pesso Boyden System Psychomotor international office, or to reach Albert Pesso directly, or to inquire about a workshop with Albert Pesso, or for the name of a psychomotor therapist in your area, please get in touch with the Psychomotor Institute, Inc., PBSP International Office in New Hampshire. The address is:

Pesso Boyden System Psychomotor
Lake Shore Drive
Franklin, NH 03235
(603) 934-5548
fax: (603) 934-0077
e-mail: pbsp1@aol.com
website: www.pbsp.com

THE PEACE AT HOME
WARNING LIST

Emotional and Economic Attacks

- Destructive Criticism/Verbal Attacks: Name-calling; mocking; accusing; blaming; yelling; swearing; making humiliating remarks or gestures.
- Pressure Tactics: Rushing you to make decisions through "guilt-tripping" and other forms of intimidation; sulking; threatening to withhold money; manipulating the children; telling you what to do.
- Abusing Authority: Always claiming to be right (insisting statements are "the truth"); telling you what to do; making big decisions; using "logic."
- Disrespect: Interrupting; changing topics; not listening or responding; twisting your words; putting you down in front of other people; saying bad things about your friends and family.
- Abusing Trust: Lying; withholding information; cheating on you; being overly jealous.
- Breaking Promises: Not following through on agreements; not taking a fair share of responsibility; refusing to help with child care or housework.
- Emotional Withholding: Not expressing feelings; not giving

support, attention, or compliments; not respecting feelings, rights, or opinions.

- Minimizing, Denying, and Blaming: Making light of behavior and not taking your concerns about it seriously; saying the abuse didn't happen; shifting responsibility for abusive behavior; saying you caused it.
- Economic Control: Interfering with your work or not letting you work; refusing to give you or taking your money; taking your car keys or otherwise preventing you from using the car; threatening to report you to welfare or other social service agencies.
- Self-Destructive Behavior: Abusing drugs or alcohol; threatening suicide or other forms of self-harm; deliberately saying or doing things that will have negative consequences (e.g., telling off the boss).
- Isolation: Preventing or making it difficult for you to see friends or relatives; monitoring phone calls; telling you where you can and cannot go.
- Harassment: Making uninvited visits or exits; following you; checking up on you; embarrassing you in public; refusing to leave when asked.

Acts of Violence

- Intimidation: Making angry or threatening gestures; use of physical size to intimidate; standing in doorway during arguments; out-shouting you; driving recklessly.
- Destruction: Destroying your possessions (e.g., furniture); punching walls; throwing and/or breaking things.
- Threats: Making and/or carrying out threats to hurt you or others.
- Sexual Violence: Degrading treatment or discrimination based on your sex or sexual orientation; using force; threats or coercion to obtain sex or perform sexual acts.
- Physical Violence: Being violent to you, your children, household pets or others; slapping; punching; grabbing; kicking; choking; pushing; biting; burning; stabbing; shooting; etc.

- Weapons: Use of weapons, keeping weapons around which frighten you; threatening or attempting to kill you or those you love.

For further information, please contact:

Peace at Home
PO Box 440044
Somerville, MA 02144
e-mail: peaceathome@aol.com
website: www.peaceathome.org
1-877-546-3737

COMMON RESPONSES
TO TRAUMA

After a trauma—either of the *little-t* (discovering a partner's infidelity) or *big-T* (witnessing a homicide) variety—individuals may display some or many of a variety of typical reactions and responses. Such reactions may be evidenced not only in people who experienced the trauma firsthand, but in those who witnessed or heard about the trauma, or who have been involved with those immediately affected. Many traumatic stress responses can be triggered by persons, places, or things associated with the trauma. Some reactions may appear totally unrelated to the original event or events.

Here is a list of common physical and emotional reactions to trauma. In some real sense, these symptoms and problems can be thought of as normal reactions to sudden, unexpected, frightening experiences that *feel* overwhelming and compromise our capacity to cope.

Emotional Reactions

1. shock and disbelief
2. fear and/or anxiety
3. grief, disorientation, denial
4. hyperalertness or hypervigilance
5. irritability, restlessness, resentment

6. overreactions, including outbursts of anger or rage
7. emotional swings—such as crying and then laughing
8. worrying or ruminating—intrusive thoughts of the trauma
9. nightmares
10. flashbacks—feeling like the trauma is happening now
11. feeling of helplessness, panic
12. increased need to control everyday experiences
13. minimizing the experience
14. attempts to avoid anything associated with trauma
15. tendency to isolate oneself
16. feelings of detachment
17. concern over burdening others with problems
18. emotional numbing or restricted range of feelings
19. an altered sense of time
20. difficulty trusting and/or feelings of betrayal
21. memory lapses or difficulty concentrating
22. feelings of self-blame and/or survivor guilt
23. shame
24. diminished interest in everyday activities or depression
25. unpleasant past memories resurfacing
26. loss of a sense of order or fairness in the world; expectation of doom and fear of the future

Physical Reactions

27. low energy
28. sudden sweating and/or heart palpitations (fluttering)
29. changes in sleep patterns, appetite, interests in sex (more or less than usual)
30. constipation or diarrhea
31. easily startled by noises or unexpected touch
32. more susceptible to colds and illnesses
33. increased use of alcohol or drugs and/or overeating

Developing problems and symptoms in the wake of severely stressful experiences is *not* a sign of personal failure, weakness, or deficiency. Many mentally well-adjusted and physically healthy people will react to awful, uncontrollable life events—either immediately or at a later point in time —with a random assortment of the responses and reactions named above. Moreover, the difficulties inherent in such situations are compounded when the trauma goes underground—when it is felt to be too shameful to discuss with anyone else, or, in some instances, too painful to remain in conscious awareness. Therefore, a vital first step on the pathway to managing the symptoms of trauma is understanding *exactly what they are*, and the range of options now available for treating them.

For further information, see:

The Trauma Center of Boston: www.traumacenter.org
International Association for Traumatic Stress Studies: www.iatss.org

SELECTED BIBLIOGRAPHY

Abramson, M. "Keeping Secrets: Social Workers and AIDS." *Social Work*, 35(2):169–173, 1990.

Allen, Jon G. *Coping with Trauma: A Guide to Self-Understanding*. Washington, D.C.: American Psychiatric Press, 1995.

American Psychiatric Association. *Diagnostic and Statistical Manual of Mental Disorders*. 4th ed. (DMS-IV). Washington, D.C.: American Psychiatric Association, 1994.

Amichai, Yehuda. *A Life of Poetry 1948–1994*. Selected and translated by Benjamin and Barbara Harshav. New York: HarperPerennial, 1994.

Amini, F., et al. "Affect, Attachment, Memory: Contributions Towards Psychobiologic Integration." *Psychiatry*, 59:213–239, 1996.

Arnsten, A. F. T. "The Biology of Being Frazzled." *Science*, 280:1711–1712, 1998.

Bach, George R., and Wyden, Peter. *The Intimate Enemy: How to Fight Fair in Love and Marriage*. New York: Avon, 1968.

Bok, Sissela. *Lying: Moral Choice in Public and Private Life*. New York: Random House, 1989.

———. *On the Ethics of Concealment and Revelation*. New York: Pantheon, 1982.

Botwin, Carol. *Men Who Can't Be Faithful*. New York: Warner, 1988.

Bradshaw, John. *Family Secrets: The Path to Self-Acceptance and Reunion*. New York: Bantam, 1995.

Bremner, J. Douglas. "Does Stress Damage the Brain?" *Biological Psychiatry*, 45:797–805, 1999.

Brown, Emily M. *Patterns of Infidelity and Their Treatment*. 2nd ed. Philadelphia: Brunner-Routledge, 2001.

Cahill, L., et al. "Beta-adrenergic Activation and Memory for Emotional Events." *Nature*, 371:702–704, 1994.

Carter, Rita. *Mapping the Mind*. Berkeley, Calif.: University of California Press, 1998.

Curran, D. *Tyranny of the Spirit: Domination and Submission in Adolescent Relationships*. Northvale, N.J.: Jason Aronson, 1996.

Damasio, Antonio R. *Descartes' Error: Emotion, Reason, and the Human Brain*. New York: Avon, 1994.

———. *The Feeling of What Happens: Body and Emotion in the Making of Consciousness*. New York: Harcourt Brace & Co., 1999.

DiBlasio, Frederick A. "Decision-based Forgiveness Treatment in Cases of Marital Infidelity." *Psychotherapy*, 37(2):149–158, 2000.

Dutton, D. *The Domestic Assault of Women*. Vancouver: UCB Press, 1995.

Dutton, D., and Painter, S. L. "Traumatic Bonding: The Development of Emotional Attachments in Battered Women and Other Relationships of Intermittent Abuse." *Victimology: An International Journal*, 6:139–155, 1981.

Eaker-Weil, Bonnie. *Adultery, the Forgivable Sin: Healing the Inherited Patterns of Betrayal in Your Family*. Seacaucus, N.J.: Carol Pub., 1993.

Edelman, Gerald M., and Changeux, Jean-Pierre, eds. *The Brain*. New Brunswick, N.J.: Transaction Pub., 2001.

Efran, J. S. "Mystery, Abstraction, and Narrative Psychotherapy." *Journal of Constructivist Psychology*, 7:219–227, 1994.

Evans, Patricia. *Verbal Abuse Survivors Speak Out: On Relationship and Recovery*. Holbrook, Mass.: Adams Media Corp., 1993.

———. *The Verbally Abusive Relationship: How to Recognize it and How to Respond*. Holbrook, Mass.: Adams Media Corp., 1996.

Everstine, Diana S., and Everstine, Louis. *The Trauma Response: Treatment for Emotional Injury*. New York: W. W. Norton, 1993.

Figley, Charles R. *Treating Stress in Families*. New York: Brunner/Mazel, 1989.

Figley, Charles R., and Kleber, Rolf J. "Beyond the 'Victim': Secondary Traumatic Stress," in R. J. Kleber, C. R. Figley, and B. P. R. Gersons, eds., *Beyond Trauma: Cultural and Societal Dynamics*. New York: Plenum Press, 1995.

Follingstad, D. R., et al. "The Role of Emotional Abuse in Physically Abusive Relationships." *Journal of Family Violence*, 5:107–120, 1990.

Ford, Charles V. *Lies! Lies!! Lies!!! The Psychology of Deceit*. Washington, D.C.: American Psychiatric Press, 1996.

Forster, E. M. *A Room with a View*. New York: Dover Pub., 1995.

Freyd, Jennifer J. *Betrayal Trauma: The Logic of Forgetting Childhood Abuse*. Cambridge, Mass.: Harvard University Press, 1996.

Friedman, Sonya. *Secret Loves: Women with Two Lives*. New York: Crown, 1994.

Geller, Janet A. *Breaking Destructive Patterns: Multiple Strategies for Treating Partner Abuse*. New York: Free Press, 1992.

Gerhardt, Pam. "The Emotional Cost of Infidelity." *Washington Post*, Health, March 30, 1999.

Glass, S. P. "Beyond Betrayal: Post-Traumatic Reactions to the Disclosure of Infidelity." *Professional Counselor*, 13(1), Feb. 1998.

Glass, S. P., and Wright, T. L. "Clinical Implications of Research on Extramarital Involvement," in Robert A. Brown and Joan R. Field, eds., *Treatment of Sexual Problems in Individual and Couples Therapy*. New York: PMA Pub., 1988.

———. "Justifications for Extramarital Relationships: The Association Between Attitudes, Behaviors, and Gender." *Journal of Sex Research*, 29(3):351–357, 1992.

———. "Reconstructing Marriages After the Trauma of Infidelity," in W. K. Halford and H. J. Markman, eds., *Clinical Handbook of Marriage and Couples Interventions*. New York: Wiley, 1997.

———. "Sex Differences in Type of Extramarital Involvement and Marital Dissatisfaction." *Sex Roles*, 12:1101–1120, 1985.

Goldner, Virginia, et al. "Love and Violence: Gender Paradoxes in Volatile Attachments." *Family Process*, 29(4):343–364, 1990.

Goleman, Daniel. *Vital Lies, Simple Truths: The Psychology of Self-Deception*. New York: Simon & Schuster, 1985.

Greenacre, Phyllis. "The Impostor." *Psychoanalytic Quarterly*, 27:359–382, 1958.

———. *Trauma, Growth, and Personality*. New York: W. W. Norton, 1952.

Greenough, W. T., Black, J. E., and Wallace, C. S. "Experience and Brain Development." *Child Development*, 58:539–559, 1987.

Grolnick, Lawrence. "Ibsen's Truth, Family Secrets, and Family Therapy." *Family Process*, 22(3):275–288, 1983.

Grotstein, J. "Nothingness, Meaninglessness, Chaos and 'the Black Hole,' II: The Black Hole." *Contemporary Psychoanalysis*, 26(3):377–407, 1990.

Herman, Judith L. *Trauma and Recovery*. New York: Basic Books, 1992.

Imber Coppersmith, Evan. "We've Got a Secret! A Non-marital Marital Therapy," in A. S. Gurman, ed., *Casebook of Marital Therapy*. New York: Guilford Press, 1985.

Imber-Black, Evan. *The Secret Life of Families: Truth-Telling, Privacy, and Reconciliation in a Tell-All Society*. New York: Bantam, 1998.

Janoff-Bulman, Ronnie. *Shattered Assumptions: Towards a New Psychology of Trauma*. New York: Free Press, 1992.

Kandel, E. R. "A New Intellectual Framework for Psychiatry." *American Journal of Psychiatry*, 155(4):457–469, 1998.

Karpel, Mark A. "Family Secrets." *Family Process*, 19(3):295–306, 1980.

Kaslow, F. "Attractions and Affairs: Fabulous and Fatal." *Journal of Family Psychotherapy*, 4:1–34, 1993.

Kendler, K. S., et al. "Stressful Life Events and Previous Episodes in the Etiology of Major Depression in Women." *American Journal of Psychiatry*, 157:1243–1251, 2000.

Kernberg, O. F. "Aggression and Love in the Relationship of the Couple." *Journal of the American Psychoanalytic Association*, 39:45–70, 1991.

Kessler, R. C., Sonnega, A., and Bromet, E. "Posttraumatic Stress Disorder in the National Comorbidity Survey." *Archives of General Psychiatry*, 52(12):1048–1060, 1995.

Kirkwood, Catherine. *Leaving Abusive Partners*. London: SAGE Pub., 1993.

Kreisman, J. J., and Straus, H. *I Hate You, Don't Leave Me: Understanding the Borderline Personality*. New York: Avon, 1989.

Krystal, H. "Trauma and Affects." *Psychoanalytic Study of the Child*, 33:81–116, 1978.

Lachkar, Joan. *The Many Faces of Abuse: Treating the Emotional Abuse of High-Functioning Women*. Northvale, N.J.: Jason Aronson, 1998.

Lawson, Annette. *Adultery: An Analysis of Love and Betrayal*. New York: Basic Books, 1988. Lecovin, K. E., and Penfold, P. S. "The Emotionally Abused Woman: An Existential-Phenomenological Exploration." *Canadian Journal of Community Health*, 15(1):30–47, 1996.

LeDoux, J. E. *The Emotional Brain: The Mysterious Underpinnings of Emotional Life*. New York: Simon & Schuster, 1996.

LeDoux, J. E., Xagoraris, A., and Romanski, L. "Indelibility of Subcortical Emotional Memories." *Journal of Cognitive Neuroscience*, 1:238–243, 1989.

Lerner, Harriet G. *The Dance of Deception: Pretending and Truth-Telling in Women's Lives*. New York: HarperCollins, 1993.

Levine, Peter A., and Frederick, Ann. *Waking the Tiger: Healing Trauma*. Berkeley, Calif.: North Atlantic Books, 1997.

Lewis, Michael, and Saarni, Carolyn, eds. *Lying and Deception in Everyday Life*. New York: Guilford Press, 1993.

Loring, Marti Tamm. *Emotional Abuse: The Trauma and the Treatment*. San Francisco, Calif.: Jossey-Bass, 1994.

Lusterman, Don-David. *Infidelity: A Survival Guide*. Oakland, Calif.: New Harbinger Pub., 1998.

Marans, Steven, and Adelman, Anne. "Experiencing Violence in a Developmental Context," in J. Osofsky, ed., *Children in a Violent Society*. New York: Guilford Press, 1997.

McDougall, Joyce. *Theaters of the Body: A Psychoanalytic Approach to Psychosomatic Illness*. New York: W. W. Norton, 1989.

———. *Theaters of the Mind: Illusion and Truth on the Psychoanalytic Stage*. New York: Brunner/Mazel, 1985.

McGaugh, J. L. "Involvement of Hormonal and Neuromodulatory Systems in the Regulation of Memory Storage." *Annual Review of Neuroscience*, 12:255–287, 1989.

———. "Significance and Remembrance: The Role of Neuromodulatory Systems." *Psychological Science*, 1:15–25, 1990.

McGoldrick, M., and Gerson, R. *Genograms in Family Assessment*. New York: W. W. Norton, 1985.

Mishkin, M., and Appenzeller, T. "The Anatomy of Memory." *Scientific American*, 256(6):80–89, 1987.

Nagy, L. M., et al. "Open Prospective Trial of Fluoxetine for Posttraumatic Stress Disorder." *Journal of Clinical Psychopharmacology*, 13:107–113, 1993.

Najavits, Lisa M. *Seeking Safety: A Treatment Manual for PTSD and Substance Abuse*. New York: Guilford Press, 2002.

Napier, Augustus Y. *The Fragile Bond: In Search of an Equal, Intimate and Enduring Marriage*. New York: Harper & Row, 1988.

Napier, Nancy J. *Getting Through the Day: Strategies for Adults Hurt as Children*. New York: W. W. Norton, 1993.

Neubeck, Gerhard. *Extramarital Relations*. Englewood Cliffs, N.J.: Prentice-Hall, 1969.

NiCarthy, Ginny. *Getting Free: A Handbook for Women in Abusive Relationships*. Seattle, Wash.: Seal Press, 1986.

Nisenbaum, L. K., et al. "Prior Exposure to Chronic Stress Results in Enhanced Synthesis and Release of Hippocampal Norepinephrine in Response to a Novel Stressor." *Journal of Neuroscience*, 11:1478–1484, 1991.

Notarius, Clifford, and Markman, Howard. *We Can Work It Out: Making Sense of Marital Conflict*. New York: Putnam, 1993.

Othmer, E., and Othmer, S. C. *Life on a Roller Coaster: Coping with the Ups and Downs of Mood Disorders*. New York: Berkley, 1989.

Ornitz, E. M. "Developmental Aspects of Neurophysiology," in M. Lewis, ed., *Child and Adolescent Psychiatry: A Comprehensive Textbook*. Baltimore, Md.: Williams & Wilkins, 1991.

Osofsky, J. D. "The Effects of Exposure to Violence on Young Children." *American Psychologist*, 50(9):782–788, 1995.

Panksepp, Jaak. *Affective Neuroscience: The Foundations of Human and Animal Emotions*. New York: Oxford University Press, 1998.

Pesso, Albert, and Crandell, John, eds. *Moving Psychotherapy: Theory and Application of Pesso System/Psychomotor Therapy*. Cambridge, Mass.: Brookline Books, 1991.

Pitman, R. K. "Post-Traumatic Stress Disorder, Hormones, and Memory." *Biological Psychiatry*, 26:221–223, 1989.

Porterfield, Kay Marie. *Violent Voices: Twelve Steps to Freedom from Verbal and Emotional Abuse*. Deerfield Beach, Fla.: Health Communications, 1989.

Reiser, Morton F. *Mind, Brain, Body: Toward a Convergence of Psychoanalysis and Neurobiology*. New York: Basic Books, 1984.

Rich, Adrienne. *On Lies, Secrets, and Silence*. New York: W. W. Norton, 1979.

Rosenbaum, A., and O'Leary, K. D. "Marital Violence: Characteristics of Abusive Couples." *Journal of Consulting and Clinical Psychology*, 49:63–71, 1981.

Rosenblum L. A., and Andrews, M. W. "Influences of Environmental Demand on Maternal Behavior and Infant Development." *Acta Paediatrica*, Supplement 397(83):57–63, 1994.

Rothschild, Babette. *The Body Remembers: The Psychophysiology of Trauma and Trauma Treatment*. New York: W. W. Norton, 2000.

———. "Defining Shock and Trauma in Body Psychotherapy." *Energy and Character*, 26(2):61–65, 1995.

Sampson, Ronald V. *The Psychology of Power*. New York: Pantheon, 1965.

Sartre, Jean Paul. *Being and Nothingness: An Essay on Phenomenological Ontology*. New York: Philosophical Library, 1956.

Schneider, J. P., Corley, M. D., and Irons, R. R. "Surviving Disclosure of Infidelity: Results of an International Survey of 164 Recovering Sex Addicts and Partners." *Sexual Addiction and Compulsivity*, 5:189–217, 1998.

Schuham, A., and Bird, H. W. "The Marriage and the Affairs of the 'Anxious' Man of Prominence." *American Journal of Family Therapy*, 18(2):141–152, 1990.

Seagull, E. A., and Seagull, A. A. "Healing the Wound That Must Not Heal: Psychotherapy with Survivors of Domestic Violence." *Psychotherapy*, 28:16–20, 1991.

Shapiro, Francine. *Eye Movement Desensitization and Reprocessing (EMDR)*. 2nd ed. New York: Guilford Press, 2001.

Shapiro, Francine, and Forrest, Margot S. *Eye Movement Desensitization and Reprocessing (EMDR)*. New York: Basic Books, 1997.

Shay, Jonathan. *Achilles in Vietnam: Combat Trauma and the Undoing of Character*. New York: Maxwell Macmillan International, 1994.

Shengold, Leonard. *Soul Murder: The Effects of Childhood Abuse and Deprivation*. New Haven, Conn.: Yale University Press, 1989.

Singer, Jefferson A., and Salovey, Peter. *The Remembered Self: Emotion and Memory in Personality*. New York: Free Press, 1993.

Southwick, S. M., et al. "Role of Norepinephrine in the Pathophysiology and Treatment of Posttraumatic Stress Disorder." *Biological Psychiatry*, 46:1192–1204, 1999.

Spanier, G. B., and Margolis, R. L. "Marital Separation and Extramarital Sexual Behavior." *Journal of Sex Research*, 19(1):23–48, 1983.

Spence, Donald P. *Narrative Truth and Historical Truth: Meaning and Interpretation in Psychoanalysis*. New York: W. W. Norton, 1982.

Sperry, L., and Maniaci, H. "The Histrionic-obsessive Couple," in L. Sperry and J. Carlson, eds., *The Disordered Couple*. Bristol, Penn.: Brunner/Mazel, 1998.

Spiegel, D., and Cardeña, E. "Disintegrated Experience: The Dissociative Disorders Revisited." *Journal of Abnormal Psychology*, 100:366–378, 1991.

Spring, Janis A., and Spring, Michael. *After the Affair: Healing the Pain and Rebuilding Trust*. New York: HarperCollins, 1996.

Squire, Larry R., "Mechanisms of Memory." *Science*, 232:1612–1619, 1986.

———. "Memory and the Hippocampus: A Synthesis from Findings with Rats, Monkeys, and Humans." *Psychological Review*, 99:195–231, 1992.

Squire, Larry R. and Kandel, Eric R. *Memory: From Mind to Molecules*. New York: Scientific American Library, 2000.

Steiner, Claude M. *Scripts People Live: Transactional Analysis of Life Scripts*. New York: Grove Press, 1974.

Stosny, Steven. *Treating Attachment Abuse: A Compassionate Approach*. New York: Springer Pub., 1995.

Straus, M. A. "Victims and Aggressors in Marital Violence." *American Behavioral Scientist*, 23(5):681–704, 1980.

Strean, Herbert S. *The Extramarital Affair*. New York: Free Press, 1980.

Subotnik, Rona, and Harris, Gloria G. *Surviving Infidelity: Making Decisions, Recovering from the Pain*. 2nd ed. Holbrook, Mass.: Adams Media Corp., 1999.

Suomi, S. J. "Early Stress and Adult Reactivity in Rhesus Monkeys," in G. Bock and J. Whelan, eds., *The Childhood Environment and Adult Disease*. New York: Wiley, 1991.

Taylor, Richard. *Having Love Affairs*. Buffalo, N.Y.: Prometheus Books, 1982.

Tolman, R. M. "Psychological Abuse of Women," in Robert T. Ammerman and Michel Hersen, eds., *Assessment of Family Violence: A Clinical and Legal Sourcebook*. New York: Wiley, 1992.

Tosone, Carol, and Aiello, Theresa, eds. *Love and Attachment: Contemporary Issues and Treatment Considerations*. Northvale, N.J.: Jason Aronson, 1999.

Uno, H., et al. "Hippocampal Damage Associated with Prolonged and Fatal Stress in Primates." *Journal of Neuroscience*, 9:1705–1711, 1989.

Van der Kolk, Bessel A. *Psychological Trauma*. Washington, D.C.: American Psychiatric Press, 1987.

Van der Kolk, Bessel A., McFarlane, Alexander C., and Weisaeth, Lars, eds. *Traumatic Stress: The Effects of Overwhelming Experience on Mind, Body, and Society*. New York: Guilford Press, 1996.

Walker, Lenore E. *The Battered Woman*. New York: Harper & Row, 1979.

Webster, Harriet. *Family Secrets: How Telling and Not Telling Affect Our Children, Our Relationships, and Our Lives*. Reading, Mass.: Addison-Wesley, 1991.

Weiner, Marcella B., and DiMele, Armand. *Repairing Your Marriage After His Affair: A Woman's Guide to Hope and Healing*. Rocklin, Calif.: Prima Pub., 1998.

Weitzman, Susan. *Not to People Like Us: Domestic Abuse in Upscale Families*. New York: Basic Books, 2000.

Wiederman, M. W. "Extramarital Sex: Prevalence and Correlates in a National Survey." *Journal of Sex Research*, 34:167–174, 1997.

Wilson, S. K., Cameron, S., Jaffe, P., and Wolfe, D. "Children Exposed to Wife Abuse: An Intervention Model." *Social Casework*, 70(3):180–184, 1989.

Winter, David G. *The Power Motive*. New York: Free Press, 1973.

Wolf, Marion E., and Mosnaim, Aron D., eds. *Posttraumatic Stress Disorder: Etiology, Phenomenology, and Treatment*. Washington, D.C.: American Psychiatric Press, 1990.

Yehuda, Rachel, ed. *Psychological Trauma*. Washington, D.C.: American Psychiatric Press, 1998.

Young, G. H., and Gerson, S. "Masochism and Spouse Abuse." *Psychotherapy*, 28(1): 30–38, 1991.

Index

—

PHOTO © JOYCE RAVID

MAGGIE SCARF, the author of *Unfinished Business*, *Intimate Partners*, and *Intimate Worlds*, is a senior fellow at the Bush Center in Child Development and Social Policy at Yale University and a member of the Advisory Board of the Poynter Fellowship in Journalism at Yale. She is currently a contributing editor to *The New Republic* and has served on the Oxygen/Markle Pulse Advisory Board; she also served as a member of the advisory board of the American Psychiatric Press for a decade (1990–2000). She has been a Ford Foundation fellow and a Nieman fellow in journalism at Harvard University, an Alicia Patterson Foundation fellow, has twice been a fellow of the Center for Advanced Study in the Behavioral Sciences at Stanford University, and is a grantee of the Smith Richardson Foundation, Inc. She has received several National Media Awards from the American Psychological Foundation. She lives in Connecticut with her husband and is the mother of three married daughters.

About the Type

This book was set in Electra, a typeface designed for Linotype by
W. A. Dwiggins, the renowned type designer (1880–1956). Electra
is a fluid typeface, avoiding the contrasts of thick and thin strokes
that are prevalent in most modern typefaces.

HOLMAN *QuickSource*™

BIBLE
DICTIONARY

HOLMAN
REFERENCE

Holman Reference
Nashville, Tennessee

Holman QuickSource Bible Dictionary
© 2005 by Holman Bible Publishers
Nashville, Tennessee
All rights reserved

Maps © 1998 by Holman Bible Publishers
Nashville, Tennessee
All rights reserved

Scripture quotations, unless otherwise noted, have been taken from
the *Holman Christian Standard Bible*®.
Copyright © 1999, 2000, 2002, 2004
Holman Bible Publishers.

Scripture quotations marked NASB are taken from the *New American Standard Bible*®.
Copyright © 1960, 1962, 1963, 1968, 1971, 1973, 1975, 1977, 1995
by the Lockman Foundation. Used by permission.

Scripture quotations marked NRSV are taken from the New Revised Standard Version.
Copyright © 1989 by the Division of Christian Education of the National Council
of the Churches of Christ in the United States of America.
Used by permission. All rights reserved.

Scripture quotations marked NIV are taken from the
Holy Bible, New International Version.
Copyright © 1973, 1978, 1984 by the International Bible Society.

Scripture quotations marked REB are taken from *The Revised English Bible.*
Copyright © Oxford University Press and Cambridge University Press, 1989.
All rights reserved. Reprinted by permission.

Dewey Decimal Classification: 220.3
Subject Heading: BIBLE--DICTIONARIES

ISBN 10: 0-8054-9446-4
ISBN 13: 978-0-8054-9446-4

Printed in the USA
2 3 4 5 6 08 07 06
DBS

EDITORIAL FOREWORD

Over two hundred years ago, Voltaire predicted that the Bible would pass from the scene within a generation and become just a historical relic. Yet as late as March 2004, Tom Brokaw reported on *NBC Nightly News* that 40 percent of Americans read the Bible once a day.

The staying power of the Bible is phenomenal. It's amazing that a collection of 66 books, written over a period of 1,500 years by 40 persons from 40 different generations, continues to be the bestseller it is.

Mortimer Adler and Charles Van Doren claimed that in Western civilization the Bible has not only been the most widely read book but the most carefully read book. It has also been the most carefully preserved and transmitted book in history. Bernard Ramm wrote,

> Jews preserved it as no other manuscript has ever been preserved. With their massora . . . they kept tabs on every letter, syllable, word and paragraph. They had special classes of men within their culture whose sole duty was to preserve and transmit these documents with practically perfect fidelity—scribes, lawyers, massoretes. Who ever counted the letters and syllables and words of Plato or Aristotle? Cicero or Seneca? (Bernard Ramm, *Protestant Christian Evidences*, Chicago: Moody Press, 1957).

The Bible is a life-changing book. It is designed by its Author to transform both individuals and whole cultures—and it has. Even those who deny the Bible's divine authority and complete truthfulness benefit from living in a civilization whose most desirable qualities have been shaped by the Bible.

The same great care is called for in reading and understanding the Bible as has been exercised in its preservation and transmission. As we grow in our understanding of the background out of which the Bible comes, so we will grow in our comprehension of what the Bible says. To this end, Holman is pleased to make available this highly portable Bible dictionary that can slip into a pocket, briefcase, purse, or backpack. Worlds of information are available in other volumes. But for starters, for those who are looking for succinct background information in a handy format, the *Holman QuickSource Bible Dictionary* will be a perfect tool.

Holman Bible Publishers

The Abana River (modern Barad River) flows through the country of Syria.

AARON Moses' brother; Israel's first high priest. His parents Amram and Jochebed were from the tribe of Levi, Israel's tribe of priests (Exod. 6:16-26). Miriam was his sister.

AARON'S ROD Aaron used a rod to demonstrate to the pharaoh that the God of the Hebrews was Lord. It became a snake when cast down (Exod. 7:8-13) and brought about the first three plagues (Exod. 7:19-20; 8:5-7,16-19). This rod was the same one used to strike the rocks at Horeb and Kadesh to bring forth water (Exod. 17:1-7; Num. 20:7-11).

ABANA or **ABANAH** (NASB) River in Syria. In his anger Naaman wanted to wash here rather than in the dirty Jordan (2 Kings 5:12).

ABBA Aramaic word for "father" used by Jesus to speak of His own intimate relationship with God, a relationship that others can enter through faith.

ABEDNEGO In Dan. 1:7 the Babylonian name given to Azariah, one of the three Hebrew youths who were conscripted along with Daniel to serve in the king's court. God delivered them from the fiery furnace (Dan. 2:48–3:30).

ABEL Though best known as the name of the second son of Adam and Eve, the word *abel* also occurs frequently meaning "vanity, breath, or vapor." See *Ecclesiastes, Book of.*

Perhaps as a personal name, Abel alludes to the shortness of life. Such was the case with Abel (Gen. 4:8). Having offered "by faith ... a better sacrifice than Cain" (Heb. 11:4 HCSB), he was murdered by Cain. Why Abel's sacrifice as a keeper of flocks was better than Cain's, whose sacrifice came from harvested fruits, is not directly stated in Gen. 4:4.

ABIATHAR Personal name meaning "father of abundance." The son of Ahimelech and the eleventh high priest in succession from Aaron through the line of Eli. He survived the slaughter of the priests at Nob and fled to David, hiding in the cave of Adullam from King Saul (1 Sam. 22). Having escaped with the ephod, Abiathar became the high priest and chief counselor for David (1 Sam. 23:6-12; 30:7).

ABIB Month of the exodus deliverance from Egypt (Exod. 13:4) and thus of the Passover festival (Exod. 23:15; 34:18; Deut. 16:1).

ABIGAIL Personal name meaning "my father rejoiced." **1.** Wife of David after being wife of Nabal. She was praised for wisdom in contrast to Nabal, her arrogant and overbearing husband, who was a large landowner and successful shepherd. **2.** Sister of David and the mother of Amasa (1 Chron. 2:16-17), married to Jether, an Ishmaelite (also called Ithra). Amasa, her son, was at one time the commander of David's army (2 Sam. 17:25).

ABIHU Personal name meaning "my father is he." The second son of Aaron; one of Israel's first priests (Exod. 6:23; 28:1). He saw God along with Moses, Aaron, his brother, and 70 elders (Exod. 24:9-10). He and his brother Nadab offered "strange fire" before God (Lev. 10:1-22), resulting in judgment. God's fire consumed them.

ABILENE Small mountainous region ruled by the tetrarch Lysanias at the time that John the Baptist began his public ministry (Luke 3:2-3). Abilene was located about 18 miles northwest of Damascus in the Anti-Lebanon mountain range. Its capital was Abila.

ABIMELECH Personal name meaning "my father is king." **1.** King of Gerar, who took Sarah for himself, thinking she was Abraham's sister rather than his wife (Gen. 20). He restored her to Abraham after a nighttime dream of God. **2.** Probably the same as 1., a king who disputed the ownership of a well at Beer-sheba with Abraham and then made a covenant of peace with him (Gen. 21:22-34). **3.** King of Philistines at Gerar related to or identical with 1. Isaac lived under his protection and fearfully passed Rebekah, his wife, off as his sister. Abimelech scolded Isaac and warned his people not to touch Rebekah. A dispute over water wells led to Isaac's leaving but finally to a treaty of peace (Gen. 26) at Beer-sheba. **4.** Son of Gideon, the judge of Israel (Judg. 8:31). **5.** Priest under David with Zadok (1 Chron. 18:16), but correct reading of text here is probably Ahimelech as in 2 Sam. 8:17. **6.** Person mentioned in title of Ps. 34, which apparently refers to 1 Sam. 21:10-15, where Achish is David's opponent. Abimelech may have been an official title for Philistine kings.

ABINADAB Personal name meaning "my father is generous." **1.** Resident of Kirjath-jearim whose house was the resting place of the ark of the covenant for 20 years after the Philistines returned it. His son Eleazar served as priest (1 Sam. 7:1-2). **2.** Son of Jesse passed over when David was selected as king (1 Sam. 16:8; 17:13). **3.** Son of King Saul killed by Philistines in battle of Mount Gilboa (1 Sam. 31:2). **4.** Solomon's official and son-in-law over Dor, the Mediterranean seaport below Mount Carmel, was the Son of Abinadab or Ben-abinadab (1 Kings 4:11).

ABIRAM Personal name meaning "my father is exalted." **1.** Leader of rebellion against Moses and Aaron, seeking priestly authority. He died when God caused the earth to open and swallow the rebels (Num. 16; 26:9-11). **2.** Son of Hiel sacrificed in foundation of rebuilt Jericho, fulfilling Joshua's warning (1 Kings 16:34).

ABISHAG Personal name meaning "my father strayed" or "is a wanderer." A young virgin or "maiden" (RSV) brought to David's bed in his last days to keep him warm (1 Kings 1:1-4). They had no sexual relations, but Solomon considered her David's wife when his brother Adonijah asked to marry her after David's death (1 Kings 2:17).

ABISHAI Personal name meaning "father exists." Son of David's sister Zeruiah and brother of Joab, David's general (1 Sam 26:6; 1 Chron. 2:15-16).

ABISHALOM Personal name meaning "my father is peace." Another spelling for Absalom (1 Kings 15:2,10). See *Absalom.*

ABLUTIONS Ceremonial washings with water to make oneself pure before worship. The practice of ablutions is one background for NT baptism. The Hebrew term *rachats* is the everyday word for washing with water, rinsing, or bathing (Gen. 18:4; Exod. 2:5; Ruth 3:3). The Greek word *louein* is similar (Acts 9:37; 16:33; 2 Pet. 2:22).

ABNER Personal name meaning "father is a lamp." The chief military officer for King Saul and Saul's uncle (1 Sam. 14:50). At Saul's death, he supported Ish-bosheth, Saul's son (2 Sam. 2:8) until Ish-bosheth accused him of treason for taking one of Saul's concubines (2 Sam. 3:7-8). Abner transferred loyalty to David. Joab, David's general, went into a jealous rage when David welcomed Abner. Joab then killed Abner, who was buried in Hebron (2 Sam. 3). See 1 Sam. 17:55-58; 20:25; 26:5, 14-15.

ABOMINATION, ABOMINATION OF DESOLATION That which is detestable to God and is particularly related to idolatry. "Abomination of desolation" is a special term in the book of Daniel and in these NT references: Matt. 24:15; Mark 13:14.

ABRAHAM Personal name meaning "father of a multitude." The first Hebrew patriarch, he became known as the prime example of faith. He was the son of Terah, a descendant of Noah's son, Shem (Gen. 11:27). His childhood was spent in Ur of the Chaldees, a prominent Sumerian city. He was known at

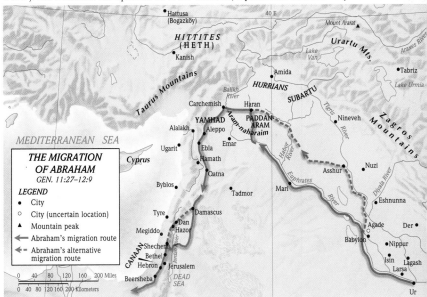

THE MIGRATION OF ABRAHAM
GEN. 11:27–12:9

LEGEND
- City
- City (uncertain location)
- Mountain peak
- Abraham's migration route
- Abraham's alternative migration route

the beginning as "Abram" ("father is exalted"), but this was changed subsequently to "Abraham" ("father of a multitude," Gen. 17:5).

Terah, his father, moved to Haran with the family (Gen. 11:31) and after some years died there. God called Abram to migrate to Canaan, assuring him that he would father a vast nation. At different times he lived in Shechem, Bethel, Hebron, and Beer-sheba. His wife Sarai's beauty attracted the pharaoh when they moved to Egypt during a famine (Gen. 12:10), but God intervened to save her. The trouble arose partly because Abram had claimed her as his sister rather than his wife, and in fact she was his half sister (Gen. 20:12). After returning to Palestine, Abram received further covenantal assurances from God (Gen. 15). He decided he could produce offspring by taking Sarai's handmaid Hagar as a concubine. Though the union produced a son, Ishmael, he was not destined to become Abram's promised heir. Even after another covenantal assurance (Gen. 17:1-21) in which the rite of circumcision was made a covenantal sign, Abram and Sarai still questioned God's promise of an heir.

Then Sarai, whose name had been changed to Sarah ("princess"), had her long-promised son, Isaac ("laughter"), when Abraham was 100 years old. Ishmael's presence caused trouble in the family, and he was expelled with his mother Hagar to the wilderness of Paran. Abraham's faith and obedience were tested by God in Moriah when he was commanded to sacrifice Isaac. God provided an alternative sacrifice, however, saving the boy's life. As a reward for Abraham's faithfulness, God renewed the covenant promises of great blessing and the growth of a mighty nation to father and son.

Subsequently, Sarah died and was buried in the cave of Machpelah (Gen. 23:19), after which Abraham sought a bride for Isaac. A woman named Rebekah was obtained from Abraham's relatives in Mesopotamia, and Isaac married her (Gen. 24:67). In old age Abraham remarried and had further children, finally dying after 175 years. Abraham recognized God as the almighty Lord of all and the author of a covenant by which the Hebrews would become a mighty nation. God Himself was known subsequently as the God of Abraham (Exod. 3:6). Through him God had revealed His plan for human salvation (Exod. 2:24). The promises to Abraham became assurance for future generations (Exod. 32:13; 33:1). Abraham became known as "God's friend forever" (2 Chron. 20:7).

John and Paul showed that descent from Abraham did not guarantee salvation (Matt. 3:9; Rom. 9). Indeed, foreigners would join Him in the kingdom (Matt. 8:11; cp. Luke 16:23-30). Lost sons of Abraham, Jesus invited to salvation (Luke 19:9). True children of Abraham do the works of Abraham (John 8:39).

For Paul, Abraham was the great example of faith (Rom. 4; Gal. 3). In Hebrews Abraham provided the model for tithing (Heb. 7) and played a prominent role in the roll call of faith (Heb. 11). James used Abraham to show that justification by faith is proved in works (James 2:21-24).

ABRAHAM'S BOSOM Place to which the angels carried the poor man Lazarus when he died. The Roman custom of reclining at meals was common among the Jews. Such positioning placed one in the bosom of the neighboring person. To be next to the host, that is to recline in the bosom of the host, was considered the highest honor. Lazarus was comforted after death by being given the place of closest fellowship with the father of the whole Hebrew nation (Luke 16:22-23). See *Heaven*.

ABRAM Personal name meaning "father is exalted." The name of Abraham ("father of a multitude") in Gen. 11:26–17:4. See *Abraham*.

ABSALOM Personal name meaning "father of peace." Third son of King David, who rebelled against his father and was murdered by Joab, David's commander (2 Sam. 3:3; 13–19). See *Abishalom*.

ABYSS Transliteration of Greek word *abussos*, literally meaning "without bottom." KJV translates "the deep" or "bottomless" pit. NASB, NIV, RSV use "abyss" to refer to the dark abode of the dead (Rom. 10:7). Abaddon rules the abyss (Rev. 9:11), from which will come the beast of the end time of Revelation (11:7). The beast of the abyss

So-called Tomb of Absalom in the Kidron Valley in Jerusalem.

faces ultimate destruction (Rev. 17:8), and Satan will be bound there during the millennium (Rev. 20:1-3). See *Hades; Hell; Sheol.*

ACACIA Hardwood with a beautiful fine grain or close grain, which darkens as it ages. Insects find the taste of acacia wood distasteful, and its density makes it difficult for water or other decaying agents to penetrate.

Moses received the instructions for building the tabernacle on Mount Sinai (Exod. 25–35), in the Arabian Desert (Gal. 4:25) where acacia is among the larger of the few timber species to be found. Items constructed for the tabernacle of acacia (shittim) wood include: the ark of the covenant and its poles, the table of showbread and its poles, the brazen altar and its poles, the incense altar and its poles, and all the poles for the hanging of the curtains and the supports (Exod. 36:20,31,36; 37; 38).

ACCO or **ACCHO** (KJV) Place-name for famous Mediterranean seaport north of Mount Carmel. Territory was assigned to tribe of Asher, but they could not conquer it (Judg. 1:31). The Greeks renamed Acco, Ptolemaïs.

ACCOUNTABILITY, AGE OF Age at which God holds children accountable for their sins. When persons come to this point, they face the inevitability of divine judgment if they fail to repent and believe the gospel.

Port of Acco from the south.

ACCURSED Translation of Hebrew *cherem*, a technical term in warfare for items captured from the enemy and devoted to God. Paul used a technical Greek term, *anathema*, to call for persons to be put under a holy ban or be accursed (Rom. 9:3; 1 Cor. 12:3; Gal. 1:8-9; cp. 1 Cor. 16:22). Paul used the term in the sense of the Hebrew *cherem*. See *Anathema; Blessing and Cursing.*

ACCUSER Legal term describing a person who claims another is guilty of a crime or a moral offense. The Hebrew word for accuser is *Satan* (cp. Ps. 109:6 in various translations). See *Satan.*

ACELDAMA or **AKELDAMA** (KJV) Judas Iscariot purchased this field where he killed himself (Acts 1:19). The name is Aramaic and means "field of blood."

ACHAIA Roman province that consisted roughly of the southern half of ancient Greece, including the Peloponnesus. Major cities in Achaia included Sparta, Athens, and Corinth, which was the administrative center. Paul preached successfully in the province (Acts 18:27-28).

ACHAN or **ACHAR** (1 Chron. 2:7). In Josh. 7:1, a Judahite whose theft of a portion of the spoil from Jericho brought divine displeasure and military defeat on the Israelite army.

ACHBOR Personal name meaning "mouse." **1.** Father of king in Edom (Gen. 36:38). **2.** Man that King Josiah commissioned to ask God the meaning of the book of the Law found in the temple (2 Kings 22:12-14). **3.** Father of Elnathan, whom Jehoiakim sent to bring back the prophet Uriah from Egypt in order to execute him (Jer. 26:22; cp. 36:12).

ACHISH Philistine personal name. **1.** King of Gath, a Philistine city, to whom David fled in fear of Saul (1 Sam. 21:10). **2.** King of Gath to whom Shimei went to retrieve his servants but in so doing violated his agreement with Solomon and lost his life (1 Kings 2:36-46).

ACHOR Place-name meaning "trouble, affliction," or "taboo." The valley in which Achan and his household were stoned to death (Josh. 7:24-26). Later, it formed part of the border of Judah. It is the subject of prophetic promises in Isa. 65:10 and Hos. 2:15. See *Joshua.*

ACHSA or **ACHSAH** (NASB, RSV, TEV) or **ACSAH** (NIV) Personal name meaning "bangle" or "ankle ornament." Daughter of Caleb offered as wife to man who conquered Kirjath-sepher (Josh. 15:16).

ACRE Translation of Hebrew *tsemed*, literally a "team" of oxen. As a measure of land, it refers to the land a team can plow in one day (1 Sam. 14:14; Isa. 5:10).

ACROSTIC Literary device by which each section of a literary work begins with the succeeding letter of the alphabet. The acrostic style helped people memorize the poem and expressed completeness of subject matter from A to Z.

ACTS OF THE APOSTLES Fifth book of the NT tracing growth of the early church. The most significant help in discovering the author of Acts is simply recognizing this book's relationship to the Gospel of Luke: both books begin with a greeting to a man named Theophilus ("friend of God"); Acts' greeting to Theophilus refers to a previous writing; the end of Luke intentionally overlaps with the beginning of Acts to provide continuity between the two volumes; and the author's writing style, vocabulary, and attention to specific themes remain constant throughout both books.

ADAM Place-name of city near Jordan River, where waters of Jordan heaped up so Israel could cross over to conquer the land (Josh. 3:16). Its location is probably Tel ed-Damieh near the Jabbok River.

ADAM AND EVE First man and woman created by God from whom all other people are descended. They introduced sin into human experience. In its most common occurrence, the word *'adam* refers to mankind in general. It has this use in Gen. 1:26-27, where it includes both male and female, those who were created in the image of God. It is also used in referring to a specific man where it occurs with the Hebrew definite article (Gen. 4:1).

In the NT Adam is used as a proper name, clearly referring to our ancestral parents. Jesus' genealogy is traced back to Adam (Luke 3:38). However, the most important NT usage treats Jesus as a second Adam (1 Cor. 15:45), where the word is used as a symbol. Furthermore, Paul in a similar manner treats Adam as a type of Christ (Rom. 5:14). As the "first Adam" brought death into the world, the "second Adam" brought life and righteousness (Rom. 5:15-19).

ADAR Twelfth month of Jewish calendar after the exile, including parts of February and March. Time of Festival of Purim established in Esther (9:21).

ADMAH Place-name meaning "red soil." City connected with Sodom and Gomorrah as border of Canaanite territory (Gen. 10:19).

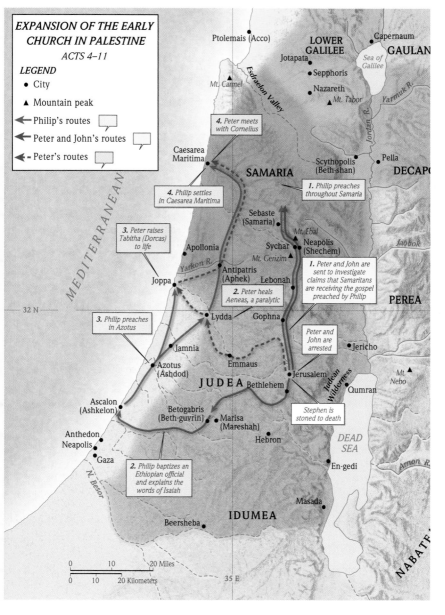

EXPANSION OF THE EARLY CHURCH IN PALESTINE
ACTS 4–11

LEGEND
- • City
- ▲ Mountain peak
- ← Philip's routes
- ← Peter and John's routes
- ◄- Peter's routes

1. Philip preaches throughout Samaria
1. Peter and John are sent to investigate claims that Samaritans are receiving the gospel preached by Philip
2. Peter heals Aeneas, a paralytic
2. Philip baptizes an Ethiopian official and explains the words of Isaiah
3. Peter raises Tabitha (Dorcas) to life
3. Philip preaches in Azotus
4. Peter meets with Cornelius
4. Philip settles in Caesarea Maritima

Peter and John are arrested
Stephen is stoned to death

ADMINISTRATION Spiritual gift that God gives to some members to build up the church (1 Cor. 12:28 NASB, NIV, RSV; HCSB "managing"), called "governments" in KJV. The Greek word *kubernesis* occurs only here in the Greek NT. It describes the ability to lead or hold a position of leadership.

ADONIJAH Personal name meaning "Yah is Lord." **1.** Fourth son of David. His mother's name was Haggith (2 Sam. 3:4). **2.** Levite that Jehoshaphat sent to teach the people of Judah the book of the law (2 Chron. 8). **3.** Leader of the Jews after the exile who signed Nehemiah's covenant to obey God's law (Neh. 10:16).

ADONIKAM Personal name meaning "the Lord has arisen."

ADONIRAM Personal name meaning "the Lord is exalted." Officer in charge of the work gangs Solomon conscripted from Israel (1 Kings 4:6; 5:14).

ADONIS God of vegetation and fertility with Syrian name meaning "lord." Worshiped in Greece and Syria.

ADONI-ZEDEK Personal name meaning "the Lord is righteous" or "the god Zedek is lord." King of Jerusalem who gathered coalition of Canaanite kings to fight Gibeon after Joshua made a peace treaty with Gibeon (Josh. 10).

ADOPTION Legal process whereby one person receives another into his family and confers upon that person familial privileges and advantages. The "adopter" assumes parental responsibility for the "adoptee." The "adoptee" is thereby considered an actual child, becoming the beneficiary of all the rights, privileges, and responsibilities afforded to all the children of the family.

References to adoption in the OT are rare. Adoption is an action of the Father (Gal. 4:6; Rom. 8:15) and is based on the love of the Father (Eph. 1:5; 1 John 3:1). The basis of this activity of God is the atoning work of Jesus Christ (Gal. 3:26). Adoption involves peacemaking (Matt. 5:9) and compels the believer to become Christlike (1 John 3:2). As an expression of the familial relationship, God as Father disciplines His children (Heb. 12:5-11). Believers are to regard all those who have come to Christ by grace through faith as members of God's family (1 Tim. 5:1-2). See *Regeneration; Salvation.*

ADRAMYTTIUM or **ADRAMYTIAN** (NASB) Place-name of a seaport on the northwest coast of modern Turkey in the Roman province of Asia. Paul used a ship whose home port was Adramyttium to make the first leg of his journey from Caesarea to Italy to appeal his case to Caesar (Acts 27:2).

ADRIA or **ADRIATIC SEA** (NASB, NIV) During Paul's time, the designated body of water between Crete and Sicily where Paul's ship was battered by gale force winds and resultant high waves for 14 days as he sailed toward Rome to appeal his case to Caesar (Acts 27:27). Later, the Adriatic Sea was extended to cover the waters between Greece and Italy.

ADULLAM Place-name meaning "sealed-off place." City five miles south of Beth-shemesh in Judah, probably modern Tell esh-Sheikh Madkur.

ADULTERY Act of unfaithfulness in marriage that occurs when one of the marriage partners voluntarily engages in sexual intercourse with a person other than the marriage partner.

Israel's covenant law prohibited adultery (Exod. 20:14) and thereby made faithfulness to the marriage relationship central in the divine will for human relationships. Jesus' teachings expanded the OT law to address matters of the heart. Adultery has its origins within (Matt. 15:19), and lust is as much a violation of the law's intent as is illicit sexual intercourse (Matt. 5:27-28). Adulterers can be forgiven (John 8:3-11); and once sanctified through repentance, faith, and God's grace, they are included among God's people (1 Cor. 6:9-11).

ADVENT Word with Latin roots, meaning "coming." Christians of earlier generations spoke of "the advent of our Lord" and of "His second advent." The first phrase refers to God's becoming incarnate in Jesus of Nazareth. The latter phrase speaks of Jesus' second coming. In a second sense "advent" designates a period before Christmas when Christians prepare for the celebration of Jesus' birth. This practice may have begun in some churches as early as the late fourth century.

ADVERSARY Enemy, either human or satanic. Psalmists often prayed for deliverance from adversaries (Pss. 38:20; 69:19; 71:13; 81:14; 109:29). The devil is the greatest adversary and must be resisted (1 Pet. 5:8-9).

ADVOCATE One who intercedes on behalf of another and is used to refer to Christ interceding with the Father on behalf of sinners. "Advocate" is the translation often given to the Greek *parakletos* in 1 John 2:1, a word found elsewhere only in John's Gospel as a title referring to the Holy Spirit, and there translated "Helper," "Comforter," "Counselor," or "Advocate" (John 14:16,26; 15:26; 16:7).

AENEAS Personal name of a paralyzed man Peter healed at Lydda (Acts 9:33-34), resulting in great evangelistic victories in the area.

AENON Place-name meaning "double spring." The location where John the Baptist was baptizing during the time that Jesus was baptizing in Judea (John 3:23).

AFFLICTION Condition of physical or mental distress. While the source and purpose of affliction may vary, the Bible describes the state of affliction with many terms. In the OT the Hebrew language uses as many as 13 words that may be translated "affliction."

As a response to affliction, the believer should pray to the Lord (Ps. 25:18; Lam. 1:9; James 5:13); comfort others (James 1:27; Phil. 4:14); remain faithful through patient endurance (2 Cor. 6:4; 1 Tim. 4:5; James 1:2,12; 1 Pet. 4:13); cultivate an attitude of joy (James 1:2); and follow the example of Jesus Christ (1 Pet. 2:19-23).

The purpose of affliction is to show the power of Christ (2 Cor. 12:8-9). The discipline of affliction produces strong faith. The end of affliction is the salvation of God's people. Christ's affliction in His atoning sacrifice and the continued affliction of His people will end in the exaltation of God and consummation of His kingdom (Col. 1:24; 2 Tim. 2:10).

AGABUS Personal name meaning "locust." Prophet in the Jerusalem church who went to visit the church at Antioch and predicted a universal famine. His prophecy was fulfilled about 10 years later in the reign of Claudius Caesar (Acts 11:27-29).

AGAG Personal name meaning "fiery one." He was king of the Amalekites, a tribal people living in the Negev and in the Sinai Peninsula. The Amalekites had attacked the Israelites in the wilderness and were therefore cursed (Exod. 17:14). In 1 Sam. 15:8, Saul destroyed all the Amalekites but King Agag. Since the Lord had ordered the complete destruction of the Amalekites, Samuel, Saul's priest, rebuked Saul for his disobedience and reported God's rejection of Saul as king. Then Samuel himself executed Agag.

AGAGITE Apparently, the term means a descendant of Agag. Only Haman, the arch villain in the book of Esther, is called an Agagite (Esther 3:1). Agagite is probably a synonym for Amalekite.

AGATE Translucent quartz with concentric bands,. "Agate" translates three words in the Bible: a stone in the breast piece of judgment (Exod. 28:19; 39:12), the material in the pinnacles of Jerusalem (Isa. 54:12; Ezek. 27:16), and the third jewel in the foundation wall of the new Jerusalem (Rev. 21:19).

AGE TO COME The expression "age to come" or "coming age[s]" is found in the Apocrypha (2 Esdras 7:113; 8:52) and several times in the NT (Matt. 12:32; Mark 10:30; Luke 18:30; Eph. 1:21; 2:7; 1 Tim. 6:19; Heb. 6:5). It is usually either explicitly or implicitly considered in opposition to "this age" or "the present age" (Matt. 12:32; Luke 16:8; 20:34-35; 1 Cor. 2:6–8; 2 Cor. 4:4; Gal. 1:4; Eph. 1:21; 2:2; 1 Tim. 6:17; 2 Tim. 4:10; Titus 2:12). The expression "the end of the age" (Matt. 13:39,40,49; 24:3; 28:20) refers to the end of the present age and therefore relates to the age to come.

AGUE KJV translation of Hebrew word meaning "burning with fever." The Hebrew term appears in Lev. 26:16 and Deut. 28:22, KJV translating "fever" in the second passage.

AGUR Personal name meaning "hired hand." Author of at least part of Prov. 30.

AHAB Personal name meaning "father's brother." The seventh king of Israel's northern kingdom, married a foreigner, Jezebel, and incited God's anger more than any of Israel's previous kings. Ahab was the son and successor of Omri. His 22-year reign (874–853 BC), while enjoying some political and military success, was marred by spiritual compromise and failure (1 Kings 16:30).

AHASUERUS Hebrew spelling for Xerxes, the king in the book of Esther (NIV, TEV).

Ruins of Ahab's Palace.

AHAVA River in Babylon and town located beside the river where Ezra assembled Jews to return to Jerusalem from exile (Ezra 8:15,21,31). Ahava was probably located near the city of Babylon, but the exact site is not known.

AHAZ 1. Evil king of Judah (735–715 BC). Ahaz, whose name means "he has grasped," was the son and successor of Jotham as king of Judah and the father of Hezekiah. Ahaz is characterized as an evil man who participated in the most monstrous of idolatrous practices (2 Kings 16:3). His 16-year reign was contemporary with the prophets Isaiah and Micah. **2.** A Benjaminite descended from Saul (1 Chron. 8:35-36; 9:42).

AHAZIAH Name of two OT kings, the king of Israel (850–840 BC) and the king of Judah (ca. 842). The name means "Yahweh has grasped."

AHIEZER Personal name meaning "my brother is help." **1.** Aide to Moses in the wilderness from the tribe of Dan (Num. 1:12; 2:25). **2.** Chief warrior who joined David at Ziklag.

AHIJAH Personal name rendered several ways in Hebrew and English meaning "my brother is Yahweh." **1.** Priest of the family of Eli in Shiloh (1 Sam. 14:3-4). **2.** Scribe of Solomon (1 Kings 4:3). **3.** Prophet from Shiloh who tore his clothes in 12 pieces and gave 10 to Jeroboam to signal God's decision to divide the kingdom after Solomon's death (1 Kings 11:29-39). **4.** Father of King Baasha of Israel from tribe of Issachar (1 Kings 15:27). **5.** Son of Jerahmeel (1 Chron. 2:25). **6.** Son of Ehud in tribe of Benjamin, an official in Geba (1 Chron. 8:7). **7.** One of David's 30 military heroes whose home was Pelon (1 Chron. 11:36). **8.** Signer of Nehemiah's covenant to obey God's law (Neh. 10:26). **9.** The Hebrew text of 1 Chron. 26:20 says Ahijah, a Levite, had charge of temple treasuries under David (KJV, RSV).

AHIKAM Personal name meaning "my brother stood up." Son of Josiah's scribe Shaphan. He took the book of the Law found in the temple to Huldah the prophetess to determine God's will (2 Kings 22:8-20).

AHILUD Personal name meaning "a brother is born." The father of Jehoshaphat, David's court recorder (2 Sam. 8:16), who retained the position under Solomon (1 Kings 4:3).

AHIMAAZ Personal name with uncertain meaning, "brother of anger" and "my brother is counselor" being suggestions. **1.** Saul's father-in-law (1 Sam. 14:50). **2.** Son of Zadok, one of David's priests (2 Sam. 15:27). He served as one of David's secret messengers from the court when Absalom rebelled and drove his father from Jerusalem (2 Sam. 15:36; 7:17). **3.** One of 12 officers over Solomon's provinces, he had charge of Naphtali. He married Solomon's daughter Basmath. He may be the same as 2. Zadok's son (1 Kings 4:15).

AHIMAN Personal name with uncertain meaning. **1.** One of the giants of Anak (Num. 13:22). Caleb drove him and his two brothers out of Hebron (cp. Judg. 1:10, where the tribe of Judah killed the three brothers). **2.** Levite and temple gatekeeper (1 Chron. 9:17).

AHINOAM Personal name meaning "my brother is gracious." **1.** King Saul's wife (1 Sam. 14:50). **2.** Wife of David from Jezreel (1 Sam. 25:43) who lived with him under the Philistines at Gath (27:3).

AHIRA Personal name meaning "my brother is a friend." Leader of tribe of Naphtali under Moses (Num. 1:15) who presented the tribe's offerings at the dedication of the altar (7:78-83) and led them in the wilderness marches.

AHIRAM Personal name meaning "my brother is exalted." Son of Benjamin who gave his name to a clan (the Ahiramites) in that tribe (Num. 26:38).

AHISAMACH Personal name meaning "my brother has supported." Father of Oholiab, the artisan who helped Bezaleel create the artwork of the wilderness tabernacle (Exod. 31:6; 35:34; 38:23).

AHISHAHAR Personal name meaning "brother of the dawn." A member of tribe of Benjamin (1 Chron. 7:10) but not listed in the genealogy of 1 Chron. 8.

AHISHAR Personal name meaning "my brother sang." Head of Solomon's palace staff (1 Kings 4:6).

AHITHOPHEL Personal name meaning "brother of folly" if it is not a scribal attempt to hide an original name including a Canaanite god such as Ahibaal. The name of David's counselor who joined Absalom's revolt against King David (2 Sam. 15:12).

AHITUB Personal name meaning "my brother is good." **1.** Priest, son of Phinehas and grandson of Eli, ministering in Shiloh (1 Sam. 14:3). He was Ahimelech's father (22:9). **2.** Father of Zadok, the high priest under David and Solomon (2 Sam. 8:17). The name occurs twice in the Chronicler's list of priests (1 Chron. 6:7-8,11-12,52; cp. 9:11). Ezra descended from Ahitub's line (Ezra 7:2).

AHLAB Place-name meaning "mountain forest" or "fertile." Probably located at Khirbet el-Macalib on the Mediterranean coast four miles above Tyre. The tribe of Asher could not conquer it (Judg. 1:31).

AHLAI Personal name meaning "a brother to me," perhaps an abbreviated form of Ahliya, "the brother is my god." Others interpret as interjection meaning "O would that." **1.** Member of clan of Jerahmeel (1 Chron. 2:31). Ahlai's father was Sheshan. **2.** Father of a valiant soldier of David (1 Chron. 11:41).

AHOAH Personal name of uncertain meaning. Grandson of Benjamin (1 Chron. 8:4), but lists in 2:25; 8:7; and evidence of early translations may point to Ahijah as the original name.

AHOHITE Clan name. In time of David and Solomon military figures of this clan or place became military leaders (2 Sam. 23:9,28; 1 Chron. 11:12,29; 27:4).

AHUZZATH Personal name meaning "that grasped" or "property." Official who accompanied Abimelech, king of Philistines, to make covenant of peace with Isaac (Gen. 26:26).

AHZAI or **AHASAI** (KJV) Personal name meaning "property" or abbreviated form of Ahzaiah, "Yahweh has grasped." A priest after the return from exile (Neh. 11:13). Sometimes said to be same as Jahzerah (1 Chron. 9:12).

AI Name means "the ruin" in Hebrew. According to the accounts of Genesis and Joshua, Ai is said to be east of Bethel (Gen. 12:8; Josh. 7:2), Bethel is very near Ai (Josh. 12:9), a mountain is said to separate Bethel and Ai (Gen. 12:8), and Ai is implied to be a small town (Josh. 7:3). Khirbet el-Maqatir (Ai) was an important military target to Joshua and the Israelites since it guarded the approach to a strategic central crossroads to the central hill country—Bethel. The topography of the account in Joshua fits with this site as does a dating of the conquest in the Late Bronze Age (ca. 1400 BC). Israel learned at Ai that they could not prevail without God. The sin of one man, Achan, affected the whole nation's conquest commission. Ai was originally in Ephraimite territory (1 Chron. 7:28) and was later occupied by Benjamites (Neh. 11:31).

AIAH Personal name imitating the cry of a hawk, then meaning "hawk." **1.** Son of Zibeon among the clans of Edom descended from Esau (Gen. 36:24). **2.** Father of Rizpah, Saul's concubine (2 Sam. 3:7) and grandfather of Mephibosheth (2 Sam. 21:8).

AIJALON Also spelled "Ajalon." Place-name meaning "place of the deer." **1.** Town and nearby valley where moon stood still at Joshua's command (Josh. 10:12). **2.** Elon, a judge of the tribe of Zebulon, was buried in a northern Aijalon (Judg. 12:12), whose location may be at Tell et-Butmeh.

AIJELETH SHAHAR Musical direction in title of Ps. 22, literally "doe of the dawn."

AIN Place-name meaning "eye" or "water spring." Often used as first part of a Place-name indicating the presence of a water source. English often used "En" as first part of such names. See *Endor*, for example. **1.** Place on eastern border of Canaan (Num. 34:11). Location is uncertain. **2.** City of southern Judah (Josh. 15:32) belonging to Simeon (Josh. 19:7) but assigned as homestead for the Levites, who had no land allotted (Josh. 21:16).

AKHENATON Egyptian pharaoh (1370–1353 B.C.) Originally named Amenhotep IV, he made a radical religious switch from worshipping Amon to serving Aton, the sun disc. During his reign he received the reports and requests from city-state rulers in Palestine that archaeologists call the Amarna letters. These show the lack of unity and harmony in Palestine that Joshua found when he entered to conquer Palestine.

AKKUB Personal name possibly meaning "protector" or "protected one." **1.** Descendant of Solomon in post-exilic Judah about 420 BC (1 Chron 3:24). **2.** Gatekeeper of the temple after the return from exile (1 Chron. 9:17; Ezra 2:42; Neh. 7:45; 11:19); he was a Levite (Neh. 12:25). **3.** Levite who helped Ezra teach the Law to God's returned people (Neh. 8:7). He may have been related to 2. **4.** The head of another family of temple staff personnel (Ezra 2:45).

ALAMOTH Musical notation meaning literally "upon or according to young woman." This apparently signifies a tune for a high voice, a song for a soprano (1 Chron. 15:20; Ps. 46 title).

ALARM Signal given by shouting or playing an instrument. The Hebrew term (*teru' ah*) literally means a shout, but musical instruments were used as the trumpets of Num. 10:1-10. The alarm called the wilderness community to march (Num. 10:5-6). Later in Israel the alarm called them to battle (10:9) and reminded them of God's presence with their armies (cp. 31:6). The alarm announcing the enemy coming in war brought shock, sadness, and fear (Jer. 4:19; Hos. 5:8). The greatest fear should come, however, when God sounds the alarm for His day (Joel 2:1).

ALDEBARAN Red star of first magnitude in eye of Taurus; brightest star in Hyades; REB, KJV reading for Arcturus (Job 9:9; 38:32).

ALEMETH Place- and personal name meaning "concealed" or "dark." **1.** City set aside for the Levites from Benjamin's allotment (1 Chron. 6:60). Known as Almon in Josh. 21:18. **2.** Grandson of Benjamin (1 Chron. 7:8). **3.** Descendant of Saul and Jonathan in tribe of Benjamin (1 Chron. 8:36).

ALEXANDER Five NT men including the son of Simon of Cyrene (Mark 15:21), a relative of Annas (Acts 4:6), a Jew of Ephesus (Acts 19:33), a false teacher (1 Tim. 1:19-20), and a coppersmith (2 Tim. 4:14).

ALEXANDER THE GREAT Succeeded his father as king of Macedonia and quickly conquered the Persian empire. Alexander the Great (356–323 BC) was one of the greatest military leaders in history. His father was Phillip of Macedon, king of a region of Greece known as Macedonia.

While Alexander is never directly named in the Bible, the culture that he brought to Palestine greatly affected the biblical world, especially during the time between the writing of the OT and NT. His empire is one element of the historical background of Daniel. See *Alexandria; Greece.*

ALEXANDRIA Capital of Egypt from 330 BC, founded by Alexander the Great as an outstanding Greek cultural and academic center.

Alexandria was designed to act as the principal port of Egypt located on the western edge of the Nile Delta. The Pharos lighthouse was visible for miles at a height of over 400 feet and is remembered today as one of the "Seven Wonders of the World."

The educated Jews of Alexandria contended with Stephen (Acts 6:9). Apollos, the great Christian orator, came from Alexandria (Acts 18:24), and Paul rode the ships of that port (Acts 27:6; 28:11). Although the Christians suffered persecution there, they produced a school with such notables as Clement and Origen in leadership. The school was noted for its allegorical approach to Scripture.

Lighthouse in the harbor at Alexandria.

ALGUM Rare wood that Solomon imported from Lebanon for the temple (2 Chron. 2:8). The exact type of wood is not known. First Kings 10:11-12 refers to "almug" wood imported from Ophir (cp. 2 Chron. 9:10-11). The rare wood was used for gateways and for musical instruments.

ALIAH Personal name meaning "height." A leader of Edom (1 Chron. 1:51), known in Gen. 36:40 as Alvah.

ALIAN Personal name meaning "high one." Descendant of Esau and thus an Edomite (1 Chron. 1:40). Known in Gen. 36:23 as Alvan.

ALIEN Person who is living in a society other than his own. Related terms are "foreigner," "stranger," and "sojourner." Israel had a special place for aliens because Israel began history in Egypt as aliens (Exod. 23:9). Special laws provided food and clothing for aliens (Deut. 24:19-20; 26:12). Aliens had rights in the courtroom (Deut. 24:17; 27:19). The ritual expectations of the alien are not always clear (Deut. 14:21; Lev. 17:15). God loves aliens (Deut. 10:19), and the alien could worship God and was supposed to keep the Sabbath (Exod. 23:12; Deut. 31:12). They could observe Passover just as any Israelite (Num. 9:14) and offer sacrifices (Lev. 17:8). They should obey sexual laws (Lev. 18:26).

ALLAMMELECH Place-name meaning "king's oak" or "royal holy tree." Border town of Asher (Josh. 19:26) whose specific location is not known.

ALLEGORY Literary device in which a story or narrative is used to convey truths about reality. The word "allegory" is taken from two Greek words: *alla* (other) and *agoreuo* (to proclaim). An allegory conveys something other than its literal meaning. Sometimes "allegory" is defined as an extended metaphor. Cicero viewed allegory as a continuous stream of metaphors.

ALLON Personal name meaning "oak." Leader of tribe of Simeon (1 Chron. 4:37).

ALLONBACHUTH or **ALLONBACUTH** Place-name meaning "oak of weeping." Burial place near Bethel of Rebekah's nurse (Gen. 35:8).

ALLOTMENT OT concept of land allocation either by God or by lot. The allotment of the land of Canaan to the tribes of Israel is recorded in Num. 32 and Josh. 13–19. God directed the process through the lot of the priest (Josh. 14:1-2). The tribes of Reuben and Gad, along with half the tribe of Manasseh, requested land east of the Jordan (Num. 32:33). Ezekiel 48 also contains a version of the allotment of the land for the Jews after the exile, revised so that each tribe received an equal share.

ALMIGHTY Title of God, translation of Hebrew *El Shaddai.* The early Greek translation introduced "Almighty" as one of several translations. Recent study has tended to see "The Mountain One" as the most likely original meaning. The name was particularly related to Abraham and the patriarchs (Gen. 17:1; 28:3; 35:11; 49:25). Job is the only book to use *El Shaddai* extensively, 31 times in all. Paul used "Almighty" once at the end of a series of OT quotations to imitate OT style and to underline divine power to bring His word to fulfillment. Revelation refers to God nine times as "Almighty," again giving a feeling of power to the vision of Revelation.

ALMODAD Personal name meaning "God is a friend." Grandson of Eber and ancestor of Arabian tribes (Gen. 10:25-26).

ALMON Place-name meaning "darkness," or "hidden," or "small road sign." City given to Levites from tribe of Benjamin, called Alemeth in 1 Chron. 6:60. The site is probably modern Khirbet Almit.

ALMOND Large, nut-bearing tree and the nuts that it bears. Noted as the first tree to bloom (January) and for its pretty white or pink blossoms. Jacob used the almond (KJV, "hazel") as a breeding device to increase his herds (Gen. 30:37). He sent almonds as one of the best fruits of the land to satisfy the Egyptian ruler (Gen. 43:11). The bowls for the tabernacle had almond-shaped decorations (Exod. 25:33-34). Aaron's rod miraculously produced ripe almonds, showing that he and his tribe were the only chosen priests (Num. 17:8).

ALMON-DIBLATHAIM Place-name meaning "road sign of the two figs." A stopping place near the end of the wilderness wandering near Mount Nebo (Num. 33:46-47).

ALMS Gifts for the poor.
Old Testament Although the Hebrew language apparently had no technical term to refer to "alms" or "almsgiving," the practice of charitable giving, especially to the poor, became a very important belief and practice within Judaism.
New Testament The NT regards alms as an expression of a righteous life. The technical term for alms (Gk. *eleemosune*) occurs 13 times in the NT. This does not include Matt. 6:1, where the preferred reading is "righteousness" (NASB, NIV) instead of "alms" (KJV). By the first century A.D. righteousness and alms were synonymous in Judaism. Although Jesus criticized acts of charity done for the notice of men (Matt. 6:2-3), He expected His disciples to perform such deeds (Matt. 6:4) and even commanded them (Luke 11:41; 12:33). Alms could refer to a gift donated to the needy (Acts 3:2-3,10) or to acts of charity in general (Acts 9:36; 10:2,4,31; 24:17).

ALOE Large tree grown in India and China, producing resin and oil used in making perfumes. Balaam used the beauty of the aloe tree to describe the beauty of Israel's camp as he blessed them (Num. 24:6). The aloe perfume gave aroma to the king's garment as he was married (Ps. 45:8). Aloe also perfumed the harlot's bed (Prov. 7:17). The beloved's garden includes aloe (Song 4:14). Nicodemus brought aloe with myrrh to perfume Jesus' body for burial (John 19:39).

ALOTH Place-name meaning "the height" if not read Bealoth (NASB, RSV), "feminine baals." Center of activity for Baana, one of Solomon's 12 district supervisors (1 Kings 4:16).

ALPHA AND OMEGA First and last letters of the Greek alphabet, used in Revelation to describe God or Christ (Rev. 1:8,17; 21:6; 22:13). "Alpha and omega" refers to God's sovereignty and eternal nature. God and Christ are "the First and the Last, the Beginning and the End" (Rev. 22:13 HCSB).

ALPHAEUS or **ALPHEUS** Personal name. **1.** Father of apostle called James the Less to distinguish him from James, the son of Zebedee and brother of John (Matt. 10:3; Mark 3:18; Luke 6:15; Acts 1:13). **2.** Father of the Apostle Levi (Mark 2:14). Comparison of Matt. 9:9 and Luke 5:27 would indicate Levi was also called Matthew.

ALTAR Structure used in worship as the place for presenting sacrifices to God or gods.

Old Testament The Hebrew word for altar that is used most frequently in the OT is formed from the verb for "slaughter" and means literally "slaughter place." Altars were used primarily as places of sacrifice, especially animal sacrifice. "Altar" is distinct from "temple." Whereas temple implies a building or roofed structure, altar implies an open structure.

New Testament The Greek word used for altar literally translates "place of sacrifice." New Testament references to altars concern proper worship (Matt 5:23-24) and hypocrisy in worship (Matt. 23:18-20). The altar of incense described in the OT (Exod. 30:1-6) is mentioned in Luke (Luke 1:11). Several NT references to altars refer back to OT altar events (Rom. 11:3; James 2:21). In Revelation, John described a golden altar (Rev. 9:13) that, like the OT bronze altar, had horns.

While direct references to altar and the sacrifice of Jesus Christ are few in the NT (Heb. 13:10), the message that Jesus Christ is the ultimate sacrifice who effects reconciliation with God is the theme of the NT.

ALTASHHETH (NASB) or **AL-TASCHITH** (KJV). Word in psalm title (Pss. 57; 58; 59; 75), transliterated letter for letter from Hebrew to English by NASB and KJV, but translated "Do not destroy" by NIV and RSV. This may indicate the tune to which the people sang the psalm.

AMALEKITE Nomadic tribe of formidable people that first attacked the Israelites after the exodus at Rephidim. Descendants of Amalek, the grandson of Esau (Gen. 36:12), they inhabited the desolate wasteland of the northeast Sinai Peninsula and the Negev.

AMANUENSIS One employed to copy manuscripts or write from dictation. Romans 16:22 identifies Tertius as the one "who penned this epistle" (cp. Col. 4:18; 1 Pet. 5:12). See *Scribe.*

AMARIAH Personal name meaning "Yahweh has spoken." Popular name, especially among priests, after the exile. Brief biblical comments make it difficult to distinguish with certainty the number of separate individuals. **1.** Priest in the line of Aaron (1 Chron. 6:7,52; Ezra 7:3). **2.** Priest in the high priestly line after Solomon's day (1 Chron. 6:11). **3.** Priestly son of Hebron in Moses' line (1 Chron. 23:19; 24:23). **4.** Chief priest and highest judge of matters involving religious law under King Jehoshaphat (2 Chron. 19:11). **5.** Priest under Hezekiah responsible for distributing resources from Jerusalem temple to priests in priestly cities outside Jerusalem (2 Chron. 31:15). **6.** Man with foreign wife under Ezra (Ezra 10:42). **7.** Priest who sealed Nehemiah's covenant to obey the law (Neh. 10:3). **8.** Ancestor of a member of tribe of Judah living in Jerusalem during Nehemiah's time (Neh. 11:4). **9.** Priest who returned to Jerusalem from exile in Babylon with Zerubbabel (Neh. 12:2). **10.** Head of a course of priests in Judah after the exile (Neh. 12:13). **11.** Ancestor of Zephaniah, the prophet (Zeph. 1:1).

AMARNA, TELL EL Site approximately 200 miles south of Cairo, Egypt, where, in 1888, 300 clay tablets were found describing the period of history when the Israelites were in bondage in Egypt. Amarna is not mentioned by name in the Bible.

The so-called Amarna Letters were written in Akkadian, the international language of that era. These letters were primarily diplomatic communications between Egypt and Egyptian-controlled territories, including Syria and Palestine. Rulers of small Palestinian city-states including Shechem, Jerusalem, and Megiddo complained of mistreatment by other rulers and asked for Egyptian aid. These letters evidence the political unrest, disunity, and instability of the period prior to or immediately following the Hebrew conquest. Reference to the *Habiru* of this time has intrigued senders, but no conclusive connection to the Hebrews is yet decisive.

AMASAI Personal name meaning "burden bearer." **1.** Levite in the line of Kohath (1 Chron. 6:25). **2.** Levite in the line of Kohath and of Heman the singer (1 Chron. 6:35), often identified with 1. **3.** The chief of David's captains, who received prophetic inspiration from the Spirit (1 Chron. 12:18). Note that he does not appear in 2 Sam. 23. **4.** Priest and musician who blew trumpets before the ark of God in David's time (1 Chron. 15:24). **5.** Levite, father of Mahath, who helped purify the temple under Hezekiah (2 Chron. 29:12).

AMASHAI or **AMASHSAI** (NASB, TEV) Personal name of priest after the exile (Neh. 11:13).

AMASIAH Personal name meaning "Yahweh has borne." One of the captains of Jehoshaphat (2 Chron. 17:16).

AMAZIAH Personal name meaning "Yahweh is mighty." **1.** A Simeonite (1 Chron. 4:34). **2.** A Levite and a descendant of Merari (1 Chron. 6:45). **3.** Priest at Bethel who sent Amos the prophet home, saying he did not have the right to prophesy against King Jeroboam II of Israel (789–746 BC) in the king's place of worship (Amos 7:10-17). **4.** Ninth king of Judah, the son of Joash and father of Uzziah (797–767 BC). He was 25 years old when he ascended the throne.

AMBASSADOR Representative of one royal court to another. Paul saw himself even in prison as an ambassador sent by the divine King to proclaim salvation through Christ to the world (Eph. 6:20; cp. 2 Cor. 5:20).

AMBER Yellowish or brownish translucent resin that takes a good polish. Also translated as gleaming bronze in RSV, but amber in NRSV, glowing metal in NASB and NIV, and bronze in TEV (Ezek. 1:4,27; 8:2).

AMEN Transliteration of Hebrew word signifying something as certain, sure and valid, truthful and faithful. It is sometimes translated "so be it." In the Gospels Jesus used "amen" to affirm the truth of His own statements. English translations often use "verily," "truly," "I tell you the truth" to translate Jesus' "amen." He never said it at the end of a statement but always at the beginning. Jesus is called "the Amen" in Rev. 3:14, meaning that He Himself is the reliable and true witness of God. Perhaps the writer had in mind Isa. 65:16 where the Hebrew says, "God of Amen."

AMETHYST Deep purple variety of stone of the aluminum oxide family. Used in the breastplate of the high priest (Exod. 28:19; 39:12) and the twelfth stone in the foundation wall of the new Jerusalem (Rev. 21:20).

AMI Personal name with uncertain meaning. A servant in the temple after the exile belonging to a group called "children of Solomon's servants" (Ezra 2:55-57). Ami is apparently called Amon in Neh. 7:59.

AMITTAI Personal name meaning "loyal," "true." Father of the prophet Jonah who lived in Gath-hepher (2 Kings 14:25).

AMMI Name meaning "my people" was given to Israel by Hosea in contrast to the name Lo-ammi (Hos. 1:9) meaning "not my people." The name Lo-ammi was given to the third child of Gomer, the wife of Hosea the prophet, to pronounce God's rejection of Israel. The name "Ammi" was the new name to be given the restored Israel in the day of redemption.

AMMIEL Personal name meaning "people of God" or "God is of my people," that is, God is my relative. **1.** Spy who represented the tribe of Dan whom Moses sent to spy out the promised land. He was one of 10 who brought a bad report and led people to refuse to enter the land (Num. 13:12). **2.** Father of Machir, in whose house Mephibosheth, son of Jonathan and grandson of Saul, lived after the death of his father and grandfather. The family lived in Lo-debar (2 Sam. 9:4; 17:27). **3.** Father of Bathshua, David's wife (1 Chron. 3:5). Second Samuel 11:3 speaks of Bathsheba, daughter of Eliam. Many Bible students think these verses are talking about the same person, whose names have been slightly altered in the process of copying the manuscripts. **4.** Gatekeeper of the temple whom David appointed (1 Chron. 26:5).

AMMIHUD Personal name meaning "my people are splendid." **1.** Father of Elishama, who represented the tribe of Ephraim to help Moses during the wilderness wandering (Num. 1:10). He presented the tribe's offerings at the dedication of the altar (7:48) and led them in marching (10:22). He was Joshua's grandfather (1 Chron. 7:26). **2.** Father of Shemuel of the tribe of Simeon, who helped Moses, Eleazar, and Joshua allot the land to the tribes (Num. 34:20). **3.** Father of Pedahel of tribe of Naphtali, who helped allot the land (Num. 34:28). **4.** Father of King of Geshur to whom Absalom fled after he killed his brother Amnon (2 Sam. 13:37). **5.** Member of tribe of Judah who returned from exile (1 Chron. 9:4).

AMMINADAB Personal name meaning "my people give freely." **1.** Aaron's father-in-law (Exod. 6:23). Father of Nahshon, who led the tribe of Judah in the wilderness (Num. 1:7). Ancestor of David (Ruth 4:19) and Jesus (Matt. 1:4; Luke 3:33). **2.** Son of Kohath in genealogy of Levites (1 Chron. 6:22), but this may be copyist's change for Izhar (Exod. 6:18,21). **3.** Head of a family of Levites (1 Chron. 15:10). He helped carry the ark of the covenant to Jerusalem (1 Chron. 15:11-29).

AMMISHADDAI Father of Ahiezer, the leader of the tribe of Dan in the wilderness (Num. 1:12). The name Ammishaddai means "people of the Almighty."

AMMIZABAD Personal name meaning "my people give." Son of Benaiah, one of captains of

David's army (1 Chron. 27:6).

AMMON, AMMONITES Territory east of the Jordan roughly equivalent to the modern state of Jordan. The Ammonites were a Semitic people living northeast of the Dead Sea in the area surrounding Rabbah who often battled with the Israelites for possession of the fertile Gilead.

AMNON Personal name meaning "trustworthy, faithful." **1.** Firstborn son of King David (2 Sam. 3:2). He raped his half sister Tamar. Tamar's brother Absalom avenged this outrage by killing Amnon (2 Sam. 13:1-20). This incident marked the beginning of the decline of David's family following his adulterous relationship with Bathsheba and the murder of Uriah. See *David.* **2.** Member of tribe of Judah (1 Chron. 4:20).

AMOK Personal name meaning "deep." A priestly family after the return from exile (Neh. 12:7,20).

AMON Personal name meaning "faithful." **1.** Governor of Samaria when Jehoshaphat was king of Judah, who followed orders from the king of Israel and put the prophet Micaiah in prison (1 Kings 22:26). **2.** King of Judah (642 BC) following his father Manasseh. He followed the infamous idolatry of his father and was killed in a palace revolt (2 Kings 21:19-23).

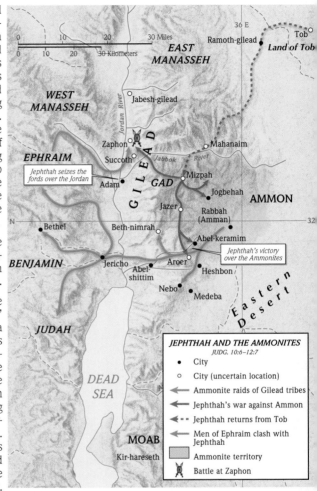

The people of Judah, in turn, killed the rebels. Good King Josiah, Amon's son, succeeded to his throne. See Matt. 1:10. **3.** Ancestor of temple staff members after the exile (Neh. 7:59), called Ami in Ezra 2:57. **4.** Egyptian god whose worship center at Thebes Jeremiah threatened with divine destruction (Jer. 46:25). KJV translates "the multitude of No."

AMORITES People who occupied part of the promised land and often fought Israel. Their history goes back before 2000 BC.

Abraham assisted Mamre the Amorite in recovering his land from four powerful kings (Gen. 14), but later the Amorites were a formidable obstacle to the Israelites' conquest and settlement of Canaan. They preferred living in the hills and valleys that flank both sides of the Jordan River. Sihon and Og, two Amorite kings, resisted the Israelites' march to Canaan as they approached east of the Jordan (Num. 21:21-35); but after the Israelite victory there, Gad, Reuben, and half of Manasseh settled in the conquered area.

AMOS Personal name meaning "burdened" or, more likely, "one who is supported [by God]." Prophet from Judah who ministered in Israel about 750 BC.

Amos was a layperson who disclaimed professional status as a prophet. He lived in a time of relative peace on the international political scene and internally, the political structures of both Israel and Judah were stable.

Morally, Israel and Judah were suffering under the corruption generated as a by-product of Canaanite and Tyrian Baalism, as well as infidelity to the Lord's covenant. Israelite society had experienced the inevitable decay that characterizes misdirected prosperity.

Exploitation of the poor occurred throughout the land (2:6; 3:10; 4:1; 5:11; 8:4-6). Justice was distorted. The dynamism of personal religious experience gave way to the superficiality of institutional religion as demonstrated in the conflict between Amos and Amaziah, the priest of Bethel (7:10-15). Amos's opposition to those moral and religious evils led him to emphasize the primary theme of the book: "let justice roll down like waters, and righteousness like an everlasting stream" (5:24 RSV).

Ruins of small building, probably dating from post-biblical times, at Tekoa, Israel, Amos's hometown.

Amos was listed as an ancestor of Jesus (Luke 3:25), but it is not known specifically if it was this prophet.

AMOS, BOOK OF One of the 12 Minor Prophets of the OT. The book of Amos may be divided into three sections. Chapters 1 and 2 are a basic section, divided into subsections that begin with a common literary introduction (1:3,6,9,11,13; 2:1,4,6). The second section of the book consists of judgment oracles directed against Israel (3:1–6:14). The third section contains the visions of Amos (7–9), which may have been the earliest revelations through the prophet. The visions were central to his call experience. Aware of the awesome reality of human sin and divine judgment, these visions shaped his prophetic messages (7:1-3,4-6,7-9; 8:1-3; 9:1-4).

AMOZ Name means "strong." Father of the prophet Isaiah (2 Kings 19:2).

AMPHIPOLIS City near the Aegean Gulf between Thessalonica and Philippi. Paul and Silas passed through it on their way to Thessalonica on Paul's second missionary journey (Acts 17:1) as they traveled the famous Egnatian Way.

AMPLIAS or **AMPLIATUS** Christian convert in Rome to whom Paul sent greetings (Rom. 16:8). Amplias was a common name often given to slaves. Paul referred to this individual as "my dear friend in the Lord" (HCSB), which may suggest a particularly warm and affectionate relationship between Amplias and the apostle. Modern translations spell the name "Ampliatus."

AMRAM Personal name meaning "exalted people." **1.** Father of Moses, Aaron, and Miriam and grandson of Levi (Exod. 6:18-20). **2.** One of the 12 sons of Bani who was guilty of marrying foreign women (Ezra 10:34). **3.** One of four sons of Dishon in 1 Chron. 1:41.

AMULETS NASB, RSV translation of rare Hebrew word for charms inscribed with oaths, which women wore to ward off evil (Isa. 3:20). NIV translates "charms," KJV, "earrings."

AMZI Personal name meaning "my strong one," or an abbreviation for Amaziah. **1.** Member of temple singer family (1 Chron. 6:46). **2.** Ancestor of Adaiah, who helped build the second temple (Neh. 11:12).

ANAB Place-name meaning "grape." Joshua eliminated the Anakim from southern Judah including Hebron, Debir, and Anab (Josh. 11:21). Joshua allotted the mountain city to Judah (Josh. 15:50). Located at modern Khirbet Anab about 15 miles southwest of Hebron.

ANAH Personal name meaning "answer." **1.** Mother of Oholibamah, a wife of Esau (Gen. 36:2), and grandmother of Jeush, Jalam, and Korah (36:14). **2.** Son of Seir and brother of Zibeon (Gen. 36:20).

ANAHARATH Place-name meaning "gorge." City on border of Issachar (Josh. 19:19) located possibly at modern Tell el-Mukharkhash between Mount Tabor and the Jordan.

ANAIAH Personal name meaning "Yahweh answered." Ezra's assistant when Ezra read the Law to the post-exilic community (Neh. 8:4). He or another man of the same name signed Nehemiah's covenant to obey God's law (Neh. 10:22).

ANAK, ANAKIM, ANAKITES (NIV) Personal and clan name meaning "long necked" or "strong necked." The ancestor named Anak had three children: Ahiman, Sheshai, Talmai (Num. 13:22). They lived in Hebron and the hill country (Josh. 11:21) before being destroyed by Joshua.

ANAMMELECH Personal name meaning "Anu is king." A god of the Sepharvites who occupied part of Israel after the northern kingdom was exiled in 721 BC. Worshipers sacrificed children to this god (2 Kings 17:31).

ANAMIM or **ANAMITES** (NIV) Tribe or nation called "son of Egypt" in Gen. 10:13. No further information is known about these people.

ANAN Personal name meaning "cloud." Signer of Nehemiah's covenant to obey God (Neh. 10:26).

ANANI Personal name meaning "cloudy" or "he heard me." Descendant of David's royal line living after the return from exile (1 Chron. 3:24).

ANANIAH Personal name meaning "Yahweh heard me." **1.** Grandfather of Azariah, who helped Nehemiah repair Jerusalem (Neh. 3:23). **2.** Village where tribe of Benjamin dwelt in time of Nehemiah (Neh. 11:32). It may be located at Bethany, east of Jerusalem.

ANANIAS Greek form of the Hebrew name Hananiah, which means "Yahweh has dealt graciously." **1.** Husband of Sapphira (Acts 5:1-6). They sold private property, the proceeds of which they were to give to the common fund of the early Jerusalem church (Acts 4:32-34). They did not give all the proceeds from the sale, as they claimed, and both were struck dead for having lied to the Holy Spirit (Acts 5:5,10). **2.** Disciple who lived in the city of Damascus (Acts 9:10-19). In response to a vision he received from the Lord, this Ananias visited Saul (Paul) three days after Saul had his Damascus road experience. Ananias laid his hands on Saul, after which Saul received both the Holy Spirit and his sight. Acts 9:18 may imply that Ananias was the one who baptized Saul. **3.** Jewish high priest from AD 47 to 58 (Acts 23:2; 24:1).

ANATH Personal name meaning "answer," or it was the name of a Canaanite god. Father of Shamgar, a judge of Israel (Judg. 3:31).

ANATHEMA Greek translation of Hebrew *cherem*; booty taken in a holy war that must be thoroughly destroyed (Lev. 27:28; Deut. 20:10-18). The total destruction of this booty showed that it was being completely turned over to God. In the NT, "anathema" has two seemingly opposite meanings. It means gifts dedicated to God (Luke 21:5 HCSB) as well as something cursed. Paul invoked such a curse on those who did not love the Lord (1 Cor. 16:22) as well as on one who preached another gospel other than the gospel of grace (Gal. 1:8-9). From these uses *anathema* has come to mean "banned or excommunicated by a religious body." Paul said he was willing to become *anathema*, cursed and cut off from the Messiah, for the benefit of his Jewish brothers (Rom. 9:3 HCSB).

ANATHOTH Personal and Place-name. **1.** City assigned to the tribe of Benjamin, located about three miles northeast of Jerusalem (Josh. 21:18). King Solomon sent Abiathar the priest there after removing him as high priest (1 Kings 2:26-27). It was also the home of Jeremiah the prophet, who may have been a priest in the rejected line of Abiathar (Jer. 1:1). **2.** The eighth of nine sons of Becher, the son of Benjamin (1 Chron. 7:8). **3.** A chief who was a family or clan leader, who along with 84 other priests, Levites, and leaders signed a covenant that the Israelites would obey the law of God given through Moses (Neh. 10:19).

ANCHOR Weight held on the end of a cable that when submerged in water holds a ship in place. Anchors were made of stone, iron, and lead during biblical times. "Anchor" is used in a figurative sense in Heb. 6:19 where the hope of the gospel is compared to "an anchor of the soul, both sure and steadfast"—that is, a spiritual support in times of trial.

ANCIENT OF DAYS Phrase used in Dan. 7:9,13,22 to describe the everlasting God. Ancient of days literally means "one advanced in (of) days" and may possibly mean "one who forwards time or rules over it."

ANDREW Disciple of John the Baptist who became one of Jesus' first disciples and led his brother Simon to Jesus. Because of John the Baptist's witness concerning Jesus, Andrew followed Jesus to His overnight lodging and became one of His first disciples. Subsequently Andrew brought his brother Simon to Jesus (John 1:40-41). He was a fisherman by trade (Matt. 4:18). He questioned Jesus about His prophesy concerning the temple (Mark 13:3). Andrew brought the lad with his lunch to Jesus, leading to the feeding of the 5,000 (John 6:8). He and Philip brought some Greeks to see Jesus (John 12:22). He is mentioned for the last time in Acts 1:13. He is believed to have been killed on an x shaped cross. See *Apostle; Disciple.*

ANDRONICUS Kinsman of Paul honored by the church. He had suffered in prison for his faith and had been a Christian longer than Paul (Rom. 16:7). Evidently he lived in Rome when Paul wrote Romans. He is referred to as an "apostle" in the broadest sense, meaning "messenger."

ANEM Place-name meaning "fountains." A city given the Levites from the territory of Issachar (1 Chron. 6:73). Joshua 21:29 lists the city as En-gannim.

ANER Personal and place-name. **1.** Ally of Abraham in the battle against the coalition of kings in Gen. 14. **2.** City from tribe of Manasseh given to Levites (1 Chron. 6:70). In Josh. 21:25 the Levites' city is called Taanach. See *Taanach.*

ANGEL Created beings whose primary function is to serve and worship God. Though some interpret the "us" in Gen. 1:26 as inclusive of God and His angelic court, the Bible does not comment as to when they were created. Unlike God, they are not eternal or omniscient. The Hebrew word in the OT is *mal'ak,* and the NT Greek word is *angelos.* They both mean "messenger" and occasionally refer to human messengers.

ANIAM Personal name meaning "I am a people," "I am an uncle," or "mourning of the people." A member of the tribe of Manasseh (1 Chron. 7:19).

ANIM Place-name meaning "springs." City given tribe of Judah (Josh. 15:50). Located at modern Khirbet Ghuwein at-Tahta, 11 miles south of Hebron.

ANISE KJV translation of the Greek term more properly translated as "dill" in Matt. 23:23.

ANKLET Ornamental rings worn above the ankles; sometimes called "ankle bracelets." The KJV has "tinkling ornaments about their feet" (Isa. 3:18; cp. 3:16). Anklets were luxury items worn by the women of Jerusalem during the days of Isaiah.

ANNA Aged prophetess who recognized the Messiah when He was brought to the temple for dedication (Luke 2:36). Anna, whose name means "grace," was the daughter of Phanuel of the tribe of Asher. After seven years of marriage, she was widowed and became an attendant of the temple. She was 84 when she recognized the Messiah, thanked God for Him, and proclaimed to all hope for the redemption of Jerusalem.

ANNAS Son of Seth; a priest at the time John the Baptist began his public preaching (Luke 3:2). Evidently, Annas, whose name means "merciful," was appointed to the high priesthood about AD 6 by Quirinius, governor of Syria. Though he was deposed in AD 15 by Gratus, he continued to exercise considerable influence. When Jesus was arrested, He was taken before Annas (John 18:13). After Pentecost, Annas led other priests in questioning Peter and the other church leaders (Acts 4:6).

ANNUNCIATION In Christian historical tradition, the annunciation refers specifically to the announcement with which the angel Gabriel notified the virgin Mary of the miraculous conception of Christ within her (Luke 1:26-38; Joseph received a similar announcement in Matt. 1:20-25).

ANOINT, ANOINTED Procedure of rubbing or smearing a person or thing, usually with oil, for the purpose of healing, setting apart, or embalming. A person can anoint himself, be anointed, or anoint another person or thing. While olive oil is the most common element mentioned for use in anointing, oils produced from castor, bay, almond, myrtle, cyprus, cedar, walnut, and fish were also used. In Esther 2:12, for example, the oil of myrrh is used as a cosmetic.

The Hebrew verb *mashach* (noun, *messiah*) and the Greek verb *chrio* (noun, *christos*) are translated "to anoint."

ANON Archaic word used in the KJV meaning "immediately."

ANTEDILUVIANS Meaning "before the Deluge"; refers to those who lived before the flood described in Gen. 6–8.

ANTHOTHIJAH Descendant of Benjamin (1 Chron. 8:24). The name may represent connection with city of Anathoth.

ANTHROPOLOGY Biblical anthropology concerns the origin, essential nature, and destiny of human beings.

ANTHROPOMORPHISM Words which describe God as if He had human features.

ANTICHRIST Describes a particular individual or a group of people who oppose God and His purpose. In the NT the only use of the term "antichrist" is in the Johannine epistles. First John 2:18 speaks of the antichrist who is the great enemy of God and, in particular, antichrists who precede that great enemy. These antichrists were human teachers who had left the church. Such antichrists deny the incarnation (1 John 4:3) and Christ's deity (1 John 2:2). In 2 Thess. 2:1-12, the antichrist figure is armed with satanic power and is fused with Belial, a satanic being (2 Cor. 6:15). In this passage the Roman government is viewed as restraining its power. In Revelation the Roman Caesar is the evil force.

Contemporary Concerns Christians today have differing views of the antichrist figure. Dispensationalists look for a future Roman ruler who will appear during the tribulation and will rule over the earth. Those in the amillennialist school interpret the term symbolically.

ANTINOMIANISM False teaching that since faith alone is necessary for salvation, one is free from the moral obligations of the law. The word "antinomianism" is not used in the Bible, but the idea is spoken of. Paul appears to have been accused of being an antinomian (Rom. 3:8; 6:1,15).

ANTIOCH Name of two NT cities, one of which was home to many Diaspora Jews (Jews living outside of Palestine and maintaining their religious faith among the Gentiles), and the place where believers, many of whom were Gentiles, were first called Christians.

One of the cities called Antioch was the third largest city of the Roman Empire after Rome in Italy and Alexandria in Egypt. Because so many ancient cities were called by this name, it is often called Antioch on the Orontes River or Antioch of Syria.

Another city called Antioch was in Pisidia, Asia Minor, west of Iconium. Paul preached in a synagogue there on his first missionary journey (Acts 13:14) and was warmly received (13:42-44).

ANTIOCHUS Name of 13 rulers of Syria-Palestine headquartered in Antioch. They were part of the Seleucid dynasty that inherited part of Alexander the Great's kingdom.

ANTIPAS Name of a martyr in Revelation and the son of Herod the Great. **1.** Tetrarch of Galilee at the time John the Baptist and Jesus began their public ministries (Luke 3:1). **2.** According to tradition the martyr of the church of Pergamum in Rev. 2:13 was roasted in a brazen bowl at Domitian's request.

The Cilician Gates through the Taurus Mountains north of Antioch of Syria where Paul would have passed on his second missionary journey.

ANTIPATRIS Place-name meaning "in place of father." City that Herod the Great built to honor his father Antipater in 9 BC. It was 40 miles from Jerusalem and 25 miles from Caesarea on the famous Via Maris, "way of the sea," international highway. Roman soldiers taking Paul from Jerusalem to Caesarea spent the night at Antipatris (Acts 23:31). It is located on the site of OT Aphek. See *Aphek*.

ANTONIA, TOWER OF Fortress near the temple built around AD 6 that served as a palace residence for King Herod, barracks for the Roman troops, a safe deposit for the robe of the high priest, and a central courtyard for public speaking. The tower of Antonia is not mentioned directly in the Bible.

ANUB Personal name meaning "grape" or "with a mustache." A member of the tribe of Judah (1 Chron. 4:8).

ANXIETY State of mind wherein one is concerned about something or someone. This state of mind may range from genuine concern (Phil. 2:20,28; 2 Cor. 11:28) to obsessions that originate from a distorted perspective of life (Matt. 6:25-34; Mark 4:19; Luke 12:22-31). Jesus did not prohibit genuine concern about food or shelter, but He did teach that we should keep things in their proper perspective. We should make God's kingdom our first priority; everything else will fall in line after we do that (Matt. 6:33).

APELLES A Christian in Rome whom Paul saluted as "approved in Christ" (Rom. 16:10), which may mean he had been tested by persecution and proved faithful.

APHEK Place-name meaning "bed of brook or river" or "fortress." **1.** City whose king Joshua defeated (Josh. 12:18), where Philistine armies formed to face Israel in days of Samuel (1 Sam. 4:1) resulting in Philistine victory and capture of Israel's ark of the covenant. **2.** Northern border city which

Joshua did not conquer (Josh. 13:4). This may be modern Afqa, 15 miles east of ancient Byblos and 23 miles north of Beirut, Lebanon. **3.** City assigned to Asher (Josh. 19:30) but not conquered (Judg. 1:31). This may be modern Tell Kerdanah, three miles from Haifa and six miles southeast of Acco. **4.** City east of Jordan near the Sea of Galilee where Benhadad led Syria against Israel about 860 BC but met defeat as a prophet predicted for Israel (1 Kings 20:26-30).

APHEKAH City that Joshua assigned to tribe of Judah (Josh. 15:53). Its location is unknown.

APHIAH Personal name meaning "forehead." An ancestor of King Saul from the tribe of Benjamin (1 Sam. 9:1).

APOCALYPTIC Occurs 18 times in the NT in the Greek noun form *apokalupsis* and 26 times in the verb form *apokalupto*. These Greek terms derive from the combination of the preposition *apo* and the verb *kalupto*, resulting in the definition "to uncover, unveil, or reveal." Such "uncovering" or "revelation" comes through visions or dreams and refers to the eschatological disclosure of secrets with reference to the last days. The use of the term "apocalyptic" is due to the opening word of Revelation, *apokalupsis*, meaning a revelation.

APOCRYPHA Jews did not stop writing for centuries between the OT and the NT. The intertestamental period was a time of much literary production. We designate these writings as Apocrypha and Pseudepigrapha. They did not attain canonical status, but some of them were cited by early Christians as almost on a level with the OT writings, and a few were copied in biblical manuscripts. Some NT authors were familiar with various noncanonical works, and the letter from Jude made specific reference to at least one of these books. They were ultimately preserved by the Christians rather than by the Jews.

APOCRYPHA, NEW TESTAMENT Collective term referring to a large body of religious writings dating back to the early Christian centuries that are similar in form to the NT (Gospels, acts, epistles, and apocalypses) but were never included as a part of the canon of Scripture. The NT Apocrypha is significant for those who study church history.

APOLLONIA Place-name meaning "belonging to Apollo." Paul visited Apollonia on his second missionary journey, though the Bible reports no activity there (Acts 17:1). The city is in northern Greece or Macedonia on the international highway called Via Egnatia, 30 miles from Amphipolis and 38 miles from Thessalonica.

APOLLOS Alexandrian Jew who came to Ephesus following Paul's first visit and was taught Christian doctrine by Priscilla and Aquila. An educated man, Apollos handled the OT Scriptures with forcefulness. However, he was lacking in a full understanding of the way of God, so Priscilla and Aquila took him aside and instructed him (Acts 18:26). In 1 Cor. 4:6 Paul placed Apollos on the same level as himself. They both sought to defeat the arrogance and superiority that comes from being self-centered rather than Christ-centered. Because of Apollos' knowledge of the OT, Luther suggested that Apollos might well be the writer of the letter to the Hebrews.

APOLLYON Greek name meaning "destroyer" (Rev. 9:11).

APOSTASY Act of rebelling against, forsaking, abandoning, or falling away from what one has believed. The English word "apostasy" is derived from a Greek word (*apostasia*) that means "to stand away from." The Greek noun occurs twice in the NT (Acts 21:21; 2 Thess. 2:3), though it is not translated as "apostasy" in the KJV. A related noun is used for a divorce (Matt. 5:31; 19:7; Mark 10:4). The corresponding Greek verb occurs nine times.

Apostasy certainly is a biblical concept, but the implications of the teaching have been hotly debated. The debate has centered on the issue of apostasy and salvation. Based on the concept of God's sovereign grace, some hold that, though true believers may stray, they will never totally fall away. Others affirm that any who fall away were never really saved. Though they may have "believed" for a while, they never experienced regeneration. Still others argue that the biblical warnings against apostasy are real and that believers maintain the freedom, at least potentially, to reject God's salvation.

Persons worried about apostasy should recognize that conviction of sin in itself is evidence that one has not fallen away. Desire for salvation shows one does not have "an evil heart of unbelief."

APOSTLE In the NT, "apostle" has three broad uses. First, it referred to the Twelve whom Jesus chose to train for the task of carrying His message to the world. The second designation of apostle is a person authorized by a local congregation with the safe delivery of specific gifts for another Christian church (2 Cor. 8:23; Phil.2:25). The third sense of apostle is those whom Jesus Christ has sent. Paul refers to a number of people as apostles in this sense (Rom. 16:7; 1 Cor. 9:1,5; 12:28; Gal. 1:17-19). See *Disciple*.

APOSTOLIC COUNCIL Meeting in Jerusalem at which the apostles and elders of Jerusalem defended the right of Paul and Barnabas to preach the gospel to the Gentiles without forcing converts to obey the Jewish laws (Acts 15).

APOSTOLIC FATHERS Group of early church writers, some of whom knew the apostles. These writers were not grouped together or called the Apostolic Fathers until the late seventeenth century. That first collection, entitled the Apostolic Fathers, included the works of Clement, Ignatius, Polycarp, Barnabas, and Hermas. Other works such as the Didache, Diognetus, and Papias often have been included in recent collections. The documents (except for Diognetus and Papias) were written between approximately AD 96 and 156, yet they were not accepted as part of the NT canon, although Codex Sinaiticus (fourth century) included the Epistle of Barnabas and the Shepherd of Hermas, and Codex Alexandrinus (fifth century) included the two epistles of Clement.

APOTHECARY KJV translation of a word translated as "perfumer" in modern versions (Exod. 30:25,35; 37:29; 2 Chron. 16:14; Neh. 3:8; Eccles. 10:1).

APPAIM Personal name meaning "nostrils." Member of clan of Jerahmeel of tribe of Judah (1 Chron. 2:30-31).

APPHIA Christian lady Paul greeted as "beloved" while writing Philemon (v. 2). Early Christian tradition identified her as Philemon's wife, a claim that can be neither proved nor disproved.

APPI FORUM KJV translation of Acts 28:15 reference to Forum of Appius or Market of Appius. See *Forum.*

APPLE OF THE EYE English expression that refers to the pupil of the eye and therefore to something very precious. Three different Hebrew words or phrases are rendered as the apple of the eye.

APRON Translation of a Hebrew word in the OT otherwise translated as girdle (1 Sam. 18:4; 2 Sam. 18:11; 20:8; 1 Kings 2:5; Isa. 3:24). In Gen. 3:7, the fig leaves sewn together by Adam and Eve are called aprons to hide their nakedness. In the OT the girdle was an inner garment wrapped around the waist. In the NT the girdle was wrapped around the waist of the outer garment. In Acts 19:12 the aprons and handkerchiefs of Paul had healing powers.

AQABA, GULF OF TEV translation in 1 Kings 9:26 to show that the part of the Red Sea meant is the eastern arm below the Dead Sea. Its northern port city is Eloth (or Elath, NIV).

AQUEDUCTS Troughs cut out of rock or soil, or pipes made of stone, leather, or bronze that were used from very early times in the Middle East to transport water from distant places into towns and cities.

Pharaoh's Island in the Gulf of Aquaba.

AQUILA AND PRISCILLA
Married couple who came from Italy to Corinth after the emperor Claudius ordered Jews expelled from Rome, became Christians, and assisted Paul in his ministry. They were tentmakers by trade (2 Tim. 4:19). They came into contact with Paul, who was a tentmaker, in Corinth (Acts 18:2). It is not clear whether they became Christians before or after meeting Paul, but they became workers in the gospel and accompanied Paul to Ephesus (Acts 18:19).

ARA Leader in tribe of Asher (1 Chron. 7:38).

ARAB Place-name meaning "ambush." **1.** City in the hill country of Judah near Hebron (Josh. 15:52). Usually identified with modern er-Rabiyeh. **2.** Member of the Semitic people of the Arabian peninsula. See *Arabia.*

ARABAH Place-name meaning "dry, infertile area" and common Hebrew noun meaning desert with hot climate and sparse rainfall. Modern usage refers specifically to the rift area below the Dead Sea to the Gulf of Elath or Aqaba, a distance of 110 miles. This was a copper-mining region and was guarded by military fortresses. Control of the Arabah along with control of the Red Sea port on its southern end meant control of valuable trade routes and sea routes connecting to southern Arabia and eastern Africa

(Deut. 2:8; 1 Kings 9:26-27).

ARABIA Asian peninsula lying between the Red Sea on the west and the Persian Gulf on the east incorporating over 1,200,000 square miles of territory.

Old Testament The Arabian peninsula, together with the adjoining lands that were home to the biblical Arabs, includes all of present-day Saudi Arabia, the two Yemens (San'a' and Aden), Oman, the United Arab Emirates, Qatar, and Kuwait, as well as parts of Iraq, Syria, Jordan, and the Sinai Peninsula. The vast Arabian Peninsula was divided into two distinct economic and social regions. Most biblical references to Arab peoples or territory are to the northern and western parts of this whole but sometimes include both the northern and southern portions.

New Testament The NT references to Arabia are fewer and less complex. The territory of the Nabatean Arabs is probably intended in each instance. The Nabateans controlled what is today southern Jordan and the Negev of Israel; for a time they controlled as far north as Damascus. Arabs heard the gospel at Pentecost (Acts 2:11). Paul went to Arabia after his conversion (Gal. 1:17).

ARABIM NASB transliteration of name of waterway mentioned in Isa. 15:7. Other translations include: "brook of the willows" (KJV); "Ravine of the Poplars" (NIV); "Valley of Willows" (TEV); "Wadi of the Willows" (NRSV). The water source indicated may be the Wadi el-Chesa at the southern end of the Dead Sea in Moab.

ARAD Two towns of significance to the OT. One town (21:1-3) is referred to in the Bible during the time of Moses, and another was inhabited during the period of the monarchy. Both are located in the dry, semidesert region known as the Negev in the southern extreme of Judah's territory.

One of the men called "Arad" was one of six sons of Beriah the Benjamite (1 Chron. 8:15-16), who was one of the major inhabitants of Aijalon. Another OT "Arad" was a Canaanite king who attacked the Israelites near Mount Hor and was defeated (Num. 21:1).

ARAH Personal name meaning "ox" or "traveler." **1.** Clan of 775 people who returned to Jerusalem with Zerubbabel from Babylonian exile about 537 B.C. (Ezra 2:5). Nehemiah 7:10 gives the number as 652. **2.** Father of Schechaniah, father-in-law of Tobiah, who led opposition to Nehemiah (Neh. 6:18). May be identical with clan head of 1. above. **3.** Member of tribe of Asher (1 Chron. 7:39).

ARAM Personal, ethnic, and geographical name. **1.** Arameans. See *Aramean.* **2.** Original ancestor of Arameans, the son of Shem and grandson of Noah (Gen. 10:22-23). **3.** Grandson of Nahor, Abraham's brother (Gen. 22:21). **4.** Member of tribe of Asher (1 Chron. 7:34).

ARAMAIC North Semitic language similar to Phoenician and Hebrew. It was the language of the Arameans whose presence in northwestern Mesopotamia is known from about 2000 B.C.

Old Testament Parts of the OT were written in Aramaic: Ezra 4:8–6:18; 7:12-26; Dan. 2:4b–7:28; Jer. 10:11. Two words in Gen. 31:47, *Jegar-sahadutha* (heap of witness) are in Aramaic. A number of Aramaic words came into common Hebrew usage, and several passages in the Hebrew Bible show Aramaic influence.

New Testament The wide diffusion of Aramaic, along with its flexibility and adaptability, resulted in the emergence of various dialects. Jewish Palestinian Aramaic words and phrases occur in the NT, such as Abba (father) (Mark 14:36), *talitha, qumi* (maiden, arise) (Mark 5:41), *lama sabachthani* (why have You forsaken Me?) (Mark 15:34 HCSB).

ARAMEAN or **ARAMAEAN** Loose confederation of towns and settlements spread over what is now called Syria as well as in some parts of Babylon from which Jacob and Abraham came (Deut. 26:5).

ARAMITESS KJV translation in 1 Chron. 7:14 for an unnamed concubine from Aram, thus an Aramaean or Syrian. She was mother of Machir, son of Manasseh.

ARAM-MAACAH Territory in Syria (1 Chron. 19:6), also called Syria-maachah, Maacah, Maachah. In 2 Sam. 10:6 only Aram-Zobah is named.

ARAM-NAHARAIM Country name meaning "Aram of the two rivers." Appears in title of Psalm 60 in KJV. Transliterated from Hebrew also in Gen. 24:10; Deut. 23:4; Judg. 3:8; and 1 Chron. 19:6 by NIV. It refers to the land between the Tigris and Euphrates rivers.

ARAM-ZOBAH Alternate name for the Aramaean town and kingdom of Zobah found in the superscription of Psalm 60. See *Zobah.*

ARAN Personal name, perhaps meaning "ibex." A Horite descended from Seir (Gen. 36:28).

ARARAT Mountainous region in western Asia. **1.** Area where the ark came to rest after the flood (Gen. 8:4). **2.** Region where Sennacherib's sons fled for refuge after murdering their father (2 Kings 19:37). **3.** Jeremiah included in a prophetic call for a war league as judgment against Babylon (Jer. 51:27). The references in Kings and Isaiah are rendered "Armenia" in KJV, following the Septuagint tradition.

This mountain in modern Turkey may be part of the Mountains of Ararat where Noah's ark came to rest after the flood.

ARAUNAH Personal name of unknown meaning. A Jebusite whose threshing floor David purchased as a site for sacrifice, following the prophetic command of God, holding back a divine plague after David disobeyed by taking a census (2 Sam. 24:15-25). Second Chronicles 3:1 and 1 Chron. 21:15-30 refer to Araunah as Ornan.

ARBA Personal name meaning "four." Father of Anak for whom Kiriath-arba was named (Josh. 14:15; 15:13). The city became known as Hebron. Arba was the outstanding warrior among the Anakim. See *Anak, Anakim.*

ARBATHITE Resident of Beth-arabah (2 Sam. 23:31). See *Beth-arabah.*

Step trench cut into the tel of Old Testament Jericho by archaeologists to uncover levels of destruction.

ARBITE Native of Arab, a village in Judah near Hebron (Josh. 15:52), identified as modern er-Rabiyeh. One of David's warriors in the Thirty was Paarai, an Arbite (2 Sam. 23:35).

ARCH KJV rendering of a Hebrew word in Ezek. 40:16-36. The KJV translates the word as "porch" elsewhere (e.g., 1 Kings 6:3; 7:12,19,21). Other versions translate the word as "porch" (NASB), "portico" and "galleries (NIV), "vestibule" and "walls" (RSV), and "entrance room" and "galleries" (TEV).

ARCHAEOLOGY AND BIBLICAL STUDY

Archaeology is the study of the past based upon the recovery, examination, and explanation of the material remains of human life, thought, and activity, coordinated with available information concerning the ancient environment. Biblical archaeology, a discipline largely developing since 1800, searches for what can be learned about biblical events, characters, and teachings from sources outside the Bible. Dealing with what ancient civilizations left behind, its goal is to give a better understanding of the Bible itself. Though the idea that archaeology can prove the Bible is frowned on by many archaeologists, it has nevertheless confirmed biblical accounts in many cases. The main function of archaeology is illumination of past cultures. The great gulf in time, language, and culture between our day and biblical times makes knowledge of archaeological discoveries essential for thorough understanding of the Bible

ARCHANGEL Chief or first angel. The English term "archangel" is a derivative of the Greek word *archangelos,* which occurs only twice in the NT.

ARCHELAUS Son and principal successor of Herod the Great (Matt. 2:22).

ARCHEVITES Group who joined Rehum the commander in writing a letter to King Artaxerxes of Persia protesting the rebuilding of Jerusalem under Zerubbabel's leadership about 537 B.C. NASB, NIV, NRSV translate Archevites as people or men of Erech.

ARCHI, ARCHITE Unknown group of people who gave their name to a border point of the tribes of Ephraim and Benjamin (Josh. 16:2).

ARCHIPPUS Personal name meaning "first among horsemen." A Christian whom Paul greeted in Col. 4:17 and Philem. 2, entreating him to fulfill the ministry God gave him. Some have suggested he was the son of Philemon and Appia, but this can be neither proved nor disproved.

ARCTURUS Constellation of stars God created (Job 9:9; 38:32) of which exact identification was not clear to the earliest Bible translators and continues to be debated. Modern translations generally use "Bear" (NASB, NIV, NRSV). TEV uses "the Dipper." Some scholars prefer "the lion." Whatever the identification, the star points to the sovereign greatness of God beyond human understanding.

ARD, ARDITE Personal name meaning "hunchbacked." **1.** Son of Benjamin and grandson of Jacob (Gen. 46:21). **2.** Grandson and clan father of Benjamin (Num. 26:40). Apparently listed as Addar in 1 Chron. 8:3.

ARDON Son of Caleb (1 Chron. 2:18).

ARELI, ARELITES Son of Gad (Gen. 46:16) and original ancestor of clan of Arelites (Num. 26:17).

AREOPAGITE Member of the highly respected Greek council which met on the Areopagus in Athens. See *Areopagus; Athens; Dionysius.*

AREOPAGUS Site of Paul's speech to the Epicurean and Stoic philosophers of Athens (Acts 17:19). It was a rocky hill about 370 feet high, not far from the Acropolis and the Agora (marketplace) in Athens, Greece. The word also was used to refer to the council that originally met on this hill. The name probably was derived from Ares, the Greek name for the god of war known to the Romans as Mars. See *Mars Hill.*

ARETAS Personal name meaning "moral excellence, power." The ruler of Damascus in NT times. He sought to arrest Paul after his conversion (2 Cor. 11:32). The name Aretas was borne by several Arabian kings centered in Petra and Damascus. Aretas IV ruled from Petra (9 BC–AD 40) as a subject of Rome. Herod Antipas married his daughter, then divorced her to marry Herodias (Mark 6:17-18). Aretas joined with a Roman officer to defeat Herod's army in AD 36.

ARGOB Personal and geographical name meaning "mound of earth." **1.** Man who might have joined Pekah (2 Kings 15:25) in murdering Pekahiah, king of Israel (742–740 BC), or possibly was killed by Pekah. **2.** Territory in Bashan in the hill country east of the Jordan River. Argob was probably in the center of the fertile tableland and was famous for its strong cities (Deut. 3:4).

ARIDAI Persian personal name, perhaps meaning "delight of Hari" (a god). Son of Haman, Esther and the Jews' archenemy. He died as the Jews reversed Haman's scheme and gained revenge (Esther 9:9).

ARIDATHA Persian personal name, perhaps meaning "given by Hari" (a god). Brother of Aridai who shared his fate. See *Aridai.*

ARIEL Personal name meaning "God's lion." **1.** Jewish leader in captivity who acted as Ezra's messenger to the Levites to send people with Ezra to Jerusalem about 458 BC (Ezra 8:16). **2.** Code name for Jerusalem in Isaiah 29.

ARIMATHEA City of Joseph, the disciple who claimed the body of Jesus following the crucifixion and in whose own new tomb the body was placed (Matt. 27:57). The location of Arimathea is not certainly known.

ARIOCH Personal, probably Hurrian, name meaning "servant of the moon god." **1.** King of Ellasar, who joined alliance against Sodom and Gomorrah (Gen. 14) but was eventually defeated by

Abraham. **2.** Commander of bodyguard of King Nebuchadnezzar (Dan. 2:14-25).

ARISAI Persian personal name. Son of Haman (Esther 9:9) who suffered his brothers' fate. See *Aridai.*

ARISTARCHUS Personal name, perhaps meaning "best ruler." Paul's companion caught by the followers of Artemis in Ephesus (Acts 19:29).

ARISTOBULUS Head of a Christian household in Rome whom Paul greeted (Rom. 16:10).

ARK Boat or water vessel and in particular one built by Noah under God's direction to save Noah, his family, and representatives of all animal life from the flood.The ark became both a symbol of a faith on the part of Noah and a symbol of grace on the part of God (Gen. 6:8,22).

ARK OF THE COVENANT

Original container for the Ten Commandments and the central symbol of God's presence with the people of Israel. Hebrews 9:1-10 shows the ark was a part of the old order with external regulations waiting for the new day of Christ to come with a perfect sacrifice able to cleanse the human conscience. Revelation 11:19 shows the ark of the covenant will be part of the heavenly temple when it is revealed.

ARM Upper limb of the human body used to symbolize power and strength.

ARMAGEDDON Middle East site of the final battle between the forces of good and evil (Rev. 16:16). The word "Armageddon" appears once in Scripture and is not found in Hebrew literature.

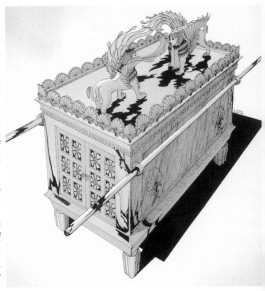

Reconstruction of the ark of the covenant drawn in the Egyptian style, reflecting the 400 years of bondage in Egypt..

ARMENIA KJV translation for land of Ararat (2 Kings 19:37). See *Ararat.*

ARMONI Personal name meaning "born in Armon." Son of Rizpah and Saul, whom David gave to the Gibeonites in revenge for Saul's earlier killing of Gibeonites (2 Sam. 21:7-9).

ARNAN Personal name meaning "quick." Person in messianic line of King David after the return from exile (1 Chron. 3:21).

ARNI Ancestor of Jesus in difficult text of Luke 3:33. NASB, NIV read Ram, correlating with list in 1 Chron. 2:10.

ARNON Place-name meaning "rushing river" or "river flooded with berries." River forming border of Moab and Amorites (Num. 21:13).

AROD or **ARODI** Personal name meaning "humpbacked." Arodi (Gen. 46:16) or Arod (Num. 26:17) was son of Gad and grandson of Jacob. He was the original ancestor of the Arodite clan.

AROER Place-name meaning "juniper." **1.** City on north rim of Arnon Gorge east of Dead Sea on southern boundary of territory Israel claimed east of the Jordan River (Josh. 13:9). **2.** City of the tribe of Gad (Josh. 13:25) near Rabbah, capital of the Ammonites. This may be the Aroer where Jephthah defeated the Ammonites (Judg. 11:33). **3.** Town in southern Judah about 12 miles southeast of Beersheba with whose leaders David divided the spoil of battle (1 Sam. 30:28). This is located at modern Khirbet Arara. The text of Josh. 15:22 may have originally read "Aroer." Two of David's captains hailed from Aroer (1 Chron. 11:44).

ARPACHSHAD or **ARPHAXAD** (NT) Third son of Shem, son of Noah, and ancestor of the Hebrew people (Gen. 10:22). He was born two years after the flood and was the grandfather of Eber.

ARPAD or **ARPHAD** City-state in northern Syria closely identified with Hamath.

ARTAXERXES Persian royal name meaning "kingdom of righteousness," belonging to four Persian rulers and forming a major piece of evidence in dating Ezra and Nehemiah. **1.** Son of Xerxes I, Artaxerxes I ruled Persia from 465 to 424 BC. He was called Longimanus or "long handed." **2.** Artaxerxes II ruled Persia 404 to 359 BC. Some Bible students identify him as ruler under whom Ezra worked. **3.** Artaxerxes III ruled 358–337 BC. **4.** Name assumed by Arses, who ruled Persia 337–336 BC.

ARTEMAS Personal name probably shortened from Artemidoros, meaning "gift of Artemis." If this is the case, then the parents worshipped the Greek goddess Artemis. Paul promised to send Artemas or Tychicus to Titus, so Titus could join Paul in Nicopolis (Titus 3:12). Artemas would apparently take over Titus' pastoral duties in Crete. Tradition says Artemas became bishop of Lystra.

ARTEMIS Name for the Greek goddess of the moon, the daughter of Zeus and Leto, whose worship was threatened by Paul's preaching of the gospel. Artemis was the goddess who watched over nature for both humans and animals. She was the patron deity of wild animals, protecting them from ruthless treatment and at the same time regulating the rules of hunting activities for humans. She was considered the great mother image and gave fertility to humankind. The most famous statue of Artemis was located in the city of Ephesus, the official "temple keeper" for Artemis. Artemis was the chief deity of Ephesus, and her temple was one of the "Seven Wonders" of the ancient world. Diana was a Roman deity somewhat similar to the more popular Artemis.

ARUBBOTH City name meaning "smoke hole" or "chimney." One of Solomon's provincial officials made headquarters there and administered over Sochoh and the land of Hepher (1 Kings 4:10).

ARUMAH Place-name meaning "exalted" or "height." Abimelech, the judge, lived there while he fought to control Shechem (Judg. 9:41).

ARVAD, ARVADITE Place-name of unknown meaning and persons from that place. It provided sailors and soldiers for Tyre (Ezek. 27:8,11). It was probably the rocky island called Rouad today, off the coast of Syria. It is related to Canaan in the family of nations (Gen. 10:18).

ARZA Personal name meaning "wood worm" or "earthiness." Steward of the house of King Baasha (908–886 BC) in Tirzah. The king was drunk in Arza's house when Zimri killed Baasha (1 Kings 16:8-10).

ASA Personal name meaning "doctor" or "healing." **1.** Son and successor of Abijam as king of Judah (1 Kings 15:8). He reigned for 41 years (913–873 BC). A pious man, he instituted several reforms to remove foreign gods and foreign religious practices from the land, even removing his mother from political power (1 Kings 15:13). **2.** Levite who returned from the exile to Jerusalem. He was the head of a family in the villages of the Netophathites near Jerusalem (1 Chron. 9:16).

ASAHEL Personal name meaning "God acted" or "God made." **1.** Brother of Joab and Abishai, David's nephew (2 Sam. 2:18). He was a commander in David's army (2 Sam. 23:24). **2.** Levite during the reign of Jehoshaphat, Asa's son. Asahel was sent out along with several princes, other Levites, and priests to teach the people of Judah the book of the law of God (2 Chron. 17:8). **3.** A Levite under Hezekiah, the king of Judah following Ahaz. **4.** Father of Jonathan who along with Jahaziah opposed Ezra's direction for the men of Judah to separate themselves from the foreign wives they had married. Ezra indicated they had sinned in marrying foreign women (Ezra 10:15).

ASAHIAH or **ASAIAH** Personal name meaning "Yahweh made." **1.** Servant of King Josiah sent with others to Huldah, the prophet, to determine the meaning of the book of the Law found in the temple about 624 BC. **2.** Leader of the tribe of Simeon who helped drive out the people of Ham from pastures of Gedor when Hezekiah was king of Judah (715–686 BC). **3.** Musical Levite in line of Merari (1 Chron. 6:30). **4.** Leader of clans from Shiloh who returned from Babylonian exile about 537 BC (1 Chron. 9:5).

ASAPH Personal name meaning "he collected." **1.** Father of court official under King Hezekiah (715–686 BC), who in sadness reported the threats of Assyria to the king (2 Kings 18). **2.** Levite musician whom David appointed to serve in the tabernacle until the temple was completed (1 Chron. 6:39). Asaph was the father of the clan of temple musicians who served through the history of the temple.

ASAREL or **ASAREEL** (KJV) Personal name meaning "God has sworn" or "God rejoiced." A member of the tribe of Judah (1 Chron. 4:16).

ASARELAH KJV, NIV, NRSV spelling of Asharelah (NASB, RSV, TEV) in 1 Chron. 25:2. This appears to be a variant of Jesharelah or Jesarelah in 1 Chron. 25:14. The person is a descendant or son of Asaph among the temple singers.

ASCENSION Movement or departure from the lower to the higher with reference to spatial location. Both OT and NT record the events of human ascension in the lives of Enoch (Gen. 5:24), Elijah (2 Kings 2:1-2), and most importantly, Jesus Christ (Acts 1:9). The ascension concluded the earthly ministry of Jesus, allowing eyewitnesses to see both the resurrected Christ on earth and the victorious, eternal Christ returning to heaven to minister at the right hand of the Father.

ASENATH Egyptian name meaning "belonging to Neith" (a goddess). Wife of Joseph and daughter of a priest in Egyptian temple at On or Heliopolis. Asenath was Pharaoh's present to Joseph (Gen. 41:45). She was mother of Ephraim and Manasseh (Gen. 41:50-51).

ASH KJV in Isa. 44:14. Some manuscripts of the Hebrew text have the word for cedar, which is very similar to the word found in the text translated by the KJV. Modern versions differ. The word is translated fir (NASB), pine (NIV), cedar (NRSV, REB), and laurel tree (TEV).

ASHAN Place-name meaning "smoke." City in western hills of tribe of Judah (Josh. 15:42) given to tribe of Simeon (Josh. 19:7). The Aaronic priests claimed Ashan as one of their cities (1 Chron. 6:59; called Ain in Josh. 21:16). Ashan was located at modern Khirbet Asan just northwest of Beersheba.

ASHBEL, ASHBELITES Personal name meaning "having a long upper lip." Son of Benjamin, grandson of Jacob, and original ancestor of Ashbelite clan (Gen. 46:21).

ASHCHENAZ or **ASHKENAZ** Personal and national name given two spellings in KJV but spelled Ashkenaz in modern translations. A son of Gomer (Gen. 10:3) and original ancestor of people called kingdom of Ashkenaz (Jer. 51:27). Usually identified with Scythians.

ASHDOD One of five principal cities of the Philistines, where the Philistines defeated Israel and captured the ark of the covenant. Ashdod was 10 miles north of Ashkelon and two and a half miles east of the Mediterranean Sea on the Philistine plain.

ASHER or **ASER** (NT Gk.), **ASHERITES** Personal, place, and tribal name meaning "fortune," "happiness." **1.** Eighth son of Jacob, born of Zilpah, the concubine (Gen. 30:13). His four sons and one daughter began the tribe of Asher (Gen. 46:17). Jacob's blessing said Asher would have rich food that he would give a king (Gen. 49:20), perhaps suggesting a period when the tribe would serve a foreign king. **2.** The tribe of Asher numbered 53,400 in the wilderness (Num. 26:47), having grown from 41,500 (Num. 1:41). They formed part of the rear guard in the wilderness marches (Num. 10:25-28). Asher's territorial allotment was in Phoenicia in the far northwest reaching to Tyre and Sidon on the Mediterranean coast (Josh. 19:24-31). **3.** Apparently a border town in Manasseh (Josh. 17:7) but possibly a reference to the border joining the tribal territories of Manasseh and Asher.

ASHERAH, ASHERIM (pl.) or **ASHEROTH** (pl.) Fertility goddess, the mother of Baal, whose worship was concentrated in Syria and Canaan, and the wooden object that represented her. The KJV translated Asherah "grove" and the proper noun "Ashtaroth."

ASHES Often associated with sacrifices, mourning, and fasting. Grief, humiliation, and repentance were expressed by placing ashes on the head or by sitting in ashes. The use of ashes to express grief and repentance continued into the NT period. Their use in purification rites is contrasted with the cleansing brought by Christ's blood. They also represent the devastating effect of God's wrath on Sodom and Gomorrah (2 Pet. 2:6).

ASHHUR Modern translation spelling of Ashur (KJV, TEV). Personal name meaning "to be black," or "belonging to Ishara." Son of Hazron, born after his father's death (1 Chron. 2:24). His title, "Father of Tekoa," may indicate he founded the city later famous for native son Amos, the prophet.

ASHIMA Syrian god made and worshiped in Hamath (2 Kings 17:30). The Hebrew word 'asham means "guilt." Hebrew writers may have deliberately written a word associated with guilt instead of the name of the god or goddess.

ASHKELON One of five principal cities of the Philistines (Pentapolis), located on the Mediterranean coast on the trade route, Via Maris, and designated for Judah in the conquest. Ashkelon was a Mediterranean coastal city 12 miles north of Gaza and 10 miles south of Ashdod. It was the only Philistine city directly on the seacoast. Its history extends into the Neolithic Period. The economic importance came from both its port and its location on the trade route, the Via Maris.

ASHNAH Place-name. **1.** City in the valley of the tribe of Judah (Josh. 15:33), possibly modern Aslin. **2.** City in the valley or shephelah of Judah (Josh. 15:43), possibly modern Idna, about eight miles northwest of Hebron.

ASHPENAZ Chief eunuch guarding the family of Nebuchadnezzar, king of Babylon (605–562 BC) (Dan. 1:3). He administered the diet and lifestyle of Daniel and his three friends, giving them new Babylonian names (Dan. 1:7). Daniel developed a close, loving relationship with him.

ASHTAROTH is the plural form of Ashtoreth, a Canaanite goddess of fertility, love, and war and the daughter of the god El and the goddess Asherah. **1.** OT uses the plural form, Ashtaroth, more than the singular form, Ashtoreth. The only references to Ashtoreth come in 1 Kings 11:5,33; 2 Kings 23:13. **2.** Egyptian documents dating from the eighteenth century BC onward refer to a city called Ashtartu or Ashtarot in the region of Bashan. Joshua 21:27 mentions a city with the name Be-eshter-ah in Bashan, while a man named Uzzia is called an Ashterathite (1 Chron. 11:44).

ASHURBANIPAL Assyria's last great king who is identified in Ezra 4:10 as the king of Assyria who captured Susa, Elam, and other nations and settled their citizens in Samaria.

ASHURITE or **ASHURI** (NIV) Apparently a tribe or clan over which Ish-bosheth, Saul's son, ruled (2 Sam. 2:9).

ASHVATH Personal name meaning "that which has been worked" (as iron). Descendant of Asher (1 Chron. 7:33).

ASIA New Testament refers to a Roman province on the west of Asia Minor whose capital was Ephesus. The Roman province of Asia comprised generally the southwest portion of Anatolia. Its first capital was Pergamum, but the capital was later changed to Ephesus.

ASIA MINOR, CITIES OF Cities located on the Anatolian peninsula (modern-day Turkey). Cities of Asia Minor important to the NT accounts included Alexandria Troas, Assos, Ephesus, Miletus, Patara, Smyrna, Pergamum, Sardis, Thyatira, Philadelphia, Laodicea, Colossae, Attalia, Antioch, Iconium, Lystra, Derbe, and Tarsus. The cities figured prominently in the Apostle Paul's missionary journeys, several of the churches receiving epistles. Among those listed are the Seven Cities of the Revelation.

ASIARCHS Somewhat general term for public patrons and leaders named by cities in the Roman province of Asia.

ASIEL Personal name meaning "God has made." A descendant of Simeon and clan leader who settled in Gedor in rich pasturelands (1 Chron. 4:35-40).

ASNAH Proper name possibly with Egyptian origins relating to the god Nah. One of the Nethanims or temple servants who returned to Jerusalem with Zerubbabel from exile about 537 BC (Ezra 2:50).

ASNAPPER KJV reading in Ezra 4:10. Modern translations read Osnappar (NASB, RSV) or Ashurbanipal (TEV, NIV).

ASP KJV translation for a dangerous, poisonous snake (Deut. 32:33; Job 20:14,16; Isa. 11:8; Rom. 3:13). Other translations use "serpent," "viper," or "cobra" at some or all of these places.

ASPATHA Persian personal name. Son of Haman killed by Jews (Esther 9:10).

ASRIEL, ASRIELITES Personal name meaning "God has made happy." A son of Gilead and clan in the tribe of Manasseh (Num. 26:31). They received a land allotment (Josh. 17:2). In 1 Chron. 7:14 KJV spells it Ashriel.

ASS "Beast of burden" and "wild animal" in KJV but translated "donkey" in most modern translations. Six different Hebrew words and two Greek words lie behind the English translations. This animal appears more than 120 times in the Bible.

ASSASSINS Organized Jewish group who attempted to win freedom from the Romans. The word in Greek is derived from the Latin term *Sicarii* and literally means "dagger men." In Acts 21:38 Paul was mistaken as a leader of 4,000 *Sicarii*. KJV calls them murderers; REB and TEV, terrorists.

ASSAYER One who tests ore for its silver and gold content. According to modern versions of Jer. 6:27, the calling of Jeremiah was to be an assayer of the people. He did not find them to be a precious metal.

ASSEMBLY Official gathering of the people of Israel and of the church.

ASSHUR, ASSHURIM, ASSHURITES (NIV) Personal and national name. **1.** Son of Shem and thus a Semite, as were the Hebrew people (Gen. 10:22). **2.** Unknown Arabian tribe (Gen. 25:3). This tribe may also be meant in Balaam's oracle (Num. 24:22-24), but a reference to Assyria is more likely. **3.** The nation Assyria and its inhabitants are generally meant by the Hebrew term *Asshur*. This is the likely meaning in Gen. 10:11; Ezek. 27:23; 32:22; Hos. 14:3. See *Assyria*.

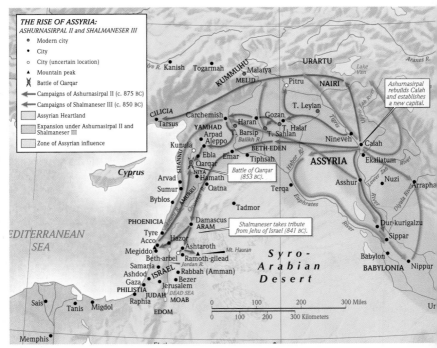

ASSYRIA Nation in northern Mesopotamia in OT times that became a large empire during the period of the Israelite kings. Assyrian expansion into the region of Palestine (about 855–625 BC) had enormous impact on the Hebrew kingdoms of Israel and Judah.

History Assyria lay north of the region of Babylonia along the banks of the Tigris River (Gen. 2:14) in northern Mesopotamia. The name Assyria (Hb., *Ashshur*) is from Asshur, its first capital, founded about 2000 BC. The foundation of other Assyrian cities, notably Calah and Nineveh, appears in Gen. 10:11-12.

ASTROLOGER Person who "divided the heavens" (literal translation of Hebrew phrase, Isa. 47:13) to determine the future. Particularly the Babylonians developed sophisticated methods of reading the stars to determine proper times for action. The Bible does not seek to describe the skills, tactics, or methods of foreign personnel engaged in various practices to determine the opportune time. Rather the Bible mocks such practices and shows that God's word to the prophets and the wise of Israel far surpasses any foreign skills.

ASUPPIM KJV interpretation in 1 Chron. 26:15,17. Modern translations read "storehouse."

ASWAN NIV, TEV in Ezek. 29:10; 30:6 for Syene.

ASYNCRITUS Personal name meaning "incomparable." Roman Christian whom Paul greeted (Rom. 16:14).

ATAD Personal name meaning "thorn." Owner of threshing floor, or part of name of Bramble Threshing Floor, east of the Jordan River where Joseph stopped to mourn the death of his father before carrying Jacob's embalmed body across the Jordan to Machpelah for burial. The place was named Abelmizraim (Gen. 50:10-11).

ATARAH Personal name meaning "crown" or "wreath." Second wife of Jerahmeel and mother of Onam (1 Chron. 2:26).

ATAROTH Place-name meaning "crowns." **1.** Town desired and built up by tribe of Gad (Num. 32:3,34). **2.** Village on border of Benjamin and Ephraim (Josh. 16:2,7).

ATAROTH-ADDAR Place-name meaning "crowns of glory." A border town in Ephraim (Josh. 16:5), bordering Benjamin (Josh. 18:13), probably modern Khirbet Attara at the foot of Tell en-Nasbeh or possibly identical with Tell en-Nasbeh and thus with biblical Mizpah.

ATER Personal name meaning either "crippled" or "left-handed." Clan of which 98 returned from Babylonian exile with Zerubbabel about 537 BC (Ezra 2:16). They were temple gatekeepers (Ezra 2:42). The head of the clan signed Nehemiah's covenant to keep God's Law (Neh. 10:17).

ATHACH Place-name meaning "attack." Town in southern Judah to which David sent spoils of victory while he fled Saul among the Philistines (1 Sam. 30:30). May be the same as Ether (Josh. 15:42), a small copying change causing the difference.

ATHAIAH Leader of tribe of Judah who lived in Jerusalem in time of Nehemiah (Neh. 11:4).

ATHALIAH Personal name meaning "Yahweh has announced His exalted nature" or "Yahweh is righteous." **1.** Wife of Jehoram, king of Judah, and mother of Ahaziah, king of Judah. She was either the daughter of Ahab and Jezebel of Israel (2 Kings 8:18) or of Omri, king of Israel (2 Kings 8:26). **2.** Son of Jeroham in tribe of Benjamin (1 Chron. 8:26). **3.** Father of Jeshaiah, who led 70 men back to Jerusalem from exile with Ezra (Ezra 8:7).

ATHARIM Hebrew word of uncertain meaning. It names a roadway the king of Arad took to attack Israel under Moses. After an initial setback, Israel prayed and found victory under God (Num. 21:1-3). KJV translates "spies" following the Septuagint, the earliest Greek translation. Modern translations simply transliterate the Hebrew. The site may be Tamar a few miles south of the Dead Sea.

ATHENS Capital of Attica, an ancient district of east central Greece, where Paul preached to the Greek philosophers (Acts 17:15-34).

ATHLAI Personal name meaning "Yahweh is exalted." A man who agreed (Ezra 10:28) under Ezra's leadership to divorce his foreign wife and return to faithfulness to Yahweh.

ATONEMENT Biblical doctrine that God has reconciled sinners to Himself through the sacrificial work of Jesus Christ. The concept of atonement spans both Testaments, every-

The Parthenon on the Acropolis at Athens.

where pointing to the death, burial, and resurrection of Jesus for the sins of the world. All are invited to find refuge in the atonement of Christ (Luke 14:16-17). The apostles plead with sinners to trust in the atoning work of Jesus (Acts 2:40; 2 Cor. 5:20). All human beings are not only invited but commanded to believe the gospel (Acts 17:30-31). This does not mean, however, that the objective accomplishment of the atonement brings about universal salvation. Jesus is Himself the One who is the propitiation of God's wrath against the world (1 John 2:2). Those who are redeemed are saved from God's judgment because they are united to Christ through faith (Eph. 1:7). On the final day of judgment, those who are not "in Christ" will bear the eternal penalty for their own sins (2 Cor. 5:10) and for the dread transgression of rejecting God's provision in Christ (John 3:19; Heb. 10:29).

ATROTH (KJV) or **ATROTH-BETH-JOAB** Place-name meaning "crowns of the house of Joab." A "descendant" of Caleb and Hur (1 Chron. 2:54), the name apparently refers to a village near Bethlehem.

ATROTH-SHOPHAN Town built by tribe of Gad of unknown location (Num. 32:35). Earliest translations spelled name various ways: Shophar, Shaphim, Shopham, Etroth Shophan.

ATTAI Personal name meaning "timely." **1.** Member of clan of Jerahmeel in tribe of Judah (1 Chron. 2:35-36). **2.** Warrior of tribe of Gad who served David in the wilderness as he fled from Saul (1 Chron. 12:11). **3.** Son of Maachah (2 Chron. 11:20), the favorite and beloved wife of King Rehoboam of Judah (931–913 BC).

ATTALIA Seaport city on northern Mediterranean coast in Asia Minor where Paul stopped briefly on first missionary journey (Acts 14:25). Modern Antalya continues as a small seaport with some ancient ruins.

AUGUSTAN COHORT Unit of the Roman army stationed in Syria from about AD 6. The cohort's place among the rest of the Roman army is indicated by the fact that it was named after the emperor. This special unit was given charge of Paul on his way to Rome (Acts 27:1). In Luke's eyes, this demonstrated the importance of Paul, and more importantly, the gospel that Paul preached.

AUGUSTUS Title meaning "reverend" that the Roman Senate gave to Emperor Octavian (31 BC–AD 14) in 27 BC. He ruled the Roman Empire, including Palestine, when Jesus was born and ordered the taxation that brought Joseph and Mary to Bethlehem (Luke 2:1). He was the adopted son of Julius Caesar.

AVA or **AVVA** People that the Assyrians conquered and settled in Israel to replace the people they took into exile (2 Kings 17:24).

AVEN Hebrew noun meaning "wickedness," used in Place-names to indicate Israel's understanding of the place as a site of idol worship. **1.** Referred to On or Heliopolis in Egypt (Ezek. 30:17). **2.** Referred to major worship centers of Israel such as Bethel and Dan (Hos. 10:8). **3.** Referred to a valley, perhaps one in place of popularly known names such as Beth-aven for Beth-el (Josh. 7:2; 18:12).

AVENGER Person with the legal responsibility to protect the rights of an endangered relative. Avenger translates Hebrew *go'el*, which in its verbal form means to redeem. Redemption applies to repossessing things consecrated to God (Lev. 27:13-31) or to God's actions for His people (Exod. 6:6; Job 19:25; Ps. 103:4; Isa. 43:1). Ultimately God is the *go'el* (Isa. 41:14).

AVIM, AVIMS, AVITES, AVVIM, AVVITE 1. People of whom nothing is known outside biblical sources. They lived on the Philistine coast before the Philistines invaded about 1200 BC (Deut. 2:23). **2.** City in the tribal territory of Benjamin (Josh. 18:23) about which nothing is known.

AVITH City name meaning "ruin." Capital city of Hadad, king of Edom, before Israel had a king (Gen. 36:35). Its location is unknown.

AWE, AWESOME Refers to an emotion combining honor, fear, and respect before someone of superior office or actions (Pss. 4:4; 33:8; 119:161 KJV) (Gen. 28:17; 1 Sam. 12:18; Matt. 9:8; Heb. 12:28 NIV). It most appropriately applies to God.

AWL Instrument or tool made of flint, bone, stone, or metal to bore holes. Biblical references refer to using the awl to pierce a servant's ear (Exod. 21:6; Deut. 15:17). Perhaps a ring or identification tag was placed in the hole. This marked the slave as a permanent slave for life. Excavators in Palestine unearth many such boring tools.

AX, AX HEAD English translation of several Hebrew terms indicating cutting instruments used in normal small industry and in war.

AYYAH Place-name meaning "ruin." In the unclear Hebrew text of 1 Chron. 7:28, modern translations read Ayyah as a city on the border of Ephraim. Some identify this with Ai. Others follow a Greek text tradition that apparently read Gaza.

AZALIAH Personal name meaning "Yahweh has reserved." Father of Shaphan, Josiah's scribe (2 Kings 22:3). See *Shaphan*.

AZANIAH Personal name meaning "Yahweh listened." Father of Levite who signed Nehemiah's covenant to obey God's law (Neh. 10:9).

AZARAEL (KJV, Neh. 13:36), **AZAREEL** (KJV) or **AZAREL** Personal name meaning "God helped." **1.** David's soldier at Ziklag, skilled with bow and arrow and able to sling stones with either hand (1 Chron. 12:6). **2.** Leader of a course of priests selected by lot under David (1 Chron. 25:18). **3.** Leader of tribe of Dan under David (1 Chron. 27:22). **4.** Priest who had married a foreign wife under Ezra (Ezra 10:41). **5.** Father of Amashai, head of a priestly family who lived in Jerusalem under Nehemiah (Neh. 11:13). **6.** Priest who played a musical instrument in time of Nehemiah (Neh. 12:36), probably the same as 5. above.

AZARIAH Personal name meaning "Yahweh has helped." **1.** Son and successor of Amaziah as king of Judah (792–740 BC). Also called Uzziah. See *Uzziah*. **2.** High priest under Solomon (1 Kings 4:2) listed as son of Zadok (1 Kings 4:2) or of Ahimaaz (1 Chron. 6:9), the son of Zadok (2 Sam. 15:27). If the latter is accurate, then son in 1 Kings 4:2 means descendant. **3.** Son of Nathan in charge of the system of obtaining provisions for the court from the 12 government provinces (1 Kings 4:5). He would have supervised the persons listed in 1 Kings 4:7-19. **4.** Great grandson of Judah (1 Chron. 2:8). **5.** Member of the clan of Jerahmeel in the tribe of Judah (1 Chron. 2:38-39). **6.** High priest, son of Johanan (1 Chron. 6:10). **7.** High priest, son of Hilkiah (1 Chron. 6:13-14) and father of Seraiah, who is listed as Ezra's father (Ezra 7:1). The list in Ezra is not complete. Apparently some generations have been omitted. **8.** Member of family of Kohath, the temple singers (1 Chron. 6:36). Apparently called Uzziah in 6:24. **9.** A priest, son of Hilkiah (1 Chron. 9:11) may be same as 7. above. **10.** Prophet, son of Oded, whose message gave King Asa (910–869 BC) courage to restore proper worship in Judah (2 Chron. 15:1-8). **11.** Two sons of Jehoshaphat, king of Judah (873–848 BC) according to 2 Chron. 21:2. Perhaps the boys had different mothers, each of whom gave the son the common name Azariah. **12.** Son of Jehoram, king of Judah (852–841) according to 2 Chron. 22:6, but the correct name is probably Ahaziah as in 2 Kings 8:29. Azariah represents a copyist's error in Chronicles. **13.** Two military commanders of 100 men who helped Jehoiada, the high priest, depose and murder Athaliah as queen of Judah and install Joash as king (835–796). **14.** High priest who led 80 priests to oppose King Uzziah of Judah (792–740 BC) when he tried to burn incense in the temple rather than let the priests. God struck Uzziah with a dreaded skin disease (2 Chron. 26:16-21). **15.** A leader of the tribe of Ephraim under Pekah, king of Israel (752–732 BC), who rescued captives Pekah had taken from Judah, cared for their physical needs, and returned them to Jericho (2 Chron. 28:5-15). **16.** Levite whose son Joel helped cleanse the temple under Hezekiah, king of Judah (715–686 BC) (2 Chron. 29:12-19). **17.** A Levite who helped cleanse the temple (2 Chron. 29:12-19). See 16. above. **18.** Chief priest under King Hezekiah who rejoiced with the king over the generous tithes and offerings of the people (2 Chron. 31:10-13). **19.** Son of Meraioth in the list of high priests and father of Amariah (Ezra 7:3). Since the list in Ezra is incomplete, this Azariah may be the same as 6. above. **20.** Helper of Nehemiah in rebuilding the wall of Jerusalem (Neh. 3:23). **21.** Man who returned from exile with Zerubbabel (Neh. 7:7) about 537 BC. He is called Seraiah in Ezra 2:2. **22.** Man who helped Ezra interpret the law to the people in Jerusalem (Neh. 8:7). **23.** Man who put his seal on Nehemiah's covenant to obey God's law (Neh. 10:2). **24.** A leader of Judah, possibly a priest, who marched with Nehemiah and others on the walls of Jerusalem to celebrate the completion of rebuilding the city defense walls (Neh. 12:33). He may be identical with any one or all of 20–23. above. **25.** Friend of Daniel renamed Abednego by Persian officials. God delivered him from the fiery furnace (Dan. 1:7; 4:1-30). See *Abednego; Daniel.* **26.** Son of Hoshaiah and leader of Jewish people who tried to get Jeremiah to give them a word from God directing them to go to Egypt after the Babylonians destroyed Jerusalem. When Jeremiah said not to go, they accused him of lying (Jer. 42:1–43:7). Hebrew text reads Jezaniah in 42:1.

AZARIAHU Long form of Azariah used by NASB, NIV in 2 Chron. 21:2 to differentiate two men named Azariah. See *Azariah*.

AZAZ Personal name meaning "he is strong." A descendant of tribe of Reuben (1 Chron. 5:8).

AZAZIAH Personal name meaning "Yahweh is strong." **1.** Levite David appointed to play the harp for the temple worship (1 Chron. 15:21). **2.** Father of leader of tribe of Ephraim under David

(1 Chron. 27:20). **3.** Overseer among the priests under Hezekiah (715–686 BC) (2 Chron. 31:13).

AZBUK Father of a Nehemiah who repaired Jerusalem under the leadership of Nehemiah, son of Hachaliah (Neh. 3:16).

AZEKAH Place-name meaning "cultivated ground." City where Joshua defeated southern coalition of kings led by Adonizedek of Jerusalem (Josh. 10:10-11), as God cast hailstones from heaven on the fleeing armies. In the battle Joshua commanded the sun and moon to stand still (Josh. 10:12).

AZEL Personal and place-name meaning "noble." **1.** Descendant of Saul in tribe of Benjamin and father of six sons (1 Chron. 8:37-38). **2.** Unclear word in Hebrew text of Zech. 14:5 may be a place-name, perhaps near Jerusalem, or a preposition meaning "near to," "beside," or a noun meaning "the side." Translations vary: "Azal" (KJV, NRSV), "the other side" (TEV), "Azel" (NASB, NIV), "the side of it" (RSV).

AZGAD Personal name meaning "Gad is strong." **1.** Clan of which 1,222 (Neh. 7:17 says 2,322) returned from exile in Babylon with Zerubbabel to Jerusalem in 537 BC (Ezra 2:12). One hundred ten more returned with Ezra about 458 BC (Ezra 8:12). **2.** Levite who signed the covenant Nehemiah made to keep God's law (Neh. 10:15).

AZIEL Short form of Jaaziel in 1 Chron. 15:20.

AZIZA Personal name meaning "strong one." Israelite who agreed under Ezra's leadership to divorce his foreign wife to help Israel remain true to God (Ezra 10:27).

AZMAVETH Personal and place-name meaning "strong as death" or "death is strong." **1.** Member of David's elite 30 military heroes (2 Sam. 23:31). He lived in Barhum or perhaps Baharum (NRSV). See *Baharum.* **2.** Descendant of Saul in tribe of Benjamin (1 Chron. 8:36). **3.** Father of two of David's military leaders (1 Chron. 12:3), probably identical with 1. above. **4.** Treasurer of David's kingdom (1 Chron. 27:25). He, too, may be identical with 1. above. **5.** City probably the same as Beth-azmaveth. Forty-two men of the city returned to Jerusalem from exile in Babylon with Zerubbabel in 537 BC (Ezra 2:24). Levites on the temple staff as singers lived there. It apparently is near Jerusalem, perhaps modern Hizmeh, five miles northeast of Jerusalem (Neh. 12:29).

AZMON Place-name meaning "bones." Place on southern border of promised land (Num. 34:4). Joshua assigned it to Judah (Josh. 15:4). It is located near Ain el-Quseimeh, about 60 miles south of Gaza. Some would identify it with Ezem.

AZNOTH-TABOR Place-name meaning "ears of Tabor." A border town of the tribe of Naphtali (Josh. 19:34). It may be modern Umm Jebeil near Mount Tabor.

AZOR Personal name of an ancestor of Jesus (Matt. 1:13-14).

AZRIEL Personal name meaning "God is my help." **1.** Head of a family of eastern part of tribe of Manasseh (1 Chron. 5:24). **2.** Head of tribe of Naphtali under David (1 Chron. 27:19). **3.** Father of royal officer commanded to arrest Baruch, Jeremiah's scribe (Jer. 36:26).

AZRIKAM Personal name meaning "my help stood up." **1.** Descendant of David after the exile (1 Chron. 3:23). **2.** Descendant of Saul of tribe of Benjamin (1 Chron. 8:38). **3.** Father of a Levite who led in resettling Jerusalem after the exile (1 Chron. 9:14). **4.** Officer in charge of palace for Ahaz, king of Judah. Zicri, a soldier in Israel's army, killed him when Israel attacked Judah about 741 BC (2 Chron. 28:7).

AZUBAH Personal name meaning "forsaken." **1.** Queen mother of Jehoshaphat (1 Kings 22:42), king of Judah (873–848 BC). **2.** First wife of Caleb, son of Hezron (1 Chron. 2:18-19).

AZZAN Personal name meaning "he has proved to be strong." Father of representative of tribe of Issachar in assigning territorial lots to the tribes after God gave Israel the promised land (Num. 34:26).

AZZUR Personal name meaning "one who has been helped." **1.** Jewish leader who sealed Nehemiah's covenant to obey God's law (Neh. 10:17). **2.** Father of Hananiah, the prophet, in Jeremiah's days (Jer. 28:1). **3.** Father of Jaazaniah, Jewish leader in Jerusalem who plotted evil in Ezekiel's day (Ezek. 11:1).

BAAL Lord of Canaanite religion and seen in the thunderstorms, Baal was worshipped as the god who provided fertility. He proved a great temptation for Israel. "Baal" occurs in the OT as a noun meaning "lord, owner, possessor, or husband," as a proper noun referring to the supreme god of the Canaanites, and often as the name of a man.

BAALAH Place-name meaning "wife, lady," or "residence of Baal." **1.** City on northern border of tribe of Judah equated with Kirjath-jearim (Josh. 15:9-11). David kept the ark there before moving it to Jerusalem (1 Chron. 13:6). **2.** Town on southern border of Judah (Josh. 15:29) that may be same as Balah (Josh. 19:3) and as Bilhah (1 Chron. 4:29). Tribe of Simeon occupied it. Its location is unknown. **3.** Mountain on Judah's northern border between Jabneel and Ekron. It may be the same as Mount Jearim.

BAALATH Place-name meaning "feminine Baal." City in original inheritance of tribe of Dan (Josh. 19:44).

BAALATH-BEER Place-name meaning "the baal of the well" or the "lady of the well." A city in the tribal allotment of Simeon (Josh. 19:8), identified with Ramath of the south (KJV) or Ramah of the Negev (NASB, NIV, NRSV). It may be identical with Baal (1 Chron. 4:33) and/or with Bealoth (Josh. 15:24).

BAAL-BERITH In Judg. 8:33 a Canaanite deity whom the Israelites began to worship following the death of Gideon. The name means "lord of covenant," and the god's temple was located at Shechem.

Statuette of Baal, the Canaanite weather god, from Minet-el-Beida (15th–14th century BC).

BAALE (KJV), **BAALE-JUDAH** (NASB, NRSV) Place-name meaning "Baals of Judah" or "lords of Judah." Second Samuel 6:2 may be read as "from the lords of Judah" or as "went from Baale-judah."

BAAL-GAD Place-name meaning "Baal of Gad" or "lord of Gad." Town representing northern limit of Joshua's conquests (Josh. 11:17) in Valley of Lebanon at foot of Mount Hermon.

BAAL-HAMON Place-name meaning "lord of abundance." Location of Solomon's vineyard according to Song 8:11.

BAAL-HANAN Personal name meaning "Baal was gracious." **1.** King of Edom prior to any king ruling in Israel (Gen. 36:38). **2.** Official under David in charge of olive and sycamore trees growing in Judean plain or Shephalah (1 Chron. 27:28).

BAAL-HAZOR Place-name meaning "Baal of Hazor." Village where David's son Absalom held celebration of sheepshearing (2 Sam. 13:23).

BAAL-HERMON Place-name meaning "Baal of Hermon" or "lord of Hermon." It marked the Hivites' southern border and Manasseh's northern border (1 Chron. 5:23).

BAALI Form of address meaning "my lord," or "my Baal." Hosea used a play on words to look to a day when Israel would no longer worship Baal (Hos. 2:16).

BAALIM Hebrew plural of Baal.

BAALIS Personal name of king of Ammon who sent Ishmael to kill Geduliah, governor of Judah immediately after Babylon captured Jerusalem and sent most of Judah's citizens into the exile (Jer. 40:14).

BAAL-MEON Place-name meaning "lord of the residence" or "Baal of the residence." City tribe of Reuben built east of Jordan (Num. 32:38), probably on the tribe's northern border.

BAAL-PEOR In Num. 25:3 a Moabite deity that the Israelites worshipped when they had illicit sexual relations with Moabite women. The guilty Israelites were severely punished for this transgression, and the incident became a paradigm of sin and divine judgment for later generations of Israelites (Deut. 4:3; Ps. 106:28; Hos. 9:10).

BAAL-PERAZIM Place-name meaning "Lord of the breakthroughs" or "Baal of the breaches." Place of David's initial victory over the Philistines after he became king of all Israel at Hebron, then captured and moved to Jerusalem (2 Sam. 5:20). The location is not known. It is probably identical with Mount Perazim (Isa. 28:21).

BAAL-SHALISHAH Place-name meaning "Baal of Shalishah" or "lord of Shalishah." Home of unnamed man who brought firstfruits to Elisha, who used them to feed a hundred men (2 Kings 4:42-44).

BAAL-TAMAR Place-name meaning "Baal of the palm tree" or "lord of the palm tree." Place where Israelites attacked and defeated tribe of Benjamin for killing concubine of traveling Levite (Judg. 20:33). It must have been near Gibeah.

BAAL-ZEBUB Deity's name meaning "lord of the flies." In 2 Kings 1:2 a Philistine deity from which the Israelite King Ahaziah sought help after injuring himself in a fall. Jesus used the name Beelzebub in reference to the prince of demons (Matt. 10:25). Beel-zebub is clearly a variation of Baal-zebub.

BAAL-ZEPHON Place-name meaning "lord of the north" or "Baal of the north." Place in Egypt near which Israel camped before miracle of crossing the sea (Exod. 14:2,9). The exact location is not known.

BAANA or **BAANAH** Personal name of uncertain meaning. Some have suggested "son of grief" or "son of Anat." English spelling variations reflect similar Hebrew spelling variations. **1.** One of Solomon's district supervisors to provide food one month a year for the court (1 Kings 4:12). **2.** Another district supervisor over Asher, the western slopes of Galilee in the north. His father Hushai may have been "David's friend" (2 Sam. 15:37). **3.** Father of Zadok, who repaired walls of Jerusalem under Nehemiah (Neh. 3:4). **4.** A captain of Ishbosheth's army after Saul died and Abner deserted to David and was killed by Joab. **5.** Father of Heleb, one of David's 30 heroes (2 Sam. 23:29). **6.** Man who returned with Zerubbabel from Babylonian captivity about 537 BC (Ezra 2:2). **7.** One who signed Nehemiah's covenant to obey God's law (Neh. 10:27).

BAARA Personal name meaning "burning" or a name intentionally changed from one honoring Baal. Wife of Shaharaim in tribe of Benjamin (1 Chron. 8:8).

BAASEIAH Personal name of unknown meaning. A Levite ancestor of Asaph (1 Chron. 6:40).

BAASHA King of Israel who was at war against Asa, king of Judah (1 Kings 15:16). Baasha reigned over Israel for 24 years (908–886 BC).

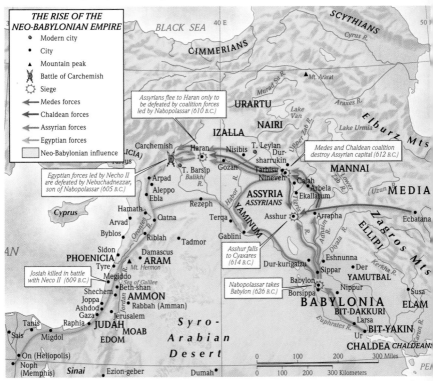

BABBLER Derogatory term the Epicureans and Stoics used against Paul in Athens (Acts 17:18). The Greek word literally means "seed picker" and was used of birds (especially crows) that lived by picking up seeds.

BABEL Hebrew word meaning "confusion," derived from a root which means "to mix." It was the name given to the city that the disobedient descendants of Noah built so they would not be scattered over all the earth (Gen. 11:4,9). Babel is also the Hebrew word for Babylon. The tower and the city which were built were intended to be a monument of human pride, for they sought to "make a name" for themselves (Gen. 11:4).

BABYLON City-state in southern Mesopotamia during OT times that eventually became a large empire. During the reign of King Nebuchadnezzar II (605–562 BC), the Babylonians invaded the nation of Judah. Jerusalem fell in August of 587 BC. The city was burned and the temple destroyed (Jer. 52:12-14). Many Judeans were taken to their exile in Babylonia (2 Kings 25:1-21; Jer. 52:1-30).

BACA Place-name meaning "Balsam tree" or "weeping." A valley in Ps. 84:6 which reflects a poetic play on words describing a person forced to go through a time of weeping who found God turned tears into a well, providing water.

BACHRITE KJV spelling of Becherites (NASB, NRSV) or Bekerite (NIV).

BACKSLIDING Term used by the prophets to describe Israel's faithlessness to God (Isa. 57:17 RSV; Jer. 3:14,22; 8:5; 31:22; 49:4; Hos. 11:7; 14:4). In these passages it is clear that Israel had broken faith with God by serving other gods and by living immoral lives.

BADGER SKINS KJV translation of the skin used to cover the tabernacle (Exod. 26:14; 36:19; 39:34), the ark, and other sacred objects (Num. 4:6-14). The leather was also used for shoes (Ezek. 16:10).

BAG Flexible container that may be closed for holding, storing, or carrying something. **1.** Large bags in which large amounts of money could be carried (2 Kings 5:23; Isa. 3:22; KJV, "crisping pins"). **2.** Small bag (purse) used to carry a merchant's weights (Deut. 25:13; Prov. 16:11; Mic. 6:11) or smaller sums of money (Prov. 1:14; Isa. 46:6). **3.** Cloth tied up in a bundle is translated as "bag" (Job 14:17; Prov. 7:20; Hag. 1:6) or "bundle" (Gen. 42:35; 1 Sam. 25:29; Song 1:13). **4.** The shepherd's bag (KJV "scrip" or "vessel"). Used by shepherds and travelers to carry one or more days' supplies, it was made of animal skins and slung across the shoulder. **5.** Large sack used to carry grain (Gen. 42:25,27,35; Josh. 9:4; Lev. 11:32). **6.** KJV translates *glossokomon* as "bag" in John 12:6; 13:29. The *glossokomon* was actually a money box.

BAGPIPE Modern translation of a musical instrument translated as "dulcimer" by the KJV (Dan. 3:5,10,15).

BAHURIM Place-name meaning "young men." Village on road from Jerusalem to Jericho in tribal territory of Benjamin.

BAJITH (KJV, Isa. 15:2) Modern translations read "temple." KJV interprets as name of Moabite worship place.

BAKBAKKAR Levite living in Judah after the exile (1 Chron. 9:15).

BAKBUK Personal name meaning "bottle." Levite who was a temple servant after returning from Babylonian exile with Zerubbabel about 537 BC (Ezra 2:51; Neh. 7:53).

BAKBUKIAH Personal name meaning "Yahweh's bottle." Leader among the Levites in Jerusalem after the exile (Neh. 11:17; 12:9,25).

BAKEMEATS Old English term for any food prepared by a baker.

BAKER'S STREET Jerusalem street known as "baker's street" where most, if not all, the bakeries of the city were located. Zedekiah promised Jeremiah, whom he had imprisoned, that he would have food for as long as bread was available on baker's street (Jer. 37:21).

BAKING OT speaks most often of the baking of bread and cakes, which were the main part of the meal for Hebrews and Canaanites alike (Gen. 19:3; Exod. 12:39;

The village baker prepares dough for baking in the stone oven on his left.

Lev. 26:26; 1 Kings 17:12-13; Isa. 44:15). The bread of the presence (Lev. 24:5) and other offerings (Lev. 2:4-6) were also baked.

BALAAM Non-Israelite prophet whom Balak, king of Moab, promised a fee if he would curse the invading Israelites (Num. 22:21-30; 2 Pet. 2:16).

BALADAN Akkadian personal name meaning "God gave a son." Father of Merodach-baladan, king of Babylon (722–711; 705–703 BC). See *Merodach-baladan.*

BALAH Place-name meaning "used, worn out." City in tribal territory of Simeon (Josh. 19:3), apparently the same as Baalah (Josh. 15:29) and Bilhah (1 Chron. 4:29). Location in southwest Judah is unknown.

BALAK In Num. 22:2 the king of Moab who sent for Balaam the prophet to pronounce a curse on the Israelites. Balaam, however, spoke no curse; and Balak was denied a military victory over Israel.

BALANCES Used to measure weights early in the development of civilization. Balances were well-known to the Hebrews and in common use in the OT (Lev. 19:36; Job 6:2; Hos. 12:7).

BALLAD SINGERS Refers to the makers and repeaters of proverbs (Num. 21:27). KJV "they that speak in proverbs" gives that sense.

BALM Aromatic resin or gum widely used in the ancient Near East for cosmetic and medical purposes.

BALM OF GILEAD Substance known in the ancient world for its medical properties. Exported from Gilead to Egypt and Phoenicia (Gen. 37:25; Ezek. 27:17). See *Balm.*

BALSAM Translation of two Hebrew words. *Baka'* is translated as "balsam trees" in the modern versions (2 Sam. 5:23-24; 1 Chron. 14:14-15; NASB, NIV, NRSV, TEV).

BAMAH Hebrew noun meaning "back, high place." Word is used frequently to describe places of worship, usually false worship of Yahweh containing Canaanite elements.

BAMOTH Place-name and common noun meaning "high places." A place in Moab where Israel stayed during the wilderness wanderings (Num. 21:19-20). Some would equate it with Bamoth-baal.

BAMOTH-BAAL Place-name meaning "high places of Baal." Mesha, king of Moab about 830 BC, mentioned it in the Moabite stone. Numbers 22:41 speaks of Bamoth or high places of Baal near the Arnon River. There Balak and Balaam could see all Israel. Joshua 13:17 lists it as a city Moses gave the tribe of Reuben. It may be modern Gebel Atarus.

BANI Personal name meaning "built." **1.** Man from tribe of Gad in David's special 30 warriors (2 Sam. 23:36). **2.** Levite descended from Merari (1 Chron. 6:46). **3.** Ancestor of Uthai of tribe of Judah who was among first Israelites to return to Palestine from Babylonian exile about 537 BC (1 Chron. 9:4). **4.** Original ancestor of clan of whom 642 returned from Babylonian exile with Zerubbabel about 537 BC (Ezra 2:10). **5.** Father of Rehum, a Levite who helped Nehemiah repair the wall of Jerusalem (Neh. 3:17)

BANNER Sign carried to give a group a rallying point. A banner was usually a flag or a carved figure of an animal, bird, or reptile. It may have been molded from bronze, as was the serpent in Num. 21:8-9. Each tribe of Israel may have had some such animal figures as their standard, or banner.

BANQUET Elaborate meal, sometimes called a "feast." In the OT and NT, banquets and feasts are prominent in sealing friendships, celebrating victories, and for other joyous occasions (Dan. 5:1; Luke 15:22-24). The idea of hospitality ran deep in the thought of those in the Near East (Gen. 18:1-8; Luke 11:5-8). In Revelation, the final victory day is described in terms of a "marriage feast of the Lamb" of God (Rev. 19:9 HCSB).

BAPTISM The Christian rite of initiation practiced by almost all who profess to embrace the Christian faith. In the NT era, persons professing Christ were immersed in water as a public confession of their faith in Jesus, the Savior. This was accomplished in direct obedience to the explicit mandate of the Lord (Matt. 28:16-20).

BAPTISM FOR THE DEAD The only biblical mention of this is 1 Cor. 15:29. Paul refers to something being practiced without commenting on it. He does not commend, condone, or condemn it.

BAR Aramaic translation of the Hebrew word *ben.* Both words mean "son of."

BARABBAS Name means "Son of the Father." A murderer and insurrectionist held in Roman custody at the time of the trial of Jesus (Mark 15:15). All four Gospels record that when Pilate offered to release Jesus or Barabbas, the crowd demanded the release of Barabbas. Pilate gave in to the demand, ordered Jesus crucified, and set Barabbas free.

BARACHEL Personal name meaning "God blessed." Father of Job's friend Elihu (Job 32:2).

BARAK Son of Abinoam whom the prophetess Deborah summoned to assume military leadership of the Israelites in a campaign against Canaanite forces under the command of Sisera (Judg. 4:6).

BARBARIAN Originally referred to stammering, stuttering, or any form of unintelligible sounds. Even the repeated syllable "bar-bar" mimics this. The term "barbarian" came to be synonymous with "foreigner," one who did not speak Greek, or one who was not a Greek.

BARHUMITE Variant Hebrew spelling for Baharumite.

BAR-JESUS Jewish magician and false prophet at Paphos (Acts 13:6). Paul the apostle denounced him, and he was struck blind. In Acts 13:8 he is called Elymas.

BAR-JONA Surname of Simon Peter (Matt. 16:17). The meaning is "son of John."

BAR-KOKHBA Means "son of the star" and was the title given by Jewish rebels to Simeon bar Kosevah, the leader of their revolt in AD 132–135. The title designated him as the Messiah (Num. 24:17). The revolt erupted because the Roman Emperor Hadrian had begun to rebuild Jerusalem as a pagan city with plans to replace the ruined Jewish temple with one dedicated to Jupiter.

BARKOS Aramaic name possibly meaning "son of Kos" (a god). The original ancestor of a clan of Nethinim or temple employees who returned to Jerusalem from exile in Babylon with Zerubbabel about 537 BC (Ezra 2:53).

BARLEY Grain for which Palestine was known (Deut. 8:8). Barley was the food of the poor (Lev. 23:22) as well as feed for horses, mules, and donkeys (1 Kings 4:28).

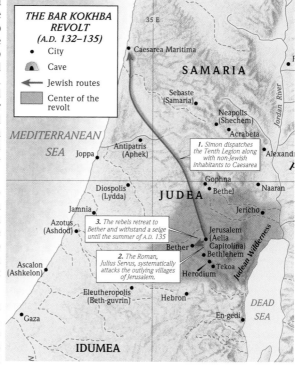

THE BAR KOKHBA REVOLT (A.D. 132–135)
- City
- Cave
- Jewish routes
- Center of the revolt

1. Simon dispatches the Tenth Legion along with non-Jewish inhabitants to Caesarea

2. The Roman, Julius Servus, systematically attacks the outlying villages of Jerusalem.

3. The rebels retreat to Bether and withstand a seige until the summer of A.D. 135

BARLEY HARVEST Began in late April or early May and preceded the wheat harvest by about two weeks (Exod. 9:31-32). At the beginning of the barley harvest (Ruth 2:23), the first fruits were offered as a consecration of the harvest (Lev. 23:10).

BARN Storage place for seed (Hag. 2:19) or grain (Matt. 13:30). Equivalent to modern granaries or silos.

BARNABAS Name probably means "son of prophecy" or one who prophesies or preaches ("son of exhortation," Acts 4:36). Barnabas was a Levite and native of the island of Cyprus, named Joseph (Joses), before the disciples called him Barnabas. The church chose Barnabas to go to Syrian Antioch to investigate the unrestricted preaching to the Gentiles there. He became the leader of the work and secured Saul as his assistant. On Paul's "first missionary journey," Barnabas seems to have been the leader (chaps. 13–14). He and Paul agreed to go on another missionary journey but separated over whether to take John Mark with them again (15:36-41).

BARREL KJV translation found in 1 Kings 17:12-16; 18:33. Modern versions translate the same word as "jar." Jars were used for carrying water and storing flour.

BARREN, BARRENNESS Term used to describe a woman who is unable to give birth to children: Sarai (Gen. 11:30), Rebekah (Gen. 25:21), Rachel (Gen. 29:31), Manoah's wife (Judg. 13:2), Hannah (1 Sam. 1:5), and Elizabeth (Luke 1:7,36). Barrenness was considered a curse from God (Gen. 16:2; 20:18; 1 Sam. 1:5).

BARSABAS or **BARSABBAS** Personal name meaning "son of the Sabbath." **1.** Name given Joseph Justus, candidate not elected when church chose replacement for Judas, the traitor (Acts 1:23). **2.** Last name of Judas, whom the Jerusalem church chose to go with Paul and Silas to Antioch after the Jerusalem council (Acts 15:22).

BARTHOLOMEW One of the 12 apostles (Mark 3:18). The name Bartholomew means "son of Talmai." Many believe Bartholomew and Nathanael are identical.

BARTIMAEUS or **BARTIMEUS** (KJV) Blind beggar near Jericho who cried to Jesus for mercy despite efforts to silence him. Jesus said that his persistent faith had made him whole. Able to see, he followed Jesus (Mark 10:46-52).

BARUCH Son of Neriah who served as Jeremiah's scribe and friend.

BARZILLAI Personal name meaning "made of iron." **1.** Man from Gilead east of the Jordan who met David at Mahanaim as he fled from Absalom. Barzillai and others gave needed supplies for David's company (2 Sam. 17:27-29). **2.** Father of Adriel whose sons David delivered to the Gibeonites for execution in payment for Saul's inhumane slaying of Gibeonites (2 Sam. 21:8). This Barzillai could be the same as 1. above. **3.** Priestly clan whose ancestor had married the daughter of 1. above and taken his name.

BASEMATH Personal name meaning "balsam." **1.** Hittite woman whom Esau married, grieving his parents, Isaac and Rebekah (Gen. 26:34-35; 27:46). **2.** Daughter of Solomon who married Ahimaaz, district supervisor providing supplies for the royal court from Naphtali (1 Kings 4:15).

BASHAN Northernmost region of Palestine east of the Jordan River. Though its precise extent cannot be determined with certainty, it was generally east of the Sea of Galilee.

BASIN (KJV, "bason") Used interchangeably with "bowl" to refer to various sizes of wide hollow bowls, cups, and dishes used for domestic or more formal purposes (John 13:5). The most common material used to make such instruments was pottery. However, basins were also made of brass (Exod. 27:3), silver (Num. 7:13), and gold (2 Chron. 4:8).

BASKET Five kinds of baskets are mentioned in the OT. The NT uses two words for basket. The smaller basket is referred to in the story of the feeding of the 5,000 (Matt. 14:20). The larger basket is mentioned in the feeding of the 4,000 (Matt. 15:37). The Apostle Paul also used the larger basket as a means of escape over the wall of Damascus (Acts 9:25).

BASTARD Illegitimate child, but not necessarily a child born out of wedlock. The term could refer to offspring of an incestuous union or of a marriage that was prohibited (Lev. 18:6-20; 20:11-20). Illegitimate children were not permitted to enter the assembly of the Lord (Deut. 23:2). According to Hebrews, those who do not have the discipline of the Lord are illegitimate children (12:8). Also translated as "a mongrel people" (Zech. 9:6 NRSV).

BAT The Hebrew word translated "bat" is the generic name for many species of this mammal found in Palestine (Isa. 2:20). Although the bat is listed among unclean birds in the Bible (Lev. 11:19; Deut. 14:18), it belongs to the mammals because it nurses its young.

BATH Liquid measure roughly equivalent to five-and-one-half gallons (U.S.). It was used to measure the molten sea in the temple (1 Kings 7:26,38) as well as oil and wine (2 Chron. 2:10; Ezra 7:22; Isa. 5:10; Ezek. 45:11,14). The bath was one-tenth of a homer.

BATHING Biblical languages make no distinction between washing and bathing primarily because the dry climate of the Middle East prohibited bathing except on special occasions or where there was an available source of water (John 9:7). Therefore, where "bathe" occurs in the biblical text, partial bathing is usually intended. However, two notable exceptions are that of Pharaoh's daughter in the Nile River (Exod. 2:5) and that of Bathsheba on her rooftop (2 Sam. 11:2).

BATH-RABBIM Place-name meaning "daughter of many." A gate of Heshbon, which was near pools of fish. Song of Songs 7:4 uses its beauty as comparison for the beauty of the beloved lady's eyes. See *Heshbon*.

BATHSHEBA Daughter of Eliam and the wife of Uriah the Hittite (2 Sam. 11:3). She was a beautiful woman with whom David the king had an adulterous relationship (2 Sam. 11:4). When David learned that she had become pregnant as a result of the intrigue, he embarked on a course of duplicity that led finally to the violent death of Uriah. David then took Bathsheba as his wife. She was the mother of Solomon and played an important role in ensuring that he be made king (1 Kings 1:11–2:19).

BATHSHUA Personal name meaning "daughter of nobility." **1.** Canaanite wife of Judah and mother of Er, Onan, and Shelah (1 Chron. 2:3 NASB, TEV, NRSV). KJV, NIV read "daughter of Shua." Genesis 38:2 says her name was Shuah, while Gen. 38:12 calls her daughter of Shuah or Bath-shua. **2.** Name for Bathsheba in 1 Chron. 3:5.

BATTALION RSV translation of one-tenth of a Roman legion, about 600 men. KJV translates "band," HCSB uses "whole company."

BAVAI or **BAVVAI** (NASB, TEV, RSV) Government official in Keilah who helped Nehemiah rebuild wall of Jerusalem (Neh. 3:18). NRSV, NIV read Binnui on basis of Neh. 3:24 and other textual evidence.

BAY KJV translation of a term referring to horses in Zech. 6:3,7. KJV took the term as referring to the color of the horses. The earliest translators had trouble with the word, as do modern versions. Recent interpreters take the Hebrew word as referring to the strength of the horses (NIV, NASB), though NRSV reads "gray" in verse 3 and "steeds" in verse 7, while REB omits the word in verse 3 and emends the text in verse 7.

BAY TREE KJV translation in Ps. 37:35. The Hebrew word (*'ezrach*) means "native" or "indigenous."

BAZAAR Section of a street given over to merchants. Ben-hadad of Damascus gave Ahab permission to set up bazaars in Damascus as Ben-hadad's father had done in Samaria (1 Kings 20:34).

BAZLITH or **BAZLUTH** Personal name meaning "in the shadow" or "onions." Original ancestor of clan of temple employees who returned from exile in Babylon with Zerubbabel in 537 BC (Neh. 7:54). Name is spelled Bazluth in Ezra 2:52, which NIV reads in Neh. 7:54.

BDELLIUM Translation of *bedolach*, a word of uncertain meaning. It has been identified as a gum or resin, pearl, or stone. Genesis 2:12 (KJV) mentions bdellium, gold, and onyx as products of Havilah. Numbers 11:7 likens manna to bdellium in appearance.

BEADS RSV translation of a term for articles of gold jewelry (Num. 31:50). The exact identification of these objects is uncertain. They are variously identified as tablets (KJV), armlets, pendants (REB, NRSV), necklaces (TEV, NIV, NASB), and breastplates.

BEALIAH Personal name meaning "Yahweh is Lord." Literally, "Yahweh is baal." Soldier who joined David at Ziklag while he fled from Saul and served the Philistines (1 Chron. 12:5).

BEALOTH Place-name meaning "female Baals" or "ladies." **1.** Town on southern border of tribal territory of Judah (Josh. 15:24). This may be the same as Baalath-beer (19:8). **2.** Region with Asher making up a district to supply food for Solomon's court (1 Kings 4:16). KJV, NIV read "in Aloth."

BEANS Leguminous plant (*Faba vulgaris*) grown in the ancient world as food. Beans mentioned in 2 Sam. 17:28 and Ezek. 4:9 were the horse or broad bean.

BEAR Large, heavy mammal with long, thick, shaggy hair. It eats insects, fruit, and flesh. The bear of the Bible has been identified with a high degree of certainty as the Syrian bear. They may grow as high as six feet and weigh as much as 500 pounds.

BEARD Hair growing on a man's face often excluding the mustache. Ancient Hebrews are often depicted in ancient Near Eastern art with full, rounded beards. This is in contrast to Romans and Egyptians who preferred clean-shaven faces.

BEAST Daniel and Revelation utilize beasts of various sorts in their symbolism. The OT used "beast" as a symbol for an enemy, and the writers of Daniel and Revelation may have built on that (Ps. 74:19; Jer. 12:9). Daniel saw four great beasts who represented four great kings arise out of the sea (Dan. 7:2-14). These four beasts would threaten God's kingdom, but God's people would prevail over them (Dan. 7:18).

The book of Revelation speaks of two beasts. The first beast arises out of the sea (Rev. 13:1), is seven headed, and derives its authority from the dragon (Rev. 12:3; 13:4). This beast has several of the characteristics of the four beasts of Dan. 7. The second beast arises out of the earth (Rev. 13:11). It serves the first beast by seeking devotees for it and is referred to as the "false prophet" (Rev. 16:13; 19:20; 20:10). Both the beast and the false prophet persecute the church but are finally judged by Christ (Rev. 19:20; 2 Thess. 2:6-12).

Mount of Beatitudes as viewed from the Sea of Galilee.

BEATITUDES Are so designated because they begin with the expression "blessed is" or "happy is" (Hb. '*ashre*; Gk *makarios*; Lat. *beatus*). The most widely known and extensive collection of such blessings introduces Jesus' Sermon on the Mount (Matt. 5:3-12; cp. Luke 6:20-26).

BEAUTIFUL GATE Scene of the healing of a lame man by Peter and John (Acts 3:2,10). Neither the OT nor other Jewish sources mention a "Beautiful Gate."

BEBAI Babylonian personal name meaning "child." **1.** Original ancestor of clan of whom 623 (628 in Neh. 7:16) returned with Zerubbabel from exile in Babylon about 537 BC (Ezra 2:11). **2.** Signer of Nehemiah's covenant to obey God's law (Neh. 10:15).

BECHER or **BEKER** (NIV) **1.** Personal name meaning "firstborn" or "young male camel." Son of Benjamin and grandson of Jacob (Gen. 46:21). He had nine sons (1 Chron. 7:8). **2.** Original ancestor of clan in tribe of Ephraim (Num. 26:35). First Chronicles 7:20 spells the name "Bered."

BECHORATH or **BECORATH** Personal name meaning "firstborn." Ancestor of King Saul (1 Sam. 9:1).

BEDAD Personal name meaning "scatter" or "be alone." Father of Hadad, king of Edom (Gen. 36:35).

BEDAN Personal name of uncertain meaning. **1.** Listed as a judge in 1 Sam. 12:11. **2.** Descendant of Machir and Manasseh (1 Chron. 7:17).

BEDEIAH Personal name meaning "Yahweh alone" or "branch of Yahweh." Man with foreign wife who divorced her under Ezra's leadership to prevent tempting Israel with foreign gods (Ezra 10:35).

BEELIADA Personal name meaning "Baal knows" or "the Lord knows." Son of David born in Jerusalem (1 Chron. 14:7). In 2 Sam. 5:16 the Baal part of the name is replaced with "El," a Hebrew word for God, becoming "Eliada."

BEELZEBUB (KJV, NIV) or **BEELZEBUL** (NASB, TEV, NRSV, HCSB) Name for Satan in NT spelled differently in Greek manuscripts. The term is based on Hebrew Baal-zebub, "lord of the flies."

BEER Place-name meaning "well." **1.** One of the camps of the Israelites during the wilderness wandering (Num. 21:16). **2.** Jotham fled to Beer when he feared his brother Abimelech would kill him (Judg. 9:21). This may be modern Bireh.

BEERA Personal name meaning "a well." A descendant of the tribe of Asher (1 Chron. 7:37).

BEERAH Personal name meaning "a well." A leader of the tribe of Reuben taken captive by Tiglath-pileser, king of Assyria, about 732 BC (1 Chron. 5:6).

BEER-ELIM Place-name meaning "well of the rams, the heroes, the terebinths, or the mighty trees." Place involved in mourning according to Isaiah's lament over Moab (Isa. 15:8).

BEERI Personal name meaning "well." **1.** Hittite father of girl Esau married, grieving his parents Isaac and Rebekah (Gen. 26:34-35; 27:46). **2.** Father of Hosea, the prophet (Hos. 1:1).

BEER-LAHAIROI Place-name meaning "well of the Living One who sees me." After Sarai had Abraham put Hagar out of the house, an angel appeared to Hagar announcing the birth of a son. Hagar interpreted this as a vision of the living God and named the well where she was Beer-lahairoi (Gen. 16:14).

BEEROTH Place-name meaning "wells." **1.** Wells of the sons of Jaakan, where Israel camped in the wilderness (Num. 33:31; Deut. 10:6). **2.** City of the Gibeonites to which Joshua and his army came to defend the Gibeonites after making a covenant with them (Josh. 9:17).

BEER-SHEBA Beer-sheba and its surrounding area factors significantly in the OT from the earliest sojourns of the patriarchs (Gen. 21; 22; 26) to the return of the Hebrew exiles with Nehemiah (Neh. 11:27,30). Since it was an important crossroad to Egypt in the geographic center of the dry, semidesert region known as the Negev, Beer-sheba also served as the administrative center of the region.

BEESHTERAH Place-name meaning "in Ashtaroth." Place east of the Jordan from territory of tribe of Manasseh set aside for the Levites (Josh. 21:27).

Tel Beer-sheba well.

BEHEMOTH Large beast known for its enormous strength and toughness. Described in detail in Job 40:15-24, this animal has been variously identified as an elephant, a hippopotamus, and a water buffalo, with the hippopotamus the most likely.

BEKA or **BEKAH** One-half a shekel. The amount contributed by each Israelite male for the use of the temple (Exod. 38:26).

BEL Name of Babylonian god, originally as city patron of Nippur, but then as a second name for the high god Marduk of Babylon. Jeremiah prophesied shame coming on Bel (Jer. 50:2). Bel would have to spit out the nations he had swallowed up (Jer. 51:44). An apocryphal book is called Bel and the Dragon.

BELA or **BELAH** Personal and place-name meaning "he swallowed." **1.** Name for Zoar. Its king joined coalition to fight off attacks from eastern kings (Gen. 14:2). See *Zoar.* **2.** King of Edom who ruled in city of Dinhabah before Israel had a king (Gen. 36:32). **3.** Son of Benjamin and grandson of Jacob (Gen. 46:21). He became original ancestor of clan of Belaites (Num. 26:38; 1 Chron. 7:7). **4.** Descendant of Reuben (1 Chron. 5:8).

BELIAL Transliteration of a Hebrew common noun meaning "useless" or "worthless." It is a term of derision (Deut. 13:13). In the NT the word occurs one time (2 Cor. 6:15), where Paul the apostle declared the mutual irreconcilability of Christ and Belial, who thus appears to be equated with Satan.

BELL Golden object fastened to the garments of the high priest that served as a signal or warning of the high priest's movements (Exod. 28:33-35; 39:25-26).

BELLOWS Instrument that blows air on a fire, making it burn hotter. The term is used only in Jer. 6:29.

BELOVED DISCIPLE Abbreviated expression used to refer to a disciple for whom Jesus had deep feelings. Church tradition and interpretation of biblical evidence appear to point to John.

BELSHAZZAR Name meaning "Bel's prince." Babylonian king whose drunken feast was interrupted by the mysterious appearance of the fingers of a human hand that wrote a cryptic message on the palace wall (Dan. 5:1).

BELTESHAZZAR Babylonian name meaning "protect the king's life." Name that the prince of eunuchs under Nebuchadnezzar, king of Babylon, gave to Daniel (Dan. 1:7).

BEN Hebrew noun meaning "son of." A Levite who became head of a clan of temple porters under David (1 Chron. 15:18 NASB, KJV).

BEN-ABINADAB Personal name meaning "son of Abinadab." The district supervisor over Dor in charge of provisions for Solomon's court one month a year. He married Solomon's daughter, Taphath (1 Kings 4:11). KJV reads "son of Abinadab."

BENAIAH Personal name meaning "Yahweh has built." **1.** Captain of David's professional soldiers (2 Sam. 8:18; 20:23), known for heroic feats such as disarming an Egyptian and killing him with his own sword as well as killing a lion in the snow (2 Sam. 23:20-23). **2.** A Pirathonite who is listed among the 30 elite warriors of David (2 Sam. 23:30). **3.** In 1 Chron. 4:36 a Simeonite prince who was involved in a defeat of the Amalekites. **4.** In 1 Chron. 15:18 a Levitical musician involved in the processional when the ark of the covenant was brought to Jerusalem. **5.** In 1 Chron. 15:24 a priest who sounded a trumpet when the ark was brought to Jerusalem. **6.** In 2 Chron. 20:14 an Asaphite, the grandfather of Jahaziel. **7.** In 2 Chron. 31:13 one of the overseers who assisted in the collection of contributions in the house of the Lord during the reign of Hezekiah. **8.** In Ezek. 11:1 the father of Pelatiah. **9.** In Ezra 10 the name of four Israelite men who put away their foreign wives.

BEN-AMMI Personal name meaning "son of my people." Son of Lot and his younger daughter after his two daughters despaired of marriage and tricked their father after getting him drunk (Gen. 19:38). Ben-ammi was the original ancestor of the Ammonites.

BEN-DEKER Personal name meaning "son of Deker" or "son of bored through." Solomon's district supervisor in charge of supplying the royal court for one month a year (1 Kings 4:9).

BENE-BERAK Place-name meaning "sons of Barak" or "sons of lightning." City of tribe of Dan (Josh. 19:45).

BENEDICTION Prayer for God's blessing or an affirmation that God's blessing is at hand. The most famous is the priestly benediction (or Aaronic blessing) in Num. 6:24-25. Most NT epistles close with benedictions as well.

BENEDICTUS Latin word meaning "blessed." The first word in Latin of Zacharias' psalm of praise in Luke 1:68-79 and thus the title of the psalm.

BENE-JAAKAN Place-name meaning "sons of Jaakan." Same as Beeroth-bene-jaakan.

BEN-GEBER Personal name meaning "son of Geber" or "son of a hero." Solomon's district supervisor in the towns northeast of the Jordan River around Ramoth-gilead (1 Kings 4:13). He provided supplies for the royal court one month a year. KJV reads "son of Geber."

BEN-HADAD Personal name or royal title meaning "son of (the god) Hadad." References to Israel's interaction with Damascus and other city-states in Syria show the power of the kings of Damascus.

BEN-HAIL Personal name meaning "son of strength." Official under King Jehoshaphat of Judah (873–848 BC), who sent him to help teach God's law in the cities of Judah (2 Chron. 17:7).

BEN-HANAN Personal name meaning "son of the gracious one." Son of Shimon in lineage of Judah (1 Chron. 4:20).

BEN-HESED Personal name meaning "son of mercy." Solomon's district supervisor over the Mediterranean coastal region between Aphek on the south and Hepher. He supplied the royal court one month a year (1 Kings 4:10).

BEN-HINNOM Place-name meaning "son of Hinnom." A valley south of Jerusalem serving as northern border of tribe of Judah (Josh. 15:8) and southern boundary of tribe of Benjamin (Josh. 18:16). Pagan child sacrifices occurred here, some kings of Judah included (Ahaz, 2 Chron. 28:3; Manasseh, 2 Chron. 33:6).

BEN-HUR Personal name meaning "son of a camel" or "son of Horus." Solomon's district supervisor over Mount Ephraim in charge of supplying the royal court one month a year (1 Kings 4:8).

BENINU Personal name meaning "our son." A Levite who sealed the covenant Nehemiah made to obey God's law (Neh. 10:13).

BENJAMIN Personal name meaning "son of the right hand" or "son of the south." The second son Rachel bore to Jacob (Gen. 35:17-18). He became the forefather of the tribe of Benjamin. The tribe of Benjamin occupied the smallest territory of all the tribes. Yet it played a significant role in Israelite history. Saul, Israel's first king, was a Benjamite. In the NT the Apostle Paul proudly proclaimed his heritage in the tribe of Benjamin (Rom. 11:1; Phil. 3:5).

BENJAMIN GATE Jerusalem gate (Jer. 37:13; 38:7). Identified by some with Nehemiah's Sheep Gate or with the Muster Gate, it could indicate a gate that led to tribal territory of Benjamin.

BENO Proper name meaning "his son." A Levite under David (1 Chron. 24:26-27).

BEN-ONI Personal name meaning "son of my sorrow."

BEN-ZOHETH Personal name meaning "son of Zoheth." Son of Ishi in the tribe of Judah (1 Chron. 4:20).

BEON Place-name of uncertain meaning. Probably a copyist's change from original Meon (Num.

32:3), a short form of Beth-meon or Beth-baal-meon.

BEOR Proper name meaning "burning." **1.** Father of Bela, king of Edom centered in Dinhabah, before Israel had a king (Gen. 36:32). **2.** Father of prophet Balaam (Num. 22:5).

BERA Personal name, perhaps meaning "with evil" or "victory." King of Sodom in days of Abraham and Lot (Gen. 14:2). He joined coalition of local kings against group of invading eastern kings.

BERACAH or **BERACHAH**(KJV) Personal name meaning "blessing." **1.** Skilled soldier able to use right or left hand with slingshot and with bow and arrows. He joined David's band in Ziklag, when David fled from Saul and joined the Philistines (1 Chron. 12:3). **2.** Valley where King Jehoshaphat of Judah (873–848 BC) and his people blessed God after He provided miraculous victory over Ammon, Moab, and Edom (2 Chron. 20:26).

BERAIAH Personal name meaning "Yahweh created." A descendant of the tribe of Benjamin (1 Chron. 8:21).

BEREA Place-name meaning "place of many waters." City in Macedonia to which Paul escaped after the Jews of Thessalonica rioted (Acts 17:10).

BERECHIAH Personal name meaning "Yahweh blessed." **1.** Descendant of David in period after Jews returned from exile in Babylon (1 Chron. 3:20). **2.** Father of Asaph (1 Chron. 6:39). **3.** Leader of the Levites after the return from exile who lived around the city of Netophah (1 Chron. 9:16). **4.** Levite in charge of the ark when David moved it to Jerusalem (1 Chron. 15:23). He could be identical with 2. above. **5.** Leader of the tribe of Ephraim who rescued prisoners of war that Pekah, king of Israel (752–732 BC), had taken from Ahaz, king of Judah (735–715 BC) (2 Chron. 28:12). **6.** Father of Meshullam, who repaired the wall with Nehemiah (Neh. 3:4). His family was tied in marriage to Tobiah, Nehemiah's enemy (Neh. 6:17-19). **7.** Father of the prophet Zechariah (Zech. 1:1; Matt. 23:35).

BERED Personal name meaning "cool." **1.** Place used to locate Beer-lahai-roi (Gen. 16:14), but a place that cannot be located today. **2.** Son of Ephraim (1 Chron. 7:20). Numbers 26:35 spells the name "Becher."

BERIAH Personal name meaning "Yahweh created." **1.** Son of Asher and grandson of Jacob (Gen. 46:17). He thus became original ancestor of clan of Beriites (Num. 26:44). **2.** Son of Ephraim born after his sons Ezer and Elead died in battle against Gath (1 Chron. 7:20-25). **3.** Clan leader of the tribe of Benjamin in the area of Ajalon. He helped drive out the inhabitants of Gath (1 Chron. 8:13). **4.** Levite under King David (1 Chron. 23:10).

BERITH Hebrew word meaning "covenant."

BERNICE Name meaning "gift." Companion of Herod Agrippa II (Acts 25:13). She was the daughter of Herod Agrippa I, born probably about AD 28.

BERODACH-BALADAN King of Babylon who wrote Hezekiah, king of Judah (2 Kings 20:12). Parallel passage in Isa. 39:1 reads Merodoch-baladan, so most Bible students think Berodach resulted from a copyist's change in the text (cp. NIV, TEV, NRSV).

BEROTHAH Place-name meaning "wells." Northern border town in Ezekiel's vision of restored promised land (Ezek. 47:16). It may be located east of the Jordan River about seven miles south of Baalbeck at Bereiten.

BEROTHAI Place-name meaning "wells." City in Syria from which David took brass as tribute after he defeated King Hadadezer (2 Sam. 8:8).

BEROTHITE Person from Beeroth (1 Chron. 11:39).

BERYL Light green precious stone closely related to emeralds and aquamarines.

BESAI Personal name of unknown meaning. A clan of temple employees who returned from exile in Babylon with Zerubbabel about 537 BC (Ezra 2:49).

BESODEIAH Personal name meaning "in Yahweh's counsel." Father of Meshullam, who helped Nehemiah repair the gate of Jerusalem (Neh. 3:6).

BESOM Broom made of twigs (KJV, Isa. 14:23).

BESOR Place-name, perhaps meaning "wadi of the good news." Brook where David left 200 weary soldiers while he and the remaining 400 pursued the Amalekites after they had burned Ziklag and captured David's wives (1 Sam. 30:9-10).

BESTIALITY Sexual intercourse between a human and an animal, punishable by death in OT legal codes (Exod. 22:19; Lev. 18:23; 20:15-16; Deut. 27:21). Israel's neighbors practiced bestiality in fertility worship and worship of animal gods.

BETAH Place-name meaning "security." City from which King David took brass after defeating King Hadadezer (2 Sam. 8:8). First Chronicles 18:8 lists Betah as Tibhath. NIV reads Tebah in 2 Sam. 8:8.

BETEN Place-name meaning "womb." Border town of tribe of Asher (Josh 19:25). It may be located at Khirbet Abtun, 11 miles south of Acco.

BETH-ABARA Place-name meaning "house of crossing." KJV reading for Bethany in John 1:28 following some Greek manuscripts.

BETH-ANATH Place-name meaning "house of Anath." A fortified city in the territory of the tribe of Naphtali (Josh. 19:38).

BETH-ANOTH Place-name meaning "house of Anath" or "house of being heard." A city of Judah (Josh. 15:59), a temple to the Canaanite goddess Anath may have been here.

BETHANY Known primarily in the Gospels as the home of Mary, Martha, and Lazarus. Ancient Bethany occupied an important place in the life of Jesus. Jesus often found Himself staying in Bethany at the home of his closest friends as He ministered in Jerusalem. Located on the Mount of Olives' eastern slope, Bethany sat "about two miles" (John 11:18 HCSB) southeast of Jerusalem.

BETH-ARABAH Place-name meaning "house of the desert." A border town of tribe of Judah (Josh. 15:6,61) also claimed as a city of Benjamin (Josh. 18:22). It may be modern Ain el-Gharbah southeast of Jericho.

View of the ancient city of Bethany, the hometown of Mary, Martha, and Lazarus.

BETH-ARBEL Place-name meaning "house of Arbel." Site of infamous battle that Hosea could use as an example of what would happen to Israel (Hos. 10:14). The battle is unknown to us.

BETH-ASHBEA Place of unknown location in Judah known for clans of linen workers, thus giving evidence of craft guilds in Israel (1 Chron. 4:21).

BETH-AVEN Place-name meaning "house of deception" or "of idolatry." **1.** City near Ai east of Bethel (Josh. 7:2). It formed a border of Benjamin (Josh. 18:12) and was west of Michmash (1 Sam. 13:5). Saul defeated the Philistines here after God used his son Jonathan to start the victory (1 Sam. 14:23). **2.** Hosea used the term as a description of Beth-el. Instead of a house of God, Beth-el had become a house of deception and idolatry (Hos. 4:15).

BETH-AZMAVETH Place-name meaning "house of the strength of death." Hometown of 42 people who returned to Palestine with Zerubbabel from exile in Babylon about 537 BC (Neh. 7:28).

BETH-BAAL-MEON Place-name meaning "house of Baal's residence." City allotted tribe of Reuben (Josh. 13:17).

BETH-BIREI or **BETH-BIRI** Place-name meaning "house of my creation." Town allotted tribe of Simeon (1 Chron. 4:31). It is apparently the same as Lebaoth (Josh. 15:32) and Beth-lebaoth (Josh. 19:6).

BETH-CAR Place-name meaning "house of sheep." Final site of battle where God thundered from heaven to defeat the Philistines for Samuel (1 Sam. 7:11).

BETH-DAGON Place-name meaning "house of Dagon." Apparently the name indicates a worship place of Philistine god Dagon. **1.** Town in tribal territory of Judah (Josh. 15:41). It is probably modern Khirbet Dajun on the road connecting Ramalleh and Joppa. **2.** Town in Asher (Josh. 19:27) without certain present location.

BETH-DIBLATHAIM Place-name meaning "house of the two fig cakes." Town in Moab on which Jeremiah prophesied judgment (Jer. 48:22).

BETH-EDEN Place-name meaning "house of bliss." Amos announced God's threat to take the royal house out of Beth-eden or the "house of Eden" (KJV) (Amos 1:5).

BETH-EKED Place-name meaning "house of shearing" (KJV, "shearing house"). Place where Jehu, after slaughtering all members of King Ahab's house in Jezreel, met representatives from King Ahaziah of Judah and killed them (2 Kings 10:12-14).

BETHEL Name meaning "house of God." **1.** Bethel was important in the OT for both geographic and religious reasons. Because of its abundant springs, the area was fertile and attractive to settlements as early as 3200 BC and first supported a city around the time of Abraham. **2.** Another city variously spelled Bethul (Josh. 19:4), Bethuel (1 Chron. 4:30), and Bethel (1 Sam. 30:27). This may be modern Khirbet el Qaryatein north of Arad. **3.** Bethel was apparently the name of a West Semitic god. Many scholars find reference to this deity in Jer. 48:13. Others would find the mention of the deity in other passages (especially Gen. 31:13; Amos 5:5).

BETHELITE Resident of Bethel (1 Kings 16:34).

BETH-EMEK Place-name meaning "house of the valley." A border town in the tribal territory of Asher (Josh. 19:27). Located at modern Tel Mimas, six and a half miles northeast of Acco.

BETHER Place-name meaning "division." A mountain range used as an emotional image in Song 2:17. NIV reads "rugged hills."

BETHESDA Name of a pool in Jerusalem where Jesus healed a man who had been sick for 38 years (John 5:2). The name, appropriately, means "house of mercy." Most ancient manuscripts identify Bethesda as the place of the pool. Some ancient manuscripts name it Bethzatha or Bethsaida.

BETH-EZEL Proper name meaning "house of the leader" or "house at the side." City Micah used in a wordplay to announce judgment on Judah about 701 BC (Mic. 1:11).

BETH-GADER City founded by or controlled by descendants of Hareph, a descendant of Caleb (1 Chron. 2:51).

BETH-GAMUL Place-name meaning "house of retaliation." City in Moab on which Jeremiah announced judgment (Jer. 48:23). Its location was modern Khirbet el-Jemeil about seven miles east of Dibon.

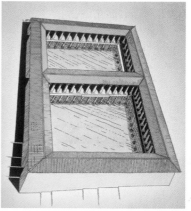

The Pool of Bethesda at Jerusalem, a spring-fed pool near the Sheep Gate where the sick used to come to receive healing. Jesus healed a man there who had been stricken with an unidentified infirmity for 38 years.

BETH-GILGAL Place-name meaning "house of the wheel or circle." A village of Levitical singers near Jerusalem whose occupants participated in the dedication of the newly built city wall under Nehemiah (Neh. 12:29).

BETH-HACCEREM or **BETH-HACCHEREM** Place-name meaning "house of the vineyard." City used to signal that enemies approached from the north (Jer. 6:1).

BETH-HAGGAN Place-name (NIV, TEV, NRSV) or common noun (KJV, NASB) meaning "house of the garden." King Ahaziah of Judah (841 BC) fled there from Jehu, but Jehu finally caught up and killed him (2 Kings 9:27). It is probably modern Jenin, southeast of Tanaach.

BETH-HANAN Place-name meaning "house of grace." A city in Solomon's second district (1 Kings 4:9 TEV).

BETH-HARAM Place-name meaning "house of the exalted one" or "house of height" (KJV, Beth-aram). A city Moses allotted to the tribe of Gad (Josh. 13:27). It is probably Tell er-Rameh though others suggest Tell Iktanu. It is probably the same as Beth-haran.

BETH-HARAN Place-name meaning "house of height." Town east of the Jordan that the tribe of Gad strengthened after Moses gave it to them (Num. 32:36). It is probably the same as Beth-haram.

BETH-HOGLAH Place-name meaning "house of the partridge." Border city between tribes of Judah and Benjamin (Josh. 15:6; 18:19,21). It is probably modern Ain Hajlah, four miles southeast of Jericho.

BETH-HORON Place-name of uncertain meaning. An important road here dominates the path to the Shephelah, the plain between the Judean hills and the Mediterranean coast. Joshua used the road to chase the coalition of southern kings led by the king of Jerusalem (Josh. 10:10).

BETH-JESHIMOTH or **BETH-JESIMOTH** (KJV) Place-name meaning "house of deserts." A town in Moab where Israel camped just before Moses died and Joshua led them across the Jordan (Num. 33:49).

BETH-LE-APHRAH Place-name meaning "place of dust." Town Micah used in a wordplay to announce judgment on Judah. The house of dust would roll in dust, a ritual expressing grief and mourning (Mic. 1:10).

BETH-LEBAOTH Place-name meaning "house of lionesses." City in territorial allotment of tribe of Simeon (Josh. 19:6).

BETHLEHEM Place-name meaning "house of bread," "...fighting," or "...Lahamu" [god]. **1.** Approximately five miles southwest of Jerusalem just off the major road from Jerusalem to the Negev lies the modern Arabic village Bethlehem. The book of Ruth takes place in the region of Bethlehem (Ruth 1:1-2,19,22; 2:4; 4:11). This story leads to the events that gave major importance to the village as the home and place of anointing of David (1 Sam. 16:1-13; 17:12,15). It is the relationship of Bethlehem to Christ that has ensured its place in Christian history. Micah 5:2 was understood to indicate that the Messiah, like David, would be born in Bethlehem not Jerusalem. **2.** Town in the territory of Zebulun, about seven miles northwest of Nazareth (Josh. 19:15), which was the burial site of Ibzan (Judg. 12:10), in modern Beit Lahm. **3.** Personal name as in 1 Chron. 2:51,54.

BETHLEHEM-EPHRATAH (KJV) or **BETHLEHEM-EPHRATHAH** (NASB, NIV, NRSV) Place-name used by Mic. 5:2 to designate birthplace of new David who would come from Bethlehem, David's birthplace, and of the clan of Ephratah, that of Jesse, David's father (1 Sam. 17:12).

BETH-MAACAH (NASB, NRSV) or **BETH-MAACHAH** (KJV) Place-name meaning "house of Maacah" or "house of pressure." Usually appears as Abel Beth-Maacah (always so in NIV). Beth-Maacah apparently appears as final stop on Sheba's trip through Israel to gain support against David (2 Sam. 20:14).

BETH-MARCABOTH Place-name meaning "house of chariots." City allotted to tribe of Simeon (Josh. 19:5). Its location is uncertain.

BETH-MEON Place-name meaning "house of residence." City in Moab on which Jeremiah pronounced judgment (Jer. 48:23). Apparently the same as Beth-baal-meon and Baal-meon.

BETH-MILLO Place-name meaning "house of fulness." **1.** Part of Shechem or a fortress guarding Shechem, where the citizens of Shechem proclaimed Abimelech king (Judg. 9:6,20). **2.** Fortification in Jerusalem where two of his servants killed King Joash (835–796 BC; 2 Kings 12:19-20). It is also called "Millo."

BETH-NIMRAH Place-name meaning "house of the panther." City east of the Jordan that tribe of Gad rebuilt after Moses allotted it to them (Num. 32:36). It provided good grazing land (Num. 32:3). It is located at either Tell Nimrin or nearby at Tell el-Bleibil, about 10 miles northeast of the mouth of the Jordan.

BETH-PAZZEZ Place-name meaning "house of scattering." Town in tribal allotment of Issachar (Josh. 19:22).

BETH-PELET Place-name meaning "house of deliverance." Southern town in tribal allotment of Judah (Josh. 15:27). After the return from exile in Babylon, the Jews lived there (Neh. 11:26). KJV spellings are Beth-palet and Beth-phelet.

BETH-PEOR Place-name meaning "house of Peor." A temple for the god Peor or Baal Peor probably stood there. Town in whose valley Israel camped as Moses delivered the sermons of the book of Deuteronomy (Deut. 3:29).

BETHPHAGE Place-name meaning "house of unripe figs." A small village located on the Mount of Olives near Bethany on or near the road between Jerusalem and Jericho (Matt. 21:1; Mark 11:1; Luke 19:29). Bethphage was where Jesus gave instruction to two disciples to find the colt on which he would ride into Jerusalem for His triumphal entry.

BETH-RAPHA Place-name meaning "house of a giant." First Chronicles 4:12 says the otherwise unknown Eshton "became the father of Beth-rapha" (NASB).

BETH-REHOB Place-name meaning "house of the market." Town near where tribe of Dan rebuilt Laish and renamed it Dan (Judg. 18:28).

BETHSAIDA Place-name meaning "house of fish." The home of Andrew, Peter, and Philip (John 1:44; 12:21), located on the northeast side of the Sea of Galilee.

BETH-SHAN, BETHSHAN, or BETH-SHEAN Place-name meaning "house of quiet." Beth-shean stood at the crossroads of the Jezreel and Jordan Valleys, commanding the routes north-south along the Jordan and east-west from Gilead to the Mediterranean Sea. Biblical references to Beth-shean relate to the period from Joshua until the United Monarchy. The city is listed among the allocations of the tribe of Manasseh, though the city was within the territory of Issachar (Josh. 17:11).

BETH-SHEMESH Place-name meaning "house of the sun." Beth-shemesh is a name applied to four different cities in the OT. The name probably derives from a place where the Semitic god Shemesh (Shamash) was worshipped. **1.** Beth-shemesh of Issachar was situated on the tribal border with Naphtali between Mount Tabor and the Jordan River (Josh. 19:22). **2.** Beth-shemesh of Naphtali was probably located in central upper Galilee because of its association with Beth-anath (Josh. 19:38; Judg. 1:33). This Canaanite town remained independent and

Beth-shan.

unconquered until the time of David. **3.** Beth-shemesh of Egypt is to be identified with Heliopolis (five miles northeast of Cairo) according to the Septuagint or early Greek translation (Jer. 43:13). **4.** Beth-shemesh of Dan is located on the south tribal border with Judah (Josh. 15:10; 19:41) overlooking the Sorek Valley about 24 miles west of Jerusalem.

BETH-SHITTAH Place-name meaning "house of Acacia." Battle scene when Gideon and his 300 men defeated the Midianites (Judg. 7:22).

BETH-TAPPUAH Place-name meaning "house of apples." Town assigned tribe of Judah in Judean hills (Josh. 15:53).

BETH-TOGARMAH Place-name meaning "house of Togarmah." Listed in the Table of Nations (Gen. 10:3) as son of Gomer and great grandson of Noah, Togarmah is a city mentioned in Assyrian and Hittite texts. It was north of Carchemish on an Assyrian trade route.

BETHUEL or **BETHUL** Place-name and personal name meaning "house of God." **1.** Nephew of Abraham and son of Nahor (Gen. 22:22). His daughter Rebekah married Isaac (Gen. 24:15,67). **2.** Town where the children of Shimei lived (1 Chron. 4:30).

BETHZATHA TEV, NSRV reading of place-name in John 5:2 based on different Greek manuscripts than those followed by other translators.

BETH-ZUR Place-name meaning "house of the rock." **1.** City allotted to tribe of Judah (Josh. 15:58). Rehoboam, Solomon's son and successor as king of Judah (931–913 BC), built it up as a defense city (2 Chron. 11:7) in view of the threat of Shishak of Egypt (2 Chron. 12:2). **2.** Son of Maon in line of Caleb (1 Chron. 2:45), apparently indicating the clan that settled the city.

BETONIM Place-name meaning "pistachios." A border town in tribal allotment of Gad (Josh. 13:26).

BETROTHAL Act of engagement for marriage in Bible times and as binding as marriage. The biblical terms, *betrothal* and *espousal,* are almost synonymous with marriage, and as binding.

BEULAH Symbolic name meaning "married," used in reference to Jerusalem (Isa. 62:4 KJV).

BEYOND THE JORDAN Often used to describe the territory on the east side of the Jordan River (also referred to as the Transjordan). Five times the phrase describes the territory on the west side of the Jordan (Gen. 50:10-11; Deut. 3:20,25; 11:30).

BEYOND THE RIVER Refers to the Euphrates River in Mesopotamia. From the perspective of those living in Palestine, "beyond the river" meant on the east side of the Euphrates River. The expression is often used when speaking of the ancestral home of the patriarchs (Josh. 24:3,14-15; KJV has "on the other side of the flood").

BEZAI Contraction of Bezaleel. **1.** Clan of 323 (Ezra 2:17) who returned from Babylonian exile with Zerubbabel about 537 BC. **2.** Man who signed Nehemiah's covenant to obey God's law (Neh. 10:18).

BEZALEEL or **BEZALEL** Personal name meaning "in the shadow of God." **1.** Son of Uri, a member of the tribe of Judah (Exod. 31:2) and great grandson of Caleb (1 Chron. 2:20). He and another man, the Danite Aholiab, were skilled craftsmen who were responsible for making the tabernacle, its furnishings, and trappings. His skill derived from his being filled with the Spirit of God. Most modern translations render the names of these men Bezalel and Oholiab. **2.** Man who followed Ezra's leadership and divorced his foreign wife (Ezra 10:30).

BEZEK Place-name meaning "lightning." Place where Judah and Simeon defeated Canaanites who were led by Adoni-bezek (literally "lord of Bezek") (Judg. 1:4).

BEZER Place-name meaning "inaccessible." A city of refuge in tribal territory of Reuben (Deut. 4:43; Josh. 20:8), set aside as a city for the Levites (Josh. 21:36).

BIBLE, FORMATION AND CANON "Bible" derives from the Greek word for "books" and refers to the OT and NT. The 39 OT books and 27 NT books form the "canon" of Holy Scripture. "Canon" originally meant "reed" and came to signify a ruler or measuring stick. In this sense the Bible is the rule or standard of authority for Christians. The concept of "canon" and process of "canonization" refers to when the books gained the status of "Holy Scripture," authoritative standards for faith and practice.

BICHRI Personal name meaning "firstborn" or clan name "of the clan of Becher." Father of Sheba, who led revolt against David after Absalom's revolt (2 Sam. 20:1).

BIDKAR Officer of Jehu who took body of Joram, king of Israel (852–841 BC), and threw it on Naboth's land after Jehu murdered the king (2 Kings 9:25). Bidkar and Jehu had originally served as chariot officers for Ahab, Joram's father.

BIER Litter or bed upon which a body was placed before burial. They were portable (2 Sam. 3:31; Luke 7:14).

BIGTHA Persian personal name possibly meaning "gift of God." A eunuch who served King Ahasuerus of Persia and took command to Queen Vashti to come to party (Esther 1:10).

BIGTHAN May be identical with Bigtha. He plotted with Teresh, another of the king's eunuchs, to assassinate King Ahasuerus of Persia (Esther 2:21). Mordecai foiled the plot, thus setting up the king's need to honor Mordecai at Haman's expense (Esther 6:1-12).

BIGVAI Persian name meaning "god" or "fortune." **1.** Leader with Zerubbabel of exiles who returned from Babylon about 537 BC (Ezra 2:2). **2.** One who sealed Nehemiah's covenant to obey God's law (Neh. 10:16).

BILDAD Proper name meaning "the Lord loved." One of the three friends of Job (Job 2:11). He is identified as a Shuhite, perhaps a member of a group of nomadic Arameans.

BILEAM City given to Levites from tribal territory of western Manasseh. It is often identified with Ibleam. Joshua 21:25, a parallel passage, reads "Gath-rimmon."

BILGAH Personal name meaning "brightness." **1.** Original ancestor of one of divisions of priesthood (1 Chron. 24:14). **2.** Priest who returned from exile with Zerubbabel about 537 BC (Neh. 12:5).

BILGAI Priest who sealed Nehemiah's covenant to obey God's law (Neh. 10:8).

BILHAH Personal name meaning "unworried." The handmaid of Rachel (Gen. 29:29). When Rachel failed to bear children to her husband Jacob, Bilhah became his concubine at Rachel's instigation. Bilhah became the mother of Dan and Naphtali (Gen. 29:29; 30:4-8).

BILHAN Personal name, perhaps meaning "afraid" or "foolish." **1.** Descendant of Seir or Edom (Gen. 36:27). **2.** Descendant of Benjamin (1 Chron. 7:10).

BILSHAN Akkadian personal name meaning "their lord." Leader of returning exiles with Zerubbabel from Babylon about 537 BC (Ezra 2:2).

BIMHAL Descendant of tribe of Asher (1 Chron. 7:33).

BINEA Descendant of the tribe of Benjamin (1 Chron. 8:37) and of King Saul (1 Chron. 9:43).

BINNUI Personal name meaning "built." **1.** Father of Noadiah, Levite who assured the temple treasures Ezra brought back from exile were correctly inventoried (Ezra 8:33). **2.** Two men who divorced foreign wives when Ezra sought to remove temptation to idolatry and purify the community (Ezra 10:30,38). **3.** Man who helped Nehemiah repair the wall of Jerusalem (Neh. 3:24). **4.** Clan leader of 648 members who returned with Zerubbabel from Babylon about 537 BC (Neh. 7:15; Ezra 2:10—spells it "Bani" with 642 people). **5.** Levite who sealed Nehemiah's covenant to obey God's law (Neh. 10:9). Could be same as any of the above. He came up with Zerubbabel from Babylonian exile (Neh. 12:8).

BIRDS The Bible contains approximately 300 references to birds, scattered from Genesis to Revelation. The Hebrew people's keen awareness of bird life is reflected in the different Hebrew and Greek names used for birds in general or for specific birds. Although bird names are difficult to translate, many birds of the Bible can be identified from the descriptions of them given in the Scriptures.

Some of the specific birds mentioned are: cock (rooster), dove (turtledove), eagle, ostrich, pigeon, quail, raven, sparrow, and vulture. See other individual bird names in the alphabetical dictionary listing.

Birds of abomination The birds of abomination are in the list of 20 birds not to be consumed by Israelites (Lev. 11:13-19). The reason for the exclusion of these birds is unclear. Some have suggested that the birds were prohibited because they were associated with the worship of idols. Others have suggested that they were excluded because they ate flesh that contained blood or because they had contact with corpses—both of which would make one ritually unclean (Lev. 7:26; 17:13-14; 21:1-4,11; 22:4; Num. 5:2-3; 6:6-11).

BIRSHA Personal name with uncertain meaning, traditionally, "ugly." King of Gomorrah who joined coalition of Dead Sea area kings against eastern group of invading kings (Gen. 14:2).

BIRTHRIGHT Special privileges that belonged to the firstborn male child in a family. Prominent among those privileges was a double portion of the estate as an inheritance. If a man had two sons, his estate would be divided into three portions, and the older son would receive two. If there were three sons, the estate would be divided into four portions, and the oldest son would receive two. The oldest son also normally received the father's major blessing.

BIRTH STOOL Object upon which a woman sat during labor (Exod. 1:16 NASB, NKJV). The birth stool may have been of Egyptian origin. The same Hebrew word ('*obnayim*) is also translated as "potter's wheel" (Jer. 18:3).

BIRZAITH or **BIRZAVITH** (KJV) Descendant of Asher (1 Chron. 7:31).

BISHLAM Personal name or common name meaning "in peace." Apparently representative of Persian government in Palestine who complained about building activities (Ezra 4:7) of the returned Jews to Artaxerxes, king of Persia (464–423 BC).

BISHOP Term that comes from the Greek noun *episkopos*, which occurs five times in the NT (Acts 20:28; Phil. 1:1; 1 Tim. 3:2; Titus 1:7; 1 Pet. 2:25). "Overseer" more accurately identifies the function of the officeholder than does the term "bishop."

BIT Metal bar fastened to the muzzle end of the horse's bridle. The bit and bridle were used figuratively in the Bible to refer to different forms of control (James 1:26; 3:2; 2 Kings 19:28; Isa. 37:29).

BITHIA (NASB) or **BITHIAH** Personal name meaning "daughter of Yahweh" or Egyptian common noun meaning "queen." Daughter of an Egyptian pharaoh whom Mered, a descendant of tribe of Judah, married (1 Chron. 4:17 NASB, RSV; 4:18 KJV, NIV).

BITHYNIA District in northern Asia Minor that Paul's missionary company desired to enter with the gospel (Acts 16:7). The Holy Spirit prevented them from doing so and directed them instead to Macedonia.

BITTER HERBS Eaten with the Passover meal (Exod. 12:8; Num. 9:11), the herbs were interpreted as symbolizing the bitter experiences of the Israelites' slavery in Egypt.

BITTERN KJV translation for an animal of desolation mentioned three times (Isa. 14:23; 34:11; Zeph. 2:14). The name "bittern" is applied to any number of small or medium-sized herons with a characteristic booming cry.

BITTER WATER A woman suspected of adultery was given bitter water to drink (Num. 5:11-31). If she was innocent, she would not be harmed and would conceive children as a blessing. If she was guilty, her "thigh would rot" and her "body swell."

BITUMEN (NRSV, RSV, ESV) Mineral pitch or asphalt (KJV has "slime"; NASB, NIV, "tar pits") found in solid black lumps in the Cretaceous limestone on the west bank of the Dead Sea (Gen. 14:10).

BIZIOTHIAH or **BIZJOTHJAH** (KJV) Place-name meaning "scorns of Yahweh." Southern town in tribal allotment of Judah (Josh. 15:28).

BIZTHA Persian personal name of uncertain meaning. One of seven eunuchs who served King Ahasuerus in matters relating to his wives (Esther 1:10).

BLAINS KJV word for "sores" in Exod. 9:9-10.

BLASPHEMY Transliteration of a Greek word meaning literally "to speak harm." In the biblical context, blasphemy is an attitude of disrespect that finds expression in an act directed against the character of God.

Old Testament Blasphemy draws its Christian definition through the background of the OT. Leviticus 24:14-16 guides the Hebrew definition of blasphemy. The offense is designated as a capital crime, and the offender is to be stoned by the community.

New Testament The NT broadens the concept of blasphemy to include actions against Christ and the church as the body of Christ. Jesus was regarded by the Jewish leaders as a blasphemer Himself (Mark 2:7). The unity of Christ and the church is recognized in the fact that persecutions against Christians are labeled as blasphemous acts (1 Tim. 1:13; 1 Pet. 4:4; Rev. 2:9). It is also important that Christians avoid conduct that might give an occasion for blasphemy, especially in the area of attitude and speech (Eph. 4:31; Col. 3:8; 1 Tim. 6:4; Titus 3:2).

The sin of blasphemy is a sin that can be forgiven. However, there is a sin of blasphemy against the Holy Spirit that cannot be forgiven (Matt. 12:32; Mark 3:29; Luke 12:10). This is a state of hardness in which one consciously and willfully resists God's saving power and grace.

BLEMISH Condition that disqualifies an animal as a sacrifice (Lev. 22:17-25) or a man from priestly service (Lev. 21:17-24). In the NT, Christ is the perfect sacrifice (without blemish, Heb. 9:14; 1 Pet. 1:19) intended to sanctify the church and remove all its blemishes (Eph. 5:27). The children of God are commanded to live lives without blemishes (Phil. 2:15; 2 Pet. 3:14).

BLESSING AND CURSING To "bless" meant to fill with benefits, either as an end in itself or to make the object blessed a source of further blessing for others. God is most often at least the understood agent of blessing in this sense. In another sense the word could mean to "praise," as if filling the object of blessing with honor and good words. Thus individuals might bless God (Exod. 18:10; Ruth 4:14; Pss. 68:19; 103:1), while God also could bless men and women (Gen. 12:23; Num. 23:20; 1 Chron. 4:10; Ps. 109:28; Isa. 61:9). Persons might also bless one another (Gen. 27:33; Deut. 7:14; 1 Sam. 25:33), or they might bless things (Deut. 28:4; 1 Sam. 25:33; Prov. 5:18).

In the NT the word "blessed" often translates *makarios*, meaning "blessed, fortunate, happy." It occurs 50 times in the NT, most familiarly in the "beatitudes" in Jesus' Sermon on the Mount (Matt. 5:3-11).

The concept of cursing was clearly more prevalent in the OT. Depending on who is speaking, one who "curses" is either predicting, praying, or causing great trouble for someone. As belonging to God and His people meant blessing, being cursed often meant separation from God and the community of faith. It thus involved the experience of insecurity and disaster.

In the NT the act of "cursing" sometimes means to wish misfortune on someone (Luke 6:28; Rom. 12:14; James 3:9-10). The concept of the "curse" is also applied to those who are outside God's blessings, which are by His grace (Matt. 25:41). They are therefore under divine condemnation, the "curse of the law" because of sin (John 7:49; Gal. 3:10,13; 1 Cor. 16:22). Especially serious is the situation of those who reject or actively oppose the work of God (Gal. 1:8-9; 2 Pet. 2:14; Rev. 16:9,11,21).

BLINDNESS Physical blindness in the biblical period was very common. The suffering of the blind person was made worse by the common belief that the affliction was due to sin (John 9:1-3). Jesus frequently healed blind persons (Matt. 9:27-31; 12:22; 20:30-34; Mark 10:46-52; John 9:1-7).

The Bible addresses spiritual blindness as the great human problem. Peter listed the qualities a person must have to have spiritual sight. Without these, a person is blind (2 Pet. 1:5-9).

BLOOD Blood is intimately associated with physical life. The Hebrews of OT times were prohibited from eating blood. Even when the OT speaks of animal sacrifice and atonement, the sacredness of life is emphasized (Lev. 17:11).

Blood of Christ—Meaning and Effects The term "blood of Christ" designates in the NT the atoning death of Christ. Atonement refers to the basis and process by which estranged people become at one with God (atonement=at-one-ment). When we identify with Jesus, we are no longer at odds with God.   In the language of sacrifice we have "propitiation" (removal of sins, Rom. 3:25 HCSB); "sprinkling with the blood of Jesus Christ" (1 Pet. 1:1-2 HCSB); redeemed "with the precious blood of Christ, like that of a lamb without defect or blemish" (1 Pet. 1:19 HCSB); "blood of Jesus His Son cleanses us from all sin" (1 John 1:7 HCSB); blood that will "cleanse our consciences" (Heb. 9:14 HCSB); and "blood of the everlasting covenant" (Heb. 13:20 HCSB).

BLOODGUILT Guilt usually incurred through bloodshed.

BLUE Hebrew word translated "blue" (*tekeleth*), also translated as "purple" (Ezek. 23:6) and "violet" (Jer. 10:9). Blue was considered inferior to royal purple but was still a very popular color. Blue was used in the tabernacle (Exod. 25:4; 26:1,4; Num. 4:6-7,9; 15:38), in the temple (2 Chron. 2:7,14; 3:14), and in the clothing of the priests (Exod. 28:5-6,8,15; 39:1).

BOANERGES Name meaning "Sons of Thunder," given by Jesus to James and John, the sons of Zebedee (Mark 3:17).

BOAZ Personal name, perhaps meaning "lively." **1.** Hero of the book of Ruth; a wealthy relative of Naomi's husband. **2.** The left or north pillar Solomon set up in the temple (1 Kings 7:21).

BOCHERU Personal name meaning "firstborn." Descendant of King Saul in the tribe of Benjamin (1 Chron. 8:38).

BOCHIM Place-name meaning "weepers." Place where angel of God announced judgment on Israel at beginning of the period of the judges because they had not destroyed pagan altars but had made covenant treaties with the native inhabitants. Thus the people cried and named the place Bochim (Judg. 2:1-5).

BOHAN Place-name and personal name meaning "thumb" or "big toe." A place on the northern border of the tribal allotment of Judah called the "stone of Bohan," "the son of Reuben" (Josh. 15:6). This was the southern border of the tribe of Benjamin (Josh. 18:17).

BOLLED KJV translation (Exod. 9:31) of a term that means "having bolls"—that is, having seedpods.

BOND Translation of several Hebrew and Greek words with the meanings of "obligation," "dependence," or "restraint." Used literally to speak of the bonds of prisoners or slaves (Judg. 15:14; 1 Kings 14:10; Ps. 107:14; 116:16; Luke 8:29; Philem. 13). Used figuratively to speak of the bonds of wickedness or sin.

BOOK OF LIFE Heavenly record (Luke 10:20; Heb. 12:23) written by God before the foundation of the world (Rev. 13:8; 17:8) containing the names of those who are destined because of God's grace and their faithfulness to participate in God's heavenly kingdom. The OT refers to a record kept by God of those who are a part of His people (Exod. 32:32; Isa. 4:3; Dan. 12:1; Mal. 3:16).

BOOK(S) Term which often refers to a scroll. A document written on parchment or papyrus and then rolled up. The "book" may be a letter (1 Kings 21:8) or a longer literary effort (Dan. 9:2).

BOR-ASHAN Place-name meaning "well of smoke" or "pit of smoke." Place in most manuscripts of 1 Sam. 30:30; others read Chor-ashan (KJV). A town of the tribe of Judah to whom David gave part of his spoils of victory. It is usually equated with Asham, the town of Judah in which Simeon lived (Josh. 15:42; 19:7).

BOTTLE Word used often in the KJV to translate several Hebrew and Greek words. Modern versions often translate these words as "skin" or "wineskin." Although glass and glass bottles were known in ancient times, ancient "bottles" were almost always made of animal skins since they were easier to carry than earthenware vessels.

BOTTOMLESS PIT Literal translation of the Greek in Rev. 9:1-2,11; 11:7; 17:8; 20:1,3. It represented the home of evil, death, and destruction stored up until the sovereign God allowed them temporary power on earth.

BOWELS Translation used in modern versions to refer to intestines and other entrails (Acts 1:18).

In the KJV "bowels" is also used to refer to the sexual reproductive system (2 Sam. 16:11; Ps. 71:6) and, figuratively, to strong emotions (Job 30:27), especially love (Song 5:4) and compassion (Col. 3:12). Both Hebrew and Greek picture the entrails as the center of human emotions and excitement.

BOX TREE KJV, REB, and NASB translation in Isa. 41:19; 60:13. The Hebrew word means "to be straight" and apparently refers to the tall, majestic cypress trees. Such wonders of nature reflect the greatness of the Creator (Isa. 41:20).

BOZEZ Place-name, perhaps meaning "white." A sharp rock marking a passage in the Wadi Suwenit near Michmash through which Jonathan and his armor bearer went to fight the Philistines (1 Sam. 14:4).

BOZRAH Place-name meaning "inaccessible." **1.** Ancestral home of Jobab, a king in Edom before Israel had a king (Gen. 36:33). **2.** City of Moab Jeremiah condemned (Jer. 48:24). It may be equated with Bezer.

BRACELET Ornamental band of metal or glass worn around the wrist (as distinct from an armlet worn around the upper arm). Bracelets were common in the ancient Near East and were worn by both women and men.

BRAMBLE Shrub (*Lycium Europaeum*) with sharp spines and runners usually forming a tangled mass of vegetation (Judg. 9:8-15; Luke 6:44). It had beautiful, attractive flowers, but its thorns gave flocks trouble.

BRASS Any copper alloy was called "brass" by the KJV translators. Brass is the alloy of copper and zinc, a combination unknown in the ancient Near East.

Serpentine bracelet.

BREAD Frequency of mention is just one indication that bread (not vegetables and certainly not meat) was the basic food of most people (except nomads and the wealthy) in Bible times. A course meal was ground from wheat (Gen. 30:14) or barley (John 6:9,13). In addition to being used as a staple food, bread was used as an offering to God (Lev. 2:4-10). It was used in the tabernacle and temple to symbolize the presence of God (Exod. 25:23-30; Lev. 24:5-9). Bread was also used in the OT to symbolize such things as an enemy to be consumed (Num. 14:9, KJV, RSV), the unity of a group (1 Kings 18:19), hospitality (Gen. 19:3), and wisdom (Prov. 9:5).

BREAD OF THE PRESENCE Also "bread of the faces." In Exod. 25:30 the Lord's instructions concerning the paraphernalia of worship include a provision that bread be kept always on a table set before the Holy of Holies. This bread was called the "bread of the Presence" or "showbread (shewbread)." It consisted of 12 loaves of presumably unleavened bread, and it was replaced each Sabbath.

BREASTPIECE OF THE HIGH PRIEST Piece of elaborate embroidery about nine inches square worn by the high priest upon his breast. It was set with 12 stones with the name of one of the 12 tribes of Israel engraved on each stone.

BREASTPLATE Piece of defensive armor. Paul used the military breastplate as an illustration of Christian virtues. Ephesians 6:14 reflects Isa. 59:17, symbolizing the breastplate as righteousness. Faith and love are symbolized in 1 Thess. 5:8. Breastplates were also strong symbols of evil (Rev. 9:9,17).

Mud-clay bricks in the ruins of the city of Ur.

BRICK Building material of clay, molded into rectangular shaped blocks while moist and hardened by the sun or fire, used to construct walls or pavement. The tower of Babel (Gen. 11:3), made of bricks, had mortar of slime, a tarlike substance. Later, the descendants of Joseph, as slaves of the pharoah in Egypt, built storehouse cities of brick in Pithom and Ramses. Both straw-made bricks and bricks of pure clay have been found there. When David conquered the Ammonites, he required that they make bricks (2 Sam. 12:31). Isaiah (65:3) condemned Israel for their paganlike practice of offering incense on altars of brick.

BRIDE Biblical writers have little to say about weddings or brides. They occasionally mention means by which brides were obtained (Gen. 24:4; 29:15-19). Ezekiel 16:8-14 describes the bride, her attire, and the wedding ceremony. The Song of Songs is a collection of love poems in which the bride describes her love for her bridegroom. In the NT, the bride imagery is used often of the church and her relationship to Christ. The bride belongs to Christ, who is the Bridegroom (John 3:29).

BRIER Translation of various Hebrew words referring to thorny plants. Used metaphorically of the enemies of Israel (Ezek. 28:24) and of land which is worthless (Isa. 5:6; 7:23-25; 55:13; cp. Mic. 7:4).

BRIMSTONE Combustible form of sulfur. Used as a means of divine retribution (Gen. 19:24; Deut. 29:23; Job 18:15; Ps. 11:6; Isa. 30:33; 34:9; Ezek. 38:22; Luke 17:29; Rev. 14:10; 19:20; 20:10; 21:8). It lies on the shore of the Dead Sea and can burst into flame when earthquakes release hot gases from the earth's interior.

BRONZE SERPENT Moses made a bronze serpent and set it on a pole in the middle of the Israelite camp (Num. 21). God had told Moses to do this so the Israelites bitten by serpents could express their faith by looking at it and be healed. Jesus made the final mention of this symbol in John 3:14. There, in His conversation with Nicodemus, Jesus compared His own purpose with that of the bronze serpent. The serpent, lifted up in the wilderness, had been God's chosen way to provide physical healing. Jesus, lifted up on the cross, is God's chosen means of providing spiritual healing for all afflicted by sin. Whoever believes in Jesus "will not perish but have eternal life" (John 3:16 HCSB).

BROOCH Class of jewelry brought by both men and women as offerings (Exod. 35:22). The Hebrew term denotes a golden pin (KJV has "bracelets"; REB, "clasp"; TEV, "decorative pins"). At a later time brooches were bow shaped and made of bronze or iron. Some recent interpreters think "nose rings" were meant.

BROOM TREE Bush that often grows large enough to provide shade (1 Kings 19:4-5). Its foliage and roots were often used as fuel (Job 30:4; Ps. 120:4).

BROTHERS In the OT the word "brother" usually refers to the blood relationship of siblings (Exod. 4:14; Judg. 9:5). The term "brother" is also used in the OT to signify kinsmen, allies, fellow countrymen. This shift of focus from blood to spiritual kinship is found in the teachings of Jesus when He designated as brothers "those who hear and do the word of God" (Luke 8:21 HCSB). The fledgling Christian community continued this emphasis on brother as expressing a spiritual relationship. In most of the NT passages "brothers" is used to designate the entire Christian community (male and female).

BROTHERS, JESUS' Jesus' Nazareth critics listed them in Mark 6:3 as James, Joses, Judas, and Simon. Their names appear again in the parallel passage of Matt. 13:55, except Joseph is used as the alternate spelling of Joses (see NASB).

BUCKLER Small rounded shield that was carried in the hand or worn on the arm. Larger shields were also used that covered the entire body.

BUKKI Personal name shortened from Bukkiah, meaning "Yahweh proved" or "Yahweh has emptied." **1.** Representative of tribe of Dan on commission to distribute the promised land among the tribes (Num. 34:22). **2.** High priestly descendant of Aaron (1 Chron. 6:5,51) and ancestor of Ezra (Ezra 7:4).

BUKKIAH Son of Herman among temple musicians David appointed (1 Chron. 25:4). He or a person of same name headed the sixth course of musicians (1 Chron. 25:13).

BUL Name of eighth month or parts of October and November meaning "harvest month." Solomon finished building the temple in this month (1 Kings 6:38).

BULL The bull was the symbol of great productivity in the ancient world and was a sign of great strength. Moses portrayed the future strength of Joseph with the term *shor* (Deut. 33:17). The king of Assyria boasted of his great strength with the term *abbir* (Isa. 10:13). The most frequent use of the bull in the OT was as a sacrificial animal.

BULRUSH In Exod. 2:3 the material used to make the basket in which the infant Moses was placed to protect him from the edict of Pharaoh requiring that every male Hebrew child be drowned. A kind of reed plant.

BUNNI Personal name meaning "built." Levite leader of worship service confessing Israel's sin in days of Ezra (Neh. 9:4). A man of same name, probably same man, signed Nehemiah's covenant to obey God's law (Neh. 10:15). His son Hasabiah was one of the Levites living in Jerusalem in time of Nehemiah (Neh. 11:15).

BURIAL Partly because of the warm climate of Palestine and partly because the corpse was considered ritually impure, the Hebrews buried their dead as soon as possible and usually within 24 hours of death (Deut. 21:23). To allow a body to decay or be desecrated above the ground was highly dishonorable (1 Kings 14:10-14; 2 Kings 9:34-37), and any corpse found by the wayside was required to be buried (2 Sam. 21:10-14).

BUTLER Translation of a Hebrew word that literally means "one who gives drink." The butler was an officer of the royal court who had charge of wines and other beverages. The butler was a trusted member of the royal court as this person helped prevent the poisoning of the king. The term that is translated "butler" (Gen. 40:1-23; 41:9) is also translated "cupbearer" (1 Kings 10:5; 2 Chron. 9:4; Neh. 1:11).

BUZ Place- and personal name meaning "scorn." **1.** Son of Nahor, brother of Abraham (Gen. 22:21). **2.** A member of tribe of Gad (1 Chron. 5:14). **3.** A land in eastern Arabia (Jer. 25:23) that Jeremiah condemned.

BUZI Personal noun meaning "scorn." Priest and father of Ezekiel, the prophet and priest (Ezek. 1:3).

BUZZARD Unclean bird, not suitable for food. Listed in the NASB and NLT in Lev. 11:13; Deut. 14:12 with the birds of abomination. Revelation 18:2 (NLT) has "filthy buzzards" nesting in the fallen Babylon.

BYWORD Object of ridicule and scorn among other peoples. Used to speak of the fate of faithless Israel (Deut. 28:37; 1 Kings 9:7; 2 Chron. 7:20; Job 17:6; 30:9; Ps. 44:14).

Byzantine street at Caesarea Maritima with two colossal statues, one possibly of the emperor Hadrian.

CABBON Place-name of uncertain meaning. Town in tribal allotment of Judah (Josh. 15:40).

CABIN KJV translation of Hebrew word appearing only in Jer. 37:16 and meaning vault, cellar, or prison cell (cistern, NRSV).

CABUL Place-name meaning "fettered" or "braided." **1.** Town on northeast border of Asher (Josh. 19:27). May be located at modern Kabul, nine miles southeast of Acco. **2.** Region of cities in Galilee Solomon gave Hiram, king of Tyre, as payment for materials and services in building the temple and the palace.

CAESAR Family name of Julius Caesar assumed as a title by the emperors who followed him.

CAESAREA Located on the Mediterranean Sea 23 miles south of Mount Carmel is the city of Caesarea, known also as Caesarea-on-the-Sea (Maritima). Herod determined to build a fine port facility and support it by a new city. The harbor, which he named Sebastos (Latin, Augustus), was a magnificently engineered project. After Archelaus was removed in AD 6, Caesarea became the capital of the province of Judea and served as the official home of the procurators.

CAESAREA PHILIPPI About 1,150 feet above sea level, Caesarea Philippi is located on a triangular plain in the upper Jordan Valley along the southwestern slopes of Mount Hermon. Caesarea Philippi seems to have been a religious center from its earliest days. The Canaanite god Baal-gad, the god of good fortune, was worshiped here in OT times. Later, in the Greek period, a shrine in the cave was dedicated to the god Pan. Near here Jesus asked His disciples the famous question about His identity. Peter, acting as the group's spokesman, replied with his famous statement that Jesus is the Christ.

CAIAPHAS Personal name meaning "rock" or "depression." High priest at the time of the trial and crucifixion of Jesus (Matt. 26:3). He was the son-in-law of Annas and a leader in the plot to arrest and execute Jesus.

CAIN Personal name meaning "acquisition." The firstborn son of Adam and Eve (Gen. 4:1). Cain was a farmer, and his brother Abel was a shepherd. When the two men each brought an offering to the Lord, Abel's was accepted, but Cain's was not. Subsequently, Cain murdered Abel his brother.

CAINAN Personal name of unknown meaning. **1.** Ancestor of Noah (Gen. 5:10-14), sometimes seen as a variant spelling of Cain (Gen. 4:17). **2.** Descendant of Noah listed in the Septuagint of Gen. 11:12 but not of Hebrew. Luke used this early Greek translation of the OT and included Cainan in Christ's ancestors (Luke 3:36).

CALAH Assyrian place-name. City that Nimrod built along with Nineveh and Rehoboth (Gen. 10:8-12).

CALAMUS Ingredient of holy anointing oil (Ezek. 30:23). It was a good-smelling spice made from an imported reed. It is also translated "fragrant cane" (NIV, NASB) or "aromatic cane" (NRSV).

CALCOL Personal name of uncertain meaning. Wise man who served as comparison for Solomon's unsurpassed wisdom (1 Kings 4:31). First Chronicles 2:6 makes him a grandson of Judah, the son of Jacob.

CALEB, CALEBITE Personal and clan name meaning "dog." Caleb, the son of Jephunneh, was one of the 12 spies sent by Moses to scout out the territory of Canaan (Num. 13:6). He was one of only two who brought back a positive report (Num. 13:30). Because of his steadfast loyalty to the Lord, God rewarded him by letting him survive the years of wilderness wandering and giving him the region of Hebron as his portion in the promised land. At the age of 85 Caleb conquered Hebron (Josh. 14).

CALENDAR OT mentions days, months, and years, the basic elements of a calendar. It was in the rabbinical period that the written treatise on Jewish traditions, *Rosh Hashanah*, a part of the Mishna, organized the biblical data into the detailed calendrical system that the Jews observe today.

CALF Young of the cow or other closely related animals. Calves were fattened in stalls to provide veal on special occasions (Gen. 18:7-8; 1 Sam. 28:24; Luke 15:23,27,30). Calves were also used in sacrificial settings (Lev. 9:2-3; Jer. 34:18; cp. Gen. 15:9-10, heifer). A calf symbolized the bullish Gentile armies (Ps. 68:30) and Egyptian mercenary soldiers (Jer. 46:21). The feet of one of the cherubim described by Ezekiel looked like those of a calf (Ezek. 1:7). One of the four creatures around the throne resembled a calf (Rev. 4:7 KJV, HCSB; other translations read "ox").

CALKERS, CALKING Those who place some substance like bitumen into the seams of a ship's planking to make it watertight (Ezek. 27:9,27).

CALNEH, CALNO Place-name of uncertain meaning. **1.** A part of the kingdom of Nimrod in Babylonia (Gen. 10:10). **2.** City in Syria under Israel's control in the days of Amos and Isaiah (around 740 BC).

CALVARY English name for the place where Jesus was crucified (Luke 23:33), derived from the Latin *Calvaria*, which is the Vulgate's translation of the Greek *Kranion*, "skull." The other three Gospels (Matt. 27:33; Mark 15:22; John 19:17) refer also to the Semitic name "Golgotha," meaning "skull" or "head."

CALVES, GOLDEN Representation of young bulls used to symbolize the god's presence in the worship place. As Moses was on Mount Sinai, Aaron formed a golden calf to use in a "feast to Yahweh" (Exod. 32:4-5). Similarly, Jeroboam placed calves in Dan and Bethel for the northern kingdom to use in its

Gordon's Calvary is one of two sites considered to be the possible location of Jesus' crucifixion.

worship of Yahweh (1 Kings 12:28) so the people would not have to go to Jerusalem, the southern capital, to worship. In both instances the calves represent the gods who brought Israel up from Egypt. Thus the sin of the calves is not worshipping the wrong god but worshipping the true God in the wrong way through images (Ps. 106:19-20).

CAMEL Large hump-backed mammal of Asia and Africa used for desert travel to bear burdens or passengers. Recent discoveries show it was domesticated before 2000 BC

Old Testament The camel, called the "ship of the desert," is adapted for desert travel with padded feet, a muscular body, and a hump of fat to sustain life on long journeys. A young camel can walk 100 miles in a day. Wealth was measured by many things, including camels (Gen. 24:35; Job 1:3).

New Testament A proverb picturing things impossible to accomplish was quoted by Jesus (Mark 10:25) when He said it is easier for a camel to pass through the eye of a needle (Matt. 19:24) than for a rich man to enter heaven.

CAMEL'S HAIR Very coarse material was woven from the hair of a camel's back and hump. A finer material was woven from the hair taken from underneath the animal. John the Baptist wore coarse camel's hair (Mark 1:6). Jesus contrasted John's cloak to the "soft raiment" (KJV) of the members of the king's court (Matt. 11:8). Wearing a hairy mantle was the mark of a prophet (Zech. 13:4; cp. 2 Kings 1:8).

CAMP, ENCAMPMENT Temporary settlement for nomadic and military people. Hence the frequent reference to "the camp" or "the camp of Israel" (Exod. 14:1,9; 16:13). Leviticus and Deuteronomy contain laws regulating life "in the camp."

CAMPHIRE KJV spelling of "camphor," Song 1:14; 4:13. Most modern versions read "henna."

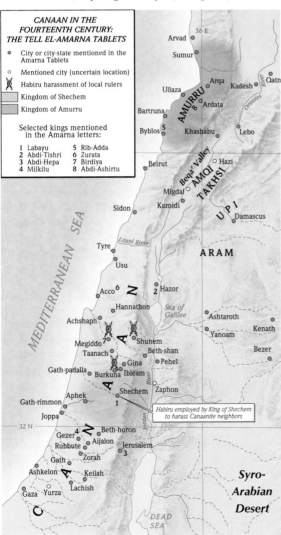

CANAAN IN THE FOURTEENTH CENTURY: THE TELL EL-AMARNA TABLETS

CANA Place-name meaning "the nest." In John 2:1 the town that was the scene of a wedding during which Jesus changed water into wine. In Cana an unnamed nobleman sought out Jesus to ask Him to heal his son in Capernaum (John 4:46). Cana was also the home of Nathanael, one of the apostles (John 21:2).

CANAAN Territory between the Mediterranean Sea and the Jordan River reaching from the brook of Egypt to the area around Ugarit in Syria or to the Euphrates. This represents descriptions in Near Eastern documents and in the OT. Apparently, Canaan meant different things at different times. Numbers 13:29 limits Canaanites to those who "are living by the sea and by the side of the Jordan" (NASB; cp. Josh. 11:3). Israel was aware of the larger "promised land" of Canaan (Gen. 15:18; Exod. 23:20; Num. 13:17-21; Deut. 1:7; 1 Kings 4:21), but Israel's basic land reached only from "Dan to Beersheba" (2 Sam. 24:2-8,15; 2 Kings 4:25). At times Israel included land east of Jordan (2 Sam. 24:5-6). Other times the land of Gilead was contrasted to the land of Canaan (Josh. 22:9). After the conquest, Israel knew "very much of the land remains to be possessed"

(Josh. 13:1 NASB). Canaan thus extended beyond the normal borders of Israel yet did not include land east of the Jordan. At times land of Canaanites and land of Amorites are identical. Whatever the land was called, it exercised extraordinary influence as the land bridge between Mesopotamia and Egypt and between the Mediterranean and the Red Sea.

CANALS Translation of a Hebrew word that refers to the branches of the Nile River (Exod. 7:19; 8:5; Isa. 19:6). The KJV uses "rivers."

CANDACE In Acts 8:27 the queen of Ethiopia whose servant became a believer in Christ and was baptized by Philip. It is generally agreed that Candace was a title rather than a proper name, though its meaning is uncertain. The title was used by several queens of Ethiopia.

CANDLE, CANDLESTICK (KJV) Candles as we know them were in use in biblical times. The reference is to "lamp" or "lampstand."

CANKER KJV translation in 2 Tim. 2:17 and James 5:3. In general, canker may refer to any source of corruption or debasement. In 2 Tim. 2:17 the reference is to gangrene, which is the local death of soft tissues due to loss of blood supply—a condition that can spread from infected to uninfected tissue. In James 5:3 the reference is to rust.

CANKERWORM KJV translation in Joel 1:4; 2:25; Nahum 3:15-16. The Hebrew refers to a type of locust. See *Insects; Locust.*

CANNEH Northern Syrian city that traded with Tyre and gained Ezekiel's mention in condemning Tyre (Ezek. 27:23). It may be variant spelling of Calneh or a city called Kannu in Assyrian documents.

CAPERNAUM Meaning "village of Nahum." Capernaum, located on the northwest shore of the Sea of Galilee about 2.5 miles west of the entrance of the Jordan, was chosen as the base of operations by Jesus when He began His ministry.

CAPHTOR Original home of the Philistines (Amos 9:7). In Jer. 47:4 and in Deut. 2:23 its inhabitants are called Caphtorim (cp. Gen. 10:14). Though several places have at times been proposed for its location, current scholarship is generally agreed that Caphtor is the island of Crete.

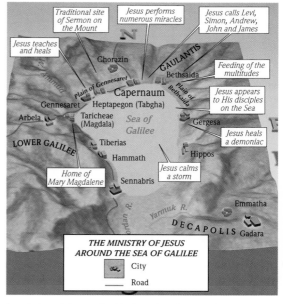

THE MINISTRY OF JESUS AROUND THE SEA OF GALILEE

CAPITAL PUNISHMENT Capital punishment, or the death penalty, refers to the execution by the state of those guilty of certain crimes. Though some have opposed capital punishment for ideological and practical reasons, it is important to note that God mandated its use. This divine mandate occurs first immediately after the Noahic flood. God instructed Noah and his sons, "Whoever sheds man's blood, by man his blood shall be shed" (Gen. 9:6 NASB). Capital punishment is reserved for the state, not the individual. There is no place for personal revenge in administration of this punishment (Rom. 12:19).

CAPPADOCIA Roman province in Asia Minor mentioned twice in the NT: Acts 2:9; 1 Pet. 1:1. Although the extent of Cappadocia varied through the centuries depending on the currently dominant empire, it lay south of Pontus and stretched about 300 miles from Galatia eastward toward Armenia, with Cilicia and the Taurus Mountains to the south. From Acts 2:9 we know that Jews from Cappadocia were in Jerusalem when Peter preached at Pentecost. Those converted to Christianity that day must have given a good witness when they returned home because in 1 Pet. 1:1 believers there are mentioned along with others in Pontus.

CAPTAIN English translation of several Hebrew words usually referring to an officer or leader; often applied to Christ.

CAPTAIN OF THE TEMPLE Officer second in authority only to the high priest. Pashhur ("chief officer in the house of the Lord," Jer. 20:1 NASB) and Seraiah ("leader of the house of God," Neh. 11:11 NASB) held this office in the OT times. In Acts it appears that one of the main functions of this officer was to keep order in the temple (Acts 4:1; 5:24,26). The plural (Luke 22:4,52) may refer to officers under the command of the captain of the temple.

CAPTIVITY Term used for Israel's exile in Babylon between 597 and 538 BC.

CARBUNCLE Precious stone used in the priest's breastpiece (Exod. 28:17 KJV) and part of the king of Tyre's apparel in the garden of Eden according to Ezekiel's ironic description (Ezek. 28:13). Equation with a stone used today is difficult if not impossible.

CARCAS Persian name meaning "hawk." One of the seven eunuchs under King Ahasuerus of Persia commanded to bring Queen Vashti to the king's party (Esther 1:10).

CARCHEMISH Fort of Chemosh; modern Jerablus. An important city on the great bend of the Euphrates River. It was on the west bank of the river, at an important river crossing point on the international trade route. Carchemish lies mostly on the Turkish side of the modern Turkish-Syrian border. Carchemish was the site of a strategic battle in 605 BC when Nebuchadnezzar defeated Egypt's Pharoah Neco II.

This victory gave Babylon authority over all of western Asia within the next few years; for this reason it ranks as one of the most decisive battles of all time.

CARMEL Place-name meaning "park, fruitful field." **1.** Village in the tribal territory assigned to Judah (Josh. 15:55). King Saul set up a monument there after he defeated the Amalekites (1 Sam. 15:12). **2.** The towering mountain (1 Kings 18:19) where Elijah confronted the prophets of Baal. The mountain is near the Mediterranean coast of Palestine between the Plain of Acco to the north and the Plain of Sharon to the south. It reaches a maximum elevation of about 1,750 feet.

The western summit of Mount Carmel overlooking the modern Israeli port city of Haifa.

CARMI Personal name meaning "my vineyard." **1.** Son of Reuben (Gen. 46:9) and thus original ancestor of a clan in the tribe of Reuben (Num. 26:6). **2.** Father of Achan (Josh. 7:1). **3.** Son of Judah (1 Chron. 4:1).

CARNAL Anything related to the fleshly or worldly appetites and desires rather than to the godly and spiritual desires. People walk either in the flesh or in the Spirit, leading to death or to life. The carnal person is hostile to God, unable to please God (Rom. 8:1-11).

CARPENTER Trade or skill lifted to a high position of honor by Jesus (Mark 6:3).

CARPUS Personal name meaning "fruit." A Christian friend with whom Paul left his cloak in Troas. He asked Timothy to retrieve it for him (2 Tim. 4:13).

CARSHENA Wise counselor of King Ahasuerus of Persia to whom the king turned for advice on how to deal with his disobedient wife Vashti (Esther 1:14).

CASIPHIA Place-name meaning "silversmith." Place in Babylon where Levites settled in exile (Ezra 8:17) and from which Ezra summoned Levites to return with him to Jerusalem. The place is unknown outside this passage.

CASLUH, CASLUHIM, CASLUHITES Clan name of "sons of Mizraim (or Egypt)" and "father" of the Philistines in the Table of Nations (Gen. 10:14).

CASSIA Bark of an oriental tree (*Cinnamomum cassia Blume*) related to cinnamon. One of the ingredients used to make anointing oil (Exod. 30:24), it was acquired through trade with Tyre (Ezek. 27:19) and was desired for its aromatic qualities (Ps. 45:8). One of Job's daughters was named Keziah (Job 42:14), a name that means "cassia."

CASTAWAY KJV translation of Greek *adokimos*, referring to battle-testing of soldiers, qualifications for office, or testing of metals to make sure they are genuine. Paul used his own example of personal discipline to ensure that his preaching proved true in life as a call to others to do the same (1 Cor. 9:27). He did not want to be cast away as impure metal or disqualified as an unworthy soldier or candidate.

CASTLE KJV translation for six Hebrew words and one Greek word. NASB uses "castle" only for one Hebrew term in 2 Kings 15:25 and Prov. 18:19. RSV uses "castle" in Prov. 18:19 and also for a different Hebrew term in Neh. 7:2. NIV does not use "castle."

CASTOR AND POLLUX Greek deities, the twin sons of Zeus, represented by the astral sign of Gemini. In Acts 28:11, Castor and Pollux were the sign or figurehead of the ship that carried Paul from Malta toward Rome.

CATERPILLAR Worm-like larvae of butterflies and moths. The term appears in different English versions to translate various Hebrew words, NIV not referring to caterpillars at all.

CATHOLIC EPISTLES NT letters not attributed to Paul and written to a more general or unidentifiable audience: James; 1 and 2 Peter; 1, 2, and 3 John; Jude. The title is from tradition.

CATTLE Domesticated quadrupeds used as livestock. In the Bible, the term commonly refers to all domesticated animals. English translations use "cattle" for at least 13 different Hebrew words and six Greek words referring to animals.

CAUDA or **CLAUDA** Small island whose name is variously spelled in the Greek manuscripts. Paul sailed by the island on his way to Malta and ultimately to Rome (Acts 27:16).

CAUL Part of the liver that appears to be left over or forms an appendage to the liver, according to KJV. Other translations refer to the "lobe" (NASB), "covering" (NIV), or "appendage" (NRSV) of the liver (Exod. 29:13).

CAVES In the Bible, caves were often used as burial places. Abraham bought the cave of Machpelah as a tomb for Sarah (Gen. 23:11-16,19). Lazarus was buried in a cave (John 11:38). David used the cave of Adullam for refuge (1 Sam. 22:1), as did five Canaanite kings at Makkedah (Josh. 10:16).

CEDAR Tree grown especially in Lebanon and valued as building material (probably *Cedrus libani*). Cedar played a still-unknown role in the purification rites of Israel (Lev. 14:4; Num. 19:6). Kings used cedar for royal buildings (2 Sam. 5:11; 1 Kings 5:6; 6:9–7:12). Cedar signified royal power and wealth (1 Kings 10:27). Still, the majestic cedars could not stand before God's powerful presence (Ps. 29:5). The cedars owed their existence to God, who had planted them (Ps. 104:16).

CEDRON (KJV, John 18:1) See *Kidron Valley.*

CELIBACY Abstention by vow from marriage. The practice of abstaining from marriage may be alluded to twice in the NT. Jesus said that some have made themselves eunuchs for the sake of the kingdom and that those who were able to do likewise should do so (Matt. 19:12). This statement has traditionally been understood as a reference to celibacy. Paul counseled the single to remain so

One of the cedars of Lebanon.

(1 Cor. 7:8). Both Jesus (Mark 10:2-12) and Paul (1 Cor. 7:9,28,36-39; 9:5), however, affirmed the goodness of the married state. One NT passage goes so far as to characterize the prohibition of marriage as demonic (1 Tim. 4:1-3).

CENCHREA or **CENCHREAE** Eastern port city of Corinth. Phoebe served in the church there (Rom. 16:1), and Paul had his head shaved there when he took a vow (Acts 18:18).

CENSER Vessel used for offering incense before the Lord (Lev. 10:1). Nadab and Abihu used it improperly and so brought God's destruction. It probably was also used for carrying live coals employed in connection with worship in the tabernacle or the temple, each priest having one (cp. Num. 16:17-18).

CENSUS Enumeration of a population for the purpose of taxation or for the determination of manpower of war.

CENTURION Officer in the Roman army, nominally in command of 100 soldiers. They were usually career soldiers, and they formed the real backbone of the Roman military force. Centurions in the NT appear in a generally favorable light.

CHAFF Husk and other materials separated from the kernel of grain during the threshing or winnowing process. It blew away in the wind (Hos. 13:3) or was burned up as worthless (Isa. 5:24; Luke 3:17).

CHALCEDONY Transliteration of Greek name of precious stone in Rev. 21:19.

CHALCOL (KJV, 1 Kings 4:31). See *Calcol.*

CHALDEA Refers either to a geographical locality (Chaldea) or to the people who lived there (Chaldeans). Chaldea was situated in central and southeastern Mesopotamia, i.e., the land between the lower stretches of the Tigris and Euphrates Rivers. Today Chaldea lies in the country of Iraq, very close to its border with Iran, and touching upon the head of the Persian Gulf.

CHALDEES Another expression for Chaldeans.

CHALKSTONE Soft stone easily crushed, used for comparison to destruction of altar (Isa. 27:9).

CHAMBER English translation of at least seven Hebrew words referring to a portion of a house or building.

CHAMBERING KJV translation of a Greek word in Rom. 13:13 rendered as "debauchery" or "sexual promiscuity" in modern versions.

CHAMBERLAIN High military or political official whose title is related to Hebrew term meaning "castrated" or "eunuch" but actually may be derived from Accadian term for royal official.

CHAMELEON Unclean animal that moves on the ground (Lev. 11:30), usually identified as the *Chamaeleo calyptratus.* A Hebrew word with the same spelling but perhaps with different historical derivation occurs in Lev. 11:18 and Deut. 14:16, where it is apparently the barn owl, *Tyto alba.*

CHAMOIS Small antelope (*rupicapra*) that stands about two feet high and is found in mountainous regions. Translated as "mountain-sheep" in modern versions (Deut. 14:5).

CHAMPAIGN Open, unenclosed land or plain (Deut. 11:30 KJV).

CHAMPION Hebrew phrase in 1 Sam. 17:4,23 is literally "the man of the space between"—that is the man (like Goliath) who fights a single opponent in the space between two armies. The Hebrew word translated "champion" in 1 Sam. 17:51 is a different word meaning "mighty one, warrior."

CHANAAN KJV form of Canaan in Acts 7:11; 13:19.

CHANCELLOR Title of a royal official of the Persian government living in Samaria and helping administer the Persian province after Persia gained control of Palestine (Ezra 4:8-9,17).

CHAPITER KJV translation of Hebrew architectural term meaning a capital made to stand on top of a pillar (1 Kings 7:16) or the base on which the actual capital is placed.

CHAPMAN Old English word for trader (2 Chron. 9:14 KJV).

CHARGER(S) 1. Large flat serving dish (Num. 7:13-85; Matt. 14:8,11 KJV). **2.** Horses used in battle to charge or attack (Nah. 2:3 NRSV; cp. TEV, REB based on early Greek translations; cp. Isa. 31:1,3; Jer. 8:6; Rev. 6:2).

CHARIOTS Two-wheeled land vehicles made of wood and strips of leather and usually drawn by horses. Egyptian chariots are the first mentioned in the Bible (Gen. 41:43; 46:29; 50:9). The iron chariots of the Philistines were fortified with plates of metal that made them militarily stronger than those of the Israelites (Judg. 1:19; 4:3,13-17; 1 Sam. 13:5-7). Chariots were used in prophetic imagery (Rev. 9:9; 18:13) and for transportation of the Ethiopian eunuch (Acts 8:26-38).

CHARITY KJV translation of Greek *agape.* NASB uses "charity" to translate Greek *ekdidomai,* "to give out" in relation to helping the poor (Luke 11:41; 12:33; Acts 9:36).

CHARRAN Greek and KJV spelling of Haran (Acts 7:2,4).

CHASTE Holy purity demanded of God's people with special reference to the sexual purity.

CHASTEN or **CHASTISEMENT** Refers to an act of punishment intended to instruct and change behavior.

CHEBAR River in Babylon where Ezekiel had visions (Ezek. 1:1; 3:15; 10:15; 43:3). This is probably to be identified with the nar Kabari, a channel of the Euphrates River southeast of Babylon.

CHEDOR-LAOMER King of Elam who joined coalition of kings against kings of Sodom and Gomorrah, leading to Abraham's involvement and victory (Gen. 14:1).

CHEESE Dairy product forming a basic part of the diet. The three occurrences of cheese in English translations reflect three different Hebrew expressions. Job 10:10 refers to cheese; 1 Sam. 17:18 speaks literally of a "slice of milk"; and 2 Sam. 17:29 uses a word usually interpreted as meaning "curds of the herd."

CHELAL Personal name of a man with foreign wife in the post-exilic community (Ezra 10:30).

CHELLUH Personal name of a man with a foreign wife in post-exilic community (Ezra 10:35).

CHELUB 1. Descendant of the tribe of Judah (1 Chron. 4:11), probably to be identified with Caleb, the hero of the spy narrative of Num. 13–14. See *Caleb, Calebite.* 2. Father of Ezri, overseer of workers on David's farms (1 Chron. 27:26).

CHELUBAI Hebrew variant of Caleb, the hero of the spy narratives (Num. 13–14).

CHEMOSH Divine name meaning "subdue." Deity the Moabites worshipped (Num. 21:29).

CHENAANAH 1. Personal name meaning "tradeswoman." Father of the false prophet Zedekiah (1 Kings 22:11). See *Zedekiah.* 2. Member of the tribe of Benjamin (1 Chron. 7:10).

CHENANI Personal name meaning "one born in month of Kanunu." A Levite who led Israel in a prayer of renewal and praise (Neh. 9:4).

CHENANIAH Personal name meaning "Yahweh empowers." 1. Chief of the Levites under David who instructed people in singing and played a leading role in bringing the ark back to Jerusalem (1 Chron. 15:22,27). 2. Levite whose family had charge of business outside the temple, including work as officials and judges (1 Chron. 26:29).

CHEPHAR-AMMONI Place-name meaning "open village of the Ammonites." A village in the tribal territory of Benjamin (Josh. 18:24).

CHEPHIRAH Place-name meaning "queen of the lions." It is located at Khirbet Kefire about four miles west of Gibeon (Josh. 9:17;18:26).

CHERAN Descendant of Seir (or Edom) listed in Gen. 36:26.

CHERETHITES, CHERETHIM People who lived south of or with the Philistines (1 Sam. 30:14). They were probably related to or paid soldiers for the Philistines. Crete may have been their original home. David used some of these soldiers as a personal bodyguard (2 Sam. 8:18). Ezekiel pronounced judgment on them (Ezek. 25:16), as did Zephaniah (Zeph. 2:5).

CHERITH Place-name meaning "cutting" or "ditch." A wadi or brook east of the Jordan River, the modern Wadi Qilt south of Jericho. Elijah pronounced God's judgment to Ahab, king of Israel, in the form of a two-year drought and then found God's protection at the brook of Cherith, where he had water to drink (1 Kings 17:3). When Cherith finally went dry, he found refuge with the widow of Zarephath.

CHERUB Man who left Tel-melah in Babylonian exile to go to Jerusalem with Zerubbabel about 537 BC. He could not provide a family list to prove he was an Israelite (Ezra 2:59).

CHERUB or **CHERUBIM** Class of winged angels. The Hebrew *cherub* (plural, *cherubim*) is of uncertain derivation. In the OT it is the name of a class of winged angels who functioned primarily as guards (Gen. 3:24) or attendants (Ezek. 10:3-22). The only NT reference to cherubim is in a description of the furnishings of the holy of holies (Heb. 9:5).

CHESALON Place-name meaning "on the hip." Village on eastern border of territory of tribe of Judah (Josh. 15:10). It is equated with Mount Jearim and is modern Kesla, about 10 miles west of Jerusalem.

CHESED Personal name meaning "one of the Chaldeans." Son of Nahor, the brother of Abraham (Gen. 22:22). His name may indicate he was the original ancestor of the Chaldeans.

CHESIL Place-name meaning "foolish." A city of the tribe of Judah (Josh. 15:30).

CHESTNUT KJV translation for plane tree in Gen. 30:37. It apparently refers to the smooth-barked *Platanus orientalis.*

CHESULLOTH Place-name meaning "on the hips." A border town of the tribe of Issachar (Josh. 19:18), probably the same as the border town of Zebulon called Chisloth-tabor in Josh. 19:12. It is the modern Iksal, four miles south of Nazareth.

CHEZIB Place-name meaning "deceiving." Birthplace of Shelah, son of Judah and Shuah, a Canaanite (Gen. 38:5).

CHICKEN Nesting, brooding bird. Both tame and wild chickens were known in Bible times. Jesus' compares His care for Jerusalem to the care of a mother hen for her nestlings (Matt. 23:37; Luke 13:34).

CHIDON Personal name meaning "crescent sword." First Chronicles 13:9 reads "Chidon" for "Nacon" in 2 Sam. 6:6. Chidon could be a place-name in the text.

CHIEF English translation of at least 13 different Hebrew words designating a leader in political, military, religious, or economic affairs.

CHILDREN (SONS) OF GOD In the OT "sons of God" can refer to spirit beings (Job 1:6; 38:7; Ps. 89:6-7), but more often refers to persons who stand in covenant relationship with God.

CHILEAB Personal name meaning "everything of the Father." David's second son (2 Sam. 3:3) born to Abigail.

CHILION Personal name meaning "sickly." One of the two sons of Elimelech and Naomi (Ruth 1:2). With his parents, he emigrated to Moab, where he married a Moabite woman named Orpah. Afterwards, he died in Moab.

CHILMAD Place-name meaning "marketplace." A trading partner of Tyre according to Hebrew text of Ezek. 27:23.

CHIMHAM Personal name meaning "paleface." **1.** Apparently the son of Barzillai, the patron of David when he fled to Mahanaim east of the Jordan before Absalom (2 Sam. 19:37). **2.** Village near Bethlehem (Jer. 41:17).

CHINNERETH Place-name meaning "harp-shaped." **1.** Sea or lake otherwise called the Sea of Galilee, Lake of Gennesaret, or Sea of Tiberias. **2.** City on the western edge of the Sea of Chinnereth, also called Chinneroth (Josh. 11:2), though this could be a reference to the Sea.

CHIOS Island with city of same name. Paul stopped here while returning from third missionary journey (Acts 20:15). The Greek poet Homer supposedly came from Chios. It lies in the Aegean Sea five miles off the coast of Asia Minor. It is now called Scio.

CHISEL English term NIV uses to translate several Hebrew expressions for working with wood and stone.

CHISLEU or **CHISLEV** Name of the ninth month of the Jewish calendar after the exile, apparently borrowed from the Babylonian name Kisliwu (Neh.1:1; Zech. 7:1).

CHISLON Personal name meaning "clumsy." Father of Elidad, who represented the tribe of Benjamin on the commission that divided the land for Israel (Num. 34:21).

CHLOE Personal name meaning "verdant." A woman whose household members informed Paul of dissension within the church at Corinth (1 Cor. 1:11). Where she lived and how her people learned of the situation in Corinth are not known.

CHOINIX Dry measure used to measure grain and was equivalent to about a quart, or a daily ration for one person (Rev. 6:6).

CHORAZIN One of the cities Jesus censured because of the unbelief of its inhabitants (Matt. 11:21). It was located in Galilee.

CHOSEN PEOPLE Israel as the elect of God. See *Election.*

CHRIST, CHRISTOLOGY "Christ" is English for the Greek *Christos,* "anointed one." The Hebrew word is *Mashiach,* Messiah. Christology is a compound of the Greek words *Christos* and *logos* (word, speech). Christology is the study of the person (who He is) and work (what He did/does) of Jesus Christ, the Son of God.

CHRISTIAN Greek word *Christianos* originally applied to the slaves belonging to a great household. It came to denote the adherents of an individual or party. A Christian is an adherent of Christ. The word is used three times in the NT (Acts 11:26; 26:28; 1 Pet. 4:16 HCSB). Agrippa responded to Paul's witness, "Are you going to persuade me to become a Christian so easily?" (Acts 26:28 HCSB).

CHRISTMAS Of the major Christian festivals, Christmas is the most recent in origin. The name, a contraction of the term "Christ's mass," did not come into use until the Middle Ages.

In the early part of the fourth century, Christians in Rome began to celebrate the birth of Christ. The practice spread widely and rapidly, so that most parts of the Christian world observed the new festival by the end of the century.

No evidence remains about the exact date of the birth of Christ. The December 25 date was chosen as much for practical reasons as for theological ones. Throughout the Roman Empire, various festivals were held in conjunction with the winter solstice. In Rome, the Feast of the Unconquerable Sun celebrated the beginning of the return of the sun. When Christianity became the religion of the Empire, the church either had to suppress the festivals or transform them. The winter solstice seemed an appropriate time to celebrate Christ's birth. Thus, the festival of the sun became a festival of the Son, the Light of the world.

CHRONICLES, BOOKS OF First and Second Chronicles are the first and second books of a four-book series that includes Ezra and Nehemiah. These four books provide a scribal (priestly) history of Israel from the time of Adam (1 Chron. 1:1) to the rebuilding of the house of God and the walls of Jerusalem and the restoration of the people in the worship of God according to the law of Moses (Neh. 13:31). Special focus is on the fortunes of God's house in Jerusalem upon which God has set His name forever (2 Chron. 7:16).

The principal purpose of 1 and 2 Chronicles is to show God's control of history to fulfill His desire to dwell among His people in a perfect relationship of holiness in which God is God and the redeemed are His people.

A second purpose is to show God's choice of a person and a people to build His house. The person is the Son of David—the Messiah. Solomon built the temple in Jerusalem, but the Son who is building and shall build to completion God's true house and the Son whose reign God will establish forever is the Lord Jesus Christ (1 Chron. 17:12; Luke 1:31-33; Acts 15:14-16).

A third purpose is to show the necessity to come to God by way of the altar of sacrifice as ministered by the Levitical priesthood. God in His merciful forgiveness of David revealed the place of the altar of sacrifice to be in Jerusalem at the threshing floor of Ornan (Araunah) (1 Chron. 21:18–22:1). There David erected the altar and built the temple according to God's directions. But most importantly, there the Son of God, our great High Priest, sacrificed Himself on the cross in our stead to bring His people into the glorious presence of God (Heb. 2:17; 5:1-10).

A fourth purpose of Chronicles is to encourage God's people to work together with God and with one another to build God's house.

CHRYSOLITE Mineral from which the seventh stone of the foundation of the New Jerusalem is made (Rev. 21:20).

CHRYSOPRASE Mineral forming the tenth stone of the foundation of the New Jerusalem (Rev. 21:20).

CHUB KJV transliteration of Hebrew name of a people in Ezek. 30:5.

CHURCH In the NT, the Greek word *ekklesia* refers to (1) any assembly, local bodies of believers, or (2) the universal body of all believers.

The Church as Body of Christ The church is not merely a sectarian religious society. Jesus speaks of personally building this new community on the confession of His lordship (Matt. 16:18-19). The apostles recognized the birth of the church at Pentecost as the work of Jesus Himself.

The description of the church as the body of Christ designates Jesus' rule over the community. As the exalted Son of David, He exercises sovereignty by His Spirit and by His Word. The body of Christ does not only refer to the universal church, but applies to each local congregation of believers. The fact that the church is the body of Christ necessarily entails that individual members belong to Christ. As such, each church must be composed of a regenerate membership, those giving evidence of faith in Jesus Christ.

The Church as Covenant Community The NT refers to the church as "the pillar and foundation of the truth" (1 Tim. 3:15 HCSB). From the beginning, the church was to serve as a confessional

body, holding to the truth of Christ as revealed by the prophets and apostles He had chosen (Eph. 2:20).
The Church and the World The Bible presents the church as sharply distinct from the world. The church is to be composed of regenerate believers called out of a world hostile to the gospel of Christ. As such, the church is called to confront the world with the reality of coming judgment and the gospel of redemption through Christ.
The Church's Commission The multinational, multiethnic character of the NT church testifies not only to the universality of the gospel message (Rom. 10:11-12) and to the personal reconciliation accomplished at the cross (Eph. 2:14-16), but also to the global extent of the coming reign of Christ (Ps. 2:8). Thus, obedience to the Great Commission (Matt. 28:16-20) is not simply a function of the church, but is essential to her identity as the people of God.

Similarly, worship is not incidental. Because God has assembled a people "to the praise of His glorious grace" (Eph. 1:6), worship is necessary to the corporate life of the church.

CHUSHAN-RISHATHAIM KJV spelling of Cushan-rishathaim, Mesopotamian king who oppressed Israel until he was defeated by Othniel the son of Kenaz (Judg. 3:8).

CHUZA Personal name meaning "seer." The steward of Herod Antipas (Luke 8:3). He was the husband of Joanna, one of the women who provided material support for Jesus.

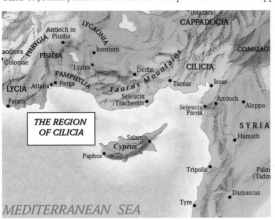

THE REGION OF CILICIA

CILICIA Geographical area and/or Roman province in southeastern Asia Minor. The region was home to some of the people who opposed Stephen (Acts 6:9). It was located on the coast of the Mediterranean Sea in the southeast part of Asia Minor. One of its important cities was Tarsus, the birthplace of Paul the apostle (Acts 21:39; 22:3). By the time of the Council of Jerusalem (Acts 15), Christianity had already penetrated Cilicia. Paul passed through the region during the course of his missionary travels (Acts 15:41; 27:5; Gal. 1:21).

CINNAMON Spice used in making fragrant oils. Such oil was used to anoint the wilderness tent of meeting (Exod. 30:23).

CIRCUMCISION Act of removing the foreskin of the male genital. In ancient Israel this act was ritually performed on the eighth day after birth upon children of natives, servants, and aliens (Gen. 17:12-14; Lev. 12:3). Circumcision was carried out by the father initially, utilizing a flint knife (cp. Josh. 5:3). Later specialists were employed among the Jewish people.
Circumcision and Christianity Controversy arose in the early church (Acts 15:1-12) as to whether Gentile converts needed to be circumcised. First-century AD Jews disdained the uncircumcised. The leadership of the Apostle Paul in the Jerusalem Council was crucial in the settlement of the dispute: circumcision was not essential to Christian faith and fellowship. Circumcision of the heart via repentance and faith were the only requirements (Rom. 4:9-12; Gal. 2:15-21).

CISTERN Translation of a Hebrew term that means "hole," "pit," or more often "well." The difference between "cistern" and "well" often is not apparent.

CITIES OF REFUGE Safe place to flee for a person who had accidentally killed another. The city provided asylum to the fugitive by sheltering and protecting him until a trial could be held to determine his guilt or innocence. If, in the judgment of the city elders, the death had occurred accidentally and without intent, the man was allowed to stay there without fear of harm or revenge by the dead man's relatives (Josh. 20:2-6).

CITIZEN, CITIZENSHIP Officially recognized status in a political state bringing certain rights and responsibilities as defined by the state. Paul raised the issue of citizenship by appealing to his right as a Roman citizen (Acts 16:37; 22:26-28).

CITY OF DAVID In the OT the phrase "the city of David" refers to Jerusalem. The name was given to the fortified city of the Jebusites after David captured it (2 Sam. 5:6-10). Its original reference may have been only to the southeastern hill and the Jebusites' military fortress there. In Luke

CITIES OF REFUGE
- ● Levitical city
- ○ Levitical city (uncertain location)
- ■ City of refuge
- ● Other city
- ▲ Mountain peak

2:4,11 the reference is to Bethlehem, the birthplace of David (John 7:42).

CITY OF MOAB City where Balak went to meet Balaam (Num. 22:36). Some identify the city as Ar.

CITY OF PALM TREES Probably to be identified with a site near Jericho where the Kenites lived (Judg. 1:16; see Deut. 34:3; Judg. 3:13; 2 Chron. 28:15). Jericho itself lay in ruins from the time of the conquest until the time of Ahab. Some identify the region with Zoar on the south side of the Dead Sea or with Tamar about 20 miles south of the Dead Sea.

CITY OF SALT City allotted to the tribe of Judah "in the desert" (Josh. 15:62). Its precise location is not known. Archaeological finds do not support identification with Qumran that some have tried to make.

CITY OF THE SUN (NRSV) Usually taken as a reference to Heliopolis (Isa. 19:18). Also translated "city of destruction."

CITY OF WATERS City in Ammon, probably to be identified with part or all of Rabbah, the capital. Joab captured it for David (2 Sam. 12:27).

CLAUDA KJV, NASB spelling of Cauda in Acts 27:16 for an island where Paul landed on his way to Rome.

CLAUDIA Woman who sent greetings to Timothy (2 Tim. 4:21).

CLAUDIUS 1. Roman emperor from AD 41 to 54. He made Judea a Roman province in AD 44. He expelled Jews from Rome in about AD 49 (Acts 18:2), probably due to conflict between Jews and Christians in Rome. **2.** Roman army captain who protected Paul from Jews who wanted to assassinate him (Acts 23:26-27).

CLAY Basic building and artistic material consisting of various types of dirt or sand combined with water to form a material that could be molded into bricks for building, sculptures, pottery, toys, or writing tablets.

CLEMENT Fellow worker in the gospel with Paul (Phil. 4:3). He was apparently a member of the church at Philippi. No other information about him is available.

CLEOPAS Follower of Jesus, who with a companion was traveling toward the village of Emmaus on the day of Christ's resurrection (Luke 24:13-25). A person whom they did not recognize joined them. Later, they discovered that the stranger was Jesus Himself.

CLEOPHAS (KJV, John 19:25) or **CLOPAS** Relative of one of the Marys who were near the cross during the crucifixion (John 19:25). "Mary, who [was] of Clopas" is the literal Greek text and has been interpreted to mean that Clopas was the husband of Mary.

CLOSET Private room in a dwelling where Jesus encouraged people to pray (Matt. 6:6). A biblical closet is an actual room, not a storage place.

CLOTH, CLOTHING Biblical and archaeological sources concur that the earliest clothing resources were the hides of wild animals (Gen. 3:21). The Bible contains little information, however, about the process of manufacturing clothes from vegetable fibers.

CLOUD, PILLAR OF Means by which God led Israel through the wilderness with His presence and still hid Himself so they could not see His face. By day Israel saw a pillar of cloud, while by night they saw a pillar of fire (Exod. 13:21-22).

CLOUT KJV translation in Jer. 38:11-12 for Hebrew word meaning "tattered clothes, rags."

CLUB Weapon of war used in close combat to strike an enemy.

CNIDUS Place-name of city in southwest Turkey. Paul's ship passed by here on the way to Rome (Acts 27:7).

COAL Charred wood used for fuel. The altar of sacrifice burned coals (Lev. 16:12), as did the blacksmith's fire (Isa. 44:12) and the baker's (Isa. 44:19).

COAST Land bordering a major body of water and used by KJV in obsolete sense of territories, borders, frontiers.

COAT OF MAIL Protective device worn from the neck to the girdle. Also called a brigandine (Jer. 46:4; 51:3 KJV) or habergeon (2 Chron. 26:14 KJV). Usually made of leather, though it may at times have been covered with metal scales of some kind. Part of the usual equipment of the soldier (1 Sam. 17:5; 2 Chron. 26:14; Neh. 4:16; Jer. 46:4; 51:3). David refused to wear Saul's coat of mail (1 Sam. 17:38). Leviathan's skin is described as a double coat of mail (Job 41:13 NRSV, NASB following early Greek translation).

COCK Strutting, crowing bird (rooster), *Zarzir motnayim* (Prov. 30:31). The crowing of the cock is probably the most well-known bird sound in the Bible. All of the NT references to the cock (except the mention of "cockcrow" in Mark 13:35) relate to Peter's denial of Christ.

COCKATRICE KJV translation of legendary serpent and poisonous snakes (Isa. 11:8; 14:29; 59:5; Jer. 8:17).

COCKLE Plant whose name derives from Hebrew word for "stink." It appears in Scripture only at Job 31:40.

COFFER Old English word for box in 1 Sam. 6:8,11,15 (KJV).

COHORT Roman military unit with capacity of 1,000 men; ten cohorts formed a legion.

COLHOZEH Personal name meaning "he sees everything" or "everyone a seer." Father whose son Shallun was ruler of part of Mizpah and who helped Nehemiah repair Jerusalem's gates (Neh. 3:15).

COLLEGE KJV translation (2 Kings 22:14) of Hebrew word meaning "repetition, copy, second," referring to the second district or division of Jerusalem (cp. Zeph. 1:10).

COLONY Only Philippi is described as a colony of Rome (Acts 16:12), though many cities mentioned in the NT were considered as such. The functioning of the local governments of Roman colonies is seen in Acts 16:12-40.

COLORS Writers of biblical literature reflected little or nothing of an abstract sense of color. Nevertheless, they made frequent references to a select group of colors when their purposes in writing so demanded it.

References to Colors Moving beyond color in the abstract sense, one does find frequent reference to certain objects that have color designations. When reference is made to a particular color or colors, it is likely made for one of two basic reasons. First, a writer may wish to use color in a descriptive sense to help identify an object or clarify some aspect about that object. A second reason for color designation in the Bible involves a more specialized usage. At times a writer may use color in a symbolic sense to convey theological truth about the subject of his writing. Color designations have general symbolic significance. For instance, white may be symbolic of purity or joy; black may symbolize judgment or decay; red may symbolize sin or life-blood; and purple may be symbolic of luxury and elegance. Color symbolism became for the writers of apocalyptic literature (Daniel, Revelation) an appropriate tool for expressing various truths in hidden language. In their writings one may find white representative of conquest or victory, black representative of famine or pestilence, red representative of wartime bloodshed, paleness (literally "greenish-gray") representative of death, and purple representative of royalty.

COLOSSIANS, LETTER TO THE
Letter from Paul to the church at Colossae. It is one of the Prison Epistles (along with Ephesians, Philemon, and Philippians). Traditional date and place of writing are AD 61 or 62 and Rome. The letter itself does not name the place where Paul was imprisoned, and Caesarea and Ephesus have been suggested as alternatives to Rome. If written from Ephesus, the time of writing would be in the mid-50's; if from Caesarea, the late 50's.

The City of Colossae Colossae was located in the southwest corner of Asia Minor in what was then the Roman province of Asia. Hierapolis and Laodicea were situated only a few miles away. All three were in the Lycus River Valley. A main road from Ephesus to the east ran through the region.

The Primary Purpose of Colossians Paul sought to correct false teachings that were troubling the church. These false teachings apparently involved the legalistic observance of "traditions," circumcision, and various dietary and festival laws (2:8,11,16,21; 3:11). The worship of angels and lesser spirits was encouraged by the false teachers (2:8,18). Asceticism, the deprivation or harsh treatment of one's "evil" fleshly body, was promoted (2:20-23). The false teachers claimed to possess special insight (perhaps special revelations) that made them (rather than the apostles or the Scriptures) the ultimate source of truth (2:18-19).

The Lycus River Valley as seen from Colossae.

To correct these false teachings, Paul describes the grandeur of the preeminent Christ (1:15-20). Though the precise meaning of some words and phrases is uncertain, there is no doubt as to Paul's intent. He meant to present Jesus as fully God incarnate (1:15,19), as supreme Lord over all creation (1:15-17), as supreme Lord of the church (1:18), and as the only Source of reconciliation (1:20).

COLT Young of various riding animals. **1.** Young camels (Gen. 32:15), noted by the Hebrew term for "sons." **2.** Young donkeys (Gen. 49:11), also "son" in Hebrew (cp. Judg. 10:4; 12:14, where Hebrew is "donkeys"). The NT uses the reference in Zech. 9:9 as a prediction of Jesus' triumphal entry into Jerusalem (Matt. 21; Mark 11; Luke 19; John 12:15).

COMFORTER Commonly used translation of the Greek word *paracletos.* The compound noun refers to "one called alongside." John's Gospel features five passages in which this word details the work and ministry of the Comforter for believers.

COMPASSION Meaning "to feel passion with someone" or "to enter sympathetically into one's sorrow and pain."

CONANIAH Personal name meaning "Yahweh has established." **1.** Levite in charge of collecting temple offerings under King Hezekiah (2 Chron. 31:12). **2.** Perhaps the grandson of 1. He and other Levites contributed 5,000 sheep and goats and 500 bulls for Josiah's Passover offering (2 Chron. 35:9).

CONCISION Archaic English noun meaning "a cutting off." KJV uses "concision" in Phil. 3:2 to describe Paul's opponents who insisted on circumcision as necessary for right relationship with God (Phil. 3:2).

CONCUBINE A wife of lower status than a primary wife. Taking of concubines dates back at least to the patriarchal period. Although the taking of concubines was not totally prohibited, monogamous marriage was more common and seems to be the biblical ideal (Gen. 2:24; Mark 10:6-9).

CONCUPISCENCE KJV translation of Greek *epithumia,* "desire, lust." The Greeks used the term to mean excitement about something in a neutral sense and then in an evil sense of wrongly valuing earthly things.

CONDEMN Act of pronouncing someone guilty after weighing the evidence. The word appears first in the context of a court of law (Exod. 22:9) where a judge hears a charge against a thief and condemns the culprit. NT usage of "condemn" is unique in its reference to the final judgment, especially in John 3:17-19. A similar teaching appears in John 5:24. Paul felt that avoiding that final condemnation was a reason for accepting the Lord's chastening in this life (1 Cor. 11:32).

CONDUIT Water channel or aqueduct in or near Jerusalem channeling water into the city (2 Kings 18:17; 20:20; Isa. 7:3).

CONEY Wild hare—*Procavia syriaca*, also called *Hyrax syriacus*. Resembled a rabbit in size and color. The badger of Exod. 23:5; 26:14 has been identified by some scholars as the Syrian coney.

CONFESSION Admission, declaration, or acknowledgment, that is a significant element in the worship of God in both OT and NT. The majority of the occurrences of the term can be divided into two primary responses to God: the confession of sin and the confession of faith.
Confession of Sin Numerous OT passages stress the importance of the confession of sin within the experience of worship.   Likewise, in the NT confession of sin is an aspect of both individual and corporate worship.
Confession of Faith Closely related to the confession of sin in the OT is the confession of faith, that is, the acknowledgment of and commitment to God. In 1 Kings 8:33,35 (as well as 2 Chron. 6:24,26) acknowledgment of the name of God results in forgiveness of sins. Such acknowledgment came to be standardized in the confessional formula known as the Shema (Deut. 6:4-5).

Such declaration of commitment to God, or particularly to Christ, is also found in the NT. One's public acknowledgment of Jesus is the basis for Jesus' own acknowledgment of that believer to God (Matt. 10:32; Luke 12:8; cp. Rev. 3:5).

CONGREGATION Assembled people of God.

CONGREGATION, MOUNT OF Mountain considered by Israel's neighbors to stand in the far north and serve as a meeting place of the gods (Isa. 14:13).

CONQUEST OF CANAAN The book of Joshua and the first chapter of the book of Judges describe the conquest of Canaan, which resulted in Israel's settlement in the land of promise.

CONSCIENCE Human capacity to reflect upon the degree to which one's behavior has conformed to moral norms. For the believer, these norms should be those established by God. The word does not occur in the OT, although clearly there are times when the concept is present (1 Sam. 25:31 NLT). In the NT two-thirds of the occurrences of the term are in Paul's writings.

CONSECRATION Persons or things being separated to or belonging to God. They are holy or sacred. They are set apart for the service of God. The Hebrew *qadesh* and Greek *hagiazo* are translated by several different English words: holy, consecrate, hallow, sanctify, dedicate.

CONSUMMATION End of history and the fulfillment of God's kingdom promises. The term comes from Dan. 9:27 speaking of the complete destruction God had decreed on the prince who threatened His sanctuary.

CONVERSION Turning or returning of a person to God, a crucial biblical and theological concept. The word itself is relatively rare in Scripture.

CONVICTION Sense of guilt and shame leading to repentance. The words "convict" and "conviction" do not appear in the KJV. The word "convince" (KJV) comes closest to expressing the meaning of "conviction."

COPPER Reddish metal that can be shaped easily by hammering and can be polished to a shining finish. While gold was probably the first metal humans used, the oldest tools and utensils recovered by archaeologists in Bible lands are of copper, usually combined with some alloy. The word "copper" appears in the KJV only in Ezra 8:27 and in the word "coppersmith" in 2 Tim. 4:14.

COR Large liquid and dry measure of unknown quantity.

CORAL Calcareous or horny skeletal deposit produced by anthozoan polyps, found exclusively in the Mediterranean and Adriatic seas (*Corallium rubrum*). Coral was among the goods of trade between Israel and Edom (Ezek. 27:16).

CORBAN Gift particularly designated for the Lord, and so forbidden for any other use (Mark 7:11) Jesus referred to some persons who mistakenly and deliberately avoided giving needed care to their parents by declaring as "corban" any money or goods that could otherwise be used to provide such care

Thus what began as a religious act of offering eventually functioned as a curse, denying benefit to one's own parents.

CORIANDER SEED Herb (*Coriandrum sativum*) of the carrot family with aromatic fruits used much as poppy, caraway, or sesame seeds are today. The manna of the wilderness period was like coriander seed either in appearance (Exod. 16:31) or taste (Num. 11:7).

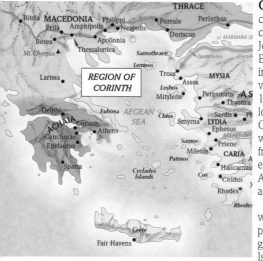

CORINTH One of four prominent centers in the NT account of the early church, the other three being Jerusalem, Antioch of Syria, and Ephesus. Paul's first extended ministry in one city was at Corinth. On his first visit to Corinth, he remained for at least 18 months (Acts 18:1-18). Paul's three longest letters are associated with Corinth. First and Second Corinthians were written to Corinth, and Romans, from Corinth. Prominent Christian leaders associated with Corinth include Aquila, Priscilla, Silas, Timothy, Apollos, and Titus.

The city of Corinth as Paul found it was a cosmopolitan city composed of people from varying cultural backgrounds. Being near the site of the Isthmian games held every two years, the Corinthians enjoyed both the pleasures of these games and the wealth that the visitors brought to the city. While their ships were being carried across the isthmus, sailors came to the city to spend their money on the pleasures of Corinth. Even in an age of sexual immorality, Corinth was known for its licentious lifestyle.

CORINTHIANS, FIRST LETTER TO THE First Corinthians is a practical letter where Paul dealt with problems concerning the church as a whole and also with personal problems.

Paul wrote 1 Corinthians to give instruction and admonition that would lead to the solving of the many problems in the congregation. Some of these problems may have arisen out of a "super spiritualist" group that had been influenced by incipient gnostic teachings. All of the problems in chapters 1–14 were grounded in egocentric or self-centered attitudes in contrast to self-denying, Christ-centered attitudes. Chapter 15 concerning the resurrection may reflect sincere misconceptions on the part of the Corinthians.

CORINTHIANS, SECOND LETTER TO THE Paul wrote 2 Corinthians to deal with problems within the church and to defend apostolic ministry in general and his apostleship in particular. In so doing, Paul revealed much about himself, his apostleship, and his apostolic ministry. Second Corinthians is relevant for today in its teachings concerning ministers and their ministries. Among these teachings are the following: (1) God was in Christ reconciling the world to Himself and has given to us a ministry of reconciliation. (2) True ministry in Christ's name involves both suffering and victory. (3) Serving Christ means ministering in His name to the total needs of persons. (4) Leaders in ministry need support and trust from those to whom they minister.

CORMORANT Large seafowl (*Phalacrocorax carbo carbo*) listed among the unclean birds (Lev. 11:17; Deut. 14:17). Other translators call it a Fisher-owl (REB).

CORN General term used by the translators of the KJV for any grain.

CORNELIUS Centurion in the Roman army who lived at Caesarea (Acts 10:1). His conversion marked the beginning of the church's missionary activity among Gentiles.

CORNER BUTTRESS (NASB, 2 Chron. 26:9) See *Turning of the Wall.*

CORNER GATE Gate of Jerusalem in the northwest corner of the city not far from the Ephraim Gate (2 Kings 14:13; 2 Chron. 25:23). It is not mentioned in Nehemiah's restoration of Jerusalem.

CORNERSTONE Stone laid at the corner to bind two walls together and to strengthen them. Used symbolically as a symbol of strength and prominence in the Bible.

CORNET KJV for several different kinds of musical instruments. See *Music, Instruments, Dancing.*

CORNFLOOR KJV for threshing floor in Hos. 9:1.

COS Island and its chief city between Miletus and Rhodes where Paul landed briefly on his return voyage after his third missionary journey (Acts 21:1). It was a center for education, trade, wine, purple dye, and ointment. Hippocrates founded a school of medicine there. It is modern Kos.

COSAM Personal name meaning "diviner." Ancestor of Jesus (Luke 3:28).

COULTER KJV word for both mattock and plowshare.

COUNCIL OF JERUSALEM Name given to the meeting described in Acts 15:6-22. The purpose of the council was to determine the terms on which Gentile converts to Christianity would be received into the church.

COUNSELOR One who analyzes a situation and gives advice to one who has responsibility for making a decision. Israelite kings seem to have employed counselors on a regular basis (2 Sam. 16:23; 1 Kings 12:6-14; Isa. 1:26; 3:3; Mic. 4:9). God is often regarded as a counselor (Pss. 16:7; 73:24) as is His Messiah (Isa. 9:6; 11:2) and the Holy Spirit (John 14:16,26; 15:26; 16:7).

COUNTENANCE One's face as an indication of mood, emotion, or character (Gen. 4:5-6; Prov. 15:13; Eccles. 7:3; Mark 10:22). To speak of God lifting up His countenance upon one is a way of speaking about being in God's presence (Ps. 21:6).

COUNTERVAIL Old English word meaning "to equal," "be commensurate with," "compensate for" in Esther 7:4.

COURIERS Members of the royal guard who carried messages throughout the kingdom (2 Chron. 30:6,10; Esther 3:13,15; 8:10,14).

COURT OF THE GUARD or **COURT OF THE PRISON** Open court in the Jerusalem palace reserved for the detention of prisoners during the day of Jeremiah (Jer. 32:8,12; 33:1; 37:21; 38:6,13,28; 39:14-15 KJV). Translated in the modern versions as "court of the guard."

COUSIN At times the KJV uses "cousin" when a distant relative is referred to (Mark 6:4; Luke 1:36,58; 2:44; 14:12). The same Greek word in all these passages means relatives, kin, or countryman.

COVENANT Oath-bound promise whereby one party solemnly pledges to bless or serve another party in some specified way. Sometimes the keeping of the promise depends upon the meeting of certain conditions by the party to whom the promise is made. On other occasions the promise is made unilaterally and unconditionally. The covenant concept is a central, unifying theme of Scripture, establishing and defining God's relationship to man in all ages.

COVET, COVETOUS Inordinate desire to possess what belongs to another, usually tangible things. While the Hebrew word for "covet" can also be translated "to desire," in the tenth commandment it means an ungoverned and selfish desire that threatens the basic rights of others.

COW Designates domestic bovine animals, especially the female.

COZBI Personal name meaning "my falsehood." A Midianite woman who was slain by Phinehas after being brought into the tent of an Israelite man named Zimri (Num. 25:15). When both she and Zimri were executed, a plague that was sweeping through the Israelite camp was stopped.

COZEBA Place-name meaning "deceptive." Home of descendants of Judah (1 Chron. 4:22). Its location is uncertain.

CRACKNEL Old English word for a hard brittle biscuit (1 Kings 14:3 KJV).

CRANE KJV translation of the Hebrew word in Isa. 38:14; Jer. 8:7. Modern translations read "swift" (NIV, NASB, REB) or "dove" (REB).

CRAWLING THINGS NRSV translation of Hebrew term in Mic. 7:17. The Hebrew word also appears in Deut. 32:24,33 where it refers to poisonous snakes.

CREATION The Bible's teaching on the creation of the universe is a central theme that runs from Genesis to Revelation. God is eternal and transcendent, creation is not (Gen. 1:1). Everything owes its creaturely existence (Isa. 44:24; 45:12; Ps. 33:6; Rev. 4:11) to the work of the Father, Son, and Holy Spirit (cp. Gen. 1:1; John 1:1; Gen. 1:2), with Christ as the preeminent agent of creation (John 1:10; Col. 1:16). Biblical teaching implies that God created the world out of nothing (Heb. 11:3).

Unlike God, any created thing can be shaken; only what He desires will continue to exist (Heb. 1:3; 12:27; Col. 1:17).

In spite of its present subjection to ethical and material corruption, God's creation still bears the original impress of its complete goodness (Gen. 1:31; 1 Tim. 4:4). The human race alone enjoys the privilege of bearing His image (Gen. 1:27—all subsequent people, though not directly created as were Adam and Eve, are regarded as God's special handiwork; Ps. 89:47; cp. Ps. 102:18). Divine purpose (Col. 1:16) and design (e.g., the marking of time by the movements of the heavenly bodies in Gen. 1:14) pervade creation. The creation speaks of the glory of God in bold contrast with man (Pss. 8; 19:1-4).

CREATURE Something having life, either animal or human. The phrase used in the Hebrew Bible *nephesh chayah* is translated by "creature," "living [thing, soul]," and "beast."

CRESCENS Personal name meaning "growing." Christian worker with Paul who had gone to Galatia when 2 Timothy was written (2 Tim. 4:10).

CRETANS, CRETES, CRETIANS Citizens of Crete.

CRETE Long, narrow, mountainous island south of mainland Greece, running 170 miles east-west but never more than about 35 miles wide.

Paul made his voyage to Rome as a prisoner on a Roman grain ship. The voyage followed the route south of Crete, which gave partial shelter from the northwest winds and avoided the peril of the lee shore on the north coast, while still involving the need to beat against largely adverse winds.

The only other references to Crete in the NT are in the epistle to Titus. Paul had left Titus in Crete to exercise pastoral supervision over the churches there (Titus 1:5). The character of

A harbor on Crete through which Paul likely passed on his journey from Caesarea Maritima to Rome.

the people is described in a quotation from a prophet of their own: "Cretans are always liars, evil beasts, lazy gluttons" (Titus 1:12 HCSB), words attributed to the Cretan seer Epimenides, who was also credited with having advised the Athenians to set up altars to unknown gods (cp. Acts 17:23).

CRIB Feeding trough for the ox (Prov. 14:4 KJV) or the ass (Isa. 1:3; cp. Job 39:9) and probably for any number of other domesticated animals.

CRICKET Hebrew term translated "cricket" (Lev. 11:22 NIV, NASB, NRSV, TEV) is difficult to identify, probably a locust or grasshopper.

CRIMSON The same Hebrew words translated as crimson are also translated "scarlet" ("red" comes from a root word from which the Hebrew word for "blood" comes and designates a different color). Crimson or scarlet thread (Gen. 38:28,30), cord (Josh. 2:18,21), and cloth (Lev. 14:4; Num. 4:8; 2 Sam. 1:24; 2 Chron. 2:7,14; 3:14; Prov. 31:21; Jer. 4:30; Nah. 2:3) are mentioned in the Bible. Crimson or scarlet along with purple were considered royal colors (Matt. 27:28; Rev. 17:3-4; 18:11-12,16). Isaiah used scarlet as the imagery to describe sins (Isa. 1:18).

CRISPING PIN KJV translation in Isa. 3:22. A crisping pin was used for curling the hair. Modern versions translate the word "handbag," or "flounced skirt" (REB).

CRISPUS Personal name meaning "curly." Leader of synagogue in Corinth (Acts 18:8) and one of few whom Paul personally baptized (1 Cor. 1:14). Church tradition says he became bishop of Aegina.

CROSS, CRUCIFIXION Method the Romans used to execute Jesus Christ. The most painful and degrading form of capital punishment in the ancient world, the cross became the means by which Jesus became the atoning sacrifice for the sins of all mankind. It also became a symbol for the sacrifice of self in discipleship (Rom. 12:1) and for the death of self to the world (Mark 8:34).

For Paul the "word of the cross" (1 Cor. 1:18 NASB) is the heart of the gospel, and the preaching of the cross is the soul of the church's mission. "Christ crucified" (1 Cor. 1:23; cp. 2:2; Gal. 3:1) is more than the basis of our salvation; the cross was the central event in history, the one moment that demonstrated God's control of and involvement in human history.

Jesus Himself established the primary figurative interpretation of the cross as a call to complete surrender to God. He used it five times as a symbol of true discipleship in terms of self-denial, taking up one's cross, and following Jesus (Mark 8:34; 10:38; Matt. 16:24; Luke 9:23; 14:27).

Closely connected to this is Paul's symbol of the crucified life. Conversion means the individual "no longer live(s)" but is replaced by Christ and faith in Him (Gal. 2:20). Self-centered desires are nailed to the cross (Gal. 5:24), and worldly interests are dead (Gal. 6:14). The Christian paradox is that death is the path to life.

CROWN Special headdress worn by royalty and other persons of high merit and honor. While most references to "crown" in the OT point to the actual headdress, in the NT it usually has a figurative significance. Paul envisioned "a crown of righteousness" for himself and others (2 Tim. 4:8), and James anticipated "the crown of life" (James 1:12).

In the book of Revelation, crowns are both realistic and figurative. The 24 elders seated around God's throne were wearing "gold crowns" (4:4), and as they worshipped, they "cast their crowns before the throne" (4:10). Later, a seven-headed dragon appeared wearing a crown on each head (12:3), but opposing all the evil forces was the "Son of Man" wearing "a golden crown" (14:14). In each case the crown symbolized power, either good or evil.

CROWN OF THORNS Crown made by the Roman soldiers to mock Jesus, the "King of the Jews" (Matt. 27:29; Mark 15:18; John 19:3; not mentioned in Luke). The identification of the plant used to plait this crown is unknown. Jesus used the imagery of "thorns" in his teaching in a negative sense (Matt. 7:16; Mark 4:7,18; Heb. 6:8).

CRUCIBLE Melting pot or "fining pot" (KJV), probably made of pottery, used in the refining of silver. The crucible is used in the Bible as a figure for testing of people (Prov. 17:3; 27:21).

CRUSE Elongated pottery vessel about six inches tall used for holding liquids such as oil (1 Kings 17:12,14,16) or water (1 Kings 19:6).

CRYSTAL Nearly transparent quartz that may be colorless or slightly tinged. "Crystal" is the modern translation of several Hebrew and Greek words used to describe something valuable (Job 28:17), a clear sky (Ezek. 1:22), a calm sea or river (Rev. 4:6; 22:1), or the radiance of the new Jerusalem (Rev. 21:11).

CUBIT Unit of measure. It was reckoned as the distance from a person's elbow to the tip of the middle finger, approximately 18 inches.

CUCKOW KJV for an unclean bird (Lev. 11:16; Deut. 14:15); also spelled "cuckoo." Since the bird in question is grouped with carrion-eating or predatory birds, the cuckoo would seem to be eliminated since it only eats insects. Modern versions read "sea gull."

CUMIN, CUMMIN Herb of the carrot family (*Cuminum cyminum* L.) mentioned with dill. Used in Bible times to season foods. Isaiah portrayed the planting and threshing of cumin (Isa. 28:25,27). Jesus faulted the Pharisees for giving attention to small things like tithing mint, dill, and cumin while ignoring the weightier matters of the law (Matt. 23:23; Luke 11:42).

CUNEIFORM Most widely used system of writing in the ancient Near East until it was supplanted by alphabetic scripts like Aramaic. The word "cuneiform" is derived from the Latin *cuneus*, "wedge," and is used to refer to characters composed of wedges. The system of writing was originated apparently by the Sumerians before 3000 BC.

CUP Drinking vessel made of pottery or various metals such as gold, silver, or bronze. In the Bible the word "cup" frequently is used in a figurative sense. The contents of the cup are accentuated, since symbolically God serves the drink. Thus the cup might represent blessings or prosperity for a righteous person (Pss. 16:5; 23:5; 116:13). Likewise, it portrayed the totality of divine judgment on the wicked (Pss. 11:6; 75:8; Isa. 51:17,22; Jer. 25:15; 49:12; 51:7; Ezek. 23:31-34; Rev. 14:10; 16:19; 17:4; 18:6). Jesus voluntarily drank the cup of suffering (Matt. 20:22; 26:39,42; Mark 10:38; 14:36; Luke 22:42; John 18:11). For Jesus, that cup was His death and everything that it involved.

The cup had a prominent place in the liturgy of the Jewish Passover meal, and so, subsequently, in the Lord's Supper. In the Christian ordinance the cup is a symbolic reminder of the atoning death of Jesus (Matt. 26:27-28; Mark 14:23-24; Luke 22:20; 1 Cor. 11:25-26).

CURSE See *Blessing and Cursing.*

CUSH 1. Member of the tribe of Benjamin about whom the psalmist sang (Ps. 7:1). Nothing else is known of him. **2.** Son of Ham and grandson of Noah (Gen. 10:8). Thus in the Table of Nations he is seen as the original ancestor of inhabitants of the land of Cush. **3.** Nation situated south of Egypt with differing boundaries and perhaps including differing dark-skinned tribes (Jer. 13:23) at different periods of history. The Hebrew word *Cush* has been traditionally translated "Ethiopia."

CUSHAN Tent-dwelling people that Habakkuk saw experiencing God's wrath (Hab. 3:7).

CUSHAN-RISHATHAIM Personal name meaning "dark one of double evil." King of Aram Naharaim to whom Yahweh gave Israel in the early period of the Judges (Judg. 3:8).

CUSHI Personal name meaning "Cushite." **1.** Father of the prophet Zephaniah (Zeph. 1:1). **2.** Ancestor of a royal official under King Jehoiakim (Jer. 36:14).

CUSHITE Citizen or inhabitant of Cush. The Hebrew word is the same as the proper name "Cushi." God has concern for and control over them just as He does for His own people (Amos 9:7). **1.** Unnamed Cushite served as Joab's messenger to bring the news of Absalom's death to David (2 Sam. 18:21-32). **2.** Eunuch under King Zedekiah who helped Jeremiah escape from a cistern into which the king had had him thrown (Jer. 38:6-12; 39:16).

CUSTODIAN Wealthy Greek and Roman families often had a slave who attended boys under the age of about 16. The major responsibilities of the custodian were to escort the boys to and from school and to attend to their behavior. The pedagogue or custodian had responsibility to discipline or punish the boy. Once the boys reached manhood, they no longer needed the services of the custodian. Often the young man rewarded the custodian by granting him freedom. Paul spoke of the law as the custodian of God's people until Christ came (Gal. 3:23-26). The law can not save; but it can bring us to the point where we could have faith in Christ by showing us our unrighteousness (Gal. 3:19; cp. Rom. 7:7-12). Of course, the law was not nullified by Christ's death nor by our becoming Christians. We are still expected to live according to the moral principles found in the law (Rom. 7:12,16; cp. Matt. 5:17-48).

CUTH, CUTHAH Place-names with two spellings in Hebrew and English. Cuthah was the center of worship of Nergal, god of death in Mesopotamia. Residents of the city were exiled by the Assyrians to live in Israel (2 Kings 17:24). Once settled, they made an idol to worship Nergal (2 Kings 17:30), thus aggravating the tendency to worship Yahweh of Israel along with other gods. Cuth was located at Tell Ibrahim, about 18 miles northeast of Babylon.

CYPRIAN Citizen or resident of Cyprus. See *Cyprus.*

CYPRUS Large island in the eastern Mediterranean Sea mentioned most prominently in Acts. In the OT scattered references refer to the island as Kittim ("Chittim," Isa. 23:1; Jer. 2:10), although in some passages the term has a wider scope and includes lands other than Cyprus lying west of Palestine (Dan. 11:30).

Cyprus is first mentioned in the NT as the birthplace of Joseph surnamed Barnabas, a Hellenistic Jewish convert who later accompanied Paul (Acts 4:36-37). As a result of the persecution associated with the martyrdom of Stephen in Jerusalem, Jewish Christians journeyed to Cyprus and preached the gospel to the Jewish community on the island (Acts 11:19-20). In AD 46 or 47 Paul undertook his first missionary journey accompanied by Barnabas and John Mark (Acts 13). Arriving at Salamis on the eastern side of Cyprus, the group crossed the island to Paphos, preaching the new faith.

CYRENE Home of a certain Simon who was compelled to carry Jesus' cross to the place of crucifixion (Matt. 27:32). Located in northern Africa, it was the capital city of the Roman district of Cyrenaica during the NT era. Cyrenaica and Crete formed one province. Simon of Cyrene may have belonged to the rather large population of Greek-speaking Jews who resided in the city during the first part of the first century AD.

CYRENIAN Citizen and/or resident of Cyrene.

CYRENIUS Roman official mentioned in Luke 2:2 as the governor of Syria when the birth of Jesus took place. Some translations of the NT use the name Cyrenius, an Anglicized form of his Greek name, while others use the Latin form Quirinius.

CYRUS Third king of Anshan, Cyrus (the Great) assumed the throne about 559 BC. According to the best histories, Cyrus was reared by a shepherd after his grandfather, Astyages, king of Media, ordered that he be killed. Apparently, Astyages had dreamed that Cyrus would one day succeed him as king before the reigning monarch's death. The officer charged with the execution instead carried the boy into the hills to the shepherds.

As an adult, Cyrus organized the Persians into an army and revolted against his grandfather and father (Cambyses I). He defeated them and claimed their throne.

Cyrus' military exploits have become legendary. However, he is best remembered for his policies of peace. His famous decree in 539 BC (2 Chron. 36:22-23; Ezra 1:1-4) set free the captives Babylon had taken during its harsh rule. Among these prisoners were the Jews taken from Jerusalem in 586 BC. They were allowed to return to rebuild the temple and city. Along with this freedom Cyrus restored the valuable treasures of the temple taken during the exile. Since the Jews had done well in Babylon financially, many of them did not want to return to the wastes of Judah. From these people Cyrus exacted a tax to help pay for the trip for those who did wish to rebuild Jerusalem.

An astute politician, Cyrus made it a practice to publicly worship the gods of each kingdom he conquered. In so doing, he won the hearts of his subjects and kept down revolt. He is referred to as Yahweh's shepherd and anointed (Isa. 44:28–45:6) because of his kindness to the Jews and worship of Yahweh.

His last years are obscure. Cyrus was killed while fighting a frontier war with the nomadic Massagetae people. His tomb is in Pasargadae (modern Murghab).

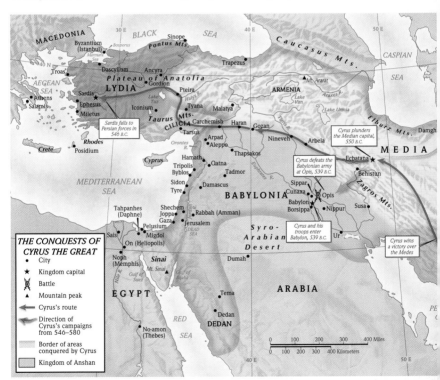

THE CONQUESTS OF
CYRUS THE GREAT
- • City
- ★ Kingdom capital
- ⚔ Battle
- ▲ Mountain peak
- ← Cyrus's route
- ← Direction of Cyrus's campaigns from 546–580
- Border of areas conquered by Cyrus
- Kingdom of Anshan

DABAREH (KJV, Josh. 21:28).See *Daberath.*

DABBASHETH or **DABBESHETH** Place-name meaning "hump." A border town of the tribe of Zebulun (Josh. 19:11). It is modern Tell esh-Shammam northwest of Jokneam.

DABERATH Place-name meaning "pasture." Border city of Zebulun near Mount Tabor (Josh. 19:12). In Josh. 21:28 it is a city given the Levites from the territory of Issachar. It is modern Daburiyeh at the northwest foot of Mount Tabor.

Wall of the New Testament period in Damascus from which Paul escaped to begin his ministry.

DAGGER KJV translation for the short, double-edged weapon of Ehud, the judge (Judg. 3:16-22). Other translations use "sword." Ehud's weapon was one cubit in length (18–22 inches), enabling him to conceal it under his cloak.

DAGON Name of a god meaning "little fish" or "dear." Dagon is a god associated with the Philistines. After the Philistines subdued Samson, they credited the victory to Dagon (Judg. 16:23). However, when Samson collapsed Dagon's temple upon himself and the Philistines, he proved the superiority of Israel's God. Likewise, the overthrow of the idol of Dagon before the ark of the covenant demonstrated God's predominance (1 Sam. 5:1-7). Nevertheless the Philistines, later, displayed the head of Saul as a trophy in the temple of Dagon (1 Chron. 10:10).

DALMANUTHA Place to which Jesus and His disciples came following the feeding of the 4,000 (Mark 8:10). Its location is not known. The parallel reference in Matt. 15:39 suggests it was in the area of Magdala.

DALMATIA Place-name referring to the southern part of Illyricum, north of Greece and across the Adriatic Sea from Italy. At the writing of 2 Timothy, Titus had left Paul to go to Dalmatia (2 Tim. 4:10). Paul had preached in Illyricum (Rom. 15:19). Illyricum included most of modern Yugoslavia and Albania.

DALPHON Personal name apparently derived from Persian word perhaps meaning "sleepless." One of 10 sons of Haman, chief enemy of Mordecai and Esther. The sons were killed when the Jews protected themselves against the Persian attack (Esther 9:7).

DAMARIS Personal name meaning "heifer." An Athenian woman who became a Christian following Paul's sermon at the Aeropagus, the highest court in Athens (Acts 17:34).

DAMASCUS Capital of important city-state in Syria with close historical ties to Israel. Apparently Damascus has been occupied continuously for a longer period of time than any other city in the world and can claim to be the world's oldest city. Its geographical location enabled Damascus to become a dominant trading and transportation center. Standing 2,300 feet above sea level, it lay northeast of Mount Hermon and about 60 miles east of Sidon, the Mediterranean port city. Both major international highways—the Via Maris and the King's Highway—ran through Damascus.

In the Bible Abraham chased invading kings north of Damascus to recover Lot, who had been taken captive (Gen. 14:15). Abraham's servant Eliezer apparently came from Damascus (Gen. 15:2). When Ahaz went to Damascus to pay tribute to Tiglath-pileser, he liked the altar he saw there and had a copy made for the Jerusalem temple (2 Kings 16:10-16). By the first century AD, Jews had migrated to Damascus and had establish synagogues there. Thus Saul went to Damascus to determine if any Christian believers were attached to the synagogues there so that he might persecute them (Acts 9). Thus the Damascus road became the sight of Saul's conversion experience and Damascus the sight of his introduction to the church. He had to escape from Damascus in a basket to begin his ministry (2 Cor. 11:32-33). Damascus gained importance, eventually becoming a Roman colony.

DAN Personal name meaning "judge." First son born to Jacob by Rachel's maid Bilhah (Gen. 30:6). He was the original ancestor of the tribe of Dan. When the Israelites entered Canaan, the tribe of Dan received land on the western coast. They could not fully gain control of the territory, especially after the Philistines settled in the area. The last chapters of Judges show Samson of the tribe of Dan fighting the Philistines. Eventually, Dan migrated to the north and was able to take a city called Laish. They renamed the city Dan and settled in the area around it. The biblical city of Dan is often mentioned in the description of the land of Israel, namely "from Dan even to Beersheba" (Judg. 20:1).

DANCING Essential part of Jewish life in Bible times. According to Eccles. 3:4, there is "a time to mourn, and a time to dance." Dances were performed on both sacred and secular occasions, though the Hebrew mind would not likely have thought in these terms. The OT employs 11 terms to describe the act of dance.

DANIEL Personal name meaning "God is judge" or "God's judge." **1.** Son of David and Abigail, the Carmelitess (1 Chron. 3:1), who is also called Chileab in 2 Sam. 3:3. **2.** Priest of the Ithamar lineage (Ezra 8:2; Neh 10:6) who returned with Ezra from the Babylonian captivity. **3.** Daniel of Ezek. 14:14,20; 28:3 is spelled differently in Hebrew from all the other forms in the OT. This Daniel was a storied figure of antiquity mentioned with Noah and Job. **4.** The most common usage of "Daniel" refers to the hero of the book of Daniel. This young man of nobility was taken captive by Nebuchadnezzar, king of Babylon, and elevated to high rank in the Babylonian and Persian kingdoms. The Babylonians sought to remove all vestiges of Daniel's nationality and religion. For this reason, they sought to

Jewish men dancing during a private ceremony in the Court of the Men at the Wailing Wall in Jerusalem.

change the name of Daniel to Belteshazzar (Dan. 1:7; 2:26; 4:8-9,18-19; 5:12; 10:1).

Daniel would probably have celebrated his one hundredth birthday during the reign of Darius. He had outstanding physical attraction. He demonstrated at an early age propensities of knowledge, wisdom, and leadership. In addition to his wisdom, he was skilled in dream interpretation. Throughout his entire life he demonstrated an unshakable faith in his God.

DANIEL, BOOK OF In the English versions, Daniel appears as the last of four major prophetic books, whereas in the Hebrew Bible it is grouped with the section of Scripture known as the *Hagiographa* or the *Writings*. The traditional position is that Daniel wrote the book in the sixth-century BC, the prophecy is historically reliable, and its predictions are supernatural and accurate.

Theological Emphases Without doubt the principal theological theme of the book is the sovereignty of God. Every page reflects the author's conviction that his God is the Lord of individuals, nations, and all of history. Daniel also emphasizes the person and work of the Messiah (e.g., 7:13-14, 9:24-27). Eschatology is another prominent theme in Daniel's prophecies. Believers will experience tribulation in the last days (7:21,25; 9:27; 12:1), but the Messiah will appear and establish a glorious, eternal kingdom (2:44-45; 7:13-14,26-27; 9:24). In this wonderful new world, the saints will be rewarded and honored (12:2-3).

Structure That the book of Daniel should be divided according to the type of literature—the stories of Daniel (1:1–6:28) and the prophecies of Daniel (7:1–12:13)—is indicated by the chronological scheme set forth by the author of the book and by the fact that the author himself grouped homogeneous literary accounts together.

DANITE Resident and/or citizen of city of Dan or member of tribe of Dan.

DAN-JAAN Place-name of uncertain meaning in 2 Sam. 24:6.

DANNAH Place-name meaning "fortress." Town assigned tribe of Judah in the hill country (Josh. 15:49). Its location is uncertain.

DAPPLED Variegated gray color of the horses in the vision in Zech. 6:3,6. KJV translates the rare Hebrew term as "bay."

DARA Hebrew reading in 1 Chron. 2:6 for Darda of 1 Kings 4:31.

DARDA Personal name possibly meaning "pearl of knowledge." Famous wise man whose father is listed as Mahol in 1 Kings 4:31 but as Zerah in what appears to be a parallel list in 1 Chron. 2:6.

DARIC Persian gold coin equivalent to four days' wages, probably introduced by Darius I (522–486 BC), and possibly the earliest coined money used by the Jews who became acquainted with it during the exile. Offerings for the reconstruction of the temple were made in darics (Ezra 2:69 ESV; Neh. 7:70,72).

DARIUS Name of several Medo-Persian kings, three of whom are mentioned in the OT. **1.** Darius the Mede (Dan. 5:31), ruler who took Babylon from Belshazzar. Against his own will, he had Daniel thrown to the lions and later decreed that "in all ... my kingdom men are to fear and tremble before the God of Daniel" (Dan. 6:26 NASB). **2.** Darius I (521–486 BC), also known as Darius Hystaspes or the Great, was both extremely cruel and generous. Darius seized power following the death of Cambyses II, son of Cyrus. This is the Darius of Ezra (Ezra 4–6;

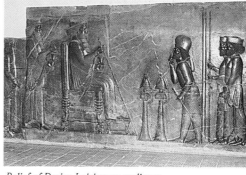
Relief of Darius I giving an audience.

Haggai; Zech. 1–8), under whom the temple in Jerusalem was reconstructed, completed in the sixth year of his reign. Darius continued Cyrus' policy of restoring disenfranchised peoples who were victims of Assyrian and Babylonian conquests. Darius reaffirmed Cyrus' authorization and also provided for maintenance of the temple. **3.** Darius the Persian (Neh. 12:22), although scholars differ as to his identity.

DARKNESS Absence of light is used in both physical and figurative senses in both the OT and NT. Darkness often has an ethical sense. Scripture speaks of ways of darkness (Prov. 2:13; 4:19), walking in darkness (John 8:12; 1 John 1:6; cp. 2 Cor. 6:14; Eph. 5:8), and works of darkness (Rom. 13:12; Eph. 5:11). In this ethical sense God has no darkness in Himself (1 John 1:5). Powers hostile to God can be termed darkness. People thus face a choice of whether to yield allegiance to God or to darkness (Luke 22:53; John 1:5; 3:19; Col. 1:13; 1 Thess. 5:5). Darkness also symbolizes ignorance, especially of God and of God's ways (Isa. 8:22; 9:2; John 12:46; Acts 26:18; 1 Thess. 5:4; 1 John 2:9). God's deliverance (either from ignorance or hostile powers) is described as lighting the darkness (Isa. 9:2; 29:18; 42:7-16; Mic. 7:8; 1 Pet. 2:9).

DARKON Personal name perhaps meaning "hard." A servant of Solomon whose descendants returned from exile with Zerubbabel about 537 BC (Ezra 2:56).

DATES Fruit of the date palm (*Phoenix dactylifera*), highly valued by desert travelers who consume dates fresh, dry them, or form them into cakes for a portable and easily storable food.

DATHAN Personal name meaning "fountain" or "warring." The son of Eliab and brother from the tribe of Reuben, Dathan and his brother Abiram were leaders of a revolt challenging Moses' authority over the Israelites. The attempted coup failed, and Dathan and Abiram, along with their families, were swallowed up by the earth (Num. 16).

A view of the excavations of the City of David led by Kathleen Kenyon.

DAVID Personal name probably meaning "favorite" or "beloved." Shepherd, musician, poet, warrior, and loyal subject of King Saul, David became Israel's second king and the first king to unite Israel and Judah. He was the first king to receive the promise of a royal messiah in his line. David was pictured as the ideal king of God's people. David ruled from about 1005 to 965 BC.

The NT tells the story of Jesus as the story of the Son of God but also as the story of the Son of David from His birth (Matt. 1:1) until His final coming (Rev. 22:16). At least 12 times the Gospels refer to Him as "Son of David." David was cited as an example of similar behavior by Jesus (Matt. 12:3), and David called Him "Lord" (Luke 20:42-44). David thus took his place in the roll call of faith given in Heb. 11:32. This was "David the son of Jesse, a man after My heart, who will carry out all My will" (Acts 13:22 HCSB).

DAVID, CITY OF Most ancient part of Jerusalem on its southeast corner representing the city occupied by the Jebusites and conquered by David (2 Sam. 5:7).

DAY OF ATONEMENT Tenth day of the seventh month of the Jewish calendar (Sept.–Oct.) on which the high priest entered the inner sanctuary of the temple to make reconciling sacrifices for the sins of the entire nation (Lev. 16:16-28). The writer of Hebrews developed images from the Day of Atonement to stress the superiority of Christ's priesthood (8:6; 9:7,11-26). Hebrews 13:11-12 uses the picture of the bull and goat burned outside the camp as an illustration of Christ's suffering outside Jerusalem's city walls. According to one interpretation, Paul alluded to the day's ritual by speaking of Christ as a sin offering (2 Cor. 5:21).

DAY OF THE LORD Time when God reveals His sovereignty over human powers and human existence. The Day of the Lord rests on the Hebrew term, *yom,* "day," the fifth most frequent noun used in the OT and one used with a variety of meanings.

The OT prophets used a term familiar to their audience, a term by which the audience expected light and salvation (Amos 5:18), but the prophets painted it as a day of darkness and judgment (Isa. 2:10-22; 13:6,9; Joel 1:15; 2:1-11,31; 3:14-15; Amos 5:20; Zeph. 1:7-8,14-18; Mal. 4:5). The OT language of the Day of the Lord is thus aimed at warning sinners among God's people of the danger of trusting in traditional religion without commitment to God and His way of life.

New Testament writers took up the OT expression to point to Christ's final victory and the final judgment of sinners. In so doing, they used several different expressions (HCSB): "day of Christ Jesus" (Phil. 1:6), "day of our Lord Jesus Christ" (1 Cor. 1:8); "Day of the Lord" (1 Cor. 5:5; 1 Thess. 5:2); "day of Christ" (Phil. 1:10; 2:16); "day of judgment" (1 John 4:17); "this day" (1 Thess. 5:4); "that day" (2 Tim. 1:12); "day of wrath" (Rom. 2:5).

DAY'S JOURNEY Customary, though inexact, measure of distance traveled in a day. The distance varied with the terrain and with the circumstances of the traveler. The typical day's journey of the Jews was between 20 and 30 miles, though groups generally traveled only 10 miles per day (Gen. 30:36; 31:23; Exod. 3:18; 8:27; Deut. 1:2; Luke 2:44).

DAYSMAN KJV term for a mediator, arbitrator, or umpire (Job 9:33). In the Near East such mediators placed their hands on the heads of the parties in a dispute.

DEACON Term "deacon" comes from the Greek noun *diakonos,* which occurs 29 times in the NT, and is most commonly translated "servant" or "minister." This noun is derived from the verb "to serve" and is used to signify various types of service.

The Dead Sea.

DEAD SEA Inland lake at the end of the Jordan Valley on the southeastern border of Canaan with no outlets for water it receives; known as Salt Sea, Sea of the Plain, and Eastern Sea. Its current English name was applied to it through writings after AD 100. It is about 50 miles long and 10 miles wide at its widest point. The surface of the sea is 1,292 feet below the level of the Mediterranean Sea.

DEAD SEA SCROLLS Discovered between 1947 and 1960 in a cave on the western Dead Sea

Dead Sea Scroll fragment.

shore near a ruin called Khirbet Qumran. Eleven caves from the Qumran area have since yielded manuscripts, mostly in small fragments. About 60 percent of the scrolls have so far been published. These were composed or copied between 200 BC and AD 70, mostly around the lifetime of Jesus, by a small community living at Qumran.

DEATH The biblical portrait of death is not that of a normal outworking of natural processes. Instead, the Bible presents human death as a reaffirmation that something has gone awry in God's created order. The Scriptures do not, however, picture death as a hopeless termination of human consciousness, but instead brim with the hope of resurrection. Biblical scholars group the Bible's teachings on death into three distinct but interrelated categories—physical, spiritual, and eternal.

DEBIR Personal and place-name meaning "back, behind." As a common noun, the Hebrew term refers to the back room of the temple, the holy of holies. **1.** King of Eglon who joined in Jerusalem-led coalition against Joshua and lost (Josh. 10:3). Nothing else about him is known. See *Eglon*. **2.** Important city in hill country of tribe of Judah whose exact location is debated by archaeologists and geographers. Joshua annihilated its residents (Josh. 10:38; cp. 11:21; 12:13). **3.** A town on the northern border of Judah (Josh. 15:7). This may be located at Thoghret ed Debr, the "pass of Debir," 10 miles east of Jerusalem. **4.** A town in Gad east of the Jordan given various spellings in the Hebrew Bible: *Lidebor* (Josh. 13:26); *Lwo Debar* (2 Sam. 9:4-5); *Lo' Debar* (2 Sam. 17:27); *Lo' Dabar* (Amos 6:13).

DEBORAH Personal name meaning "bee." Deborah is the name of two women in the Bible, Rebekah's nurse (Gen. 35:8) and a leader of pre-monarchic Israel (Judg. 4–5).

DECAPOLIS Place-name meaning "10 cities." A group of Greek cities referred to in Matt. 4:25; Mark 5:20; 7:31, originally 10 in number but including more cities at a later time.

DECISION, VALLEY OF (Joel 3:14) See *Jehoshaphat, Valley of*.

DEDAN Personal and place-name of unknown meaning. **1.** The original ancestor of an Arabian tribe listed in the Table of Nations as a son of Cush (Gen. 10:7). See *Cush*. **2.** Grandson of Abraham (Gen. 25:3). Here, as in 10:7, Dedan's brother is Sheba. Three otherwise unknown Arabian tribes descended from Dedan, according to Gen. 25:3. **3.** Arabian tribe centered at al-Alula, 70 miles southwest of Tema and 400 miles from Jerusalem.

DEDANIM or **DEDANITE** Resident or citizen of the tribe of Dedan.

DEDICATION, FEAST OF Term for Hanukkah in John 10:22.

DEEP, THE English translation of the Hebrew term *tehom*. The deep constitutes the primeval waters of creation in Gen. 1:2. The waters of the deep can be destructive or constructive, curse or blessing. When the waters of the deep burst their bounds, the result is a flood (Gen. 7:11). On the other hand, the waters of the deep are a blessing, without which life could not continue. Deuteronomy 8:7 describes the promised land as a land of brooks, fountains, and deeps, which irrigate the land so that grain and fruit can be grown (Ezek. 31:4).

The Greek Bible or Septuagint translated *tehom* as "abyss," bringing it into relationship with the pit, the abode of the dead (Rom. 10:7) and place of evil spirits (Luke 8:31), including the beast of the apocalypse (Rev. 17:8).

DEER Antlered animal (all male and some female have antlers) with two large and two small hooves. It is believed that three species of deer lived in Palestine in Bible times: red, fallow, and roe.

DEFILE To make ritually unclean.

DEGREES, SONG OF KJV phrase used in the titles of 15 psalms (Pss. 120–134). Modern speech translations render the phrase "Song of Ascents." Though the origin of the phrase is obscure, the generally accepted view is that the Hebrew term *ma'alot* (goings up) is a reference to pilgrims going up to Jerusalem for the three required festivals (Pss. 42:4; 122:4).

DEHAVITE KJV transliteration of Aramaic text in Ezra 4:9. Modern translators read the text as two Aramaic words—*di-hu'*— meaning "that is."

DEKAR KJV reads "son of Dekar" in 1 Kings 4:9, where modern translations transliterate the Hebrew text to read "Ben-deker."

DELAIAH Personal name meaning "the Lord rescued." **1.** Head of one of the 24 divisions of the priestly order organized by David (1 Chron. 24:18). **2.** Son of Shemaiah and a courtier who counseled Jehoiakim not to burn Jeremiah's scroll (Jer. 36:12,25). **3.** One of the exiles who returned under

Zerubbabel to Jerusalem (Ezra 2:60; Neh. 7:62). **4.** Descendant of David and son of Elioenai (1 Chron. 3:24). **5.** Contemporary of Nehemiah (Neh. 6:10).

DELILAH Personal name meaning "with long hair hanging down." A woman from the valley of Sorek who was loved by Samson (Judg. 16:4).

DEMAS Companion and coworker of Paul the apostle (Col. 4:14). Though in Philem. 24 Paul identified Demas as a "coworker," 2 Tim. 4:10 indicates that this man later deserted Paul, having "loved this present world."

DEMETRIUS Personal name meaning "belonging to Demeter, the Greek goddess of crops." **1.** Silversmith in Ephesus who incited a riot directed against Paul because he feared that the apostle's preaching would threaten the sale of silver shrines of Diana, the patron goddess of Ephesus (Acts 19:24-41). **2.** Apparently a convert from the worship of Demeter, the god worshipped in the mystery religion at Eleusis near Athens. John commended him, saying, he "has a good testimony from everyone, and from the truth itself" (3 John 12 HCSB).

DEMONIC POSSESSION Demons are identified in Scripture as fallen angels who joined Satan in his rebellion. They follow Satan, doing evil and wreaking havoc. They have limited power and like Satan are already defeated (Col. 2:15).

The NT distinguishes between demonic possession and physical disease. Matthew 4:24 states that Jesus healed "all those who were afflicted, those suffering from various diseases and intense pains, the demon-possessed, the epileptics, and the paralytics" (HCSB).

The cure for demonic possession was faith in the power of Christ. Never were magic or rituals used to deliver one from demonic possession. The exorcisms of Jesus were accomplished by the power of His speech. He issued simple commands, such as "be quiet, and come out of him!" (Mark 1:25), or "you mute and deaf spirit, I command you: come out of him and never enter him again!" (Mark 9:25 HCSB).

DENARIUS Coin representing a typical day's wage for an ordinary laborer (Matt. 20:2). KJV translates it "penny." This unit of Roman currency is the most frequently mentioned coin in the NT.

DEN OF LIONS Place where lions live, at times a thicket (Jer. 50:44) or cave (Nah. 2:12). See *Lion.*

DEPUTY Official of secondary rank (1 Kings 22:47); KJV term for a Roman proconsul (Acts 13:7; 18:12; 19:38).

DERBE Important city in region of Lycaonia in province of Galatia in Asia Minor. It is apparently near modern Kerti Huyuk. The residents of Derbe and Lystra spoke a different language from the people to the north in Iconium. Paul visited Derbe on his first missionary journey (Acts 14:6), fleeing from Iconium. Persecution in Lystra led to a successful preaching mission in Derbe (14:20-21). On the second journey Paul returned to Derbe (Acts 16:1). He apparently visited again on the third journey (18:23). Paul's fellow minister Gaius was from Derbe (20:4).

DESCENT Path down a mountain (Luke 19:37); a genealogy, line of ancestors (Heb. 7:3,6).

DESERT Areas with little rainfall to the east and south of Palestine and inhabited by nomads with flocks and herds. Three major deserts figure in biblical events: the plateau east of the mountains to the east of the Jordan River; the area south of Edom; and the triangle bordered by Gaza, the Dead Sea, and the Red Sea.

Wasteland of the northern Negev in southern Israel.

DESIRE OF ALL NATIONS Phrase that Haggai used in his prophecy of a renewed temple (Hag. 2:7). Some translations (KJV, NIV) interpret the underlying Hebrew as a prophecy of the coming Messiah. Other translations render the phrase "treasure" (TEV, NRSV, REB) or "wealth" (NASB) of all nations in parallel to the gold and silver of 2:8.

DESTINY Word used in modern translations for God's act in electing or predestinating people and nations.

DEUEL Personal name meaning "God knows." In Num. 1:14 the father of Eliasaph, the leader in the wilderness of the tribe of Gad.

DEUTERONOMY, BOOK OF English name of fifth book of OT taken from Greek translation meaning "second law." The title used in the Hebrew Bible, "these (are) the words" (two words in Hebrew), follows an ancient custom of using words from the first line of the text to designate a book.

Deuteronomy is the last of five books of Law and should not be read in isolation from the other four books (Genesis, Exodus, Leviticus, Numbers). Pentateuch (five books) is the familiar title associated with these five books of Law, the first and most important division of the Hebrew Bible. By longstanding tradition these books have been associated with Moses, the human instrument of God's deliverance of Israel from bondage in Egypt and the negotiator of the covenant between God and Israel.

The approaching death of Moses put urgency into his appeal for covenant renewal. He called for obedience through love to Yahweh, the loving God, who had established the covenant with Israel. Moses was convinced that only through a renewed relationship with God could the new generation of Israelites hope to succeed under Joshua's leadership in possessing the land. Deuteronomy is either quoted or alluded to nearly 200 times in the NT. Jesus resists Satan's three temptations in the wilderness by quoting from Deuteronomy.

Deuteronomy calls for a complete and undivided devotion to God. It sets forth the consequences of obedience and recognizes the inclination of God's people to forget who He is and what He has done for them. For that reason, Moses urges the people to continually be on guard against forgetting God and not to allow their children to be ignorant of Him and His expectations.

DEVIL, SATAN, EVIL, DEMONIC Evil appears early in Genesis with the serpent figure (Gen. 3:1-5). While Genesis does not identify this figure as "Satan," Revelation alludes to him as such (Rev. 12:9). The Scriptures portray Satan as a personal being in direct opposition to God and his purposes. Satan is not equal to God nor does he threaten God's power (Isa. 45:5-7).

DEW Moisture that forms into drops of water on the earth during a cool night. Dew is used in the Bible as a symbol of refreshment (Deut. 32:2; Ps. 133:3); a symbol of the loving power of God that revives and invigorates (Prov. 19:12); a symbol of the sudden onset of an enemy (2 Sam. 17:12); a symbol of brotherly love and harmony (Ps. 133:3); a symbol of God's revelation (Judg. 6:36-40); and a symbol of God's blessing (Gen. 27:28).

DIADEM English translation of three Hebrew terms designating a head covering symbolizing authority and honor.

DIAMOND Precious stone used in jewelry and engraving. It is the hardest mineral known, formed of pure carbon crystals. Two Hebrew words stand behind English "diamond." *Yahelom* is a stone on the high priest's breastplate (Exod. 28:18; NIV, "emerald"; NRSV, "moonstone") and among the jewels of the king of Tyre (Ezek. 28:13). *Shamir* is the stone used on the point of an engraving tool to cut into stone surfaces (Jer. 17:1; NIV, "flint"; others suggest "emery"). The term also appears in Ezek. 3:9 and Zech. 7:12 as the hardest stone known.

DIANA Roman goddess with similar characteristics to the Greek Artemis. KJV reads "Diana" in Acts, where Greek and most modern translations read "Artemis."

DIASPORA Scattering of the Jews from the land of Palestine into other parts of the world. The term "dispersion" is also often used to describe this process.

DIBLAH or **DIBLATH** Place-name with variant manuscript spellings and English transliterations in Ezek. 6:14. The Hebrew term may mean "cake of figs."

DIBLAIM Personal or place-name meaning "two fig cakes." Hosea 1:3 lists Diblaim as a parent of Gomer, Hosea's harlot wife.

DIBON or **DIBON-GAD** Place-name possibly meaning "pining away" or "fence of tubes." **1.** Capital city of Moab captured by Moses (Num. 21:21-31). **2.** In Nehemiah's day (about 445 BC)

Jews lived in a Dibon in Judah. This may be the same as Dimonah.

DIBRI Personal name meaning "talkative" or "gossip." Father of an Israelite woman who had a son with an Egyptian father. The son cursed God's name and was stoned to death (Lev. 24:10-23).

DIDRACHMA Greek coin worth two drachmas or a Jewish half shekel, the amount of the temple tax paid by every male Jew above age 19 (Matt. 17:24).

DIDYMUS Personal name meaning "twin." An alternative name for the Apostle Thomas (John 11:16). It appears only in John's Gospel.

DIETING The book of Proverbs cautions that excessive eating and drinking is the mark of a fool (Prov. 23:20-21; cp. Eccles. 5:18; 9:7; 1 Cor. 15:32) and urges bodily restraint (Prov. 23:2; 25:16). The writer of Ecclesiastes noted that one who is blessed "eats at a proper time—for strength and not for drunkenness" (Eccles. 10:17). Daniel and his friends refused the rich foods of Babylon in favor of vegetables and water (Dan. 1:5-16) and were healthier as a result.

New Testament teaching holds that a person's body is the temple of the Holy Spirit (1 Cor. 6:19) and that it must therefore be subdued (1 Cor. 9:27) and cared for in a way that honors God (1 Cor. 6:20). For this reason, excessive eating is contrary to Christian discipline (Phil. 3:19).

DIGNITIES KJV translation of Greek *doxas* (literally, "glorious ones") in 2 Pet. 2:10. The people whom Peter condemned in his second letter willingly blasphemed the "dignities," who are either good angels or evil angels (cp. Jude 8).

DIKLAH Personal name apparently meaning "date palm." Grandson of Eber (Gen. 10:27).

DILEAN Place-name meaning "protrusion" or "ledge." Village in tribal territory of Judah (Josh. 15:38).

DILL Spice cultivated in Israel (Isa. 28:25-27). KJV translates "fitches"; NIV, "caraway." It was probably black cumin, *Nigella satina*. Jesus accused the scribes and Pharisees of tithing their dill but neglecting justice, mercy, and faith (Matt. 23:23).

DIMNAH Place-name meaning "manure." Town in tribal territory of Zebulun given to Levites (Josh. 21:35). First Chronicles 6:77 appears to refer to the same city as Rimmon (cp. Josh. 19:13). A scribe copying the text could easily confuse the two names.

DIMON Place-name perhaps meaning "blood." City in Moab on which Isaiah announced judgment (Isa. 15:9).

DIMONAH Place-name related to Hebrew word for blood. A town on southeast border of tribal allotment of Judah (Josh. 15:22). Some have suggested its location at Tell ed-Dheib near Aroer. It may be the same as Dibon mentioned in Neh. 11:25.

DINAH Personal name meaning "justice" or "artistically formed." The daughter of Jacob and Leah (Gen. 30:21). According to Gen. 34 she was sexually assaulted by a man named Shechem, who wished to marry her. Simeon and Levi, her brothers, took revenge by killing the male residents of the city of Shechem.

DINAITE KJV transliterations of Aramaic word in Ezra 4:9. Modern translations translate the word as "judges."

DINHABAH City name of unknown meaning. Residence of one of earliest kings of Edom in period prior to Saul in Israel (Gen. 36:32). Nothing else is known of the city.

DIONYSIUS Athenian aristocrat who was converted to Christianity through the preaching of Paul the apostle (Acts 17:34). He was a member of the Areopagus, an elite and influential group of officials.

DIOTREPHES Personal name meaning "nurtured by Jove." An individual whose self-serving ambition is cited unfavorably (3 John 9). The writer of the letter declared that Diotrephes rejected his (the writer's) authority.

DIPHATH NRSV, NASB reading of great grandson of Noah in 1 Chron. 1:6. KJV, NIV follow other Hebrew manuscripts and versions and Gen. 10:3 in reading Riphath.

DIRECTIONS The OT uses all the cardinal directions in several passages. God tells Abraham to look north and south, east and west (that is, in all directions), and all that land will be his and his descendants (Gen. 13:14). In the NT, ones from all directions, east and west, north and south, will sit at the table in God's kingdom (Luke 13:29).

DIRGE Modern translation term for lamentation.

DISCERNING OF SPIRITS One of the gifts of the Spirit (1 Cor. 12:10). It apparently refers to the God-given ability to tell whether a prophetic speech came from God's Spirit or from another source opposed to God.

DISCHARGE Modern translation term for bodily excretion that rendered one ceremonially unclean (Lev. 15:2-33: Num. 5:2; KJV, "issue"). A discharge rendered unclean the person and anything or anyone coming into contact with the source of uncleanness.

DISCIPLE Follower of Jesus Christ, especially the commissioned Twelve who followed Jesus during His earthly ministry. The term "disciple" comes to us in English from a Latin root. Its basic meaning is "learner" or "pupil." The term is virtually absent from the OT, though there are two related references (1 Chron. 25:8; Isa. 8:16).

DISCIPLINE In the Bible discipline has a positive and essential place in the lives of God's people. God had prescribed a way of life for His people. They had to learn how to be obedient. The process by which God's people learned obedience was the "discipline of the Lord" (Deut. 11:2 NIV). Discipline, biblically understood, results in blessing. God's people learn how to serve Him. Through praise and correction, their lives are shaped into a pattern of consistent obedience and love. Within "the discipline of the Lord," expressed in and through the Lord Jesus Christ, one can live the kind of life that is pleasing to God and of benefit to others.

DISEASES Physical and/or mental malfunctions that limit human functions and lessen the quality of life. Successful treatment of disease depends primarily on prompt, correct diagnosis, and the use of effective therapeutic agents. Unfortunately, people living in biblical times had limited means to diagnose and treat illness. The best-educated people in biblical times had a meager understanding of human anatomy and physiology and even less knowledge about the nature of disease and its effect on the body. No one knew about bacteria and viruses. This fact hampered diagnosis. Illness was often attributed to sin or to a curse by an enemy. The main diagnostic tools were observation and superficial physical examination. The physician had few aids to use in his work.

Jesus and the Treatment of Disease One of the major ministries of Jesus was the healing of ill persons. They flocked to Him in large numbers, often after having tried all the remedies available in their day. They were desperate for help.

Jesus did not believe that all illness is the direct result of sin (John 9:1-3). He had the power, however, both to forgive sin and to heal (Matt. 9:1-8; cp. Mark 2:1-12; Luke 5:17-26). Ordinarily, He did not use any kind of secondary means to treat the afflicted, although on several occasions He used spittle (Mark 7:32-35; 8:22-25; John 9:6-7). Some of the illnesses treated by Jesus probably had a psychosomatic basis; but many others undoubtedly had organic causes, including birth defects, accidental injuries, and infections.

Regardless of the cause of their distress, people found that Jesus could truly help. There can be no doubt that the ability of Jesus to perform miracles is seen most vividly in His healing ministry. The blind, the deaf, the lame, and sufferers of all varieties found in Him the help that was often not available through regular medical channels.

DISHAN Personal name meaning "bison" or "antelope." This may be a variant spelling/pronunciation of Dishon. A Horite chief and son of Seir (Gen. 36:21,28,30).

DISHON Name of Horite chief of Edom (Gen. 36:21,25-26,30). The name may be the same as Dishan with the variant spelling used to identify the separate individuals.

DISPENSATION An arrangement or management in which God places responsibility on mankind. As it is related to Jesus Christ, who had not been revealed for a long time (Eph. 3:5), the dispensation is new with regards to time. Paul indicated earlier in the epistle that there is coming a "dispensation of the fullness of the times" (1:10 KJV; cp. HCSB, NASB), which appears as a future phenomenon. Colossians 1:25-29 indicates that there existed a previous dispensational arrangement different from the present one. This suggests that in Paul's thought at least three dispensations of God's dealings with mankind are evident: past, present, and future.

DISSIPATION Deceptive desires leading to a lifestyle without discipline resulting in the dizzy hangovers of drunkenness. The Greek word *apate* means "deception" caused by riches (Matt. 13:22) and sin (Heb. 3:13).

DISTAFF Part of the spindle used in spinning wool (Prov. 31:19).

DIVES Name sometimes given to the rich man of whom Jesus spoke in Luke 16:19-31. *Dives* actually is the Latin word for "rich" used in Luke 16:19 in the Vulgate translation. The idea that this was the name of the man emerged in medieval times.

DIVIDED KINGDOM Two political states of Judah and Israel that came into existence shortly after the death of Solomon (1 Kings 11:43) and survived together until the fall of Israel in 722 BC. The northern kingdom, known as Israel, and the southern kingdom, known as Judah, were operated as separate countries from approximately 924 BC until 722 BC (1 Kings 12).

DIVINATION AND MAGIC Practice of making decisions or foretelling the future by means of reading signs and omens. Several types of divination are mentioned in the Bible. God condemned divination and magic in every form. The law of Moses repeatedly condemns the practice. In Exod. 22:18 and Lev. 20:27 it brings the death penalty. People are exhorted to listen to God's prophets instead.

DIVINE FREEDOM One of God's unique attributes is freedom. Scripture declares, "Our God is in heaven and does whatever He pleases" (Ps. 115:3 HCSB). God's actions are always voluntary. God cannot be compelled to act by any other person or exterior force. Only His nature and will are determinative for His actions (Isa. 42:21; Eph. 1:11).

DIVINE RETRIBUTION Repayment without stipulation of good or evil. The application of the word in theology is, however, almost always viewed as the response of a just and holy God to evil. Like other prominent theological terms (i.e., Trinity, etc.), the word is not found in the Bible, but the idea of God's repayment for evil is prominent in at least three ways.

First, the law of sowing and reaping is part of God's economy (Gal. 6:7-8). Second, coming judgment at the end of history includes repayment from God for rebellion. Finally, the justice of God's condemnation of sinners gives rise to the necessity of the grace of God in salvation and the substitutionary death of Jesus on the cross. God in His grace extends to sinners an offer of pardon rather than the retribution they deserve, because Jesus paid the price for human sin in His vicarious death, making it possible for the Father to be both "just" and still the "justifier" of the sinner who places his faith in Jesus (Rom. 3:26).

DIVINERS' OAK Place visible from the gate of Shechem (Judg. 9:35,37).

DIVORCE Breaking of the marriage covenant. An action contrary to the pattern of "one man, one woman, one lifetime" revealed by God in Gen. 1:27; 2:21-25. The root idea implied a cutting of the marriage bond. While ancient cultures differed in details, most had a concept of marriage and a corresponding concept of divorce.

The NT also sheds light on the subject of divorce. The Lord Jesus stated that divorce, except in the case of sexual immorality, would cause complications for remarriage. An improper divorce would make the divorced wife and her future husband adulterers in their relationship (Matt. 5:31-32). In Matt. 19:3-12, Jesus stated that God did not intend for divorce to occur. Further, He stated that the Mosaic law allowed for divorce only because of the hardness of Israelite hearts. Jesus' disciples considered this a hard saying and said so; nevertheless, He affirmed His position on divorce (Matt. 19:7-12; Mark 10:4-12).

DIZAHAB Place-name meaning "place of gold." Place east of Jordan River used in Deut. 1:1 to locate where Moses spoke to Israel. Nothing else is known of it. It may be located in Moab in modern ed-Dhebe.

DOCTRINE Christian truth and teaching passed on from generation to generation as "the faith that was delivered to the saints" (Jude 3 HCSB).

DODAI Personal name related to Hebrew word meaning "favorite" or "beloved."

DODANIM Great grandson of Noah and son of Javan in the Table of Nations (Gen. 10:4).

DODAVAH or **DODAVAHU** Personal name meaning "beloved of Yahweh." Father of Eliezer the prophet (2 Chron. 20:37).

DODO Personal name meaning "his beloved." **1.** Grandfather of Tola, the judge (Judg. 10:1). **2.** Father of Eleazar, one of David's three mighty men (2 Sam. 23:9). In 1 Chron. 27:4 he is called Dodai. **3.** Citizen of Bethlehem and father of Elhanan, one of David's warriors (2 Sam. 23:24).

DOE Modern translation where KJV has "hind" or "roe."

DOEG Personal name meaning "full of fear." An Edomite in the service of King Saul (1 Sam. 21:7)

DOG Considered an unclean animal; often wild, scavenger animal that ran in packs (Pss. 22:16-21; 59:6), but sometimes kept as domestic pet. Metaphorically, "dog" was a term of contempt (1 Sam. 17:43) and self-abasement (1 Sam. 24:14). Jesus used dogs to teach people to be discriminating in whom they chose to teach (Matt. 7:6). In Mark 7:27, Jesus probably was referring to the small dogs that people kept as pets. Jews contemptuously called Gentiles "dogs." Paul insulted his Judaizing opponents, calling them dogs (Phil. 3:2; cp. 2 Pet. 2:22; Rev. 22:15).

DOPHKAH Place-name perhaps meaning "(animal) drive." Station in the wilderness between Wilderness of Sin and Rephidim where Israel camped (Num. 33:12).

DOR Place-name meaning "dwelling." Canaanite city located at modern Khirbet el-Burj, 12 miles south of Mount Carmel. Dor lay in the territory assigned Asher, but the tribe of Manasseh claimed it (Josh. 17:11).

DORCAS Personal name meaning "gazelle." A Christian woman of Joppa who was known for her charitable works (Acts 9:36). She was also called Tabitha, an Aramaic name.

DOTHAN Place-name of uncertain meaning, also known as Dothaim. A city of the tribe of Manasseh, west of the Jordan, northeast of Samaria, southeast of Megiddo, and now identified as Tell Dotha. It was located in an area less productive for agriculture and was traversed by roads used for commerce. Dothan is the area to which Joseph traveled to find his brothers (Gen. 37:17).

View of the ancient harbor at Dor in Israel.

DOVE The term "dove" is applied rather loosely to many of the smaller species of pigeon. Because of the gentleness of the dove and because of its faithfulness to its mate, this bird is used as a descriptive title of one's beloved in the Song of Songs (2:14; 5:2; 6:9). In Matt. 10:16 the dove symbolizes innocence. All four Gospels describe the Spirit of God descending like a dove upon Jesus after His baptism (Matt. 3:16; Mark 1:10; Luke 3:22; John 1:32).

DOVE'S DUNG An item sold as food for an incredible price (2 Kings 6:25) during the siege of Samaria.

DOWRY Marriage present that ensured the new wife's financial security against the possibility her husband might forsake her or might die. The husband-to-be or his father paid the dowry or bride price to the bride's father to be kept for the bride.

DOXOLOGY Brief formula for expressing praise or glory to God. Biblical doxologies are found in many contexts, but one of their chief functions seems to have been as a conclusion to songs (Exod. 15:18), psalms (Ps. 146:10), and prayers (Matt. 6:13), where they possibly served as group responses to solo singing or recitation.

DRACHMA Greek term used to refer to silver coins (Luke 15:8-9). It was a Greek unit of silver coinage that, during the time of the NT, was considered equivalent to the Roman denarius. In 300 BC a sheep cost one drachma, but apparently by NT times the drachma was worth much less.

DRAGNET Large fishing net equipped with a weighted bottom edge for touching ("dragging") the river or lake bottom and a top with wooden floats allowing the net to be spread across the water (Isa. 19:8). Jesus compared the kingdom of God to a dragnet, containing both good and bad fish until the time of separation and judgment (Matt. 13:47).

DRAGON Symbol of Satan in the NT. Revelation described it as a great, red monster with seven heads and ten horns. As in the OT texts, the dragon is put under guard (Rev. 20:1-3; Job 7:12) and later released for final destruction (Rev. 20:7-10; Isa. 27:1).

DRAWERS OF WATER Water carriers (Josh. 9:21,23,27).

DRESSER OF SYCAMORE TREES One of the occupations of the prophet Amos (Amos 7:14). The tending involved slitting the top of each piece of fruit to hasten its ripening and to produce a sweeter, more edible fruit.

DRIED GRAPES Raisins. Grapes were dried in clusters for a food that was easily stored and transported (1 Sam. 25:18; 30:12; 2 Sam. 16:1; 1 Chron. 12:40). Nazarites were prohibited from eating dried grapes (Num. 6:3).

DROMEDARY One-humped species of camel.

DROPSY Edema, a disease with fluid retention and swelling. Thus the TEV speaks of a man whose arms and legs were swollen (Luke 14:2).

DRUNKENNESS Result of consuming a quantity of alcohol; the outcome being the impairment of faculties. This impairment may be mild (deep sleep) to severe (dizziness, vomiting, hallucination, and death). There are many cases of drunkenness in the OT. In the NT the Lord explicitly warned against the use of alcohol (Luke 21:34). In Paul's letters there are numerous warnings against the indulgence of alcohol (1 Cor. 5:11; 6:10; Gal. 5:21; Eph. 5:18).

DRUSILLA Wife of Felix, the Roman governor of Judea who heard Paul's case. Drusilla was a Jew and listened to Paul's arguments with her husband (Acts 24:24).

DULCIMER Apparently a Greek word used to name a musical instrument in Dan. 3:10. Many think the bagpipes are meant here (NASB). NRSV translates "drum."

DUMAH Place-name meaning "silence" or "permanent settlement." **1.** Son of Ishmael and the original ancestor of the Arabian tribe (Gen. 25:14) centered in the oases of Dumah, probably modern el-Gof, also called Dumat el-Gandel, meaning Dumah of the Rocks. **2.** City of the tribe of Judah (Josh. 15:52). It is probably modern Khirbet ed-Dome about nine miles southwest of Hebron. It may be mentioned in the Amarna letters.

DUNG Excrement of man or beast. "Dung" translates several different Hebrew and Greek words. An ash heap or rubbish heap was used to convey the haunt of the destitute (1 Sam. 2:8; Luke 14:35).

DUNG GATE Jerusalem landmark in the time of Nehemiah (Neh. 2:13; 3:13-14; 12:31). Located at the southwest corner of the wall, the gate was used for the disposal of garbage that was dumped into the Hinnom Valley below. Referred to as the Refuse Gate by KJV, NASB, and Rubbish Gate by TEV.

DURA Akkadian place-name meaning "circuit wall." Plain in Babylonia where King Nebuchadnez- zar set up a mammoth golden image of a god or of himself (Dan. 3:1). The common place-name does not lend itself to an exact location.

DYEING Process of coloring materials. The dying process is not mentioned in Scripture, though dyed material is.

DYSENTERY Disease characterized by diarrhea, painful bowel spasms, and ulceration and infection of the bowels resulting in blood and pus in the excreta. Modern speech translations of Acts 28:8 render the "bloody flux" of the KJV as dysentery.

The Dung Gate in old Jerusalem.

EAGLE The term "eagle" refers to several large birds of prey active in the daytime rather than at night. The Hebrew term translated "eagle" (*nesher*) also sometimes is translated "vulture." In Exod. 19:4 and Deut. 32:11 the eagle is used figuratively of God's protection and care.

EAR Physical organ of hearing. The ears appear in a variety of expressions in both Testaments. To incline the ear was to listen (2 Kings 19:16) or even to obey (Jer. 11:8). To give ear was to pay careful attention (Job 32:11). Sometimes

The mountainous landscape of the land of Edom.

the functions of the mind were attributed to the ear. Thus the ear exercised judgment (Job 12:11) and understanding (13:1).

EARNEST Sincerity and intensity of purpose (Luke 22:44; Jude 3) or a deposit paid to secure a purchase (2 Cor. 1:22; 5:5; Eph. 1:14).

EARTHQUAKE Shaking or trembling of the earth due to volcanic activity or, more often, the shifting of the earth's crust. Severe earthquakes produce such side effects as loud rumblings (Ezek. 3:12-13 RSV), openings in the earth's crust (Num. 16:32) and fires (Rev. 8:5).The Bible mentions an earthquake during the reign of Uzziah (Amos 1:1; Zech. 14:5). The oracles of Amos are dated two years before this earthquake.

EAST GATE This designation refers to three different gates. **1.** KJV refers to the East Gate of Jerusalem as leading to the Hinnom Valley (Jer. 19:2). **2.** The East Gate of the outer court of the temple. Since the temple faced east, this gate was the main entrance to the temple complex (Ezek. 47:1). **3.** The East Gate of the inner court of the temple. This gate was closed on the six working days but open on the Sabbath (Ezek. 46:1).

EAST SEA Ezekiel's expression for the Dead Sea (Ezek. 47:18).

EASTER The special celebration of the resurrection at Easter is the oldest Christian festival, except for the weekly Sunday celebration. In the early centuries the annual observance was called the *pascha*, the Greek word for Passover, and focused on Christ as the paschal Lamb.

EBAL Personal name and place-name possibly meaning "bare." **1.** Grandson of Seir and son of clan leader Shobal among the Horite descendants living in Edom (Gen. 36:23). **2.** Son of Joktan in line of Shem (1 Chron. 1:22). He is called Obal in Gen. 10:28 through a scribal copying change. **3.** Mountain near Shechem on which Moses set up the curse for the covenant ceremony (Deut. 11:29; 27:13).

EBED Personal name meaning "servant." **1.** Father of Gaal, who led revolt in Shechem against Abimelech (Judg. 9:26-40). **2.** Clan leader who returned from exile under Ezra (Ezra 8:6).

EBED-MELECH Personal name meaning "servant of the king." An Ethiopian eunuch in the service of King Zedekiah of Judah (Jer. 38:7).

EBENEZER Personal name meaning "stone of help." The name of a site near Aphek where the Israelites camped before they fought in battle against the Philistines (1 Sam. 4:1).

EBER Personal name meaning "the opposite side." **1.** The ancestor of Abraham and the Hebrew people, and a descendant of Shem (Gen. 10:21-25; 11:14-17). **2.** A member of the tribe of Gad, called Heber by KJV (1 Chron. 5:13). The name entered Israel's record about 750 BC (v. 17). **3.** Clan leader in tribe of Benjamin (1 Chron. 8:12). **4.** Another clan leader of Benjamin (1 Chron. 8:22). **5.** Head of priestly family of Amok (Neh. 12:20) in days of Jehoiakim (609–597 BC).

EBIASAPH Personal name meaning "my father has collected or taken in." A Levite descended from Kohath (1 Chron. 6:23).

EBLA Major ancient site located in Syria about 40 miles south of Aleppo. The discovery of over 17,000 clay tablets in the mid-1970's revealed a major Syrian civilization in the mid-third millennium and brought the site worldwide prominence by the late 1970s. Valuable general information can be gleaned from Ebla for the study of the Bible. Ebla was a major religious center, and over 500 gods are mentioned in the texts. The chief god was Dagon, a vegetation deity associated in the Bible with the Philistines (1 Sam. 5:2).

EBRON City in territory of Asher (Josh. 19:28), spelled Hebron in KJV. Several manuscripts in Josh. 19:28 plus the lists in Josh. 21:30; 1 Chron. 6:74 have Abdon.

ECBATANA Modern translation spelling of Achmetha. Capital of the ancient Median empire, located in the Zagros Mountains in western Iran (Ezra 6:2).

ECCLESIASTES, BOOK OF Classified along with Job and Proverbs as one of the OT wisdom books. Traditionally Solomon has been identified as the author of Ecclesiastes.
Theme Probably no biblical book is so dominated by one leading theme as is Ecclesiastes. In 1:2 the author declares that "everything is meaningless" (NIV) or better, "vanity" (KJV, NRSV, NASB, NKJV, ASV). The Hebrew word translated "meaningless" or "vanity" is *hevel* (literally, "breath"), the key word in the book.
Interpretation Of all the books in the Bible, Ecclesiastes is usually considered to be the most problematic. The work has been called pessimistic, shocking, unorthodox, and even heretical. For example, certain statements in the book have been interpreted to deny life-after-death (3:18-21; 9:5-6,10). Yet, when these passages are considered in light of the overall theme of the book, it becomes clear that the author is not denying the existence of the human spirit after death but is stating an obvious fact: at death earthly life (life "under the sun") with its joys, sorrows, and opportunities is over. Earthly possessions and mere worldly endeavors are temporary and have no eternal value for believers or nonbelievers. Only what is done for God will endure (12:13-14).

ED Place-name meaning "witness." Altar that the tribes assigned territory east of the Jordan built as a witness that Yahweh is God of both the eastern and western tribes. The building resulted in a dispute between the two groups of tribes, but Phinehas, the priest, helped settle the dispute, ensuring the altar was a symbol and would not be used for burnt offering (Josh. 22:34). NASB, NIV, NRSV read "witness."

EDEN Garden of God. "Eden" appears 20 times in the OT but never in the NT. Fourteen appearances refer to the idyllic place of creation. In Genesis (2:8,10,15; 3:23-24; 4:16) the reference is to the region in which a garden was placed. Though details seem precise, identification of the rivers that flow from the river issuing forth from Eden cannot be accomplished with certainty. The Euphrates and the Tigris can be identified, but there is no agreement on the location of the Pishon and the Gihon.

EDER Place- and personal name meaning "water puddle" or "herd." **1.** Tower near Bethlehem (Gen. 35:21; cp. v. 19). The exact location is not known. Micah referred to Jerusalem as the "tower of the flock," the same Hebrew expression as in Genesis (Mic. 4:8). **2.** A town in the southern limits of the tribal territory of Judah near Edom (Josh. 15:21). Its location is not known. **3.** A Levite of the clan of Merari (1 Chron. 23:23; 24:30). **4.** A leader of the tribe of Benjamin (1 Chron. 8:15); KJV spelling is Ader.

EDOM Area southeast and southwest of the Dead Sea, on opposite sides of the Arabah, was known as Edom in biblical times and was the home of the Edomites. The name "Edom" derives from a Semitic root that means "red" or "ruddy" and characterizes the red sandstone terrain of much of the area in question. The Israelites regarded the Edomites as close relatives, even more closely related to them than the Ammonites or Moabites. According to the biblical writers, enmity between Israel and Edom began with Jacob and Esau (when the former stole the latter's birthright) and was exacerbated at the time of the Israelite exodus from Egypt (when the Edomites refused the Israelites passage through their land). Be that as it may, much of the conflict also had to do with the fact that Edom was a constant threat to Judah's frontier and moreover blocked Judean access to the Gulf of Aqaba.

EDREI Place-name of unknown meaning. **1.** Royal city of Og, king of Bashan (Josh. 12:4). Invading Israel defeated Og there (Num. 21:33-35). It is also known from Egyptian records. Its location is modern Dera, halfway between Damascus and Amman. The clan of Machir in the tribe of Manasseh laid claim to the city (Josh. 13:31). **2.** Fortified city in the tribal territory of Naphtali (Josh. 19:37).

EGLAH Personal name meaning "heifer, young cow." David's wife and mother of his son Ithream (2 Sam. 3:5).

EGLAIM Place-name meaning "two cisterns." Place in Moab used by Isaiah to describe far limits of Moab's distress. It is modern Rugm el-Gilimeh, southeast of el-Kerak. It is distinct in location and Hebrew spelling from En-eglaim (Ezek. 47:10).

EGLATH-SHELISHIYAH Place-name meaning "the third heifer." Place apparently in Moab where Moab fugitives fled in Isaiah's description of disaster (Isa. 15:5).

EGLON 1. Moabite king who oppressed the Israelites (Judg. 3:12). Aided by the Amalekites and Ammonites, Eglon dominated Israel for 18 years. He was finally slain by the Benjamite judge Ehud, who ran the obese monarch through with a short sword. **2.** Canaanite city whose king entered an alliance with four other Canaanite rulers against Gibeon (Josh. 10:3).

EGYPT Land in northeastern Africa, home to one of the earliest civilizations, and an important cultural and political influence on ancient Israel.

Egypt lies at the northeastern corner of Africa, separated from Palestine by the Sinai wilderness. In contrast to the modern nation, ancient Egypt was confined to the Nile River Valley, a long, narrow ribbon of fertile land (the "black land") surrounded by uninhabitable desert (the "red land"). Egypt proper, from the first cataract of the Nile to the Mediterranean, is some 750 miles long.

From the Middle Kingdom (2040–1786 BC) onward, Egyptian history is contemporary with biblical events. Abraham's brief sojourn in Egypt (Gen. 12:10-20) during

Air view of the Nile Valley taken near Thebes. Notice the dramatic difference between the lands nourished by the Nile River and the deserts that surround the valley.

this period may be understood in light of a tomb painting at Beni Hasan showing visiting Asiatics in Egypt about 1900 BC.

Six centuries later, documents from Akhetaton, the Amarna Letters, represent diplomatic correspondence between local rulers in Egypt's sphere of influence and pharaoh's court. They especially illuminate the turbulent situation in Canaan which, depending upon one's preference for a fifteenth or thirteenth century date for the exodus, could be a century after or prior to the Israelite invasion.

EHI Personal name meaning "my brother." A son of Benjamin (Gen. 46:21), but he does not appear in the lists of Benjamin's sons in Num. 26:38-40; 1 Chron. 8:1-2.

EHUD Personal name meaning "unity, powerful." **1.** A left-handed Benjamite whom the Lord raised up to deliver the Israelites from Moabite oppression (Judg. 3:15). By a ruse he gained access to the Moabite King Eglon and assassinated him. **2.** Great grandson of Benjamin and clan leader in that tribe (1 Chron. 7:10). **3.** Clan leader in tribe of Benjamin who originally lived in Geba but were deported by someone unknown to Manahath (1 Chron. 8:6).

EKER Personal name meaning "root" or "offspring." Son of Jerahmeel and grandson of Hezron in the tribe of Judah (1 Chron. 2:27).

EKRON Northernmost of the five major Philistine cities known as the Pentapolis. Judges 1:18 reports that Judah captured Ekron along with other parts of the Philistine coast, but Ekron was certainly in Philistine hands at the time the ark was captured (1 Sam. 5:10). It was also the place to which the Philistines retreated after David slew Goliath (1 Sam. 17:52). Ahaziah, the son of King Ahab of Israel, called on the god of Ekron, Baal-zebub, when he was sick (2 Kings 1:2-16).

EL One of several words for God found in biblical Hebrew and the name of the high god among the Canaanites. The word is common to Hebrew, Aramaic, and Arabic, yet the origin and root from which the word was derived are obscure. "*El*" is a general term that expresses majesty or power. It occurs 238 times in the OT, most frequently in Psalms and Job. "El" is a synonym for the more frequent noun for God: Elohim. "El" refers to the God of Israel and in other passages to one of the pagan gods. "El" was frequently combined with nouns or adjectives to express the name for God with reference to particular attributes or characteristics of His being.

ELA Personal name of unknown meaning, perhaps related either to *'el*, Hebrew word for God, or to Elah, a slightly different Hebrew spelling not noted in KJV. Father of one of Solomon's district superintendents (1 Kings 4:18).

ELAH Personal name and place-name meaning "oak," "mighty tree," or "terebinth." **1.** Clan chief descended from Esau (Gen. 36:41) and thus an Edomite. **2.** A valley where Saul and his army set up battle lines against the Philistines (1 Sam. 17:2). The valley runs east and west just north of Socoh. There David defeated Goliath (1 Sam. 21:9). **3.** King of Israel (732–723 BC), killed while he was drunk during rebellion that Zimri, his general, led successfully (1 Kings 16:6-14). **4.** Father of Hoshea, who led a revolt and became king of Israel (732–723 BC) (2 Kings 15:30). **5.** Son of Caleb and father of Kenaz among clans of Judah (1 Chron. 4:15). **6.** Head of a clan from Benjamin who settled in Jerusalem after the exile (1 Chron. 9:8).

ELAM Personal name and place-name. **1.** Elam was a son of Shem, one of the sons of Noah (Gen. 10:22; 1 Chron. 1:17). He may have given his name to the region known as Elam. **2.** The region of Elam is on the western edge of ancient Persia, modern Iran. **3.** Clan head of tribe of Benjamin living in Jerusalem (1 Chron. 8:24). **4.** Priestly gatekeeper under David (1 Chron. 26:3). **5.** Two clan leaders among the exiles who returned to Jerusalem with Zerubbabel in 537 BC (Ezra 2:7,31; cp. 8:7; 10:2,26). **6.** Post-exilic leader who signed Nehemiah's covenant to obey God (Neh. 10:14). **7.** Priest who helped Nehemiah lead the people in celebrating the completion of the Jerusalem wall (Neh. 12:42).

ELASAH Personal name meaning "God has made." **1.** Son of Shaphan, the royal scribe. He took Jeremiah's message to the exiled community in Babylon while on a mission for King Zedekiah (Jer. 29:3). **2.** Descendant of Jerahmeel in tribe of Judah (1 Chron. 2:39-40); spelled "Eleasah" in English translations. **3.** Descendant of Saul and Jonathan in tribe of Benjamin (1 Chron. 8:37; cp. 9:43); spelled "Eleasah" in English translations. **4.** Priest with a foreign wife who agreed to divorce her to avoid temptation of foreign gods in the time of Ezra (Ezra 10:22).

ELATH or **ELOTH** Place-name meaning "ram," "mighty trees," or "terebinth." Port city on northern end of Red Sea. Israel passed through it on way through Edom in wilderness (Deut. 2:8).

EL-BERITH Name of a god meaning "god of the covenant." A god worshipped in a temple at Shechem. It had a stronghold or citadel guarding it. There the citizens of Shechem sought protection when Abimelech attacked them, but Abimelech set the citadel on fire (Judg. 9:46-49). KJV translates "god Berith."

EL-BETHEL Place-name meaning "god of the house of El (god)." Either Bethel or place in or near Bethel, where Jacob built an altar to God as memorial to his previous visit to Bethel when he had seen a vision of God (Gen. 35:7; cp. 28:10-19). Apparently the name used for God was used as a place-name.

ELDAAH Personal name meaning "God has called," "God has sought," or "God of wisdom." Son of Midian and grandson of Abraham thus original ancestor of clan of Midianites (Gen. 25:4).

ELDAD Personal name meaning "God loved." Along with Medad, he was one of 70 elders of Israel that God selected to help Moses, but the two did not meet at the tabernacle with the others. Still the Spirit came upon Eldad and Medad in the camp, and they prophesied. Joshua attempted to stop them, but Moses prayed that all God's people might have the Spirit (Num. 11:16-29).

ELDER Prominent member of both Jewish and early Christian communities. In the OT, "elder" usually translates the Hebrew word *zaqen* from a root that means "beard" or "chin." In the NT, the Greek word is *presbuteros*, which is transliterated in English as "presbyter" and from which the word "priest" was derived.

ELEAD Personal name meaning "God is a witness." Member of tribe of Ephraim killed by men of Gath for stealing their cattle (1 Chron. 7:21).

ELEADAH Personal name meaning "God adorned Himself." Modern translation spelling for KJV Eladah, a descendant of Ephraim (1 Chron. 7:20).

ELEALEH Moabite place-name meaning "God went up" or "high ground." Town that tribe of Reuben requested from Moses and strengthened (Num. 32:3,37). Isaiah announced judgment on the town (Isa. 15:4; 16:9; cp. Jer. 48:34).

ELEASAH Personal name meaning "God acted," or "God made," using same Hebrew spelling as Elasah. **1.** Member of clan of Jerahmeel in tribe of Judah (1 Chron. 2:39-40). **2.** Descendant of Saul and Jonathan in tribe of Benjamin (1 Chron. 8:37; 9:43).

ELEAZAR Personal name meaning "God helps." **1.** The third son of Aaron (Exod. 6:23) and high priest of Israel (Num. 20:28). **2.** Son of Abinadab who was sanctified by the men of Kirjath-jearim to have responsibility for the ark of the Lord (1 Sam. 7:1). **3.** One of David's renowned warriors, the son of Dodo (2 Sam. 23:9). **4.** Son of Mahli who died having had no sons, but only daughters (1 Chron. 23:21-22). **5.** Son of Phinehas who assisted in weighing out the silver and gold utensils in the house of God (Ezra 8:33). **6.** One of the sons of Parosh in a list of persons who had married foreign wives. He later put away his wife because of Ezra's reform banning foreign marriage (Ezra 10:25). **7.** Musician involved in the dedication of the wall of Jerusalem (Neh. 12:42). **8.** Son of Eliud and father of Matthan. He was an ancestor of Joseph the husband of Mary (Matt. 1:15).

ELECT LADY Recipient of John's second letter (2 John 1) sometimes understood to be an individual, but the phrase probably is a way of referring to a local church congregation.

ELECTION God's plan to bring salvation to His people and His world. The doctrine of election is at once one of the most central and one of the most misunderstood teachings of the Bible. At its most basic level, election refers to the purpose or plan of God whereby He has determined to effect His will. Thus election encompasses the entire range of divine activity from creation, God's decision to bring the world into being out of nothing, to the end time, the making anew of heaven and earth. The word "election" itself is derived from the Greek word, *eklegomai*, which means, literally, "to choose something for oneself." This in turn corresponds to the Hebrew word, *bachar*. The objects of divine selection are the elect ones, a concept found with increasing frequency in the later writings of the OT and at many places in the NT (Matt. 22:14; Luke 18:7; Col. 3:12; Rev. 17:14). The Bible also uses other words such as "choose," "predestinate," "foreordain," "determine," and "call" to indicate that God has entered into a special relationship with certain individuals and groups through whom He has decided to fulfill His purpose within the history of salvation.

EL-ELOHE-ISRAEL Divine name meaning "God, the God of Israel." Name that Jacob gave the altar he set up in the land he bought near Shechem (Gen. 33:20).

ELEMENTS, ELEMENTARY SPIRITS Greek term (*ta stoicheia*) used in a number of ways in ancient sources and in the NT.

First, "elements" could refer to the primary or elementary points of learning, especially for a religion or philosophy. Second, the term could refer to the four basic elements out of which all other materials were thought to have emerged: fire, air, water, and earth. Finally, the term came to be used in association with "elementary spirit-beings" who were thought by some to exercise a certain amount of control over the heavenly bodies—either for good or evil.

ELEPHANTS While elephants are not specifically referred to in the Bible, ivory is mentioned in connection with King Solomon, that ivory was among the riches he imported (1 Kings 10:22). Ivory tusks were used in trading among nations in Ezek. 27:15, and in Rev. 18:12 ivory is again mentioned among products traded or bought. See *Ivory*.

ELHANAN Personal name meaning "God is gracious." The Bethlehemite who slew the brother of Goliath (2 Sam. 21:19).

ELI Personal name meaning "high." The priest at Shiloh who became the custodian of the child Samuel (1 Sam. 1:3). He was the father of Hophni and Phinehas. Eli's death was precipitated by the news of the death of his sons and the capture of the ark of God by the Philistines (1 Sam. 4:18).

ELI, ELI, LAMA SABACHTHANI This cry of Jesus on the cross, traditionally known as the "fourth word from the cross," means "My God, My God, why have You forsaken Me?" (Matt. 27:46; Mark 15:34 HCSB). It is a quotation from Ps. 22:1. The Markan form, *Eloi*, is closer to

Aramaic than Matthew's more Hebraic *Eli.*

ELIAB Personal name meaning "God is father." **1.** Leader of tribe of Zebulun under Moses (Num. 1:9). He brought the tribe's offering at the dedication of the altar (Num. 7:24). **2.** Member of tribe of Reuben and father of Dathan and Abiram. **3.** First son of Jesse to pass by and be rejected when Samuel searched for king to replace Saul (1 Sam. 16:6). **4.** Levite in the line of Kohath and ancestor of Samuel (1 Chron. 6:27). The same person is apparently called Elihu in 1 Sam. 1:1 and Eliel in 1 Chron. 6:34. **5.** Levite appointed as a temple musician under David (1 Chron. 15:18,20; 16:5). **6.** Military leader from the tribe of Gad under David (1 Chron. 12:9).

ELIADA Personal name meaning "God has known." **1.** Son born to David after he established his rule in Jerusalem (2 Sam. 5:16). In 1 Chron. 14:7 he is listed as Beeliada ("Baal has known" or "the lord has known"). **2.** Father of Rezon, who established himself as king of Damascus after David conquered Zobah (1 Kings 11:23). **3.** Military commander of the tribe of Benjamin (2 Chron. 17:17) under King Jehoshaphat (873–848 BC).

ELIAHBA Personal name meaning "God hides in safety" or "my god is Chiba." A leading soldier in David's army (2 Sam. 23:32).

ELIAKIM Personal name meaning "God will raise up." **1.** Son of Hilkiah who was in charge of the household of King Hezekiah of Judah (2 Kings 18:18). **2.** Son of Josiah who was placed on the throne of Judah by Pharaoh Neco of Egypt (2 Kings 23:34). **3.** Priest who was involved in the dedication of the wall of Jerusalem (Neh. 12:41). **4.** Ancestor of Joseph, the husband of Mary (Matt. 1:13). **5.** Son of Melea, mentioned in Luke's genealogy of Jesus (Luke 3:30).

ELIAM Personal name meaning "God is an uncle or relative" or "God of the people." **1.** Father of Bathsheba (2 Sam. 11:3). The two parts of his name are reversed in 1 Chron. 3:5, becoming Ammiel. **2.** Leading warrior under David (2 Sam. 23:34).

ELIASAPH Personal name meaning "God has added." **1.** Leader of the tribe of Gad under Moses (Num. 1:14). **2.** Levite of the family of Gershon (Num. 3:24).

ELIASHIB Personal name meaning "God repays or leads back." **1.** Descendant of David in Judah after the return from exile in Babylon (1 Chron. 3:24). **2.** Leading priest under David (1 Chron. 24:12). **3.** High priest in time of Nehemiah who led in rebuilding the sheep gate in the Jerusalem wall (Neh. 3:1). **4.** Priest in the time of Nehemiah who administered the temple storerooms and provided a place for Tobiah, Nehemiah's strong opponent (Neh. 13:4-9). This may be the Eliashib of Ezra 10:6. **5.** Levite and temple singer in Ezra's day who agreed to divorce his foreign wife to avoid tempting Israel to worship other gods (Ezra 10:24). **6.** Two Israelites who agreed to divorce their foreign wives under Ezra's leadership (Ezra 10:27,36).

ELIATHAH Personal name meaning "my God has come." A temple musician appointed under David to play and prophesy (1 Chron. 25:4).

ELIDAD Personal name meaning "God loved" or "My God is uncle or friend." The name in Hebrew is a variant spelling of Eldad. Representative of tribe of Benjamin on committee that God chose to help Joshua and Eleazar divide the land of Canaan among the tribes (Num. 34:21).

ELIEHOENAI Personal name meaning "to Yaho are my eyes" (cp. Ps. 123:2). **1.** One of the temple porters or gatekeepers under David (1 Chron. 26:3). **2.** One of the 12 clan heads who returned to Jerusalem from Babylon with Ezra (Ezra 8:4).

ELIEL Personal name meaning "my God is God" or "my God is El." **1.** Clan leader in the tribe of Manasseh east of the Jordan River (1 Chron. 5:23-24). **2.** Levite and ancestor of the singer Heman (1 Chron. 6:34). **3.** Member of the tribe of Benjamin (1 Chron. 8:20). **4.** Another Benjaminite (1 Chron. 8:22). **5.** Military leader under David (1 Chron. 11:46), not listed in 1 Sam. 23. **6.** Another military leader under David not listed in 1 Sam. 23 (1 Chron. 11:47). **7.** Warrior from the tribe of Gad who served under David in the wilderness (1 Chron. 12:11). **8.** Chief Levite in the time of David (1 Chron. 15:9,11). **9.** Overseer of temple offerings among the Levites (2 Chron. 31:13) under King Hezekiah (715–686 BC).

ELIENAI Abbreviated form of the Hebrew personal name Eliehoenai. The abbreviated form's literal meaning is "my God my eyes." A member of the tribe of Benjamin (1 Chron. 8:20).

ELIEZER Personal name meaning "God helps." **1.** Servant of Abram who would have been the patriarch's heir if Abram had remained childless (Gen. 15:2). **2.** Second son of Moses and Zipporah (Exod. 18:4). **3.** One of the sons of Becher the Benjamite (1 Chron. 7:8). **4.** One of the priests who blew the trumpets when the ark of the covenant was brought to Jerusalem (1 Chron. 15:24). **5.** A ruler of the Reubenites (1 Chron. 27:16). **6.** Son of Dodavah, who prophesied against Jehoshaphat (2 Chron. 20:37). **7.** One of the leaders whom Ezra sent for (Ezra 8:16). **8.** Priest who put away his foreign wife (Ezra 10:18). **9.** Levite who put away his foreign wife (Ezra 10:23). **10.** Member of the clan of Harim who put away his foreign wife (Ezra 10:31). **11.** Son of Jorim mentioned in the genealogy of Jesus (Luke 3:29).

ELIHOREPH Personal name meaning "my God repays," or "my God is the giver of the autumn harvest," or borrowed from Egyptian, "Apis is my God." One of Solomon's two royal scribes with his brother Ahijah (1 Kings 4:3).

ELIHU Personal name meaning "he is God." **1.** Son of Barachel the Buzite who addressed Job after the latter's first three friends had ended their speeches (Job 32:2). **2.** Samuel's great grandfather (1 Sam. 1:1). **3.** Member of tribe of Manasseh who defected to David (1 Chron. 12:20). **4.** Mighty military hero under David (1 Chron. 26:7). **5.** David's brother in charge of the tribe of Judah (1 Chron. 27:18).

ELIJAH Personal name meaning "my God is Yah." The prophet from the ninth century BC from Tishbe of Gilead in the northern kingdom has been called the grandest and the most romantic character that Israel ever produced (1 Kings 17:1–2 Kings 2:18). He was a complex man of the desert who counseled kings. His life is best understood when considered from four historical perspectives that at times are interrelated: his miracles, his struggle against baalism, his prophetic role, and his relationship to Messiah. Elijah appeared along with Moses on the Mount of Transfiguration with Jesus to discuss His "departure."

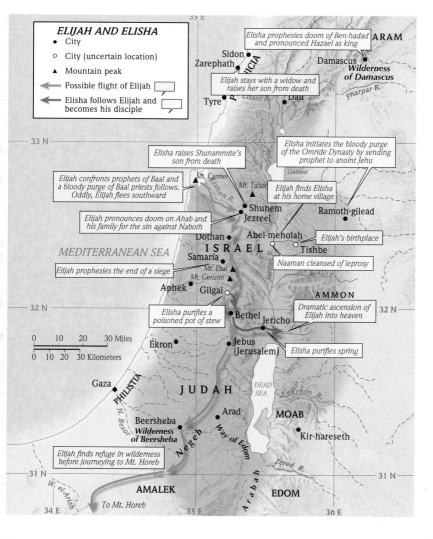

ELIJAH AND ELISHA

- City
- City (uncertain location)
- ▲ Mountain peak
- ← Possible flight of Elijah
- ← Elisha follows Elijah and becomes his disciple

Elisha prophesies doom of Ben-hadad and pronounced Hazael as king

Elijah stays with a widow and raises her son from death

Elisha raises Shunammite's son from death

Elisha initiates the bloody purge of the Omride Dynasty by sending prophet to anoint Jehu

Elijah confronts prophets of Baal and a bloody purge of Baal priests follows. Oddly, Elijah flees southward

Elijah finds Elisha at his home village

Elijah pronounces doom on Ahab and his family for the sin against Naboth

Elijah's birthplace

Naaman cleansed of leprosy

Elijah prophesies the end of a siege

Elisha purifies a poisoned pot of stew

Dramatic ascension of Elijah into heaven

Elisha purifies spring

Elijah finds refuge in wilderness before journeying to Mt. Horeb

ELIKA Personal name meaning "my God has arisen" or "my God has vomited." One of David's military heroes from the village of Harod (2 Sam. 23:25).

ELIM Place-name meaning "trees." One of the encampments of the Israelites after the exodus from Egypt (Exod. 15:27). It was the first place where they found water.

ELIMELECH Personal name meaning "my God is king." Husband of Naomi, who led his family from Bethlehem to Moab to escape famine and then died in Moab. This prepared the scene for the book of Ruth (Ruth 1:2-3; cp. 4:3).

ELIOENAI Personal name meaning "to Yo [Yahweh] are my eyes," a Hebrew spelling variant of Eliehoenai. **1.** Post-exilic descendant of David, maintaining Israel's royal line (1 Chron. 3:23-24). **2.** Clan leader of the tribe of Simeon (1 Chron. 4:36). **3.** Grandson of Benjamin and thus great grandson of Jacob (1 Chron. 7:8). **4.** Priest who agreed under Ezra's leadership to divorce his foreign wife to protect the community from false worship (Ezra 10:22). **5.** Israelite who agreed to divorce his foreign wife (Ezra 10:27). **6.** Priest who led in the service of dedication and thanksgiving for the completion of repairs of the wall around Jerusalem (Neh. 12:41).

ELIPHAL Personal name meaning "God has judged." Military hero under David (1 Chron. 11:35). In 2 Sam. 23:34 the name appears as Eliphelet.

ELIPHAZ Personal name meaning "my god is gold." **1.** Son of Esau by his wife Adah, the daughter of Elon the Hittite (Gen. 36:4). **2.** One of three men who visited Job and engaged the sufferer in dialogue (Job 2:11). He is identified as a Temanite, meaning he was from Teman in Edom.

ELIPHELEH (KJV) or **ELIPHELEHU** Personal name meaning "God treated him with distinction." Levite and musician in temple under David (1 Chron. 15:18,21).

ELIPHELET Personal name meaning "God is deliverance." **1.** David's son born in Jerusalem (2 Sam. 5:16). He is apparently listed twice in both 1 Chron. 3:6,8 and 14:5,7, with an abbreviated Hebrew spelling in 14:5. **2.** Descendant of Saul and Jonathan in the tribe of Benjamin (1 Chron. 8:39). **3.** Clan leader who accompanied Ezra on his return from exile in Babylon (Ezra 8:13). **4.** Man who divorced his foreign wife under Ezra's leadership to avoid false worship among God's people (Ezra 10:33). **5.** Famous warrior under David (2 Sam. 23:34).

ELISABETH Personal name meaning "my God is good fortune" or "my God has sworn an oath." A woman descended from Aaron who was the wife of Zacharias the priest (Luke 1:5) and mother of John the Baptist.

ELISHA Personal name meaning "my God is salvation." A ninth century BC Israelite prophet, son of Shaphat of Abel-meholah (1 Kings 19:16). Elisha was plowing one day when "Elijah passed over to him and threw his mantle on him" (1 Kings 19:19 NASB). This action symbolically manifested God's plan to bestow the prophetic powers of Elijah upon Elisha. The chosen one understood the call of God for "he left the oxen and ran after Elijah" (1 Kings 19:20). That Elisha felt the call of prophetic succession is again clear following Elijah's dramatic ascent into heaven. There Elisha "took up the mantle of Elijah that fell from him" (2 Kings 2:13).The beginning of Elisha's ministry should be dated to the last years of King Ahab's rule (1 Kings 19) or approximately 850 BC.

ELISHAH Place-name of unknown meaning. Elishah, or Alashiya as it appears in Hittite, Akkadian, and Ugaritic texts, is a name for all or part of the island of Cyprus, which exported copper and purple cloth.

ELISHAMA Personal name meaning "God heard." **1.** Leader of the tribe of Ephraim under Moses in the wilderness (Num. 1:10). **2.** David's son born after he captured and moved to Jerusalem (2 Sam. 5:16). He is apparently listed twice in 1 Chron. 3:6,8, though 1 Chron. 14:5 reads the first Elishama as Elishua, as in 2 Sam. 5:15. **3.** Royal scribe under King Jehoiakim (609–597 BC). Baruch's scroll of Jeremiah's preaching was stored in Elishama's room before it was taken to be read to the king (Jer. 36:12-21). **4.** Ancestor with royal bloodlines of Ishmael, the person who murdered Gedaliah and took over political control of Judah immediately after Babylon had destroyed Jerusalem (2 Kings 25:25). **5.** Descendant of the clan of Jerahmeel in the tribe of Judah (1 Chron. 2:41). **6.** Priest under King Jehoshaphat (873–848 BC). He taught the book of the law to the people of Judah at the king's request (2 Chron. 17:7-9).

ELISHAPHAT Personal name meaning "God had judged." Military captain who helped Jehoiada the priest, overthrow Queen Athaliah and establish Joash (835–796 BC) as king of Judah (2 Chron. 23:1).

ELISHEBA Personal name meaning "God is good fortune." Wife of Aaron, the high priest (Exod. 6:23).

ELISHUA Personal name meaning "God is salvation." David's son born after he captured and moved to Jerusalem (2 Sam. 5:15).

ELIUD Personal name meaning "God is high and mighty." Great, great grandfather of Joseph, the earthly father of Jesus (Matt. 1:14-15).

ELIZABETH Americanized spelling used in modern translations of KJV Elisabeth.

ELIZAPHAN Personal name meaning "God has hidden or treasured up." **1.** Clan leader among the sons of Kohath among the Levites in the wilderness with Moses (Num. 3:30; cp. 1 Chron. 15:8; 2 Chron. 29:13). **2.** Representative of tribe of Zebulun on the council to help Joshua and Eleazar divide the land among the tribes (Num. 34:25).

ELIZUR Personal name meaning "God is a rock." Leader of tribe of Reuben under Moses in the wilderness (Num. 1:5). He presented the tribe's offerings at the dedication of the altar (Num. 7:30-35).

ELKANAH Personal name meaning "God created." **1.** One of the sons of Korah, the priest (Exod. 6:24). **2.** Son of Jeroham. He became the father of Samuel (1 Sam. 1:1). **3.** Person named in a list of Levites (1 Chron. 6:23-26). **4.** Father of Asa who is mentioned in a list of Levites (1 Chron. 9:16). **5.** Benjaminite warrior who deserted Saul and joined David (1 Chron. 12:6). **6.** One of two gate-keepers for the ark of the covenant (1 Chron. 15:23). **7.** An official in the service of King Ahaz of Judah who was assassinated by Zichri the Ephraimite (2 Chron. 28:7).

ELKOSH Place-name of unknown meaning. Home of Nahum the prophet (Nah. 1:1). Although several traditions exist that identify various places as the site of Elkosh, its location remains unknown. That it was in Judea is fairly likely.

ELLASAR Babylonian place-name of unknown meaning. The capital city of King Arioch, who joined the eastern coalition against Sodom and Gomorrah, resulting in Abraham's involvement in war (Gen. 14:1).

ELMADAM or **ELMODAM** (KJV) Personal name of unknown meaning. An ancestor of Jesus Christ (Luke 3:28).

ELNAAM Personal name meaning "God is a delight." Father of military leaders under David (1 Chron. 11:46). He is not listed in 2 Sam. 23.

ELNATHAN Personal name meaning "God has given." **1.** Father of King Jehoiachin's mother (2 Kings 24:8). **2.** Possibly to be identified with 1. He was the member of King Jehoiakim's advisory staff who brought the prophet Uriah back to the king from Egypt for punishment (Jer. 26:22-23). He tried to prevent the king from burning Baruch's scroll of Jeremiah's preaching (Jer. 36:12-26). **3.** Three men of the same name plus a "Nathan" are listed in Ezra 8:16 as part of the delegation Ezra sent to search for Levites to return from Babylon to Jerusalem with him. Many Bible students feel that copying of the manuscripts has introduced extra names into the list.

ELOI Greek transliteration of Aramaic *'elohi*, "my God."

ELON Personal name and place-name meaning "great tree" or "tree of god" (cp. Gen. 12:6; Judg. 9:6,37). **1.** Son of Zebulun and grandson of Jacob (Gen. 46:14). A clan in Zebulun was thus named for him (Num. 26:26). **2.** Judge from the tribe of Zebulun (Judg. 12:11-12). **3.** City in tribal territory of Naphtali (Josh. 19:33), often transliterated into English as Allon. **4.** Site where Deborah, Rebekah's nurse, was buried, called "Allon-bachuth" or "the oak of weeping" (Gen. 35:8). **5.** A leader in the tribe of Simeon (1 Chron. 4:37).

A different Hebrew spelling underlies other examples of Elon in English translations. **1.** The Hittite father of Esau's wife Bashemath (Gen. 26:34). **2.** The Hittite father of Adah, Esau's wife (Gen. 36:2), Bashemath being listed as Ishmael's daughter (36:3). **3.** City in tribal territory of Dan (Josh. 19:43). It may be located at Khirbet Wadi Alin. It is probably the same place as Elon-beth-hanan (1 Kings 4:9), though some read Ajalon and Bethhanan or "Elon, and Beth-hanan" (REB).

ELPAAL Personal name meaning "God has made." A clan name in the tribe of Benjamin, mentioned twice in 1 Chron. 8 (vv. 11-12,18).

ELPARAN Place-name meaning "tree of Paran." The place where the eastern coalition of kings extended its victory over the Horites (Gen. 14:6). It is apparently a place in or near Elath.

ELPELET David's son born after he captured and moved to Jerusalem (1 Chron. 14:5). This is apparently an abbreviated spelling of Eliphelet.

ELTEKE or **ELTEKEH** Place-name meaning "place of meeting," "place of hearing," or "plea for rain." A city in Dan (Josh. 19:44) assigned to the Levites (21:23).

ELTEKON Place-name meaning "securing advice." Village in tribal territory of Judah in southern hill country (Josh. 15:59).

ELTOLAD Place-name meaning "plea for a child." Village in tribal territory of Judah (Josh 15:30), given to tribe of Simeon (Josh. 19:4).

ELUL Sixth month of Hebrew year, name taken over from Akkadian. It included parts of August and September. See Neh. 6:15.

ELUZAI Personal name meaning "God is my strength." A member of King Saul's tribe of Benjamin, who became a military leader for David, while he lived as a fugitive in Ziklag (1 Chron. 12:5).

ELYMAS Personal name possibly meaning "wise." A magician and false prophet also known as Bar-jesus (Acts 13:6-11). At Paphos on the island of Cyprus, Elymas tried to dissuade the deputy Sergius Paulus from listening to the words of Barnabas and Paul. He was denounced by Paul and stricken temporarily blind.

ELZABAD Personal name meaning "God made a gift." **1.** Soldier who fought for David while he was a fugitive in Ziklag (1 Chron. 12:12). **2.** Levite and grandson of Obed-edom, identified as a valiant man (1 Chron. 26:7). He was a porter or gatekeeper in the temple.

ELZAPHAN Personal name meaning "God has hidden or treasured up." An abbreviated form of Elizaphan. A son of Uzziel, Aaron's uncle (Exod. 6:22). He helped carry the dead bodies of Nadab and Abihu out of the wilderness camp after God punished them (Lev. 10:4-5).

EMBALMING Process of preserving bodies from decay. Embalming originated in Egypt and was seldom used by the Hebrews. The practice is rarely mentioned in the Bible, and the human remains unearthed in Palestinian tombs generally show no signs of having been embalmed. In Gen. 50:2-3 it is recorded that Joseph ordered the embalming of Jacob's body and that "physicians" required 40 days to perform the process.

EMEK-KEZIZ Place-name meaning "the cut-off valley" or "the valley of gravel." It is listed as one of the cities assigned to the tribe of Benjamin (Josh. 18:21). Its location is not known.

EMERODS Archaic form of the word "hemorrhoids" used by the KJV for the disease(s) in Deut. 28:27 and 1 Sam. 5–6.

EMIM or **EMITES** (NIV) National name meaning "frightening ones." They lost a war to the eastern coalition of kings (Gen. 14:6) and are identified with a place in northern Moab, Shaveh Kiriathaim.

EMMAUS Place-name meaning "hot baths." A village that was the destination of two of Jesus' disciples on the day of His resurrection (Luke 24:13). As they traveled, they were joined by a person whom they later realized was the risen Christ. Emmaus was about 60 furlongs (approximately seven miles) from Jerusalem.

EMPEROR WORSHIP Practice of assigning the status of deity to current or deceased rulers. A specific NT example of emperor worship is the worship of the beast in the book of Revelation. Revelation 13 speaks of a beast that is given ruling authority. An image is made of the beast, and all are commanded to worship it (13:4,12,14-15; see also Dan. 8:4,8-12).

ENAIM or **ENAM** Place-name meaning "two eyes or springs." A village near Timnah, where Tamar seduced Judah (Gen. 38:14). It is probably the same as Enam in the tribal territory of Judah (Josh. 15:34).

ENAN Personal name meaning "eyes or springs." Father of Ahira, the leader of the tribe of Naphtali under Moses (Num. 1:15).

ENDOR Place-name meaning "spring of Dor," that is, "spring of settlement." **1.** Home of witch who brought up Samuel from the grave (1 Sam. 28:7). Psalm 83:10 says Jabin died there (cp. Judg. 4–5). It is modern Khirbet Safsafe, three miles south of Mount Tabor. **2.** City tribe of Manasseh claimed but could not conquer (Josh. 17:11; cp. Judg. 1:27).

EN-EGLAIM Place-name meaning "spring of the two calves." A spring near the Dead Sea where Ezekiel predicted a miracle, the salt waters being made fresh and becoming a paradise for fishing (Ezek. 47:10).

EN-GANNIM Place-name meaning "the spring of gardens." **1.** Town in the tribal territory of Judah located in the Shephalah (Josh. 15:34). It has been located at modern Beit Jemal, about two miles south of Beth-shemesh or at 'umm Giina one mile southwest of Beth-shemesh. **2.** Town in tribal territory of Issachar designated as city for Levites (Josh. 19:21; 21:29).

EN-GEDI Place-name meaning "place of the young goat." A major oasis along the western side of the Dead Sea about 35 miles southeast of Jerusalem. The springs of En-gedi are full, and the vegetation is semitropical. Both biblical and extra-biblical sources describe En-gedi as a source of fine dates, aromatic plants used in perfumes, and medicinal plants (Song 1:14). When David was fleeing from Saul, he hid in the area of Engedi (1 Sam. 23:29). Saul was in a cave near En-gedi when David cut off a piece of his robe but spared his life (1 Sam. 24).

This natural waterfall, rare in Israel, is located at Engedi on the west side of the Dead Sea.

ENGINE Catapult or battering ram.

ENGRAVE To impress deeply, to carve. Many materials were engraved including clay writing tablets (Isa. 8:1), metal, precious gems, stone (Zech. 3:9), and wood. Engraving was frequently done with an iron pen, a stylus, sometimes with a diamond point (Job 19:24; Jer. 17:1).

EN-HADDAH City in tribal lot of Issachar (Josh. 19:21). It is apparently el-Hadetheh about six miles east of Mount Tabor.

EN-HAKKORE Place-name meaning "spring of the partridge" or "spring of the caller." Place where God gave Samson water from the jawbone he had used to kill a thousand Philistines (Judg. 15:18-19). It is near Beth-shemesh.

EN-HAZOR Place-name meaning "spring of the enclosed village." A fortified city in the tribal territory of Naphtali (Josh. 19:37).

EN-MISHPAT Place-name meaning "spring of judgment." Another name for Kadesh, where the eastern coalition of kings defeated the Amalekites and Amorites.

ENOCH Personal name meaning "dedicated." **1.** The son of Jared who was taken up to God without dying (Gen. 5:18). He became the father of Methuselah. **2.** Son of Cain for whom Cain built a city and named it (Gen. 4:17-18).

ENON CITY TEV translation of Hazar-enan (Ezek. 47:17).

ENOS or **ENOSH** Personal name meaning "humanity" or "a man." Son of Seth and therefore the grandson of Adam (Gen. 4:26). The period following his birth is identified as the time when people began to worship Yahweh. See Gen. 5:6-11.

EN-RIMMON Place-name meaning "spring of the pomegranate." A town in Judah (Neh. 11:29) where people lived in Nehemiah's day (about 445 BC).

EN-ROGEL Place-name meaning "spring of the fuller" or "spring of the foot." A border town between the tribal territory of Judah (Josh. 15:7) and that of Benjamin (Josh. 18:16).

EN-SHEMESH Place-name meaning "spring of the sun." Town on border between tribal territories of Judah (Josh. 15:7) and Benjamin (18:17).

EN-TAPPUAH Place-name meaning "spring of apple." A spring near the town of Tappuah which marked the border of the tribe of Manasseh and Ephraim (Josh. 17:7).

ENVY Painful or resentful awareness of another's advantage joined with the desire to possess the same advantage. The advantage may concern material goods (Gen. 26:14) or social status (30:1).

EPAENETUS Personal name meaning "praise." The first Christian convert in Achaia and thus a friend with special meaning for Paul (Rom. 16:5).

EPAPHRAS Personal name meaning "lovely." A Christian preacher from whom Paul learned of the situation of the church in Colossae (Col. 1:7). He was a native of Colossae whose ministry especially involved Colossae, Laodicea, and Hierapolis. Later he was a companion of Paul during the latter's imprisonment.

EPAPHRODITUS Personal name meaning "favored by Aphrodite or Venus." A friend and fellow worker of Paul the apostle (Phil. 2:25). He had delivered to Paul a gift from the church at Philippi while the apostle was in prison. While he was with Paul, Epaphroditus became seriously ill. After his recovery, Paul sent him back to Philippi, urging the church there to receive him "with all gladness" (Phil. 2:29).

EPHAH Personal name meaning "darkness." **1.** Son of Midian and grandson of Abraham (Gen. 25:4). **2.** Concubine of Caleb and mother of his children (1 Chron. 2:46). **3.** Son of Jahdai and apparently a descendant of Caleb (1 Chron. 2:47).

EPHAI Personal name meaning "bird." Father of men who joined Ishmael in revolt against and murder of Gedaliah, the governor of Judah after Babylon captured and destroyed Jerusalem in 586 BC (Jer. 40:8). Ephai was from Netophah near Bethlehem.

EPHER Personal name meaning "young deer." **1.** Son of Midian, grandson of Abraham through his wife Keturah, and clan father among the Midianites (Gen. 25:4). **2.** Descendant of Caleb in the tribe of Judah (1 Chron. 4:17). **3.** Original ancestor of clan in tribe of Manasseh (1 Chron. 5:24).

EPHES-DAMMIM Place-name meaning "end of bloodshed." Town between Shocoh and Azekah where Philistines gathered to fight Saul (1 Sam. 17:1) preceding David's killing of Goliath.

EPHESIANS, LETTER TO THE While it is not the longest of the Pauline Epistles, Ephesians is the one that best sets out the basic concepts of the Christian faith.

A traditional view is that Ephesians is one of four letters Paul wrote during his imprisonment in Rome, AD 61–62. The other three letters are Colossians, Philemon, and Philippians.

Paul's motive for writing this letter was the challenge that Christianity faced in confrontation with other religions and philosophies of the day. Paul was convinced that the religion he proclaimed was the only way of redemption from sin and sonship to God.

Ephesians, like other letters of Paul, begins with theological affirmation and transitions to ethical implications of that theology. Paul opens the letter by praising God for His grace and His plan of redemption that is seen in Jesus' death, resurrection, and ascension to the Father's right hand. God's Spirit takes this word of truth about what God has done in Christ and applies it to individuals. The Spirit takes up residence in each believer and becomes the down payment of final and complete redemption. This redemption is not just an individual matter. God incorporates believers into the church, the body of Christ, a holy sanctuary in the Lord. It also brings reconciliation between Jews and Gentiles.

What God has done has consequences for personal life, calling for a complete transformation from the life-styles of unbelievers. Without faith the individual is devoted to selfish lust and earthly dissipation. The believer becomes like God in holiness, purity, and righteousness. A central element of this is human speech, speaking the truth and saying that which helps build up others. Anger and malice must turn to love, compassion, and forgiveness. Walking in the light means pleasing God and showing the sinfulness of evil deeds. This is the wise path avoiding spirits that make one drunk but turning to the one Spirit who leads to praise and worship. This changes one's role at home. Submission to one another becomes the key, a submission motivated by loyalty to Christ and love to

he marital partner. That love follows the example of Christ's love for His church. Parents expect
honor from children while training children in the Lord's way of love. Similarly, masters and servants
respect and help one another.

To complete his letter, Paul called his readers to put on God's armor to avoid Satan's temptations.
This will lead to a life of prayer for self and for other servants of God. This will lead to concern for
and encouragement from other Christians. As usual, Paul concluded his letter with a benediction,
praying for peace, love, faith, and grace for his beloved readers.

EPHESUS One of the largest and most impressive cities in the ancient world, a political, religious, and commercial center in Asia Minor. Associated with the ministries of Paul, Timothy, and the Apostle John, the city played a significant role in the spread of early Christianity. Ephesus and its inhabitants are mentioned more than 20 times in the NT.

Location The ancient city of Ephesus, located in western Asia Minor at the mouth of the Cayster River, was an important seaport.

The Great Theater at Ephesus as viewed from the Harbor Road.

Situated between the Maeander River to the south and the Hermus River to the north, Ephesus had excellent access to both river valleys that allowed it to flourish as a commercial center. Due to the accumulation of silt deposited by the river, the present site of the city is approximately five to six miles inland.

EPHLAL Personal name meaning "notched" or "cracked." Descendant of Jerahmeel in tribe of Judah (1 Chron. 2:37).

EPHOD Priestly garment connected with seeking a word from God and used in a wrong way as an idol. The exact meaning and derivation of the term "ephod" are not clear. In early OT history there are references to the ephod as a rather simple, linen garment, possibly a short skirt, apron, or loincloth. It is identified as a priestly garment (1 Sam. 14:3; 22:18). It was worn by Samuel (1 Sam. 2:18) and by David when he danced before God on the occasion of the transfer of the ark of the covenant to David's capital city of Jerusalem (2 Sam. 6:14).

EPHPHATHA Aramaic expression that Jesus spoke when He healed a person who was deaf and had a speech impediment. It is translated "be opened." When Jesus had said it, the individual was healed (Mark 7:34).

EPHRAIM Personal and tribal name meaning "two fruit land" or "two pasture lands." The younger son of Joseph by the Egyptian Asenath, daughter of the priest of On (Gen. 41:52). Ephraim played an important role in Israelite history.

Joshua was an Ephraimite (Josh. 19:50). Samuel was an Ephraimite (1 Sam. 1:1). Jeroboam I was an Ephraimite (1 Kings 12:25).

EPHRAIM, FOREST OF Densely wooded site of the battle between the forces of King David and the rebel army of Absalom (2 Sam. 18:6,8).

EPHRAIM GATE Entrance to Jerusalem located 400 cubits (about 200 yards) from the Corner Gate (2 Kings 14:13). The section of wall between these two gates was destroyed by King Jehoash of Israel in the eighth century BC. In Nehemiah's time the city square at the Ephraim Gate was one of the sites where booths for the celebration of the Feast of Tabernacles were set up (Neh. 8:16).

EPHRAIM, MOUNT KJV designation for the hill country belonging to Ephraim.

EPHRAIN KJV reading of city in 2 Chron. 13:19 following the earliest Hebrew scribal note. Hebrew text reads "Ephron," as do most modern translations.

EPHRATAH or **EPHRATH** or **EPHRATHAH** Place and personal name meaning "fruitful."
1. Town near which Jacob buried his wife Rachel (Gen. 35:16-19; usually translated in English as Ephrath, NRSV). Genesis 35:16 seems to indicate that Ephrath(ah) must have been near Bethel. This is supported by 1 Sam. 10:2; Jer. 31:15, which place Rachel's tomb near Ramah on the border

between the tribal territories of Ephraim and Benjamin. Genesis 35:19, however, identifies Ephrath(ah) with Bethlehem (cp. Gen. 48:7). **2.** Caleb's wife (1 Chron. 2:50; spelled Ephrath in 2:19; cp. 4:4).

EPHRON Personal name and place-name meaning "dusty." **1.** Hittite who sold the cave of Machpelah to Abraham (Gen. 23:8-20). **2.** Mountain marking the tribal border of Judah with Benjamin (Josh. 15:9). It is located northwest of Jerusalem near Mozah at el-Qastel. **3.** City that King Abijah of Judah (913–910 BC) took from King Jeroboam of Israel (926–909 BC), according to spelling of Hebrew text (2 Chron. 13:19).

EPICUREANISM School of philosophy that emerged in Athens about 300 BC. The school of thought was founded by Epicurus who was born in 341 BC on the Greek island of Samos. Epicurus founded his school (The Garden) in Athens. Paul met Epicureans as he preached about Jesus and the resurrection in Athens (Acts 17:18). Epicurean philosophy centered on the search for happiness. Pleasure is the beginning and fulfillment of a happy life. To Epicurus, happiness could only be achieved through tranquility and a life of contemplation. The goal of Epicureanism was to acquire a trouble-free state of mind, to avoid the pains of the body, and especially mental anguish.

EPILEPSY Disorder marked by erratic electrical discharges of the central nervous system resulting in convulsions. In ancient times epilepsy was thought to be triggered by the moon. The term in Matt. 4:24, translated as "epileptics" by most modern translations, is literally "moonstruck." The KJV term "lunatick" from the Latin *luna* (moon) assumes the same cause for the disorder. Many interpreters understand the symptoms of the boy in Mark 9:17-29 (inability to speak, salivation, grinding teeth, rigid body, convulsions) as expressions of epilepsy.

EPIPHANY Term "epiphany" comes from a Greek word which means "appearance" or "manifestation." In Western Christianity the festival of Epiphany, observed on the sixth of January, celebrates the manifestation of Christ to the Gentiles, the coming of the Magi to see the child Jesus (Matt. 2:1-12).

In much of Eastern Christianity, Epiphany is a celebration of the baptism of Jesus, a recognition of His manifestation to humanity as the Son of God (Mark 1:9-11).

ER Personal name meaning "protector" or "watchful." **1.** Oldest son of Judah and grandson of Jacob (Gen. 38:3). He married Tamar but was so wicked that God killed him (Gen. 38:6-7). **2.** Grandson of Judah (1 Chron. 4:21).

ERAN Personal name meaning "of the city" or "watchful." Some of the earliest translations and the Samaritan Pentateuch read "Eden" rather than Eran. Eran was grandson of Ephraim and a clan leader in the tribe of Ephraim (Num. 26:36).

ERASTUS Personal name meaning "beloved." **1.** Disciple Paul sent with Timothy from Ephesus to Macedonia to strengthen the churches during his third missionary journey (Acts 19:22). **2.** City financial officer of Corinth who joined Paul in greeting the church at Rome (Rom. 16:23). **3.** Disciple who remained at Corinth and was not with Paul when he wrote Timothy (2 Tim. 4:20). He may have been identical with either of the other men named Erastus or may be a separate individual.

ERECH Hebrew transliteration of Akkadian place-name: Uruk, one of the oldest Sumerian cities founded before 3100 BC. Genesis' Table of Nations reports that Nimrod, the mighty hunter, included Erech in his kingdom (Gen. 10:10).

ERI Personal name meaning "of the city of" or "watchful." A son of Gad and grandson of Jacob (Gen. 46:16). Original ancestor of clan of Erites (Num. 26:16).

ESAIAS KJV transliteration of Greek spelling of Isaiah in the NT.

ESARHADDON Assyrian royal name meaning "Ashur (the god) has given a brother." King of Assyria (681–669 BC).

ESAU Personal name whose meaning is not known. Son of Isaac and Rebekah; elder twin brother of Jacob (Gen. 25:24-26; 27:1,32,42; 1 Chron. 1:34); father of the Edomite nation (Gen. 26:34; 28:9; 32:3; Deut. 2:4-29; Mal. 1:2-3).

ESCHATOLOGY Derived from the combination of the Greek *eschatos*, meaning "last," and *logos*, meaning "word" or "significance." Refers to the biblical doctrine of last things. The doctrine of last things normally focuses on a discussion of the return of Christ at the end of the age, the coming judgments, various expressions of the kingdom of heaven and the kingdom of God, the nature of the glorified body, and the prospects for eternal destiny.

The Great Plain of Esdraelon viewed from near Megiddo.

ESDRAELON Greek translation of the word "Jezreel," indicating the low-lying area that separates the mountains of Galilee from the mountains of Samaria.

Esdraelon, also called the Great Plain of Esdraelon or the Plain of Jezreel, is the area assigned to Zebulun and Issachar (Josh. 19:10-23). It extends from the Mediterranean Sea to the Jordan River at Beth-shean. Included are the Valley or Plain of Megiddo in the east and the Valley of Jezreel in the west. Esdraelon is mentioned in the NT as Armageddon or har-Megiddon, meaning hill or city of Megiddo. Revelation 16:16 echoes the OT portrayal of Esdraelon as a place of war and tragedy. The final battle of the Lord will be waged there (Rev. 16:14-16; 19:19).

ESEK Place-name meaning "strife." A well that Isaac's servants dug in the valley near Gerar to find water for their herds (Gen. 26:18-24).

ESHAN or **ESHEAN** (KJV) Place-name meaning "I lean on." Town in the hill country of Judah assigned to tribe of Judah (Josh. 15:52).

ESH-BAAL Personal name meaning "man of Baal." Son of Saul, the first king of Israel (1 Chron. 8:33; 9:39). In 2 Sam. 2:8 the name is Ish-bosheth, "man of shame," apparently an intentional corruption in the Hebrew tradition to avoid the name of the Canaanite god and to characterize the person with such a name.

ESHBAN Personal name of unknown meaning. An Edomite listed as a descendant of Seir the Horite (Gen. 36:26).

ESHCOL Place-name meaning "valley of grapes" or "cluster." **1.** A valley in Canaan that was explored by the 12 Israelites sent to spy out the land (Num. 13:23). From the valley of Eshcol they brought back an exceptionally large cluster of grapes. **2.** Brother of Mamre and Aner (Gen. 14:13). He and his brothers were Amorites who were allies of Abram in the defeat of Chedorlaomer.

ESHEK Personal name meaning "oppression" or "strong." A member of the tribe of Benjamin descended from King Saul (1 Chron. 8:39).

ESHTAOL Place-name meaning "asking (for an oracle)." Town in lowlands of Shephelah of Judah allotted to the tribe of Judah (Josh. 15:33) but also to the tribe of Dan (Josh. 19:41). Near there, God's Spirit stirred Samson of the tribe of Dan (Judg. 13:25).

ESHTEMOA Place-name and personal name meaning "being heard." The name may indicate an ancient tradition of going to Eshtemoa to obtain an oracle or word of God from a prophet or priest. **1.** City in tribal allotment of Judah (Josh. 15:50, with variant Hebrew spelling). God set it aside for the Levites (Josh. 21:14). While living in exile in Ziklag, David sent some of the plunder from his victories to Eshtemoa (1 Sam. 30:28). **2.** Member of clan of Caleb in tribe of Judah (1 Chron. 4:17), probably listed as the clan father of those who settled in Eshtemoa.

ESHTEMOH Variant Hebrew spelling of Eshtemoa (Josh. 15:50).

ESHTON Personal name of uncertain meaning. Member of the tribe of Judah (1 Chron. 4:11-12).

ESLI Personal name of unknown meaning. Ancestor of Jesus (Luke 3:25), spelled Hesli in NASB. Some scholars equate him with Elioenai (1 Chron. 3:23).

ESSENES Members of a Jewish sect that existed in Palestine during the time of Christ. They are not mentioned in the NT.

The ruins of ancient Qumran probably inhabited by Essenes from 130 BC until AD 70.

They were ascetics who practiced community of goods, generally shunned marriage, refrained from attending worship in the temple, and attached great importance to the study of the Scriptures. Many scholars associate the Dead Sea Scrolls discovered in 1947 with an Essene community.

ESTHER Persian personal name meaning "a star." Since this is not the biblical Esther's given name at birth (Esther 2:7), some have suggested that this name is linked to the planet Venus and the goddess Ishtar.

ESTHER, BOOK OF Placed by the Jews in the third section of the Hebrew Bible known as the Writings. While some debate over the book occurred due to the lack of inclusion of the name of God, the activity of the Lord was so obvious in the book that this objection was overruled.

The book of Esther provides the historical background for the feast of Purim. In plotting against the Jews, Haman cast lots (*purim* from Assyrian *puru*) to determine their fate (9:24-28). The story of God's preservation of His people through the courageous action of Queen Esther is a reminder of His covenant with Abraham that He will not only bless those who bless His people, but He will also curse those who curse them. The preservation of the Jews kept alive messianic expectations in the intertestamental period. Esther's husband, King Ahasuerus, is usually identified with Xerxes I (486–465/64 BC).

ETAM Place-name meaning "place of birds of prey." **1.** Rocky crag where Samson camped during his battles with the Philistines (Judg. 15:8-13), conferring there with men of Judah who wanted to bind him and hand him over to the Philistines. **2.** Town in territorial allotment of tribe of Judah according to earliest Greek translation of the OT but omitted from present Hebrew manuscripts (Josh. 15:59 REB). **3.** Member of tribe of Judah and apparently clan father of town of same name associated with Jezreel (1 Chron. 4:3). **4.** Village assigned to Simeon (1 Chron. 4:32), though it is not listed in Simeon's tribal territory in Josh. 19:7. It may be modern Aitun, about 11 miles southwest of Hebron.

ETERNAL LIFE Life at its best, having infinite duration characterized by abiding fellowship with God. This important term in the NT is emphasized in the Gospel of John but also appears in the other Gospels and in Paul's writings. Eternal life in the NT eliminates the boundary line of death. Death is still a foe, but the one who has eternal life already experiences the kind of existence that will never end.

Yet, in this expression, the emphasis is on the quality of life rather than on the unending duration of life. Probably some aspects of both quality and duration appear in every context, but some refer primarily to quality of life and others point to unending life or a life to be entered into in the future.

In terms of quality, life is (1) life imparted by God; (2) transformation and renewal of life; (3) life fully opened to God and centered in Him; (4) a constant overcoming of sin and moral evil; and (5) the complete removal of moral evil from the person and from the environment of that person.

ETHAM Place-name meaning "fort." The second station in Israel's wilderness wandering out of Egypt (Exod. 13:20; Num. 33:6-8). The nearby wilderness was called the wilderness of Etham (Num. 33:8).

ETHAN Personal name meaning "long-lived." **1.** Man so famous for his wisdom that Solomon's outstanding wisdom could be described as exceeding Ethan's (1 Kings 4:31). **2.** Levite and temple singer (1 Chron. 6:42,44; 15:17) and instrumentalist (1 Chron. 15:19). He is associated with Pss. 88 and 89 in their titles.

ETHANIM Canaanite name of the seventh month taken over by Israel (1 Kings 8:2), who also called the month Tishri. This was the first month of the civil year. Ethanim means "always flowing with water" and refers to the flooding streams fed by heavy fall rains.

ETH-BAAL Personal name meaning "with him is Baal." King of Sidon and father of Jezebel (1 Kings 16:31), who married Jeroboam II, king of Israel (793–753 BC). Through her influence Baal worship pervaded the northern kingdom.

ETHER Place-name meaning "smoke of incense." **1.** Town in tribal territory of Judah (Josh. 15:42). **2.** Town occupied by tribe of Simeon (Josh. 19:7).

ETHICS Study of good behavior, motivation, and attitude in light of Jesus Christ and biblical revelation.

ETHIOPIA Region of Nubia just south of Egypt, from the first cataract of the Nile into the Sudan. Confusion has arisen between the names Ethiopia and Cush. The OT Hebrew (and Egyptian) name for the region was Cush. In some passages such as Gen. 2:13 and Isa. 11:11, various English versions alternate between Cush and Ethiopia. See *Cush*.

The biblical Ethiopia should not be confused with the modern nation of the same name somewhat further to the southeast. In biblical times Ethiopia was equivalent to Nubia, the region beyond the first cataract of the Nile south, or upstream, of Egypt.

The Ethiopian eunuch to whom Philip explained the gospel was a minister of "Candace, queen of the Ethiopians" (Acts 8:27 HCSB). Candace should be understood as a title rather than a personal name.

ETHKAZIN Place-name perhaps meaning "time of the chieftain." Town in tribal territory of Zebulun (Josh. 19:13).

ETHNAN Personal name meaning "gift." Member of tribe of Judah (1 Chron. 4:7).

ETHNI Personal name meaning "I will give." Levite, ancestor of Asaph (1 Chron. 6:41).

EUBULUS Personal name meaning "good counsel." Companion of Paul who sent greetings to Timothy (2 Tim. 4:21).

EUNICE Personal name meaning "victorious." The mother of Timothy (2 Tim. 1:5). Paul commended both her and her mother Lois for their faith. She was a Jewish woman whose husband was a Gentile. No details are known about her conversion to Christianity.

EUNUCH A male deprived of the testes or external genitals. Such men were excluded from serving as priests (Lev. 21:20) and from membership in the congregation of Israel (Deut. 23:1). Part of Isaiah's vision of the messianic era was a picture of the eunuch no longer complaining of being "a dry tree," one without hope of descendants, because God would reward the faithful eunuch with a lasting monument and name in the temple which would be far better than sons or daughters (Isa. 56:45).

A eunuch for the sake "of the kingdom of heaven" (Matt. 19:12 HCSB) is likely a metaphor for one choosing single life in order to be more useful in kingdom work (cp. 1 Cor. 7:32-34).

EUODIA or **EUODIAS** Female leader in the church at Philippi whose disagreement with Syntyche concerned Paul (Phil. 4:2-3). The name Euodia means either prosperous journey or pleasant fragrance.

EUPHRATES AND TIGRIS RIVERS

Two of the greatest rivers of Western Asia. They originate in the mountains of Armenia and unite about 90 miles from the Persian Gulf to form what is now called the Shatt-al-Arab that flows into the gulf. In ancient times the Tigris flowed through its own mouth into the gulf. The Euphrates and Tigris were included among the four rivers of Paradise (Gen. 2:14).

Euphrates River.

EURAQUILO NASB transliteration of Greek name for northeast wind in Acts 27:14.

EUROCLYDON Noun meaning "southeast wind raising mighty waves." KJV reading of traditional Greek text in Acts 27:14, but most modern translations follow other Greek texts that read *Eurakulon*, the northeast wind.

EUTYCHUS Personal name meaning "good fortune." A young man who listened to Paul the apostle preach in Troas (Acts 20:9-10). Overcome with sleep, Eutychus fell from a third floor windowsill and was picked up dead. Paul, however, embraced the youth, and Eutychus was restored to life.

EVANGELISM Active calling of people to respond to the message of grace and commit oneself to God in Jesus Christ.

EVE Personal name meaning "life." The first woman created and thus original ancestor of all people (Gen. 3:20; cp. 4:1-2,25). She also faced the serpent's temptation first (3:1; 2 Cor. 11:3; 1 Tim. 2:13-14). Her fall illustrates the ease with which all persons fall into sin (2 Cor. 11:3).

EVERLASTING PUNISHMENT God's unending punishment of sinners beyond this life is known as eternal punishment. The Bible teaches that unrepentant, unforgiven sinners will be punished (Dan. 12:2; Matt. 10:15; John 5:28-29; Rom. 5:12-21).

Two common reasons are typically offered as grounds for denying everlasting punishment. One of these is that everlasting punishment denies God's eternal love. For God to allow His creatures to exist in eternal torment is a contradiction of His loving nature. Another argument against everlasting punishment is that endless torment contradicts God's sovereignty because He allows unbelievers to exist for eternity. As significant as these points are, they both seem to lack any support from the Bible.

God's intention for humanity is to live eternally in bliss and fellowship with God. Those who pervert this intention will and must experience the eternal consequences of that act.

EVI Personal name of uncertain meaning, perhaps "desire." King of Midian killed in battle by Israelites during wilderness wanderings (Num. 31:8). He apparently ruled as a vassal of Sihon (Josh. 13:21).

EVIL-MERODACH Babylonian royal name meaning "worshipper of Marduk." Babylonian king (562–560 BC) who treated Jehoiachin, king of Judah, with kindness (2 Kings 25:27). The Babylonian form of the name is Amel-Marduk. He was the son of Nebuchadnezzar.

EXACTOR KJV term for a taskmaster or a tax collector used only at Isa. 60:17 (ruler, HCSB).

EXCOMMUNICATION Practice of temporarily or permanently excluding someone from the church as punishment for sin or apostasy.

EXECRATION Act of cursing; an object of cursing. The term appears in the KJV twice (Jer. 42:18; 44:12), both times in reference to the fate of the remnant who disobeyed God's word and sought safety in Egypt.

EXHORTATION Argument (Acts 2:40) or advice intended to incite hearers to action.

EXILE Events in which the northern tribes of Israel were taken into captivity by the Assyrians (beginning about 734 BC) and the southern tribes of Judah were taken into captivity by the Babylonians (beginning in 598 BC).

The prophets Hosea and Amos had prophesied the fall of Israel. These two prophets proclaimed that Israel's fall was due to moral and spiritual degeneration rather than to the superior military might of the Assyrian nation. Assyria was only the "rod of mine anger"' (Isa. 10:5).

More than a hundred years before the Babylon exile, Isaiah, the prophet, had predicted Judah's fall (Isa. 6:11-12; 8:14; 10:11). In addition, the prophets Micah, Zephaniah, Jeremiah, Habakkuk, and Ezekiel agreed that Judah would fall.

EXODUS Israel's escape from slavery in Egypt and journey towards the promised land under Moses. Historically and theologically this is the most important event in the OT. More than a hundred times in all parts of the OT except the Wisdom Literature, Yahweh is proclaimed as "the one who brought you up from the land of Egypt, out of the house of bondage."

The Bible stresses that the exodus was the work of God. God brought the plagues on Egypt (Exod. 7:1-5). The miracle at the sea was never treated merely as a natural event or as Israel's victory alone. In the earliest recorded response to the event Miriam sang, "Sing to the LORD, for He is highly exalted; the horse and his rider He has hurled into the sea" (Exod. 15:21 NASB).

The Date of the Exodus The Bible does not give an incontrovertible date for the exodus. The most commonly accepted early date (among conservatives) is 1446 BC. This is based on the following passage of I Kings 6:1, "In the four hundred and eightieth year after the sons of Israel came out of the land of Egypt, in the fourth year of Solomon's reign over Israel, in the month of Ziv which is the second month, that he began to build the house of the LORD" (NASB).

Some scholars cite a combination of biblical and archaeological evidence to place the Exodus about two hundred years later.

The Pharaoh of the Exodus The pharaoh of the exodus is tied directly to the interpretation of the data for the dating of the exodus/conquest. If one takes the late exodus date (ca. 1270 BC), the pharoah of the oppression would have been Seti I and the pharaoh of the exodus would have been Ramesses II (1304–1237 BC). However, taking the early exodus date (ca. 1446 BC), the pharaoh of the oppression was Thutmose III and the pharaoh of the exodus was Amenhotep II (1450–1425 BC).

If the statistics are correct that males over the age of twenty make up approximately 25 percent of the total population, then the Israelites numbered well over two million people at both the beginning and the end of the wilderness wanderings.

The exodus was the work of God. It was a historical event involving a superpower nation and an oppressed people. God acted redemptively in power, freedom, and love. When the kingdom of God did not come, the later prophets began to look for a second exodus. That expectation was fulfilled spiritually in Christ's redemptive act.

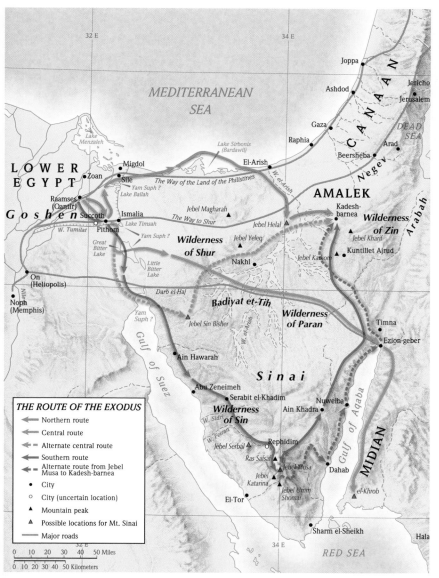

Jebel Musa, the traditional site of Mount Sinai.

EXODUS, BOOK OF Central book of the OT, reporting God's basic saving act for Israel in the exodus from Egypt and His making of His covenant with the nation destined to be His kingdom of priests.

The book of Exodus is the second book of the OT and of the Pentateuch. Exodus takes up the story of the children of Jacob in Egypt, now under a new pharaoh and seen as feared foreigners instead of welcomed deliverers from famine. Israel thus became slave laborers in Egypt (chap. 1). Exodus is the account of how God raised up Moses as His instrument for delivering His people from slavery. The miracle of the Red Sea (or perhaps more literally, the Sea of Reeds) became the greatest moment in Israel's history, the moment

God created a nation for Himself by delivering them from the strongest military power on earth as He led them through the divided waters of the sea and then flooded the sea again as the Egyptians tried to follow (chap. 14).

Three months after Israel was delivered from Egypt, they came to Sinai, where God called them to become His covenant people, a holy nation to carry out Abraham's mission of blessing the nations. God gave the Ten Commandments and other laws central to the covenant (chaps. 19–23), and then confirmed the covenant in a mysterious ceremony (chap. 24). Moses went to the top of the mountain to receive the remainder of God's instructions, especially instructions for building the sacred place of worship, the tabernacle (chaps. 24–31). Impatient Israel got Aaron to build an object of worship they could see, so he made the golden calf. The people began worshipping. This angered God, who sent Moses back down to the people. Moses prayed for the people despite their sin but then saw the people's sinful actions and threw the tablets with the law to the ground, breaking them. Moses again went up and prayed for the people. God punished them but did not destroy them as He had threatened. God showed His continued presence in the Tent of Meeting and in letting His glory pass by Moses (chaps. 32–33). God then gave Moses the law on two new tablets of stone and renewed the covenant with the people, providing further basic laws for them. Such intense communication with God brought radiance to Moses' face (chap. 34). Moses then led Israel to celebrate the Sabbath and to build the tabernacle (chaps. 35–39). Moses set up the tabernacle and established worship in it. God blessed the action with His holy glorious presence (chap. 40). This provided the sign for Israel's future journeys, following God's cloud and fire.

EXORCISM Practice of expelling demons by means of some ritual act. Although the Hebrew Bible does make reference to demonic beings (Lev. 17:7; Deut. 32:17; Isa. 13:21; 34:14; 2 Chron. 11:15; Ps. 106:37 NRSV), there is no account of demons being cast out of a person or a place. In the NT the demons were earthly powers or spirits allied with Satan. Jesus' power to exorcise is demonstrated in the Synoptic Gospels of His power over Satan (Matt. 15:21-28; Mark 1:23-38; 5:1-20; 7:24-30; 9:14-29). See *Demonic Possession.*

EXPIATION, PROPITIATION Terms that elaborate the meaning of atonement for sins. Expiation is the process by which sins are nullified or covered. Propitiation involves the satisfaction of an offended party—in this case—God. Sin evokes God's wrath, His eternal opposition to evil. Sin can't be expiated or covered until a prior issue has been addressed. Because God is just, He punishes sin. God is also compassionate, loving those who sin. Jesus' atonement for sin, His bearing the just punishment for sin, makes it possible for God to be "righteous and declare righteous" those who sin but who have faith in Jesus Christ (Rom. 3:26). Because Jesus is first the propitiation for sin, He can also be its expiation. Expiation without propitiation leaves God's righteousness in question.

EYELIDS OF THE MORNING Phrase meaning "the glow of dawn" used to describe the eyes of Leviathan (Job 41:18).

EZBAI Personal name of unknown meaning. Father of one of David's military leaders (1 Chron. 11:37).

EZBON Personal name perhaps meaning "bare." Son of Gad and grandson of Jacob (Gen. 46:16).

EZEKIAS KJV spelling of Ezekiel in the NT following the Greek spelling there.

EZEKIEL Personal name meaning "God will strengthen." Ezekiel was a sixth-century BC prophet who ministered to the Judean exiles in Babylon. All that is known of Ezekiel derives from his book. He was a son of Buzi (1:3), taken captive to Babylon in 597 BC, along with King Jehoiachin and 10,000 others, including political and military leaders and skilled craftsmen (2 Kings 24:14-16). Ezekiel lived in his own house near the river Chebar, an irrigation canal that channeled the Euphrates River into surrounding arid areas. He was married and ministered from his own home (3:24; 8:1; 33:30-33). His wife died suddenly (24:18), but he was not allowed to mourn the loss.

Sunrise ("eyelids of the morning") over the Mediterranean Coast of Israel.

EZEKIEL, BOOK OF Classified with the major prophets and placed in the OT canon following Lamentations. Ezekiel is a series of oracles delivered in a number of identifiable literary forms such as woe oracle, judgment oracle, riddle, and other. Unlike Jeremiah, the order of Ezekiel is approximately chronological.

Ezekiel has sometimes been described as emotionally unstable, a victim of neurotic and psychotic abnormalities. Today scholars recognize that he was not a man on the verge of a breakdown but used deliberate rhetorical tactics to get his message across to a hardened and resistant audience. No prophet was as creative as Ezekiel in the strategies employed to communicate his message. Inspired by God, he crafted powerful word pictures (17:1-24; 19:1-14; 27:1-9), demolished populist slogans with impeccable logic (11:1-21; 18:1-32), played the role of prosecuting attorney (16:1-63; 23:1-49), and, like watchman on the wall, warned them of certain doom (3:16-21; 7:1-27; 33:1-9). Once the judgment had fallen, he assumed a sympathetic stance, like a pastor (34:1-31), a bearer of good news (6:8-10; 36:16-38; 37:1-14), and like a second Moses, heralding a new constitution (40–48). But he also performed symbolic acts to expose the condition of the nation and her kings (chaps. 4–5; 12:1-20). Later he used the same strategy to declare his message of hope (37:15-28), but this was more than "street theatre." In his own body Ezekiel bore his message of doom (2:8–3:3; 3:22-27; 24:15-27; 33:21-22).

To evaluate Ezekiel's effectiveness we must look to the events that followed his book. According to the internal evidence, Ezekiel delivered his last oracle in 571 BC (29:1), more than two decades after his call. Even then, there was no hint of positive response among the exiles. However, the following three decades witnessed a remarkable development: when Cyrus issued a decree in 538 BC, permitting the Judeans to return home and rebuild the temple, more than 40,000 people returned, totally weaned off idolatry and eager to rebuild (Ezra 2:64). Most likely they came through the ministry of Ezekiel, having experienced a widespread spiritual revival. Whether he lived long enough to witness these developments, we do not know. The preservation of his prophecies testifies to his impact on the exiles.

EZEL Place-name of uncertain meaning, perhaps, "disappearance." Rock where David hid from Saul and watched for Jonathan's signal (1 Sam. 20:19).

EZEM Place-name meaning "mighty" or "bone." Town in Judah's tribal territory but settled by tribe of Simeon (Josh. 15:29; 19:3; 1 Chron. 4:29). KJV spells Azem in Joshua.

EZER English spelling of two Hebrew names with different spellings and meanings. The first Hebrew meaning is "gathering" or "pile." Ezer was a leader in Edom and a descendant of Esau (Gen. 36:21,27,30). He was a Horite and lived in Seir or Edom.

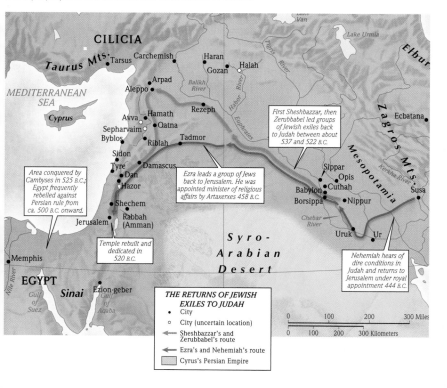

THE RETURNS OF JEWISH EXILES TO JUDAH
- City
- ○ City (uncertain location)
- Sheshbazzar's and Zerubbabel's route
- Ezra's and Nehemiah's route
- Cyrus's Persian Empire

First Sheshbazzar, then Zerubbabel led groups of Jewish exiles back to Judah between about 537 and 522 B.C.

Ezra leads a group of Jews back to Jerusalem. He was appointed minister of religious affairs by Artaxerxes 458 B.C.

Area conquered by Cambyses in 525 B.C.; Egypt frequently rebelled against Persian rule from ca. 500 B.C. onward.

Temple rebuilt and dedicated in 520 B.C.

Nehemiah hears of dire conditions in Judah and returns to Jerusalem under royal appointment 444 B.C.

The second Hebrew meaning is "help" or "hero." **1.** Descendant of Judah (1 Chron. 4:4) in the clan of Caleb. **2.** Son of Ephraim and grandson of Jacob. With his brother Elead, he was killed as he tried to take cattle from the inhabitants of Gath (1 Chron. 7:21). **3.** Member of tribe of Gad who joined David's wilderness army before he became king (1 Chron. 12:9). **4.** Person who helped Nehemiah repair the Jerusalem wall. His father had political authority over Mizpah (Neh. 3:19). **5.** Temple musician who helped Nehemiah dedicate the completion of the Jerusalem wall (Neh. 12:42, with a slightly different Hebrew spelling).

EZION-GABER (KJV, Num. 33:35-36; Deut. 2:8; 2 Chron. 20:36) or **EZION-GEBER** Port city of Edom located on the northern shore of the Gulf of Aqaba. It is first mentioned in the Bible among the cities on the route of the exodus (Num. 33:35-36; Deut. 2:8). Solomon utilized this city for ship-building purposes. During this time it was a port from which ships manned by Phoenician sailors sailed to Ophir for gold and other riches (1 Kings 9:26-28; 10:11,22; 2 Chron. 8:17).

EZNITE Word of uncertain meaning describing the family or tribal relationship of Adino (2 Sam. 23:8).

EZRA Priest and scribe of the fifth century BC. He descended from Aaron through Phinehas and later Zadok (Ezra 7:1-5; 1 Chron. 6:4-14). Ezra was sent with a large company of Israelites to Jerusalem by King Artaxerxes of Persia in 458 BC (Ezra 7:7). His mission was "to study the law of the LORD, and to practice it, and to teach His statutes and ordinances in Israel" (7:10 NASB).

Ezra was the main instigator of reform just after Israel's return from exile and one of the most important preservers and teachers of law in Jewish history. (He was probably the author of the books of Chronicles and Ezra and the final editor of the OT.) Additionally, he is the main source of information about the first return from exile.

EZRA, BOOK OF Name "Ezra" means "Yahweh helps." Several had the name: a family head in Judah (1 Chron. 4:17), a priest in the return with Zerubbabel (Neh. 12:1,13), and a prince at the dedication of Jerusalem's walls built by Nehemiah (Neh. 12:32-33). The most famous is the chief character in the book of Ezra.

The book of Ezra is intimately connected with Chronicles and Nehemiah. The connection is so obvious that possibly one person wrote and compiled all three. This unknown person is referred to as the Chronicler. Ezra and Nehemiah were actually one book in the ancient Hebrew and Greek OT. Each book contains materials found in the other (e.g., the list in Ezra 2 is also in Neh. 7). Each book completes the other; Ezra's story is continued in Nehemiah (chaps. 8–10).

The book chronicles two major events, that of Zerubbabel and the group of returnees who rebuilt the temple (chaps. 1–6), and that of Ezra (chaps. 7–10, completed in Neh. 8–10).

There he read from "the book of the law of Moses, which the LORD had commanded to Israel" (Neh. 8:1). A great revival resulted.

Ezra's greatest contribution was his teaching, establishing, and implementing "the book of the law of the LORD" (Neh. 9:3) among the Jews. Ezra evidenced strong theology; he believed in the sovereignty of God, who could use a Cyrus, an Artaxerxes, and a Darius to accomplish His purposes. He believed in the faithfulness of God, who brought home the exiles who wanted to return. He believed in the sacredness and practicality of the Scriptures; he read them to his people and insisted that their teachings be carried out. He was a person of prayer; note his long confessional prayers (Ezra 9:5-15; Neh. 9:6-37). He was a preacher: he used a pulpit (Neh. 8:4); he publicly read the Scriptures; and he helped to interpret them to his congregation (8:8).

EZRAH Modern translation spelling of Ezra in 1 Chron. 4:17 to reflect different final letter in Hebrew spelling. This Ezra is a descendant of Judah about whom nothing else is known. The spelling of his name may be a Hebrew form, whereas the more common spelling is Aramaic.

EZRAHITE Term used to describe the family relationships of Ethan, a famous wise man (1 Kings 4:31). The precise meaning of the Hebrew word is debated. It may mean one born in the land with full citizenship rights and point to a Canaanite origin for Ethan. A related word appears in Exod. 12:19,49; Lev. 17:15; Josh. 8:33, and other places.

EZRI Personal name meaning "my help." Supervisor of royal farm labor under David (1 Chron. 27:26).

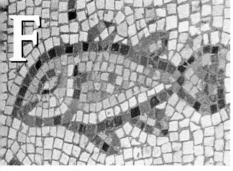

FABLE Short, fictitious story that uses animals or inanimate objects as characters to teach an ethical or practical lesson. Fables are rarely found in the Bible, but there are two clear examples in the OT. The fable of the trees of the forest selecting a king (Judg. 9:8-15) is designed to warn Israel of the dangers in selecting a weak and ruthless king. In 2 Kings 14:8-10 (2 Chron. 25:17-19), there is a fable addressed to Amaziah, king of Judah, about the folly of arrogance. In this story a thistle thinks that it is equal to the giant cedars of Lebanon and gets trampled by a wild beast of the forest.

Floor mosaic of fish from church in Galilee, Israel.

FACE The word "face" has a variety of meanings. It is used literally to refer to the face of man or animals (Gen. 30:40), seraphim (Isa. 6:2), and the face of Christ (Matt. 17:2). Figuratively, it is used in reference to the face of the earth (Gen. 1:29), waters (Gen. 1:2), sky (Matt. 16:3), and moon (Job 26:9). Also, the word "face" is used theologically with regard to the "presence of God" (Gen. 32:30).

FAIR HAVENS An open bay on the southern coast of Crete near the city of Lasea. Protected only by small islands, it did not appear to be a safe harbor for winter, so the sailors of the ship carrying Paul to Rome decided to try to reach Phoenix. They refused to listen to Paul's warnings and were caught in a ferocious storm (Acts 27:8-20).

FAIRNESS Prerequisite for wisdom (Prov. 2:9-10) and therefore an important value for life (Ps. 99:4; Prov. 1:2-3). The prophets linked fairness with righteousness (Isa. 11:4; cp. Ps. 98:9) and saw that when fairness was lacking, life became tenuous and uncertain (Isa. 59:9-11; Mic. 3:9-12). Biblical persons who exhibited fairness in their words or actions include Jacob (Gen. 31:38-41), Solomon (1 Kings 3:16-27), Jesus (John 7:53–8:11) and the thief on the cross (Luke 23:40-41).

FAITH, FAITHFULNESS Faith is essentially trust and faithfulness is dependability or trustworthiness. Throughout the Scriptures faith is the trustful human response to God's self-revelation via His words and His actions. God initiates the relationship between Himself and human beings. He expects people to trust Him; failure to trust Him was in essence the first sin (Gen. 3:1-7).

God's *modus operandi* during the OT and NT periods was to make Himself knowable through words about how people can relate properly to Him. Those words are not the object of the believer's faith; God is the object. But His words mediate faith in Him. His words guide people to Him. Without the words, no one would know how to respond properly to Him. Old Testament believers praised God for revealing His word of salvation (Ps. 56:4).

FALL Traditional name for the first sin of Adam and Eve that brought judgment upon both nature and mankind.

Sin had immediate results in the couple's relationship; the "self-first" and "self-only" attitude displayed toward God affected the way they looked at one another. The couple also felt compelled to hide from God when they heard Him walking in the garden. When loving trust characterized the couple's attitude, they were apparently comfortable in God's presence. After their sin, shame appropriately marked their relationships—both human and divine (Gen. 3:8).

The NT writers assumed the fallen state of both humans and nature. Both groan for redemption (Rom. 8:19-23). When comparing Adam and Christ, Paul declared that sin and death gained entrance into the world through Adam and that sin and death are now common to all people (Rom. 5:12; 6:23). Adam is pictured as a representative of mankind, all of whom share in his penalty (Rom. 5:19).

FALLOW GROUND Virgin soil or else soil that has not recently been planted (Jer. 4:3; Hos. 10:12).

FALSE APOSTLES Designation for Paul's opponents in 2 Cor. 11:13; also designated deceitful workers (11:13) and servants of Satan (11:15).

FALSE CHRISTS Imposters claiming to be the Messiah (Christ in Greek). Jesus associated the appearance of messianic pretenders with the fall of Jerusalem (Matt. 24:23-26; Mark 13:21-22). Jesus warned His followers to be skeptical of those who point to signs and omens to authenticate their false messianic claims. Jesus also urged disbelief of those claiming the Messiah was waiting in the wilderness or was in "the inner rooms" (perhaps a reference to the inner chambers of the temple complex).

FALSE PROPHET Person who spreads false messages and teachings, claiming to speak God's words. While the term "false prophet" does not occur in the OT, references to false prophets are clear. The pages of the OT are filled with men and women who fit the description of a false prophet given in Jer. 14:14. Jesus and the apostles spoke many times about false prophets. In the Sermon on the Mount, Jesus taught about the marks of a false prophet and the consequences of being one (Matt. 7:15-23). The apostles instructed believers to be diligent in faith and understanding of Christian teachings, in order to discern false prophets when they arise (2 Pet. 1:10; 1:19-2:1; 1 John 4:1). The tests of a prophet are: (1) Do their predictions come true (Jer. 28:9)? (2) Does the prophet have a divine commission (Jer. 29:9)? (3) Are the prophecies consistent with Scripture (2 Pet. 1:20-21; Rev. 22:18-19)? (4) Do the people benefit spiritually from the prophet's ministry (Jer. 23:13-14,32; 1 Pet. 4:11)?

Punishments for false prophets were just as severe in the NT as they were in the OT. Paul caused a false prophet to be stricken with blindness (Acts 13:6-12), but most other punishments were more permanent in nature. Jesus said the false prophets would be cut down and burned like a bad tree (Matt. 7:19). Second Peter 2:4 describes being cast into pits of darkness. The ultimate punishment appears in Rev. 19:20; 20:10—the false prophet, the beast, and the devil will be thrown into a lake of fire and brimstone and be tormented forever.

FALSE WORSHIP Broad category of acts and attitudes that includes worship, reverence, or religious honoring of any object, person, or entity other than the one true God. It also includes impure, improper, or other inappropriate acts directed toward the worship of the true God.

FAMILY A group of persons united by the ties of marriage, blood, or adoption, enabling interaction between members of the household in their respective social roles. God has ordained the family as the foundational institution of human society.
Old Testament The importance of the family unit in Israel is suggested by the fact that about half of the capital crimes were family related, including adultery, homosexuality, incest, persistent disobedience to or violence against one's parents, and rape (Lev. 20; Deut. 21–22). The basis for the family unit was the married couple (Gen. 2:4–5:1). From the union of the husband and wife the family expanded to include the children, and also various relatives such as grandparents, and others.

Along with paternal authority over the family came responsibility to provide for and protect the family. The father was responsible for the religious and moral training of his children (Deut. 6:7,20-25; Exod. 12:26-27; Josh. 4:6-7), and before the law he acted as the family priest (Gen. 12:7-8; Job 1:2-5). After establishment of the Levitical priesthood the father led the family in worship at the sites designated by God with the priests performing the sacrifices (1 Sam. 1). Moral purity was stressed for men and women in Israel with severe penalties for either party when sin occurred (Lev. 18; Prov. 5). The father was to give his daughter in marriage (Deut. 22:16; 1 Sam. 17:25; Jer. 29:6) to only an Israelite man, usually one from his own tribe. A daughter found to have been promiscuous before she married was to be stoned on her father's doorstep (Deut. 22:21).

Contrary to the practices of the surrounding nations, wives were not considered property. Though most marriages in the OT were arranged, this does not mean that they were loveless. The Song of Songs extols the joys of physical love between a husband and wife. God is used as an example of the perfect husband who loves His "wife" Israel (Hos. 1–2) and delights to care for her and make her happy.

A mother gave birth and reared the children, ran the home under her husband's authority, and generally served as her husband's helper (Gen. 2:18; Prov. 31:10-31). The importance of children in ancient Israel may be inferred from the law of Levirate marriage, which provided for the continuance of the family line (Deut. 25:5-10; Ps. 127:3-5). They were also the instruments by which the ancient traditions were passed on (Exod. 13:8-9,14; Deut. 4:9; 6:7). God delights to be praised by children (Ps. 8:2). Children were taught to respect their mothers as well as their fathers (Exod. 20:12; Deut. 5:16; 21:13; 27:16; Prov. 15:20; 23:22,25; 30:17) and to heed their instruction (Prov. 1:8; 6:20). Discipline was one way of showing love to one's children (Prov. 3:11-12; 13:24).

Polygamy (more specifically "polygyny") was one of the abnormal developments of the family in the OT and was first practiced by Lamech, a descendant of Cain. It is never cast in a positive light in Scripture but is a source of rivalry and bickering, as is seen in the lives of Abraham and Jacob (Gen. 16; 29–30). The exception was in the case of "Levirate marriage," that is, an unmarried male's marriage to the childless widow of his deceased brother.
New Testament Much of the NT teaching on the family is found in Paul's writings. Household ethics are described in Eph. 5–6 and Col. 3–4. In these texts husbands are responsible for the physical, emotional, religious, and psychological health of wives. A wife's submission is in the marriage context.

Wives are called to be household administrators. As household managers wives are responsible to give the family guidance and direction. Paul states that performing these tasks will inhibit gossiping and other unprofitable activities (1 Tim. 5:14). Thus any decision made within the family without the counsel and guidance of the wife is unwise.

Family roles in the NT also include children, who are commanded to obey their parents (Eph. 6:1-4). Each member of the family has responsibilities. Jesus affirms the importance of children and their importance to him in Matt. 18:2-14; 19:13-14; Mark 10:14-16.

FAMINE AND DROUGHT Famine is an extreme shortage of food, and drought is an excessive dryness of land. The Bible reports or predicts the occurrence of several famines and droughts. While the Bible states that some famines and droughts are the judgment of God (2 Sam. 21:1; 1 Kings 17:1; 2 Kings 8:1; Jer. 14:12; Ezek. 5:12; Amos 4:6), not all such disasters are connected to divine punishment (Gen. 12:10; 26:1; Ruth 1:1; Acts 11:28). When God did send drought and famine on His people, it was for the purpose of bringing them to repentance (1 Kings 8:35-36; Hos. 2:8-23; Amos 4:6-8). Moreover, the OT contains promises that God will protect His faithful ones in times of famine (Job 5:20,22; Pss. 33:18-19; 37:18-19; Prov. 10:3).

FAN KJV term for a long wooden fork used to toss grain into the air so that the chaff is blown away. Shovels were also used for this purpose (Isa. 30:24). Modern translations render the underlying Hebrew and Greek terms "shovel," "winnowing fork," or "winnowing shovel."

FASTING Refraining from eating food. The Bible describes three main forms of fasting. The *normal fast* involves the total abstinence of food. Luke 4:2 reveals that Jesus "ate nothing"; afterwards "He was hungry." Jesus abstained from food but not from water. In Acts 9:9 we read of an *absolute fast* where for three days Paul "did not eat or drink" (HCSB). The abstinence from both food and water seems to have lasted no more than three days (Ezra 10:6; Esther 4:16). The *partial fast* in Dan. 10:3 emphasizes the restriction of diet rather than complete abstinence. The context implies that there were physical benefits resulting from this partial fast. However, this verse indicates that there was a revelation given to Daniel as a result of this time of fasting.

Fasting is to be done with the object of seeking to know God in a deeper experience (Isa. 58; Zech. 7:5). Fasting relates to a time of confession (Ps. 69:10). Fasting can be a time of seeking a deeper prayer experience and drawing near to God in prevailing prayer (Ezra 8:23; Joel 2:12). The early church often fasted in seeking God's will for leadership in the local church (Acts 13:2). When the early church wanted to know the mind of God, there was a time of prayer and fasting.

FATE That which must necessarily happen. The OT speaks of death as the common fate of humankind (Pss. 49:12; 81:15; Eccles. 2:14; 3:19; 9:2-3). The OT similarly speaks of violent death as the destiny of the wicked (Job 15:22; Isa. 65:12; Hos. 9:13).

FATHERLESS Person without a male parent, often rendered orphan by modern translations. Orphans are often mentioned with widows as representatives of the most helpless members of society (Exod. 22:22; Deut. 10:18; Ps. 146:9). God, however, has a special concern for orphans and widows (Deut. 10:18; Pss. 10:14-18; 146:9; Hos. 14:3) evidenced in the title "a father of the fatherless" (Ps. 68:5). Old Testament law provided for the material needs of orphans and widows who were to be fed from the third year's tithe (Deut. 14:28-29; 26:12-13), from sheaves left forgotten in the fields (24:19), and from fruit God commanded to be left on the trees and vines (24:20-21). Orphans and widows were to be included in the celebrations of the worshipping community (Deut. 16:11,14). God's people were repeatedly warned not to take advantage of orphans and widows (Exod. 22:22; Deut. 24:17; 27:19; Ps. 82:3; Isa. 1:17). In the NT James defined worship acceptable to God as meeting the needs of orphans and widows (1:27).

FATHOM Measure of depth equaling six feet (Acts 27:28).

FATLINGS, FATTED Generally a young animal penned up to be fed for slaughter. Sometimes a general reference to the strongest or to the choice among a flock or herd is intended. In the parable of the loving father, a son is welcomed home with a banquet of a fatted calf (Luke 15:23,27,30). Fattened animals were used as a symbol for slaughter. In the NT James pictured the oppressive rich as fattening their hearts for a day of slaughter, perhaps a reference to God's judgment on them (5:5).

FAWN Young deer; term used in modern translations for KJV's "hind" and "roe."

FEAR Natural emotional response to a perceived threat to one's security or general welfare. It ranges in degree of intensity from a sense of anxiety or worry to one of utter terror. It can be a useful emotion when it leads to appropriate caution or measures that would guard one's welfare. On the other hand, fear can be a hindrance to the enjoyment of life if it is induced by delusion or if it lingers and overpowers other more positive emotions such as love and joy, perhaps leading to an inability to engage in the normal activities of life. In the Bible, however, fear is perhaps more often than in popular culture regarded not as pure emotion but as wise behavior.

Attitude of Respect and Submission In some cases, "fear" carries with it the expectation of obedience. Respect or honor may be the sense in which Israel "feared" Solomon when they saw evidence that he possessed God's wisdom (1 Kings 3:28). Respect or reverence is also the proper attitude toward God's sanctuary (Lev. 19:30). Fear can be the opposite of treating someone or something as common, insignificant, irrelevant, or otherwise unworthy of attention (Esther 5:9).

Fear of God Any of these senses—terror, honor, submission—may be involved when God is the object of fear, with the additional sense of worship. For those who are enemies rather than followers of the Lord, terror is most appropriate (Jer. 5:22). Such terror is limited by the fact that God is not capricious but acts consistently according to His righteous character and revealed will. Nevertheless, those guilty of idolatry and injustice have every reason to fear His coming wrath in judgment (Ps. 90:11; Isa. 13:6-11; 30:30-33; Zeph. 1:18; Heb. 10:26-31). Terror is the only reasonable response when confronted by a Being whose knowledge and power have no limits, unless one's safety has been assured. The Bible contains many cases of a divine or angelic appearance to which fear is the natural response (Exod. 3:6; 20:18-20; Dan. 10:10-12; Luke 1:12-13,30). Following the resurrection of Christ, for example, an angelic appearance caused the guards at the tomb to faint with fear, but the believing women were told they had nothing to fear (Matt. 28:4-5).

The proper attitude of believers toward God is often said to be respect, reverence, or awe rather than fear. The biblical terminology, however, is the same, and God's character remains unchanged. The description of God often translated "awesome" is literally "feared" or "fearful" (Exod. 15:11; Neh. 1:5; Job 37:22; Ps. 89:7; Dan. 9:4). Confining the believer's attitude toward God to "reverence" or "awe" rather than "fear" may lose sight of those aspects of the divine character that compel obedience—His perfect holiness and righteousness and His unlimited knowledge and power. Knowing that God's wrath has been satisfied in Christ relieves the believer from the fear of condemnation, but not from accountability to a holy God (2 Cor. 5:10-11; 7:1; 1 Tim. 5:20; 1 Pet. 1:17).

FEAR OF ISAAC Name or title that Jacob used in referring to God (Gen. 31:42; cp. 31:53; 46:1). Evidently the patriarchs used various names to refer to God until He revealed His personal name to Moses (Exod. 6:3). Some scholars translate the Hebrew expression "Kinsman of Isaac" or "Refuge of Isaac."

FELIX Procurator of Judea at the time Paul the apostle visited Jerusalem for the last time and was arrested there (Acts 23:24).

FELLOES (KJV, REB) Rim of a wheel (1 Kings 7:33).

FENCED CITY KJV term for a fortified or walled city.

FERRET White European polecat mentioned by KJV in Lev. 11:30. Other translations read "gecko."

FESTIVALS Regular religious celebrations remembering God's great acts of salvation in the history of His people. Traditionally called "feasts" in the English Bibles, these can conveniently be categorized according to frequency of celebration. Many of them were

Fenced city: city walls and buildings outside Hazor.

timed according to cycles of seven. The cycle of the week with its climax on the seventh day provided the cyclical basis for much of Israel's worship; as the seventh day was observed, so was the seventh month (which contained four of the national festivals), and the seventh year, and the fiftieth year (the year of Jubilee), which followed seven cycles each of seven years.

Sabbath The seventh day of each week was listed among the festivals (Lev. 23:1-3). It functioned as a reminder of the Lord's rest at the end of the creation week (Gen. 2:3) and also of the deliverance from slavery in Egypt (Deut. 5:12-25). The Sabbath day was observed by strict rest from work from sunset until sunset (Exod. 20:8-11; Neh. 13:15-22). Each person was to remain in place and not engage in travel (Exod. 16:29; Lev. 23:3). Despite such restrictions even as kindling a fire (Exod. 35:3) or any work (Exod. 31:14; 35:2), the Sabbath was a joyful time (Isa. 58:13-14).

New Moon This festival was a monthly celebration characterized by special offerings, great in quantity and quality (Num. 28:11-15), and blowing of trumpets (Num. 10:10; Ps. 81:3). According to Amos 8:5, business ceased. The festivals of the new moon and Sabbath are often mentioned together in the OT (Isa. 1:13; 66:23; Ezek. 45:17; 46:1,3).

Passover The first of the three annual festivals was the Passover. It commemorated the final plague in Egypt when the firstborn of the Egyptians died and the Israelites were spared because of the blood smeared on their doorposts (Exod. 12:11,21,27,43,48). Passover took place on the fourteenth day (at evening) of the first month (Lev. 23:5).

During NT times large crowds gathered in Jerusalem to observe this annual celebration. Jesus was crucified during the Passover event. He and His disciples ate a Passover meal together on the eve of His death. During this meal Jesus said, "This is My body," and "this cup is the new covenant in My blood" (Luke 22:17,19-20 HCSB). The NT identifies Christ with the Passover sacrifice: "For Christ our Passover has been sacrificed" (1 Cor. 5:7 HCSB).

Feast of Weeks The second of the three annual festivals was Pentecost, also called the Feast of Weeks (Exod. 34:22; Deut. 16:10,16; 2 Chron. 8:13), the Feast of Harvest (Exod. 23:16), and the day of firstfruits (Num. 28:26; cp. Exod. 23:16; 34:22; Lev. 23:17). It was celebrated seven complete weeks, or 50 days, after Passover (Lev. 23:15-16; Deut. 16:9); therefore, it was given the name Pentecost.

Essentially a harvest celebration, the term "weeks" was used of the period of grain harvest from the barley harvest to the wheat harvest, a period of about seven weeks. In the NT the Holy Spirit came upon the disciples at Pentecost (Acts 2:1-4), at the festive time when Jews from different countries were in Jerusalem to celebrate this annual feast.

The Day of Atonement The third annual festival came on the tenth day of the seventh month (Tishri-Sept./Oct.) and the fifth day before the Feast of Tabernacles (Lev. 16:1-34; Num. 29:7-11). According to Lev. 23:27-28, four main elements comprise this most significant feast. First, it was to be a "holy convocation," drawing the focus of the people to the altar of divine mercy. The holy One of Israel called the people of Israel to gather in His presence and give their undivided attention to Him. Second, they were to "humble their souls" ("afflict your souls," Lev. 23:27 KJV). This was explained by later tradition to indicate fasting and repentance. Israel understood that this was a day of mourning over their sins. The seriousness of this requirement is reiterated in Lev. 23:29, "If there is any person who will not humble himself on this same day, he shall be cut off from his people" (Lev. 23:29 NASB). Third, offerings are central to the Day of Atonement. The Bible devotes an entire chapter (Lev. 16) to them; they are also listed in Num. 29:7-11. In addition to these, when the day fell on a sabbath, the regular Sabbath offerings were offered. The fourth and final element of the day involved the prohibition of labor. The Day of Atonement was a "sabbath of rest" (Lev. 23:32), and the Israelites were forbidden to do any work at all. If they disobeyed, they were liable to capital punishment (Lev. 23:30).

The center point of this feast involved the high priest entering the holy of holies. Before entering, the high priest first bathed his entire body, going beyond the mere washing of hands and feet as required for other occasions. This washing symbolized his desire for purification. Rather than donning his usual robe and colorful garments (described in Exod. 28 and Lev. 8), he was commanded to wear special garments of linen. Also, the high priest sacrificed a bullock as a sin offering for himself and for his house (Lev. 16:6). After filling his censer with live coals from the altar, he entered the holy of holies where he placed incense on the coals. Then he took some of the blood from the slain bullock and sprinkled it on the mercy seat ("atonement cover," Lev. 16:13 NIV) and also on the ground in front of the ark, providing atonement for the priesthood (Lev. 16:14-15). Next he sacrificed a male goat as a sin offering for the people. Some of this blood was then also taken into the holy of holies and sprinkled there on behalf of the people (Lev. 16:15). Then he took another goat, called the "scapegoat" (for "escape goat"), laid his hands on its head, confessed over it the sins of Israel, and then released it into the desert where it symbolically carried away the sins of the people (Lev. 16:8,10). The remains of the sacrificial bullock and male goat were taken outside the city and burned, and the day was concluded with additional sacrifices.

According to Heb. 9–10 this ritual is a symbol of the atoning work of Christ, our great high Priest, who did not need to make any sacrifice for Himself but shed His own blood for our sins. As the high priest of the OT entered the holy of holies with the blood of sacrificial animals, Jesus entered heaven itself to appear on our behalf in front of the Father (Heb. 9:11-12). Each year the high priest repeated his sin offerings for his own sin and the sins of the people, giving an annual reminder that perfect and permanent atonement had not yet been made; but Jesus, through His own blood, accomplished eternal redemption for His people (Heb. 9:12). Just as the sacrifice of the Day of Atonement was burned outside the camp of Israel, Jesus suffered outside the gate of Jerusalem so that He might redeem His people from sin (Heb. 13:11-12).

Feast of Tabernacles The fourth annual festival was the Feast of Tabernacles (2 Chron. 8:13; Ezra 3:4; Zech. 14:16), also called the Feast of Ingathering (Exod. 23:16; 34:22), the feast to the Lord (Lev. 23:39; Judg. 21:19). Sometimes it was simply called "the feast" (1 Kings 8:2; 2 Chron. 5:3; 7:8; Neh. 8:14; Isa. 30:29; Ezek. 45:23,25) because it was so well known. Its observance combined the ingathering of the labor of the field (Exod. 23:16), the fruit of the earth (Lev. 23:39), the ingathering of the threshing floor and winepress (Deut. 16:13), and the dwelling in booths (or "tabernacles"), which were to be joyful reminders to Israel (Lev. 23:41; Deut. 16:14). The "booth" in Scripture is not an image of privation and misery, but of protection, preservation, and shelter from heat and storm (Pss. 27:5; 31:20; Isa. 4:6). The rejoicing community included family, servants, widows, orphans, Levites, and sojourners (Deut. 16:13-15).

The feast began on the fifteenth day of Tishri (the seventh month), which was five days after the Day of Atonement. It lasted for seven days (Lev. 23:36; Deut. 16:13; Ezek. 45:25).

Feast of Trumpets Modern *Rosh Hashanah* is traced back to the so-called "Feast of Trumpets," the sounding of the trumpets on the first day of the seventh month (Tishri) of the religious calendar year (Lev. 23:24; Num. 29:1). The trumpet referred to here was the *shofar*, a ram's horn. It was distinctive from the silver trumpets blown on the other new moons.

This day evolved into the second most holy day on the modern Jewish religious calendar. It begins the "ten days of awe" before the Day of Atonement. According to Lev. 23:24-27 the celebration consisted of the blowing of trumpets, a time of rest, and "an offering by fire." The text itself says nothing specifically about a New Year's Day, and the term itself (*rosh hashanah*) is found only one time in Scripture (Ezek. 40:1) where it refers to the tenth day.

Purim Purim, commemorating the deliverance of the Jews from genocide through the efforts of Esther (Esther 9:16-32), derives its name from the "lot" (*pur*) which Haman planned to cast in order to decide when he should carry into effect the decree issued by the king for the extermination of the Jews (Esther 9:24). In the apocryphal book of 2 Maccabees (15:36) it is called the Day of Mordecai. It was celebrated on the fourteenth day of Adar (March) by those in villages and unwalled towns and on the fifteenth day by those in fortified cities (Esther 9:18-19). No mention of any religious observance is connected with the day; in later periods, the book of Esther was read in the synagogue on this day. It became a time for rejoicing and distribution of food and presents.

A Jewish mother and child celebrate the Jewish tradition of lighting of the candles at Hanukkah.

Hanukkah The other postexilic holiday was Hanukkah, a festival that began on the twenty-fifth day of Kislev (Dec.) and lasted eight days. Josephus referred to it as the Feast of Lights because a candle was lighted each successive day until a total of eight was reached. The festival commemorates the victories of Judas Maccabeus in 167 BC At that time when temple worship was reinstated after an interruption of three years, a celebration of eight days took place. The modern celebration does not greatly affect the routine duties of everyday life. This feast is referred to in John 10:22, where it is called the Feast of Dedication.

Two festivals occurred less often than once a year, the Sabbatical year and the Year of Jubilee.

Sabbatical Year Each seventh year Israel celebrated a sabbath rest for its fields. This involved a rest for the land from all cultivation (Exod. 23:10,11; Lev. 25:2-7; Deut. 15:1-11; 31:10-13). Other names for this festival were sabbath of rest (Lev. 25:4), year of rest (Lev. 25:5), year of release (Deut. 15:9), and the seventh year (Deut. 15:9). The Sabbatical Year, like the Year of Jubilee, began on the first day of the month Tishri. This observance is attested by 1 Maccabees 6:49,53 and Josephus.

Laws governing this year of rest included the following: (1) the soil, vineyards, and olive orchards were to enjoy complete rest (Exod. 23:10,11: Lev. 25:4-5); (2) the spontaneous growth of the field or trees (Isa. 37:30) was for the free use of the hireling, stranger, servants, and cattle (Exod. 23:10 11; Lev. 25:6-7), fruitful harvest was promised for the sixth year (Lev. 25:20-22); (3) debts were released for all persons, with the exception of foreigners (Deut. 15:1-4) (probably this law did not for bid voluntary payment of debts, no one was to oppress a poor man); (4) finally, at the Feast of Tabernacles during this year, the law was to be read to the people in solemn assembly (Deut. 31:10-13).

Jewish tradition interpreted 2 Chron. 36:21 to mean that the 70 years' captivity was intended to make up for not observing sabbatical years. After the captivity this Sabbatical Year was carefully observed.

Year of Jubilee This was also called the Year of Liberty (Ezek. 46:17). Its relation to the Sabbatical Year and the general directions for its observance are found in Lev. 25:8-16,23-55. Its bearing on lands dedicated to the Lord is given in Lev. 27:16-25.

After the span of seven sabbaths of years, or seven times seven years (49 years), the trumpet was to sound throughout the land; and the Year of Jubilee was to be announced (Lev. 25:8-9). The law states three respects in which the Jubilee Year was to be observed: rest for the soil—no sowing, reaping, or gathering from the vine (Lev. 25:11); reversion of landed property (Lev. 25:10-34; 27:16-24)—all property in fields and houses located in villages or unwalled towns, which the owner had been forced to sell through poverty and which had not been redeemed, was to revert without payment to its original owner or his lawful heirs (exceptions noted in Lev. 25:29-30; 27:17-21); and redemption of slaves—every Israelite, who through poverty had sold himself to another Israelite or to a foreigner settled in the land, if he had not been able to redeem himself or had not been redeemed by a kinsman, was to go free with his children (Lev. 25:39-41).

FESTUS Successor of Felix as procurator of Judea (Acts 24:27); assumed this office at Nero's appointment in AD 60. He held it until his death in AD 62. Paul the apostle appealed to Porcius Festus for the opportunity of being tried before Caesar, and Festus granted that request.

FETTER Translation of several Hebrew and Greek terms referring to something that constrains, especially a shackle for the foot. Fetters were made of wood, bronze (Judg. 16:21; 2 Chron. 33:11), or iron (Ps. 149:8).

FEVER Elevated body temperature or disease accompanied by such symptoms. The "burning ague" (Lev. 26:16) is an acute fever marked by regular periods of fever, sweating, and then chills.

FIELD Unenclosed land. In the Hebrew definition of field, both the use of land (pasture, Gen. 29:2; 31:4; cropland, Gen. 37:7; 47:24; hunting ground, Gen. 27:3,5) and the terrain (land, Num. 21:20, literal translation, "field of Moab"; Judg. 9:32,36) were insignificant. The crucial distinction is between what is enclosed and what is open.

FIG, FIG TREE Important fruit and tree of the Holy Land. Adam and Eve used leaves from the plant to make clothing (Gen. 3:7). Jesus cursed a fig tree because it was without fruit (Mark 11:13-14,20-21).

FINGER OF GOD Picturesque expression of God at work. The finger of God writing the Ten Commandments illustrated God's giving the law without any mediation (Exod. 31:18; Deut. 9:10). Elsewhere the finger of God suggests God's power to bring plagues on Egypt (Exod. 8:19) and in making the heavens (Ps. 8:3). Jesus' statement, "If I drive out demons by the finger of God, then the kingdom of God has come to you" (Luke 11:20 HCSB), means that since Jesus cast out demons by the power of God, God's rule had become a reality among His hearers.

FINING POT KJV term for a crucible (NRSV, NIV) or smelting pot (REB), a vessel used to heat metal to a high temperature as part of the refining process (Prov. 17:3; 27:21).

FIR TREE KJV term for a tree most often identified with the pine (NIV, REB, TEV). Others have identified the tree with the juniper (NASB at Isa. 41:19 and 60:13 only) or cypress (NRSV, NASB elsewhere).

FIRE The word "fire" in our English Bibles normally translates the Hebrew word 'esh in the OT and the Greek word pur (the root from which such English terms as "pyromaniac" and "pure" are derived) in the NT. Both terms signify the physical manifestations of burning: heat, light, and flame.

Throughout both the OT and NT, "fire" functions as a significant theological symbol. It is frequently associated with such important concepts as God's presence, divine judgment, and purification. In fact, in the OT, fire served as the primary means by which God manifested His presence and exercised judgment. Because of the sacrificial system, fire was an important aspect of early Israelite worship; it was the means by which animal sacrifices were offered up to God as a "pleasing aroma" (Gen. 1:8; Exod. 29:18,25,41).

The NT continues to portray God's presence in the form of fire especially in the person of the Holy Spirit. The outpouring of the Spirit at Pentecost was signaled by the appearance of fire on each believer's head (Acts 2:3). In his first letter to the Thessalonians, Paul warns believers not to "quench the

Holy Spirit" (1 Thess. 5:19 NASB). The word "quench" normally refers to extinguishing a fire. Since God so frequently indicated His presence by means of fire, fire became a metaphor for God emphasizing both His holiness and His retributive justice (Deut. 4:24; Heb. 12:29).

FIREPAN Utensil made of bronze (Exod. 27:3) or gold (1 Kings 7:50, KJV, "censers") used to carry live coals from the altar of burnt offering (Exod. 27:3; 38:3), as censers for burning incense (Num. 16:6,17), and as trays for collecting the burnt wicks from the tabernacle lamps (Exod. 25:38; 37:23; the "snuffdishes" of the KJV).

FIRKIN Unit of liquid measure (John 2:6). Firkin is an archaic English word that was used to translate a Greek term referring to a measure of approximately 10 gallons.

FIRMAMENT Great vault or expanse of sky that separates the upper and lower waters. God created the firmament on the second day to separate the "waters from the waters" (Gen. 1:6-7).

FIRSTBORN First son born to a couple and required to be specially dedicated to God. The firstborn son of newly married people was believed to represent the prime of human vigor (Gen. 49:3, Ps. 78:51). In memory of the death of Egypt's firstborn and the preservation of the firstborn of Israel all the firstborn of Israel, both of man and beast, belonged to Yahweh (Exod. 13:2,15; cp. 12:12-16). This meant that the people of Israel attached unusual value to the eldest son and assigned special privileges and responsibilities to him. The birthright of a firstborn included a double portion of the estate and leadership of the family. As head of the house after his father's death, the eldest son customarily cared for his mother until her death, and he also provided for his sisters until their marriage

FIRST RAIN KJV term at Deut. 11:14 for the early rain.

FISH, FISHING Animals living in water and breathing through gills; the profession and/or practice of catching fish to supply a family or society's need for food. Methods of catching fish included angling with a hook (Job 41:1), harpoons and spears (Job 41:7), use of dragnets (John 21:8), and thrown hand nets (Matt. 4:18).

Fishing boats on the Nile River in Egypt.

Old Testament Fish are mentioned often but not by the different kinds. Fish were a favorite food and a chief source of protein (Num. 11:5; Neh. 13:16). The law regarded all fish with fins and scales as clean. Water animals that did not have fins and scales were unclean (Lev. 11:9-12).

Fish abounded in the inland waters of Palestine as well as in the Mediterranean.

References to fishing as an occupation are rare in the OT because, for the most part, in OT time the Mediterranean coast was controlled by the Philistines and Phoenicians. The Israelites depended largely on foreign trade for their fish (Neh. 13:16). Two OT texts (Song 7:4 KJV; Isa. 19:10 KJV) speak of fishpools and fishponds, possibly an indication of commercially raised fish or of fish farming.

The most famous OT fish was the great fish of the book of Jonah (1:17), one that God prepared especially for the occasion and one whose species the OT does not indicate.

New Testament During NT times commercial fishing businesses were conducted on the Sea of Galilee by fishermen organized in guilds (Luke 5:7,11). Fishermen were hard workers, crude in manner, rough in speech and in their treatment of others (John 18:10). Fishermen owned their ships, took hirelings into their service, and sometimes joined to form companies (Mark 1:20; Luke 5:7).

Fish provided food for the common people (Matt. 14:17; 15:34). The risen Lord ate fish with the disciples in Jerusalem (Luke 24:42) and by the Sea of Galilee (John 21:13). The primary method of preparing fish was broiling (John 21:9). The most famous NT fish was the one used to pay the temple tax for Jesus and Peter (Matt. 17:27).

Theological In early Christian churches the Greek word for fish (*ichthusro*) came to be interpreted as a cipher for Jesus. Combining the first letter of each successive Greek word for "Jesus Christ, Son of God, Savior" spells *ichthus*. We do not know when this cipher was first used; but once the identification was made, the fish became a standard Christian symbol.

FISH GATE A north gate of the second quarter of Jerusalem (Zeph. 1:10) mentioned in connection with fortifications built by Manasseh (2 Chron. 33:14). The gate was rebuilt during the time of Nehemiah (Neh. 3:3; 12:39). The name is perhaps derived from the proximity of the gate to the fish market (cp. Neh. 13:16-22).

FISHHOOK Curved or bent device of bone or iron used in biblical times for catching or holding fish (Job 41:1-2; Isa. 19:8 KJV, "angle"; Matt. 17:27). Habakkuk described God's people as helpless fish who would be captured by hooks (1:15) and nets. Amos 4:2 refers to the practice of ancient conquerors of leading captives with hooks through their lips. Such was the fate of Manasseh according to one interpretation (2 Chron. 33:11 NASB, NIV, TEV).

FITCHES KJV term for two different plants. The first is black cummin (Isa. 28:25,27). Ezekiel 4:9 refers to either spelt, an inferior type of wheat (NASB, NIV, TEV), or else vetches (REB), a plant of the bean family.

FLAG KJV term for a water plant generally translated as "reed" (Exod. 2:3,5; Job 8:11) or rush (Isa. 19:6) by modern translations.

FLAGON Large, two-handled jar for storing wine (Isa. 22:24 KJV; Exod. 25:29; 37:16 REB, NRSV).

FLAX Plant (*Linum usitatissimumro*) used to make linen. The fibers of the flax stem are the most ancient of textile fibers. Flax was cultivated by the Egyptians before the exodus (Exod. 9:31) and by the Canaanites before the conquest (Josh. 2:6).

FLEET Group of ships. Solomon built a fleet of ships at Ezion-geber with the help of Hiram of Tyre (1 Kings 9:26-27; 10:11,22). KJV translated "fleet" as "navy" or "navy of ships." Solomon's fleet was used for commercial rather than military purposes.

FLESH The term "flesh," while prevalent in older English translations of the Bible such as the KJV and ASV (1901), has largely been replaced by numerous other terms in most modern English translations. Undoubtedly this shift is due to the wide variety of nuances the word "flesh" can have in the biblical context that are better rendered by other words in a modern setting. Nonetheless, such seemingly unrelated terms as "skin," "food," "meat," "relatives," "humankind," and "sinful nature" in modern English translations often render the same single word in the original languages: *basar* in Hebrew and *sarx* in Greek. Due to the obvious flexibility of the word, each of its primary meanings is listed below followed by an explanation and biblical examples.

"Flesh" as a Designation for the Body or Parts of the Body "Flesh" frequently refers to the skin or the body—all the material that covers the skeleton of humans and animals. For example, "flesh" clearly refers to the body as a whole in Lev. 14:9 where cleansed lepers are commanded to bathe "their flesh" in water. The psalmist also uses "flesh" in reference to his whole body when he says "my flesh trembles in fear of you" (Ps. 119:120 NIV).

Flesh as a Designation for Mankind or Blood Relatives Scripture occasionally uses the term "flesh" as a general designation for all living things. In Gen. 6:17, God warned that the flood He was about to bring upon the earth would destroy "all flesh." This included animals and human beings alike. More narrowly, "flesh" can be used as a designation for all humanity. The famous prophecy in Joel 2:28-32 which is quoted and fulfilled in Acts 2:17-21 promised that God's Spirit would be poured out on "all flesh." Clearly, in this case, only humanity is in view.

In an even narrower sense, "flesh" can refer to one's relatives. Leviticus 18:6, for example, employs the terms in prohibitions against sexual intimacy with close family members.

Flesh as a Designation for the Sinful Nature In the NT, especially in the Pauline epistles, the term "flesh" takes on a specialized theological meaning. Paul consistently uses the term "flesh" in reference to the fallen human nature that is incapable of conforming to God's holy expectations (Rom. 7:5,18; 8:3-9; Gal. 3:3). In this sense, "flesh" is unaided human effort—mere human strength without the power of the Holy Spirit. It is this "flesh" that offers sin a foothold in a believer's life (Rom. 8:3-4,9; Gal. 3:3; 5:16-17). Paul explains that the flesh and the Spirit are in conflict with each other within believers, necessitating the believer's denial of sinful desires and cooperation with the Holy Spirit (Rom. 8:13; Gal. 2:19-21; Col. 3:5).

Unfortunately, many have misunderstood Paul's specialized use of the term "flesh" and have taken the passages mentioned above to mean that our bodies are inherently evil. Nothing, however, could have been further from Paul's mind. Paul taught that Christ Himself came in the flesh and yet lived a sinless life (Rom. 1:3; 1 Tim. 3:16). Furthermore, the body is God's creation and therefore is good when it is devoted to God in holy service (1 Tim 4:4). In fact, Paul referred to the believer's body as the temple of the Holy Spirit, indicating its sacred nature and purpose (1 Cor. 6:19-20). The notion that the physical body is inherently evil and therefore an obstacle to spirituality came not from Paul but from Plato.

FLOOD Genesis 6-9 tells the story of the flood that covered the whole earth, and of Noah, the man used by God to save the world of men and beasts. Both OT and NT texts seem clearly to teach that the flood was universal (Gen. 7:19-24; 2 Pet. 3:6,20). But that does not mean that any one way of arguing for a universal flood, such as the catastrophist approach, for instance, is the last word on the matter. Much work remains to be done. What can be said is that the scientific evidence for a flood, even for a universal flood, is strong and growing daily.

FLOWERS Colorful blooms containing a plant's reproductive organs. Flowers grew abundantly during springtime in Palestine. Flowers grew mostly in open fields, since flower gardens as we now know them were not cultivated. Flowers grew in crop fields and in groves of trees around houses. Numerous kinds of wild flowers could be found in the plains and mountains of Palestine. The words "flower" and "flowers" refer to colorful blossoms, towering plants, open flowers, and flourishing flowers. In Palestine the warm spring temperatures joined with the winter rains to produce beautiful, blooming plants and flowers.

Almond blossoms (Gen. 43:11; Exod. 25:33-34; 37:19-20; Num. 17:8; Eccles. 12:5). The almond tree, a member of the rose family, had beautiful pink blossoms that the Israelites used as models for engravers to adorn the cups of the golden lampstand.

Bulrush (Exod. 2:3; Job 8:11; Isa. 18:2; 35:7). Sometimes referred to as "flag," "papyrus" (NIV), "reed" (NASB), or "rush" (NEB). This tall, slender reed-like plant grew along the banks of the Nile River and provided the earliest known material for making paper and covering the frames of boats (Isa. 18:2).

Calamus leaves (Exod. 30:23; Song 4:14; Isa. 43:24; Jer. 6:20; Ezek. 27:19). The leaves from this plant were a sweet-smelling cane or ginger grass. The leaves, when crushed, gave a much relished ginger smell. It was apparently imported from India for use in worship (Jer. 6:20). Several Hebrew expressions lie behind "calamus." The basic Hebrew term *qaneh* means "cane." It is modified in Exod. 30:23 by the word for balsam, apparently referring to sweet cane or *Cymbopogon*. A similar plant may be meant by *qaneh tob* in Jer. 6:20, *tob* meaning either "good" or "perfumed." Elsewhere, *qaneh* occurs without modification and may refer to different types of cane. For example, in 1 Kings 14:15 the giant reed *Arundo donax* may be meant (cp. Job 40:21; Isa. 19:6; 35:7).

Cyclamen is one of the flowers found in Israel. The flowers appear between December and early May, but there is a single region near Jericho where the plants flower in the autumn.

Israel's Star of Bethlehem flower.

Camphire flowers (sometimes referred to as Henna) (Song 1:14; 4:13; 7:11; see REB). The camphire was a small plant or shrub that bore beautiful cream-colored flowers that hung in clusters like grapes and were highly scented. It was used for orange dye.

Caperberry flowers (Eccles. 12:5 NASB). The caperberry was a prickly shrub that produced lovely flowers and small, edible berries as it grew in rocks and walls. It was supposed to stimulate sexual desires and powers. KJV, NRSV, NIV, TEV translate the Hebrew term as "desire" in Eccles. 12:5, but REB and NASB follow recent Hebrew dictionaries in translating it "caperberry" or "caper-buds."

Cockle flowers (Job 31:40). Purplish red flowers of a noxious weed called the "cockle" or "darnel" (*Lolium tenulentumro*). This plant grew abundantly in Palestinian grain fields. Its Hebrew name is spelled like the Hebrew word for "stink" and thus is translated "stinkweed" by NASB.

Crocus (Song 2:1; Isa. 35:1). Spring flowering herb with a long yellow floral tube tinged with purple specks or stripes. It is sometimes translated as rose. Technically, it was probably the asphodel (Isa. 35:2 REB).

Fitch (Isa. 28:25-27). KJV calls this flower the "fitch," but the better designation is probably the nutmeg flower. This flower was a member of the buttercup family and grew wildly in most Mediterranean lands. The plant was about two feet high and had bright blue flowers. The pods of the plant were used like pepper. Technically the plant is probably dill (NRSV, NASB, REB) or more precisely black cummin (*Nigella sativaro*). NIV translates "caraway." See *Fitches*.

Leek (Num. 11:5). Member of the lily family, a bulbous biennial plant with broad leaves. The bases of the leaves were eaten as food. The bulbs of this plant were used as seasoning. Israel relished the memory of leeks (*Allium porrumro*) from Egypt.

Lily (1 Kings 7:19,22,26; 2 Chron. 4:5; Songs 2:1-2,16; 5:13; 6:2-3; 7:2; Hos. 14:5). The term "lily" covered a wide range of flowers. The most common was *Lilius candidum*. The lily mentioned in Song 5:13 refers to a rare variety of lily that had a bloom similar to a glowing flame. The "lily of the valley" (Song 2:1-2,16) is known as the Easter lily. The lily mentioned in Hos. 14:5 is more akin to an iris. The beautiful water lily or lotus was a favorite flower in Egypt and was used to decorate Solomon's temple (1 Kings 7:19,22,26; 2 Chron. 4:5). The "lilies of the field" (Matt. 6:28; Luke 12:27; HCSB, wildflowers) were probably numerous kinds of colorful spring flowers such as the crown anemone.

Mandrake (Gen. 30:14-16; Song 7:13). The mandrake, an herb of the nightshade family, had a rosette of large leaves and mauve flowers during winter and fragrant and round yellow fruit during spring. The mandrake grew in fields and rough ground. It was considered to give sexual powers and probably can be identified as *Atropa Mandragora*, often used for medicine in ancient times.

Mint (Matt. 23:23; Luke 11:42). Aromatic plant with hairy leaves and dense white or pink flowers, probably *jucande olens*. Mint was used to flavor food. The Jews scattered it on the floors of houses and synagogues for its sweet smell.

Myrtle branches (Neh. 8:15; Isa. 41:19; 55:13; Zech. 1:8-11). Myrtle bushes (*Myrtus communisro*), which grew on Palestinian hillsides, had fragrant evergreen leaves and scented white flowers. The flowers on the myrtle branches were used as perfumes.

Pomegranate blossoms (Exod. 28:33; Num. 13:23; 1 Sam. 14:2; 1 Kings 7:18). Blossoms from the pomegranate tree (*Punica granatumro*) had dark green leaves with large orange-red blossoms. Decorators carved pomegranates on public buildings. The fruit symbolized fertility and was used to tan leather and for medicine.

Rose (Song 2:1; Isa. 35:1). Several varieties of roses could be found in Palestine. The rose was a member of the crocus family. Traditionally, what is considered a rose is not the flower mentioned in Scripture. The "rose" is more generally considered an asphodel. See *Crocus* above.

The blossoms and fruit of a pomegranate tree growing in Israel. The pomegranate is one of the seven species with which the land of Israel is blessed (Deut. 8:8). It is a frequent theme in Jewish art and is found atop the columns on the façade to the temple.

Saffron (Song 4:14) (*Curcuma longa* or *Crocus sativasro*). A species of crocus. In ancient times the petals of the saffron flower were used to perfume banquet halls. The type meant in Song 4:14 may be an exotic plant imported from India.

Other Though not specifically mentioned by kind in the Bible, other varieties of flowers grew in Palestine. Appearing as early as January were the pink, white, and lilac blossoms of the cyclamen. Dominating many landscapes were the various shades of reds and pinks of the crown anemones, poppies, and mountain tulips. Some short-lived summer flowers were the yellow and white daisy-like chrysanthemums.

FODDER Feed for domestic animals. The Hebrew suggests a mixed feed, either of several grains (though barley was the common grain for livestock, Judg. 19:19; 1 Kings 4:28) or a mix of finely cut straw, barley, and beans formed into balls. Silage refers to fodder that has been moistened and allowed to ferment slightly (Isa. 30:24 NRSV). Fodder was salted to satisfy the animals' need for salt and to give a tastier feed.

FOOD There were only two main meals for the Jewish family. Breakfast was taken informally soon after getting up and normally consisted of a flat bread cake and a piece of cheese, dried fruit, or olives. Sometimes the bread was wrapped around the appetizer, and sometimes the bread was split open to make a bag where the morsels might be placed.

After the midday rest, the evening meal was prepared on the fire; a vegetable or lentil stew was made in the large cooking pot, herbs and salt being used to add to the flavor. Only on special occasions such as a sacrifice or festival day was any meat added to the stew, and only on very rare occasions was the meat roasted or game or fish eaten. At the close of the meal, fruit would be eaten and the wine would be drunk.

FOOL, FOOLISHNESS, AND FOLLY Translations of several uncomplimentary words that appear approximately 360 times throughout the OT and NT to describe unwise and ungodly people. The words are especially predominant in the Wisdom Literature of the OT.

FOOT Part of the human and animal body used for walking. In Scripture "foot" refers mainly to the human foot (Exod. 12:11; Acts 14:8). It may also be used of the feet of animals (Ezek. 1:7) or, anthropomorphically, of God's feet (Isa. 60:13).

FOOTMAN KJV translation of two unrelated Hebrew terms. The first refers to foot soldiers as distinguished from cavalry (2 Sam. 8:4), to soldiers in general (1 Sam. 4:10; 15:4), or to men of military age (Exod. 12:37). The second term refers to a runner who served in the honor guard that ran ahead of the king's chariot (1 Sam. 8:11; 2 Sam. 15:1), to the king's guards in general (1 Kings 14:27-28; 2 Kings 10:25), or to royal couriers (Esther 3:13,15).

FOOTSTOOL Piece of furniture for resting the feet, especially for one seated on a throne (2 Chron. 9:18; James 2:3). The footstool of Tutankhamen of Egypt was carved with pictures of his enemies. Other Pharaohs were portrayed with their feet on their enemies' heads. In Ps. 110:1 God makes the messianic King triumph over His enemies, who are then made His footstool.

FOOTWASHING An act necessary for comfort and cleanliness for any who have traveled dusty Palestinian roads wearing sandals. Customarily, a host provided guests with water for washing their own feet (Judg. 19:21; Luke 7:44, where the complaint was that Simon had not provided water). Footwashing was regarded as so lowly a task that it could not be required of a Hebrew slave.

FOREKNOW, FOREKNOWLEDGE Scripture reveals God as being omniscient, that is, having exhaustive knowledge of all things—past, present, and future. Both the OT and the NT testify to God's comprehensive knowledge. Nothing is hidden from God's sight (Heb. 4:13). God's foreknowledge is that aspect of God's omniscience that relates to the future. Scripture clearly indicates that God's knowledge is not limited to the past and present. He is the One who announces events before they occur, and He makes known the end from the beginning (Isa. 42:9; 46:10a). It is this knowledge of the future, among other things, that distinguishes God from the false gods (Isa. 44:6-8; 48:14). It was not the prophets' clairvoyance but God's foreknowledge that made possible their predictions.

FORERUNNER Greek term *prodromos* (one who runs ahead) occurs only once in the NT (Heb. 6:20) where it serves as a designation for Christ. In secular Greek the term was frequent as a military term for advanced scouts or cavalry that prepared for a full assault. In English, forerunner indicates one who precedes and indicates the approach of another. In this sense John the Baptist is termed the forerunner of Jesus, though the NT does not use this term of John.

FOREST Large, naturally wooded areas, characteristic of the central hill country, the Galilee, and the Bashan. Large expanses of forest covered the majority of the hills in Palestine during the OT period. Large portions of the forests around Jerusalem were destroyed during the Roman siege of the city in AD 70.

FORGIVENESS Term used to indicate pardon for a fault or offense; to excuse from payment for a debt owed. God is characterized early in the life of Israel as a God who both forgives and holds the guilty accountable (Exod. 34:7; cp. Neh. 9:17). He is the source of forgiveness for Israel at Sinai (Exod. 32:2; 34:9). He provides forgiveness for sin through the sacrificial system (Lev. 4:20,26,28,31; 5:10,13,16,18; 6:7; 19:22). The prophets held this same covenant grace out to Israel if she would only repent from her presumption on God's grace and her election (Dan. 9:9; Isa. 33:74; Jer. 33:8; Mic. 7:8). The psalms reveal the God of Israel as the same God found in the Torah. He does not allow the guilty to go unpunished, yet He is a God of forgiveness.

Forgiveness is a vital idea for NT theology. John's baptism was for repentance and the forgiveness of sins (Mark 1:4; Luke 1:76-77). The idea is found in the confession of the Christ child's destiny

(Matt. 1:21; Luke 1:77). It is the blood of Jesus' atonement that yields eternal forgiveness of sins (Matt. 26:28; Heb. 10:11-12; Lev. 16; 17:11). Jesus places enormous emphasis on horizontal (human to human) forgiveness. Because Christians have been redeemed, they are obligated to forgive as they have been forgiven (Col. 3:13).

The NT also speaks of a sin that will not be forgiven (Mark 3:29; Luke 12:10). Presumably the sin of indignantly categorizing the spirit of Jesus, whom Jesus identifies as the Holy Spirit, as demonic reveals the desire to vilify God and to deny Him any place as sovereign.

FORK Two types of forks (pronged implements) are mentioned in Scripture: an implement used in the sacrificial cult and a farm tool used to winnow grain.

FORNICATION Various acts of sexual immorality, especially being a harlot or whore.

Masada, the site of a palace built by Herod the Great, provides its own natural fortification.

FORT, FORTIFICATION Walled structures built for defense against enemy armies. Cities of the ancient world were fortified for defensive purposes as far back as archaeological records exist. The oldest fortifications in Israel are at Jericho, where a Neolithic stone tower and part of a wall have been dated to 7000 BC.

FORTUNATUS Corinthian Christian who together with Stephanus and Achaicus ministered to Paul at Ephesus (1 Cor. 16:17).

FORUM The open place of a market town or the town itself. The Appii Forum (Acts 28:15) or market town of Appius was located 43 miles to the southeast of Rome on the Appian Way.

FOUNTAIN Spring of water flowing from a hole in the earth. The limestone rock of Palestine is especially suited for the formation of springs. In semi-arid country springs are highly prized as water sources and often determine the location of settlements. The goodness of Canaan was seen in its abundant water supply, "a land of brooks of water, of fountains and springs, flowing forth in valleys and hills" (Deut. 8:7 NASB).

FOWLER One who traps birds. All biblical references are figurative. A variety of means are mentioned in Scripture: snares (Pss. 91:3; 124:7); traps (Ps. 141:9; Jer. 5:26-27); ropes (Job 18:10 KJV, "snare"); and nets (Hos. 7:12). God is praised as One who delivers from the fowler's snare (Pss. 91:3; 124:7), an image of the power of the wicked.

FOX Dog-like carnivorous mammal, smaller than the wolf with shorter legs (Neh. 4:3). It has large erect ears and a long bushy tail (Judg. 15:4). It is referenced as cunning and crafty (cp. Luke 13:32).

FRANKINCENSE Ingredient used in making the perfume for the most holy place in the tabernacle (Exod. 30:34). It is a resinous substance derived from certain trees in the balsam family. Frankincense was one of the gifts presented to the child Jesus by the magi (Matt. 2:11).

Fountain in the center of Cisterna, a possible site for Three Taverns.

FREEWILL OFFERING Gift given at the impulse of the giver (Exod. 35:21-29; 36:3-7; Lev. 7:16). The distinctive marks of the freewill offering were the "stirred hearts" and "willing spirits" of the givers. The tabernacle was constructed using materials given as freewill offerings (Exod. 35:29).

FRIEND, FRIENDSHIP Close trusting relationship between two people. Nowhere does the Bible present a concise definition of "friend" or "friendship." Friendship may be simple association (Gen. 38:12; 2 Sam. 15:37) or loving companionship, the most recognizable example being that between David and Saul's son, Jonathan (1 Sam. 18:1,3; 20:17; 2 Sam. 1:26).

Friendship, however, was not limited to earthly associates. The OT also affirms friendship between God and human persons. The relationship between God and Moses (Exod. 33:11) is likened to friendship because they conversed face to face.

In the NT, the predominant word for friend is *philos*. A derivative, *philia*, is often used for friendship. Jesus is described as the "friend of ... sinners" (Matt. 11:19 HCSB). He called His disciples "friends" (Luke 12:4; John 15:13-15).

FRINGE Tassels of twisted cords fastened to the four corners of the outer garment, worn by observant Jews as a reminder of covenant obligations (Num. 15:38,39; Deut. 22:12; cp. Zech. 8:23). The woman suffering from chronic hemorrhage touched the tassel of Jesus' cloak (Matt. 9:20; Luke 8:44).

FROG Amphibious animal specifically used by God as a plague against Pharaoh and his people (Exod. 8:2-15).

A modern orthodox Jewish man praying at the Wailing Wall in Jerusalem wearing his frontlet.

FRONTLETS Objects containing Scripture passages worn on the forehand and between the eyes, primarily at prayer times. Jews followed scriptural commands, literally, writing Exod. 13:1-16; Deut. 6:4-9; 11:13-21 on small scrolls, placing these in leather containers and placing these on their forehead and left arm (Exod. 13:9,16; Deut. 6:8; 11:18).

By NT times, the frontlets were known as phylacteries (Matt. 23:5).

FULFILL Verb used in three senses that merit special attention: an ethical sense of observing or meeting requirements; a prophetic sense of corresponding to what was promised, predicted, or foreshadowed; and a temporal sense related to the arrival of times ordained by God.

FULLER One who thickens and shrinks newly shorn wool or newly woven cloth; also one who washes or bleaches clothing.

FURNITURE Equipment in a home used for rest, beautification, storage, and workspace.
Sacred Furniture Biblical interest in furniture focuses on the sacred furnishings of the tabernacle and the temple. We have in Exod. 25–27; 30; 37–38 a full description of the tabernacle with all its objects of furniture.

Common Furniture But this is not the case regarding the furniture of the common people living out their daily lives in their tents and houses. The Bible occasionally refers to basic furniture items such as beds, chairs, etc., but we have virtually nothing about manufacturers, building materials, designs, or appearances.

The Sea of Galilee as viewed from the northwest.

GAAL Personal name meaning "abhorrence," "neglect," or perhaps "dung-beetle." Man who usurped Abimelech's leadership in Shechem but met sudden defeat from Abimelech and left the city (Judg. 9:26-41).

GAASH Personal name meaning "rising and falling noisily." A height in the hill country of Ephraim that cannot be located any more precisely. Joshua was buried there (Josh. 24:30). Hiddai, one of David's 30 military heroes, came from the brooks of Gaash (2 Sam. 23:30).

GABBAI Personal name traditionally interpreted as meaning "tax collector." Member of tribe of Benjamin who settled in Jerusalem in time of Nehemiah (Neh. 11:8).

GABBATHA English transliteration of Greek transliteration of Aramaic place-name meaning "elevation." A platform in front of the praetorian's, or governor's palace in Jerusalem, where Pilate sat in judgment over Jesus (John 19:13), pronouncing the sentence to crucify Jesus.

GABRIEL Personal name meaning "strong man of God." The heavenly messenger who interpreted to Daniel the meaning of the vision of the ram and the goat. He appears four times in the Bible, each time bringing to human beings a message from the Lord. Twice he appeared to Daniel (8:15-27; 9:20-27). In the NT he appeared to announce the births of John the Baptist (Luke 1:8-20) and Jesus (Luke 1:26-38).

GAD Personal name meaning "good fortune." **1.** Seventh son of Jacob and the progenitor of the tribe of Gad (Gen. 30:9-11). His mother was Leah's maid Zilpah. **2.** Syrian god known from inscriptions from Phoenicia and Palmyra and used in biblical names such as Baal-gad (Josh. 11:17) and Migdal-gad (Josh. 15:37). **3.** Prophet who advised David as he fled from Saul (1 Sam. 22:5) and who brought God's options for punishment after David took a census of Israel (2 Sam. 24:11-14).

GADARA Place-name for home of Gadarenes used in TEV (Matt. 8:28).

GADARENE Resident of Gadara, one of the cities of Decapolis (Mark 5:1; Gerasenes, HCSB).

GADDI Personal name meaning "my good fortune." Spy from the tribe of Manasseh sent by Moses to examine the land of Canaan prior to Israel's conquest (Num. 13:11).

GADDIEL Personal name meaning "God is my good fortune." Spy from tribe of Zebulun that Moses sent to examine Canaan, the land to be conquered (Num. 13:10).

GADFLY (Jer. 46:20 NIV, NRSV) Stinging insect (stinging fly, TEV), either a horsefly (*Tabanidae*, NASB) or a botfly (*Oestridae*).

GADI Personal name meaning "my good fortune." A variant Hebrew spelling of Gaddi using same word as Gadite. Father of Menahem, king of Israel (752–742 BC) (2 Kings 15:14,17).

GADITE Member of tribe of Gad.

GAHAM Personal name meaning "flame." Son of Nahor, Abraham's brother, by his concubine Reumah (Gen. 22:24).

GAHAR Personal name meaning "drought" or "small in spirit" or "red-faced." Clan head of family of temple servants who returned from Babylonian captivity with Zerubbabel about 537 BC (Ezra 2:47).

GAIUS Greek form of Latin name *Caius* meaning "I am glad, rejoice." **1.** Macedonian Christian who was one of Paul's traveling companions (Acts 19:29). **2.** Christian from Derbe who accompanied Paul the apostle into Asia (Acts 20:4). **3.** Paul the apostle's host in Corinth (Rom. 16:23). According to 1 Cor. 1:14 he was one of the individuals in Corinth whom Paul personally had baptized. **4.** The Christian John loved and to whom he addressed 3 John (3 John 1).

GALAL Personal name meaning "roll" or "turtle." **1.** Levite among those who settled in Jerusalem after the exile (1 Chron. 9:15). **2.** Grandfather of Adda, a Levite who led in Nehemiah's thanksgiving (Neh. 11:17).

GALATIA Geographical name derived from Gaul because its inhabitants were Celts or Galli (Gauls). The original settlement was in central Asia Minor. Paul visited Galatia (Acts 16:6; 18:23), though his precise route is not clear. It is not known whether he visited Phrygian-dominated cities or the true Galatians in the countryside or whether his letter was addressed to the original territory in the north or to the Roman province with its southern additions (cp. 1 Cor. 16:1; 2 Tim. 4:10, where some manuscripts have Gaul, and 1 Pet. 1:1).

GALATIANS, LETTER TO THE Galatians is Paul's most intense letter. His anger at their situation is evidenced by the omission of his usual expression of praise after the salutation. The Galatian churches were founded by Paul (4:13-15), but others, probably from Jerusalem, visited the Galatians espousing views contrary to what Paul had taught. Their teachings centered on the need to supplement faith in Christ with obedience to the law of Moses. Circumcision was required, since it marked the "conversion" of a Gentile male to Judaism. The false teachers were referred to as "Judaizers."

The letter can be divided into three main sections. In the first (Gal. 1:10–2:21) Paul defends his apostleship as given directly by God through Christ, not dependent on Jerusalem or those who were apostles before him. Paul concludes this section by stating the main argument of the epistle: Justification is by faith in Christ and the works of the law must not be added. Faith is living one's life in constant submission to Christ and in relationship to Christ. In fact, Paul says, "Christ lives in me."

In the second section (3:1–5:12) he supports his thesis by appeals to the Galatians' own experience, inheritance practices, and the experiences of Abraham. Paul reminds them that Abraham was declared righteous when he was uncircumcised. He, too, had simply believed God and this faith was credited to him as righteousness (3:6-9). Reliance on the law placed one under the curse of the law (3:10-14). The purpose of Christ's work was to free (redeem) from the curse.

The third major section (5:13–6:10) contains Paul's appeal to live by the Spirit. They must not lose their spiritual freedom by giving in to sin. Life in the Spirit does not rule out moral absolutes. Paul's emphasis on justification by faith was an argument for the Galatians to live out their freedom. That freedom, however, must not be taken as meaning there is no moral accountability. The command that they not live by the law of Moses is not inconsistent with directions on how to live. The "works of the flesh" are obvious and must be avoided. They must nurture the fruit of the Spirit (5:22-23a) and act in love toward each other. In this way they will fulfill the law of Christ.

The closing section is written in Paul's own hand and again challenges them not to return to dependence upon the law (6:11-18).

GALEED Place-name meaning "pile for witness." Place where Jacob and his father-in-law Laban made a formal agreement or covenant determining the boundary line between their peoples and agreeing not to harm one another (Gen. 31:43-52). The place was also called Sahadutah and Mizpah.

GALILEAN Person who lived in Galilee. Dialect distinguished them from Jews in Jerusalem and Judah, particularly the difficulty in distinguishing the sounds of the gutturals that are important in Hebrew and Aramaic. Peter's Galilean style of speech set him apart from the courtyard crowd during Jesus' trial (Mark 14:70; cp. Acts 2:7).

GALILEE Place-name meaning "circle" or "region." The northern part of Palestine above the hill country of Ephraim and the hill country of Judah (Josh. 20:7). The term "Galilee" apparently was used prior to Israel's conquest, being mentioned in Egyptian records. It was used in Israel but

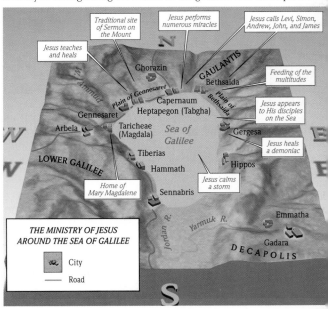

THE MINISTRY OF JESUS AROUND THE SEA OF GALILEE

not as a political designation. The tribes of Naphtali, Asher, Issachar, Zebulun, and Dan occupied the territory which covered approximately the 45-mile stretch between the Litani River in Lebanon and the Valley of Jezreel in Israel north to south and from the Mediterranean Sea to the Jordan River west to east.

In the time of Jesus' Galilee, Herod Antipas governed Galilee and Perea. Jesus devoted most of His earthly ministry to Galilee, being known as the Galilean (Matt. 26:69). After the fall of Jerusalem in AD 70, Galilee became the major center of Judaism, the Mishnah and Talmud being collected and written there.

GALILEE, SEA OF Place-name meaning "circle." A freshwater lake nestled in the hills of northern Palestine. Its surface is nearly 700 feet below the level of the Mediterranean, some 30 miles to the west. The nearby hills of Galilee reach an altitude of 1,500 feet above sea level. To the east are the mountains of Gilead with peaks of more than 3,300 feet. To the north are the snow-covered Lebanon Mountains. Fed chiefly by the Jordan River, which originates in the foothills of the Lebanon Mountains, the Sea of Galilee is 13 miles long north and south and eight miles wide at its greatest east-west distance. Because of its location, it is subject to sudden and violent storms that are usually of short duration. In the OT this sea is called Chinnereth. In NT times it was also called the "lake of Gennesaret." Once John called it the "Sea of Tiberias" (6:1).

Capernaum, which played a major role in the ministry of Jesus, was a center of that industry. The other lake towns of importance were Bethsaida, which means "the fishing place," and Tiberias, a Gentile city constructed by Herod Antipas when Jesus was a young man.

GALL 1. Bitter, poisonous herb (perhaps *Citrullus colocynthis*), the juice of which is thought to be the "hemlock" poison that Socrates drank. Gall was frequently linked with wormwood (Deut. 29:18; Jer. 9:15; 23:15; Lam. 3:19; Amos 6:12) to denote bitterness and tragedy. **2.** Expressed by two different Hebrew words, used in three senses in connection with the liver: (1) as an organ, either the liver or the gallbladder, through which a sword might pass when one was run through (Job 20:25); (2) as bile, a sticky, yellow-greenish, alkaline fluid secreted by the liver, which might be poured out on the ground when one was disemboweled (Job 16:13); (3) in a figurative sense (Job 13:26) for bitterness (bitter things, NASB, NIV, NRSV; bitter charges, REB, TEV).

GALLIM Place-name meaning "piles." Village near Anathoth in tribal territory of Benjamin. Saul gave his daughter Michal as wife to a citizen of Gallim after taking her away from David (1 Sam. 25:44; cp. 2 Sam. 3:14-15).

GALLIO Personal name of unknown meaning. The deputy or proconsul of Achaia headquartered in Corinth, where his judgment seat has been discovered. Certain Jews brought Paul before Gallio seeking to get Roman punishment of him. They charged that Paul advocated an unlawful religion (Acts 18:12-17).

GALLON Word used by modern translations to transfer Greek *metretes* into modern terminology. A *metretes* contained about nine gallons (cp. John 2:6; KJV reads "firkins").

GALLOWS English translation referring to the platform on which a person was hanged. The Hebrew term translated "gallows" in Esther (2:23; 7:9-10; 9:25) is the word for "tree." It is frequently suggested that tree should be understood as "stake" and that those executed by the Persians were impaled rather than hung.

GAMALIEL Personal name meaning "God rewards with good." **1.** Son of Pedahzur; a leader of the tribe of Manasseh who helped Moses take the census in the wilderness (Num. 1:10; cp. 7:54-59). **2.** Highly regarded Pharisee who was a member of the Sanhedrin (Acts 5:34). He squelched a plan by the Sanhedrin to kill the apostles by reminding the members that interference with what the apostles were doing might prove to be opposition to God. **3.** A leading Jewish rabbi in the late first and early second centuries AD He was the grandson of the Gamaliel mentioned in the book of Acts. He is credited with many of the adaptations in Judaism necessitated by the destruction of the temple in AD 70.

The interior of the traditional site of the tomb of Gamaliel.

GAMES Archaeological finds from the ancient Near East provide ample evidence for the existence in antiquity of numerous types of games, including early forms of checkers and chess. Likewise, various children's toys found in Palestine confirm that Hebrew children, like their counterparts in nearly every culture and era, played recreational games. There is, however, no specific mention of organized games of any kind in the OT.

Children in present-day Jerusalem playing a game in the street on the Via Dolorosa..

By the first century, Jews in Palestine and in the Diaspora, and of course Gentiles throughout the Mediterranean world, were familiar with competitive games. In the NT there are direct references to games and competitions, particularly in Paul's epistles. For those living in first-century Corinth, illustrations from competitive games would be easily understood not only from everyday life, but also because it was the site of the Isthmian games (AD 51), an event second only to the Olympics in prestige. Both Paul and the writer of Hebrews found illustrations of the Christian life in the competitive games of the first century.

GAMUL Personal name meaning "receiver of good deeds." Head of one of the priestly divisions in the temple under David and Solomon (1 Chron. 24:17).

GANGRENE Greek *gangraina* (2 Tim. 2:17) can refer either to gangrene, a death of soft tissue resulting from problems with blood flow (NASB, NRSV, REB) or to an ulcer (canker, KJV; open sore, TEV). In 2 Timothy *gangraina* is used figuratively for false teachings that destroy people who accept them.

GARDEN In biblical times an enclosed plot of ground on which flowers, vegetables, herbs, and fruit and nut trees were cultivated (Gen. 2:8; 1 Kings 21:2; Esther 1:5; Isa. 51:3; John 18:1-2).

The garden of Eden (Gen. 2:8; 3:23-24) was planted by God (2:8) and entrusted to Adam for cultivating and keeping (2:15). Following their sin, Adam and Eve were banished from the garden; but "Eden, the garden of God" (Ezek. 28:13) continued as a symbol of blessing and bounty (Ezek. 36:35; Joel 2:3). The "king's garden" in Jerusalem was located near a gate to the city that provided unobserved exit or escape (2 Kings 25:4; Neh.

The Garden of Gethsemane looking west toward the city wall of old Jerusalem.

3:15; Jer. 39:4; 52:7). The "garden" (John 18:1) called Gethsemane (Matt. 26:36; Mark 14:32) was a place where Jesus often met with His disciples (John 18:2) and where He was betrayed and arrested.

GAREB Personal name and place-name meaning "scabby." **1.** Member of David's personal army (2 Sam. 23:38). **2.** Hill in Jerusalem marking point of city wall which Jeremiah promised would be rebuilt (Jer. 31:39).

GARLAND In modern translations two Hebrew terms and one Greek term, all referring to wreaths worn on the head. Garlands symbolized instruction or the benefit of wisdom (Prov. 1:8-9; 4:7-9).

GARMITE Title or designation meaning "my bone" used for Keilah in the line of the tribe of Judah (1 Chron. 4:19). The Hebrew text and the exact meaning of Garmite are obscure.

GARNER KJV term for a barn, storehouse, or granary (Ps. 144:13; Joel 1:17; Matt. 3:12; Luke 3:17). To garner (Isa. 62:9 NASB, NRSV) means to gather (a crop) for storage.

GASH In modern translations to cut the skin as a sign of mourning (NASB, Jer. 41:5; 47:5; 48:37) or in the worship of pagan deities (1 Kings 18:28).

GASHMU Aramaic form of *Geshem* used in Neh. 6:6.

GATAM Personal name of uncertain meaning. Son of Eliphaz and grandson of Esau (Gen. 36:11). He headed a clan of Edomites (Gen. 36:16).

GATE A gate, like a door, a wall, or a threshold, sets a boundary between that which is inside and that which is outside. "Gate" is the more prominent term since it provided the most common access into towns and villages, temples, and even houses. In reality a gate serves both to allow access and to limit access. Open gates allowed entrance, though gatekeepers were often employed to ascertain that only authorized persons gained entry (1 Chron. 9:22). Shut gates offered protection and safety for those inside (Josh. 2:5). Because the gate was the primary means of entry, it was often the site where enemies assembled for attack or forced entry (Jer. 1:15).

The Bible has several figurative or symbolic allusions to gates. Jacob, after his dream at Bethel, describes the place as "the house of God, ... the gate of heaven" (Gen. 28:17 NASB). In effect for Jacob this spot marked a symbolic boundary between heaven and earth. Both Job and the psalmist speak of the gates of death (Job 38:17; Ps. 107:18). The gates of death mark the boundary between life and death. King Hezekiah in the book of Isaiah

The Damascus Gate at Jerusalem as seen from outside the old city walls.

speaks of being consigned to the gates of Sheol the rest of his days, a clear reference to his death (Isa. 38:10). Jesus says of the church "the gates of Hades shall not overpower it" (Matt. 16:18 NASB). Hades, the realm of the underworld and the dead, has no power over Christ's church.

GATH One of the five cities that comprised the Philistine city-state system (1 Sam. 6:17). The inhabitants of Gath were referred to as the Gittites (1 Sam. 17:4; 2 Sam. 6:10-11). In addition to Gath, the other towns of the Philistine city-state system were Ekron, Ashdod, Ashkelon and Gaza (1 Sam. 6:17). We may reasonably assume that Gath was the principal city among the five and served as the hub of the Pentapolis.

GATH-HEPHER Place-name meaning "winepress on the watering hole." A city on the eastern border of Zebulun's tribal allotment (Josh. 19:13). The prophet Jonah came from Gath-hepher (2 Kings 14:25). It is located at modern el-Meshed or nearby Khirbet ez-Zurra, three miles northeast of Nazareth.

GATH-RIMMON Place-name meaning "winepress on the pomegranate tree." Town in tribal territory of Dan (Josh. 19:45) and set aside for Levites (21:24).

GAZA Place-name meaning "strong." Philistine city on the coastal plain about three miles inland from the Mediterranean Sea. It was the southernmost town of the Philistine city-state system, which also included Ashkelon, Ashdod, Ekron, and Gath (1 Sam. 6:17).

GAZELLE Fleet-footed animal noted for its attractive eyes. Native to the Middle East, this animal resembles an antelope but is smaller. They were considered clean by the Israelites and thus were permitted as food (Deut. 12:15,22).

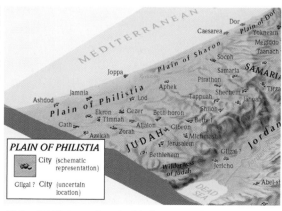

Plain of Philistia touches the Mediterranean Sea.

GAZER KJV spelling of Gezer based on Hebrew accented form (2 Sam. 5:25; 1 Chron. 14:16).

GAZEZ Personal name meaning "sheepshearing." Name both of Caleb's son and grandson (1 Chron. 2:46). As other names in the list represent cities in southern Judah occupied by the clan of Caleb, Gazez may also be a city, though nothing else is known about it.

GAZZAM Personal name meaning "caterpillar" or "bird of prey." Leader of a clan of temple servants who returned from Babylonian captivity with Zerubbabel (Ezra 2:48).

GEAR Context of Acts 27:17 indicates that the Greek term underlying "gear" (RSV) refers to some type of nautical equipment or apparatus.

GEBA Place-name meaning "hill," and variant Hebrew spelling of Gibeah, with which it is sometimes confused, though the two represent different towns in the territory of Benjamin. Geba was given to Benjamin (Josh. 18:24) but set aside for the Levites (21:17).

GEBAL Place-name meaning "mountain." **1.** Seaport known to Greeks as Byblos whose help for Tyre Ezekiel described (Ezek. 27:9). **2.** Member of a coalition against Israel that the psalmist lamented (Ps. 83:7). It is the northern part of Arabia near Petra in the mountainous country south of the Dead Sea. The Genesis Apocryphon from the Dead Sea Scrolls also mentions it.

GEBALITE Citizens of Gebal.

GEBER Personal name meaning "young man" or "hero." Solomon's district governor for Gilead beyond the Jordan (1 Kings 4:19) was the son of Uri. He collected provisions to supply the royal court. The district governor over Ramoth-gilead was Ben-geber or the son of Geber.

GEBIM Place-name meaning "water ditch." It lay on the line of the march that conquerors took against Jerusalem (Isa. 10:31).

GEDALIAH Personal name meaning "Yahweh has done great things." **1.** Son of Ahikam who was appointed ruler of Judah by Nebuchadnezzar of Babylon in 587 BC (2 Kings 25:22). **2.** Royal official under King Zedekiah (597–586 BC) who was with the group that got the king's permission to imprison Jeremiah in a cistern (Jer. 38). **3.** Temple singer and prophet who played the harp with his father Jeduthan and five brothers (1 Chron. 25:3). He headed one of the 24 divisions of temple servants (1 Chron. 25:9).

GEDEON KJV transliteration of Greek for Gideon in Heb. 11:32.

GEDER Place-name meaning "stonewall." City whose king Joshua killed (Josh. 12:13).

GEDERAH Place-name meaning "sheepfold" or "stonewall." A village in the Shephalah or valley of Judah (Josh. 15:36). Villagers were noted for skill in making pottery, much of which was made for the king (1 Chron. 4:23).

GEDERITE Citizen of Geder.

GEDEROTH Place-name meaning "walls." City in tribal allotment of Judah in the Shephelah or valley (Josh. 15:41).

GEDEROTHAIM Place-name meaning "two walls" or common noun referring to sheepfolds (cp. REB translation, namely both parts of Gederah). A town in the valley or Shephelah of Judah allotted to Judah (Josh. 15:36).

GEDOR Place-name meaning "wall." **1.** Town in hill country of Judah allotted to tribe of Judah (Josh. 15:58). It is located at Khirbet Judur three miles north of Hebron and Beth-zur and west of Tekoa. **2.** In 1 Chron. 4:18 Jered is the father of Gedor. **3.** The Gedor in 1 Chron. 4:39 probably represents an early copyist's change from Gerar, which is quite similar in appearance in Hebrew and appears in the earliest Greek translation.

GEHARASHIM Place-name meaning "valley of the handcrafts workers." A member of the genealogy of Judah and Caleb in 1 Chron. 4:14, a list which often includes place-names. It is listed as a place where members of the tribe of Benjamin lived in the time of Nehemiah (Neh. 11:35).

GEHAZI Personal name meaning "valley of vision" or "goggle-eyed." Servant of the Prophet Elisha (2 Kings 4:12). The Bible portrays him as a man of questionable character.

GEHENNA English equivalent of the Greek word (*geena*) derived from the Hebrew place-name (*gehinnon*) meaning "valley of Hinnom" and used in NT times as a word for hell. The valley south of Jerusalem now called the Wadi er-Rababi (Josh. 15:8; 18:16; 2 Chron. 33:6; Jer. 32:35) became the place of child sacrifice to foreign gods. The Jews later used the valley for the dumping of refuse

View of the Valley of Genenna (Hinnom Valley) looking northeast toward the new city of Jerusalem.

the dead bodies of animals, and executed criminals. The NT uses "Gehenna" to speak of the place of final punishment.

GELILOTH Place-name meaning "circles" or "regions." Border point north of Jerusalem in tribal allotment of Benjamin (Josh. 18:17). It appears to correspond to Gilgal in the description of Judah (Josh. 15:7).

GEMALLI Personal name meaning "my camel" or "camel driver." Spy who represented tribe of Dan in searching out the land of Canaan (Num. 13:12).

GEMARIAH Personal name meaning "Yahweh has completed or carried out." **1.** Messenger King Zedekiah (597–586 BC) sent to Babylon. He carried a letter from Jeremiah to the exiles (Jer. 29:3). **2.** Son of Shaphan, the court scribe, who had a room in the temple, where Baruch read from Jeremiah's sermons to the congregation (Jer. 36:10). Later, Gemariah sought to keep the king from burning Jeremiah's scroll (v. 25).

GENEALOGIES Written or oral expressions of the descent of a person or persons from an ancestor or ancestors. Genealogies are presented in two forms: in concise lists or within narratives that will contain additional information. Biblical genealogies do not always name all the members of the family line. They serve a selective function, depending on the purpose(s) of the author.

GENERAL With reference to Sisera (Judg. 4:7) and Joab (1 Chron. 27:34), a general (NRSV) is the highest-ranking officer in command of an army. General, commander, and (chief) captain are used interchangeably for such an officer in English translations. KJV consistently translates "captain" or "chief captain."

GENERATION Period of time and its significant events comprising the life span of a person but also used to talk of a more indefinite time span. Two Hebrew words are at times translated "generation." The more significant of these is *toledot*, derived from the Hebrew verb, meaning "to bear children."

In the NT "generation" refers to a specific contemporary audience. Jesus often used the term to describe the evil nature of the people He addressed (Matt. 11:16; 12:39; Luke 17:25). The message of the NT can be summarized: "to Him be glory in the church and in Christ Jesus to all generations, forever and ever" (Eph. 3:21 HCSB).

GENESIS, BOOK OF The first book of the Bible and the first of five written by Moses. Genesis describes the creation of all things by the mighty acts of the one true God, human rebellion, punishment, and restoration (Gen. 1–11:9). The remainder explains the origins of the people of God, Israel, and their place in God's plan of redemption (Gen. 11:10–50:26).

God is the central character of Genesis. He is sovereign Lord and Creator of all things. Genesis assumes the fact of divine creation but does not try to prove it. Genesis does not specify when creation occurred or exactly how long it took. Genesis eloquently teaches that God created all things, including Adam and Eve, by special creation for fellowship with Himself. They were created innocent and with free wills. Freely they chose to disobey God, fell from innocence, and lost their freedom. Their fallen nature was passed to every other human being. The freedom of human wills is limited by fallen human nature. Humans are moral agents who make choices, but their wills are not free to obey God. Death came because of sin, and humanity was so corrupt that God wiped them out and started over with Noah. The second humanity also proved corrupt, and God confused their languages and scattered them. God's plan of redemption began to unfold by His calling of one man to found a family, one family chosen from among all the families of the earth. That family would be the source of blessing and salvation for all peoples. Through each generation in Genesis God demonstrated that the promise depended only on His sovereign power and that no circumstance, person, family, or nation could thwart His purposes. Human sin could not destroy God's plan, but rather provided Him opportunity to demonstrate His glory. Joseph may lie dead in a casket in Egypt, but his dying command was that his bones be carried home to Canaan when, not if, God brought His people again into the land He promised Abraham, Isaac, and Jacob.

GENNESARET Another name for the Sea of Galilee.

GENTILES People who are not part of God's chosen family at birth and thus can be considered "pagans." Though not synonymous in English, "Gentiles," "nations," "pagans," and "heathens" are variants chosen by translators to render *goyim* in Hebrew and *ethnoi* in Greek.

GENUBATH Personal name meaning "theft" or "foreign guest." Son of Hadad, king of Edom, and the sister of Tahpenes, the wife of Egypt's pharaoh (1 Kings 11:19-20). The name of the Egyptian pharaoh is not known.

GERA Personal name meaning "stranger," "alien," or "sojourner." **1.** Son of Benjamin and grandson of Jacob (Gen. 46:21). **2.** Grandson of Benjamin (1 Chron. 8:3,5). Son of Ehud and clan head in Geba who was exiled to Manahath (1 Chron. 8:6-7). **3.** Father of Ehud (Judg. 3:15, see 1. above). **4.** Father of Shimei, who cursed David (2 Sam. 16:5).

GERAH Smallest biblical measure of weight equaling one-twentieth of a shekel. Archaeological discoveries show a gerah weighed about half a gram.

GERAR Place-name possibly meaning "drag away." City located between Gaza and Beersheba. Abraham and Isaac made treaties with the king of Gerar (Gen. 20; 26).

GERASA Two places bear this name. One of them is referred to in the Bible; the other is not. According to some excellent ancient manuscript evidence, Mark 5:1 and Luke 8:26 located the healing of the demon-possessed man who lived among the tombs in "the country of the Gerasenes (Gadarenes)" ("Gerasenes" in NIV, NASB). This would point to a place-named Gerasa.

The other Gerasa was located some 26 miles north of present-day Amman in Jordan. Its ruins are among the most excellently preserved in the Middle East.

GERASENES Citizens of Gerasa.

GERGESENES KJV reading in Matt. 8:28. Modern translations read "Gadarenes."

GERIZIM AND EBAL Closely related place-names meaning "cut off ones" and "stripped one" or "baldy." Two mountains that form the sides of an important east-west pass in central Israel known as the valley of Shechem.

When the Israelites conquered central Israel, Joshua carried out the directive given by Moses and placed half of the tribes on Mount Gerizim to pronounce the blessing (Deut. 27:12) and the other half on Mount Ebal to pronounce the curses (Deut. 11:29; Josh. 8:30-35). Joshua built an altar on Ebal (Josh. 8:30).

GERSHOM Personal name meaning "sojourner there," "expelled one," or "protected of the god Shom." **1.** Firstborn son of Moses and Zipporah (Exod. 2:22). **2.** Son of Levi and head of a clan of Levitic priests (1 Chron. 6:16-20,43,62,71; 15:7). First Chronicles 23:14 shows that Moses' sons had been incorporated into the line of Levites (cp. 1 Chron. 26:24). **3.** Man who accompanied Ezra on the return from Babylon to Jerusalem (Ezra 8:2).

The ruins of ancient Gerasa located in the modern country of Jordan.

GERSHOMITES NRSV term for "sons of Gershom" (1 Chron. 6:62,71).

GERSHON Personal name meaning "expelled" or "bell." Eldest son of Levi (Gen. 46:11). He was the progenitor of the Gershonites, who had specifically assigned responsibilities regarding the transporting of the tabernacle during the years of Israel's nomadic existence in the wilderness (cp. Exod. 6:16-17; Num. 3:17-25; 4:22-41; 7:7; 10:17; 26:57; Josh. 21:6,27).

GERSHONITE Descendant of Gershon.

GERUTH Part of a place-name meaning "hospitality" (Jer. 41:17) translated differently—KJV "habitation of Chimham"; NASB, NRSV: "Geruth Chimham"; REB: "Kimham's holding."

GESHAM Personal name with variant spellings, perhaps meaning "rain." Son of Jahdai (1 Chron. 2:47).

GESHEM Personal name meaning "rain." Arabian ruler of Kedar who joined Sanballat and Tobiah in opposing Nehemiah's efforts to rebuild the wall of Jerusalem (Neh. 2:19; 6:1-19).

GESHUR Place-name perhaps meaning "bridge." Small Aramean city-state between Bashan and Hermon. It served as a buffer between Israel and Aram. David married Maacah, daughter of the king of Geshur, who became mother of Absalom (2 Sam. 3:3), which caused the two lands to be on friendly terms.

GETHER Aramean tribal name of uncertain meaning. They are Semites, their original ancestor being the grandson of Shem and great grandson of Noah (Gen. 10:23).

Looking toward the Garden of Gethsemane with the Church of All Nations in the center of the photo.

GETHSEMANE Place-name meaning "olive press." Place where Jesus went after the Last Supper, a garden outside the city, across the Kidron on the Mount of Olives (Matt. 26:36-56; Mark 14:32-52; Luke 22:39-53; John 18:1-14).Gethsemane was probably a remote walled garden (Jesus "entered" and "went out") where Jesus went often for prayer, rest, and fellowship with His disciples.

GEUEL Personal name meaning "pride of God." Spy from tribe of Gad whom Moses sent to inspect the land before conquering it (Num. 13:15).

GEZER An important city in the biblical period, located on a main juncture of the Via Maris, the Way of the Sea. It guarded the Aijalon Valley and the route from the coast up to Jerusalem and the Judean Hills. Joshua defeated the king of Gezer who was part of a Canaanite coalition (Josh. 10:33). Gezer remained in Canaanite hands throughout the period of the judges (Josh. 16:10; Judg. 1:29). David fought against the Philistines near Gezer (2 Sam. 5:25; 1 Chron. 20:4).

GHOST KJV uses "ghost" in two senses, for the human life force and for God's Holy Spirit. KJV never uses "ghost" for the disembodied spirits of the dead. All 11 OT references involve the phrase "give up the ghost" (for example, Gen. 25:8; 35:29), which means to cease breathing or simply to die. This phrase occurs eight times in the NT (Matt. 27:50; Acts 5:5; 12:23). The predominant NT use is for the Holy Spirit.

GIAH Place-name meaning "bubbling." Place where David's general Joab confronted Abner, Saul's general, after Abner killed Joab's brother Asahel (2 Sam. 2:24).

GIANTS Persons of unusual stature who often are reputed to possess great strength and power. The earliest biblical reference to giants is to the *nephilim* born to the "daughters of men" and the "sons of God" (Gen. 6:1-4).

A second class of giants who inhabited pre-Israelite Palestine was the *repha'im.* Their last survivor was Og, king of Bashan (Deut. 3:11,13).

GIBBAR Personal name meaning "young, powerful man." A man, 95 of whose descendants returned from Babylonian captivity with Zerubbabel in 537 BC (Ezra 2:20). The corresponding list in Neh. 7:25 has Gibeon.

GIBBETHON Place-name meaning "arched," "hill," or "mound." City in the tribal territory of Dan (Josh. 19:44) but assigned to the Levites (Josh. 21:23).

GIBEA Personal name meaning "hill." Son of Caleb by his concubine Maacah (1 Chron. 2:49).

GIBEAH Place-name meaning "a hill," closely related to names of Geba and Gibeon. Gibeah or Gibeath was the name of four different places in the OT. **1.** City in hill country of Judah allotted to tribe of Judah (Josh. 15:57). **2.** City closely connected with Phinehas, the high priest and grandson of Aaron. Phinehas buried his father Eleazar there (Josh. 24:33). **3.** The ark was lodged on a hill (Hb.

Gibeah) during the period between its return by the Philistines and David's initial effort to move it to Jerusalem (2 Sam. 6:3-4). **4.** The most significant Gibeah was the city in the tribal territory of Benjamin (Josh. 18:28). A bloody civil war between Benjamin and the other Israelite tribes broke out when the men of Gibeah raped a traveling Levite's concubine (Judg. 19:1–21:25).

GIBEATH Alternative Hebrew spelling for Gibeah (Josh. 18:28) preserved in KJV spelling.

GIBEATH-ELOHIM Place-name meaning "hill of God."

GIBEATH-HAARALOTH Place-name meaning "hill of foreskins." KJV translates the place-name in Josh. 5:3, while modern translations transliterate it. Joshua used traditional flint stone knives rather than more modern metal ones to circumcise the Israelite generation about to conquer Canaan.

GIBEON Place-name meaning "hill place." This "great city" (Josh. 10:2) played a significant role in OT history, especially during the conquest of Canaan. Archaeology has demonstrated that the city was a thriving industrial area that made it a primary community in Canaan.

GIDDALTI Personal name meaning "I brought from there" or "I made great, praised." Son of Heman to whom David gave the task of prophesying through playing musical instruments (1 Chron. 25:4). He became a leader of a clan of temple musicians (1 Chron. 25:29).

GIDDEL Personal name meaning "he made great, praised." **1.** Clan leader of a group of temple servants who returned from the Babylonian captivity with Zerubbabel about 537 BC (Ezra 2:47). **2.** Original clan father of a group of royal servants who returned from the Babylonian exile with Zerubbabel about 537 BC (Ezra 2:56).

GIDEON Personal name meaning "one who cuts to pieces." The fifth major judge of 12th century Israel. He was also called Jerubbaal and was the son of Joash of the tribe of Manasseh. He judged for 40 years (Judg. 6:11–8:35). Gideon was given the task of delivering the Israelites from the Midianites and Amalekites, desert nomads who repeatedly raided the country. Gideon was not a willing volunteer, but God gave him more than enough evidence that he was being called to this task. God then gave Gideon a strategy for getting the job done. Although Gideon is counted among the men and women of faith (Heb. 11:32), some of his actions in later life had the result that Gideon's family did not follow his God (Judg. 8:33).

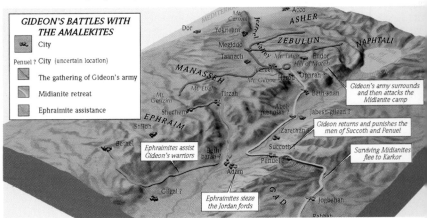

GIDEONI Personal name meaning "one who cuts down or cuts to pieces." Father of Abidan, a leader of the tribe of Benjamin during the encampment in the wilderness (Num. 1:11; 2:22; 7:60; 10:24).

GIDOM Place-name meaning "cleared land." Place where tribes of Israel punished tribe of Benjamin by killing 2,000 of Benjamin's soldiers (Judg. 20:45) for grossly mistreating a traveling Levite and his concubine.

GIFT, GIVING Favor or item bestowed on someone. Gifts were given on numerous occasions for a variety of purposes: as dowry for a wife (Gen. 34:12); as tribute to a military conqueror (2 Sam. 8:2); as bribes (Exod. 23:8; Prov. 17:8; Isa. 1:23); as rewards for faithful service and to insure future loyalty (Dan. 2:48); and as relief for the poor (Esther 9:22).

Both OT and NT witness to God as the giver of every good gift (1 Chron. 29:14; James 1:17).

Human life is God's gift (Job 1:21), as are all things necessary for physical life.

Scripture also witnesses to God's gifts as evidence of a special providence. In the OT such gifts include the promised land (Gen. 12:7), including its successful conquest (Deut. 2:36), possessing its cities (Deut. 6:10) and its spoils (Deut. 20:14); the Sabbath (Exod. 16:29); the promises (1 Kings 8:56); the covenants (2 Kings 17:15); the law (Exod. 24:12); and peace (Lev. 26:6). In the NT God's special providence is especially evident in the gift of God's Son (John 3:16) and of God's Holy Spirit (Luke 11:13).

God makes relationship with Himself possible by giving His people wisdom (1 Kings 4:29), understanding (1 Kings 3:9), a new heart (1 Sam. 10:9), and a good Spirit to teach them (Neh. 9:20). The NT expresses these gifts as the power to become children of God (John 1:12), justification from sin (Rom. 3:24; 5:15-17), and eternal life (John 10:28; Rom. 6:23).

Both Testaments witness to God's gift of leadership to God's people as: priests (Num. 8:19; Zech. 3:7); Davidic kings (2 Chron. 13:5); deliverers (2 Kings 13:5); shepherds with God-like hearts (Jer. 3:15); apostles, prophets, evangelists, and pastor-teachers (Eph. 4:11-12). Paul spoke of God's giving the ministry of reconciliation (2 Cor. 5:18), authority for building up the church (2 Cor. 10:8), and grace for sharing the gospel with the Gentiles (Eph. 3:8). The NT also stresses God's gift of spiritual abilities to every believer (Rom. 12:6; 1 Cor. 12:4; 1 Pet. 4:10).

God's gifts should prompt the proper response from the recipients. This response includes not boasting (1 Cor. 4:7; Eph. 2:8); amazement at God's inexpressible goodness (2 Cor. 9:15); the using of gifts for the furtherance of Christ's kingdom (1 Tim. 4:14; 2 Tim. 1:6-11); and a life of good works (Eph. 2:10).

GIHON Place-name meaning "gushing fountain." The primary water supply for Jerusalem and one of the four rivers into which the river of Eden divided (Gen. 2:13). The river cannot be identified with any contemporary river.

During the OT period the spring of Gihon was the primary water supply for the city of Jerusalem. The name comes from a Hebrew word meaning "a bursting forth" and is descriptive of the spring that is located in the Kidron Valley. It does not produce a steady flow, but gushes out at irregular intervals, twice a day in the dry season to four or five times in the rainy season. Water issues from a crack 16 feet long in the rock. At some point in the ancient past a wall was built at the eastern end of the crack, diverting water into a cave at the other end.

In the Jebusite period before David, a shaft went from the spring to a pool under the city. Water jugs were let down into the pool through another vertical shaft. This probably was the way Joab entered into the city and captured it for David (2 Sam. 5:8; 1 Chron. 11:6). During the early Israelite occupation, water was collected outside the city walls in an open basin called the "upper pool" (Isa. 7:3). An open aqueduct carried water from there to the "old pool" at the southern end of the city (Isa. 22:11; cp. Isa. 8:6). Along this conduit Isaiah confronted Ahaz (Isa. 7:3), and later Sennacherib's army demanded the city's surrender (2 Kings 18:17). Before Sennacherib's arrival, Hezekiah plugged the aqueduct and dug his famous water tunnel (2 Kings 20:20; 2 Chron. 32:30).

The pool of Siloam in Jerusalem. The pool was built in the 8th century BC by King Hezekiah to bring water from the Gihon Spring into Jerusalem.

GILALAI Personal name perhaps meaning "rolled away." Temple musician who helped Nehemiah lead the thanksgiving service for the completion of the Jerusalem wall (Neh. 12:36).

GILBOA Place-name of uncertain meaning, perhaps, "hill country" or "bubbling fountain." Location of an Israelite encampment (1 Sam. 28:4). The Israelites under Saul were preparing to do battle against the Philistines. At Mount Gilboa Saul and his three sons were slain (1 Sam. 31:8). David sang a lament over the Gilboa tragedy (2 Sam. 1:17-27). Mount Gilboa has been identified with modern Jebel Fuqus, on the eastern side of the Plain of Esdraelon.

GILEAD Place and personal name meaning "raw" or "rugged." **1.** The north-central section of the Transjordanian highlands. The name may originally have applied to a very small area. Usage of the name then grew and could be applied in different contexts depending on present political situations (cp. Judg. 10:17; Hos. 6:8). Physically, Gilead is a rugged country; the Hebrew name *Gil'ad* may be translated "rugged." Some of its peaks reach over 3,500 feet. It also has plains with grassland suitable

The rugged hill country of Gilead.

for cattle, and in antiquity the northern half of the region particularly was heavily forested. The King's Highway, an important international trade route, passed through Gilead. Gilead was an agriculturally significant region as well. It was famous especially for its flocks and herds and also for the balm of Gilead, an aromatic and medicinal preparation, probably derived from the resin of a small balsam tree. **2.** Great grandson of Joseph and original clan leader in tribe of Manasseh (Num. 26:28-32; 36:1).

GILGAL Place-name meaning "circle" and probably referring to a circle of stones or a circular altar. Such a circle of stones could be found almost anywhere in Palestine and led easily to naming towns "Gilgal." The many references to Gilgal in the OT cannot thus be definitely connected to the same town, since several different Gilgals may well have existed. **1.** Gilgal is most closely associated with Joshua, but the number of Gilgals involved continues an unsolved question. After crossing the Jordan, Joshua established the first camp at Gilgal (Josh. 4:19). There Joshua took 12 stones from the bed of the river to set up a memorial for the miraculous crossing. Gilgal, the first foothold on Palestinian soil, became Israel's first worship place, where they were circumcised and observed the Passover. There God appeared to Joshua and affirmed his mission (Josh. 5). **2.** Elijah and Elisha were associated closely with Gilgal. At one time Elisha made his headquarters there (2 Kings 4:38), where Elijah was taken up into heaven (2 Kings 2:1). This was apparently Tell Jiljulieh about three miles southeast of Shiloh, though it could still be Joshua's original Gilgal. **3.** Gilgal of the nations is mentioned as a royal city near Dor (Josh. 12:23).

GILO RSV, TEV spelling of Giloh to refer to Gilonite (2 Sam. 23:34).

GILOH Place-name meaning "uncovered" or "revealed." Town in tribal allotment of Judah in Judean hills (Josh. 15:51). David's counselor Ahithophel came from Giloh (2 Sam. 15:12). Some scholars locate it at Khirbet Jala in the suburbs of Jerusalem, but most think Giloh was actually further south.

GIMZO Place-name of uncertain meaning. Town in the Shephelah or valley of Judah which the Philistines captured from King Ahaz of Judah (735–715 BC), leading him to ask Assyria for help and to pay tribute to them (2 Chron. 28:18).

GIN KJV term for a trap or snare. With the exception of Amos 3:5, all scriptural uses are figurative, either of the fate of the wicked (Job 18:9; Isa. 8:14) or of the schemes of the wicked (Pss. 140:5; 141:9).

GINATH Place-name or personal name meaning "wall" or "enclosure." Father of Tibni, the favorite of half of Israel for kingship when Omri became king about 885 BC (1 Kings 16:21).

GINNETHO KJV spelling in Neh. 12:4 of Levite who returned from Babylonian captivity with Zerubbabel about 537 BC. Hebrew texts have various spellings followed by modern translations: Ginnethon (NIV; REB); Ginnethoi (NASB, TEV, NRSV).

GIRDLE Several items of clothing in KJV. **1.** An ornate sash worn by the officiating priests (Exod. 28:4,40) and by the wealthy of Jerusalem (Isa. 3:24). **2.** A decorated band (NRSV), woven belt (TEV, NASB), or waistband (NIV, REB) for the high priest's ephod (Exod. 28:8,27-28). **3.** A belt on which a sword or bow might be carried (1 Sam. 18:4; 2 Sam. 20:8; perhaps Isa. 5:27); a leather belt forming part of the proverbial garb of the prophets (2 Kings 1:8; Matt. 3:4). **4.** An undergarment (Job 12:18; Jer. 13:1-11), often rendered "waistcloth" or "loincloth."

To gird up one's loins means literally to tuck the loose ends of one's outer garment into one's belt. Loins were girded in preparation for running (1 Kings 18:46), for battle (Isa. 5:27), or for service for a master (Luke 12:35). The call to "gird up your minds" (1 Pet. 1:13 NASB) means to be spiritually alert and prepared.

GIRGASHITE or **GIRGASITE** Tribal name possibly meaning "sojourner with a deity." One on the list of original tribal groups inhabiting Canaan, traced back to Canaan, son of Ham and grandson of Noah (Gen. 10:16). The Ugaritic texts from Ras Shamra also apparently mention them.

GISHPA or **GISPA** (KJV) Personal name of uncertain meaning. Supervisor of temple servants in days of Nehemiah (Neh. 11:21). It does not appear in the lists in Chronicles and Ezra, so some Bible students think the name is a copyist's change from Hasupha, which the Jews would pronounce similarly (Ezra 2:43; Neh. 7:46).

GITTAH-HEPHER KJV spelling for Gath-hepher (Josh. 19:13) based on a variant Hebrew spelling in the text.

GITTAIM Place-name meaning "two winepresses." City to which people of Beeroth fled after Israel entered Canaan. The Bible does not tell the precise time (2 Sam. 4:3). After the exile, part of the tribe of Benjamin settled there (Neh. 11:33). This could be the same as the Gath of 1 Chron. 7:21; 8:13, but that is not certain.

GITTITH Word of uncertain meaning used in the titles of Pss. 8; 81; 84. It may represent a musical instrument resembling a Spanish guitar, a musical tune, or a rite or ceremony as part of a festival.

GIZONITE Citizen of Gizah or Gizon, a place not otherwise mentioned. It may be modern Beth-giz southwest of Latrun. David had military leaders from there (1 Chron. 11:34), though Gizonite does not appear in the parallel in 2 Sam. 23:34.

GIZRITE Citizen of Gezer. REB reading in 1 Sam. 27:8 for Girzite.

GLAD TIDINGS KJV phrase for good news (Luke 1:19). A synonym for "gospel" as the news Jesus brought of God's kingdom (Luke 8:1; Acts 13:32; Rom. 10:15).

GLASS Amorphous substance, usually transparent or translucent. Glass has a long history in the Middle East. Transparent glass was not made until NT times as a luxury item. Corinth became known for the production of glass after the time of Paul. John probably had the transparent variety of glass in mind when he wrote Revelation. He described the walls and streets of the new Jerusalem being made of pure gold. The gold of the walls and streets was so pure that it was as clear as glass (Rev. 21:18,21). John also described the sea as being like glass (Rev. 4:6; 15:2). Here the reference is probably not so much to transparency as to calmness.

GLEANING Process of gathering grain or produce left in a field by reapers or on a vine or tree by pickers. Mosaic law required leaving this portion so that the poor and aliens might have a means of earning a living (Lev. 19:9-10; 23:22; Deut. 24:19-21; cp. Ruth 2).

GLEDE KJV term for an unclean bird of prey (Deut. 14:13).

GLORY Weighty importance and shining majesty that accompany God's presence. The basic meaning of the Hebrew word *kavod* is heavy in weight (cp. 1 Sam. 4:18; Prov. 27:3). The NT uses *doxa* to express glory and limits the meaning to God's glory. In classical Greek *doxa* means opinion, conjecture, expectation, and then praise. The NT carries forward the OT meaning of divine power and majesty (Acts 7:2; Eph. 1:17; 2 Pet. 1:17). The NT extends this to Christ as having divine glory (Luke 9:32; John 1:14; 1 Cor. 2:8; 2 Thess. 2:14). Divine glory means that humans do not seek glory for themselves (Matt. 6:2; John 5:44; 1 Thess. 2:6). They only look to receive praise and honor from Christ (Rom. 2:7; 5:2; 1 Thess. 2:19; Phil. 2:16).

GLOSSOLALIA Technical term for speaking in tongues (Gk. *glossa*).

GLUTTON One habitually given to greedy and voracious eating. Gluttony was associated with stubbornness, rebellion, disobedience, drunkenness, and wastefulness (Deut. 21:20).

GNASHING OF TEETH Grating one's teeth together. In the OT gnashing of teeth was an expression of anger reserved for the wicked and for one's enemies (Job 16:9; Pss. 35:16; 37:12; Lam. 2:16). In the NT gnashing of teeth is associated with the place of future punishment (Matt. 8:12; 13:42,50).

GNOSTICISM Modern designation for certain dualistic religious and philosophical perspectives that existed prior to the establishment of Christianity and for the specific systems of belief characterized by these ideas, which emerged in the second century and later. The term "Gnosticism" is derived from the Greek word *gnosis* (knowledge) because secret knowledge was such a crucial doctrine in Gnosticism.

GOAD Rod, generally about eight feet long, with a pointed end used to control oxen.

GOAH Place-name meaning "low" (as in a sound made by a cow) or "bellow." A place, apparently on the west side of Jerusalem, where Jeremiah promised the walls would be restored after the Babylonian destruction (Jer. 31:39).

GOAT Hollow-horned, cud-chewing mammal with long, floppy ears, usually covered with long, black hair. Sometimes, they were speckled. One type of goat mentioned in the Bible has been identified as the Syrian or Mamber goat.

GOATH KJV and REB transliteration of Hebrew in Jer. 31:39 for Goah.

GOATSKIN Hide of goats that desert dwellers used for clothing (Heb. 11:37) and for containers for water (Gen. 21:14) and wine (Josh. 9:4).

GOB Place-name meaning "back" or "mountain crest." Site where David and his men fought two battles with the Philistines, killing Philistine giants (2 Sam. 21:18-19).

GOBLET KJV term for a bowl-shaped drinking vessel without handles (Song 7:2).

GOD Personal Creator and Lord of the universe, the Redeemer of His people, the ultimate author and principal subject of Scripture, and the object of the church's confession, worship, and service.

Knowledge of God At the heart of the biblical presentation of God is that God alone is the personal Creator and Lord, and that if He is to be known truly by His creatures, He must take the initiative in making Himself known to us (1 Cor. 2:10-11; Heb. 1:1-2). No doubt His existence and power are disclosed in the created order, even though that order has been deeply scarred by human rebellion and its consequences (Ps. 19:1-2; Rom. 1:19-20; Gen. 3:18; Rom. 8:19-22). But Scripture is also very clear that apart from God's own gracious self-disclosure, both in Word and action, we could not know Him in any true sense. In truth, God is incomprehensible, one that we cannot totally fathom (Pss. 139:6; 145:3; Rom. 11:33-36). But this in no way implies that we cannot know God truly. For in creating us in His image and giving us a Word, revelation of Himself, even though we cannot know God fully, we may know Him truly (Deut. 29:29).

Nature of God God is both transcendent over and immanent in His world. God is presented as the Lord who is exalted above and over His world, that is, transcendent (Pss. 7:17; 9:2; 21:7; 97:9; 1 Kings 8:27; Isa. 6:1; Rev. 4:3). Second, God is infinite, sovereign, and personal. By infinite, Scripture presents God as having every attribute or quality to the most perfect degree as well as not being bound by any of the limitations of space or time that apply to us, His creatures. Third, God is Triune. Distinctive to biblical theism is the conviction that the covenant Lord is as truly three as He is one. Although the word "trinity" is not found in Scripture, theologians have employed it to do justice to the biblical teaching that God is not only one in nature, but also three in person. As one follows the self-revelation of God in redemptive history, we discover not only the oneness of God (Deut. 6:4-5; Isa. 44:6), but also the affirmation that the Father is God (John 20:17), the Son is God (John 1:1,14; Rom. 9:5; Col. 2:9), and the Holy Spirit is God (Gen. 1:2; Acts 5:3-4; 1 Cor. 3:16).

Character of God Throughout Scripture, in God's dealings with human beings, we see God's character fully revealed and displayed. There are at least two statements that must be affirmed concerning the character of God.

First, God's character is holy love. It is important never to separate the holiness of God from the love of God. God is holy (Lev. 11:44; Isa. 6:3; Rev. 4:8). In the first instance, the word "holy" conveys the meaning of separateness and transcendence. However, it is the secondary meaning of "holiness" that speaks of God's moral purity in the sense of God's separateness from sin. In this latter sense, as the holy one, God is pure, righteous, and just. That is why Scripture repeatedly emphasizes that our sin and God's holiness are incompatible. His eyes are too pure to look on evil and He cannot tolerate wrong (Exod. 34:7; Rom. 1:32; 2:8-16). Thus, our sins effectively separate us from Him, so that His face is hidden from us (Isa. 59:1-2). Closely related to God's holiness is His wrath, that is, His holy reaction to evil (Rom. 1:18-32; John 3:36). The wrath of God, unlike the holiness of God, is not one of the intrinsic perfections of God; rather, it is a function of His holiness against sin. Where there is no sin, there is no wrath, but there will always be holiness.

Nevertheless, God is also love. Often divine holiness and love are set over against one another, but in Scripture this is never the case. This is best seen in the context of the affirmation, "God is love" (1 John 4:8). John, in this context, does not view the love of God as mere sentimentality or a blind overlooking of our sin; rather, He views divine love as that which loves the unlovely and undeserving. In fact, the supreme display of God's love is found in the Father giving His own dear Son as our propitiatory sacrifice that turns back God's holy anger against us and satisfies the demands of justice on our behalf (1 John 4:8-10). Thus, in the cross of Christ we see the greatest demonstration of both the holiness and love of God fully expressed, where justice and grace come together, and God remains both just and the justifier of those who have faith in Christ Jesus (Rom. 3:21-26).

Second, God's character is that of moral perfection. In all of God's dealings with His creation and with His people, God displays the wonder, beauty, and perfection of His own character. Ultimately the purpose of human existence, and especially of God's redeemed people, the church, is to live before this great and glorious God in adoration, love, and praise and to find in Him alone our all in all (Ps. 73:23-28; Rom. 11:33-36).

GOD FEARER The term used to describe the Gentiles mentioned in Acts who were drawn to the Jewish religion, perhaps for ethical and moral reasons or because they were attracted to Jewish monotheism and worship practices. "God fearers" took part in Jewish practices such as tithing and regular prayers (Acts 10:2-4) and were apparently welcome to take part in some synagogue services.

GODHEAD Word used with reference to God when one speaks of God's divine nature or essence or of the three persons of the Trinity.

GODLESSNESS Attitude and style of life that excludes God from thought and ignores or deliberately violates God's laws. Romans 1:20-32 is a classic characterization of godlessness.

GODLINESS The term appears most frequently in the writings of Paul, specifically the Pastoral Epistles. Paul encouraged Timothy to pursue "godliness" in an active manner (1 Tim. 6:11). He emphasized the value of godliness by contrasting it to physical training (1 Tim. 4:8). Whereas physical training has benefit for this life, Paul noted that godliness would benefit the believer in this life and in the life to come.

GOD OF THE FATHERS Technical phrase used as a general designation of the God of the patriarchs—Abraham, Isaac, and Jacob.

GOG AND MAGOG In Ezek. 38–39 Gog of the land of Magog is the leader of the forces of evil in an apocalyptic conflict against Yahweh. In Rev. 20:8 Gog and Magog appear together in parallel construction as forces fighting for Satan after his 1,000-year bondage. The identity of Gog and Magog has been the subject of an extraordinary amount of speculation. In general, however, attempts to relate these figures to modern individuals or states have been unconvincing.

GOIIM Proper name meaning "nation," particularly a "Gentile, foreign nation." **1.** Land where King Tidal joined the eastern coalition against a coalition from Sodom and Gomorrah. This action led to a war in which Abraham became involved (Gen. 14:1). **2.** Joshua 12:23 lists a king of Goiim in Gilgal as one Joshua conquered. **3.** Isaiah 9:1 also refers to Galilee of the nations. This may represent the Hebrew way of referring to Assyria's governmental district that the Assyrians called Megiddo.

GOLAN Place-name meaning "circle" or "enclosure." It was a city of refuge for people who unintentionally killed someone and was located in Bashan for the part of the tribe of Manasseh living east of the Jordan River (Deut. 4:43). It was also a city for the Levites (Josh. 21:27). It was located at modern Sahem el-Jolan on the eastern bank of the River el-Allan.

GOLDEN CALF See *Calves, Golden.*

GOLDEN RULE Name usually given to the command of Jesus recorded in Matt. 7:12 (cp. Luke 6:31)—"whatever you want others to do for you, do also the same for them" (HCSB). The designation "Golden Rule" does not appear in the Bible, and its origin in English is difficult to trace. The principle of the Golden Rule can be found in many religions, but Jesus' wording of it was original and unique.

GOLGOTHA See *Calvary.*

GOLIATH In 1 Sam. 17:4 the huge Philistine champion who baited the Israelite army under Saul in the valley of Elah for 40 days. He was slain by the youthful David.

GOMER Personal name meaning "complete, enough," or "burning coal." **1.** Daughter of Diblaim and wife of Hosea the prophet (Hos. 1:3). She is described in Hos. 1:2 as "a wife of harlotry" (NASB). **2.** Son of Japheth and grandson of Noah in the Table of Nations (Gen. 10:2).

GONG Loud percussion instrument, perhaps like a type of cymbal used in the temple worship (1 Cor. 13:1; KJV, brass). The Greek is literally "noisy brass," referring to the metal from which the instrument was made.

GOOD In contrast to the Greek view of "the good" as an ideal, the biblical concept focuses on concrete experiences of what God has done and is doing in the lives of God's people.

Azekah in the Valley of Elah where young David killed Goliath.

GOODMAN KJV term for a husband or for the head of a household.

GOPHER WOOD In Gen. 6:14 the material out of which Noah was instructed to construct the ark.

The fertile land of Goshen in the delta country of northern Egypt.

GOSHEN 1. The phrase, "land of Goshen," appears in the general description of territory occupied by Joshua's forces (Josh. 10:41; 11:16). **2.** The "land of Goshen" may have been named after the city of Goshen located in the district of Debir (Josh. 15:51). **3.** Goshen is primarily recognized as an area in the northeast sector of the Nile Delta. It was occupied by the Hebrews from the time of Joseph until the exodus.

GOSPEL The term "gospel" occurs frequently in the NT in both noun and verb forms, literally meaning "good news" or "proclaiming good news." The gospel in the NT is the message about the kingdom of God established in the life, death, and resurrection of Jesus the Messiah, who is enthroned as Lord of all. This good news describes events to which all Scripture points and declares that all principalities and powers are defeated once and for all by Jesus the Messiah. Finally, all of humanity will be judged according to their reception or rejection of this good news.

GOSPELS, SYNOPTIC The collective name for the Gospels of Matthew, Mark, and Luke. The term "synoptic" means "with the same eye," thus "with the same viewpoint."

GOURD Inedible fruit with a hard rind of the genera *Lagenaria* or *Cucurbita.* Gourd motifs were used in the ornamentation of the interior of the temple (1 Kings 6:18 NASB; KJV, knops) and of the rim of the bronze sea (1 Kings 7:24).

GOVERNOR Generally an appointed civil official charged with the oversight of a designated territory.

GOZAN Place-name of uncertain meaning, possibly, "quarry." A Syrian city-state to which the Assyrians exiled many of the people from Israel after they defeated Israel in 732 BC (1 Chron. 5:26) and 722 BC (2 Kings 17:6; 18:11).

GRACE Undeserved acceptance and love received from another. Although the biblical words for "grace" are used in a variety of ways, the most characteristic use is to refer to an undeserved favor granted by a superior to an inferior. When used of divine grace toward mankind, it refers to the undeserved favor of God in providing salvation for those deserving condemnation. In the more specific Christian sense it speaks of the saving activity of God that is manifested in the gift of His Son to die in the place of sinners.

Storage facilities at Knossos, Crete. Oil, wine, and grain were stored here.

GRANARY Storage facility for threshed and winnowed grain.

GRASS Herbage suitable for consumption by grazing animals (Job 6:5). English translations use "grass" to translate at least five Hebrew words.

GRATE, GRATING Framework of crisscrossed bars. The grating of the tabernacle altar was made of bronze and held rings through which carrying poles could be inserted (Exod. 27:4-7; 35:16; 38:4-5,30; 39:39).

GRAVE Pit or cave in which a dead body is buried. In Hebrew thought, graves were not simply places to deposit human remains. They were in a sense extensions of Sheol, the place of the dead. Since the realm of Sheol was threatening and since each grave was an individual expression of Sheol, the Israelites avoided burial sites when possible and treated them with circumspection. They performed purification rites when contact was unavoidable.

GRAVING TOOL Sharp implement used to finish shaping the rough form of a statue cast from a mold (Exod. 32:4) or used for engraving tablets with writing (Jer. 17:1).

GRAY Usually a reference to hair color (Prov. 16:31; 20:29).

GRECIAN Proper adjective referring to things or to people with origins in Greece. In the NT this refers to Jews who had adopted the Greek culture and language. They formed a significant part of the early church and created problems because of prejudice within the church (Acts 6:1; 9:29).

Looking through a gate into the ancient city of Corinth.

GREECE Located between the Italian Peninsula and Asia Minor, Greece itself is a peninsula with the Adriatic and Ionian Seas on the west and the Aegean Sea on the east. Very few references to Greece appear in the OT with most of them being found in the book of Daniel (Dan. 8:21; 10:20; 11:2; Zech. 9:13). This is not true of the NT, however, especially in regard to Paul's ministry. Some of his most fruitful work was done in Greek cities: Philippi, Thessalonica, Berea, Athens, and Corinth.

The Greek influence on the NT and Christianity is immeasurable. Koine, the Greek of the streets, is the language of the NT. At least five NT books are written to churches in Greek cities (Philippians, 1 and 2 Thessalonians, 1 and 2 Corinthians). All the other books in the NT are written in the Greek language. As the Christian gospel moved out into the Mediterranean world, it had to communicate its values to people who were steeped in Greek culture and religion. Both gained from the relationship, with people being transformed by the gospel and Christianity gaining a vehicle for its spread.

GREED Excessive or reprehensible desire to acquire; covetousness.

GREETING A salutation on meeting; an expression of good wishes at the opening (or in Hellenistic times, also the close) of a letter. Among Semitic peoples the usual greeting was and is "peace": "Peace be to you, and peace be to your house, and peace be to all that you have" (1 Sam. 25:5-6 NASB; cp. Luke 10:5).

GREYHOUND (KJV, Prov. 30:31). Modern translations read "strutting cock" or rooster.

GRIDDLE Flat surface on which food is cooked by dry heat (Lev. 2:5; 6:21; 7:9 modern translations; KJV, pan).

GRIEF AND MOURNING Practices and emotions associated with the experience of the death of a loved one or of another catastrophe or tragedy. After Jesus watched Mary and her friends weeping, we are told, "Jesus wept" (John 11:35). Weeping was then, as now, the primary indication of grief. Tears are repeatedly mentioned (Pss. 42:3; 56:8). The loud lamentation (wail) was also a feature of mourning, as the prophet who cried, "Alas! My brother!" (1 Kings 13:30; cp. Exod. 12:30; Jer. 22:18; Mark 5:38).

Sometimes they tore either their inner or outer garment (Gen. 37:29,34; Job 1:20; 2:12). They might refrain from washing and other normal activities (2 Sam. 14:2), and they often put on sackcloth. Mourners would typically sit barefoot on the ground with their hands on their heads (Mic. 1:8; 2 Sam. 12:20; 13:19; Ezek. 24:17) and smear their heads or bodies with dust or ashes (Josh. 7:6; Jer. 6:26; Lam. 2:10; Ezek. 27:30; Esther 4:1). They might even cut their hair, beard, or skin (Jer. 16:6; 41:5; Mic. 1:16), though disfiguring the body in this way was forbidden since it was a pagan practice (Lev. 19:27-28; 21:5; Deut. 14:1). Fasting was sometimes involved, usually only during the day (2 Sam. 1:12; 3:35), typically for seven days (Gen. 50:10; 1 Sam. 31:13). Food, however, was brought by friends since it could not be prepared in a house rendered unclean by the presence of the dead (Jer. 16:7).

Not only did the actual relatives mourn, but they might hire professional mourners (Eccles. 12:5;

Amos 5:16). Reference to "the mourning women" in Jer. 9:17 suggests that there were certain techniques that these women practiced. Jesus went to Jairus's house to heal his daughter and "saw the flute players and a crowd lamenting loudly" (Matt. 9:23 HCSB).

GRISLED KJV term for dappled (spotted) grey (Gen. 31:10,12).

GROVE In Gen. 21:33 a tree planted in Beersheba by Abraham. More than likely it was a tamarisk. The KJV also uses the word "grove" to translate the term *Asherah*.

GUARDIAN Adult responsible for the person and property of a minor (2 Kings 10:1,5). The Greek term *epitropos*, translated "guardian" at Gal. 4:2 (KJV, tutor), is a general word for a manager.

GUDGODAH Place-name of uncertain meaning. A stop on the Israelites' wilderness journey (Deut. 10:7).

GUILE Crafty or deceitful cunning; treachery; duplicity; deceit. Jesus pronounced Nathanael "a true Israelite in whom is no deceit (guile)" (John 1:47 HCSB; cp. John 1:51 with Gen. 28:12). Paul encouraged Christians to be "guileless as to what is evil" (Rom. 16:19 NRSV; cp. 1 Pet. 2:1), that is, innocent or naive when it comes to evil.

GUILT Responsibility of an individual or a group for an offense or wrongdoing. The Bible teaches that the violation of God's moral law (that is, sin; 1 John 3:4), whether in act or attitude, results in an immediate state of culpability before God requiring either punishment or expiation. Sin results in guilt whether or not the sinner is a member of God's redemptive community. Whereas this covenant community is further accountable to obey God's written law, all men are accountable to God's moral law (Rom. 2:14-15).

God's righteousness demands that the guilt resulting from sin cannot just be overlooked (Prov. 11:21; Hab. 1:13). The "wages" for sin is death (Rom. 6:23), and God cannot leave the guilty unpunished and still be righteous (Exod. 34:7). The only way God can forgive sin in us is to impute that sin to Christ and punish it in Him: "He presented Him to demonstrate His righteousness at the present time, so that He would be righteous and declare righteous the one who has faith in Jesus" (Rom. 3:26; see also Isa. 53:6,12; John 1:29). The result is that one who is "in Christ" by faith has been freed of his guilt so that there is "no condemnation" (Rom. 8:1).

The presence or absence of the feeling or realization of one's guilt is not a reliable indication of true guilt, because the heart is more deceitful than anything else (Jer. 17:9). Some who are "self righteous," that is, with no sense of guilt, may nevertheless be guilty (Matt. 5:20; 9:10-13), and those plagued by self-doubt may nevertheless be right with God (cp. 1 Cor. 8:7). On the other hand, the Bible gives several examples of the emotional anguish caused by sin (Pss. 32:1-5; 38; 51; Matt. 27:3-5; Luke 22:62). See *Atonement; Christ; Expiation, Propitiation; Forgiveness; Reconciliation; Sin.*

GULF Term used by the KJV and REB for the gorge or pit (HCSB, chasm) separating the rich man's place of torment from Lazarus's place of comfort in the presence of Abraham (Luke 16:26).

GUM Yellow to yellowish-brown product formed from the excretions of certain plants. Gum was an item of the Ishmaelites' caravan trade with Egypt (Gen. 37:25; KJV, spicery) and was regarded as one of the choice products of the land (Gen. 43:11).

GUNI Personal name meaning "black-winged partridge." **1.** Son of Naphtali and grandson of Jacob (Gen. 46:24), thus head of the Gunite clan (Num. 26:48). **2.** Member of tribe of Gad (1 Chron. 5:15).

GUNITE Descendant of Guni and member of clan originated by Guni.

GUR Place-name meaning "foreign sojourner" or "young animal." An unidentified mountain road near Ibleam where Jehu's men caught up with and mortally wounded Ahaziah, king of Judah (841 BC) (2 Kings 9:27).

GUR-BAAL Place-name meaning "foreign sojourner of Baal" or "young animal of Baal." An Arabian or Bedouin city where God helped King Uzziah of Judah (792–740 BC) attack (2 Chron. 26:7).

GUTTER KJV translation of two Hebrew terms. That in Gen. 30:38,41 is rendered (drinking) "troughs" (NIV, REB, NRSV TEV) or "runnels," "a small stream" (RSV). The term used at 2 Sam. 5:8 is rendered "water shaft" (NIV, NRSV) or "water tunnel" (NASB, TEV).

Jewish men of the orthodox tradition are prohibited from cutting off the hair above their ears.

HAAHASHTARI Personal and national name in Persian language meaning "kingdom." Member of tribe of Judah and clan of Caleb (1 Chron. 4:6).

HABAIAH Personal name meaning "Yahweh hides, keeps safe." Clan leader of exiled priests who returned from Babylon to Jerusalem with Zerubbabel about 537 BC (Ezra 2:61).

HABAKKUK Prophet of the late seventh century BC, contemporary to Jeremiah. One explanation has his name based on a root meaning "to embrace." The Greek OT spelling "Hambakoum" suggests a root meaning "plant" or "vegetable."

Other than his work as a prophet, nothing for certain of a personal nature is known about Habakkuk. Tradition makes him a priest of the tribe of Levi.

HABAKKUK, BOOK OF One of the 12 Minor Prophets. After a brief statement identifying the prophet (1:1), the book falls into three distinct divisions: (1) Prophet's Questions and the Lord's Answers (1:2–2:5); (2) Five Woes against Tyrants (2:6-20); (3) Prayer of Habakkuk (3:1-19).

The first question, Why does violence rule where there should be justice? (1:2-5), expressed the prophet's sense of dismay, either about conditions within his own land caused by Jehoiakim or by the oppression of weak countries by stronger powers. In light of what follows, internal injustice seems to have been the object of his concern. In response, the Lord told the prophet that He was at work sending the Chaldeans as the instrument of His judgment (1:5-11).

The prophet shrank from such an idea and posed another question: Lord, how can you use someone more sinful than we are to punish us? (1:12-17). When the answer was not forthcoming immediately, he took his stand in the watchtower to wait for it. It was worth the wait: "Behold, as for the proud one, his soul is not right within him; but the righteous will live by his faith" (2:4 NASB). The term "faith" has more of the sense of faithfulness or conviction that results in action.

Habakkuk had a significant influence on the Apostle Paul. Habakkuk's declaration that "the righteous (just) will live by his faith" (2:4) was taken by Paul as a central element in his theology. As he did with many OT passages, he used it with a slightly different emphasis. Through Paul, this passage came alive for an Augustinian monk named Martin Luther, setting off the Protestant Reformation, one of history's greatest religious upheavals. Thus a so-called "Minor" prophet had a major influence on those who followed him.

HABAZINIAH or **HABAZZINIAH** Personal name meaning "Yahweh inflated or caused to make merry." Grandfather of Jaazaniah, the Rechabite leader Jeremiah tested with wine (Jer. 35:3).

HABERGEON Short coat of mail covering the neck and shoulder worn as defensive armor.

HABITATION Dwelling place; home; KJV translation of 10 different Hebrew words.

HABOR Akkadian river name. A major tributary of the Euphrates River (2 Kings 17:6).

HACALIAH or **HACHALIAH** (KJV) Personal name meaning "wait confidently on Yahweh." Father of Nehemiah.

HACHMON Clan name meaning "wisdom." Original ancestor of an Israelite clan called the Hachmonites (1 Chron. 27:32).

HADAD Personal name meaning "mighty." **1.** An Edomite king (Gen. 36:35). The name Hadad was borne by several members of the royal household of Edom. **2.** Hadad was also the name of the chief deity of the Ugaritic pantheon. This deity was identified as a storm-god.

HADAD-EZER Syrian royal name meaning "Hadad (god) helps" (2 Sam. 8:3-13).

HADAD-RIMMON Names of two Syrian gods combined into one word (Zech. 12:11).

HADAR Apparently a copyist's change of the name Hadad, a Syrian god, in Gen. 36:39 and in some manuscripts of Gen. 25:15.

HADAR-EZER Copying change in some manuscripts for Hadad-ezer.

HADASHAH Town name meaning "new" (Josh. 15:37).

HADASSAH Personal name meaning "myrtle." In Esther 2:7, another name for Esther.

HADATTAH Place-name meaning "new." Part of name Hazor-hadattah (Josh. 15:25).

HADES The Greek noun *hades* is used 61 times in the Greek OT (Septuagint) to translate the Hebrew term *sheol*, which refers to the grave or the realm of the dead (Gen. 37:35; 1 Sam. 2:6; Prov 15:24; cp. Ps 16:10 and Acts 2:27,31). The picture generally presented by *Sheol* is the tomb, where the bodies of the dead lie in silence.

Hades in the NT, on the other hand, can represent a place of torment for the wicked. Jesus use the term in this way in His condemnation of Capernaum in Matt. 11:23 (parallel Luke 10:15) and in the parable of the rich man and Lazarus in Luke 16:23 where the rich man is said to be "in torment in Hades."

HADID Place-name meaning "fast" or "sharpened." Home of people returning from exile with Zerubbabel (Ezra 2:33).

HADLAI Personal name meaning "quit" or "fat sack." Leader in tribe of Ephraim and father of Amasa (2 Chron. 28:12).

HADORAM Personal and tribal name perhaps meaning "Hadad (god) is exalted." **1.** Arabic tribe descended from Shem through Eber and thus distantly related to Hebrews according to the Table of Nations (Gen. 10:27). **2.** Son of Tou, city-state ruler in Hamath of Syria. Hadoram brought tribute to David after David had defeated Hadad-ezer of Zobah (1 Chron. 18:10). **3.** "Taskmaster over the forced labor" (2 Chron. 10:18 NRSV) under Rehoboam, Solomon's son and successor as king of Judah.

HADRACH City-state name of uncertain meaning. Zechariah 9:1 claims this Syrian city-state will become a part of God's territory, though the precise meaning of the verse is difficult to interpret.

HAELEPH Place-name meaning "the ox." KJV reads the initial "h" as the Hebrew definite article and thus has "Eleph." Some interpreters combine the preceding town name in Josh. 18:28 to read "Zelah Haeleph" as one town, following early Greek manuscript evidence.

HAFT KJV term for the hilt or handle of a dagger (Judg. 3:22).

HAGAB Personal name meaning "grasshopper" or "chamberlain." Clan of temple servants who returned to Jerusalem from Babylonian exile with Zerubbabel (Ezra 2:46).

HAGABA Clan of temple servants who returned home from Babylonian exile with Zerubbabel about 537 BC (Ezra 2:45).

HAGAR Personal name meaning "stranger." The personal servant of Sarah who was given as a concubine to Abraham and became the mother of Ishmael (Gen. 16:1-16; 21:8-21; 25:12; Gal. 4:24-25).

HAGARITE Name of nomadic tribe whom the tribe of Reuben defeated east of the Jordan River (1 Chron. 5:10,19-20).

HAGGADAH and **HALAKAH** In Judaism, rabbinic teaching is divided into two categories halakah and haggadah (also spelled aggadah). Both of these terms refer to the oral teaching of the rabbis. Halakah refers to the legal teachings that are considered authoritative for religious life Haggadah refers to the remaining non-legal teachings.

HAGGAI Personal name of one of the "postexilic" (sixth-century) prophets and of the book preserving his preaching. The name probably means that he was born on one of the Jewish feast days He and the Prophet Zechariah roused the people of Judah to finish the Temple under Zerubbabel leadership.

HAGGAI, BOOK OF One of the so-called Minor Prophets (also collectively known as "the Twelve"). It consists of four addresses the prophet delivered to the postexilic community of Judah and its leaders, Zerubbabel the governor and Joshua the high priest. The addresses are precisely dated according to the year of the Persian ruler and the month and day of the Jewish calendar.

Historical Background The Persian ruler Cyrus had freed the Jews to return from Babylonian exile shortly after he conquered Babylon in October, 539 BC. He had also promised to help them rebuild their temple in Jerusalem that the Babylonians had destroyed in 586 BC. The temple foundation was laid fairly quickly under Zerubbabel's leadership, who eventually replaced Sheshbazzar as governor

This initial success was met not only with celebration but also with sadness when this temple was compared with Solomon's (Ezra 1–3; Hag. 2:3; Zech. 4:10). This is the first hint that perhaps this restoration would not satisfy entirely the prophetic announcements of Israel's glorious restoration.

Message and Purpose The leaders and people of Judah allowed external opposition, discouragement, and self interest to keep them from completing the task of rebuilding the Lord's temple (1:2-4; 2:3). So they and their offerings to the Lord were defiled and displeasing to Him (2:14). The Lord's command through Haggai was to "build the house" for the pleasure and glory of God (1:8). Toward that end the Lord exhorted them not to fear but to "be strong . . . and work" (2:4-5). Finally, by a parable Haggai instructed them of the need to dedicate themselves and their work to the Lord (2:11-16). The Lord called upon them to recognize His chastisement in the deprivation they had been experiencing (1:5-6,9-11; 2:16-17). He also informed the people that the completion of the temple would bring Him pleasure and glory (1:8). He further assured them of their success because of His presence (1:13-14; 2:4-5). He promised them that He would reward their renewed work and dedication to Him by glorifying the temple and granting them peace (2:6-9) and blessing (2:18-19). Finally, He promised to restore the Davidic throne on the earth through a descendant of Zerubbabel (2:20-23).

HAGGEDOLIM Personal name meaning "the great ones." Zabdiel, a leading priest, was the son of Haggedolim (Neh. 11:14; KJV, "the great men"; TEV, "a leading family").

HAGGERI KJV transliteration of Hebrew for Hagarite in 1 Chron. 11:38.

HAGGI Personal name meaning "my festival," indicating birth on a holy day. Son of Gad and grandson of Jacob and thus original ancestor of clan of Haggites (Gen. 46:16; Num. 26:15).

HAGGIAH Personal name meaning "Yahweh is my festival." A Levite in the line of Merari (1 Chron. 6:30).

HAGGITE Member of clan of Haggi.

HAGGITH Personal name meaning "festival." Wife of David and mother of Adonijah, who was born at Hebron (1 Sam. 3:4).

HAGIOGRAPHA Greek term meaning "holy writings," used as a designation for the third and final major division of the Hebrew Bible. The Hagiographa in their Hebrew order include: Psalms, Proverbs, and Job; the "five scrolls" (*Megilloth*) read at major festivals, namely, Song of Songs, Ruth, Lamentations, Ecclesiastes, and Esther; Daniel; and Ezra-Nehemiah and Chronicles. These books were the last portion of the Hebrew Bible to be recognized as canonical. Luke 24:44 uses "psalms" as a designation for these writings.

HAGRI Tribal or personal name probably referring to the Hagarites (1 Chron. 11:38) or a miscopying of "the Gaddite" from 2 Sam. 23:36.

HAHIROTH Reading of some manuscripts and translations for Pi-hahiroth in Num. 33:8.

HAIR Covering of the human head and of animals. Ordinarily human hair is meant in biblical references (Num. 6:5), though animal hair (wool) may be in mind (Matt. 3:4). Beautiful hair has always been desirable for both women and men (Song 5:11). In OT times both men and women wore their hair long. Both Samson and Absalom were greatly admired for their long locks (Judg. 16:13; 2 Sam. 14:25-26). In the NT era, men wore their hair much shorter than women did (1 Cor. 11:14-15). Gray hair and white hair were respected signs of age (Prov. 20:29). But baldness could be considered embarrassing or even humiliating (2 Kings 2:23; Ezek. 7:18).

HAKELDAMA NASB, NRSV spelling for Aceldama or Akeldama (Acts 1:19).

HAKKATAN Personal name meaning "the small one, the lesser." Father of the clan leader who accompanied Ezra from Babylon to Jerusalem about 458 BC (Ezra 8:12).

HAKKORE TEV reading of En-hakkore (Judg. 15:19), translating *En* as spring.

HAKKOZ Personal and clan name meaning "the thorn." **1.** Clan leader in tribe of Judah (1 Chron. 4:8). **2.** Clan of priests (1 Chron. 24:10; cp. Neh. 3:4,21).

HAKUPHA Personal name meaning "bent." Original ancestor of clan of temple servants (Ezra 2:51).

HALAH City-state or region in northern Mesopotamia to which Assyrians exiled some leaders of the northern kingdom after capturing Samaria in 722 BC (2 Kings 17:6).

HALAK Place-name meaning "barren" or "naked." Mountain marking southern extent of Joshua's conquests (Josh. 11:17; 12:7). It is identified with Jebel Halak, about 40 miles southwest of the Dead Sea in Edom.

HALF TRIBE Used to designate a segment of the tribe of Manasseh that received territory on both sides of the Jordan River. The term usually refers to that part of Manasseh dwelling to the east of the Jordan along with Reuben and Gad (Num. 32:33; Deut. 3:13; Josh. 1:12; 4:12; 22:1).

HALF-SHEKEL TAX Temple tax required annually of every Israelite 20 years of age and upwards (Exod. 30:13,15; 38:26). Such payment brought atonement, but atonement price was equal for all (30:15). At Matt. 17:24 this tax is called the *didrachma* ("the two drachma") tax. The coin in the fish's mouth was a stater, a coin worth four drachmas or the temple tax for two (17:27).

HALHUL Place-name perhaps meaning "circles." Town in hill country of Judah assigned to the tribe of Judah (Josh. 15:58).

HALI Place-name meaning "jewel." Border town assigned to tribe of Asher (Josh. 19:25).

HALL Large, usually imposing building, often used for governmental functions; the chief room in such a structure. NIV uses hall for the main room of the temple (1 Kings 6:3,5,17,33). Other translations have house (KJV), nave (NASB, NRSV), or sanctuary (REB).

HALLEL Song of praise. The name derives from the Hebrew "Praise Thou." The singing of psalms of praise was a special duty of the Levites (2 Chron. 7:6; Ezra 3:11). The "Egyptian" Hallel (Pss. 113–118) was recited in homes as part of the Passover celebration (cp. Ps. 114:1; Matt. 26:30). The "Great Hallel" was recited in the temple as the Passover lambs were being slain and at Pentecost, Tabernacles, and Dedication. Scholars disagree as to the original extent of the "Great Hallel" with some limiting the Hallel to Ps. 136, some including Ps. 135, and still others including the "Songs of Ascents" (Pss. 120–134).

HALLELUJAH Exclamation of praise that recurs frequently in the book of Psalms meaning "Praise Yahweh!"

HALLOHESH Personal name meaning "the exorcist." Father of Shallum, who helped Nehemiah repair the Jerusalem wall (Neh. 3:12; 10:24).

HALLOW To make holy; to set apart for holy use; to revere.

HALT Term that KJV sometimes uses as alternate translation for "lame" (Matt. 18:8; Mark 9:45; Luke 14:21; John 5:3).

HAM Personal name meaning "hot." Second of Noah's three sons (Gen. 5:32). Following the flood, he discovered Noah, his father, naked and drunken and reported it to Shem and Japheth (Gen. 9:20-29). When Noah learned of the incident, he pronounced a curse on Canaan the son of Ham. Ham became the original ancestor of the Cushites, the Egyptians, and the Canaanites (Gen. 10:6).

HAMAN Personal name meaning "magnificent." The Agagite who became prime minister under the Persian king Ahasuerus (Esther 3:1). He was a fierce enemy of the Jews, and he devised a plot to exterminate them. In particular, he had a gallows erected on which he hoped to hang Mordecai because Mordecai would not bow to him. Through the intervention of Esther, however, his scheme was unmasked, and he was hanged on the gallows he had designed for Mordecai the Jew.

HAMATH Place-name meaning "fortress" or "citadel." City-state located in the valley of the Orontes River, roughly 120 miles north of Damascus. The southern boundary of Hamath served as the northern boundary of Israel during the reigns of Solomon (1 Kings 8:65; 2 Chron. 8:4) and Jeroboam II (2 Kings 14:25,28). The "entrance of Hamath" was treated as the northern border of Israel (Num. 34:8; Josh. 13:5; Ezek. 47:15-17,20; 48:1) and served as an accepted geographical expression (Num. 13:21; Judg. 3:3).

HAMATH-ZOBAH Place-name meaning "hot place of Zobah." City that Solomon captured in Syria (2 Chron. 8:3). Both Hamath and Zobah are cities in Syria that David controlled (2 Sam. 8).

HAMMATH Place-name meaning "hot spot," probably due to hot spring, and personal name meaning "hot one." **1.** Fortified city in the tribal territory of Naphtali (Josh. 19:35); probably the same as the Levitical town of Hammoth-dor (21:32). **2.** Original ancestor of Kenites and Rechabites (1 Chron. 2:55; KJV reads "Hamath"; TEV, REB see a verbal construction meaning "intermarried" or "connected by marriage").

HAMMEDATHA Personal name meaning "given by the god." Father of Haman, the villain of the book of Esther (Esther 3:1).

HAMMELECH According to KJV, personal name translated "the king" (Jer. 36:26; 38:6). Modern translations read "son of the king."

HAMMER A striking tool. Mallets of bone and wood were used (Judg. 5:26), though these have not normally been preserved. Hammers were used in cutting stone (1 Kings 6:7), working common and precious metals (Isa. 41:7; 44:12), and for woodworking (Jer. 10:4). The hammer was a symbol of power. God's word is pictured as a hammer (Jer. 23:29). Babylon is mocked as a hammer whose strength has failed (Jer. 50:23).

HAMMOLEKETH (KJV, NIV, REB) Personal name meaning "queen." Sister of Gilead in genealogy of Manasseh in the unparalleled list of 1 Chron. 7:18.

HAMMON Place-name meaning "hot spot," probably from a hot spring. Town in tribal allotment of Asher (Josh. 19:28).

HAMMUEL Personal name meaning "El is my father-in-law" or "God is hot with anger." Member of tribe of Simeon (1 Chron. 4:26).

HAMMURABI King of Babylon about 1700 BC who issued a famous code of law. The Hammurabi code resembles Hebrew law in form, style, and general content. Thus some scholars believe the Hebrews were influenced by Hammurabi's code through the Canaanites among whom they settled.

Whatever the similarities, important differences are obvious. First, the Hammurabi code presupposes an aristocratic class system that did not prevail in Israel. Second, Israel could never have viewed the state as the custodian of the law. Third, Hebrew law is characterized by a more humane spirit. Fourth, Hebrew law maintains a high ethical emphasis. Fifth, the pervading religious fervor makes the Hebrew code unique. Sixth, Hebrew law is set within a covenant relationship.

HAMON-GOG Place-name meaning "horde of Gog." Place where Ezekiel predicted burial of defeated army of Gog (Ezek. 39:11,15).

HAMONAH Place-name meaning "horde." Town in valley of Hamon-gog where Israel would bury the defeated army of Gog (Ezek. 39:16).

HAMOR Personal name meaning "donkey" or "ass." In Gen. 33:19, the father of Shechem.

HAMRAN Personal name of uncertain meaning perhaps "vineyard." Member of family of Esau (1 Chron. 1:35,41). KJV spells the name "Amram."

HAMSTRING To cripple by cutting the leg tendons. Horses captured in war were frequently hamstrung (KJV, hough) (Josh. 11:6,9; 2 Sam. 8:4; 1 Chron. 18:4). The hamstringing of oxen (Gen. 49:6 modern translations) is an example of rash anger.

HAMUL Personal name meaning "pitied, spared" or "El is father-in-law" or "El is hot, angry." Son of Pharez and grandson of Judah (Gen. 46:12) and thus a clan leader in Judah (Num. 26:21).

HAMUTAL Personal name meaning "father-in-law or kindred of the dew." Mother of King Jehoahaz (2 Kings 23:31) and King Zedekiah (2 Kings 24:18) of Judah.

HANAMEEL Personal name meaning "God is gracious." Uncle of Jeremiah from whom the prophet bought the field in Anathoth (Jer. 32:7-12). Jeremiah's act symbolized God's long-range plans to restore the people to the land after exile.

HANAN Personal name meaning "gracious." Personal name probably originally connected to divine name such as El, Yahweh, or Baal. **1.** Clan or guild of prophets or priests living in the temple. Jeremiah used their temple chamber for his meeting with the Rechabites (Jer. 35:4). **2.** Clan of temple servants who returned to Jerusalem from Babylonian exile with Zerubbabel about 537 BC (Ezra 2:46). **3.** Man that Nehemiah appointed as assistant temple treasurer to receive and disperse tithes brought to care for the Levites (Neh. 13:13). **4.** One of David's military heroes (1 Chron. 11:43). **5.** Levite who instructed the people in the Lord's law while Ezra read it (Neh. 8:7). **6.** Levite who sealed Nehemiah's covenant to obey God's law (Neh. 10:10). **7.** Another signer of Nehemiah's covenant (Neh. 10:22). **8.** Another who signed Nehemiah's covenant (Neh. 10:26). **9.** Member of tribe of Benjamin (1 Chron. 8:23). **10.** Descendant of Saul in tribe of Benjamin (1 Chron. 8:38).

HANANEEL (KJV) or **HANANEL** Place-name meaning "God is gracious." Tower marking northern wall of Jerusalem. Jeremiah predicted its rebuilding in the day of the Lord to come (Jer.

31:38; cp. Zech. 14:10).

HANANI Personal name meaning "my grace" or a shortened form of "Yahweh is gracious." **1.** Father of Prophet Jehu (1 Kings 16:1,7; 2 Chron. 19:2). **2.** Man who agreed under Ezra's leadership to divorce his foreign wife to protect the Jews from temptation to worship idols (Ezra 10:16-20,44). **3.** Nehemiah's brother who reported the poor conditions in Jerusalem to him while Nehemiah was still in Persia (Neh. 1:2). **4.** Priest musician at dedication of Jerusalem walls (Neh. 12:36). **5.** Temple musician and descendant of Heman (1 Chron. 25:4). Some would equate him with 4. above. **6.** Original leader of one course of temple musicians (1 Chron. 25:25). **7.** Prophetic seer who condemned King Asa of Judah (910–869 BC) for paying tribute to King Ben-hadad of Damascus rather than relying on God (2 Chron. 16:7). Asa imprisoned Hanani (2 Chron. 16:10).

HANANIAH Personal name with two Hebrew spellings meaning "Yah(weh) is gracious." **1.** Prophet from Gibeon who opposed Jeremiah by promising immediate deliverance from Babylon. Jeremiah could combat this false prophecy only by telling the people to wait until they saw it fulfilled in history (Jer. 28:8-9). **2.** Father of Zedekiah, a court official, in time of Jeremiah (Jer. 36:12). **3.** Grandfather of captain of guard who arrested Jeremiah as he left Jerusalem (Jer. 37:13). **4.** Jewish name of Daniel's friend Shadrach (Dan. 1:7). **5.** Son of Zerubbabel in the royal line of David (1 Chron. 3:19). **6.** Clan head in tribe of Benjamin living in Jerusalem (1 Chron. 8:24). **7.** Son of Heman among the priestly musicians in the temple (1 Chron. 25:4). **8.** Military leader under King Uzziah of Judah (792–740 BC) (2 Chron. 26:11). **9.** Man who followed Ezra's leadership and divorced his foreign wife to protect Judah from the temptation to worship foreign gods (Ezra 10:16-20,44). **10.** A member of the perfumers' guild who helped Nehemiah repair the Jerusalem wall (Neh. 3:8 NASB). **11.** Man who helped Nehemiah repair the Jerusalem wall (Neh. 3:30). **12.** Ruler of the temple fortress under Nehemiah (Neh. 7:2 NASB). **13.** Man who signed Nehemiah's covenant to obey God's law; perhaps the same as 12. above (Neh. 10:23). **14.** A priest immediately after the time of return from Babylonian exile (Neh. 12:12) when Joiakim was high priest. **15.** Priest musician who helped Nehemiah celebrate the completion of the Jerusalem wall (Neh. 12:41).

HAND The Greek and Hebrew words that are translated by the English word "hand" appear approximately 1,800 times. Of these occurrences to which "hand" is referred, the literal sense is intended some 500 times, and the figurative sense some 1,300 times.

HANDBREADTH Ancient measurement equal to the width of the hand at the base of the fingers (about three inches). Ezekiel's long cubit was six handbreadths, one more than the common cubit (Ezek. 40:5). In Ps. 39:5 "a few handbreadths" illustrates the shortness of life.

HANDSTAVE Wooden staff used as a weapon by foot soldiers. KJV used "handstave" to translate a weapon at Ezek. 39:9.

HANES Egypt place-name. City to which Israel sent ambassadors in time of Isaiah to seek military and economic help (Isa. 30:4).

HANGING A method of ridiculing, shaming, and desecrating an enemy. Hanging was not regarded as a means of capital punishment according to biblical law, although it was practiced by the Egyptians (Gen. 40:19,22) and the Persians (Esther 7:9). The Israelites, after putting an enemy or criminal to death, might hang them on a gibbet or tree for public scorn as added degradation and warning (Gen. 40:19; Deut. 21:22; Josh. 8:29; 2 Sam. 4:12), but biblical law demanded that the corpses be taken down and buried the same day (Deut. 21:22-23). Hanging oneself is mentioned only once in the OT (2 Sam. 17:23) and once in the NT (Matt. 27:5).

HANNAH Personal name meaning "grace." One of the wives of Elkanah and mother of Samuel (1 Sam. 1:2). Because she had been barren for many years, she vowed to the Lord that if she should give birth to a son, she would dedicate the child to God (1 Sam. 1:11). Subsequently, she gave birth to the child Samuel. She fulfilled her vow by bringing her son to the sanctuary at Shiloh, where he served the Lord under the direction of Eli. Later on, Hannah had other sons and daughters.

HANNATHON Place-name meaning "grace." Town on northern border of tribal territory of Zebulun (Josh. 19:14).

HANNIEL Personal name meaning "God is gracious." **1.** Representative of tribe of Manasseh on council that helped Joshua and Eleazar divide the land among the tribes (Num. 34:23). **2.** Member of tribe of Asher (1 Chron. 7:39).

HANOCH Personal name with same Hebrew spelling as Enoch meaning "dedicated" or "vassal." **1.** Son of Reuben and grandson of Jacob (Gen. 46:9) and thus a clan leader in Israel (Exod. 6:14;

Num. 26:5). **2.** Son of Midian and grandson of Abraham and thus one of the Midianites (Gen. 25:4).

HANUKKAH An eight-day festival that commemorated the cleansing and rededication of the temple following the victories of Judas Maccabeus in 167/165 BC. It is the only Jewish festival not specified in the Hebrew Bible. Hanukkah, also called the Feast of Dedication, begins on the 25th day of Kislev (December). One candle is lit each day until a total of eight are lit. Jesus was in Jerusalem once during this festival (John 10:22) also called Feast of Lights.

HANUN Personal name meaning "blessed" or "favored." **1.** King of Ammon whom David sought to honor and with whom he sought to renew the peace treaty (2 Sam. 10). **2.** Man who repaired the Valley Gate of Jerusalem under Nehemiah (Neh. 3:13). **3.** Another man who worked under Nehemiah to repair the Jerusalem wall (Neh. 3:30).

HAPHRAIM (KJV) or **HAPHARAIM** Place-name meaning "two holes" or "two wells." Town in tribal territory of Issachar (Josh. 19:17-19).

HAPPIZZEZ Personal name meaning "the shattered one." Leader of one course of the priests (1 Chron. 24:6-7,15) and thus the original ancestor for that priestly clan. KJV, REB spell the name Aphses.

HAR-HERES NRSV reading in Judg. 1:35 for Mount Heres, NRSV transliterating *har*, Hebrew word for "mountain."

HAR-MAGEDON NASB, NRSV transliteration of Greek transliteration from Hebrew in Rev. 16:16 for place-name other English translations transliterate as Armageddon.

HARA Place-name of uncertain meaning. City or region in northern Mesopotamia where, according to 1 Chron. 5:26, the Assyrians under Tiglath-pileser settled some of the exiles from east of the Jordan in the northern kingdom in 734 BC.

HARADAH Place-name meaning "quaking" or "terror." Station in Israel's wilderness journey (Num. 33:24-25).

HARAN Personal and place-name meaning "mountaineer" or "caravan route." Three men and an important city of northern Mesopotamia located on the Balik River. **1.** Terah's son and Lot's father (Gen. 11:26-29,31). **2.** Son of Caleb's concubine (1 Chron. 2:46). **3.** Son of Shimei and a Levite (1 Chron. 23:9). **4.** The city became Abraham's home (Gen. 11:31-32; 12:4-5) and remained home for his relatives like Laban (Gen. 27:43).

HARAR Geographical name perhaps related to Hebrew word for "mountain." The word appears in slightly difficult forms in its appearances in the Hebrew Bible. Three of David's military heroes are related to Harar (2 Sam. 23:11,33; 1 Chron. 11:34-35). Harar can either be a town, a region, a tribe, or a general reference to mountain country.

Vista of Haran (4) from Crusader's Castle.

HARBEL TEV reading of place-name in Num. 34:11, usually translated Riblah but spelled in Hebrew with beginning "h," which can be the Hebrew definite article.

HARBONA Persian personal name perhaps meaning "barren." A eunuch on the staff of King Ahasuerus of Persia (Esther 1:10; 7:9).

HARBONAH Alternate spelling of Harbona, based on Hebrew text's alteration between Hebrew and Aramaic spelling.

HARD SAYING Teaching difficult to understand or accept (John 6:60).

HARDNESS OF HEART The action or state of resistance to and rejection of the Word and will of God.

HARE Long-eared member of the rabbit family (*Leporhyidae*), especially those born with open eyes and fur. Hares were regarded as unclean (Lev. 11:6; Deut. 14:7) and were forbidden for Israelites to eat.

HAREPH Personal name meaning "clever" or "reproach." Descendant of Caleb and thus member of tribe of Judah (1 Chron. 2:51).

HARETH Place-name meaning "woodland." Forest where David went at advice of Gad, the prophet, as he hid from Saul (1 Sam. 22:5).

HARHAIAH Personal name of uncertain meaning. Member of goldsmiths' guild whose son helped Nehemiah repair the wall of Jerusalem (Neh. 3:8).

HARHAS Foreign name of uncertain meaning. Grandfather of the husband of Huldah, the prophet (2 Kings 22:14).

HARHUR Personal name meaning "glow, burn," possibly describing fever of mother at birth. A temple servant who returned from Babylonian exile with Zerubbabel about 537 BC (Ezra 2:51).

HARIM Personal name meaning "dedicated." **1.** Clan leader from Bethlehem whose family returned from Babylonian exile with Zerubbabel about 537 BC (Ezra 2:32). **2.** Head of one course of priests appointed under David's leadership (1 Chron. 24:8; cp. Ezra 2:39; Neh. 12:15). **3.** Another Israelite clan with members having to divorce foreign wives under Ezra (Ezra 10:31). **4.** Priest who signed Nehemiah's covenant to obey God's law (Neh. 10:5). **5.** Clan leader who signed Nehemiah's covenant (Neh. 10:27).

HARIPH Personal name meaning "sharp" or "fresh." **1.** Israelite clan whose members accompanied Zerubbabel in returning from Babylonian exile about 537 BC (Neh. 7:24). **2.** Leader of people who signed Nehemiah's covenant to obey God's law (Neh. 10:19).

The Harod Spring at Ainharod at the foot of the Gilboa Mountain range. This is where Gideon gathered his men before fighting the Midianites.

HARLOT One who is a prostitute. The most famous harlot in the Bible is Rahab of Jericho, who saved the Israelite spies sent by Joshua to scout out the promised land (Josh. 2).

HARMON Place-name of uncertain meaning in Amos 4:3 as translated by NRSV, NASB, NIV.

HARNEPHER Egyptian personal name meaning "Horus (god) is good." Member of tribe of Asher (1 Chron. 7:36).

HAROD Place-name meaning "quake," "terror," or "intermittent spring." Place where God led Gideon to test his troops to reduce their numbers before fighting Midian (Judg. 7:1).

HAROEH Personal name meaning "the seer." Descendant of Caleb in tribe of Judah (1 Chron. 2:52).

HAROSHETH Place-name meaning "forest land." Home of Sisera, captain of the army of Jabin of Hazor (Judg. 4:2).

HARSHA Personal name meaning "unable to talk, silent" or "magician, sorcerer." Clan of temple servants who returned with Zerubbabel from Babylonian exile about 537 BC (Ezra 2:52).

HART Adult male deer (Ps. 42:1; Isa. 35:6).

HARUM Personal name meaning "the exalted." A member of the tribe of Judah (1 Chron. 4:8).

HARUMAPH Personal name meaning "split nose." Father of worker who helped Nehemiah rebuild the wall of Jerusalem (Neh. 3:10).

HARUZ Personal name meaning "gold" or "industrious." Maternal grandfather of Amon, king of Judah (642–640 BC).

HARVEST Festive occasion for gathering the crops, usually marked by important religious festivals. Among the more important crops grown were wheat, grapes, and olives. Other crops included barley, flax, and various vegetables and fruits. Crops that had been planted were harvested at various times.

HARVEST, FEAST OF Alternate name for Pentecost or the Feast of Weeks (Exod. 23:16; 34:22).

HASADIAH Personal name meaning "Yahweh is gracious." Son of Zerubbabel and descendant of David (1 Chron. 3:20).

HASHABIAH Personal name meaning "Yahweh has reckoned or imputed," appearing in longer and shorter Hebrew spellings. **1.** Ancestor of Merari among the Levite leaders (1 Chron. 6:45). **2.** Another member of the Merari priesthood (1 Chron. 9:14; Neh. 11:15). **3.** Temple musician and Levite under David (1 Chron. 25:1,3,6,19). **4.** Family of Levites from Hebron given authority to carry out God's business in the service of the king west of the Jordan (1 Chron. 26:30). This shows the close connection between temple and palace, religious and political activity in Israel. **5.** Leader of the tribe of Levi possibly connected with taking the ill-fated census under David (1 Chron. 27:17). He may be identical with 4. above. **6.** Levite leader under Josiah who provided animals for the Levites to celebrate Passover (2 Chron. 35:9). **7.** Levite leader Ezra conscripted to return to Jerusalem with him from Babylonian exile about 458 BC (Ezra 8:19). **8.** Israelite called to divorce his foreign wife to protect the people from temptation to false worship according to Greek manuscripts of Ezra 10:25 (NRSV). **9.** Levite with administrative duties over city of Keilah who joined Nehemiah in repairing wall of Jerusalem (Neh. 3:17). He could be the same as both 7. and 8. above. **10.** Ancestor of chief Levite in Jerusalem in Nehemiah's day (Neh. 11:22). **11.** Priest one generation after the return from exile (Neh. 12:21).

HASHABNAH Personal name perhaps meaning "reckoning." Signer of Nehemiah's covenant to obey God's law (Neh. 10:25).

HASHABNEIAH or **HASHABNIAH** (KJV) Personal name meaning "Yahweh has imputed to me." **1.** Father of man who helped Nehemiah repair the Jerusalem wall (Neh. 3:10). **2.** Levite who led worship in Nehemiah's covenant ceremony in which people reaffirmed their commitment to obey God (Neh. 9:5).

HASHBADANA (KJV) or **HASHBADDANAH** Personal name of uncertain meaning. A member of the community leaders who stood with Ezra as he read the law to the people (Neh. 8:4).

HASHEM Personal name meaning "the name." Father of some of David's heroes (1 Chron. 11:34) and said to be a Gizonite. The parallel passage in 2 Sam. 23:32 may preserve the original spelling: Jashen.

HASHMONAH A station in Israel's wilderness journey (Num. 33:29-30).

HASHUBAH Personal name meaning "highly treasured." Son of Zerubbabel in the royal line of David (1 Chron. 3:20).

HASHUM 1. Personal name meaning "flat-nosed." Clan leader of group returning from Babylonian exile with Zerubbabel about 537 BC. Some clan members divorced their foreign wives under Ezra's leadership to rid the community of religious temptations (Ezra 10:33). **2.** Community leader who stood with Ezra while he read the law to the people (Neh. 8:4).

HASMONEAN Name given to the dynasty that ruled ancient Judea for almost a century, from the Maccabean wars (that ended in approximately 145 BC) until Roman occupation of ancient Palestine in 63 BC.

HASRAH Personal name perhaps meaning "lack."

HASSENAAH Personal or place-name perhaps meaning "the hated one." Apparently the same name without "h," the Hebrew definite article, appears as Senaah, a clan who returned with

Zerubbabel from Babylonian exile about 537 BC (Ezra 2:35). Members of the clan helped Nehemiah rebuild the Fish Gate of the Jerusalem wall (Neh. 3:3).

HASSENUAH Personal name meaning "the hated one." Leader in tribe of Benjamin (1 Chron. 9:7). The name without the Hebrew article "h" appears in Neh. 11:9 as father of a leader in post-exilic Jerusalem from the tribe of Benjamin.

HASSHUB Personal name meaning "one to whom He has imputed or reckoned." **1.** Man who helped Nehemiah repair the Jerusalem wall (Neh. 3:23). **2.** Man who helped repair the bakers' ovens and apparently two parts of the wall (Neh. 3:23).

HASSOPHERETH Personal name meaning "the scribe" or "scribal office." Ezra 2:55 indicates it was either a family name of persons returning from Babylonian exile with Zerubbabel about 537 BC or a guild of scribes who returned.

HASUPHA Personal name meaning "quick." A clan returning with Zerubbabel from Babylonian exile about 537 BC (Ezra 2:43).

HAT Article of clothing for the head (Dan. 3:21). The root word is similar to the Akkadian term for a helmet or cap. The NASB rendered the term "cap"; NIV, "turban."

HATACH Personal name perhaps of Persian origin meaning "runner." A eunuch serving King Ahasuerus in the Persian court whom the king assigned as Esther's servant (Esther 4:5-6). Esther assigned him to find why Mordecai was troubled, thus initiating Esther's appearances before the king to save her people.

HATHATH Personal name meaning "weakling." Son of Othniel in the family line of Caleb and the tribe of Judah (1 Chron. 4:13).

HATIPHA Aramaic personal name meaning "robbed." Clan who returned from Babylonian exile with Zerubbabel about 537 BC (Ezra 2:54).

HATITA Aramaic personal name meaning "bored a hole" or "soft" or "festival." Clan of temple gatekeepers who returned from Babylonian exile with Zerubbabel about 537 BC (Ezra 2:42).

HATTIL Personal name meaning "talkative, babbling" or "long-eared." Clan of temple servants who returned from Babylonian exile with Zerubbabel about 537 BC (Ezra 2:57).

HATTUSH Personal name of uncertain meaning. **1.** Man in David's royal line after the return from exile (1 Chron. 3:22). **2.** Priest who signed Nehemiah's covenant to obey God (Neh. 10:4). It is not impossible that this was the same as 1. above. **3.** Priest who returned from Babylonian exile with Zerubbabel about 537 BC (Neh. 12:2). **4.** Man who helped Nehemiah repair the Jerusalem walls (Neh. 3:10).

HAURAN Geographical name of uncertain meaning. One of four or five provinces through which the Assyrians and their successors administered Syria. Ezekiel promised it would be in the restored promised land (Ezek. 47:16,18).

HAVEN Place that offers safe anchorage for ships (Gen. 49:13; Ps. 107:30; Isa. 23:10 NRSV, NIV).

HAVILAH Place-name meaning "sandy stretch." Biblical name for the sand-dominated region to the south covering what we call Arabia without necessarily designating a particular geographical or political area. The river from Eden is described as flowing "around the whole land of Havilah" (Gen. 2:11 NASB), a land noted for gold and other precious stones.

HAVOTH-JAIR or **HAVVOTH-JAIR** Place-name meaning "tents of Jair." Villages in Gilead east of the Jordan which Jair, son of Manasseh, captured (Num. 32:41).

HAWK Bird of prey considered unclean (Lev. 11:16; Deut. 14:15) and not to be eaten. God reminded Job that He created the hawk to soar (Job 39:26).

HAZAEL Personal name meaning "El (a god) is seeing." A powerful and ruthless king of the Syrian city-state of Damascus during the last half of the eighth century BC. While an officer of Ben-hadad, king of Syria, Hazael was sent to Elisha the prophet to inquire about the king's health (2 Kings 8:7-15).

HAZAIAH Personal name meaning "Yahweh sees." Member of tribe of Judah and ancestor of Jerusalem descendants in Nehemiah's day (Neh. 11:5).

HAZAR Hebrew term meaning a court or enclosed space. *Hazar* is a common element in place-names.

HAZAR-ADDAR Place-name meaning "threshing floor." Station on Israel's wilderness journey (Num. 34:4) near Kadesh, possibly Ain Qedesh.

HAZAR-ENAN Place-name meaning "encampment of springs." Site marking northeastern border of promised land (Num. 34:9-10; Ezek. 47:17).

HAZAR-ENON Variant Hebrew spelling of Hazar-enan in Ezek. 47:17 and reflected in NRSV. TEV calls the place Enon City.

HAZAR-GADDAH Place-name meaning "village of good luck." Town in tribal territory of Judah of unknown location near Beersheba (Josh. 15:27).

HAZAR-HATTICON Place-name meaning "middle village." Ezekiel named it as the border of the future Israel (47:16).

HAZAR-MAVETH Place-name meaning "encampment of death." Name in the Table of Nations for son of Joktan in the line of Eber and Shem (Gen. 10:26).

HAZAR-SHUAL Place-name meaning "encampment of the foxes." Town near Beersheba in tribal territory of Judah (Josh. 15:28) but allotted to tribe of Simeon (Josh. 19:3; 1 Chron. 4:28).

HAZAR-SUSAH or **HAZAR-SUSIM** Place-name meaning "encampment of a horse." Town in tribal allotment of Simeon (Josh. 19:5).

HAZAZON-TAMAR Place-name meaning "grave dump with palms." Home of Amorites who fought eastern coalition led by Chedorlaomer (Gen. 14:7).

HAZEL KJV translation of a term meaning "almond" rather than "hazelnut" (Gen. 30:37).

HAZELELPONI Personal name meaning "Overshadow my face." Daughter of Etam in the tribe of Judah (1 Chron. 4:3 NASB; NIV, TEV, REB, NRSV). KJV follows Hebrew text, which reads "these the father of Etam."

HAZERIM KJV interpretation and transliteration of Hebrew word meaning "villages" or "hamlets" in Deut. 2:23.

HAZEROTH Place-name meaning "villages" or "encampments." Wilderness station on Israel's journey from Egypt (Num. 11:35). There Aaron and Miriam challenged Moses' sole authority, using his Cushite wife as an excuse (Num. 12).

HAZIEL Personal name meaning "God saw." A leading Levite in the time of David (1 Chron. 23:9).

HAZO Abbreviated form of personal name Haziel meaning "God saw." Son of Abraham's brother Nahor (Gen. 22:22).

HAZOR Place-name meaning "enclosed settlement." **1.** Hazor was located in upper Galilee on the site now known as Tell el-Qedah, 10 miles north of the Sea of Galilee and 5 miles southwest of Lake Huleh. Hazor was the dominant and largest city-state in ancient Canaan. Joshua defeated the Canaanite forces, slew the leaders, including Jabin, and burned the city of Hazor. Modern archaeology lends support to this biblical account. First Kings 9:15 mentions that Solomon rebuilt the walls of Hazor, Megiddo, and Gezer. Excavations have discovered conclusive evidence to support this short portion of

Overview of the excavations at Tel el-Qedah (ancient Hazor) north of the Sea of Galilee.

Scripture. **2.** Town in tribal inheritance of Judah (Josh. 15:23), probably to be read with earliest Greek translation as Hazor-Ithnan. This may be modern el-Jebariyeh. **3.** Town in southern part of tribal inheritance of Judah, probably to be read as Hazor-Hadattah (Josh. 15:25) with most modern translations. This may be modern el-Hudeira near the Dead Sea's southern end. **4.** Town identified with Hezron (Josh. 15:25). **5.** Town where part of tribe of Benjamin lived in time of Nehemiah (Neh. 11:33). **6.** Name of "kingdoms" that Nebuchadnezzar of Babylon threatened (Jer. 49:28-33).

HAZOR-HADDATTAH Place-name meaning "new Hazor." Town in tribal territory of Judah (Josh. 15:25). Its location is not known.

HAZZOBEBAH NIV rendering of the name of the son of Coz (or Kos) and grandson of Helah (1 Chron. 4:8).

HE Fifth letter of the Hebrew alphabet; it carries the numerical value five. In Judaism *he* is used as an abbreviation for the divine name Yahweh (Tetragrammaton).

HEAD Literally, the uppermost part of the body, considered to be the seat of life but not of the intellect; and figuratively for first, top, or chief. The Jewish notion was that the heart was the center or seat of the intellect. "Head" meant the physical head of a person (Gen. 48:18; Mark 6:24) or of animals, such as a bull's head (Lev. 1:4). It was often used to represent the whole person (Acts 18:6). Achish made David "keeper of mine head" (KJV), that is, his bodyguard (1 Sam. 28:2).

HEAD OF THE CHURCH Title for Christ (Eph. 4:15; Col. 1:18). Christ's headship includes the idea of His authority (1:22; 5:23) and of the submission required of the church (5:24). Also in view is the character of Christ's relationship with the church. Unlike self-seeking human lords (Luke 22:25), Christ exercises His authority for the church (Eph. 1:22 NRSV, NIV), nourishing and caring for the church as one cares for one's own body (5:29).

HEADSTONE KJV term for a top stone (NASB) or capstone (NIV) at Zech. 4:7. New Testament writers spoke of Christ as a stone rejected by the builders that has become the head of the corner (Acts 4:11; 1 Pet. 2:7). Here, head of the corner refers either to a capstone (coping), a keystone of an arch, or to a cornerstone.

HEALING, DIVINE God's work through instruments and ways He chooses to bring health to persons sick physically, emotionally, and spiritually. Nearly one-fifth of the Gospels report Jesus' miracles and the discussions they occasioned. The Gospels record 14 distinct instances of physical and mental healing. Jesus commissioned His disciples to continue His basic ministry, including healing (Matt. 10:5-10; Mark 6:7-13; Luke 9:1-6). In the book of Acts the healing ministry continued.

HEART Center of the physical, mental, and spiritual life of humans. The word "heart" refers to the physical organ and is considered to be the center of the physical life. Eating and drinking are spoken of as strengthening the heart (Gen. 18:5; Judg. 19:5; Acts 14:17). The believer is commanded to love God "with all your heart" (Mark 12:30; cp. Deut. 6:5). Paul taught that the purpose of God's command is love that comes from a "pure heart" (1 Tim. 1:5 HCSB). The heart is spoken of in Scripture as the center of the moral and spiritual life. The conscience, for instance, is associated with the heart.

On the negative side, depravity is said to issue from the heart: "The heart is more deceitful than all else and is desperately sick; who can understand it?" (Jer. 17:9 NASB). Jesus said that out of the heart come evil thoughts, murder, adultery, fornication, theft, false witness, slander (Matt. 15:19). In other words, defilement comes from within rather than from without.

Because the heart is at the root of the problem, this is the place where God does His work in the individual. For instance, the work of the law is "written on their hearts," and conscience is the proof of this (Rom. 2:15 HCSB). The heart is the field where seed (the Word of God) is sown (Matt. 13:19; Luke 8:15).

The heart is the dwelling place of God. Two persons of the Trinity are said to reside in the heart of the believer. God has given us the "down payment [of the Spirit] in our hearts" (2 Cor. 1:22 HCSB). Ephesians 3:17 expresses the desire that "the Messiah may dwell in your hearts through faith" (HCSB). The love of God "has been poured out in our hearts through the Holy Spirit who was given to us" (Rom. 5:5 HCSB).

HEATH Shrubby, evergreen plant of the heather family, used by the KJV (Jer. 17:6; 48:6). Various translations have been offered: juniper (NASB); bush (NIV); shrub (NRSV, 17:6).

HEAVE OFFERING See *Sacrifice and Offerings*.

HEAVEN Part of God's creation above the earth and the waters including "air" and "space" and serving as home for God and His heavenly creatures. The word "heaven" occurs more frequently in

Revelation than in any other NT book. The Revelation addresses heaven from the standpoints of the struggle between good and evil and of God's rule from heaven. The most popular passage dealing with heaven is Rev. 21:1–22:5. In this passage, heaven is portrayed in three different images: (1) the tabernacle (21:1-8), (2) the city (21:9-27), and (3) the garden (22:1-5). The image of the tabernacle portrays heavenly life as perfect fellowship with God. The symbolism of the city portrays heavenly life as perfect protection. The image of the garden shows heavenly life as perfect provision.

HEBER Personal name meaning "companion." **1.** Grandson of Asher and great grandson of Jacob (Gen. 46:17). He was the original clan ancestor of the Heberites (Num. 26:45). **2.** Kenite related to family of Moses' wife (Judg. 4:11). **3.** A member of the tribe of Judah in a Hebrew text (1 Chron. 4:18), which apparently lists two mothers of Heber, one an Egyptian. **4.** A member of the tribe of Benjamin (1 Chron. 8:17). **5.** A different Hebrew word lies behind Eber (1 Chron. 5:13; 8:22), which KJV spells Heber. The Heber in Luke 3:35 (KJV) is the Eber of Gen. 11:15.

HEBREW A descendant of Eber. It differentiates early Israelites from foreigners. After David founded the monarchy the term "Hebrew" seems to disappear from the Hebrew language. The designation apparently begins with Abraham (Gen. 14:13).

HEBREW LANGUAGE The language in which the canonical books of the OT were written, except for the Aramaic sections in Ezra 4:8–6:18; 7:12-26; Dan. 2:4b–7:28; Jer. 10:11, and a few other words and phrases from Aramaic and other languages. The language is not called "Hebrew" in the OT. Rather, it is known as "the language (literally, 'lip') of Canaan" (Isa. 19:18) or as "Judean" (NASB), that is, the language of Judah (Neh. 13:24; Isa. 36:11).

HEBREWS, LETTER TO THE Both the author of Hebrews and the historical situation that prompted its writing are matters of speculation. Although Paul's name is included in the title in some manuscripts, the author never mentions his name. Nor does the author identify his recipients or their location. The date of the letter is also uncertain. The author labeled himself and his audience as "second generation" Christians, who heard the word from those who had known Jesus (Heb. 2:3b).

The main theme of Hebrews is found early in chapter one. The God who spoke to the Israelites is the same God who spoke through Jesus (1:1-2). And when God speaks, His people ought to listen, a message reiterated in the climactic warning passage of the letter: "See

The Gezer Calendar is believed to be the oldest Hebrew inscription found to date. The inscription is on a limestone tablet and dates from 925 BC.

that you do not reject the One who speaks …" (12:25 HCSB). Related to this is the warning against apostasy. This issue is present in all the warning passages, but the focal point of discussion usually is 6:4-8. The passage leaves no doubt that those who fall away will be punished for their disobedience. What is often overlooked, however, is that the text is far from explicit about what they are falling away from and what the punishment will be.

The most common assumption is that they have fallen away from salvation and the burning (6:8) refers to eternal destruction. However, Herschel Hobbs' contention that these believers were in danger of falling away from God's world mission and the punishment will be loss of opportunity is credible. The theme of God's mission can be seen in other passages, such as the failed attempt at Kadesh-barnea to enter the promised land to fulfill their calling (chaps. 3 and 4). Another often suggested solution looks at those who fall away as phenomenological believers; in other words, they appeared to be believers but were not. A difficulty with this position is the strong language the author used in 6:4-5 to describe these people.

In what may be the climax of the whole letter (13:10-16), the author reintroduced the themes of high priest, altar, and Day of Atonement sacrifice, all of which were central images in chapters 8–10.

In this passage these images were used to call the hearers outside their security zone. The synagogue might represent physical security for the audience, but Jesus was outside, suffering for the people. His people needed to be outside with Him.

Other theological themes give support to the call to obedience. One such theme is the nature of Christ: Jesus is God's ultimate, superior revelation of Himself. He is superior to angels, Moses, and the earthly priests, and His sacrifice is superior to anything offered in the temple. Through careful exposition of OT passages the author points out the temporal nature of the priesthood, the temple sacrificial system, and the initial covenant between God and His people. Jesus as the perfect high priest offered a once-for-all sacrifice that initiated the new covenant foretold by Jeremiah.

The mosque of the patriarchs at Hebron built over the traditional site of the Cave of Machpelah.

HEBRON Place-name and personal name meaning "association" or "league." A major city in the hill country of Judah about 19 miles south of Jerusalem and 15 miles west of the Dead Sea.

After his separation from Lot, Abraham moved to Hebron. At that time the area was known as Mamre and was associated with the Amorites (Gen. 13:18; 14:13; 23:19). Abraham apparently remained at Mamre until after the destruction of Sodom and Gomorrah. When Sarah died, the place was called Kirjath-arba; and the population was predominantly Hittite (Gen. 23:2; Josh. 14:15; 15:54; Judg. 1:10). From them Abraham purchased a field with a burial plot inside the Cave of Machpelah. Abraham and Sarah, Isaac and Rebekah, and Jacob and Leah were buried there (Gen. 23:19; 25:9; 35:29; 49:31; 50:13).

Four centuries later, when Moses sent the 12 spies into Canaan, the tribe of Anak lived in Hebron. After the death of Saul, David settled in the city (2 Sam. 2:3) and made it his capital during the seven years he ruled only Judah (1 Kings 2:11). His son, Absalom, launched an abortive revolt against David from Hebron (2 Sam. 15:10).

HEDGEHOG NASB, NRSV translation of the Hebrew *qippod*, a term of uncertain meaning (Isa. 14:23; 34:11; Zeph. 2:14). The term either refers to the hedgehog (or porcupine) or else to a type of bird.

HEEL, LIFTED HIS To lift one's heel against someone is to turn one's back and join rank with the enemies. Jesus applied the expression to Judas, who accepted Jesus' hospitality but then plotted His arrest (John 13:18).

HEGAI Persian name of unknown meaning. Eunuch in charge of King Ahasuerus's harem who befriended Esther (Esther 2:8-9,15).

HEGE KJV spelling of Hegai in Esther 2:3 based on variant spelling in Hebrew text.

HEGLAM NRSV interpretation of Hebrew text in 1 Chron. 8:7, taking as a proper name giving a second name to Gera what other translations translate as "who deported them."

HEIFER Young cow, especially one that has not yet calved.

HELAH Personal name meaning "jewelry for the neck." Wife of Ashur in the tribe of Judah (1 Chron. 4:5,7).

HELAM Place-name meaning "their army." Helam is the region, rather than a city, where David defeated the army of Hadadezer and thus gained control of Syria (2 Sam. 10:15-19).

HELBAH Place-name meaning "forest." City in tribal territory of Asher that Asher could not drive out (Judg. 1:31).

HELBON Place-name meaning "forest." City known for its trade in wine mentioned in Ezekiel's lament over Tyre (Ezek. 27:18).

HELDAI Personal name meaning "mole." **1.** Officer in charge of David's army for the twelfth month of the year (1 Chron. 27:15). **2.** Man who returned from exile in Babylon, apparently with a gift of silver and gold, which God told Zechariah to take and have made into a crown for Joshua, the high priest (Zech. 6:10).

HELEB Personal name meaning "fat" or "the best." One of David's military heroes (2 Sam. 23:29).

HELEK Personal name meaning "portion." Son of Gilead from the tribe of Manasseh and original clan ancestor of the Helekites (Num. 26:30). The clan received an allotment in the tribe's share of the promised land (Josh. 17:2).

HELEM Personal name meaning "beat, strike." Member of tribe of Asher (1 Chron. 7:35).

HELEPH Place-name meaning "replacement settlement" or "settlement of reeds." Border city of the tribal allotment of Naphtali (Josh. 19:33).

HELEZ Personal name perhaps meaning "ready for battle." **1.** David's military hero (2 Sam. 23:26) in charge of the army for the seventh month (1 Chron. 27:10). **2.** Member of the family of Caleb and Jerahmeel in the tribe of Judah (1 Chron. 2:39).

HELI Hebrew personal name meaning "high." The son of Matthat and father of Joseph, Jesus' earthly father (Luke 3:23-24).

HELIOPOLIS 1. Greek name for Egyptian city that meant "city of the sun." Its name in Egyptian means "pillar town" and was rendered in Akkadian as *Ana* and in Hebrew as *On* or *Awen* (Gen. 41:45; 46:20; Ezek. 30:17). **2.** Ancient city of Baalbek ("Lord of the Valley") located in the Beqaa Valley of Lebanon about 50 miles east of Beirut. Although it was a very ancient city, it was renamed Heliopolis in the third or second century BC.

HELKAI Personal name meaning "my portion." Priest when Joiakim was high priest one generation after the return from the exile under Zerubbabel (Neh. 12:15).

HELKATH Place-name meaning "flat place." Border town in the tribal allotment of Asher (Josh. 19:25) given to the Levites (21:31).

HELKATH-HAZZURIM Place-name meaning "field of flint stones" or "field of battle." Site of "play" (2 Sam. 2:14) battle between young warriors of Saul and those of David leading to defeat of Ish-bosheth's army (2:12-17).

HELL Usually understood as the final abode of the unrighteous dead wherein the ungodly suffer eternal punishment; the term translates one OT word and several NT words.

HELLENISM Used to describe any influence of classical Greek thought on Western heritage. The Hellenistic culture of Alexandria strongly impacted Jewish and Christian communities. The Koine Greek language became the *lingua franca*, an influence seen in the Greek terms used to name the Jewish "synagogue" (*sunagoge*) and the NT "church" (*ekklesia*). In about 275 BC Jewish scholars produced the first translation of the

Harbor at Alexandria. In Alexandria the Septuagint was translated about 275 BC.

Hebrew Scriptures, the Greek Septuagint (LXX). The Greek language was crucial in the spread of the gospel. NT authors used and quoted from the Septuagint and the NT was written in Koine Greek. Some passages in the NT seem to reflect Greek thought as well as Greek terminology. Greek influence shows in the use of *logos* in John 1:1-14, a term Stoic philosophers used to describe the creative order of the universe.

HELLENISTS Group of early Christians whose language and culture were Greek rather than Hebrew. One of the first conflicts among believers in the early church was between those with a Greek background and those who had grown up in the Hebrew tradition (Acts 6:1; 9:29).

HELON Personal name meaning "powerful." Father of the leader of the tribe of Zebulun under Moses (Num. 1:9).

HELPER NASB translation of *parakletos*, a distinctive title for the Holy Spirit in the Gospel of John (14:16,26; 15:26; 16:7). Other versions translate the term "Comforter" (KJV), "Advocate" (NEB), or "Counselor" (HCSB, RSV, NIV).

HELPMEET KJV term for woman as a helper precisely adapted to man (Gen. 2:18). Modern translations supply various equivalents: help suitable for him (NASB, NIV); help as his partner (NRSV); a suitable companion for him (TEV). The noun translated "help" or "partner" does not suggest subordination. Elsewhere the term is used of God as Help (1 Chron. 12:18; Pss. 30:10; 54:4; 121:1) or of military allies (Jer. 47:4; Nah. 3:9). The adjective "meet" (translated "suitable," "comparable," or "corresponding") stresses that woman, unlike the animals (Gen. 2:20), can be truly one with man (2:24), that is, enjoy full fellowship and partnership in humanity's God-given task (Gen. 1:27-28) of rule and dominion.

HELVE KJV term used for the handle of an ax (Deut. 19:5).

HEMAM Personal name of uncertain meaning. Descendant of Seir (Gen. 36:22).

HEMAN Personal name meaning "faithful." **1.** In Gen. 36:22, one of the sons of Lotan mentioned among the descendants of Esau. **2.** In 1 Kings 4:31, a notable sage to whose wisdom that of Solomon is compared. **3.** In 1 Chron. 6:33, the son of Joel, a Kohathite.

HEMDAN Personal name meaning "beauty, charm." Descendant of Seir and thus an Edomite (Gen. 36:26).

HEMLOCK KJV translation of two Hebrew terms. Modern translations agree in translating that in Hos. 10:4 as poisonous weed(s). The term at Amos 6:12 is translated as "bitterness" (NASB margins, NIV), "poison" (REB), and "wormwood" (NRSV, NASB).

HEMORRHAGE Heavy or uncontrollable bleeding. The KJV translates the underlying Hebrew and Greek terms as "issue of blood" (Lev. 12:7; Matt. 9:20) or "fountain of blood" (Mark 5:29).

HEMORRHOIDS Mass of dilated veins and swollen tissue in the vicinity of the anus. The KJV translators understood the affliction of Deut. 28:27; 1 Sam. 5:6,9,12 as hemorrhoids (or emerods).

HENA Place-name of uncertain meaning. City Sennacherib, king of Assyria, captured prior to threatening Hezekiah and Jerusalem in 701 BC (2 Kings 18:34).

HENADAD Personal name meaning "grace of Hadad (the god)." Clan of Levites who supervised the rebuilding of the temple under Zerubbabel after 537 BC (Ezra 3:9). Clan members also helped Nehemiah rebuild Jerusalem's walls (Neh. 3:18,24) and signed Nehemiah's covenant of obedience (Neh. 10:10).

HEPHER Personal name meaning "well" or "shame." **1.** Original family ancestor in clan of Gilead and father of Zelophehad (Num. 26:28-37). He belonged to the tribe of Manasseh (Josh. 17:1-2). **2.** A hero in David's wilderness army (1 Chron. 11:36). **3.** Member of the tribe of Judah (1 Chron. 4:6).

HEPHZIBAH Personal name meaning "my delight is in her." **1.** In 2 Kings 21:1 the mother of Manasseh, king of Judah. **2.** In Isa. 62:4 it is used as a symbolic name for Jerusalem.

HERBS, BITTER Salad of bitter herbs was eaten as part of the Passover observance (Exod. 12:8; Num. 9:11).

HERES Place-name meaning "sun." A mountain pass over which Gideon traveled in returning from his battle with the Midianites (Judg. 8:13).

HERESH Personal name meaning "unable to speak." Levite who lived near Jerusalem after the return from exile about 537 BC (1 Chron. 9:15).

HERESY Opinion or doctrine not in line with the accepted teaching of a church; the opposite of orthodoxy. Our English word is derived from a Greek word that has the basic idea of "choice."

HERETH Modern translation spelling of Hareth; place-name meaning "cut in to." Forest in which David hid from Saul after settling his parents with the king of Moab (1 Sam. 22:4-5).

HERMAS Christian to whom Paul sent greetings (Rom. 16:14). His name, the variant spelling of the Greek god Hermes, may indicate he was a slave, since many slaves were named for gods.

HERMES In Acts 14:12 the Greek deity for whom the superstitious people at Lystra took Paul. KJV uses the god's Latin name, Mercurius. Hermes was known as a messenger of the gods and was associated with eloquence. Paul's role as chief speaker made the Lystrans think of Hermes.

HERMOGENES Personal name meaning "born of Hermes." Follower who deserted Paul, apparently while he was in prison in Ephesus (2 Tim. 1:15). Paul's statement indicates acute disappointment in Hermogenes but does not say he became an apostate.

HERMON, MOUNT Place-name meaning "devoted mountain." At 9,100 feet above sea level, Hermon is the highest mountain in Syria. It can be seen from as far away as the Dead Sea—120 miles. The range is approximately 28 miles in length and reaches a width of 15 miles. Its peak is covered with snow two-thirds of the year. The mount is significant for four reasons. (1) It was the northern border of the Amorite kingdom (Deut. 3:8; 4:48). (2) It marked the northern limits of Joshua's victorious campaigns (Josh. 11:17; 12:1; 13:5). (3) It has always been regarded as a sacred mountain. (4) Some scholars believe the transfiguration of Jesus occurred on Hermon.

View of Mount Hermon from the ancient city-mound of Hazor in northern Galilee.

This aqueduct built by Herod the Great brought fresh water to Caesarea Maritima.

HEROD Name given to the family ruling Palestine immediately before and to some degree during the first half of the first Christian century. The most prominent family member and ruler was called Herod the Great, an Idumaean who was appointed king of the Jews in 40 BC and ruled until his death in 4 BC. Herod was ruler of Judea when Jesus was born (Matt. 2:1).

HERODIAN Member of an aristocratic Jewish group who favored the policies of Herod Antipas and thus supported the Roman government. Apparently they lived in Galilee, where Antipas ruled, and joined the Jerusalem religious authorities in opposing Jesus (Matt. 22:15-22; Mark 12:13-17).

HERODIAS Wife of Herod Antipas (Mark 6:17).

HERODION Christian man to whom Paul the apostle sent a greeting (Rom. 16:11). Paul referred to him as a kinsman.

HERODIUM A fortress-palace built by Herod the Great about four miles southeast of Bethlehem. Herod was buried there.

HERON Any of a family of wading birds with long necks and legs (*Areidae*), which were regarded as unclean (Lev. 11:19; Deut. 14:18).

HESED Personal name meaning "grace" or "covenant love." Father of one of Solomon's district governors (1 Kings 4:10 KJV).

HESHBON Place-name meaning "reckoning." City in Moab ruled by Sihon and captured by Moses (Num. 21:21-30).

HESHMON Place-name meaning "flat field." Town in tribal territory of Judah (Josh. 15:27).

HETH Personal name of unknown meaning. Son of Canaan, great grandson of Noah, and original ancestor of the Hittites, some of the original inhabitants of Palestine (Gen. 10:15).

HETHLON Place-name of unknown meaning on the northern border of Israel's promised land, according to Ezekiel's vision (Ezek. 47:15).

HEW To cut with blows from a heavy cutting instrument. The references to "hewers of wood" together with "drawers of water" (Josh. 9:21,23,27; Deut. 29:11) probably refer to those who gathered firewood. Such work was a despised task relegated to foreigners and slaves.

HEXATEUCH Modern designation for the first six books of the OT viewed as a literary unity.

The Gihon Spring in the Kidron Valley. King Hezekiah built a tunnel from the spring to the pool of Siloam that he also built to provide water for Jerusalem.

HEZEKIAH Son and successor of Ahaz as king of Judah (716/15–687/86 BC). Hezekiah began his reign when he was 25 years old. Hezekiah died in 687/86 BC. Manasseh, his son, succeeded him, although Manasseh had become co-regent with Hezekiah about 696 BC.

In 711 BC, just a few years after Hezekiah had become king, Sargon II of Assyria captured Ashdod. Hezekiah anticipated the time when he would have to confront Assyrian armies. Hezekiah fortified the city of Jerusalem and organized an army. Knowing that a source of water was crucial, Hezekiah constructed a tunnel through solid rock from the spring of Gihon to the Siloam pool. The city wall was extended to enclose this important source of water.

Hezekiah consistently demonstrated both faith in and obedience to God. "Not one of the kings of Judah was like him, either before him or after him" (2 Kings 18:5 HCSB).

HEZION Personal name meaning "vision." Grandfather of King Ben-hadad of Damascus (1 Kings 15:18).

HEZIR Personal name meaning "wild pig." Ugaritic texts apparently show that the name came from the profession of herding swine **1.** Leader of one of the 24 courses of priests (1 Chron. 24:15). **2.** Levite who signed Nehemiah's covenant to obey God's law (Neh. 10:20).

HEZRAI or **HEZRO** Personal name meaning "his stalk" or "stem." KJV reading of name of one of David's warriors (2 Sam. 23:35).

HEZRON Personal and place-name meaning "camping place" or "reeds." **1.** Son of Reuben, grandson of Jacob (Gen. 46:9), and original clan ancestor of Hezronites (Num. 26:6). **2.** Grandson of Judah, great grandson of Jacob (Gen. 46:12), original clan ancestor of Hezronites (Num. 26:21) through whom David was born (Ruth 4:19).

HIDDAI Personal name, perhaps a short form for Hodai, meaning "my majesty." One of David's warriors (2 Sam. 23:30).

HIDDEKEL Hebrew name for the third river flowing from the garden of Eden (Gen. 2:14). Most modern translations translate it as Tigris.

HIEL Personal name meaning "God lives" or, following the Greek translation, a short form of Ahiel, "brother of God." Man from Bethel who rebuilt Jericho at the price of the life of two of his sons

Mineral deposits from the hot springs of Hierapolis used as a health spa during the Roman period.

(1 Kings 16:34), fulfilling the divine curse Joshua issued when he destroyed Jericho (Josh. 6:26).

HIERAPOLIS Place-name meaning "sacred city." Site of early church where Epaphras worked (Col. 4:13). The city was 12 miles northwest of Colossae.

HIGGAION Transliteration of Hebrew word meaning "whispering" (Lam. 3:62 NASB) or "meditation" (Ps. 19:14) or musical sound a stringed instrument produces (Ps. 92:3). It appears as a worship notation with uncertain meaning in Ps. 9:16. It may mean to play quietly or to pause for meditation.

HIGHEST KJV designation for God (Luke 1:32,35,76; 6:35). Modern translations prefer "Most High" (NASB, NIV, NRSV) or "Most High God" (TEV).

HIGH GATE, HIGHER GATE KJV designations for a gate of the Jerusalem temple (2 Kings 15:35; 2 Chron. 23:20; 27:3).

HIGH HEAPS KJV translation of a Hebrew term that occurs only at Jer. 31:21. Modern translations render the term as guideposts (NASB, NIV, NRSV) or signpost (REB).

HIGH PLACE Elevated site, usually found on the top of a mountain or hill; most high places were Canaanite places of pagan worship.

HIGH PRIEST One in charge of the temple (or tabernacle) worship. A number of terms are used to refer to the high priest: the priest (Exod. 31:10); the anointed priest (Lev. 4:3); the priest who is chief among his brethren (Lev. 21:10); chief priest (2 Chron. 26:20); and high priest (2 Kings 12:10). The high priesthood was a hereditary office based on descent from Aaron (Exod. 29:29-30; Lev. 16:32). Normally, the high priest served for life (Num. 18:7; 25:11-13;

Stone fragments of what is probably an altar base at the high place in Lachish.

35:25,28; Neh. 12:10-11), though as early as Solomon's reign a high priest was dismissed for political reasons (1 Kings 2:27).

During the Roman period, Annas (high priest AD 6–15) was clearly the most powerful priestly figure. Even when deposed by the Romans, Annas succeeded in having five of his sons and a son-in-law, Joseph Caiaphas (high priest AD 18–36/37) appointed high priests.

HIGHWAY A road, especially an elevated road (Isa. 62:10). In addition to literal uses, there are figurative uses, especially in Isaiah.

HILEN Place-name, perhaps meaning "power." City in tribal territory of Judah given to Levites (1 Chron. 6:58).

HILKIAH Personal name meaning "Yah's portion." **1.** Father of Amaziah (1 Chron. 6:45). He was a Levite who lived before the time of David the king. **2.** Levite and temple servant who lived during the time of David (1 Chron. 26:11). **3.** Father of Eliakim, who was in charge of the household of King Hezekiah (2 Kings 18:18). **4.** Father of Jeremiah the prophet (Jer. 1:1). **5.** Father of Gemariah, who was an emissary from Zedekiah to Nebuchadnezzar, king of Babylon (Jer. 29:3). **6.** High priest who aided in Josiah's reform movement (2 Kings 22:4). **7.** Person who stood with Ezra the scribe at the reading of the law (Neh. 8:4). **8.** Priest who was among the exiles that returned (Neh. 12:7).

HILL OF GOD (Hb. *Gibeat-elohim*) Site of a Philistine garrison and of a place of worship. Here Saul met a band of ecstatic prophets and joined them in their frenzy (1 Sam. 10:5).

HILL OF THE FORESKINS (Hb. *Gibeat-haaraloth*) Place near Gilgal where Joshua circumcised the Israelites born during the wilderness wandering (Josh. 5:3).

HILLEL Personal name meaning "praise." **1.** Father of the judge Abdon (Judg. 12:13). **2.** Influential rabbi and Talmudic scholar who flourished just prior to the time of the ministry of Jesus. He and his colleague Shammai presided over the two most important rabbinic schools of their time.

HIN Unit of liquid measure reckoned as one sixth of a bath (Exod. 29:40). It would have been approximately equivalent to a gallon.

HIND Female deer; doe (Prov. 5:19). "To make my feet like hinds' feet" (KJV, NASB) is a common expression (2 Sam. 22:34; Ps. 18:33; Hab. 3:19) of God's care in dangerous situations.

HINNOM, VALLEY OF Place-name of uncertain meaning; also called the valley of the son(s) of Hinnom. The valley lies in close proximity to Jerusalem (2 Kings 23:10), just south of the ancient city (Josh. 15:8). The valley had a somewhat unglamorous history during the OT period. The worshippers of the pagan deities, Baal and Molech, practiced child sacrifice there (2 Kings 23:10).

HIP Part of the body where the thigh and torso connect. Jacob's hip came out of socket when he wrestled with God at the Jabbok (Gen. 32:25). The Israelites commemorated this encounter by not eating the thigh muscle on the hip socket (Gen. 32:32).

HIPPOPOTAMUS Large, thick-skinned, amphibious, cud-chewing mammal of the family *Hippopotamidae*. The Hebrew *behemoth* (Job 40:15-24) is sometimes understood as the hippopotamus (NASB, TEV margins).

HIRAH Personal name of unknown meaning. A friend of Judah, the son of Jacob, whom Judah was visiting when he met Shuah, who bore three of his sons (Gen. 38:1-12).

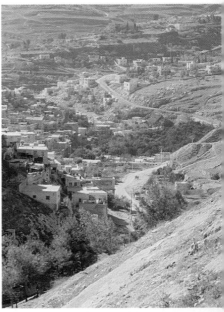

The Hinnom (or Gehenna) Valley in Jerusalem, just south of the ancient city.

HIRAM Personal name apparently meaning "brother of the lofty one." **1.** King of Tyre, associated with David and Solomon in building the temple. **2.** Craftsman who did artistic metal work for Solomon's temple (1 Kings 7:13-45). He lived in Tyre, his father's hometown, but had a widowed Jewish mother from the tribe of Naphtali.

HISS Sound made by forcing breath between the tongue and teeth in mockery or to ward off demons. In the OT an army or nation hissed at their enemy's city or land that suffered defeat or disaster (Jer. 19:8).

HITTITES Non-Semitic minority within the population of Canaan who frequently became involved in the affairs of the Israelites. Hittites, along with the Hivites, were people of Indo-European origin, identified within the population of Canaan (as "sons" of Canaan) in the Table of Nations (Gen. 10:15,17).

HIVITES A name that occurs 25 times in the Bible though not in texts outside the Bible. Most frequently the name appears in the list of nations God would drive out of the land during the Israelite conquest (e.g., Deut. 7:1).

HIZKI Personal name meaning "my strength" or a shortened form of "Yah is my strength." Modern translation spelling of Hezeki, a Benjaminite (1 Chron. 8:17).

HIZKIAH Personal name meaning "Yah is my strength." **1.** Abbreviated form in Hebrew for Hezekiah and used as alternate spelling of the king's name (2 Kings 18; Prov. 25:1). **2.** Apparently the Hebrew name of a clan that returned from Babylonian exile with Zerubbabel about 537 BC. **3.** A descendant of David living after the return from exile (1 Chron. 3:23).

HIZKIJAH KJV spelling of Hizkiah in Neh. 10:17. Modern translations usually use "Hezekiah."

HOARFROST or **HOAR FROST** KJV terms for frost from "hoar" (white) and "frost" (Exod. 16:14; Job 38:29; Ps. 147:16).

HOBAB Personal name meaning "beloved" or "cunning." Father-in-law of Moses (Num. 10:29; Judg. 4:11). Some uncertainty exists concerning the identity of Moses' father-in-law. Jethro (Exod. 3:1; 18:2) and Reuel (Exod. 2:18) are also given as names for the father-in-law of the great lawgiver.

HOBAH Place-name probably meaning "guilt" in Hebrew but "land of reeds" in Akkadian. Town in Syria to which Abraham pursued the coalition of eastern kings who kidnapped Lot (Gen. 14:15).

HOBAIAH Personal name meaning "Yah hides." Clan of priests in time of Zerubbabel who did not have family records to prove their descent from pure priestly lines and were excluded from the priesthood (Ezra 2:61; Neh. 7:63).

HOD Personal name meaning "majesty." Member of tribe of Asher (1 Chron. 7:37).

HODAIAH KJV, REB spelling of Hodaviah (1 Chron. 3:24).

HODAVIAH Personal name meaning "praise Yah." **1.** The final generation of the sons of David that the Chronicler listed (1 Chron. 3:24). **2.** Original ancestor of clan in half-tribe of Manasseh living east of the Jordan (1 Chron. 5:24). **3.** A member of the tribe of Benjamin (1 Chron. 9:7). **4.** A clan of Levites who returned to Judah under Zerubbabel about 537 BC (Ezra 2:40).

HODESH Personal name meaning "new moon." Wife of Shaharaim of the tribe of Benjamin who bore children in Moab (1 Chron. 8:9).

HODEVAH Transliteration of Hebrew text in Neh. 7:43 for original "Hodaviah."

HODIAH Personal name meaning "Yah is majestic." **1.** Member of tribe of Judah (1 Chron. 4:19). **2.** A Levite who helped Ezra explain the meaning of the Law to the people (Neh. 8:7; note KJV spelling, Hodijah) and had a leading part in Israel's confession of sin and worship (Neh. 9:5).

HOGLAH Personal name meaning "partridge." Daughter of Zelophehad in tribe of Manasseh (Num. 26:33). Her marriage to a son of her father's brothers helped ensure the family land inheritance remained within the tribe (Num. 36:11).

HOHAM Personal name of uncertain meaning, perhaps related to "unlucky." King of Hebron who joined forces with the king of Jerusalem to punish Gibeon for making an alliance with Joshua (Josh. 10:3).

HOLM TREE Small, holly-like, evergreen oak (*Quercus ilex*). The identity of the tree of Isa. 44:14 is disputed: cypress (NASB, NIV); ilex (REB); holm oak or tree (NASB margin, NRSV); oak (TEV).

HOLON Place-name meaning "sandy spot." **1.** Town in the hill country of Judah allotted to tribe of Judah and given as city for Levites (Josh. 15:51; 21:15). **2.** City of Moab that Jeremiah condemned (Jer. 48:21). Its location is not known.

HOLY Biblical use of the term "holy" has to do primarily with God's separating from the world that which He chooses to devote to Himself. As God's redemptive plan unfolded through the OT, the "holy" became associated with the character of God's separated people conforming to His revealed law. When the time became ripe for the saving work of Jesus Christ, His redeemed people came to be known as saints (literally, "holy ones"). The cross made this possible by inaugurating the fulfillment of the preparatory OT teachings on the holy, opening the way for God's Holy Spirit to indwell His people.

God's people are to be holy because God is holy. In this sense, God's holiness is the complete perfection of His attributes such as power and goodness. God's holiness is a humbling and even terrifying thing when revealed to weak and sinful men (e.g., Isa. 6:5; Luke 5:8; Rev. 1:17).

HOLY CITY Designation for Jerusalem (Neh. 11:1,18; Isa. 48:2; 52:1; Dan. 9:24; Matt. 4:5; 27:53; Rev. 11:2) and for the new, heavenly Jerusalem (Rev. 21:2,10; 22:19) because the holy God lived there.

HOLY OF HOLIES Innermost sanctuary of the temple. Separated from the other parts of the temple by a thick curtain, the holy of holies was specially associated with the presence of Yahweh. In the early years of the existence of the temple the holy of holies contained the ark of the covenant.

HOLY ONE OF ISRAEL In Isa. 1:4, a designation for Yahweh. The title stresses God's nature as holy and His unique relationship to Israel.

HOLY PLACE Courts, inner room, and outer room of the tabernacle (Exod. 26:33). Later the expression was used in reference to the temple and its environs. It was a holy place in the sense of being a place set apart for Yahweh.

HOLY SPIRIT Third person of the Trinity through whom God acts, reveals His will, empowers individuals, and discloses His personal presence in the OT and NT. See *God; Spirit.*

HOLY SPIRIT, SIN AGAINST THE Attributing the work of the Holy Spirit to the devil (Matt. 12:32; Mark 3:29; Luke 12:10).

HOMAN Personal name perhaps meaning "confusion." Hebrew text name for grandson of Seir (1 Chron. 1:39). The parallel passage reads "Hemam" (Gen. 36:22).

HOMER Unit of dry measure (Lev. 27:16). According to Ezek. 45:11, it was equal to 10 ephahs. In liquid measure this was 10 baths. The actual volume represented by the term has been variously estimated between 3.8 and 6.6 bushels. It was the same volume as the cor (Ezek. 45:14).

HOMOSEXUALITY Sexual relations between people of the same sex. When discussing homosexuality, the biblical emphasis is on behavior, and the verdict is always that it is sinful.

Paul argues in Rom. 1:18-32 that homosexuality is one consequence of rejecting God as creator and His created order. Paul indicates that both male homosexuality and female lesbianism result from a denial of God.

In 1 Cor. 6:9-11 "homosexuals" appears in a similar vice list and Paul comments that anyone who continues in these sins will not inherit the kingdom of God. *Arsenokoites* refers to the active partner in the homosexual act. However, in addition to "homosexuals" in 1 Cor. 6:9, Paul adds a second word, "effeminate" (*malakoi*). *Malakoi* refers to the passive member in the homosexual relationship. The point is that both passive and active kinds of "homosexual" behavior are sinful, ungodly, and disqualify one from entrance into the kingdom of God.

However ungodly and undeserving of heaven any homosexual might be, there is the opportunity to be forgiven, changed, and declared righteous through Jesus Christ. Paul continues in 1 Cor. 6:11 (HCSB) to say, "some of you were like this." The homosexual who repents and believes receives the same cleansing, sanctification, and justification as every other believer who turns from sin to Christ.

HONESTY Fairness and straightforwardness of conduct. KJV frequently used "honesty" or cognates where modern translations use other words: "honorable/honorably" (Rom. 13:13; Phil. 4:8; Heb. 13:18; 1 Pet. 2:12); "noble" (Luke 8:15; Rom. 12:17); "dignity" (1 Tim. 2:2); "properly" (1 Thess. 4:12). Men of "honest report" (Acts 6:3) are men of good standing (NRSV).

HOOF Curved covering of horn protecting the front of or enclosing the digits of some mammals. According to Mosaic law, ritually clean animals are those that both chew the cud and have cloven (divided) hooves (Deut. 14:6-7).

HOOPOE Any of the Old World birds of the family *Upupidae*, having a plumed head crest and a long, slender, curved bill. The identity of the unclean bird of Lev. 11:19 (Deut. 14:18) is disputed: lapwing (KJV); hoopoe (modern English translations); waterhen (earliest Greek); woodcock (Targum).

HOPE Trustful expectation, particularly with reference to the fulfillment of God's promises. Biblical hope is the anticipation of a favorable outcome under God's guidance. More specifically, hope is the confidence that what God has done for us in the past guarantees our participation in what God will do in the future. This contrasts to the world's definition of hope as "a feeling that what is wanted will happen."

Christians live in hope for two basic reasons. The first reason is because of what God has done in Christ. Especially important is the emphasis the NT places on the resurrection by which Christ has defeated the power of sin and death. "According to His great mercy, He has given us a new birth into a living hope through the resurrection of Jesus Christ from the dead" (1 Pet. 1:3 HCSB).

The second reason is the indwelling of the Holy Spirit. "The Spirit Himself testifies together with our spirit that we are God's children" (Rom. 8:16 HCSB).

HOPHNI AND PHINEHAS Personal names meaning "tadpole" and "dark-skinned one" in Egyptian. In 1 Sam. 1:3, sons of Eli and priests at Shiloh. They were disreputable men who were contemptuous of sacred matters. They were slain in battle against the Philistines (1 Sam. 4:4). The news of their deaths precipitated the death of their father Eli (1 Sam. 4:18).

HOPHRA Egyptian divine name meaning "the heart of Re endures." Egyptian pharaoh (589–569 BC).

HOR, MOUNT Place-name, perhaps an ancient variant of Hebrew common noun, *har*, "mountain." **1.** Place where Aaron, the high priest, died, fulfilling God's word that he would be punished for rebelling at the water of Meribah (Num. 20:22-29; 33:38-39). **2.** Mountain marking northern boundary of promised land (Num. 34:7-8). The location is unknown, though some would see Hor as a variant name for Mount Hermon.

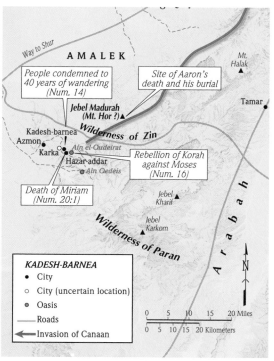

HOR-HAGGIDGAD or **HOR-HAGIDGAD** (KJV) Place-name perhaps meaning "hill of crickets." Station on Israel's wilderness journey (Num. 33:32-33).

HORAM Personal name perhaps meaning "high, exalted." King of Gezer whose attempt to deliver Lachish from Joshua resulted in his death and the annihilation of his army (Josh. 10:33), though his city remained a Canaanite stronghold (Josh. 16:10; cp. 1 Kings 9:16).

HOREB Alternative name for Mount Sinai (Exod. 3:1-12; 17:6-7; Deut. 1:19; 5:2; 1 Kings 19:8).

HOREM Place-name meaning "split rock" but sounding like the word for "war booty under the ban." City in tribal allotment of Naphtali (Josh. 19:38).

HORESH Place-name meaning "forest," KJV interpreting the term as a common noun. As David hid there from Saul, Jonathan, Saul's son, came out to help him and made a covenant of mutual help (1 Sam. 23:15-18).

HORI Personal name meaning "bleached," "lesser," or "Horite." **1.** Edomite descended from Seir (Gen. 36:22). **2.** Father of the leader of tribe of Simeon under Moses in the wilderness (Num. 13:5).

HORIM (KJV) or **HORITES** Pre-Edomite inhabitants of Mount Seir in the southern Transjordan.

HORMAH Place-name meaning "split rock" or "cursed for destruction." City marking the limit of the Canaanite route of the Israelites after the failed Israelite attempt to invade Canaan that followed the report of the 12 spies (Num. 14:45).

HORN Curved bone-like structures growing from the heads of animals such as deer or goats and vessels or instruments made from or shaped like such horns. In Scripture "horn" refers to trumpets, vessels, topographical features, and figurative symbols.

Metaphorically, horn signified the strength and honor of people and brightness and rays. Such references are used in Scripture as emblems of the power of God (Heb. 3:4) and other physical or spiritual entities. There is an apocalyptic use of the word in Dan. 7:7. Horns budding or sprouting is a figurative language indicating a sign of revival of a nation or power.

Christ is called "a horn of salvation" (Luke 1:69 HCSB), which is a metaphorical use of the word signifying strength.

HORNED OWL Species of owl having conspicuous tufts of feathers on the head. NIV reckons the horned owl an unclean bird (Lev. 11:16; Deut. 14:15). The precise identity of the bird is unclear.

Other possibilities include: desert owl (REB), owl (KJV), and ostrich (NASB, NRSV).

HORNED SNAKE Venomous viper (*Cerastes cornutus*) of the Near East having a horny protrusion above each eye. Dan is compared to a horned snake (Gen. 49:17 NASB, REB).

HORONAIM Place-name meaning "twin caves." Prominent town in Moab upon which Isaiah (15:5) and Jeremiah (48:3,5,34) pronounced laments, warning of coming destruction.

HORSE Four-legged, solid-hoofed animal used for transportation and in war. The horse is mentioned more than 150 times in the Bible, with the earliest reference being found in Gen. 47:17. The number of horses owned by Solomon was as many as 12,000. They were used to draw chariots (1 Kings 4:26; 10:26). Since the Mosaic law forbade the breeding of horses, Solomon imported horses from Egypt (Deut. 17:16; 2 Chron. 1:16). Likely, because of the superiority of the horse for warfare, this law was later ignored. The ruins of Solomon's well-known horse stables at ancient Megiddo are today marked as a historical and archeological site. In Megiddo what appear to be stalls and feeding troughs from King Ahab's time have been discovered. These were sufficient for about 450 horses.

Horses are often used as symbols of swiftness (Jer. 4:13), strength (Job 39:19), and surefootedness (Isa. 63:13). The most detailed description of a horse is found in Job 39:19-25. In prophecy horses also play an important role as in Joel 2:4-5 and Rev. 6:1-8 where four horses of different colors are associated with different tragedies.

HORSE GATE Gate on east side of city wall of Jerusalem near the temple. Jeremiah promised its rebuilding (Jer. 31:40), and the priests under Nehemiah rebuilt it (Neh. 3:28).

HOSAH Personal name and place-name perhaps meaning "seeker of refuge." **1.** Coastal city in tribal territory of Asher (Josh. 19:29). **2.** Gatekeeper of the sanctuary under David (1 Chron. 16:38).

HOSANNA Cry with which Jesus was greeted on the occasion of His triumphal entrance into Jerusalem (Mark 11:9). "Hosanna" is a Hebrew or Aramaic word that is best translated as a prayer: "Save now," or "Save, we beseech Thee."

HOSEA Personal name meaning "salvation." In Hebrew the name is the same as that of Joshua's original name (Num. 13:16; Deut. 32:44) and of the last king of Israel (2 Kings 17:1), who lived at the same time as the prophet. One of David's officers bore the name (1 Chron. 27:20) as did a clan chief in the time of Nehemiah (Neh. 10:23). English translators have often chosen to spell the prophet's name Hosea to distinguish him from the others whose names they spell "Hoshea."

HOSEA, BOOK OF Title of the first book in the section of the Hebrew Bible called the Book of the Twelve, named after its prophetic hero who lived in the northern kingdom of Israel. The small prophetic books that make up this section frequently are designated Minor Prophets. This title is not an assessment of worth but a description of size as compared to Isaiah, Jeremiah, and Ezekiel.

The two broad divisions of the book of Hosea are "Hosea's Marriage" (Hos. 1–3) and "Hosea's Messages" (Hos. 4–14). A pattern of judgment followed by hope recurs in each of the first three chapters. A similar pattern is discernible in the oracles of Hosea (Hos. 4–14) though the pattern is not balanced as neatly nor revealed as clearly. Certainly the book ends on a hopeful note (Hos. 14), but most of the oracles in chapters 4–13 are judgmental in nature. The dominant theme of the book is love (covenant fidelity), God's unrelenting love for His wayward people and Israel's unreliable love for God.

HOSHAIAH Personal name meaning "Yah saved." **1.** Father of Jewish leader who led delegation requesting Jeremiah's prayer support (Jer. 42:1) and then rejected Jeremiah's word from God (Jer. 43:2). **2.** Leader of Jewish group in celebration upon the completion of the Jerusalem wall under Nehemiah (Neh. 12:32).

HOSHAMA Personal name, an abbreviated form of Jehoshama, "Yahweh heard." Descendant of David during the exile (1 Chron. 3:18).

HOSPITALITY To entertain or receive a stranger (sojourner) into one's home as an honored guest and to provide the guest with food, shelter, and protection. This was not merely an oriental custom or good manners but a sacred duty that everyone was expected to observe.

HOST OF HEAVEN Army at God's command, composed of either heavenly bodies (such as sun, moon, and stars) or angels.

"Host" is basically a military term connected with fighting or waging a war. The most frequent use of the word is to designate a group of men organized for war. In this sense, the Hebrew word often refers to a human army (Gen. 21:22,32; Judg. 4:2,7; 9:29; 1 Sam. 12:9; 2 Sam. 3:23; Isa. 34:2; Jer. 51:3).

HOSTAGE Person held as security against rebellion or aggression. When King Joash of Israel defeated King Amaziah of Judah, he took hostages (2 Kings 14:14; 2 Chron. 25:24).

HOTHAM Personal name meaning "seal" or "lock." **1.** Member of tribe of Asher (1 Chron. 7:32). **2.** Father of two warriors in David's army (1 Chron. 11:44; KJV, Hothan). Their home was Aroer.

HOTHIR Personal name meaning "he caused to be a remnant." Priestly musician in the clan of Heman under David (1 Chron. 25:4). He led the twenty-first course of Levites (1 Chron. 25:28).

HOUGH KJV term meaning "hamstring" (Josh. 11:6,9; 2 Sam. 8:4; 1 Chron. 18:4).

HOUR Appointed time for meeting or for religious festival; a brief moment of time; one twelfth of the day or of the night; and in the Gospel of John the significant period of Jesus' saving mission on earth from His triumphal entry until His death and resurrection.

HOUSE OF THE FOREST OF LEBANON A designation for a great hall Solomon constructed as part of his palace complex in Jerusalem (1 Kings 7:2-5), so called because of the extensive use of cedar for the pillars, beams, and roofing material.

HOUSE OF THE HEROES (NIV) or **HOUSE OF THE WARRIORS** Mentioned in Neh. 3:16. Thought possibly to be a type of museum to honor heroes or warriors of the past. "House of the mighty" in KJV.

HOUSE OF THE ROLLS Place mentioned in Ezra 6:1 where records of the king's decrees and actions were kept.

HOWLING CREATURES Identity of the "howling creature" (NRSV) of Isa. 13:21 is disputed. Suggestions include: the jackal (NIV), owl (NASB, KJV, TEV), porcupine (REB), and the laughing hyena.

HOZAI Personal name meaning "seer." NASB literal transliteration of Hebrew text of 2 Chron. 33:19 making Hozai a prophet who recorded the reign of King Manasseh.

HUBBAH NIV, NRSV reading of Jehubbah (1 Chron. 7:34).

HUKKOK or **HUKOK** Place-name meaning "hewn out." **1.** Town on border of tribal allotment of Naphtali between Mount Tabor and the border of Zebulun (Josh. 19:34). **2.** The same Hebrew word names a Levitical city in the tribe of Asher (1 Chron. 6:75).

HUL Personal name meaning "ring." A son of Aram, son of Shem, and grandson of Noah in the Table of Nations (Gen. 10:23).

HULDAH Personal name meaning "mole." Prophetess, the wife of Shallum (2 Kings 22:14). She was consulted after Josiah the king of Judah saw a copy of the book of the law that was found as preparations were being made to restore the temple. She prophesied judgment for the nation but a peaceful death for Josiah the king.

HUMAN SACRIFICE Ritual slaying of one or more human beings to please a god. This was widely practiced by many cultures in antiquity. However, although Israelite law specifically forbade human sacrifice (Lev. 18:21; 20:2-5), persistent references to the practice occur, especially between 800 and 500 BC. Both Ahaz and Manasseh burned their sons as an offering in times of national peril (2 Kings 16:3; 21:6). The sacrifices were made in the valley of Hinnom that protected Jerusalem from the west and south. The term *Molech* occurs frequently in connection with human sacrifice. In the Bible and elsewhere Molech apparently was used in two ways: as the name or title of a god to whom sacrifice was made (1 Kings 11:7) and as a specific type of sacrifice that involved the total consummation of a person, usually a child, by fire. Both usages of the term may be reflected in the OT. Both Jeremiah and Ezekiel condemn such offerings as an abomination to God (Jer. 7:31-32; 19:5-6; Ezek. 16:20-21; 20:31).

HUMANITY Genesis 1–2 is foundational for understanding humanity as created by God. Humankind was created directly by God (Gen. 1:26) and did not evolve from lower forms of life. Empirical evidence favors the sudden appearance of full humanity, which is consistent with Scripture.

Man was created in the image of God. God also created humanity male and female, both bearing the image of God (Gen. 1:27) and having equal standing before God. God's creation of humanity as male and female is the foundation of the biblical teaching concerning marriage, divorce, the family, and homosexuality (Gen. 2:18-25; Matt. 19:3-6; Rom. 1:26-27).

Man was also created by God as body and soul (Gen. 2:7). Man has a material part suited to life in this world and an eternal, immaterial part that survives physical death (2 Cor. 5:1-8).

The sin of the first couple caused a profound change in humanity and humanity's relationship with God (Rom. 5:12). The image of God remained, but it is marred and distorted. Humanity continued to procreate as male and female, though relationships with others were deeply and immediately affected by sin (Gen. 4). Man remained body and soul, but his inmost being was particularly impacted by sin. Man's heart, the core of his being, is sinful (Gen. 6:5; Jer. 17:9; Mark 7:20-23) and his mind is darkened (Eph. 4:17-19). Man's will is in bondage to sin (Rom. 3:10-11; 2 Tim. 2:25-26), his conscience is defiled (Titus 1:15), and his desires are twisted (Eph. 2:3; Titus 3:3). Simply put, humanity is universally dead in sin (Eph. 2:1), in a state of hostility toward God (Rom. 5:10), and subject to physical death followed by eternal judgment (Rom. 5:12-21; 8:10; 14:12; Heb. 9:27).

God in His grace did not leave humanity to perish eternally but provided for redemption. Humanity's participation in salvation begins at the individual level, when one places conscious faith in Jesus Christ. Saving faith includes a recognition of who Jesus is (fully divine and human Son of God), trust in the merits of His atoning death, and submission of the will to Him. This is all made possible by God who, according to His eternal and gracious purpose, enables sinful humanity to believe (Eph. 2:4-9; 1 Tim. 1:14; Titus 3:5).

Humanity's participation in salvation will be consummated at the end of the age with resurrection and entry into the eternal state (1 Cor. 15:50-57). Scripture emphasizes the perfect conformity of the believer to Christ (1 John 3:2), his eternal fellowship with God (John 14:2-3), and the joyful, worshipful assembly of all the redeemed (Rev. 7:9). This, of course, does not include all of humanity. Those who do not believe in Jesus Christ will spend an eternity suffering the just wrath of God (John 3:36; 2 Thess. 1:9).

HUMILITY The personal quality of being free from arrogance and pride and having an accurate estimate of one's worth.

HUMP Fleshy mound on the back of a camel where food is stored in the form of fat. Isaiah 30:6 refers to burdens carried on camels' humps (KJV, bunches).

HUMTAH Place-name meaning "lizards." Town in hill country of Judah in tribal territory of Judah (Josh. 15:54). Its exact location is not known.

HUNCHBACK One with a humped (curved or crooked) back. According to the Holiness Code, a hunchback was excluded from priestly service though allowed to eat the priests' holy food (Lev. 21:20). REB translates the unique Hebrew term, "misshapen brows."

HUNDRED, TOWER OF (KJV "Tower of Meah") Tower located on the north wall of Jerusalem that was restored by Nehemiah (Neh. 3:1; 12:39). The name perhaps refers to the height of the tower (100 cubits), the number of its steps, or the number of troops in its garrison. It may have been part of the temple fortress (Neh. 2:8).

HUNDREDWEIGHT Unit of weight equal to 100 pounds (Rev. 16:21 REB, RSV).

HUNT, HUNTER To pursue game for food or pleasure. Hunting was an important supplementary food source, especially in the semi-nomadic stage of civilization. Genesis mentions several hunters by name, none of whom are Israelite ancestors (Nimrod, 10:9; Ishmael, 21:20; Esau, 25:27), perhaps suggesting that hunting was more characteristic of Israel's neighbors than of Israel. Hunting was, however, regulated by Mosaic law. The blood of captured game was to be poured out on the ground (Lev. 17:13). Deuteronomy 14:3-5 outlines what game was permitted as ritually clean food.

HUPHAM Original ancestor of clan of Benjamin in the wilderness (Num. 26:39).

HUPPAH Personal name meaning "shelter" or "roof" or "bridal chamber." Leader of thirteenth course of priests under David (1 Chron. 24:13).

HUPPIM Personal name of unknown meaning. Son of Benjamin and grandson of Jacob (Gen. 46:21).

HUR Personal name of uncertain meaning, perhaps "white one" or "Horite" or perhaps derived from the name of the Egyptian god "Horus." **1.** Israelite leader who accompanied Moses and Aaron to the top of the mountain in the fight against the Amalekites (Exod. 17:10-12). **2.** King of Midian whom Israel slew as they moved toward the promised land (Num. 31:8). **3.** District governor under Solomon over Mount Ephraim in charge of providing the royal table with provisions one month a year (1 Kings 4:8). His name may also be translated Ben-hur. **4.** Administrator over half the district of Jerusalem under Nehemiah or father of the administrator (Neh. 3:9).

HURAI Variant reading in 1 Chron. 11:32 for David's warrior Hiddai in the parallel passage (2 Sam. 23:30).

HURAM Personal name probably shortened from Ahuram meaning "exalted brother." **1.** Chronicler's spelling of Hiram, king of Tyre (2 Chron. 2). **2.** Descendant of Benjamin, often identified with Hupham of Num. 26:39.

HURAMABI Personal name perhaps meaning "my father is an exalted brother." NASB, NIV, NRSV name for Huram/Hiram, the skilled artisan that Hiram, king of Tyre, sent to Solomon to help build the temple (2 Chron. 2:13).

HURI Personal name of uncertain meaning, perhaps "white one," "linen maker," "Horite," or "my Horus" (Egyptian god). A member of tribe of Gad (1 Chron. 5:14).

HUSBANDMAN KJV term for one who tills the soil; a farmer.

HUSHAH Personal name and place-name meaning "hurry." Member of tribe of Judah (1 Chron. 4:4).

HUSHAI Personal name meaning "quick," "from Hushah," or "gift of brotherhood." The clan became a part of Israel as a clan of the tribe of Benjamin living in Archi southwest of Bethel (Josh. 16:2).

HUSHAM Personal name, perhaps meaning "large-nosed" or "with haste." One of the early kings of Edom (Gen. 36:34) from Teman.

HUSHIM Personal name meaning "hurried ones." **1.** Son of Dan and grandson of Jacob (Gen. 46:23). **2.** Member of tribe of Benjamin (1 Chron. 7:12). **3.** Wife of Shaharaim of tribe of Benjamin (1 Chron. 8:8) and mother of Abitub and Elpaal (1 Chron. 8:11).

HUT Modern translations' rendering for a lean-to or temporary shelter; shack (Isa. 1:8; 24:20). The image of Isa. 1:8 stresses the isolation of Jerusalem, the sole survivor of the cities of Judah (1:7-9). Isaiah 24:20 illustrates God's power in judgment in the picture of the earth's swaying like an unstable hut before the Lord.

HYACINTH Stone regarded as precious in ancient times. The hyacinth is sometimes identified with the sapphire (Rev. 9:17 NRSV, TEV) or turquoise (Exod. 28:19; Rev. 9:17; 21:20 REB; Exod. 28:19; Rev. 21:20 TEV). Others identify the hyacinth with zircon, a brown to grayish gem, or essonite, a yellow to brown garnet.

HYENA Any of a group of stocky built, carnivorous mammals of the genus *Hyaena*, located zoologically between the felines and canines. It is a striped scavenger looking much like a fox.

HYKSOS Racial name from the Greek form of an Egyptian word meaning "rulers of foreign lands" given to kings of the Fifteenth and Sixteenth Dynasties of Egypt.

HYMENAEUS or **HYMENEUS** (KJV) Personal name of the Greek god of marriage. Name of a fellow worker of Paul whose faith weakened and whose lifestyle changed, leading Paul to deliver him to Satan (1 Tim. 1:20). That probably means Paul led the church to dismiss Hymenaeus from the membership to purify the church, remove further temptation from the church, and to lead Hymenaeus to restored faith, repentance, and renewed church membership. Along with Philetus, Hymenaeus taught that the resurrection had already occurred (2 Tim. 2:17-18; cp. 1 Cor. 5).

HYMN A song of praise to God.

HYPOCRISY Pretense to being what one really is not, especially the pretense of being a better person than one really is.

HYRAX Small mammal making its home in the rock cliffs (Ps. 104:18; Prov. 30:26 NIV, HCSB).

HYSSOP Small (about 27 inches), bushy plant, probably *Origanum Maru L.*, the Syrian marjoram. Stalks of hyssop bear numerous small white flowers in bunches. Hyssop was thus well suited for use as a "brush" to dab the lintels of Israelite homes with the blood of the Passover lambs (Exod. 12:22).
    A branch of hyssop bore the sponge used to offer vinegar to Christ at His crucifixion (John 19:29; Matt. 27:48 and Mark 15:36 mention a reed).

IBEX Species of wild goat with large curved horns, native to high mountain areas. The ibex has been identified as the wild goat of the Bible (1 Sam. 24:2; Ps. 104:18).

IBHAR Personal name meaning "he elected." Son born to David after he moved to Jerusalem (2 Sam. 5:15).

IBLEAM Place-name meaning "he swallowed the people." City in tribal territory of Issachar but given to tribe of Manasseh (Josh. 17:11).

IBNEIAH Personal name meaning "Yah builds." Benjaminite who returned from exile and settled in Jerusalem (1 Chron. 9:8).

IBNIJAH Personal name meaning "Yah builds," a variant spelling of Ibneiah. Ancestor in tribe of Benjamin of one of persons returning from exile and living in Jerusalem (1 Chron. 9:8).

A vase handle in the shape of a beautiful winged ibex.

IBRI Personal name meaning "Hebrew." A Levite under King David (1 Chron. 24:27).

IBSAM Personal name akin to balsam, meaning "sweet smelling" in modern translations. KJV spelling is Jibsam. Member of tribe of Issachar (1 Chron. 7:2).

IBZAN Personal name, perhaps meaning "quick, agile." Judge of Israel from Bethlehem who participated in royal practice of marrying children to foreigners (Judg. 12:8-10).

ICHABOD Personal name meaning "where is the glory?" The son of Phinehas, Eli's son (1 Sam. 4:21). His birth seems to have been precipitated by the news of the death of his father and the capture of the ark of the covenant in battle against the Philistines. The mother of Ichabod died immediately after the child's birth.

ICONIUM City of Asia Minor visited by Barnabas and Paul during the first missionary journey (Acts 13:51). Paul endured sufferings and persecution at Iconium (2 Tim. 3:11).

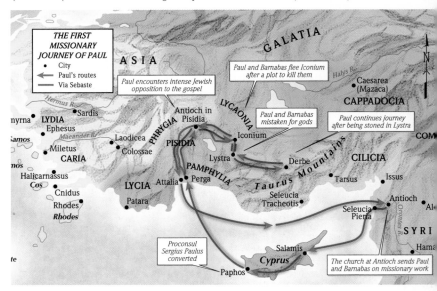

IDALAH Place-name of uncertain meaning, perhaps "jackal" or "memorial." Town in tribal territory of Zebulun (Josh. 19:15).

IDBASH Personal name meaning "sweet as honey." Son of Etam in the tribe of Judah (1 Chron. 4:3).

IDDO English spelling of four different Hebrew personal names. **1.** Name of uncertain meaning. Person with authority in the exilic community during the Persian period to whom Ezra sent messengers to secure Levites to join him in the return to Jerusalem (Ezra 8:17-20). **2.** Personal name, perhaps meaning "his praise." Leader of the eastern half of the tribe of Manasseh under David (1 Chron. 27:21). **3.** Name, perhaps meaning "Yahweh adorns Himself." A prophet whose records the chronicler refers to for more information about Solomon and Jeroboam (2 Chron. 9:29), Rehoboam (2 Chron. 12:15), and Abijah (2 Chron. 13:22). **4.** Grandfather of Zechariah, the prophet (Zech. 1:1,7 with different Hebrew spellings). Ezra 5:1; 6:14 put Zechariah as Iddo's son, using "son" to mean descendant, as often in Hebrew. **5.** Father of Solomon's district supervisor who supplied the royal court provisions for one month a year in the area of Mahanaim (1 Kings 4:14). **6.** A Levite (1 Chron. 6:21).

IDLE Not engaged in earning a living; depending on the labor and generosity of others for support. Scripture distinguishes between those unwilling to work who should not eat (2 Thess. 3:10) and those unable to earn a living (e.g., "true" widows, 1 Tim. 5:9) for whom the community of faith is responsible.

IDOL Physical or material image or form representing a reality or being considered divine and thus an object of worship. In the Bible various terms are used to refer to idols or idolatry: "image," either graven (carved) or cast, "statue," "abomination." Both Testaments condemn idols, but with idols the OT expresses more concern than the NT, probably reflecting the fact that the threat of idolatry was more pronounced for the people of the OT (Exod. 20:4-5 NASB).

IDUMEA In Isa. 34:5 a nation destined for judgment. "Idumea" is the term used in the Greek version of the OT and in the writings of the Jewish historian Josephus for Edom. The region was southeast of the Dead Sea. The Herods came originally from Idumea. Crowds from Idumea followed Jesus early in His ministry (Mark 3:8).

IEZER Personal name meaning "where is help" or a short form of "my father is help." (Hb. *Aviezer*, Josh. 17:2). Son of Gilead in tribe of Manasseh and original clan ancestor of Iezerites (Num. 26:30). KJV, REB spelling is Jeezer.

IGAL Personal name meaning "he redeems." **1.** Spy representing tribe of Issachar whom Moses sent to investigate the land of Canaan (Num. 13:7). **2.** One of David's heroic warriors, apparently a foreigner from

Allat, the moon goddess of Syria and later northern Arabia.

Zobah (2 Sam. 23:36), though his name is spelled Joel, and he is the brother, not son, of Nathan in 1 Chron. 11:38. **3.** Descendant of David in the postexilic community (about 470 BC) and thus bearer of the messianic line and hope (1 Chron. 3:22).

IGDALIAH Personal name meaning "Yahweh is great." Ancestor of the prophets whose chamber in the temple Jeremiah used to test the Rechabites' loyalty to their oath not to drink wine (Jer. 35:4).

IIM Place-name meaning "ruins." **1.** Town on southern border of tribal territory of Judah (Josh. 15:29). **2.** Used in Num. 33:45 (KJV) as abbreviation for Iye-abarim.

IJON Place-name meaning "ruin." Place in northern Israel captured by King Ben-hadad of Damascus. This was a result of his agreement with King Asa of Judah (910–869 BC) to break the treaty between Damascus and Baasha, king of Israel (1 Kings 15:20).

IKKESH Personal name meaning "perverted, false." Father of one of David's 30 heroes from Tekoa (2 Sam. 23:26).

ILAI Personal name of uncertain meaning. One of David's military heroes (1 Chron. 11:29), apparently the same as Zalmon (2 Sam. 23:28).

ILLYRICUM Place-name of uncertain meaning. A district in the Roman Empire between the Danube River and the Adriatic Sea. The Romans divided it into Dalmatia and Pannonia. It includes modern Yugoslavia and Albania. Illyricum represented the northeastern limits of Paul's missionary work as he wrote the Romans (Rom. 15:19), though the Bible nowhere mentions his work there.

THE ROMAN EMPIRE IN THE EARLY SECOND CENTURY (ca. A.D. 117)
- • City
- ▲ Mountain peak
- Roman Empire under Flavian Dynasty
- Territory added by Trajan
- Territory added by Hadrian
- —— Territory under Roman control

IMAGE OF GOD Biblical designation for the unique nature, status, and worth of all human beings as created by God. See *Humanity.*

IMAGERY, CHAMBER OF KJV phrase (Ezek. 8:12) understood as "room of his carved images" (NASB) or "shrine of his own idol" (NIV). The picture of the representatives of Israel worshipping idols within the Jerusalem temple in Ezekiel's vision (8:3,12) symbolizes the people's unfaithfulness to God.

IMAGINATION KJV term for thought as the prelude to action, frequently in the sense of plotting or devising evil; can also refer to stubbornness from the Hebrew words meaning "formed" or "twisted."

IMLA or **IMLAH** Personal name meaning "he fills," appearing in different spelling in Kings and Chronicles. Father of the prophet Micaiah (1 Kings 22:8).

IMMANUEL Personal name meaning "God with us." Name of son to be born in Isaiah's prophecy to King Ahaz (Isa. 7:14) and fulfilled in birth of Jesus (Matt. 1:22-23).

IMMER Personal name probably meaning "lamb." **1.** Father of Pashhur, the priest and temple administrator (Jer. 20:1). **2.** Priest whose son Zadok helped Nehemiah repair Jerusalem's walls (Neh. 3:29). **3.** Leader of priestly division under David (1 Chron. 24:14).

IMMORALITY Any illicit sexual activity outside of marriage. Both in the OT and in the NT the word has a figurative meaning as well, referring to idolatry or unfaithfulness to God.

IMMORTALITY Quality or state of being exempt from death. In the true sense of the word, only God is immortal (1 Tim. 1:17; 6:16; 2 Tim. 1:10), for only God is living in the true sense of the word. Humans may be considered immortal only insofar as immortality is the gift of God.

IMMUTABILITY OF GOD The unchangeability of God. In biblical theology God is described as unchanging in His nature and in His character. This includes God's being (essence), purposes, and promises.

IMNA Personal name meaning "he defends." A member of the tribe of Asher (1 Chron. 7:35).

IMNAH Personal name meaning "he allots for" or "on the right hand, good fortune." **1.** Son of

Asher and original ancestor of the Imnites (Num. 26:44; KJV, Jimna). **2.** Levite in the time of King Hezekiah (2 Chron. 31:14).

IMPEDIMENT IN SPEECH Disturbance of the vocal organs resulting in the inability to produce intelligible sounds (Mark 7:32). In Jesus' healing of a man who "had a speech difficulty" (HCSB; NIV, "hardly talk"), the crowds recognized a fulfillment of Isa. 35:5-6.

IMPERISHABLE Not subject to decay; ever-enduring. Imperishable (KJV, incorruption) describes the spiritual resurrection body that, unlike the physical body, is not subject to the decay associated with death (1 Cor. 15:42-54).

IMPORTUNITY Troublesome urgency; excessive persistence. In Luke 11:8 importunity results in a favorable response to a midnight request for bread (KJV, RSV).

IMPOTENT Lacking power, strength, or vigor; helpless. Impotence in the KJV never refers to sexual inability. Modern translations replace "impotent" with other terms: "cripple" (Acts 4:9 NIV); "disabled" (John 5:3 NIV); "invalid" (John 5:3 NRSV); "sick" (John 5:3,7; Acts 4:9 NASB).

IMPRECATION, IMPRECATORY PSALMS Act of invoking a curse. In the Imprecatory Psalms the author calls for God to bring misfortune and disaster upon the enemies (Pss. 5; 11; 17; 35; 55; 59; 69; 109; 137; 140). Some of the theological principles underlying these psalms are (1) the principle that vengeance belongs to God (Deut. 32:35; Ps. 94:1), which excludes personal retaliation and necessitates appeal to God to punish the wicked (cp. Rom. 12:19); (2) the principle that God's righteousness demands judgment on the wicked (Pss. 5:6; 11:5-6); (3) the principle that God's covenant love for the people of God necessitates intervention on their part (Pss. 5:7; 59:10,16-17); and (4) the principle of prayer that believers trust God with all their thoughts and desires.

IMPUTE, IMPUTATION Setting to someone's account or reckoning something to another person. God reckoned righteousness to believing Abraham (Gen. 15:6). This means that God credited to Abraham that which he did not have in himself (Rom. 4:3-5). The imputation of righteousness lies at the heart of the biblical doctrine of salvation. This righteousness is seen in Christ who purchased redemption. God grants righteousness to those who have faith in Christ (Rom. 1:17; 3:21-26; 10:3; 2 Cor. 5:21; Phil. 3:9). This righteousness imputed or reckoned to believers is, strictly speaking, an alien righteousness. It is not the believer's own righteousness but God's righteousness imputed to the believer. So, as Luther said, believers are simultaneously righteous and sinful.

IMRAH Personal name meaning "he is obstinate." Member of tribe of Asher (1 Chron. 7:36).

IMRI Short form of personal name "Amariah" meaning "Yah has spoken." **1.** Ancestor of clan from tribe of Judah living in Jerusalem after the return from exile (1 Chron. 9:4). **2.** Father of Zaccur, who helped Nehemiah rebuild Jerusalem's wall (Neh. 3:2).

INCANTATIONS Chants used by magicians to control evil spirits and thus heal the sick or afflict enemies. Mosaic law prohibited the casting of spells (Deut. 18:10-11). The complaint that the wicked are like a snake, immune to the cunning enchanter, perhaps refers to the futility of incantations (Ps. 58:3-5). The Babylonians hoped to gain success and terrorize their enemies by means of incantations (Isa. 47:12). Isaiah warned their incantations would be of no avail (47:9). The tongue muttering wickedness perhaps refers to incantations (Isa. 59:3). The books of magic of Acts 19:19 were likely collections of incantations.

INCARNATION God's becoming human; the union of divinity and humanity in Jesus of Nazareth. Incarnation (Lat. *incarnatio*, being or taking flesh), while a biblical idea, is not a biblical term. Its Christian use derives from the Latin version of John 1:14 and appears repeatedly in Latin Christian authors from about AD 300 onward.

As a biblical teaching, incarnation refers to the affirmation that God, in one of the modes of His existence as Trinity and without in any way ceasing to be the one God, has revealed Himself to humanity for its salvation by becoming human. Jesus, the Man from Nazareth, is the incarnate Word or Son of God, the focus of the God-human encounter. As the God-Man, He mediates God to humans; as the Man-God, He represents humans to God. By faith-union with Him, men and women, as adopted children of God, participate in His filial relation to God as Father.

Formulation of the Doctrine The problem of the incarnation begins with John's assertion, "the Word became flesh" (1:14). Clear expression of the relation of the Word to the flesh, of divinity to humanity within the person of Jesus, became a matter of major concern during the first five centuries of the Christian era. The unsystematized affirmations of the NT were refined through controversy, a process that culminated in the ecumenical councils of Nicaea (AD 325), Constantinople (AD 381),

Ephesus (AD 431), and Chalcedon (AD 451).

The mystery of the incarnation continues, and the statements of the first four councils of the Christian church preserve that mystery. Jesus, God incarnate, was one Person in two natures—fully divine and fully human. See *Christ.*

INCENSE Mixture of aromatic spices prepared to be burned in connection with the offering of sacrifices (Exod. 25:6). The incense used in worship was to be prepared according to exacting specifications and was to be offered only by the high priest. According to Luke 1:8-20, Zacharias was burning incense in the temple when he was visited by the angel Gabriel.

INCEST Sexual intercourse between persons too closely related for normal marriage. The twofold theological rationale for the prohibition of incestuous unions is the divine claim "I am the LORD your God" (Lev. 18:2,4,6) and the note that such behavior characterized the Egyptians and Canaanites whom God judged (Lev. 18:3,24-25).

Penalties for various forms of incest included childlessness (Lev. 20:20-21), exclusion from the covenant people (Lev. 18:29; 20:17-18; cp. 1 Cor. 5:2,5), and death (Lev. 20:11-12,14). In patriarchal times marriage to a half-sister (Gen. 20:12) and marriage to rival sisters (Gen. 29:21-30) were permissible, though such marriages proved troublesome to both Abraham and Jacob. Scriptural accounts of incest include Gen. 19:31-35; 35:22; and 2 Sam. 13.

INCH A unit of measure equal to a twelfth of a foot. Eighteen inches (Gen. 6:16 NIV, TEV) is the equivalent of a cubit.

INCONTINENCY, INCONTINENT KJV term for the lack of self-control (1 Cor. 7:5). Incontinent (2 Tim. 3:3) means lacking self-control (NASB), profligate (NRSV), or even violent (TEV).

INDIA Eastern boundary of the Persian Empire of Ahasuerus (Xerxes) (Esther 1:1; 8:9). Biblical references to India refer to the Punjab, the area of Pakistan and northwest India drained by the Indus River and its tributaries. India was possibly a port of call for Solomon's fleet (1 Kings 10:22). Trade between India and the biblical lands began before 2000 BC.

INFANT BAPTISM Rite of initiation performed on infants born into Christian families, also called "paedobaptism." While there is no explicit record of infant baptism in the NT, it was an established practice in the church by the third century.

Adherents of believer's baptism argue against paedobaptism on the basis that: (1) the clear pattern in the NT is that baptism is preceded by repentance and faith (e.g., Acts 2:38; 8:12; 18:8); (2) it is not clear that household baptisms included infants; and (3) the NT parallel to circumcision is not baptism but circumcision of the heart (Rom. 2:29; Col. 2:11), which points to an inward spiritual reality based upon a confession of faith that is impossible for infants.

INFLAMMATION Response to cellular injury characterized by redness, infiltration of white blood cells, heat, and frequently pain. Inflammation was one of the curses upon those disobedient to the covenant (Deut. 28:22; cp. Lev. 13:28).

INGATHERING, FEAST OF Alternate name for the Feast of Tabernacles (Booths) (Exod. 23:16; 34:22). See *Festivals.*

INHERITANCE Legal transmission of property after death. The Hebrew Bible has no exclusive term for "inheritance." The words often translated "inherit" mean more generally "take possession." Only in context can they be taken to mean "inheritance." The Greek word in the NT does refer to the disposition of property after death, but its use in the NT often reflects the OT background more than normal Greek usage.

INK Writing fluid. Ink for writing on papyrus (a plant product) was made of soot or lampblack mixed with gum arabic (Jer. 36:18; 2 Cor. 3:3; 2 John 12; 3 John 13). Red ink was made by replacing lampblack with red iron oxide. Because such ink did not stick well to parchment (a leather product), another ink was made from nutgalls mixed with iron sulfate.

INKHORN KJV term for a case in which ingredients for making ink were kept (Ezek. 9:2-3,11). A scribe customarily carried his inkhorn in his belt.

INLET Bay or recess in the shore of a sea or lake. When Deborah and Barak went to battle against Sisera, the tribe of Asher stayed at home "by his inlets" ("landings," NRSV, Judg. 5:17).

INN Different kinds of shelters or dwellings. In the OT the Hebrew word translated "inn" or "lodging place" might refer to a camping place for an individual (Jer. 9:2), a family on a journey (Exod.

4:24), an entire caravan (Gen. 42:27; 43:21), or an army (Josh. 4:3,8). In these passages (with the possible exception of the reference in Jeremiah) the presence of a building is not implied. Often the reference is only to a convenient piece of ground near a spring. It is doubtful that inns in the sense of public inns with a building existed in OT times.

By the time of Christ, the situation is quite different. Public inns existed in Greek times and throughout the Roman period. The Greek word for "inn" in the NT implies some type of stopping place for travelers. At times it refers to a public inn. Such an inn of the first century consisted primarily of a walled-in area with a well. A larger inn might have small rooms surrounding the court. People and animals stayed together.

INNKEEPER One who serves as the host or hostess at an inn. The innkeeper of Luke 10:35 was responsible for providing food and medical care. A Targum (early Aramaic Free translation) on Josh. 2:1 identifies Rahab as an innkeeper.

INSCRIPTION Words or letters carved, engraved, or printed on a surface (Mark 15:26; Luke 23:38; superscription, KJV). Pilate likely intended the inscription above the cross in a derogatory sense: "See the defeated King of the Jews." According to John 19:21, the Jewish leadership found the inscription offensive. The Gospel writers saw in Pilate's mockery the truth about Jesus who in His suffering and death fulfilled His messianic role.

INSECTS Air-breathing arthropods that make up the class *Hexapoda.* Representatives are found on land and in water. They have three distinct body

Hieroglyphic inscriptions on a temple wall at Karnak in Egypt.

parts (head, thorax, and abdomen) as well as three pairs of legs, one pair of antennae, and usually one or two pairs of wings. Insects are found often in the story of God's dealings with His people. These occurrences help the reader to understand the life of an ancient people. Insects are a part of the Bible because they were a part of life. Yet, the references to these small creatures do more than give information. From them the reader can learn much about God.

God's sovereignty is reflected in His use of hornets to accomplish His divine purpose of driving Israel's enemies out of Canaan. He also could chasten the chosen people with a locust if they should disobey. The absence of advanced methods of insect control reminds us of Israel's utter dependence upon God. The Lord would inspire His servants to use the lowly ant and locust as examples for mankind to follow. The wisdom writers would use even the disgusting fly larva to remind humanity of its mortality.

INSPECTION GATE Jerusalem city gate (Neh. 3:31 NASB, NIV). The KJV refers to the gate as the Miphkad Gate.

INSPIRATION OF SCRIPTURE "All Scripture is inspired by God" (2 Tim. 3:16 HCSB). Paul's Greek suggests that Scripture is a divine "spiration" (that which God has breathed out, the product of His creative breath). Paul's point, then, is not that Scripture is inspiring to read (it is that), nor that the authors were inspired (they were), but that Scripture's origin means it is the very Word of God. **Theories of Inspiration** Historically, biblical inspiration has been reckoned in four ways. (1) The Bible is only inspired like other good books with human authors. This is neither what Scripture says nor what the church has believed. (2) The Bible is only partially inspired by God. Proponents hold that only the theological (not the scientific or historical) portions of Scripture are inspired, or that Scripture is just a record of God's saving historical acts, or that the Bible contains the word of God rather than being that word. But inspiration ensures that Scripture itself is the revealed word of God, not only testifying of God's redemptive work but also interpreting it. (3) The Bible is divinely inspired without use of human authors. Mechanical dictation theory renders Scripture analogous to myths regarding the origins of the Koran or Book of Mormon, and runs contrary to what the Bible says of its origins. (4) The Bible is divinely inspired because God concurrently worked with human authors to produce the very written message He desired. This classical view teaches the Holy Spirit superintended more than 40 authors from widely divergent backgrounds (shepherds, kings, prophets, fishermen, etc.), spanning a period of approximately a millennium and a half, to produce with supernatural congruity not just the thoughts but the very words of God to mankind.

INSTRUCTION Teaching or exhortation on aspects of Christian life and thought directed to persons who have already made a faith commitment. Instruction (*didache*) is frequently distinguished from missionary preaching (*kerugma*). Matthew's Gospel says of Jesus, "He was teaching them like one who had authority" (Matt. 7:29 HCSB). The Sermon on the Mount (Matt. 5–7) in particular is the rock-solid foundational teaching for Christian life (7:24-27). Jesus Himself admonished His disciples to make disciples, baptizing them in the name of the Father, the Son, and the Holy Spirit, "teaching them to observe everything I have commanded you" (28:20 HCSB).

INSTRUMENT KJV term for a tool, utensil (1 Chron. 28:14), weapon (Gen. 49:5; 1 Chron. 12:33,37), or musical instrument (1 Chron. 15:16; 16:42; 23:5).

INSULT To treat with insolence, indignity, or contempt. The term does not appear in the KJV but becomes increasingly frequent in more recent translations, such as the NIV, where it replaces such terms as *abuse, mock, revile, reproach,* or *ridicule.*

INTEGRITY Faithful support of a standard of values. Terms that occur in parallel with integrity (Hb. *tom, tomim*) suggest its shades of meaning: righteousness (Ps. 7:8); uprightness (Ps. 25:21); without wavering (Ps. 26:1 NRSV, NASB, NIV); blameless (Ps. 101:2 NRSV, Hebrew uses *tom* twice in verse, otherwise translated "integrity"). In the NT, integrity occurs only at Titus 2:7 (NRSV, NIV, REB) in reference to teaching. The idea of singleness of heart or mind is frequent (Matt. 5:8; 6:22; James 1:7-8; 4:8).

INTERCESSION Act of intervening or mediating between differing parties, particularly the act of praying to God on behalf of another person. In the OT the Hebrew verb *paga'* is used of such pleading or interceding (Gen. 23:8; Isa. 53:12; 59:16; Jer. 7:16; 15:11; 27:18; 36:25). More general terms such as *palal,* "pray," or *chalah,* "appease," are also sometimes translated "intercede" (1 Sam. 7:5; 1 Kings 13:6). In the NT the Greek term is *entungkano* and its derivatives (Rom. 8:26-27,34; 1 Tim. 2:1; Heb. 7:25).

INTEREST Sum of money a borrower pays for use of loaned capital. Mosaic law prohibited the charging of interest to fellow Israelites (Exod. 22:25; Lev. 25:36-37; Deut. 23:19). Interest could be charged to foreigners (Deut. 23:20). The motive in loaning without interest to fellow Israelites was to prevent the formation of a permanent underclass in Israel.

INTERTESTAMENTAL HISTORY AND LITERATURE Events and writings originating after the final prophet mentioned in the OT (Malachi, about 450 BC) and before the birth of Christ (about 4 BC). The Intertestamental Period can be divided into three sections: The Greek Period, 323 BC to 167 BC; the Period of Independence, 167–63 BC; and the Roman Period, 63 BC through the time of the NT.

Literature The Jews produced many writings during the Intertestamental Period. These writings can be divided into three groups. The Apocrypha are writings that were included, for the most part, in the Greek translation of the OT, the Septuagint. They were translated into Latin and became a part of the Latin Vulgate, the authoritative Latin Bible. A second group of writings is the Pseudepigrapha. It is a larger collection than the Apocrypha, but there is no final agreement as to which writings should be included in it. Fifty-two writings are included in the two volumes, *The Old Testament Pseudepigrapha,* edited by James H. Charlesworth. The final group of writings from this period is the Qumran scrolls, popularly known as the Dead Sea Scrolls. The first knowledge of these came with the discovery of manuscripts in a cave above the Dead Sea in 1947. During subsequent years, fragments of manuscripts have been found in at least 11 caves in the area. These writings include OT manuscripts, writings of the Qumran sect, and writings copied and used by the sect that came from other sources. These writings show us something of the life and beliefs of one group of Jews in the last two centuries before Jesus.

IPHDEIAH or **IPHEDEIAH** Personal name meaning "Yah redeems." Member of tribe of Benjamin who lived in Jerusalem (1 Chron. 8:25).

IPHTAH Place-name meaning "he opened." Town in tribal territory of Judah in the Shephelah (Josh. 15:43).

IPHTAHEL Place-name meaning "God opens." Valley separating tribal territories of Zebulun and Asher (Josh. 19:14,27).

IR Personal name meaning "city" or "donkey's calf." Member of tribe of Benjamin (1 Chron. 7:12).

IRA Personal name meaning "city" or "donkey's colt." **1.** Priest under David (2 Sam. 20:26). **2.** Two of David's military heroes were named Ira (2 Sam. 23:26,38). Ira from Tekoa was also an officer in charge of the sixth month's "national guard" army (1 Chron. 27:9).

IRAD Personal name of uncertain meaning. Son of Enoch (Gen. 4:18).

IRAM Personal name of uncertain meaning. Tribal leader in Edom (Gen. 36:43).

IRI Personal name meaning "my city" or "my donkey's colt." Leader in tribe of Benjamin (1 Chron. 7:7).

IRIJAH Personal name meaning "Yah sees." Army captain who accused Jeremiah of treason and turned him over to the authorities for punishment (Jer. 37:13) about 586 BC.

IRNAHASH Place-name meaning "city of the snake" or "city of bronze." First Chronicles 4:12 lists it as a personal name in the descendants of Judah, using the Table of Nations (Gen. 10) and other passages of listing cities by original ancestors in the form of a genealogy.

IRON Metal that was a basic material for weapons and tools in the biblical period. The Iron Age began in Israel about 1200 BC, though introduction of this metal into daily life occurred slowly. The Bible mentions iron in conjunction with Moses and with the Canaanite conquest, but at this time iron was rare and used mainly for jewelry. The availability of iron was a sign of the richness of the promised land (Deut. 8:9), and articles of iron were indications of wealth (Deut. 3:11; Josh. 6:19).

IRON Place-name meaning "fearful." Town in tribal territory of Naphtali (Josh. 19:38), sometimes spelled Yiron (RSV, TEV, NASB).

IRONSMITH One who works with iron, either one who smelts ore or one who works cast pieces. Barzillai (2 Sam. 17:27-29; 19:31-39), whose name means "man of iron," perhaps served as David's ironsmith.

IRPEEL Place-name meaning "God heals." Town in tribal territory of Benjamin (Josh. 18:27). Location is not known.

IRRIGATION Transportation of water by man-made means such as canals, dams, aqueducts, and cisterns. The dry climate of the ancient Near East made the transportation of water, often across long distances, a necessity. Large canal systems crossed the lands of Egypt and Mesopotamia, providing the vast amounts of water necessary to support crops during the dry months of March to October. In Egypt, the second highest official, the vizier, oversaw the maintenance of canals and the alloca-

At the second cataract of the Nile River a scene of tion of water to the provinces.
primitive irrigation with the use of manpower.

IRSHEMESH Place-name meaning "city of the sun." Town in tribal territory of Dan (Josh. 19:41) on the border of the tribe of Judah (Josh. 15:10, called Beth-shemesh or house of the sun).

IRU Personal name meaning "donkey's colt" or "they protect." Son of Caleb (1 Chron. 4:15).

ISAAC Personal name meaning "laughter." Only son of Abraham by Sarah and a patriarch of the nation of Israel.
Old Testament Isaac was the child of a promise from God, born when Abraham was 100 years old and Sarah was 90 (Gen. 17:17; 21:5). After waiting years for the fulfillment of God's promise of a son, God tested Abraham's faith once again by commanding him to sacrifice Isaac (Gen. 22:1-19).

Isaac married Rebekah (Gen. 24), who bore him twin sons, Esau and Jacob (Gen. 25:21-28). Though less significant than Abraham and Jacob, Isaac was revered as one of the Israelite patriarchs (Exod. 3:6; 1 Kings 18:36; Jer. 33:26).

New Testament In the NT Isaac appears in the genealogies of Jesus (Matt. 1:2; Luke 3:34), as one of the three great patriarchs (Matt. 8:11; Luke 13:28; Acts 3:13), and as an example of faith (Heb. 11:20). Isaac's sacrifice by Abraham (Heb. 11:17-18; James 2:21), in which he was obedient to the point of death, serves as a type looking forward to Christ and as an example for Christians. Paul reminded believers that "you, brothers, like Isaac, are children of promise" (Gal. 4:28 HCSB).

ISAIAH Personal name meaning "Yahweh saves." Isaiah ministered primarily to the southern kingdom of Judah, although he was interested in the affairs of the northern kingdom of Israel during its time of demise and ultimate fall in 722/21 BC. According to Isa. 1:1, the prophet ministered under the Judahite kings of Uzziah, Jotham, Ahaz, and Hezekiah. Neither the beginning nor closing dates of Isaiah's prophesying can be discerned with certainty. Isaiah 6 dates the temple vision of Isaiah to the year of Uzziah's death in 740 BC. The close of Isaiah's ministry cannot be dated with certainty. The last datable prophecy records the Sennacherib crisis of 701 BC (chaps. 36–37), although the prophet may have continued to minister beyond this point. The Assumption of Isaiah, an apocryphal book, preserves the tradition that the prophet was sawn in half at the command of Manasseh, who began to reign around 689 BC.

Isaiah was the son of Amoz (1:1). Jewish tradition mentions Amoz as the brother of King Amaziah of Judah. If this assumption is correct, Isaiah and Uzziah were cousins, thus making Isaiah a member of the nobility. This family connection would explain the impact of Uzziah's death (chap. 6) on the prophet as well as the apparent ready access Isaiah had to the kings to whom he ministered.

Isaiah was married to "the prophetess" (8:3) and had at least two sons, Shear-jashub, "A remnant will return" (7:3) and Maher-shalal-hash-baz, "Speed the spoil; hasten the prey" (8:3). The sons' names were symbolic and served as warnings to Isaiah's generation of God's coming judgment against Judah's rebellion.

ISAIAH, BOOK OF The book of Isaiah stands at the head of the classical prophetic books both in the order of the English canon and the Hebrew canon. The English division of Scripture into the "Major Prophets" and the "Minor Prophets" places Isaiah first among the Major Prophets. In the Hebrew canon Isaiah appears first among the "Latter Prophets," the section including also the books of Jeremiah, Ezekiel, and "The Twelve" (that is, the "Minor Prophets").

Division of the Book Of particular scholarly interest is the question of the division of the book and the related issues of authorship. In the late 18th century, different theories regarding the authorship of Isaiah began to emerge. The issue of authorship is directly related to the division of the book into sections. Different sections of Isaiah do contain different emphases, issues, vocabulary, style, and even historical perspectives. However, whether these differences demand different authors for the book is debated.

Isaiah 1–39 The issues and events found in Isa. 1–39 clearly relate to the times of Isaiah as an eighth-century prophet. In fact, in some of the oracles, Isaiah relates the story in first person (chaps. 6 and 8). Other oracles, although told in third person, refer to incidents in Isaiah's lifetime (chaps. 20; 36–39). The historical background of Isa. 1–39 involves Assyrian aggression and attempts on the part of Assyria to expand control into the areas of Israel and Judah. Isaiah 7 and 8 clearly have Assyrian interference in the region as their historical basis. Assyria is mentioned specifically in chapter 10, as well as chapters 20 and 36–37. Assyria is the major international power in the region in chapters 1–39.

Another indication that Isa. 1–39 comes from the time of the Prophet Isaiah is the frequent occurrence of the prophet's name (occurs 16 times in 1–39). Isaiah interacts with various people on several occasions in these chapters. The clear intent of the text is to show Isaiah acting and prophesying during the first 39 chapters.

A major emphasis in this section of the book is the prediction of exile because of the nation's rebellion against God. The clearest statement of this is Isa. 39:5-7. In the early chapters of Isaiah, judgment has not yet come upon the people, but it is predicted.

Isaiah 40–66 The situation changes in Isa. 40–66. The prophet's name does not appear at all nor is any indication given that the prophet is acting or speaking. Of greater importance is the change in the major world power. Assyria is no longer the emphasis; Babylon is now the power. Babylon and Babylon's gods receive attention (Isa. 46–48). The mention of Cyrus (45:1), the Persian king who conquered Babylon, presumes a Babylonian background.

The judgment upon God's people for their sin that was prophesied in Isa. 1–39 is depicted as having already happened in Isa. 40–66. Jerusalem had received God's judgment (40:2) and was in ruins (44:26,28). God had given Judah into Babylon's hand (47:5-6). Jerusalem had drunk the cup of God's wrath (51:17). The temple had been destroyed (63:18; 64:10-11). The historical perspective of chapters 40–66 seems clearly different from the perspective found in 1–39. The explanation for this, some argue, is that Isaiah prophesied extensively about these future events; others, that someone(s) later appended what befell Judah as the consummation of what the prophet had earlier predicted. Clearly, the latter chapters need to be interpreted in the light of the events of the sixth-century exile to Babylon and return while the earlier chapters need to be interpreted based on events in the eighth century.

Although many scholars would divide the book of Isaiah among two or more authors, other scholars hold to single authorship of the book. The designation as "single author" may be misleading. Few would argue that Isaiah personally penned every word. Rather, this view holds that the messages themselves derive from the Prophet Isaiah, leaving open the possibility that Isaiah's disciples later organized or put the prophet's oracles in writing.

The NT includes quotations and allusions from Isaiah on several occasions. In each instance, no indication is given that the book should be divided. For example, John 12:38-40 alludes to both Isa. 53:1 and Isa. 6:10, indicating both were spoken by Isaiah. Likewise, the Dead Sea Scrolls shed light on the unity of the book. Among the discoveries at Qumran was a complete copy of Isaiah. The particular placement of Isa. 40 is interesting. Chapter 39 ends on the next to the last line on the page. Chapter 40 begins on the last line. If a break ever existed between chapters 39 and 40, the copyists at Qumran did not indicate it.

Messiah is a key theme in Isaiah. The messiah of Isaiah is an enigmatic figure. Sometimes this image is a branch (11:1), other times a kingly figure (9:6-7), and other times a suffering servant (50:6; 53:3-6). Isaiah, however, never made a distinct connection between the messianic passages dealing with kingship and those having the suffering servant motif. The messiah and the suffering servant themes seem contradictory, at least initially. The messiah would rule while the servant suffered and died for the nation. From the NT perspective, one can easily see how Jesus fulfilled both images in His ministry. The church, knowing how Jesus suffered, yet believing He would also return to rule, combined the concepts into the ministry of the ultimate Messiah, the Christ.

ISCAH Personal name, perhaps meaning "they look." Daughter of Haran and sister of Milcah (Nahor's wife) and Lot (Gen. 11:29).

ISCARIOT Personal name transliterated from Hebrew into Greek and meaning "man of Kerioth," or perhaps a name derived from Latin and meaning "assassin" or "bandit." Surname of both the disciple Judas who betrayed Jesus (Mark 3:19) and of his father Simon (John 6:71).

ISH-BOSHETH Personal name meaning "man of shame." Son of Saul and his successor as king of Israel (2 Sam. 2:8). After Saul's death, Abner the commander of Saul's army proclaimed Ish-bosheth king. He reigned for two years. His own captains finally murdered him (2 Sam. 4:1-7).

ISHBAH Personal name meaning "he soothes." Member of tribe of Judah known as father of town of Eshtemoa (1 Chron. 4:17).

ISHBAK Personal name meaning "come before, excel." Son of Abraham and Keturah (Gen. 25:2).

ISHBIBENOB Personal name meaning "inhabitant of Nob." Philistine who tried to kill David in battle (2 Sam. 21:16-17).

ISHHOD Personal name meaning "man of vigor and vitality." Member of tribe of Manasseh, east of the Jordan (1 Chron. 7:18).

ISHI Personal name meaning "my deliverer or salvation." **1.** Descendant of Jerahmeel in tribe of Judah (1 Chron. 2:31). **2.** Member of tribe of Judah (1 Chron. 4:20). **3.** Father of military leaders of tribe of Simeon who successfully fought the Amalekites (1 Chron. 4:42). **4.** Clan leader in tribe of Manasseh, east of the Jordan (1 Chron. 5:24). **5.** Transliteration of Hosea's wordplay between "my man" or "my husband" (Hb. *ishi*) and "my master" or "my lord" (Hb. *baali*) (Hos. 2:16 KJV, NASB). Hosea looked to the day when Israel would quit worshipping or even pronouncing the name of Baal and would be totally faithful to Yahweh as "her man" and "her master."

ISHMA Short form of Ishmael meaning "God hears." Member of tribe of Judah (1 Chron. 4:3).

ISHMAEL Personal name meaning "God hears." Son of Abraham by the Egyptian concubine Hagar (Gen. 16:11). He became the progenitor of the Ishmaelite peoples. The description in Gen. 16:12 points to an unruly and contentious disposition. Genesis 21:20 explains that God was with Ishmael and that he became an archer.

ISHMAELITE Tribal name for descendants of Ishmael. According to Gen. 25:12-16, Ishmael was the father of 12 sons. The Ishmaelites were regarded as an ethnic group, generally referring to the nomadic tribes of northern Arabia.

ISHMAIAH Long and short form of personal name meaning "Yah(weh) hears." **1.** Military hero from Gibeon in charge of David's select "30" warriors (1 Chron. 12:4). **2.** Head of tribe of Zebulun under David (1 Chron. 27:19).

ISHMERAI Short form of personal name meaning "Yah protects." Member of tribe of Benjamin (1 Chron. 8:18).

ISHPAH Personal name, perhaps meaning "baldhead." Member of tribe of Benjamin (1 Chron. 8:16).

ISHPAN Personal name of uncertain meaning. Member of tribe of Benjamin (1 Chron. 8:22).

ISHTAR Mesopotamian goddess of fertility and war. The goddess is perhaps the "Queen of heaven" of Jer. 7:18; 44:17-19,25; Ezek. 8:14.

ISHTOB Personal name meaning "man of good" or "man of Tob." KJV follows early translations in interpreting this as a proper name (2 Sam. 10:6,8).

ISHVAH Personal name meaning "he is equal" or "he satisfies." Son of Asher (Gen. 46:17).

ISHVI Personal name meaning "he is equal," "he satisfies," or "he rules." Son of Asher (Gen. 46:17) and original clan ancestor of Ishvites (Num. 26:44).

ISLAND Tract of land surrounded by water. The Hebrews were not a seafaring people and so easily equated the Mediterranean islands with the ends of the earth. Scripture mentions many islands by name.

ISMACHIAH Personal name meaning "Yahweh supports." Priest and administrator in the temple under Cononiah and Shimei when Hezekiah was king of Judah (2 Chron. 31:13).

ISRAEL 1. Name of northern kingdom after Jeroboam led the northern tribes to separate from the southern tribes and form a separate kingdom (1 Kings 12). **2.** Personal name meaning "God strives," "God rules," "God heals," or "he strives against God." Name that God gave Jacob after he wrestled with the divine messenger (Gen. 32:28).

ISRAEL, LAND OF The most common name in the OT for the land where the history of Israel takes place is Canaan. It occupies about 9,500 square miles, an area about the size of the state of Vermont, the upstate of South Carolina, or the country of Belgium. Canaan, or Palestine, reaches from the Mediterranean Sea on the west, to the Great Arabian Desert on the east, to the Lebanon and Anti-Lebanon Mountains on the north, and the Sinai Desert on the south. It is about 150 miles from

THE KINGDOMS OF ISRAEL AND JUDAH

- City
★ Capital city
○ City (uncertain location)
▲ Mountain peak
▢ Israel
▢ Judah
— International roads
— Local roads

north to south and 75 miles from east to west. The very location of Israel profoundly affected what was to happen to her over the centuries, for she sat uncomfortably in the middle of the "Fertile Crescent" (including Egypt, Palestine, Mesopo-tamia, Anatolia, and Armenia, or to use modern names: Egypt, Lebanon, Syria, Turkey, Jordan, Iraq, and Iran). This area was the very matrix of human-kind, a veritable cradle for civilization.

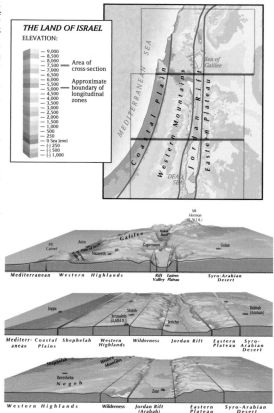

Due to its strategic location, it served as a land bridge between Asia and Africa, a meeting place, and a contested battlefield for many ancient powers, including Egypt, Assyria, Babylonia, Medo-Persia, Greece, and Rome. To this day it remains one of the most geopoliti-cally sensitive and important areas of the world.

From west to east the topograph-ical features are the coastal plain, Galilee and the central hill country, flowing in a southerly direction from the Lebanon range; the Jordan Rift Valley, continuous with the Bekaa Valley, continuing south to the Dead Sea in the Arabah; and the Transjordanian highlands as the southern continuation of the Anti-Lebanon Mountains in Phoenicia/Lebanon on into the Moab-Edom plateau. It is an arid and exotic land of great variety. Mountains in the north are in stark contrast to the Arabah and the lowest point on the earth, the Dead Sea, some 1,300 feet below sea level.

ISRAEL, SPIRITUAL The phrase "spiritual Israel" is often used as a description of the Church in contrast to national or ethnic Israel. It refers to all believers in all times regardless of ethnic identity. Some interpreters see Paul's language of "Israel according to the flesh" (1 Cor. 10:18) as necessarily implying its antithesis, "Israel according to the Spirit," and thus, "spiritual Israel." While Paul's phrase may be suggestive, it is not conclusive. The idea of a "spiritual Israel" must rest on the basis of evidence drawn from texts viewed together.

ISSACHAR Personal name meaning "man for hire" or "hireling." Ninth son of Jacob, the fifth borne by Leah (Gen. 30:18). He became the progenitor of the tribe of Issachar.

ISSARON Transliteration of Hebrew word meaning "a tenth." A dry measure equal to one tenth of an ephah (Exod. 29:40; Lev. 14:10,21; 23:13,17; 24:5; Num. 15:4) or about two quarts. KJV translates a tenth deal.

ISSHIAH Personal name meaning "let Yahweh forget." In Hebrew the name appears in a longer form in 1 Chron. 12:6. **1.** Leader in the tribe of Issachar (1 Chron. 7:3). **2.** Soldier from Saul's tribe of Benjamin who joined David at Ziklag while he hid from Saul (1 Chron. 12:6). **3.** Member of the Kohath branch of Levites (1 Chron. 23:20; 24:24-25). **4.** Descendant of Moses among the Levites (1 Chron. 24:21; cp. 23:13-17).

ISSHIJAH Personal name meaning "let Yahweh forget." Same Hebrew name as Isshiah. Israelite who had married a foreign wife, threatening Israel's total allegiance to Yahweh in the time of Ezra (Ezra 10:31).

ISSUE KJV term referring to offspring (Gen. 48:6; Isa. 22:24; Matt. 22:25; cp. 2 Kings 20:18; Isa. 39:7) or to a bodily discharge (Lev. 15:2-30; Matt. 9:20).

ITALIAN COHORT Name of the archery unit of the Roman army to which the Gentile centurion Cornelius belonged (Acts. 10:1).

ITALY Boot-shaped peninsula between Greece and Spain that extends from the Alps on the north to the Mediterranean Sea on the south. Italy is named in the NT in Acts 18:2; 27:1,6 and Hebrews 13:24.

ITHAI Personal name, perhaps meaning "with me." A member of David's elite "30" military heroes (2 Sam. 23:29 NIV; NASB, Ittai).

ITHAMAR Personal name of uncertain meaning, perhaps "island of palms," or "where is Tamar," or shortened form of "father of Tamar (palms)." Fourth son of Aaron the priest (Exod. 6:23; 38:21).

ITHIEL Personal name meaning "with me is God." **1.** Member of the tribe of Benjamin in the time of Nehemiah after the return from exile (Neh. 11:7). **2.** Person to whom Prov. 30 is addressed, following standard Hebrew text (KJV, NASB, NIV, HCSB).

ITHLAH Place-name, perhaps meaning "he hangs." Town in tribal territory of Dan (Josh. 19:42).

ITHMAH Personal name meaning "orphan." Moabite soldier in David's army (1 Chron. 11:46).

ITHNAN Place-name meaning "flowing constantly." Town on southern border of tribal territory of Judah (Josh. 15:23).

ITHRA Personal name meaning "remnant" or "abundance." He was the father of Amasa, and the general that Absalom appointed to replace David's general Joab when he revolted against his father (2 Sam. 17:25).

ITHRAN Personal name meaning "remnant" or "abundance." **1.** A Horite leader who lived in Edom (Gen. 36:26). **2.** Leader in the tribe of Asher (1 Chron. 7:37). He may be the same as the similarly spelled Jether (1 Chron. 7:38).

ITHREAM Personal name meaning "remnant of the people." David's son born in Hebron to Eglah, David's wife (2 Sam. 3:5).

ITHRITE Clan name meaning "of Jether." Descendants of Jether or Jethro (Exod. 4:18) or a clan whose home was Kiriath-jearim (1 Chron. 2:53). The latter may have been Hivites (cp. Josh. 9:7,17). Two of David's valiant "30" warriors were Ithrites (2 Sam. 23:38).

ITTAI Personal name meaning "with God." **1.** Gittite (from Gath) soldier who demonstrated loyalty to David by accompanying the latter in flight from Jerusalem after the outbreak of a rebellion led by David's son Absalom (2 Sam. 15:19-22). **2.** One of the "30" of David's army (2 Sam. 23:29) and son of Ribai of Gibeah from the tribe of Benjamin.

ITURAEA or **ITUREA** Place-name meaning "related to Jetur." Region over which Herod Philip was governor when John the Baptist began his public ministry (Luke 3:1). It was located northeast of Galilee between the Lebanon and Anti-Lebanon mountains, though its precise boundaries are almost impossible to determine.

IVORY English translation of the Hebrew word that means "tooth." Ivory was used for decoration on thrones, beds, houses, and the decks of ships (1 Kings 10:18; 22:39; 2 Chron. 9:17; Ps. 45:8; Ezek. 27:6,15; Amos 3:15; 6:4). Archaeologists in Palestine have unearthed numerous articles made of ivory: boxes, gaming boards, figurines, spoons, and combs.

IYE-ABARIM Place-name meaning "ruins of the crossings." Station in the wilderness wanderings (Num. 21:11) near Moab.

IYIM Modern translations spelling of Iim (Num. 33:45), a shortened form of Iye-abarim.

IZHAR Personal name meaning "olive oil" or "he sparkles." **1.** Son of Kohath and grandson of Levi, thus original ancestor of a priestly clan (Exod. 6:18). He was father of Korah (Num. 16:1; cp. 1 Chron. 23:18). **2.** Written Hebrew text of 1 Chron. 4:7 names Izhar as a member of the tribe of Judah.

IZHARITE Clan of Levites descended from Izhar.

IZLIAH Personal name meaning "long-lived" or "Yahweh delivers." Leader in tribe of Benjamin living in Jerusalem after the return from exile (1 Chron. 8:18).

IZRAHIAH Personal name meaning "Yahweh shines forth." Member of tribe of Issachar (1 Chron. 7:3).

IZRAHITE Clan name in 1 Chron. 27:8 for which the text tradition gives several variants: Harorite (1 Chron. 11:27 KJV); Harodite (2 Sam. 23:25 KJV).

IZRI Clan leader of fourth course of temple musicians (1 Chron. 25:11). He is probably the same as Zeri (25:3), the name change occurring in copying the text.

IZZIAH Personal name meaning "Yah sprinkled." Priest who repented of marrying a foreign woman and thus tempting Israel with foreign gods in the time of Ezra (Ezra 10:25).

The Jabbok River between Jerash and Amman. Near this river Jacob wrestled with the angel.

JAAKAN Personal name meaning "to be fast." Descendant of Esau and thus tribal ancestor of Edomites (1 Chron. 1:42).

JABAL Personal name meaning "stream." Son of Lamech by Adah (Gen. 4:20). A descendant of Cain, he was the first nomad, the progenitor of tent dwellers and herdsmen.

JABBOK Place-name meaning "flowing." River near which Jacob wrestled through the night with God (Gen. 32:22). A tributary of the Jordan River, some sections of the Jabbok served as the western boundary of Ammon.

JABESH or **JABESH-GILEAD** Place-name meaning "dry, rugged" or "dry place of Gilead." City whose residents, with the exception of 400 virgins, were put to death by an army of Israelites (Judg. 21:8-12). The 400 women who were spared became wives for the Benjaminites. King Saul's rescue of the people of Jabesh-gilead from Nahash the Ammonite marked the effective beginning of the Israelite monarchy (1 Sam. 11:1-11).

JABEZ Personal and place-name with a connotation of pain, hurt, and sorrow. **1.** Home of scribes whose location is not known (1 Chron. 2:55). **2.** Israelite who asked God for blessing and received it (1 Chron. 4:9-10). He illustrates the power of prayer.

JABIN Personal name meaning "he understands." **1.** Leader of northern coalition of kings who attacked Joshua at the water of Merom and met their death (Josh. 11:1-11). **2.** Many scholars believe that a dynasty of kings in Hazor carried the name Jabin.

JACHIN AND BOAZ Proper names meaning "he establishes" and "agile." In 1 Kings 7:21 the names of two bronze pillars that stood on either side of the entrance to Solomon's temple. They may have been 27 feet high and 6 feet in diameter with a 10-foot capital on top. See *Temple.*

JACINTH Semiprecious stone. Some English translations give "jacinth" as a gem in the high priest's breastplate (Exod. 28:19 NASB, NIV, NRSV), the color of one of the riders' breastplates (Rev. 9:17 KJV), and the eleventh foundation stone of the new Jerusalem (Rev. 21:20 HCSB, KJV, NASB, NIV, NRSV).

JACKAL A carnivorous mammal resembling the wolf but smaller. The same Hebrew word is translated both "jackal" and "fox" (Judg. 15:4, REB has "jackals"; NIV has "foxes"). Most biblical references associate jackals with desert ruins. For a city or nation to be made the haunt or lair of jackals

TRAVELS OF JACOB
- City
- ○ City (uncertain location)
- ← Jacob's journey
- ←- - Jacob's sons seek pasturage
- ← Esau's journey

is for it to be utterly destroyed (Isa. 13:22; Jer. 9:11).

JACOB Personal name built on the Hebrew noun for "heel" meaning "he grasps the heel" or "he cheats, supplants" (Gen. 25:26; 27:36). Original ancestor of the nation of Israel and father of the 12 ancestors of the 12 tribes of Israel (Gen. 25:1–Exod. 1:5). He was the son of Isaac and Rebekah, younger twin brother of Esau, and husband of Leah and Rachel (Gen. 25:21-26; 29:21-30). God changed his name to "Israel" (Gen. 32:28; 49:2).

Living up to his name, Jacob cheated his older brother Esau out of his birthright, or the inheritance rights of the older son. Rebekah had to arrange for Jacob to flee to her ancestral home in Paddan-aram to escape Esau's wrath (27:41–28:5). A lonely night in Bethel, interrupted by a vision from God, brought reality home to Jacob. Life had to include wrestling with God and assuming responsibility as the heir of God's promises to Abraham (28:10-22). Jacob made an oath, binding himself to God.

In Aram with his mother's family, the deceiver Jacob met deception. Laban tricked him into marrying Leah, the elder daughter, before he got his beloved Rachel, the younger. He labored fourteen years for his wives (29:1-30). Six more years of labor let Jacob return the deception and gain wealth at the expense of his father-in-law, who continued his deception, changing Jacob's wages 10 times (31:7,41). Amid the family infighting, both men prospered financially, and Jacob's family grew. Eventually he had twelve children from four different wives (29:31–30:24). Prosperous and confident, he made plans to return to his home in Canaan with his wives, children, and livestock.

As Jacob approached his homeland, a band of angels met him at Mahanaim (32:1-2). They probably symbolized God's protection and encouragement as he headed southward to meet his brother Esau for the first time in 20 years. Esau's seemingly hostile advance prompted a call for clear evidence of God's protection. Shrewdly, Jacob sent an enormous gift to his brother. After crossing the Jabbok River, Jacob met One who wrestled with him until daybreak (chap. 32). The two struggled without one gaining advantage, until the Opponent dislocated Jacob's hip. Jacob refused to release his Antagonist. Clinging to Him, he demanded a blessing. The Opponent emphasized His superiority by renaming Jacob. He became Israel, the one on whose behalf God strives. Jacob named the place Peniel (face of God), because he had seen God face to face and his life had been spared (32:30).

Jacob's fear of meeting Esau proved groundless. Esau was willing to forget the wrongs of the past. So Jacob set out for Shechem. From Shechem, he returned to Bethel. Once again he received the promises that God had originally given to Abraham. Losses and grief characterized this period of his life. The death of his mother's nurse (35:8; 24:59) was followed by the death of his beloved wife Rachel while giving birth to Benjamin at Ephrath (35:19; 48:7). About the same time Reuben forfeited the honor of being the eldest son by sexual misconduct (35:22). Finally, the death of Jacob's father, who had been robbed of companionship with both sons, brought Jacob and Esau together again at the family burial site in Hebron.

When severe famine gripped Canaan, Jacob and his sons set out for Egypt. At Beer-sheba Jacob received further assurance of God's favor (46:1-4). Jacob lived in the land of Goshen until his death. Jacob bestowed the blessing not only upon his favorite son Joseph, but also upon Joseph's two oldest sons, Ephraim and Manasseh. He was finally laid to rest at Hebron in the cave Abraham had purchased as a burial site (50:12-14).

God did not choose Jacob because of what he was but because of what he could become. His life is a long history of discipline, chastisement, and purification by affliction. Not one of his misdeeds went unpunished. He sowed deception and reaped the same, first from Laban and then from his own sons. But God was at work in his life, building a nation through him and his descendants.

JACOB'S WELL Place in Samaria where Jesus stopped to rest as He traveled from Judea to Galilee (John 4:6). There He met and conversed with a Samaritan woman on the subject of living water.

JAEL Personal name meaning "mountain goat." Wife of Heber the Kenite (Judg. 4:17), she assassinated the Canaanite leader Sisera. Her action is celebrated in the Song of Deborah (Judg. 5:24-27).

JAH Short form of divine name Yahweh in Ps. 68:4 (KJV) and in many proper names.

The traditional site of Jacob's Well in the city of Sychar.

JAHAZIEL Personal name meaning "Yah looks." **1.** Benjaminite military hero who supported David against Saul (1 Chron. 12:4). **2.** Priest whom David appointed to blow the trumpet before the ark (1 Chron. 16:6). **3.** Levite of the clan of Hebron (1 Chron. 23:19; 24:23). **4.** Levite and a son of Asaph who received the Spirit of the Lord and prophesied (2 Chron. 20:14-19). **5.** Clan leader who led 300 men among the exiles returning to Jerusalem with Ezra (Ezra 8:5).

JAIR Abbreviated place-name meaning "Jah shines forth." **1.** Son of Manasseh who took possession of a number of villages in Gilead (Num. 32:41). **2.** A Gileadite who judged Israel for 22 years (Judg. 10:3-5). **3.** Father of El-hanan (1 Chron. 20:5) whose name comes from a different Hebrew word possibly meaning "Jah protects." **4.** Benjamite who was the ancestor of Mordecai, Esther's guardian (Esther 2:5).

JAIRUS Greek form of Hebrew personal name "Jair" meaning "Jah will enlighten." Synagogue official who came to Jesus seeking healing for his daughter (Mark 5:22). Taking the girl by the hand, Jesus restored her to life, showing His power over death.

JAMES The name of three men of the NT. **1.** James, the son of Zebedee and brother of John (Matt. 4:21; 10:2; Mark 1:19; 3:17; Luke 5:10). As one of the 12 disciples of Jesus (Acts 1:13), he, with Peter and John, formed Jesus' innermost circle of associates. These three were present when Jesus raised Jairus's daughter (Mark 5:37; Luke 8:51), witnessed the transfiguration (Matt. 17:1; Mark 9:2), and were summoned by Christ for support during His agony in Gethsemane (Matt. 26:36-37; Mark 14:32-34). Perhaps because of James's and John's fiery fanaticism, evidenced as they sought to call down fire from heaven on the Samaritan village refusing to receive Jesus and the disciples (Luke 9:52-54), Jesus called the brothers "Boanerges" or "sons of thunder" (Mark 3:17). James's zeal was revealed in a more selfish manner as he and John (their mother, on their behalf, in Matt. 20:20-21) sought special positions of honor for the time of Christ's glory (Mark 10:35-40). James was the first of the 12 to be martyred (Acts 12:2). His execution (about AD 44), by order of King Herod Agrippa I of Judea, was part of a larger persecution in which Peter was arrested (Acts 12:1-3). **2.** James, the son of Alphaeus, one of the 12 disciples of Jesus (Matt. 10:3; Acts 1:13). He is not distinguished by name in any occasion reported in the Gospels or Acts. He may be "James the younger," whose mother, Mary, was among the women at Jesus' crucifixion and tomb (Matt. 27:56; Mark 15:40; 16:1; Luke 24:10). **3.** James, the half brother of Jesus. During the Lord's ministry, the brothers of Jesus (Matt. 13:55) were not believers (John 7:3-5; cp. Luke 8:19-21). Paul specifically mentioned a resurrection appearance by Jesus to James (1 Cor. 15:7). After the resurrection and ascension, the brothers are said to have been with the Twelve and the other believers in Jerusalem (Acts 1:14). In time, James assumed the leadership of the Jerusalem church. In a Jerusalem conference called regarding Paul's Gentile mission, James presided as spokesman for the Jerusalem church (Acts 15).

JAMES, LETTER FROM Letter from James belongs to the section of the NT usually described as the "General Epistles." The letter is one of exhortation for practical Christianity. The author stated principles of conduct and then frequently provided poignant illustrations. The author's concerns were clearly more practical and less abstract than those of any other NT writer.

JANNES AND JAMBRES Two men who opposed Moses and Aaron (2 Tim. 3:8). Though the names do not appear in the OT, rabbinic tradition identified Jannes and Jambres as being among those Egyptian magicians who sought to duplicate for Pharaoh the miracles performed by Moses (Exod. 7:11).

JAPHETH Personal name meaning "may he have space." One of Noah's three sons (Gen. 5:32). Genesis 10:2 identifies Japheth's sons as Gomer, Magog, Madai, Javan, Tubal, Meshech, and Tiras. These names point to Japheth as having been the progenitor of the Indo-European peoples who lived north and west of Israel. See *Noah; Table of Nations.*

JAPHIA Place-name and personal name meaning "place situated high above" or "may He bring shining light." **1.** Border town of tribal territory of Zebulun (Josh. 19:12). **2.** King of Lachish who joined southern coalition against Joshua and met death by cave of Makkedah (Josh. 10:1-27,31-32). **3.** Son born to David in Jerusalem by unnamed wife (2 Sam. 5:15).

JASHAR, BOOK OF An ancient written collection of poetry quoted by Bible authors (Josh. 10:12–13).

JASHOBEAM Personal name meaning "the uncle (or people) will return." Warrior of Saul's tribe of Benjamin who supported David at Ziklag as he fled from King Saul (1 Chron. 12:6).

JASON Personal name often used by Jews as a substitute for Hebrew Joshua or Joseph and also used by Gentiles. **1.** Paul's host in Thessalonica (Acts 17:5). He was brought up on charges before the city officials when the angry Jewish mob was unable to find Paul (Acts 17:6-7). The Jason mentioned in Rom. 16:21 may have been the same person. **2.** Jewish high priest during the final years of Seleucid control of Palestine.

JASPER Green chalcedony. Jasper commonly translates two Hebrew terms and one Greek term. The first term is used for the sixth stone in the headdress of the king of Tyre (Ezek. 28:13). The second term is used for a stone in the high priest's breastplate (Exod. 28:20; 39:13). The third term describes the face of the One seated on the throne (Rev. 4:3) and the glory of the new Jerusalem (Rev. 21:11,18-19).

JAVAN Personal name meaning "Greece." Son of Japheth (Gen. 10:2) and father of Elishah, Tarshish, Kittim, and Dodanim (Gen. 10:4), thus the original ancestor of Greek peoples. Elsewhere in the OT, the name Javan is used to denote Greece.

JAVELIN Light spear thrown as a weapon (1 Sam 18:10–11).

JAZER Place-name meaning "May He help." Amorite city-state that Israel conquered while marching across the land east of the Jordan River toward the promised land (Num. 21:32). The tribe of Gad rebuilt and settled Jazer (Num. 32:35; cp. Josh. 13:25). Joshua assigned it to the Levites (Josh. 21:39).

JEALOUSY Used in three senses in Scripture: (1) as intolerance of rivalry or unfaithfulness; (2) as a disposition suspicious of rivalry or unfaithfulness; and (3) as hostility toward a rival or one believed to enjoy an advantage, a sense of envy. God is jealous for His people Israel in the first sense. That is, He is intolerant of rival gods (Exod. 20:5; Deut. 4:24; 5:9). One expression of God's jealousy for Israel is God's protection of His people from enemies.

JEALOUSY, ORDEAL OF Test to determine guilt or innocence of a wife suspected of adultery but who had not been caught in the act (Num. 5:11-31). The ordeal consisted of two parts: "a grain offering of memorial, a reminder of iniquity" (5:15 NASB) and "the water of bitterness that brings a curse" (5:18). See *Bitter Water.*

JEBUS Place-name meaning "trodden under foot." Name of tribe originally occupying Jerusalem and then of the city of Jebus (Judg. 19:10; cp. Josh. 18:28; 1 Chron. 11:4). See *Jebusi or Jebusites; Jerusalem.*

JEBUSI (Josh. 18:16,28 KJV) or **JEBUSITES** Clan who originally controlled Jerusalem before David conquered the city. In the time of the judges, Jerusalem was attacked and burned by the men of Judah (Judg. 1:8), but the Jebusites were not expelled. In later years David captured the city and made it his capital. David purchased a stone threshing floor from a Jebusite named Araunah (2 Sam. 24:16-24), and this later became the site of Solomon's temple. The remnants of the Jebusites became bondservants during Solomon's reign (1 Kings 9:20-21).

JEDUTHUN Personal name meaning "praise." Prophetic musician and Levite in the service of King David (1 Chron. 25:1). Three psalms (39; 62; 77) include his name in their titles. The exact nature of Jeduthun's relationship to these psalms is uncertain.

JEHOAHAZ Personal name meaning "Yahweh grasps hold." Two kings of Judah and one king of Israel bore this name. **1.** In 2 Chron. 21:17 the son and successor of Jehoram as king of Judah (841 BC). He is more frequently referred to as Ahaziah. **2.** In 2 Kings 10:35 the son and successor of Jehu as king of Israel (814–798 BC). His reign is summarized in 2 Kings 13. **3.** In 2 Kings 23:30 the son and successor of Josiah as king of Judah (609 BC). He is also known as Shallum.

JEHOASH Personal name meaning "Yahweh gave." Variant spelling of Joash. See *Joash.*

JEHOIACHIN Personal name meaning "Yahweh establishes." Son and successor of Jehoiakim as king of Judah (2 Kings 24:6). He was 18 years old when he came to the throne late in 598 BC, and he reigned for three months in Jerusalem before being taken into captivity by Nebuchadnezzar of Babylon. Jehoiachin's original name seems to have been Jeconiah or Coniah. He retained the title "king of Judah" even in exile, but he never returned to Judah to exercise rule. Nevertheless, he was ultimately released from prison by Evil-merodach of Babylon and accorded some honor in the land of his captivity (2 Kings 25:27-30).

JEHOIADA Personal name meaning "Yahweh knows" or "Yahweh concerns Himself for." **1.** Priest who led the coup in which Queen Athaliah, who had usurped the throne of Judah, was slain and Joash (Jehoash), the legitimate heir to the monarchy, was enthroned (2 Kings 11:4). Since Joash was only seven years old, Jehoiada evidently acted as regent for a number of years. He influenced the young king to restore the temple. **2.** Father of Benaiah, David's military leader (2 Sam. 8:18). **3.** Leading priest in the time of Jeremiah (Jer. 29:25-26).

JEHOIAKIM Personal name meaning "Yahweh has caused to stand." Son of Josiah who succeeded Jehoahaz as king of Judah (609–597 BC). Jehoiakim was a throne name given to him by Pharaoh Neco of Egypt, who deposed his brother Jehoahaz. His original name had been Eliakim (2 Kings 23:34). After reigning for 11 years, Jehoiakim was succeeded by his son Jehoiachin.

JEHONADAB Personal name meaning "Yahweh incites" or "Yahweh offers Himself freely." Son of Rechab who supported Jehu in the latter's bloody purge of the house of Ahab (2 Kings 10:15). He was representative of a group of austere ultraconservatives known as the Rechabites. See *Rechabites.*

JEHORAM Personal name meaning "Yahweh is exalted." Alternate form of Joram. See *Joram.*

JEHOSHABEATH Variant form of Jehosheba. See *Jehosheba.*

JEHOSHAPHAT Personal name meaning "Yahweh judged." **1.** Son and successor of Asa as king of Judah (1 Kings 15:24). He occupied the throne for 25 years (873–848 BC). He was an able ruler and a faithful worshipper of Yahweh (1 Kings 22:42-43). Nevertheless, he made an alliance with Ahab, king of Israel, which proved to be disastrous. This alliance involved a marriage between Jehoshaphat's son Jehoram and Ahab's daughter Athaliah. Athaliah's influence in Judah finally proved to be horrific.

Valley of Jehoshaphat (Kidron Valley) in Jerusalem showing the Church of All Nations.

2. Father of Jehu (2 Kings 9:2,14). **3.** Official at David's court (2 Sam. 8:16), called the "recorder" or "secretary of state" (REB). **4.** Solomon's official in tribal territory of Issachar in charge of providing provisions for the royal court one month a year (1 Kings 4:17).

JEHOSHAPHAT, VALLEY OF Place-name meaning "valley where Yahweh judged." Place to which the Lord summons the nations for judgment (Joel 3:2).

JEHOSHEBA Personal name meaning "Yahweh is fullness or fortune." Sister of King Ahaziah who, after his death, took young Joash and protected him from Queen Athaliah (2 Kings 11:2).

JEHOSHUA (Num. 13:16 KJV) See *Joshua*.

JEHOVAH English transliteration of Hebrew text's current reading of divine name Yahweh.

JEHOVAH-JIREH Place-name meaning "Yahweh will provide." The name Abraham gave to the place where the Lord provided a sacrifice in place of Isaac (Gen. 22:14).

JEHOVAH-NISSI Transliteration of place-name meaning "Yahweh is my banner." Name Moses gave to the altar he built after defeating the Amalekites (Exod. 17:15).

JEHOVAH-SHALOM Place-name meaning "Yahweh is peace." Name Gideon gave to the altar he built at Ophrah (Judg. 6:24).

JEHOVAH-SHAMMA Transliteration of a Hebrew name (Ezek. 48:35, margin) meaning "The LORD is there." The Jerusalem of Ezekiel's vision was known by this name (cp. Isa. 60:19-20; Rev. 21:3).

JEHOVAH-TSIDKENU Hebrew name meaning "The LORD [is] our righteousness" (Jer. 23:6; 33:16, margin). The name is applied to a future Davidic king who would lead his people in righteousness and thus bring peace (23:6).

JEHU Personal name meaning "Yah is He." **1.** Son of Jehoshaphat and king of Israel (841–814 BC). He was a commander of the army when Elisha the prophet sent one of the sons of the prophets to Ramoth-gilead to anoint him as king (2 Kings 9:1-10). Jehu embarked on a violent and bloody course that finally led him to the throne. He was responsible for the deaths of Joram, king of Israel; Ahaziah, king of Judah; Jezebel, still powerful former queen of Israel, and some 70 surviving members of the household of Israel's late

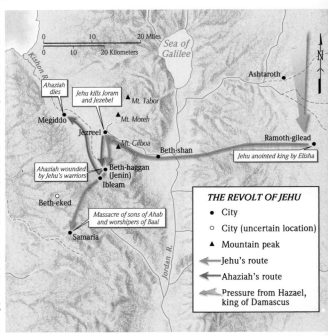

King Ahab. Jehu established a strong dynasty in Israel. He and his descendants held the throne for approximately a century. **2.** Prophet who proclaimed God's judgment on King Baasha of Israel (1 Kings 16:1-12). **3.** Member of David's army at Ziklag (1 Chron. 12:3). **4.** Leader of tribe of Simeon (1 Chron. 4:35).

JEPHTHAH Personal name meaning "he will open." One of Israel's judges about 1100 BC (Judg. 11:1–12:7). A Gileadite, he was driven from his home because he was "the son of a harlot" (Judg. 11:1). He lived and raided in the land of Tob with a band of outlaws, becoming known as a "mighty warrior." When the Ammonites moved against Israel, Jephthah's people asked him to return and lead them. His victory over the Ammonites came about after a vow he made to offer as a burnt offering the first living thing he saw upon his return from the battle. Even though it was his daughter who greeted him, Jephthah did fulfill his vow. Jephthah is hailed by the author of Hebrews as a hero of faith (Heb. 11:32).

JERASH Modern Arabic name of Gerasa. See *Gerasa*.

JERBOA Any of several species of leaping rodents having long hind legs and long tails. The REB

Sunset at Jerash (ancient Gerasa).

includes the jerboa among the unclean animals of Lev. 11:29.

JEREMIAH, THE PROPHET Jeremiah was called to be a prophet in the 13th year of King Josiah (627/6 BC) (Jer. 1:2). He was active under the Kings Jehoahaz/Shallum (609 BC) (22:11), Jehoiakim (609–597 BC) (Jer. 1:3; 22:18; 26:1; 35:1; 36:1,9), Jehoiachin/Jeconiah/Coniah (597 BC) (22:24; 24:1; 27:20; 28:4; 29:2; 37:1), and Zedekiah (597–586 BC) (1:3; 21:1; 27:1-12; 28:1; 32:1; 34:2; 37–38; 39:4; 52:8). When Jerusalem was destroyed by the Babylonians in 587 BC, Jeremiah moved to Mizpah, the capital of Gedaliah, the newly appointed Jewish governor of the Babylonian province of Judah (40:5). When Gedaliah was assassinated (41:1-2), Jeremiah was deported to Egypt against his will by Jewish officers who had survived the catastrophes (42:1–43:7). In Egypt he continued to preach against the Egyptians (43:8-13) and his compatriots (44:1-30).

Jeremiah recommended national surrender to the rule of the Babylonian Empire and called Nebuchadnezzar, Babylon's emperor and Judah's most hated enemy, the "servant of the Lord" (25:9; 27:6). He even incited his compatriots to desert to the enemy (21:8-9). He was accused of treason and convicted (37:12-13; 38:1-6), and yet the most aggressive oracles against Babylon are attributed to him (50–51). Enemies challenged his prophetic honesty and the inspiration of his message (43:1-3; 29:24), and yet kings and nobles sought his advice (21:1-2; 37:3; 38:14; 42:1-2).

He constantly proclaimed God's judgment upon Judah and Jerusalem, and yet he was also a prophet of hope, proclaiming oracles of salvation, conditioned (3:22–4:2) or unconditioned (30–31; 32:36-38; 33:6; 34:4). God forbade him to intercede for his people (7:16; 11:14; 14:11; cp. 15:1); yet he interceded (14:7-9,19-22). God ordered him to live without marriage and family (16:2). He had to stay away from the company of merrymakers (15:17) and from houses of feasting (16:8). He complained to and argued with God (12:1-17), complaining about the misery of his prophetic office (20:7-18). At the same time he sang hymns of praise to God (20:13).

JEREMIAH, BOOK OF A prophetic book of the OT, written by the Prophet Jeremiah, which stimulates the search for the will of God in moments when all the institutions and religious representatives normally in charge of administrating His will are discredited. The nation of Judah would fall to the Babylonians, the prophet emphasized, unless they turned back from their idolatry to worship the one true God.

Jeremiah declared that God's justice and righteousness cannot be usurped by His people. He can be a stumbling block even for His prophet (Jer. 12:1-6; 20:7-12). Execution of judgment and destruction is not God's delight. God Himself suffers pain because of the alienation between Himself and His people (2:1-37). Better than the prophet was able to admit, the apostate members of God's people remembered a correct notion of the nature of God. He continued to be their Father, and His anger would not last forever (3:4,12-13). Judah and Jerusalem would be carried away as captives to a foreign land. But this was not God's last word. His faithfulness prevails and creates new hope where all hope is lost (chaps. 30–33).

JERICHO Place-name meaning "moon." Apparently the oldest city in the world and the first city Israel conquered under Joshua. Jericho is situated in the lower Jordan Valley, which, according to Gen. 13:10, "was well-watered everywhere . . . like the LORD's garden" (HCSB). The OT town lies beneath Tell es-Sultan near one of Palestine's strongest springs. The combination of rich alluvial soil, the perennial spring, and constant sunshine made Jericho an attractive place for settlement. Jericho could be called "city of palms" (Deut. 34:3; Judg. 1:16; 3:13; 2 Chron. 28:15) and has plenty of palm trees today. Only about 6.4 inches of rain fall there per year. Jericho was an oasis situated in a hot plain.

New Testament Jericho, founded by Herod the Great, was about one and one-half miles south of the location of OT Jericho. In NT times Jericho was famous for its balm (an aromatic gum known for its medicinal qualities). This, along with its being the winter capital, made it a wealthy city.

JEROBOAM Personal name possibly meaning "he who contends for justice for the people" or "may the people multiply." **1.** First king of the northern kingdom Israel about 926–909 BC Jeroboam managed the laborers Solomon had conscripted for his huge building projects

Reconstruction of Herod the Great's winter palace at Jericho. The palace had a commanding view of New Testament Jericho and the arid, fertile Jordan River.

(1 Kings 11:28). During Solomon's reign Ahijah, a prophet from Shiloh, predicted that Jeroboam would become king over 10 of the 12 tribes. Seizing upon the people's resentment toward Solomon's high-handed policies at his death, Jeroboam led the 10 northern tribes to revolt against the house of David. They then crowned Jeroboam king. Jeroboam became the example of evil kings in Israel because he built temples in Dan and Bethel with golden calves representing God's presence. **2.** Powerful king of Israel in the dynasty of Jehu about 793–753 BC (2 Kings 14:23-29). He managed to restore prosperity and territory to a weak nation but continued the religious practices of Jeroboam I and thus met condemnation from the biblical writers.

JERUBBAAL Personal name meaning "Baal judges." Another name for Gideon (Judg. 6:32). See *Gideon*.

Round Neolithic (New Stone Age) defense tower at Old Testament Jericho.

JERUSALEM Jerusalem is a city set high on a plateau in the hills of Judah, considered sacred by Judaism, Christianity, and Islam. Its biblical-theological significance lies in its status as Yahweh's chosen center of His divine kingship and of the human kingship of David and his sons, Yahweh's vice-regents. Besides the name "Jerusalem," the city is also called "the City of David" and "Zion" (originally referring to a part of the city, the "stronghold of Zion" that David captured from the Jebusites; see 2 Sam. 5:6-10).

The city (known earlier as Jebus for its inhabitants, the Jebusites; see Judg. 19:10-11) was captured in Joshua's time (Judg. 1:8), but the Jebusites were not driven out (Josh. 15:63; Judg. 1:21). After David captured it and made it Israel's capital (1 Chron. 11:4-9), David brought the ark of the covenant into Jerusalem (2 Sam. 6:17) and made it the seat of his kingdom. Jerusalem came to be "the city of our God," "the city of the great King," "the city of Yahweh of hosts" (Ps. 48). Under Solomon, the temple was constructed in Jerusalem (2 Chron. 3-7) and the nation reached its political and economic zenith with Jerusalem at the center (2 Chron. 9).

Since the people abandoned God, He eventually abandoned His chosen city to the Babylonians in 586 BC (2 Kings 23:26-27). Yet judgment was not His final word. The Persian king Cyrus (decree in 538 BC) was the Lord's servant in facilitating the return of many exiles and the rebuilding of the city and the temple (Isa. 44:26-28; 45:13; Ezra 6; Neh. 1–6). Moreover, the future salvation of Jerusalem would exceed the temporal restoration of the postexilic community. All peoples would come to it (Isa. 2:2-4; Jer. 3:17). God's new work for Jerusalem would usher in nothing less than a new age (Isa. 65:18-25; Zech. 14:8-21).

The NT portrays the various Jerusalem-related prophecies as fulfilled in and through Jesus, Israel's Messiah. In the Gospels, Jerusalem takes on ironic, contrasting roles. On one hand, it is "the city of the great King" (Matt. 5:35) and "the holy city" (Matt. 4:5; 27:53). On the other hand, it is the city "who kills the prophets and stones those who are sent to her" (Luke 13:34 HCSB). While there were those who longed for "the redemption of Jerusalem" (Luke 2:38), the city and its inhabitants will face judgment because they did not recognize the time of divine visitation by Jesus (Luke 19:41-44). Indeed Jesus' mission ended in His rejection by Jerusalem's rulers and His death outside the city walls (Mark 8:31; 10:32-34).

The promises of the Lord's reign ("the kingdom of God") and of the salvation of His people, both Jews and Gentiles, find their fulfillment in Jesus' death and resurrection and in the dawning of the new heaven and new earth. Biblical hope is now focused on "the city of the living God, the heavenly Jerusalem" (Heb. 12:22).

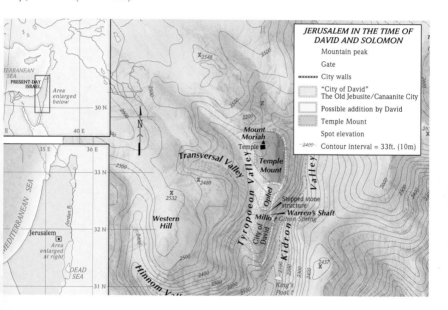

Jerusalem in the time of Jesus.

JESHURUN Proper name meaning "upright" or "straight." Poetic name for Israel (Deut. 32:15; 33:5,26; Isa. 44:2).

JESSE Personal name meaning "man" or "manly." Father of David the king (1 Sam. 16:1). He was a Judahite who lived in Bethlehem, the son of Obed and the grandson of Boaz and Ruth (1 Sam. 16:1; Ruth 4:17). He is mentioned in the genealogies of Jesus in the Gospels of Matthew and Luke.

JESUS CHRIST Jesus' proper name derives from the Hebrew "Joshua," meaning "Yahweh saves" or "salvation is from Yahweh" (Matt. 1:21). *Christ* is the Greek term for "anointed," equivalent to the Hebrew *Messiah*. This anointed Savior is also Immanuel, "God is with us" (Matt. 1:23; Isa. 7:14). Paul's favorite term for Jesus was *kurios*, "Lord," and the earliest Christian confession was that "Jesus is Lord." The sublime introduction of Jesus in the prologue to John's Gospel presents Him as the *logos*, the "Word" who created all things (1:3) and who became flesh and dwelt among us (1:14). He is the Life (1:4) and the Light of mankind (1:4); the Glory of God (1:14); the only begotten Son of God who makes the Father known (1:18).

The Gospels record Jesus' own self designation as Son of Man, the title He frequently used to speak of His humiliation, His identification with sinful mankind, His death on behalf of sinners, and His glorious return. While Jesus was the Son of Man in respect to His ministry and passion, He is also Son of God, the uniquely begotten one sent from God Himself (Mark 1:1; John 3:16). The book of Hebrews shows Jesus as God's great high priest (3:1; 4:14) who both makes sacrifice for His people and who is Himself the sacrifice (10:10-14). Hebrews also presents Jesus as the creator of all things (1:2), the perfect representation of God (1:3), and the apostle of our confession (3:1). The metaphors used of Jesus, particularly in John's Gospel, speak poignantly to the indispensable need for a person to know Jesus. He is the water of life (John 4:14), the bread of life (6:41), the light (8:12), the door (10:7), the way, the truth, and the life (14:6).

Jesus was fully human. He was not partially human nor did He function at times as a human and at times as God nor did He merely appear to be human. He was at once both man and God. The evidence for Jesus' humanity in Scripture is abundant. He displayed physical symptoms that all humans experience: fatigue (John 4:6), sleep (Matt. 8:24), hunger (Matt. 21:18), and suffering (Luke 22:43-44). Jesus also experienced the emotional reactions of mankind: compassion (Luke 7:13), weeping (Luke 19:41), anger and indignation (Mark 3:5), grief (Matt. 26:37), and joy (John 15:11).

Yet Jesus was not just a real man; He was also a unique person. He differed from all other people in two ways. First, He was born to a virgin; He had no human father. He was conceived by the Holy Spirit in Mary's womb (Matt. 1:18-25). Second, unlike any other person, Jesus was without sin. He claimed to be sinless (John 8:46) and there is never a record of His confessing sin, though He told us to confess ours (Matt. 6:12). Other biblical writers ascribe sinlessness to Jesus. Paul said that Jesus became sin for us but that He personally knew no sin (2 Cor. 5:21). The writer of Hebrews says that Jesus never sinned (Heb. 4:15), and Peter affirmed that Jesus the righteous died for the unrighteous (1 Pet. 3:18).

Throughout the centuries few people have denied the existence of the man Jesus. A fierce battle has always raged, however, over the supernatural nature of Jesus. If Jesus was virgin born and sinless, then a supernatural element is already introduced into His nature that sets Him apart from all other people. Further, His resurrection denotes that this is a person who transcends time and space. The Gospel accounts record many eyewitnesses to the resurrected Christ (Matt. 28:1-10; John 20:19-31), and all attempts to refute such accounts fall short. However, the NT goes beyond these implicit references to deity and clearly states that Christ is divine.

The demands of loyalty from His followers (Luke 9:57-62) and the claims that He will judge the world (John 5:27) sound strange if they come from a mere man. He also claimed that He could forgive sins (Mark 2:5), and He declared that in the judgment people will be condemned or approved according to their attitude toward the people who represent Him (Matt. 25:31-46). Scripture says that Jesus created (John 1:3) and now sustains all things (Col. 1:17). He even has the power to raise the dead (John 5:25). Angels and people worship Him (Heb. 1:6; Matt. 2:2). He possesses equality with the persons of the Trinity (John 14:23; 2 Cor. 13:14).

Beyond these assertions, the NT provides even clearer evidence regarding the deity of Christ. He is called God in Heb. 1:8. John's prologue (1:1-18) affirms that Jesus is from the beginning, that He is "with" (literally "face to face") God, and that He is God. The Gospel of John declares Jesus to be equal in nature with God the Father but distinct in person. Another important passage is John 5:16-29. During a controversy with the Jews about healing a man on the Sabbath, the Jews sought to kill Him because He blasphemed in making Himself equal with God. Rather than correcting them for mistaking His identity, Jesus went on to make even further claims regarding His deity: He has power to give life to people (v. 21), all judgment is handed over to Him (v. 22), and all should honor the

Son with the same honor they bestow upon the Father (v. 23).

Jesus was a master teacher. Crowds that claimed no loyalty to Him were forced to admit, "No man ever spoke like this" (John 7:46 HCSB). At the close of His compelling Sermon on the Mount, the multitudes were amazed at how He taught (Matt. 7:29). He taught mainly about His Father and the kingdom that He had ushered in. He explained what that kingdom is like and the absolute obedience and love His followers are to have as citizens of the kingdom. His teaching often enraged the religious leaders of His day because they did not understand that He was the promised Messiah who appeared to usher in the kingdom through His death, resurrection, and second coming. He stressed that the kingdom, though inaugurated at His first appearing, will find its consummation in His second coming (Matt. 24–25). Until then, His disciples are to conduct themselves as salt and light in a dark, sinful world (Matt. 5–7). Often He spoke in parables, helping people to understand by using common things to illustrate spiritual truths.

Jesus' mighty works validated His unique and divine nature. He backed up His claims to deity by demonstrating His power over sickness and disease, over nature, and over life and death itself. One great miracle that demonstrates conclusively His claim to deity is His resurrection from the dead. Death could not hold Him. He rose from the dead and showed Himself alive by many "convincing proofs" (Acts 1:3). Despite rigorous attempts by liberalism to expunge the miracles from the Gospels, it is impossible to eliminate these supernatural elements from Jesus' life without damaging the credibility of the Gospel records about Him.

Christianity affirms that Jesus is the only way to God (John 14:6; Acts 4:12). This view seems intolerant in light of our pluralistic, relativistic age. Yet, one must deal with Jesus Christ either as the Lord God whom He claimed to be or as an imposter who somehow was deceived as to His own identity.

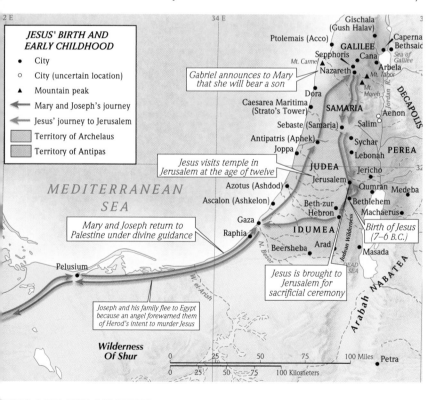

JESUS' BIRTH AND EARLY CHILDHOOD
- • City
- ○ City (uncertain location)
- ▲ Mountain peak
- ← Mary and Joseph's journey
- ← Jesus' journey to Jerusalem
- ▨ Territory of Archelaus
- ▨ Territory of Antipas

Gabriel announces to Mary that she will bear a son

Jesus visits temple in Jerusalem at the age of twelve

Mary and Joseph return to Palestine under divine guidance

Joseph and his family flee to Egypt because an angel forewarned them of Herod's intent to murder Jesus

Jesus is brought to Jerusalem for sacrificial ceremony

Birth of Jesus (7–6 B.C.)

MEDITERRANEAN SEA

Wilderness Of Shur

JESUS, LIFE AND MINISTRY The story of Jesus begins abruptly in the Gospel of Mark when He presented Himself at the Jordan River to the desert prophet John the Baptist as a candidate for baptism. All that is said about His origin is that He came to the river "from Nazareth" (Mark 1:9). "Jesus of Nazareth" was a designation that followed Him to the day of His death (John 19:19). Matthew's Gospel demonstrates that although Nazareth was Jesus' home when He came to John for baptism, He was not born there. Rather, He was born (as the Jewish messiah must be) in Bethlehem, the "city of David," as a descendant of David's royal line (Matt. 1:1-17; 2:1-6). However, He grew up in Nazareth.

The traditional site on the Jordan River where Jesus was baptized.

Even after the momentou[s] events associated with Jesu[s'] baptism in the Jordan River— the descent of God's Spirit o[n] Him like a dove and the voi[ce] from heaven announcing, "Yo[u] are My beloved Son; in You [I] take delight!" (Mark 1:10-1[1] HCSB)—His identity as Son [of] God remained hidden fro[m] those around Him. We have n[o] evidence that anyone excep[t] Jesus, and possibly John th[e] Baptist, either heard the voi[ce] or saw the dove. Ironically, th[e] first intimation after the baptis[m] that He was more than simpl[y] "Jesus of Nazareth" came n[ot] from His family or friends [or] from the religious leaders [of] Israel, but from the devil!

Twice the devil challenged him: "If You are the Son of God, tell this stone to become bread" (Luk[e] 4:3), and (on the pinnacle of the temple in Jerusalem), "If You are the Son of God, throw Yourself dow[n] from here" (Luke 4:9). Jesus made no attempt to defend or make use of His divine sonship but appeale[d] instead to an authority to which any devout Jew of His day might have appealed—the holy Scriptures– and through them to the God of Israel.

Two things about this temptation story have a special bearing on the ministry of Jesus as a whol[e]

First, the God-centered character of His message continued in the proclamation He began i[n] Galilee when He returned home from the desert: "The time is fulfilled, and the kingdom of God ha[s] come near. Repent and believe in the good news!" (Mark 1:15 HCSB). Mark called this proclam[a]tion "the good news of God" (Mark 1:14). John's Gospel presented Jesus as reminding His hearer[s] again and again that He had come not to glorify or proclaim Himself, but solely to make known "th[e] Father," or "Him who sent me" (John 4:34; 5:19, 30; 6:38; 7:16-18,28; 8:28,42,50; 14:10,28).

Second, the issue of Jesus' identity continued to be raised first by the powers of evil. Just as th[e] devil challenged Jesus in the desert as "Son of God," so in the course of His ministry the demons (o[r] the demon-possessed) confronted Him with such words as "What do You have to do with us, Jesus– Nazarene? ... I know who You are—the Holy One of God" (Mark 1:24), or "What do You have [to] do with me, Jesus, Son of the Most High God?" (Mark 5:7).

The mystery of Jesus' person emerged in pronouncements of this kind, but Jesus seemed not t[o] want the question of His identity raised prematurely. He silenced the demons (Mark 1:25,34; 3:12[)] and when He healed the sick, He frequently told the people who were cured not to speak of it t[o] anyone (Mark 1:43-44; 7:36a). The more He urged silence, however, the faster the word of His hea[l]ing power spread (Mark 1:45; 7:36b). The crowds appear to have concluded that He must be th[e] Messiah, the anointed King of David's line expected to come and deliver the Jews from Roman rul[e.] If Jesus was playing out the role of Messiah, the Gospels present Him as a strangely relucta[nt] Messiah.

At one point, when the crowds tried to "take Him by force to make Him king, He withdrew aga[in] to the mountain by Himself" (John 6:15 HCSB). Seldom, if ever, did He apply to Himself the cu[s]tomary terms "Messiah" or "Son of God." He had instead a way of using the emphatic "I" when [it] was not grammatically necessary and a habit sometimes of referring to Himself indirectly and my[s]teriously as "Son of Man." In the Aramaic language Jesus spoke, "Son of Man" meant simply "a ce[r]tain man," or "someone."

Though He made no explicit messianic claims and avoided the ready-made titles of honor that th[e] Jews customarily applied to the Messiah, Jesus spoke and acted with the authority of God Himsel[f.] He gave sight to the blind and hearing to the deaf; He enabled the lame to walk. When He touche[d] the unclean, He made them clean. He even raised the dead to life. In teaching the crowds that gat[h]ered around Him, He did not hesitate to say boldly, "You have heard that it was said ... but I tell you[" (Matt. 5:21-22,27-28,31-34,38-39,43-44). So radical was He toward the accepted traditions that H[e] found it necessary to state at the outset: "Don't assume that I came to destroy the Law, or th[e] Prophets. I did not come to destroy but to fulfill" (Matt. 5:17).

Jesus' primary mission was to reach the lost sheep of Israel. Through their carelessness about the law, the religious leaders had become the enemies of God; but God loved His enemies. Jesus' conviction was that both He and His disciples must love them, too (Matt. 5:38-48). Jesus was challenged on one occasion for enjoying table fellowship with social outcasts (known to the religious Jews as "sinners") in the house of Levi, the tax collector in Capernaum. He replied to this criticism: "Those who are well don't need a doctor, but the sick do need one. I didn't come to call the righteous, but sinners" (Mark 2:17 HCSB). Such an exuberant celebration of divine mercy must have seemed to religious leaders a serious lowering of ancient ethical standards and a damaging compromise of the holiness of God.

We have little evidence that Jesus included non-Jews among the "sinners" to whom He was sent. Despite the reference in Luke 4:25-27 to Elijah and Elisha and their ministry to foreigners, Jesus explicitly denied that He was sent to Gentiles or Samaritans (Matt. 15:24). Yet the principle, "not to the righteous, but to sinners," made the extension of the good news of the kingdom of God to the Gentiles after Jesus' resurrection a natural one. Even during Jesus' lifetime, He responded to the initiatives of Gentiles seeking His help (Matt. 8:5-13; Luke 7:1-10), sometimes in such a way as to put Israel to shame (Matt. 8:10).

The Gospel accounts of Jesus' last days in Jerusalem correspond in broad outline to His predictions of His death. He seems to have come to Jerusalem for the last time in the knowledge that He would die there. Though He received a royal welcome from crowds who looked to Him as the long-expected Messiah (Mark 11:9-10; John 12:13), no evidence points to this as the reason for His arrest. Rather, His action in driving the money-changers out of the Jerusalem temple (Matt 21:12-16; Mark 11:15-17), as well as certain of His pronouncements about the temple, aroused the authorities to act decisively against Him.

During His last week in Jerusalem, Jesus had predicted the temple's destruction (Matt. 24:1-2; Luke 21:5-6) and claimed that "I will demolish this sanctuary made by hands, and in three days I will build another not made by hands" (Mark 14:58 HCSB). Jesus' intention to establish a new community as a "temple," or dwelling place of God (Matt. 16:18; John 2:19), was perceived as a threat to Judaism and to the temple that stood as its embodiment. On this basis He was arrested and charged as a deceiver of the people.

During a hearing before the Sanhedrin, or Jewish ruling council, Jesus spoke of Himself as "Son of Man seated at the right hand of the Power and coming with the clouds of heaven" (Mark 14:62 HCSB). Though the high priest called this blasphemy and the Sanhedrin agreed that such behavior deserved death, the results of the hearing seem to have been inconclusive. The high priest and his cohorts apparently found no formal charges they could make stick. The Sanhedrin decided, therefore, to send Jesus to Pontius Pilate, the Roman governor, with charges against Him that the Romans

Painting from the 15th or 16th century showing the burial of Jesus, seen at the Church of the Holy Sepulchre in Jerusalem.

would take seriously: "We found this man subverting our nation, opposing payment of taxes to Caesar, and saying that He Himself is the Messiah, a King" (Luke 23:2 HCSB). Jesus' execution is therefore attributable neither to the Jewish people as a whole, nor to the Sanhedrin, but rather to a small group of priests who manipulated the Romans into doing what they were not able to accomplish within the framework of their law.

Though Pilate pronounced Jesus innocent three times (Luke 23:4,14,22), he was maneuvered into sentencing Jesus with the thinly veiled threat: "If you release this man, you are not Caesar's friend. Anyone who makes himself a king opposes Caesar!" (John 19:12 HCSB). Consequently, Jesus was crucified between two thieves, fulfilling His own prediction that "as Moses lifted up the serpent in the wilderness, so the Son of Man must be lifted up" (John 3:14). Most of His disciples fled at His arrest; only a group of women and one disciple, called the disciple whom He loved, were present at the cross when He died (John 19:25-27).

The story did not end with the death of Jesus. His body was placed in a new tomb that belonged to a secret disciple named Joseph of Arimathea (John 19:38-42). Two days later, the morning after the Sabbath, some of the women who had remained faithful to Jesus came to the tomb. They discovered the stone over the entrance to the tomb rolled away and the body of Jesus gone. According to Mark, a young man was there (16:5; tradition calls him an angel) and told the women to send word to the rest of the disciples to go and meet Jesus in Galilee, just as He had promised them (Mark 16:7; 14:28). According to Matthew, the young man's word was confirmed to the women by the risen Jesus Himself. When they brought word to the 11 disciples (the Twelve minus Judas, the betrayer), the disciples went to a mountain in Galilee, where the risen Jesus appeared to them as a group. He commanded them to make more disciples, teaching and baptizing among the Gentiles (Matt. 28:16-20).

According to Luke, the risen Jesus appeared to the gathered disciples already in Jerusalem on the same day He was raised and before that to two disciples walking to the neighboring town of Emmaus. According to John, there was an appearance in Jerusalem on Sunday to one of the women Mary Magdalene, another on the same day to the gathered disciples, another a week later (still in Jerusalem) to the same group plus Thomas, and a fourth appearance, at an unstated time, by the lake of Galilee, in which Jesus reenacted the initial call of the disciples by providing them miraculously with an enormous catch of fish.

Luke adds in the book of Acts that the appearances of the risen Jesus went on over a period of 40 days in which He continued to instruct them about the kingdom of God. The disciples' experience of the living Jesus transformed them from a scattered and cowardly band of disillusioned visionaries into the nucleus of a coherent movement able to challenge and change forever the Roman Empire within a few short decades.

Even today, the story of Jesus is not over; He continues to fulfill His mission wherever His name is confessed and His teaching is obeyed. Christians believe that He will do so until He comes again.

JETHRO Personal name meaning "excess" or "superiority." Priest of Midian and the father-in-law of Moses (Exod. 3:1). In Exod. 2:18 his name is Reuel; in Num. 10:29 it is Hobab. The deity whom he served is not explicitly identified; in Exod. 18:11, however, he declared Yahweh to be greater than all gods.

JEWISH PARTIES IN THE NEW TESTAMENT Judaism in NT times included several different groups, or parties, including the Pharisees, Sadducees, Herodians, and Zealots.

Pharisees The term *Pharisee* means "separated ones." Perhaps it means that they separated themselves from the masses or that they separated themselves to the study and interpretation of the law. They saw the way to God as being through obedience to the law. They were the progressives of the day, willing to adopt new ideas and adapt the law to new situations. The Pharisees accepted all the OT as authoritative. They affirmed the reality of angels and demons. They had a firm belief in life beyond the grave and a resurrection of the body. They were missionary, seeking the conversion of Gentiles (Matt. 23:15). They had little interest in politics. The Pharisees opposed Jesus because He refused to accept their interpretations of the oral law.

Sadducees The Sadducees were the party of the wealthy and of the high priestly families. They were in charge of the temple, its services, and concessions. They claimed to be descendants of Zadok, high priest of Solomon. They stood in opposition to the Pharisees. They were social conservatives, seeking to preserve the practices of the past. They opposed the oral law, accepting the Pentateuch as the ultimate authority. The Sadducees were materialistic in their outlook. They did not believe in life after death or rewards or punishment beyond this life. They denied the existence of angels and demons. They did not believe that God is concerned with what people do. Rather, people are totally free. The Sadducees were politically oriented, supporters of ruling powers, whether Seleucids or Romans. They tolerated no threats to their position and wealth, so they strongly opposed Jesus.

Herodians The Herodians are mentioned only three times in the NT (Matt. 22:16; Mark 3:6; 12:13). In Mark they joined the Pharisees in a plot to kill Jesus. The other references are to Pharisees and Herodians together asking Jesus about paying taxes to Caesar. They were Jews who supported Herod Antipas or sought to have a descendant of Herod the Great given authority over Palestine. At this time Judea and Samaria were under Roman governors.

Zealots The Zealots were the extreme wing of the Pharisees. In contrast with other Pharisees, they believed only God had the right to rule over the Jews. They were willing to fight and die for that belief. For them nationalistic patriotism and religion were inseparable. Simon, one of the disciples, is called Zealot (Luke 6:15).

JEZEBEL Personal name meaning "Where is the prince?" perhaps derived from Phoenician name meaning "Baal is the prince." Wife of King Ahab of Israel (874–853 BC), who brought the worship of Baal from Sidon where her father Ethbaal was king (1 Kings 16:31). Jezebel tried to destroy all God's prophets in Israel (1 Kings 18:4) while installing prophets of Baal and Asherah (1 Kings 18:19) as part of the royal household. Jezebel was killed by her own servants when Jehu overthrew the dynasty of Ahab (2 Kings 9:30-37). Jezebel's name became so associated with wickedness that the false prophetess in the church at Thyatira was labeled "Jezebel" (Rev. 2:20).

JEZREEL Personal and place-name meaning "God sows." **1.** The Valley of Jezreel that separates Galilee from Samaria, including the valley of Esdraelon. **2.** Northern city of Jezreel and the site of the royal residence of Omri and Ahab (1 Kings 21). **3.** The southern city of Jezreel located in the vicinity of Ziph (1 Sam. 25:43). **4.** Name given by Hosea to his son as a symbol to indicate the evil nature of the dynasty of Jehu (Hos. 1:4-5; 1:10–2:1).

The Valley of Jezreel (Esdraelon or Megiddo) as viewed from the top of the Megiddo tel.

JOAB Personal name meaning "Yahweh is father." Military commander during most of David's reign. He was loyal to David and ruthless in achieving his objectives. Joab successfully led David's armies against the Ammonites (2 Sam. 10). During this campaign David sent his infamous order to have Uriah, the husband of Bathsheba, killed (2 Sam. 11). When Absalom led a rebellion, Joab remained loyal to David. Joab killed Absalom against the clear orders of David (2 Sam. 18:14). Joab murdered Amasa, whom David had named commander (2 Sam. 20:10). He opposed David's plan for a census but carried it out when ordered to do so (2 Sam. 24:1-9). When David was dying, Joab supported Adonijah's claim to the throne (1 Kings 1). David named Solomon king and told him to avenge Abner and Amasa by killing Joab. Although Joab fled to the tabernacle for sanctuary, Solomon ordered Benaiah to kill Joab (1 Kings 2).

JOANNA Personal name meaning "Yahweh's gift." **1.** One of the women who came to Jesus' tomb on the Sunday following the crucifixion and reported to the 11 that He had risen (Luke 8:3). **2.** The son of Rhesa mentioned in the genealogy of Jesus (Luke 3:27 KJV).

JOASH Personal name meaning "Yahweh gives." **1.** Father of Gideon (Judg. 6:11). **2.** A son of Shelah (1 Chron. 4:21-22). **3.** A son of Becher (1 Chron. 7:8). **4.** One of David's warriors (1 Chron. 12:3). **5.** One of David's officers who was in charge of the stores of oil (1 Chron. 27:28). **6.** A son of Ahab king of Israel and one of those to whom Micaiah the prophet was handed over (1 Kings 22:26). **7.** Infant son of King Ahaziah of Judah who survived the bloodbath carried out by Athaliah, the queen mother, following the murder of Ahaziah (2 Kings 11:2). Joash was hidden by Jehosheba his aunt for six years, then proclaimed as the legitimate ruler of Judah in a move instigated by Jehoiada. Athaliah was executed, and Joash took the throne at the age of seven. **8.** Son and successor of Jehoahaz as king of Israel (2 Kings 13:10). He ruled for 16 years during the early part of the eighth century BC. His son Jeroboam II succeeded him on the throne.

JOB, BOOK OF This OT book is most frequently pictured as a drama that deals with the age-old question of human suffering. It consists of a series of debates between Job and his three friends, with Job searching for answers on why he, who claimed to be a righteous man, lost all his possessions, his children, and his health. Through his ordeal, Job learns that God still controls the world, even a world with unexplainable suffering. The human mind cannot have perfect understanding, but God can be trusted to treat us with justice and fairness. In the final analysis, He is sovereign, and He does not owe us an explanation for His actions.

JOCHEBED Personal name meaning "Yahweh's glory." Wife of Amram and the mother of Miriam, Aaron, and Moses (Exod. 6:20).

JOEL Personal name meaning "Yah is God." **1.** Son of Samuel who became an evil judge (1 Sam. 8). **2.** Levite (1 Chron. 6:36). **3.** Member(s) of tribe of Reuben (1 Chron. 5:4,8). **4.** Leader among the Levites under David (1 Chron. 15:7,11,17). **5.** Member of tribe of Simeon (1 Chron. 4:35). **6.** Leader of tribe of Gad (1 Chron. 5:12). **7.** Leader of tribe of Issachar (1 Chron. 7:3). **8.** Military hero under David (1 Chron. 11:38). **9.** Leader of the western half of the tribe of Manasseh under David (1 Chron. 27:20). **10.** Levite who helped King Hezekiah cleanse the temple (2 Chron. 29:12). **11.** Israelite whom Ezra condemned for having a foreign wife (Ezra 10:43). **12.** Leader of the people from tribe of Benjamin living in Jerusalem in time of Nehemiah (Neh. 11:9). **13.** Prophet whose preaching ministry produced the book of Joel.

JOEL, BOOK OF This OT book describes a terrible locust plague that devastated the land of Israel. The prophet interpreted this disaster as a symbol of the coming day of God's judgment. Then when the people repented of their sin and turned to the Lord, He answered that He would show pity and remove their plague (2:18-27). The clear message of the book is that the Creator of the universe is in complete control of nature and can use calamities to bring His people to repentance. Joel also predicted a time when God's Spirit would fall upon His people. On the day of Pentecost the apostle Peter proclaimed that this new day of Spirit-filled people predicted by the prophet Joel had arrived (Acts 2:17-21).

JOHN THE APOSTLE A disciple of Jesus, brother of James, and leader in the early church. John is always mentioned among the first four apostles in the lists of the Twelve (Mark 3:17). John is also among the "inner three" (the other two were Peter and James) who were with Jesus on special occasions in the Synoptic Gospels: the raising of Jairus's daughter (Mark 5:37), the transfiguration (Mark 9:2), and the garden of Gethsemane (Mark 14:32-33). The Apostle John appears four times in the book of Acts, and each time he is with Peter (1:13; 3:1-11; 4:13-20; 8:14). After Peter healed the man, they were arrested, imprisoned, and then released. They were "uneducated and untrained men" (Acts 4:13 HCSB), but they answered their accusers boldly (Acts 4:20).

Five books of the NT have been attributed to John the apostle: the Gospel, three letters, and Revelation. In each case, the traditional view that the apostle was the author of these books can be traced to writers in the second century. Neither the Gospel nor the letters identify their author by name.

JOHN THE BAPTIST Prophet from a priestly family who preached a mes-

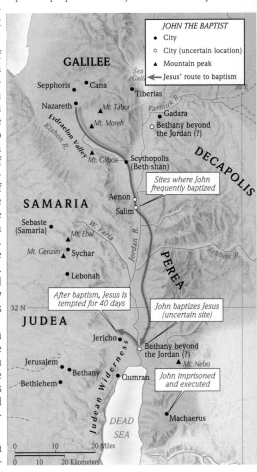

JOHN THE BAPTIST
- ● City
- ○ City (uncertain location)
- ▲ Mountain peak
- ← Jesus' route to baptism

GALILEE
Sepphoris ● Cana
Sea of Galilee
Tiberias
Nazareth ● Mt. Tabor
Yarmuk R.
Gadara
Mt. Moreh
Bethany beyond the Jordan (?)
Esdraelon Valley
Kishon R.
Mt. Gilboa
Scythopolis (Beth-shan)
DECAPOLIS
Sites where John frequently baptized
Aenon
SAMARIA
Salim
Sebaste (Samaria)
Mt. Ebal
W. Faria
Mt. Gerizim ● Sychar
Jordan R.
PEREA
Jabbok R.
● Lebonah
After baptism, Jesus is tempted for 40 days
John baptizes Jesus (uncertain site)
32 N
JUDEA
Jericho
Bethany beyond the Jordan (?)
Jerusalem ●
Judean Wilderness
Mt. Nebo
● Bethany
John imprisoned and executed
Bethlehem ●
Qumran
DEAD SEA
Machaerus
0   10   20 Miles
0   10   20 Kilometers

sage of repentance, announced the coming of the Messiah, baptized Jesus, and was beheaded by Herod Antipas. Luke 1:5-80 records the birth of John. Zechariah, his father, was a priest. The angel Gabriel announced John's birth while Zechariah was burning incense in the temple. According to Gabriel, John would not drink wine or strong drink. He would be filled with the Holy Spirit, and as a prophet he would have the spirit and power of Elijah. His role would be to prepare the Lord's people for the coming of the Messiah.

Machaerus, Herod's fortress-palace where John the Baptist was imprisoned and beheaded.

Mark 1:3-4 records that John was in the wilderness until the time of his public ministry. There he ate locusts and wild honey. He wore the dress of a prophet, camel's hair and a leather girdle (Matt. 3:4; cp. 2 Kings 1:8).

According to the Gospel of Luke, John began his ministry around the Jordan River in the 15th year of the reign of Tiberius Caesar (Luke 3:1-3), which must have been AD 26 or 27. John's preaching emphasized the coming judgment, the need for repentance, and the coming of the Messiah. Jesus was baptized by John at the beginning of His public ministry

According to the Gospel of John, the ministry of Jesus overlapped with that of John (3:22-24), and some of Jesus' first disciples had also been disciples of John the Baptist (John 1:35-37). Jesus even identified John with the eschatological role of Elijah (Mark 9:12-13). John was vigorous in his attacks on Herod Antipas, Roman ruler over Palestine, because of his sensual lifestyle. Herod had him arrested and eventually executed. John's death is recorded in detail in Mark 6:14-29.

JOHN, GOSPEL OF The fourth Gospel in the NT, noted for its distinctiveness when compared with the Synoptic Gospels—Matthew, Mark, and Luke. Unlike the other three Gospels, John emphasizes the deity of Jesus from the beginning of his Gospel. The prologue to his Gospel affirms that Jesus is the eternal Word (*logos*) who was both with God and was God. Jesus is the Word incarnate (John 1:14). Jesus uses the significant phrase "I am" seven times in John, claiming the personal name of God as His own.

Knowing and *believing* are key terms for John. Knowledge of God comes from believing and knowing Jesus. Both these words occur over 90 times in this Gospel and are always used as verbs. Jesus' teaching reminds us that knowing God and believing in Jesus are expressed in action. John wrote his Gospel to assure fearful believers that they must believe Jesus and the words that He spoke. Further, he calls on others who sense a spiritual thirst to come to the One who gives the life-giving water. In Him one finds light, life, and love.

JOHN, LETTERS FROM Three short letters in the New Testament that are attributed to John, the apostle of Jesus.

First John This letter was written to a church or group of churches in crisis—churches which were being attacked by false teaching (cp. 2:18-28; 4:1-6; 5:6-7). False teachers had compromised the person and work of Jesus Christ. They did not confess Jesus of Nazareth as the Christ (2:22) and denied that Jesus had come in the flesh (4:2-3). John affirmed that Jesus had indeed come to earth in human form because he had seen Him with his own eyes (1:1-2). To know Christ, according to John, is to keep His commandments, or to walk in the light of His truth (2:6). Furthermore, a person cannot be in the light and hate his brother or love the world (2:7–17).

Second John Only 245 words in the Greek text, Second John is an excellent example of hortatory (or exhortation) discourse. The "elect lady," to whom the letter is addressed (v. 1)—most likely a reference to a local church—must continue to walk in the truth, love one another, and be on guard against false teachers (the deceiver and the antichrist of v. 7). The church must not extend hospitality to those who deny "the coming of Jesus Christ in the flesh" (v. 7 HCSB).

Third John This is a personal letter that revolves around three individuals: Gaius (the recipient), Diotrephes (the troubler), and Demetrius (probably the bearer of the letter). It contains a word of exhortation to Gaius encouraging him not to imitate the bad example of Diotrephes but to continue the good work he is doing of receiving and supporting the traveling teachers/missionaries.

JOKTAN Personal name meaning "watchful" or "he is small." Son of Eber in line from Shem in the Table of Nations (Gen. 10:25-26).

JONAH Personal name meaning "dove." God used Jonah to deliver a warning of God's judgment to the pagan citizens of Nineveh, capital of the Assyrian Empire. Jonah also prophesied in the northern kingdom during the time of Jeroboam II (793–753 BC; see 2 Kings 14:25).

JONAH, BOOK OF This OT book tells about how God used a prejudiced and narrow-minded prophet to show that His grace extends to all people, Gentiles as well as Jews. At first Jonah refused to answer God's call to preach God's message of judgment and repentance to the citizens of Nineveh, capital city of the cruel Assyrian Empire. God mercifully delivered him from drowning by having Jonah swallowed by a great fish and delivered on dry land. Finally, Jonah did preach to the Ninevites, only to sulk and pout when the people repented and turned to the Lord. The message of the book is that God is concerned for all human beings (1 Tim. 2:1–6) and has the right to show mercy to whomever He wills (Rom. 9:15).

JONATHAN Personal name meaning "Yahweh gave." **1.** Levite who served as priest of Micah in Ephraim and later with tribe of Dan (Judg. 17–18). **2.** Eldest son of King Saul and friend of David. Jonathan made a covenant with David and warned him about his father's plot against David's life (1 Sam. 9:1–2). Jonathan was killed by the Philistines in a battle at Mt. Gilboa (1 Sam. 31:1–2). In later years, after David became king of Judah, he showed kindness to Jonathan's son, Mephibosheth (2 Sam. 9:1–13). **3.** Son of Abiathar the priest in service to David (1 Kings 1:42-43). **4.** An uncle of David who functioned as counselor and scribe in the royal court (1 Chron. 27:32). **5.** Son of Shimea who killed a Philistine giant (1 Chron. 20:7). **6.** One of David's 30 mighty men (2 Sam. 23:32-33). **7.** A royal treasurer in reign of David; called Jehonathan (KJV) in 1 Chron. 27:25. **8.** House of a scribe or secretary where Jeremiah was imprisoned (Jer. 38:26). **9.** Son of Kareah, "Johanan"; possibly same as 8. (Jer. 40:8). **10.** Father of Ebed, a returned exile (Ezra 8:6). **11.** Priest during high priesthood of Joiakim (Neh. 12:14). **12.** Priest, son of Joiada (Neh. 12:11). **13.** Priest who played musical instruments (Neh. 12:35). **14.** Son of Asahel who supported foreign marriages in time of Ezra (Ezra 10:15). **15.** Descendant of Jerahmeel (1 Chron. 2:32-33).

The ancient seaport of Joppa (Jaffa).

JOPPA Place-name meaning "beautiful." Situated on the Mediterranean coast, Joppa is located about 35 miles northwest of Jerusalem. In Joppa, Simon Peter was praying on the flat roof of a house when he saw in a trance what seemed to be "a large sheet being lowered to the earth by its four corners" (HCSB). Through this encounter with God, he learned that the Gentile world was a fit audience for the gospel (Acts 10:9-16).

JORAM Personal name meaning "Yahweh is exalted." Name of a king of Israel (849–843 BC) and a king of Judah

Traditional house of Simon the Tanner in Joppa where Peter received a vision from God.

(850–843 BC). Joram of Judah was succeeded on the throne by his son, whose name was Ahaziah; Joram of Israel came to the throne at the death of his brother, who was also named Ahaziah. The account of the reign of Joram (Jehoram) of Israel is found in 2 Kings 3. He led a coalition with Judah and Edom, advised by Elisha, to defeat Moab. The reign of Joram of Judah is treated in 2 Kings 8. He married the daughter of Ahab of Israel and brought Baal worship to Judah.

JORDAN RIVER Place-name meaning "the descender." River forming geographical division separating eastern and western tribes of Israel. It is the longest and most important river of Palestine. The first mention of the Jordan in the Bible occurs in the story of Abram and Lot. Upon his separation from Abram, Lot chose for himself "all the valley of the Jordan" (Gen. 13:11 NASB). Under the leadership of Joshua, Israel crossed the Jordan "on dry ground" (Josh. 3:15-17). During the period of the judges and the

The Jordan River flows south from Mount Hermon through Israel, finally emptying into the Dead Sea.

early monarchy, the possession of the fords of the Jordan more than once meant the difference between defeat and victory. The Jordan was a strong line of defense, not to be easily forded. The Jordan River is also featured in the miracles of Elijah and Elisha.

The essential story of the Gospels begins at the Jordan River. It was there that John the Baptist came preaching the coming kingdom of heaven. The most important NT event relating to the Jordan is the baptism of Jesus, which was performed by John the Baptist (Mark 1:9).

JOSEPH Personal name meaning "adding." **1.** Son of Jacob by Jacob's favorite wife, Rachel. As the child of Jacob's old age, Joseph became his favorite son. This and dreams which showed his rule over his family inspired the envy of his brothers, who sold Joseph to a caravan of Ishmaelites (Gen. 37). Joseph was taken to Egypt, where he eventually became second in command to the pharaoh because of his prediction of a coming famine and his recommendation on how to solve this problem (Gen. 41:39-45). Later, under Joseph's patronage, his father Jacob moved the rest of his family to Egypt (Gen. 46:1–47:12). Joseph died in Egypt but was embalmed and later buried in Shechem (Gen.

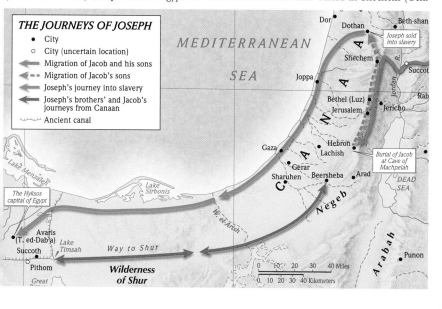

50:26; Josh. 24:32). While in Egypt, Joseph became the father of two sons, Manasseh and Ephraim (Gen. 41:50-52), who were counted as sons of Jacob (48:5-6) and whose tribes dominated the northern nation of Israel. The name Joseph is used later in the OT as a reference to the tribes of Ephraim and Manasseh (1 Kings 11:28) or as a designation for the whole northern kingdom (Zech. 10:6). **2.** A spy from the tribe of Issachar (Num. 13:7). **3.** A Levite of the sons of Asaph (1 Chron. 25:2). **4.** A contemporary of Ezra with a foreign wife (Ezra 10:42). **5.** A priest in the days of high priest Joiakim (Neh. 12:14). **6.** Husband of Mary, mother of Jesus. Upon learning of Mary's pregnancy, he sought to put her away without public disgrace. But after assurances from the Lord in a dream, he took Mary to his ancestral home, Bethlehem, was with her at Jesus' birth, and shared in the naming, circumcision, and dedication of the child (Luke 2:8-33). Joseph does not appear later in the Gospels, and it is likely that he died before Jesus launched His public ministry. **7.** Joseph of Arimathea, a rich member of the Sanhedrin and a secret disciple of Jesus. After the crucifixion, he requested Jesus' body from Pilate and laid it in his own unused tomb (John 19:38-42). **8.** Two different Josephs mentioned in the genealogy of Jesus (Luke 3:24,30). **9.** Another name for both Barsabbas (Acts 1:23) and Barnabas (Acts 4:36).

JOSES Personal name. **1.** One of the brothers of Jesus (Mark 6:3). **2.** The brother of James the Less (Mark 15:40).

JOSHUA Personal name meaning "Yahweh delivered." **1.** Moses' successor who led the Israelites to take control of the promised land. Joshua was on Mt. Sinai when Moses received the Law (Exod. 32:17). He was also one of the 12 spies Moses sent to investigate Canaan (Num. 13:8). He and Caleb returned with a positive, minority report. Of all the adults alive at that time, only the two of them were allowed by God to live to enter the land of Canaan (Num. 14:28-30,38). **2.** High priest of community who returned from Babylonian exile in 538 BC.

JOSHUA, BOOK OF This OT book points backward to the exodus as well as forward to the time of the judges and the monarchy. The book is named after the successor to Moses and one of the greatest military leaders of the OT, Joshua the son of Nun. However, the central character of the book is not Joshua but God. He fights for Israel and drives out the enemy before them. He is a faithful God who desires a true covenant relationship with His chosen people.

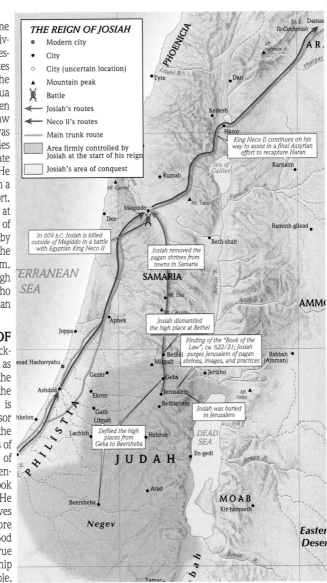

THE REIGN OF JOSIAH

- Modern city
- City
- ○ City (uncertain location)
- ▲ Mountain peak
- ✕ Battle
- ← Josiah's routes
- ← Neco II's routes
- ⋯ Main trunk route
- Area firmly controlled by Josiah at the start of his reign
- Josiah's area of conquest

King Neco II continues on his way to assist in a final Assyrian effort to recapture Haran

In 609 B.C. Josiah is killed outside of Megiddo in a battle with Egyptian King Neco II

Josiah removed the pagan shrines from towns in Samaria

Josiah dismantled the high place at Bethel

Finding of the "Book of the Law", ca. 622/21; Josiah purges Jerusalem of pagan shrines, images, and practices

Josiah was buried in Jerusalem

Defiled the high places from Geba to Beersheba

God promised that He would give Israel the land that He had pledged to their fathers (Gen. 15:18-21; Exod. 3:8). The book of Joshua documents how God fulfilled this promise.

JOSIAH Personal name meaning "Yahweh heals." Judah's king from about 640 to 609 BC who led the people to renew their loyalty to the Lord. Anointed king at the age of eight, he began to seek the God of David (34:3). Josiah initiated a religious purge of Judah during his 12th year on the throne (34:3-7). This purge included tearing down the Canaanite worship centers that had been taken over by Judah. In his 18th year as king, a "book of the Law" was discovered while repairs were being made on the temple. Upon hearing the message of the book, Josiah tore his clothes, a sign of repentance, and humbled himself before God. The reading of this book prompted Josiah to instigate the most far-reaching religious reforms in Israel's history.

JOTHAM Personal name meaning "Yahweh has shown Himself to be perfect." **1.** Son of Gideon who survived the mass killing of Gideon's sons by Abimelech, their half brother (Judg. 9:5). Afterwards, when Abimelech had been hailed as king at Shechem, Jotham addressed a fable to the people of Shechem designed to mock the idea of Abimelech acting as a king. **2.** Son and successor of Uzziah (750–732 BC) as king of Judah (2 Kings 15:32). His reign was marked by building projects, material prosperity, and military successes.

JOY State of delight and well-being that results from knowing and serving God. Joy is the fruit of a right relation with God. It is not something people can create by their own efforts. God Himself knows joy, and He wants His people to know joy. Psalm 104:31 speaks of God Himself rejoicing in His creative works. Isaiah 65:18 speaks of God rejoicing over His redeemed people who will be to Him "a joy." Joy is a fruit of a Spirit-led life (Gal. 5:22). When a person walks with the Lord, he can continue to rejoice even when troubles come. Jesus spoke of those who could rejoice even when persecuted and killed (Matt. 5:12).

JUBAL Personal name meaning "a ram," as a "ram's horn" used as a musical instrument. Son of Lamech and full brother of Jabal (Gen. 4:19-21). He is associated with the invention of musical instruments.

JUBILEE See *Festivals*.

JUDAH Personal, tribal, and territorial name meaning "Praise Yahweh" but may have originally been related to the mountain of Jehud. **1.** Fourth son of Jacob and progenitor of the tribe of Judah (Gen. 29:35). His mother was Leah. Though Judah is prominent in the Genesis narratives, he seldom occupies center stage. Genesis 49:8-12 preserves the blessing of Judah by Jacob. Through Judah ran the genealogical line that led to Jesus. **2.** The tribe of Judah occupied the strategically important territory

THE TRIBAL ALLOTMENTS OF ISRAEL
- City
- City (uncertain location)
- Mountain peak

west of the Dead Sea. The city of Jerusalem was on the border between Judah and Benjamin. David was from the tribe of Judah. **3.** When the kingdom was divided following the death of Solomon, the southern kingdom took the name Judah. **4.** The province set up by the Persian government to rule a conquered Judean kingdom (Neh. 5:14; Hag. 1:1). **5.** Priest whose sons helped Zerubbabel and Joshua restore the temple (Ezra 3:9; cp. Neh. 12:8). **6.** Levite whom Ezra condemned for having foreign wife (Ezra 10:23). **7.** Member of tribe of Benjamin who lived in Jerusalem after the return from exile (Neh. 11:9). **8.** Priestly musician who helped in Nehemiah's celebration (Neh. 12:36).

JUDAS Greek transliteration of Hebrew personal name Judah meaning "Praise Yahweh." **1.** Half brother of Jesus (Mark 6:3). **2.** Judas of Galilee, who was killed in a revolt against the Romans. **3.** A man in Damascus visited by Paul (Acts 9:7-12). **4.** Judas, surnamed Barsabbas, was one of those chosen by the church of Jerusalem to go with Paul and Barnabas to deliver the letter from James to the church at Antioch concerning the important matter of Gentile salvation (Acts 15:22). **5.** An apostle of Jesus, also called Lebbaeus Thaddaeus (Matt. 10:3; Mark 3:18). **6.** Judas Iscariot, who betrayed Jesus. All of the Gospels place him at the end of the list of disciples because of his role as betrayer. *Iscariot* is an Aramaic word that means "man of Kerioth," a town near Hebron. He was the only disciple from Judea. He acted as treasurer for the disciples but was known as a miser and a thief (John 12:4-6).

JUDE, EPISTLE OF A NT letter of only twenty-five verses that addresses the problem of false teachings in the early church. Jude emphasized that the Lord will judge evil intruders who are attempting to corrupt the true faith. The message of judgment strikes many in our world as intolerant, unloving, and contrary to the message of love proclaimed elsewhere in the NT. But some of the most beautiful statements about God's sustaining grace are found in Jude (vv. 1,24-25), and they shine with a greater brilliance when contrasted with the false teachers who have departed from the true Christian faith. Jude called on believers to contend for the faith that was transmitted to them (v. 3) and not to abandon God's love.

JUDEA Place-name meaning "Jewish." In Ezra 5:8 the Aramaic designation of a province that varied in size with changing political circumstances, but always included the city of Jerusalem and the territory surrounding it. The area, formerly called Judah, was first given the name Judea following the Babylonian exile.

JUDGE (OFFICE) 1. An official with authority to administer justice by trying cases. **2.** One who usurps the prerogative of a judge. **3.** A military deliverer in the

Sunset over the Judean hills.

period between Joshua and David. Moses served as the judge of Israel, both deciding between persons and teaching Israel God's statutes (Exod. 18:15-16). Elders of a community frequently served as judges at the city gate (Deut. 22:15; 25:7). During the monarchy the king served as the supreme judge (2 Sam. 15:2-3) and appointed local judges (2 Chron. 19:5), along with an appeals process (2 Chron. 19:8-11). Following the exile King Artaxerxes of Persia gave the priest Ezra the authority to appoint judges in Judea (Ezra 7:25). God is the ultimate Judge of all the earth (James 4:12). As God's representative, Christ functions as Judge as well (1 Pet. 4:5).

JUDGES, BOOK OF A historical book of the OT that describes a dark period in the life of Israel. The nation fell into worship of pagan gods and refused to follow the commands of the Lord. God would punish the people by sending a foreign nation to oppress them. Then they would repent and cry out for deliverance. God would respond by sending a judge, or military deliverer, to overthrow the enemy. This cycle of sin-oppression-repentance-deliverance occurs throughout the book (4:1–3). The best-known judges of the book of Judges are Gideon (6:1–8:35) and Samson (13:1–16:31).

JUDGING The interpretation of Matt. 7:1 that Christians should not make value judgments of the behavior of others is shown to be erroneous by multiple commands in Scripture to do exactly that (e.g., Matt. 7:15-20; 1 Tim. 3:10). But Christians are to judge others constructively with humility and gentleness (Gal. 6:1). We are forbidden to judge hypocritically, that is, when such judgment entails intolerance of another's sin coupled with blindness of one's own (Matt. 7:1-5; Rom. 2:1-4) or when human judgment impinges on God's prerogative as judge (1 Cor. 4:5). Instructions on proper exercise of judgment include (1) the call to judge reputed prophets by their fruits (Matt. 7:15-17),

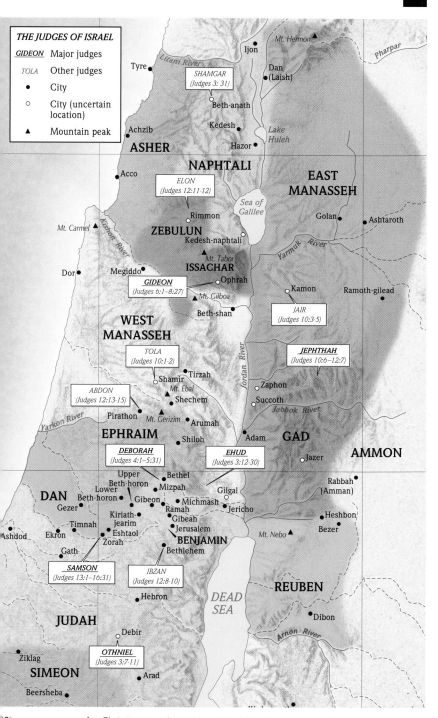

THE JUDGES OF ISRAEL

GIDEON Major judges
TOLA Other judges
● City
○ City (uncertain location)
▲ Mountain peak

SHAMGAR (Judges 3:31)
ELON (Judges 12:11-12)
GIDEON (Judges 6:1–8:27)
JAIR (Judges 10:3-5)
TOLA (Judges 10:1-2)
JEPHTHAH (Judges 10:6–12:7)
ABDON (Judges 12:13-15)
DEBORAH (Judges 4:1–5:31)
EHUD (Judges 3:12-30)
SAMSON (Judges 13:1–16:31)
IBZAN (Judges 12:8-10)
OTHNIEL (Judges 3:7-11)

encouragement for Christians to arbitrate between fellow believers who have a dispute rather than going to pagan law courts (1 Cor. 6:1-6), and (3) instructions regarding church cases (Matt. 18:15-20). First Corinthians 5:3-5 illustrates the function of a church court.

JUDGMENT DAY Appointed time in the future when God will intervene in history for the purpose of judging the wicked and upholding the righteous. In OT texts nations are pictured as being judged during this time. Yet in the NT the judgment seems to be more for individuals. In the OT Yahweh is pictured as the Judge, while the Judge is Christ in the NT. Generally the NT understands the day of judgment as being closely associated with the second coming of Christ, resurrection of the dead, and the coming kingdom of God. The day of judgment is often referred to as the "day of Christ" (Phil. 1:10; 2:16) or "day of the Lord" (1 Cor. 5:5). The Gospels point to Christ as the agent who will judge mankind (Matt. 16:27; 19:28; 25:31; Luke 9:26; 17:24; 22:69). The day of judgment will be a time when all mankind throughout eternity will be judged. On this day the living and dead of all humanity shall stand and make an account to God (1 Pet. 4:5).

JULIUS A Roman centurion assigned the responsibility of escorting Paul to Rome (Acts 27:1).

The temple of Jupiter at Baalbek (Heliopolis).

JUPITER Latin name of Zeus, king of Greek gods. The people of Lystra responded to Paul's healing of a crippled man by claiming the gods had come to earth. They referred to Barnabas as Zeus, or Jupiter (Acts 14:12-13 KJV).

JUSTICE Order that God seeks to reestablish in His creation where all people are treated fairly and impartially. As the sovereign Creator of the universe, God is just (Gen. 18:25; Deut. 32:4), particularly as the defender of all the oppressed of the earth (Jer. 49:11). Justice thus is universal (Ps. 9:7-9) and applies to each covenant or dispensation. Jesus affirmed for His day the centrality of the OT demand for justice (Matt. 23:23). Justice is the work of the NT people of God (James 1:27). God's justice is not a distant external standard. It is the source of all human justice (2 Chron. 19:6,9). Justice is grace received and grace shared (2 Cor. 9:8-10). Various needy groups are the recipients of justice. These groups include widows, orphans, resident aliens (also called "sojourners" or "strangers"), wage earners, the poor, prisoners, slaves, and the sick (Job 29:12-17; Mal. 3:5).

JUSTIFICATION Divine, forensic act of God, based on the work of Christ upon the cross, whereby a sinner is pronounced righteous by the imputation of the righteousness of Christ. The doctrine of justification is developed most fully by the Apostle Paul as the central truth explaining how both Jew and Gentile can be made right before God on the exact same basis—faith in Jesus Christ.

The term *justification* does not mean "to subjectively change into a righteous person" but instead "to declare righteous" upon the act of faith based upon the work of another—the divine substitute Jesus Christ. Justification then involves both the forensic, legal declaration of the righteousness of the believer and the imputation of the righteousness of Christ as the grounds and basis of their acceptance. The fact that it is the righteousness of Christ which is imputed to the believer accounts for the resulting perfection of the relationship between the believer and God: "Therefore, since we have been declared righteous by faith, we have peace with God through our Lord Jesus Christ" (Rom. 5:1 HCSB). Justification is wholly the work of God, obtained solely by faith alone (3:28).

JUSTUS Common Jewish personal name. **1.** Surname of Joseph Barsabbas, one of two men put forward to replace Judas Iscariot among the Twelve (Acts 1:23). **2.** A pious man, probably a Roman citizen, whose home adjoined the synagogue in Corinth (Acts 18:7). Paul left the synagogue and moved into the home of Titius Justus. **3.** Surname of a fellow minister with Paul (Col. 4:11).

JUVENILE DELINQUENCY God expects parents to control their children and children to obey their parents (Eph. 6:1-4). But even in the Bible, this did not always happen. The sons of Eli (1 Sam. 2:22-25), the boys who jeered at Elisha (2 Kings 2:23-24), and the prodigal son (Luke 15:12-13) are all examples of juvenile delinquency. The Mosaic law categorized striking (Exod. 21:15), cursing (Exod. 21:17) and dishonoring (Deut. 27:16) one's parents as acts of familial rebellion and mandated that a son who refused correction should be stoned in public (Deut. 21:18-21).

In spite of the responsibility placed on parents for child rearing (Deut. 6:7), the Bible recognizes that ultimately, children are responsible for their own actions (Ezek. 18:10-13). Jesus used the example of the prodigal son to teach that everyone stands delinquent before God and must come to him for forgiveness (Luke 15:11-32).

KADESH or **KADESH-BARNEA** Place-name meaning "consecrated." The site where the Hebrews stayed for most of the 38 years after leaving Mount Sinai and before entering the promised land. Moses sent out the 12 spies into Canaan from Kadesh-barnea (Num. 13:3-21,26). The Hebrews also attempted their abortive southern penetration into Canaan from there (Num. 13:26; 14:40-45).

KARKOR Place-name meaning "soft, level ground." A mountainous village in the eastern region of Gilead during the period of the judges. Gideon and three hundred Israelite men conducted their second surprise attack on the Midianites at Karkor.

Iron Age fortress in the area of ancient Kadesh-Barnea.

KEDAR Personal name meaning "mighty" or "swarthy" or "black." The second son of Ishmael and a grandson of Abraham (Gen. 25:13; 1 Chron. 1:29). The name occurs later in the Bible presumably as a reference to a tribe that took its name from Kedar. Apparently the descendants of Kedar occupied the area south of Palestine and east of Egypt (Gen. 25:18).

KEDESH Place-name meaning "sacred place" or "sanctuary." **1.** A city in the southern part of Judah (Josh. 15:23), probably the same as Kadesh-barnea. **2.** Canaanite town in eastern Galilee defeated by Joshua (Josh. 12:22). **3.** City in Issachar allotted to the Gershonite Levites (1 Chron. 6:72).

KEILAH Personal and place-name, perhaps meaning "fortress." **1.** Descendant of Caleb (1 Chron. 4:19). **2.** Fortified city in the lowland plain (Shephelah) of the territory of Judah. David rescued the city from a Philistine attack but later withdrew, fearing the populace would hand him over to Saul (1 Sam. 23:1-13).

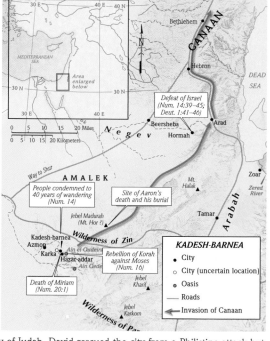

KENITES Nomadic tribe, probably of blacksmiths, whose land, along with that of the Kadmonites and Kenizzites, was promised to Abraham by the Lord (Gen. 15:19). Their home was the southeastern hill country of Judah. Balaam pronounced doom and captivity for them (Num. 24:21-22). Moses' father-in-law Jethro is described as a Kenite (Judg. 1:16). This association suggests a close relationship between the Kenites and Midianites.

KENIZZITE Clan name of uncertain meaning. God promised Abraham that the Israelites would dispossess this group (Gen. 15:19). The Kenizzites lived in the Negev, the southern desert region of Judah, before the conquest of the land by Joshua. The tribe of Judah absorbed some of the Kenizzites while Edom absorbed others. The Kenizzites probably derived their name from Kenaz—a descendant of Esau (Gen. 36:11,15).

KENOSIS View asserting that the eternal Son of God by virtue of the incarnation gave up some or all of the divine attributes which were incommensurate with a fully human existence. This view is primarily based on Phil. 2:5-11, especially verse 7, which states that Christ "emptied Himself." The idea of self-emptying is taken from the Greek verb *kenoo* which means "make empty." Although the kenosis view of Christ sought to do full justice to the real humanity of Jesus, in reality it is a serious assault on the true deity of Jesus Christ. Most evangelicals have resisted the kenotic view and have replaced it with what may be termed a sub-kenotic view stating that what Christ laid aside in the incarnation was not some or all of the divine attributes such as omniscience, omnipotence, and omnipresence. Instead, what Christ "emptied Himself" of was the independent use of these attributes in order to live a normal human life. See *Incarnation*.

KERIOTH Place-name meaning "cities." A fortified city of Moab (Jer. 48:24,41; Amos 2:2, KJV, Kirioth). Judas, the disciple who betrayed Jesus, may have been from Kerioth. Many scholars take the designation "Iscariot" to be derived from the Hebrew meaning "man of Kerioth."

KERYGMA Transliteration of the Greek *kerugma*, "the content of what is preached"; "the message"; closely connected with the act of preaching. Repentance comes, God saves those who believe (1 Cor. 1:21), and believers are strengthened and confirmed (Rom. 16:25) through the message preached (Matt. 12:41; Luke 11:32).

KETURAH Personal name meaning "incense" or "the perfumed one." In Gen. 25:1 Keturah is called Abraham's wife, while 1 Chron. 1:32 calls her a concubine. She was Abraham's second wife, apparently taken after Sarah's death. Keturah bore six sons to Abraham, the most notable being Midian. The list of Keturah's children substantiates the link between the Hebrews and the tribes that inhabited the areas east and southeast of Palestine. As children of a second wife, they were viewed as inferior to Isaac, Sarah's son.

KEY(S) An instrument for gaining access (Judg. 3:25). In the OT the holder of the keys had the power to admit or deny entrance to the house of God (1 Chron. 9:22-27; Isa. 22:22). In late Judaism this key imagery was extended to angelic beings and to God as keepers of the keys of heaven and hell. In the NT keys are used only figuratively as a symbol of access (Luke 11:52) or of authority, particularly the authority of Christ over the final destiny of persons. The risen Christ holds the key of David and controls access to the New Jerusalem (Rev. 3:7). By overcoming death He has the keys to the world of the dead (Rev. 1:18).

KIBROTH-HATTAAVAH Place-name meaning "graves of craving, lust, gluttony." The first stopping place of the Israelites after they left Sinai (Num. 33:16). The Israelites craved meat, which the Lord gave them (Num. 11:31), but because they overindulged, an epidemic broke out and many Israelites died. The dead were buried there, giving the place its name (Num. 11:34; Deut. 9:22; Ps. 78:30-31).

KIBZAIM Place-name meaning "double gathering" or "double heap." One of the Levitical cities in the tribal territory of Ephraim also designated as a city of refuge (Josh. 21:22).

KIDNEYS The kidneys are often associated with the heart as constituting the center of human personality (Pss. 7:9; 26:2; Rev. 2:23). The Hebrews believed the kidneys were the seat of the emotions (Job 19:27; Ps. 73:21; Prov. 23:16). The kidneys were also used figuratively as the source of the knowledge and understanding of the moral life (Ps. 16:7; Jer. 12:2).

KIDRON VALLEY Place-name meaning "turbid, dusky, gloomy." Deep ravine beside Jerusalem separating the temple mount and the city of David on the west from the Mount of Olives on the east. David crossed the brook of Kidron when he fled Jerusalem to escape from Absalom (2 Sam. 15:23). After the Last Supper Jesus went through the Kidron Valley on His way to the Mount of Olives (John 18:1).

KINDNESS In the OT this word is a translation of the Hebrew term *chesed*. Throughout the OT the idea of *chesed* is that of compassion and faithfulness to one's obligations as well as to relatives, friends, and even to slaves (Gen. 21:23; 39:21; 1 Sam. 15:6). Kindness can be in the form of kind deeds done for another person. In the NT kindness is translated from the Greek word *chrestotes*. This word can describe gentleness, goodness, uprightness, generosity, and graciousness. The NT describes kindness as an attribute of God (Titus 3:4; HCSB, love). The Lord's people should possess kindness and not refuse to dispense it to others (Matt. 5:7; 1 Tim 5:9).

KING, CHRIST AS Biblical teaching that Jesus of Nazareth fulfilled the OT promises of a perfect King and reigns over His people and the universe. The OT hope for the future included a vision of a new king like David, called "the anointed one," or "the Messiah" (2 Sam. 7:16; 22:51). When Jesus Christ was born, His birth was announced in these categories. His earthly ministry then amplified these themes (Matt. 4:17; Luke 1:32-33). Similarly, John the Baptist proclaimed the presence of God's kingdom in the coming of Jesus (Matt. 3).

KING, KINGSHIP Male monarch of a major territorial unit; especially one whose position is hereditary and who rules for life. From the time of Joshua to the time of Saul, the judges led Israel. Their leadership was temporary and local in nature, their main function being to lead those parts of

Israel threatened by some outside force until the threat was gone. As Israel became more settled in Canaan, the people began to feel a need for a hereditary and totalitarian leadership. The first national leader was King Saul.

Israel, unlike most other nations, placed limitations on the power of its kings (1 Sam. 8:10-18). It was normal for the elders of the nation to make a covenant with the king (2 Sam. 5:3; 2 Kings 11:17) in which the rights and duties of the king were recorded and deposited in the sanctuary—possibly at the time of the anointment ceremony (1 Sam. 10:25). It was clearly understood that the king was not exempt from observing civil laws (1 Kings 21:4), nor was the king the absolute lord of life and death. The prophetic denunciation of certain kings demonstrates that they were subject to the law (2 Sam. 12:1-15; 1 Kings 21:17-24; cp. Deut. 17:14-20). Israel's faith included the confession that God was its ultimate King. The earthly king derived his authority from God as the Lord's anointed (1 Sam. 16:6; 2 Sam. 1:14).

KINGDOM OF GOD Concept of God's kingly or sovereign rule, encompassing both the realm over which rule is exerted (Matt. 24:7) and the exercise of authority to reign (Rev. 17:12,17-18). God rules sovereignly over all His works as King. He desires His rule to be acknowledged in a bond or relationship of love, loyalty, spirit, and trust. The fullest revelation of God's divine rule is in the person of Jesus Christ. His birth was heralded as the birth of a king (Luke 1:32-33). The crucifixion was perceived as the death of a king (Mark 15:26-32). Jesus preached that God's kingdom was at hand (Matt. 11:12). His miracles, preaching, forgiving sins, and resurrection are an inbreaking of God's sovereign rule in this dark, evil age.

KINGS, BOOKS OF Covering the time frame between the final days of King David and the end of the nation of Judah, the books of 1 and 2 Kings are a vital part of the history of Israel. The title of these books is indicative of their contents: the kings and the kingdoms of Israel and Judah. The historical beginning point for the narrative of 1 Kings is approximately 970 BC. The final event in 2 Kings—Evil-Merodach's release of King Jehoiachin from prison—occurs in approximately 560 BC. Thus, the narrative of 1 and 2 Kings spans 410 years of history. These 410 years witness monumental changes within the nation of Israel, including the division of the kingdom in 930 BC, the height of the monarchy under Solomon (970–930 BC), and the exiles of both Israel and Judah (722 BC and 587/586 BC).

The author of 1 and 2 Kings gave a qualitative judgment regarding how well each king followed God's covenant. All of the kings of the northern kingdom of Israel were wicked kings, while the kings of Judah continued the dynasty of King David and were generally more obedient to the commands of the Lord. While the history of God's people was fraught with failure, God remained faithful to His promise. Even though both nations went into exile, God remembered His covenant with Abraham, and He preserved His people. God would bring His ultimate redemption to pass in the future in the person of His Son, Jesus Christ.

KING'S GARDEN Place in Jerusalem adjacent to and probably irrigated by the overflow of the pool of Shelah (Siloam) (Neh. 3:15).

KING'S HIGHWAY Major transportation route east of the Jordan River. Literally "the way of the king," this highway has been in continuous use for over 3,000 years. It runs from Damascus to the Gulf of Aqabah and is the main caravan route for the Transjordan. It is mentioned in Num. 20:17 and 21:22 as the route Moses and the Israelites would take through Edom and the land of Sihon.

KING'S POOL Probably the same as the Pool of Shelah, a reservoir in the king's garden in Jerusalem (Neh. 2:14). It was rebuilt by Shallum, ruler of the district of Mizpah (Neh. 3:15).

"INTERNATIONAL ROUTES"
- City
— International Coastal Highway
— King's Highway
— Sea routes
— Other routes

KINSMAN This term usually refers to a blood relative. Certain obligations were laid on the kinsman. In the case of an untimely death of a husband without a son, the law of levirate marriage specified that the husband's brother was obligated to marry his widow to raise up a male descendant for his deceased brother and thus perpetuate the family name and inheritance. The living brother was the dead brother's *go'el*—his redeemer (Gen. 38:8; Deut. 25:5-10; Ruth 3:9-12).

The kinsman was also the blood avenger. A wrong done to a single member of the family was considered a crime against the entire tribe or clan. The clan had an obligation, therefore, to punish the wrongdoer. In the case of a murder committed, the kinsman should seek vengeance. The kinsman was also responsible to redeem the estate that his nearest relative might have sold because of poverty (Lev. 25:25; Ruth 4:4). It was the kinsman's responsibility also to ransom a kinsman who had sold himself into slavery (Lev. 25:47-48).

KIRIATH Place-name meaning "city" in tribal territory of Benjamin (Josh. 18:28 NASB, NIV; KJV, Kirjath). The same as Kiriath-jearim (Josh. 18:28 NRSV, REB, TEV).

KIRIATHAIM Place-name meaning "double city" or "two cities." **1.** Levitical city and city of refuge in the tribal territory of Naphtali (1 Chron. 6:76; KJV, Kirjathaim). **2.** City taken from the Emim by Chedorlaomer (Gen. 14:5, Shaveh-kiriathaim means "the plain of Kiriathaim"). Later the Israelites took it from the Amorites and assigned it to the tribe of Reuben (Num. 32:37; Josh. 13:19).

KIRIATH-ARBA Place-name meaning "city of Arba" or "city of four." The ancient name for the city of Hebron, the chief city in the hill country of Judah (Josh. 15:54). It was both a Levitical city (Josh. 21:11) and a city of refuge (Josh. 20:7). Caleb captured the city for Israel (Josh. 15:13-14).

KIRIATH-JEARIM Place-name meaning "city of forests." After the Philistines returned the ark of the covenant to the Israelites, it was kept at Kiriath-jearim for a time (1 Sam. 6:21-7:2). David attempted to move the ark to Jerusalem from there, but because he did so improperly, God struck Uzzah dead (2 Sam. 6:1-8).

KISHON Place-name meaning "curving, winding." A small river that flows through the Valley of Jezreel. It was at the Kishon that Deborah and Barak defeated the Canaanite Sisera when his chariots became mired in the river marshes (Judg. 4:7,13; 5:21). Later the river was the place where Elijah brought the prophets of Baal to be executed following God's display and victory on Mount Carmel (1 Kings 18:40).

KISS The touching of the lips to another person's lips, cheeks, shoulders, hands, or feet as a gesture of friendship, acceptance, respect, and reverence. The location of the kiss carried different meanings as Jesus made clear in the episode of the woman kissing his feet (Luke 7:36-50). With the exception of three occurrences (Prov. 7:13; Song 1:2; 8:1), the term is used without any erotic overtones. The holy kiss was widely practiced among the early Christians as a manner of greeting, a sign of acceptance, and an impartation of blessing. This custom could well have been used to express the unity of the Christian fellowship. The kiss still survives in the Near Eastern culture as a sign of love, respect, and reverence.

KITE Bird of prey, best described as a scavenger of the hawk family. It was medium-sized with red coloring (Deut. 14:13; Isa. 34:15). This bird was considered unclean and not for human consumption.

Limassol, a modern city on the southern coast of Cyprus. Kittim or Chittim was the tribal name of Cyprus.

KITTIM Tribal name for the island of Cyprus, sometimes spelled Chittim. Genesis 10:4 traces the roots of the people of Kittim to Noah's son Japheth. Jeremiah and Ezekiel both mention it in their prophecies (Jer. 2:10; Ezek. 27:6; cp. Isa. 23:1,12).

KNEAD, KNEADING BOWL Process of making bread dough by mixing flour, water, and oil along with a piece of the previous day's dough with the hands in a kneading bowl or trough. The mixture was allowed to stand in the bowl to rise and ferment (Exod. 12:34).

KNEEL Common posture when requesting a blessing from a person believed able to bestow the blessing. The Hebrew word for *kneel* comes from the same root as the word for *bless*. Kneeling is also considered a sign of reverence, obedience, or respect. Kneeling was the posture of prayer (Dan. 6:10; Eph. 3:14), acknowledging a superior (Mark 1:40), or worship of God (1 Kings 8:54), Jesus (Phil. 2:10), or idols (1 Kings 19:18).

KNIFE Small instrument made of flint, copper, bronze, or iron used mainly for domestic purposes. Knives were used most commonly for killing and skinning animals and for killing sacrificial animals (1 Sam. 9:24).

KNOB Ornamental detail on the seven-branched lampstand in the tabernacle (Exod. 25:31-36). Some suggest that the knob was an imitation of the almond. The word may also refer to the capital of a column (Zeph. 2:14).

Large, wide-bladed knife from the Roman era.

KNOP An element of the candles that were part of the lampstand in the tabernacle (Exod. 25:31-36). It may have resembled the fruit of the almond.

KNOWLEDGE God knows all things (Job 21:22; Ps. 139:1-18); His understanding is beyond measure (Ps. 147:5). He knows the thoughts of our minds and the secrets of our hearts (Pss. 44:21; 94:11). He knows past events (Gen. 30:22), present happenings (Job 31:4), and future events (Zech. 13:1; Luke 1:33). The Bible also speaks often about human knowledge. Knowledge of God is the greatest knowledge (Prov. 9:10) and is the chief duty of mankind (Hos. 6:6). In the OT the Israelites know God through what He does for His people (Deut. 4:32-39; Hos. 2:19-20). In the NT one knows God through knowledge of Jesus Christ (John 8:19; Col. 2:2-3). The Apostle Paul closely connected knowledge to faith. Knowledge gives direction, conviction, and assurance to faith (2 Cor. 4:14).

KOHATH Personal name of unknown meaning. The second son of Levi (Gen. 46:11) and father of Amram, Izhar, Hebron, and Uzziel (Exod. 6:18), who became the heads of the Kohathite branch of the Levitical priesthood.

KOHATHITES Descendants of Kohath, the son of Levi (Exod. 6:16). Since Kohath was the grandfather of Aaron, Moses, and Miriam (Exod. 6:20; Num. 26:59), the Kohathites were considered the most important of the three major Levitical families: Kohathites, Gershonites, and Merarites. The Kohathites, along with the Gershonites and Merarites, were placed around the tabernacle and were charged with caring for and moving it. David appointed 120 Kohathites to bring the ark to Jerusalem (1 Chron. 15:5).

KOHELETH English transliteration of the Hebrew title of Ecclesiastes (also spelled Qoheleth). Koheleth is a Hebrew word that is translated as preacher (KJV, RSV, NASB), teacher (NIV, NRSV), speaker (REB), or philosopher (TEV) in Eccles. 1:1.

KOPH Nineteenth letter of Hebrew alphabet. Used as a heading for Ps. 119:145-152. Each verse in this section begins with the letter Koph (KJV), Qoph (NASB, NIV), or Qof (HCSB).

KOR A dry measure equal to a homer or to about 6.3 imperial bushels, though estimates vary greatly. It apparently represented the load a donkey could carry.

KORAH Personal name meaning "bald." **1.** Son of Esau (Gen. 36:5,14) who became chief of a clan of Edom (Gen. 36:18). **2.** Grandson of Esau, son of Eliphaz, and chief of a clan of Edom (1 Chron. 1:36). **3.** Leader of rebellion against Moses and Aaron while Israel was camped in the wilderness of Paran (Num. 16). Korah, Dathan, and Abiram led a confederacy of 250 princes of the people against Aaron's claim to the priesthood and Moses' claim to authority in general. The rebels contended that the entire congregation was sanctified and therefore qualified to perform priestly functions. As punishment for their insubordination, God caused the earth to open and swallow the leaders and their property. A fire from the Lord consumed the 250 followers. **4.** Levite descended from Izhar, of the family of Kohath (Exod. 6:21), probably to be identified with 3. above. The sons of Korah and Asaph were the two most prominent groups of temple singers (cp. 2 Chron. 20:19). Many of the psalms with the heading "A Psalm of the Sons of Korah" may have been taken from their hymnbook (Pss. 42; 44-49; 84-85; 87-88). **5.** Son of Hebron in the lineage of Caleb (1 Chron. 2:43). **6.** Possibly a town in Judah near Hebron. The five Korahites who joined David at Ziklag may have been persons from this town (1 Chron. 12:6).

The definitive line of a wall at Lachish running from the south going northeast up to the high place.

LABAN Personal name meaning "white." Rebekah's brother (Gen. 24:29) and father of Leah and Rachel (Gen. 29:16). Laban agreed to give his daughter, Rachel, as payment for Jacob's seven years of labor. But Laban deceived Jacob, making him marry the older daughter, Leah. After Jacob worked an additional seven years, Laban allowed him to marry Rachel (Gen. 29:15-30).

LACE Ornamental braid used as a trim. Blue or purple cords were used to fasten the high priest's breastpiece to the ephod (Exod. 39:21) and the golden plate to his turban (Exod. 28:37).

LACHISH An important OT city located in the Shephelah ("lowlands") southwest of Jerusalem. The Israelites under Joshua's command killed the king of Lachish and conquered his city (Josh. 10:5,23,32-33). Later, Lachish was apportioned to the tribe of Judah (Josh. 15:39). The "Lachish Letters"—a group of messages in ancient Hebrew inscribed with ink on pottery shards dating to around 590 BC—are among the most significant finds from Lachish. They provide important linguistic and historical information about this period.

LAISH Personal and place-name meaning "strong" or "lion." **1.** Father of Paltiel (Phalti in KJV) and father-in-law of Michal, King Saul's daughter (1 Sam. 19:11-12; 25:44). **2.** Originally a Canaanite city in northern Palestine known for its quiet, isolated lifestyle (Judg. 18:7). It was spied out by the Danites as a place to live after the Philistines forced them from the coastal region. The Danites renamed the city and area Dan. **3.** Town apparently in tribal territory of Benjamin mentioned by Isaiah (Isa. 10:30).

LAMB OF GOD Title bestowed on Jesus by John the Baptist (John 1:29). The expression comes from the important place that the "lamb" occupied in the sacrifices of the Jewish people. A lamb was used for sacrifice during the annual Passover (Exod. 12:1-36) as well as in the daily sacrifices of Israel (Lev. 14:12-21). Christ fulfilled the promise made by the Prophet Isaiah (see Isa. 53) that God would provide a sacrifice who would bear the curse of sin and provide salvation for the world.

LAME, LAMENESS Physical condition in which walking is difficult or impossible. A proverb excluding the blind and lame from "the house" (that is, the temple) is traced to the assault on Jerusalem (2 Sam. 5:8). In the NT the healing of the lame was an important part of Jesus' messianic work (Matt. 15:29-31). By healing the lame in the temple, Jesus restored these excluded ones to full participation in the worshipping community (Matt. 21:14).

LAMECH Personal name meaning "powerful." The son of Methuselah and father of Noah (Gen. 4:18; 5:25,29). His two sons are credited with the rise of the nomadic way of life, music, and metalworking.

LAMED Twelfth letter of the Hebrew alphabet used as a heading for Ps. 119:89-96. Each verse in this section of the psalm begins with the letter *lamed*.

LAMENTATIONS, BOOK OF An OT book consisting of poetic laments over the destruction of Jerusalem and the temple in 587 BC (Lam. 2:7) and over the pitiable condition of the people of Judah that resulted (Lam. 2:11). The misery after the destruction is all the more deplorable compared to the glory beforehand (Lam. 1:1). The author calls on the people to recognize that because of their sin God is just in what He has done (Lam. 1:5), so the people should turn to Him, repent, and appeal for mercy (Lam. 2:18). It was probably written by the Prophet Jeremiah. The fall of Jerusalem is recorded in 2 Kings 25 and Jer. 52. Lamentations expresses the deep emotions that issued from this tragedy.

LAMPS, LIGHTING, LAMPSTAND Archaeologists have discovered numerous examples of these lighting implements used in ancient times. These lamps were of the open-bowl design with a pinched spout to support the wick. Lamps burned olive oil almost exclusively (Exod. 25:6). A golden lampstand with three branches extending from either side of the central tier was placed in the tabernacle (Exod. 25:31-40). Each branch may have had a seven-spouted lamp (Zech. 4:2). This seven-branched candelabrum (menorah), supporting seven lamps, became symbolic of the nation of Israel.

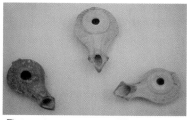

First-century B.C pottery oil lamps.

LANCE, LANCET Weapon consisting of a long shaft with a metal head; javelin; spear (Judg. 5:8 NASB; 1 Kings 18:28 RSV; Jer. 50:42 KJV).

LANDMARK Pillar or heap of stones serving as a boundary marker (Gen. 31:51-52). Moving the landmark meant changing the traditional land allotments (Josh. 13–19) and cheating a poor landowner of what little land he owned.

LANGUAGES OF THE BIBLE The OT was first written in Hebrew with the exceptions of much of Ezra 4–7 and Daniel 2:4b–7:28, which appear in Aramaic. The NT was written in Greek, though Jesus and the early believers may have spoken Aramaic.

Hebrew is a Semitic language related to Phoenician and the dialects of ancient Canaan. Semitic languages have the ability to convey abundant meaning through few words. Importance rests on the verb, which generally comes first in the sentence because action is the most significant element. Similarly, modifiers (such as adjectives) follow nouns, lending greater weight to the nouns.

Aramaic is similar to Hebrew and shares a considerable vocabulary with it. It began as the language of Syria and was gradually adopted as the language of international communication. After about 600 BC it replaced Hebrew as the spoken language of Palestine. Hebrew then continued as the religious language of the Jews, but the Aramaic alphabet was borrowed for writing it.

Greek belongs to the Indo-European language group. It spread throughout the Mediterranean world after about 335 BC with the conquests of Alexander the Great. The NT is written in a dialect called *koine* (meaning "common") which was the dialect of the common person. New Testament Greek is heavily infused with Semitic thought modes, and many Aramaic words are rendered with Greek letters (e.g., *talitha koum*, Mark 5:41; *ephphatha*, Mark 7:34; *Eloi, Eloi, lema sabachthani*, Mark 15:34; *maranatha*, 1 Cor. 16:22). So also are such Latin words as *kenturion* (centurion) and *denarion* (denarius). Greek's accurateness of expression and widespread usage made it the ideal tongue for the early communication of the gospel.

LAODICEA City in southwest Asia Minor on an ancient highway running from Ephesus to Syria ten miles west of Colossae and six miles south of Hierapolis. Christian communities existed in all three cities (Col. 2:1; 4:13-16). Laodicea was well known in the ancient world for its textile industry, the production of black wool, and its banking industry. As one of the seven churches of Asia minor, the church at Laodicea was criticized for its spiritual lethargy, or lukewarmness (Rev. 3:16-16).

An unexcavated Roman theater, smaller of the two theaters at ancient Laodicea.

LAPWING Bird with a short bill and a crest of feathers on its head. The lapwing is known for its irregular flapping flight and shrill cry. KJV included the lapwing among the unclean birds (Deut. 14:18). Modern translations generally identify this bird as the hoopoe.

LASCIVIOUSNESS KJV term for an unbridled expression of sexual urges (2 Cor. 12:21; Gal. 5:19). RSV translates the underlying Greek as "licentiousness"; NASB, "sensuality." Other translations use a variety of terms: "debauchery," "indecency," "lewdness."

LASHARON Place-name meaning "belonging to Sharon." One of the towns whose king was killed by Joshua during his conquest of Canaan (Josh. 12:18).

LAST SUPPER The last meal Christ shared with His disciples before the crucifixion (Mark 14:12-

31). The event marked the institution of the Lord's Supper, which is to be celebrated until Christ returns. The meal focuses on Jesus' impending death and anticipates His resurrection. The bread served to His disciples by Jesus is a symbol of His body to be broken for His people. The wine is a symbol of His blood of the covenant to be poured out on the cross for the forgiveness of sins.

LATCHET KJV term for a leather thong or strap that fastened sandals. Untying sandals was a slave's task that could not be required of a disciple. John the Baptist thus claimed for himself a position lower than that of a slave before Jesus (John 1:27).

LATRINE Receptacle, generally a pit, used as a toilet (2 Kings 10:27; KJV, draught house). Jehu demonstrated his utter contempt for Baal by ordering that his temple be destroyed and converted into a latrine.

LAUGH To express joy or scorn with a chuckle or explosive sound. Laughter is central to the account of the birth of Isaac. Both Abraham (Gen. 17:17) and Sarah (Gen. 18:12) laughed in contempt and disbelief at God's promise that Sarah would bear a son. The name Isaac (from the Hebrew word for laughter) served as a joyful reminder that the last laugh was on those slow to believe (Gen. 21:3,6).

The public latrine of ancient Ephesus.

LAVER Large basin or bowl used in purification rites. The priests used the laver for washing their hands and feet before priestly service (Exod. 40:30-31). Levites also used water from this laver to purify themselves (Num. 8:7). Solomon's temple featured a large laver, the molten sea (1 Chron. 4:2-5), and 10 smaller lavers (1 Kings 7:38-39).

LAW, TEN COMMANDMENTS, TORAH Few expressions in the Bible are more significant yet more misunderstood than "law." Biblical interpreters apply the word to specific commandments, customs, legal judgments, collections of regulations/ordinances, the book of Deuteronomy (which means "second law"), the entire complex of regulations revealed at Sinai, the Pentateuch (in contrast to the Prophets), and the OT as a whole as opposed to the NT.

The contrast between the OT, in which God's people were under the law, as opposed to the NT, where God's people are under grace, seems to determine many peoples' understanding of Scripture. Appeal is sometimes made to John 1:17, "For the law was given through Moses; grace and truth came through Jesus Christ" (HCSB). However, a closer look at the biblical evidence raises questions about the common perception of the old covenant as a works-oriented system.

It is important to remember that God and Moses perceived obedience to the laws, not as a way of or precondition to salvation, but as the grateful response of those who had already been saved. God did not reveal the law to the Israelites in Egypt and then tell them that as soon as they had measured up to this standard He would rescue them. On the contrary, by grace alone, through faith they crossed the Red Sea to freedom. All that was required was belief in God's promise that He would hold up the walls of water on either side and see them safely through to the other shore.

In the OT obedience to the law was an expression of covenant relationship. Israel's primary commitment was not to a code of laws but to the God who graciously called Israel to Himself. They were to obey "His voice." In fact, He did not reveal His will to the people until He heard their declaration of complete and unconditional servitude to Him as covenant lord (Exod. 19:8).

God's revelation of the law to Israel was a supreme act of grace and a unique sign of privilege (Deut. 4:6-8). In contrast to the nations who worshiped gods of wood and stone who never spoke (4:28; Ps. 115:4-8), Israel's God had spoken, clearly revealing to His people what He deemed an acceptable response to Him. Accordingly, for the genuinely faithful in Israel, obedience to the law was not a burden but a delight because of their deep gratitude for God's saving grace and covenant relationship (Ps. 24:3-6).

The laws were perceived as comprehensible and achievable (Deut. 30:11-20) by those whose hearts were right with God. God did not impose upon His people an impossibly high standard but revealed to them in great detail a system of behavior that was righteous and gracious (Deut. 4:6-8). At the same time there is a recognition of human depravity and the need for divine enablement for covenant faithfulness. Jeremiah anticipated a future new covenant when all Israel will love God and demonstrate with their lives that His law or *tora* has been written on their hearts (Jer. 31:31-34). God had a realistic view of His people. Recognizing their propensity to sin, within the law He graciously provided a way of forgiveness and communion through the sacrificial and ceremonial ritual.

Of course, these facts about the law did not prevent the Israelites from perverting obedience to the law into a condition for blessing and a condition for salvation. The prophets constantly railed against their people for substituting external rituals prescribed by the law for true piety, which is demonstrated first in moral obedience (Isa. 1:10-17; Hos. 6:6; Mic. 6:6-8). In every age Israelites misused the law, thinking that performance of rituals obligated God to receive them favorably. They imagined that God looked upon their hearts through the lenses of their sacrifices. They persisted in violating the moral laws even while they continued to observe the ceremonial regulations (Isa. 1; Jer. 7). In the end, Moses' predictions of disaster in Deut. 4 and 29–30 proved true in the exile of Judah in 586 BC.

Like Moses and the psalmists, the NT views God's original revelation of the law to Israel as a climactic moment of grace. Accordingly, when Jesus and Paul appear to be critical of the law, we should ask whether their struggle was with the law itself or with misuse of the law. From the beginning Israelites had perverted the law by treating the law as a precondition of entrance into the kingdom of God rather than as a response to His grace. They also misrepresented the law by adhering to the law's legal requirements as a matter of duty rather than a grateful expression of heartfelt covenant love for God and one's neighbor. In addition, they treated physical descent from Abraham and membership in the Jewish nation as a guarantee of divine favor, rather than spiritual descent by faith as the precondition to blessing. It is to these abuses that many of the critical words concerning the law are addressed in the NT.

With Christ's first coming, many aspects of the law are brought to complete fruition. As the eschatological fulfillment of the old covenant, in His person Jesus brings to an end the ceremonial sacrifices and festivals and transforms old covenant customs into new covenant realities. Baptism, the sign of the covenant made with the church, appears to replace circumcision, the sign of the covenant made with physical Israel. The Lord's Supper replaces the Passover meal (Luke 22:13-20) and anticipates the eschatological covenant meal (Rev. 19:6-10). But other aspects of the law were to remain in force until Christ's return. When we read the OT law, we should always be open to both continuities and discontinuities with NT demands.

As God's Son who fulfills the law and as the Lord of the covenant originally made with Israel at Sinai, Jesus has the perfect perspective on the law and the authority to declare its intention. He declared that God's demands cannot be reduced to a list of rules, but involve the commitment of one's whole being to Him and a genuine concern for the well-being of others.

The writings of Paul are the source of most of the confusion on the NT's view of the law. He spoke of the law as a way of death, in contrast to the Spirit that gives life (Rom. 7:10), and the law as a curse from which Christ has redeemed us (Gal. 3:13). He contrasted the letter (of the old covenant), which kills, with the Spirit (of the new covenant), that delivers life (2 Cor. 3:6). Such statements are difficult to reconcile with Moses' and the psalmists' celebration of the law as the supreme gift of grace and the way of life for God's people. But when we understand Paul correctly, we will discover his perspective to be in line with that of Moses.

Paul agrees with Moses in affirming the law, declaring that without it we would not know what sin is (Rom. 7:7), evaluating it as holy, just, and good (1 Tim. 1:8), and rooting his understanding of the ethical implications of the gospel firmly in the Torah (2 Cor. 6:14-18). Furthermore, Paul, like Jesus, captures the spirit of the OT law by reducing its demands to love for God and one's neighbor (Gal. 5:13).

Paul declared that the problem was not with the law, but with himself, because the law of sin inside him constantly waged war against the law of God. The glorious news of the gospel is that God through Christ lifts the curse of sin, which the law says we deserve. But this does not mean that the law has been suspended as a fundamental statement of God's moral will. The law served as a reflection of God's very nature. Since His nature does not change, neither does His moral will. Accordingly, those who fulfill the "Law of Christ," and those who love God with all their hearts and their neighbors as themselves will fulfill the essence of the law.

LAWLESS, LAWLESSNESS Terms that describe people not restrained or controlled by law, especially God's law. As rebellion against God, sin is lawlessness (1 John 3:4). Those responsible for Christ's death are characterized as lawless (Acts 2:23), as are Gentiles in their idolatry (1 Pet. 4:3). The leader of the eschatological (end-time) rebellion is called the man of lawlessness (2 Thess. 2:3). The lawless one is already at work but is presently restrained (2 Thess. 2:6-7). The lawless one will be revealed before the return of Christ, who will destroy him with His breath (2 Thess. 2:8).

LAWYER An interpreter of the Mosaic law. Characterization of the lawyers is especially harsh in Luke's Gospel: they rejected God's purpose by refusing John's baptism (Luke 7:30); they burdened others without offering any relief (Luke 11:45-46); and they refused God's offer of salvation and hindered others from accepting it (Luke 11:52-53).

LAYING ON OF HANDS Symbolic ceremonial act used to invoke a divine blessing or establish a connection for the purpose of sacrifice, ordination, or to impart spiritual gifts. In the OT this ceremony was associated with priestly sacrifices (Lev. 16:21). Moses laid his hands on Joshua to identify him as Moses' successor and to symbolize that he was imparting his authority to Joshua (Num 27:18-23). In the NT laying on of hands also signified the appointment of persons to specific tasks such as the ordination of the "seven" in Acts 6:6. It was used in the commissioning of Barnabas and Saul for their mission (Acts 13:3). First Timothy 4:14 speaks of Timothy receiving a spiritual gift from elders who laid their hands on him. Paul mentions the spiritual gift that Timothy received "through the laying on of my hands" (2 Tim. 1:6). These references show that Timothy received authority, the spirit of power, love, and self-discipline, through the laying on of hands (2 Tim. 1:7).

LAZARUS Personal name meaning "one whom God helps." **1.** One of the principal characters in a parable Jesus told to warn the selfish rich that justice will eventually prevail (Luke 16:19-31). **2.** Lazarus of Bethany, a personal friend of Jesus and the brother of Mary and Martha (John 11:1-3). Jesus raised Lazarus from the dead after he had been in the tomb for four days to show the glory of God. Lazarus was at the Passover celebration in Bethany six days later. He was targeted for murder by the chief priests because of his notoriety (John 12:9-11).

LEAH Personal name meaning "wild cow" or "gazelle." Older daughter of Laban (Gen. 29:16) and Jacob's first wife. Jacob had asked for the younger Rachel's hand but was tricked by her father Laban into marrying Leah. Leah bore six sons to Jacob (Reuben, Simeon, Levi, Judah, Issachar, Zebulun) (Gen 29:31-35) and a daughter (Dinah). Her handmaid, Zilpah, bore two sons to Jacob (Gad, Asher) (Gen 30:9-13).

LEANNOTH Transliteration of Hebrew word in title of Ps. 88 possibly meaning "to sing" or "for the poor," "for the sick." It may be part of the title of a tune to which the psalm was sung. Its meaning is uncertain.

The traditional site of the tomb of Lazarus in Bethany.

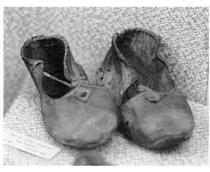

A child's leather shoes from Egypt (Roman era).

LEATHER Animal skins tanned and used for clothing. Elijah the prophet was recognized by his hairy garment and leather belt or girdle (2 Kings 1:8). The similar dress of John the Baptist marked him as a prophet (Matt. 3:4; Mark 1:6).

LEAVEN Small portion of fermented dough used to ferment other dough and often symbolizing a corruptive influence. The common bread of OT times was made with leaven. Unleavened bread was also prepared in times of haste (1 Sam. 28:24) and was required for the Feast of Unleavened Bread that was celebrated in conjunction with the Passover festival (Lev. 23:4-8). This unleavened bread reminded the Israelites of their hasty departure from Egypt and warned them against corruptive influences (Exod. 12:14-20). In the NT leaven is a symbol of any evil influence. Jesus warned His disciples against the leaven of the Pharisees, or their teaching and hypocrisy (Luke 12:1).

LEBANON Place-name meaning "white" or perhaps "white mountain." A small country at the eastern end of the Mediterranean Sea and the western end of Asia. Lebanon is often mentioned in the OT as the northern boundary of Palestine (Josh. 1:4), dividing it from Phoenicia and Syria. It was a proverbially lush land, noted for its magnificent forests (Isa. 60:13), especially the "cedars of Lebanon" (Isa. 2:13). These cedars, as well as other woods of Lebanon, were used in great abundance in the construction of David's palace and Solomon's temple and palace buildings (1 Kings 7:2).

LEEKS An Egyptian food eaten by the Hebrews during their captivity. After a steady diet of manna in the wilderness, they were ready to return to slavery and the foods of servitude (Num. 11:5).

LEES Solid matter that settles out of wine during the fermentation process. In Palestine wine was allowed to remain on the lees to increase its strength and flavor. Such wine "on the lees" was preferred to the newly fermented product. To drink dregs or lees is to endure the bitterness of judgment or punishment (Ps. 75:8).

LEGION In the NT a term referring to a collection of demons (Luke 8:30) and the host of angels (Matt. 26:53). Behind this usage was a Roman military term. Legions were made up of the best soldiers in the army. At different times in Rome's history, the legion numbered between 4,500 and 6,000 soldiers.

LEHI Place-name meaning "chin" or "jawbone." City where Samson killed 1,000 Philistines with the jawbone of a donkey and where God provided water from the jawbone (Judg. 15).

LEISURE TIME The Bible recognizes the need for regularly scheduled breaks from work. The weekly Sabbath (Exod. 20:8-11) and several yearly festivals (Deut. 16:1-17) were intended to focus on Israel's spiritual needs but also provided breaks from physical labor. The Bible cautions against the misuse of leisure time, which leads to idleness (Prov. 19:15), excessive partying (Isa. 5:11-12), or troublemaking (Prov. 6:10-15).

LEMUEL Personal name meaning "devoted to God." A king who received words of wisdom from his mother concerning wine, women, and the legal rights of the weak and poor (Prov. 31:1-9).

LEOPARD Large cat with yellow fur containing black spots. Known for its gracefulness and speed, it was common in Palestine in OT times, especially in the forests of Lebanon. Two sites in the OT suggest habitats of leopards—Beth-nimrah ("leopards' house," Num. 32:36) and "waters of Nimrim" ("waters of leopards," Jer. 48:34). The lurking, noiseless movement of the leopard symbolizes God's wrath (Hos. 13:7).

LEPROSY Generic term applied to a variety of skin disorders, ranging from psoriasis to true leprosy. Its symptoms ranged from white patches on the skin to running sores and even the loss of fingers and toes. For the Hebrews leprosy was a dreaded malady that rendered its victims ceremonially unclean, or unfit to worship God (Lev. 13:3). Anyone who came in contact with a leper was also considered unclean. Therefore, lepers were isolated from the rest of the community. Even houses and clothing could have "leprosy" and, thus, be unclean (Lev. 14:33-57). Jesus did not consider this distinction between clean and unclean valid. He touched and healed lepers (Mark 1:40-45) and even commanded His disciples to do so (Matt. 10:8). See *Diseases*.

LEVI Personal name meaning "a joining." **1.** Third son of Jacob and Leah (Gen. 29:34) and original ancestor of Israel's priests. He is characterized in Scripture as savage and merciless, avenging the rape of his sister, Dinah, by annihilating the male population of an entire city (Gen. 34:25-31). Later, Jacob spoke harshly of Levi rather than blessing him (Gen. 49:5-7). After the people of Israel sinned in the wilderness by making the molten calf, Moses commanded the people of Levi to slaughter those who had participated in the debacle (Exod. 32:28). Levi's descendants became a tribe of priests. **2.** Name of two of Jesus' ancestors (Luke 3:24,29). **3.** A tax collector in Capernaum who became a follower of Jesus (Mark 2:14); another name for Matthew.

LEVIATHAN Name of an ancient sea creature that means "coiled one." Isa. 27:1 refers to leviathan as "the dragon that is in the sea." The psalmist in 74:14 mentions a many-headed leviathan among the supernatural enemies of God dwelling in the sea. Job 3:8; 41:1-9 present the sea creature as a formidable foe that should not be aroused. Yet, leviathan was created by God and subject to Him (Ps. 104:24-30).

LEVIRATE LAW, LEVIRATE MARRIAGE Legal provision requiring a dead man's brother (levirate) to marry his childless widow and father a son who would carry on the family name (Deut. 25:5-10). The practice is an important element in the story of Ruth (Ruth 4:1-11).

LEVITES Assistants to the priests in Israel's sacrificial system. Originally, Israel's priests and temple personnel were to be drawn from the firstborn of every family in Israel (Exod. 13:11-15). Later God chose the tribe of Levi to carry out this responsibility for Israel (Num. 3:11-13). The Levites were not given a tribal inheritance in the promised land, since God was considered their inheritance. They were placed in 48 Levitical cities throughout the land (Num. 18:20; 35:1-8). The tithe of the rest of the nation was used to provide for their material needs (Num. 18:24-32).

During the wilderness journey, the Levites were in charge of taking down the tabernacle, transporting it, setting it up, and conducting worship at the tent where God dwelt (Num. 1:47-54; 3:14-39). In some passages (Deut. 17:9,18; 24:8) the terms "priest" and "Levite" (or Levitical priests) seem identical, but in Exod. 28 and Lev. 8–10 it is clear that only the family of Aaron fulfilled the priestly duties of offering sacrifices in the tabernacle. Because there appears to be a different way of handling the relationship between the priests and the Levites in these texts, interpreters differ in the way they understand the Levites. Although it is possible that the role of the Levites changed or that the distinction between the priests and Levites was not maintained in each period with equal strictness, the interpretation that maintains a general distinction between the priests and Levites seems to fit most texts.

The Levites assisted the priests in their responsibilities (Num. 16:9) by preparing grain offerings and the showbread, by purifying all the holy instruments used in the temple, by singing praises to the Lord at morning and evening offerings, by assisting the priests with burnt offerings on Sabbaths and feast days, and by taking care of the temple precinct and the chambers of the priests (1 Chron. 6:31-48; 2 Chron. 29:12-19). See *Levitical Cities*.

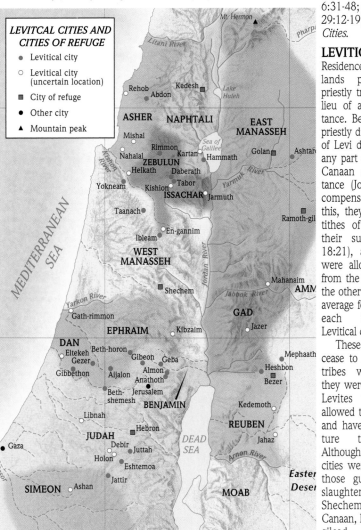

LEVITICAL CITIES

Residence and pasture-lands provided the priestly tribe of Levi in lieu of a tribal inheritance. Because of their priestly duties, the tribe of Levi did not receive any part of the land of Canaan as an inheritance (Josh. 18:7). To compensate them for this, they received the tithes of Israelites for their support (Num. 18:21), and 48 cities were allotted to them from the inheritance of the other tribes. On the average four cities from each tribe were Levitical cities.

These cities did not cease to belong to the tribes within which they were located. The Levites were simply allowed to live in them and have fields to pasture their herds. Although 6 of the 48 cities were asylums for those guilty of manslaughter (Kedesh, Shechem, Hebron in Canaan, Bezer, Ramoth-gilead, and Golan), Levitical cities and cities of refuge were not synonymous. The privilege of asylum for persons who had committed manslaughter was not extended to all 48 Levitical cities. Living among the tribes in these cities meant the Levites could better infiltrate each of the tribes to instruct them in God's covenant. Since the Levites had no steady income, the cities were also provided for their economic relief and support. See *Cities of Refuge.*

LEVITICUS, BOOK OF Third book of the OT containing instructions for priests and worship. These regulations are referred to as the ceremonial law—how to observe the rituals and regulations that were considered important acts of worship for God's people, the nation of Israel. Leviticus describes the establishment of the priesthood through Aaron, his sons, and their successors. The priests were to preside at the tabernacle and temple when various sacrifices were presented by the people to offer thanksgiving to their Creator and to atone for their sins. One of the most important themes of Leviticus is holiness. God's people were to be different than pagan worshippers and wholly dedicated to God's service. They worshipped a holy God, and He expected His people to be holy.

LEWDNESS Lust; sexual unchastity; licentiousness. Lewdness sometimes refers to an especially heinous crime such as brutal gang rape resulting in murder (Judg. 19:25-27), murder by priests (Hos. 6:9), or any vicious crime (Acts 18:14). Most often lewdness is used figuratively for idolatry (Hos. 2:10).

LIBERTINE KJV transliteration of Greek for "freedmen" (Acts 6:9).

LIBERTY, LIBERATION Freedom from physical, political, and spiritual oppression. One of the dominant themes of the OT is that Yahweh is the God who liberated the Israelites from their bondage in Egypt. In the NT God liberates people from bondage to sin through Jesus Christ.

LIBYA Large land area between Egypt and Tunisia. The people who inhabited the territory in biblical days are referred to variously as Chub (Ezek. 30:5), Put (Nah. 3:9), Phut (Ezek. 27:10), and Libyans (Acts 2:10). Pharaoh Shishak I (about 950 BC) is thought to have been a Libyan.

LIFE The animating force in both animals and humans (Gen. 1:20). Only God has life in the absolute sense. He is the living God (Matt. 16:16). All other life depends on Him for its creation and maintenance (Acts 17:25). God is spoken of as the God of life or as life-giving (Deut. 32:40). In contrast to God, the idols are dead (Jer. 10:8-10,14), and so are those who depend on these pagan symbols for life (Ps. 135:18).

No possibility of life exists when God withholds His breath or spirit (Job 34:14-15). Thus, God is Lord of both life and death (James 4:15). Life is something that only God can give (Ps. 139:13-14) and sustain (Ps. 119:116). Thus every life is solely the possession of God. Jesus warned that "one's life is not in the abundance of his possessions" (Luke 12:15 HCSB). He brought wholeness into physical life.

We come to God to receive life. We walk in fellowship with God, and in His light we see life. Otherwise, we are devoid of life and cannot see. The proper response to life as the gift of God is to live life in service to God (Isa. 38:10-20) by obeying the Law (Lev. 18:5), doing God's will (Matt. 7:21), and feeding on God's Word (Matt. 4:4). Only that life which lives in obedience to God deserves to be called life in the true sense of the word (Ezek. 18:1-32).

The genuine life that comes from Jesus to those who obey God is true or eternal life. Just as physical life is the gift of God, so is eternal life (Rom. 6:23). Eternal life refers as much to the quality of life one has as to the quantity of life. According to the Bible, all people will have an endless duration of life either in the blessing of God's presence or in the damnation of God's absence (John 5:28-29). The thing that distinguishes the life of these two groups of people is not its duration but its quality.

LIFE, BOOK OF Heavenly document mentioned in Ps. 139:16 and further defined in the NT (Rev. 13:8). In it are recorded by God the names and deeds of righteous people.

LIFE, ORIGIN OF The Bible teaches that all matter (John 1:3), including living matter, was created by God *ex nihilo* (out of nothing—Heb. 11:3) through a series of decisive acts (Ps. 148:5; Rev. 4:11). Plants and animals were created in self-reproducing "kinds" (Gen. 1:11-12,21,24). God created people to bring glory to Himself (Isa. 43:7). The psalmist stood in wonder at the intricate design of the human body and saw it as testimony of God's creative power (Ps. 139:13-15).

LIFE SPAN The life expectancy in industrialized western countries closely approximates the natural life span of mankind according to Ps. 90:10: "Our lives last seventy years or, if we are strong, eighty years." While modern medicine, improved health care, and a healthy diet can increase this natural limit somewhat, it is unreasonable to assume that people can ever live as long as several centuries, which was the case with the patriarchs before the flood (Gen. 5:3-31). After the flood the recorded life span of the descendants of Noah gradually decreased so that the patriarchs lived only twice today's normal span (Gen. 25:7-8; 47:28; 50:26).

LIFE SUPPORT (ARTIFICIAL) The Bible does not speak directly to the issue of life support by artificial means, but it does provide principles relevant to the time of one's death. Only God gives life, and only God should take life away (Exod. 20:13; Job 1:21). Human life is a sacred and precious gift because each person is created in the image of God (Ps. 8:5). These principles suggest that extreme measures to artificially prolong life encroach upon the prerogative of God to control life and death. For the same reason, any and all forms of euthanasia are contrary to the teaching of Scripture. Yet there comes a God-appointed time for everyone to die (Eccles. 3:2). Although Christians value life highly, they need not fear death (Heb. 2:14-15).

LIGHT, LIGHT OF THE WORLD Light is one of the Bible's most complex symbols. Light is linked with instruction (Ps. 119:105,130), truth (Ps. 43:3), good (Isa. 5:20), salvation (Isa. 49:6), life (Job 33:28,30), peace (Isa. 45:7), rejoicing (Ps. 97:11), covenant (Isa. 42:6), justice and righteousness (Isa. 59:9), God's presence and favor (Ps. 89:15), and the glory of Yahweh (Isa. 60:1-3). Apocalyptic visions of the end are associated with the extinguishing of light (Matt. 24:29). In the new age, the new Jerusalem "does not need the sun or the moon to shine on it, because God's glory illumines it, and its lamp is the Lamb" (Rev. 21:23 HCSB).

On the first day God created light (Gen. 1:3), which implies that light existed before the sun and other luminaries (Gen. 1:14-18). God Himself is the source of light (Ps. 104:2). This light probably signified the divine presence in the same way as the luminous cloud of the Shekinah glory (Exod. 24:15-18).

The identification of light with the divine presence of the Shekinah glory sheds light on the meaning of light in the Gospel of John and 1 John. In the person of Jesus, "the true light, who gives light to everyone, was coming into the world" (John 1:9 HCSB). The only begotten God, who is in the bosom of the Father, has made the Father known (John 1:18) because he "became flesh and took up residence among us" (John 1:14).

In Jesus God was made manifest because in Him the Shekinah glory had returned to reside among us, and this glory consisted of fullness of grace and truth (John 1:16-17). Light thus signifies Jesus' glory, which is fullness of grace and truth. Jesus is "the light of the world," and His followers will have "the light of life" (the truth that brings life; John 8:12). Jesus, who is the light, the embodiment of grace and truth, also brings salvation (John 12:35-36,46-47) and the doing of God's works (John 9:4-5). This salvation and doing of God's works comes from guidance and instruction from the light (John 12:35,47).

The attribution of God (rather than the Word) as light in 1 John 1:5 falls into place in this line of interpretation. Not only is the only begotten God characterized by fullness of grace and truth, His Father, whom He makes known as characterized by fullness of grace and truth, is as well (John 1:17-18). John can thus affirm that those who do not do the truth do not have fellowship with God, who is light (1 John 1:6).

LIGHTNING Flash of light resulting from a discharge of static electricity in the atmosphere. God is the Maker of lightning and thunder (Job 28:26), which reveal God's power and majesty (Ps. 77:18). Lightning and thunder frequently accompany a revelation of God (Ezek. 1:13-14). In poetic language God's voice is identified with the thunder (Job 37:3-5). Lightning serves as an illustration of Christ's clearly visible coming (Matt. 24:26-27) and of Satan's fall (Luke 10:18).

LIKENESS Quality or state of being like; resemblance. Old Testament passages center on two truths: (1) God is wholly other and cannot be properly compared to any likeness (Isa. 40:18). (2) Humanity is created in the image and likeness of God (Gen. 1:26). The first truth forms the basis for the prohibition of making any graven images (Deut. 4:16-18). Interpreters have identified the image of God in man with the ability to think rationally, to form relationships with other humans and with God or with the exercise of dominion over creation (Ps. 8:5-8). See *Image of God*.

LILY Any of a number of distinctive flowers ranging from the lotus of the Nile (1 Kings 7:19) to wild field flowers in Palestine (Matt. 6:28). See *Flowers*.

LIME White, caustic solid consisting primarily of calcium oxide obtained by heating limestone or shells to a high temperature. Lime was used as a plaster (Deut. 27:2,4). Burning someone's bones to lime amounts to complete annihilation (Isa. 33:12) and was regarded as an especially heinous crime (Amos 2:1).

LINE Tool used for measuring length or distance; a plumb line; a cord; a row. References to a plumb line refer to judgment (Isa. 34:11) upon those who failed to meet God's high standards (Isa. 28:17).

Line is used in the sense of a cord in the story of Rahab and the spies (Josh. 2:18,21).

LINEN Most common fabric used in the ancient Near East. It was spun from the flax plant and bleached before being woven into clothing, bedding, curtains, and burial shrouds. The tabernacle curtains (Exod. 26:1) and the high priest's garments (Exod. 28:6) were of finely woven linen. See *Flax*.

LINTEL Wooden crossbeam over a doorway. The people of Israel were to avoid the death angel sent by the Lord by sprinkling the blood of the sacrificial lamb on the lintel and the doorposts (Exod. 12:22-23).

The Lion of Amphipolis, a statue erected to look over the burial site of battle casualties.

LION Large flesh-eating cat that was once common in Palestine (Judg. 14:18; 1 Sam. 17:34-35) but is no longer found in the Middle East.

LIPS In the OT lips frequently show the character of a person. There are flattering and lying lips (Ps. 12:2); joyful lips (Ps. 63:5); righteous lips (Prov. 16:13); and fearful lips (Hab. 3:16). Uncircumcised lips (Exod. 6:12 KJV) probably refer to stammering lips or lack of fluency in speech (Exod. 4:10).

LITTLE OWL Any species of owl other than the great owl; included in the unclean birds of Lev. 11:17. See *Owl*.

LIVER According to the NASB, the lobe of the liver was offered to God with the other choice parts of the burnt offering (Lev. 3:4,10,15). The ancients examined livers to discern the future. The only scriptural mention of the practice concerns the king of Babylon (Ezek. 21:21).

LIVING BEINGS, LIVING CREATURES

Creatures in Ezekiel's first vision (Ezek. 1:5,13-15,19-20,22; 3:13; 10:15,17,20) later identified as cherubim (10:20). There were four creatures, each having a human form but with four faces. Perhaps the best interpretation views the creatures as a pictorial representation of the total sovereignty of God. The book of Revelation develops a similar image to portray God's total sovereignty (Rev. 4:1-8).

LO-AMMI Symbolic personal name meaning "not my people." Son of Hosea the prophet whose name God gave to symbolize Israel's lost relationship with Him because of their sin and broken covenant (Hos. 1:9).

LOAN Because of Israel's experience as slaves in Egypt, its moral code made special provision for the poor (Exod. 22:21-24). Thus loans were to be gestures of generosity, not acts for profit at the expense of the poor (Lev. 25:35-37). The OT forbade charging interest to fellow Israelites (Lev. 25:35-38), but sojourners or foreigners could be charged interest (Deut. 23:20). Laws for collateral focused on protecting the debtor. The pledge must not threaten the debtor's dignity (Deut. 24:10-11), livelihood (Deut. 24:6), or family (Job 24:1-3,9). Years of release and the Jubilee Year (Exod. 23:10-11) provided a systematic means for addressing long-term economic hardship by returning family property, freeing slaves, and canceling debts.

LOCUST An insect similar to the grasshopper that periodically multiplies to astronomical numbers in the Middle East. As the swarm moves across the land, it devours all vegetation. The locust plague is a symbol of God's judgment (Joel 2:1,11,25). The image of the locust plague also symbolized being overwhelmed by a large and powerful army (Judg. 6:5).

LOD Place-name of unknown meaning, later called Lydda, 11 miles southeast of Joppa. Returning Jewish exiles settled there about 537 BC (Neh. 11:35). See *Lydda*.

LOGOS John in his Gospel deliberately used *logos* (translated "Word") to describe Jesus (John 1:1). The Greek word *logos* ("word") ordinarily refers to an explanation or reason for something otherwise meaningless. But the OT concept of the "word" (*davar*) of God is foundational for understanding John's usage of this word in reference to Jesus. The Hebrews saw the word of God not as merely words but as a powerful and effectual means of accomplishing God's purposes (Isa. 40:8). By His word God spoke the world into existence (Gen. 1:3-31). God communicated His word directly to persons, especially in the Law (Deut. 5:4-5) and the Prophets (Jer. 1:4,11). The wise person lives in accordance with the word of God (Ps. 106:24).

Writing under the inspiration of the Holy Spirit, John poured new meaning into the concept of *Logos*. In relation to God, Jesus as the *Logos* was not merely an angel or created being who was the agent of creation, nor another word from God or wisdom from God; rather He was God Himself (John 1:1-4). In relation to humanity, Jesus the *Logos* was not an impersonal principle, but He was a personal Savior who took on human flesh in the incarnation (John 1:4-14). By depicting Jesus as the *Logos*, John portrays Him as the pre-existent Creator of the universe, with God, and identical to God. From this perspective of Jesus' divinity and eternity, any view of Jesus as a mere prophet or teacher is impossible (Col. 1:13-20; Rev. 19:13).

In other NT texts, *logos* refers to Scripture, particularly as proclaimed in gospel preaching (Heb. 4:12). The preaching of the gospel brings order and meaning to lives shattered by sin. Those who put faith in Jesus, the *Logos*, will be welcomed into the family of God (John 1:11-12).

LOINS Midsection of the human body. The OT sometimes speaks of the loins as the seat of physical strength (Nah. 2:1). Tying up the long, lower garments about the waist or loins indicated readiness for travel (1 Kings 18:46). In the NT to gird up one's loins is used in the figurative sense of preparedness (Eph. 6:14).

LOIS Personal name, perhaps meaning "more desirable" or "better." The mother of Eunice and grandmother of Timothy (2 Tim. 1:5).

LOOKING GLASS KJV term for a hand mirror (Exod. 38:8). Mirrors were made of polished metal (Job 37:18), which yielded a distorted image (1 Cor. 13:12).

LOOM Implement used for weaving thread into cloth. The weaving of cloth was an important industry in the ancient world. Job compared the brevity of life to the speed of the weaver's shuttle (Job 7:6). See *Cloth, Clothing*.

LOOPS The inner and outer coverings of the tabernacle were made of two large curtains held together by 50 clasps that passed through curved sections of blue cord for the inner tent or of leather for the outer tent (Exod. 36:11-12,17).

LORD English rendering of several Hebrew and Greek words. Generally, the term refers to one who has power or authority. *Jehovah* (or Yahweh; Hebrew *YHWH*, "self-existent") is the name of God most frequently used in the Hebrew Scriptures. This word or title is commonly represented by LORD (in small capital letters) in English translations of the Bible. The Jews meticulously avoided every mention of this name and substituted another word, *'Adonai*.

The importance of this name of God cannot be overstated. Exodus 3:14 furnishes a clue to the meaning of the word. When Moses through the burning bush received his commission to be the deliverer of Israel, God communicated to him the name to give as the credentials of his mission: "God said to Moses, 'I AM WHO I AM'; and He said, 'Thus you shall say to the sons of Israel, "I AM has sent me to you"'" (NASB). The root idea behind this name is uncreated existence. When it is said that God's name is "I am," more than simple existence is affirmed. He *is* in a sense in which no other being is. He is, and the cause of His being is in Himself. *He is because He is.* This name affirms God's lordship over His people (Exod. 34:23), as well as His power over the whole creation (Josh. 3:13). By this name God avows His superiority over all other gods (Deut. 10:17).

'Adonai is another important designation for God as Lord in the OT. It derives from the Hebrew word *'Adon*, an early word denoting ownership, hence, absolute control. *'Adon* is not properly a divine title as it is used of humans in some places. It is applied to God as the owner and governor of the whole earth (Ps. 114:7). It is sometimes used as a term of respect (like our "sir") but with a pronoun attached ("my lord"). It often occurs in the plural. *'Adonai* is, in the emphatic form, "the Lord."

Kurios is the word normally used in the NT to speak of Jesus as Lord. The word, however, has a wide range of reference, being used of God (Acts 2:34), of Jesus (Luke 10:1), of humans (Acts 16:19), and of angels (Acts 10:4). When characters in the Gospels speak of Jesus as Lord, they often mean no more than "sir." At other times the designation *kurios* expresses a full confession of faith, as in Thomas' declaration, "My Lord and my God!" (John 20:28 HCSB). "The Lord" came to be used as a simple yet profound designation of Christ in Luke and Acts. "The Lord Jesus" was used frequently in Acts as well (4:33) to speak of faith in Christ as Lord (16:31) and to identify baptism as being performed in the name of the Lord Jesus (8:16; 19:5). The phrase "Jesus is Lord" was the earliest Christian confession of faith. Peter declared that God had made Jesus both Lord and Christ (Acts 2:36).

Paul often used a fuller phrase to speak of Jesus' lordship: "the Lord Jesus Christ." It is significant that he used this in conjunction with the mention of God the Father and the Holy Spirit (2 Cor. 13:14). At other times Paul used the simpler formulas "the Lord Jesus" (2 Thess. 1:7) and "our Lord Jesus" (1 Thess. 3:13). In contrast to the many false gods and lords of pagans, there is for Christians one God, the Father, and one Lord, Jesus Christ (1 Cor. 8:5-6).

LORD'S DAY Designation for Sunday, the first day of the week (Rev. 1:10). Because the first day of the week was the day on which the early Christians celebrated the Lord's Supper, it became known as the Lord's Day, the distinctively Christian day of worship. The earliest account of a first-day worship experience is found in Acts 20:7-12. Here Paul joined the Christians of Troas on the evening of the first day of the week for the breaking of bread (probably a reference to the Lord's Supper). Sunday became the standard day for Christian worship, probably because the resurrection of Jesus took place on that day.

LORD'S PRAYER Words Jesus used to teach His followers to pray. Jesus' prayer life caused one of His disciples to ask for instruction in prayer. What followed (Luke 11:2-13) was a teaching on prayer in which the disciples were told why to pray and what to pray for. The Lord's Prayer is a model of how believers should pray. To pray in this way is a distinguishing mark of Jesus' disciples. The Lord's Prayer is a community's prayer: "*Our* Father"; "Give *us*"; Forgive *us*"; "Deliver *us*." It is the prayer of the community of Jesus' disciples. This model prayer for Christians is not praise, thanksgiving, meditation, or contemplation, but petition. It is asking God for something. A prayer of petition assumes a certain view of God. A God to whom one prays in this way is assumed to be in control; He is able to answer. He is also assumed to be good; He *wants* to answer.

LORD'S SUPPER

Church ordinance where unleavened bread and the fruit of the vine memorialize the death of the Lord Jesus and anticipate His second coming. Jesus established the Lord's Supper before His crucifixion while observing the Passover with His disciples (Matt. 26:26-29). Paul used the phrase "Lord's Supper" in 1 Cor. 11:20. In observing the Lord's Supper, church members eat unleavened bread and drink the "fruit of the

Stone relief of the Lord's Supper.

vine" to symbolize the body and blood of Christ. This memorial meal is to be observed until Christ comes again.

LO-RUHAMAH Symbolic personal name meaning "without love." Name that God gave Hosea for his daughter to symbolize that Israel, by rebelling against God and serving foreign gods, had rejected God's love (Hos. 1:6).

LOT Personal name meaning "concealed." Nephew of Abraham (Gen. 11:27). When Abraham left Haran for Canaan, he was accompanied by Lot and Lot's household (Gen. 12:5). After traveling throughout Canaan and into Egypt, Abraham and Lot finally settled in Canaan between Bethel and Ai, about 10 miles north of Jerusalem (Gen. 13:3). Abraham and Lot acquired herds and flocks so large that the land was unable to support both (Gen. 13:2,5-6). Abraham suggested that they separate, and he allowed Lot to take his choice of the land. Lot chose the well-watered Jordan Valley where the city of Sodom was located (13:8-12).

Some time after this, two angels visited Lot in the city of Sodom. They warned Lot to leave the city because God intended to destroy Sodom and its sister city Gomorrah because of the wickedness of the people (Gen. 18:20). When the townsmen heard that two strangers were staying with Lot, they wanted to have sexual relations with them. Lot protected his guests and offered them his daughters instead. The angels urged Lot to take his family into the nearby hills to escape the judgment that God promised to send upon the city. During their flight from Sodom, Lot's wife looked at the destruction and turned to a pillar of salt (Gen. 19:1-29).

After Sodom and Gomorrah were destroyed, Lot's daughters began to fear they would never have children, so they tricked their father into having intercourse with them. The son of the elder daughter was called Moab, and he became the father of the Moabites. The son of the younger daughter was named Ben-ammi, and he became the father of the Ammonites (Gen. 19:30-38). These two tribes became enemies of the Israelites in later years. In the NT, the story of Lot is used to show the faithfulness of God to rescue His people (2 Pet. 2:7-9).

LOTS Objects used to determine God's will. Matthias was chosen as Judas's successor by casting lots (Acts 1:26). The apostles' prayer immediately before they cast the lots shows the belief that God would express His will through this method. In the OT Saul was chosen as Israel's first king through the use of lots (1 Sam. 10:20-24). When Joshua summoned the people to stand before the Lord to find the guilty party after the defeat at Ai, he may have used lots (Josh. 7:10-15). God commanded that the promised land be divided by lots (Num. 26:52-56).

LOVE Unselfish, loyal, and benevolent intention and commitment toward another person. The concept of the love of God is deeply rooted in the Bible. The Hebrew term *chesed* refers to covenant love. Jehovah is the God who remembers and keeps His covenants in spite of the treachery of people. His faithfulness in keeping His promises proves His love for Israel and all humanity.

In NT times three words for love were used by the Greek-speaking world. The first is *eros*, referring to erotic or sexual love. This word is not used in the NT or in the Septuagint. It was commonly used in Greek literature of the time. The word *phileo* refers to tender affection, such as toward a friend or family member. It is very common in the NT. It is used to express God the Father's love for Jesus (John 5:20), God's love for an individual believer (John 16:27), and Jesus' love for a disciple (John 20:2).

The word *agapao* (and its cognate *agape*) was used by believers to denote the unconditional love of God and is used interchangeably with *phileo* to designate God's love for Jesus (John 3:35), God's love for an individual believer (John 14:21), and Christ's love for a disciple (John 13:23). Biblical love has God as its object, true motivator, and source. Love is a fruit of the Holy Spirit (Gal. 5:22) and is not directed toward the world or the things of the world. The ultimate example of God's love is the Lord Jesus Christ, who said, " I give you a new commandment: that you love one another. Just as I have loved you, you should also love one another" (John 13:34 HCSB). The definitive statement on love in Paul's writings occurs in 1 Cor. 13. Paul declared that rhetorical ability, preaching, knowledge, mountain-moving faith, charity towards the poor, and even martyrdom are nothing without *agape*.

LOVE FEAST Fellowship meal that the Christian community celebrated with joy in conjunction with the Lord's Supper. It served as a practical expression of the *koinonia* or communion that characterized the church's life. The only explicit NT reference to the *agape* meal is found in Jude 12, but allusions to the practice may be seen in other NT texts. Acts 2:46 mentions that the early believers, while celebrating the Lord's Supper, took their food "with gladness and simplicity of heart," implying a social meal was connected with this celebration.

LOVING-KINDNESS Occasional translation of the Hebrew, *chesed*. The OT's highest expression for love. It is variously called God's election, covenant-keeping, or steadfast love. It is a love that remains constant regardless of the circumstances. See *Kindness; Love*.

LUBIM Racial name of uncertain meaning apparently applied to all white North Africans, especially the inhabitants of Libya (Dan. 11:43). Many English translations read "Libyans." See *Libya*.

LUCIFER Latin translation (followed by the KJV) of the Hebrew word for "day star" in Isa. 14:12, where the word is used as a title for the king of Babylon, who had exalted himself as a god. The prophet taunted the king by calling him "son of the dawn" (NIV, NASB), a play on a Hebrew term which could refer to a pagan god but normally indicated the light that appeared briefly before dawn.

LUCIUS Personal name of uncertain meaning. **1.** Christian prophet from Cyrene who helped lead the church at Antioch to set apart Saul and Barnabas for missionary service (Acts 13:1). **2.** Relative of Paul who sent greetings to the church at Rome (Rom. 16:21).

LUD Racial name for person from Lydia (pl. Ludim). **1.** Son of Egypt in the Table of Nations (Gen. 10:13) and apparently a people living near Egypt or under the political influence of Egypt. **2.** Son of Shem and grandson of Noah in Table of Nations (Gen. 10:22). See *Lydia*.

LUKE Author of the Third Gospel and the book of Acts in the NT; traveling companion of the Apostle Paul. Many scholars believe Luke wrote his Gospel and the book of Acts while in Rome with Paul during the apostle's first Roman imprisonment. Apparently Luke remained nearby or with Paul also during the apostle's second Roman imprisonment. Shortly before his martyrdom, Paul wrote that "only Luke is with me" (2 Tim. 4:11). Paul identified Luke as a physician (Col. 4:14) and distinguished Luke from those "of the circumcision" (Col. 4:11), perhaps meaning that he was a Gentile.

LUKE, GOSPEL OF Third Gospel and longest book in the NT. Luke is the first of a two-part work dedicated to the "most honorable Theophilus" (Luke 1:3 HCSB; Acts 1:1). The book of Acts is a sequel to Luke, with the author explaining in Acts that Luke dealt in his Gospel with "all that Jesus began to do and teach until the day He was taken up" (Acts 1:1-2 HCSB). It was written by Luke the physician (Col 4:14), a missionary associate of the Apostle Paul.

Luke wrote his Gospel to confirm for Theophilus the certainty of the things Theophilus had been taught (Luke 1:1-4). His target audience was Gentile inquirers and Christians who needed strengthening in the faith. His Gospel emphasized the universal redemption available to all people through Christ. Samaritans enter the kingdom (17:11-19) as well as Gentiles (23:47). Publicans, sinners, and outcasts (7:37-50) are welcome along with Jews (1:33) and respectable people (11:37). Both the poor (6:20) and rich (23:50) can have redemption. Luke especially notes Christ's high regard for women. Mary and Elizabeth are central figures in chapters 1 and 2. Luke included the story of Christ's kind dealings with the widow of Nain (7:11-18) and the sinful woman who anointed Him (7:36-50). He also related Jesus' parable of the widow who persevered (18:1-8).

LUKEWARM Tepid; neither hot nor cold (Rev. 3:16). The city of Laodicea received its water from an aqueduct several miles long. The lukewarm water that arrived at the city served as an appropriate illustration of a tasteless, good-for-nothing Christianity.

LUNATIC Term for epilepsy or insanity (Matt. 17:15). The term *lunacy* derives from the Latin *luna* (moon) and reflects the popular notion that the mental state of the "lunatic" fluctuated with the changing phases of the moon.

LUST A strong craving or desire, especially sexual desire. The unregenerate (pre-conversion) life is governed by deceitful lusts or desires (Eph. 4:22). Following conversion such fleshly desires compete with spiritual desires for control of the individual (2 Tim. 2:22). Part of God's judgment on sin is to give persons over to their own fleshly desires (Rom. 1:24). Only the presence of the Holy Spirit in the life of the believer makes victory over sinful desires possible (Rom. 8:1-2). See *Concupiscence.*

LUTE Stringed instrument with a large, pear-shaped body and a neck. NRSV used "lute" to translate two Hebrew terms (Pss. 92:3; 150:3). NASB translated the first term as "10-stringed lute" and the second as "harp." The KJV translated both terms as psaltery. See *Music, Instruments, Dancing.*

LUZ Place-name meaning "almond tree." **1.** Original name of Bethel (Gen. 28:19). **2.** City in the land of the Hittites founded by a man who showed the tribe of Joseph how to conquer Bethel (Judg. 1:25-26).

LYCAONIA Roman province in the interior of Asia Minor including cities of Lystra, Iconium, and Derbe (Acts 14:1-23).

LYCIA Place-name indicating the projection on the southern coast of Asia Minor between Caria and Pamphylia (Acts 27:5).

LYDDA Place-name of uncertain meaning. Known as Lod in the OT (1 Chron. 8:12), Lydda was located at the intersection of the caravan routes from Egypt to Babylon and the road from Joppa to Jerusalem. The church spread to Lydda early (Acts 9:32) as the result of Peter's ministry.

LYDIA A place-name and personal name of uncertain meaning. **1.** Country in Asia Minor whose citizens were named by Ezekiel as "men of war" or mercenaries who fought to defend Tyre (27:10) and who made an alliance with Egypt (30:5). **2.** The first convert to Christ under the preaching of Paul at Philippi (Acts 16:14). Her name originally might have been the designation of her home, "a woman of Lydia." She hosted Paul and his entourage in Philippi after her conversion.

LYE A cleaning substance similar to soap (Jer. 2:22).

LYSANIAS Personal name of unknown meaning. Roman tetrarch of Abilene at the beginning of John the Baptist's ministry about AD 25–30 (Luke 3:1). See *Abilene.*

LYSIAS Second name or birth name of Roman tribune or army captain who helped Paul escape the Jews and appear before Felix, the governor (Acts 23:26). See *Claudius.*

LYSTRA City in south central Asia Minor where Paul healed a crippled man (Acts 14:8-10). It was probably the home of Timothy, one of Paul's missionary associates (Acts 16:1).

The south city gate (possibly Hellenistic) at Perga of Pamphylia, the port from which Mark returned home.

MACEDONIA A mountainous country north of Greece to which the Apostle Paul was beckoned by the vision of a man pleading, "Come over into Macedonia and help us" (Acts 16:9). Responding to the vision, Paul and his missionary associate, Silas, went to the city of Philippi. They were received by Lydia, a God fearer from Thyatira, and founded the first Christian community in Europe (Acts 16:14-15).

MACHIR Personal name meaning "sold." **1.** Head of the family called the Machirites (Num. 26:29). Machir was allotted the territory of Bashan and Gilead, east of the Jordan River (Josh. 17:1). **2.** Member of the tribe of Manasseh who provided assistance for Mephibosheth, the son of Jonathan (2 Sam. 9:4-5), and David during Absalom's rebellion (2 Sam. 17:27-29).

MACHPELAH Place-name meaning "the double cave." A field and cave located near Hebron purchased by Abraham that became the burial site for Sarah (Gen. 23:19), Abraham (25:9), Isaac, Rebekah, Jacob, Leah, and probably other members of the family. Jacob requested burial there before he died in Egypt and was returned there by his sons (Gen. 49:29-30; 50:13).

MAGADAN Site on the Sea of Galilee (Matt. 15:39). At Mark 8:10 most translations follow other Greek manuscripts reading Dalmanutha. KJV follows the received text of its day in reading Magdala. The location of Magadan, if it is a correct reading, is not known.

MAGDALA Place-name, perhaps meaning "tower." City on the western shore of the Sea of Galilee and home of Mary Magdalene, or "Mary of Magdala" (Matt. 27:56).

MAGGOT Soft-bodied, legless grub that is the intermediate stage of some insects (Isa. 14:11). The term emphasizes human mortality.

MAGI Eastern wise men, priests, and astrologers who were expert in interpreting dreams and other "magic arts." The phrase is used of those men who came to Palestine to find and honor Jesus, the newborn King (Matt. 2). They may have been from Babylon, Persia, or the Arabian Desert. Matthew gives no number, names, or royal positions to the magi.

MAGISTRATE Government official with administrative and judicial responsibilities. In the OT the term perhaps signified a judge (Ezra 7:25). In the NT magistrates were military commanders and civil officials of a Greek city (Acts 16:20,22,35-36,38).

MAGNIFICAT Latin word meaning "magnify." The first word in Latin of Mary's psalm of praise that she would be the earthly mother of Jesus (Luke 1:46-55) and thus the title of the psalm.

MAGOG See *Gog and Magog.*

MAHALATH-LEANNOTH A phrase in the title of a psalm perhaps giving a choreographic instruction or referring to an antiphonal performance by two groups answering and responding to each other (Ps. 88).

MAHANAIM Place-name meaning "two camps." Levitical city in the hill country of Gilead on the border of Gad and eastern Manasseh (Josh. 13:26,30; 21:38). It served as a refuge for Ishbosheth after Saul's death (2 Sam. 2:8-9) and for David when Absalom usurped the throne (2 Sam. 17:24-27).

MAHER-SHALAL-HASH-BAZ Personal name meaning "quick to the plunder, swift to the spoil" (Isa. 8:1). Symbolic name Isaiah gave his son to warn Judah of the danger posed by the nations of Syria and Israel. The context of Isaiah's prophecy was that these two enemies of Judah would be destroyed before they could attack the southern kingdom. Assyria defeated Syria in 732 BC and Israel in 722 BC.

MAHLON Personal name meaning "sickly." One of the two sons of Elimelech and Naomi (Ruth 1:2,5), and the husband of Ruth the Moabitess (4:9-10). Mahlon died while the family was sojourning in Moab to escape a famine in their homeland of Israel.

MAID, MAIDEN A young, unmarried woman, especially of the servant class (Ruth 2:8). The word for "maid" sometimes refers to a female slave or a virgin.

MAIMED Mutilated, disfigured, or seriously injured, especially by loss of a limb (Matt. 18:8). The maimed had difficulty finding work and relied on the generosity of others (Luke 14:13). Christ, the Good Shepherd, cared for the maimed in His healing ministry (Matt. 15:30-31).

MAKKEDAH Place-name meaning "place of shepherds." A Canaanite city where Joshua defeated the combined forces of five Canaanite kings (Joshua 10:10). Joshua captured the city, killing all its inhabitants (10:28).

MALACHI, BOOK OF The last prophetic book of the OT. Malachi prophesied during the dark days after the exile when the Jewish captives had returned from the exile and resettled their homeland. It was a time of indifference and spiritual apathy. Blaming their economic and social troubles on the Lord's supposed unfaithfulness to them, the people were treating one another faithlessly (especially husbands treating their wives) and were profaning the temple by marrying pagan women. They were also withholding their tithes from the temple. Malachi calls the people to turn from their spiritual apathy and correct their wrong attitudes of worship by trusting God with genuine faith as living Lord. This includes honoring the Lord's name with tithes and offerings and being faithful to covenants made with fellow believers, especially marriage covenants.

MALCAM or **MALCHAM** Name meaning "their King." **1.** A Benjaminite (1 Chron. 8:9). **2.** Chief god of the Ammonites (Zeph. 1:5, KJV; Malcam, RSV and NASB margins). The Hebrew *malcam* is sometimes seen as a deliberate scribal misspelling of Milcom (cp. Jer. 49:1,3; Zeph. 1:5), the common name for the god of the Ammonites (Zeph. 1:5).

MALCHUS Personal name meaning "king." High priest's servant whose ear was cut off by Peter (John 18:10).

MALEFACTORS KJV word that denotes the two criminals who were crucified beside Jesus (Luke 23:32-33,39).

MALICE Vicious intention or desire to hurt someone. Malice is characteristic of pre-conversion life in opposition to God (Rom. 1:29). Christians are called upon to rid their lives of malice (Eph. 4:31-32).

MALLOW Two plants mentioned in the Bible: **1.** A salt marsh plant and unpleasant food (Job 30:4). **2.** A flowering plant whose fading petals provide an image for the unrighteous, according to one interpretation of Job 24:24 (NRSV, REB).

MAMMON Aramaic word for "money," "worldly goods," or "profit." Jesus declared, "Ye cannot serve God and mammon" (KJV), meaning that no one can be a slave of God and worldly wealth at the same time. Concentration on making money is incompatible with total devotion to God and His service (Col. 3:5).

MAMRE Place-name meaning "grazing land." Abraham and his family sojourned in Canaan in this area. Mamre was famous for its oak trees. Abraham purchased a cave (Machpelah) for a family burial plot just east of Mamre (Gen 23:9–18).

MAN OF LAWLESSNESS or **MAN OF SIN** (KJV) Ultimate opponent of Christ (2 Thess. 2:3). Modern translations follow other manuscripts in reading "man of lawlessness."

MANAEN Greek form of Menahem ("Comforter"). A prophet and teacher in the early church at Antioch (Acts 13:1).

MANASSEH Personal name meaning "God has caused me to forget" (trouble). **1.** A son of Joseph (Gen. 41:50-51). Along with Joseph's other son Ephraim, Manasseh became one of the 12 tribes of Israel and received a portion of the land. Half of the tribe of Manasseh settled on the east bank of the Jordan River and half on the west. **2.** King of Judah (696–642 BC) who led the people into worship of false gods. Second Kings blames Manasseh for Judah's ultimate destruction and exile (2 Kings 21:10-16).

MANDRAKE Small plant viewed as an aphrodisiac and fertility drug. It is often called love apple or devil's apple. A barren Rachel bargained with Reuben (Leah's oldest son) for mandrakes that he had found (Gen. 30:14-16).

MANGER Feeding trough used for livestock. The place where Jesus was laid after his birth (Luke

2:16). Archaeologists have discovered stone mangers in the horse stables of King Ahab of Israel at Megiddo. Other ancient mangers were made of masonry.

MANNA Grainlike substance, considered to be food from heaven, which sustained the Israelites in the wilderness and foreshadowed Christ, the true Bread from heaven. The small round grains or flakes, which appeared around the Israelites' camp each morning with the dew, were ground and baked into cakes or boiled (Exod. 16:13-36). The name *manna* may have come from the question the Israelites asked when they first saw it: "What is it (*man hu*)?"

MANOAH Personal name meaning "rest." A member of the tribe of Dan and the father of Samson (Judg. 13). Manoah asked God for a son when his wife could not produce an heir.

MANSERVANT KJV, RSV word for a male servant or slave.

MANSLAYER One guilty of involuntary manslaughter; one who accidentally causes another's death (Deut. 19:1-10). English translations distinguish manslayer from murderer although the underlying Hebrew term (*ratsach*) is the same (cp. Exod. 20:13).

MANTLE Robe, cape, veil, or loose-fitting tunic worn as an outer garment. Many of the prophets wore mantles (1 Kings 19:13). The transference of the mantle from Elijah to Elisha signified the passing of prophetic responsibility and God's accompanying power.

MAONITES A tribal group that oppressed Israel during the period of the judges (Judg. 10:12). These Maonites were perhaps the Meunites, a band of marauding Arabs from south of the Dead Sea in the vicinity of Ma'an. After the period of the judges, the Meunites were attacked by King Hezekiah (1 Chron. 4:41) and King Uzziah (2 Chron. 26:7) of Judah.

MARA Personal name meaning "bitter," chosen by Naomi to reflect God's bitter dealings with her in the death of her husband and sons (Ruth 1:20-21).

MARAH Place-name meaning "bitter." Place in the Wilderness of Shur, so named because of the bitter water found there by the wandering Israelites (Exod. 15:23). At God's command Moses cast a tree into the water to make it miraculously sweet and drinkable.

MARANATHA Aramaic expression meaning "Our Lord, come" or "Our Lord has come" (1 Cor. 16:22), depending on the way the word is divided. The phrase probably reveals the expectant hope in which early Christians lived, watching for the imminent return of Christ.

MARCUS Latin form of Mark ("large hammer") used by the KJV at Col. 4:10; Philem. 24; and 1 Peter 5:13. See *Mark, John*.

MARDUK Chief god of Babylon, sometimes called Merodach or Bel, the Babylonian equivalent of Baal, meaning "lord." He was credited with creation, a feat reenacted each new year and celebrated with a festival. The prophets mocked Marduk and his worshippers as products of human craftsmen who would lead Babylon to defeat and exile (Isa. 46:1; Jer. 51:47).

MARK, JOHN Author of the Second Gospel and an early missionary leader. John Mark, as Luke calls him in Acts, was the son of Mary, in whose house the church was meeting when Peter was miraculously freed from prison in Acts 12. Commonly called by his Greek name, Mark, in the NT, John was probably his Jewish name. Mark was a cousin of Barnabas (Col. 4:10) and a companion of Barnabas and Paul on their first missionary journey. On the first missionary journey Mark ministered with the group on Cyprus, the home territory of Barnabas and also a place with family connections for Mark. However, when they left for Pamphylia, Mark returned to Jerusalem.

Mark was the cause of the split between Paul and Barnabas when Mark's participation in the second missionary journey was debated (Acts 15:39). Barnabas sided with his cousin, while Paul refused to take Mark since he had left them on the first journey. Later, however, Paul indicated that Mark was with him (in Rome likely) as Paul sent letters to the Colossians (Col. 4:10) and Philemon (Philem. 24). Mark was also summoned to be with Paul in 2 Tim. 4:11. Whatever rift existed earlier had been healed and their friendship renewed.

Mark is closely related to Peter. In 1 Pet. 5:13 Peter refers to Mark, his "son," as being with him in Rome (Babylon). Early church tradition supports the strong association between Peter and Mark. In the early second century, Papias mentioned that Mark was Peter's interpreter. Other early church figures associate Mark with Peter and note that the Gospel of Mark was based upon Peter's preaching.

MARK, GOSPEL OF Second book of the NT and shortest Gospel account of the ministry of Jesus. According to early church tradition Mark—also known as John Mark— recorded and arranged the "memories" of Peter, producing a Gospel based on apostolic witness. Mark became an important assistant to both Paul and Peter, preaching the good news to Gentiles and preserving the gospel message for later Christians. Mark wrote his Gospel for Gentile Christians. He explains Jewish customs in detail for the benefit of readers unfamiliar with Judaism (Mark 7:3-4; 12:18).

Mark has been called the "Gospel of action." Jesus is constantly on the move. Mark apparently had more interest in the work of Jesus than in His words. Thus he omitted the Sermon on the Mount. Jesus taught as He moved from region to region, using the circumstances of His travel as valuable lessons for His disciples (8:14-21). Geographical references serve only to trace the expansive parameters of His ministry. According to Mark's "motion" picture, Jesus moved quickly—as if He were a man whose days were numbered.

MARKETPLACE Narrow streets and clustered buildings of most towns and villages in ancient Palestine left little room for a public marketplace. Shops were built into private residences or clustered in the gate area to form bazaars (1 Kings 20:34). Merchants operated booths just inside the city gate or hawked their merchandise outside the gate area in an open space or square. This area also served as a marshaling place for troops (2 Chron. 32:6) and the site for public meetings (Neh. 8:1), victory celebrations (Deut. 13:16), and the display of captives (2 Sam. 21:12).

Modern produce vendors at a busy market in Tel Aviv.

MARRIAGE The sacred, covenantal union of one man and one woman formed when the two swear before God an oath of lifelong loyalty and love to each other. God instituted the first marriage in the garden of Eden when He gave Eve to Adam as his wife (Gen. 2:18-25). That later marriages were to follow the pattern of the first is indicated by the concluding divine instruction (see Matt. 19:4-6): "This is why a man leaves his father and mother and bonds with his wife, and they become one flesh" (Gen. 2:24). A unique unity between Adam and Eve was seen in that the two became "one flesh." The oneness of marriage separated the couple from others as a distinct family unit.

If man's main purpose is to glorify God and enjoy our relationship with Him forever (1 Cor. 10:31), clearly this is the chief purpose of marriage. Paul explains in Eph. 5:21-33 that the marriage relationship is to be patterned after that of Christ and the church. A husband and wife are to display in their relationship the nature of our relationship with Christ, our divine Husband, as His bride, the church. This same principle may also be inferred from the OT, where the marriage relationship was one of the key analogies used to describe Yahweh's relationship with Israel (Jer. 2:1; 3:6; 31:32; Hos. 1–3). Marriage is also God's unique gift to provide the framework for intimate companionship, as a means for procreation of the human race, and as the channel of sexual expression according to biblical standards.

The Bible describes the marriage that pleases God in terms of mutual submission empowered by the Holy Spirit (Eph. 5:18-21; see also Phil. 2:1-4). Such a marriage also provides the marital fulfillment and companionship God intends. However, mutual submission is to be expressed differently by the husband and the wife. The husband is to practice self-denying, nurturing love patterned after that of Christ (Eph. 5:25-33). He is the initiator and is responsible for leading his wife with wisdom and understanding. He is also to protect, provide for, and honor her (Col. 3:19). A wife, on the other hand, is to express her submission by following her husband's leadership with respect (Eph. 5:22-24,33), maintaining a pure and reverent life with "a gentle and quiet spirit" (1 Pet. 3:1-6).

MARROW Soft tissue within bone cavities. The image of the dividing of joints and marrow pictures the power of Scripture to penetrate a person's thoughts and motives (Heb. 4:12).

MARS HILL Prominent hill overlooking the city of Athens where the philosophers of the city gathered to discuss their ideas.

Mars Hill, where Paul was invited to address the intellectuals of Athens at the Areopagus.

Paul discussed religion with the leading minds of Athens on Mars Hill. He used the altar to an "unknown god" to present Jesus to them (Acts 17:22).

MARTHA Personal name meaning "lady [of the house]" or "mistress." Sister of Mary and Lazarus of Bethany and follower of Jesus. True to her name, Martha is portrayed as a person in charge: she welcomed Jesus as a guest in her home (Luke 10:38); she was concerned with meeting the obligations of a hostess, whether preparing food (John 12:2) or greeting guests (John 11:20). Luke 10:38-42 contrasts Martha's activist discipleship with Mary's contemplative discipleship. Jesus' gentle rebuke of Martha serves as a perpetual reminder not to major on minor matters.

MARTYR Transliteration of the Greek word *martus*, meaning "witness." The messages and oracles of God were often rejected, resulting in the messenger's maltreatment or death (1 Kings 19:2). Witnesses also bear testimony about moral, religious, or spiritual truths so important that one would give his life for those truths. The NT refers three times to a martyr in this sense (Acts 22:20; Rev. 2:13; 17:6).

"Mary's House" in Ephesus where tradition says that Mary the mother of Jesus lived out her last days.

MARY Personal name of seven women in the NT. **1.** Mary, the earthly mother of Jesus. Mary was a young woman, a virgin, living in Nazareth, and a relative of Elizabeth, mother of John the Baptist (Luke 1:5; 2:26). She had been pledged to marry a carpenter named Joseph. The angel Gabriel appeared to her, announcing she would give birth to "the Son of the Most High" who would sit on "the throne of His father David" (Luke 1:32 HCSB). When Mary raised the issue of her virginity, the angel indicated the conception would be supernatural (Luke 1:34-35). Subsequently, Mary visited Elizabeth (Luke 1:39-45). Later, after journeying to Bethlehem and giving birth to Jesus (Luke 2:1-20), Mary and Joseph presented the baby to the Lord at the temple (Luke 2:22-38). Matthew indicates that Mary, Joseph, and Jesus lived in Bethlehem until the visit of the magi, when the threat posed by Herod forced them to take refuge in Egypt (Matt. 2:1-18). The family then lived in Nazareth in Galilee (Matt. 2:19-23). Mary was present at the cross when Jesus committed her care to John, who took her into his home (John 19:26-27). After the ascension Mary and her sons were with the disciples in Jerusalem as they waited for the promised coming of the Holy Spirit (Acts 1:14). **2.** Mary Magdalene, one of the women who followed and supported Jesus (Mark 15:41). She was from Magdala in Galilee. She experienced dramatic healing when seven demons came out of her (Luke 8:2). She was a key witness to Jesus' death (Matt. 27:56), burial (Mark 15:47), and the empty tomb (Luke 24:1-10), and was the first to encounter the risen Christ (John 20:1-18). She has been identified as a sinful woman, perhaps a prostitute and the "sinful woman" of Luke 7:36-50. However, there is no evidence for this assumption. **3.** Mary of Bethany, sister of Martha and Lazarus. Jesus commended Mary for her interest in His teaching (Luke 10:38-42). Mary later anointed the feet of Jesus with perfume (John 12:1-8). **4.** Mother of James the Younger, Joses, and Salome. This Mary is also identified as an eyewitness to the death, burial, and resurrection of Jesus (Mark 15:40–16:1). **5.** Wife of Clopas. This Mary also was a witness to the death of Jesus and may be the same Mary as No. 4 (John 19:25). **6.** Mother of John Mark. When Peter was freed from prison in Acts 12, he went to the house of Mary, mother of John Mark, where the disciples were meeting. **7.** A believer in Rome greeted by Paul (Rom. 16:6).

MASKIL A word of uncertain meaning in the titles of Pss. 32; 42; 44; 45; 52–55; 74; 78; 88; 89; 142. The word may have given directions for the melody in which these psalms were to be sung.

MASONS Building craftsmen using brick or stone. The professional mason in Israel first appears in the Bible in David's time. The Bible suggests that no Israelites were skilled in the art of quarrying, squaring, and setting fine building stones in David's time. David relied upon the king of Tyre for craftsmen (1 Chron. 22:2-4,14-18).

Examples of Herodian masonry are visible around the Temple Mount in Jerusalem.

MASSAH Place-name meaning "to test, try." Stopping place near Mt. Sinai where the people put God to the test by demanding water (Exod. 17:7). Massah became a reminder of Israel's disobedience or hardness of heart (Ps. 95:8).

MATTANIAH Personal name meaning "gift of Yah." **1.** Tabernacle musician in David's time (1 Chron. 25:4). **2.** Ancestor of Jahaziel (2 Chron. 20:14). **3.** Levite who participated in King Hezekiah's religious reforms (2 Chron. 29:13). **4.** Original name of King Zedekiah of Judah (2 Kings 24:17). **5.** Asaphite who returned from exile (1 Chron. 9:15). **6.** Levitic leader of the temple choir in Zerubbabel's time (Neh. 11:17,22). **7.** Levitic temple gatekeeper (Neh. 12:25). **8.** Father of the Levite Shemaiah (Neh. 12:35). **9.** Grandfather of Hanan (Neh. 13:13). **10.–13.** Four men who returned from exile with foreign wives (Ezra 10:26-27,30,37). Some of 5–13 may be identical.

MATTHEW Personal name meaning "the gift of Yahweh." A tax collector who became an apostle of Jesus (Matt. 9:9; 10:3). Matthew is the same person as Levi (Luke 5:27). From earliest times Christians affirmed that Matthew wrote the Gospel that bears his name.

MATTHEW, GOSPEL OF Opening book of the NT that was written to show the Jewish people that Jesus was the Messiah promised in the OT. In Matthew's genealogy of Jesus, he traces Him to two of the greatest personalities in the history of the Jewish people—Abraham (Matt. 1:2) and David (Matt. 1:6). Another purpose of this Gospel was to show that Jesus had the power to command His disciples to spread His gospel throughout all the world (Matt. 28:16–20). Matthew also contains the teachings of Jesus known as the Sermon on the Mount (Matt. 5:1–7:29). It includes His teachings on such subjects as true happiness (5:2-12), prayer and fasting (6:1–18), and building life on a secure foundation (7:24-27).

MATTHIAS Shortened form of Mattathias ("gift of Yah"). Follower of Jesus who was chosen by lot to succeed Judas as an apostle (Acts 1:20-26). This selection was regarded as necessary to fulfill Scripture concerning the band of apostles (Ps. 69:25).

MAW KJV term for the fourth stomach of a cud-chewing animal. The maw was among the choice cuts of meat reserved for the priests (Deut. 18:3). Modern translations render as "stomach" (HCSB, NASB, REB, NRSV) or "inner parts" (NIV).

MAZZAROTH Puzzling term in Job 38:32. Either a proper name for a constellation (KJV, NRSV), a collective term for the 12 signs of the Zodiac (KJV margin, REB), or a general term meaning constellation or stars (NASB, NIV, TEV).

MEADOW Tract of grassland, especially moist, low-lying pasture. In modern translations "meadows" illustrate God's blessing (Ps. 65:13 NASB, NIV, NRSV [pastures, HCSB]; Isa. 30:23; 44:4 NIV). Meadows are also used in pictures of God's judgment (Jer. 25:37 NIV; Hos. 9:13 NASB; Zeph. 2:6 NRSV).

MEASURING LINE Cord used to measure length (2 Chron. 4:3). References to a measuring line point to the restoration of Jerusalem (Zech. 2:1).

MEASURING REED Ezekiel's measuring reed was a cane about 10 feet long used as a measuring tool (Ezek. 40:3,5-8).

MEAT OFFERING KJV term for a food offering in contrast to a drink offering, or libation (1 Chron. 21:23). Modern translations render the term as "grain offering."

MEAT TO IDOLS Offerings of animal flesh sacrificed to a pagan god. Most religions of the ancient Near East had laws regarding offering sacrifices to the gods. A problem arose in the church when Gentile converts ate meat that had been offered to idols. The Jerusalem council decided that Christians should abstain from eating meat offered to idols so as not to cause weak believers to stumble (Acts 15:29). Paul echoed this sentiment (1 Cor. 8:13).

MEDEBA A Moabite town captured by the Amorites, then by the Israelites (Num. 21:23–30), and allotted later to the tribe of Reuben (Josh. 13:9,16).

MEDES, MEDIA Inhabitants of an ancient kingdom west of Assyria who descended from Japheth, the grandson of Noah (Gen 10:2). The Medes were first reported in history by King Shalmaneser III of Assyria about 850 BC. At this time they were a group of nomadic tribes rather than a state or kingdom. After the Assyrian Empire fell to the Babylonians, Babylon and Media divided the Assyrian Empire with Media taking the land east and north of the Tigris River. The Medes turned their attention to the north and toward Asia Minor. The end of the Median kingdom came with the rise of Cyrus II, founder of the Persian Empire. Though conquered by the Persians, the Medes continued to hold a place of honor in the Persian Empire. Media was the second most important portion of the Empire after Persia itself.

Biblical references frequently combine "the Medes and the Persians" (Dan. 5:28). The kings of the Persian Empire are called "the kings of Media and Persia" (Dan. 8:20). The most famous Mede in Scripture was Darius the Mede (Dan. 5:31; 9:1). Media is sometimes referred to as the instrument of God, especially against Babylon (Jer. 51:11,28), but the Medes also had to drink the cup of God's judgment (Jer. 25:25). Their final appearance in Scripture is the presence of Jews or Jewish converts from there at Pentecost (Acts. 2:9).

MEDIATOR One who stands between two or more parties to negotiate and establish agreement. The idea of a mediator or the need for mediation is prevalent throughout the OT. Abraham entered into negotiations with God for mercy toward Sodom (Gen. 18:22-32), and Joab mediated between David and Absalom (2 Sam. 14:1-23). Most commonly it was the prophet, priest, or king who stood in this role. The prophets were representatives of God to the people and often had the task of pronouncing God's judgment or good news to the Israelites. Priests mediated for man in the presence of God (Lev. 9:7).

God the Son became incarnate as a man and fulfilled the role as the perfect mediator between God and man. Paul declares that man is unable to commune with God unless he come to Him through Jesus because there is only one mediator "between God and man, a man, Christ Jesus" (1 Tim. 2:5 HCSB). Christ, who is superior to Moses (Heb. 3:1-6), mediates a new covenant (Heb. 8:6) based upon His "once for all" substitutionary death on the cross that guarantees a better covenant (Heb. 7:22).

MEDITATION Deep thought or reflection upon some truth or supposition. A righteous person contemplates God or His great spiritual truths (Pss. 63:6; 143:5). He hopes to please God by meditation (Ps. 19:14). Thus meditation by God's people is a reverent act of worship. Through it they commune with God and are renewed spiritually. Meditation is an important part of the Christian's relationship with Christ.

Sunset over the Mediterranean Sea.

MEDITERRANEAN SEA Most of the important nations of ancient times were either on the shores of the Mediterranean Sea or operated in its 2,200 miles of water. These included Israel, Syria, Greece, Rome, Egypt, Philistia, and Phoenicia. The Mediterranean Sea served as the western border for the land of Canaan (Num. 34:6) and the territory of Judah (Josh. 15:12). Following the conquest of Palestine by Pompey in 63 BC, traffic on the Mediterranean increased. This development helped to make possible the missionary activity of Paul, Silas, Barnabas, and others. Paul made three missionary journeys across the Mediterranean. Under Roman arrest, Paul made his final voyage across the Mediterranean Sea and shipwrecked (Acts 27). Paul's work involved such Mediterranean cities as Caesarea, Antioch, Troas, Corinth, Tyre, Sidon, Syracuse, Rome, and Ephesus. Designated in the OT and the NT simply as "the sea" (Acts 10:6), the Mediterranean was also called the "Western Sea" (Deut. 11:24 RSV, NIV), and the "Sea of the Philistines" (Exod. 23:31).

MEDIUM A person possessed by (Lev. 20:6) or consulting (Deut. 18:11) a ghost or spirit of the dead, especially for information about the future. Acting as a medium was punishable by stoning (Lev. 20:27); consulting a medium, by exclusion from the congregation of Israel (Lev. 20:6). The transformation of King Saul from a person who expelled mediums (1 Sam. 28:3) to one who consulted a medium at En-dor (1 Sam. 28:8-19) graphically illustrates his fall.

MEEKNESS Humility and gentleness, usually exhibited during suffering and accompanied by faith in God. While God can be described as "meek" or "gentle" in His dealings with humanity (Ps. 18:35), meekness is primarily a character trait associated with people (Prov. 22:4). In the OT God often promises deliverance or salvation to the "meek," who are righteous persons suffering injustice, poverty, or oppression (Pss. 25:9; 147:6; Isa. 11:4). In the NT Jesus is presented as the supreme example of meekness (Matt. 11:29). Humble and faithful ("meek") disciples, although suffering the same rejection as their Messiah, will one day be vindicated by God (Matt. 5:5,11-12). Meekness is part of the "fruit of the Spirit," which is produced in believers by the Holy Spirit (Gal. 5:23). See *Humility.*

MEGIDDO Place-name, perhaps meaning "place of troops." One of the most strategic cities of Canaan since it guarded the main pass through the Carmel mountain range. This range was an obstacle along the international coastal highway that connected Egypt with Mesopotamia. After the conquest of Canaan by the Israelites, the city was allotted to Manasseh (Josh. 17:11), but it was not secured by the tribe. By the time of Solomon, though, the city was firmly Israelite, since he fortified the city (1 Kings 9:15), including his mighty six-chambered gate that followed the pattern of his other two key fortress cities of Hazor and Gezer. The Mount of Megiddo (har-Megiddon thus "Armageddon") will be where the kings of the world are gathered for the final battle in the last day of the Lord (Rev 16:16).

MEHUNIM KJV form of Meunim or Meunites, an Arab tribe whose name probably comes from the city of Ma'an about 12 miles southeast of Petra. The Meunites raided Judah during the reign of Jehoshaphat (873–849 BC)

Megiddo overlooking the valley of Jezreel.

according to 2 Chron. 20:1 (NASB, NIV, REB, NRSV). The Meunites are listed as temple servants in the postexilic period (Neh. 7:52). They were perhaps the descendants of prisoners of war.

MELCHIZEDEK Personal name meaning "Zedek is my king" or "My king is righteousness." Mysterious priest and king of Salem who blessed Abraham in the name of "God Most High." In return, Abraham gave Melchizedek a tenth of everything (Gen. 14:20). Melchizedek and Abraham both worshipped the one true God. Abraham also appeared to recognize the role of Melchizedek as a priest. The writer of Hebrews made several references in chapters 5–7 to Jesus' priesthood being of the "order of Melchizedek" as opposed to Levitical in nature. Only Jesus, whose life could not be destroyed by death, fit the description of a priest of "the order of Melchizedek."

MEM Thirteenth letter of the Hebrew alphabet that serves as the heading for Ps. 119:97-104. Each of these verses begins with this letter.

MEMORIAL Something that serves as a reminder. God's covenant name (Yahweh) was to be a "memorial name" (Exod. 3:15 NASB), a reminder of God's liberation of His people. The Passover served as a similar reminder (Exod. 13:9). In the NT the Lord's Supper serves as a reminder of Christ's sacrificial death and an assurance of His future coming (Matt. 26:13; 1 Cor. 11:25-26).

MEMPHIS Place-name meaning "the abode of the good one." An ancient capital of Egypt (Jer. 46:19) located just south of modern Cairo on the west bank of the Nile River. For over 300 years Memphis was the principal city of Egypt. Gradually, other cities grew in importance, and Memphis was eclipsed as the seat of power. Many of the royal pyramids of the Egyptian kings and the famous Spinx are located near Memphis.

One of several small sphinxes located at Memphis on the Nile River in Egypt.

MENAHEM Personal name meaning "consoler." King of Israel (reigned 752–742 BC) who assassinated Shallum to take the throne (2 Kings 15:10-14). After becoming king Menahem attacked and destroyed one of Israel's cities because it resisted his rule (2 Kings 15:16). He paid tribute to Tiglath-pileser III, the king of Assyria. This is the first mention of the Assyrian monarch in the biblical record. It is possible that Menahem obtained the throne of Israel with Tiglath-pileser's help. See *Tiglath-pileser.*

MENE,MENE,TEKEL,UPHARSIN Strange inscription written on the palace wall of King Belshazzar of Babylon that was interpreted by the prophet Daniel. He told the king that it meant "numbered, weighed, and divided," or Nebuchadnezzar and his kingdom had been weighed in the balance and found wanting. The kingdom would be divided and given to his enemies, the Medes and Persians. The overthrow occurred that very night (Dan. 5:30).

MENORAH Candelabrum used in Jewish worship, specifically the seven-branched lampstand used in the tabernacle (Exod. 25:31-35).

MEPHIBOSHETH Personal name meaning "shame destroyer" or "image breaker." **1.** Son of Jonathan and grandson of King Saul. Crippled at age five after his father was killed by the Philistines, Mephibosheth was granted special position and privilege in David's court (2 Sam. 9). **2.** Son of King Saul who was delivered by David to the Gibeonites to be hanged, in retaliation for Saul's earlier slaughter of a band of Gibeonites (2 Sam. 21:1-9).

MERAB Personal name from the root "to become many." Eldest daughter of King Saul (1 Sam. 14:49), who was twice promised to David in exchange for killing Goliath (1 Sam. 17:25) and for fighting the Lord's battles against the Philistines (1 Sam. 18:17-19). Saul reneged on his promise and gave Merab to another man.

MERARI Personal name meaning "bitterness" or "gall." Third son of Levi (1 Chron. 23:6) and ancestor of a division of priests, the Merarites.

MERARITES Major division of priests descended from Merari, the third son of Levi. The Merarites and Gershonites were responsible for the set up, breakdown, and transport of the tabernacle (Num. 10:17). The Merarites received an allotment of 12 cities from the tribes of Reuben, Gad, and Zebulun, including Ramoth-gilead, a city of refuge (1 Chron. 6:63,77-81). Representatives of the Merarites participated in David's move of the ark to Jerusalem (1 Chron. 15:6), served as tabernacle musicians (1 Chron. 15:17,19) and gatekeepers (1 Chron. 26:10,19), shared in Hezekiah's (2 Chron. 29:12) and Josiah's (2 Chron. 34:12) reforms, and returned from exile to assist in building the new temple (Ezra 8:19).

Trajan's Market in Rome, a large second-century AD "shopping center" where merchants sold their wares.

MERCHANT Buyer and seller of goods for profit. With the exception of the period of Solomon (1 Kings 10:15,22), Israel was not known as a nation of merchants. The majority of OT references to merchants are to nations other than Israel. Businessmen of Tyre sold fish and all kinds of merchandise in postexilic Jerusalem (Neh. 13:16). Tyre's trading partners included 22 nations or peoples encompassing Asia Minor, Palestine, Syria, Arabia, and Mesopotamia. Some merchants generated great wealth. The prophets railed against the pride that accompanied their material successes (Ezek. 27).

MERCURIUS Roman name for the pagan god Mercury. The people of Lystra referred to the apostle Paul by this name (Acts 14:12).

MERCY SEAT Slab of pure gold measuring about 45 inches by 27 inches that sat atop the ark of the covenant. It was the base for the golden cherubim (Exod. 25:17-19,21) and symbolized the throne from which God ruled Israel (Lev. 16:2; Num. 7:89). On the Day of Atonement the high priest sprinkled the blood of a sacrificial lamb on the mercy seat as a plea for forgiveness for the sins of the nation (Lev. 16:15). The Hebrew word for "mercy seat" means literally "to wipe out" or "cover over."

MERCY An attribute of God. On the human level it is best described as a person's consideration of the condition and needs of his fellow man. It is an essential disposition of a covenant people, especially Israel and the church. In the OT God's mercy was not primarily given to people outside His covenant community but was expressed mainly toward His people Israel. It also became the expected attitude and action of the people of Israel toward one another. This expectation was passed on to the church and became a chief characteristic of the lifestyle of believers. Jesus made it an essential part of His Christian manifesto in the Sermon on the Mount (Matt. 5:7).

Mercy as given by God is the foundation of forgiveness. God is not seen as displaying an emotion called mercy but as taking merciful action. This action was taken as Israel was in need: provisions such as manna in the wilderness (Exod. 13:31-35), protection such as the Shepherd who keeps Israel and does not sleep (Ps. 121), and deliverance (Ps. 56:12-23) as Yahweh who delivered His people from Egypt (1 Sam. 10:18). Mercy has never been the benefit of God's people because of their merit but is always the gift of God.

MERIBBAAL Personal name meaning perhaps "opponent of Baal" or "Baal defends." The original name of Mephibosheth, Jonathan's son (1 Chron. 8:34).

MERODACH Hebrew form of Marduk, the chief god of Babylon, also called Bel, corresponding to the Semitic Baal or "Lord" (Jer. 50:2). Merodach is an element in the names of the Babylonian kings Merodach-baladan (2 Kings 20:12; Isa. 39:1) and Evil-Merodach (2 Kings 25:27; Jer. 52:31).

MERODACH-BALADAN Personal name meaning "god Marduk gave an heir." King of Babylon who sent envoys to King Hezekiah of Judah (2 Kings 20:12-13). Hezekiah showed these agents the palace treasure house and treasuries, an action condemned by the prophet Isaiah (2 Kings 20:12–19).

MEROM Place-name meaning "high place." Place in Galilee where Joshua led Israel to defeat a coalition of Canaanite tribes under King Jabin of Hazor (Josh. 11:1-7).

MESHA Personal and place-name. **1.** Ruler of Moab who led a rebellion against the northern kingdom of Israel (2 Kings 3:4-27). Mesha succeeded in seizing Israelite border towns and in fortifying towns on his frontier. An alliance of Israel, Judah, and Edom, however, outflanked his defenses and attacked Mesha from the rear. Mesha retreated to Kir-hareseth, where he sacrificed his firstborn son to his god Chemosh on the city walls. In response the Israelites lifted their siege and returned home. **2.** Descendant of Benjamin living in Moab (1 Chron. 8:9). **3.** Descendant of Caleb (1 Chron. 2:42). **4.** City in the territory of the Joktanites (Gen. 10:30).

MESHACH Personal name. One of Daniel's friends exiled to Babylon after the fall of Jehoiakim in 597 BC (Dan. 1:6-7). His Hebrew name was Mishael ("Who is what God is") but was changed to Meshach (perhaps "Who is what Aku is") to mock Israel's God. Declining the rich food of the king's table, he and his friends proved that the simple fare of vegetables and water was superior to the king's rich food. After refusing to bow to the king's golden image, he, Shadrach, and Abednego were thrown into a flaming furnace but were delivered by God (Dan. 3).

MESOPOTAMIA The area between the Tigris and Euphrates rivers. This region was the homeland of the patriarchs (Gen. 11:31–12:4; 28:6). A Mesopotamian king subdued Israel for a time during the period of the judges (Judg. 3:8). Mesopotamia supplied mercenary chariots and cavalry for the Ammonites' war with David (1 Chron. 19:6; superscription of Ps. 60). Both the northern kingdom of Israel (1 Chron. 5:26) and the southern kingdom of Judah (2 Kings 24:14-16) went into exile in Mesopotamia.

MESSENGER One sent with a message. The Hebrew and Greek terms for "messenger" are frequently rendered "angel," the heavenly messengers of God. The prophets (Isa. 44:26; Hag. 1:13) and priests (Mal. 2:7) are termed messengers in their role as bearers of God's message for humanity. Sometimes messengers made advance travel arrangements for their master (Luke 9:52). The Gospel writers applied this preparatory function to John the Baptist (Mark 1:2).

MESSIAH Transliteration of Hebrew word meaning "anointed one" that was translated into Greek as *Christos*. "Christ" or Messiah is a name that expresses the church's link with Israel through the OT and the faith that sees Jesus Christ as the bearer of salvation for the world. "Anointed" carries several senses in the OT. All have to do with installing a person in an office in a way that the person will be regarded as accredited by Yahweh, Israel's God. Prophets such as Elisha were set apart in this way (1 Kings 19:16). Israelite kings were particularly hailed as Yahweh's anointed (Judg. 9:8), beginning with Saul (1 Sam. 9–10 NIV) and especially referring to David (2 Sam. 2:4; 5:3) and Solomon (1 Kings 1:39). The king in Israel thus became a sacred person to whom loyalty and respect were to be accorded (1 Sam. 24:6,10).

The king, especially in the Psalms, became idealized as a divine son (Ps. 2:2,7) and enjoyed God's protecting favor (Ps. 18:50). His dynasty would not fail (Ps. 132:17), and the people were encouraged to pray to God on his behalf (Ps. 84:9). The fall of Jerusalem in 586 BC led to great confusion, especially when Yahweh's anointed was taken into exile as a prisoner (Lam. 4:20) and his authority as king rejected by the nations (Ps. 89:38,51).

After the exile the Israelite priesthood came into prominence. In the absence of a king, the high priest took on a central role in the community. The rite of anointing was the outward sign of his authority to function as God's representative. This authority was traced back to Aaron and his sons (Exod. 29:7-9). The high priest was the anointed-priest (Lev. 4:3,5,16) and even, in one place, a "messiah" (Zech. 4:14). In the exilic and postexilic ages, the expectation of a coming Messiah came into sharper focus, beginning with Jeremiah's and Ezekiel's vision of a Messiah who would combine the traits of royalty and priestly dignity (Jer. 33:14-18; Ezek. 46:1-8).

A question posed about Jesus in John 4:29 is: "Could this be the Messiah?" (HCSB). The issue of the Messiah's identity and role was much debated among the Jews in the first century. In the Synoptic Gospels the way Jesus acted and spoke led naturally to the dialogue at Caesarea Philippi. Jesus asked His disciples, "Who do you say that I am?" a question to which Peter replied, "You are the Messiah" (Mark 8:29 HCSB). Mark made clear that Jesus took an attitude of distinct reserve and caution to this title since it carried overtones of political power. Jesus, therefore, accepted Peter's confession with great reluctance since with it went the disciple's objection that the Messiah could not suffer (Mark 9:32). For Peter, Messiah was a title of a glorious personage both nationalistic and victorious in battle. Jesus, on the other hand, saw His destiny in terms of a suffering Son of man and Servant of God (Mark 10:33-34).

The course of Jesus' ministry is one in which He sought to wean the disciples away from the traditional notion of a warrior Messiah. Instead, Jesus tried to instill in their minds the prospect that the road to His future glory was bound to run by way of the cross, with its experience of rejection, suffering, and humiliation. After the trial before His Jewish judges (Matt. 26:63-66) He went to the cross as a crucified Messiah because the Jewish leaders failed to perceive the nature of messiahship as Jesus understood it. Pilate sentenced Him as a messianic pretender who claimed (according to the false charges brought against Him) to be a rival to Caesar (John 19:14-15). It was only after the resurrection that the disciples were in a position to see how Jesus was truly a king Messiah and how Jesus then opened their minds to what true messiahship meant (Luke 24:45-46). The national title "Messiah" then took on a broader connotation, involving a kingly role that was to embrace all peoples (Luke 24:46-47). See *Christ, Christology; Jesus Christ.*

MESSIANIC SECRET Term that Bible students use to describe Jesus' commands not to reveal who He was after His performance of messianic wonders. Mark used the unveiling of the messiahship of Jesus as the unifying theme of his Gospel. Demons demonstrated that they recognized Jesus immediately: "I know who You are—the Holy One of God!" (Mark 1:24-25,34 HCSB); nevertheless, Jesus suppressed their confession. He prohibited public profession by those who experienced miraculous healing (Mark 8:26). The parables of Jesus were offered in order to keep "outsiders" from learning the secret (Mark 4:11-12). Even the disciples, once they related that they understood the "secret of the kingdom of God" (Mark 4:11), were sworn to silence (Mark 9:9).

Perhaps Jesus avoided the title because of the popular messianic expectations of the people. They were looking for a political deliverer. Some believe that Jesus prohibited messianic proclamation so He could continue to move about freely in public. The only parable of Jesus that Mark recorded exclusively may provide a clue to the purpose of the messianic secret. Jesus introduced the parable of the secret growing seed (Mark 4:26-29) with the proverb: "For nothing is concealed except to be revealed, and nothing hidden except to come to light" (4:22 HCSB). Like the seed that is covered by ground, the secret of Jesus' identity would be concealed for a season. The disciples needed time to recognize Jesus as Messiah (Mark 4:41; 6:52; 8:17-21). They also needed time to come to terms with the fact that His messianic suffering would precede messianic glory (Mark 9:31-32). Complete human understanding of the messianic secret would only be possible after the resurrection (Mark 9:9-10). See *Christ, Christology; Jesus Christ; Messiah.*

METHUSELAH Personal name meaning either "man of the javelin" or "worshipper of Selah." A son of Enoch and grandfather of Noah (Gen. 5:21,26-29) who died at the age of 969 (Gen. 5:27), making him the oldest man in the Bible.

MEZUZAH Hebrew word for "doorpost." Ancient doors pivoted on posts set in sockets. The blood of the Passover lamb was to be applied to doorposts (Exod. 12:7,22-23). Today the word *mezuzah* refers to small scrolls inscribed with Deut. 6:4-9 and 11:13-21 and placed in a container attached to the doorjambs of Jewish homes.

MICAH Abbreviated form of the personal name Micaiah, meaning "Who is like Yahweh?" **1.** Ephraimite whose home shrine was the source of Dan's idolatrous worship (Judg. 17–18). **2.** Descendant of Reuben (1 Chron. 5:5). **3.** Descendant of King Saul (2 Sam. 9:12 KJV, Micha). **4.** Leader of a family of Levites in David's time (1 Chron. 23:20). **5.** Father of Abdon, a contemporary of King Josiah of Judah (2 Kings 22:12, Micaiah). **6.** Prophet of the eighth century BC who came from Moresheth (NRSV, HCSB), which probably should be identified with Moresheth-gath. Micah prophesied during the reigns of Jotham (750–732 BC), Ahaz (735–715 BC), and Hezekiah (715–686 BC), kings of Judah. Even though Micah ministered in Judah, some of his messages were directed toward the northern kingdom of Israel.

MICAH, BOOK OF A short prophetic book of the OT in which the prophet Micah condemned the rich for oppressing the poor, criticized unjust business practices, denounced the idolatry of the people, and predicted the destruction of Judah as an act of God's judgment. At the same time he proclaimed messages of hope. Judgment would come, but afterwards God would restore a remnant of the people devoted to Him (7:14-20). Perhaps Micah is best known for its prediction that the Messiah would be born in Bethlehem (Mic. 5:2). Matthew saw in Micah's hope for a new ruler a description of Christ (Matt. 2:6).

MICAIAH Personal name meaning "Who is like Yahweh?" **1.** Prophet who predicted the death of King Ahab and the scattering of Israel's forces at Ramoth-gilead (1 Kings 22:7-28). **2.** Form of Michaiah preferred by modern translations.

MICHAEL Personal name meaning "Who is like God?" **1.** Father of one of the 12 Israelite spies (Num. 13:13). **2–3.** Two Gadites (1 Chron. 5:13-14). **4.** Ancestor of Asaph (1 Chron. 6:40). **5.** Leader of the tribe of Issachar (1 Chron. 7:3). **6.** Leader of the tribe of Benjamin (1 Chron. 8:16). **7.** Manassite who defected to David's army (1 Chron. 12:20). **8.** Son of King Jehoshaphat (2 Chron. 21:2). **9.** Ancestor of one of those who returned from exile with Ezra (Ezra 8:8). **10.** Archangel who served as the guardian of the nation of Israel (Dan. 12:1). Together with Gabriel, Michael fought for Israel against the prince of Persia. In Rev. 12:7 Michael commands the forces of God against the forces of the dragon in a war in heaven. See *Angel.*

MICHAL Personal name meaning "Who is like God?" King Saul's daughter (1 Sam. 14:49), given to David in marriage for killing 100 Philistines (1 Sam. 18:20-29). Michal criticized King David for dancing before the ark of the covenant as he brought the sacred chest to Jerusalem. As punishment Michal was never allowed to bear children (2 Sam. 6:16-23).

MICHMASH Place-name meaning "hidden place." City in Benjamin about seven miles northeast of Jerusalem that served as a staging area, first for King Saul (1 Sam. 13:2) and then for the Philistine army. Before the battle began, Jonathan and his armor bearer sneaked into the Philistine camp, killed 20 sentries, and set off great confusion, resulting in the Philistines fighting one another (1 Sam. 14:20).

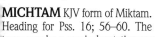
View of the gorge at Michmash.

MICHTAM KJV form of Miktam. Heading for Pss. 16; 56–60. The term may be a musical notation or a title for psalms connected with expiation of sin.

MIDDLE WALL Term found in Eph. 2:14 and variously translated as "middle wall of partition" (KJV); "dividing wall of hostility" (HCSB, NRSV, NIV); "barrier of the dividing wall" (NASB); "barrier of enmity which separated them" (REB). There are several possible interpretations of this word. **1.** The wall that separated the inner and outer courts of the temple and prevented Jews and Gentiles from worshipping together. **2.** The curtain that separated the holy of holies from the rest of the temple. This curtain was torn at the death of Jesus (Mark 15:38) and is representative of the separation of all humanity from God. **3.** The "fence" consisting of detailed commandments and oral interpretations erected around the law by its interpreters to ensure its faithful observation. **4.** The cosmic barrier that separates God and people, people themselves, and other powers in the universe (Eph. 1:20-21)—angels, dominions, principalities. **5.** Echoing Isa. 59:2, the term refers to the separation of humanity from God as a result of sin.

No one interpretation is sufficient by itself. The writer of Ephesians emphasized that every conceivable barrier that exists between people and between God and humanity has been destroyed by Jesus Christ.

MIDIAN, MIDIANITES Personal and clan name meaning "strife." Midian was the son of Abraham by his concubine Keturah (Gen. 25:2). Abraham sent him and his brothers away to the east, leading to the association of the Midianites with the "children of the east" (Judg. 6:3). The people of Israel had both good and bad relationships with the Midianites. When Moses fled from Pharaoh, he went east to Midian (Exod. 2:15). Here he met Jethro, the priest of Midian, and married his daughter. In the time of the judges the Midianites along with the Amalekites began to raid Israel. Gideon drove them out and killed their leaders (Judg. 6–8). They never again threatened Israel, but Midian did harbor Solomon's enemy Hadad (1 Kings 11:18).

MIDRASH Jewish interpretations of the OT included a form called Midrash. The word was used to denote the process of biblical interpretation or the written expression of that interpretation. According to early rabbinic tradition, Hillel the Elder formulated seven rules that guided Jewish biblical interpretation. These rules were sensible guidelines for understanding the Bible. Examples of the application of each rule appear in the NT. Later rabbis formulated many other rules that resulted in wild, fanciful interpretations that lost all connection with the literary and historical context of the passage under discussion.

The NT contains midrash and is midrashic in the sense that many portions of the NT offer interpretations of specific OT texts that follow the normal patterns of exegesis suggested by ancient rabbis. The study of midrash may offer the interpreter of Scripture insight into the methods of interpretation used throughout Jewish history. As the student examines the strengths and weaknesses of these approaches to interpretation, he may learn how a person's culture and worldview impact his understanding of the Bible and how he may more "accurately interpret the word of truth."

MIDWIFE Woman who assisted in the delivery of a baby (Exod. 1:15-21). The duties of the midwife likely included cutting the umbilical cord, washing and salting the infant, and wrapping the child in cloths (Ezek. 16:4).

MIGHTY MEN As applied to the descendants of the Nephilim, "mighty men" likely indicates men of great size (Gen. 6:4). Elsewhere the phrase refers to valiant warriors, especially to the elite groups of three and thirty who served David (1 Kings 1:10,38).

MILCOM Name of a pagan god meaning "king" or "their king." Apparently this was a form created by Hebrew scribes to avoid pronouncing the name of the national god of Ammon (1 Kings 11:5,7), who may have been identified with Chemosh, the god of Moab. Solomon built sanctuaries to Milcom on the Mount of Olives at the request of his foreign wives, reviving the ancient cult (1 Kings 11:5,33). See *Chemosh; Moab; Molech.*

MILDEW Fungus causing a whitish growth on plants. The Hebrew term rendered "mildew" means "paleness." The term may refer to the yellowing of leaves as a result of drought rather than to a fungus (1 Kings 8:37). Mildew is one of the agricultural plagues God sent to encourage repentance.

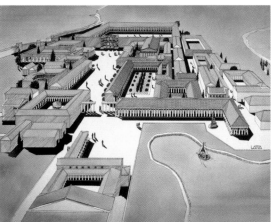

Reconstruction of the Asian city of Miletus as it appeared in the first century AD

MILETUM (KJV) or **MILETUS** Ancient city on the west coast of Asia Minor that served as the port for Ephesus. Paul met with the elders of the church at Ephesus in Miletus (Acts 20:15-17). See *Ephesus.*

MILK Nourishing liquid and its by-products, a staple of the Hebrew diet. Most often milk came from sheep and goats (Deut. 32:14); cow's milk was also known (Isa. 7:21-22). Butter and cheese were known among the ancients (1 Sam. 17:18) as well as curdled, sour milk, which still forms one of the main foods of the poorer classes in Arabia and Syria. This soured milk was carried by travelers who mixed it with meat, dried it, and then dissolved it in water to make a refreshing drink such as that set before his visitors by Abraham (Gen. 18:8).

Rotary mills at Capernaum.

MILL Two circular stones used to grind grain. The grain is fed into a hole in the upper stone and gradually works down between the stones for grinding. It was forbidden to take millstones as a pledge because they were essential for sustaining life (Deut. 24:6).

MILLENNIUM This expression, taken from Latin words, means 1,000 years. The Bible passage that mentions the "thousand years" is Rev. 20:1-7, where the word appears six times. There are three schools of thought about the millennium: amillennialism, premillennialism, and postmillennialism. The prefixes "a," "pre," and "post" suggest different views of the timing of the Lord Jesus Christ's second coming in relation to the "thousand years."

Postmillennialists argue that Christ returns *after* the thousand years. Premillennialists argue that Christ comes *before* the thousand years. Amillennialists, much like postmillennialists, also contend that the Lord comes after the thousand years, but they understand the thousand years differently. For the amillennialist, as the prefix suggests, there really is no literal thousand years. Instead, the whole inter-advent period between the first and second comings of Christ is taken to be the "millennium." Some postmillennialists argue with the amillennialists that the millennium may not be a literal thousand years, yet they generally agree with the premillennialists that the millennium is yet future. There are many variations even among adherents to the same broad view of the millennium.

Despite differences on the details, all evangelicals are firmly committed to the literal second coming of Jesus Christ.

MILLET A small cereal grain. Millet makes a poor quality bread and is normally mixed with other grains (Ezek. 4:9).

MILLO Hebrew word meaning "filling" that describes a stone terrace system used in ancient construction. **1.** A Canaanite sanctuary built upon an artificial platform or fill and thus named "House of the Filling" (Judg 9:6, 20). **2.** A tower built by David near Jerusalem for defensive purposes (2 Sam. 5:9). It was improved by King Solomon because of a threat from Assyria (1 Kings 9:15).

MIND The seat of human reflection, understanding, reasoning, feeling, and decision making. Philippians 1:27 says believers are to be of "one mind (soul)." Hebrews 12:3 urges believers not to faint in your minds (souls)." These passages show that the mind is considered to be the center of the human personality. The mind can be evil. It is described as "reprobate" (Rom. 1:28 KJV), "fleshly" (Col. 2:18), "vain" (Eph. 4:17), "corrupt" (2 Tim. 3:8), and "defiled" (Titus 1:15). On the other hand, believers are commanded to love God with all their mind (Matt. 22:37). This is possible because the mind can be empowered by the Holy Spirit (Rom. 12:2) and because God's laws under the new covenant are put into our minds (Heb. 8:10).

MINERALS AND METALS Inorganic elements or compounds found naturally in nature. A number of precious stones, minerals, and metals are mentioned in the Bible.

Precious Stones The Bible contains three extensive lists of precious stones: the 12 stones in Aaron's breastpiece (Exod. 39:10-13), the treasures of the king of Tyre (Ezek. 28:13), and the stones in the foundation of the new Jerusalem (Rev. 21:18-21). Other lists are found in Job 28:15-19; Isa. 54:11-12; and Ezek. 27:16. The precise identification of some of the terms is unclear, and they are rendered differently in various English translations of the Bible.

Adamant This Hebrew word is sometimes translated "diamond" (Jer. 17:1 KJV, NRSV, REB, NASB). The stone was "harder than flint" (Ezek. 3:9) and may be emery (Ezek. 3:9 NASB) or an imaginary stone of impenetrable hardness. It is perhaps best translated "the hardest stone" (Ezek. 3:9 NRSV).

Agate Multicolored and banded form of chalcedony. It was on Aaron's breastpiece (Exod. 28:19) and by some translations is the third stone in the foundation of the new Jerusalem (Rev. 21:19 NRSV).

Amethyst (Exod. 28:19; 39:12; Rev. 21:20) Identical with modern amethyst, a blue-violet form of quartz.

Beryl Most translations indicate beryl is the first stone in the fourth row of Aaron's breastpiece (Exod. 28:20; 39:13; REB "topaz"; NIV "chrysolite"). The word also occurs in the list of the king of

Tyre's jewels (Ezek. 28:13; RSV, NIV "chrysolite"; NRSV "beryl"; REB "topaz").

Carbuncle In KJV, RSV the third stone in Aaron's breastpiece (Exod. 28:17; 39:10; REB "green feldspar"; NASB, NRSV "emerald"; TEV "garnet"; NIV "beryl") and material for the gates of the restored Jerusalem (Isa. 54:12; REB "garnet"; NIV "sparkling jewels").

Carnelian (KJV and sometimes RSV, NASB "sardius") A clear to brownish red variety of chalcedony. NRSV reading for one of the stones of the king of Tyre (Ezek. 28:13; NASB, TEV, NIV "ruby"; REB "sardin") and the sixth stone in the foundation of the new Jerusalem wall (Rev. 21:20; cp. 4:3).

Mineral deposits from the hot minera[l] springs at Hierapolis.

Chalcedony Alternate translation for agate as the third stone in the foundation of the nev[w] Jerusalem (Rev. 21:19 HCSB, KJV, NASB, REB, NIV). This non-crystalline form of quartz has man[y] varieties, including agate, carnelian, chrysoprase, flint, jasper, and onyx.

Chrysolite (Rev. 21:20) Represents various yellowish minerals. It replaces the KJV renderin[g] "beryl" frequently in the RSV (Ezek. 1:16; 10:9; 28:13) and throughout the NIV but not in NRS[V] REB reads "topaz."

Chrysoprase or Chrysoprasus (KJV) Apple-green variety of chalcedony, the tenth stone i[n] the foundation of the new Jerusalem (Rev. 21:20).

Coral (Job 28:18; Ezek. 27:16) Calcium carbonate formed by the action of marine animals. NRS[V] REB, NASB translated a second word as coral (Lam. 4:7 KJV, NIV "rubies").

Crystal Refers to quartz, the two Hebrew words so translated being related to "ice." In Job 28:1[8] KJV has "pearls", the NIV "jasper", but NRSV, NASB read "crystal," while REB has "alabaster." Th[e] glassy sea (Rev. 4:6) and river of life (Rev. 22:1) are compared to crystal.

Diamond Stone in the high priest's breastpiece (Exod. 28:18; 39:11; REB "jade"; NIV "emer[-] ald") and one of the jewels of the king of Tyre (Ezek. 28:13; NRSV, REB "jasper"; NIV "emerald"[)] It is not clear, however, if diamonds were known in the ancient Near East, and the translation i[s] uncertain.

Emerald Bright green variety of beryl. A stone in the high priest's breastpiece and one of th[e] stones of the king of Tyre (Exod. 28:18; 39:11; Ezek. 28:13; REB "purple garnet"; NASB, NIV, NRS[V] "turquoise"), with NRSV translating another word as "emerald" in Ezek. 28:13. The rainbow aroun[d] the throne is compared to an emerald (Rev. 4:3), which was also a stone in the foundation of th[e] new Jerusalem (Rev. 21:19).

Jacinth Transparent red to brown form of zirconium silicate. It appears in Aaron's breastpiec[e] (Exod. 28:19; 39:12; KJV "ligure"; REB, TEV "turquoise") and the foundation of new Jerusalen[m] (Rev. 21:20).

Jasper (Exod. 28:20; 39:13; Rev. 21:11,18-19) A red, yellow, brown, or green opaque variety o[f] chalcedony. In the RSV at Ezekiel 28:13, "jasper" translates the word elsewhere rendered "diamond[" (REB "jade"), but NRSV reads "moonstone" with the sixth stone jasper as in other translations.

Lapis Lazuli Not one mineral but a combination of minerals that yields an azure to green-blu[e] stone popular in Egypt for jewelry. It is an alternate translation for sapphire (NASB in Ezek. 28:13[NIV marginal notes).

Onyx A flat-banded variety of chalcedony; sardonyx includes layers of carnelian. Onyx was use[d] on the ephod (Exod. 25:7; 28:9; 35:27; 39:6) and in the high priest's breastpiece (Exod. 28:2[0] 39:13). It was provided for the settings of the temple (1 Chron. 29:2) and was one of the preciou[s] stones of the king of Tyre (Ezek. 28:13).

Pearl (Job 28:18 NASB, NRSV; KJV, NIV "rubies"; REB "red coral") Formed around foreign ma[t-] ter in some shellfish. In the NT, "pearl" is a simile for the kingdom of God (Matt. 13:46), a metaph[or] for truth (Matt. 7:6), and a symbol of immodesty (1 Tim. 2:9). Pearl is also material for the gates [of] the new Jerusalem (Rev. 21:21).

Ruby Red variety of corundum, or aluminum oxide. The first stone of Aaron's breastpiece is some[-] times translated "ruby" (Exod. 28:17; 39:10 NASB, NIV; KJV, RSV, REB "sardius"; NRSV "ca[r-] nelian"). It also appears as a stone of the king of Tyre (Ezek. 28:13 NASB, NIV; REB, KJV "sardius[" NRSV "carnelian").

Sapphire (Exod. 24:10; Lam. 4:7; Rev. 21:19) The Hebrew *sappir* is a blue variety of corundum[. It is possible that *sappir* refers to lapis lazuli (NIV marginal notes) rather than true sapphire.

Topaz Stone in Aaron's breastpiece (Exod. 28:17; 39:10); also mentioned in the wisdom list (Jo[b] 28:19) and the list of the king of Tyre's precious stones (Ezek. 28:13). True topaz is an aluminu[m] floro silicate and quite hard, but the OT topaz may refer to peridot, a magnesium olivine. The ninth decorative stone of the new Jerusalem wall foundation is topaz (Rev. 21:20). See *Beryl, Chrysolite* above.

Turquoise Sky-blue to bluish-green base phosphate of copper and aluminum was mined in the Sinai by the Egyptians and was a highly valued stone in antiquity. Turquoise is sometimes substituted for emerald (Exod. 28:18 NASB, NIV) or jacinth (Exod. 28:19; 39:11 REB, TEV).

The following minerals are mentioned in the Bible.

Alabaster A fine-grained gypsum, but Egyptian alabaster was crystalline calcium carbonate with a similar appearance. Alabaster may be mentioned once in the Song of Songs (5:15 NRSV, NASB; KJV, REB, NIV "marble"). In the NT (Mark 14:3) it refers to containers for precious ointment.

Brimstone Refers to sulfur (NRSV, NIV). Burning sulfur deposits created extreme heat, molten flows, and noxious fumes, providing a graphic picture of the destruction and suffering of divine judgment (Isa. 30:33; Luke 17:29).

Salt Sodium chloride is an abundant mineral, used as a seasoning for food (Job 6:6) and offerings (Ezek. 43:24). As a preservative, salt was symbolic of covenants (2 Chron. 13:5). Both meanings are present in Jesus' comparison of the disciples to salt (Matt. 5:13). Salt was also a symbol of desolation and barrenness, perhaps because of the barrenness of the Dead Sea, the biblical Salt Sea.

Soda (Prov. 25:20 NASB, NIV; Jer. 2:22 REB, NIV), or **nitre** (KJV), is probably sodium or potassium carbonate. Other translations prefer lye (Jer. 2:22 NRSV, NASB). In Prov. 25:20 the Hebrew text refers to vinegar or lye or soda, but some modern translations follow the earliest Greek translation in reading "vinegar on a wound" (NRSV, REB; TEV "salt in a wound").

The following metals are mentioned in the Bible.

Brass Relatively modern alloy of copper and tin. Brass in the KJV should be rendered "copper" or "bronze." RSV substitutes bronze, retaining brass only in a few places (Lev. 26:19; Deut. 28:23; Isa. 48:4; NRSV using brass only in Isa. 48:4). NIV does not use brass.

Bronze Usual translation of the Hebrew word that can indicate either copper or bronze. An alloy of copper and tin, and stronger than both, bronze was the most common metal used to make utensils in the ancient Near East. The Bible mentions armor (1 Sam. 17:5-6), shackles (2 Kings 25:7), cymbals (1 Chron. 15:19), gates (Isa. 45:2), and idols (Rev. 9:20), as well as other bronze objects.

Copper Usually alloyed with tin to make bronze, which had greater strength. The KJV uses copper only in Ezra 8:27 (NRSV, NIV "bronze"). See *Ezion-gaber*.

Gold Valued and used because of its rarity, beauty, and workability. A number of Israel's worship objects were solid gold or gilded (Exod. 37). Gold occurs in the Bible more frequently than any other metal, being used for jewelry (1 Tim. 2:9), idols, scepters, worship utensils, and money (Matt. 10:9; Acts 3:6). The new Jerusalem is described as made of gold (Rev. 21:18,21).

Iron A more difficult metal to smelt than copper, it did not come into widespread use until about the time of Israel's conquest of Canaan. The Canaanites' "chariots of iron" (Judg. 4:3) represented a technological advantage over Israel, while the Philistines may have enjoyed an iron-working monopoly (1 Sam. 17:7). Iron was used where strength was essential and became a symbol of hardness and strength (Ps. 2:9).

Lead Gray metal of extremely high density (Exod. 15:10) used for weights, heavy covers (Zech. 5:7-8), and plumb lines (Amos 7:7-8). Lead is quite pliable and useful for inlays such as lettering in rock (Job 19:24). It was also used in the refining of silver (Jer. 6:27-30).

Silver Silver was a measure of wealth (Zeph. 1:18). By Solomon's day it was common in Israel (1 Kings 10:27) and was the standard monetary unit, being weighed in shekels, talents, and minas (Exod. 21:32). Silver was used for objects in Israel's worship (Exod. 36:24), idols (Ps. 115:4), and jewelry (Song 1:11).

Tin (Num. 31:22; Ezek. 22:18,20) Sometimes confused with lead; articles of pure tin were rare. It was principally used in making bronze, an alloy of tin and copper.

MINGLED PEOPLE KJV term for foreigners who are perhaps of mixed race and are associated with a dominant population (Ezek. 30:5).

MINISTER, MINISTRY One who serves another. God's call to Abram (Gen. 12) contains the foundations of ministry. God's promise was to begin with Abram and Sarai and from them make a nation that would be a blessing to all nations. For Christians Jesus is the supreme model of a minister. In His inaugural sermon in the synagogue at Nazareth, Jesus read from the Prophet Isaiah, summarizing the purpose of His ministry (Luke 4:18-19). Although Jesus had all authority in heaven and on earth, His style of leadership and ministry was not one of dominating His followers (Mark 10:42) but one of service. On one occasion when James and John sought prominent places in Jesus' kingdom, He reminded them, "For even the Son of Man did not come to be served, but to serve, and to give His life—a ransom for many" (Mark 10:45 HCSB).

Jesus' intention was that His ministry would continue through His people, the church. God through the Holy Spirit gives a variety of roles and gifts to those in the church for the purpose of ministry. These include preaching, evangelism, teaching, pastoral care, and administration.

MINSTREL KJV term for musician (Matt. 9:23). Modern translations have "flute players" or "musicians." Professional musicians were hired to assist in mourning at funerals. See *Grief and Mourning.*

MINT AND CUMIN Mint is a sweet-smelling herb for seasoning food. Cumin is a caraway-like herb used in seasonings and in medicine (Matt. 23:23).

MIRACLES, SIGNS, WONDERS Events that involve an immediate and powerful action of God designed to reveal His character or purposes. Words used in the Scriptures to describe the miraculous include "sign," "wonder," "work," "mighty work," "portent," and "power." The basic nature of a sign is that it points people to God. "Wonders" describe God's supernatural activity, a special manifestation of His power (Exod. 7:3). New Testament writers also used *dunamis*, power or inherent ability, to refer to activity of supernatural origin or character (Mark 6:2; Heb. 2:4). "Work" (*ergon*) is also used in the NT in the sense of "miracle." John the Baptist heard of the "works" of Jesus while he was in prison (Matt. 11:2).

Contemporary philosophical and theological arguments over the possibility of the miraculous reflect the altered worldview of the last several centuries—from a theistic to a non-theistic concept of the universe. We live in a world that seems intent on squeezing the supernatural out of the realm of reality. The people of the Bible did not face this problem. The biblical perspective on the universe is that it is created, sustained, and providentially governed by God. The Bible makes no clear-cut distinction between the natural and supernatural. In the "natural" event the Bible views God as working providentially; whereas, in the miraculous, God works in striking ways to call attention to Himself or His purposes.

One's view of the miraculous is related to one's view of the universe. A mechanistic perspective believes the world is controlled by unalterable natural laws and cannot allow for the possibility of miracles. Christians in every century have refused to have their universe so limited. They have affirmed the continuing miraculous work of God in the universe He created, continues to care for, uses to reveal Himself, and has promised to redeem.

MIRIAM Personal name meaning "bitter," "God's gift," "beloved," or "defiant." **1.** Sister of Moses and Aaron. She played a key role in the rescue of the baby Moses (Exod. 2:4-8) and in the experience of the exodus and the wilderness community. After crossing the Red Sea, she assumed the role of prophetess and led the women in singing a song of victory (Exod. 15:20-21). Miriam sided with Aaron in an act of rebellion against Moses. God chastened her by striking her with leprosy, but granted healing following Moses' intercessory prayer and a seven-day quarantine (Num. 12:15). **2.** Member of the clan of Caleb (1 Chron. 4:17).

MIRROR Polished or smooth surface that produces images by reflection. In Bible times mirrors were made of polished metal (Job 37:18). The Apostle Paul spoke of the unclear reflections seen in such mirrors (1 Cor. 13:12).

MISHNAH A term that refers to the teaching about the oral law (*halakah*) passed on by a particular teacher (rabbi). According to the Mishnah itself, oral tradition and its teachings go all the way back to Moses, who received the halakah from God on Mt. Sinai and passed it on to subsequent generations. The Mishnah has helped scholars reconstruct specific elements in the Judaism of Palestine at the time of Jesus. It has also been helpful in understanding the development of Judaism during the period of establishment and growth of the early Christian church.

MISSION(S) Task on which God sends a person whom He has called, particularly a mission to introduce another group of people to salvation in Christ. In the Christian context the person sent is called a missionary. The mission of the churches is to send missionaries to all parts of the world until everyone has had the opportunity to hear the message of Jesus and accept Him as Lord. Mission is an important OT concept. Its foundation lies in the

Bronze mirror with a bone handle from the Etruscan culture (ca 350 BC).

understanding that the transcendent God is also the God who is involved in history. He is the God who acts. The record of His involvement in history indicates that His work is both revelatory and redemptive. People know who God is by what He has done. Since the fall (Gen. 3), God's primary activity has been redemptive (Josh. 24:2-15). God sends His messengers to the house of Israel and His prophets as His spokesmen to all nations.

God's mission concern is inclusive, not exclusive. His interest has been in all people, not just in Israel. When God called Abraham and his descendants, they were chosen, not to be exclusive vessels, but to be a means of blessing "all families of the earth" (Gen. 12:1-3). Later God told Israel that they had been elected as God's chosen people (Exod. 19:3-6). They were to be the recipient and guardian of God's special revelation (Heb. 1:1-3) and the channel through which the Redeemer would enter the stream of human history (Isa. 49:1-10).

The NT brings to a crescendo the Bible's symphonic theme of mission. The mission begins with Jesus who was sent to earth to reveal the Father (John 1:18), to glorify Him (John 13:31), to bring the kingdom of God on earth (Matt. 12:22-32), and to make God's love and mercy known to a lost world. He came to seek and save the lost (Luke 19:10). Through His teachings Jesus made clear that His mission was to continue after He ascended. Each of the Gospels and Acts contain an account of His mandate to His followers, telling them to go to all the world, make disciples, baptize them, and preach the gospel (Matt. 28:19-20; Mark 16:15-16; Luke 24:46-49; John 20:21-22; Acts 1:8). Jesus assumed that the church would reach out beyond itself. The church was to cross all barriers—to reach out to all ethnic groups, clans, tribes, social classes, and cultures. The message of salvation was to be shared with all people everywhere.

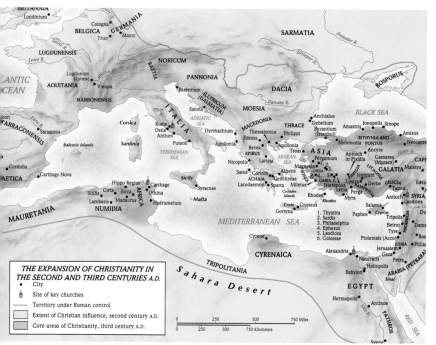

THE EXPANSION OF CHRISTIANITY IN THE SECOND AND THIRD CENTURIES A.D.
- • City
- ⛪ Site of key churches
- ----- Territory under Roman control
- ☐ Extent of Christian influence, second century A.D.
- ☐ Core areas of Christianity, third century A.D.

MIST The mist of Gen. 2:6 refers to subterranean waters welling up and watering the ground. In Job 36:27 rain distills from the mist or fog rising from the earth. Mist is often symbolic of something that disappears quickly (James 4:14; 2 Pet. 2:17).

MITRE KJV term for a type of headdress, probably a turban. The mitre was part of the high priest's distinctive clothing (Exod. 28:4,36-39) and was required dress on the Day of Atonement (Lev. 16:4).

MITYLENE Place-name meaning "purity." Chief city of the Aegean island of Lesbos southeast of Asia Minor. Paul stopped at Mitylene on his return trip to Syria from Achaia during his third missionary journey (Acts 20:14).

MIXED MULTITUDE Term for foreigners who associate themselves with a dominant ethnic group. The term is used for those foreigners who joined the Israelites in the exodus from Egypt (Exod.

12:38), who became associated with the people of Judah during the exile (Neh. 13:3), or who were associated with the Egyptians (Jer. 25:20) or Babylonians (Jer. 50:37). See *Mingled People*.

MIZPAH or **MIZPEH** Place-name meaning "watchtower" or "lookout." **1.** Place in Gilead where Laban and Jacob made a covenant and set up a pillar (Gen. 31:49). This Mizpah was also the hometown of Jephthah, a judge of Israel (Judg. 11). **2.** A district near Mt. Hermon (Josh. 11:3–8). **3.** A city in the lowland plain of Judah (Josh 15:38). **4.** A city of Benjamin where Saul was first presented to Israel as its new king (1 Sam. 10:17).

MIZRAIM Hebrew word for Egypt (Gen. 12:10; 25:18). **1.** Son of Ham (Gen. 10:6,13). **2.** The Mushri, a people of Cilicia in southeastern Asia Minor (possibly 1 Kings 10:28; 2 Kings 7:6; 2 Chron. 1:16-17 TEV; NIV note). See *Egypt*.

MNASON Personal name meaning "remembering"; variant of Jason. Native of Cyprus, and Paul's host during his final trip to Jerusalem in about AD 60 (Acts 21:16).

MOAB AND THE MOABITE STONE

Personal and national name and monument that the nation left behind. The narrow strip of land east of the Dead Sea was known in biblical times as "Moab." The history of the Moabites was intertwined with that of Israel. Moreover, the Israelites regarded the Moabites as close relatives, as implied by Gen. 19:30-38. There were peaceful interchanges as well as conflicts between the Israelites and Moabites during the time of the judges. The story of Ruth illustrates peaceful relations, while the episode of Ehud and Eglon illustrates conflict (Judg. 3:12-30).

King Saul of Judah is reported to have fought against the Moabites (1 Sam. 14:47). David, a descendant of the Moabitess Ruth according to the biblical genealogies (Ruth 4:18-22), placed his parents under the protection of the king of Moab while he was on the run from Saul (1 Sam. 22:3-4). Yet he is reported to have defeated the Moabites in battle later on and to have executed two-thirds of the Moabite prisoners by arbitrary selection (2 Sam. 8:2). Moab was represented among Solomon's wives, and the worship of Chemosh, the Moabite god, accommodated in Solomon's Jerusalem (1 Kings 11:1-8).

The Moabite Stone found at Dibon. In the inscription, Mesha, king of Moab, gives thanks to Chemosh for delivering Moab out of the hands of Israel.

Our major source of information about ancient Moab is the Moabite Stone. This stone, which bears an inscription from the reign of the same King Mesha mentioned in 2 Kings 3, was discovered in 1868, near the ruins of ancient Dibon. The monument reports the major accomplishments of King Mesha's reign. He boasts especially of having recovered Moabite independence from Israel and of having restored Moabite control over northern Moab.

MODERATION Self-control; calmness; temperateness (Phil. 4:5). Modern translations read "forbearance" (RSV), "forbearing spirit" (NASB), "gentleness" (NIV, NRSV), and "consideration of others" (REB).

MOLE Large rodent. In Lev. 11:30 some translate the Hebrew word as "chameleon" (NIV, NASB, RSV). Others translate "mole" in Lev. 11:29 (NASB, NEB) or in Isa. 2:20 (NASB, RSV, KJV).

MOLECH A pagan Ammonite god to whom human sacrifices were made. Leviticus 20:5 condemns those who "commit whoredom with Molech." But some Israelites fell into false worship and made their children "go through the fire to Molech" (Lev. 18:21), apparently a reference to the sacrifices of children in the Valley of Hinnom at a site known as Topheth.

MOLTEN SEA Large bronze basin with water for the ceremonial washing of priests that stood in the courtyard southeast of Solomon's temple (1 Kings 7:23-26). The basin was cast by Hiram of Tyre who was responsible for all the bronze work in the temple (1 Kings 7:13-14). This basin was over 14 feet in diameter, over 7 feet high, and over 43 feet in circumference. It held about 12,000 gallons. After the fall of Jerusalem in 587 BC, the basin was broken up and taken to Babylon (Jer. 52:17).

MONEY CHANGERS Persons who sold or exchanged foreign money for Jewish money acceptable in temple worship. Some exchangers profited greatly from this business and loaned their money along with what others invested with them. Money changers set up tables in the temple court of the Gentiles in the time of Jesus to provide this service for worshippers. In anger at this corruption of the purpose of the temple, Jesus drove them, along with the sellers of sacrificial animals, out of the temple court (Matt. 21:12).

MONKEY Small, long-tailed primate. TEV, REB include monkeys among the exotic animals brought as gifts to King Solomon (2 Chron. 9:21). NIV, NRSV note read "baboons." KJV, NASB, NRSV render the Hebrew term "peacocks."

MONOTHEISM/POLYTHEISM Competing systems of religious belief that only one god exists or that many gods exist. The first commandment demanded of the Israelites, "Do not have other gods besides Me" (Exod. 20:3 HCSB). This requirement seems to assume that other gods besides Yahweh existed. However, it was only acknowledging that most people believed in the existence of many gods, and it also demanded that the people who followed the Mosaic commandments should reject such beliefs. The Lord who brought Israel out of the land of Egypt would allow no compromise in the loyalty of the people. That kind of belief system is commonly called henotheism.

In contrast to Israel's strict commitment to the Lord alone, the surrounding nations believed in numerous gods whose activities influenced their lives. A good example of this is the Canaanite religious system. Principal among the gods of the Canaanite pantheon were El, the great father figure, and Baal, the younger hero, along with several other gods. The Canaanites believed that the fertility of the land depended on the fertility of Baal and his consort.

A move away from henotheism and polytheism appears first in the OT among the prophets. Competition between the people of Israel and the people of Phoenicia was highlighted by a competition for loyalty of the people between the Lord and Baal. That competition came to its sharpest focus in the contest between Elijah, the Lord's prophet, and the prophets of Baal on Mount Carmel, with Yahweh emerging victorious (1 Kings 18).

The pressure of the exile challenged Yahweh's claim as the only God. If the Lord is really God, how could the people of the Lord lose their independence and their land to a foreign people? Would the success of the Babylonians not suggest that the Lord, the God of the Judeans, had been defeated by Marduk, the god of the Babylonians? The prophets' response was that the exile was the result of Israel's own God using the Babylonians as an instrument of punishment against the Lord's own people since they had violated the terms of the covenant. This opened the door for a theological position that asserted the existence of only one God who is Lord not only of Israel but also of all the rest of the world. This is known as monotheism.

The beautiful poetry of Isa. 40–66 represents the height of Israel's monotheism. For the first time in the OT literature, a prophet argued that no other gods exist (Isa. 45:5-6 NASB). With that poetry, Israel reached a fully developed monotheism.

MOON Light in the night sky created by God and controlling the calendar (Gen. 1:14-19). Two of Israel's greatest festivals were celebrated at the beginning of the full moon: the Passover in the spring and the Feast of Booths in the fall. Each month they celebrated the "new moon" with a little more festivity than a regular Sabbath (Num. 28:11-15 NIV). Still the OT strongly teaches against worshiping the moon (Deut. 4:19) as did Israel's neighbors. The moon was nothing more than an object created by Yahweh and had no power over people.

MORAL DECLINE The Bible teaches that in the latter days the world will be gripped by an unprecedented decline in morals. False teaching will allow wickedness to grow, resulting in apathy (Matt. 24:12) and hostility (2 Tim. 3:1-5) toward the things of Christ. Religion will become a pretense for personal gain rather than an expression of true devotion to God (2 Tim. 3:5), and as a result the standards of moral behavior rooted in the Bible will be held to be irrelevant. These are the kind of activities that people have always done in opposition to God, but they will be more intense and worldwide in scope.

MORDECAI Personal name meaning "little man." **1.** Esther's cousin and the mastermind behind her rise to power and subsequent victory over the evil Haman. A descendant of the Amalekite king Agag, Haman sought to destroy the Jewish race. Mordecai, a descendant of King Saul's family, led Esther to thwart the attempt. Haman was hanged on the gallows he had built for Mordecai. **.** A man who returned from Babylon to Jerusalem with Zerubbabel (Ezra 2:2; Neh. 7:7).

MOREH Place-name meaning "instruction" or "archers." **1.** Abraham's first encampment in the land of Canaan. Here he built an altar after God had appeared to him and entered into covenant

The hill of Moreh.

(Gen. 12:6-7). In later years, God set forth at Moreh the blessings and curses on Israel regarding their keeping of the commandments (Deut. 11:26-30). Joshua set up a memorial stone under the oak at Moreh as a reminder of the covenant between God and His people (Josh. 24:26). **2.** Hill in tribal territory of Issachar where Gideon reduced his troops by testing the way they drank water (Judg. 7:1).

MORESHETH or MORESHETH-GATH Place-name meaning "inheritance of Gath." Home of the prophet Micah (Mic. 1:1). The city was apparently located near Philistine Gath. This may be the Gath which King Rehoboam fortified (2 Chron. 11:8).

MORIAH Rocky outcropping in Jerusalem located north of the ancient city of David. It was on this rock that Abraham would have sacrificed Isaac as a burnt offering, but God intervened and provided a ram (Gen. 22:2,13). Centuries later, King Solomon built the temple on this site (1 Chron. 28:3-6).

MORTAR A vessel used to crush grain, herbs, and olives (Num. 11:8). Mortar was also a clay-like building material (Exod. 1:14), used to secure brick or stone.

MOSES Personal name meaning "drawn out of the water." Leader of the Israelites in their exodus from Egyptian slavery and oppression and their later sojourn in the wilderness as they journeyed toward the promised land.

The story of Moses begins in Exod. 1 with an account of events in Egypt that affected Moses' people. Since the Israelites had grown to be so numerous, the Egyptian pharaoh feared their power. To control them he

A stone mortar for grinding grain or other substances at Lachish.

launched an official policy of oppression. When the oppression failed to curb their population growth, he decreed that all male Hebrew babies were to be cast into the Nile River (Exod. 1:22). Moses was born after this decree was issued, so his life began under the pharaoh's judgment of death.

His mother acted to protect her baby from the pharaoh's death decree. She placed Moses in a basket in the river. The pharaoh's own daughter came to the river, found the ark, and recognized the child as a Hebrew. Eventually she adopted the baby as her own child and hired Moses' own mother to take care of him (Exod. 2:10).

Rock traditionally considered the Rock of Rephidim that Moses struck to get water for the Israelites.

Moses grew to maturity in the palace of the Egyptian king. But he was forced to flee to the land of Midian when he killed an Egyptian supervisor who was brutalizing a Hebrew slave (Exod. 2:14-15). Soon after arriving in Midian, Moses witnessed the aggression of male shepherds against female shepherds who had already drawn water for their sheep. Moses saved the oppressed shepherds, whose father, the priest of Midian, invited him to live and work under the protection of the Midianite's hospitality. Eventually one of the Midianite's daughters became Moses' wife. In the idyllic peace of the Midianite's hospitality, Moses took care of Jethro's sheep, fathered a child, and lived at a distance from his own people (Exod. 18:3-4).

The event at the burning bush while Moses worked as a shepherd introduced him to the critical character of his heroic work. The burning bush caught Moses' attention. There Moses met the God of the fathers who offered Moses a distinctive name as the essential key for Moses' authority—"I am who I am." This strange formulation played on God's promise to Moses to be present with him in his special commission. God sent Moses back to the Egyptian pharaoh to secure the release of his people from oppression.

The negotiation narratives depict Moses in one scene of failure after another. Moses posed his demands to the pharaoh, announced a sign that undergirded the demands, secured some concession from the pharaoh on the basis of the negotiations, but failed to win the release of the people. The final scene is hardly a new stage in the negotiations. To the contrary, God killed the firstborn of every Egyptian family, passing over the Israelite families. In the agony of this death scene, the Egyptians drove the Israelites out of Egypt (Exod. 12:30-36).

Moses led the people into the wilderness, only to have the pursuing Egyptians trap the Israelites at the Red Sea. But God, who had promised divine presence for the people, defeated the enemy at the sea. Then God proved His presence with His people. He met their needs for food and water in the hostile wilderness. Even the serpents and the Amalekites failed to frustrate the wilderness journey of the Israelites under Moses' leadership. Exodus 17:8-13 shows Moses to be faithful in the execution of his leadership responsibilities. Numbers 12:1-16 shows Moses to be meek, a leader of integrity who fulfilled the duties of his office despite opposition from members of his own family.

Stream in the Wilderness of Zin that local tradition says was formed when Moses and Aaron hit the rock.

At Mount Sinai, also known as Mt. Horeb, God delivered the law through Moses that would serve as the instruction book for His people (Exod. 20:1-24). The law showed each new generation how to follow Moses' teaching in a new setting in the life of the people. The law of Moses became a model for Israelite society. Indeed, Israel's historians told the entire story of Israel under the influence of the Moses model and suggested that the Davidic kings should have constructed their leadership for Israel under the influence of the Moses model.

The death of Moses is marked by tragic loneliness, yet graced with God's presence. Because of Moses' sin (Num. 20:1-13), God denied Moses the privilege of entering the promised land. Deuteronomy 34 reports the death scene. Moses left his people to climb another mountain. Atop that mountain, away from the people whom he served so long, Moses died (Deut. 34:1-8). God attended this servant at his death. Indeed, God buried him. Only God knows where the burial place is.

The Moses saga served as a model for future leaders in Israel. Jeroboam I created a new kingdom, distinct from the Davidic kingdom centered in Jerusalem. The sign of his kingship included the golden calves of Aaron. Josiah modeled a reformation in Jerusalem on the basis of the Mosaic model. As the new Moses, he almost succeeded in uniting the people of the south with the people of the north. Perhaps the most important OT figure that must be interpreted as a new Moses is the servant of Isa. 40–66, the model for understanding Jesus in the NT.

MOST HIGH Translation of the Hebrew word *'Elyon*. It is used in conjunction with other divine names such as El (Gen. 14:18) and Yahweh (Ps. 7:17) to speak of God as the Supreme Being. See *Names of God.*

MOTE Archaic English word (KJV) referring to a small particle or speck. Jesus used the word in His Sermon on the Mount to contrast a slight moral fault one may enjoy pointing out in others, while neglecting one's own more heinous fault, represented by the "log," "plank," or "beam" in one's own eye (Matt. 7:3-5).

MOTH Literally "consumer" or "waster," an insect whose destructive power illustrates the result of sin (Ps. 39:11) and the judgment of God (Hos. 5:12). The moth's weakness speaks of the frailty of man (Job 4:19). Jesus urged His followers to avoid the temptation to accumulate wealth on earth where the moth could destroy it but to lay up treasures in heaven (Matt. 6:19-20). See *Insects.*

MOTHER The Bible refers to every aspect of motherhood: conception (Gen. 4:1), pregnancy (Luke 1:24), the pain of childbirth (Gen. 3:16), and nursing (1 Sam. 1:23). A new mother was considered to be ritually unclean, and an offering was prescribed for her purification (Lev. 12; cp. Luke 2:22-24). The book of Proverbs (31:1) indicates that even in ancient times mothers shared with fathers the responsibility for instructing and disciplining children. Mothers have the same right to obedience and respect as fathers (Lev. 19:3), and in OT times death was the fate of those who cursed or assaulted parents (Deut. 21:18-21). Jesus enforced the fifth commandment and protected it against scribal evasion (Matt. 15:3-6).

Motherly virtues are often extolled: compassion for children (Isa. 49:15), comfort of children

(Isa. 66:13), and sorrow for children (Jer. 31:15, quoted in Matt. 2:18). The fact that God would use a human mother to bring His Son into the world has bestowed upon motherhood its greatest honor. Jesus set an example for all to follow by the provision He made for His mother (John 19:25-27). Jesus made it plain, however, that devotion to God must take precedence over that of a mother (Matt. 12:46-50). Even the OT (Gen. 2:24) indicated that a man's devotion to his wife supercedes that to his mother.

In addition to the literal sense, the word *mother* is often used metaphorically. Israel is compared to an unfaithful mother (Isa. 50:1). Revelation 17:5 calls Babylon (Rome) the mother of harlots (those who are unfaithful to God). A city is the "mother" of her people (2 Sam. 20:19). Deborah was the "mother" (or deliverer) of Israel. In a more positive vein, the heavenly Jerusalem is the "mother" of Christians (Gal. 4:26). Jesus spoke of His compassion for Jerusalem as being like that of a mother hen for her chicks (Matt. 23:37). Paul compared his ministry to a mother in labor (Gal. 4:19) and a nursing mother (1 Thess. 2:7).

Church of the Beatitudes on the traditional site of the Sermon on the Mount by the Sea of Galilee.

Lightning strikes over the traditional location for Mt. Sinai, Jebel Musa. The monastery of St. Catherine, built on the traditional spot where Moses saw the burning bush, is in the center of the photograph.

MOUNT OF THE BEATITUDES The "Horns of Hattin" near Capernaum that tradition identifies as the site of the Sermon on the Mount (Matt. 5:1–7:29).

MOUNTAIN The geography of Palestine featured high mountains and deep rifts. Many important events in the Bible took place on or near mountains. God called Moses to His work at Mount Horeb, sometimes called "the mountain of God." A part of God's call was the promise that the Israelite people would worship there upon their escape from Egypt (Exod. 3:1-12). After the exodus God commanded Moses to gather the people at Mount Sinai (probably identical to Horeb). There God gave the law including the Ten Commandments to Moses. Other OT mountain episodes include Aaron's death on Mount Hor (Num. 33:38), the death of Moses on Mount Nebo (Deut. 34:1-8), and Elijah's defeat of the prophets of Baal on Mount Carmel (1 Kings 18:15-40). The term *mountain* is also used symbolically. It is a natural image for stability (Ps. 30:7), obstacles (Zech. 4:7), and God's power (Ps. 121:1-2). God will remove all obstacles when His redemption is complete "and every mountain and hill be made low" (Isa. 40:4 NASB).

MOUSE Rodent listed among the unclean animals (Lev. 11:29). Mice were apparently feared as carriers of the plague (1 Sam. 6:4).

MOUTH The word *mouth* is often used as a synonym for lips (2 Kings 4:34). The phrase "the mouth of the LORD has spoken" serves as a frequent reminder of the reliability of a prophetic message (Jer. 9:12). Fire (2 Sam. 22:9) or a sword (Rev. 1:16) proceeding from the mouth of God pictures the effectiveness of God's word of judgment.

MUFFLER KJV term for a scarf (Isa. 3:19, NRSV). The item was part of the finery of Jerusalem socialites.

MULE Hybrid animal produced by the union of a male ass and a female horse. Since the Mosaic law forbade crossbreeding (Lev. 19:19), the Israelites imported mules (Ezek. 27:14). They were used as war animals, for riding, and for carrying burdens (2 Kings 5:17). They were especially good for moving heavy burdens in mountainous areas. David chose a mule to symbolize royalty for Solomon's coronation (1 Kings 1:33), possibly because the Israelites did not have horses.

MURDER Intentional taking of human life. People are created in the image of God, and human life is viewed as a sacred trust. It is because of this that taking human life is viewed as a serious crime in the Bible. The prohibition against murder is found in the Ten Commandments, the heart of Hebrew law (Exod. 20:13). The OT (Gen. 9:6) prescribed that a murderer should be prepared to forfeit his own life. In Num. 35:16-31 careful attention is given to determining whether a killing is to be classified as murder. According to Jesus, murder in the heart is also a serious matter (Matt. 5:21-22). Murder really begins when one loses respect for another human being. Spitting in the face of another, looking with contempt upon another, and unleashing one's anger are signs that a murderous spirit is present.

MUSIC, INSTRUMENTS, DANCING Expression of the full range of human emotions vocally or instrumentally through music was an important part of the lives of biblical people. Celebration through dance found a natural place in both the religious and secular life of ancient Israel.

Music The first reference to music in the Bible occurs in Gen. 4:21. Lamech's son, Jubal, "was the father of all those who play the lyre and pipe" (NASB). Jubal brought the advent of music to the portrayal of cultural advance. The name Jubal is related to the Hebrew word for "ram" (*yovel*), the horns of which served as a signaling instrument in ancient Israel. The joy of music is evidenced by its prominent role in the celebrations of life. A farewell might be said "with joy and with songs, with timbrel and with lyre" (Gen. 31:27 NASB); a homecoming welcomed "with tambourines and with dancing" (Judg. 11:34). Victory in warfare provided impetus for numerous songs. The song of Miriam, one of the oldest poetic verses in the OT, celebrated the defeat of Pharaoh at the Sea (Exod. 15:21).

The establishment of the monarchy about 1025 BC brought a new dimension to the musical tradition of ancient Israel. Professional musicians took their place at court (1 Kings 1:34,39-40) and in religious ritual. Worship featured trumpet calls (cp. Num. 10:10) and songs of thanksgiving, expressions of praise and petition sung after the offering of sacrifices (2 Chron. 29:20-30).

The psalms show not only the emotional range of music from lament to praise but also provide words for some of the songs used in temple worship. Guilds of musicians, known through reference to their founders in some psalm headings (for example, "the sons of Korah"), were devoted to the discipline of liturgical music.

Musical Instruments Pictorial representations as well as remains from instruments discovered through archaeology give us information about ancient musical instruments. The most common musical instrument in the Bible is the "shofar" (ram's horn). It was a signaling instrument in times of peace and war (Judg. 3:27).The shofar announced the new moons and Sabbaths, warned of approaching danger, signaled the death of nobility, and was sounded in national celebrations (1 Kings 1:34). Other musical instruments mentioned in the Bible are the trumpet, known as the instrument of the priests (Num. 10:2-10); the lyre, a rectangular stringed instrument (2 Sam. 6:5); the harp, another stringed instrument (2 Chron. 9:11); the flute, also called "pipes," a wind instrument best described as a primitive clarinet (1 Kings 1:39-40); and the timbrel or tambourine, a percussion instrument (Ps. 150). The cymbal, another percussion instrument, is mentioned in the NT (1 Cor. 13:1).

Dancing Dancing had a prominent place in the life and worship of Israel. Pictured in the homecoming welcome of victorious soldiers by women, dancing could be accompanied by song and instrumental music (1 Sam. 18:6).

MUSTARD Large plant whose seeds were once thought to be the smallest in the plant world. Jesus used the mustard plant in a parable to symbolize the rapid growth of the kingdom of God (Matt. 13:31-32), and its seed as a simile for faith (Matt. 17:20).

MUTENESS Inability to speak. God made Ezekiel mute (Ezek. 3:26) in response to Israel's failure to listen to his message. Daniel became speechless in response to the appearance of a heavenly messenger (Dan. 10:15). Zechariah's muteness (Luke 1:20,22) served as a sign of the truthfulness of Gabriel's message as well as a punishment for Zechariah's unbelief. Symbolically, to be mute means to hold one's peace (Isa. 53:7), especially in the face of injustice.

MUTH-LABBEN Hebrew phrase in the title of Ps. 9 that means "death of the son." The phrase likely refers to the tune to which the psalm was sung.

MYRA A city in the province of Lysia in southeastern Asia Minor. Myra was a stopping point on Paul's voyage to Rome (Acts 27:5-6).

MYRRH Aromatic resin used as an ingredient in anointing oil (Exod. 30:23), applied as perfume (Esther 2:12), placed in clothes to deodorize them (Ps. 45:8), given as a gift (Matt. 2:11), and used to embalm bodies (John 19:39).

MYSIA Northwest region of Asia Minor (Acts 16:7). Hindered from mission work in Bythinia, Paul passed through Mysia before embarking on his mission to Macedonia (Acts 16:6-11).

The Treasury building of ancient Petra, the Nabatean capital.

NAAM Personal name meaning "pleasantness." Descendant of Caleb (1 Chron. 4:15).

NAAMAH Name *meaning* "pleasant" or "delightful." **1.** Sister of Tubal-cain (Gen. 4:22). **2.** Ammonite wife of Solomon and mother of Rehoboam (1 Kings 14:21,31; 2 Chron. 12:13). **3.** Village in the Shephelah district of Judah (Josh. 15:41).

NAAMAN Personal name meaning "pleasantness." Syrian general cured of leprosy under the direction of the Prophet Elisha (2 Kings 5). Naaman's leprosy apparently was not contagious nor was it seen as the result of some moral sin. Following his cleansing he professed faith in Israel's God.

NAAMATHITE Title meaning "resident of Na'ameh," given to Zophar, one of Job's three friends (Job 2:11; 11:1; 20:1; 42:9).

NAAMITES Family of Benjaminites descended from Naaman (Num. 26:40).

NAARAH Name meaning "girl" or "mill." **1.** Wife of Ashur (1 Chron. 4:5-6). **2.** Form of Naarath preferred by modern translations.

NAARAI Personal name meaning "attendant of Yah." One of David's 30 elite warriors (1 Chron. 11:37). The parallel account gives the name Paarai (2 Sam. 23:35).

NAARAN City allotted to Ephraim, likely identical with Naarah (1 Chron. 7:28; cp. Josh. 16:7).

NAARATH KJV form of Naarah, a city in the tribal territory of Ephraim just north of Jericho (Josh. 16:7)

NABAL Personal name meaning "fool" or "rude, ill-bred."

NABATEANS Arabic people whose origins are unknown. Although not mentioned in the Bible they greatly influenced Palestine during intertestamental and NT times. They appear to have infiltrated ancient Edom and Moab from a homeland southeast of Petra. That city later became their capital.

NABONIDUS Personal name meaning "Nabu is awe-inspiring." Last king of the Neo-Babylonian Empire (555–539 BC).

NABOPOLASSAR Personal name meaning "Nabu, protect the son." King (626–605 BC) who revolted from the Assyrians and established the Neo-Babylonian Empire. He rebelled in 627 BC and established his capital in Babylon.

NABOTH Personal name, perhaps meaning "sprout." Owner of a vineyard in the Jezreel Valley adjacent to the country palace of King Ahab, who desired the property for a vegetable garden. Naboth refused to sell on the grounds that the property was a family inheritance (1 Kings 21:3-4). Hebrew law only allowed farmland to be leased for the number of crops until the Jubilee Year (Lev. 25:15-16). Farmland was not to be sold in perpetuity (Lev. 25:23). Jezebel, who had no regard for Israel's laws, plotted Naboth's judicial murder on the charge that he had blasphemed God and the king (1 Kings 21:8-14). Naboth's murder evoked God's judgment on Ahab and his family (1 Kings 21:17-24).

NACON Place-name meaning "firm" or "prepared." Threshing floor between Baal-judah (Kiriath-jearim) and Jerusalem (2 Sam. 6:6).

NADAB Personal name meaning "willing" or "liberal." **1.** Aaron's eldest son (Exod. 6:23; Num. 3:2; 1 Chron. 6:3), who participated in the ratification of the covenant (Exod. 24:1,9), served as a priest (Exod. 28:1), and was consumed by fire along with his brother Abihu for offering unholy fire before the Lord (Lev. 10:1-7; Num. 26:61). **2.** Descendant of Judah and Tamar (1 Chron. 2:28,30). **3.** Descendant of Benjamin and great-uncle of Saul (1 Chron. 8:30; 9:36). **4.** Son of Rehoboam (1 Kings 14:20) and idolatrous king of Israel (901–900 BC).

NAG HAMMADI Modern Egyptian village 300 miles south of Cairo and about 60 miles north of Luxor or ancient Thebes. Because of the close proximity of Nag Hammadi to the site of an important discovery of ancient documents relating to Gnosticism, the collection of documents is usually referred to as the Nag Hammadi Documents or Library.

NAGGAI or **NAGGE** (KJV) Personal name, perhaps meaning "splendor of the sun." Ancestor of Jesus (Luke 3:25).

NAHALAL Place-name meaning "pasture" with alternate forms: Nahallal (Josh. 19:15 KJV); Nahalol (Judg. 1:30). Town Zebulun's territory allotted to the Levites (Josh. 19:15; 21:35). The Israelites did not drive out the Canaanite inhabitants of the city (Judg. 1:30).

NAHALIEL Place-name meaning "palm grove of God," "torrent valley of God," or less likely, "God is my inheritance." One of Israel's stopping places in Transjordan (Num. 21:19).

NAHAM Personal name meaning "consolation." Either the brother (KJV, REB) or brother-in-law (NASB, NIV, NRSV) of Hodiah (1 Chron. 4:19).

NAHAMANI Personal name meaning "comfort." Exile who returned with Zerubbabel (Neh. 7:7). The name does not appear in the parallel list (Ezra 2:2).

NAHARAI or **NAHARI** (KJV) Personal name meaning "intelligent" or "snorting." One of David's 30 elite warriors who served as armor-bearer to Joab (2 Sam. 23:37; 1 Chron. 11:39).

NAHASH Personal name meaning "serpent" or perhaps "magnificence." **1.** Ammonite ruler whose assault of Jabesh-Gilead set the stage for Saul's consolidation of power as king (1 Sam. 11:1-11). **2.** Parent of Abigail (2 Sam. 17:25).

NAHATH Personal name meaning "descent," "rest," "quietness," or even "pure, clear." **1.** Edomite clan chief (Gen. 36:13,17; 1 Chron. 1:37). **2.** Levite (1 Chron. 6:26), possibly identical with Toah (1 Chron. 6:34) and Tohu (1 Sam. 1:1). **3.** Overseer in Hezekiah's time (2 Chron. 31:13).

NAHBI Personal name meaning "hidden" or "timid." Naphtali's representative among the 12 spies sent to survey Canaan (Num. 13:14).

NAHOR Personal name meaning "snore, snort." **1.** Son of Serug, father of Terah, and grandfather of Abraham (Gen. 11:22-26). **2.** Son of Terah and brother of Abraham (Gen. 11:26). **3.** City in Mesopotamia where Abraham's servant sought and found a wife for Isaac (Gen. 24:10).

NAHSHON Personal name meaning "serpent." Leader of the tribe of Judah during the wilderness years (Num. 1:7; 2:3; 7:12,17; 10:14), brother-in-law of Aaron (Exod. 6:23), and an ancestor of King David (Ruth 4:20-22) and of Jesus (Matt. 1:4; Luke 3:32).

NAHUM, BOOK OF Personal name "Nahum" means "comfort, encourage." He was a Hebrew prophet and the OT book that bears his name contains some of his messages. Very little biographical information is known about the Prophet Nahum. He is called an Elkoshite (1:1), but the location of Elkosh is unknown.

The date of the prophet's ministry can be placed between 600 and 700 BC by two events mentioned in his book. Nahum 3:8 refers to the destruction of the Egyptian capital, No-amon or Thebes, in 663 BC and indicates that the prophet was active after this time. In chapter 2 he looked forward to the destruction of Nineveh, which took place in 612 BC Nahum, therefore, prophesied after 650 BC, probably close to the time of the fall of Nineveh.

Historical Background Since about 730 BC Israel and Judah had been Assyrian vassals. Almost a century later the Assyrian Empire began its decline. Many vassal nations revolted along with Josiah of Judah (2 Kings 22–23). A coalition of Medes, Babylonians, and Scythians attacked Assyrians and in 612 BC destroyed the capital, Nineveh. The Assyrians formed a coalition with the Egyptians, but in 605 BC they were defeated.

The Prophet's Message The Assyrian oppression caused the people to ask how God could allow such inhumanity to go unanswered. Nahum responded to Assyrian tyranny with a message marked by its vivid language. Assyria's might had been heavy upon Judah, but Nahum announced that God would destroy them.

While the book of Nahum is harsh and deals with the unpleasantness of war, it served to give hope to the people of Judah. They had been subjected to the cruel domination of Assyria for over a century, but now their faith in God to act on their behalf could be bolstered through God's response. God's justness was reaffirmed.

NAIL 1. Keratinous covering of the top ends of fingers and toes. If an Israelite desired to marry a

Nails from Roman times.

prisoner of war, she was to cut her nails either as a sign of mourning for her parents or as part of her purification on entering the community of Israel (Deut. 21:12). **2.** Metal fasteners used in construction and for decoration (1 Chron. 22:3; 2 Chron. 3:9; Isa. 41:7; Jer. 10:4). The earliest nails were made of bronze. With the introduction of iron, larger nails were made of iron. Smaller nails continued to be made of bronze. Nails were sometimes plaited with precious metal and nail heads decorated with gold foil when used for ornament (cp. 2 Chron. 3:9). The nails used in the crucifixion of Jesus were likely iron spikes five to seven inches long (John 20:25). **3.** KJV used nail (pin) as an alternate translation for a Hebrew term modern translations consistently render "peg" (Exod. 35:18; Judg. 4:21-22; Zech. 10:4).

NAIN Place-name meaning "pleasant." Village in southwest Galilee where Jesus raised a widow's son (Luke 7:11-15). The ancient town sat on a hillside overlooking the Plain of Esdraelon.

NAIOTH Place-name meaning "dwelling." The name refers either to a building or district in the city of Ramah that housed the prophetic school that Samuel led (1 Sam. 19:18-24). David sought refuge from Saul at Naioth. Three groups of royal messengers and finally Saul himself fell victim to prophetic frenzy when they attempted to capture David there.

NAKED Being without clothes (Gen. 2:25; Job 1:21; Eccles. 5:15; Amos 2:16; Mic. 1:8) or else poorly clothed (Deut. 28:48; Matt. 25:36-44; James 2:15). The phrase "to uncover the nakedness of" means to have sexual intercourse (Lev. 18:6-19; 20:11,17-21). Nakedness frequently occurs in conjunction with shame (Gen. 3:7; 9:21-27; Isa. 47:3; Ezek. 16:8,36-37).

NAMES OF GOD The name of God holds an important key to understanding the doctrine of God and the doctrine of revelation. The name of God is a personal disclosure and reveals His relationship with His people. His name is known only because He chooses to make it known. To the Hebrew mind, God was both hidden and revealed, transcendent and immanent. Even though He was mysterious, lofty, and unapproachable, He bridged the gap with mankind by revealing His name.

NAMES OF GOD

Name	Reference	Meaning
Hebrew Names		
Adonai	Ps. 2:4	Lord, Master
El-Shaddai	Gen. 17:1-2	All Powerful God
El-Elyon	Gen. 14:18-20	Most High God/Exalted One
El-Olam	Gen. 21:33	The Eternal God
El-Berith	Judg. 9:46	God of the Covenant
El-Roi	Gen. 16:13	God Who Sees Me
Qedosh Yisra'el	Isa. 1:4	The Holy One of Israel
Shapat	Gen. 18:25	Judge/Ruler
Yahweh-Jireh	Gen. 22:14	Yahweh Provides
Yahweh-Nissi	Exod. 17:15	Yahweh My Banner
Yahweh-Mekaddesh	Exod. 31:13	Yahweh Sanctifies
Yahweh-Shalom	Judg. 6:24	Yahweh My Peace
Yahweh-Sabaoth	1 Sam. 1:3	Yahweh of Armies
Yahweh-Rohi	Ps. 23:1	Yahweh My Shepherd
Yahweh-Shammah	Ezek. 48:35	Yahweh Is There
Yahweh-Tsidkenu	Jer. 23:6	Yahweh Our Righteousness
Aramaic Names		
Attiq yomin	Dan. 7:9	Ancient of Days
Illaya	Dan. 7:25	Most High

NAMING In biblical tradition the task of naming a child generally fell to the mother (Gen. 29:31–30:24; 1 Sam. 1:20) but could be performed by the father (Gen. 16:15; Exod. 2:22) and in exceptional cases by non-parental figures (Exod. 2:10; Ruth 4:17). Naming could be attributed to God originating through a divine birth announcement (Gen. 17:19; Luke 1:13). Naming took place near birth in the OT and on the eighth day accompanying circumcision in NT narratives (Luke 1:59; 2:21).

The biblical concept of naming was rooted in the ancient world's understanding that a name expressed essence. To know the name of a person was to know that person's total character and nature. Revealing character and destiny, personal names might express hopes for the child's future. Changing of name could occur at divine or human initiative, revealing a transformation in character or destiny (Gen. 17:5,15; 32:28; Matt. 16:17-18).

NAOMI Personal name meaning "my pleasantness." Wife of Elimelech and mother-in-law to Orpah and Ruth (Ruth 1:2,4). Naomi suffered the deaths of her husband and two sons while in Moab. Her matchmaking between Ruth and Boaz was successful, and she became a forebearer of David, Israel's greatest king (Ruth 4:21-22).

NAPHATH-DOR Designation of the region surrounding the coastal city of Dor about 15 miles west of Megiddo (Josh. 12:23; 1 Kings 4:11).

NAPHISH Personal name meaning "refreshed." A son of Ishmael and ancestor of a northwest Arabian tribe of the same name (Gen. 25:15; 1 Chron. 1:31). The tribe dwelt in Transjordan before being displaced by Reuben, Gad, and the half-tribe of Manasseh (1 Chron. 5:19).

NAPHOTH-DOR RSV alternate form of Naphath-Dor (Josh. 11:2). The NIV consistently uses the form Naphoth Dor (Josh. 11:2; 12:23; 1 Kings 4:11).

NAPHTALI Personal name meaning "wrestler." Sixth son of Jacob and second son by his concubine Bilhah (Gen. 30:6-8). In blessing him Jacob likened Naphtali to a hind let loose (49:21), probably a reference to unbridled energy. The tribe that bears his name inhabited a territory north of the Sea of Galilee that extended along the northwest side of Jordan beyond Lake Huleh (Josh. 19:32-39).

NAPHTUHIM Residents of Naphtuh, an unidentified geographic area (Gen. 10:13; 1 Chron. 1:11; Naphtuhites, NIV and REB). The Naphtuhim were most likely residents of the Nile Delta or else inhabitants of the oases to the west of the Nile Valley.

NARCISSUS Common name among both slaves and freedmen meaning "daffodil." The Narcissus of Rom. 16:11 headed a household, perhaps including slaves and/or associated freedmen, which included some Christians.

NARD Expensive fragrance derived from the roots of the herb *nardostachys jatamansi*. The term appears twice in the Song of Songs (1:12 ESV; 4:13-14) and in two of the Gospel accounts of the woman anointing Jesus at Simon's house in Bethany (Mark 14:3; John 12:3; "spikenard," KJV). The disciples rebuked her for this action, stating that the ointment could have been sold for a sizeable sum and the proceeds donated to the poor.

NATHAN Personal name meaning "gift." **1.** Prophet in royal court during reign of David and early years of Solomon. **2.** Son of David, born in Jerusalem (2 Sam. 5:14; 1 Chron. 14:4). His mother was Bathsheba (Bath-shua) (1 Chron. 3:5). He is in the genealogy of Jesus Christ (Luke 3:31). **3.** Nathan of Zobah, father of Igal, one of David's mighty men (2 Sam. 23:36). He may be the same as Nathan the brother of Joel (1 Chron. 11:38), within another list of David's mighty men. **4.** The two Nathans mentioned as fathers of Azariah and Zabud may be the same man and identified as the Prophet Nathan (1 Kings 4:5) during Solomon's reign. **5.** Returning exile whom Ezra sent on a mission to secure ministers for God's house (Ezra 8:15-17). He may be the same exile who had married a foreign wife and put her away (Ezra 10:39).

NATHAN-MELECH Personal name meaning "The king has given" or perhaps "Melech [the god Molech] has given." Nathan-Melech served as an official of King Josiah (2 Kings 23:11).

NATHANAEL Personal name meaning "giver of God." An Israelite whom Jesus complimented as being guileless (John 1:47) and who, in turn, confessed the Lord as being the Son of God and King of Israel (v. 49). Nathanael was from Cana of Galilee (John 21:2) and apparently became one of the inner core of disciples who followed Jesus.

NATIVES Term used by several modern translations (NASB, REB, NRSV) to designate the inhabitants of Malta (Acts 28:2). Barbarous people (KJV) reflects the Greek *barbaroi*, which designates the islanders as non-Greek speaking. NIV reads "islanders," HCSB "local people."

NATURAL According to nature. **1.** Natural use (Rom. 1:26-27 KJV; natural relations, RSV) refers to heterosexual relations, thus "natural intercourse" (NRSV, REB). **2.** Natural affection refers specifically to affection for family members. Those lacking natural affection (*astorgoi*) are unloving to their families or generally inhuman or unsociable (Rom. 1:31; 2 Tim. 3:3). **3.** Natural branches refer to original or native branches as opposed to engrafted ones (Rom. 11:21,24). **4.** Natural or unspiritual person (1 Cor. 2:14) is one not open to receiving gifts from God's Spirit or to discerning spiritual matters (contrast 2:15). This contrast between the spiritual and natural is also evidenced by James 3:15 (NASB) and Jude 19 (NIV). **5.** The natural face (James 1:23) is literally the face of one's birth. To see one's natural face is to see oneself as one actually is.

NAUM KJV form of Nahum, an ancestor of Christ (Luke 3:25).

NAVE 1. Term used by some modern translations (NASB, NRSV) for the main room of the temple between the vestibule and the holy of holies (1 Kings 6:3,5,17; 7:50; 2 Chron. 3:4-5,13; 4:22). KJV referred to this room as the temple or house. **2.** KJV used "nave" for the center of a wheel through which an axle passes (1 Kings 7:33). Modern translations render the underlying Hebrew as "rim."

NAVEL 1. Depression in the middle of the belly marking the place where the umbilical cord was formerly attached. Ezekiel 16:4 graphically portrays Jerusalem's hopeless state before God's adoption in the image of a child whose umbilical cord (navel string) is not cut. **2.** Hebrew expression for "midst of the land" or "center of the earth" (NRSV) in Judg. 9:37; Ezek. 38:12.

An overview of modern Nazareth from the southwest.

NAZARETH, NAZARENE Place-name meaning "branch." Nazareth did not enjoy a place of prominence until its association with Jesus. It does not appear in the OT. As He became known as "Jesus of Nazareth" (Matt. 26:71; Luke 18:37; 24:19; John 1:45; Acts 2:22; 3:6; 10:38), His hometown became fixed in Christian memory. Nazareth was located in lower Galilee about halfway between the Sea of Galilee and the Mediterranean Sea.

Nazareth did not possess a good reputation, as reflected in the question of Nathanael, himself a Galilean (John 1:46). The early church received similar scorn as the Nazarene sect (Acts 24:5). Such lack of respect was likely due to an unpolished dialect, a lack of culture, and quite possibly a measure of irreligion and moral laxity. Jesus was rejected by His townspeople near the beginning of His public ministry, being cast out of the synagogue at Nazareth (Luke 4:16-30; Matt. 13:54-58; Mark 6:1-6).

NAZIRITE Member of a class of individuals especially devoted to God. The Hebrew term means consecration, devotion, and separation. Two traditional forms of the Nazirite are found. One was based on a vow by the individual for a specific period; the other was a lifelong devotion following the revelatory experience of a parent that announced the impending birth of a child.

The lifelong Nazirites in biblical tradition included Samson (Judg. 13), Samuel (1 Sam. 1), and John the Baptist (Luke 1:15-17). In the NT Paul took the Nazirite vow for a specific period of time (Acts 18:18; 21:22-26). Amos 2:12 shows an ethical concern for protecting the status of the Nazirite.

NEAH Place-name meaning "settlement." Border town in the tribal territory of Zebulun (Josh. 19:13).

NEAPOLIS Name meaning "new city," of the seaport of Philippi (Acts 16:11). Neapolis (modern Kavala) is located about 10 miles from Philippi in northeastern Macedonia. The city sits on a neck of land between two bays, both of which serve as harbors.

NEARIAH Personal name, perhaps meaning "Yah's young man." **1.** Descendant of David (1 Chron. 3:22-23). **2.** Commander of Hezekiah's forces who defeated the Amalekites (1 Chron. 4:42-43).

NEBAI Personal name meaning "projecting" or "fruitful." One of the witnesses to Ezra's renewal of the covenant (Neh. 10:19).

NEBAIOTH or **NEBAJOTH** (KJV) Personal name meaning "fruitfulness." Son of Ishmael and ancestor of an Arab tribe of the same name (Gen. 25:13; 28:9; 36:3). KJV used the alternate form Nebajoth in 1 Chron. 1:29; Isa. 60:7.

NEBALLAT Place-name, perhaps meaning "blessed with life." The name perhaps derives from Nabu-uballit, the personal name of an Assyrian governor of Samaria. Neballat was resettled by Benjaminites after the exile (Neh. 11:34).

NEBAT Personal name meaning "God has regarded." Father of Jeroboam I (1 Kings 11:26; 12:2,15). Nebat was from Zeredah about 10 miles west of Shiloh.

NEBO Place-name and divine name meaning "height." **1.** Babylonian god of speech, writing, and water. Worship of Nebo was popular during the Neo-Babylonian era (612–539 BC). Isaiah mocked parades featuring the idol of Nebo (Isa. 46:1). **2.** Moabite city located southwest of Heshbon. The tribes Reuben and Gad requested the area around Nebo for their flocks (Num. 32:2-3). It was held by Israel until recaptured by King Mesha about 850 BC. **3.** Town reinhabited by exiles returning from Babylon (Ezra 2:29). The site has been identified with Nob. **4.** Mountain about 12 miles east of the mouth of the Jordan River from which Moses viewed the promised land (Deut. 32:49). It rises over 4,000 feet above the Dead Sea and gives an excellent view of the southwest, west, and as far north as Mount Hermon.

The Jordan Valley from the top of Mount Nebo looking toward Jericho.

NEBUCHADNEZZAR Personal name meaning "Nabu protects." King of Babylon 602–562 BC. He was the son of Nabopolassar and inherited the throne upon the death of his father. Nebuchadnezzar served as a general under his father and was a brilliant strategist. His victory over the Egyptian forces at Carchemish (605) signaled the completion of Babylon's conquest of Palestine (Jer. 46:1-2).

NEBUSHASBAN, NEBUSHAZBAN Variant transliterations of personal name meaning "Nabu save me." High official of Nebuchadnezzar involved in the fall of Jerusalem (Jer. 39:13).

NEBUZARADAN Personal name meaning "Nebo has given offspring." An officer in the Babylonian army during King Nebuchadnezzar's reign. His title is given as "captain of the guard" (bodyguard, Jer. 39:13), a designation which is uncertain. He led his troops in a siege of Jerusalem in 587 BC (2 Kings 25:8-9), burned the city's buildings, tore down its walls, and carried away the people into exile. Four years later he returned and deported still more citizens (Jer. 52:30).

NECHO KJV form of Neco (2 Chron. 35:20,22; 36:4). KJV used the hyphenated form Pharaoh-necho at Jer. 46:2.

NECHOH KJV alternate form of Neco. This form always occurs in the hyphenated form Pharaoh-nechoh (2 Kings 23:29,33-35).

NECK Portion of the body connecting the head to the torso. To put one's feet on the neck of an enemy is a sign of complete victory (Josh. 10:24). A yoke placed on the neck is a frequent emblem of servitude (Gen. 27:40; Deut. 28:48; Isa. 10:27). To fall upon someone's neck with weeping or kissing is a special sign of tenderness (Gen. 33:4; 45:14; cp. Luke 15:20). To be stiff-necked or to harden one's neck is a common picture of stubborn disobedience (Exod. 32:9; 33:3,5).

NECKLACE Ornament worn around the neck (Song 1:10; Ezek. 16:11). The gift of a gold necklace is sometimes the sign of installation to a high office (Gen. 41:42; Dan. 5:29).

NECO Second Pharaoh (609–594 BC) of the 26th dynasty of Egypt whose forces killed Josiah in battle (2 Kings 23:29-35; 2 Chron. 35:20-24) and who installed Jehoiakim as king of Judah in his place (2 Kings 23:34-35).

NECROMANCY Conjuring the spirits of the dead to predict or influence future events.

NEDABIAH Personal name meaning "Yah is generous." Son of Jeconiah, the exiled king of Judah (1 Chron. 3:18).

NEEDLE Small slender instrument used in sewing with an eye at one end through which thread is passed. The needles of NT times were similar in size to modern needles with the exception of our smallest needles. Needles were most often made of bronze, though bone and ivory were also used. Jesus' teaching that "it is easier for a camel to go through the eye of a needle than for a rich person to enter the kingdom of God" (Matt. 19:24 HCSB; cp. Mark 10:25; Luke 18:25) illustrates the impossibility of a rich person's being saved apart from the intervention of God who does the impossible (Matt. 19:26).

NEEDLEWORK Decorative work sewn upon cloth. Needlework was used in the decoration of the screens for the tabernacle door (Exod. 26:36; 36:37) and for the gate to its court (Exod. 27:16; 38:18) as well as for Aaron's girdle (Exod. 28:39; 39:29).

NEESINGS KJV term meaning "sneezings" or "sneezes" (Job 41:18).

NEGEB or **NEGEV** (preferred sp.) Place-name meaning "dry" and referring to an arid region in southern Palestine and coming to mean "south." During biblical times it was more populated than today, indicating either more rainfall then or better conservation of the resources. It was the land of the Amalekites during Abraham's day (Gen. 14:7). There he exiled Hagar (21:14). The Israelites wandered in the Negev after a futile attempt to enter Canaan (Num. 14:44-45). David incorporated it into his kingdom, and Solomon established fortresses in the region.

View of the Negeb from Beer-sheba, the most important city of the Negeb.

NEGINAH, NEGINOTH Neginoth, the plural form of Neginah, is used as a technical term in the superscriptions of several psalms (Pss. 4; 6; 54–55; 61; 67; 76) and as the subscription of Hab. 3:19. The term is generally understood to specify the instrumentation needed for performance "with stringed instruments" (cp. Isa. 38:20; Lam. 5:14). Other references suggest that *neginah* designates a taunt song (Job 30:9; Ps. 69:12; Lam. 3:14).

NEHELAM, NEHELAMITE Either a family name or a reference to the home of the false prophet Shemaiah (Jer. 29:24,31-32). The name is perhaps a play on the Hebrew word for dreamer (cp. Jer. 23:25,32).

Cross-sectional view of the Negeb in relation to the Dead Sea, Judah, and the Mediterranean Sea.

NEHEMIAH Personal name meaning "Yah comforts or encourages" and name of OT book featuring work of Nehemiah. **1.** Leader who was among the first to return with Zerubbabel from exile to Judah in about 538 BC (Ezra 2:2; Neh. 7:7). **2.** Son of Azbuk, "the ruler of the half part of Bethzur" (Neh. 3:16), one who helped Nehemiah son of Hachaliah with rebuilding the walls of Jerusalem. **3.** Nehemiah, the son of Hachaliah, is the main character in the book that bears his name. He was a contemporary of Ezra and Malachi, Socrates in Greece (470–399 BC).

NEHEMIAH, BOOK OF Nehemiah and Ezra were one book in the ancient Hebrew and Greek OT and probably were not divided until after the interbiblical period. Jewish tradition says Ezra or Nehemiah was the author. Because of the close connection between Chronicles and Ezra-Nehemiah, one person might have written or compiled all three books. Those who follow this argument refer to the author as the Chronicler.

The literary style of Nehemiah is similar to that in Ezra. There are many lists (chaps. 3; 10:1-27; 11; 12:1-26). The author/compiler wove Ezra's and Nehemiah's stories together, Ezra being featured in Neh. 8.

The book has four major sections: the rebuilding of Jerusalem's walls (chaps. 1–7), the Great Revival (chaps. 8–10), population and census information (chaps. 11–12), and the reforms of Nehemiah (chap. 13). Nehemiah made two visits from King Artaxerxes to Jerusalem (2:1-6; 13:6-7). His first, 445 BC, was to repair the walls; they were in a state of disrepair almost a century after the first arrival from exile in 538 BC. The second was a problem-solving trip in the 32nd year of Artaxerxes (13:6), 432 BC.

NEHILOTH Technical musical term in the superscription of Ps. 5. The term is generally understood to specify the instrumentation for the psalm, "with flutes."

NEHUSHTA Personal name meaning "serpent" or "bronze." Mother of King Jehoiachin of Judah (2 Kings 24:8). As queen mother she was among those deported in the first exile (24:12,15).

NEHUSHTAN Name of a "brazen serpent" destroyed by King Hezekiah as part of an attempt to reform Judah's life and worship (2 Kings 18:4). The object was believed to be the one Moses fashioned to relieve a plague in the Israelite camp during the exodus (Num. 21:8-9).

NEIEL Name meaning "dwelling place of God." Town assigned to Asher (Josh. 19:27).

NEIGH Loud, prolonged cry of a horse used as a figure of approaching battle (Jer. 8:16) or of unbridled sexual desire (Jer. 5:8; 13:27; 50:11).

NEKEB KJV transliteration of a Hebrew term meaning tunnel, shaft, or mine (Josh. 19:33).

NEKODA Personal name meaning "speckled." **1.** Family of temple servants returning to Jerusalem after the exile (Ezra 2:48; Neh. 7:50). **2.** Family who returned from exile but were unable to establish their Israelite descent (Neh. 7:62).

NEMUEL 1. Ancestor of a family of Simeonites, the Nemuelites (Num. 26:12; 1 Chron. 4:24); this Nemuel is also called Jemuel (Gen. 46:10; Exod. 6:15) **2.** A Reubenite (Num. 26:9).

NEPHEG Personal name meaning "boaster." **1.** A Levite (Exod. 6:21). **2.** Son born to David in Jerusalem (2 Sam. 5:15; 1 Chron. 3:7; 14:6).

NEPHEW 1. The son of one's brother or sister. KJV never used "nephew" in this sense, but NASB and NIV used it in this sense for Lot (Gen. 12:5; 14:12). **2.** When KJV translation was being made, "nephew" was used in the broader sense of a lineal descendant, especially a grandson (Judg. 12:14; Job 18:19; Isa. 14:22; 1 Tim. 5:4).

NEPHILIM Transliteration of a Hebrew word that designates a class of beings mentioned in Gen. 6:4 and Num. 13:33. Some interpreters believe the word is related to *naphal* meaning "to fall." In Gen. 6:4 the term refers to "heroes of old" (NRSV) so some have concluded that these are beings that have fallen from heaven and married the daughters of men. However, the text does not state that explicitly. At most it says that the Nephilim were on the earth during the days when the sons of God married the daughters of men. When the 12 spies were sent to Canaan, they saw giants whom they called the Nephilim, beside whom they seemed small, as "grasshoppers." There is no attempt to relate these people to the Nephilim of Gen. 6.

NEPHISIM Family of temple servants who returned from exile (Ezra 2:50), probably identical with the Nephushesim (Nephishesim, KJV) of Neh. 7:52.

NEPHTHALIM Greek form of Naphtali used by the KJV (Matt. 4:13,15; Rev. 7:6).

NEPHTOAH Name meaning "opening," found only in the phrase "Waters of Nephtoah." Boundary marker for Judah and Benjamin (Josh. 15:9; 18:15).

NER Personal name meaning "light." Father of Saul's general Abner and grandfather of Saul (1 Sam. 14:51; 26:5,14; 2 Sam. 2:8; 1 Chron. 9:36).

NEREUS Personal name borrowed from Greek mythology where Nereus is the sea god who fathers the Nereids (sea nymphs). The NT Nereus was a Roman Christian, possibly the son of Philogus and Julia (Rom. 16:15).

NERGAL Name, perhaps a form of "Ne-uru-gal" (Lord of the great city). Following the fall of the northern kingdom of Israel, the Assyrians resettled Samaria with Mesopotamian peoples who brought their gods, including Nergal, with them (2 Kings 17:30).

NERGAL-SHAREZER A personal name meaning "Nergal, protect the king." He is mentioned as being among the officers of Nebuchadnezzar's court who helped destroy Jerusalem in 586 BC (Jer. 39:3,13). He was a son-in-law of Nebuchadnezzar who usurped the Babylonian throne following the death of Evil-merodach.

NERI Personal name meaning "lamp." An ancestor of Jesus (Luke 3:27).

NERIAH Personal name meaning "Yahweh is light." Father of two men who assisted Jeremiah: Baruch the scribe (Jer. 32:12; 36:4-19) and Seraiah the quartermaster (Jer. 51:59).

NERO Personal name meaning "brave." Roman emperor AD 54–68. Nero became emperor in AD 54 at the age of 17. During Nero's rule the Great Fire broke out in Rome (AD 64). Much of the city was destroyed, including Nero's palace. The story, probably true in part, goes that Nero fiddled while

Rome burned. Nero took measures to provide relief for those affected by the fire. Still he could not dispel the rumor that he had the fire set. People knew that he planned to build a much larger palace for himself and they reasoned that he used the fire to clear off the land. Nero felt the need to divert suspicion to another group. He selected the Christians as his scapegoats. He claimed that they had set the fire. A systematic persecution of the Christians followed. Because of his lifestyle and the persecution, many Christians viewed him as the antichrist.

NEST Hollow container fashioned by a bird to contain its eggs and young. Nest is often used as a simile or metaphor for a human dwelling (Num. 24:21; Job 29:18; Hab. 2:9; Prov. 27:8). The term translated "nest" (Matt. 8:20; Luke 9:58) suggests a leafy "tent" rather than a nest.

NET 1. Loosely woven mesh of twine or cord used for catching birds, fish, or other prey. **2.** Netting or network refers to grillwork used as part of the ornament of the altar of burnt offering (Exod. 27:4-5; 38:4) and of the capitals of the temple columns (1 Kings 7:17-20).

NETAIM Name meaning "plantings." Site of a royal pottery works (1 Chron. 4:23).

NETHANEEL or **NETHANEL** Personal name meaning "given by God." **1.** Leader of the tribe Issachar and a son of Zuar (Num. 1:8). He commanded an army of 54,400 men (2:5-6). **2.** Fourth son of Jesse and brother of King David (1 Chron. 2:14). **3.** One of several priests to blow the trumpet before the ark of God (1 Chron. 15:24). **4.** Prince of Judah whom King Jehoshaphat sent out with others to teach the law of God in the cities of Judah (2 Chron. 17:7-9). **5.** Levite and father of Shemaiah who recorded the names and order of the people who would minister in the temple (1 Chron. 24:6). **6.** Fifth son of Obed-edom who was a gatekeeper in the temple (1 Chron. 26:4). **7.** Levite who contributed to the Passover offering when Josiah was king (2 Chron. 35:9). **8.** Priest and son of Pashur who had married a foreign wife while exiled in Babylon (Ezra 10:22). He might have participated in the dedication of the wall around Jerusalem (Neh. 12:36). **9.** Head of the priestly family of Jedaiah when Joiakim was high priest (Neh. 12:21). **10.** Priest, one of Asaph's associates, who played a trumpet, in dedicating the rebuilding of Jerusalem's wall (Neh. 12:36). Some identify him with 8.

NETHANIAH Personal name meaning "given of Yah." **1.** Son of Asaph who served in a company of prophets established by David. They issued their message with harps, psalteries, and cymbals (1 Chron. 25:1-2). **2.** Levite sent along with Jehoshaphat's princes to teach from the book of the law of God in all the cities of Judah (2 Chron. 17:7-9). **3.** Father of Jehudi sent to Baruch by the princes of Jehoiakim (Jer. 36:14). **4.** Father of Ishmael who killed Gedaliah (2 Kings 25:23-25; Jer. 40:8,14-16; 41).

NETHINIM Name meaning "those given (to the priests and Levites)," which Ezra and Nehemiah apply to persons of foreign extraction who performed menial tasks in the temple. Representatives of the Nethinim returned from exile with Zerubbabel in 538 BC (Ezra 2:43-54; Neh. 7:46-56). The lists of returnees contain many foreign names suggesting their origin as prisoners of war. Despite their foreign origin, the Nethinim appear to be accepted as part of the people of Israel. They were prohibited from mixed marriages with the people of the land (Neh. 10:28-30) and shared in the responsibility for repair of the Jerusalem city walls (Neh. 3:26; contrast Ezra 4:1-3). The Nethinim resided in the Ophel district of Jerusalem, likely near the water gate (Neh. 3:26), a site conducive with their task as water bearers.

NETOPHAH Name meaning "dropping." A village and surrounding district in the hill country of Judah (2 Sam. 23:28-29; 1 Chron. 11:30; 27:13; Neh. 7:26).

NETTLE Two different Hebrew words are sometimes translated "nettle" (other times "weeds," "thistles" [HCSB]). Nettles are coarse plants with stinging hairs belonging to the family *Urtica*; generally, any prickly or stinging plant (Job 30:7; Prov. 24:31; Isa. 34:13; Hos. 9:6; Zeph. 2:9). Nettles are used as a sign of desolation and judgment.

NEW BIRTH Term referring to God's impartation of spiritual life to sinners. It is synonymous with regeneration, and finds its origin in John 3:1-10. There Jesus told Nicodemus, "Unless someone is born again, he cannot see the kingdom of God" (v. 3 HCSB). Jesus indicated that the idea of the new birth is rooted in the OT when He chastised Nicodemus for his dismay at this teaching: "Are you a teacher of Israel and don't know these things?" (v. 10; cp. Ezek. 36:26-27). The new birth is caused by the gracious and sovereign act of God apart from man's cooperation (John 1:13; Eph. 2:4-5). God brings the new birth about through the preaching of the word of God (1 Pet. 1:23; James 1:18). The result of the new birth is a changed life (2 Cor. 5:17), which includes saving faith and repentance (Eph. 2:8; Acts 11:18; 16:14) and obedience to God's law (1 John 3:9).

NEW GATE A gate of the Jerusalem temple (Jer. 26:10; 36:10), which should perhaps be identified with the Upper Gate that Jothan built (2 Kings 15:35) and/or with the Upper Benjamin Gate (Jer. 20:2).

NEW TESTAMENT Second major division of the Christian Bible with 27 separate works (called "books") attributed to at least eight different writers. Four accounts of Jesus' life are at the core. The first three Gospels (called "Synoptic") are very similar in content and order. The Fourth Gospel has a completely different perspective. A history of selected events in the early church (Acts) is followed by 20 letters to churches and individuals and one apocalypse. The letters deal mainly with the interpretation of God's act of salvation in Jesus Christ. Matters of discipline, proper Christian behavior, and church polity also are included. The apocalypse is a coded message of hope to the church of the first century that has been reinterpreted by each succeeding generation of Christians for their own situations.

NEZIAH Personal name meaning "faithful" or "illustrious." Head of a family of temple servants (Nethinim) who returned from exile (Ezra 2:54; Neh. 7:56).

NEZIB Name meaning "garrison," "idol," "pillar," or "standing place." Village in the Shephelah district of Judah (Josh. 15:43).

NIBHAZ Deity worshipped by the residents of Avva whom the Assyrians used to resettle the area about Samaria after the fall of that city in 722 BC (2 Kings 17:31).

NIBSHAN Name meaning "prophesy." Town assigned to the tribe of Judah (Josh. 15:62).

NICANOR Personal name meaning "conqueror." One of seven Hellenists "full of faith and the Holy Spirit" (HCSB) chosen to administer food to the Greek-speaking widows of the Jerusalem church (Acts 6:5).

NICODEMUS Personal name meaning "innocent of blood." John identifies Nicodemus as a Pharisee, "a ruler of the Jews" (John 3:1), that is, a member of the Sanhedrin, the Jewish ruling council, and as "a teacher of Israel" (John 3:10), that is, an authority on the interpretation of the Hebrew Scriptures. Nicodemus's coming at night suggests his timidity and his trek from the darkness of his own sin and ignorance to the light of Jesus (John 3:2).

True to his name, Nicodemus defended Christ before his peers (John 7:51), who were unaware that one of their number might have believed in Him (v. 48). Their response is a twofold rebuke that may be paraphrased "Are you a Galilean peasant?" and "Are you ignorant of the Scriptures?" (v. 52).

The reference to Nicodemus's initial coming at night highlights his later public participation in Jesus' burial (John 19:39-41). Nicodemus's contribution was enough aloes and spices to prepare a king for burial, and so he did. On one level the burial was a simple act of Pharisaic piety (cp. Tobit 1:17). On a deeper level it recognized that in His suffering and death Christ fulfilled His role as King of the Jews.

NICOLAITANS Heretical group in the early church who taught immorality and idolatry. They are condemned in Rev. 2:6,15 for their practices in Ephesus and Pergamum. Thyatira apparently had resisted the false prophecy they preached (Rev. 2:20-25). The Nicolaitans have been linked to the type of heresy taught by Balaam (Num. 25:1-2; 2 Pet. 2:15), especially the pagan feasts and orgies that they apparently propagated in the first-century church.

NICOLAS Personal name meaning "conqueror of people." One of seven Hellenists "full of faith and the Holy Spirit" chosen to administer food to the Greek-speaking widows of the Jerusalem church (Acts 6:5).

NICOPOLIS Place-name meaning "city of victory," shared by many cities in the ancient world. The site in which Paul most likely wintered (Titus 3:12) was Nicopolis in Epirus in northwest Greece.

NIGER Latin nickname meaning "black." Surname of Simeon (KJV, Symeon), one of the teacher-prophets of the early church at Antioch (Acts 13:1).

NIGHT MONSTER Translation (NASB, ASV) of the Hebrew term *Lilith* (Isa. 34:14 NRSV). The term occurs only here in Scripture unless textual emendations are accepted (Job 18:15; Isa. 2:18).

NIGHT WATCH Ancient division of time (Pss. 90:4; 119:148; Lam. 2:19; Matt. 14:25). According to the later Jewish system, the night was divided into three watches (evening, midnight, and morning). The Greco-Roman system added a fourth (crowing of the rooster, HCSB) between midnight and morning (Mark 13:35). The fourth watch (Matt. 14:25; Mark 6:48) designates the time just before dawn.

NILE RIVER Major river considered the "life" of ancient Egypt. The Egyptian Nile is formed by the union of the White Nile that flows out of Lake Victoria in Tanzania and the Blue Nile from Lake Tana in Ethiopia. These join at Khartum in the Sudan and are later fed by the Atbara. Thereafter the Nile flows 1,675 miles northward to the Mediterranean Sea without any further tributary.

The Nile is the basis of Egypt's wealth, indeed of its very life. It is the only river to flow northwards across the Sahara. Egypt was unique as an agricultural community in not being dependent on

Sunrise over the Nile from Minia.

rainfall. The secret was the black silt deposited on the fields by the annual flood caused when the Blue Nile was swollen by the run-off from the winter rains in Ethiopia. This silt was remarkably fertile. Irrigation waters, raised laboriously from the river, let the Egyptians produce many varieties of crops in large quantities (Num. 11:5; Gen. 42:1-2). If the winter rains failed, the consequent small or nonexistent inundation resulted in disastrous famine: some are recorded as lasting over a number of years (cp. Gen. 41).

NIMRAH Place-name meaning "clear (water)." Alternate form of Beth-nimrah (Num. 32:36) used at Num. 32:3.

NIMRIM Place-name meaning "leopards" or "basins of clear waters." The name occurs in the phrase "Waters of Nimrim" (Isa. 15:6; Jer. 48:34), the stream upon which Moab's agricultural productivity depended.

NIMROD Personal name meaning "we shall rebel." Son of Cush or Ethiopia (Gen. 10:8-10; 1 Chron. 1:10). A hunter and builder of the kingdom of Babel whom some Bible students have linked to Tukulti-ninurta, an Assyrian king (about 1246–1206 BC).

NIMSHI Personal name meaning "weasel." Grandfather of Jehu (2 Kings 9:2,14). Elsewhere Jehu is called the son of Nimshi (1 Kings 19:16; 2 Kings 9:20; 2 Chron. 22:7). Either "son" is used loosely in the sense of descendant, or a variant tradition is involved.

Restored gate at the site of the ancient city of Nineveh of Assyria.

NINEVE (KJV, Luke 11:32) or **NINEVEH** Greatest of the capitals of the ancient Assyrian Empire, which flourished from about 800 to 612 BC It was located on the left bank of the Tigris River in northeastern Mesopotamia (Iraq today). Nineveh is first mentioned in the OT as one of the cities established by Nimrod (Gen. 10:9-12). It was the enemy city to which God called the reluctant Prophet Jonah in the eighth century BC The book of Jonah calls it "that great city" (1:2; 4:11), and "an exceeding great city" (3:3). The final biblical references are from Nahum, who prophesied the overthrow of the "bloody city" by the attack of the allied Medes and Chaldeans in 612 BC. By 500 BC the prophet's words (Nah. 3:7) "Nineveh is devastated" (NASB) were echoed by the Greek historian Herodotus who spoke of the Tigris as "the river on which the town of Nineveh formerly stood."

NIPPUR City located in Mesopotamia, approximately 50 miles southeast of the ancient city of Babylon and approximately 100 miles south of modern Baghdad, Iraq.

NISAN Foreign term used after the exile for the first month of the Hebrew calendar (Neh. 2:1; Esther 3:7). This month that falls within March and April was formerly called Abib.

NISROCH God worshiped by the Assyrian king Sennacherib (2 Kings 19:37; Isa. 37:38).

NOADIAH Personal name meaning "Yah has met." **1.** Levite who returned from exile and served as a temple treasurer (Ezra 8:33). **2.** Prophetess who discouraged Nehemiah's building of the walls of

Jerusalem (Neh. 6:14).

NOAH Personal name of uncertain meaning, related to "rest." **1.** Son of Lamech, a descendant of Adam in the line of Seth, and a survivor of the flood. A good and righteous man, Noah was the father of Shem, Ham, and Japheth who were born when he was 500 years old. God warned Noah that He was going to wipe mankind from the face of the earth. Because Noah walked with God and stood blameless among the people of that time, God gave him specific instructions for building the ark by which Noah and his family would survive the coming flood. Hebrews 11:7 affirms Noah's actions of faith in building the ark. The references to Noah in 1 Pet. 3:20 and 2 Pet. 2:5 speak of Noah and those of his family who were saved in the flood. **2.** One of Zelophehad's five daughters (Num. 26:33). Of the tribe of Manasseh, these daughters received an inheritance in the land in their father's name even though he was dead with no male offspring (27:1-11). This was most unusual in that time.

NOB City in Benjamin likely situated between Anathoth and Jerusalem (Neh. 11:31-32; Isa. 10:32).

NOBAH Personal name meaning "barking" or "howling." **1.** Leader of the tribe of Manasseh who conquered Kenath in Gilead (Num. 32:42). **2.** Town in Gilead, formerly Kenath (Num. 32:42). Site is perhaps identical with Kanawat about 60 miles east of the Sea of Galilee. **3.** Town in Gilead (Judg. 8:10-11) to the east of Succoth and Penuel and west of the king's highway (KJV, "the way of them that dwell in tents"; NRSV, "caravan route").

NOD Place-name meaning "wandering." After murdering his brother Abel, Cain was condemned to be "a fugitive and a wanderer on the earth" (Gen. 4:12,14 NRSV). Nod is located "away from the presence of the LORD" and "east of Eden" (Gen. 4:16). The text is not so much interested in fixing the physical location of Nod as in emphasizing the "lostness" of the wanderer Cain.

NODAB Name meaning "nobility." Tribe conquered by Reuben, Gad, and the half tribe of Manasseh (1 Chron. 5:19).

NOGAH Personal name meaning "brilliance" or "luster." Son born to David in Jerusalem (1 Chron. 3:7; 14:6).

NOHAH Personal name meaning "quiet." Son of Benjamin (1 Chron. 8:2). The name is omitted from the parallel list (Gen. 46:21).

NOON Middle of the day, specifically 12 o'clock noon. Noon is frequently associated with death and destruction (2 Sam. 4:5; 1 Kings 20:16; 2 Kings 4:20; Ps. 91:6; Jer. 6:4; 15:8; 20:16; Zeph. 2:4). Noon is also associated with blessings and vindication (Job 11:17; Ps. 37:6; Isa. 58:10).

NOOSE Loop of rope used as a trap (Job 18:10 NASB, NIV; Prov. 7:22 NIV).

NOPH Variant form of Moph, the Hebrew term for Memphis (Isa. 19:13; Jer. 2:16; 44:1; 46:14,19; Ezek. 30:13,16).

NOPHAH Place-name meaning "blast." Nophah passed from Moabite to Ammonite to Israelite control (Num. 21:30).

NORTH GATE Designation of two gates in Ezekiel's vision of the renewed temple, a gate entering the outer court (Ezek. 8:14; 44:4; 46:9; 47:2) and a gate entering the inner court (Ezek. 40:35,40,44).

NOSE Part of the face between the eyes and mouth that bears the nostrils and covers the nasal cavity. Jewelry was worn in the nose (Gen. 24:47; Isa. 3:21; Ezek. 16:12). Prisoners of war were sometimes led captive with hooks in their noses (2 Kings 19:28; Isa. 37:29).

NUBIANS Residents of an ancient kingdom along the Nile River in southern Egypt and northern Sudan (Dan. 11:43 NIV; also NRSV margin).

NUMBER SYSTEMS AND NUMBER SYMBOLISM The Hebrews did not develop the symbols to represent numbers until the postexilic period (after 539 BC). In all preexilic inscriptions, small numbers are represented by individual strokes (for example, //// for four). Larger numbers were either represented with Egyptian symbols, or the name of the number was written out ("four" for the number 4).

Biblical passages show that the Hebrews were well acquainted with the four basic mathematical operations of addition (Num. 1:20-46), subtraction (Gen. 18:28-33), multiplication (Num. 7:84-86), and division (Num. 31:27). The Hebrews also used fractions such as a half (Gen. 24:22), a third (Num. 5:6), and a fourth (Exod. 29:40).

In addition to their usage to designate specific numbers or quantities, many numbers in the Bible came to have a symbolic meaning. Thus seven came to symbolize completeness and perfection.

Multiples of seven frequently had symbolic meaning. The Year of Jubilee came after the completion of every 49 years. Jesus sent out the 70 (Luke 10:1-17). Seventy years is specified as the length of the exile (Jer. 25:12, 29:10; Dan. 9: 2). The messianic kingdom was to be inaugurated after a period of 70 weeks of years had passed (Dan. 9:24).

After seven the most significant number for the Bible is undoubtedly 12. The Sumerians used 12 as one base for their number system. Both the calendar and the signs of the zodiac reflect this 12-base number system. The tribes of Israel and Jesus' disciples numbered 12. Multiples of 12 are also important. There were 24 divisions of priests (1 Chron. 24:4) and 24 elders around the heavenly throne (Rev. 4:4). Seventy-two elders, when one includes Eldad and Medad, were given a portion of God's spirit that rested on Moses, and they prophesied (Num. 11:24-26). An apocryphal tradition holds that 72 Jewish scholars, six from each of the 12 tribes, translated the OT into Greek, to give us the version we call today the Septuagint. The 144,000 servants of God (Rev. 7:4) were made up of 12,000 from each of the 12 tribes of Israel.

Three as a symbolic number often indicated completeness. The created cosmos had three elements: heaven, earth, and underworld. Three Persons make up the Godhead: Father, Son, and Holy Spirit.

Four was often used as a sacred number. Significant biblical references to four include the four corners of the earth (Isa. 11:12), the four winds (Jer. 49:36), four rivers that flowed out of Eden to water the world (Gen. 2:10-14), and four living creatures surrounding God (Ezek. 1; Rev. 4:6-7). God sent forth the four horsemen of the Apocalypse (Rev. 6:1-8) to bring devastation to the earth. The most significant multiple of four is 40, which often represented a large number or a long period of time. Rain flooded the earth for 40 days (Gen. 7:12). For 40 days Jesus withstood Satan's temptations (Mark 1:13). Forty years represented approximately a generation. Thus all the adults who had rebelled against God at Sinai died during the 40 years of the Wilderness Wandering period. By age 40 a person had reached maturity (Exod. 2:11; Acts 7:23).

NUMBERS, BOOK OF Fourth in the chronological series of the Torah, Numbers carries the title *Bemidhbar* ("in the wilderness") in the original Hebrew text. The book carries the title Numbers in English translations as a result of the early Greek title *ARIOMOI* and the Latin title *Numeri*. In both instances, the title reflects a focus on the censuses taken to account for the number of fighting men in each tribe.

Numbers is a book of transition, in which the conditional nature of the Sinaitic covenant is most clearly demonstrated to the generation of adults who escaped Egyptian bondage. The older generation chose disobedience, which carried a death sentence in the wilderness. More time elapses historically in this book than the other books combined that relate to the exodus from Egypt (Exodus, Leviticus, Deuteronomy). The nearly 40 years of wandering take place in Numbers as a result of Israel's disobedience and lack of faith in the covenant God, *YHWH* (Yahweh).

This book is essential for understanding the reasons for the second giving of the commandments (see Exod. 20 and Deut. 5). Were it not for the death sentence on the adults, it would not have been necessary for Moses to reintroduce the Law and the commandments to another generation who would take the promised land.

Numbers also records historical details that are only alluded to by other biblical writers. In Ps. 95 for example, the writer gives the command "Do not harden your hearts as at Meribah, as on that day at Massah in the wilderness" (HCSB). The context indicates a reference to Israel's choice to accept the spies' majority report (Num. 14). Another incident found in Numbers is the fashioning of the bronze snake (Num. 21). Jesus refers to this event during His instruction of Nicodemus.

NUN 1. Father of Joshua (Exod. 33:11; Num. 11:28; 13:8,16). **2.** Fourteenth letter of the Hebrew alphabet that serves as a heading for Ps. 119:105-112. Each verse of this section begins with "nun."

NYMPHA or **NYMPHAS** Christian host of a house church, likely in Laodicea (Col. 4:15). Because the name occurs only in the accusative case, it is not possible to determine whether it is masculine or feminine.

Ancient oil lamp decorated with two human figures.

OARSMEN NIV term for those who row a galley (Ezek. 27:8,26).

OATHS Statements by which a person promises or guarantees that a vow will be kept or that a statement is, in fact, true. In the OT the name of God was invoked as the One Who would guarantee the results or veracity of a statement. Oaths were often accompanied and evidenced by the raising of a hand or hands toward heaven or by placing the hand under the thigh (Gen. 14:22; 24:2-3; Dan. 12:7).

Jesus did not use oaths to confirm the authority of His teaching. He pointed to a higher ethic that rests upon the integrity of the child of God as one not needing to prove his veracity by affirming an oath. So in the Sermon on the Mount Jesus exhorts His followers to refrain from oaths, and, "But let your word 'yes' be 'yes' and your 'no' be 'no.' Anything more than this is from the evil one" (Matt. 5:33-37 HCSB).

The admonition of Jesus to His followers to have honesty in their speech does not discount the use of oaths in the NT. Though Jesus did not use oaths when Caiaphas placed Him under oath, He accepted the challenge and declared Himself to be the promised Messiah of Israel (Matt. 26:63-64).

OBADIAH Personal name meaning "Yahweh's servant." **1.** Person in charge of Ahab's palace. He was devoted to Yahweh and saved Yahweh's prophets from Jezebel's wrath. He was the go-between for Elijah and Ahab (1 Kings 18:3-16). **2.** Descendant of David through Hananiah (1 Chron. 3:21). **3.** Son of Izrahiah of the tribe of Issachar (1 Chron. 7:3). **4.** Son of Azel of the tribe of Benjamin (1 Chron. 8:38; 9:44). **5.** Levite who returned to Jerusalem with the first of the Babylonian exiles (1 Chron. 9:16). **6.** Gadite who joined David, along with Ezer and Eliab. Obadiah was second in command behind Ezer (1 Chron. 12:8-9). **7.** Father of Ishmaiah, an officer from the tribe of Zebulun who served in David's army (1 Chron. 27:19). **8.** One of five officials Jehoshaphat sent throughout the cities of Judah to teach "the book of the law of the LORD" (2 Chron. 17:7-9). See *Jehoshaphat.* **9.** Levite descended from Merari appointed by Josiah to oversee the repairing of the temple (2 Chron. 34:12). See *Josiah.* **10.** Priest who returned from Babylonian exile to Jerusalem with Ezra (Ezra 8:9). He joined other priests along with princes and Levites in putting his seal upon the covenant (Neh. 9:38) made between the people and God (Neh. 10:5). **11.** Gatekeeper and guardian of "the ward" (KJV), "the storehouses of the gates" (NASB) during the leadership of Ezra and Nehemiah (Neh. 12:25).

OBADIAH, BOOK OF Shortest book of the Minor Prophets, preserving the message of the Prophet Obadiah.

Historically, the book belongs to the early postexilic period at the end of the sixth century BC. Its central section, verses 10-14, deals with the fall of Jerusalem to the Babylonians in 586 BC., concentrating on the part the Edomites played in that tragic event. Edom was a state to the southeast of Judah. Despite treaty ties ("brother," v. 10) the Edomites, along with others, had failed to come to Judah's aid and had even helped Babylon by looting Jerusalem and handing over refugees. Moreover, the Edomites filled the vacuum caused by Judah's exile by moving west and annexing the Negev to the south of Judah and even its southern territory (cp. v. 19).

Judah reacted with a strong sense of grievance. Obadiah's oracle responded to an underlying impassioned prayer of lament, like Pss. 74; 79; or 137, in which Judah appealed to God to act as providential trial Judge and Savior to set right the situation.

Like the book of Revelation, which proclaims the downfall of the persecuting Roman Empire, the aim of Obadiah is to sustain faith in God's moral government and hope in the eventual triumph of His just will. It brings a pastoral message to aching hearts that God is on the throne and cares for His own.

OBAL Personal name meaning "stout." Son of Joktan and ancestor of an Arab tribe (Gen. 10:28). At 1 Chron. 1:22 the name takes the alternate form Ebal.

OBED Personal name meaning "serving." **1.** Son of Boaz and Ruth (Ruth 4:13-17), father of Jesse, and grandfather of King David. He was an ancestor of Jesus Christ (Matt. 1:5; Luke 3:32). **2.** Son of Ephal and father of Jehu (1 Chron. 2:37-38). **3.** One of David's mighty men (1 Chron. 11:47). **4.** Gatekeeper in Solomon's temple (1 Chron. 26:7). **5.** Father of Azariah, a commander assisting in coronation of King Josiah (2 Chron. 23).

OBED-EDOM Personal name meaning "serving Edom." **1.** Philistine from Gath who apparently was loyal to David and Israel. At Obed-edom's house David left the ark of the covenant following the death of Uzzah at the hand of God (2 Sam. 6:6-11). **2.** Levite who served as both gatekeeper and musician in the tabernacle in Jerusalem during David's reign (1 Chron. 15:18,24; 16:5). His duties related especially to the ark of the covenant. A guild of Levites may have adopted the name "Obed-edom" as their title as keepers of the ark. **3.** Member of the Korhites (1 Chron. 26:1,4-8) who kept the south of the temple (v. 15). **4.** Keeper of the sacred vessels of the temple. Joash of Israel took with him the sacred vessels to Samaria following his capture of Jerusalem and of Amaziah king of Judah (2 Chron. 25:23-24).

OBEDIENCE To hear God's Word and act accordingly. The word translated "obey" in the OT means "to hear" and is often so translated. In the NT several words describe obedience. One word means "to hear or to listen in a state of submission." Another NT word often translated "obey" means "to trust."

The person's obedient response to God's Word is a response of trust or faith. Thus, to really hear God's Word is to obey God's Word (Exod. 19:5; Jer. 7:23).

OBEISANCE To bow down with one's face to the ground as a sign of homage and submission. KJV and RSV translate the Hebrew *shachah* as "obeisance" when the object of homage is a person but as "worship" when the object of homage is God or other gods (84 times in the RSV).

OBIL Personal name of uncertain meaning, perhaps "camel driver," "tender," or "mourner." Overseer in charge of David's camels (1 Chron. 27:30).

OBLATION Gift offered at an altar or shrine, especially a voluntary gift not involving blood.

OBOTH Place-name meaning "fathers" or "water skins." A wilderness station (Num. 21:10-11; 33:43-44).

OBSCENE OBJECT REB translation for an object the queen mother Maacah erected for the worship of Asherah, a fertility goddess (1 Kings 15:13; 2 Chron. 15:16).

OBSCURITY KJV term for gloom or darkness (Isa. 29:18; 58:10; 59:9).

OBSERVER OF TIMES KJV term for a soothsayer (Deut. 18:10,14; cp. Lev. 19:26; 2 Kings 21:6; 2 Chron. 33:6).

OCHRAN (NASB, REB, NRSV) or **OCRAN** (KJV, NIV) Personal name meaning "troubler." Father of Pagiel, a leader of the tribe of Asher (Num. 1:13; 2:27; 7:72,77; 10:26).

ODED Personal name of uncertain meaning, perhaps "counter," "restorer," or "timekeeper." **1.** Father of the Prophet Azariah (2 Chron. 15:1). **2.** Prophet in the time of Ahaz who urged the Israelites to release the people of Judah they had taken as prisoners of war (2 Chron. 28:8-15).

ODOR Scent of fragrance, usually in the phrase "pleasing odor" (KJV, "sweet savour"). A synonym for a burnt offering (Num. 28:1-2).

OFFAL NIV term for the waste remaining from the butchering of a sacrificial animal (Exod. 29:14; Lev. 4:11; 8:17; 16:27; Num. 19:5; Mal. 2:3). Other translations render the underlying Hebrew as "dung."

OFFENSE Translates several Hebrew and Greek terms. The following two senses predominate. **1.** That which causes indignation or disgust (Gen. 31:36). Here offense approximates crime (Deut. 19:15; 22:26), guilt (Hos. 5:15), trespass (Rom. 5:15,17-18,20), or sin (2 Cor. 11:7). Christ is said to be a rock of offense in this sense (Rom. 9:33; Gal. 5:11; 1 Pet. 2:8). What was especially offensive was the claim that an accursed one was the Messiah and that faith in this crucified one and not works was necessary for salvation. **2.** That which serves as a hindrance (Matt. 16:23) or obstacle (2 Cor. 6:3). This hindrance is often temptation to sin (Matt. 18:7; Luke 17:1).

OFFSCOURING That which is removed by scouring: the dregs, filth, garbage, refuse, or scum (Lam. 3:45; 1 Cor. 4:13).

OG Amorite king of Bashan defeated by the Israelites before they crossed the Jordan (Num. 21:33-35; Deut. 1:4; 3:1-13).

OHAD Personal name meaning "unity." Son of Simeon (Gen. 46:10; Exod. 6:15). The name is omitted in parallel lists (Num. 26:12-14; 1 Chron. 4:24).

OHEL Personal name meaning "tent," "family (of God)," or "(God is) shelter." Descendant of David (1 Chron. 3:20).

OHOLAH Personal name meaning "tent dweller." A woman's name Ezekiel used to portray Samaria (Ezek. 23:1-10).

OHOLIAB Personal name meaning "father's tent." Danite craftsman, designer, and embroiderer who assisted Bezalel in supervision of the construction of the tabernacle and its equipment (Exod. 31:6; 35:34; 36:1-2; esp. 38:23).

OHOLIBAH Personal name meaning "tent worshipper." Younger sister in the allegory of Ezek. 23 identified with Jerusalem (23:4,11-49). The sexual misconduct of these sisters represents Israel's and Judah's embrace of idolatry.

OHOLIBAMAH Personal name meaning "tent of the high place" or "tent dweller of the false cult." **1.** Hivite daughter of Anah and wife of Esau (Gen. 36:2). **2.** Edomite leader descended from Esau (Gen. 36:41).

OIL Indispensable commodity in the ancient Near East for food, medicine, fuel, and ritual. Oil was considered a blessing given by God (Deut. 11:14), and the olive tree was a characteristic of the land that God gave to Israel (Deut. 8:8).

OINTMENT Perfumed unguents or salves of various kinds used as cosmetics, medicine, and in religious ceremonies. The use of ointments and perfumes appears to have been a common practice in the ancient Near East including the Hebrews.

OLD GATE KJV, NASB, NRSV designation for a Jerusalem city gate repaired in Nehemiah's time (Neh. 3:6; 12:39). This rendering is doubtful on grammatical grounds (the adjective and noun do not agree).

OLD TESTAMENT First part of the Christian Bible, taken over from Israel. It tells the history of the nation of Israel and God's dealings with them to the return from exile in Babylon. For Jews it is the complete Bible, sometimes called Tanak for its three parts (Torah or Law, Nebiim or Prophets, Kethubim or Writings). Christians see its complement in the NT, which reveals Jesus Christ as the fulfillment of OT prophecy. The OT has three major divisions: Law, Prophets (Former and Latter), and Writings.

OLD TESTAMENT QUOTATIONS IN THE NEW TESTAMENT Influence of the OT is seen throughout the NT. The NT writers included approximately 250 express OT quotations, and if one includes indirect or partial quotations, the number jumps to more than 1,000. It is clear that the writers of the NT were concerned with demonstrating the continuity between the OT Scriptures and the faith they proclaimed. They were convinced that in Jesus the OT promises had been fulfilled.

The western slope of the Mount of Olives on which Jesus gave His Olivet discourse.

OLIVES, MOUNT OF Two-and-a-half-mile-long mountain ridge that towers over the eastern side of Jerusalem, or more precisely, the middle of the three peaks forming the ridge. Heavily covered with olive trees, the ridge juts out in a north-south direction (like a spur) from the range of mountains running down the center of the region.

Both the central Mount of Olives and Mount Scopus, the peak on its northern side, rise over 200 feet above the Temple Mount across the Kidron Valley. It provided a lookout base and signaling point for armies defending Jerusalem.

David crossed the Mount of Olives when fleeing Absalom (2 Sam. 15:30). Ezekiel saw the cherubim chariot land there (Ezek. 11:22-23). Zechariah described how the Mount of Olives would move to form a huge valley on the Day of the Lord (Zech. 14:3-5). Many crucial events in Jesus' life occurred on the Mount of Olives (Matt. 26:30; Mark 11:1-2; Luke 4:5; 22:39-46; Acts 1:9-12).

OLIVET DISCOURSE Jesus' major sermon preached on the Mount of Olives; Jesus gave instructions concerning the end of the age and the destruction of Jerusalem. The discourse (Matt. 24–25; Mark 13) is in part an apocalypse because it uses symbolic, visionary language that makes it a difficult passage to understand. Parts of it appear scattered throughout Luke 12–21.

OLYMPAS Perhaps a shortened form of Olympiodorus (gift of Olympus). Christian whom Paul greeted in Rom. 16:15. Olympas was apparently a member of a house church including the others mentioned in 16:15.

OMAR Personal name meaning "talkative." Son of Eliphaz and ancestor of an Edomite clan of the same name (Gen. 36:11,15; 1 Chron. 1:36).

OMEGA Last letter in the Greek alphabet. Together with the first letter, alpha, omega designates God and Christ as the all-encompassing "Reality" (Rev. 1:8; 21:6; 22:13).

OMEN 1. Sign used by diviners to predict the future. The Israelites were prohibited from interpreting omens (Deut. 18:10 NASB, NIV). **2.** Sign indicating a future event. Ahab's reference to Ben-hadad as "my brother" was understood as an omen or sign of Ahab's favor (1 Kings 20:33 NASB, NRSV).

The faithful witness of Christians in the face of opposition is likewise an omen or sign pointed to the salvation of believers and the destruction of God's enemies (Phil. 1:28).

OMER 1. Unit of dry measure equal to one tenth of an ephah or a little more than two quarts (Exod. 16:13-36). See *Weights and Measures*. **2.** First sheaf (omer) of the barley harvest that was elevated as an offering (Lev. 23:9-15).

OMNIPOTENCE State of being all-powerful, which is true only of God. Scripture often affirms that all power belongs to God (Ps. 147:5), that all things are possible for God (Luke 1:37; Matt. 19:26), and that God's power exceeds what humans can ask or think (Eph. 3:20).

OMNIPRESENCE Being present everywhere at once, a unique attribute of God.

OMNISCIENCE Having all knowledge, a unique attribute of God. God knows us intimately (Ps. 139:1-6; Matt. 6:4,6,8). Such knowledge is cause for alarm for the unrighteous but for confidence for God's saints (Job 23:10; Pss. 34:15-16; 90:8; Prov. 15:3; 1 Pet. 3:12).

OMRI Personal name meaning "pilgrim" or "life." **1.** King of Israel 885–874 BC and founder of the Omride dynasty, which ruled the northern kingdom until 842. **2.** Officer of the tribe of Issachar under David (1 Chron. 27:18). **3.** Grandson of Benjamin (1 Chron. 7:8). **4.** Grandfather of a member of the tribe of Judah who returned to Jerusalem from exile about 537 BC.

ON 1. Egyptian place-name meaning "city of the pillar," called in Greek Heliopolis or "city of the sun" and in Hebrew Beth-shemesh, "city of the sun" (Jer. 43:13), and Aven. It was the cult center for the worship of the sun-god, Re (Atum).

ONAM Personal name meaning "vigorous." **1.** Ancestor of an Edomite subclan (Gen. 36:23; 1 Chron. 1:40). **2.** Ancestor of a family of Jerahmeelites, a subclan of Judah (1 Chron. 2:26,28).

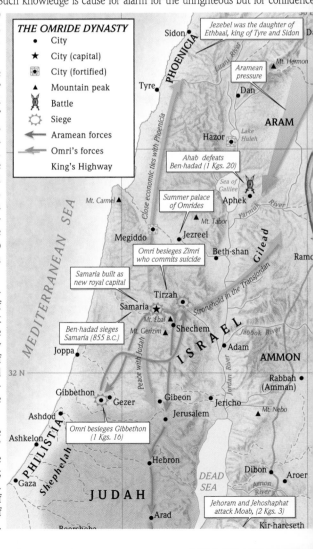

THE OMRIDE DYNASTY
- • City
- ★ City (capital)
- ▣ City (fortified)
- ▲ Mountain peak
- Battle
- Siege
- ← Aramean forces
- ← Omri's forces
- King's Highway

Jezebel was the daughter of Ethbaal, king of Tyre and Sidon

Aramean pressure

Ahab defeats Ben-hadad (1 Kgs. 20)

Summer palace of Omrides

Omri besieges Zimri who commits suicide

Samaria built as new royal capital

Ben-hadad sieges Samaria (855 B.C.)

Omri besieges Gibbethon (1 Kgs. 16)

Jehoram and Jehoshaphat attack Moab, (2 Kgs. 3)

PHOENICIA · ARAM · ISRAEL · JUDAH · AMMON · PHILISTIA · Shephelah · Gilead

MEDITERRANEAN SEA · DEAD SEA

Sidon · Tyre · Dan · Mt. Hermon · Hazor · Lake Huleh · Sea of Galilee · Aphek · Yarmuk River · Mt. Carmel · Mt. Tabor · Jezreel · Beth-shan · Megiddo · Tirzah · Samaria · Mt. Ebal · Mt. Gerizim · Shechem · Adam · Jabbok River · Rabbah (Amman) · Joppa · Gibbethon · Gezer · Gibeon · Jericho · Mt. Nebo · Jerusalem · Ashdod · Ashkelon · Hebron · Dibon · Aroer · Gaza · Arad · Kir-hareseth · Beersheba · Jordan River · Arnon River

Close economic ties with Phoenicia · Peace with Judah · Stronghold in the Transjordan

32 N

ONAN Personal name meaning "power." A son of Judah and his Canaanite wife, Shuah (Gen. 38:2-8). Following the death of his older brother, Er, Onan was to have married the widow and produced a son who would carry on Er's name. Onan repeatedly failed to complete the responsibilities of the marriage and therefore God killed him (38:8-10).

ONESIMUS Personal name that may mean "profitable." The slave for whom Paul wrote his letter to Philemon. Later, Onesimus accompanied Thychius in bearing Paul's letter to the church at Colossae (Col. 4:7-9).

ONESIPHORUS Personal name meaning "profit bearing." Ephesian Christian praised for his effort to seek out the place of Paul's arrest, his disregard of the shame connected with befriending one in chains, and his past service in Ephesus (2 Tim. 1:16-18).

ONO Name meaning "grief." Benjaminite town about seven miles southeast of Joppa.

ONYCHA Spice probably derived from the closing flaps or the shell of a Red Sea mollusk that was used in the incense reserved for the worship of Yahweh (Exod. 30:34).

OPHEL Place-name meaning "swelling," "fat," "bulge," or "mound." It became the proper name of a portion of the hill on which the city of David was built (2 Chron. 27:3).

OPHIR Place-name and personal name meaning "dusty." Place famous in the ancient Near East for its trade, especially in gold. Solomon's ships with help from Phoenician sailors brought precious goods from Ophir (1 Kings 9:28; 10:11; cp. 1 Kings 22:48).

OPHNI Name meaning "high place." Town allotted to Benjamin (Josh. 18:24).

OPHRAH Name meaning "fawn." **1.** Descendant of Judah (1 Chron. 4:14). **2.** City in Benjamin (Josh. 18:23), likely north of Michmash (1 Sam. 13:17-18). **3.** Town associated with the Abiezer clan of Manasseh who settled west of the Jordan (Judg. 6:11,24; 8:32). This Ophrah was the home of Gideon.

ORACLES Communications from God. The term refers both to divine responses to a question asked of God and to pronouncements made by God without His being asked. In one sense oracles were prophecies since they often referred to the future; but oracles sometimes dealt with decisions to be made in the present. Usually in the Bible the communication was from Yahweh, the God of Israel. In times of idol worship, however, Israelites did seek a word or pronouncement from false gods (Hos. 4:12). Many of Israel's neighbors sought oracles from their gods.

ORCHARD Grove of fruit (Neh. 9:25; Eccles. 2:5) or nut trees (Song 6:11). An enclosed orchard is sometimes called a garden or park.

ORDINANCES See *Baptism; Lord's Supper.*

ORDINATION, ORDAIN Appointing, consecrating, or commissioning of persons for special service to the Lord and His people. Four primary examples provide OT precedents for ordination: the consecration of Aaron and his sons as priests to God (Exod. 28–29; Lev. 8–9), the dedication of the Levites as servants of God (Num. 8:5-14), the appointment of 70 elders to assist Moses (Num. 11:16-17,24-25), and the commissioning of Joshua as Moses' successor (Num. 27:18-23). The NT practice of ordination is generally associated with the laying on of hands, but other appointments, consecrations, and commissionings must be considered even if they lack formal investiture.

OREB AND ZEEB Personal names meaning "raven" and "wolf." Two Midianite princes captured and executed by the Ephraimites following Gideon's rout of their forces (Judg. 7:24–8:3).

OREN Personal name meaning "cedar." Member of the Jerahmeelite clan of Judah (1 Chron. 2:25).

ORGAN KJV term for a musical instrument that modern translations identify as a pipe or shrill flute (Gen. 4:21; Job 21:12; 30:31; Ps. 150:4).

ORION Constellation bearing the name of a giant Greek hunter who, according to myth, was bound and placed in the heavens. Job 38:31 perhaps alludes to this myth. God is consistently portrayed as the creator of the Orion constellation (Job 9:9; Amos 5:8). The plural of the Hebrew term for Orion is rendered "constellations" at Isa. 13:10.

ORNAN Personal name meaning "prince." Alternate name of Araunah (1 Chron. 21:15,18,20-25,28; 2 Chron. 3:1).

ORONTES RIVER Principal river of Syria which originates east of the Lebanon ridge, rises near

Heliopolis (Baalbek) in the Beka Valley of Lebanon, and flows north some 250 miles through Syria and Turkey before turning southwest into the Mediterranean south of Antioch-on-the-Orontes (Antakya) to reach the coast just south of ancient Seleucia, the seaport of Antioch.

ORPAH Personal name meaning "neck," "girl with a full mane," or "rain cloud." Daughter-in-law of Naomi who returned to her people and gods after Naomi twice requested that she go (Ruth 1:4-15).

ORYX Large, straight-horned antelope.

OSEE Greek form of Hosea used by KJV (Rom. 9:25).

OSHEA KJV alternate form of Hoshea (Joshua) at Num. 13:8,16.

OSNAPPAR or **OSNAPPER** Assyrian king who repopulated Samaria with foreigners following its capture in 722 BC (Ezra 4:10). Osnappar is most often identified with Ashurbanipal. KJV used the form Asnapper.

OSPRAY, OSPREY Large, flesh-eating hawk included in lists of unclean birds (Lev. 11:13; Deut. 14:12 KJV, NRSV).

OSSIFRAGE English applies "ossifrage" to three birds: the bearded vulture; the osprey; and the giant petrel. The KJV included the ossifrage among the unclean birds (Lev. 11:13; Deut. 14:12).

OSTIA Roman city at the mouth of the Tiber about 15 miles from Rome that, following construction of an artificial harbor by Claudius (AD 41–54), served as the principle harbor for Rome.

OSTRACA Potsherds (pottery fragments), especially fragments used as an inexpensive writing material.

OSTRICH The ostrich, the largest of birds, is a swift, flightless fowl. One passage in Job (39:13-18) describes some of the characteristic habits of the ostrich.

OTHNI Personal name, perhaps meaning "force" or "power." Levitic gatekeeper (1 Chron. 26:7).

OTHNIEL Name meaning "God is powerful." **1.** First of Israel's judges or deliverers. Othniel received Caleb's daughter Achsah as his wife as a reward for his capture of Kiriath-sepher (Debir) (Josh. 15:15-19; Judg. 1:11-15). **2.** Clan name associated with a resident of Netophah (1 Chron. 27:15).

OUCHES KJV term for (filigree) settings for precious stones (Exod. 28:11,13-14,25; 39:6,13,16,18).

OUTCAST Scripture never employs "outcast" in the now common sense of one rejected by society. "Outcasts" often has the technical sense of Diaspora. NASB employs "outcast" for one excommunicated from the synagogue (John 16:2).

OUTLANDISH KJV term meaning "foreign" (Neh. 13:26).

OVEN Device used for baking food, especially bread (Lev. 2:4; Exod. 8:3). Ancient ovens were cylindrical structures of burnt clay two to three feet in diameter. A fire was built on pebbles in the oven bottom. Bread was baked by either placing the dough against the oven walls or upon the heated pebbles. Dried grass (Matt. 6:30; Luke 12:28), thorny shrubs, and animal dung were often used as fuels.

OVERLIVE KJV term meaning "outlive" (Josh. 24:31).

OVERPASS KJV term (Jer. 5:28) meaning either "surpass" previous limits or bounds (NASB, NIV, RSV, TEV) or else "pass over" in the sense of overlook (NASB margin, REB).

OVERRUN Term meaning "outrun" (2 Sam. 18:23; Ps. 105:30 HCSB).

OVERSEER Superintendent or supervisor. Various translations use "overseer" for a variety of secular

Large domed oven.

positions. HCSB, NASB, and NIV employ "overseer" for the bishop of the KJV, NRSV (Phil. 1:1; 1 Tim. 3:1-2; Titus 1:7).

OWL Bird of prey belonging to the order *Strigiformes,* which are generally nocturnal. Hebrew terms for various bird species cannot be identified precisely with English terms.

OWNERSHIP Possession of property. Two general principles guided Israelite laws of ownership: (1) all things ultimately belong to God, and (2) land possession is purely a business matter. After the division of the land among the 12 tribes, individual plots were given to family groups or clans. If the occasion demanded it, the land could be redivided at a later time. Land sales and transfers were recorded by scribes on leather or papyrus scrolls, on clay tablets, or in the presence of witnesses with the symbolic removal of a sandal (Ruth 4:7) or the stepping onto the land by the new owner. Land passed from father to son but could be given to a daughter. Private lands ultimately reverted to the king if not used for several years (2 Kings 8).

Private ownership continued in much the same fashion during the NT era. Bills of sale and land deeds written on papyrus scrolls from this period have been discovered, attesting to the exchange of private lands. Often the sale of private land was subject to royal approval. The Romans oversaw the control of lands in Palestine, requiring heavy taxes from owners. The early Christian community existed through the generosity of those members who sold many of their possessions to help poorer believers.

OX Large, often domesticated, bovine. In the OT it was extremely valuable as a work animal. Permitted as food, they were also offered as sacrifices (Deut. 14:4-6; Lev. 17:3-4).

OZEM Personal name meaning "irritable" or "strength." **1.** Sixth son of Jesse (1 Chron. 2:15). **2.** Fourth son of Jerahmeel (1 Chron. 2:25).

OZIAS Greek form of Uzziah used by KJV (Matt. 1:8-9).

OZNI Personal name meaning "my hearing" or "attentive." Ancestor of a Gadite family, the Oznites (Num. 26:16).

The altar of Zeus, the highest god in the Greek pantheon.

PAARAI Personal name meaning "revelation of Yahweh." One of David's 30 elite warriors (2 Sam. 23:35) designated an Arbite, a resident of Arbah (Josh. 15:52). The parallel list has the name "Naarai" (1 Chron. 11:37).

PADAN-ARAM (KJV) or **PADDAN-ARAM** Place-name, perhaps meaning "way of Syria," "field of Syria," or "plow of Syria." The land from where Abraham journeyed to Canaan. One of the principal cities was Haran. Later Abraham sent his steward to Paddan-aram (Gen. 25:20) to seek a wife for Isaac (Gen. 24:1-9), and Jacob fled there and married into Laban and Rebekah's branch of the patriarchal family (28:2-5).

PADDLE KJV term for a digging tool (Deut. 23:13). Modern translations render the term as something to dig with (NIV), spade (NASB), stick (RSV, TEV), or trowel (NRSV, REB). The Israelites were required to respect God's presence in their camp by burying their excrement.

PADON Personal name meaning "redemption." Ancestor of a family of postexilic temple servants (Ezra 2:44; Neh. 7:47).

PAGANS Those who worship a god or gods other than the living God to whom the Bible witnesses. NIV, REB, and RSV sometimes use "pagans" as the translation of the Greek *ethnoi* (1 Cor. 5:1; 10:20), which is generally translated "Gentiles" (so KJV, NASB). In English, "Gentile" relates to ethnic background while "pagan" refers to religious affiliation.

PAGIEL Personal name meaning "fortune of God," "God is entreated," or "God meets." Wilderness leader of the tribe of Asher (Num. 1:13; 2:27; 7:72,77; 10:26).

PAHATH-MOAB Title meaning "governor of Moab." A family of returned exiles likely descended from the Hebrew governor of Moab in the time of David (2 Sam. 8:2; Ezra 2:6; 8:4; 10:30; Neh. 7:11; 10:14).

PAI Place-name meaning "groaning." Alternate form of Pau used at 1 Chron. 1:50 (cp. Gen. 36:39).

PAINT Mixture of pigment and liquid used to apply a closely adhering, colorful coat to a surface. Most scriptural references are to painting the eyes.

PALACE Residence of a monarch or noble. KJV often used "palace" in passages where modern translations have substituted a term more appropriate to the context.

PALAL Personal name meaning "God comes to judge." One of those assisting in Nehemiah's repair of the wall (Neh. 3:25).

PALANQUIN REB, RSV term for an enclosed seat or couch carried on servants' shoulders (Song 3:9). Other translations include: carriage (NIV), chariot (KJV), and sedan chair (NASB).

PALESTINA KJV alternate name for Philistia (Exod. 15:14; Isa. 14:29,31).

PALESTINE Geographical designation for the land of the Bible, particularly land west of Jordan River that God allotted to Israel for an inheritance (Josh. 13–19). Various terms have been used to designate that small but significant land known in the early OT era as "Canaan" (Gen. 12:5) and often referred to as the promised land (Deut. 9:28). The area was designated "Israel" and "Judah" at the division of the kingdoms in 931 BC. By NT times the land had been divided into provincial designations: Judea, Samaria, Galilee, and others. Generally the region was considered to be a part of Syria. See *Israel*

Palestine is derived from the name *Pelishtim* or "Philistines." The Greeks, familiar primarily with the coastal area, applied the name "Palestine" to the entire southeastern Mediterranean region. Although the word "Palestine" (or "Palestina") is found four times in the KJV (Exod. 15:14; Isa. 14:29,31; Joel 3:4), these are references to the territory of the Philistines and so properly designate only the strip of coastland occupied by that people.

Climate Palestine lies in the semitropical belt between 30 degrees 15 feet and 33 degrees 15 feet north latitude. Temperatures are normally high in the summer and mild in the winter, but these generalizations are modified by both elevation and distance from the coast. Variety is the necessary word in describing Palestinian weather, for in spite of its relatively small size, the geographical configuration of the area produces a diversity of conditions. Because of the Mediterranean influence, the coastal plain has an average annual temperature of 57 degrees at Joppa. Jerusalem, only 35 miles away, has an annual average of 63 degrees. Its elevation of 2,500 feet above sea level causes the difference. Jericho is only 17 miles further east, but it is 3,400 feet lower

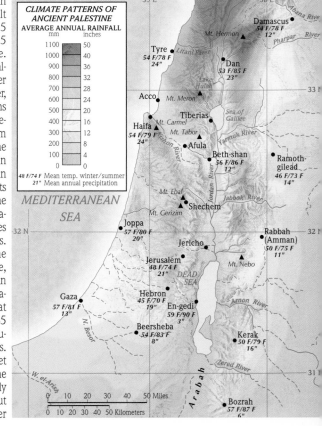

CLIMATE PATTERNS OF ANCIENT PALESTINE
AVERAGE ANNUAL RAINFALL

mm	inches
1100	50
1000	40
900	36
800	32
700	28
600	24
500	20
400	16
300	12
200	8
100	4
0	0

48 F/74 F Mean temp. winter/summer
21" Mean annual precipitation

(900 feet below sea level), consequently having a tropical climate and very low humidity. Here bitterly cold desert nights offset rather warm desert days. Similarly, much of the area around the Sea of Galilee experiences temperate conditions, while the Dead Sea region is known for its strings of 100 degrees-plus summer days.

Palestine is a land of two seasons, a dry season and a rainy season, with intervening transitional periods. The dry season lasts from mid-May to mid-October. From June through August no rain falls except in the extreme north. Moderate, regular winds blow usually from the west or southwest. The breezes reach Jerusalem by noon, Jericho in early afternoon, and the Transjordan plateau by mid afternoon. The air carries much moisture, but atmospheric conditions are such that precipitation does not occur. However, the humidity is evident from the extremely heavy dew that forms five nights out of six in July.

With late October the "early rain" so often mentioned in Scripture begins to fall. November is punctuated with heavy thunderstorms. The months of December through February are marked by heavy showers, but it is not a time of unrelenting rain. Rainy days alternate with fair days and beautiful sunshine. The cold is not severe, with occasional frost in the higher elevations from December to February. In Jerusalem snow may fall twice during the course of the winter months.

All of Palestine experiences extremely disagreeable warm conditions occasionally. The sirocco wind (the "east wind" of Gen. 41:6 and Ezek. 19:12) blowing from the southeast during the transition months (May—June, September—October) brings dust-laden clouds across the land. It dries vegetation and has a withering effect on people and animals. On occasion the temperature may rise 30 degrees Fahrenheit and the humidity fall to less than 10 percent.

Along the coastal plain, the daily temperature fluctuation is rather limited because of the Mediterranean breezes. In the mountains and in Rift Valley the daily fluctuation is much greater.

PALLET Small, usually straw-filled mattress light enough to be carried. All biblical references are found in accounts or summaries of the healing of invalids (Mark 2:4-12; John 5:8-12; Acts 5:15). The "bedridden" man of Acts 9:33 was one who had lain on a pallet for eight years.

PALLU Personal name meaning "conspicuous," "wonder," or "distinguished." Second son of Reuben (Gen. 46:9; Exod. 6:14; Num. 26:5,8; 1 Chron. 5:3). KJV used the alternate spelling Phallu in Genesis.

PALMERWORM Caterpillar stage of a species of locust (Joel 1:4; 2:25; Amos 4:9). See *Insects*.

PALMS Date palm (*Phoenix dactylifera*) was among the earliest cultivated trees. Five thousand-year-old inscriptions from Mesopotamia give instruction for their cultivation. Palms are characteristic of oases and watered places (Exod. 15:27; Num. 33:9). The fruit of the date palm is highly valued by desert travelers since it may be consumed fresh or else dried or made into cakes for a portable and easily storable food. Palms were used in the construction of the booths for the Festival of Booths (Lev. 23:40; Neh. 8:15). In John 12:13 the crowd used palm branches to welcome Jesus to Jerusalem.

Palm trees in the Wadi Feiran on the Sinai Peninsula.

PALMS, CITY OF Alternate name for Jericho (Deut. 34:3; Judg. 1:16; 3:13; 2 Chron. 28:15).

PALSY KJV term for paralysis (Matt. 4:24; 9:2; Luke 5:18; Acts 8:7).

PALTI Personal name meaning "my deliverance." **1.** Benjamin's representative among the 12 spies sent to survey Canaan (Num. 13:9). **2.** Second husband of Michal, King Saul's daughter who had previously been given in marriage to David (1 Sam. 25:44; KJV, Phalti).

PALTIEL Personal name meaning "God is (my) deliverance." **1.** Leader of Issachar whom Moses appointed to assist Joshua and Eliezer in distribution of land to the tribes west of the Jordan (Num. 34:26). **2.** Fuller form of the name of Saul's son-in-law (2 Sam. 3:15-16).

PALTITE Title meaning "resident of Beth-pelet," given to Helez, one of David's 30 elite warriors (2 Sam. 23:26). The parallels in 1 Chronicles read Pelonite (11:27; 27:10).

PAMPHYLIA One of the provinces of Asia Minor. Located in what is now southern Turkey,

Pamphylia was a small district on the coast. It measured about 80 miles long and 20 miles wide. One of the chief cities was Perga, where John Mark left Paul and Barnabas during the first missionary journey (Acts 13:13).

PAPER, PAPYRUS Popular writing material invented by the Egyptians and used by scribes from 2500 BC to AD 700.

The English word "paper" is derived from the word *papyrus*. The papyrus plant once grew in abundance along the Nile delta ("Can the papyrus grow tall where there is no marsh?" [Job 8:11 NIV]), providing the Egyptians with an inexpensive writing material that was exported throughout the Mediterranean world.

The road north from Antalia to Isparta in the Roman province of Pamphylia (modern Turkey).

A modern variety of the ancient papyrus plant from whose stalks writing material was made.

By AD 100 papyrus was used to make codices (books). The codex format—a stack of papyrus sheets, bound at one end—proved to be more economical than the roll since a scribe could only write on one side of the roll. A codex was also less cumbersome, considering the transportation of rolls and the difficulty of cross referencing. Eventually, papyrus was replaced by the more expensive and yet more durable parchment (animal skins). Aged papyrus became brittle, literally causing words to fall off the page. Furthermore, unlike papyrus, parchment could be "erased" and used again. The only biblical reference to papyrus paper is found in 2 John 12, where the Elder writes: "Having many things to write unto you, I would not write with *paper* and ink" (author's italics).

New Testament manuscripts produced before the fourth century were written exclusively on papyrus; after the fourth century almost all NT documents were preserved on parchment.

PAPHOS Town on the southwest side of Cyprus and capital of the island during NT times. Paul, Barnabas, and John Mark came to the city on their first missionary journey and possibly led the proconsul, Sergius Paulus, to Christ (Acts 13:6-12).

PAPS KJV term used for a woman's breasts (Ezek. 23:21; Luke 11:27) or a man's chest (Rev. 1:13).

PARABLES Stories, especially those of Jesus, told to provide a vision of life, especially life in God's kingdom. Parable means a putting alongside for purposes of comparison and new understanding. Parables utilize figures of speech such as metaphors and similes and frequently extend them into a brief story to make a point or disclosure. Parables are not allegories although some parables bear close resemblance to allegories.

Common Theme of Jesus' Parables Jesus' great thesis centers on the kingdom of God (Mark 1:15). Jesus lifted the theme to new heights and through His parables portrayed the nature of the kingdom (Mark 4:26-29), the grace of the kingdom (Luke 18:9-17), the crisis of the kingdom (Luke 12:54-56) and the conditions of the kingdom such as commitment (Luke 14:28-30), forgiveness (Matt. 18:23-35), and compassion (Luke 10:25-37).

The parables further proclaim the kingdom as ethical, experiential or existential, eschatological and evangelistic. Several parables accentuate ethical concerns such as attitude toward one's fellow (Luke 18:9-14; 15:25-32; Matt. 18:23-35). Jesus insisted on being religious through relationships. The rousing call to repentance embodied in many parables requires a moral and spiritual reorientation of life around the kingdom.

Many parables reach the water table of common experience and illumine existence or life. Jesus could expose a pale or petrified life. He could convey the moving experience of being lost in the far country and then to come to oneself and go home (Luke 15:17). His parables exposed the inauthentic life as aggressively self-centered and greedy (Luke 12:13-21; 16:19-31).

PARACLETE Transliteration of the Greek word literally meaning "called beside or alongside to help." John exclusively used the term in the NT. He described the Spirit as another "Paraclete" who teaches (John 14:16), reminds the disciples of what Jesus taught (John 14:26), testifies (John 15:26), and convicts of sin (John 16:7-8). John also described Jesus as the first "Paraclete" (John 14:16) or advocate (1 John 2:1).

PARADISE Old Persian term that means literally "enclosure" or "wooded park," used in the OT to speak of King Artaxerxes's forest (Neh. 2:8), and twice of orchards (Eccles. 2:5; Song 4:13). All three NT occurrences (Luke 23:43; 2 Cor. 12:4; Rev. 2:7) refer to the abode of the righteous dead (heaven).

PARAH Place-name meaning "heifer" or "young cow." Village in territory of Benjamin about five miles northeast of Jerusalem, identified with modern Khirbet el-Farah (Josh. 18:23). The Hebrew *parat*, often translated Euphrates (KJV, NASB, NRSV), may refer to the spring 'Ain Farah at Jer. 13:4-7 (cp. NASB, NRSV margin, "Parah"). NIV, REB simply transliterate the term.

PARAMOUR Illicit sexual partner (Ezek. 23:20 KJV, NASB, NRSV; Hos. 3:1 RSV). Other translations read: lovers (NIV); male prostitutes (REB); and oversexed men (TEV).

PARAN 1. Wilderness area south of Judah, west of Edom, and north of Sinai. Israel camped there after leaving Sinai during the exodus and sent spies to scout out the promised land from Kadesh, a location in Paran (Num. 10:11-12; 13:3,26. **2.** Mount Paran appears as a poetic parallel to Mount Sinai (Deut. 33:2; cp. Hab. 3:3) as the place of revelation. If not the same place as Sinai, the location is unknown.

PARCHED GRAIN Common food prepared by roasting grains in a pan or by holding heads of grain over a fire (Lev. 23:14; Josh. 5:11; Ruth 2:14; 1 Sam. 17:17; 25:18; 2 Sam. 17:28).

South end of the Wilderness of Paran where Israel wandered (photo taken in sand storm).

Mosaic law prohibited the eating of parched grain before the first fruits of the grain had been offered to God.

PARDON Authoritative act reversing a sentence given under a guilty verdict. Prayer for God's pardon for sin is based on the greatness of God's covenant love and on the long history of God's acts of forgiveness (Num. 14:19; Mic. 7:18).

PARE To trim or shave off. The paring of nails served as a sign of mourning for lost parents (Deut. 21:12 KJV, REB, NRSV). An Israelite desiring to marry a female prisoner of war was required to allow her to cut her hair and pare her nails first. These actions perhaps symbolized purification on entering the covenant community.

PARMASHTA Personal name, probably of Persian origin, possibly meaning "strong-fisted" or "the very first." One of Haman's 10 sons (Esther 9:9).

PARMENAS Personal name meaning "faithful" or "constant." One of the seven chosen by the Jerusalem congregation to distribute food to the Greek-speaking widows of that church (Acts 6:5).

PARNACH Persian personal name of uncertain meaning. Father of Elizaphan (Num. 34:25).

PAROSH Personal name meaning "flea." **1.** Ancestor of a postexilic family (Ezra 2:3; 8:3; KJV, Pharosh; 10:25; Neh. 7:8). **2.** One of the witnesses to Ezra's renewal of the covenant (Neh. 10:14), possibly the father of Pedaiah (Neh. 3:25). This Parosh was likely the chief member of the family above.

PAROUSIA Transliteration of Greek word which means "presence" or "coming." In NT theology it encompasses the events surrounding the second coming of Christ.

PARSHANDATHA Personal name, probably of Persian origin, possibly meaning "inquisitive." One of Haman's 10 sons (Esther 9:7).

PARTHIANS Tribal people who migrated from Central Asia into what is now Iran. In 53 BC the Romans invaded Parthia but were defeated on several occasions. They did not gain control of Parthia until AD 114. Some Parthians were among those in Jerusalem on the Day of Pentecost who heard the gospel in their own language (Acts 2:9-11).

PARTRIDGE Stout-bodied, medium-size game bird with variegated plumage. David likened his life as a fugitive from Saul to a hunted partridge (1 Sam. 26:20).

PARUAH Personal name meaning "blossoming," "joyous," or "increase." Father of Jehoshaphat (1 Kings 4:17).

PARVAIM Source of gold for Solomon's decoration of the temple (2 Chron. 3:6). The place is perhaps el Farwaim (Farwa) in Yemen, or else a general term for the East.

PARZITES KJV alternate form of Perezites (Num. 26:20).

PASACH Personal name, perhaps meaning "divider." Member of the tribe of Asher (1 Chron. 7:33).

PASCHAL Adjective expressing relation to the Passover.

PASDAMMIN Place-name meaning "boundary of blood." Scene of David's victory over the Philistines (1 Chron. 11:13). The site is probably between Socoh and Azekah, the same as Ephes-dammin (1 Sam. 17:1).

PASEAH Personal name meaning "lame." **1.** Member of the tribe of Judah (1 Chron. 4:12). **2.** Ancestor of a family of temple servants (Neh. 7:51; KJV "Phaseah"). **3.** Father of Joiada (Neh. 3:6).

PASHUR Personal name meaning "son of (the god) Horus." **1.** Chief officer in the Jerusalem temple in the last years before Nebuchadnezzar's victory over the city. He had Jeremiah beaten and imprisoned (Jer. 20:1-2). He or another Pashur was the father of Gedaliah (Jer. 38:1). **2.** Man in Zedekiah's court in Jerusalem (Jer. 21:1). As the Babylonian army approached, Pashur asked Jeremiah for a word from the Lord. Jeremiah prophesied the destruction of the city (21:1-7; cp. 38:1-3). **3.** Forebear of a priestly family (1 Cor. 9:12) who returned from the exile (Ezra 2:38) and who later gave up their foreign wives (10:22; cp. Neh. 10:3; 11:12).

PASSION 1. Any bodily desire that leads to sin (Rom. 6:12; Gal. 5:24; Eph. 2:3). Passion is especially used for strong sexual desire (Rom. 1:26-27; 1 Cor. 7:9; 1 Thess. 4:5). **2.** KJV twice used the phrase "like passions" (Acts 14:15; James 5:17) to mean "shared human nature." **3.** The suffering of Jesus during the last two days of His life. Luke uses a word translated "passion" only in Acts 1:3 (KJV, after His passion). The root is the Greek verb *pascho*, "to suffer." Acts 17:3 and 26:23 use *pathein* to speak specifically of Christ's suffering—Jesus foretold His sufferings a number of times and yet His disciples rejected this possibility (Matt. 16:21; Mark 9:12; Luke 17:25).

PASSOVER Hebrew feast, commemorating their deliverance from Egyptian bondage. See *Festivals.*

PASTOR Common translation of the Greek noun (Eph. 4:11) and its verb form; also the Hebrew *ra'ah* (Jer. 3:15; 10:21; 12:10; 22:22 KJV). Literally, a shepherd (or one who keeps animals, Gen. 4:2; 13:7; 46:32,34; Exod. 2:17; Isa. 13:20; Jer. 6:3; Luke 2:8,15,18,20), but used figuratively of those called by God to feed (Jer. 3:15; John 21:16), care for (Acts 20:28), and lead (1 Pet. 5:2) His people, who are His "flock." In the NT pastor (shepherd) appears to depict aspects, or functions, of the responsibilities of the overseer/elder (1 Pet. 2:25, where the two are put together in Christ).

PASTORALS First and Second Timothy and Titus are called the Pastoral Epistles, a title first used by Anton in 1753.

PASTURE Open land surrounding towns and villages, regarded as common property to be freely used by village shepherds and herdsmen (Num. 35:2,7; Josh. 14:4; 21:11). The same Hebrew term designates open space around a city or the sanctuary (Ezek. 27:28; 45:2; 48:17).

PATH A walkway. Two contrasting paths are a common image for rival ways of life in Hebrew wisdom literature. The path of the wicked (Prov. 4:14) who forget God (Job 8:13) is crooked (Prov. 2:15). This approach to life contrasts with the path of righteousness (Ps. 23:3; Prov. 2:13,20).

PATHROS Hebrew transliteration of Egyptian term for Upper (southern) Egypt. Upper Egypt included the territory between modern Cairo and Aswan. The NIV translates the term; other translations transliterate (Isa. 11:11; Jer. 44:1,15; Ezek. 29:14; 30:14).

PATHRUSIM Son of Mizraim (Egypt) and ancestor of the inhabitants of upper (southern) Egypt who bore his name (1 Chron. 1:12).

PATIENCE Active endurance of opposition, not a passive resignation. "Patience" and "patient" are used to translate several Hebrew and Greek words.

PATMOS Small island (10 miles by 6 miles) in the Aegean Sea located about 37 miles southwest of Miletus. The Romans used such places for political exiles. John's mention of the island in Rev. 1:9

The island of Patmos on which John was probably exiled by the Romans.

probably means that he was such a prisoner, having been sent there for preaching the gospel. Eusebius (an early church father) wrote that John was sent to Patmos by Emperor Domitian in AD 95 and released after one and one-half years.

PATRIARCHS Israel's founding fathers—Abraham, Isaac, Jacob, and the 12 sons of Jacob (Israel). The word "patriarch" comes from a combination of the Latin word *pater*, "father," and the Greek verb *archo*, "to rule." A patriarch is thus a ruling ancestor who may have been the founding father of a family, a clan, or a nation.

PATROBAS Personal name meaning "life of (or from) father." Member of a Roman house church whom Paul greeted (Rom.16:14).

PAU Edomite city meaning "they cry out." Hadar's (Hadad) capital (Gen. 36:39). The parallel in 1 Chron. 1:50 gives the name as Pai.

PAUL Outstanding missionary, theologian, and writer of the early church. Paul is a very important figure in the NT and in the history of Christianity. He wrote 13 epistles that comprise almost one-fourth of the NT. Approximately 16 chapters of the book of Acts (13–28) focus on his missionary labors. Thus Paul is the author or subject of nearly one-third of the NT and the most important interpreter of the teachings of Christ and of the significance of His life, death, and resurrection.

Early Life and Training (AD 1–35) *Birth and Family Background* Paul was born in a Jewish family in Tarsus of Cilicia (Acts 22:3), probably sometime during the first decade of the first century. Paul's family was of the tribe of Benjamin (Phil. 3:5), and he was named for the most prominent member of the tribe—King Saul. Paul probably came from a family of tentmakers or leatherworkers and, according to Jewish custom, was taught this trade by his father. Apparently the business thrived and Paul's family became moderately wealthy.

Paul was born a Roman citizen. Many speculate that Paul's father or grandfather was honored with citizenship because of some special service rendered to a military proconsul.

Rabbinic Training Acts 22:3 shows that Paul grew up in Jerusalem. Paul used this fact to prove that he was no Diaspora Jew who was more influenced by Gentile culture than Jewish ways. He was educated in Jerusalem in the Jewish religion according to the traditions of his ancestors (Acts 22:3). Acts 22 says that Paul was trained by Rabbi Gamaliel I, the member of the Sanhedrin mentioned in Acts 5:33-39. Gamaliel was a leading Jewish teacher in Paul's day. In Acts 26:5 Paul identifies himself with the sect of the Pharisees. His father had also been a Pharisee (Acts 23:6).

Persecution of Christians As an ideal Pharisee Paul was probably active as a Jewish missionary winning Gentiles as proselytes. He may have been like the Pharisees Jesus described who traveled "over land and sea to make one convert" (Matt. 23:15 HCSB).

Paul was probably in his thirties when he, with authorization from the chief priest, began to imprison believers first in the synagogues of Jerusalem and then later in Damascus. Paul's initial and adamant rejection of Jesus as the Messiah may largely have been motivated by Jesus' ignoble death. Death by crucifixion was indicative of divine curse (Deut. 21:23). Certainly the Messiah could not have died under the curse of God. But when Paul wrote his first epistle, this death curse was recognized as the grounds for substitutionary atonement (Gal. 3:10-14). In 1 Cor. 1 Paul explained that the idea of a crucified Messiah was a stumbling block to the Jews. Probably Paul was speaking from his own past experience.

Paul's Conversion (AD 35) While Saul was on his way to Damascus to arrest and imprison believers there, the resurrected and glorified Christ appeared to him with blinding radiance. Christ's words "It is hard for you to kick against the goads" indicate that God had already begun His convicting work earlier. At the appearance of Christ, Saul immediately surrendered to His authority and went into the city to await further orders. There his blindness was healed, and he received the Holy Spirit and accepted believer's baptism.

Paul's Missionary Travels (AD 35–61) *Early Travels* Soon after his conversion, Paul traveled to Arabia where he began evangelization of the Nabatean Arabs (Gal. 1:17; 2 Cor. 11:32-33) and probably experienced his first opposition to the gospel from political authorities. He then returned to Damascus where he began to go into the synagogues to preach the message that had been revealed to him on the Damascus road: Jesus is the Son of God and the promised Messiah. The Jews in

PAUL'S CONVERSION
AND EARLY MINISTRY
- City
- ▲ Mountain peak
- ⋈ Pass
- ← Paul sent to Damascus
- ← ••• Paul spends time in Arabia
- ← ⋅⋅ Paul returns to Jerusalem
- ← Paul flees from Hellenists
- ← Paul and Barnabas travel to Antioch
- ← ⋅⋅ Paul and Barnabas sent to Jerusalem
- ← Paul and Barnabas return to Antioch
- ▨ Kingdom of Agrippa I

COMMAGENE

Cilician Gates
Tarsus
Issus
Amanus Mts.
Syrian Gates

6. Paul and Barnabas establish a strong church where believers were first called Christians

Antioch
Aleppo
Seleucia Pieria
Euphrates R.

7. Paul and Barnabas travel to Jerusalem with aid for famine

SYRIA

Cyprus
Paphos

Hamath
Emesa

8. Paul and Barnabas return to Antioch

Palmyra (Tadmor)

Tripolis

Orontes R.

MEDITERRANEAN
SEA

Byblos
Litani R.
COELE-SYRIA

3. Paul baptized and preaches about his newfound faith

Sidon
Mt. Hermon ▲
PHOENICIA
Damascus

2. Paul has a vision of Jesus and converts

5. Paul returns to his hometown of Tarsus

Tyre
Caesarea-Philippi
Capernaum
Gamala
Canatha (Kenath)
▲ Mt. Hauran

Ptolemais (Acco)
Tiberias
Bostra

Caesarea Maritima
Scythopolis
Pella

4. Paul flees to Arabia then returns to Jerusalem

Antipatris
Joppa
JUDEA
abbok R.
Philadelphia (Amman)

Azotus (Ashdod)
Jericho

Gaza
Jerusalem
Raphia
IDUMEA

DEAD SEA

Arabah
NABATEA

N

Syro-Arabian Desert

1. Paul sanctioned to arrest followers in Damascus

0 25 50 75 100 Miles
0 25 50 75 100 Kilometers

Damascus watched the city gates in order to kill Paul, and he had to escape through a window in the wall by being lowered in a basket (Acts 9:22-25).

Paul then traveled to Jerusalem. Church leaders were initially suspicious of Paul but Barnabas intervened in his behalf (Acts 9:26-30 and Gal. 1:18). After 15 days in Jerusalem, visiting with Peter and James, the Lord's brother, Paul returned to Tarsus, evangelizing Syria and Cilicia for several years. While in Syria, Barnabas contacted Paul and invited him to become involved in the Antioch church where large numbers of Gentiles were responding to the gospel.

First Missionary Journey Paul and Barnabas soon began their first missionary journey, traveling through Cyprus and Anatolia probably during the years AD 47–48. The missionary team carried the gospel to the cities of Pisidian Antioch, Iconium, Lystra, and Derbe. These cities were located in the Roman province of Galatia, and it is probably these churches in south Galatia to which the epistle to the Galatians is addressed. Galatians was probably written during this journey.

Jerusalem Council When Paul returned to Antioch from the first missionary journey, he found himself embroiled in controversy over requirements for Gentile salvation. Peter and even Barnabas were vacillating on the issue of Jew-Gentile relationships. Even worse, some false teachers from the Jerusalem church had infiltrated congregations in Antioch and were teaching, "Unless you are circumcised according to the custom taught by Moses, you cannot be saved." The church appointed Paul and Barnabas to go to Jerusalem and settle the matter. A council was convened in AD 49 that included the missionary team, those who insisted upon circumcision as a requirement for salvation, and the apostles. The Apostle Peter and James the brother of Jesus spoke in defense of Paul's Law

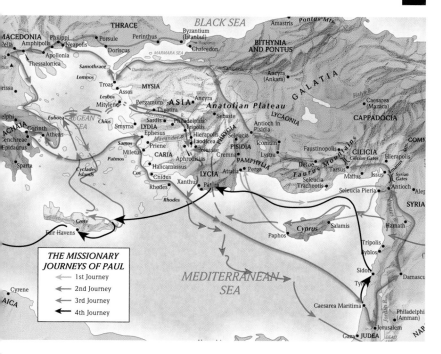

THE MISSIONARY
JOURNEYS OF PAUL
← 1st Journey
← 2nd Journey
← 3rd Journey
← 4th Journey

ree gospel and a letter was sent to the Gentile churches confirming the official view. Paul returned to Antioch and remained there from 49 to 51.

Second Missionary Journey The second missionary journey carried Paul through Macedonia and Achaia in AD 50–52. Paul and Barnabas parted company early in this journey in a disagreement about the participation of Barnabas' nephew John Mark. Mark had abandoned the team on the first journey (Acts 15:38). Paul took Silas and established churches in Philippi, Thessalonica, and Berea. Barnabas went with John Mark. Paul also spent 18 months in Corinth strengthening a fledgling church there. Four of Paul's letters are addressed to churches known from this second journey. Most scholars believe that 1 and 2 Thessalonians were written during this journey.

Third Missionary Journey Paul's third missionary journey (AD 53–57) focused on the city of Ephesus where Paul spent the better part of three years. Toward the end of this journey Paul worked hard to collect another relief offering for Jerusalem believers. Paul wrote 1 and 2 Corinthians and Romans during this journey.

Final Years Paul carried the relief offering to Jerusalem. While he was in the temple performing a ritual to demonstrate his Jewish faithfulness to some of the Jerusalem believers, Jewish opponents incited a riot and Paul was arrested (AD 57). Paul was sent to Caesarea to stand trial before the procurator Felix. After two years of procrastination on the part of his detainers, Paul finally appealed to the Roman emperor for trial. After arriving in Rome Paul spent two years under house arrest awaiting his trial. Paul wrote Philemon, Colossians, Ephesians, and Philippians during this first Roman imprisonment.

The record of Acts ends at this point so information as to the outcome of the trial is sketchy. Early church tradition suggests that Paul was acquitted (ca. AD 63) or exiled and fulfilled the dream expressed in Rom. 15:23-29 of carrying the gospel to Spain (AD 63–67). Paul probably wrote 1 and 2 Timothy and Titus during the period between his acquittal and a second Roman imprisonment. According to church tradition Paul was arrested again and subjected to a harsher imprisonment. He was condemned by the Emperor Nero and beheaded with the sword at the third milestone on the Ostian Way, at a place called Aquae Salviae, and lies buried on the site covered by the basilica of St. Paul Outside the Walls. His execution probably occurred in AD 67.

Paul's Gospel Paul's gospel indicted all humanity for the crime of rejecting God and His rightful authority. Under the influence of Adam's sin, mankind plunged into the depths of depravity so that they were utterly unable to fulfill the righteous demands of God (Rom. 1:18-32; 3:9-20; 9:12-19) and deserved only the wrath of God (Rom. 1:18; 2:5-16). The sinner was alienated from God and at enmity with Him (Col. 1:21). Consequently, the sinner's only hope was the gospel that embodied God's power to save those who had faith in Christ (Rom. 1:16). The focus of Paul's gospel was Jesus Christ (Rom. 1:3-4). Paul affirmed Jesus' humanity and His deity. Christ was a physical descendent

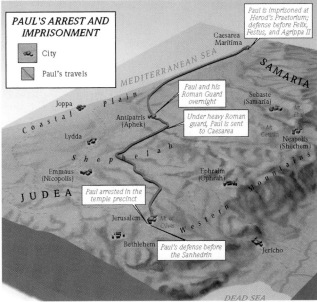

PAUL'S ARREST AND IMPRISONMENT

- City
- Paul's travels

MEDITERRANEAN SEA

SAMARIA

Caesarea Maritima

Paul is imprisoned at Herod's Praetorium; defense before Felix, Festus, and Agrippa II

Joppa

Coastal plain

Sebaste (Samaria)

Mt. Ebal

Paul and his Roman Guard overnight

Antipatris (Aphek)

Lydda

Under heavy Roman guard, Paul is sent to Caesarea

Mt. Gerizim

Neapolis (Shechem)

Shephelah

Emmaus (Nicopolis)

Ephraim (Ophrah)

Western Mountains

JUDEA

Paul arrested in the temple precinct

Jerusalem

Mt. of Olives

Bethlehem

Paul's defense before the Sanhedrin

Jericho

DEAD SEA

from the line of David (Rom. 1:2), came in the likeness of sinful man (Rom. 8:3), and had assumed the form of a humble obedient servant (Phil. 2:7-8). Yet He was the visible form of the invisible God (Col. 1:15), all the fullness of deity living in bodily form (Col. 2:9), the very nature of God (Phil. 1:6), and possessed the title "Lord" (Greek title for the God of the OT), the name above all names (Phil. 2:9-11). Paul believed that by virtue of His sinlessness, Jesus was qualified to be the sacrifice which would make sinners right with God (2 Cor. 5:21). In His death on the cross Jesus became the curse for sin (Gal. 3:10-14), and the righteous died for the unrighteous (Rom. 5:6-8). Salvation is a free gift granted to believers and grounded solely in God's grace. Salvation is not dependent upon human merit, activity, or effort, but only upon God's undeserved love (Eph. 2:8-10; Rom. 6:23). Those who trust Jesus for their salvation, confess Him as Lord, and believe that God raised Him from the dead (Rom. 10:9) will be saved from God's wrath, become righteous in God's sight (Rom. 5:9), be adopted as God's children (Rom. 8:15-17), and be transformed by the Spirit's power (Gal. 5:22-24). At the coming of Christ believers will be resurrected (1 Cor. 15:12-57), will partake fully of the Son's righteous character (Phil. 3:20-21), and will live forever with their Lord (1 Thess. 4:17). By his union with Christ through faith, the believer participated spiritually in Christ's death, resurrection, and ascension (Rom. 6:1-7:6; Eph. 2:4-5). Consequently, the believer has been liberated from the power of sin, death, and the Law. He is a new, though imperfect, creation that is continually being made more Christlike (Col. 3:9-10; 2 Cor. 5:17). Although the believer is no longer under the authority of the written Law, the Holy Spirit functions as a new internal law that leads him to naturally and spontaneously fulfill the Law's righteous demands (Rom. 8:1-4). As a result, the Law-free gospel does not encourage unrighteous behavior in believers. Such behavior is contrary to their new identity in Christ. The union of believers with Christ brings them into union with other believers in the body of Christ, the church. Believers exercise their spiritual gifts in order to help each other mature, to serve Christ, and to glorify Him, which is the church's highest purpose (Eph. 3:21; 4:11-13). Christ now rules over the church as its Head, its highest authority (Eph. 1:22). When Christ comes again, His reign over the world will be consummated and all that exists will be placed under His absolute authority (Phil. 2:10-11; 4:20; Eph. 1:10). He will raise the dead: unbelievers for judgment and punishment; believers for glorification and reward (2 Thess. 1:5-10).

Reconstruction of Caesarea Maritima where Paul was imprisoned for two years (Acts 23:31–26:32).

PAVILION Large, often richly decorated tent.

PEACE OFFERING See *Sacrifice and Offering.*

PEACE A condition or sense of harmony, well-being, and prosperity. The biblical concept means more than the absence of hostility, and it is more than a psychological state.

Old Testament The Hebrew word *shalom* and its derivatives have been said to represent "one of the most prominent theological concepts in the OT." (The word group occurs about 180 times in the

OT.) It was not a negative or passive concept but involved wholeness and completeness.

New Testament The term translated "peace" in the NT is *eirene*. It occurs in every NT book except 1 John (most frequently in Luke, 14 times; followed by Romans, 10; then Ephesians, 8). Outside the Bible the Greek word was likely to mean just the opposite of war, but its use to translate *shalom* in the Septuagint may have been what broadened its usage. Like *shalom*, the term in the NT could refer not only to the absence of hostility, strife, and disorder (1 Cor. 14:33) but also to the condition and sense of being safe and secure (Acts 9:31). Christ made peace between believing Jew and Gentile by making them into one new man in Him (Eph. 2:14-15). The term could also describe a state of either physical or spiritual well-being.

PEACEMAKERS Those who actively work to bring about peace and reconciliation where there is hatred and enmity. God blesses peacemakers and declares them to be His children (Matt. 5:9). Those who work for peace share in Christ's ministry of bringing peace and reconciliation (2 Cor. 5:18-19; Eph. 2:14-15; Col. 1:20).

PEACOCK KJV translated two Hebrew words as "peacock." Modern translations replace "peacock" with "ostrich" at Job 39:13. NASB, NRSV read "peacock" with KJV at 1 Kings 10:22 and 2 Chron. 9:21. Other translations read "monkey" (REB, RSV) or "baboon" (NIV, NRSV margin).

PEDAHEL Personal name meaning "God delivers." Leader of the tribe of Naphtali whom Moses appointed to assist Joshua and Eliezer in the distribution of land to the tribes living west of the Jordan (Num. 34:28).

PEDAHZUR Personal name meaning "(the) Rock redeems." Father of Gamaliel (Num. 1:10; 2:20; 7:54,59; 10:23).

PEDAIAH Personal name meaning "Yah redeems." **1.** Maternal grandfather of King Jehoiakim (2 Kings 23:36). **2.** Father (1 Chron. 3:18-19) or uncle (Ezra 3:2,8; 5:2; Neh. 12:1; Hag. 1:1,12,14; 2:2,23) of Zerubbabel. First Chronicles presents Pedaiah and Shealtiel as brothers. **3.** Manassite father of Joel (1 Chron. 27:20). **4.** Son of Parosh assisting in Nehemiah's repair of the wall (Neh. 3:25). **5.** Witness to Ezra's renewal of the covenant (Neh. 8:4), perhaps identical with 4. **6.** Benjaminite father of Joed (Neh. 11:7). **7.** Levite whom Nehemiah appointed as temple treasurer (Neh. 13:13).

PEDDLER One who sells goods, usually on the street or door-to-door. Paul denied being a peddler of God's word (2 Cor. 2:17). Here Paul either emphasized that he did not preach for pay (1 Cor. 9:12,15) or that he did not use tricks to gain converts (2 Cor. 4:2; 12:16).

PEG Small, cylindrical, or tapered piece of wood (or some other material). Pegs were used: to secure tents (Judg. 4:21-22; 5:26); to hang articles (Isa. 22:23,25; Ezek. 15:3); to weave cloth (Judg. 16:14); even to dig latrines (Deut. 23:13).

PEKAH Personal name meaning "open-eyed." Officer in Israel's army who became king in a bloody coup by murdering King Pekahiah (2 Kings 15:25).

PEKAHIAH Personal name meaning "Yah has opened his eyes." King of Israel 742–740 BC He succeeded his father, Menahem, as a vassal of the Assyrian throne (2 Kings 15:23).

PEKOD Hebrew for "punishment" or "judgment" that plays on the name Puqadu, an Aramean tribe inhabiting the area east of the mouth of the Tigris (Jer. 50:21; Ezek. 23:23).

PELAIAH Personal name meaning "Yahweh is wonderful (or performs wonders)." **1.** Descendant of David (1 Chron. 3:24). **2.** Levite assisting in Ezra's public reading of the Law (Neh. 8:7). **3.** Levite witnessing Nehemiah's covenant (Neh. 10:10), perhaps identical to 2.

PELALIAH Personal name meaning "Yahweh intercedes." Ancestor of a priest in Ezra's time (Neh. 11:12).

PELATIAH Personal name meaning "Yahweh delivers." **1.** Descendant of David (1 Chron. 3:21). **2.** One of the Simeonites destroying the remaining Amalekites at Mount Seir (1 Chron. 4:42). **3.** Judean prince who offered "wicked counsel," perhaps appealing to Egypt for help in a revolt against the Babylonians (Ezek. 11:1,13; cp. Jer. 27:1-3; 37:5,7,11). **4.** Witness to Nehemiah's covenant (Neh. 10:22).

PELEG Personal name meaning "division" or "watercourse." Descendant of Shem (Gen. 10:25), ancestor of Abraham (Gen. 11:16-19; 1 Chron. 1:19,25) and Jesus (Luke 3:35).

PELET Personal name derived from a root meaning "escape." **1.** Descendant of Caleb (1 Chron. 2:47).

2. Benjaminite warrior who defected from Saul to David (1 Chron. 12:3).

PELETH Personal name meaning "swift." **1.** Father of On (Num. 16:1). The name is possibly a textual corruption of Pallu (Gen. 46:9; Num. 26:5,8), whose descendants are also associated with the Korah rebellion (Num. 26:9-10). **2.** A Jerahmeelite (1 Chron. 2:33).

PELETHITES Family name meaning "courier." Foreign mercenaries King David employed as bodyguards and special forces. Their leader was Benaiah (2 Sam. 8:18).

PELICAN Any member of a family of large, web-footed birds with gigantic bills having expandable pouches attached to the lower jaw. The Hebrew term translated "pelican" in Lev. 11:18; Deut. 14:17, however, suggests a bird that regurgitates its food to feed its young.

PELLA City just east of the Jordan River and southeast of the Sea of Galilee. It received a large part of the Jerusalem church when they fled there before the Roman destruction of the Holy City in AD 66.

PENINNAH Personal name, perhaps meaning "woman with rich hair," "coral," or "pearl." It may be an intentional wordplay meaning "fruitful." Elkanah's second wife and rival of barren Hannah (1 Sam. 1:2,4).

PENKNIFE Another name for a scribe's knife.

PENTAPOLIS League of five Philistine city-states that banded together to oppose the Israelite occupation of Canaan: Ashdod, Gaza, Ashkelon, Gath, and Ekron (1 Sam. 6:17).

PENTATEUCH The expression derives from two Greek words, *penta*, "five," and *teuchos*, "vessel, container," and refers to the first five books of OT. This designation dates to the time of Tertullian (ca. AD 200), but Jewish canons label these books collectively as the Torah, which means "Teaching, Instruction." In English Bibles these first five books are commonly called "Law." This designation is misleading because it misrepresents the content of the Pentateuch. Large portions are not law at all; they are actually inspiring narratives (virtually all of Genesis; Exod. 1–11; 14–20; 32–34; Lev. 8–10; Num. 1:1–3:4,7,9-14,16-17,20-28,31-33). Although *Deuteronomium* means "second law," the book presents itself as preaching, Moses' final pastoral addresses.

The Samaritan Pentateuch at Nablus. Samaritans consider only the Pentateuch as canonical.

The Plot of the Pentateuch The pivotal event of the Pentateuch is God's revelation of Himself at Sinai. Everything before is prologue, and all that comes after is epilogue. This is evident from the redundant highlighting of the place in Deut. 19:1-3, and also from the explicit anticipation of Exod. 3:12, where Yahweh told Moses that Israel's service to God at Mount Sinai would prove Yahweh had sent him. This is confirmed by Moses' demands to Pharaoh that he let Israel go to serve Yahweh in the desert (4:23; 5:1,3; 6:11; 7:16; 8:1,25-28; 9:13; 10:3,7,9,24-26). The Patriarchal narratives also look forward to Sinai. In Gen. 12:2 God promises Abraham that he would be a blessing to the whole world. Later we learn that this would involve being the recipient of the divine revelation (cp. Deut. 4:5-8), being a kingdom of priests, a holy nation, a special treasure "among all the peoples, for all the earth is mine" (Exod. 19:5-6).

The narratives describing Israel's journey from Sinai to the Plains of Moab are told against the backdrop of Yahweh's covenant with Israel and Israel's promise to do "all that Yahweh had told them." Numbers 28:6 explicitly refers to the Sinai revelation. But the book of Deuteronomy, virtually in its entirety, represents Moses' exposition of the Sinai covenant. However, remember that the primary character is not human; this is a record of God's relationship with those He created in His own image, whom He elected, redeemed, and commissioned to be His agents on the earth.

PENTATEUCH, SAMARITAN See *Samaritan Pentateuch*.

PENTECOST See *Festivals (Feast of Weeks)*.

PENUEL Name meaning "face of God." **1.** Descendant of Judah and founder (father) of Gedor (1 Chron. 4:4). **2.** A Benjaminite (1 Chron. 8:25). **3.** Site on Jabbok River northeast of Succoth where Jacob wrestled with the stranger (Gen. 32:24-32; cp. Hos. 12:4).

PEOPLE OF GOD Group elected by God and committed to be His covenant people. Scripture repeatedly defines who is included in the people of God. The history of revelation shows God electing Israel by grace.

PEOR Name, perhaps meaning "opening." **1.** Mountain in Moab opposite the wilderness of Judah. Balak brought Balaam there to curse the camp of the Israelites, which was visible from the site (Num. 23:28; 24:2). **2.** Abbreviated form of Baal-Peor (lord of Peor), a god whom the Israelites were led to worship (Num. 25:18; 31:16; Josh. 22:17). **3.** Site in Judah identified with modern Khirbet Faghur southwest of Bethlehem (Josh. 15:59 REB, following the earliest Greek translation).

PERDITION Describes the eternal state of death, destruction, annihilation, or ruin.

PEREA Roman district in Transjordan that became a part of Herod the Great's kingdom. The capital was Gadara where Jesus drove demons out of a man. Perea was the area through which the Jews traveled to avoid going through Samaria. Although not referred to by name in the NT, it is mentioned as "Judea beyond the Jordan" in several texts (Matt. 19:1; Mark 10:1 RSV).

PERESH Personal name meaning "separate." A Manassite (1 Chron. 7:16).

PEREZ Personal name meaning "breach." One of the twins born to the illicit affair between Judah and his daughter-in-law, Tamar (Gen. 38).

PEREZ-UZZA (NASB, RSV) or **PEREZ-UZZAH** Place-name meaning "breach of Uzzah." Site of the threshing floor of Nacon (or Chidon) west of Jerusalem on the Kiriath-jearim road where the anger of the Lord "broke out" against Uzzah, who touched the ark to steady it (2 Sam. 6:8; 1 Chron. 13:11).

PERFECT To be whole or complete; also referred to as "mature." Throughout the Bible, especially in the OT, God is referred to as being "perfect" (Ps. 18:32). He is complete and lacks nothing. In the Sermon on the Mount, Jesus commanded, "Be perfect, therefore, as your heavenly Father is perfect" (Matt. 5:48). The perfection demanded of Christians is a state of spiritual maturity or completeness.

PERFUME, PERFUMER Modern translation of a word translated as "apothecary" by the KJV (Exod. 30:25,35; 37:29; 2 Chron. 16:14; Neh. 3:8; Eccles. 10:1). Perfumes mentioned in the Bible include aloes, balsam (or balm), bdellium, calamus (or sweet or fragrant cane), camel's thorn, cinnamon (or cassia), frankincense, galbanum, gum, henna, myrrh, nard (or spikenard), onycha, saffron, and stacte.

PERGA Ancient city in the province of Pamphylia, about eight miles from the Mediterranean Sea. Settlement at Perga dates to prehistory. Alexander the Great passed through the town during his campaigns and used guides from there. A temple to Artemis was one of the prominent buildings. Paul, Barnabas, and John Mark came to Perga from Paphos (Acts 13:13). There young John left the team to return home.

The south Hellenistic gate of the ancient city of Perga in Pamphylia (modern Turkey).

PERGAMOS KJV, Rev. 1:11; 2:12) or **PERGAMUM** Place-name meaning "citadel." A wealthy ancient city in the district of Mysia in Asia Minor.

PERIDA Personal name meaning "unique" or "separated." Head of a family of Solomon's servants, some of whom returned from exile (Neh. 7:57; cp. Peruda, Ezra 2:55).

PERIZZITES Group name meaning "rustic." One of the groups of people who opposed the Israelite occupation of Canaan (Josh. 9:1-2). They dwelled in the land as early as Abraham's time (Gen. 13:7).

The temple of Athena at ancient Pergamum.

PERJURY False statement given voluntarily under oath. Perjury involves either false witness to past facts or the neglect of what has been previously vowed. Mosaic law prohibited false swearing (Lev. 19:12; Exod. 20:7) and giving false witness (Exod. 20:16).

PERSECUTION Harassment and suffering that people and institutions inflict upon others for being different in their faith, worldview, culture, or race. Persecution seeks to intimidate, silence, punish, or even kill people. Jesus was persecuted and finally killed by the religious and political establishments of His day (Mark 3:6; Luke 4:29; John 5:16; Acts 3:13-15; 7:52; passion stories). Whole epistles and books like 1 Peter, Hebrews, and Revelation were written to encourage Christians in a situation of persecution (1 Pet. 3:13-18; 4:12-19; 5:6-14; Heb. 10:32-39; 12:3; Rev. 2–3). Something like a theology of persecution emerged, which emphasized patience, endurance, and steadfastness (Rom. 12:12; 1 Thess. 2:14-16; James 5:7-11); prayer (Matt. 5:44; Rom. 12:14; 1 Cor. 4:12); thanksgiving (2 Thess. 1:4); testing (Mark 4:17) and the strengthening of faith (1 Thess. 3:2-3); experiencing the grace of God (Rom. 8:35; 2 Cor. 4:9; 12:10); and being blessed through suffering (Matt. 5:10-12; 1 Pet. 3:14; 4:12-14).

PERSEVERANCE Maintaining Christian faith through the trying times of life. As a noun the term "perseverance" occurs in the NT only at Eph. 6:18 (*proskarteresis*) and Heb. 12:1 (*hupomone*). The idea is inherent throughout the NT in the great interplay of the themes of assurance and warning.

PERSIA As a nation Persia corresponds to the modern state of Iran. As an empire Persia was a vast collection of states and kingdoms reaching from the shores of Asia Minor in the west to the Indus River Valley in the east. It reached northward to southern Russia and in the south included Egypt and the regions bordering the Persian Gulf and the Gulf of Oman. In history the empire defeated the Babylonians and then fell finally to Alexander the Great.

Politically the Persian Empire was the best organized the world had ever seen. The Persian Empire had considerable influence on the Jews and biblical history. Babylon had conquered Jerusalem and destroyed the temple in 586 BC When Cyrus conquered Babylon, he allowed the Jews to return to Judah and encouraged the rebuilding of the temple (Ezra 1:1-4). The work was begun but not completed. Then, under Darius I, Zerubbabel and the high priest, Joshua, led the restored community with the support and encouragement of the Persians. (Ezra 3–6 tells of some of the events while Haggai's and Zechariah's prophecies were made during the days of the restoration.) Despite some local opposition Darius supported the rebuilding of the temple, which was rededicated in his sixth year (Ezra 6:15). In addition, both Ezra and Nehemiah were official representatives of the Persian government. Ezra was to teach and to appoint judges (Ezra 7). Nehemiah may have been the first governor of the province of Yehud (Judah). He undoubtedly had official support for his rebuilding of the walls of Jerusalem.

Column with inscription in Old Persian script ascribed to Cyrus the Great.

The Jews had trouble under Persian rule, too. Although Daniel was taken into exile by the Babylonians (Dan. 1), his ministry continued through the fall of the Babylonians (Dan. 5) into the time of the Persians (Dan. 6). His visions projected even further. Daniel 6 shows a stable government but one in which Jews could still be at risk. His visions in a time of tranquility remind readers that human kingdoms come and go. Esther is a story of God's rescue of His people during the rule of the Persian emperor, Ahasuerus (also known as Xerxes I). The story shows an empire where law was used and misused. Jews were already, apparently, hated by some. Malachi, too, was probably from the Persian period. His book shows an awareness of the world at large and is positive toward the Gentiles and the government.

PERSIS Personal name meaning "Persian woman." Leader in the Roman church whom Paul greeted and commended for diligent service (Rom. 16:12).

PERVERSE Translation of one Greek and several Hebrew terms with the literal meaning "bent," "crooked," or "twisted," applied to persons involved in moral error.

PESHITTA Common Syriac version of the Scriptures. The OT was likely translated between AD 100 and 300. The NT translation dates from before AD 400. The Peshitta lacked those books rejected by the Syriac-speaking churches (2 Peter; 2 and 3 John; Jude; Revelation).

PESTILENCE Devastating epidemic that OT writers understood to be sent by God (Exod. 9:15; Jer. 15:2; Hab. 3:5; Amos 4:10), sometimes by means of a destroying angel (2 Sam. 24:16; 1 Chron. 21:15). God sent pestilence as punishment for persistent unbelief (Num. 14:12) and failure to fulfill covenant obligations (Deut. 28:21) as well as to encourage repentance (Amos 4:10).

PESTLE Small, club-shaped tool used to grind in a mortar (Prov. 27:22).

PETER Derived from the Greek *petros*, meaning "rock." The name occurs 183 times in the NT. Simon was his personal name; Peter was given to him by Jesus (Matt. 16:18). Though Peter is dominant, there are three other names: the Hebrew Simeon (Acts 15:14), Simon, and Cephas (Aramaic for rock), used mostly by Paul (1 Cor. 1:12; 3:22; 9:5; 15:5; Gal. 1:18; 2:9,11,14) and one other time (John 1:42).

Church of St. Peter in Gallicantu that honors the traditional site of Peter's weeping after his denial of Jesus.

Peter's Family The Gospels provide information about Peter and his family. He was called Barjona (Aramaic for "son of Jona," Matt. 16:17) or son of John (Gk. for Barjona, Luke 1:42). Peter and his brother Andrew came from Bethsaida (John 1:44) and were Galilean fishermen (Mark 1:16; Luke 5:2-3; John 21:3) in business with James and John (Luke 5:10). Peter was married (Mark 1:30) and lived in Capernaum (Mark 1:21-31). Peter and Andrew were associated with John the Baptist prior to becoming disciples of Jesus (John 1:40).

Peter's Role Among the Disciples Peter was leader and spokesman for the 12 disciples (Mark 8:29; Matt. 17:24). Peter often posed questions to Jesus representing concerns of the others (Matt. 15:15; 18:21; Mark 11:21; Luke 12:41). Sometimes he was spiritually perceptive (Matt. 16:16; John 6:68) and other times slow to understand spiritual matters (Matt. 15:15-16). Once he walked on water with Jesus, but his faith waned and he began to sink (Matt. 14:28-31). The greatest example of Peter's inconsistency was his confession "You are the Messiah" (Matt. 16:16 HCSB) opposed to his denial "I don't know this man" (Mark 14:71). After Pentecost (Acts 2:1) Peter was bold when persecuted. On two occasions Peter was arrested and warned to refrain from preaching about Jesus (Acts 4:1-22; 5:12-40). Herod imprisoned Peter with intent to execute him (Acts 12:3-5). Peter, however, was freed and delivered by an angel (Acts 12:6-11).

Peter's Role in the Early Church and His Legacy Though Peter led the disciples and took a prominent role in the early church (Acts 1–5), he did not emerge as the leader. Peter helped establish the Jerusalem church, but James the brother of Jesus assumed the leadership of the Jerusalem church (Acts 15). Though Peter was active in the spread of the gospel to the Gentiles (Acts 11–12), Paul became "the apostle to the Gentiles" (Acts 14; 16–28). Peter served as a bridge to hold together the diverse people of the early church (Acts 15). Peter became the "apostle to the Jews," preaching throughout Palestine. Peter died as a martyr in Rome under Nero, probably in AD 64 or 65 (1 Clement 5:1–6:1).

PETER, FIRST LETTER FROM First Peter is addressed to churches in Asia Minor experiencing persecution. Peter reminded them of their heavenly hope and eternal inheritance so that they would be strengthened to persevere in the midst of suffering. He emphasized that believers are called to holiness and a life of love. Believers are called upon to glorify God in their daily lives and to imitate Christ who suffered on the cross for the sake of His people. Peter sketched what it means to live as a Christian, how believers relate to governing authorities, to cruel masters, and to unbelieving husbands. He warned believers that suffering may be intense, but believers should rely upon God's grace, knowing there is a heavenly reward.

If we accept Petrine authorship, the letter was likely written in the early 60s, before the composition of 2 Peter. The first verse of the letter indicates that the letter was written to various churches in the northern part of Asia Minor (present-day Turkey). The courier of the letter, presumably Silvanus, probably traveled in a circle in reading the letter to the various churches. The purpose of the letter was to fortify the churches and give them hope as they experienced persecution.

PETER, SECOND LETTER FROM In his second epistle Peter wrote in response to false teachers who denied the second coming of the Lord Jesus Christ and advocated a libertine lifestyle. Peter maintained that God's grace is the foundation for a godly life and that living a life of godliness is necessary to obtain an eternal reward. Such a claim does not amount to works-righteousness, for such works do not merit salvation but are a result of God's transforming grace. Peter also vigorously defended the truth of Christ's second coming, which was anticipated in the transfiguration and promised in God's word. Those who reject Christ's coming deny God's sovereignty. They reject God's intervention in the world and remove any basis for ethical living. Peter urged his readers to grow in grace and knowledge until the day of salvation arrives.

The date of 2 Peter depends upon one's view of authorship. Probably Peter wrote the letter shortly before his death in the mid 60s. The letter was most likely written to the same readers who received 1 Peter (cp. 3:2), and hence it was probably sent to churches in Asia Minor.

PETHAHIAH Personal name meaning "Yahweh opens." **1.** Ancestor of a postexilic priestly family (1 Chron. 24:16). **2.** Royal advisor to the Persian king, either at his court or as his representative in Jerusalem (Neh. 11:24). **3.** Levite participating in Ezra's covenant renewal (Neh. 9:5). **4.** Levite with a foreign wife (Ezra 10:23), perhaps identical with 3.

PETHOR Place-name meaning "soothsayer." City in upper Mesopotamia identified with Tell Ahmar, 12 miles south of Carchemish near the confluence of the Sajur and Euphrates Rivers. Home of Balaam (Num. 22:5; Deut. 23:4).

PETHUEL Personal name meaning "vision of God" or "youth of God." Father of the Prophet Joel (1:1).

PETRA Capital city of the Nabatean Arabs located about 60 miles north of the Gulf of Aqaba. Petra is sometimes identified with Sela (Judg. 1:36; 2 Kings 14:7; Isa. 16:1; 42:11) because both names mean "rock." Lack of archaeological evidence of Edomite settlement in the basin suggests that Sela is better identified with Um el Bayyarah on the mountain plateau overlooking Petra. The Nabatean king Aretas IV (2 Cor. 11:32-33) reigned from Petra.

PEULLETHAI or **PEULTHAI** (KJV) Personal name meaning "recompense." A Levitical gatekeeper (1 Chron. 26:5).

PHANUEL Alternate form of the personal name Penuel meaning "face of God." Father of the Prophetess Anna (Luke 2:36).

PHARAOH Title meaning "great house" for the ancient kings of Egypt. Egyptians applied "pharaoh" to the royal palace and grounds in the fourth dynasty (about 2500 BC). The title Pharaoh came to be applied to the king from about 1500 BC until the Persian domination, about 550 BC.

References to 10 pharaohs can be clearly distinguished in the OT: the pharaoh of Abraham, Gen.

A view from the front of the Treasury building of the narrow entryway into the Nabatean city of Petra.

12:10-20; of Joseph, Gen. 39–50; of the Oppression, Exod. 1; of the exodus, Exod. 2:23–15:19; of 1 Chron. 4:18; of Solomon, 1 Kings 3–11; of Rehoboam, called Shishak, king of Egypt, 1 Kings 14:25; of Hezekiah and Isaiah, 2 Kings 18:21; Isa. 36; of Josiah, 2 Kings 23:29; of Jer. 44:30 and Ezek. 29:1-16.

PHARISEES Largest and most influential religious-political party during NT times. See *Jewish Parties in the New Testament.*

PHARPAR River associated with Damascus (2 Kings 5:12). The river is perhaps the Nahr el 'A'waj, which flows from Mount Hermon, passing about 10 miles

The funerary mask of King Tut (Pharaoh Tutankhamun) of Egypt.

south of Damascus, or else the Nahr Taura.

PHICHOL (KJV) or **PHICOL** Personal name meaning "mighty." The chief captain of the Philistine army under King Abimelech (Gen. 21:22). He witnessed covenants between his commander and Abraham (21:32) and Isaac (26:26-28).

Temple ruins at the site of the ancient city of Philadelphia in Asia Minor (modern Turkey).

PHILADELPHIA Place-name meaning "love of brother." A Hellenistic city in the province of Lydia in western Asia Minor. See *Asia Minor, Cities of; Revelation, Book of.*

PHILEMON, LETTER TO Personal name meaning "affectionate" and 18th book of the NT. Philemon owed his conversion to the Christian faith to the Apostle Paul (v. 19). This conversion took place during Paul's extended ministry in Ephesus (Acts 19:10). There is no evidence that Paul ever visited Colossae where Philemon lived. Paul and Philemon became devoted friends. Paul referred to Philemon as a "dear friend and co-worker" (v. 1 HCSB).

Paul's only letter of a private and personal nature included in the NT was written to Philemon in AD 61. This letter concerned a runaway slave. The slave Onesimus had robbed Philemon and escaped to Rome. There Onesimus found the Apostle Paul, who was imprisoned. Paul wrote to Philemon concerning Onesimus. Paul sent both the letter and Onesimus back to Colossae. The letter states that Onesimus was now a Christian. Paul requested that Philemon forgive and receive Onesimus not as a slave but as a brother (v. 16). This request was not made from Paul's apostolic authority but tenderly as a Christian friend. Paul wrote, "Accept him as you would me" (v. 17 HCSB).

PHILETUS Personal name meaning "beloved." Heretical teacher who asserted that the (general) resurrection had already occurred (2 Tim. 2:17-18), perhaps in a purely spiritual sense.

PHILIP Personal name meaning "fond of horses." **1.** A respected member of the church at Jerusalem who was chosen as one of the seven first deacons (Acts 6:5). Following Stephen's martyrdom, Philip took the gospel to Samaria, where his ministry was blessed (Acts 8:5-13). Subsequently, he was led south to the Jerusalem-Gaza road where he introduced the Ethiopian eunuch to Christ and baptized him (Acts 8:26-38). He was then transported by the Spirit to Azotus (Ashdod) and from there conducted an itinerant ministry until he took up residence in Caesarea (Acts 8:39-40). Then, for nearly 20 years, we lose sight of him. He is last seen in Scripture when Paul lodged in his home on his last journey to Jerusalem (Acts 21:8). He had four

Philip's Martyrium at Hierapolis, built to commemorate the tradition that Philip the apostle was martyred here.

unmarried daughters who were prophetesses (Acts 21:9). See *Deacon.* **2.** One of 12 apostles (Matt. 10:3). From Bethsaida he called Nathanael to "come and see" Jesus (John 1:43-51). Jesus tested Philip concerning how to feed the multitude (John 6:5-7). He and Andrew took inquiring Gentiles to Jesus (John 12:21-22). Philip asked Jesus to show them the Father (John 14:8-9), opening the way for Jesus' teaching that to see Him is to see the Father. See *Disciple.* **3.** Tetrarch of Ituraea and Trachonitis (Luke 3:1).

PHILIPPI City in the Roman province of Macedonia. Paul did missionary work in Philippi (Acts 16:12) and later wrote a letter to the church there (Phil. 1:1).

Paul and Philippi Paul first visited Philippi on his second missionary journey in response to his Macedonian vision (Acts 16:9). They and his companions sailed from Troas across the Aegean Sea to Neapolis, on the eastern shore of Macedonia (Acts 16:11). Then they journeyed a few miles inland to "Philippi, a Roman colony, which is a leading city of that district of Macedonia" (Acts 16:12 HCSB).

On the Sabbath Paul went to a prayer meeting on the riverbank. When Paul spoke, Lydia and others opened their hearts to the Lord (Acts 16:13-15).

The Roman character of the city is apparent from Paul's other experiences in Philippi. He healed

Overlooking ruins of Philippi from atop the theater.

a possessed slave girl whose owners charged that Jews troubled the city by teaching customs unlawful for Romans to observe (Acts 16:20-21). The city magistrates ordered Paul and Silas to be beaten and turned over to the jailer (Acts 16:20,22-23). After Paul's miraculous deliverance and the jailer's conversion, the magistrates sent the jailer word to release Paul (Acts 16:35-36). Paul informed the messengers that he was a Roman citizen. Since he had been beaten and imprisoned unlawfully, Paul insisted that the magistrates themselves come and release him (Acts 16:37). The very nervous magistrates went to the jail. They pled with Paul not only to leave the jail but also to leave town (Acts 16:38-40).

PHILIPPIANS, LETTER TO THE Eleventh book of the NT, written by Paul to the church at Philippi, the first church he established in Europe. It is one of the Prison Epistles (along with Ephesians, Colossians, and Philemon). The traditional date and place of writing is AD 61/62 from Rome.

Content of the Letter Philippians is structured much like a typical personal letter of that day. The introduction identifies the sender(s): Paul and Timothy, and the recipients: the saints, overseers, and deacons.

This typical letter form, however, is filled with Christian content. Paul expresses thanksgiving for the Philippian church's faithful participation in the work of the gospel (1:3-8), and a prayer that they may be blessed with an ever growing, enlightened, Christian love (1:9-11). The body of the letter begins with Paul explaining his current situation (1:12-26).

When Paul returned to Philippi, he hoped to find a church united in Christ. Philippians 1:27–4:9 is a multifaceted call for unity in the church. Those who follow Christ must follow him in selfless service to others (2:5-11).

Philippians 2:6-11 is known as the *kenosis* passage (from the Greek word translated "emptied" in 2:7 RSV). The language and structure of the passage have convinced most commentators that Paul was quoting a hymn that was already in use in the church. The purpose of the pre-Pauline hymn was probably to teach the believer about the nature and work of Christ. Preexistence, incarnation, passion, resurrection, and exaltation are all summarized in a masterful fashion.

General exhortations to rejoice and to remain faithful (4:4-9) led to Paul's expression of gratitude for the Philippians' faithful support of him and of the ministry (4:10-20). The letter closes in typical Pauline fashion, with an exchange of greetings and a prayer for grace.

PHILISTIA Coastal plain of southwestern Palestine that was under the control of the Philistines (Exod. 15:14; Pss. 60:8; 87:4; 108:9; Isa. 14:29-31). KJV sometimes referred to Philistia as Palestina (Exod. 15:14; Isa. 14:29-31). See *Gaza; Pentapolis.*

PHILISTIM (KJV, Gen. 10:14) or **PHILISTINES** One of the rival groups the Israelites encountered as they settled the land of Canaan. According to biblical references, the homeland of the Philistines was Caphtor (Amos 9:7; Jer. 47:4). See *Caphtor.*

Philistines are first mentioned in the patriarchal stories (Gen. 21:32,34). The most dramatic phase of Philistine history begins in the period of the Judges when the Philistines were the principal enemy of and the major political threat to Israel. This threat is first seen in the stories of Samson (Judg. 13–16). During the time of Samuel the Israelites defeated the Philistines at times (1 Sam. 7:5-11; 14:16-23), but, generally speaking, their advance against the Israelites continued. Saul not only failed to check their intrusion into Israelite territory but in the end lost his life fighting the Philistines at Mount Gilboa (1 Sam. 31:1-13). David finally checked the Philistine advance at Baal-perazim (2 Sam. 5:17-25).

PHILO JUDAEUS Early Jewish interpreter of Scripture known for use of allegory. Also known as Philo of Alexandria, he lived about the same time as Jesus (about 20 BC to AD 50).

PHILOLOGUS Personal name meaning "lover of words," either in the sense of "talkative" or of "lover of learning." Member, perhaps the head, of a Roman house church whom Paul greeted (Rom. 16:15). Philologus was perhaps the husband of Julia and father of Nereus and Olympas.

PHINEHAS Personal name meaning "dark-skinned" or "mouth of brass." **1.** Grandson of Aaron and high priest who, on several occasions, aided Moses and Joshua. **2.** One of Eli the priest's worthless sons. He engaged in religious prostitution (1 Sam. 2:22) and led the people to follow.

PHLEGON Personal name meaning "burning," perhaps in the sense of "zealous." Member of a Roman house church whom Paul greeted (Rom. 16:14).

PHOEBE Personal name meaning "bright." "Servant," "minister" (REB), "deaconess" (NASB, NIV note), or "deacon" (NRSV) of church at Cenchrea whom Paul recommended to church at Rome (Rom. 16:1-2).

PHOENICIA Place-name meaning "purple" or "crimson," translation of Hebrew *Canaan*, "land of purple." The narrow land between the Mediterranean Sea and the Lebanon Mountains between Tyre in the south and Arvad in the north. New Testament Phoenicia reached south to Dor. Great forestland enabled the people to build ships and become the dominant seafaring nation. The forests also provided timber for export, Phoenician cedars being the featured material of Solomon's temple (1 Kings 5:8-10).The Phoenician princess Jezebel imported devotion to Baal to Israel.

Harbor at Tyre showing ancient Phoenician harbor (facing northwest).

Growth of Assyrian power about 750 BC led to Phoenicia's decline. The Persian Empire gave virtual independence to Phoenicia, using the Phoenician fleet against Egypt and Greece. Alexander the Great put an end to Phoenician political power, but the great cities retained economic power.

New Testament Jesus' ministry reached Tyre and Sidon (Matt. 15:21). Persecution, beginning with Stephen's death, led the church to spread into Phoenicia (Acts 11:19; cp. 15:3; 21:2-3).

PHOENIX Place-name, perhaps meaning "date palm." Port on the southeast coast of Crete that Paul and the ship's crew hoped to reach for winter harbor (Acts 27:12).

PHRYGIA Place-name meaning "parched." During Roman times Phrygia was a subregion of Galatia, and her people often were slaves or servants. Some of the Phrygians were present in Jerusalem on the Day of Pentecost and heard the gospel in their native language (Acts 2:10; cp. 16:6; 18:23).

PHYGELUS Personal name meaning "fugitive." Christian who deserted Paul (2 Tim. 1:15). The contrast with Onesiphorus, who was not ashamed of the imprisoned Paul (1:16-17), suggests that Phygelus abandoned Paul in prison.

PI-BESETH Egyptian city, name meaning "house of Bastet," located on the shore of the old Tanite branch of the Nile about 45 miles northeast of Cairo. Ezekiel mentions this city in his oracle against Egypt (Ezek. 30:17).

PICTURE KJV term in three passages where modern translations use a term better suited to the context. **1.** Carved stone figures (Num. 33:52). **2.** Settings (NASB, NIV, NRSV) or filigree (REB) (Prov. 25:11). **3.** Sailing craft or vessel (Isa. 2:16).

PIECE OF MONEY 1. Translation of the Hebrew *qesitah*, a coin of uncertain weight and value (Gen. 33:19; Job 42:11 KJV, NASB, NRSV). NIV reads "pieces of silver." **2.** KJV translation of the Greek term *stater* (Matt. 17:27). Modern translations read: stater (NASB); four drachma coin (NIV); shekel (RSV); coin (NRSV, REB).

PIETY Translation of a Hebrew expression and several Greek terms. **1.** NIV used "piety" to translate the Hebrew idiom "the fear [or reverence] of the Lord" (Job 4:6; 15:4; 22:4; cp. REB). **2.** NRSV used piety to translate the Greek term meaning "righteousness" (Matt. 6:1), where the concern was with an external show of religion (Matt. 6:2-6). **3.** Piety translates two Greek terms for fear or reverence for God (Acts 3:12 NASB, NRSV; Heb. 5:7 NASB). **4.** Piety represents the religious duty of caring for the physical needs of elderly family members (1 Tim. 5:4 KJV, NASB).

PIGEON "Pigeon" is a general term referring to any of a widely distributed subfamily of fowl (*Columbinae*). The term "pigeon" basically is employed when referring to the use of these birds for sacrificial offerings.

PIHAHIROTH Hebrew place-name derived from the Egyptian, "house of Hathor," and interpreted in Hebrew as "mouth of canals." The Israelites encamped at Pihahiroth in the early days of the exodus (Exod. 14:2,9; Num. 33:7).

The only known extrabiblical mention of Pilate's name is shown here in a Latin dedicatory inscription on a stone slab found at Caesarea Maritima.

PILATE, PONTIUS Roman governor of Judea remembered in history as a notorious anti-Semite and in Christian creeds as the magistrate under whom Jesus Christ "suffered" (1 Tim 6:13). The NT refers to him as "governor," while other sources call him "procurator" or "prefect" (an inscription found in Caesarea in 1961).

PILDASH Personal and clan name, perhaps meaning "powerful." Sixth son of Nahor (Gen. 22:22), probably the ancestor of an otherwise unknown north Arabian tribe.

PILFER To steal secretly, usually little by little (John 12:6 NASB, REB; Titus 2:10 NASB, REB, NRSV).

PILHA Personal name meaning "millstone." Lay leader witnessing Ezra's covenant renewal (Neh. 10:24).

PILLAR Stone monuments (Hb. *matstsevah*) or standing architectural structures (Hb. *amudim*). **1.** Stones set up as memorials to persons. Jacob set up a pillar on Rachel's grave as a memorial to her (Gen. 35:20). Because Absalom had no son to carry on his name, he set up a pillar and carved his name in it (2 Sam. 18:18). **2.** Shrines both to the Lord and to false gods. Graven images often were pillars set up as gods. **3.** As structural supports pillars were used extensively. The tabernacle used pillars for the veil (Exod. 26:31-32), the courts (27:9-15), and the gate (27:16). The temple in Jerusalem used pillars for its support (1 Kings 7:2-3), and the porch had pillars (7:6). Figuratively, pillars were believed to hold up heaven (Job 26:11) and earth (1 Sam. 2:8). **4.** God led Israel through the wilderness with a pillar of cloud by day and a pillar of fire by night (Exod. 13:21; cp. 14:19-20). These pillars were symbols of God's presence with Israel as much as signs of where they were to go. **5.** Solomon's temple had two freestanding brass pillars (1 Kings 7:15).

PILTAI Short form of personal name meaning "(Yah is) my deliverance." Head of a family of postexilic priests (Neh. 12:17).

PINNACLE Highest point of a structure. NRSV referred to the pinnacles of the temple or the city of Jerusalem (Isa. 54:12). The pinnacle (literally, "little wing") of the temple (Matt. 4:5; Luke 4:9) is not mentioned in the OT, intertestamental literature, or rabbinic sources.

PINON Edomite clan chief (Gen. 36:41; 1 Chron. 1:52), whose descendants perhaps settled Punon (Num. 33:42-43).

PIRAM Personal name, perhaps meaning "wild ass." King of Jarmuth southwest of Jerusalem and member of a coalition of five Amorite kings who battled Joshua unsuccessfully (Josh. 10:3,23).

The traditional "pinnacle of the temple."

PIRATHON, PIRATHONITE Place-name meaning "princely" or "height, summit" and it inhabitants. The town in the hill country of Ephraim was the home of the judge Abdon (Judg 12:13,15) and of Benaiah, one of David's elite warriors (2 Sam. 23:30 1 Chron. 11:31). The site is identified with Far'ata about five miles southwest of Shechem.

PISGAH Place-name, perhaps meaning "the divided one." Mountain in the Abarim range across the Jordan River from Jericho. Some Bible scholars believe it was part of Mount Nebo. God allowed Moses to view the promised land from the heights of Pisgah (Deut. 34:1) but would not let him cross into Canaan.

PISHON Name meaning "free-flowing," designating one of the rivers of Eden (Gen. 2:11). The identity of the river is unknown. Some suggest the "river" was a canal connecting the Tigris and Euphrates or another body of water, such as the Persian Gulf.

The snow-capped mountains of the ancient Roman province of Pisidia in Asia Minor (modern Turkey).

PISIDIA Small area in the province of Galatia in southern Asia Minor bounded by Pamphylia, Phrygia, and Lyconia. Only in 25 BC did the Romans gain control over the region through economic diplomacy. Antioch was made the capital, although some historians contend that the city was not actually in Pisidia. Paul and Barnabas came through Antioch (Acts 13:14) after John Mark left them in Perga (v. 13).

PISPA, PISPAH Personal name of unknown meaning. Member of the tribe of Asher (1 Chron. 7:38).

PITHOM AND RAMESES Egyptian cities located in northern Egypt (Nile Delta) in or near the Wadi Tumilat. They were built by the Israelites while in Egypt (Exod. 1:11) as supply hubs for royal, military, and religious purposes and were located near palaces, fortresses, and temples.

PITHON Personal name of unknown meaning. Descendant of Saul (1 Chron. 8:35; 9:41).

PITY Sympathetic sorrow toward one facing suffering or distress. Pity moved Jesus to heal (Matt. 20:34). Jesus used a compassionate Samaritan as an unexpected example of active pity (Luke 10:33). Such active concern for those in need serves as evidence that one is a child of God (1 John 3:17).

PLAGUES Disease interpreted as divine judgment, translation of several Hebrew words. The 10 plagues in the book of Exodus were the mighty works of God that gained Israel's release and demonstrated God's sovereignty and were called "plagues" (Exod. 9:14; 11:1), "signs" (Exod. 7:13), and "wonders" (Exod. 7:3; 11:9). They showed the God of Moses was sovereign over the gods of Egypt, including Pharaoh, who was considered a god by the Egyptians.

PLAISTER KJV variant form of plaster (Isa. 38:21). Here plaster refers to a fig poultice (cp. NIV, REB, NASB, NRSV).

PLAIT KJV term meaning "to braid" (1 Pet. 3:3). See *Hair*.

PLANKS Long, flat pieces of timber, thicker than boards, used in shipbuilding (Ezek. 27:5; Acts 27:44) and for the flooring of Solomon's temple (1 Kings 6:15 KJV). The "thick planks upon the face of the porch" in Ezekiel's vision of the renewed temple (Ezek. 41:25 KJV) likely refers to some type of canopy (NRSV; overhang, NIV; covering, TEV; cornice, REB) or to a threshold (NASB).

PLANTATION KJV term (Ezek. 17:7) to designate a bed (NASB, REB, NRSV) or plot (NIV) where plants are planted.

PLASTER Pastelike mixture, usually of water, lime, and sand, that hardens on drying and is used for coating walls and ceilings. Mosaic law included regulations for treating homes in which mold or rot appeared in the plaster (Lev. 14:41-48). Writing was easy on a surface of wet plaster (Deut. 27:2-4).

PLATE 1. Shallow vessel from which food is eaten or served. 2. Sheet of metal (Exod. 28:36; Num. 16:38).

PLATTER Large plate. The platter bearing the head of John the Baptist was likely of gold or silver (Matt. 14:8,11 and parallels). Ceramic platters were in common use (Luke 11:39 NASB).

PLEDGE Something given as down payment on a debt. The OT regulated this practice. An outer garment given in pledge was to be returned before night since it was the only protection the poor had from the cold (Exod. 22:26; Deut. 24:12-13).

PLEIADES Brilliant grouping of six or seven visible stars located in the shoulder of the constellation Taurus (Job 9:9; 38:31; Amos 5:8).

PLUMB LINE Cord with a weight (usually metal or stone) attached to one end. The plumb line would be dangled beside a wall during its construction to assure vertical accuracy. Prophets spoke of the measurement God would use on the nation (Isa. 28:17; Amos 7:7-8). Israel had been built straight, but, because it was out of line, it would be destroyed.

POCHERETH-HAZZEBAIM Personal name signifying an official office, "binder (or hunter) of Gazelles." Head of a family of Solomon's servants included in those returning from exile (Ezra 2:57; Neh. 7:59). KJV takes "Zebaim" as a place-name.

PODS Dry coverings split in the shelling of beans and similar plants. The pods of Luke 15:16 (NASB, NIV, REB, NRSV; husks, KJV; bean pods, TEV) were likely the pods of the carob tree that served as a common feed for livestock. These sweet-tasting pods may reach one foot in length.

POETRY "Poetry" calls to mind a Western pattern of balanced lines, regular stress, and rhyme. Hebrew manuscripts do not distinguish poetry from prose in such a clear-cut way. Hebrew poetry has three primary characteristics—parallelism, meter, and the grouping of lines into larger units called stanzas. Each of the three elements mentioned may be found to a lesser extent in prose. One third of the OT is cast in poetry.

POLL 1. KJV term for "to cut off" or "to trim" hair (2 Sam. 14:26; Ezek. 44:20; Mic. 1:16). Priests were permitted to "poll" their hair but not to shave their heads. Polling one's hair could be understood as a sign of mourning. **2.** KJV term for "the head," especially that part on which hair grows. To count every male "by their polls" (Num. 1:2; cp. 1 Chron. 23:3,24) is to count "heads."

POLLUX One of the twin brothers in the constellation Gemini (Acts 28:11).

POMEGRANATE Small tree, the fruit of which has a thick shell, many seeds, and a red pulp.

POMMELS KJV term for the bowl-shaped capitals topping the temple pillars (2 Chron. 4:12-13).

POND At Exod. 7:19; 8:5, "pond" renders the Hebrew '*agam* meaning "marsh" or "muddy pool." The term is usually translated "pool."

PONTUS Province just south of the Black Sea in Asia Minor. Christianity spread to Pontus early. First Peter was addressed to the elect there (1:1-2). Citizens of Pontus were in Jerusalem on the Day of Pentecost (Acts 2:9).

POOL Collection of water, natural or artificial. Small pools were commonly seen as a place to collect rainwater from the roof that was used for irrigation or drinking. These reservoirs were important sources of water supply in the arid climate of the Middle East.

The pomegranate is one of the many fruits found in the Middle East.

POOR IN SPIRIT Not those who are spiritually poor, that is, lacking in faith or love, but those who have a humble spirit and thus depend on God (Matt. 5:3). Luke's parallel speaks simply of the poor (Luke 6:20). That God has "chosen those who are poor in the eyes of the world to be rich in faith and to possess the kingdom" was regarded as a well-established fact (James 2:5 REB).

POOR, ORPHAN, WIDOW Three groups of people of the lower social classes in need of legal protection from the rich and powerful who sometimes abused them (Job 24:3-4). God's promise of care for the poor, the orphans, and the widows was a tremendous source of hope during times of severe difficulty.

PORATHA Persian personal name meaning "bounteous." One of Haman's 10 sons (Esther 9:8).

PORCUPINE Large rodent, sometimes called a hedgehog, that has stiff, sharp bristles mixed with its hair. Disagreement exists about the translation of the Hebrew word. Some feel "porcupine" is the correct translation (Isa. 14:23; 34:11 NKJV, NLT). NASB uses "hedgehog" in Isaiah and Zeph. 2:14. Others have various translations (NIV, owl; KJV, bittern; NEB, bustard).

PORPHYRY Rock composed of feldspar crystals embedded in a dark red or purple groundmass (Esther 1:6; KJV, "red marble").

PORPOISE Any of several species of small-toothed whales. NASB uses porpoise skins for a covering over the tabernacle (Exod. 25:5; Num. 4:6; KJV, NKJV, badger; NIV, sea cow) and "sandals of porpoise skin" in Ezek. 16:10. See *Sea Cow*.

PORTER KJV term for a gatekeeper or doorkeeper. Such persons served at city gates (2 Sam. 18:26; 2 Kings 7:10), temple gates (1 Chron. 9:22,24,26), the doors of private homes (Mark 13:34), and even the gate of a sheepfold (John 10:3).

PORTION Allotment, allowance, ration, share. Portion is frequently used in the literal sense of a share in food, clothing, or property as well as in a variety of figurative senses. Wisdom writings often designate one's lot in life as one's portion (Job 20:29; 27:13; Eccles. 9:9).

POTENTATE KJV term in 1 Tim. 6:15 meaning "ruler" (NIV) or "sovereign" (NASB, NRSV, REB), used as a title for God.

POTIPHAR Personal name meaning "belonging to the sun." Egyptian captain of the guard who purchased Joseph from the Midianite traders (Gen. 37:36; 39:1).

POTIPHERA or **POTIPHERAH** Priest in the Egyptian city of On (Heliopolis) where the sun god, Re, was worshipped. Joseph married his daughter, Asenath, at the pharaoh's command (Gen. 41:45). Potipherah and Potiphar are the same in Egyptian, leading some to believe that one name was slightly changed in Hebrew to distinguish between the captain of the guard and the priest.

POTSHERD Fragment of a baked, clay vessel, "potsherd" (more commonly called a "sherd" by archaeologists) is used in the OT with both a literal and symbolic or figurative meaning. Job used a potsherd (2:8) to scrape the sores that covered his body; the underparts of the mythological monster Leviathan are said to be "jagged potsherds" (41:30 NIV).

POTTAGE Thick soup usually made from lentils and vegetables and spiced with various herbs. Jacob served pottage and bread to the famished Esau in return for the birthright (Gen. 25:29-34). Elisha added meal to a tainted recipe of pottage at Gilgal (2 Kings 4:38-41).

POTTER'S FIELD Tract of land in the Hinnom Valley outside Jerusalem used as a cemetery for pilgrims to the Holy City since the interbiblical era. The field was bought with the money paid for

Pile of pottery sherds at Banias.

betraying Jesus (Acts 1:18). Matthew 27:3-10 records that the priests bought the field with the money Judas returned. Their reasoning was that the money had been used to bring about bloodshed and could not be returned to the temple treasury.

A modern Middle Eastern potter fashioning pottery in the same manner used in biblical times.

POTTERY Everyday household utensils whose remains form the basis for modern dating of ancient archaeological remains. The few statements about the preparation of the clay, "the potter treads clay" (Isa. 41:25), and the potter's failure and success on the wheel (Jer. 18:3-4) hardly hint at the importance and abundance in antiquity of "earthen vessels" (Lev. 6:21; Num. 5:17; Jer. 32:14), the common collective term for pottery in the Bible. However, the work of the potter in shaping the worthless clay provided the imagery the biblical writers and prophets used in describing God's creative relationship to human beings (Job 10:8-9; Isa. 45:9).

POUND See *Weights and Measures*.

POWDERS, FRAGRANT Pulverized spices used as a fragrance (Song 3:6).

The front of the praetorium at the palace of the Roman emperor Hadrian.

PRAETORIAN GUARD Roman military branch assigned to personal security for the imperial family and to represent and protect the emperor's interests in the imperial provinces. The term is used in Phil. 1:13 with regard to a unit of the Praetorian guard. Greetings from "those from Caesar's household" (Phil. 4:22 HCSB) do not prove Paul was in Rome when he wrote Philippians. The term "Caesar's household" was applied often to the Praetorian guard, and units were dispersed throughout the Roman Empire. *Praetorion* is used in Mark 15:16 in reference to the headquarters where Jesus was taken and subsequently mocked by Roman soldiers prior to His crucifixion. The NT locates the praetorium in Jerusalem as the palace of the Roman governor, the Tower of Antonia, located adjacent to the temple on the northwestern corner (Matt. 27:27; Mark 15:16; John 18:28,33; 19:9) of Temple Mount.

PRAISE One of humanity's many responses to God's revelation of Himself. The Bible recognizes that men and women may also be the objects of praise, either from other people (Prov. 27:21; 31:30) or from God Himself (Rom. 2:29), and that angels and the natural world are likewise capable of praising God (Ps. 148). Nevertheless, human praise of God is one of Scripture's major themes.

PRAYER Dialogue between God and people, especially His covenant partners.
Old Testament Israel is a nation born of prayer. Abraham heard God's call (Gen. 12:1-3), and God heard the cries of the Hebrew children (Exod. 3:7). Moses conversed with God (Exod. 3:1–4:17) and interceded for Israel (Exod. 32:11-13; Num. 11:11-15). God worked miracles through the prayers of Elijah and Elisha (1 Kings 17:19-22; 18:20-40).

The book of Psalms teaches that variety and honesty in prayer are permissible; the psalms proclaim praise, ask pardon, seek such things as communion (63), protection (57), vindication (107), and healing (6). Psalm 86 provides an excellent pattern for prayer. Daily patterned prayer becomes very important to exiles denied access to the temple (Dan. 6:10).
New Testament Jesus' example and teaching inspire prayer. Mark emphasized that Jesus prayed in crucial moments, including the disciples' appointment (3:13), their mission (6:30-32), and the transfiguration (9:2). The Lord's Prayer (Matt. 6:9-13; Luke 11:2-4) is taught to disciples who realize the kingdom is present but still to come in all its fullness. Significantly the disciples asked Jesus to teach them to pray after watching Him pray (Luke 11:1). The prayer also provides a contrast to hypocritical prayers (Matt. 6:5). Although it is permissible to repeat this prayer, it may be well to remember Jesus was emphasizing how to pray, not what to pray.

Jesus' teaching on persistence in prayer is linked to the inbreaking kingdom (Luke 11:5-28; 18:1-8). God is not like the reluctant neighbor, even though Christians may have to wait for answers (Luke 11:13; 18:6-8). The ironies of prayer are evident: God knows our needs, yet we must ask; God is ready to answer, yet we must patiently persist. Children of the kingdom will have their requests heard (Matt. 6:8; 7:7-11; 21:22; John 14:13; 15:7,16; 16:23; cp. 1 John 3:22; 5:14; James 1:5), particularly believers gathered in Jesus' name (Matt. 18:19).

Dialogue is what is essential to prayer. Prayer makes a difference in what happens (James 4:2). Our understanding of prayer will correspond to our understanding of God. When God is seen as desiring to bless (James 1:5) and sovereignly free to respond to persons (Jon. 3:9), then prayer will be seen as dialogue with God. God will respond when we faithfully pursue this dialogue. Prayer will lead to a greater communion with God and a greater understanding of His will.

PREEXILIC Period in Israel's history before the exile in Babylon (586–538 BC).

PREMARITAL SEX Engaging in sexual intercourse prior to marriage. The Song of Songs is an extended poem extolling the virtue of sexual fidelity between a king and his chosen bride. Sexual desire runs strong throughout the song as the king and his beloved anticipate their union together. At intervals the poet repeats a refrain counseling sexual restraint: "Young women of Jerusalem, charge you, by the gazelles and the wild does of the field: do not stir up or awaken love until the appropriate time" (Song 2:7 HCSB; 3:5; 8:4).

PREPARATION DAY Sixth day of week in which Jews prepared life's necessities to avoid work on the Sabbath (cp. Exod. 20:8-11; Matt. 12:1-14; John 9:14-16). John explicitly identified the day of preparation as the day of Jesus' execution (John 19:14,31,42) and placed the Last Supper before

Passover (John 13:1). The Synoptic Gospels, however, dated the Last Supper on the day of Passover (Matt. 26:17; Mark 14:12; Luke 22:7). This apparent contradiction in dating may depend on whether the Gospel writers were referring to the preparation day for the Sabbath or to the preparation day for the Passover.

PRESBYTER See *Elder*.

PRIDE Undue confidence in and attention to one's own skills, accomplishments, state, possessions, or position. It is the opposite of humility, the proper attitude one should have in relation to God. Pride is rebellion against God because it attributes to oneself the honor and glory due to God alone.

PRIESTHOOD OF BELIEVERS Christian belief that every believer has direct access to God through Jesus Christ and that the church is a fellowship of priests serving together under the lordship of Christ. The concept of priesthood is integral to both the OT and the NT and is fulfilled in Christ as Mediator and great high priest.

PRIESTHOOD OF CHRIST That work of Christ in which He offers Himself as the supreme sacrifice for the sins of humankind and continually intercedes on their behalf.

PRIESTS Persons who represent God to human beings and human beings to God. Priests performed numerous roles, the most important of which was officiating at sacrifices and offerings at worship places, particularly the tabernacle and temple. Aaron and his descendants of the tribe of Levi served in the tabernacle and temple as priests. Members of the tribe of Levi not related to Aaron assisted the priests but did not offer sacrifices. Priests were supported by offerings and Levites were supported by tithes (Num. 18:20-24).

PRINCE More frequently designates the position and authority of a ruler, not just the limited sense of a male heir of a sovereign or noble birth (cp. Zeph. 1:8, which distinguishes princes and king's sons).

PRINCESS Two Hebrew constructions are translated "princess." **1.** "Daughter of a king." Solomon's 700 wives were princesses married to seal political ties with their fathers (1 Kings 11:3). Lamentations 1:1 pictures the reversal of Jerusalem's fortune in the image of a princess turned servant. **2.** Feminine form of the common word for leader or ruler applied to a king's wife (Ps. 45:13 NIV, NRSV) and to the leading women of Judah (Jer. 43:6 NRSV). See *Prince*.

PRINCIPALITIES Supernatural spiritual powers, whether good or evil. Principalities were created by and are thus subject to Christ (Col. 1:16). Neither principalities nor any other force can separate a believer from God's love found in Christ (Rom. 8:38).

PRISCA or **PRISCILLA** See *Aquila and Priscilla*.

PRISON GATE KJV designation for a gate in Jerusalem (Neh. 12:39). Modern translations refer to the Gate of the Guard or Guardhouse Gate. The gate is perhaps identical with the Miphkad (Muster) Gate (Neh. 3:31).

Interior of the Mamertinum Prison in Rome, believed to be the place where Paul was held prior to his execution.

PRISON, PRISONERS Any place where persons accused and/or convicted of criminal activity are confined and the persons so confined or captured in war.

PRIZE Award in an athletic competition. Paul used the image to illustrate the goal of the Christian life (Phil. 3:14; cp. 1 Cor. 9:24).

PROCHORUS Personal name meaning "leader of the chorus (or dance)." One of the 7 selected to assist in distribution of food to the Greek-speaking widows of the Jerusalem church (Acts 6:5).

PROCONSUL Office in the Roman system of government. Proconsuls oversaw the administration of civil and military matters in a province. They were responsible to the senate in Rome. The NT refers to two proconsuls: Sergius Paulus in Cyprus (Acts 13:7) and Gallio in Achaia (Acts 18:12; cp. Acts 19:38).

PROCURATOR Roman military office that developed into a powerful position by NT times. Three procurators are named in the NT: Pilate (Matt. 27:2; some question whether Pilate was a procurator), Felix (Acts 23:24), and Festus (Acts 24:27).

PROMISE God's announcement of His plan of salvation and blessing to His people, one of the unifying themes integrating the message and the deeds of the OT and NT. God's promise begins with a declaration by God; it covers God's future plan for not just one race but all the nations of the earth. It focuses on the gifts and deeds that God will bestow on a few to benefit the many.

PROPHECY, PROPHETS Reception and declaration of a word from the Lord through a direct prompting of the Holy Spirit and the human instrument thereof.

Old Testament Moses, perhaps Israel's greatest leader, was a prophetic prototype (Acts 3:21-24). He appeared with Elijah in the transfiguration (Matt. 17:1-8). Israel looked for a prophet like Moses (Deut. 34:10).

Elijah and Elisha offered critique and advice for the kings. The prophets did more than predict the future; their messages called Israel to honor God. Their prophecies were not general principles but specific words corresponding to Israel's historical context.

Similarly the classical or writing prophets were joined to history. Israel's political turmoil provided the context for the writing prophets. The Assyrian rise to power after 750 BC furnished the focus of the ministries of Amos, Hosea, Isaiah, and Micah. The Babylonian threat was the background and motive for much of the ministry of Jeremiah and Ezekiel. The advent of the Persian Empire in the latter part of the sixth century set the stage for prophets such as Obadiah, Haggai, Zechariah, and Malachi. Thus the prophets spoke for God throughout Israel's history.

New Testament The word *prophetes* means "to speak before" or "to speak for." Thus it refers to one who speaks for God or Christ. Prophets were also called "pneumatics"(*pneumatikos*), "spiritual ones" (1 Cor. 14:37). The prophets played a foundational role in the early church (1 Cor. 12:28-31; Eph. 4:11; 2:20). Due to the presumed prophetic silence in the time between the Testaments, the coming of Jesus is seen as an inbreaking of the Spirit's work especially visible in prophecy. Jesus called Himself a prophet (Luke 13:33). His miracles and discernment were rightly understood as prophetic (John 4:19). He taught not by citing expert rabbis but with His own prophetic authority (Mark 1:22; Luke 4:24).

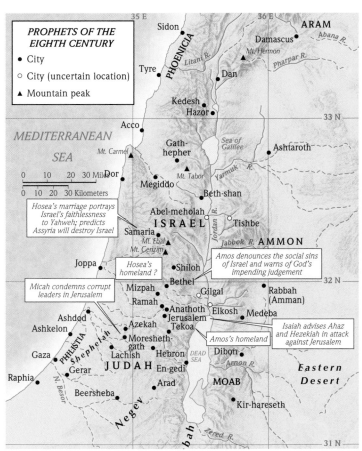

The early believers saw the outpouring of the Spirit (Acts 2:17) as a fulfillment of Joel's prediction that all God's people, young and old, male and female, would prophesy. New Testament prophecy was limited (1 Cor. 13:9); it was to be evaluated by the congregation (1 Cor. 14:29; 1 Thess. 5:20-21). One may even respond inappropriately to prophecy (Acts 21:12). The supreme test for prophecy is loyalty to Christ (1 Cor. 12:3; Rev. 19:10).

PROPHETESS 1. Female prophet; women serving as God's spokesperson. Five women are explicitly identified as prophetesses: Miriam (Exod. 15:20), Deborah (Judg. 4:4), Huldah (2 Kings 22:14), Noadiah, a "false" prophetess (Neh. 6:14), and Anna (Luke 2:36). **2.** The wife of a prophet (Isa. 8:3).

PROPITIATION See *Expiation, Propitiation.*

PROVENDER Grains and grasses used as animal feed (Isa. 30:24 KJV, RSV). Other translations use fodder or silage.

PROVERBS, BOOK OF The book of Proverbs contains the essence of Israel's wisdom. It provides a godly worldview and offers insight for living. Proverbs 1:7 provides the perspective for understanding all the proverbs: "The fear of the LORD is the beginning of knowledge; fools despise wisdom and instruction." "Fear of the LORD" is biblical shorthand for an entire life in love, worship, and obedience to God.
Date and Composition Though the title of Proverbs (1:1) seems to ascribe the entire book to Solomon, closer inspection reveals that the book is composed of parts and that it was formed over a period of several hundred years. It is difficult to know precisely the role Solomon and his court may have had in starting the process that culminated in the book of Proverbs. This process may be compared to the way psalms of Davidic authorship eventually led to the book of Psalms.
Themes and Worldview In spite of being a collection of collections, Proverbs displays a unified, richly complex worldview. Proverbs 1–9 introduces this worldview and lays out its main themes. The short sayings of Proverbs 10–31 are to be understood in light of the first nine chapters. The beginning and end of wisdom is to fear God and avoid evil (1:7; 8:13; 9:10; 15:33). The world is a battleground between wisdom and folly, righteousness and wickedness, good and evil.

God has placed in creation a wise order that speaks to mankind of good and evil, urging humans toward good and away from evil. This is not just the "voice of experience," but God's general revelation, found throughout the Bible, that speaks to all people with authority. The world is not silent but speaks of the Creator and His will (Pss. 19:1-2; 97:6; 145:10; 148; Job 12:7-9; Acts 14:15-17; Rom. 1:18-23; 2:14-15).

PROVIDENCE God's benevolent and wise superintendence of His creation. God attends not only to apparently momentous events and people but also to those that seem both mundane and trivial. Thus, while He holds the lives of both kings and nations in His hand (cp. Isa. 40:21-26; Jer. 18:1-6), God also concerns Himself with the welfare of the lowly and meek (cp. Pss. 104:10-30; 107:39-43). Indeed, so all-encompassing is God's attention to events within creation that nothing—not even the casting of lots—happens by chance (cp. Prov. 16:33).

With regard to God's role in the course of earthly events, one must avoid the error of deism on the one hand and that of fatalism on the other. Deism is the view that God created the universe as a sort of colossal machine, set it in motion according to various natural laws (which, perhaps, He Himself established), and now simply sits back and watches events unfold in accordance with those laws. Fatalism is the view that every event that happens had to happen. Since Scripture clearly indicates that humans do face real choices and are in general responsible for their actions (cp. Deut. 30:11-20), fatalism is false.

PROVINCE Roman political region.

PSALMIST Writer of psalms or hymns. Second Samuel 23:1 calls David the "sweet psalmist of Israel." Superscriptions ascribe about one half of the psalms to David.

PSALMS, BOOK OF The Hebrew title of the book means "praises." The English title (Psalms) comes from the Septuagint, the ancient Greek translation of the Hebrew Old Testament. The Greek word *psalmoi* means "songs," from which comes the idea, "songs of praise" or "praise songs."
The individual psalms of the book came from several authors. David, the sweet psalmist of Israel (2 Sam. 23:1), wrote approximately half of the 150 psalms in the book. David's psalms became the standard followed by others, thereby imprinting a Davidic character to the entire book. Other authors include Asaph (12), the sons of Korah (10), Solomon (two), Moses (one), Heman (one), and Ethan (one). Approximately 48 psalms are anonymous.
The book of Psalms contains individual psalms covering a thousand-year period from the time of

Moses (15th century BC) to the postexilic period (fifth century BC). Most of the psalms were written in the time of David and Solomon (1010–930). The final editor of the work was probably Ezra (450).

PSALTER 1. Alternate name for the book of Psalms. **2.** Any collection of psalms used in worship.

PSEUDEPIGRAPHA Intertestamental literature not accepted into the Christian or Jewish canon of Scripture and often attributed to an ancient hero of faith. Ongoing discovery and research provide differing lists of contents. A recent publication listed 52 writings. They give much information about the development of Jewish religion and culture.

PSEUDONYMITY Text is pseudonymous when it is not authored by the person whose name it bears. Such works are written after the purported author's death by another person or during his life by someone who is not commissioned to do so. Pseudonymous writings are not the same as anonymous texts. The former works make definite claims to authorship; the latter do not.

Many critical scholars believe that pseudonymity exists in the OT (e.g., Daniel) and the NT (e.g., the Pastoral Epistles). Some scholars argue that the early church was really only concerned about the content of works and not pseudonymity. However this theory does not explain the exclusion from the church's canon of several pseudonymous writings which were orthodox in their content (e.g., the Preaching of Peter, the Apocalypse of Peter, the Epistle of the Apostles, the Correspondence of Paul and Seneca, the extant Epistle to the Laodiceans, etc.).

Evidence is lacking to support pseudonymity in the Scriptures.

PTOLEMIES Dynastic powers that emerged in Egypt following the conquests of Alexander the Great.

PUAH 1. Personal name meaning "girl." Hebrew midwife who disobeyed Pharaoh's orders to kill male Hebrew infants (Exod. 1:15). **2.** Personal name meaning "red dye." Father of the judge Tola (Judg. 10:1) and an alternate form of Puvah (1 Chron. 7:1).

PUBLICAN Political office created by the Romans to help collect taxes in the provinces. Actually, the title "tax collector" is more correct than the older term "publican" in referring to the lowest rank in the structure.

PUBLIUS Personal name meaning "pertaining to the people." The highest official, either Roman or local, on Malta (Acts 28:7-8).

PUDENS Personal name meaning "modest." Roman Christian who greeted Timothy (2 Tim. 4:21). This Pudens is sometimes identified with the friend of the Roman poet Martial.

PUL 1. Alternate name of the Assyrian king Tiglath-Pileser III (2 Kings 15:19; 1 Chron. 5:26). The name is perhaps a contraction of Pileser. See *Assyria.* **2.** The Hebrew Pul in Isa. 66:19 is likely a textual corruption of Put.

PULPIT KJV, RSV term for a raised platform (NRSV, REB, NIV, TEV) on which a speaker stood (Neh. 8:4); not a lectern or high reading desk behind which a reader stands.

PULSE General term for peas, beans, and lentils (Dan. 1:12,16). Modern translations read "vegetables." The Hebrew is literally "things which have been sown," a designation including grains in addition to vegetables.

PUNITES Descendants of Puvah (Num. 26:23). Some manuscripts read "Puvanites" or "Puvites."

PUR or **PURIM** See *Festivals.*

PURAH Personal name meaning "beauty" or nickname meaning "metal container." Gideon's servant (Judg. 7:10-11). KJV used the form Phurah.

PURGE To cleanse from impurity, frequently in the figurative sense of cleansing from evil (Deut. 13:5), guilt (Deut. 19:13), idolatrous worship (2 Chron. 34:3), and sin (Ps. 51:7).

PURITY, PURIFICATION State of being or process of becoming free of inferior elements or ritual uncleanness. The primary Hebrew root word for pure (*tahar*) often refers to pure or flawless gold (1 Kings 10:21; Job 28:19; Ps. 12:6). *Tahar* and other Hebrew words for "pure" are used to describe other objects such as salt (Exod. 30:35), oil (Exod. 27:20), and incense (Exod. 37:29). Thus, a basic OT meaning is that of "refined, purified, without flaw, perfect, clean" (cp. Lam. 4:7).To be ritually pure means to be free of some flaw or uncleanness which would bar one from contact with holy objects or places, especially from contact with the holy presence of God in worship. God is the ideal of purity, and those who are to come in contact with God's presence are also to be pure. Hab. 1:13

indicates that God's eyes are too pure to look upon evil.

Most NT uses of words for purity relate to cleanness of some type. Old Testament meanings are often reflected. Perfection is the meaning in Mark 14:3; this is mixed with religious purity in Heb. 10:22; 1 John 3:3.

Ethical purity dominates in the NT. The person who is in right relationship with God is to live a life of purity (2 Tim. 2:21-22; Titus 1:15 and references to a pure heart—Matt. 5:8; 1 Tim. 1:5; Heb. 9:14; James 4:8; 1 Peter 1:22). Purity is also listed among virtues (2 Cor. 6:6; Phil. 4:8; 1 Tim. 4:12; cp. Mark 7:15).

Purification through sacrifice is also mentioned in the NT and applied to the death of Christ, a purification which does not need repeating and thus is on a higher level than OT sacrifices (Heb. 9:13-14). The sacrifice of Christ brings purification; Christ cleansed as a part of the work of the high priest and His blood cleanses from sin (1 John 1:7).

PURLOIN KJV term meaning "to misappropriate" (Titus 2:10). Modern translations use "pilfer" or "steal."

PURPLE GARNET REB designation of a precious stone (Exod. 28:18; 39:11) that other translations identify as an emerald or turquoise.

PURSLANE Fleshy-leafed, trailing plant used as a potherb or in salads, which the RSV of Job 6:6 used as an illustration of tasteless food.

PUT Personal name and a geographic designation, perhaps derived from the Egyptian *pdty* meaning "foreign bowman." **1.** Son of Ham (Gen. 10:6; 1 Chron. 1:8) in "Table of Nations" and thus ancestor of inhabitants of Put. **2.** Designation for a region of Africa bordering Egypt (Jer. 46:9; Ezek. 27:10; 30:5; 38:5; Nah. 3:9; and, by emendation, Isa. 66:19).

PUTHITES Family of Judahites (1 Chron. 2:53; KJV, Puhites).

PUTIEL Personal name meaning "he whom God gives" or "afflicted by God." Father-in-law of the priest Eleazar (Exod. 6:25).

PUVAH NASB (Num. 26:23) and NRSV (Gen. 46:13; Num. 26:23) form of the name of a son of Issachar. Other renderings include: Pua (KJV, REB); Puah (NIV, TEV); and Phuvah (KJV).

PYGARG KJV term for a white-rumped antelope (Deut. 14:5). Most modern translations identify the underlying Hebrew term with the ibex. The REB has "white-rumped deer."

PYRE Pile of material to be burned, especially that used in burning a body as part of funeral rites (Isa. 30:33 NASB, NRSV; pile, KJV; fire pit, NIV, REB). God's preparation of a funeral pyre for the Assyrian king highlights the certainty of God's judgment.

PYRRHUS Personal name meaning "fiery red." Father of Paul's companion Sopater (Acts 20:4).

PYTHON 1. Large constricting snake. **2.** A spirit of divination (*python*, Gk., Acts 16:16).

Q Abbreviation of the German *Quelle*, meaning "source," used to designate the hypothetical common source of over 200 verses found in Matthew and Luke but not in Mark.

QOHELETH See *Koheleth*.

QUAIL The Hebrew term translated "quail" in the OT is found only in connection with God's provision of food for Israel in the wilderness (Exod. 16:13; Num. 11:31-32; Ps. 105:40).

QUARTERMASTER Officer charged with receipt and distribution of rations and supplies (Jer. 51:59 NASB, NRSV, REB).

QUARTUS Latin personal name meaning "fourth." Christian, most likely from Corinth, who sent greetings to the Roman church through Paul (Rom. 16:23). Quartus and Tertius, whose name means "third" (Rom. 16:22), were possibly the fourth and third sons of the same family.

QUATERNION KJV term for a squad composed of four soldiers (Acts 12:4; cp. John 19:23). By translating the underlying Greek as simply "squad," NASB and RSV failed to convey the size of the guard.

QUEEN Wife or widow of a monarch and the female monarch reigning in her own right. Queen mother refers to the mother of a reigning monarch.

QUEEN OF HEAVEN Goddess that women in Judah worshipped to ensure fertility and material stability (Jer. 7:18; 44:17). Forms of worship included making cakes (possibly in her image as in molds found at Mari), offering drink offerings, and burning incense (Jer. 44:25).

Famous bust of Queen Nefertiti (from about 1356 BC), wife of Pharaoh Akhenaton of Egypt.

QUEEN OF SHEBA See *Sabean*.

QUICK, QUICKEN KJV terms meaning "living, alive" and "make alive, revive, refresh" (Pss. 55:15; 119:25; John 5:21; Acts 10:42).

QUICKSANDS KJV translation of the Greek *surtis* meaning "sandbar" (Acts 27:17). Modern translations take *surtis* as a proper name for the great sandbars off the west coast of Cyrene (modern Libya). NIV and REB paraphrase "sandbars of Syrtis," which conveys the sense.

QUILT NASB translation of a Hebrew term in 1 Sam. 19:13,16. Other possible translations include net (NRSV), pillow (KJV, RSV), and rug (REB).

QUIRINIUS Latin proper name which the KJV transliterated as Cyrenius. Modern versions prefer the Latin spelling. See *Cyrenius*.

QUIVER Leather case, hung over one's shoulder, for carrying arrows.

QUMRAN Archeological site near the caves where Dead Sea Scrolls were discovered and center of Jewish Essene community.

The limestone cliffs of the Qumran region showing the caves in which the Dead Sea Scrolls were discovered.

QUOTATIONS IN THE NEW TESTAMENT See *Old Testament Quotations in the New Testament.*

QUMRAN CAVES AND THE DEAD SEA SCROLLS

Docus) · OT Jericho (T. es-Sultan)

Chozba

NT Jericho (Tulul Abu el-Alayiq)

W. Nusariyat

Site of several caves where Dead Sea Scrolls were discovered

Jerusalem

Middin

Area enlarged above

Secacah · W. Qumran · Khirbet Qumran

Khirbet Mird (Hyrcania) · Ras Feshkha · Ain Feshkha

W. Kidron

Nibsharka · Khirbert Mazin

Ain Ghuweir

Jordan R.

Judean Wilderness

DEAD SEA

Callirrhoe

W. Zarqa Main

En-gedi

W. Arugot

Nahal Hever

Arnon R.

Nahal Ze'elim

Masada

LEGEND
· City

0   2   4   6   8   10 Mile
0 2 4 6 8 10 Kilometers

The traditional location of Rachel's tomb in Bethlehem.

RAAMA or **RAAMAH** Son of Cush (Gen. 10:7) and ancestor of Sheba and Dedan. Arab tribes occupying southwest and west-central Arabia (1 Chron. 1:9). Raamah and Sheba were trading partners of Tyre (Ezek. 27:22).

RAAMIAH Returning exile (Neh. 7:7). Variant form of Reelaiah (Ezra 2:2).

RAAMSES Alternate form of place-name "Rameses" (Exod. 1:11).

RAB-MAG Title of the Babylonian official Nergal-sharezer (Jer. 39:3,13). If associated with the root for "magi," the Rab-mag was likely the officer in charge of divination (cp. Ezek. 21:21).

RABBAH Place-name meaning "greatness." **1.** Village near Jerusalem (Josh. 15:60) assigned to tribe of Judah but apparently in territory of Benjamin. Its location is uncertain. **2.** Capital of Ammon that Moses apparently did not conquer (Deut. 3:11; Josh. 13:25), located about 23 miles east of the Jordan River.

RABBATH (KJV, Deut. 3:11; Ezek. 21:20) See *Rabbah*.

RABBI Title meaning "my master," applied to teachers and others of an exalted and revered position. During the NT period the term "rabbi" came to be more narrowly applied to one learned in the law of Moses, without signifying an official office.

RABBIT (*Oractolagus cuniculus*) Small, long-eared furry mammal related to the hare but differing in giving birth to naked young. NASB, NIV, and TEV use "rabbit" for an unclean animal in Lev. 11:6; Deut. 14:7 where other English translations use "hare."

RABBITH Unidentified site in territory of Issachar (Josh. 19:20). Rabbith is possibly a corruption of Daberath, a site included in other lists of Issachar's territory (Josh. 21:28; 1 Chron. 6:72) but missing in Josh. 19.

RABBONI An Aramaic honorary title, and variant spelling of "rabbi," meaning "teacher" that was used by blind Bartimaeus and Mary Magdalene to address Jesus (Mark 10:51; John 20:16). The term "Rabboni" possibly connotes heightened emphasis or greater honor than the almost synonymous expression "rabbi."

RABSARIS Assyrian court position with strong military and diplomatic powers. The OT records that the rabsaris was sent on two occasions to deal with the Israelite kings (2 Kings 18:17; Jer. 39:3).

RABSHAKEH Assyrian title, literally, "chief cupbearer." The position probably began as a mere butler but developed into a highly influential post by the time of its mention in the Bible. The official who dealt with Hezekiah spoke for the Assyrian king much as an ambassador would. He urged the people of Jerusalem to make peace with Assyria rather than believing King Hezekiah that God would protect Judah (2 Kings 18:17-32).

RACA Word of reproach, meaning "empty" or "ignorant," that the Hebrew writers borrowed from the Aramaic language. Jesus used it in Matt. 5:22 as a strong term of derision, second only to "fool." He placed it in the context of anger and strongly condemned one who would use it of another person.

RACAL Unidentified site in southern Judah (1 Sam. 30:29).

RACHEL Personal name meaning "ewe." Younger daughter of Laban, the second wife and cousin of Jacob, and the mother of Joseph and Benjamin. In flight from his brother Esau, Jacob met Rachel when she brought the sheep to water. She immediately became the object of his attention.

RADDAI Personal name meaning "Yahweh rules." Son of Jesse and brother of David (1 Chron. 2:14).

RAFT King Hiram's means of transporting timber for the temple by lashing logs together and floating them down the coast from Tyre to Joppa (1 Kings 5:9; 2 Chron. 2:16).

RAHAB Name meaning "arrogant, raging, turbulent, afflicter." **1.** Primeval sea monster representing the forces of chaos that God overcame in creation (Job 9:13; 26:12; Ps. 89:10; Isa. 51:9; cp.

Ps. 74:12-17). **2.** Symbolic name for Egypt (Ps. 87:4). Isaiah 30:7 includes a compound name Rahab-hem-shebeth. Translations vary: "Rahab who sits still" (NRSV); "Rahab who has been exterminated" (NASB); "Rahab the Do-Nothing" (NIV); "Rahab the Subdued" (REB). **3.** The plural appears in Ps. 40:4 for the proud, arrogant enemies. **4.** Personal name meaning "broad." Harlot in Jericho who hid two Hebrew spies that Joshua sent there to determine the strength of the city (Josh. 2:1). Matthew named Rahab as Boaz's mother (1:5) in his genealogy of Christ, making her one of the Lord's ancestors. Some interpreters think, however, that the Rahab in Matthew was a different woman. Hebrews 11:31 lists Rahab among the heroes of faith.

RAHAM Personal name meaning "mercy, love." Descendant of Judah (1 Chron. 2:44).

RAIL KJV term meaning "revile," "deride," "cast contempt upon," or "scold using harsh and abusive language" (1 Sam. 25:14; 2 Chron. 32:17; Mark 15:29; Luke 23:39).

RAIN Moisture from heaven providing nourishment for plant and animal life. Palestine was a land dependent upon the yearly rains to ensure an abundant harvest and an ample food supply for the coming year. Thus, the presence or absence of rain became a symbol of God's continued blessing or displeasure with the land and its inhabitants. See *Palestine.*

RAINBOW Caused by the reflection and refraction of sunlight by droplets of rain, a rainbow often appears after the passing of a thunderstorm, marking its end. The bow is colored by the division of sunlight into its primary colors. The rainbow served to remind Israel and her God of His covenant with Noah to never again destroy the earth by flooding (Gen. 9:8-17).

RAISIN CAKES Food prepared by pressing dried grapes together. David gave raisin cakes ("flagon," KJV) to those who accompanied the ark to Jerusalem (2 Sam. 6:19; 1 Chron. 16:3 NRSV). Hosea 3:1 (NRSV) links raisin cakes with the worship of pagan deities (cp. Jer. 7:18).

RAKEM Personal name meaning "variegated, multicolored." Grandson of Manasseh (1 Chron. 7:16).

RAKKATH Place-name meaning "spit," "narrow," or "swamp." Fortified town in the territory of Naphtali (Josh. 19:35).

RAKKON Place-name possibly meaning "swamp" or "narrow place." Village in the vicinity of Joppa allotted to Dan (Josh. 19:46).

RAM Personal name meaning "high, exalted." **1.** Ancestor of David (Ruth 4:19; 1 Chron. 2:9) and Jesus (Matt. 1:3-4). **2.** Jerahmeel's eldest son (1 Chron. 2:25,27), the nephew of 1. **3.** Head of the family to which Job's friend Elihu belonged (Job 32:2).

RAMA (KJV, Matt. 2:18) or **RAMAH** Place-name meaning "high," applied to several cities located on heights, especially military strongholds. **1.** Border town in tribal territory of Asher (Josh. 19:29). The precise location of the city is unknown, although most scholars would place it in the vicinity of Tyre. **2.** Fortified city of tribal territory of Naphtali (Josh. 19:36); this town is probably to be identified with present-day er-Rameh. **3.** Ramah of Gilead usually called Ramoth-gilead (cp. 2 Kings 8:28-29; 2 Chron. 22:6). See *Ramoth-gilead.* **4.** City in the inheritance of Benjamin listed along with Gibeon, Beeroth, Jerusalem, and others (Josh. 18:25). It is to be identified with modern er-Ram five miles north of Jerusalem. **5.** City of the Negev, the arid desert south of Judea, in the tribal inheritance of Simeon (Josh. 19:8). David once gave presents to this town following his successful battle with the Amalekites (1 Sam. 30:27). **6.** Birthplace, home, and burial place of Samuel (1 Sam. 1:19; 2:11; 7:17; 8:4; 15:34; 25:1).

RAMATH Place-name meaning "height, elevated place." An element of several names: Ramath-lehi meaning "height of the jawbone," site of Samson's victory over the Philistines (Judg. 15:17).

RAMATHAIM (NIV) or **RAMATHAIM-ZOPHIM** Birthplace of Samuel (1 Sam. 1:1). The first element in the name means "twin peaks." The final element distinguishes this Ramath from others. Zophim is perhaps a corruption of Zuph, the home district of Samuel (1 Sam. 9:5).

RAMATHITE Resident of Ramah (1 Chron. 27:27).

The gateway to the city of Rameses (Tanis).

RAMESES Egyptian capital city and royal residence during the 19th and 20th Dynasties (about 1320–1085 BC). See *Pithom and Rameses*.

RAMIAH Personal name meaning "Yahweh is exalted." Israelite having a foreign wife (Ezra 10:25).

RAMOTH-GILEAD Place-name meaning "heights of Gilead." One of the cities of refuge Moses appointed for unintentional killers (Deut. 4:43; cp. Josh. 20:8) and Levitical cities (Josh. 21:38). Solomon made Ramoth-gilead a district capital (1 Kings 4:13). After the division of the kingdom about 922 BC, the city fell to Syria (1 Kings 22:3) and remained there for almost 70 years. Ahab attempted to retake the city but was mortally wounded in the battle (1 Kings 22:29-40). Joram did recapture the city (2 Kings 9:14; cp. 8:28). In Ramoth-gilead Elisha anointed Jehu as king over Israel (2 Kings 9:1-6). In 722 BC the region was taken by Assyria.

RAMPART Outer ring of fortifications, usually earthworks. The underlying Hebrew term is literally "encirclement" and can be applied to moats and walls as well as earthworks (2 Sam. 20:15; Ps. 122:7; Lam. 2:8). Because Jerusalem was ringed by steep valleys, only its north side had extensive ramparts.

RANGE KJV term for a rank or row of soldiers (2 Kings 11:8,15; 2 Chron. 23:14).

RAPE Crime of engaging in sexual intercourse with another without consent, by force and/or deception. Mosaic law required a man who had seduced a virgin to pay the bride price and offer to marry her (Exod. 22:16-17). The rape of an engaged woman was a capital offense (Deut. 22:25-27).The Mosaic code highlighted the victim's rights, both to monetary compensation and to recovery of dignity. This quest for dignity was a driving force behind acts of retaliatory violence recorded in the narrative texts. These texts, however, suggest the ease with which the victim is forgotten in the spiral of vengeful violence.

RAPHA Personal name meaning "He has healed." **1.** Fifth son of Benjamin (1 Chron. 8:2). The parallel in Gen. 46:21 gives the name "Naaman." **2.** KJV form of Raphah (1 Chron. 8:37).

RAPHAH Personal name from a root meaning "heal." A descendant of Saul (1 Chron. 8:37). Raphah is identified with Rephaiah of 1 Chron. 9:43.

RAPHU Personal name meaning "healed." Father of the Benjaminite representative among the 12 spies sent to survey Canaan (Num. 13:9).

RAPTURE God's taking the church out of the world instantaneously. The Latin term *rapio*, which means to "snatch away" or "carry off," is the source of the English word. While there are differing views of the millennium (Rev. 20:2-7) in relation to Christ's second coming (e.g., premillennial, postmillennial, and amillennial), nevertheless, all evangelicals affirm a literal return of Christ to the earth preceding the eternal state. In premillennialism, however, the distinct event of the rapture is often emphasized.

The main biblical passage for the rapture (Gk. *harpazo*) of the church is 1 Thess. 4:15-17. Other texts often used to support the doctrine of the rapture are John 14:1-3 and 1 Cor. 15:51-52.

There are three main approaches to understanding the rapture in premillennialism: (1) In the *pretribulational* view Christ raptures the church before any part of the seven-year tribulation begins (Dan. 9:24-27; Matt. 24:3-28; Rev. 11:2; 12:14). Upon Christ's coming in the air, which is distinct from and that precedes His coming to the earth, believers will be "caught up together . . . in the clouds to meet the Lord in the air" (1 Thess. 4:17 HCSB). In this view, believers are delivered "from the coming wrath" (1 Thess. 1:10; Rev. 3:10) by being taken out of the world. (2) A *midtribulational* view also sees the rapture as a distinct event that precedes Christ's second coming and that delivers believers from the last half of the seven-year period, the "great tribulation" (Matt. 24:15-28; Rev. 16-18). (3) A *posttribulational* view holds that the rapture and the second coming occur at the same time. Therefore, the church remains on earth during "the time of Jacob's distress" (Jer. 30:7 NASB). Unlike the world, however, believers who go through the tribulation will be protected from the devastating outpouring of God's wrath and judgment (1 Thess. 5:9).

RAT Large rodent listed among the unclean animals (Lev. 11:29), but they were eaten by a disobedient people (Isa. 66:17).

RAVEN The raven, conspicuous because of its black color (Song 5:11), is a member of the crow family. The raven acts as a scavenger and is listed among the unclean birds (Lev. 11:15; Deut. 14:14).

RAVEN, RAVIN KJV term for "prowl for food" or "feed greedily" (Ps. 22:13; Ezek. 22:25,27).

KJV used "ravin" both as a verb meaning "to prowl for food" (Gen. 49:27) and as a noun meaning "something taken as prey" (Nah. 2:12).

REAIA (KJV, 1 Chron. 5:5) or **REAIAH** Personal name meaning "Yahweh has seen." **1.** Member of the tribe of Judah (1 Chron. 4:1-2). **2.** Member of the tribe of Reuben (1 Chron. 5:5). **3.** Head of a family of temple servants returning from exile (Ezra 2:47; Neh. 7:50).

REAP To harvest grain using a sickle (Ruth 2:3-9). Reaping is used as a symbol of recompense for good (Hos. 10:12; Gal. 6:7-10) and evil (Job 4:8; Prov. 22:8; Hos. 8:7; 10:13), of evangelism (Matt. 9:37-38; Luke 10:2; John 4:35-38), and of final judgment (Matt. 13:30,39; Rev. 14:14-16).

REBA Personal name from a root meaning "lie down." Midianite king whom Israel defeated in the time of Moses (Num. 31:8). Joshua 13:21 connects the defeat of the Midianite kings with that of the Amorite king Sihon (Num. 21:21-35).

REBECCA New Testament form of "Rebekah," Rom. 9:10; Greek transliteration used by KJV, NKJV, NRSV, RSV, REB, NJB, TEV.

REBEKAH Personal name, perhaps meaning "cow." Daughter of Bethuel, Abraham's nephew (Gen. 24:15); Isaac's wife (24:67); and mother of Jacob and Esau (25:25-26).

RECAB, RECABITES NIV form of Rechab, Rechabites.

RECAH Unidentified site in Judah (1 Chron. 4:12). Early Greek manuscript has Rechab in place of Recah.

RECHAB Personal name meaning "rider" or "charioteer." **1.** Leader, together with his brother, of a band of Benjaminite raiders. He and his brother murdered Saul's son Ish-bosheth, thinking to court David's favor. His response was their execution (2 Sam. 4:1-12). **2.** Father or ancestor of Jehonadab, a supporter of Jehu's purge of the family of Ahab and other worshippers of Baal (2 Kings 10:15,23). **3.** Father or ancestor of Malchijah, who assisted in Nehemiah's repair of Jerusalem's walls (Neh. 3:14), possibly identical with 2.

RECHABITES Descendants of Jehonadab ben Rechab, who supported Jehu when he overthrew the house of Ahab (2 Kings 10:15-17). About 599 BC the Rechabites took refuge from Nebuchadnezzar in Jerusalem (Jer. 35).

RECONCILIATION Bringing together of two parties that are estranged or in dispute. Jesus Christ is the one who brings together God and man, with salvation as the result of the union. Several themes are essential to a biblical understanding of reconciliation. First is a recognition of the need for reconciliation (Rom. 5:10; Eph. 2:12; Col. 1:21). Sin has created the separation and alienation between God and man. Reconciliation assumes there is a need for separation to be bridged and for God and humanity to be restored in right relationship. Second, God is the Reconciler; reconciliation is His work. The incarnation is God's declaration that the initiative for reconciliation resides exclusively with Him (2 Cor. 5:19). Third, the death of Jesus Christ is the means by which God accomplishes reconciliation (Rom. 5:10). Fourth, reconciliation is a completed work but is still being fulfilled. Although the substitutionary sacrifice of Christ has already procured reconciliation, human beings still receive God's reconciling work and gracious gift by grace through faith in Jesus Christ. Fifth, the divine-human act of reconciliation serves as the basis for authentic person-to-person reconciliation. Finally, God's reconciling work is in large measure the ministry of the church. Believers have been commissioned by the resurrected Lord to have a message and ministry of reconciliation. In this sense reconciliation is not only a reality of life for believers, but it is also a purpose of their kingdom ministry.

RED KJV used "red" as the translation of several Hebrew terms where modern translations substitute another meaning: "foaming" or "blended" (Ps. 75:8); "pleasant" or "delight" (Isa. 27:2); and "porphyry" (Esther 1:6).

RED HEIFER Function of the red heifer ceremony was production of ash for the water used to remove ritual impurity contracted through contact with a corpse, bones, or a grave (Num. 19). The rite involved: slaughter of a sacrificially acceptable heifer outside the camp; sprinkling blood toward the tent of meeting seven times; burning the entire heifer, including its blood and dung, together with cedarwood, hyssop, and scarlet thread (cp. Lev. 14:4); and storing the ash in a clean place outside the camp.

Hebrews 9:14 uses the image of the red heifer ceremony to picture Christ's cleansing believers of the effect of "dead works." Dead works refer either to acts that lead to death (NIV), "useless rituals" n view of salvation (TEV), or works produced prior to being made alive in Christ (cp. Heb. 6:1).

RED SEA (REED SEA) Body of water God divided in the exodus. Red Sea is a common translation of two Hebrew words *yam suph*. *Yam* means "sea," but *suph* does not normally mean "red." *Suph* often means "reeds" (Exod. 2:3,5; Isa. 19:6) or "end," "hinder part" (Joel 2:20; 2 Chron. 20:16; Eccles. 3:11). *Yam suph* could be translated "Sea of Reeds" or "Sea at the end of the world."

The Red Sea.

No one knows the exact location of the place where Israel crossed the "Red Sea" on the way out of Egypt. Four primary theories have been suggested as to the place of the actual crossing of the isthmus of Suez: (1) the northern edge of the Gulf of Suez; (2) a site in the center of the isthmus near Lake Timsah; (3) a site at the northern edge of the isthmus and the southern edge of Lake Menzaleh; and (4) across a narrow stretch of sandy land which separates Lake Sirbonis from the Mediterranean Sea. Although no one knows the exact site of the crossing, the weight of the biblical evidence is on the side of suggested site number two. See *Exodus*.

REDEEM, REDEMPTION, REDEEMER The first term means to pay a price in order to secure the release of something or someone. It connotes the idea of paying what is required in order to liberate from oppression, enslavement, or another type of binding obligation. The redemptive procedure may be legal, commercial, or religious.

In the OT two word groups convey the idea of redemption. The verb *ga'al* and its cognates mean "to buy back" or "to redeem." When *ga'al* is used of God, the idea is redemption from bondage or oppression, typically from one's enemies. In the Exodus account Yahweh declares to Moses: "I am the LORD ... and I will redeem you with an outstretched arm and with mighty acts of judgment" (Exod. 6:6 NIV).

In the NT two word groups convey the concept. The first consists of *lutron* and its cognates. They mean "to redeem," "to liberate," or "to ransom." The idea of ransom suggests the heart of Jesus' mission (Mark 10:45). His life and ministry culminated in His sacrificial death. His death served as the ransom to liberate sinners from their enslaved condition.

Another word family, *agorazein*, means "to buy at the market" or "to redeem." This group is used several times to express God's redemptive activity in Christ. For example, God's redemption of fallen humanity is costly (1 Cor. 6:20). Believers are liberated from the enslaving curse of the law (Gal. 3:13; 4:5). God's redemptive mission among the nations is cause for eschatological worship (Rev. 5:9; 14:3-4).

Paul provides the fullest explanation in the NT, connecting the redemptive work of Christ with the legal declaration of the sinner's pardon (justification) and the appeasement of God's wrath against sin (propitiation, Rom. 3:24; 1 Cor. 1:30).

REELAIAH Personal name meaning "Yahweh has caused trembling." Exile who returned with Zerubbabel (Ezra 2:2); identical to Raamiah (Neh. 7:7).

REFINE To reduce to a pure state; often used figuratively of moral cleansing.

REFORMATION Translation of the Greek *diorthosis* (Heb. 9:10). The term refers either to the new order for relating to God established by Christ (NIV) or else to the process of establishing the new order (NRSV, TEV).

REGEM Personal name meaning "friend." Descendant of Caleb (1 Chron. 2:47).

REGEM-MELECH Personal name meaning "friend of the king." Delegate whom the people of Bethel sent to Jerusalem to inquire about continuing to fast in commemoration of the destruction of the Jerusalem temple (Zech. 7:2). The prophet repeated the word of previous prophets: God desires moral lives rather than fasts (7:9-10).

REGENERATION Special act of God in which the recipient is passive. God alone awakens the person spiritually through the power of His Holy Spirit. Both the OT and NT also speak of the renewing of the individual. In a technical sense the act of regeneration takes place at the moment of conversion as the individual is spiritually awakened.

The term "regeneration" is a translation of the Greek word *palingenesia* (used only in Matt. 19:28

of creation and Titus 3:5). The Titus text refers to the regeneration of the individual: "He saved us—not by works of righteousness that we had done, but according to His mercy, through the washing of regeneration and renewal by the Holy Spirit" (HCSB). The Bible expresses the concept in numerous places with other terms like "born again," "renewed," "re-made," and "born of God." For instance, in John 3:3-8 Jesus tells Nicodemus that in order to enter the kingdom of God, he must be born again.

REGIMENT NIV term for "cohort," a tenth of a legion (Acts 10:1; 27:1).

REGISTER KJV term for a record of names, a genealogical registry (Ezra 2:62; Neh. 7:5,64). Modern translations use "register" more often in the verbal sense, to record in formal records (NASB: Num. 1:18; 11:26; 2 Sam. 24:2,4; Neh. 12:22-23; Ps. 87:6). See *Census.*

REHABIAH Personal name meaning "Yahweh has made wide." Son of Eliezer and ancestor of a group of Levites (1 Chron. 23:17; 24:21; 26:25).

REHOB Personal and place-name meaning "broad or open place." **1.** Father of a king of Zobah, an Aramean city north of Damascus (2 Sam. 8:3,12). **2.** Witness to Nehemiah's covenant (Neh. 10:11). **3.** Town in the vicinity of Laish in upper Galilee (Num. 13:21) See *Beth-rehob.* **4.** Town in the territory of Asher (Josh. 19:28,30). Asher was not able to drive out the Canaanite inhabitants (Judg. 1:31).

REHOBOAM Personal name meaning "he enlarges the people." One of Solomon's sons and his successor to the throne of the united monarchy (1 Kings 11:43). He reigned about 931–913 BC. While at Shechem for his crowning ceremony as king over Israel (1 Kings 12), the people asked Rehoboam if he would remove some of the tax burden and labor laws that his father had placed on them. Instead of taking the advice of the older men, he acted on the counsel of those who wanted to increase the burden further. The Northern tribes revolted and made the rebel Jeroboam their king. Rehoboam was left with only the tribes of Judah and Benjamin. He continued the pagan ways that Solomon had allowed (14:21-24) and fought against Jeroboam and Shishak of Egypt. Some of his fortifications may be those at Lachish and Azekah.

REHOBOTH Place-name meaning "broad places." **1.** Rehoboth-Ir, "broad places of the city," likely denotes an open space within Nineveh or its suburbs (Gen. 10:11) rather than a separate city between Nineveh and Calah. **2.** Site of a well dug and retained by Isaac's men in the valley of Gerar (Gen. 26:22). The name affirms that God had made room for them following confrontations over rights to two previous wells. **3.** Unidentified Edomite city (Gen. 36:37; 1 Chron. 1:48).

REHUM Personal name meaning "merciful, compassionate." **1.** One returning from exile with Zerubbabel (Ezra 2:2); the parallel (Neh. 7:7) reads "Nehum." **2.** Persian official with oversight of the Trans-Euphrates territory, including Judah. His protest of the rebuilding of the Jerusalem temple and city walls resulted in suspension of the project (Ezra 4:8-24). **3.** Levite engaged in Nehemiah's repair of the wall (Neh. 3:17). **4.** Witness to Nehemiah's covenant (Neh. 10:25). **5.** Priest or priestly clan (Neh. 12:3), perhaps a corruption of Harim.

REI Personal name meaning "friendly." David's officer who sided with Solomon in his succession struggle with Adonijah (1 Kings 1:8).

REINS KJV term for kidneys, used both in a literal anatomical sense and in a figurative sense for the seat of the emotions. The substitutions made by the NRSV are illustrative of those of other modern translations: literal sense as "kidneys" (Job 16:13), "inward parts" (Ps. 139:13), and "loins" (Isa. 11:5); figurative sense as "heart" (Job 19:27; Pss. 7:9; 16:7; 26:2; 73:21; Jer. 11:20) with the exception of Prov. 23:16 ("soul").

REKEM Personal and place-name meaning "maker of multicolored cloth." **1.** One of five Midianite kings whom Israel defeated in Moses' time (Num. 31:8; Josh. 13:21). Rekem was apparently the earlier name of Petra. See *Reba.* **2.** Descendant of Caleb (1 Chron. 2:43-44). **3.** Ancestor of a family living in Gilead (1 Chron. 7:16). **4.** Unidentified site in Benjamin (Josh. 18:27).

RELEASE, YEAR OF Hebrew expression that occurs only twice (Deut. 15:9; 31:10 KJV, RSV) both times in reference to the Sabbatical Year as a year of release from debt. Some confusion results from modern translations using the verb "release" in connection with both the Sabbatical Year and the Year of Jubilee.

REMALIAH Personal name meaning "may Yahweh be exalted" or "Yahweh adorned." Father of Pekah who murdered King Pekahiah of Israel and reigned in his stead (2 Kings 15:25; Isa. 7:1).

REMETH Place-name meaning "height." Town in Issachar's territory (Josh. 19:21), likely identical with Ramoth (1 Chron. 6:73) and Jarmuth (Josh. 21:29).

REMISSION Release, forgiveness. RSV used "remission" only in the sense of refraining from exacting a tax (Esther 2:18). Other modern translations avoided the term. KJV frequently used the expression, "remission of sins," to mean release from the guilt or penalty of sins.

REMMON KJV variant of Rimmon (Josh. 19:7). RSV reads "En-rimmon." Other modern translations follow the KJV in understanding two cities: Ain and Rimmon.

REMMON-METHOAR KJV took Remmon-methoar as a proper name (Josh. 19:13).

REMNANT Something left over, especially the righteous people of God after divine judgment. Noah and his family may be understood as survivors, or a remnant, of a divine judgment in the flood (Gen. 6:5-8; 7:1-23). The same could be said of Lot when Sodom was destroyed (Gen. 18:17-33; 19:1-29), Jacob's family in Egypt (Gen. 45:7), Elijah and the 7,000 faithful followers of the Lord (1 Kings 19:17-18), and the Israelites going into captivity (Ezek. 12:1-16). They were survivors because the Lord chose to show mercy to those who had believed steadfastly in Him and had been righteous in their lives.

The remnant doctrine was so important to Isaiah that he named one of his sons Shear-jashub, meaning "a remnant shall return" (7:3). The faithful would survive the onslaughts of the Assyrian army (4:2-6; 12:1-6) as illustrated by the remarkable deliverance of the few people in Jerusalem from the siege of the city by the Assyrians (chaps. 36–38).

In the NT Paul quoted (Rom. 9:25-33) from Hosea and from Isaiah to demonstrate that the saving of a remnant from among the Jewish people was still part of the Lord's method of redeeming His people. There would always be a future for anyone among the covenant people who would truly turn to the Lord for salvation (chaps. 9–11).

REPENTANCE Change of mind; also can refer to regret or remorse accompanying a realization that wrong has been done or to any shift or reversal of thought.

Old Testament The concept of a whole-hearted turning to God is widespread in the preaching of the OT prophets. Terms such as "return," "turn," and "seek" are used to express the idea of repentance.

New Testament Repentance was the keynote of the preaching of John the Baptist, referring to a complete turn from self to God. The emphasis upon a total life change continues in the ministry of Jesus. The message of repentance was at the heart of His preaching (Mark 1:15). When describing the focus of His mission, Jesus said, "I have not come to call the righteous, but sinners to repentance"(Luke 5:32 HCSB).

REPENTANCE OF GOD Old Testament description of God's reaction to human situations. The Hebrew verb (*nacham*) expresses a strong emotional content, perhaps with a reference to deep breathing of distress or relief. It should be noted that "repent" is not always the best translation for *nacham* but was the translation used by the KJV. The scope of possible translations includes "repent" (Jer. 18:8,10 RSV), "grieve" (Gen. 6:7 NIV), "pity" (Judg. 2:18 NASB), "change of mind" (Ps. 110:4 REB), and "relent" (Ps. 106:45 NASB). God's repentance plays an important role in our understanding about the role of prayer and about certain attributes of God, such as immutability, timelessness, and impassability. The God who repents is free to answer prayer and to interact with people. This freedom is part of His being the same forever.

REPHAEL Personal name meaning "God heals." Temple gatekeeper (1 Chron. 26:7).

REPHAH Personal name meaning "overflow." An Ephraimite (1 Chron. 7:25).

REPHAIAH Personal name meaning "God healed." **1.** Descendant of David (1 Chron. 3:21). **2.** Simeonite living at Mount Seir (1 Chron. 4:42). **3.** Warrior from the tribe of Issachar (1 Chron. 7:2). **4.** Descendant of Saul (1 Chron. 9:43). **5.** One helping with Nehemiah's repair of the wall who had oversight of one half of the administrative district embracing Jerusalem (Neh. 3:9).

REPHAIM 1. Residents of Sheol, often translated "shades" or "the dead" (Job 26:5 NRSV; Ps. 88:10; Prov. 9:18; 21:16; Isa. 14:9; 26:14,19). See *Sheol.* **2.** Ethnic designation of the pre-Israelite inhabitants of Palestine, equivalent to the Anakim, the Moabite term *Emim* (Deut. 2:10-11), and the Ammonite term *Zanzummim* (2:20-21).

REPHAITES NIV alternate translation for the Hebrew *Rephaim* when applied to the pre-Israelite inhabitants of Canaan. See *Rephaim.*

REPHAN Term for a foreign, astral deity (Acts 7:43; NASB, Rompha). Acts 7 follows the earliest Greek OT translation reading at Amos 5:26. The Hebrew Masoretic text reads "Kaiwan," the Babylonian name for Saturn.

REPHIDIM Site in the wilderness where the Hebrews stopped on their way to Canaan just prior to reaching Sinai (Exod. 17:1; 19:2). There the people complained of thirst, and God commanded Moses to strike the rock out of which would come water. While the Hebrews were encamped at Rephidim, the Amalekites came against them and were defeated by Israel under Joshua's leadership. Moses' father-in-law, Jethro, came to Rephidim and helped the leader delegate his authority over the people (18:13-26). The exact location is unknown.

REPROACH Term used to indicate disgrace, dishonor, or to discredit someone or something.

REPROBATE KJV term used in two senses: that which fails to meet a test and is thus rejected as unworthy or unacceptable, as impure silver (Jer. 6:30) or persons (2 Cor. 13:5-7; Titus 1:16); and that which is depraved or without morals (Rom. 1:28; 2 Tim. 3:8). NASB and RSV used "reprobate" to mean "one rejected by God" (Ps. 15:4; cp. HCSB, REB, TEV).

REPTILES Animals that crawl or move on the belly or on small short legs. This category of animals includes alligators, crocodiles, lizards, snakes, and turtles. It is generally agreed that in many instances the reptiles in the Bible cannot be specifically determined. Many times the same Hebrew word is translated in different ways.

RESEN Place-name meaning "fountain head." City that Nimrod founded between Nineveh and Calah (Gen. 10:12). Probably modern Salemijeh (in Iraq), two and a half miles northwest of Nimrud.

RESERVOIR Place for catching and storing water for later use, either agricultural (2 Chron. 26:10; Eccles. 2:6) or as an urban supply in anticipation of a siege (2 Kings 20:20; Isa. 22:8b-11). Reservoirs were a necessity in most of Palestine where seasonal rains were the major water source.

RESH Twentieth letter in the Hebrew alphabet, which the KJV used as heading for the eight verses of Ps. 119:153-160 that each begin with this letter.

RESHEPH Personal name meaning "flame." An Ephraimite (1 Chron. 7:25).

RESIN NIV translation of "bdellium" (Gen. 2:12; cp. Num. 11:7).

RESTITUTION Act of returning what has wrongfully been taken or replacing what has been lost or damaged, and the divine restoration of all things to their original order.

RESURRECTION Future, bodily rising from the dead of all persons. Believers in Christ rise to eternal life and bliss with God; unbelievers to eternal torment and separation from God.

Resurrection is different from resuscitation. A resuscitation, like that of Lazarus, is a return to life but eventually physical death comes again. Those resurrected will not die again.

RESURRECTION OF JESUS THE CHRIST Historical event whereby Jesus came back from physical death to newness of life with a glorified body, never to die again. The bodily resurrection of Jesus is one of the central tenets of the Christian faith. His bodily resurrection validates the claim that He is both Lord and Christ. It substantiates the proposition that His life and death were not just the life and death of a good man, but that He indeed was God incarnate, and that by His death we have forgiveness of sin.

The four Gospels are selective in the events they report surrounding the resurrection. Each emphasizes the empty tomb, but each is somewhat different in the post-resurrection appearances recounted.

The oldest account of the resurrection is found in 1 Cor. 15. In that passage Paul recounted a number of post-resurrection appearances. He established that the believer's future resurrection is based on the historicity of Christ's bodily resurrection.

RETINUE NASB, REB, NRSV, REB term for the attendants of the queen of Sheba (1 Kings 10:2; KJV, train; NIV, caravan).

REU Personal name meaning "friend, companion." Descendant of Shem (Gen. 11:18-21; 1 Chron. 1:25), possibly the ancestor of a Semitic tribe associated with Ra'ilu, an island in the Euphrates below Anat.

REUBEN, REUBENITES Eldest son of Jacob, born to Leah (Gen. 29:32) while the couple was living with her father, Laban, in Paddan-aram, and the clan or tribe descended from him. Among his acts recorded in the Bible, Reuben found mandrakes (out of which a love potion probably was made for his mother to use with Jacob, 30:14,16-17) and had sexual relations with one of his father's con cubines (35:22), for which he later was chastised (49:4). Reuben felt compassion for young Joseph when his brothers wanted to kill the brash dreamer (37:21-22) and was willing to be responsible to his father for Benjamin's welfare when the unrecognized Joseph commanded that the youngest brother be brought to Egypt (42:37).

The tribe that was named for Reuben held a place of honor among the other tribes. The territory the tribe inherited was just east of the Dead Sea and was the first parcel of land to be bestowed Num. 32).

REUEL Personal name meaning "friend of God." **1.** Son of Esau and ancestor of several Edomite clans (Gen. 36:4,10,13,17; 1 Chron. 1:35,37). **2.** Exodus 2:18 identifies Reuel as the "father" of Zipporah, Moses' wife. Numbers 10:29 presents Reuel as the father of Hobab, Moses' father-in-law. Elsewhere Moses' father-in-law is called Jethro. The tradition is also divided regarding the background of Moses' father-in-law, either Midianite (Exod. 2:16; 3:1) or Kenite (Judg. 1:16; 4:11). **3.** A Gadite (Num. 2:14). **4.** A Benjaminite (1 Chron. 9:8).

REUMAH Personal name meaning "coral." Nahor's concubine, an ancestress of several Aramean tribes living northwest of Damascus (Gen. 22:24).

REVELATION OF GOD Content and process of God's making Himself known to people. All knowledge of God comes by way of revelation. Human knowledge of God is revealed knowledge, since God, and He alone, gives it. He bridges the gap between Himself and His creatures, disclosing Himself and His will to them. By God alone can God be known.

Theologians make a distinction between general revelation and special revelation. General revelation is universal in the sense that it is God's self-disclosure of Himself in a general way to all people at all times in all places. General revelation occurs (1) through nature, (2) in our experience and in our conscience, and (3) in history. God's general revelation is often misinterpreted because sinful and finite humans are trying to understand a perfect and infinite God. Men and women suppress God's truth because they do not like the truth about God. General revelation does not bring one into a saving relationship with God; it does reveal God to His creatures and they are, therefore, responsible for their response.

In contrast to God's general revelation, which is available to all people, God's special revelation is available to specific people at specific times in specific places. Special revelation is particular. God reveals Himself to His people. These people of God are the children of Abraham, whether by natural (Gen. 12:1-3) or spiritual descent (Gal. 3:16,29). Special revelation is primarily redemptive and personal. In recognition of the human predicament God chose at the very beginning to disclose Himself in a more direct way. Within time and space God has acted and spoken to redeem the human race from its own self-imposed evil. Through calling people, miracles, the exodus, covenant making, and ultimately through Jesus Christ, God has revealed Himself in history.

REVELATION, BOOK OF Last book in the Bible. Its title is from its first word, *apokalupsis*, meaning to "unveil," "disclose," or "reveal." Revelation 1:1 gives the theme of the book: it is a revelation "of," "from," and "about" Jesus Christ.

Four times the author identifies himself as John (1:1,4,9; 22:8). Early Christian traditions attribute the Gospel of John, the three letters from John, and the book of Revelation. Revelation is the only one claiming to be written by someone named John. Though the author does not claim to be the Apostle John, it seems unlikely that any other first-century Christian leader would have had the authority or was associated closely enough with the churches of Asia Minor to have referred to himself simply as John.

John's situation was one of suffering. He was a "brother and partner in the tribulation" that is "in Jesus," and because of his testimony to Jesus, was exiled to the island of Patmos (1:9 HCSB).

Revelation was written late in the first century. Early tradition dated the book during the reign of the Roman emperor Domitian (AD 81–96). An alternative view dates it shortly after the reign of Nero AD 54–68).

To encourage faithfulness, Revelation points to the glorious world to come, a world where "death will exist no longer; grief, crying, and pain will exist no longer" (21:4 HCSB; cp. 7:16) at the reappearing of the crucified and risen Jesus. The enthroned Lord will return to conclude world history with the destruction of God's enemies, the final salvation of His people, and creation of a new heaven and a new earth (21–22). The intensity of John's experience is matched only by the richness of the apocalyptic symbolism employed to warn his readers of impending disasters and temptations that would require steadfast allegiance to the risen Lord. To be sure, the Lord will come in power and glory, but not before His enemies have exercised a terrible but limited (by divine mercy) attack on those who "hold to the testimony of Jesus" (cp. 1:9; 6:9; 12:11).

John concluded his prophecy by declaring the utter faithfulness of his words. Those who heed his prophecy will receive the blessings of God. Those who ignore the warnings will be left outside the gates of God's presence (22:6-15). Solemnly and hopefully praying for the Lord to come, John closed his book (22:17,20). The churches must have ears to hear what the Spirit has said (22:16). The people of God must, by His grace (22:21), persevere in the hour of tribulation, knowing their enthroned Lord will return in triumph.

REVERENCE Respect or honor paid to a worthy object. In Scripture, reverence is paid: to father and mother (Lev. 19:3; Heb. 12:9); to God (1 Kings 18:3,12; Heb. 12:28); to God's sanctuary (Lev. 19:30; 26:2); and to God's commandments (Ps. 119:48). The failure to revere God (Deut. 32:51) and the act of revering other gods (Judg. 6:10) have dire consequences. Reverence for Christ is expressed in mutual submission within the Christian community (Eph. 5:21). Christian persecution takes on new meaning as suffering becomes an opportunity for revering Christ (1 Pet. 3:14-15).

REZEPH Place-name meaning "glowing coal." Town the Assyrians conquered, most likely under Shalmaneser III (about 838 BC), and which the Assyrians used as a warning to King Hezekiah of Judah in 701 BC against relying on God to deliver him from them (2 Kings 19:12; Isa. 37:12).

REZIN King of Syria about 735 BC during the reigns of Pekah in Israel and Ahaz in Judah. When Ahaz refused to join Rezin and Pekah in fighting against Assyria, Rezin persuaded Pekah to ally with him against the Judean king (2 Kings 15:37; 16:5). Ahaz appealed for help to Tiglath-pileser of Assyria, who came against Rezin and Pekah and destroyed their kingdoms. Rezin died in 732 BC when Damascus fell to the Assyrians.

REZON Personal name meaning "prince." An Aramean leader who led a successful revolt against Solomon and established an independent state with its capital at Damascus (1 Kings 11:23-25).

RHEGIUM Place-name either derived from the Greek *rhegnumi* (rent, torn) or from the Latin *regium* (royal). Port located at the southwestern tip of the Italian boot about seven miles across the Strait of Messina from Sicily. Paul stopped there en route to Rome (Acts 28:13).

RHESA Ancestor of Jesus (Luke 3:27).

RHODA Personal name meaning "rose." Rhoda's relationship to the household of Mary, the mother of John Mark, is not clear. She was most likely a servant, though it is possible that she was a family member or a guest at the prayer service. In her great joy at finding Peter at the door, Rhoda failed to let him in. Her joy in rushing to tell the disciples and their response accusing her of madness recall details of Luke's resurrection narrative (Acts 12:13; cp. Luke 24:9-11).

RHODES Island off the southwest coast of Asia Minor in the Mediterranean Sea associated with the Dodanim (NASB, KJV; Gen. 10:4; Ezek. 27:15). When the Apostle Paul stopped over on his voyage from Troas to Caesarea (Acts 21:1), Rhodes was only a minor provincial city.

The city and harbor area of the island of Rhodes.

RIBAI Personal name meaning "Yahweh contends." Father of Ittai, one of David's 30 elite warriors (2 Sam. 23:29; 1 Chron. 11:31).

RIBBAND KJV form of ribbon (Num. 15:38). Modern translations read "cord" (NASB, NIV, NRSV) or "thread" (REB).

RIBLAH 1. Syrian town located near Kadesh on the Orontes near the border with Babylonia. There Pharaoh Neco imprisoned King Jehoahaz of Judah after the young monarch had reigned only three months (2 Kings 23:31-33). Later, when Zedekiah rebelled against Nebuchadnezzar of Babylon, he was taken to Riblah as a prisoner and viewed the execution of his sons before having his eyes put out (25:4-7). 2. Otherwise unknown town on eastern border of Canaan (Num. 34:11). Earliest translations read "Arbelah."

RIDDLE Enigmatic or puzzling statement, often based on the clever use of the ambiguities of language. The classic biblical example of a riddle is that posed by Samson to the Philistines (Judg. 14:12-14).

RIGHT MIND Sound mind, mentally healthy (Mark 5:15; Luke 8:35). Elsewhere, the underlying

Greek term is rendered "sober judgment" (Rom. 12:3 NRSV) or "self-controlled" (Titus 2:6 NRSV).

RIGHTEOUSNESS Biblical terminology used to denote the term "righteousness" is from one basic word group. The Hebrew *tsadiq* is translated by the Greek *dikaiosune* and its various forms in both the LXX and the NT. Psalms 111–112 provide a holistic picture of the righteousness of God and the righteous man. Righteousness itself is grounded in the character of God (Exod. 9:27; Deut. 32:4; Judg. 5:11; 1 Sam. 12:7; Mic. 6:4; cp. Ps. 103:6; Dan. 9:16; 2 Chron. 12:6; Ezra 9:15; Neh. 9:8; Pss. 119:137; 129:4). He is righteous, His law is righteous, and He alone credits righteousness to man.

In the NT, like the OT, God and all that comes from Him is righteous. His judgments are righteous (2 Thess. 1:5-6; Rev. 16:7; 19:2; 2 Tim. 4:8), as He Himself is as a judge (John 17:23). All God's revealed will in Jesus' teachings is righteousness (Matt. 6:23; John 16:8-10).

Paul utilizes the idea of righteousness more than other writers in the NT. God demonstrates His righteousness perfectly in the propitiatory death of His Son (Rom. 3:21,25-26). Jesus' death on the cross was ordained by God, is in conformity with His character, and accomplishes God's righteous purposes with sinners (Rom. 5:16,18).

RIMMON Place-name and divine name meaning "pomegranate." **1.** Chief god of Syria, also called Hadad. Naaman worshipped Rimmon in Damascus (2 Kings 5:18). **2.** Town allotted to tribe of Judah (Josh. 15:32) but then given to Simeon (19:7; cp. 1 Chron. 4:32). **3.** Levitical city in Zebulun (Josh. 19:13; 1 Chron. 6:77), probably the original reading for present Dimnah (Josh. 21:35). **4.** Rock near Gibeah to where the people of Benjamin fled from vengeful Israelites (Judg. 20:45-47), modern Rammun four miles east of Bethel. **5.** Father of Rechab and Baanah, who killed Saul's son Ish-Bosheth (2 Sam. 4:2,9).

RIMMON-PAREZ (KJV) or **RIMMON-PEREZ** Place-name meaning "pomegranate of the pass." Campsite during Israel's wilderness wanderings (Num. 33:19-20).

RIMMONO Place-name meaning "his Rimmon." NIV, NASB, NRSV reading of Rimmon in 1 Chron. 6:77 (cp. Josh. 19:13; 21:25).

RINNAH Personal name meaning "ringing cry." Descendant of Judah (1 Chron. 4:20).

RIPHATH Personal name of foreign origin. Son of Gomer, likely the ancestor of an Anatolian tribe (Gen. 10:3). The name is likely a scribal corruption of Diphath (1 Chron. 1:6).

RISHATHAIM Mesopotamian king, Cushan-rishathaim, who conquered and oppressed Israel (Judg. 3:8). Cushan may relate to Guzana or Tell Halaf. KJV uses Chushan-rishathaim.

RISSAH Place-name possibly meaning "dewdrop," "rain," or "ruins." Campsite during Israel's wilderness wanderings (Num. 33:21-22), modern Sharma, east of Gulf of Aqaba.

RITHMAH Place-name meaning "broom plant." Campsite during Israel's wilderness wanderings (Num. 33:18-19), possibly valley called er-Retame, east of Gulf of Aqaba.

RIZIA Personal name meaning "delight." Head of a family within the tribe of Asher who was a renowned warrior (1 Chron. 7:39-40).

RIZPAH Personal name meaning "glowing coals" or "bread heated over coals or ashes." Saul's concubine whom Abner took as wife in what amounted to a claim to the throne (2 Sam. 3:7; cp. 1 Kings 2:22). Rizpah is best known for her faithful vigil over the bodies of her executed sons (2 Sam. 21:10-14) until David commanded their burial.

ROCK Use of rocky sites as places of refuge (Num. 24:21; Judg. 15:8; 20:47) led to the frequent image of God as a rock, that is, a source of protection. Titles of God include: the "Stone of Israel" (Gen. 49:24 NASB); the Rock (Deut. 32:4); the Rock of salvation (32:15); the Rock who begot Israel (32:18); "a rock that is high above me" (Ps. 61:2 HCSB). Isaiah 8:13-14 pictures the Lord of hosts as a "rock to stumble over" (NASB) to the unholy people of Israel and Judah. Paul identified Christ as the spiritual Rock that nourished Israel in the wilderness (1 Cor. 10:4).

ROCK BADGER (NRSV) Maybe the hyrax, a mammal somewhat resembling a shrew (Lev. 11:5; Ps. 104:18; Prov. 30:26).

ROD, STAFF "Rod" designates a straight, slender stick growing on (Jer. 1:11) or cut from (Gen. 30:37-41) a tree. "Rod" is sometimes used interchangeably with "staff" (Isa. 10:5; Rev. 11:1). Elsewhere, rod designates a shorter, clublike stick (Ps. 23:4). Rods and staffs were used as walking sticks (Gen. 32:10), for defense (Ps. 23:4), for punishment (Exod. 21:20; Num. 22:27; Prov. 13:24;

1 Cor. 4:21), and for measurement (Rev. 11:1). Rods and staffs were also used as symbols of prophet ic (Exod. 4:2-4; 7:8-24; Judg. 6:21), priestly (Num. 17:1-10), and royal (Gen. 49:10 NRSV; Judg 5:14 NRSV; Jer. 48:17; Rev. 2:27) offices.

RODANIM Inhabitants of Rhodes (1 Chron. 1:7 NRSV). The parallel in Gen. 10:4 (KJV) reads "Dodanim" which should be preferred as the more difficult reading. Rhodians, however, fits well in the general geographic context.

ROE, ROEBUCK (*Capreolus capreolus*) One of the smallest species of deer, measuring about 26 inches at the shoulder (2 Sam. 2:18; Deut.12:15 KJV). Other translations use "gazelle" or "deer."

ROGELIM Place-name meaning "[place of] the fullers." City on the Jabbok River in Gilead (2 Sam 17:27-29; 19:31). The site is perhaps Zaharet's Soq'ah. Tell Barsina lacks evidence of occupation in David's time.

ROHGAH Personal name, perhaps meaning "cry out." Leader of the tribe of Asher (1 Chron 7:34).

ROLLER KJV term for something wrapped around the arm (Ezek. 30:21) as a bandage (NASB REB, NRSV) or splint (NIV).

ROMAMTI-EZER Personal name meaning "I have exalted help." Temple musician (1 Chron 25:4,31). Some scholars recognize a prayer of praise behind the names of the temple musicians Hananiah through Mahazioth (25:4).

ROMANS, LETTER TO THE Longest and most intensely theological of the 13 NT letters writ ten by Paul. This letter is also the most significant in the history of the church. Martin Luther was studying Romans when he concluded that a person becomes righteous in the sight of God through faith alone. His discovery led to the Reformation battle cry, *sola fide*, "by faith alone."

Where and When Did Paul Write Romans? Romans 15:25-29 indicates Paul wrote Romans shortly before a trip to Jerusalem. He went to Jerusalem to present money collected by Gentile churches in Macedonia and Achaia for poor believers in Jerusalem (15:26). Paul hoped to travel from Jerusalem through Rome to Spain to "evangelize where Christ has not been named" (HCSB). This fits well with Luke's description of Paul's travels at the close of the third missionary journey (Acts 19:21; 20:16).

What Is the Message of Romans? Romans 1:16-17 expresses the theme of the letter. Paul is not ashamed to proclaim the gospel because the gospel is God's saving power that accomplishes salva tion for all who believe, whether they are Jews or Gentiles. The gospel reveals God's righteousness both His justice and His activity of justifying sinners (Rom. 3:21-26). Salvation by faith was not new but was the message of the OT prophets (Rom. 1:17; Hab. 2:4).

Gentiles deserve God's wrath because their sins are not committed in ignorance but involve sup pression of the truths about God that are apparent to all. Jews as well as Gentiles deserve God's wrath. Though they preach and teach the law, they have failed to obey the law, thereby dishonoring God and blaspheming His name. Circumcision grants no protection against divine judgment.

Both the Law and the Prophets testify that God declares sinners who have failed to keep the law to be righteous in His sight if they believe in Jesus Christ. This righteous standing is granted freely by divine grace and based on the atoning sacrifice of Christ.

This righteousness was also credited to Abraham before the Mosaic law was given, further demon strating that God grants this righteousness on the basis of faith and not law-keeping.

Because of justification, believers are at peace with God and joyfully anticipate full and final trans formation. Through Jesus' sacrificial and substitutionary death, believers who were formerly God's enemies and deserved His wrath have been reconciled to God.

The impact of Adam's disobedience on the human race offers a negative parallel to the impact of Christ's obedience on believers. Just as the effects of Adam's disobedience were universal, the effects of Christ's obedience are also universal. The law did not introduce death into the world. It did offer Adam's descendants explicit commandments to defy just as Adam had done. This made sin more rampant and more heinous. This only served to magnify the abundance and greatness of God's grace

One should not conclude from this that sin should be continued. The believer's union with Christ in His death, burial, and resurrection is inconsistent with a sinful lifestyle. The old person died with Christ. Now the believer has been liberated from sin's mastery. Eventually, the believer's union with Christ will result in his resurrection and complete liberation from sin. Believers should live now in light of the fact that sin's mastery has been broken.

The law aggravates and arouses sin in unbelievers, but this does not mean the law is bad. The law is holy, righteous, and good, but the sinful nature uses the law to destroy sinners. The law still serve a positive function. It demonstrates man's utter corruption and slavery to sin. However, it can not liberate him from that slavery. Paul illustrated this by describing his own frustration in trying to fulfill the law's demands. Paul had been caught in a tug-of-war between delighting in God's law and being dominated by sin. Paul confessed that this conflict would end only through the bodily resurrection. Yet the believer can enjoy victory over sin. The Spirit accomplishes for the believer what the law can not. The Spirit liberates the believer from slavery to sin and moves him to fulfill naturally and spontaneously the law's righteous demands. The Spirit exercises the same power that He used to raise Jesus from the dead in order to produce new life in the believer. Those who live by God's Spirit are God's children and thus heirs who will share in God's glory. The whole creation longs for this glory. The believer longs for adoption through the redemption of the body.

God presently works through every circumstance for the spiritual good of the believer. God's eternal purpose will not be thwarted, and he will unfailingly make those whom He loved from eternity past become like His Son. The completion of the believer's salvation through justification at final judgment and his glorification is certain because it is grounded in God's undying love.

The rejection of Christ by Israel, God's chosen people, might seem to contradict the infallibility of God's promises and shake the believer's hopes. However, God's promises to Israel have not failed. Not all physical descendants of Abraham are true Israelites. God's promises apply to those whom He has chosen. This choice is based not on human character or behavior but God's mysterious purpose.

Still, Israel is fully responsible for its spiritual condition. Gentiles obtained true righteousness by faith. Israel sought righteousness but attempted to establish her own righteousness through obedience to the law rather than faith in Christ. Israel did not find true righteousness despite all her efforts because the law is fulfilled only through faith in Christ. Salvation comes only through faith in Christ as the OT demonstrates.

Gentiles should not assume they have favored status with God. After all elect Gentiles have been saved, God will shift His focus to national Israel again. Great masses of Jews will be saved, because God's gifts and call are irrevocable. God has displayed His mysterious wisdom by using Gentiles and Jews to prompt one another to believe in Christ.

Believers respond to God's mercy by devoting themselves completely to Him and by renewed minds that know God's will. The renewed mind recognizes the interdependency of the members of the church and does not establish a hierarchy based on spiritual gifts. The renewed mind is characterized by love. This love expresses itself through forgiveness, sympathy, harmony, humility, and kindness.

Believers should submit themselves to governing authorities. Governmental authority is appointed by God, preserves order, and thwarts lawlessness. For this reason, believers pay their taxes and show respect for political leaders.

Believers should fulfill the law by expressing love for others. Expressing love to others and living righteously are especially important since we are approaching Christ's return. Believers should accept one another in love even when they disagree over issues of conscience, even as they follow their own consciences. They should be careful not to allow their behavior to disturb other believers who hold different convictions. They should be especially careful not to encourage other believers to do something they do not believe is right. It is wrong to eat, drink, or do anything that disturbs one's conscience.

Jewish and Gentile believers, the weak and the strong, should live in unity and try to build up one another. They should learn to glorify God with one heart and one voice. Jesus himself came into the world as a servant to the Jews, fulfilling the promises to the Jews, and yet including Gentiles in God's plan so that they might glorify God as the OT foretold.

ROME AND THE ROMAN EMPIRE

International rule that the government in Rome, Italy, exercised after 27 BC when the Republic of Rome died and the Roman Empire was born. The first several emperors ruled at the time of the beginning of the Christian movement in the Roman Empire.

Jesus was born during the reign of Augustus (27 BC to AD 14) and conducted His ministry during the reign of Augustus's successor, Tiberius (AD 14 to 37; cp. Luke 3:1). The latter's image was stamped on a silver denarius that Jesus referred to in a discussion about taxation (Luke 20:20-26). In about AD 18 Herod Antipas, the son of Herod the Great,

The famous Colosseum at Rome was built in the latter years of the first century AD.

The Egnatian Way, shown here near Neapolis, was part of the extensive Roman road system.

built his capital on the western shore of the Sea of Galilee and named it Tiberias after the emperor. Tiberius was an extremely able military commander and a good administrator, leaving a large surplus in the treasury when he died. He followed Augustus' example of not expanding the borders of the empire and thus avoiding war. The *pax Romana* (peace of Rome) that Augustus had inaugurated was preserved, providing easy, safe travel throughout the empire. Paul undoubtedly referred to this in Gal. 4:4 when he wrote: "When the completion of the time came, God sent His Son" (HCSB). Tiberius was never popular with the senate and chose to leave Rome at the first opportunity, choosing after AD 26 to rule the empire from his self-imposed seclusion on the Isle of Capri. In this year Pontius Pilate was appointed governor of Judea, a post he held until AD 36, just prior to the death of Tiberius in AD 37.

Tiberius was succeeded by his mentally unbalanced grandnephew, Gaius (Caligula), who proved to be a disaster. During his reign (AD 37–41) and that of his successor, his aging uncle Claudius (AD 41–54), most of the ministry of the Apostle Paul took place. Claudius is reported to have expelled Jews from Rome who were creating disturbances because of Christ (cp. Acts 18:2). Initially, his contemporaries viewed Claudius as inept, but he proved to have considerable hidden talents of administration and turned out to be one of Rome's more proficient emperors. His fourth wife, Agrippina, is mentioned on a recently discovered sarcophagus in the Goliath family cemetery on the western edge of Jericho. She poisoned Claudius in AD 54 to speed up the succession of Nero, her son by a previous marriage.

Nero (AD 54–68) was in some respects worse than Caligula. He was a man without moral scruples or interest in the Roman populace except for exploitation of them. Both Paul and Peter seem to have been martyred during Nero's reign, perhaps in connection with the burning of Rome by Nero in AD 64, an event that he blamed on Christians. The Roman historian Tacitus wrote that when the fire subsided, only four of Rome's 14 districts remained intact. Yet Paul wrote, "All the saints greet you, but especially those from Caesar's household" (Phil. 4:22 HCSB). Nero's hedonism and utter irresponsibility led inevitably to his death. The revolt of Galba, one of his generals, led to Nero's suicide.

Galba, Otho, and Vitellius, three successive emperor-generals, died within the year of civil war (AD 68–69) that followed Nero's death. Vitellius's successor was Vespasian, one of the commanders who had taken Britain for Claudius and who was in Judea squelching the first Jewish revolt. He was declared emperor by the Syrian and Danube legions and returned to Rome to assume the post, leaving his son Titus to finish the destruction of Jerusalem with its holy temple in the next year (AD 70). This event was prophesied by Jesus toward the end of His life when He said: "When you see Jerusalem surrounded by armies, then know that its desolation has come near" (Luke 21:20 HCSB).

The aristocratic Julio-Claudian dynasties that had reigned until the death of Nero were happily replaced by the Flavian dynasty, which issued from the rural middle class of Italy and reflected a more modest and responsible approach to the use of power. Vespasian's reign (AD 69–79) was succeeded by the brief tenure of his son Titus (AD 79–81), who at his death gave way to the rule of his brother Domitian (AD 81–96). The fourth century historian Eusebius reported that the Apostle John was exiled to Patmos (cp. Rev. 1:9) in the reign of Domitian. Eusebius also claimed that in Nerva's reign the senate took away Domitian's honors and freed exiles to return home, thus letting John return to Ephesus.

Nerva's reign was brief, lasting little more than a year (AD 96–98). He was succeeded by Trajan (AD 98–117), who bathed the empire red in the blood of Christians. His persecution was more severe than that instituted by Domitian. Irenaeus wrote in the second century that John died in Ephesus in the reign of Trajan. The persecution of the church, depicted in the book of Revelation, probably reflects the ones initiated by Trajan and Domitian. Trajan, the adopted son of Nerva, was the first emperor of provincial origin. His family roots were in the area of Seville, Spain. Marcus Aurelius, a later emperor of Spanish descent (AD 161–180), also persecuted the church.

ROOT Part of a plant buried in and gaining nourishment through the ground. In Scripture "root" generally appears in a figurative sense. Root of Jesse (Isa. 11:10; Rom. 15:12) and root of David (Rev. 5:5; 22:16) serve as titles of the Messiah. In Paul's allegory of the grapevine, Israel is the root of the plant, the church is the branches (Rom. 11:16-18).

ROSH Personal name meaning "head" or "chief." Seventh son of Benjamin (Gen. 46:21).

ROYAL CITY City having a monarchical government. Gibeon (Josh. 10:2) was compared in size and strength to cities with kings, such as Ai and Jericho. Gath (1 Sam. 27:5) was one of five Philistine cities ruled by kings or lords. Rabbah (2 Sam. 12:26) served as capital of the Ammonite kingdom.

RUDDY Having a healthy, reddish color (1 Sam. 16:12; 17:42; Song 5:10; Lam. 4:7; cp. Gen. 25:25).

RUE (*Ruta graveolens*) Strong-smelling shrub used as a condiment, in medicines, and in charms (Luke 11:42). Dill appears in the Matthean parallel (Matt. 23:23).

RUFUS Personal name meaning "red haired." **1.** Son of Simon of Cyrene and brother of Alexander (Mark 15:21). **2.** Recipient of Paul's greetings in Rom. 16:13. If Mark was written from Rome, both references likely refer to the same person.

RUHAMAH Personal name meaning "pitied." Name Hosea used to symbolize the change in Israel's status before God following God's judgment (2:1; cp. 1:6). First Peter 2:10 applies Hosea's image to Christians who have experienced God's mercy in Christ.

RUMAH Place-name meaning "elevated place." Home of Jehoiakim's mother (2 Kings 23:36), possibly identified with Khirbet Rumeh near Rimmon in Galilee or with Arumah.

RUSH, RUSHES English terms used to translate several types of reedlike plants.

RUST Coating produced by the corrosive effects of air and water on metal, especially iron. Rust on a copper cooking pot symbolized Jerusalem's persistent wickedness in Ezek. 24:6,12-13.

RUTH, BOOK OF OT book whose principal character is a Moabite woman named Ruth, an ancestor of David and Jesus. Given the nature of later Judaism with its denigration of women and its contempt for outsiders, it is remarkable that a biblical book was named for a Moabite woman. This is all the more striking since Ruth is not as important as Boaz and Naomi, and that the book's significance is linked directly to Boaz, as shown in the concluding genealogy.

After reading the book of Judges, which paints a dark and depressing picture of Israel, the reader is relieved to encounter Ruth. One learns that while Israel was in a state of severe moral and spiritual decline, Bethlehem represented an oasis of covenant loyalty in an otherwise barren landscape. Many have recognized in Ruth a supreme literary masterpiece, a delightful short story with a classical plot that moves from crisis (famine and death threaten the existence of a family), to complication (the introduction of a primary but less desirable candidate to resolve the crisis), to resolution (the desirable candidate rescues the family line). With great skill the narrator draws the reader into the minds of the characters (successively Naomi, Ruth, and Boaz), inviting us to identify with their personal anxieties and joys and in the end to celebrate the movement from emptiness and frustration to fulfillment and joy. In the course of the narrative, each of the main characters proves to be a person of extraordinary courage and covenant love (*chesed*, "lovingkindness, faithfulness, loyalty," is the key word in the book: 1:8; 2:20; 3:10). These are people whose spiritual commitment is demonstrated clearly in godly living.

From the perspective of the author, the events of Ruth have significance, primarily because of the critical place these events have in the history of the Davidic line. One of the questions the book answers is, "How can David, the man after God's own heart, emerge from the dark and demoralized period of the judges (cp. 1:1)?" The answer is, "Because of the providential hand of God on this family in Bethlehem."

Ultimately the book of Ruth is about the Messiah. Although the author may not have recognized the full significance of these events, when Matthew begins his Gospel with a long genealogy of Jesus the Messiah, the son of David and Abraham, the names of Boaz and Ruth appear (Matt. 1:5). Three other women in this genealogy (Tamar, v. 3; Rahab, v. 5; Bathsheba, v. 6) are also tainted. The theological significance of these women in this list of men is obvious: Jesus the Messiah represents all the peoples of the earth, and if God can accept Gentiles like Ruth, and incorporate them into His plan of salvation, then there is hope for all (cp. Matt. 28:18-20).

RYE (*Secale cereale*) Hardy grass grown as a cereal (Exod. 9:32 KJV) and cover crop (Isa. 28:25 KJV, NASB). Other translations render the underlying Hebrew as "spelt."

Iron Age sacrificial altar located at the site of ancient Arad.

SABAOTH An intensive title describing God as all-powerful. He is the God without equal (Ps. 89:8) who is present with His people (Ps. 46:7,11). *See Names of God.*

SABBATH Day of rest, considered holy to God because of His rest on the seventh day after creation and viewed as a sign of the covenant relation between God and His people. The day became a time for sacred assembly and worship (Lev. 23:1-3), a token of Israel's covenant with God (Exod. 31:12-17). Jesus' failure to comply with the minute restrictions of the Pharisees about the Sabbath brought conflict (John 5:1-18). At first, Christians also met on the Sabbath with the Jews in the synagogues to proclaim Christ (Acts 13:14). Their holy day, the day that belonged especially to the Lord, was the first day of the week, the day of Jesus' resurrection (Rev. 1:10). They viewed the Sabbath and other matters of the law as a shadow of the reality that had now been revealed (Col. 2:16-23), and the Sabbath became a symbol of the heavenly rest to come (Heb. 4:1-11). See *Lord's Day.*

SABBATH DAY'S JOURNEY Distance a Jew in Jesus' day could walk on the Sabbath without violating its sanctity. The distance was probably just over one-half mile. This phrase appears only once in the Bible (Acts 1:12), describing the distance from the Mount of Olives to Jerusalem.

SABBATICAL YEAR Every seventh year when farmers rested their land from bearing crops to renew the soil (Lev. 25:1-7). Just as the law reserved the seventh day as holy to God, so was the seventh year set aside as a time of rest and renewal. This assured the continued fertility of the land by allowing it to lie fallow, and it also helped the poor. Peasants were allowed to eat from the natural abundance of the untended fields. It is possible that only a portion of the land was allowed to rest each Sabbath year, and the remainder was farmed as usual.

SABEAN Two Hebrew national names. **1.** Descendants of Seba, son of Cush (Gen. 10:7), who were expected to bring gifts signifying loyalty to Jerusalem (Isa. 45:14). God could use the Sabeans to "pay for" Israel's ransom from captivity (Isa. 43:3). **2.** Descendants of Sheba, the son of Raamah (Gen. 10:7b) or Joktan (Gen. 10:28). The rich queen of Sheba visited Solomon (1 Kings 10). Sabeans destroyed Job's flocks and herds and servants (Job 1:15).

SACKBUT A musical instrument (Dan. 3:5 KJV), identified in modern translations as zither (TEV), lyre (NIV), trigon (NASB, NRSV), or triangle (REB). It was apparently a triangular harp with four or more strings.

SACKCLOTH Garment of coarse material fashioned from goat or camel hair and worn as a sign of mourning or anguish (Isa. 58:5). See *Grief and Mourning.*

SACRAMENT Religious rite or ceremony regarded as an outward sign of an inward, spiritual grace. The Roman Catholic Church practices seven sacraments: confirmation, penance, ordination, marriage, last rites, baptism, and the Eucharist. Protestant churches recognize only two: baptism and the Lord's Supper, and these are generally referred to as ordinances rather than sacraments. Unlike sacraments, ordinances are not understood to convey some type of grace. They commemorate the death, burial, and resurrection of Christ. The ordinance of baptism is a believer's public profession of faith and serves as an initiatory rite of entrance into the community of faith. The Lord's Supper denotes a believer's continuing commitment to Christ. The idea that outward signs show spiritual realities is taught in the Bible, but the notion that sacraments convey grace is contrary to Scripture. Grace comes through faith, not works (Rom. 4:3).

SACRIFICE AND OFFERING Physical elements the worshipper brings to God to express devotion, thanksgiving, or the need for forgiveness. Sacrifice was practiced in early OT times. Cain and Abel brought offerings to the Lord from the produce of the land and from the firstborn of the flock (Gen. 4). Upon disembarking from the ark after the great flood, Noah built an altar and offered burnt sacrifices (Gen 8:20). The accounts of the patriarchs in Gen. 12–50 are filled with instances of sacrifice to God. But an organized system of sacrifice does not appear in the OT until after the exodus of Israel from Egypt. In the instructions given for the building of the tabernacle and the establishment of a priestly organization, sacrifices were to be used in the consecration or ordination of the priests (Exod. 29). Leviticus 1–7 gives the most detailed description of Israel's sacrificial system, including five types of sacrifices.

1. Burnt offering This sacrifice was offered in the morning and in the evening, as well as on special days such as the Sabbath, the new moon, and the yearly feasts (Ezra 3:3-6). Rituals performed after childbirth (Lev. 12:6-8), for an unclean discharge (Lev. 15:14-15) or hemorrhage (Lev. 15:29-30), or after a person who was keeping a Nazirite vow was defiled (Num. 6:10-11) required a burnt offering. The animal for this sacrifice could be a young bull, lamb, goat, turtledove, or young pigeon. The person bringing the offering was to lay a hand on the animal, indicating that the animal was taking the person's place, and then he was to kill it. Then the priest burned the animal as a sacrifice. The person who made this sacrifice did so to restore his relationship with God and to atone for his sin.

2. Grain offering ("meat offering," KJV) This sacrifice came from the harvest of the land, and it was the only offering that required no bloodshed. It was composed of fine flour mixed with oil and frankincense. Sometimes it was cooked into cakes before it was taken to the priest. Only a portion of this offering was burned on the altar, with the remainder going to the priests. While no reason is given for the grain offering, it may have recognized the blessings of God, who provided the harvest for the sustenance of life.

3. Peace offering This sacrifice consisted of a bull, cow, lamb, or goat that had no defect. As with the burnt offering, the worshipper killed the animal. The priests then sprinkled its blood around the altar. Only certain parts of the internal organs were burned. The priest received the breast and the right thigh (Lev. 7:28-36), but the person who offered the sacrifice was given much of the meat to prepare as a meal of celebration (Lev. 7:11-21). A peace offering was to be brought in response to an unexpected blessing (a "thank offering") or an answer to prayer (a "vow offering"), or for general thankfulness (a "freewill offering"). The idea of thanksgiving was associated with the peace offering. The "wave offerings" and the "heave offerings" were associated with the peace offerings. They were portions presented or lifted up before the Lord, mentioned first as part of the priestly ordination ceremony (Exod. 29:24-27).

4. Sin offering This sacrifice was made to purify the sanctuary from sin that had been committed unintentionally. If the priest or the congregation of Israel sinned, then a bull was required. A leader of the people had to bring a male goat, while anyone else sacrificed a female goat or a lamb. The poor were allowed to bring two turtledoves or two young pigeons. The same internal organs that were designated for burning in the peace offering were likewise designated in this sacrifice. The rest of the animal was taken outside the camp and burned.

5. Guilt offering This offering was concerned with restitution. It seems to overlap or relate to the sin offering (Lev. 4–5). In Lev. 5:6-7 the guilt offering is called a sin offering. A person who took another's property illegally was expected to repay it in full plus 20 percent of the value and then bring a ram for the guilt offering. Other instances in which the guilt offering was prescribed included the cleansing of a leper (Lev. 14), having sexual relations with the female slave of another person (Lev. 19:20-22), and the renewing of a Nazirite vow that had been broken (Num. 6:11-12).

The NT describes Christ's death in sacrificial terms. Christ is portrayed as the sinless high priest who offered Himself up as a sacrifice for sinners (Heb. 7:27). Christ's sacrifice is superior to the Levitical system because His sacrifice—His death—had to be offered only once.

SADDUCEES See *Jewish Parties in the New Testament*.

SAINTS Holy people, a title for all God's people but applied in some contexts to a small group considered most dedicated to Him. In the OT to be holy is to separate oneself from evil and to dedicate oneself to God. This separation reflects God's character, since He is holy (Lev. 19:2). Holiness is portrayed as an encounter with the living God, which results in holiness of lifestyle (Isa. 6). Therefore, holiness is more than a one-time separating and uniting activity. It is a way of life (Dan. 7:18-28).

In the NT, saints are believers in Christ, or those who name Jesus as Lord. In the book of Revelation, however, where the word "saints" occurs 13 times, the meaning is further defined. Saints not only name Jesus as Lord, but they are faithful and true witnesses for Jesus. To believe in Jesus demands obedience and conformity to His will. A saint bears true and faithful witness to Christ in speech and lifestyle.

SALAMIS Most important city on the island of Cyprus where Barnabas and Paul preached during the first missionary journey (Acts 13:5). See *Cyprus*.

SALEM Abbreviated form of Jerusalem (Gen. 14:18). See *Jerusalem; Melchizedek*.

SALIM Place-name meaning "peace." Town near the site where John the Baptist baptized (John 3:23).

SALMON Personal and place-name meaning "coat." **1.** Father of Boaz and ancestor of David (Ruth 4:21; Matt. 1:5). **2.** KJV spelling of Zalmon (Ps. 68:14).

SALOME Personal name meaning "pacific." Wife of Zebedee and mother of James and John (if one combines Mark 16:1 and Matt. 27:56). She became a disciple of Jesus and was among the women at the crucifixion who helped prepare His body for burial.

SALUTATION Act of greeting, blessing, or welcoming by gestures or words, especially in the opening and closing of letters. The typical greeting in Greek letters was the infinitive "to rejoice." Paul fused the Greek word for the typical Hebrew blessing, "Peace," with the noun form of the Greek blessing, "Grace," to yield the distinctly Christian salutation, "Grace and peace." This salutation invoked mercy from God ("grace") and eternal well-being from God's presence ("peace").

SALVATION Rescue from sin and death. The need for salvation is demonstrated in the first three chapters of the Bible. Adam and Eve disobeyed God in the garden of Eden. Sin entered into God's created order, but God promised salvation through the seed of the woman (Gen. 3:15). Even though male and female were created in the image of God, now God's image was marred in all humankind. The results of sin included death and separation from God.

In the NT salvation by grace alone through faith in the person and work of Jesus Christ is the dominant theme. Salvation begins with the initiating love of God (Eph. 1:3-6). God's eternal purpose is to save sinners through Jesus' atoning death on the cross. Thus, Christology is a vital component of the NT and relates directly to the doctrine of salvation. Jesus' nature as the God-man and His substitutionary death on the cross are the key elements of salvation.

The NT identifies several other key doctrines or elements as part of a complete concept of salvation. The Holy Spirit convicts a person of sin and brings about the new birth. "Conversion" is the term generally used to describe when a person actually receives salvation. This is the point when a person repents and believes. Faith and repentance are the conditions of salvation, according to the NT (Mark 1:15). Repentance means turning from self and sin to God and holiness while faith is believing the historic facts about Jesus and trusting Him alone to forgive sin and to grant eternal life (Heb. 11:1-6).

At the moment of conversion the sinner becomes a saint, not free from sin in this life but free from the death penalty brought on by sin. A lifelong process of growth in Christlikeness called "sanctification" through the work of the Holy Spirit now begins. Thus, salvation is a free gift from God that rescues the believer from sin and its consequences, renews the believer to a holy life, and restores the believer to a right relationship with God for all eternity. See *Conversion; Forgiveness; Grace; Justification; New Birth; Reconciliation; Redeem, Redemption, Redeemer; Repentance; Sanctification.*

SAMARIA, SAMARITANS Place-name of a city and a region meaning "mountain of watching" and the residents of this region. The city of Samaria was founded by Omri, the sixth king of Israel (885–874 BC), when he purchased the hill of Samaria for his royal residence. The name of this city eventually became associated with the surrounding region, or the tribal territories of Manasseh and Ephraim. Finally, "Samaria" became synonymous with the entire northern kingdom (Jer. 31:5).

The name "Samaritans" originally was identified with the Israelites of the northern kingdom (2 Kings 17:29). When the Assyrians conquered Israel and exiled 27,290 Israelites, a "remnant of Israel"

Long colonnaded street built by the emperor Severus at New Testament Sebaste, which was the Old Testament city of Samaria.

remained in the land. Assyrian captives from distant places also settled there (2 Kings 17:24). This led to the intermarriage of Jews of this region with Gentiles and to widespread worship of foreign gods. In the days of Christ, the relationship between the Jews and the Samaritans—whom the Jews considered half breeds and idol worshippers—was strained (John 8:48). The animosity was so great that the Jews bypassed Samaria as they traveled between Galilee and Judea.

Yet Jesus rebuked His disciples for their hostility to the Samaritans (Luke 9:55-56), healed a Samaritan leper (Luke 17:16), honored a Samaritan for his neighborliness (Luke 10:30-37), praised a Samaritan for his gratitude (Luke 17:11-18), asked for a drink of water from a Samaritan woman (John 4:7), and preached to the Samaritans (John 4:40-42). Then in Acts 1:8 Jesus challenged His disciples to witness in Samaria. Philip, a deacon, opened a mission in Samaria (Acts 8:5).

SAMARITAN PENTATEUCH Canon or "Bible" of the Samaritans, who revere the Torah as God's revelation to Moses on Mount Sinai and do not regard the rest of the Hebrew Bible as authoritative. Their Scripture includes Genesis through Deuteronomy with many variant readings from the Masoretic Text or Hebrew text currently used by scholars.

SAMOS An island of Greece visited by the Apostle Paul (Acts 20:15).

Samaritan priests with a copy of their Scripture—the Samaritan Pentateuch.

SAMOTHRACE or **SAMOTHRACIA** Place-name, perhaps meaning "height of Thrace." Mountainous island in the Aegean Sea visited by the Apostle Paul during his second missionary journey (Acts 16:11).

SAMSON Personal name meaning "of the sun." Last of the major judges of Israel about 1100 BC (Judg. 13:1–16:31). Before he was born Samson was dedicated by his parents to be a lifelong Nazirite (Judg. 13:3-7), a person especially consecrated to the Lord. Part of the vow included letting the hair grow and abstaining from wine and strong drink. Samson's legendary strength did not come from his long hair but from the "Spirit of the LORD," who enabled him to perform amazing feats of physical strength against the Philistines, enemies of Israel (Judg. 14:6,19; 15:14).

Samson was a headstrong young man with little self-control who failed to live up to his Nazirite vow. Every major crisis in his life was brought on by his relationships with Philistine women. Samson's fascination with Delilah finally brought his downfall. The Philistine leaders offered her money to find out the source of Samson's strength. She finally coaxed the truth from him, and Samson was captured by his enemies. In his death Samson killed more Philistines than he had killed during his life (Judg. 16:30). He is listed with the heroes of faith in Heb. 11:32 because his strength came from God and he demonstrated his faith in his dying act.

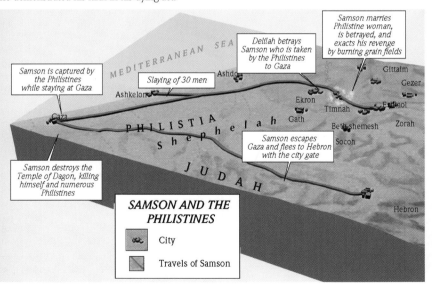

SAMSON AND THE PHILISTINES

SAMUEL Personal name meaning "name of God." Priest and prophet who linked the period of the judges with the monarchy (about 1066–1000 BC). Born in answer to his barren mother's prayer (1 Sam. 1:10), Samuel was dedicated to the Lord before his birth (1 San. 1:11). The priest Eli raised Samuel at the central sanctuary in Shiloh (1 Sam. 2:11). The sins of Eli's sons and the Philistine threat led the elders of Israel to appeal to Samuel to appoint a king for the nation (1 Sam. 8:3,5,20). Samuel warned Israel of the dangers of a monarchy before anointing Saul as Israel's first king (1 Sam. 10:1). Samuel's recording of the rights and duties of kingship (1 Sam. 10:25) set the stage for later prophets to call their monarchs to task for their disobedience of God's commands.

King Saul's stubbornness and disobedience brought Samuel's declaration of God's rejection of his kingship. At God's command, Samuel anointed David as the new king (1 Sam. 16:13). Samuel's death brought national mourning (1 Sam. 25:1; 28:3), and it also left Saul without access to God's word. In desperation he acknowledged Samuel's power and influence by seeking to commune with Samuel's spirit (1 Sam. 28). Thus in life and death Samuel cast a long shadow over Israel and its early experience with an earthly king.

SAMUEL, BOOKS OF Two historical books of the OT named for the Prophet Samuel, the major figure of its opening section. Samuel anointed King Saul as the first king of the nation of Israel and then later anointed David to the same position when Saul proved unworthy. Thus, the books detail the transition of the nation from a loose confederation of tribes to a united kingdom under the leadership of a human king.

SANBALLAT Governor of Samaria around 407 BC who, along with Tobiah and Shemaiah, opposed Nehemiah's rebuilding of Jerusalem (Neh. 4:7-8; 6:1-4).

SANCTIFICATION Process of being made holy and growing into the likeness of Jesus Christ. The idea behind the word is to stand in awe of something or someone. God is separate, or holy, and people dedicated to Him are also to be separate from the world and to reflect His holy nature. In the OT the priests and Levites who functioned in the sanctuary were sanctified to the Lord by the anointing of oil (Exod. 40:12-15). Additionally, the Nazirite was consecrated to God (Num. 6:8), although only for a specified period of time. Finally, the nation of Israel was sanctified to the Lord as a holy people (Deut. 26:19). This holiness was closely identified with obedience to the law of holiness in Lev. 17–26, which includes both ritual and ethical commands.

In the prophets especially, the ethical responsibility of being holy in conduct was prominent. In the NT sanctification is linked to salvation and is concerned with the moral and spiritual obligations assumed in that experience. Believers are set apart to God in conversion, and they live out this dedication to God in holiness (2 Thess. 2:13).

SANCTUARY Place set aside as sacred and holy, especially a place of worship. On sites where the patriarchs had erected altars, the people of Israel later built shrines and temples to commemorate their encounters with God. The tabernacle and the temple in Jerusalem were revered as sanctuaries.

The sandaled foot on a Roman statue.

SANDALS, SHOES Two types of shoes existed: slippers of soft leather and the more popular sandals with a hard leather sole. Thongs secured the sandal across the insole and between the toes. The removal of the sandals of guests and the washing of their dusty feet was the job of the lowliest servant. The Prophet Isaiah walked barefooted to symbolize the impending poverty of Israel before the judgment of God (Isa. 20:2). See *Footwashing.*

SANHEDRIN Highest Jewish council in NT times. The word *Sanhedrin* is usually rendered "council" in English translations of the Bible. The council had 71 members and was presided over by the high priest. The Sanhedrin included representatives from the two main Jewish parties, Pharisees and Sadducees. During the first century the Sanhedrin exerted authority under the watchful eye of the Romans. Generally, the Roman governor allowed the Sanhedrin considerable autonomy and authority. But the trial of Jesus shows that the Sanhedrin did not have the authority to condemn people to death (John 18:31). The Gospels describe the role of the Sanhedrin in the arrest, trials, and condemnation of Jesus. Under the leadership of Caiaphas the high priest, this body plotted to have Jesus killed (John 11:47-53). After His arrest they brought Jesus into the council (Luke 22:66) and used false witnesses to condemn Him (Mark 14:55-56). They sent Him to Pilate and pressured him into pronouncing the death sentence against Jesus (Mark 15:1-15).

SAPPHIRA Personal name meaning "beautiful" or "sapphire." See *Ananias.*

SARA or **SARAH** Variant Hebrew form of name Sarai. See *Sarai.*

SARAI Personal name meaning "princess." Wife of Abraham (Gen. 11:29–25:10) who was barren for many years before giving birth to Isaac. First called Sarai, she was Abraham's half sister, since she had the same father as Abraham. Marriages with half brothers were not uncommon in her time. Sarai traveled with Abraham from Ur to Haran. In her grief over her barrenness, Sarai gave her maid Hagar to Abraham in the hope of a son; but she expressed resentment when Hagar conceived. When Sarai was almost 90 years old, God changed her name to Sarah and promised her a son. A year later, she bore Isaac. At the age of 127, Sarah died at Hebron, where she was buried in the cave in the field of Machpelah near Mamre.

SARDIS City of Asia Minor where one of the seven churches addressed in Rev. 3:1-6 was located. The church was condemned as being "dead," perhaps a reference to its ineffectiveness as a witness in the world.

SARGON King of Assyria who destroyed Samaria and deported the people of Israel to Media and other parts of the Middle East. He was succeeded by his son, Sennacherib.

SATAN Transliteration of Hebrew word meaning "adversary." The Hebrew term appears in Num. 22:22,32; 1 Sam. 29:4; 2 Sam. 19:22; 1 Kings 5:4; 11:14,23,25; Ps. 109:6, normally translated in English as adversary or accuser. In Job 1–2; Zech. 3:2; and 1 Chron. 21:1 the same term is translated as a proper name.

Ruins of the Roman gymnasium at the ancient city of Sardis in Asia Minor (modern Turkey).

SATAN, SYNAGOGUE OF Term used in Revelation (2:9; 3:9) to describe Jewish worshippers who persecuted the church.

SATRAP, SATRAPY Political official who governed a province of the Persian Empire. A satrap's territory was called a satrapy (Ezra 8:36). These officials aided the people of Israel in rebuilding Jerusalem and the temple. See *Persia*.

SATYR Hairy, demonic figure with the appearance of a goat. The Israelites apparently sacrificed to such desert-dwelling demons, although they had a law forbidding such sacrifice (Lev. 17:7). King Jeroboam I of Israel (926–909 BC) appointed priests to serve these demons (2 Chron. 11:15).

SAUL Personal name meaning "asked for." **1.** First king of Israel who reigned about 1020–1000 BC.

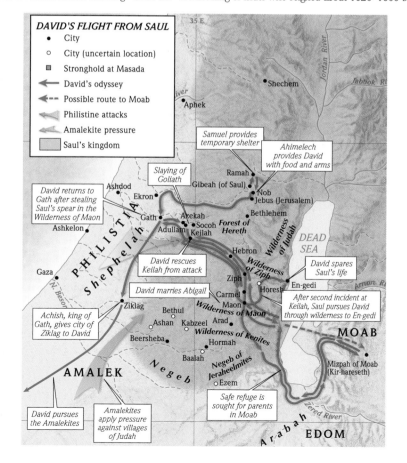

DAVID'S FLIGHT FROM SAUL

- • City
- ○ City (uncertain location)
- ▣ Stronghold at Masada
- ← David's odyssey
- ◄--- Possible route to Moab
- ◄ Philistine attacks
- ◄ Amalekite pressure
- ▢ Saul's kingdom

35 E

Jordan River

Jabbok R.

Shechem

Aphek

Samuel provides temporary shelter

Ahimelech provides David with food and arms

Slaying of Goliath

Ramah

Gibeah (of Saul)

David returns to Gath after stealing Saul's spear in the Wilderness of Maon

Ashdod

Ekron

Nob

Jebus (Jerusalem)

Bethlehem

Gath

Azekah

Socoh

Forest of Hereth

Ashkelon

Adullam

Kyilah

PHILISTIA

Shephelah

DEAD SEA

Wilderness of Judah

Hebron

David rescues Keilah from attack

Wilderness of Ziph

Ziph

Horesh

En-gedi

David spares Saul's life

Gaza

Maon

Carmel

David marries Abigail

Arnon R.

After second incident at Keilah, Saul pursues David through wilderness to En-gedi

Achish, king of Gath, gives city of Ziklag to David

Ziklag

Bethul

Ashan

Kabzeel

Arad

Wilderness of Maon

Beersheba

Wilderness of Kenites

Hormah

MOAB

Negeb

Baalah

Negeb of Jerahmeelites

Ezem

Mizpah of Moab (Kir-haresheth)

AMALEK

David pursues the Amalekites

Amalekites apply pressure against villages of Judah

Safe refuge is sought for parents in Moab

Zered River

Arabah

EDOM

Saul got off to a good start, but his presumptuous offering (1 Sam. 13:8-14) and violation of a holy war ban led to his break with Samuel and rejection by God (1 Sam. 15:7-23). The Spirit of the Lord left Saul and was replaced by an evil spirit that tormented him. David soothed the king by playing the lyre (1 Sam. 16:14-23). After David defeated the giant Goliath, Saul became jealous and fearful of David (1 Sam. 18:6-9,12), eventually making several attempts on his life (1 Sam. 18:10-11,25; 19:1,9-11). His final wretched condition is betrayed by his consultation of the witch at Endor (28:7-8). The following day Saul and three sons were killed by the Philistines on Mount Gilboa (1 Sam. 31). **2.** King of Edom (Gen. 36:37-38). **3.** Son of Simeon (Gen. 46:10). **4.** Kohathite Levite (1 Chron. 6:24). **5.** Hebrew name of the Apostle Paul. See *Paul.*

Sunset over the site of ancient Azekah near the location of a battle between Sau and the Philistines.

SAVIOR One who saves by delivering, preserving, healing, or providing (2 Sam. 22:2-7). God is the only true Savior (Isa. 45:15,21-22). Jesus is also the Savior because He is God incarnate, fully human and fully divine. Christianity is unique among world religions because it portrays salvation by the grace of a savior.

SCALL KJV term for a skin disease (Lev. 14:54). The disease caused head sores, itching, and hair thinning. Modern translations render this word as *scale* or *itch.*

SCAPEGOAT Animal that carried away the sins of the people into the wilderness on the Day of Atonement (Lev. 16:8,10,26). On this one day of the year when the high priest went into the holy of holies to offer sacrifices for the sins of his family and for all the people, two goats were brought before him. One goat was killed as a sin offering and the second was designated for "Azazel." This word is usually rendered as "scapegoat." By laying his hands on the goat's head, the priest transferred the sins of the people to it and then had the goat led away into the desert to symbolize the removal of their sins.

SCARLET Color used especially in clothing, often designating royal honor (Dan. 5:7,16,29).

SCEPTER Official staff or baton of a king that symbolized his authority. The scepter was extended to a visitor or dignitary (Esther 5:2) to signal approval of the visit and allow the person to approach the throne.

SCEVA Jewish "high priest" in Ephesus with seven sons who tried unsuccessfully to exorcise demons in Jesus' name as Paul had done (Acts 19:14). The evil spirit jumped on them instead.

SCHOOL Place and agency for education, particularly of children. Until the exile in Babylon (586 BC) the education of children was centered in the home. During their years of captivity, the exiles assembled on the Sabbath for prayer and worship. As time went by, buildings were erected where the people could meet. These little gatherings were the origin of the synagogue, which ultimately became the center of Jewish religious life after the exile. In the synagogue the scribes taught the law to the people. By AD 200, a school specifically for the education of elementary-age children had become firmly established in the synagogue. Known as Beth-hasepher, the "house of the book," this school was devoted to study of the Jewish written law. Knowledge of the written word, in school as in the home, had the religious goal of bringing about obedience to the law.

SCORN, SCORNFUL Contempt and derision. Scorn is often expressed by laughter (2 Chron. 30:10). In deep trouble, psalmists often felt themselves scorned (Ps. 123:4). When His people are unfaithful to Him, God can scorn them and their worship (Lam. 2:7).

SCORPION Small invertebrate animal known for the venom and sting in its tail. In the wilderness God protected Israel from scorpions (Deut. 8:15).

SCOURGE Severe form of corporal punishment involving whipping and beating. The victim was usually tied to a post or bench, and the beating was administered by a servant of the synagogue (for religious reasons) or by a slave or soldier. Jesus was scourged before His crucifixion (John 19:1).

SCRIBE Person trained in writing skills (1 Chron. 24:6). During the exile in Babylon, educated scribes apparently became the experts in God's written word, copying, preserving, and teaching the law. A professional group of such scribes developed by NT times (Mark 2:16). They interpreted the law, taught it to disciples, and were experts in cases where people were accused of breaking the law of Moses. They led in plans to kill Jesus (Luke 19:47) See *Jewish Parties in the New Testament*.

SCRIPTURE Sacred writings considered God's instruction for believers. New Testament writers often used formulas like "God says" to introduce OT passages. For the NT authors, Scripture was the record of God speaking and revealing Himself to His people. Thus Scripture and God are so closely joined together that these writers could speak of Scripture doing what it records God as doing (Rom. 9:17). Because of their belief in the Scripture's divine origin and content, the NT writers described it as "strongly confirmed" (2 Pet. 1:19 HCSB), "deserving of full acceptance" (1 Tim. 1:15), and "confirmed" (Heb. 2:3). The Bible was written for "instruction" and "encouragement" (Rom. 15:4), to guide people toward godliness (2 Tim. 3:16), and to equip believers for good works (2 Tim. 3:17).

A Torah scroll being held in its wooden case at a celebration in Jerusalem.

Scripture, comprised of 66 books, written by over 40 authors spanning almost 1,500 years, reveals to God's people the unifying history of His redeeming words and acts. The ultimate focus of Scripture is the incarnation and redemptive work of Jesus Christ. He is the center to which everything in Scripture is united and bound together. See *Bible, Formation and Canon; Inspiration of Scripture*.

Dead Sea Scroll fragment.

SCROLL Roll of papyrus (a paper-like material made of the papyrus plant) or parchment (specially treated leather) used as a writing material (Luke 4:17).

SCYTHIANS Nomadic, Indo-European people, referred to in the OT as Ashchenaz (Gen. 10:3).

SEA COW Aquatic herbivorous mammal related to the manatee whose skin is mentioned as a covering for the tabernacle (Exod. 25:5).

SEAL Signet containing a distinctive mark that represented the authority of the person who owned it. Joseph was given the Egyptian pharaoh's ring with his royal stamp of authority, or seal, when Joseph was placed in command of the country (Gen. 41:42). This showed that Joseph had the right to act for the king.

North Syrian and Hittite stamp-type seals.

SECOND COMING Biblical teaching that Christ will return visibly and bodily to the earth to render judgment and complete His redemptive plan. The concept of the second coming originally derived from the OT teachings about a coming Messiah. The prophets foretold the Lord would send One from within the nation of Israel (Jer. 23:5-6) who would not only be God's anointed, but would in fact be God Himself (Mic. 5:2). The NT clearly distinguishes between two comings of Jesus Christ, the Messiah: the first in the incarnation and the second at the end of this present age. The earliest instructions of this second coming are recounted in the Gospels where Christ Himself explicitly claimed He would come again. He urged people to be prepared because He would come unexpectedly, like a thief (Luke 21:34-36). He also promised to return in order to claim His people and reward them (Matt. 25:31-46).

Later, other NT writers expanded Christ's teachings. They taught that He would come in glory to judge unbelievers, Satan, and even the earth itself (Rev. 19:20–20:3). Likewise, He would come in the heavens to gather all believers to Himself by resurrecting the dead, catching them up along with the living into the air to meet Him on His return, and then reward them for their faithfulness (1 Thess. 4:13-17). Because the second coming promised both vindication and salvation, it was a motivation for godly living and became the blessed hope of the early church (1 John 3:2-3).

SECOND DEATH Eternal separation from God. The concept is referred to in Rev. 2:11; 20:6,14; and 21:8. According to Rev. 20:15, it includes being "thrown into the lake of fire. See *Death; Resurrection.*

SECT Group having established their own identity and teachings over against the larger group to which they belong, especially the different parties making up Judaism in NT times.

SECUNDUS Personal name meaning "second." A believer who accompanied Paul when he carried the churches' contributions to the Jerusalem church (Acts 20:4).

SECURITY OF THE BELIEVER Teaching that God protects believers for the completion of their salvation. The Bible teaches that salvation does not depend upon human effort. God is the author of salvation (John 3:16). God justifies sinners who receive Christ in faith (Rom. 3:21-26). Security does not come by absolutions, church attendance, good works, reciting Scripture, or performances of penance. God who has begun the work of salvation in Christians also provides the necessary assurance to bring His work to its completion in the day of Christ (Phil. 1:6). God in Christ protects and keeps believers (2 Thess. 3:3). We do not have the strength to secure ourselves.

The biblical view of assurance or security is rooted in the conviction that when Jesus left the disciples, He did not leave them without support. He promised Christians that he would provide them with a companion Spirit (the Comforter or Paraclete) who would be within them—as much a part of them as their breath (John 14:16-18). The Spirit would be their sense of peace and security, their witness about Jesus, their attorney with the world, and their guide or teacher into all truth (John 14:25-30; 16:8-15).

In raising His Son Jesus, God provided Christians with the sign of the destinies and the basis for their security. As we identify with the power of Christ in the resurrection, we will experience the meaning of the security of the believer in the triumph of God (1 Cor. 15:20-28).

SEIR, MOUNT Place-name meaning "hairy" and thus "thicket." A mountain range that runs the length of biblical Edom. This region was home to Esau and his descendants (Josh. 24:4). Edom was sometimes referred to as Seir (Gen. 36:8). See *Edom.*

SELAH Term of unknown meaning appearing in psalms, outside the book of Psalms only in Hab. 3. The word probably called for a pause or an intensification of instruments or voices in worship.

SELEUCIA A city of Syria visited by Paul during his first missionary journey (Acts 13:4).

SELF-CONTROL Mastery of personal desires and passions. Believers are admonished to exercise self-control (2 Pet. 1:6). Freedom in Christ calls for a self-disciplined life, following Christ's example of being in the world but not of the world.

SELF-ESTEEM Acceptance of oneself as a person created in the divine image. Every person is of great value to God (1 Cor. 6:20) and supremely loved by Him (1 John 4:10). Christians have a new nature that allows them to be self-confident, but only through Christ (2 Cor. 3:5). Paul taught that Christians should strive for a balanced self-esteem that enables them to minister to the needs of others (Rom. 12:3).

SELF-WILLED To do something arbitrarily without divine permission; to act on one's own decision rather than considering the needs of others and the purpose of God. Jacob rebuked Simeon and Levi for wanton, undisciplined actions (Gen. 49:6).

SEMITE A person who claims descent from Noah's son Shem (Gen. 5:32; 10:21-31). Genesis 10:21-31 lists the descendants of Shem. These people spread geographically from Lydia to Syria, to Assyria, to Persia. Armenia formed the northern boundary while the Red Sea and Persian Gulf formed the southern boundary. The Elamites, Assyrians, Lydians, Arameans, and numerous Arab tribes are said to have been descendants of Shem.

SENIR Mountain name meaning "pointed." Amorite name for Mount Hermon (Deut. 3:9). Song of Songs 4:8 may indicate that Senir was a different peak than Hermon in the Anti-Lebanon mountain range or that it indicated the entire range. See *Hermon, Mount.*

SENNACHERIB Assyrian royal name meaning "Sin (the god) has replaced my brother." King of Assyria (704–681 BC) who overran all the fortified cities of Judah except Jerusalem and then demanded tribute payments from King Hezekiah of Judah (2 Kings 18:13–16). See *Assyria.*

Ahab's palace in Samaria. Sennacherib conquered Samaria in 722 BC

SENTRY Government official with responsibility for guarding a prison (Acts 5:23; 12:6) or possibly a captain over such a guard (Jer. 37:13).

SEPARATION Term used for the period when a woman is ritually unclean during menstruation (Lev. 12:2,5) or for a time of refraining from certain activities because of a vow (Num. 6). KJV term for water used to make a person ritually pure or clean (Num. 19).

SEPHARVAIM Racial name of foreign origin. Foreign peoples whom the Assyrians conquered and resettled in Israel to replace the Israelites they deported in 722 BC (2 Kings 17:24).

SEPTUAGINT Title meaning "the 70." Oldest Greek translation of the Hebrew OT. It also contains several apocryphal books. Most NT quotations of the OT are from the Septuagint.

SEPULCHRE Tomb or grave (Gen. 23:6). Sepulchres usually were carved out of the walls in natural caves. Jesus was buried in such a cave (Mark 15:46).

SERAPHIM Literally "the burning ones," seraphim (a plural word) were winged beings who attended God's throne. Isaiah envisioned the seraphim as agents of God who prepared him to proclaim the Lord's message (Isa. 6:2).

SERGIUS PAULUS Proconsul of the island of Cyprus converted to Christ under the preaching of Paul during his first missionary journey (Acts 13:6-12).

SERMON ON THE MOUNT The first of five major discourses by Jesus in the Gospel of Matthew (Matt. 5–7). An exposition of the law and how it meshes with the new covenant in Christ, the sermon also offers a stinging indictment of Pharisaic legalism and cold, formal self-righteousness. Jesus emphasizes His demands for disciples and issues a call to demonstrate a righteousness of heart that the law cannot produce.

The sermon opens with the beatitudes (Matt. 5:3-12) and then moves to describe the witness Christ's disciples are to bear in the world (5:13-16). Jesus' relationship to and interpretation of the

Sea of Galilee at Nof Ginnosar looking across the Sea to the Mount of Beatitudes, traditional site of the Sermon on the Mount.

law follows (5:17-48); then He enumerates some specific acts of righteousness—including the model prayer (6:1-18). The heart attitudes Jesus requires of His disciples comes next (6:19–7:12), and the sermon closes with a challenge to live as true disciples (7:13-27). Jesus addressed His Sermon on the Mount primarily to His disciples, but the rest of the crowd heard it with interest. They marveled at His teaching because, unlike their teachers of the law, He spoke with authority (Matt. 7:28-29).

SERPENT English translation of several biblical words for *snake,* a symbol of evil and Satan. God gave Moses a sign showing His control of the feared serpents (Exod. 4:3; 7:9-10). Jesus accused the Pharisees of being as evil and deadly as serpents (Matt. 23:33).

SERVANT OF THE LORD Title Jesus took up from the OT, especially Isa. 40–55. The term is applied to many leaders of God's people: to Moses over 30 times, to David over 70 times, and to Israel as a nation a number of times. Isaiah 42 gives a remarkable picture of the ideal Servant of the Lord and the great work that God intends Him to accomplish. He is to bring God's justice to all the nations (vv. 1,4). He will move forward with absolute confidence. He will have such an understanding of His power that He can be meek and gentle as He does His work (vv. 2-4).

The Lord Himself called attention to the inability of the nation of Israel to fulfill the picture of the ideal Servant. In verse 19 He says, "Who is blind but My servant, or so deaf as My messenger whom I send?" Israel had a responsibility to fulfill this ideal, but to do so was far beyond its power. Perhaps not all Israel could be meant, because some were blasphemers and idolaters. Could part of Israel be the real Servant? Or might it point to One who must come out of Israel—One who could represent Israel in accomplishing the task?

The NT pictures Jesus as the Suffering Servant fulfilling the glorious descriptions of Isaiah. In refusing to let disciples reveal His true identity, Jesus was the Servant who did not strive or cry out (Matt. 12:14-21). In the resurrection and ascension, God glorified Jesus the Servant (Acts 3:13). The apostles prayed that as God's servants they would speak with boldness and perform miracles through the name of "Your holy Servant Jesus" (Acts 4:29-30). See *Jesus Christ; Slave, Servant.*

SERVICE Work done for other people or for God and the worship of God. Jacob worked for Laban seven years for each of his wives (Gen. 29:15-30). Service could be slave labor (Exod. 5:11), farm work (1 Chron. 27:26), or daily labor on the job (Ps. 104:23). It could be service of earthly kingdoms (2 Chron. 12:8), of God's place of worship (Exod. 30:16), of God's ministers (Ezra 8:20), and of God (Josh. 22:27). Service at its best is worship. This involves the service of temple vessels (1 Chron. 9:28), of worship actions (2 Chron. 35:10), of bringing offerings (Josh. 22:27), and of priestly work (Num. 8:11). The NT speaks of forced service (Matt. 27:32), sacrificial living (Rom. 12:1), slave labor done for Christ's sake (Eph. 6:7), worship (Heb. 12:28), offerings (Rom. 15:31), and personal ministry (1 Tim. 1:12).

SETH Personal name meaning "He set or appointed" or "replacement." Third son of Adam and Eve, born after Cain murdered Abel (Gen. 4:25; 5:3). He was an ancestor of Jesus (Luke 3:38).

SEVEN CHURCHES OF ASIA Original recipients of book of Revelation (Rev. 1:4). See *Asia Minor, Cities of.*

SEVEN WORDS FROM THE CROSS Statements that Jesus made during the six agonizing hours of His crucifixion. (1) He asked forgiveness for those who crucified Him (Luke 23:34). (2) He promised the penitent thief he would meet the Lord in paradise that very day (Luke 23:43). (3) He made provision for the care of His mother by the apostle John (John 19:26-27). (4) His fourth statement was a cry of isolation, quoting Ps. 22:1 (Mark 15:34). (5) His physical agony was expressed in the fifth statement, when He acknowledged His thirst (John 19:28). (6) "It is finished" (John 19:30) was a cry of victory, not defeat. (7) Jesus quoted Ps. 31:5 as He committed His spirit to God (Luke 23:46).

SEVEN, SEVENTH Number of completeness. See *Number Systems and Number Symbolism.*

SEVENTY WEEKS Time spoken of in Dan. 9:24-27, usually understood as 70 weeks of years or 490 years. A prophetic approach to this passage sees the 490 years as a reference to the future coming of Jesus Christ, the Messiah.

SEVENTY YEARS Prophetic and apocalyptic period pointing to the time of Israel's exile in Babylon and to the end of the nation's suffering in Daniel's vision. The prophet Jeremiah predicted that Judah would serve Babylon 70 years (Jer. 25:11). Second Chronicles 36:21 saw the completion of the 70 years in the coming of King Cyrus of Persia to power after his defeat of the Babylonians (538 BC). Daniel meditated on Jeremiah's prophecy (Dan. 9:2) and learned that 70 weeks of years were intended (v. 24).

SEX, BIBLICAL TEACHING ON God created human beings as male and female, both in His own image (Gen. 1:27). Thus, gender is not a biological accident or social construction. The contrast and complementarity between the man and the woman reveal that gender is part of the goodness of God's creation. Modern efforts to redefine or redesign gender are contrary to the Bible's affirmation of maleness and femaleness as proper distinctions. Throughout the Bible, a complementary pattern of relation between man and woman, particularly within the institution of marriage, is presented as the divine intention. Both are equal in dignity and status, but a pattern of male leadership in the home and in the church is enforced by both descriptive and prescriptive passages (1 Tim. 2:8-3:7; 1 Cor. 14:34-38). The Bible places sex and sexual activity within the context of holiness and faithfulness, presenting an honest explanation of God's design for sex and its place in human life and happiness. The biblical writers affirm the goodness of sexuality as God's gift. The Song of Songs is an extended love poem with explicit erotic imagery and language. Sex is affirmed as a source of pleasure and shared intimacy between husband and wife. The Bible also places sexual activity within the context of the marital covenant. Sexual relations are limited to this covenant relationship. All forms of extramarital sexual activity are condemned, including premarital sex (fornication) and adultery (Exod.

20:14; 1 Cor. 6:9-10). At the same time, the husband and wife are ordered to fulfill their marital duties to each other and not to refrain from sexual union (1 Cor. 7:2-5). As human beings we are sexual creatures, and as sexual creatures we are called to honor God with our bodies (1 Cor. 6:15-20). Within the context of the marital covenant, the husband and wife are free to express love for each other, to experience pleasure, and to join in the procreative act of sexual union. This is pleasing to God and is not to be a source of shame.

SHADDAI Transliteration of a Hebrew name for God, often translated "Almighty" (Exod. 6:3). See *Almighty; Names of God.*

SHADRACH Babylonian name of Hananiah, one of Daniel's three friends thrown into a fiery furnace for refusing to worship a graven image set up by King Nebuchadnezzar. The Lord miraculously delivered them (Dan. 3:30). See *Abednego; Daniel; Meshach.*

SHALLUM Personal name meaning "replacer" or "the replaced." **1.** King of Israel (752 BC). He assassinated Zechariah and was, in turn, assassinated by Menahem a month later (2 Kings 15:10-15). **2.** Another name for King Jehoahaz of Judah. **3.** Husband of Huldah (2 Kings 22:14). **4.** A temple gatekeeper (1 Chron. 9:17,19,31). This may be the same as Shelemiah (1 Chron. 26:14) and Meshelemiah 1 Chron. 26:1-14). **5.** A chief priest (Ezra 7:2). **6.** Descendant of Judah (1 Chron. 2:40). **7.** Jeremiah's uncle (Jer. 32:7). **8.** Temple doorkeeper (Jer. 35:4). **9.** Descendant of Simeon (1 Chron. 4:25). **10.** Descendant of Naphtali (1 Chron. 7:13). **11.** Father of Jehizkiah (2 Chron. 28:12). **12.** Porter who agreed to divorce his foreign wife (Ezra 10:24). **13.** Israelite with a foreign wife (Ezra 10:42). **14.** Supervisor of half of Jerusalem who helped Nehemiah rebuild the city walls (Neh. 3:12).

SHALMANESER Personal name meaning "Shalmanu (the god) is the highest ranking one." **1.** Assyrian king who ruled 1274–1245 BC. Records of his military exploits set a precedent that succeeding kings followed. **2.** Shalmaneser II ruled Assyria 858–824 BC. He fought a group of small kingdoms, including Israel, in the battle of Qarqar in 853 BC. Despite claiming victory, Shalmaneser proceeded no farther. **3.** Shalmaneser V ruled Assyria 726–722 BC. He completed the attack on Samaria begun by his predecessor, Tiglath-pileser III. In 722 Israel fell to Shalmaneser (2 Kings 17:6), thus ending the northern kingdom.

Replica of the Black Obelisk of Shalmaneser III (858–824 BC). The obelisk was found in 1846 during excavations at Nimrud, an ancient site south of Baghdad, Iraq.

SHAME AND HONOR Honor and shame were values that shaped everyday life in biblical times. Honor, the primary measure of social status, was based upon ascribed honor and acquired honor. *Ascribed* honor was social standing due to being part of a social unit, principally the family. *Acquired* honor was gained through meritorious deeds or public performance. The public forum provided challenges for gaining or losing honor. A challenge might show the superiority of one person or group over another. A challenge could be ignored if not worthy of response due to social distance between the parties, but a true honor challenge required response. The party recognized as winning gained honor and the other lost honor or social standing.

Shame was not simply the opposite of honor; both positive and negative shame existed. Shame could be handled positively by knowing how to keep matters out of public awareness. For example, a woman could bear shame well by remaining covered in public and by avoiding male dominated areas. Shame could also designate dishonor or loss of honor. When people claimed an undeserved place of honor, shame resulted (Luke 14:7-11).

Perhaps the most vivid honor/shame text in the Bible is Phil. 2:5-11. Jesus had unquestionable ascribed honor; yet He gave it all up and took the most humble of all honor bases (a slave) and died the most shameful of all deaths, crucifixion. But God gave Him the highest of all honor positions and a name above all names on the honor scale, causing everyone to bow before Him. The honor code thus defined by God instead of men.

SHAMGAR Judge of Israel who killed 600 Philistines with an ox goad, a metal-tipped pole (Judg. 3:31).

SHAPHAN Personal name meaning "coney." Scribe and treasurer under King Josiah of Judah who delivered the book of the law that had been discovered in the temple to the king's palace (2 King 22:14).

SHARD Pottery fragment found in archaeological excavations and used for dating.

SHARON, PLAIN OF Geographical name meaning "flat land" or "wetlands." **1.** Fertile coasta plain between Mt. Hermon and the city of Joppa along the Mediterranean Sea (1 Chron. 27:29) **2.** Area of uncertain location east of the Jordan River inhabited by the tribe of Gad (1 Chron. 5:16)

SHEAF Harvested grain bound together into a bundle. Joseph's dream featured sheaves still in the field (Gen. 37:7). The prophets used sheaves as figures of judgment (Zech. 12:6).

SHEAR-JASHUB Symbolic personal name meaning "a remnant shall return." Name given by the Prophet Isaiah to his first son, probably to show that a remnant would survive the fall of Judah to foreign power (Isa. 7:3–4). See *Isaiah*.

SHEATH Protective holder for sword attached to a belt.

SHEBA, QUEEN OF Ruler of the Sabeans who visited King Solomon of Judah (1 Kings 10) to test his wisdom, learn about his God, and enhance trade relations.

SHECHEM Personal name and place name meaning "shoulder" or "back." District and city in the hill country of Ephraim in north central Palestine Shechem makes its earliest appearance in biblical history in connection with Abram's arrival in the land of Canaan (Gen. 12:6-7). When Jacob returned from Paddan-aram, he settled down at Shechem and purchased land from the sons of Hamor (33:18-19). In Gen. 33–3 Shechem was the name of the city and also of the prince of the city. When the Israelites conquered Canaan, Joshua buil an altar on Mount Ebal (Josh. 8:30-35 Shechem was a city of refuge (Josh. 20:7

Shechem. Here between Mount Gerazim and Mount Ebal, Joshua led Israel to renew their commitment to the Law of Moses.

and a Levitical city (Josh. 21:21). Joshua led Israel to renew its covenant with God there (Josh. 24:1-17

Rehoboam, successor to King Solomon, went to Shechem to be crowned king over all Israe (1 Kings 12:1). Later, when the nation divided into two kingdoms, Shechem became the first cap tal of the kingdom of Israel (1 Kings 12:25). Samaria eventually became the permanent political cap ital of the northern kingdom, but Shechem retained its religious importance. It apparently was a sanc tuary for worship of God in the prophet Hosea's time about 750 BC (Hos. 6:9).

SHEEP A prominent animal in the sacrificial system of Israel. Sheep are first mentioned in Gen. 4: where Abel is identified as a keeper of sheep. The sheep of the Bible usually are the broad-tailed var ety. The tail, weighing as much as 15 pounds, was sometimes offered as a sacrifice. Sheep were als a source for food and clothing. Symbolically, sheep portrayed people without leadership (1 King 22:17), innocent people not deserving of punishment (1 Chron. 21:17), and helpless people facin slaughter (Ps. 44:11,22). Straying sheep illustrate human sin (Isa. 53:6), but the silent lamb facin slaughter prepares the way for Christ's sacrifice (Isa. 53:7). The search for one lost sheep depict God's love for His people (Luke 15).

SHEEPFOLD Place where sheep were kept (Gen. 49:14).

SHEET English translation of Greek word meaning "a linen cloth" and usually used for ships' sail Such a cloth held all the clean and unclean animals in the vision that taught Peter that God offe salvation to all people, not just the Jews (Acts 10:11).

SHEKEL Hebrew weight of about four-tenths of an ounce. This became the name of a silver coi of that weight. See *Weights and Measures*.

SHEKINAH Transliteration of a Hebrew word that speaks of God's presence. The term mean "that which dwells," and is implied throughout the Bible whenever it refers to God's nearnes (Exod. 13:21).

SHEM Personal name meaning "name." Noah's oldest son and original ancestor of Semitic people including the Israelites (Gen. 5:32). Through his line came Abraham and the covenant of blessing.

SHEMA Transliteration of a Hebrew imperative meaning "hear" (Deut. 6:4) and a name for the central statement of the Jewish law. The Shema became for the people of God a confession of faith by which they acknowledged the one true God and His commandments. Later worship practice combined Deut. 6:4-9; 11:13-21; and Num. 15:37-41 into the larger Shema as the summary of Jewish confession. When Jesus was asked about the "greatest commandment," He answered by quoting the Shema (Mark 12:29).

SHEMAIAH Personal name meaning "Yahweh heard." **1.** Prophet in the days of King Rehoboam of Judah whose message from God prevented war between Israel and Judah about 930 BC (1 Kings 12:22). His preaching humbled Rehoboam and the leaders of Judah, leading God not to permit Shishak of Egypt to destroy Jerusalem (2 Chron. 12). **2.** False prophet among Babylonian exiles who opposed Jeremiah (Jer. 29:24-32). **3.** Descendant of David and Zerubbabel (1 Chron. 3:22). **4.** Member of tribe of Simeon (1 Chron. 4:37). **5.** Member of tribe of Reuben (1 Chron. 5:4). **6.** A Levite (Neh. 11:15). **7.** A Levite (1 Chron. 9:16). **8.** Head of one of the six Levitical families under David (1 Chron. 15:8,11). **9.** Levitical scribe who recorded the priestly divisions under David (1 Chron. 24:6). **10.** Head of an important family of gatekeepers (1 Chron. 24:4-8). **11.** Levite in time of King Hezekiah of Judah. (2 Chron. 29:14). **12.** Head of a family that returned with Ezra from Babylonian exile (Ezra 8:13). **13.** Priest married to a foreign woman (Ezra 10:21). **14.** Man married to a foreign woman (Ezra 10:31). **15.** Keeper of east gate who helped Nehemiah repair Jerusalem's wall about 445 BC (Neh. 3:29). **16.** Prophet whom Tobiah and Sanballat hired against Nehemiah (Neh. 6:10-12). **17.** Original ancestor of a priestly family (Neh. 10:8; 12:6,18). **18.** Leader of Judah who participated with Nehemiah in dedicating the rebuilt walls of Jerusalem (Neh. 12:34). **19.** Priest who helped Nehemiah dedicate the walls (Neh. 12:42). **20.** Priest whose grandson helped Nehemiah dedicate the walls (Neh. 12:35). **21.** Levitical musician who helped Nehemiah dedicate the walls (Neh. 12:36). **22.** Father of the Prophet Urijah (Jer. 26:20). **23.** Father of an official at King Jehoiakim's court (Jer. 36:12). **24.** Levite in days of King Jehoshaphat who taught God's law to the people (2 Chron. 17:8). **25.** Levite in days of King Josiah (2 Chron. 35:9).

SHEMER Personal name meaning "protection, preservation." **1.** Head of clan from the tribe of Asher (1 Chron. 7:34). **2.** Original owner of the hill for whom the city of Samaria was named (1 Kings 16:24). See *Samaria, Samaritans.*

SHEMINITH Musical direction meaning "the eighth," used in titles of Pss. 6; 12; and in 1 Chron. 15:21. It may designate the instrument to be used in worship.

SHEOL Abode of the dead, both righteous and wicked, in Hebrew thought. It was thought to be deep within the earth (Amos 9:2) and was entered by crossing a river (Job 33:18). Sheol is pictured as a city with gates (Isa. 38:10), a place of ruins (Ezek. 26:20), or a trap (2 Sam. 22:6). It is sometimes personified as a hungry beast (Hab. 2:5) with an open mouth and an insatiable appetite. Sheol is described as a place of dust (Ps. 30:9) and of gloom and darkness (Job 10:21).

Though the overall picture of Sheol is grim, the OT nevertheless affirms that God is there (Ps. 139:8) and that it is impossible to hide from God in Sheol (Job 26:6). The OT also affirms that God has power over Sheol and is capable of ransoming souls from its depths (Job 33:18,28-30). In the majority of these passages a restoration to physical life is clearly intended, though several (e.g., Ps. 49:15 with its image of God's receiving the one ransomed from Sheol) point the way toward the Christian understanding of afterlife with God.

SHEPHERD Keeper of sheep. The Hebrew word for shepherding is often translated "feeding." Shepherds led sheep to pasture and water (Ps. 23) and protected them from wild animals (1 Sam. 17:34-35). Shepherds took care of their sheep and even carried weak lambs in their arms (Isa. 40:11). The word *shepherd* came to designate not only persons who herded sheep but also kings (2 Sam. 5:2) and God Himself (Ps. 23:1). The prophets referred to Israel's leaders as shepherds (Ezek. 34). Humble shepherds were the first people to visit Jesus at His birth (Luke 2:8-20). Jesus spoke of Himself as "the good shepherd" who would lay down His life for His sheep (John 10:7-18).

SHESHBAZZAR Babylonian name probably meaning "may Shamash (sun god) protect the father." Jewish leader who accompanied the first group of exiles from Babylon to Jerusalem in 538 BC (Ezra 1:8). King Cyrus of Persia apparently appointed Sheshbazzar governor of restored Judah and supplied his company of people with provisions and many of the treasures that the Babylonians had taken from Jerusalem. He attempted to rebuild the temple (Ezra 5:16).

SHETHAR-BOZENAI or **SHETHAR-BOZNAI** (KJV) Persian name, perhaps meaning "Mithra is deliverer." Persian provincial official who questioned Zerubbabel's right to begin rebuilding the temple in Jerusalem (Ezra 5:3,6).

SHEWBREAD Sacred bread that was set before the Lord in the tabernacle and temple as a continual sacrifice (Exod. 25:30). The old bread that it replaced was then eaten by the priests (Lev. 24:5-9).

SHIBBOLETH Hebrew password meaning "ears," "twigs" or "brook." People of Gilead east of the Jordan River used it to detect people of the tribe of Ephraim from west of the Jordan since the Ephraimite dialect evidently did not include the *sh* sound. The Ephraimites always said, "Sibboleth," a word not used elsewhere in Hebrew (Judg. 12:6).

SHIGGAION Technical term used in psalm titles (Ps. 7), possibly calling for an increased tempo in singing.

SHILOH Place-name, perhaps meaning "tranquil" or "secure." City about 30 miles north of Jerusalem that served as Israel's religious center for more than a century after the conquest of Canaan. At the tabernacle in Shiloh, Hannah vowed that if the Lord would give her a son she would give him back to God (1 Sam. 1). After the birth of Samuel, Hannah brought him to Shiloh in gratitude to God (1 Sam. 1:24-28). Shiloh became home for Samuel as he lived under the care of Eli, the high priest of Israel. Eventually Jerusalem became the capital city of Judah and the city where the ark was kept. The Bible gives no information on

Ruins of an ancient synagogue at the site of the city of Shiloh.

what happened to Shiloh. According to archaeological evidence, Shiloh apparently was destroyed about 1050 BC by the Philistines. Supporting this theory is the fact that when the Philistines returned the ark of the covenant to Israel, it was housed at Kiriath-jearim rather than Shiloh (1 Sam. 7:1). The prophet Jeremiah warned Jerusalem that it might suffer the same destruction as Shiloh (7:12).

SHIMEI Personal name meaning "my being heard." **1.** Grandson of Levi and head of a Levitical family (Num. 3:18). **2.** A Levite (1 Chron. 23:9). **3.** A relative of King Saul who cursed and opposed David as he fled from Absalom (2 Sam. 16). When David returned after Absalom's death, Shimei met him and pleaded for forgiveness and mercy, which David granted because of the festive occasion (2 Sam. 19). Solomon followed David's advice and had Shimei executed (1 Kings 2). **4.** Court personality who refused to support Adonijah against Solomon in the struggle for the kingship (1 Kings 1:8). **5.** District supervisor in territory of Benjamin responsible for supplying Solomon's court one month each year (1 Kings 4:18); he could be identical with 4. above. **6.** Ancestor of Mordecai, the cousin of Esther (Esther 2:5). **7.** Brother of Zerubbabel (1 Chron. 3:19). **8.** Member of tribe of Simeon (1 Chron. 4:26). **9.** Member of tribe of Reuben (1 Chron. 5:4). **10.** A Levite (1 Chron. 6:29). **11.** A Benjaminite (1 Chron. 8:21). **12.** Temple musician under David (1 Chron. 25:17). **13.** Supervisor of David's vineyards (1 Chron. 27:27). **14. and 15.** Two Levites under King Hezekiah (2 Chron. 31:12-13). **16.** Levite married to a foreign wife (Ezra 10:23). **17. and 18.** Two Jews married to foreign women (Ezra 10:33,38).

SHIN Next to last letter of Hebrew alphabet used as title for Ps. 119:161-168. Each verse of the section begins with this letter.

SHINAR, PLAIN OF Place-name of uncertain meaning. In the Bible it refers to Mesopotamia (Gen. 10:10). The tower of Babel was built in Shinar (Gen. 11:2-9).

SHIPHRAH Personal name meaning "beauty." Israelite midwife in Egypt who disobeyed Pharaoh and saved the baby Moses (Exod. 1:15-21).

SHIPMASTER Captain in charge of a ship (Jon. 1:6).

SHISHAK Egyptian royal name of unknown meaning. A pharaoh of Egypt who invaded Jerusalem and took away the temple treasures (1 Kings 14:25-26). Some equate him with the pharaoh whose daughter married King Solomon (1 Kings 3:1) and who later burned Gezer and gave it to his daughter (1 Kings 9:16). See *Egypt*.

The yellow blooms of a modern variety of the acacia (shittim) tree in Israel.

SHITTIM Transliteration of a Hebrew word for acacia trees. **1.** Area in Moab where the Israelites camped before crossing into the promised land. **2.** In Joel 3:18 the symbolic meaning of acacias (note NASB) comes to the fore in the messianic picture of fertility for the Kidron Valley.

SHOA National name meaning "help!" A nation used by the Lord to punish His people (Ezek. 23:23).

SHOBACH Personal name of uncertain meaning. Commander of the Syrian army killed by David's troops (2 Sam. 10:16,18).

SHOPHAR Ceremonial ram's horn used to call the people of Israel together (Exod. 19:16). The shophar was to be blown on the Day of Atonement in the Jubilee Year to signal the release of slaves and of people from indebtedness. It was also used as a war trumpet.

SHOSHANNIM Transliteration of Hebrew word meaning "lotuses." Technical term used in titles of Pss. 45; 60; 69; 80, perhaps referring to the tune or melody to which these psalms were to be sung.

SHOVEL Instrument used to remove ashes from the altar in the tabernacle (Exod. 27:3).

SHRINE Small building devoted to the worship of a pagan god. Sometimes shrines were located in larger temples, set apart by a partition or niche in a wall. An Ephraimite, Micah, had a shrine in Israel during the days of the judges (Judg. 17:5).

SHROUD Long pieces of cloth wound around a body for burial. Spices were placed within the folds of the shroud. After His crucifixion, Jesus' body was buried in this manner by Joseph of Arimathea (Matt. 27:59-61).

SHULAMITE or **SHULAMMITE** Description of woman in Song 6:13, either as from Shunem; or from Shulam, an otherwise unknown town; or Solomonite, referring to a relationship to Solomon; or a common noun meaning "the replaced one."

SHUNEM, SHUNAMMITES Place-name and clan name of uncertain meaning. The town of *Shunem* was located southeast of Mount Carmel in the territory of Issachar. The Israelites controlled it under Joshua (Josh. 19:18). As David lay dying, Abishag the *Shunammite* was hired to minister to the king (1 Kings 1:3). The Prophet Elisha stayed often at the home of a Shunammite couple, prophesied that a son would be born to them, and raised the boy from the dead (2 Kings 4).

The Wilderness of Shur.

SHUR, WILDERNESS OF Place-name meaning "wall." Region on Egypt's northeastern border where the Israelites made their first stop after crossing the Red Sea (Exod. 15:22).

SHUSHAN Persian place-name meaning "lily" or "lotus." The throne city of King Ahasuerus of Persia, generally referred to as *Susa* in modern translations. Shushan was the Persian king's winter residence (Esther 1:2).

SIBLING RIVALRY Tensions and fighting among brothers or sisters, including Cain and Abel (Gen. 4:1-16); Shem, Ham, and Japheth (Gen. 9:20-27); Jacob and Esau (Gen. 25:22–28:9); Leah and Rachel (Gen. 29:16–30:24); Joseph and his brothers (Gen. 37; 39–45); Er and Onan (Gen. 38:1-10); Moses, Aaron, and Miriam (Num. 12:1-15); Abimelech and Jotham (Judg. 9:1-57); David and Eliab (1 Sam. 17:28-30); Absalom and Amnon (2 Sam. 13:1-39); and Solomon and Adonijah (1 Kings 1:5-53). In each case one, or usually both, of the siblings attempted to gain status or favor over the other. The psalmist praised the goodness and pleasantness of brothers who are able to dwell together in unity (Ps. 133:1-3).

SICKLE Curved blade of flint or metal used to cut down stalks of grain. The sickle is often used symbolically to speak of coming judgment. Revelation 14 uses the analogy of Christ reaping the harvest of mankind at the great judgment.

SIDON AND TYRE Phoenician cities located on the coastal plain between the mountains of Lebanon and the Mediterranean Sea (Gen. 10:15). Sidon and Tyre were ancient cities, having been founded long before the Israelites entered Canaan. Sidon seems to have been the more dominant of the two cities during the early part of their histories, but Tyre eventually surpassed Sidon. Both cities were known for their maritime exploits and as centers of trade. Israel had relations with the two cities, but especially with Tyre. David employed Tyrian stonemasons and

The harbor at Sidon in the modern state of Lebanon.

carpenters and used cedars from that area in building his palace. (2 Sam. 5:11). The construction of the temple in Jerusalem during Solomon's reign depended heavily on the materials and craftsmen from Tyre.

SIEGE Battle tactic in which an army surrounded a city and cut off all supplies so the enemy army was forced to surrender for lack of food and water. Judah suffered siege from King Sennacherib of Asssyria (2 Kings 18–19) and from King Nebuchadnezzar of Babylon (2 Kings 24–25).

SIEGEWORKS Platforms or towers built by an army around and above the city walls of a city under siege. This allowed the besieging army to shoot arrows and throw missiles of war into the city.

SIEVE Instrument used to remove foreign matter from sand or grain. Pebbles or straw remained in the sieve, while the sand or grain passed through. God warned Israel that He would place them in a sieve of judgment from which no one would escape (Amos 9:9).

SIGN Symbol, action, or occurrence that points to something beyond itself. In the OT signs often refer to miraculous intervention by God. They can point to knowledge of God, such as the events of the exodus (Deut. 4:34). Signs can reinforce faith through remembrance of His mighty deeds, such as memorial stones from the Jordan River (Josh. 4:6). Signs can also point to God's covenant with His people. These include the rainbow (Gen. 9:12), circumcision (Gen. 17:11), the Sabbath (Exod. 31:13), and the wearing of phylacteries on the wrist and forehead (Deut. 11:18).

In the NT Luke records signs at the birth of Jesus. The "baby wrapped snugly in cloth" (HCSB) was a sign to the shepherds that verified the angels' announcement (Luke 2:12), and Simeon prophesied that Jesus Himself was a sign, one who would be opposed by many people (Luke 2:34). While signs can point to God's work, Jesus condemned the demand of the Pharisees for signs to prove that God was working through Him (Matt. 12:39). The only sign they would be given was the sign of Jonah, a reference to His death and resurrection. In the Gospel of John, Jesus tells those following Him after the feeding of the 5,000, "You are looking for Me, not because you saw signs, but because you ate the loaves and were filled" (John 6:26). They saw the signs Jesus performed but did not perceive their significance that He was the Son of God. While signs point to God and His Son Jesus, they are not enough by themselves to bring a person to saving faith.

SIHON Amorite personal name of unknown meaning. Amorite king who opposed Israel's passage through his country as they journeyed toward the promised land. He was defeated when he attacked the Israelites (Num. 21:21–30).

SILAS, SILVANUS A leader in the early Jerusalem church, Silas carried news of the Jerusalem conference to the believers at Antioch (Acts 15:22). He and Paul left Antioch together on a mission to Asia Minor (15:40-41) and later to Macedonia. In Philippi they were imprisoned (16:19-24), but they later won the jailer and his family to the Lord after God delivered them from prison. Later in his ministry Silas teamed with Peter on missions to Pontus and Cappadocia. He also served as Peter's scribe, writing the first letter from Peter and perhaps other letters.

SILENCE Silence is a sign of reverence to God (Hab. 2:20), a symbol of death (Ps. 94:17), a symbol of Sheol (Ps. 115:17), and an expression of despair (Lam. 2:10).

SILK Cloth made from thread that came from the Chinese silkworm. Some interpreters feel that the Hebrew word translated "silk" should be "fine linen" or "expensive material" (Ezek. 16:10), the Hebrew indicating something glistening white.

SILOAM Place-name possibly meaning "sending" or "sent." This place is easily confused with the

waters of *Shiloah* mentioned in Isa. 8:6. *Siloam* was the pool created by King Hezekiah's tunnel that diverted the waters of Shiloah from the Siloam spring to a point inside the city walls of Jerusalem. John 9:7,11 uses the etymological significance of the term "Siloam" for a play on words to press the point that the blind man was "*sent*" to Siloah by one who was Himself the One who was "*sent.*" To gain his sight, the blind man obeyed the Sent One. The pool of Siloam is still in use today.

SILVANUS See *Silas, Silvanus.*

SILVER A precious metal. The Bible refers to the process of refining silver (Prov. 17:3). In most of the OT it is given a priority over gold. Only in Chronicles and Daniel is gold considered to have more worth. Silver coins were first minted after 700 BC, but weight was the most common standard for determining their value. In the NT period, the drachma, a silver coin, was required for the temple tax. Figuratively, refining silver refers to the testing of human hearts (Isa. 48:10) and the purity of God's word (Ps. 12:6). Wisdom is declared to be of more value than silver (Job 28:10-15).

The Siloam Pool in Jerusalem.

SILVERSMITH Person who works with silver, either refining silver from the ore or making refined silver into the finished product (Acts 19:23-41). Silver was used for making money and religious images (Judg. 17:4) and many of the utensils used in the tabernacle and temple (Num. 7:13).

SIMEON Personal name meaning "hearing" or possibly "little hyena beast." **1.** One of Jacob's 12 sons (Gen. 29:33). Joseph held his brother Simeon as a prisoner to ensure that the other brothers would bring Benjamin to Egypt (Gen. 42:24). **2.** Devout Jew who was promised by the Lord that he would not die before seeing the Christ (Luke 2:25). When Joseph and Mary brought Jesus to the temple for the purification rites, Simeon announced God's plan for the boy (2:34). **3.** Ancestor of Jesus (Luke 3:30). **4.** Prophet and teacher in church at Antioch (Acts 13:1). **5.** Alternate form in Greek for *Simon,* original Greek name of Peter.

SIMON Greek personal name meaning "flat-nosed." Used in NT as Greek alternative for the Hebrew "Simeon." **1.** The father of Judas Iscariot (John 6:71). **2.** One of Jesus' disciples; a son of Jonah (Matt. 16:17) and brother of Andrew. After he confessed Jesus as the Christ, the Lord changed his name to Peter (v. 18). See *Peter.* **3.** Pharisee who hosted Jesus at a dinner (Luke 7:36-40). Simon learned valuable lessons about love, courtesy, and forgiveness after a sinful woman anointed Jesus at this event. **4.** Native of Cyrene who was forced to carry Jesus' cross to Golgotha (Mark 15:21). **5.** Tanner of animal skins who lived in the seaport of Joppa. Peter stayed at his house (Acts 9:43), where he received a visionary message from God declaring all foods to be fit for consumption (10:9-16). **6.** Jesus' disciple, also called "the Canaanite" (Matt. 10:4) or the Zealot (Luke 6:15). **7.** Half brother of Jesus (Matt. 13:55). **8.** Leper who hosted Jesus and saw a woman anoint Jesus with costly ointment (Matt. 26:6-13). **9.** Magician from Samaria who believed Philip's preaching, was baptized, and then tried to buy the power of the gospel (Acts 8:9-24).

The traditional area of the home of Simon the tanner in ancient Joppa (modern Jaffa near Tel Aviv).

SIN Actions by which humans rebel against God and miss His purpose for their lives. The cause of estrangement from God is sin, the root cause of humanity's problems. The Bible describes sin as rebellion against God. Rebellion was at the root of the problem for Adam and Eve (Gen. 3) and has been at the root of humanity's plight ever since.

The OT affirms that God established the law as a standard of righteousness, so any violation of this standard is defined as sin. Breach of the covenant between God and man is also caused by sin (Deut. 29:19-21). The OT also pictures sin as a violation of the righteous nature of God. As the righteous and holy God, He sets forth as a criterion for His people a righteousness like His own. (Lev. 11:45). Any deviation from God's righteousness is viewed as sin.

In the NT sin is defined against the backdrop of Jesus as the standard for righteousness. His life exemplifies perfection. The exalted purity of His life creates the norm for judging what is sinful. Sin is also viewed as a lack of fellowship with God. Jesus taught that sin is a condition of the heart. He traced sin to inner motives, stating that the sinful thought leading to the overt act is the real sin. Anger in the heart is the same as murder (Matt. 5:21-22). The impure look is tantamount to adultery (Matt. 5:27-28). The real defilement in a person stems from the inner person (heart), which is sinful (Matt. 15:18-20). Sin, therefore, is understood as involving the essential being of a person—the essence of human nature.

The NT also interprets sin as unbelief—not just the rejection of a dogma or a creed but rejection of that spiritual light that has been revealed in Jesus Christ. The outcome of such rejection is judgment. The only criterion for judgment is whether a person has accepted or rejected the revelation of God as found in Jesus Christ (John 16:8-16). Death is a by-product of sin. Continual, consistent sin will bring spiritual death to any person who has not come under the lordship of Christ through repentance and faith (Rom. 6:23). Christ has negated the power of Satan and has freed people from slavery to sin and death (Heb. 2:14-15.)

The desolate country of the Wilderness of Sin.

SIN, WILDERNESS OF Barren region in the Sinai Peninsula where the Israelites stopped on their journey from Egypt to the promised land (Exod. 16:1). Here God provided manna and quail for them to eat.

SINAI, MOUNT Mountain in northwestern Arabia where God made many revelations of Himself and His purposes to Israel, including the giving of the Ten Commandments to Moses (Exod 19:1–3). The Bible uses the term *Sinai* for both the mountain and the entire wilderness area where the Israelites settled for a time after the exodus from Egypt (Lev. 7:38). The term *Horeb* is often used to refer to Sinai. Since Horeb means "waste" or "wilderness area," it seems best to think of Horeb as the general term for the area and Sinai as the specific peak where God revealed Himself to Moses. The modern name for the traditional site of Sinai is Jebel Musa (the mount of Moses). However, several other mountains in different locations have been suggested as the site of biblical Sinai.

Above: Jebel Musa, the traditional site of Mount Sinai, in the southern Sinai Peninsula. Left: a view of the surrounding rugged landscape.

SINEW Tendons and tissue that connect muscles to bone. Isaiah spoke of sinew in a figurative way to show rebellion against God (Isa. 48:4). The angel who wrestled with Jacob struck the sinew of his thigh. To commemorate this event, the Jews cut away this sinew from meat and did not eat it (Gen. 32:24-32).

SINNER Person who has missed God's mark for life, rebelling against Him. The Bible considers every person a sinner (Rom. 3:23). In the OT people who do not live by the law were considered sinners (Ps. 1). Paul spoke of sinners as those separated from God (Rom. 5:8). See *Law; Salvation; Sin.*

SIRION Sidonian name for Mount Hermon (Deut. 3:9). See *Hermon, Mount.*

SISERA Personal name meaning "mediation." **1.** Military leader of Jabin, king of Canaan (Judg. 4:2) who was killed by Heber's wife, Jael (v. 21). **2.** Nethinim descendant who returned to Judah with Zerubbabel (Neh. 7:55).

SISTER A general term for any close female relative, including a sister or stepsister (2 Sam. 13:2). The word *sister* was also used of people held in special esteem as a counterpart to brotherly affection (Song 4:9). See *Family; Woman.*

SITNAH Well dug by Isaac's servants near the city of Gerar (Gen. 26:21). The well was seized by the servants of Abimelech; therefore the name meaning "hatred" or "opponent."

SIVAN Third month (May–June) of the Hebrew calendar, the time of wheat harvest and Pentecost.

SKIN The human skin is often mentioned in relation to disease (Lev. 13). God made clothing from animal skin for Adam and Eve (Gen. 3:21). Animal skins were also used to make containers for liquids (Matt. 9:17). The skin is spoken of in several proverbial sayings: "Skin for skin" (Job 2:4), "the skin of my teeth" (Job 19:20), and "Can the Ethiopian change his skin?" (Jer. 13:23).

SLANDER To speak critically and maliciously of another person (Lev. 19:16). In a court of law, it means to accuse another person falsely (Deut. 5:20). Slander is a mark of the unregenerate world (1 Pet. 3:16). Jesus called Satan "a liar and the father of liars" (John 8:44 HCSB).

SLAVE, SERVANT In the first Christian century, one out of three persons in Italy and one out of five elsewhere were slaves. Many were domestic and civil servants. Some slaves were highly intelligent and held responsible positions. A person could become a slave as a result of capture in war, default on a debt, being sold as a child by destitute parents, conviction of a crime, or kidnapping and piracy.

Slavery laws appear in Exod. 21:1-11; Lev. 25:39-55; and Deut. 15:12-18. A Hebrew sold to another Hebrew or a resident alien because of indebtedness was to be released after six years of service. A Hebrew who sold himself to another Hebrew or resident alien was to be released during the Jubilee Year. A slave could be redeemed at any time by a relative. A Hebrew girl sold by her father to another Hebrew to become his wife was to be released if that man or his son did not marry her. A slave permanently maimed by his or her master was to be freed (Exod. 21:26-27).

In the New Testament Paul and Peter insisted that Christian slaves should be obedient to their masters (Eph. 6:5-8; 1 Pet. 2:18-21) and not seek freedom because of their conversion (1 Cor. 7:20-22). Masters were urged to be kind to their slaves (Col. 4:1). Neither Jesus nor the apostles condemned slavery. Slavery was so much a part of their society that to call for abolition would have resulted in violence and bloodshed. But Jesus and the apostles did set forth principles of human dignity and equality that eventually led to abolition of the practice.

Jesus adopted a servant's role (Mark 10:45) and indicated that His disciples should do the same (Luke 17:10). Paul referred to himself as a slave or servant of Jesus Christ (Phil. 1:1).

SLEEP Regenerative rest (Ps. 4:8). God causes "deep sleep," sometimes for revelation (Job 4:13) and sometimes to prevent prophetic vision (Isa. 29:10). Sleep is also spoken of metaphorically as a sign of laziness (Prov. 19:15) and physical death (1 Cor. 15:51). See *Death; Eternal Life.*

SLING, SLINGERS, SLINGSTONES Weapon consisting of two long straps with a piece between them at the end to hold a stone. Shepherds and professional soldiers used slings.

SLOTHFUL Loose, undisciplined. The slothful person becomes subjected to another's rule (Prov. 12:24). The wise, hardworking ant illustrates the opposite of sloth (Prov. 6:6). Jesus condemned an evil, lazy slave (Matt. 25:26) but praised and rewarded the "good and faithful slave" (Matt. 25:23 HCSB).

SMYRNA Major city on the west coast of Asia Minor and site of one of the seven churches addressed in Rev. 2:8-11. See *Asia Minor, Cities of.*

SNAIL Animal whose name apparently means "moist one." It illustrates the brevity of life (Ps. 58:8; HCSB, "slug").

SNARE Trap for birds and animals. Figuratively,

Ruins of the forum at the site of the ancient city of Smyrna in Asia Minor (modern Turkey).

snares spoke of danger and destruction (Ps. 18:5). See *Fowler; Hunt, Hunter.*

SNOW Palestine rarely has snow, although one snowfall is recorded in the Bible (2 Sam. 23:20). The word is used figuratively of whiteness (Isa. 1:18), cleanness (Job 9:30), and refreshing coolness (Prov. 25:13).

SNUFFERS Two different instruments—tongs and cutting tools—used to tend the lamps in the tabernacle and temple (Exod. 25:38).

SOAP Cleaner used to wash the body (Jer. 2:22) and to launder clothes (Mal. 3:2).

SOBER Characterized by self-control, seriousness, and sound moral judgment (1 Pet. 1:13). The KJV at 2 Cor. 5:13 used "sober" to mean in one's right mind.

SODOM AND GOMORRAH Place-names of uncertain meaning. Two cities in Canaan at the time of Abraham that were destroyed by the Lord because of their wickedness. Sodom and Gomorrah were probably situated in the Valley of Siddim (Gen. 14:3,8,10-11) near the Dead Sea. Abraham's nephew Lot settled in Sodom (Gen. 19:1). Despite Abraham's plea (18:22-32), not even 10 righteous men could be found in Sodom, and the cities were destroyed by the Lord (Gen. 19:24). The unnatural lusts of the men of Sodom (Gen. 19:4-8; Jude 7) have given us the modern term *sodomy.* The memory of the

Bab Edh Dhra, believed by many archaeologiests to be ancient Sodom and Gomorrah.

destruction of these two cities provided a picture of God's judgment (Jer. 49:18) and made them an example to be avoided (Deut. 29:23-25).

SODOMITE Originally a citizen of the town of Sodom, a city destroyed by the Lord because of its wickedness (Gen. 13:12). The term came to mean a male who has sexual relations with another male. The wickedness of Sodom became proverbial (Gen. 19:1-11). See *Homosexuality.*

SOLDIER In early Israelite history every male was called on to fight when the tribes were threatened. David was the first to assemble a national army made up of professional soldiers. The NT warrior was usually the Roman soldier. See *Centurion.*

SOLOMON David's son and successor as king of Israel. He is remembered most for his wisdom, his building program—including the temple in Jerusalem—and his wealth generated through trade and administrative reorganization. In addition to building the temple (1 Kings 5–8), Solomon fortified a number of cities that helped provide protection to Jerusalem, built "store-cities" for stockpiling the materials required in his kingdom, and established military bases for charioteers (1 Kings 9:15-19). Solomon divided the country into administrative districts and had the districts provide provisions for the central government. This system made it possible for Solomon to accumulate vast wealth.

Solomon had faults as well as elements of greatness. His "seven hundred wives, princesses, and three hundred concubines" came from many of the kingdoms with which Solomon had treaties (1 Kings 11:1,3). He apparently allowed his wives to worship their native gods and even had altars to these gods constructed in Jerusalem (1 Kings 11:7-8). Rebellions led by the king of Edom, Rezon of Damascus, and Jeroboam, one of Solomon's own officers, indicates that Solomon's reign was not without its turmoil. His oppressive taxation policies led the northern tribes to rebel and establish their own nation known as the northern kingdom of Israel (1 Kings 12:1–17).

SOLOMON'S PORCH The raised outermost part of the temple in Jerusalem during NT times (Acts 3:11). It is called "the portico of Solomon" (NASB, NRSV, REB) and "Solomon's Colonnade" (HCSB, NIV), since Solomon's workers constructed at least the oldest portico on the east side. See *Temple of Jerusalem.*

SON OF GOD Term used to express the deity of Jesus as the one, unique Son of God. Jesus conceived of His divine sonship as unique, as indicated by such assertions as "the Father and I are one" (John 10:30 HCSB) and "the Father is in Me and I in the Father" (John 10:38). He frequently referred to God as "My Father" (John 15:15). At Jesus' baptism and transfiguration, God the Father identified Jesus as His Son. The term "Son of God" is closely associated with Jesus' royal position as Messiah.

Paul emphasized the salvation that Jesus provided (Rom. 1:4), and the author of Hebrews focused on Jesus' priesthood (Heb. 5:5). All of these are related to His position as Son of God.

SON OF MAN

Expression found in both the OT and the NT. "Son of Man" is used in these ways: (1) as a poetic synonym for "man" or "human," as in Pss. 8:4 and 80:17; (2) in Ezekiel as the title by which God regularly addresses the prophet (2:1,3; 3:1,3); and (3) in Dan. 7 as the identity of the glorious person whom the prophet sees coming with the clouds of heaven to approach the Ancient of Days. "The Son of Man" is a designation of Christ found frequently in the NT. It was Jesus' favorite designation of Himself to imply both His messianic mission and His full humanity.

SONG OF SONGS, SONG OF SOLOMON

Collection of romantic

SOLOMONS
BUILDING ACTIVITIES
● City
○ City (uncertain location)
● City (modern name)
Hazor City built or rebuilt by Solomon
● Cities and towns showing building/
rebuilding in the 10th century B.C.
▢ Fortified by Solomon
■ Fortified enclosures
—— Major routes
—— Other routes
▨ Territory ceded to Hiram of Tyre

Source of timbers used in construction of Temple of Yahweh

Casting of bronze vessels

Construction of the temple of Yahweh, palace and city

Built fortress and agricultural settlements

Built fortress, port and ships

poetry that may have been written by King Solomon or on behalf of him. Solomon or "king" is mentioned in the book several times (1:1,4-5,12; 3:7,9,11; 7:5; 8:11-12), but scholars remain uncertain about its author. This book has been interpreted allegorically or symbolically in the past, but most modern scholars prefer a literal reading of the Song. Like Gen. 2:23-25, the Song celebrates God's gift of physical love between man and woman. Here the Creator's wisdom and bounty are displayed. The Song is an example of Israel's wisdom poetry (see Prov. 5:15-20; 6:24-29; 7:6-27; 30:18-20).

SONS OF THE PROPHETS Members of a band or guild of prophets. "Sons of" refers to membership in a group or class and does not imply a family relationship. This phrase occurs often in the book of 2 Kings, where the prophet Elisha is portrayed as the leader of the prophetic guild. The sons of the prophets functioned either as witnesses (2 Kings 2:3,5,7,15) or as agents of Elisha's ministry (2 Kings 9:1-3).

SOP A small piece of bread that could be dipped in a dish or wine (John 13:26-30 KJV). A host honored a guest by dipping a piece of bread into the sauce of the main dish and handing it to the guest. Most interpreters feel that Jesus was making His last appeal to Judas to change his mind about betraying Him when He handed Judas a piece of bread at the Last Supper. See *Judas*.

SOPATER Personal name meaning "sound parentage." A believer who accompanied Paul on his final trip to Jerusalem (Acts 20:4). Some feel he is the same as "Sosipater" in Rom. 16:21.

SORCERER Person who practices sorcery or divination.

SORROW Emotional, mental, or physical pain or stress. Trouble and sorrow were not meant to be part of the human experience. Humanity's sin brought sorrow into the world (Gen. 3:16-19). Sorrow can lead a person to a deeper faith in God; or it can cause a person to live with regret, centered on the experience that caused the sorrow. Jesus gave believers words of hope to overcome trouble and sorrow "In the world you have suffering. Be courageous! I have conquered the world" (John 16:33 HCSB).

SOSIPATER Personal name meaning "to save one's father." A kinsman of Paul who sent greetings to the Christians at Rome (Rom. 16:21). "Sopater . . . from Beroea" (Acts 20:4 HCSB) may be the same person.

SOSTHENES Personal name meaning "of safe strength." A ruler of a synagogue in Corinth who was beaten by a mob when the Apostle Paul was arrested (Acts 18:17).

SOUL The word *soul* has had a varied and complex constellation of meanings. Though it is often used to refer to the inner part of the person, or the non-physical aspect of being, it is used in other ways in Scripture. In the OT soul means primarily "life" or "possessing life." It is used of both animals (Ezek. 47:9) and humans (Gen. 2:7). The word sometimes indicates the whole person, as for instance in Gen. 2:7 where God breathes breath into the dust and thus makes a "soul." A similar usage is found in Gen. 12:5 where Abram takes all the "souls" (persons) who were with him in Haran and moves to Canaan. The word is also used in the OT to refer to the inner life, psychological or spiritual state of the human person (Ps. 42:12). The word also refers to the source of emotion in Job 30:25: "Was not my soul grieved for the needy."

In the NT the soul is often equated with the total person (Rom. 13:1). Soul also indicates the emotions or passions (John 10:24). The soul is also referred to as something that is distinguishable from the physical existence of a person (Matt. 10:28). Scripture clearly teaches that persons continue to exist consciously after physical death. Jesus pointed out that as the God of Abraham, Isaac, and Jacob He is the God of the living. These people still live, their souls having returned to God (Eccles. 12:7). In addition, Paul equated being absent from the body with being present with Christ. Whether it is the "immaterial" aspect of the soul that is consciously alive with God after death, awaiting resurrection completeness, or whether believers exist in some kind of physical form, uninterrupted existence is certain (2 Cor. 5:1-10).

SOVEREIGNTY OF GOD Biblical teaching that God possesses all power and is the ruler of all things (Dan. 4:34-35). God works according to His eternal purpose, even through events that seem to contradict His rule. Scripture testifies to God's rule over His creation (Rom. 8:20-21), including Christ's sustaining and governing of all things (Heb. 1:3). The Bible affirms also that God rules human history according to His purpose, from ordinary events in the lives of individuals (Prov. 16:9,33) to the rise and fall of nations (Acts 17:26). Scripture also depicts redemption as the work of God alone. God takes the initiative in the provision and application of salvation and in enabling man's willing acceptance (2 Tim. 1:9-10). See *God; Providence.*

An Arab farmer near Bethlehem sowing seeds on his land.

SOWER Person who sowed seed, as in the parable of the sower told by Jesus (Matt. 13:3-9; Luke 8:4-8).

SPAIN Country still known by that name in the south west corner of Europe. Paul wanted to go to Spain (Rom. 15:24,28). See *Tarshish.*

SPAN Half a cubit. A cubit is the length of the arm from the elbow to the tips of the fingers—about 18 inches See *Weights and Measures.*

SPARROW A small bird. Jesus used sparrows (Luke 12:7) to show how God loves human beings. The God who cares for all of His creation, even the insignificant sparrow, certainly cares for people.

SPECK Modern translation of KJV "mote." See *Mote.*

SPELT Wheat of poor quality. Spelt had not sprouted when the plagues struck Egypt (Exod. 9:32) Spelt illustrates the farmer's planning, placing it on the outer edge of the field to retard the intrusion of weeds (Isa. 28:25).

SPICES Aromatic, pungent substances used in the preparation of foods, sacred oils for anointings, incense, perfumes, and ointments used for personal hygiene and for burial of the dead. Expensive and highly prized, spices were brought into Palestine from India, Arabia, Persia, Mesopotamia, and Egypt. Solomon had an extensive commercial venture with Hiram, king of Tyre, dealing in spices and other commodities. Some of the most important spices were:

Aloe Spice used to perfume garments and beds (Ps. 45:8). The extract from its leaves was mixed with water and other spices to make ointment for the anointing of the dead.

Balsam This product of Gilead was exported to Egypt and Tyre. The resin from this desert plant was used for medicinal and cosmetic purposes (Jer. 46:11).

Cassia The dried bark or blooms of this plant were used in the preparation of the anointing oil; the pods and leaves were used as medicine (Exod. 30:24).

Cinnamon Highly prized plant, used as a condiment, in the preparation of perfumes (Prov. 7:17) and in the holy oil for anointing (Exod. 30:23).

Coriander Aromatic seed used as a spice in food; its oil was used in the manufacture of perfume. The Israelites compared the manna to the coriander seed (Num. 11:7).

Cumin This seed was used as a spice in bread. (Isa. 28:23-28).

Dill Seed and leaves of this plant were used to flavor foods and as medicine to wash skin wounds (Matt. 23:23; KJV, "anise").

Frankincense Resin of a tree that produced a strong aromatic scent. Frankincense was used in the preparation of the sacred oil for anointing of kings and priests and for the sacrifices in the temple. The wise men from the East presented frankincense to Jesus (Matt. 2:11).

Galbanum Fragrant resin that was one of the ingredients of the holy incense (Exod. 30:34).

Henna Plant used as a cosmetic; its leaves produced a dye (Song 4:13; KJV, "camphire").

Mint Leaves of the mint plant were used as a condiment (Luke 11:42).

Myrrh Resinous gum of a plant that was included in the preparation of the holy anointing oil (Exod. 30:23). It was also used for its aromatic properties (Ps. 45:8) and for female purification (Esther 2:12). Myrrh was given to Jesus at His birth as a gift (Matt. 2:11) and as a drink when He was on the cross (Mark 15:23).

Onycha A type of cress used in holy incense (Exod. 30:34).

Rue Herb used as a condiment. Valued for its medicinal properties, its leaves were used to treat insect bites (Luke 11:42).

Saffron Substance of a plant that produced a yellow dye and was used to color foods. When mixed with oil, it was used as medicine and perfume (Song 4:14).

Spikenard Expensive fragrant oil used in perfumes and ointments. Also translated as "perfume" and "nard." A woman anointed Jesus with this expensive perfume (John 12:3).

Stacte Small tree which produced a resin used in the sacred incense (Exod. 30:34).

SPIDER Animal known for spinning a web. The spider's web is cited as a sign of frailty (Job 8:14).

SPINDLE In spinning, the stick around which spun thread was wrapped (Prov. 31:19, KJV). See *Cloth, Clothing.*

A bedouin woman spinning wool into yarn.

SPINNING AND WEAVING Making thread and cloth were familiar processes in biblical times. Thread was spun from raw fibers. Flax (Ezek. 40:3) and wool (Lev. 13:47) were the major fibers used. Raw fibers were pulled into a loose strand and twisted to form a continuous thread. A spindle (2 Sam. 3:29 NRSV) was a slender stick that could be twirled to twist drawn-out fibers caught in a hook or slot at the top. The finished product could then be used for weaving cloth (Exod. 35:25-26). Weaving was done on looms (Judg. 16:13-14). Weavers apparently were professionals who specialized in particular types of work. The OT differentiates between ordinary weavers, designers, and embroiderers (Exod. 35:35).

SPIRIT The word *spirit* is used of both God and human beings. In His conversation with Nicodemus (John 3), Jesus said that the Spirit is like the wind because a person cannot see it but can see its effects. This is true of both the Spirit of God and the spirit of a human being. At the beginning of creation, the Spirit of God hovered over the waters (Gen. 1:3). The Spirit of God is everywhere. The psalmist sensed that no matter where he was, God's Spirit was there (Ps. 139:7). Moses realized that the Spirit of God was on him, and he desired that God's Spirit be on all of His people (Num. 11:29). During the period of the Judges, the Spirit of the Lord came to people and empowered them to accomplish specific tasks (Judg. 11:29). Likewise, the Spirit came upon David when Samuel anointed him as king (1 Sam. 16:13).

Each of the four Gospels has numerous references to the Spirit of God or the Holy Spirit. The Spirit was the agent of Jesus' miraculous conception (Matt. 1:18,20), came down on Jesus at His baptism (Matt. 3:16), led Him into the wilderness where He was tempted by the devil (Matt. 4:1), and enabled Him to heal diseases and cast out demons (Matt. 12:28). Jesus promised the Spirit to His followers as He prepared to leave the world. The Spirit would serve as Comforter and Counselor, continuing to teach Jesus' followers and reminding them of what He had said to them (John 14:25-26). Not many days after Jesus' ascension, the promised Spirit came upon His followers during the Feast of Pentecost. The advent of the Spirit was accompanied by a sound that was like a mighty wind. The Holy Spirit empowered and guided the followers of Jesus in their mission to the world (Acts 11:12).

In both the OT and NT, *spirit* is associated with a wide range of human functions, including thinking and understanding, emotions, attitudes, and intentions. Elihu told Job it was spirit in a person, the breath of God, that gave understanding (Job 32:8). Caleb had a different spirit than most of his contemporaries because he followed the Lord wholeheartedly (Num. 14:24). A person's spirit can be contrite (Ps. 34:18), steadfast (Ps. 51:10), willing (Ps. 51:12), broken (Ps. 51:17), and haughty (Prov. 16:18).

SPIRITS IN PRISON First Peter 3:19 declares that Christ "went and made a proclamation to the spirits in prison" (HCSB). Peter further says that they "in the past were disobedient, when God patiently waited in the days of Noah." These must have been people whom God destroyed in the flood and who were in hell or hades. Christ probably preached to these persons "in the spirit" through Noah while they were still alive.

SPIRITUAL GIFTS God-granted empowerment of believers for carrying out the work of ministry in the church. In the two lengthiest discussions of these *gifts,* Paul emphasizes the diversity that is to be found in the church, the body of Christ, as reflected in the various spiritual gifts (1 Cor. 12:1-31; Rom. 12:3-8).

Some gifts are spectacular in their manifestation. Gifts of miracles (1 Cor. 12:28-29) refer to the power by which the lordship of Christ over all of reality is demonstrated. "Message of wisdom" (1 Cor. 12:8 HCSB) has to do with the ability to speak a word of wise counsel in any difficult situation. Many in the NT demonstrated remarkable gifts of healing, and these manifestations were among "the signs of an apostle" (2 Cor. 12:12). "Distinguishing between spirits" (1 Cor. 12:10) may refer to the ability to detect evil spirits (Acts 16:16-18) or the ability to have a discerning heart in dealing with spiritual needs (1 Cor. 2:14).

Other gifts are more "normal" and might not seem to come directly from God. These include teaching, service, administration, helping, and mercy. But Paul makes it clear in his analogy of the body that these "less honorable" (1 Cor. 12:23) gifts are just as important as the more visible and spectacular gifts. Though the gifts are many, the Spirit who grants them is one. God has given many different gifts to the church, since the needs of the Christian community are complex. Gifts entail ministry. All Christians have tasks to perform in the service of the Lord in the church.

SPIT, SPITTLE Spitting at or on someone is a sign of contempt. The soldiers who mocked Jesus before His crucifixion spat on Him (Matt. 27:30). But Jesus used spittle to heal a blind man (John 9:6).

SPOIL Items taken from the enemy by a victorious army. In ancient warfare a soldier could take anything he could carry that had belonged to a foe. Holy war laws dedicated all such booty to God (Deut. 20).

SPOON Shallow dish or bowl in which incense was burned in the tabernacle and temple (Num. 7:14 KJV).

SPORTS Several games of skill are alluded to in the Bible. Jacob's combat at Peniel may have been a wrestling match between two skilled fighters (Gen. 32:24-32). The fight at the pool of Gibeon between the soldiers of Abner and the soldiers of Joab may have begun as a show of strength through wrestling (2 Sam. 2:12-17). Foot races are alluded to in Ps. 19:5. Paul mentions Greco-Roman gladiatorial bouts, the most gruesome of all entertainment events (1 Cor. 15:32). The NT uses various games as figures of the Christian life. Paul often spoke of his work on behalf of the gospel as "running" (Gal. 2:2; 5:7) and compared the spiritual discipline required for successful living to that required for winning foot races and boxing matches (1 Cor. 9:24-27).

SPOT Skin blemish that made a person ceremonially unclean (Lev. 13:1-8). In the sacrificial system, only animals "without spot" (Num. 28:3 KJV) could be used for an offering to God. See *Sacrifice and Offering.*

STABLE Place where animals are sheltered. King Solomon kept large numbers of horses in stalls, or stables (1 Kings 4:26). Jesus was born in a stable, perhaps a cave where animals were kept (Luke 2:7). See *Manger.*

STACHYS Personal name meaning "head of grain." A fellow believer in Rome greeted by Paul (Rom. 16:9 HCSB).

STACTE Gum of the storax tree which was combined with other elements to make the incense burned in the tabernacle (Exod. 30:34). See *Incense.*

STAG Modern translation of "hart," an adult male deer.

STAIRS Steps on which a person can climb to another level. Houses in Palestine usually had stairs to the roof on the outside. The steps in Jacob's dream about a ladder may have been stairs (Gen. 28:12).

STAKE Wooden peg used to anchor a tent. It was used figuratively of Jerusalem (Isa. 33:20).

STALL Place where animals were kept and fed.

STANDARD Flag or banner used to identify groups of soldiers or a central flag to rally all the soldiers at one time (Num. 1:52; 2:2). This word is also used figuratively of God (Isa. 59:19).

STARS Constellations, planets, and all heavenly bodies except the sun and the moon. God is acknowledged to be the Creator of the stars (Gen. 1:16) as well as the One who knows their names and numbers (Ps. 147:4). Probably the most famous of all the stars mentioned in Scripture is the star of Bethlehem (Matt. 2). Scripture does not name the star. It is one of many miracles that attest to the power of God. In the final book of the Bible, the Lord Jesus is called "the Bright Morning Star" (Rev. 22:16 HCSB).

STATUTE Law or commandment. Different divine statutes were given by Moses to God's people (Exod. 15:25-26).

STEADFASTNESS Patient endurance. A steadfast person is reliable, faithful, and true to the end (Rom. 15:3-5). Trials that test our faith produce steadfastness (James 1:3 KJV).

STEEL KJV translation of a word that most modern versions translate as "bronze" (2 Sam. 22:35).

STEPHANAS Greek name meaning "crown." A believer in Corinth baptized by Paul (1 Cor. 1:16).

STEPHEN Personal name meaning "crown." The first Christian martyr. Stephen was so mighty in the Scriptures when he argued that Jesus was the Messiah that his Jewish opponents could not refute him (Acts 6:10). He accused the Jewish leaders of rejecting God's way as their forefathers had done (Acts 6:12–7:53). Saul of Tarsus heard Stephen's speech to the Jewish Sanhedrin and saw him die a victorious death. Stephen may have been the human agency that God used to transform Paul into the great Christian missionary.

St. Stephen's Gate (Lion's Gate) at Jerusalem.

STEWARDSHIP Responsibility to manage all the resources of life for the glory of God. The biblical concept of stewardship, beginning with Adam and Eve and developed more fully in the NT, is that God is owner and provider of everything. Since all belongs to Him, it should be used for His purposes. A collective responsibility was given to mankind to have dominion over the earth, care for it, and manage it for His glory. The believer is to seek the mind and will of God for every decision, whether financial resources, property, time, or influence. God not only expects us to return a portion of what He gives us as tithes and offerings; He expects us to use all that we have to His glory.

STOCKS Wooden frame which secured the feet and hands of prisoners (Job 33:11). The Romans often added chains along with the stocks.

STONE Hardened mineral matter comprising much of the earth. Palestine is a stony country. Often it was necessary to clear a field of stones to prepare it for cultivation (Isa. 5:2). An enemy's fields were marred by throwing stones on them. Stones were used for construction, including city walls (Neh.

4:3), dwellings (Lev. 14:38-40), palaces (1 Kings 7:1,9), temples (1 Kings 6:7), pavement in court yards, and columns (Esther 1:6). The Israelites often heaped up stones to commemorate some great spiritual event or encounter with God (Gen. 31:46). Symbolically, a stone denotes hardness or insen sibility (1 Sam. 25:37). The followers of Christ were called living stones that were built up into the spiritual temple of Christ. Christ Himself became the chief cornerstone (1 Pet. 2:4-8).

Storage rooms, or storehouse, excavated at Tel Beersheba in the Negev.

STOREHOUSE, STORAGE CITY Storehouses were built early in human history to protect harvested crops. Special sections of Israelite towns were designated as storage areas, with several storehouses lining the streets. During the divided kingdom period, royal storage facilities were established in regional capitals to collect tax payments made in flour, oil, grain, or wine. A full storehouse was a symbol of God's blessing (Mal. 3:10).

STORK Long-legged bird noted for its care of its young and for returning each year to the same nesting area. It was ceremonially unclean (Lev. 11:19). See *Birds*.

STRAIGHT STREET A street in Damascus where Paul stayed after his dramatic conversion (Acts 9:10-12).

STRANGER See *Alien*.

STRAW Stalks left after the grain has been stripped. Straw was usually used as bedding for animals. The Israelites were forced to make bricks without straw in Egypt (Exod. 5:6-13).

STREETS The layout of city streets was often determined by the shape of the defensive walls. In some cities a wide street followed the line of the wall. In other

The street called Straight in Damascus, Syria.

towns, streets radiated from a main plaza or thoroughfare. Streets were often paved with large, flat stones, although dirt paths were not uncommon. During the NT era, Roman engineers designed cities throughout the empire with wide, straight streets, usually leading to a central plaza or temple. Paul lodged in a house on Straight Street in Damascus after his conversion (Acts 9:11).

STRONG DRINK Intoxicating drink made from grain. It was denied to priests (Lev. 10:8-9) and those who took the Nazirite vow (Num. 6:3).

STUMBLING BLOCK Anything that causes a person to stumble or fall. The term is usually used metaphorically. Paul warned Christians not to let their freedom become a stumbling block to other believers (1 Cor. 8:9). The disobedient are warned that Jesus Himself could be a stumbling block (Rom. 9:32-33).

SUBMISSION, SUBORDINATION Voluntary placement of oneself under the authority and leadership of another. First Corinthians 11:3-10 teaches the headship of the husband in marriage and bases this instruction on the creation account. Ephesians 5:22-33 instructs wives to submit to the authority of their husbands, while husbands should love their wives. Peter also exhorts the wife to submit to her husband and cautions that the husband's authority should be exercised with understanding and honor toward his wife (1 Pet. 3:1-7). This structure, when balanced with Gen. 1:26-27, demonstrates that men and women are equal before God but different in their role and function

The relationship between Christ and the church is a paradigm for submission and authority in marriage (Eph. 5:22-33). The church willingly submits herself to Christ, her designated head (Col. 1:18). Christ loves the church and gave Himself for her (Eph. 5:25-27). All human beings are required to submit to God (Isa. 45:23). The Bible also teaches submission to God-appointed leaders (1 Pet. 5:1-5). Human beings are required to submit to governmental authorities (Rom. 13:1-7). Children should submit to their parents (Eph. 6:1-4).

SUBURBS Pastureland around cities that were used as common lands, or open range, for the grazing of livestock (Lev. 25:34 KJV).

SUCCOTH Place-name meaning "booths." **1.** A town whose leaders were punished by Gideon for not helping him in a campaign against the Midianites (Judg. 8:5-7,13-16). **2.** Place where the Israelites camped upon leaving Egypt (Num. 33:5-6).

SUFFERING The Bible asserts that suffering is inevitable in a fallen world (Acts 14:22). People have always asked, "Why does God allow suffering?" Scripture gives no comprehensive explanation. God's reasons and purposes transcend human knowledge, and we cannot always understand suffering. At times we must trust God without understanding (Job 42:2-3). We will not have complete answers until eternity (Rom. 8:18).

One cause of suffering is sinfulness (Hos. 8:7). Misuse of God's gift of freedom, beginning with the fall of Adam and Eve and continuing in all persons, brings devastating consequences (Rom. 3:23). However, the assumption that suffering is always the direct result of sin is wrong (John 9:1-3). Some evil and suffering transcend human depravity and are caused by Satan and demonic forces (Eph. 6:10-13). Another explanation for suffering is that God either sends or allows suffering to discipline and bring maturity to His people. Suffering reminds us of our finitude and teaches us to trust God (Job 1:9-12). Believers should not suffer with resignation but with hope (1 Pet. 5:8-11). Through hope in the resurrection, Christians can endure their suffering victoriously (Rom. 8:17-39). The ultimate solution to suffering comes in heaven (Rev. 21:4-5). Our suffering as believers is a shadow compared to the glory yet to come (Rom. 8:17-18).

SUICIDE The Bible records several instances of suicide (Abimelech—Judg. 9:54; Samson—Judg. 16:29-30; Saul—1 Sam. 31:4; Saul's armor-bearer—1 Sam. 31:5; Ahithophel—2 Sam. 17:23; Zimri—1 Kings 16:18; and Judas—Matt. 27:5). The deaths of Abimelech and Saul could be called "assisted" suicide. With the possible exception of Samson (whose death may be better termed a martyrdom), the Bible presents each person who committed suicide as an individual whose behavior is not to be emulated. While the Bible does not specifically prohibit suicide, it does proclaim the sanctity of life (Ps. 8:5) and declares that God's people should choose life over death (Deut. 30:15,19). The right to give life and to take it away belongs to God (Job 1:21).

SUMER A region between the Tigris and Euphrates rivers referred to as Shinar (Gen. 10:10) or Chaldea (Jer. 50:10), now the southern part of modern Iraq. Archaeologists believe the inhabitants of ancient Sumer developed humanity's first high civilization about 3000 BC. Perhaps the most important Sumerian contribution to civilization was the invention of cuneiform writing, a wedge-shaped script formed by pressing a reed stylus into wet clay tablets. The Babylonians and other surrounding peoples adapted the cuneiform script to their own languages. For many centuries, cuneiform was the dominant mode of writing in ancient Mesopotamia. These tablets have given scholars information about life in this part of the world in Bible times.

SUN Ancient people often viewed the sun as a god, but the Bible views the sun as the "greater light" that God created to rule the day (Gen. 1:16). Thus, God was superior to, and separate from, the sun. The Psalms compared the sun's brightness to God's glory by which it will one day be replaced (Ps. 84:11).

SUNDIAL Device used to measure time by the position of a shadow cast by the sun. The root of the Hebrew word translated "dial" (2 Kings 20:11) means "to go up" and usually refers to stairs. Most interpreters thus understand King Ahab's sundial to be a staircase on which a shadow went up as the day progressed (2 Kings 20:11).

SUPERSCRIPTION Usually the Romans identified a person's crime by writing it on a sign and nailing it to the person's cross. All four Gospels mention such a superscription in connection with Jesus' crucifixion (Matt. 27:37; Mark 15:26; Luke 23:38; John 19:19). The word *superscription* is also used for the titles of some psalms that give information about the writer and the context of the psalm.

SURETY Person who is legally responsible for the debt of another. Should default occur, the surety would have to pay the debt or even be enslaved until the debt was paid. Judah became surety for his brother Benjamin to Joseph (Gen. 43:9). Proverbs warns against being surety for a person you do not know well (11:15). In a positive sense, Jesus is surety for the faithful under the new covenant (Heb. 7:22). See *Loan; Pledge*.

SUSA Winter capital of the ancient Persian Empire. King Cyrus made Susa a capital city along with Ecbatana and Babylon. Some believe Susa to be the place where Queen Esther and King Ahasuerus ruled (Esther 1:2). See *Esther, Book of; Persia*.

SUSANNA Personal name meaning "lily." A woman who followed Jesus and supported Him financially (Luke 8:2-3).

SWADDLING CLOTHES A long piece of linen used to wrap babies (Luke 2:7,12) and broken limbs. The cloth or band of cloth was wrapped tightly around the body to prohibit movement.

SWALLOW Bird that made nests in the temple (Ps. 84:3) and was often seen with the common sparrow. See *Birds*.

SWAN An unclean water bird (Deut. 14:16 KJV). Other versions translate as "desert owl" or "pelican" (NRSV) or "the white owl" (HCSB, NIV, NASB). See *Owl*.

An Arab mother watches her baby who i[s] wrapped in swaddling clothes.

SWEAT Perspiration, caused by physical exertion, sickness, or mental or emotional excitement (Luke 22:44).

SWIFT Bird similar to a swallow (Jer. 8:7 NASB, NIV). Other versions translate "swallow" (KJV, NRSV).

SWINE The swine of the Bible, in most instances, probably were wild pigs, still common in Palestine. The Mosaic law classified this animal as unclean and unfit for eating (Lev. 11:7). The fact that the prodigal son resorted to tending swine points to the extreme humiliation he experienced.

Sword dating from the Middle Kingdom of Egypt.

SWORD Close-range offensive weapon. Symbolically, the sword represented war (Matt. 10:34), divine justice (Rev. 1:16), the tongue (Ps. 57:4), and the word of God (Heb. 4:12). The sword of the Spirit, which is the word of God, is part of the Christian's armament in the fight against evil (Eph. 6:17).

SYCAMORE Combination "fig" and "mulberry" tree; the fig tree in the Jordan Valley that had leaves like our mulberry tree. Its fruit was inferior to the fig tree and had to be punctured to make the fruit edible. The prophet Amos was employed as "one who took care of sycamore-fig trees" (Amos 7:14 NIV).

SYCHAR Village in Samaria where Jesus talked with the Samaritan woman at Jacob's well (John 4:5-6).

SYMBOL Token or sign. The Bible is rich in symbolism and symbolic language. The universal and supreme symbol of Christian faith is the cross, an instrument of execution. For Christians this hideous object is a sign of God's love for human beings. Baptism is a picture of the death, burial, and resurrection of Christ. In being baptized, a person says to the world that he is identifying with the saving act being pictured, dying to sin and rising to walk in new life with God as the center of life. The Lord's Supper uses the ordinary elements of bread and wine to picture Christ's broken body and His blood shed for humanity's sin.

Several symbols in the OT are related to NT truths. For example, the sacrificial lamb in the OT points to the sacrificial death of Christ. The parables of Jesus are rich in symbols: grain, weeds, various kinds of soil, a lost sheep, a lost coin, and a lost son. Jesus used symbolic language in talking about Himself and His relationship to persons: bread of life, light of the world, good shepherd, water of life, and the door.

SYNAGOGUE Local meeting place and assembly of the Jewish people during late intertestamental and NT times. The synagogue had its roots in the time after Solomon's temple was destroyed and the people of Judah went into Babylonian exile. Local worship and instruction became necessary. Even after Jews returned to Jerusalem and rebuilt the temple, places of local worship continued

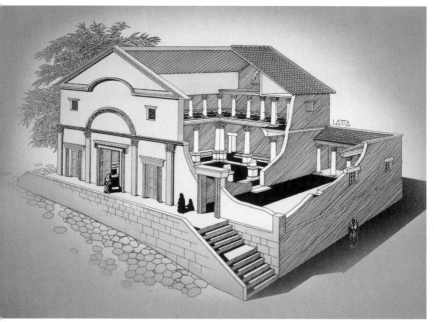

Reconstruction of a typical synagogue of the first century AD showing the large inner room where the men gathered and its loft above where the women gathered. This particular drawing is patterned after the synagogue at Capernaum.

A third-century synagogue at Capernaum.

By the first century these local meeting places were called synagogues.

SYNOPTIC GOSPELS See *Gospels, Synoptic.*

SYNTYCHE Personal name meaning "pleasant acquaintance" or "good luck." Woman in the church at Philippi exhorted by Paul to settle her disagreement with another woman named Euodia (Phil. 4:2).

SYRACUSE Major city on the island of Sicily where Paul stayed during his trip to Rome (Acts 28:12).

SYRIA Region or nation directly north of Palestine in the northwest corner of the Mediterranean Sea. The area covered by ancient Syria is roughly equal to the modern states of Syria and Lebanon with small portions of Turkey and Iraq. In most English versions of the OT "Syria" and "Syrian" translate the Hebrew word *'Aram*, which refers to the nations or territories of the Arameans, a group akin to Israel (Deut. 26:5). The Arameans began to settle in Syria and northern Mesopotamia around the beginning of the Iron Age (about 1200 BC), establishing a number of independent states. The OT mentions the Aramean kingdoms of Beth-eden in north Syria, Zobah in south-central Syria, and Damascus in the south. In NT times Judea was made part of a procuratorship within the larger Roman province of Syria (Matt. 4:24), the latter being ruled by a governor (Luke 2:2). Syria played an important role in the early spread of Christianity. Paul was converted on the road to Damascus (Acts 9:1-9) and subsequently evangelized in the province (Acts 15:41). Antioch, where believers were first called "Christians" (Acts 11:26), became the base for his missionary journeys (Acts 13:1-3).

SYROPHENICIAN (KJV) or **SYROPHOENICIAN** Combination of Syria and Phoenicia. The word reflects the joining of the two areas into one district under Roman rule. Jesus encountered in this district a woman whose daughter was possessed by a devil (Mark 7:26).

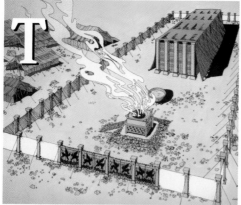

Reconstruction of the Israelite tabernacle and its court. The court was formed by curtains attached to erect poles. In front of the tent was placed the altar of burnt offerings and the laver. The tabernacle was always erected to face the east.

TAANACH Place-name of uncertain meaning. One of the sites along the northern slope of the Mount Carmel range protecting the accesses from the Plain of Esdraelon to the region of Samaria.

In the Bible Taanach is only mentioned seven times, usually in lists such as tribal allotments (Josh. 17:11; 1 Chron. 7:29), administrative districts (1 Kings 4:12), Levitical towns (Josh. 21:25), or conquered cities (Josh. 12:21; Judg. 1:27). The most famous biblical reference to Taanach is that of the battle fought at "Taanach near the waters of Megiddo" (NASB) where the Hebrew forces under Deborah and Barak defeated the Canaanites under Sisera (Judg. 5:19).

TAANATH-SHILOH Place-name likely meaning "approach to Shiloh." Village located about seven miles southeast of Shechem between Michmethath and Janoah (Josh. 16:6).

TABBAOTH Personal name meaning "signet ring." Head of a family of temple servants (Nethinim) returning from exile (Ezra 2:43; Neh. 7:46).

TABBATH Place-name, perhaps meaning "sunken." Site in the mountains of Gilead east of the Jordan where Gideon ended his pursuit of the Midianites (Judg. 7:22).

TABEEL Aramaic personal name meaning "God is good." **1.** Father of a man whom King Rezin of Damascus and King Pekah of Israel hoped to install as puppet king of Judah rather than Ahaz (Isa. 7:6). Alternately, Tabeel designates a region in northern Transjordan and home of the potential puppet. Spelling has been slightly changed in Hebrew to mean "good for nothing." **2.** Persian official in Samaria who joined in a letter protesting the reconstruction of the Jerusalem temple (Ezra 4:7).

TABERAH Place-name meaning "burning." Unidentified site in the wilderness wandering. The name commemorates God's "burning anger," which broke out in fire against the ever-complaining Israelites (Num. 11:3; Deut. 9:22). The name does not appear in the itinerary of Num. 33.

TABERING KJV term meaning "beating" (Nah. 2:7).

TABERNACLE, TENT OF MEETING Sacred tent, portable and provisional sanctuary, where God met His people (Exod. 33:7-10). Two compound phrases ('*ohel mo'ed* and '*ohel ha'eduth)* are used to designate this tent: "the tabernacle of the congregation" (Exod. 29:42,44), literally the "tent of meeting" (NRSV, NIV, NASB, REB) and "the tabernacle of witness" (Num. 17:7) or "tent of witness." In both cases it was the place where the God of Israel revealed Himself to and dwelled among His people. The basic Hebrew term (*mishkan*) translated as "tabernacle" (Exod. 25:9) comes from a verb that means "to dwell." In this sense it is correctly translated in some instances as "dwelling," "dwelling place," "habitation," and "abode."

The OT mentions three tents or tabernacles. First, after the sin of the golden calf at Mount Sinai the "provisional" tabernacle was established outside the camp and called the "tent of meeting" (Exod. 33:7). Second, the "Sinaitic" tabernacle was built in accordance with directions given to Moses by God (Exod. 25–40). Unlike the tent of meeting, it stood at the center of the camp (Num. 2). Third, the "Davidic" tabernacle was erected in Jerusalem for the reception of the ark (2 Sam. 6:17).

TABERNACLES, FEAST OF See *Festivals.*

TABITHA Aramaic personal name meaning "gazelle," which serves as the counterpart to the Greek name Dorcas (Acts 9:36).

TABLE OF NATIONS Genesis 10 lists the descendants of Noah's sons to explain the origin of the nations and peoples of the known world. The account is unique for several reasons. First, a new chapter begins in biblical history at this point: humanity has a new beginning through Noah and his three sons. Second, the account highlights the ethnic makeup of the ancient world, listing some 70 different ethnic groups that formed the basis of the known world. Third, despite our lack of

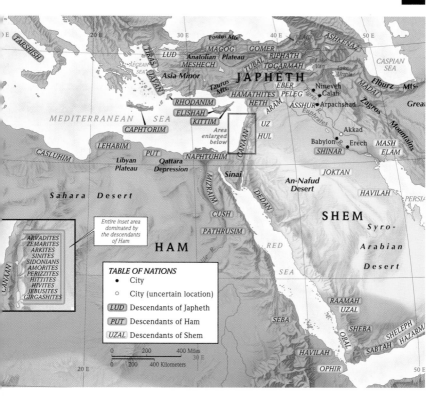

knowledge about many of the groups listed in the chapter, Gen. 10 underlines the fact that the Bible is based on historical events. Fourth, Gen. 10 provides the basis for understanding Abraham, introducing his world and his relationship to that world. The account of the Table of Nations, with a few variations, also appears in 1 Chron. 1:5-23.

The Table of Nations has three basic divisions. The people and lands of the known world fit into one of three families, the family of Shem, Ham, or Japheth. The names that appear in each of the families are names that come from several different categories: racial descent, geographical location, language differences, or political units.

Japheth's descendants (Gen. 10:2-5) inhabited the Aegean region and Anatolia or Asia Minor. The descendants of Ham (Gen. 10:6-20) were located especially in the regions of North Africa and the coastal regions of Canaan and Syria. The descendants of Shem (Gen. 10:21-31) are especially important because Abraham comes from the line of Shem. Thus Abraham is a Shemite or Semite. Because he is also a descendant of Eber, he is called a Hebrew (Gen. 11:14-32). The descendants of Shem were located generally in north Syria, that is, the region of the upper part of the Euphrates River, and Mesopotamia, especially the eastern part.

TABLET Usually a flat surface used for writing. **1.** *Law tablets.* Scripture names the stone objects bearing the Ten Commandments the tablets (or tables) of the law (Exod. 24:12), testimony (Exod. 31:18), and covenant (Deut. 9:9). These tablets were perhaps small steles such as those other nations used to publicize their laws. **2.** *Writing tablets.* Writing was often done on clay tablets (Ezek. 4:1) or wood tablets covered with wax (Luke 1:63). The heart is often described as a tablet upon which God writes His law (Prov. 3:3; Jer. 17:1; 2 Cor. 3:3).

Mount Tabor located a few miles southeast of Nazareth.

TABOR Place-name of uncertain meaning, perhaps "height." **1.** Mountain in the valley of Jezreel. About six miles east of Nazareth, it has played an important role in Israel's history since the period of the conquest. Tradition holds that Tabor was the site of Jesus' transfiguration (Mark 9:2), although no evidence exists to validate the claim. **2.** Levitical city (1 Chron. 6:77), apparently replacing Nahalal in the earlier list (Josh. 21:35). It may be Khirbet Dabura. **3.** The "Plain of Tabor" (1 Sam. 10:3) was apparently near Gibea.

TABOR, OAK OF NASB, NRSV designation of a site between Rachel's tomb (near Bethlehem) and Gibeah of Saul (1 Sam. 10:3). Other translations read "plain" (KJV), "great tree" (NIV), or "terebinth" (REB) of Tabor.

TABRIMMON Personal name meaning "Rimmon is good." Father of King Ben-hadad of Damascus (1 Kings 15:18). Rimmon was the Akkadian god of thunder.

TACHES KJV term meaning "hooks" or "clasps" (Exod. 26:6,11,33) used to connect the individual curtains of the tabernacle into one tent.

TACKLING KJV form of tackle, that is, gear used to handle cargo and rigging to work a ship's sails (Isa. 33:23; Acts 27:19).

TADMOR Place-name of uncertain meaning. A city in northern Palestine built by Solomon (2 Chron. 8:4), probably to control a caravan route. The site has been identified with Palmyra, a great Arabian city, located about 120 miles northeast of Damascus.

TAHAN Personal name meaning "graciousness." **1.** Third son of Ephraim (Num. 26:35). The parallel list gives Tahath as Ephraim's third son (1 Chron. 7:20). **2.** Ephraimite ancestor of Joshua (1 Chron. 7:25).

TAHANITES Member of the Ephraimite clan descended from Tahan (Num. 26:35).

TAHASH Personal name meaning "porpoise" or "dugong." Third son of Nahor and Reumah (Gen. 22:24) and ancestor of an Arab tribe.

TAHATH Personal name and place-name meaning "beneath, low" or "substitute, compensation." **1.** A Levite (1 Chron. 6:24,37). **2.** Two descendants of Ephraim (1 Chron. 7:20). See *Tahan.* **3.** Stopping place during the wilderness wandering (Num. 33:26-27).

TAHCHEMONITE or **TAHKEMONITE** (NIV) Title of one of David's 30 elite warriors (2 Sam. 23:8), likely a scribal altering of the Hebrew *ha Hachmonite* (REB), which occurs in the parallel list (1 Chron. 11:11).

TAHPANHES Hebrew transliteration of an Egyptian place-name meaning "fortress of Penhase" or "house of the Nubian." City in the Nile Delta near the eastern border of Egypt (Jer. 2:16). Following the destruction of Jerusalem and continuing unrest in Judah, a large group of Jews took Jeremiah with them and fled to Tahpanhes (Jer. 43:7; 44:1). Jeremiah argued against the move (Jer. 42:19) warning that Nebuchadnezzar would again reach Tahpanhes (Jer. 46:14).

TAHPENES Egyptian royal consort; title for queen of Egypt in 1 Kings 11:19-20. Her sister was given in marriage to Hadad the Edomite, an enemy of David, and later of Solomon.

TAHREA Alternate form of Tarea (1 Chron. 9:41).

TAHTIM-HODSHI Site in northern Israel that David's census takers visited (2 Sam. 24:6).

TALENT Hebrew weight of about 76 pounds (about 3,000 shekels). In the NT, a talent was a large sum of money. See *Weights and Measures.*

TALITHA CUMI Transliteration of Aramaic phrase meaning "damsel, arise." Jesus' words to Jairus's daughter (Mark 5:41).

TALMAI Personal name meaning "plowman" or else derived from the Hurrian word for "big." **1.** One of three Anakim (giant, pre-Israelite inhabitants of Canaan) residing in Hebron (Num. 13:22). **2.** King of Geshur, father of David's wife Maacah and grandfather of Absalom (2 Sam. 3:3; 1 Chron. 3:2).

TALMON Personal name meaning "brightness." **1.** Levite whom David and Samuel appointed as a gatekeeper (1 Chron. 9:17), ancestor of a family of temple gatekeepers who returned from exile (Ezra 2:42; Neh. 7:45). **2.** Leader of the postexilic gatekeepers (Neh. 11:19; 12:25).

TALMUD Jewish commentaries. Talmud means "study" or "learning" and refers in rabbinic Judaism to the opinions and teachings that disciples learn from their predecessors particularly with regard to the development of oral legal teachings (*halakah*). The word "Talmud" is most commonly used in Judaism to refer specifically to the digest of commentary on the Mishnah. The Mishnah codification of oral legal teachings on the written law of Moses) was probably written down at Javneh in Galilee at about AD 220. Between AD 220 and 500 the rabbinic schools in Palestine and Babylonia amplified and applied the teachings of the Mishnah for their Jewish communities. Two documents came to embody a large part of this teaching: the Jerusalem Talmud and the Babylonian Talmud.

TAMAR Personal name meaning "date palm." **1.** Daughter-in-law of Judah, wife of his eldest son, Er (Gen. 38:6). **2.** Daughter of David raped by her half brother, Amnon (2 Sam. 13:14). **3.** Absalom named his only daughter Tamar. She is called "a beautiful woman" (2 Sam. 14:27). **4.** City built by Solomon "in the wilderness" (1 Kings 9:18). **5.** Fortified city at the southern end of the Dead Sea, marking the ideal limit of Israel (Ezek. 47:19; 48:28).

TAMARISK Shrublike tree (*Tamarix syriaca*) common to the Sinai and southern Palestine with small white or pink flowers. Abraham planted a tamarisk at Beer-sheba (Gen. 21:33), and Saul was buried beneath one at Jabesh-gilead (1 Sam. 31:13).

TAMMUZ Sumerian god of vegetation. The worship of Tammuz by women in Jerusalem was revealed as one of the abominations in Ezekiel (8:14-15).

TANHUMETH Personal name meaning "comforting." Father of Seraiah, a captain of forces remaining with Gedaliah in Judah following the deportation of Babylon (2 Kings 25:23; Jer. 40:8). A Lachish stamp witnesses to the name as does an Arad inscription.

TAPHATH Personal name meaning "droplet." Daughter of Solomon and wife of Ben-abinadab, a Solomonic official (1 Kings 4:11).

TAPPUAH Personal name meaning "apple" or "quince." **1.** A Calebite, likely a resident of a town near Hebron (1 Chron. 2:43). **2.** City in the Shephelah district of Judah (Josh. 15:34), possibly Beit Nettif about 12 miles west of Bethlehem. **3.** City of the north border of Ephraim (Josh. 16:8) whose environs were allotted to Manasseh (17:7-8), likely the Tappuah of Josh. 12:17 and 2 Kings 15:16.

TARAH KJV form of "Terah," the wilderness campsite (Num. 33:27-28).

TARALAH Place-name meaning "strength." Unidentified site in Benjamin, likely northwest of Jerusalem (Josh. 18:27).

TAREA Personal name of unknown derivation. Descendant of Saul (1 Chron. 8:35; "Tahrea" 1 Chron. 9:41).

TARES KJV term for grassy weeds resembling wheat, generally identified as darnel (*genus Lolium*) (Matt. 13:25-30,36-40).

TARGUM Early translations of the Bible into Aramaic, the native language of Palestine and Babylon in the first century AD. Targum, in its verbal Hebrew form, means "to explain, to translate."

TARPELITES KJV transliteration of an Aramaic title in Ezra 4:9. Most modern translations render the term "officials" (NIV, "men of Tripolis").

TARSHISH Personal name and place-name of uncertain derivation, either meaning "yellow jasper," as in the Hebrew of Exod. 28:20; Ezek. 28:13, or else derived from an Akkadian term meaning "smelting plant." **1.** Son of Javan (Gen. 10:4; 1 Chron. 1:7) and ancestor of an Aegean people. **2.** Benjaminite warrior (1 Chron. 7:10). **3.** One of seven leading officials of King Ahasuerus of Persia (Esther 1:14). This name possibly means "greedy one" in Old Persian. **4.** Geographic designation, most likely of Tartessus at the southern tip of Spain but possibly of Tarsus in Cilicia. Jonah sailed for Tarshish, the far limit of the western world, from the Mediterranean port of Joppa in his futile attempt to escape God's call (Jon. 1:3). Tarshish traded in precious metals with Tyre, another Mediterranean port (Isa. 23:1; Jer. 10:9; Ezek. 27:12). **5.** References to Tarshish in 1 Kings and 2 Chronicles suggest a non-geographic meaning. Solomon's (1 Kings 10:22; 2 Chron. 9:21) and Jehoshaphat's (1 Kings 22:48; 2 Chron. 20:36) fleets were based at Ezion-geber on the Red Sea. Solomon's cargo suggests east African trading partners. Thus "ships of Tarshish" may designate seagoing vessels like those of Tarshish or else ships bearing metal cargo like those of Tarshish (cp. Isa. 2:16, where "ships of Tarshish" parallels "beautiful crafts").

TARSUS Birthplace of Paul (Acts 9:11) and capital of Roman province of Cilicia.

TARTAK Deity worshipped by the Avvites, whom the Assyrians made to settle in Samaria after 722 BC (2 Kings 17:31).

TARTAN Title of the highest ranking Assyrian officer under the king; commander in chief; supreme commander (2 Kings 18:17; Isa. 20:1).

The Cleopatra Gate at Tarsus commemorating Mark Antony's meeting of Cleopatra at this ancient city.

TASKMASTER Oppressive overseers of forced labor gangs employed by monarchies for large public works projects (Egyptian: Exod. 1:11; 3:7; 5:6-14; Israelite: 2 Sam. 20:24; 1 Kings 4:6; 5:16; 12:18; 2 Chron. 10:18).

TATNAI (KJV) or **TATTENAI** Contemporary of Zerubbabel, governor of the Persian province "across the (Euphrates) River," which included Palestine (Ezra 5:3,6; 6:6,13).

TAU Twenty-second and final letter of the Hebrew alphabet, which the KJV used as a heading for Ps. 119:169-176, each verse of which begins with the letter.

TAXES Regular payments to rulers. Early Israel only paid taxes to support the tabernacle and the priests. Terms in the OT that refer to taxes were: "assessment," "forced labor," "tribute," and "toll." During David's reign, an army was maintained by tribute paid by conquered tribes. Taxes increased under Solomon's rule. Tradesmen and merchants paid duties; subject peoples paid tribute; farmers paid taxes in kind of oil and wine; and many Israelites did forced labor on the temple. The burden of taxation contributed to the rebellion following Solomon's death (1 Kings 12). Soon, Israel became a vassal state, paying tribute—a compulsory tax—to Assyria, and, eventually, to Rome.

In the NT era Herod the Great levied a tax on the produce of the field and a tax on items bought and sold. Other duties owed to foreign powers were a land tax, a poll tax, a kind of progressive income tax (about which the Pharisees tested Jesus, Matt. 22:17), and a tax on personal property. In Jerusalem a house tax was levied. These taxes were paid directly to Roman officials.

Export and import customs paid at seaports and city gates were farmed out to private contractors who paid a sum in advance for the right to collect taxes in a certain area. Such were Zacchaeus (Luke 19) and Matthew (Matt. 9).

The Israelites resented most deeply the duties paid to the occupying powers. Many zealous Jews considered it treason to God to pay taxes to Rome. When questioned about paying the poll tax, Jesus surprised His questioners by saying that the law should be obeyed (Mark 12:13).

TEBAH Personal name meaning "slaughter." Son of Nahor and ancestor of an Aramaean tribe (Gen. 22:24).

TEBALIAH Personal name meaning "Yahweh has dipped, that is, purified," or "loved by Yahweh," or "good for Yahweh." Postexilic Levitic gatekeeper (1 Chron. 26:11).

TEBETH Tenth month (December–January) of the Hebrew calendar (Esther 2:16). The name derives from an Akkadian term meaning "sinking" and refers to the rainy month.

TEHAPHNEHES Alternate form of Tahpanhes (Ezek. 30:18).

TEHINNAH Personal name meaning "supplication" or "graciousness." Descendant of Judah responsible for founding Irnahash (1 Chron. 4:12).

TEIL TREE KJV term meaning "lime" or "linden tree," used to translate a Hebrew term generally rendered oak or terebinth (Isa. 6:13).

TEKOA Place-name meaning "place of setting up a tent." A city in the highlands of Judah six miles south of Bethlehem and ten miles south of Jerusalem; home of the Prophet Amos. God called Amos

Modern Tekoa.

from among the shepherds of Tekoa to preach to the northern kingdom of Israel (Amos 1:1). The priest tried to send him back to Tekoa (7:12).

TEL-ABIB Place-name meaning "mound of the flood" or "mound of grain." Tel-abib on the Chebar Canal near Nippur in Babylon was home to Ezekiel and other exiles (Ezek. 3:15). The Babylonians may have thought it was the ruined site of the original flood.

TEL-ASSAR Place-name meaning "mound of Asshur." City in northern Mesopotamia that the Assyrians conquered (2 Kings 19:12 KJV, "Thelasar"; Isa. 37:12).

TEL-HARSA (KJV, Ezra 2:59) or **TEL-HARSHA** Place-name meaning "mound of the forest" or "mound of magic." Home of Babylonian Jews unable to demonstrate their lineage (Ezra 2:59; Neh. 7:61).

TEL-MELAH Place-name meaning "mound of salt." Babylonian home of a group of Jews unable to demonstrate their lineage (Ezra 2:59; Neh. 7:61).

TELAH Personal name meaning "breach" or "fracture." An ancestor of Joshua (1 Chron. 7:25).

TELAIM Place-name meaning "young speckled lambs." City in southern Judah where Saul gathered forces to battle the Amalekites (1 Sam. 15:4).

TELEM Personal name and place-name meaning "brightness" or "lamb." **1.** Levite with a foreign wife (Ezra 10:24). **2.** City in southern Judah (Josh. 15:24), a variant form of Telaim.

TELL Semitic term meaning "mound," applied to areas built up by successive settlements at a single site. "Tell" or "tel" is a common element in Near Eastern place-names.

TEMA Personal name and place-name meaning "south country." Tema, a son of Ishmael (Gen. 25:15; 1 Chron. 1:30), is associated with Tema (modern Teima), a strategic oasis located on the Arabian Peninsula 250 miles southeast of Aqaba and 200 miles north-northeast of Medina.

TEMAH Family of temple servants (Nethinim) returning from exile (Ezra 2:53; Neh. 7:55).

TEMAN Personal name and place-name meaning "right side," that is, "southern." **1.** Edomite clan descended from Esau (Gen. 36:11,15; 1 Chron. 1:36). **2.** City of area associated with this clan (Jer. 49:7,20; Ezek. 25:13; Amos 1:12; Obad. 1:9; Hab. 3:3). Teman has often been identified with Tawilan, 50 miles south of the Dead Sea just east of Petra.

TEMANI (KJV) or **TEMANITES** Descendants of Teman or residents of Teman, the southern area of Edom. The land of the Temanites designates (southern) Edom (Gen. 36:34 KJV "Temani"; 1 Chron. 1:45). The Temanites were renowned for their wisdom (Job 2:11; cp. Jer. 49:7).

TEMENI Personal name, perhaps meaning "on the right hand," that is, "to the south." Descendant of Judah (1 Chron. 4:6).

TEMPLE OF JERUSALEM Place of worship, especially the temple of Solomon built in Jerusalem for national worship of Yahweh. When David built for himself a cedar palace, he thought it only proper he should build one for Yahweh, too (2 Sam. 7:1-2). Nathan at first approved his plan, but the Lord Himself said He had been used to living

Reconstruction of Herod's temple (20 BC–AD 70) at Jerusalem as viewed from the southeast. The drawing reflects archaeological discoveries made since excavations began in 1967 along the south end of the Temple Mount platform.

A Christian monastery on the Mount of Temptation marks the traditional site of Jesus' temptation.

in a tent since the exodus from Egypt. He would allow David's son to build Him a house (temple), but He would build for David a house (dynasty, 2 Sam. 7:3-16). This covenant promise became exceedingly significant to the messianic hope fulfilled in the coming of the ideal king of the line of David.

There were three historical temples in succession, those of Solomon, Zerubbabel, and Herod in the pre-exilic, postexilic, and NT periods. Herod's temple was really a massive rebuilding of the Zerubbabel temple, so both are called the "second temple" by Judaism. All three were located on a prominent hill north of David's capital city, which he conquered from the Jebusites (2 Sam. 5:6-7). David had acquired the temple hill from Araunah the Jebusite at the advice of the Prophet Gad to stay a pestilence from the Lord by building an altar and offering sacrifices on the threshing floor (2 Sam. 24:18-25). Chronicles identifies this hill with Mount Moriah, where Abraham had been willing to offer Isaac (2 Chron. 3:1; Gen. 22:1-14). So the temple mount today in Jerusalem is called Mount Moriah, and the threshing floor of Araunah is undoubtedly the large rock enshrined within the Dome of the Rock, center of the Muslim enclosure called Haram es-Sharif (the third holiest place in Islam, after Mecca and Medina). This enclosure is basically what is left of Herod's enlarged temple platform, the masonry of which may best be seen in its Western Wall, the holiest place within Judaism since the Roman destruction of Herod's temple.

TEMPTATION Broadly defined, temptation is the enticement to do evil. Satan is the tempter (Matt. 4:3; 1 Thess. 3:5). Beginning with Eve, Satan successfully tempted Adam, Cain, Abraham, and David to sin. He was less successful with Job, and Jesus was "tested in every way as we are, yet without sin" (Heb. 4:15 HCSB). James explains that God cannot be tempted by evil, and He does not tempt anyone (James 1:13). Temptation may be for the purpose of destroying a person through sin leading to death and hell. This is Satan's intent. God may allow testing for the purpose of bringing forth faith and patience, which ultimately honor Him, as in the case of Job. James further explains that a blessing awaits the one who endures temptation (James 1:12).

TEMPTATION OF JESUS Jesus was tempted by the devil in the wilderness subsequent to His baptism by John. Matthew and Luke describe in some detail three encounters between Jesus and Satan. The foremost difference between the accounts is the reversal of the order of the final two temptations. Matthew connects the first two with a connective particle that can have chronological implications. Luke's interest in Jerusalem and the temple (1:9; 2:22,25,37,41-50) make it more likely that he used the third temptation as a climax to the temptations.

Forty days in the wilderness is reminiscent of the fasts of Moses (Exod. 34:28; Deut. 9:9) and Elijah (1 Kings 9:8), and the 40 years of the Israelites in the desert (Num. 14:33; 32:13). The only parallel developed, however, is the wilderness wanderings of Israel. As God led Israel in the wilderness, likewise the Spirit led Jesus into the wilderness. God tested Israel in the wilderness and they failed. God allowed Jesus to be tempted by the devil and He succeeded in resisting. Angels ministered to Jesus after the temptations. Luke is the only evangelist to note that Satan's departure was not the end of the conflict (4:13), but the intensity was not repeated until Gethsemane (22:40,46,53) and Golgotha (23:35-36,39).

Several significant features stand out as one contemplates Jesus' temptation in the wilderness. His encounter with the devil in the wilderness is a source of encouragement and instruction to believers as they battle temptation (Heb. 2:18; 4:15). His commitment to the Father's will, use of Scripture and resolve to resist the devil (James 4:7) are helpful examples for battling temptation.

TEN COMMANDMENTS Although many people refer to the "Decalogue" as "the Ten Commandments," this is unfortunate for several reasons. First, it obscures the fact that this is not what the OT calls them. Wherever it is referred to by title it is identified as *aseret haddebarim,* "the Ten Words" (Exod. 34:28; Deut. 4:13; 10:4). This sense is captured precisely in the Greek word *decalogos.* Second, in both the original context in which the Decalogue was given (Exod. 20:1) and

Moses' remembrance of the event in Deut. 4:12 and 5:22, the Decalogue is presented as a set of spoken words rather than a written set of laws. Third, "Ten Commandments" obscures the fact that the Decalogue is a covenant document, whose form follows ancient Near Eastern treaty tradition. Fourth, as a code of laws the Decalogue is virtually unenforceable. For all these reasons, although the 10 statements are in the form of commands, we should follow the lead of the biblical texts and refer to them as the "Ten Words/Declarations," the 10 fundamental principles of covenant relationship. The stipulations revealed in the "Book of the Covenant," the "Holiness Code," and other parts of the Pentateuch represent clarifications and applications of these principles. Presumably the stipulations of the covenant were reduced to 10 principles so they could be easily memorized.

Apart from Moses' citation of the Decalogue in Deut. 5, the OT gives little if any evidence of giving the Decalogue greater authority than any of the other laws revealed at Sinai. This does not mean that these tablets were not treated as special. On the contrary, Moses notes that the Decalogue contained the only revelation that was communicated by God directly to the people (Deut. 4:12-13; 5:22) and committed to writing on tablets of stone by God's own hand (Exod. 24:12; 31:18; 34:1; Deut. 4:13; 5:22; 10:1-4). All subsequent revelation at Sinai was communicated indirectly through Moses, the covenant mediator. The special status of the tablets is reflected in the fact

St. Catherine's Monastery as seen from atop Mount Sinai where Moses received the Ten Commandments.

that these tablets (and these alone) were deposited inside the ark of the covenant (Deut. 10:5; 1 Kings 8:9).

The Decalogue may legitimately be interpreted as a Bill of Rights, perhaps the world's first Bill of Rights. Yet unlike modern bills of rights, this document seeks not to secure my rights but to protect the rights of others. I am perceived as a potential violator of the other person's rights. Understood this way, the significance of the 10 declarations may be summarized as follows:

1. God's right to exclusive allegiance (Exod. 20:3; Deut. 5:7).
2. God's right to self-definition (Exod. 20:4-6; Deut. 5:8-10).
3. God's right to proper representation by His people (Exod. 20:7; Deut. 5:11).
4. God's right to His people's time (Exod. 20:8-11); a household's right to humane treatment by the head of the house (Deut. 5:12-15).
5. My parents' right to respect (Exod. 20:12; Deut. 5:16).
6. My neighbor's right to life (Exod. 20:13; Deut. 5:17).
7. My neighbor's right to a secure marriage (Exod. 20:14; Deut. 5:18).
8. My neighbor's right to personal property (Exod. 20:15; Deut. 5:19).
9. My neighbor's right to an honest hearing in court (Exod. 20:16; Deut. 5:20).
10. My neighbor's right to secure existence in the community (Exod. 20:17; Deut. 5:21).
The first four statements protect the rights of the covenant Lord; the last six protect the rights of the covenant community. The Decalogue calls on the redeemed to respond to the grace they have experienced in salvation with covenant commitment, first to God, and then to others. This is the essence of "love" (*'ahab*) as understood in both the OT and NT.

TENDERHEARTED KJV used "tenderhearted" in two senses: of timidity (2 Chron. 13:7) and of compassion (Eph. 4:32).

TENON KJV, NASB, REB, RSV translation of a Hebrew term meaning "hands," applied to projections designed to fit into a mortise or socket to form a joint (Exod. 26:17,19; 36:22,24). Other translations employ "projections" (NIV, TEV) or "pegs" (NRSV).

TERAH Personal name, perhaps meaning "ibex." **1.** The father of Abraham, Nahor, and Haran (Gen. 11:26). Along with a migration of people from Ur of the Chaldees, Terah moved his family, following the Euphrates River to Haran (11:31). He intended to continue from Haran into Canaan but died in Mesopotamia at the age of 205 (11:32). A debate has centered on Terah's religious practices, for Josh. 24:2 apparently points to his family when it claims records that the father worshipped gods other than Yahweh. **2.** Wilderness campsite (Num. 33:27-28).

TERAPHIM Transliteration of a Hebrew word for household idols of indeterminate size and shape. They were also referred to as "gods" (cp. Gen. 31: 19,30-35; 1 Sam. 19:13).

TEREBINTH Large, spreading tree whose species is uncertain so that translations vary in reading the Hebrew 'elah into English (cp. 2 Sam. 18:9; Isa. 1:30; 6:13). The tree had religious connections as a place under which pagan gods were worshiped (Hos. 4:13; Ezek. 6:13) that were at times taken up in Israel's religion (Gen. 35:4; Josh. 24:26; Judg. 6:11; 1 Kings 13:14).

TERESH Personal name meaning "firm, solid," or derived from an Old Persian term meaning "desire." One of two royal eunuchs who plotted an unsuccessful assassination of the Persian king Ahasuerus. Following their exposure by Mordecai, the two were hung (Esther 2:21-23).

TERTIUS Latin personal name meaning "third [son]." Paul's amanuensis (secretary) for the writing of Romans who included his own greeting at Rom. 16:22. Some suggest that Quartus, whose name means "fourth," is perhaps Tertius' younger brother (Rom. 16:23).

TERTULLUS Diminutive of the personal name Tertius, meaning "third" (Acts 24:1-8). Tertullus was the prosecutor opposing Paul before Felix, the Roman governor of Judea.

TETH Ninth letter of the Hebrew alphabet that KJV used as a heading for Ps. 119:65-72, each verse of which begins with this letter.

TETRARCH Political position in the early Roman Empire. It designated the size of the territory ruled (literally the "fourth part") and the amount of dependence on Roman authority. Luke 3:1 names one of the tetrarchs who served in the year of Jesus' birth.

TEXTUAL CRITICISM The art and science of reconstructing the text of a work that no longer exists in its original form. The word "criticism" is not a negative term in this context. It refers to methods of careful study and analysis whose aim is to determine the original text of each book with the greatest possible degree of detail and accuracy through the careful study and comparison of all extant manuscripts.

TEXTUS RECEPTUS Term that is generally applied to certain printed editions of the Greek NT but sometimes extended to refer also to the ben Chayim edition of the Hebrew OT.

THADDAEUS Personal name, perhaps meaning "gift of God" in Greek but derived from Hebrew or Aramaic meaning "breast."

THEBEZ Likely Tubas, 13 miles northeast of Shechem where the roads from Shechem and Dothan converge to lead down to the Jordan Valley. During the siege of Thebez, a woman of the city fatally wounded Abimelech by throwing an upper millstone on his head (Judg. 9:50-53; 2 Sam. 11:21).

THEOCRACY Form of government in which God directly rules. As the Sovereign King, God may rule directly through unmediated means, or He may choose to use various mediators to manifest His rule. In either case, God Himself is the Sovereign Ruler.

The theocracy of God is revealed progressively in the Scripture. The giving of the Mosaic law by God to the Israelites gave the Hebrew people a unique theocratic structure. The next step in the development of the theocratic state was the taking of promised land (the conquest) and the period of the judges (conflict). Under Joshua's capable leadership, the Israelites were able to enter and conquer Canaan according to the promises of God. In this act, the people of God were provided a land in which to build a theocratic state.

The people soon asked for a king. The existence of a human king, however, did not ideally conflict with the theocracy. The king, as chosen by God, would not be a despotic, selfish dictator, but rather a man who would walk in the light of the Lord and seek God's guidance in all matters. Thus, the rule of the human monarch would glorify God and manifest the theocratic ideal.

The theocratic ideal experience declined among the Israelites following the division of the monarchy and the exilic/postexilic periods. There is a sense, however, in which the ideal of a theocracy is resumed in the NT. Christ, as the Messiah and the Davidic King, is the person in whom the kingdom of God resides. With His preaching and earthly ministry, He gave evidence that "the kingdom of God is at hand." Further, following His resurrection, He declared to His followers: "All authority has been given to Me in heaven and on earth. Go, therefore, and make disciples of all nations" (Matt 28:18-20, HCSB). With this declaration, the risen King commissioned His followers to go and to proclaim the existence of His kingdom. As Christians individually and corporately submit and propagate the Lordship of Christ, in a sense they experience and express the theocratic ideal of God's direct governance. Thus, a NT church should endeavor to realize and appropriate the direct rule of the Sovereign King in all areas.

THEOLOGY, BIBLICAL Discussion of what the Bible itself teaches about God and His dealings with human beings and the rest of creation. Biblical theology opens up the unity of the Bible by exposing and collecting its major themes. It demonstrates the many ways in which diverse books and material are united by the character of God the Father, Son, and Holy Spirit.

THEOPHANY Physical appearance or personal manifestation of God to a person. There are some five forms of theophanies: in human form (Gen. 32:30; Exod. 24:10), in visions (Isa. 6; Ezek. 1; Dan. 7:9), by the Angel of the Lord (Gen. 16:7-13), not in human form (as at the burning bush, Exod. 3:2–4:17, and in the guidance through the wilderness, 13:21; cp. Acts 7:30), and as the name of the Lord (God's sacred name represented His presence, Deut. 12:5; Isa. 30:27; 59:19). The glory of the Lord appears to people in numerous passages. God's presence is in a cloud (Exod. 16:10; 33:9-10; Ezek. 10:4). God was also manifest in nature and history (Isa. 6:3; Ezek. 1:28; 43:2).

The incarnate Christ was not, and indeed is not, a theophany. The phenomena of theophanies were temporary, for the occasion that required them, and then disappeared. On the other hand, in the incarnate Christ His deity and humanity were joined, not for time alone, but for eternity.

THEOPHILUS Personal name meaning "friend of God;" the person to whom the books of Luke and Acts were written (Luke 1:3; Acts 1:1).

THESSALONIANS, FIRST LETTER TO THE Thessalonica was the largest city in first-century Macedonia and the capital of the province. It was a free city. Paul, Silas, and Timothy evangelized the city against the strong opposition of the Jews; but, though their stay was short, they were successful in establishing a church (Acts 17:4). There was not time to give much instruction to the new converts, so it is not surprising that questions arose as to the meaning of some aspects of the Christian faith and of the conduct demanded of believers.

Among the problems the Thessalonian church faced were persecution by pagans (2:14) and a temptation for believers to accept pagan sexual standards (4:4-8). Some of the Christians seem to have given up working and to have relied on the others to supply their needs (4:11-12). There was uncertainty about the fate of believers who had died, and some of the Thessalonians appear to have thought that Christ would come back soon and take them all to be with Him. What would happen to those who had died before the great event (4:13-18)? Paul's reply to this gives us information about Christ's return that we find nowhere else. Again, some of the believers seem to have been concerned about the time of Jesus' return (5:1-11). So Paul wrote this pastoral letter to meet the needs of inexperienced Christians and to bring them closer to Christ.

THESSALONIANS, SECOND LETTER TO THE The exact date of Paul's mission to Thessalonica is not known, and the same is true of his letters to the very young church there. Most scholars agree that 2 Thessalonians must have been written not more than a year or two after Paul and Silas left the city. The church was apparently enthusiastic, but clearly the believers had not as yet matured in their faith. Paul wrote to committed Christians who had not progressed very far in the Christian life.

We see the enthusiasm and excitement of the Thessalonians expressed in the riots when the first Christian preachers visited them. Such a riot broke out in Thessalonica (Acts 17:5-8,13). Those who became Christians during this time did so with verve and enthusiasm. However, they had not yet had the time to come to grips with all that being a Christian means.

Second Thessalonians is not a long letter and does not give us a definitive outline of the whole Christian faith. Paul wrote to meet a present need, and the arrangement of his letter focuses on local circumstances. Perhaps we can say that there are four great teachings in this letter:
(1) the greatness of God,
(2) the wonder of salvation in Christ,
(3) the second coming, and
(4) the importance of life and work each day.

THESSALONICA Name of modern-day Thessaloniki, given to the city about 315 BC by Cassander, a general of Alexander the Great. When the Apostle Paul visited the city, it was larger than Philippi and reflected a predominantly

The Triumphal Arch of the Emperor Galerius built over the Egnatian Way in Thessalonica.

Roman culture. Thessalonica was a free city, having no Roman garrison within its walls and maintaining the privilege of minting its own coins. Like Corinth, it had a cosmopolitan population due to the commercial prowess of the city. The recent discovery of a marble inscription, written partly in Greek and partly in a Samaritan form of Hebrew and Aramaic, testifies to the presence of Samaritans in Thessalonica. The book of Acts testifies to the presence of a Jewish synagogue there (17:1).

THEUDAS Personal name meaning "gift of God." Acts 5:36 refers to a Theudas who was slain after leading an unsuccessful rebellion of 400 men prior to the census (AD 6).

THIGH Side of the lower torso and the upper part of the leg. Sometimes the reference is simply physical (Judg. 3:16; Ps. 45:3; Song 3:8; 7:1). More often Scripture regards the thigh as the seat of vital functions, especially procreation. English translations often obscure this connection.

THOMAS Personal name from Hebrew meaning "a twin." One of the first 12 disciples of Jesus (Mark 3:18). His personality was complex, revealing a pessimism mixed with loyalty and faith (John 11:16). Thomas sought evidence of Jesus' resurrection (John 20:25) but, when convinced of the miracle, made a historic confession of faith (20:28).

THORN IN THE FLESH Greek word *skolops* occurred in classical Greek as a stake or sharp wooden shaft used to impale. Because false teachers in Corinth claimed receiving divine revelation, Paul shared his vision of the "third heaven" as miraculous evidence of his apostolic calling. Paul's revelation was balanced by a "thorn in the flesh" (2 Cor. 12:7). During this era physical ailments were a constant problem. As a result, most patristic writers perceived Paul's affliction as either a painful chronic physical problem or ongoing persecution.

In the Middle Ages, the "thorn" was taken as carnal temptation. The Vulgate encouraged the perception of the thorn as a sexual temptation. In the Reformation, Luther and Calvin rejected the idea of sexual temptation. Calvin interpreted the "thorn in the flesh" as a variety of physical and spiritual temptations. Luther interpreted the thorn as physical illness.

Four modern theories concern Paul's thorn in the flesh. The most common theory is some sort of recurring physical illness, possibly malaria, based on a perceived relationship to Paul's bodily illness of Gal. 4:13. Some hold that Paul suffered from an eye disease (*ophthalmia*), pointing to Gal. 4:13-15, where Paul confirmed that the Galatians would have given him, if possible, their eyes. Further, in Gal. 6:11 Paul indicates he wrote in large script, which is logical for a person with eye trouble. A third common theory was sorrow and pain because of Jewish unbelief (Rom. 9:1-3). A fourth theory is that of a "messenger of Satan," rather than a physical ailment, given as a redemptive judgment of God on Paul for the purpose of humility.

Other theories were hysteria, hypochondria, gallstones, gout, rheumatism, sciatica, gastritis, leprosy, lice, deafness, dental infection, neurasthenia, a speech impediment, and remorse for persecuting the Church.

THREE TAVERNS Rest stop on the Appian Way, 33 miles southeast of Rome and 10 miles northwest of the Forum of Appius, where Roman Christians met Paul on his trip to Rome (Acts 28:15).

THYATIRA City in the Lycus River Valley. Thyatira was the center of a number of trade guilds that used the natural resources of the area to make it a very profitable site. Thyatira had a Jewish contingent out of which grew a NT church. One of Paul's first converts from the European continent, Lydia, was a native of Thyatira (Acts 16:14). She probably was a member of a guild there that dealt in purple dye. The church at Thyatira was praised for its works of charity, service, and faith (Rev. 2:19), but criticized for allowing the followers of Jezebel to prosper in its midst (2:20).

The ruins of Thyatira in ancient Asia Minor (modern Turkey).

TIAMAT Sumerian-Akkadian goddess viewed by the Babylonians as one of the major gods of their pantheon.

TIBERIAS Mentioned only in John 6:23 (cp. 6:1;

Modern Tiberias, built over the ancient city of Tiberias, overlooks the Sea of Galilee.

21:1), Tiberias is a city located on the western shore of the Sea of Galilee encompassing today what in ancient times were two separate cities, Tiberias and Hammath, each surrounded by its own wall.

TIBERIUS CAESAR Person who had the unenviable task of following Augustus as Roman emperor. See *Rome and the Roman Empire.*

TIBHATH Place-name meaning "place of slaughter." City from which David took spoils (or received tribute) of bronze (1 Chron. 18:8). The site is likely in the vicinity of Zobah north of Damascus. The parallel in 2 Sam. 8:8 reads "Betah."

TIBNI Personal name meaning "intelligent" or "straw." Likely an army officer who struggled with Omri over succession to the throne of Israel following Zimri's suicide (1 Kings 16:21-22).

TIDAL One of four kings allied against five in Gen. 14:1,9. The name is similar to Tud'alia, the name of several Hittite kings, suggesting the king's origin in eastern Asia Minor. The king is perhaps Tudhalia I (about 1700–1650 BC).

TIGLATH-PILESER Personal name meaning "My trust is the son of Esarra (the temple of Asshur)." King of Assyria from 745 to 727 BC (2 Kings 16:7), also known as Tilgath-pilneser 1 Chron. 5:6; 2 Chron. 28:20) and Pul (2 Kings 15:19; 1 Chron. 5:26). See *Assyria.*

The Tigris River flows through Iraq (ancient Mesopotamia).

TIGRIS RIVER See *Euphrates and Tigris Rivers.*

TIKVAH Personal name meaning "hope, expectation." **1.** Father-in-law of Huldah, the prophetess (2 Kings 22:14; 2 Chron. 34:22). **2.** Father of Jahaziah who opposed Ezra's call for Israelites to divorce their foreign wives (Ezra 10:15).

TIKVATH KJV alternate form of Tikvah (2 Chron. 34:22), perhaps representing original form of foreign name written in Hebrew as Tikvah.

TILGATH-PILNESER Alternate form of Tiglath-pileser (1 Chron. 5:6; 2 Chron. 28:20).

TILON Personal name of uncertain meaning. Descendant of Judah (1 Chron. 4:20).

TIMAEUS Personal name meaning "highly prized" (Mark 10:46). Bartimaeus is Aramaic for "son of Timaeus."

TIMBREL KJV term for a tambourine.

TIME, MEANING OF God is Lord over time, because He created and ordained time (Gen. 1:4-5,14-19). God Himself is timeless and eternal, not bound by space or time (Exod. 3:14-15; 1 Chron. 16:36; Pss. 41:13; 90:1-2; 93:2; 146:10; Isa. 9:6; John 1:1-18; 8:58; Heb. 13:8; 2 Pet. 3:8; Jude 1:25). On the other hand, God is not removed from time. Through His providential care and especially in the incarnation of Jesus Christ, God enters into time without being limited by the constraints of time.

Because of His foreknowledge, only God knows and foreordains events in time (Dan. 2:20-22; Mark 13:31-32; Acts 1:7; 2:22-23). God sees all things in time from a perspective of eternity, sees the end from the beginning. Humans, however, are trapped in time, and sometimes cannot discern the meaning and significance of time in their own day (Eccles. 3:1-11; 9:12; Ps. 90:9-10; Luke 12:54-56; James 4:13-16). Being bound by the remorseless march of time is a telling reminder of human finitude and temporality.

TIMNA Personal name meaning "holding in check" or "she protects." **1.** Sister of the Horite clan chief Lotan (Gen. 36:22; 1 Chron. 1:39), concubine of Esau's son Eliphaz, and mother of Amalek (Gen. 36:12). **2.** Son of Eliphaz (1 Chron. 1:36; Gen. 36:16 "Teman") and Edomite clan chief (Gen. 36:40; 1 Chron. 1:51). Timna is associated with either Timna in southern Arabia or, following Gen. 36:16, Teman in southern Edom. It is the name of the capitol of Qataban. **3.** Modern name for an ancient copper mining site 14 miles north of Elath.

The modern name Timna refers to a large copper-mining area north of the Gulf of Aqaba.

TIMNAH Place-name meaning "allotted portion."

Overview of Tell Batash (site of the ancient city of Timnah).

1. Town assigned to Dan (Josh. 19:43), located on the southern border with Judah (Josh. 15:10). **2.** Village in the hill country of Judah (Josh. 15:57). This Timnah was the likely scene of Judah's encounter with Tamar (Gen. 38:12-14).

TIMNATH-HERES or **TIMNATH-SERAH** Place of Joshua's inheritance and burial (Judg. 2:9; Josh. 19:50; 24:30). Timnath-heres means "portion of the sun," suggesting a site dedicated to sun worship (Judg. 2:9); Timnath-serah means "remaining portion," pointing to land given to Joshua following distribution of land to the tribes (Josh. 19:50; 24:30).

TIMON Personal name meaning "honorable." One of seven chosen to supervise distribution of food to the Greek-speaking widows of the Jerusalem church (Acts 6:5).

TIMOTHY Personal name meaning "honoring God." Friend and trusted coworker of Paul. When Timothy was a child, his mother Eunice and his grandmother Lois taught him the Scriptures (2 Tim. 1:5; 3:15). A native of Lystra, he may have been converted on Paul's first missionary journey (Acts 14:6-23). Paul referred to Timothy as his child in the faith (1 Cor. 4:17; 1 Tim. 1:2; 2 Tim. 1:2). This probably means that Paul was instrumental in Timothy's conversion. When Paul came to Lystra on his second journey, Timothy was a disciple who was well respected by the believers (Acts 16:1-2). Paul asked Timothy to accompany him. Timothy not only accompanied Paul but also was sent on many crucial missions by Paul (Acts 17:14-15; 18:5; 19:22; 20:4; Rom. 16:21; 1 Cor. 16:10; 2 Cor. 1:19; 1 Thess. 3:2,6).

TIMOTHY, FIRST LETTER TO First of two letters Paul wrote to Timothy. The letter was written in approximately AD 63, following Paul's first imprisonment in Rome. It is likely that Paul left Rome and traveled to Ephesus. There is some debate concerning the place of writing. Rome and Macedonia have been offered as possibilities. Perhaps, in light of 1 Tim. 1:3, Macedonia could be the better choice. The letter was addressed to Timothy in Ephesus. Paul had urged Timothy to remain in Ephesus and lead this important church as its pastor (1:3).
Purpose Paul had hoped to visit Timothy in Ephesus but was fearful of a delay. If he were delayed, he wanted Timothy to "know how people ought to act in God's household" (3:14-15 HCSB). The epistle contains instructions concerning order and structure in the church and practical advice for the young pastor. One important theme in this and the other two Pastoral Epistles (2 Timothy and Titus) is sound teaching. Paul urged Timothy and Titus to confront the false teaching by sound or healthy teaching. This word occurs eight times in these three letters (1 Tim. 1:10; 6:3; 2 Tim. 1:13; 4:3; Titus 1:9,13; 2:1-2).

TIMOTHY, SECOND LETTER TO Second of Paul's letters to Timothy, pastor of the church in Ephesus. The letter was the last letter of which we have a record written by Paul. He wrote this letter from his jail cell during his second imprisonment in Rome. He was awaiting trial for his faith. It is clear that he felt he would not be released (4:6). If Nero executed Paul and if Nero was killed in AD 68, then Paul had to have been executed sometime before. The letter can be dated between AD 63 and 67. Timothy was the recipient of Paul's letter. He had been the apostle's representative in the city of Ephesus for some time.
Purpose The letter contains Paul's stirring words of encouragement and instruction to his young disciple. Paul longed to see Timothy (1:4) and asked him to come to Rome for a visit. It is generally believed that Timothy went. Paul asked him to come before winter (4:21) and bring the winter coat Paul left in Troas (4:13). Timothy was also asked to bring the scrolls and the parchments so Paul could read and study (4:13).

TINKLING ORNAMENTS (KJV) Anklets making a tinkling noise as one walked. Part of the finery of the affluent women of Jerusalem (Isa. 3:16,18).

TIPHSAH Place-name meaning "passage, ford." **1.** City on the west bank of the Euphrates about 75 miles south of Carchemish, representing the northeastern limit of Solomon's kingdom (1 Kings 4:24). **2.** Site near Tirzah in Samaria (2 Kings 15:16), possibly a corruption of Tappuah, the reading of the earliest Greek translation that REB, RSV, TEV follow.

TIRAS Division of the descendants of Japheth who are all seagoing peoples (Gen. 10:2; 1 Chron. 1:5). Traditionally, they have been related to Turscha, part of the sea peoples Ramesses II

(1198–1166 BC) fought. Some have identified them with the Etruscans of Italy.

TIRATHITES Family of Kenite scribes (1 Chron. 2:55).

TIRE KJV term meaning "turban" (Ezek. 24:17,23).

TIRHAKAH Egyptian pharaoh of the 25th Dynasty (689–664 BC) who supported Hezekiah's revolt against the Assyrian king Sennacherib (2 Kings 19:8-9; Isa. 37:9).

TIRHANAH Personal name of uncertain meaning. Son of Caleb and Maacah (1 Chron. 2:48).

TIRIA Personal name meaning "fear." Descendant and family of Judah (1 Chron. 4:16).

TIRSHATHA Title of honor designating respect for an official, sometimes translated "your excellence" (Ezra 2:63; Neh. 7:65,70; 8:9; 10:1).

TIRZAH Personal name and place-name meaning "she is friendly." **1.** Daughter of Zelophehad who inherited part of tribal land allotment of Manasseh since her father had no sons. **2.** Originally a Canaanite city noted for its beauty (Song 6:4) but captured in the conquest of the promised land (Josh. 12:24).

TISHBITE Resident of an unidentified village, Tishbe, used as a title of Elijah (1 Kings 17:1; 21:17,28; 2 Kings 1:3,8; 9:36). Tishbite is possibly a corruption of Jabeshite or a class designation (cp. the Hebrew *toshav*, which designates a resident alien, Lev. 25:6).

TITHE Tenth part, especially as offered to God. Abraham presented a tithe of war booty to the priest-king of Jerusalem, Melchizedek (Gen. 14:18-20). Jacob pledged to offer God a tithe of all his possessions upon his safe return (Gen. 28:22). The tithe was subject to a variety of legislation. Some scholars think the differences in legislation reflect different uses of the tithe at various stages of Israel's history. Malachi 3:8 equates neglect of the tithe with robbing God. Jesus, however, warned that strict tithing must accompany concern for the more important demands of the law, namely, for just and merciful living (Matt. 23:23; Luke 11:42).

TITTLE A point (Matt. 5:18; Luke 16:17), the minute point or stroke added to some letters of the Hebrew alphabet to distinguish them from others that they resemble; hence, the very least point.

TITUS Gentile companion of Paul (Gal. 2:3) and recipient of the NT letter bearing his name. Titus may have been converted by Paul, who called him "my true child in our common faith" (Titus 1:4 HCSB). As one of Paul's early associates, Titus accompanied the apostle and Barnabas to Jerusalem (Gal. 2:1), probably on the famine relief visit (Acts 11:28-30).

Though Acts does not mention Titus, he was quite involved in Paul's missionary activities as shown in the Pauline letters. He was evidently known to the Galatians (Gal. 2:1,3), possibly from the first missionary journey to that region. Titus also seems to have been a very capable person, called by Paul "my partner and coworker" (2 Cor. 8:23 HCSB). He was entrusted with the delicate task of delivering Paul's severe letter (2 Cor. 2:1-4) to Corinth and correcting problems within the church there (2 Cor. 7:13-15). Titus's genuine concern for and evenhanded dealing with the Corinthians (2 Cor. 8:16-17; 12:18) no doubt contributed to his success which he reported in person to Paul, anxiously awaiting word in Macedonia (2 Cor. 2:13; 7:5-6,13-15). Paul responded by writing 2 Corinthians, which Titus probably delivered (2 Cor. 8:6,16-18,23).

Paul apparently was released after his first Roman imprisonment and made additional journeys, unrecorded in Acts. One of these took him and Titus to Crete, where Titus remained behind to oversee and administer the church (Titus 1:5). It was to Crete that Paul wrote his letter, asking Titus to join him in Nicopolis on the west coast of Greece (Titus 3:12). Following Paul's subsequent re-imprisonment, Titus was sent to Dalmatia (2 Tim. 4:10). According to church tradition, Titus was the first bishop of Crete.

TITUS, CAESAR Roman emperor AD 79–81, eldest son of Vespasian. Titus, like his father, was a soldier. He served in Germany and Britain and later in the Middle East. When Vespasian left his Middle East command to become emperor in AD 69, he left Titus in charge of crushing the Jewish revolt. In AD 70 his troops captured the temple in Jerusalem. They took the last stronghold, Masada, in AD 73. His victory over the Jews was vividly depicted on the Triumphal Arch erected in Rome that still stands today.

Titus was deeply admired by his soldiers; when he later became emperor, the populace loved him. He was considered an honest ruler and an efficient administrator. An adherent of Stoic philosophy, he believed that the Roman emperor was the servant of the people. He and his father before him (the so-called Flavian emperors) struggled after the excesses of Nero to reestablish stability in the empire and in the government. They managed to return the empire to sound financial footing.

Titus was constantly plagued by the activities of his younger brother, Domitian. Even though he did not believe that Domitian was worthy to be his successor, he would not dispose of him. See *Rome and the Roman Empire*.

TITUS, LETTER TO

Paul the apostle wrote to Titus, a trusted Gentile co-worker. See *Titus*. The circumstances of the writing of Titus are similar to those of the first letter to Timothy. After his first Roman imprisonment (AD 60–62), Paul returned to the East for missionary work. Apparently after Paul and Titus had evangelized Crete, Titus was

TITUS' CAMPAIGNS
- • City
- ○ City (uncertain location)
- ▲ Mountain peak
- ✿ Siege
- ← Titus's campaign
- ← Roman pressure
- ☐ Area of Jewish revolt

Titus assembles two legions to attack Jerusalem

Caesarea Maritima

Scythopolis (Beth-shan)
Pella

SAMARIA

Sebaste (Samaria)
Mt. Ebal ▲ Neapolis (Shechem)
Mt. Gerizim ▲ Coreae
Antipatris (Aphek)
Acrabeta
Alexandrium
Joppa
Yarkon R.
Thamna
Bethel
Lydda
Gophna
Legions from Jericho and Emmaus join Titus
JUDEA
Jericho
Azotus (Ashdod)
Jamnia
Emmaus
Gibeah
Cyprus
Qumran
Roman troops torch the temple August 28, A.D. 70 and gain complete control by late September
Jerusalem
Area enlarged below
Hyrcania
Herodium
Ascalon (Ashkelon)
Capharabis
Caphartobas
DEAD SEA
Betogabris
Anthedon
Caparorsa
Hebron
Judean Wilderness
Gaza
IDUMEA
En-gedi
Masada falls A.D. 73–74
Masada

left behind to set the churches in order, appointing elders in every city (Titus 1:5). Paul probably wrote this letter on the way to Nicopolis from Crete around AD 63–65. Just as in the first letter to Timothy, Paul warned against false teachers and issued instructions to various groups regarding proper Christian behavior. Furthermore, he instructed Titus to join him in Nicopolis whenever a replacement arrived (3:12).

TIZITE Title of Joha, one of David's 30 elite warriors (1 Chron. 11:45), designating his hometown or home region, which is otherwise unknown.

TOAH Personal name, perhaps meaning "humility." A Kohathite Levite (1 Chron. 6:34). The parallel lists read Nahath (1 Chron. 6:26) and Tohu (1 Sam. 1:1).

TOB Place-name meaning "good." Syrian city in southern Hauran to which Jephthah fled from his brothers (Judg. 11:3-5). Tob contributed troops to an unsuccessful alliance against David (2 Sam. 10:6-13). Tob is perhaps identical with Tabeel (Isa. 7:6).

TOBADONIJAH Personal name meaning "Yah, my Lord, is good." Levite whom Jehoshaphat sent to teach the people of Judah (2 Chron. 17:8).

TOBIAH Personal name meaning "Yah is good."

A closeup of the interior of the Arch of Titus in the Roman Forum showing the spoils of war taken during the First Jewish Revolt. The scene shows furnishings of the Jerusalem temple, including the seven-branch candlestick (the Menorah), plundered from the temple before it was destroyed.

1. One of the major adversaries to Nehemiah's rebuilding efforts at Jerusalem, Tobiah was a practicing Jew who lived in a residence chamber in the temple (Neh. 2:10,19). **2.** Ancestor of clan who returned from exile but could not show they were Israelites (Ezra 2:60)

TOBIJAH Alternate form of Tobiah. **1.** Levite whom Jehoshaphat sent to teach the people (2 Chron. 17:8). **2.** Returned exile who apparently brought a gift of gold from Babylon for the Jerusalem community. Zechariah used him as a witness for his crowning of Joshua, the high priest, and to preserve the crowns in the temple (Zech. 6:9-14).

TOCHEN Place-name meaning "measure." An unidentified village in Simeon (1 Chron. 4:32). The parallel lists in Josh. 15:42; 19:7 have "Ether."

TOGARMAH Son of Gomer and name of a region of Asia Minor (Gen. 10:3; 1 Chron. 1:6; cp. Beth-togarmah, Ezek. 38:6) inhabited by his descendants. Togarmah was famed for its horses (Ezek. 27:14).

TOHU Ancestor of Samuel (1 Sam. 1:1). Parallel lists read "Nahath" (1 Chron. 6:26) and "Toah" (6:34) in the corresponding position.

TOI Personal name meaning "error." King of Hammath on the Orontes who sent tribute to David following his defeat of their mutual foe, Hadadezer of Zobah (2 Sam. 8:9-10; Tou, 1 Chron. 18:9-10).

TOKEN KJV term meaning "sign" (Gen. 9:12-17; Pss. 65:8; 135:9).

TOKHATH Alternate form of Tikvah (2 Chron. 34:22).

TOLA Personal name meaning "crimson worm." **1.** Issachar's firstborn son (Gen. 46:13; Num. 26:23; 1 Chron. 7:1-2). **2.** Judge who governed Israel for 23 years from Shamir, likely at or near Samaria (Judg. 10:1).

TOLAD Alternate form of Eltolad (1 Chron. 4:29).

TOLAITE Division of Issachar descended from Tola (Num. 26:23-25).

TOMB OF JESUS According to the NT accounts, the tomb of Jesus was located in a garden in the place where Jesus was crucified (John 19:41) outside the city walls of Jerusalem (19:20). It was a "new tomb" that had been "cut into the rock" by Joseph of Arimathea (Matt. 27:60 HCSB; cp. Luke 23:50-56), who had apparently prepared it for his own family's use.

The Garden Tomb is one site offered by tradition as the burial place of Jesus' body.

TONGS Pinchers for holding coals (1 Kings 7:49; 2 Chron. 4:21; Isa. 6:6). KJV used "tongs" at Exod. 25:38; Num. 4:9 where modern translations read "snuffers" (HCSB, NASB, NRSV) or "wick trimmers" (NIV).

TONGUES, GIFT OF The NT deals with the practice of speaking in tongues both by example and instruction in Acts and the first letter to the Corinthians. There is also a brief mention of it in the long ending of Mark.

Tongues in the NT has three functions—to show the progress of the gift of the Spirit to the various people groups in the book of Acts in a salvation-history context, as a way of revealing the content of the NT revelation, and as a means of communicating cross-linguistically. The first two purposes would no longer be applicable, since the gospel has now gone out to the entire world and the NT revelation has been given. As regards the third purpose, no one would wish to limit God's ability to grant such a gift. There are even stories of such events from the mission field, though undoubtedly some of them have been embellished. It is also the case that all Pentecostal groups that send missionaries send them for language training first.

TOPHEL Place near the site of Moses' farewell speech to Israel (Deut. 1:1), identified with et-Tafileh about 15 miles southeast of the Dead Sea between Kerak and Petra.

TOPHET or **TOPHETH** Name for a place in the Hinnom Valley outside Jerusalem derived from Aramaic or Hebrew meaning "fireplace" but altered by Hebrew scribes to mean "shameful thing" because of the illicit worship carried on there (Jer. 7:31-32; KJV, "Tophet"). Child sacrifice was practiced at Topheth, leading the prophet to declare a slaughter of people there when God would come in vengeance (Jer. 19:6-11).

TORAH Hebrew word normally translated "law," which eventually became a title for the Pentateuch, the first five books of the OT.

TORCH Long pole with cloths dipped in oil wrapped around one end used as a light. The Greek *lampas* is generally rendered "torch" (John 18:3; Rev. 4:5; 8:10), unless the context suggests the translation "lamp" (Acts 20:8). The lamps of the wise and foolish virgins (Matt. 25:1-8) were perhaps torches.

TOU Alternate form of Toi (1 Chron. 18:9-10).

TOW Short, broken fibers of flax, known to be easily broken and highly flammable, used as a figure for weakness and transience (Judg. 16:9; Isa. 1:31; 43:17).

TOWER Tall edifice erected so watchmen could guard pastures, vineyards, and cities. Towers ranged from small one-room structures to entire fortresses. Archaeological remains confirm the wide usage of towers from the earliest times. Most were made of stones although some wooden towers have been unearthed. The word is used figuratively of God's salvation in 2 Sam. 22:51, indicating the strength of the Lord's action.

Watchtower overlooking grainfields near the valley of Lebonah.

TRACHONITIS Place-name meaning "heap of stones." A political and geographic district in northern Palestine on the east side of the Jordan River (Luke 3:1).

TRADITION Teaching or ritual that is handed down. The term "tradition" has several usages. The term is often used to speak of denominations or distinct theological viewpoints, such as the Baptist tradition or the Reformed tradition. The term is also commonly used to refer to liturgical consistency or to historical practice, as in a tradition of the church. Tradition also is used to speak of legend material, such as the tradition of Peter asking to be crucified upside-down. From a technical standpoint, the term is used to describe two distinct groups of theological material: biblical material prior to its being written down as Scripture and writings that are not part of the Bible but are still esteemed by the church.

TRAIN Used to refer to the part of a robe that trails behind the wearer (Isa. 6:1 KJV, NASB, NIV).

TRANCE Translation of the Greek term that literally means a change of place. Trance is descriptive of an experience in which a person received a revelation by supernatural means (Acts 10:10; 11:5; 22:17; HCSB, "visionary state"). In these instances, the author of Acts, in reference to the experiences of Peter and Paul, seemed to be interested in showing that the trance was only a vehicle for a revelation from God. Luke illustrated that the trances that Peter and Paul experienced "happened" to them and were not self-induced. The distinctions between "trance," "dream," and "vision" are not always clear.

TRANSFIGURATION Transformation of Jesus in His appearance with Moses and Elijah before Peter, James, and John (Matt. 17:1-13; Mark 9:1-13; Luke 9:28-36; cp. 2 Pet. 1:16-18). This event took place shortly after the confession at Caesarea Philippi, the first passion prediction, and a discourse on the cost of

Mount Hermon, one possible site of the Transfiguration.

discipleship. Jesus took Peter, James, and John to a mountain where the event took place. Jesus' personal appearance and that of His garments were changed. Moses and Elijah appeared and talked with Jesus.

The Place The traditional site is Mount Tabor in lower Galilee, but it is not a high mountain (only 1,850 feet) and was probably fortified and inaccessible in Jesus' day. Much more likely is Mount Hermon (9,100 feet) to the north of Caesarea Philippi.

Meaning A mountain in the Bible is often a place of revelation. Moses and Elijah represented the law and the prophets respectively, which testify to but must give way to Jesus. Clouds represent divine presence. The close connection of the transfiguration with the confession and passion prediction is significant. The Messiah must suffer, but glorification and enthronement, not suffering, is His ultimate fate. These involve resurrection, ascension, and return in glory. The disciples needed the reassurance of the transfiguration as they contemplated Jesus' death and their future sufferings.

TRANSGRESSION Image of sin as overstepping the limits of God's law.

TRANSJORDAN Area immediately east of the Jordan River settled by Reuben, Gad, half of Manasseh, Edom, Moab, and Amon. The most prominent topographical feature of Palestine is the Jordan River Valley, referred to in the OT as the "Arabah" and called today, in Arabic, the *Ghor*.

Transjordan included the River Jabbok, scene of the account of Jacob's wrestling on his return from Aram (Gen. 32:22-32); the Plains of Moab, where the Israelites are said to have camped following their exodus from Egypt and where Balaam prophesied; and Mount Nebo, from which Moses viewed the promised land (Num. 22:1–24:25; Deut. 34). Three Transjordanian kingdoms (Ammon, Moab, and Edom) were contemporary with the two Hebrew kingdoms (Israel and Judah), sometimes as allies, sometimes as enemies (1 Sam. 11; 14:47; 2 Sam. 8:12; 10; 2 Kings 3; Amos 1:11–2:3). The Prophet Elijah was from Tishbe, a town in the Transjordanian territory of Gilead (1 Kings 17:1). Other Israelite prophets and poets often referred to the territories and peoples of the Transjordan. See, for example, the allusions in Amos 4:1 and Ps. 22:12 to the cows and bulls of Bashan.

By NT times a cluster of Greco-Roman-oriented cities with primarily Gentile populations (the so-called "Decapolis" cities) had emerged in the northern Transjordan (earlier Bashan, Gilead, and Ammon). The southern Transjordan (earlier Moab and Edom) was dominated, on the other hand, by the Nabateans, a people of Arab origin who established a commercial empire along the desert fringe with its capital at Petra.

TRANSLATE 1. KJV term meaning "to transfer," used of the transfer of Saul's kingdom to David (2 Sam. 3:10) and the transfer of believers from the power of darkness to the sphere of Christ's control (Col. 1:13). **2.** KJV term meaning "to take up," used of Enoch's being taken up into God's presence without experiencing death (Heb. 11:5). **3.** Converting text from one language to another, retaining the original meaning or putting words in simpler terms.

TREE OF KNOWLEDGE Plant in the midst of the garden of Eden whose fruit was forbidden to Adam and Eve (Gen. 2:17). The tree of knowledge was Adam and Eve's opportunity to demonstrate obedience and loyalty to God, but the serpent used it to tempt Eve to eat and to become like God, "knowing good and evil" (Gen. 3:5). When Adam joined Eve in eating the forbidden fruit, the result was shame, guilt, exclusion from the garden, and separation from the tree of life and from God. The result for mankind was disaster as they failed the test and fell to the temptation.

TREE OF LIFE Plant in the garden of Eden symbolizing access to eternal life. Also, a metaphor used in Proverbs. For the biblical writer the tree of life was an important consideration only after Adam and Eve disobeyed. Their relationship to God changed radically when they disobeyed the command not to eat of the tree of knowledge. Chief among the radical changes was that they no longer had access to the tree of life (Gen. 3:22-24). The "tree of life" appears in Proverbs four times (Prov. 3:18; 11:30; 13:12; 15:4) and in Rev. 2:7; 22:2,14.

TRIAL OF JESUS Two systems of justice combined to produce a sentence of death for Jesus. Jewish religious leaders accused Jesus of blasphemy, a capital offense under Jewish law (Lev. 24:16). The Jewish leaders at Jesus' trial manipulated procedures to coerce Jesus into an admission that He was God's Son (Luke 22:66-71). For them this constituted blasphemy. Roman leaders allowed conquered people such as the Jews to follow their own legal system so long as they did not abuse their privileges. The Romans did not give the Jews the right of capital punishment for the accusation of blasphemy. The Jews had to convince a Roman judge that their demand for capital punishment was justified.

The Roman trial of Jesus also had three phases: first appearance before Pilate, appearance before Herod Antipas, and second appearance before Pilate. The Jewish leaders asked Pilate to accept their verdict against Jesus without investigation (John 18:29-31). Pilate refused this, but he offered to let them carry out the maximum punishment under their law, probably beating with rods or imprisonment. They insisted that they wanted death.

The Jews knew that Pilate would laugh at their charge of blasphemy. They fabricated three additional charges against Jesus that would be of concern to a Roman governor (Luke 23:2). Pilate concerned himself only with the charge that Jesus had claimed to be a king. This charge sounded like treason. The Romans knew no greater crime than treason.

Pilate interrogated Jesus long enough to be convinced that He was no political rival to Caesar (John 18:33-37). He returned to the Jews to announce that he found Jesus no threat to Rome and hence not deserving of death (John 18:38). The Jews responded with vehement accusations against Jesus' actions in Judea and Galilee (Luke 23:5). When Pilate learned that Jesus was from Galilee, he sent Jesus to Herod Antipas of Galilee who was then in Jerusalem (Luke 23:6-12). The king and his soldiers mocked and ridiculed Jesus, finally sending Him back to Pilate.

When Herod returned Jesus to Pilate, the Roman governor announced that he still found Jesus innocent of charges of treason. Three times Pilate tried to release Jesus. First, Pilate offered to chastise or beat Jesus and then to release him (Luke 23:16). Second, he offered to release either Jesus or Barabbas, a radical revolutionary. To Pilate's surprise the crowd chanted for Barabbas' release (Luke 23:17-19). Third, he scourged Jesus. Soldiers flailed at Jesus' bare back with a leather whip. The whip had pieces of iron or bone tied to the ends of the thongs. Pilate then presented the bleeding Jesus, who was wearing a crown of thorns and a mock purple robe, to the crowd as their king. He hoped that this spectacle would lead them to release Jesus out of pity. Again they chanted for crucifixion (John 19:4-6).

When Pilate seemed to waver one more time concerning crucifixion, the Jews threatened to report his conduct to Caesar (John 19:12). That threat triggered Pilate's action. After symbolically washing his hands of the entire affair (Matt. 27:24), he delivered Jesus for crucifixion (John 19:16).

THE 12 TRIBES OF ISRAEL

The 12 tribes of Israel descended from the 12 sons of the patriarch Jacob, whom God later renamed Israel. The land assignment and relative importance of each tribe reflected the birth order, birth mother, and individual actions of each son.

Record of the sons' births
Genesis 29:31–30:24; 35:16-20.

Key historical incidents in the sons' lives
Genesis 34:25-31 Simeon and Levi kill the men of Shechem.
Genesis 35:21-22 Reuben sleeps with his father's concubine.
Genesis 37:2-11 Joseph is hated by his brothers but the favorite of his father.
Genesis 48:1-20 Jacob blesses Joseph's two children, Ephraim and Manasseh, and "adopts" them as his own.
Genesis 49:1-28 Jacob gives a prophetic blessing to each of his sons.

Tribal allotments in the land of Israel
Numbers 32:1-42 Allotment for Reuben, Gad, and one-half of Manasseh
Joshua 15:1-63 Allotment for Judah
Joshua 16:1–17:18 Allotment for Ephraim and one-half of Manasseh
Joshua 18:11-28 Allotment for Benjamin
Joshua 19:1-9 Allotment for Simeon
Joshua 19:10-16 Allotment for Zebulun
Joshua 19:17-23 Allotment for Issachar
Joshua 19:24-31 Allotment for Asher
Joshua 19:32-39 Allotment for Naphtali
Joshua 19:40-48 Allotment for Dan
Joshua 21:1-42 Allotment for Levi

TRIBES OF ISRAEL Social and political groups in Israel claiming descent from one of the 12 sons of Jacob. The tribal unit played an important role in the history of the formation of the nation of Israel.

The ancestral background of "the tribes of Israel" went back to the patriarch Jacob, whose name was changed to "Israel." The nation of Israel was identified as "the children of Israel," or more literally "the sons of Israel." According to the biblical account, the family of Jacob, from which the tribes came, originated in north Syria during Jacob's stay at Haran with Laban his uncle. Eleven of the 12 sons were born at Haran, while the 12th, Benjamin, was born after Jacob returned to Canaan. The birth of the sons came through Jacob's wives Leah and Rachel and their maids Zilpah and Bilhah. The sons of Leah included Reuben, Simeon, Levi, Judah (Gen. 29:31-35), Issachar, and Zebulun, as well as one daughter named Dinah (Gen. 30:19-21). Rachel's sons were Joseph (Gen. 30:22-24), who became the father of Ephraim and Manasseh (Gen. 41:50-52), and Benjamin (Gen. 35:16-18). Jacob's sons through Zilpah, Leah's maid, were Gad and Asher (Gen. 30:9-13), while Bilhah, the maid of Rachel, bore Dan and Naphtali (Gen. 30:1-8).

This family of families or family of tribe

occupied the focal point in the history of the development of Israel as a nation. While there are details of that history that we do not clearly understand and other groups simply referred to as "an ethnically diverse crowd" (Exod. 12:38 HCSB) that were perhaps incorporated into the nation, the central focus is always on the "tribes of Israel," the descendants of Jacob.

TRIBULATION Generally refers to the suffering and anguish of the people of God. According to the NT, tribulations are an expected reality among the followers of Christ.

The Bible teaches several important truths concerning the tribulations of believers. First, the tribulations of Christ are the pattern for the sufferings of believers. As tribulation was inevitable and expected in the messianic ministry of Jesus, so tribulation will be present among His followers (Matt. 13:21; John 16:33; Acts 14:22; Rom. 8:35; 12:12; 1 Thess. 3:3; 2 Thess. 1:4; Rev. 1:9). Second, the tribulations of believers are in a sense participation in the sufferings of Christ (Col. 1:24; 2 Cor. 1:5; 4:10; Phil. 3:10; 1 Pet. 4:13). Third, the tribulations of believers promote transformation into the likeness of Christ (Rom. 5:3; 2 Cor. 3:18; 4:8-12,16). Tribulation teaches Christ's followers to comfort and encourage others in similar situations, enabling those suffering to persevere and persist (2 Cor. 1:4; 4:10; Col. 1:24; 1 Thess. 1:6).

Another biblical understanding of tribulation is eschatological. The expression "great tribulation" refers to the time of trouble that will usher in the second coming of Christ (Matt. 24:21; Rev. 2:22; 7:14). Jesus warned that the great tribulation will be so intense that its calamities will nearly decimate all of life (Matt. 24:15-22). Jesus' words in Matt. 24:29 may refer to Dan. 12:1, "a time of distress such as never occurred since there was a nation until that time" (NASB). This allusion suggests an eschatological view of the great tribulation.

One's millennial view usually determines the interpretation of the time and nature of this period of intense tribulation. Postmillennialists and amillennialists consider the great tribulation as a brief, indefinite period at the end of this age, usually identifying it with the revolt of Gog and Magog in Rev. 20:8-9. Dispensational premillennialists identify the tribulation with the 70th week of Daniel's prophecy (Dan. 9:27), a period of seven years whose latter half is the great tribulation. The rapture of the church precedes a literal, seven-year tribulation, which is followed by the second coming of Christ. Historical premillennialists (posttribulationalists) assert that the tribulation is a horrific period of trouble immediately preceding the millennium and typically teach that believers and unbelievers will both undergo this tribulation.

Although this event should rightly be regarded as a future occurrence, attempts to connect the time of tribulation with specific events or persons have proved futile. Believers are exhorted to watch for Christ and fix their hope on Him, not upon events surrounding His coming (1 John 3:3).

TRIBUNE Commander of an ancient Roman cohort, a military unit ideally comprising 1,000 men.

TRIBUTE Any payment exacted by a superior power, usually a state, from an inferior one. The weaker state, called a vassal state, normally contributed a specified amount of gold, silver, or other commodities on a yearly basis.

TRIGON Small, three-cornered harp with four strings (Dan. 3:5,7,10; KJV "sackbut"; HCSB, "lyre").

TRINITY Theological term used to define God as an undivided unity expressed in the threefold nature of God the Father, God the Son, and God the Holy Spirit. While the term "trinity" does not appear in Scripture, the trinitarian structure appears throughout the NT to affirm that God Himself is manifested through Jesus Christ by means of the Spirit. The following four statements summarize the truths inherent in the Christian understanding of the Trinity.

1. God is One. The God of the OT is the same God of the NT. His offer of salvation in the OT receives a fuller revelation in the NT in a way that is not different but more complete. The doctrine of the Trinity does not abandon the monotheistic faith of Israel.

2. God has three distinct ways of being in the redemptive event, yet He remains an undivided unity. That God the Father imparts Himself to mankind through Son and Spirit without ceasing to be Himself is at the very heart of the Christian faith. A compromise in either the absolute sameness of the Godhead or the true diversity reduces the reality of salvation.

3. The primary way of grasping the concept of the Trinity is through the threefold participation in salvation. The approach of the NT is not to discuss the essence of the Godhead, but the particular aspects of the revelatory event that includes the definitive presence of the Father in the person of Jesus Christ through the Holy Spirit.

4. The doctrine of the Trinity is an absolute mystery. It is primarily known, not through speculation, but through experiencing the act of grace through personal faith. See *God; Holy Spirit; Jesus Christ.*

TRIUMPHAL ENTRY Term used for the entry of Jesus into the city of Jerusalem on the Sunday prior to His crucifixion. Due to the fact that palm branches were placed before Him, this day is often called "Palm Sunday." The event is recorded in Matt. 21:1-9; Mark 11:1-10; Luke 19:28-38; John 12:12-15. All accounts agree in substance with each adding certain detail.

A section of the ruins of the theater at Troas.

TROAS City in northwest Asia Minor visited by Paul during his second and third missionary journeys (Acts 16:8,11; 20:5-6; 2 Cor. 2:12; 2 Tim. 4:13).

TROGYLLIUM Promontory on the west coast of Asia Minor less than one mile across the strait from Samos, a stopping place on Paul's return to Jerusalem according to the Western text of Acts 20:15.

TROPHIMUS Personal name meaning "nutritious." Gentile Christian from Ephesus who accompanied Paul to Jerusalem for the presentation of the collection (Acts 20:4; 21:29).

TRUTH Statements accurately reflecting facts, such as accurate and trustworthy witnesses (Prov. 12:17; cp. 1 John 2:21). Lying is the opposite of truth (Jer. 9:3; cp. Gen. 42:16). The people of God are to speak truth to one another (Zech. 8:16; Eph. 4:25). Jesus stresses the authority and certainty of His message in saying, "I tell you the truth" (Luke 9:27 HCSB; cp. Luke 4:24; John 16:7). John stresses he is telling the truth about Jesus (John 19:35), and Paul emphasizes he is not lying (Rom. 9:1; cp. 2 Cor. 7:14; 1 Tim. 2:7; Acts 26:25).

For Moses, the covenant God abounds in truth (Exod. 34:6). His truth is eternal (Ps. 117:2). Human testimony can swear to truth by nothing higher than God (1 Kings 22:16; Isa. 65:16). Since God is true, so is His word (Ps. 119:160; cp. John 17:17; 2 Sam. 7:28; Pss. 43:3; 119:142,151). Scripture is this very word of truth and thus should be handled carefully (2 Tim. 2:15). The gospel is equated with the truth (Gal. 2:5,14; Eph.1:13), and the truth is equated with the gospel (Gal. 5:7).

TRYPHAENA AND TRYPHOSA Personal names meaning "dainty" and "delicate." Two women whom Paul greeted as those "who have worked hard in the Lord" (Rom. 16:12 HCSB). The two were perhaps deacons serving the Roman church (cp. Phoebe in Rom. 16:1) or else "marketplace" evangelists like Priscilla (Acts 18:26; Rom. 16:3). The similarity of their names suggests the two were perhaps (twin) sisters.

TUBAL Son of Japheth (Gen. 10:2; 1 Chron. 1:5) and ancestor of a people known for their metalworking ability, likely of Cappadocia or Cilicia in Asia Minor (Isa. 66:19; Ezek. 27:13; 32:26; 38:2-3; 39:1).

TUBAL-CAIN Son of Lamech, associated with the origin of metalworking (Gen. 4:22). The two elements in his name mean "producer" and "smith."

TUNIC Loose-fitting, knee-length garment worn next to the skin (Matt. 10:10; Mark 6:9).

TURBAN Headdress formed by wrapping long strips of cloth around the head. A distinctive headdress formed part of the garb of the high priest (Exod. 28:4,37,39; 29:6; 39:28,31; Lev. 8:9; 16:4). Removal of one's turban was a sign of mourning or shame (Isa. 3:18-23; Ezek. 24:17,23).

TURNING OF THE WALL Expression used in the KJV, elsewhere translated as "the corner buttress" (NASB), "the Angle" (NRSV), "the escarpment" (REB), and "the angle of the wall" (NIV). One segment of the Jerusalem ramparts probably located

Relief of two Roman men wearing tunics partially visible beneath their outer togas.

near the palace. It was fortified by Uzziah (2 Chron. 26:9) and rebuilt by Nehemiah (Neh. 3:19-20,24). Not to be confused with "the corner" (Neh. 3:31) nor associated with the corner gate.

TYCHICUS Personal name meaning "fortunate." One of Paul's fellow workers in the ministry. A native of Asia Minor (Acts 20:4), he traveled with the apostle on the third missionary journey. Tychicus and Onesimus carried the Colossian letter from Paul (Col. 4:7-9) and were to relate to the church Paul's condition. Paul also sent Tychicus to Ephesus on one occasion (2 Tim. 4:12) and possibly to Crete on another (Titus 3:12). Tradition holds that he died a martyr.

TYPOLOGICAL INTERPRETATION Seeing persons, event, actions, and objects in the Old Testament as foreshadowing persons, events, actions, and objects in the New Testament. Typological interpretation is different than allegorical interpretation. See *Allegory.*

TYRANNUS Latin form of the Greek term *turannos,* a ruler with absolute authority. After Paul withdrew from the synagogue in Ephesus, he preached for two years at the lecture hall of Tyrannus (Acts 19:9). Tyrannus was either the owner of the hall or a prominent philosopher associated with it.

TYRE See *Sidon and Tyre.*

TYROPOEON VALLEY Narrow depression between Jerusalem's Ophel (Hill of David) and the western or upper hill of the city. It was much deeper in ancient times but has been filled up with debris through the centuries, especially since the destruction of the city by the Romans in AD 70. When David captured the city, the valley served as one of the natural defensive barriers. During Hellenistic times it was included within the city walls. During Herod's building campaign, he constructed bridges across the valley to connect the palace area with the temple complex.

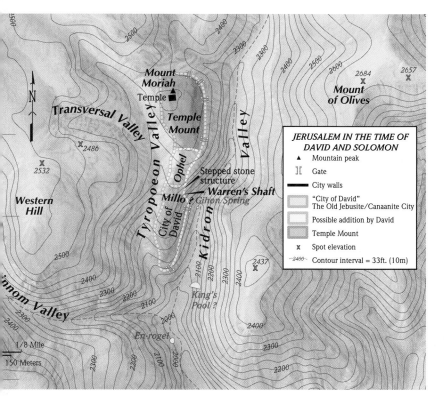

The excavated areas of Ugarit which have yielded much material about Canaan and Canaanite religion.

UCAL Personal name meaning "I am strong" or "I am consumed." Pupil of Agur, the wisdom teacher responsible for Prov. 30 (v. 1). REB followed the earliest Greek translation in rendering the proper names Ithiel and Ucal as "I am weary, God, I am weary and worn out" (cp. HCSB, NRSV).

UEL Personal name meaning "will of God," or a contraction of Abiel meaning "God is father." Contemporary of Ezra with a foreign wife (Ezra 10:34; KJV, Juel).

UGARIT Important city in Syria whose excavation has provided tablets giving the closest primary evidence available for reconstructing the Canaanite religion Israel faced. Ruins of the ancient city of Ugarit lie on the Mediterranean coast about nine miles north of Latakia. The contemporary name is Ras Shamra, "head [land] of fennel."

ULAI Canal connecting the Kerkha and Abdiziful Rivers just north of Susa (Dan. 8:2,16).

ULAM Personal name meaning "first" or "leader." **1.** Descendant of Manasseh (1 Chron. 7:16-17). **2.** Leader of a family of Benjaminite archers (1 Chron. 8:39-40).

ULLA Personal name meaning "burden" or "yoke." Descendant of Asher (1 Chron. 7:39). Scholars suggest a variety of emendations.

UMMAH Place-name meaning "kin." Town in Asher (Josh. 19:30). The name is perhaps a copyist's change from Acco as may be indicated by Greek manuscript evidence.

UNCTION KJV term meaning "anointing" (1 John 2:20,27).

UNDEFILED Ritually clean, frequently used for moral cleanness.

UNICORN KJV word for several related Hebrew terms that modern translations render as "wild ox" (Num. 23:22; 24:8; Deut. 33:17).

UNLEAVENED BREAD Bread baked without using leaven, a substance such as yeast that produces fermentation in dough. Unleavened bread was often served to guests (Gen. 19:3; Judg. 6:19; 1 Sam. 28:24). The eating of unleavened bread took on special significance through the Feast of Unleavened Bread celebrated in connection with Passover (Exod. 12:8,15,20; 13:3,6-7).

UNNI or **UNNO** Personal name, perhaps meaning "afflicted" or "answered." **1.** Levitical harpist in David's time (1 Chron. 15:18,20). **2.** Levite returning from exile with Zerubbabel (Neh. 12:9).

UNPARDONABLE SIN All three Synoptic Gospels (Matt. 12:31-32; Mark 3:28-29; Luke 12:10) refer to this concept. The context is identical in Matthew and Mark, following an exorcism by Jesus, including the accusation that Jesus casts out demons by Beelzebub's (Satan's) authority. The warning includes the statement that blasphemy against the Son of Man, while a sin, can be forgiven. This would be a rejection of the gospel, the good news of God's salvation in Jesus. In light of the context, the unpardonable sin can be defined as rejecting the power and authority of the Holy Spirit working in Jesus and crediting that authority to Satan. The Pharisees' false accusation prompts the warning but Jesus never explicitly says that they have crossed the

The traditional site of the upper room, or Hall of the Coenaculum, in Jerusalem.

line and committed the unpardonable sin. Perhaps this indicates that the unpardonable sin occurs when one knowingly credits the power and authority of the Holy Spirit to Satan. If so, some Pharisees may or may not have been guilty of making a charge against Jesus that they knew was false.

UPHAZ Unidentified source of fine gold (Jer. 10:9; Dan. 10:5) or else a term for fine gold. A related Hebrew term is translated "best gold" (1 Kings 10:18; Isa. 13:12). "Uphaz" is possibly a copyist's change for "Ophir" at Jer. 10:9 as indicated by early versions.

UPPER ROOM Upstairs room chosen by Jesus in which to hold a final meal with His disciples before His arrest (Mark 14:14-15).

The excavations at Ur showing the palace foundations in the foreground with the ziggurat in the distance.

UR Place-name meaning "fire oven." An ancient city in lower Mesopotamia that is mentioned as Abraham's birthplace. Ur was an important population center in Sumerian and Babylonian civilization. Abraham's family home is alluded to in Gen. 12:1 and Acts 7:2. The site associated with Ur is located in present-day Iraq, in the lower eastern portion of the Fertile Crescent.

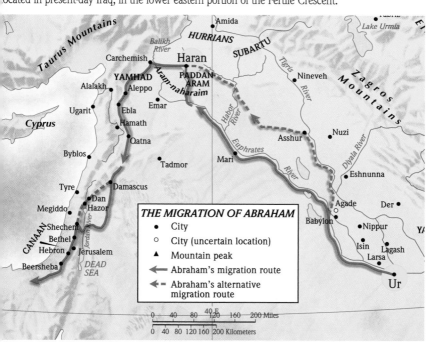

THE MIGRATION OF ABRAHAM
- • City
- ○ City (uncertain location)
- ▲ Mountain peak
- ← Abraham's migration route
- ◄- Abraham's alternative migration route

URBANE (KJV) or **URBANUS** Personal name meaning "of the city," that is, "elegant, refined." Roman Christian whom Paul greeted as a "co-worker in Christ" (Rom. 16:9 HCSB).

URI Personal name meaning "fiery." **1.** Father of the tabernacle artisan Bezalel (Exod. 31:2; 35:30). **2.** Father of Geber, one of Solomon's officers charged with providing the royal household food for a month (1 Kings 4:19). **3.** Postexilic, Levitical singer with a foreign wife (Ezra 10:24).

URIAH Personal name meaning "fire of Yah." **1.** Hittite mercenary or native, perhaps noble Israelite of Hittite ancestry, in David's army (2 Sam. 11), a member of David's elite warriors (23:39). He was the husband of Bathsheba, the woman with whom David committed adultery. The sin led to the eventual murder of Uriah after the king could cover the affair no longer. The Dead Sea Scrolls and Josephus report that Uriah was Joab's weapon-bearer. Uriah displayed more character and morality than did the king. **2.** High priest in Jerusalem temple under King Ahaz who followed the king's instructions in setting up an altar in the temple according to a Syrian pattern (2 Kings 16:10-16). He apparently served as a witness for Isaiah (8:2). **3.** Priest in time of Ezra and Nehemiah (Ezra 8:33; Neh. 3:4,21). **4.** Person who helped Ezra in informing the people of God's word (Neh. 8:4).

URIEL Personal name meaning "God is light" or "flame of God." **1.** Chief of the Levites assisting in David's transport of the ark to Jerusalem (1 Chron. 6:24; 15:5,11). **2.** Grandfather of King Abijah of Judah (2 Chron. 13:2).

URIJAH Personal name meaning "flame of Yahweh." Variant spelling of Uriah. **1.** Chief priest who complied with Ahab's order to build an Assyrian-style altar for the Jerusalem temple (2 Kings 16:10-16). **2.** Prophet who joined Jeremiah in preaching against Jerusalem. When King Jehoiakim ordered his execution, Urijah fled to Egypt. He was, however, captured, returned to Jerusalem, and executed (Jer. 26:20-23).

URIM AND THUMMIM Objects Israel, and especially the high priest, used to determine God's will. Little is known about the Urim and Thummim. They are first mentioned in Exodus as being kept by the high priest in a "breastplate of judgment" (Exod. 28:15-30). Later on, Moses gave the tribe of Levi special responsibility for their care (Deut. 33:8).

USURY Sum of money charged for a loan. OT laws prohibited a Jew from charging another Jew usury but permitted it when money was loaned to a Gentile (Deut. 23:19-20). Although the word has negative connotations today, it was not so in biblical days when usury simply was the interest charged for a loan. Excessive usury was condemned.

UTHAI Personal name meaning "Yahweh is help" or "He has shown Himself supreme." **1.** Postexilic descendant of Judah (1 Chron. 9:4). **2.** Head of a family of those returning from exile (Ezra 8:14).

UZ Personal name and place-name, perhaps meaning "replacement." **1.** Unspecified territory, most likely in Hauran south of Damascus (Jer. 25:20) or else between Edom and northern Arabia (Job 1:1 Lam. 4:21). **2.** Descendant of Shem's son Aram (Gen. 10:23; 1 Chron. 1:17) and progenitor of an Aramaean tribe. **3.** Descendant of Abraham's brother Nahor (Gen. 22:21). **4.** Descendant of Esau (Gen. 36:28) and member of the Horite branch of Edomites.

UZAI Personal name meaning "hoped for" or "he has heard." Father of one helping with Nehemiah's repair of the wall (Neh. 3:25).

UZAL Son of Joktan and ancestor of an Arabian tribe (Gen. 10:27; 1 Chron. 1:21). Scholars have linked the tribe with Izalla in northeastern Syria and Azalla near Medina. Ezekiel 27:19 includes them among Tyre's trading partners.

UZZA Personal name meaning "strength." **1.** Descendant of Benjamin (1 Chron. 8:7). **2.** Descendant of Levi (1 Chron. 6:29). **3.** Head of a family of postexilic temple servants or Nethinims (Ezra 2:49). **4.** Owner of the garden in which Manasseh and Amon were buried (2 Kings 21:18,26). **5.** Variant English spelling of "Uzzah."

UZZAH Personal name meaning "he is strong." **1.** One of the drivers of the cart carrying the ark of the covenant when David began moving it from the house of Abinadab in Gibeah to Jerusalem (2 Sam. 6:3). When the ark started to slip from the cart, Uzzah put out his hand to steady it, and God struck him dead for touching the holy object (6:6-7). **2.** Ancestor of exiles who returned to Jerusalem from Babylon (Ezra 2:49). **3.** Name of garden in which kings Manasseh and Ammon were buried. This distinguished them from other kings who "slept with their fathers," that is, were buried in the royal tomb. Uzzah may have been a noble who owned the garden burial plot or may have been a variant spelling of the Canaanite god Attar-melek. **4.** Member of tribe of Benjamin (1 Chron. 8:7). **5.** Family of temple servants who returned from exile with Zerubbabel (Ezra 2:49). **6.** A Levite (1 Chron. 6:29).

UZZEN-SHEERAH Place-name meaning "ear of Sheerah." Village that Ephraim's daughter Sheerah founded (1 Chron. 7:24). The site is perhaps Beit Sira, three miles south of lower Beth-horon.

UZZI Personal name; an abbreviated form of "Yahweh is my strength." **1.** Aaronic priest (1 Chron. 6:5-6,51; Ezra 7:4). **2.** Family of the tribe of Issachar (1 Chron. 7:2-3). **3.** Descendant of Benjamin (1 Chron. 7:7; 9:8). **4.** Overseer of Jerusalem Levites after the exile (Neh. 11:22). **5.** Postexilic priest (Neh. 12:19). **6.** Musician involved in Nehemiah's dedication of Jerusalem's walls (Neh. 12:42).

UZZIA Personal name meaning "Yahweh is strong." One of 16 whom the Chronicler added to the list of David's 30 elite warriors (1 Chron. 11:44).

UZZIAH Personal name meaning "Yahweh is [my] strength." **1.** Descendant of Levi (1 Chron. 6:24). **2.** Father of one of David's treasurers (1 Chron. 27:25). **3.** Also known as Azariah (2 Kings 15:1,6-8,17,23,27); son and successor of King Amaziah of Judah. **4.** Postexilic priest with a foreign wife (Ezra 10:21). **5.** Descendant of Judah and father of a postexilic resident of Jerusalem (Neh. 11:4).

UZZIEL Personal name meaning "God is strength." **1.** Descendant of Levi (Exod. 6:18; Num. 3:19; 1 Chron. 6:2,18) and ancestor of a subdivision of Levites, the Uzzielites (Num. 3:27; 1 Chron. 15:10; 26:23). **2.** One captain in the successful Simeonite attack on the Amalekites of Mount Seir (1 Chron. 4:42). **3.** Descendant of Benjamin (1 Chron. 7:7). **4.** Levitical musician (1 Chron. 25:4). **5.** Levite involved in Hezekiah's reform (2 Chron. 29:14). **6.** Goldsmith assisting in Nehemiah's repair of the Jerusalem walls (Neh. 3:8).

UZZIELITE Member of Levitical clan of Uzziel.

VAIZATHA or **VAJEZATHA** Persian personal name, perhaps meaning "the son of the atmosphere." One of Haman's 10 sons the Jews killed after Esther gained permission to retaliate against Haman's deadly plan (Esther 9:9).

VALLEY Depression between mountains, a broad plain or plateau, a narrow ravine, or a low terrain. "Valleys" of varying shapes and sizes mark Palestine's landscape. "Valley" is often used symbolically to refer to the difficulties of life. The classic example of this is Ps. 23:4.

VANIAH Personal name possibly meaning "worthy of love." Man who married a foreign wife (Ezra 10:36).

VASHNI Personal name, perhaps meaning "weak." Samuel's son according to Hebrew text of 1 Chron. 6:28 (KJV).

VASHTI Personal name meaning "the once desired, the beloved." Wife of King Ahasuerus and queen of Persia and Media (Esther 1:9). The king called for her to show off her beauty to a group he was entertaining, but she refused. Vashti was deposed as queen (1:19), and a beauty contest was arranged to select a new queen. Esther was chosen as the new queen (2:16).

VEIL (KJV "vail") Cloth covering. **1.** *Womens' veils* Rebekah veiled herself before meeting Isaac (Gen. 24:65). Her veil was perhaps the sign that she was a marriageable maiden. At Isa. 47:2 the removal of one's veil is again a sign of shamelessness. Paul regarded the wearing of veils as necessary for women praying or preaching ("prophesying") in public (1 Cor. 11:4-16). **2.** *Moses' veil* Moses spoke to God with his face unveiled and then delivered God's message to the people with his face still unveiled. Afterwards, Moses veiled his face (Exod. 34:33-35). **3.** *Imagery* The "veil which is stretched over the nations" (Isa. 25:7 NASB) is likely an image for death, which is also swallowed up (25:8). The veil possibly includes reproach as well. **4.** *Temple veil* This curtain separated the most holy place from the holy place (2 Chron. 3:14). Only the high priest was allowed to pass through the veil and then only on the Day of Atonement (Lev. 16:2). At Jesus' death the temple veil was ripped from top to bottom, illustrating that in Christ God had abolished the barrier separating humanity from the presence of God (Matt. 27:51; Mark 15:38; cp. Luke 23:45). Hebrews 10:20 uses the tabernacle veil, not as the image of a barrier, but of access. Access to God is gained through the flesh of the historical Jesus (cp. John 10:7).

VENGEANCE The restoration of community integrity seems to have expected some deed(s) of retaliation or punishment by God. The range of meanings in this community motif go beyond "vengeance" as punishment. They include the positive side as well, "vengeance" as "deliverance" for the people of God.

Human revenge against one's enemies is expressed in a variety of situations in the OT (Gen. 4:23-24; Jer. 20:10). Thus, Samson's reaction to his enemies was described as "vengeance" in Judg. 15:7. Such "vengeance" was a just punishment directed at an adulterer (Prov. 6:32-34). It might also be directed against a whole ethnic group like the Philistines (1 Sam. 18:25). Sometimes, this human "vengeance" is sought against Israel by her enemies (Ezek. 25:12,15,17).

In the context of loving one's neighbor, human revenge toward a fellow Hebrew was strictly forbidden (Lev. 19:17-18; Deut. 32:35). On occasion, however, the word *naqam* was used of legitimate punishment administered by humans on humans for wrongs having been done (Exod. 21:20,23-25; Lev. 24:19; Deut. 19:21). As an act of God on behalf of His people, the term is best understood as just retribution (Judg. 11:36) rather than emotion-driven vengeance.

New Testament The motif of "vengeance" in the NT occurs infrequently and is kept in perspective by a strong emphasis on "compassion" and "forgiveness."

Interestingly, Luke is the only Gospel writer who used both the verb and noun forms. He used them in Jesus' parable of the unjust judge/persistent widow. Vengeance against her enemies was reluctantly granted (Luke 18:1-8)

Paul forbade human "vengeance" much like Deut. 32:35 (cp. Lev. 19:18), asserting that God is the one who avenges wrong (Rom. 12:19; 1 Thess. 4:6-7). He utilized both the noun and verb forms in the Corinthian correspondence to speak of a "punishment" designed to bring about repentance (2 Cor. 7:10-11; 10:5-6). He also wrote of the eschatological wrath (vengeance/judgment) of God (2 Thess. 1:7-8; cp. Isa. 66:15; Ps. 79:6).

VENISON Flesh of a wild animal taken by hunting (Gen. 25:28; "game," NASB, NRSV; "wild game," NIV, HCSB). The word is only used in the narrative of Jacob's stealing Esau's birthright. Isaac preferred Esau because of his love of wild game.

VENOM Poisonous secretion from an animal such as a snake, spider, or scorpion that is released into its victim by a bite or sting. Venom is a translation of *ro'sh* (Deut. 32:33; Job 20:16). The same Hebrew term is used for a dangerous, poisonous plant (Deut. 29:18; Hos. 10:4, among others).

VESPASIAN Emperor of Rome AD 69–79. He was born into a wealthy family and became a military hero as commander of a legion under Emperor Claudius. After becoming commander of three legions, he was ordered to quell the Jewish revolt in Palestine in AD 66. Three years into the war, he answered the call of the army to become emperor. Vespasian left his command to his son, Titus, and went to Rome. He sought to establish a dynasty, but it lasted only through his two sons, Titus and Domitian.

VIA DOLOROSA Literally, "way of suffering." Christian pilgrims from the time of the Crusaders have retraced the alleged path of Jesus from the Fortress of Antonia to the cross. This journey assumes the trial took place at the Antonian Fortress, which is debatable. Even if the fortress was the location of Jesus' trial before Pilate, the centuries of remains have filled in and changed the streets from Jesus' time. Thus, the 14 "stations" of the cross are based on tradition.

VIAL Vessel that held oil, usually for anointing purposes (1 Sam. 10:1 KJV, NRSV; NASB, NIV, "flask"). The same word is used a number of times in the book of Revelation (5:8; 15:7; 16:1-4,8,10,12,17; 17:1; 21:9; HCSB, NASB, NIV, NRSV, "bowls") See *Anoint; Oil.*

One of the stations on the Via Dolorosa (the Way of Sorrow) in Jerusalem.

VILLAGE OT distinguishes between city and village. The city was usually walled and much larger, while the village was characterized by no wall and usually homes consisting of one room (Lev 25:29,31). The village had little or no organized government. Archaeology shows Israelite villages built around the circumference with house walls joining to form the only defense system and open community space left in the middle. Many villages had 20 to 30 houses. The cattle were kept in the inner open space where grain was stored. The main job in the villages was farming. Small craft manufacturing was practiced. Usually a common threshing floor was available. Shepherds often gathered around villages. The pastureland was seen as the possession of the village (1 Chron. 6:54-60).

VINE Any plant having a flexible stem supported by creeping along a surface or by climbing a natural or artificial support. While ancient Israel grew different types of plants that produced vines, such as cucumbers and melons (Num. 11:5; Isa. 1:8), the word "vine" almost always refers to the grapevine or vineyard. The climate of Palestine was well suited for growing vineyards. Along with the olive and fig trees, the grapevine is used throughout the OT to symbolize the fertility of the land (Deut. 6:11 Josh. 24:13; 1 Sam. 8:14; 2 Kings 5:26; Jer. 5:17 40:10; Hos. 2:12).

Grapes growing on the vine.

The Bible frequently uses "vine" and "vineyard" as symbols. Vine is often used in speaking of Israel. Thus Israel is said to have been brought out of Egypt and planted as a vine on the land but was forsaken (Ps. 80:8-13; cp. Isa. 5:1-7). Israel was planted a "choice vine" but became a "wild vine" (Jer. 2:21; cp. Hos. 10:1). As the dead wood of a vine is good for nothing but fuel, so the inhabitants of Jerusalem would be consumed (Ezek. 15:1-8; 19:10-14).

On the other hand, the abundance of vines and vineyards was seen as an expression of God's favor. The fruit of the vine gladdens the heart of mankind (Ps. 104:15; Eccles. 10:19) and suppresses pain and misery (Prov. 31:6-7). Israel was "like grapes in the wilderness" when God found them (Hos. 9:10), and the remnant surviving the exile is compared to a cluster of grapes (Isa. 65:8). Finally, an abundance of the vine symbolizes the glorious age to come when the treader of the grapes will overtake the one who sows the seed (Amos 9:13-15; cp. Gen. 49:10-12).

In the NT Jesus often used the vineyard as an analogy for the kingdom of God (Matt. 20:1-16). Those who hope to enter the kingdom must be like the son who at first refused to work in his father's vineyard but later repented and went (Matt. 21:28-32 and parallels). Ultimately, Jesus Himself is described as the "true vine" and His disciples (Christians) as the branches (John 15:1-11).

VINEGAR Literally, "that which is soured," related to Hebrew term for "that which is leavened" and referring to a drink that has soured, either wine or beer from barley (Num. 6:3). In biblical times vinegar was most commonly produced by pouring water over the skins and stalks of grapes after the juice had been pressed out and allowing the whole to ferment. However, any fruit could be used for making wine or vinegar. In the NT it is mentioned only in connection with the crucifixion. The first instance, which Jesus refused, was a mixture used to deaden the sense of the victim and nullify the pain. Possibly the vinegar mentioned in the second instance, which Christ accepted, was the customary drink of a peasant or soldier called *posca*, a mixture of vinegar, water, and eggs. Vinegar was most commonly used as a seasoning for food or as a condiment on bread (Ruth 2:14). Solomon figuratively used vinegar to describe the irritation caused by a lazy man's attitude.

VIOLENCE Use of force to injure or wrong. The OT affirms that God hates violence (Mal. 2:16). The flood was God's response to a world filled and corrupted by violence (Gen. 6:11,13). The exile was likewise God's response to a Jerusalem filled with violence (Ezek. 7:23). The Wisdom literature often warns that those who live lives of violence will meet violent ends (Ps. 7:16; Prov. 1:18-19; 21:7; cp. Matt. 26:52). Through the prophets God demanded an end to violence (Jer. 22:3; Ezek. 45:9). Such violence was especially evidenced in the oppression of the poor by the rich (Pss. 55:9,11; 73:6; Jer. 22:17; Mic. 6:12; James 5:1-6). The servant of the Lord models a nonviolent response to violence (Isa. 53:9; cp. 1 Pet. 2:23; James 5:6). Isaiah anticipated the end of violence in the Messianic age (60:18).

Matthew 11:12 is one of the most difficult texts in the NT. Does the kingdom of heaven suffer violence (HCSB, KJV, NASB, REB, NRSV), or does the kingdom come "forcefully" (NIV)? The violence which John the Baptist (Matt. 14:3-10) and believers (Matt. 5:10-11; 10:17; 23:34) suffer argues for the former.

Candidates for church leadership should be nonviolent persons (1 Tim. 3:3; Titus 1:7).

VIPER Poisonous snake. Several species of snakes are called vipers, and the various words used in the Bible for them probably do not designate specific types. Jesus spoke of the wicked religious leaders as vipers (Matt. 3:7) because of their venomous attacks on Him and their evil character in leading the people astray. Paul was bitten by a viper (Acts 28:3) but suffered no ill effect from it.

VIRGIN, VIRGINAL CONCEPTION (OR VIRGIN BIRTH) The event that initiated the incarnation of Christ whereby He was supernaturally conceived in the womb of a virgin without the participation of a human father. The NT texts that deal with the virgin birth are Matt. 1:18-25 and Luke 1:26-35.

Theological Relevance The virginal conception affects two major areas of theology. First, it relates to the truthfulness of Scripture. The NT clearly states that Jesus was born of a virgin, and to deny this is to question the veracity and authenticity of the text. Second, the virgin conception is linked to the deity of Christ, for through this event He simultaneously retained His divine nature and received a sinless human nature. Scripture reveals it as a critical aspect of the incarnation.

A viper partially hidden in the surrounding grass and wildflowers.

VISION Experience in the life of a person whereby a special revelation from God was received. The revelation from God had two purposes. First, a vision was given for immediate direction, as with Abram in Gen. 12:1-3; Lot, Gen. 19:15; Balaam, Num. 22:22-40; and Peter, Acts 12:7. Second, a vision was given to develop the kingdom of God by revealing the moral and spiritual deficiencies of the people of God in light of God's requirements for maintaining a proper relationship with Him. The visions of prophets such as Isaiah, Amos, Hosea, Micah, Ezekiel, Daniel, and John are representative of this aspect of revelation.

VOPHSI Personal name of uncertain meaning. Father of Nahbi of the tribe of Naphtali (Num. 13:14). Nahbi was one of the spies Moses sent into Canaan.

VOWS Voluntary expressions of devotion usually fulfilled after some condition had been met. Vows in the OT usually were conditional. A common formula for vows was the "if . . . then" phrase (Gen. 28:20; Num. 21:2; Judg. 11:30). The one making the religious vow proposed that if God did something (such as give protection or victory), then he or she in return would make some act of devotion.

Not all vows, however, were conditional. Some, such as the Nazirite vow (Num. 6), were made out of devotion to God with no request placed upon God. Whether conditional or not, the emphasis in the Bible is on keeping the vow. A vow unfulfilled is worse than a vow never made. While vows do not appear often in the NT, Paul made one that involved shaving his head (Acts 18:18).

VULGATE Latin translation of the Bible by Jerome about AD 400.

A mosaic in the chapel of Jerome's Room, the traditional site where Jerome translated the Latin Vulgate, located under the Church of the Nativity in Bethlehem.

VULTURE Both carrion vulture and vulture are listed separately in the unclean bird lists (Lev. 11:13-19; Deut. 14:12-18 RSV).

The wadi through the limestone cliffs at Qumran near the Dead Sea.

WADI Transliteration of Arabic word for a rocky watercourse that is dry except during rainy seasons. These creek beds can become raging torrents when especially heavy rains fall. Wadis are numerous in the Middle East.

WAGES Terms of employment or compensation for services rendered encompass the meaning of the Hebrew and Greek words. Their usage in the text applies to commercial activities and labor service, as well as judgmental recompense for one's actions in life.

WAGON Vehicle of transportation with two or four wooden wheels. The two-wheeler was usually called a cart. Wagons were used to transport people and goods (Gen. 45:17-21). Sometimes wagons were used as instruments of war (Ezek. 23:24). Wagons were usually pulled by oxen.

WALK Slower pace contrasted with running. It is used literally (Exod. 2:5; Matt. 4:18) and figuratively to mean a person's conduct or way of life (Gen. 5:24; Rom. 8:4; 1 John 1:6-7).

WALLS Outside vertical structures of houses and the fortifications surrounding cities. In ancient times the walls of cities and houses were constructed of bricks made of clay mixed with reed and hardened in the sun. Archaeologists estimate that the walls of Nineveh were wide enough to drive three chariots abreast and the walls of Babylon were wide enough to drive six chariots abreast on the top.

In scriptural language a wall is a symbol of salvation (Isa. 26:1; 60:18), of the protection of God (Zech. 2:5), of those who afford protection (1 Sam. 25:16; Isa. 2:15), and of wealth of the rich in their own conceit (Prov. 18:11). A "fortified wall of bronze" (NRSV) is symbolic of prophets and their testimony against the wicked (Jer. 15:20). The "wall of partition" (Eph. 2:14 KJV; HCSB, dividing wall of hostility) represented temple worship and Jewish practice separating Jew from Gentile.

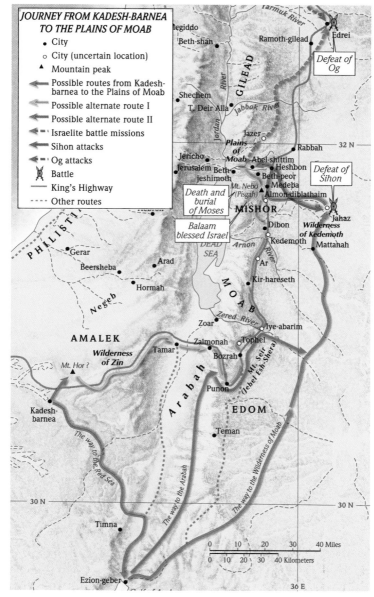

JOURNEY FROM KADESH-BARNEA TO THE PLAINS OF MOAB
- • City
- ○ City (uncertain location)
- ▲ Mountain peak
- Possible routes from Kadesh-barnea to the Plains of Moab
- Possible alternate route I
- Possible alternate route II
- Israelite battle missions
- Sihon attacks
- Og attacks
- Battle
- King's Highway
- Other routes

WANDERINGS IN THE WILDERNESS Israel's movements from Egypt to the promised land under Moses, including the place-names along the routes. A reconstruction of the Israelites' wilderness wanderings is more complex than a casual reading of the biblical account at first would seem to indicate.

WATCH Division of time in which soldiers or others were on duty to guard something. They are listed as "evening," "midnight," "crowing of the rooster," and "morning" (Mark 13:35 HCSB). Nehemiah set watches that may mean armed persons or just citizens on guard (4:9; 7:3). The OT seems to have had three watches rather than four. There was the "beginning of the night watches" (Lam. 2:19), the "middle watch" (Judg. 7:19), and the "morning watch" (Exod. 14:24).

WATCHMAN One who stands guard. Ancient cities had watchmen stationed on the walls. Their responsibility was to sound a warning if an enemy approached (2 Kings 9:17; Ezek. 33:2-3). Israel's prophets saw themselves as watchmen warning the nation of God's approaching judgment if the people did not repent. Vineyards and fields also had watchmen, especially during harvest. Their responsibility was to guard the produce from animals and thieves.

WATCHTOWER Tower on a high place or built high enough to afford a person to be able to see for some distance. The person doing the watching might be a soldier or a servant (2 Kings 9:17; Isa. 5:2; Mark 12:1). See *Tower*.

WATER The Bible speaks of water in three different ways: as a material resource, as a symbol, and as a metaphor.

A Material Necessity That God Provides Water as a material resource is necessary for life. God made water a part of His good creation, and He exercises sovereignty over it (Gen. 1–2; Isa. 40:12). He controls the natural processes of precipitation and evaporation, as well as the courses of bodies of water (Job 5:10; 36:27; 37:10; Pss. 33:7; 107:33; Prov. 8:29). God normally assures the provision of water for human needs (Deut. 11:14). However, water is sometimes used in punishment for sin, as with the flood of Noah's day (Gen. 6:17) or the drought proclaimed by Elijah (1 Kings 17:1). The divine control of water teaches people obedience to and dependency upon God.

An ancient watchtower remains relatively unchanged in an open field in Israel.

Many of the great acts of God in history have involved water, such as the parting of the sea (Exod. 14:21), the provision of water for the Israelites in the wilderness (Exod. 15:25; 17:6), and the crossing of the Jordan River (Josh. 3:14-17). Water was also involved in several of Jesus' miracles (Matt. 14:25; Luke 8:24-25; John 2:1-11).

Water was a crucial element in God's gift of the promised land to Israel (Deut. 8:7). Palestine contains several natural sources of water: rain, springs, wells, and a few short, perennial streams. The average annual rainfall in Palestine is about 25 inches, all of which normally falls between November and April. The dry months of May to October made necessary the use of cisterns and pools for water storage. Several famous biblical cities had pools, such as Gibeon (2 Sam. 2:13), Hebron (2 Sam. 4:12), Samaria (1 Kings 22:38), and Jerusalem (2 Kings 20:20). See *Palestine*.

A Theological Symbol and Metaphor The OT contains laws for the use of water in rituals as a symbol of purification. Priests, sacrificial meat, and ritual utensils were washed before involvement in rituals (Lev. 1:9; 6:28; 8:6). Unclean people and things were also washed as a symbol of ritual cleansing (Lev. 11:32-38; 14:1-9; 15:1-30; Num. 31:23). The book of Genesis uses water as a symbol of instability before the completion of creation (1:2), and Ezekiel spoke of water as a symbol of renewal in the age to come (47:1-12).

The Bible contains dozens of metaphorical usages of water. For example, in the OT, water is a metaphor or simile for fear (Josh. 7:5), death (2 Sam. 14:14), sin (Job 15:16), God's presence (Ps. 72:6), marital fidelity (Prov. 5:15-16), the knowledge of God (Isa. 11:9), salvation (Isa. 12:3), the Spirit (Isa. 44:3-4), God's blessings (Isa. 58:11), God's voice (Ezek. 43:2), God's wrath (Hos. 5:10) and justice (Amos 5:24). Among the metaphorical uses of water in the NT are references to birth (John 3:5), the Spirit (John 4:10), spiritual training (1 Cor. 3:6), and life (Rev. 7:17).

An Arab man drinks from the spout of a multi-spouted waterpot as he would have done in biblical times.

WATERPOT Vessel made for carrying water, usually made of clay although some were made of stone (John 2:6). Large pots stored water (1 Kings 18:33; John 2:6); a woman could carry smaller pots on her shoulder (John 4:28). Small pitchers were used for pouring water (Luke 22:10; Jer. 19). Water was also carried in animal skins. See *Pottery; Skin*.

WAVE OFFERING See *Sacrifice and Offering*.

WAW Sixth letter in the Hebrew alphabet. Heading of Ps. 119:41-48 (KJV, Vau) in which each verse begins with the letter.

WEALTH AND MATERIALISM Physical possessions having significant value, such as land, livestock, money, and precious metals, and the practice of valuing such possessions more highly than they ought to be valued, especially when this results in the misalignment of ones' priorities and undermines one's devotion to God.

Wealth To understand the biblical view of wealth, one must understand the biblical account of creation. On that account, God created the universe—and everything therein—"out of nothing" (Gen. 1:1-27). Thus, in virtue of being the absolute Creator, God's claim on the universe and everything therein is absolute—everything ultimately belongs to Him and to Him alone (cp. Ps. 50:10-12).

Since everything belongs ultimately to God, whatever one possesses—and thus owns—comes as a trust from Him; for this reason, one's right of ownership is never absolute—one's property always belongs first and foremost to God Himself. Second, since it comes as a trust from God, ownership of property carries with it significant responsibilities. For instance, God holds those to whom He has entrusted wealth responsible for giving to His work (cp. Num. 18:20-32; Deut. 14:28-29; Mal. 3:8-10; 2 Cor. 9:6-14; 1 Tim. 5:18-18) and for caring for the poor among them (cp. Prov. 29:7; Amos 5:11-12; Matt. 19:21; 1 Tim. 5:3-5). In addition, they are accountable to God for how they use the rest of their resources.

God has blessed some with abundant wealth. Abram, Isaac, Solomon, and Job were each blessed with great riches (cp. Gen. 13:2; 26:12-14; 1 Kings 3:13; Job 42:12). This does not mean, however, that poverty is a sign of God's disfavor. According to Scripture, God takes special interest in the poor (Ps. 72:12-15). Moreover, Job was righteous when God allowed him to become impoverished (Job 1:1,13-19).

Materialism Scripture warns against valuing one's wealth too highly. Riches can prevent one from bearing spiritual fruit (cp. Luke 8:14). Perhaps awareness of this lay behind Agur's plea that he not be given riches lest he deny God (Prov. 30:8-9). A generous spirit accompanies righteousness. Zacchaeus responded to Jesus not only by restoring fourfold what he had gained dishonestly, but also by giving freely to the poor (Luke 19:8), and the members of the church in Jerusalem shared their possessions with one another (Acts 2:44-45; 4:32-35). Such generosity characterizes those who have been freed from love of money and have sought to store up for themselves treasure in heaven rather than on earth (Matt. 6:19-21).

WEAPONS Since mankind's beginnings, the desire to impose one's will upon another person(s) or being has led to active conflict using many types of weapons. Human history shows marked means by which the implements were advanced technologically through the past six millennia.

The implements of warfare and defense are known from three sources: excavations; pictorial representations in murals, reliefs, and models; and written documents. Tombs of Egypt contained actual weapons and models. Assyrian reliefs depicted great battles in detail. Excavations have uncovered numerous examples of stone and metal weapons; and biblical and inscriptional sources provide names of objects, strategy and tactics, and methods of construction.

Military action has been defined in terms of ability to achieve supremacy over the enemy in three fields: mobility, firepower, and security. Mobility is exemplified by the chariot and cavalry; firepower by bow, sling, spear, ax, and sword; and security by shield, armor, and helmet.

WEASEL Unclean animal (Lev. 11:29); a small mammal related to the mink.

Reconstruction of a Roman siege tower with battering ram (first century AD).

Reconstruction of a Roman battering ram (first century AD).

WEB 1. A fabric usually woven on a loom (Judg. 16:13-14). See *Loom*. **2.** The weaving of a spider that looks like thread. The spider's web is used figuratively for that which is impermanent and untrustworthy (Job 8:14).

WEDDINGS In biblical times the father selected the bride for his son. Abraham sent his servant to Haran to find a wife for his son Isaac (Gen. 24). In arranging a marriage, the bridegroom's family paid a price (Hb. *mohar*) for the bride (cp. Gen. 34:12; Exod. 22:16; 1 Sam. 28:25). When the marriage had been arranged, the couple entered the betrothal period, usually lasting a year and much more binding than the engagement of today.

The wedding was largely a social event during which a blessing was pronounced on the bride: "May you, our sister, become thousands of ten thousands, and may your descendants possess the gate of those who hate them" (Gen. 24:60). The blessing reflected the concept of God's blessing, namely, a large family and victory over one's enemies. The marriage itself was secured by the formalizing of a marriage contract.

The parable of the 10 virgins is rich with explanation of the Jewish wedding (Matt. 25:1-13). The wedding ceremony began with the bridegroom bringing home the bride from her parents' house to his parental home. The bridegroom, accompanied by his friends and amid singing and music, led a procession through the streets of the town to the bride's home (cp. Jer. 16:9). Along the way friends who were ready and waiting with their lamps lit would join in the procession (Matt. 25:7-10). Veiled and dressed in beautifully embroidered clothes and adorned with jewels, the bride, accompanied by her attendants joined the bridegroom for the procession to his father's house (Ps. 45:13-15). Isaiah 61:10 describes the bridegroom decked out with a garland and the bride adorned with jewels. The bride's beauty would be forever remembered (Jer. 2:32). The bride and groom were considered king and queen for the week. Sometimes the groom even wore a gold crown.

Once at the home, the bridal couple sat under a canopy amid the festivities of games and dancing which lasted an entire week—sometimes longer (Song 2:4). Guests praised the newly married couple; songs of love for the couple graced the festival. Sumptuous meals and wine filled the home or banquet hall (John 2:1-11). Ample provision for an elaborate feast was essential—failure could bring a lawsuit (John 2:3). The bridal couple wore their wedding clothes throughout the week; guests also wore their finery, which was sometimes supplied by wealthy families (Matt. 22:12).

WEEK For the Jews, any seven consecutive days ending with the Sabbath (Gen. 2:1-3). The Sabbath began at sunset Friday and lasted until sunset Saturday. The Christians moved their day of worship to Sunday, the first day of the week. In this way they called attention to the resurrection of their Lord Jesus Christ (Luke 24:1-7). The week is of ancient Semitic origin. It was shared with the ancient world through the Bible and the religious practice of both Jews and Christians.

WEIGHTS AND MEASURES Systems of measurement. In the ancient Near East weights and measures varied. The prophets spoke against merchants who used deceitful weights (Mic. 6:11).Weights and measures in biblical times are seldom precise enough to enable one to calculate exact metric equivalents, but the Lord set forth an ideal for "just" balances, weights, and measures. Different standards in surrounding Near Eastern countries affected biblical standards. Sometimes there were two standards operating at the same time, such as short and long, light and heavy, common and royal. There is enough evidence to figure approximate metrological values for the biblical weights and measures.

WELL Source of water created by digging in the earth to find available water. In the semiarid climate of ancient Israel, the availability of water was a constant concern, and the Bible contains many references to the sources used for obtaining it.

"Well" is also used figuratively of a "forbidden woman" (Prov. 23:27 HCSB) and of a wicked city (Jer. 6:7). Elsewhere it is used as a metaphor for sexual pleasure (Prov. 5:15; Song 4:15).

A chaduf for raising well water near ancient Lystra in south central Asia Minor (modern Turkey).

WHALE Large aquatic mammal that resembles a large fish (Ezek. 32:2; Jon. 1:17; Matt. 12:40). The Greek word translated "whale" in Matt. 12:40 (KJV) is also called "a great fish" (Jon. 1:17), "great creature" (Gen. 1:21; Ps. 148:7 NIV), "monster" (Job 7;12; Ezek. 32:2 NIV). The exact identification of the animal is impossible with present knowledge.

WHEAT Staple grain of the ancient Near East (Num. 18:12). Wheat has been raised in this region since at least neolithic times (8300–4500 BC). Many species exist, and exact types cannot be determined from the biblical words. It became the major crop after the nomads began settling into agrarian societies. It is used as an analogy to speak of God's judgment (Matt. 3:12) and His care (Ps. 81:16). Wheat was used to make bread and was also parched (Lev. 23:14). KJV often translated "wheat" by the word "corn" (Mark 4:28). Wheat harvest was an ancient time reference (Exod. 34:22) and was celebrated by the Feast of Weeks. Wheat was said to have been harvested (1 Sam. 6:13), threshed (Judg. 6:11), and winnowed (Matt. 3:12).

WHEEL Disk or circular object capable of turning on a central axis. Archaeologists and historians believe that the wheel was probably invented in Mesopotamia before 3000 BC.

The Bible describes both a functional use and symbolic meaning for the wheel. The wheel was indispensable for transportation. It was used on wagons, carts, and chariots, and the word "wheel" could be a synonym for any of these vehicles (Ezek. 23:24; 26:10; Nah. 3:2). In Solomon's temple there were 10 stands upon which rested 10 lavers. Each of the stands was adorned with four wheels (1 Kings 7:30-33).

A burned Roman wagon wheel.

Ezekiel's vision of the great wheel in the sky (1:4-28; 10) was a symbol of God's presence. There were four cherubim around the throne. Beside each there was a wheel which "sparkled like chrysolite" (1:16 NIV). Ezekiel described the rims of the wheel as "high and awesome" and "full of eyes" (v. 18). The exact meaning of these mysterious images is unknown. Perhaps they represented the wheels of God's invisible chariot moving across the sky ("chariots of the sun," 2 Kings 23:11) or the wheels of God's throne (Dan. 7:9).

Other symbolic uses of the wheel are a whirlwind (Ps. 77:18 HCSB, NIV, NRSV, NASB) and God's judgment, as a wheel is driven over the wicked (Prov. 20:26). Jeremiah described God's redemption as the reshaping of marred clay on a potter's wheel (18:13).

WHELP Lion's cub, used figuratively in the OT (Gen. 49:9; Jer. 51:38; Nah. 2:11). See *Lion.*

A small whirlwind in the desert of the Wadi Arabah.

WHIRLWIND English translation of four Hebrew words that designate any windstorm that is destructive. Only Ps. 77:18 uses a term indicating circular motion. True whirlwinds and tornadoes are rare in Palestine. They usually occur near the coast where the cool breezes of the Mediterranean Sea collide with the hot wind from the desert. Lesser whirlwinds are seen as whirling dust is thrown up into the air. The Lord used the raging wind to take Elijah to heaven (2 Kings 2:1,11) and to talk with Job (38:1; 40:6). The prophets used the "storm wind" as a figure for judgment (Isa. 5:28; Jer. 4:13; Hos. 8:7; Amos 1:14; Zech. 7:14). God comes to deliver His people riding the stormy winds (Zech. 9:14).

WILD BEASTS Designation of any wild animal in contrast to domesticated animals, translating different Hebrew words. Most often the Hebrew is *chayyah* indicating living creatures (Gen. 1:24) including wild animals (Gen. 1:25). The same Hebrew form indicates humans as "living" beings (Gen. 2:7). The context shows the precise type creature meant.

WILD GOURD Poisonous plant, probably *Citrillus colocynths* (2 Kings 4:39).

WILDERNESS Holy Land areas, particularly in the southern part, with little rainfall and few people. The words for "wilderness" in the OT come close to our word "desert," because they usually mean a rocky, dry wasteland.

Geographically the wilderness lay south, east, and southwest of the inhabited land of Israel in the Negev, Transjordan, and the Sinai. A particular wilderness, closer to home, lay on the eastern slopes of the Judean mountains in the rain shadow leading down to the Dead Sea.

Historically the wilderness was particularly connected with the wandering of the Hebrews after their miraculous escape from Egypt and just prior to the conquest of Transjordan. This was remembered in their retelling of the story as "the great and terrible wilderness" (Deut. 1:19 HCSB; 8:15).

The prophets felt that most of Israel's religious troubles began with the settlement of Canaan and apostasy to Canaanite idolatry, but they also looked forward to a renewed pilgrimage in the wilderness (Hos. 2:14-15; 9:10, cp. Deut. 32:10; Jer. 2:2-3; 31:2-3). There would be a new exodus after the Babylonian exile through the north Syrian Desert to make the Lord their king and "prepare his way" (Ezek. 20:30-38; Isa. 40:3-5). John the Baptist appeared in the wilderness of Judea as the promised

The Wilderness of Judea.

prophetic forerunner (Matt. 3:1-3; Mark 1:2-4; Luke 3:2-6; John 1:23). Not only did Jesus overcome the tempter in the wilderness, but He fed the 4,000 in a desolate place east of the Sea of Galilee (Mark 8:1-9).

WILL OF GOD God's plan and purpose for His creation and for each individual. God does whatever He pleases (Ps. 135:6) and desires that all people do His will. Only people fully mature in Christ are able to do God's will consistently (Col. 4:12; cp. Ps. 40:8). God's will is always good, acceptable and perfect (Rom. 12:2). Doing God's will sustained Jesus for life (John 4:34). Sometimes, however, the will of God leads to suffering (Rom. 8:28; James 1:2-4; 1 Pet. 3:17), as it did for Jesus (Isa. 53:10; Matt. 26:39,42).

Christians are to strive to know the will of God for their lives (Ps. 143:10; Eph. 5:17; Col. 1:9; cp. Rom. 1:10). Christians are to discern God's will through prayer (Col. 1:9) and also pray that God's will for the world be done (Matt. 6:10). Jesus counted those who did God's will as His own family members (Matt. 12:50). They, like Jesus, will live forever (1 John 2:17).

WILLOW Tree usually found where water is plentiful, particularly along the Jordan River. Often the willow and the poplar are found together. The willow can grow up to 40 feet high. Willow branches were used to make the booths for the Feast of Tabernacles (Lev. 23:40). In Babylonian captivity the Jews hung their harps on willow trees because they did not feel like singing about Jerusalem in a foreign land (Ps. 137:1-4). NIV often translated willow as "poplar."

WIMPLE Covering that women wore around their head and neck (Isa. 3:22). Other translations use "cloaks."

WIND Natural force that represents in its extended meaning the breath of life in human beings and the creative, infilling power of God and His Spirit. Two words in the Bible—the Hebrew *ruach* and the Greek *pneuma*—bear the basic meaning of wind but are often translated as spirit. Some understanding of the development of the latter word clarifies this transfer in meaning and enriches the concept. See *Spirit.*

A limestone window grill from Tel el-Amarna in Egypt dating from the Eighteenth Dynasty, 1570 to 1320 BC.

WINDOW English translation of several Hebrew and Greek terms indicating holes in a house. Such holes served several purposes: as a chimney for smoke to escape (Hos. 13:3); holes in places were doves live (Isa. 60:8); holes in heaven through which rain falls (Gen. 7:11; 8:2; Mal. 3:10; cp. 2 Kings 7:2). The Hebrew term indicates holes in the wall for air and light (Gen. 8:6; Josh. 2:15; Judg. 5:28). Recessed windows with lattice work marked elaborate public buildings such as the temple (1 Kings 6:4) and the royal palace (2 Kings 9:30). A third Hebrew term relate to enabling something to be seen (1 Kings 7:4).

WINE Beverage made from fermented grapes. Grapes grew throughout ancient Palestine. Even in areas with limited rainfall, enough dew fell at night to support thriving vineyards. Wine was produced by pressing the juice from the grapes in large stone vats with a small drain at one end. The juice was collected in troughs, poured into large jars, and allowed to ferment while stored in cool, rock cisterns. In NT times wine was kept in skin flasks and often diluted with water. It was also used as a medicine and disinfectant. Scripture condemns drunkenness and overindulgence but pictures wine as a part of the typical ancient meal.

WINEPRESS Machine used for making wine from grapes. In OT times the presses for making

Reconstruction of a first-century winepress

wine were usually cut or hewed out of rock (Isa. 5:2) and were connected by channels to lower rock-cut vats where the juice was allowed to collect and ferment. The juice was squeezed from the grapes by treading over them with the feet (Job 24:11; Amos 9:13). Both royal presses and cellars are mentioned in 1 Chron. 27:27 and Zech. 14:10. Other activities besides the making of wine could go on at a press site (Judg. 6:11; 7:25). By the NT period both beam presses and presses with mosaic pavements were in use. The harvesting and treading of the grapes was a time of joy and celebration (Isa. 16:10; Jer. 48:33; Deut. 16:13-15), and the image of the abundance of wine is used to speak of God's salvation and blessing (Prov. 3:10; Joel 3:18; Amos 9:13). But God's judgment is also vividly portrayed as the treading of the winepress (Isa. 63:2-3; Rev. 14:19-20).

WING Specialized part of the bird that allows flight (Gen. 1:21). The word is most often used figuratively: of God's help (Ruth 2:12), of God's judgment (Jer. 48:40), of strength to return from exile (Isa. 40:31).

WINNOWING A step in the processing of grain whereby the grain is separated from the inedible parts. The stalks are thrown into the air, and the wind blows away the chaff and the straw, letting the heavier pure grain fall back to the ground (Isa. 30:24). John the Baptist used winnowing as an analogy of God's judgment, when the Lord would separate the sinful from the righteous (Matt. 3:12).

Arabs winnowing grain in the ancient way with wooden winnowing forks.

WINTER Season between fall and spring, usually short and mild in Palestine. Winter is also the rainy season for that land (Song 2:11).

WINTER HOUSE Part of a palace or a separate home of the rich that is heated and thus warmer than the rest of the house (Jer. 36:22) or built in a warmer part of the country. Amos spoke of the destruction of the winter house because of Israel's sin against God (3:15).

WISDOM LITERATURE A genre of writing featuring wise sayings and astute observations. These writings teach how to live according to such principles as intelligence, understanding, common sense, statecraft, and practical skills. With regard to the Bible, the term refers to the books of Job, Proverbs, and Ecclesiastes. Portions of other biblical books—such as Esther, Psalms, Song of Songs, and Daniel—can also be classified as Wisdom literature, as can the apocryphal books Sirach and the Wisdom of Solomon. Ancient Egypt and Babylon also produced Wisdom literature, but biblical Wisdom literature is unique, teaching that the fear of God is the foundation of true wisdom (Prov. 9:10) and ultimate success (Ps. 25:12-13; Eccles. 8:12-13).

WITCH Female whose work was in divination and magic.

WITNESS, MARTYR Refers generally to something or someone who bears testimony to things seen, heard, transacted, or experienced.

Old Testament The words translated "witness" and "testimony" derive from three Hebrew words: *'ed*, a legal witness, and *mo'ed*, or sometimes *'edah*, meaning agreement or appointment.

Legal The chief usage of "witness" is in the legal sphere, referring to facts or personal experiences (Lev. 5:1; Num. 23:18; Isa. 8:2). It also denotes the proof or evidence presented in a court case, primarily by the prosecution (Num. 5:13; 35:30; Deut. 17:6-7; 19:15). False, unrighteous, and overhasty witnesses are disdained and subject to reprisals (Deut. 19:16-21; Exod. 23:1; Pss. 26:12; 34:11; Prov. 6:19; 12:17; 19:5; 21:28). Examples of a witness to an agreement are found in Ruth 4:9-10 and Jer. 39:10,25,44. God may be invoked as a witness to one's integrity (Job 16:19). In an accusatory sense the Israelites stand self-accused if they return to idolatry (Josh. 24:22). Israel is also a witness to the uniqueness, reality, and deity of God on the basis of their experience of election by God (Isa. 43–44).

Memorial Inanimate objects sometimes served as witnesses to promises, pacts, and covenants. Altars (Josh. 22), piles of stones (Gen. 31:44; Josh. 24:27), and even God's law (Exod. 25:22) are examples. *Mo'ed* is used over 100 times for "witness" in the phrase "Tent of Witness" (*'ohel mo'ed*), meaning the appointed place where God met Moses (Exod. 25:22).

Moral This ideological nuance of witness involves the proclamation of certain truths, views, and internal convictions one holds by faith, and for which one would willingly die. This sense is not as distinct in the OT as it later became in the NT and early church. A firm case cannot be made for any kind of martyr theology in the OT.

New Testament ***Legal*** In the judicial sense "witness" refers to a person who gives testimony and/or to the content of that testimony (John 1:7; 3:28; 1 Pet. 5:12; Matt. 18:16; cp. Deut. 19:15), whether true or false (Matt. 26:60-68). Jesus tells the scribes and Pharisees they are self-accusing witnesses (Matt. 23:31).

Personal Witness is used to mean "reputation" (Luke 4:22, Acts 6:3; 1 Tim. 3:7; Rev. 3:1) and may also refer to one's own life or person (as John the Baptist; John 1:6-7). Jesus, throughout John's Gospel, was a witness to God's love and gift of eternal life to believers and was an accusing witness to non-believers (John 20:30-31; 21:24).

Evangelistic Especially in the Lukan material, "witness" is used in an active, evangelistic sense. Christians proclaim the gospel (*kerugma*) in an active, insistent way, encouraging listeners to receive and respond to their message (Acts 2:40; 18:5; 1 Thess. 2:11-12).

Mortal The word *martus* refers to a martyr, one who is deprived of life as a result of one's testimony for Jesus Christ. This term is only used three times in the NT (Acts 22:20; Rev. 2:13; 17:6). See *Martyr*.

WOLF Largest of wild carnivorous canines (*Canis lupus*; *Canis pallipes*) that include dogs, foxes, and jackals. It is thought to be the primary ancestor of the domestic dog. The wolf is known for its boldness and fierceness of attack (Luke 10:3). It often killed more than it could eat because the taste of blood put it into a frenzy. Shepherds knew the wolf as the greatest enemy of sheep. The wolf was well-known in biblical days (John 10:12), yet nearly every reference to wolves is in a figurative sense. Its name is used symbolically to describe deceitful and greedy people (Gen. 49:27; Jer. 5:6; Ezek. 22:27; Zeph. 3:3; Acts 20:29). Jesus used the figure of the false prophet as a wolf in sheep's clothing (Matt. 7:15). One of the signs of the messianic age is that the "wolf and the lamb will feed together" (Isa. 65:25).

WOMAN The Bible's paradigm for womanhood, while allowing for diversity and uniqueness, is nevertheless entirely consistent in its presentation of the Creator's plan for the nature and purposes of womanhood.

The Origin of the Woman The woman came after the man as his acknowledged offshoot, having a nature like his but her own unique existence. She is the only creature said to be "built" by God (Hb. *banah*, "made" in 2:22, literally "built"). God "built" the woman from raw resources derived from the man (Gen. 2:22). According to the rabbis, the wife "builds" the home and her children as her responsibility in marriage.

Man and woman are created "in the image of God" and their position in Christ eliminates any possibility of inferiority of either to the other. Yet, because they are complementary, they cannot be identified one as the other. Equal dignity prohibits the despising of one by the other; complementary interaction of one with the other requires that differences be honored.

Together man and woman are equipped to continue the generations and to exercise dominion over the earth and its resources. Yet the divine order calls for a reciprocity exhibited in male servant leadership and female submission, both of which are modeled in Jesus Himself.

Old Testament Israelite women managed the household and performed the duties of wives and mothers (Prov. 31:10-31). They had a measure of anonymity in life and were subordinate to their husbands. Beauty is associated with women in the Bible but without detail as to what makes them beautiful (Gen. 12:11; 26:7; 29:17; 2 Sam. 11:2; Song 4:2-3). Inner beauty, defined as "the fear of the Lord" and a "gentle and quiet spirit," is elevated over an attractive countenance (Prov. 31:30; 1 Tim. 2:9-10; 1 Pet. 3:3-4). Women were expected to meet their husbands' sexual needs, but their own needs were also to be met (Song 1:2; 2:3-6,8-10; 8:1-4; 1 Cor. 7:3,5).

The husband was the patriarch of his family or clan, and the wife became part of her husband's family. Women were an integral part of the community and were to be protected therein. Marriage was the ideal (Gen. 2:24); a good wife was usually praised and honored (Prov. 31:10-31); godly women were admired and their contributions greatly valued (e.g., Deborah, Hannah, Abigail, Naomi, Ruth, Esther); widows were to be protected (Deut. 24:19-22; 26:12).

A woman's legal position in Israel was weaker than a man's. Though a husband could divorce h wife for "some uncleanness in her," no law is given suggesting that a wife could divorce her husband Deut. 24:1-4). Wives could be required to take a jealousy test if they were suspected of unfaithfulness to their husbands, but no law is given permitting a wife to require the same of her husband Num. 5:11-31).

Hebrew laws did offer protection for women. If a husband added a second wife, he was not allowed to ignore the needs of his first wife (Exod. 21:10). Even a woman taken captive in war had rights (Deut. 21:14), and a man found guilty of raping a woman was stoned to death (Deut. 22:23-27). Although men usually owned property, daughters could receive the inheritance from their fathers if there were no sons in the family (Num. 27:8-11). Often the importance of the dowry to women is overlooked. Since theoretically the dowry belonged to the bride, some have suggested that this gift represented the daughter's share of her father's estate. She received her "inheritance" upon marriage, while her brothers had to wait to receive their shares until the father's death.

The Bible identifies women who were active in ancient society: Deborah, a prophetess and judge; Esther, a queen whose skills in diplomacy saved the Jews from extinction; Lydia, a tradeswoman with a thriving business. Just because the placement of women in civil and business pursuits is the exception rather than the rule does not lessen the valuable role of women in society. From the ancient world until now, society stands or falls according to its infrastructure, that is, the family, over which the wife and mother is to preside.

Children were to respect both mother and father equally (Exod. 20:12), even though they were the mother's special charge (Exod. 21:15; Prov. 1:8; 6:20; 20:20). The names of mothers appeared in biographies of successive kings (2 Chron. 24:7; 27:6). To disobey or curse either parent was punishable by stoning (Deut. 21:18-21). If a man and a woman were caught in the act of adultery, both were to be stoned (Deut. 22:22).

The husband exercised his spiritual leadership by presenting the sacrifices and offerings for the family (Lev. 1:2), but only women offered a sacrifice after the birth of a child (Lev. 12:6). Women also participated in worship, but they were not required, as the men, to appear before the Lord (Deut. 29:10; Neh. 8:2; Joel 2:16). This optional participation may have been because of their responsibilities as wives and mothers (1 Sam. 1:3-5,21-22).

New Testament Jesus offered women new roles and equal status in His kingdom. A woman was the first to bear witness of His resurrection (Matt. 28:8-10). Women followed Jesus with the multitudes (Matt. 14:21), and Jesus featured women and used things associated with them in His parables and illustrations (Matt. 13:33; 25:1-13; Luke 13:18-21; 15:8-10; 18:1-5).

In the NT the birth and infancy narratives note a remarkable number of women. Matthew includes four—Tamar, Rahab, Ruth, and Bathsheba—in his genealogy of Christ (Matt. 1:3,5-6). Through these women to whom God extended His forgiveness, Messiah would come. Jesus spoke to women John 4) and taught them individually and privately (Luke 10:38-42). A company of women often traveled with Him (Luke 8:1-3), and He often spoke highly of women (Matt. 9:20-22; Luke 21:1-4). He safeguarded the rights of women, especially in His teachings on marriage and divorce (Matt. 5:27-32; 19:3-9). For Jesus to expend time and energy in teaching women indicates that He saw in them not only intellectual acumen but also spiritual sensitivity.

Jesus treated men and women as equal in spiritual privilege, but as different in spiritual activity. No woman was among the 12 disciples nor among the 70 he sent out (Luke 10:1-12); the Lord's Supper was instituted within a group of men (Matt. 26:26-29). Jesus' selectiveness by no means minimized the ministries He gratefully received from godly women—words of encouragement, hospitality, gifts to undergird His work. Jesus elevated domestic responsibilities that women used in ministering to Him to a new importance.

The Kingdom of Christ Scripture affirms that women functioned in the early church with service, influence, leadership, and teaching. Mark's mother Mary and Lydia of Thyatira opened their homes for meetings of believers and practiced hospitality (Acts 12:12; 16:14-15). Paul mentioned Phoebe with favor (Rom. 16:1-2), and he employed women in kingdom service (Phil. 4:3). Priscilla, with her husband Aquila, instructed Apollos in individual ministry (Acts 18:26). Women offered themselves in special ministries to Jesus (John 12:1-11).

Some women are identified as prophetesses: Miriam, who led the women of Israel (Exod. 15:20); Huldah, whose only prophecy in Scripture was to a man who consulted her at home (2 Kings 22:14-20); Noadiah, who was labeled a false prophet (Neh. 6:1-14); Anna, who prophesied in the temple Luke 2:36-40); and the daughters of Philip (Acts 21:9). God also reserves the right to interdict history with the unexpected or extraordinary by His own divine fiat, such as calling Deborah to be a judge of Israel (Judg. 4–5).

No evidence exists of suppressing women in kingdom ministries. Rather, they are encouraged to work within the divinely given framework based upon the natural order of creation and appropriateness of function. Paul commended learning for women (1 Tim. 2:11). He exhorted spiritually mature women to instruct the younger women and outlined what they were to teach (Titus 2:3-5). Women are admonished to share the gospel (1 Pet. 3:15), and mothers and fathers are to do lifestyle teaching to their children (Deut. 6:7-9). Women may pray and prophesy in the church (1 Cor. 11:5), but they are given boundaries within which to exercise their gifts. Only two restrictions are given: teaching men and ruling over men—and that within two spheres, the home and church (1 Tim. 2:11-15).

WOODWORKER Person who worked with wood in some sense—cutting trees in a forest (1 Kings 5:6), bringing the logs to where they were needed (v. 9), building the house and the furniture needed for it (2 Kings 22:6), and making beautiful objects of art from wood.

WOOL Thick hair, forming the coat of sheep and some other animals. It was made into thread and used to make clothing, blankets, and other articles. It was one of the major economic factors in Israel and the surrounding countries. Gideon used a piece of wool to determine God's will for his life (Judg. 6:35-40). Wool was also used as a symbol of whiteness and purity (Isa. 1:18).

WORD Utterance or saying that may refer to a single expression, the entire law, the gospel message, or even Christ.

Old Testament *Davar* is the primary Hebrew expression for "word." It has various meanings and can refer to a spoken utterance, a saying, a command, a speech, or a story—linguistic communication in general. *Davar* can also mean a thing, event, or action (Gen. 18:14).

New Testament *Logos* and *rhema* are the two primary Greek words meaning "word." They are used interchangeably and variously as with the OT *davar*. The NT can use these words to apply to Jesus' message, the message about Jesus, and Jesus Himself.

Jesus' message of the coming kingdom can be called a "word" (Mark 2:2; 4:33; Luke 5:1), as can His individual sayings (Matt. 26:75; Luke 22:61; John 7:36). Significantly, Jesus avoided citing rabbinic authorities or using the traditional language of a prophet who would claim "that the word of the Lord came to me" or declare "thus says the Lord." Perhaps these phrases did not significantly honor His special relationship with the Father and His own authority (Matt. 11:27; cp. 5:21-26; Mark 3:28-29). As in the OT, so also Jesus' word demanded decision on the part of the hearers (John 8:51; 12:47).

The message concerning Jesus can also be called "a word." Paul spoke of "the message about God that you heard from us" that is mediated by his human words (1 Thess. 2:13 HCSB). Jesus Himself is the Word—the living Word. The preexistent Word who was with God "in the beginning" has now become flesh (John 1:1-18). Scholars have frequently claimed that John used *logos* in a philosophical sense to refer to the world's controlling rational principle (Stoicism) or to the created intermediary between God and His world (*Philo*). However, John's word is not a principle or divine characteristic. It is a preexistent, life-giving person. John opposed Greek philosophy by arguing that salvation comes not by mankind's escape from this world but by God entering and redeeming creation. More probably *logos* was chosen because of its meaning in the OT, its Greek translation, and contemporary Hebrew literature, where the concepts of "wisdom" and "word" were being spoken of as a distinct manifestation of God. John saw that the same agent of God who gave life in the first creation was also giving life in the new creation inaugurated by Jesus' coming. The creative Word of God became flesh; being divine He embodied divine communication. Now the Word dwells among us revealing the glory of God (John 1:14).

Power of the Word It is often assumed that in Hebrew thought words had a mysterious binding authority. For example, when Isaac discovered he had been deceived and had wrongly given his blessing to Jacob, he declared that his blessing had been given and Jacob would be blessed (Gen. 27:33). Isaac's word seems conclusive—like an arrow once shot, it could not be recalled. Caution must be exercised here. Actually, only God's word has this type of irresistible potency (Isa. 55:11) and absolute creative power (Gen. 1:3-31; Luke 1:32-35; cp. Isa. 9:8; 31:2; 45:23). Most occurrences like Isaac's may be explained in terms of their social custom. Following a prescribed social custom, a person could form a bond, or a will, by speaking a word. Even today a couple can make or create a marriage by saying "I do." We must also note that Scripture teaches that a person's word is often powerless (1 Cor. 2:4; 4:19-20) and frequently fails (Matt. 21:28-32).

Words are capable of great good and great evil (Matt. 12:36; James 3:5-6,8). Words can deeply injure (Prov. 12:18; 18:14) or revive (Prov. 12:18,25; 16:24). Words can have a widespread influence: words from the wicked are like "a scorching fire" (Prov. 16:27-28 HCSB); words from the righteous can be "a fountain of life" (Prov. 10:11; 12:14).

WORK, THEOLOGY OF Refers to the significance of work in light of the nature of God. God is a personal being whose manifold activities and works not only bestow blessings upon His crea-ures, but even infuse the act of work with meaning and divine significance, enjoining upon humans an obligation to engage in work even as God works.

Genesis opens with the image of a working, collaborative Creator, whose primal work constitutes an investment of His creativity, intelligence, words, breath, and "hands" (the image of the Son and Spirit as the two "hands of God" is a later second-century theological development).

God's purpose for humans, who are the pinnacle of His creation, was to work, specifically in Eden, to till the soil (Gen. 2:15) and to manage the garden as good stewards. Despite the perfection of God's creation, human disobedience marred the image of God in them, resulting in a curse on the ground (Gen. 3:17-19). Henceforth, the cooperative relationship between humans and the rest of creation turned work from a pleasant task into toil and hardship. This state will continue until that eschatological time when the curse is lifted and all creation is redeemed (Rom. 8:19-23). In the intervening time both the OT and NT teach that work (no longer restricted to agriculture but expanded to include business dealings, household obligations, and any employment in which people find themselves) brings to humans a sense of joy, satisfaction, dignity and respect (Eccles. 3; 4). God's people are not only to put forth their best efforts to accomplish their tasks; they are also called upon to maintain the highest moral and ethical standards. Transacting business with integrity, working with all diligence, and treating one's employees well are admired and praised (Boaz in Ruth 2:4), while dishonesty, laziness, and slothfulness are abhorred (Prov. 6).

In the NT creaturely labor is somehow sanctified because the Son of God also worked. Jesus and His disciples exemplified a life of working in various occupations (fishing, carpentry), and through many of His parables Jesus taught kingdom principles by using illustrations involving work (fairness and generosity in dealing with employees: Matt. 18:23-35; 20:1-16; resourcefulness in investing: Matt. 25:14-30; shrewdness and prudence: Luke 16:1-13). In general, the Gospels and the Pauline literature portray work positively and exhort God's people to labor faithfully, honestly, fruitfully and with a view to pleasing God more than earthly masters. Diligence receives praise while idleness draws censure (Eph. 6:5-9; 1 Thess. 2:9; 4:11-12; 2 Thess. 3:6-12).

WORKS Refers to acts, deeds, or accomplishments of both God and human beings. The Gospels asserted that believers demonstrate by good works that God is active in their lives (Matt. 5:16; John 5:28-29; 14:12).

Much debate exists concerning the relationship of faith and works in the salvation process. Paul stated that justification comes from faith alone apart from works (Rom. 4:2-3,9-10; Gal. 3:9-11; Eph. 2:8-9; Phil. 3:7-9). James, however, seems to affirm a closer relationship (James 2:14-24). This apparent contradiction has troubled many, especially Luther, who called James "an epistle of straw" and declared its message to be "flatly against St. Paul and all the rest of Scripture in ascribing justification to works."

There is a credible solution to the apparent contradiction. Paul, often dealing with Jewish legalists, used the term to describe "works of the law," which legalists believed would earn salvation. Paul rejects these "works" as insufficient. However, he freely acknowledged the inevitability of good works by those genuinely converted by faith (Eph. 2:10). Conversely, James' argument is that any "faith" that cannot be seen by the evidence of "works" is not true saving faith (2:14). The definite article in the text (*ha pistis*) indicates James is not speaking of genuine saving faith, but rather of a particular fictitious faith, proven to be such by a lack of good deeds. Paul and James are speaking from two sides of the same coin. Works of the law are insufficient to earn one's salvation, while good works are a natural consequence of saving faith. As Calvin put it: "Faith alone saves, but the faith that saves is not alone!"

WORLD A term that has a number of different meanings in the Bible.

"World" often refers to the universe or the cosmos. Biblical writers often use "world" when talking about the planet earth and more specifically dry land, as opposed to the sea and other bodies of water (notice the three categories: heavens, earth, and sea—Neh. 9:6 and Exod. 20:11).

Mankind was often referred to in Scripture as the "world" or "earth," because mankind is the most important part of God's creation. John 3:16, "God loved the world in this way: He gave His One and Only Son" (HCSB), that is, the world of human habitation. Sin entered the world of mankind through one man's transgression and brought death with it (Rom. 5:12).

The Scriptures use the term "world" to describe that environment or spirit of evil and enmity toward God and the things of God. It may also refer to those people who manifest this attitude because they do not know Christ. Particularly in John, "world" takes on this sinister meaning.

Scriptures often use "world" as an equivalent to the word "age" denoting a distinction between the temporality of this present evil world (Gal. 1:4; 1 John 2:17; Ps. 102:25-26; 1 Cor. 7:31) and the world to come.

WORM Small, slender, soft-bodied animal without a backbone, legs, or eyes. *Worm* is also used in the Bible as a figure of lowliness or weakness (Ps. 22:6; Job 17:14; Isa. 41:14). Both the OT and the NT speak of the place of the ungodly and unbeliever as being where the worm is always alive and working (Isa. 66:24; Mark 9:44,48).

WORMWOOD Nonpoisonous but bitter plant common to the Middle East. Wormwood often used in analogy to speak of bitterness and sorrow. OT prophets pictured wormwood as the opposite of justice and righteousness (Amos 5:7; Jer. 23:15). Revelation describes as wormwood one of the blazing stars that brings destruction (8:10-11).

WORSHIP Term used to refer to the act or action associated with attributing honor, reverence, worth to that which is considered to be divine by religious adherents. Christian worship is often defined as the ascription of worth or honor to the triune God. Worship is more fully understood an interrelation between divine action and human response: worship is the human response to the self-revelation of the triune God. This includes: (1) divine initiation in which God reveals Himself, His purposes and His will; (2) a spiritual and personal relationship with God through Jesus Christ the part of the worshipper; and (3) a response by the worshipper of adoration, humility, submission, and obedience to God.

Two central features of Christian worship are the ordinances of baptism (Matt. 28:19; Acts 2:38,41) and the Lord's Supper (Luke 22:19; 1 Cor. 11:17-34). Since there is no order of worship prescribed in the NT, it seems best to conclude that Christian worship should draw from the several models of worship in the Bible while employing the various elements of worship that are more clearly defined in Scripture.

WRATH, WRATH OF GOD Used to express several emotions, including anger, indignation, vexation, grief, bitterness, and fury. It is the emotional response to perceived wrong and injustice. Both humans and God express wrath. When used of God, wrath refers to His absolute opposition to sin and evil. When used of humans, however, wrath is one of those evils that is to be avoided.

God is a personal moral being who is unalterably opposed to evil and takes personal actions against it. Wrath is the punitive righteousness of God by which He maintains His moral order, which demands justice and retribution for injustice. Moreover, God's wrath is inextricably related to the doctrine of salvation. If there is no wrath, there is no salvation. If God does not take action against evil and sinners, there is no danger from which sinners are to be saved. The good news of the gospel is that sinners who justly deserve the wrath of God may be delivered from it. Through the atoning death of Christ, God is propitiated, and His anger is turned away from all those who receive Christ (Rom. 3:24-25). Therefore, those who have faith in Christ's blood are no longer appointed to wrath but are delivered from it and appointed "to obtain salvation" (1 Thess. 1:10; 5:9).

WRITING Human ability to record and communicate information through etching signs on stone, drawing them on skins or papyrus. Present knowledge shows that writing began in the ancient Near East about 3500 BC.

Several writing systems were in use in Syria-Palestine by the time of Moses and Joshua. Many Bible texts refer to Moses being directed to write down accounts of historical events (Exod. 17:14), laws and statutes (Exod. 34:1-9), and the words of the Lord (Exod. 24:4). Joshua wrote on stones a copy of the law of Moses (Josh. 8:32) and later wrote down statutes and ordinances in the book of law of God (Josh. 24:26). Gideon had a young man of Succoth to write down the names of the officials and elders of that town (Judg. 8:14). Samuel wrote down the rights and duties of kings (1 Sam. 10:25). David could write his own letter to his general (2 Sam. 11:14). Kings engaged in international correspondence (2 Chron. 2:11). Many references to the chronicles of the kings of Israel and Judah perhaps indicate court diaries or annals (1 Kings 14:19). The prophets wrote, or dictated, their oracles (Isa. 8:1,16; 30:8; Jer. 30:1-2; 36:27-28). By at least 800 BC court scribes were tallying the payment of taxes (cp. the *Samaria Ostraca*). Commemorative and memorial inscriptions were in use (cp. the Siloam inscription and the Siloam tomb inscription). Nehemiah as an official under Persian appointment wrote down the covenant to keep the law of God (Neh. 9:38), to which several men set their seals as witnesses (Neh. 10:1-27).

Similarly, in the NT period literacy was widespread. Jesus could both read (Luke 4:16-21) and write (John 8:6). The writers of the Gospels and Paul wrote in excellent Greek, with Paul regularly using an amenuensis or scribe.

The various kinds of documents and writings mentioned in the Bible were letters (personal and official), decrees (religious and civil), legal documents, deeds of sale, certificates of divorce, family registers, topographical descriptions, and books of scrolls containing laws, court records, and poetic works.

XYZ

XERXES Persian king who reigned 486–464 BC, known in the book of Esther as Ahasuerus. He was the son of Darius the Great and grandson of Cyrus the Great. He campaigned militarily against the Greeks, avenging the loss at Marathon in 490. However, his armada suffered a crippling defeat in the Bay of Salamis in 480.

YAH Shortened form of *Yahweh*, the Hebrew name for the God of the covenant. See *God; Jehovah; Lord; YHWH.*

YEAR OF JUBILEE See *Festivals.*

YELLOW Two Hebrew words are translated "yellow." *Cheruts* (Ps. 68:13) refers to gold strongly alloyed with silver or the sallow color of sick skin (Lev. 13:49). *Tsahov* (Lev. 13:30,32,36) refers to the color of hair in a patch of skin that lets the priest know it is leprous. The basic meaning of *tsahov* is "shining" and represents bright red or gold.

YHWH Known by the technical term *Tetragrammaton* (Gk., meaning "four letters"), these are the four consonants that make up the divine name (Exod. 3:15; found more than 6,000 times in the OT). The written Hebrew language did not include vowels; only the consonants were used; thus readers supplied the vowels as they read (this is true even today in Hebrew newspapers). Reverence for the divine name led to the practice of avoiding its use lest one run afoul of commandments such as Exod. 20:7 or Lev. 24:16. In time it was thought that the divine name was too holy to pronounce at all. Thus the practice arose of using the word *Adonai:* "Lord." Many translations of the Bible followed this practice. In most English translations YHWH is recognizable where the word LORD appears in caps.

A latinized form of this was pronounced "Jehovah," but it was actually not a real word at all. From the study of the structure of the Hebrew language most scholars today believe that YHWH was probably pronounced Yahweh (Yah´ weh). See *God*

YOD Tenth letter of the Hebrew alphabet used as title of Ps. 119:73-80 (KJV, "Jod"), in which all verses begin with this letter.

YOKE Wooden frame placed on the backs of draft animals to make them pull in tandem. The simple yokes consisted of a bar with two loops either of rope or wood that went around the animals' necks. More elaborate yokes had shafts connected to the middle with which the animals pulled plows or other implements. The word is used most often to speak of slavery, bondage, and hardship (1 Kings 12:4; Jer. 27:8). Positive usages include the yoke of Christ (Matt. 11:29-30) and the joint nature of the church's work (Phil. 4:3).

An ox and a donkey yoked together and pulling a wooden plow.

ZAANAIM KJV, TEV spelling of Zaanannim (Judg. 4:11) following written Hebrew text rather than scribal note and Josh. 19:33.

ZAANAN Place-name, possibly meaning "sheep country" or "outback." Unidentified city in southernmost Judah (Mic. 1:11), probably identical with Zenan (Josh. 15:37).

ZAANANNIM Place-name of uncertain meaning. Town on northeastern corner of tribal allotment of Naphtali near Kadesh (Josh. 19:33; Judg. 4:11). The "plain of Zaanaim" (Judg. 4:11 KJV) is literally translated "great tree in Zaanannim" (NIV) or "oak in Zaanannim" (NASB; note transliterations of REB, NRSV). This probably indicates a "sacred tree" associated with a worship center.

ZAAVAN Personal name meaning "tremble or quake." Son of Ezer (Gen. 36:27).

ZABAD Place-name meaning "He has given" or "gift." **1.** Member of the tribe of Judah (1 Chron. 2:36-37). **2.** An Ephraimite (1 Chron. 7:21). **3.** One of David's 30 elite warriors (1 Chron. 11:41); the first of 21 names which the Chronicler appended to a list paralleling that of 2 Sam. 23:24-39. **4.** Assassin of King Joash (2 Chron. 24:26), called Jozacar in 2 Kings 12:21. **5.** Three postexilic laymen ordered to divorce their foreign wives (Ezra 10:27,33,43).

ZABBAI Abbreviated personal name, perhaps meaning "pure." **1.** Son of Bebai who promised Ezra he would put away his foreign wife (Ezra 10:28). **2.** Father of Baruch who worked on the wall of Jerusalem with Nehemiah (3:20). Some say that 1. and 2. may be the same person. The early scribal note (*qere*) in Nehemiah writes the name Zaccai.

ZABBUD Personal name meaning "gift." Descendant of Bigvai who returned to Jerusalem with Ezra after the exile (Ezra 8:14) according to written Hebrew text. Scribal note (*qere*) has Zaccur.

ZABDI Personal name meaning "my gift" or short form of "Yah gives." **1.** Son of Zerah of the tribe of Judah (Josh. 7:1). **2.** Man of the tribe of Benjamin (1 Chron. 8:19). **3.** Man in charge of the wine cellars of David (1 Chron. 27:27). **4.** Son of Asaph who led in thanksgiving and prayer (Neh. 11:17).

ZABDIEL Personal name meaning "God gives gifts" or "My gift is God." **1.** Descendant of David (1 Chron. 27:2). **2.** Overseer in Jerusalem during the time of Nehemiah (Neh. 11:14).

ZABUD Personal name meaning "endowed." Son of Nathan, a priest and Solomon's friend (1 Kings 4:5).

ZACCAI Personal name meaning "pure" or "innocent." One whose descendants returned to Jerusalem with Zerubbabel (Ezra 2:9; Neh. 7:14).

ZACCHAEUS or **ZACCHEUS** Greek form of Hebrew name meaning "innocent." A corrupt tax collector in first-century Jericho (Luke 19:2-9). Out of curiosity he went to hear Jesus. Because of his short stature, he had to climb a tree to catch a glimpse of the Lord. To his surprise Jesus called him by name to come down and He went home with Zacchaeus. There the official believed and was converted. As a result of his newfound faith, he restored with interest the money he had taken illegally.

ZACCHUR or **ZACCUR** Personal name meaning "well remembered." **1.** Father of Shammua of the tribe of Reuben (Num. 13:4). **2.** Descendant of Mishma of the tribe of Simeon (1 Chron. 4:26). **3.** Descendant of Merari among the Levites (1 Chron. 24:27). **4.** Son of Asaph (1 Chron. 25:2; Neh. 12:35). **5.** Son of Imri who helped Nehemiah rebuild the walls of Jerusalem (3:2). **6.** One who sealed the covenant of reform during the time of Ezra and Nehemiah (10:12). Father of Hanan, one of the treasurers appointed by Nehemiah (13:13).

ZADOK, ZADOKITES Personal name meaning "righteous," a short form of Zedekiah, "the Lord is righteous." See *Zedekiah.* **1.** Son of Ahitub and father of Ahimaaz, descended from Aaron through Eleazar and was a priest in the time of David (2 Sam. 8:17; 1 Chron. 6:3-8). As a reward for Zadok's loyalty to Solomon and as punishment for the sins of Eli's sons, Zadok's descendants (the line of Eliezer) replaced the descendants of Ithamar as the leading priests. The developing role of Jerusalem as the exclusive center of Israel's worship furthered the position of the Zadokites. In later days Ezekiel declared that the priests who were sons of Zadok were the only faithful ones at the time of the exile and that they only would be allowed to serve in the ideal future temple. This statement agrees with the genealogies of Chronicles that list only two families as far as the captivity—David of Judah and Zadok the descendant of Aaron through Eleazar. **2.** Grandfather of Jotham, king of Judah (2 Kings 15:33). **3.–4.** Men who helped Nehemiah rebuild the Jerusalem wall (Neh. 3:4,29). **5.** Leader who signed Nehemiah's covenant (Neh. 10:21). **6.** A faithful scribe whom Nehemiah appointed as a treasurer (Neh. 13:13).

ZAHAM Personal name meaning "fatness" or "loathing." Son of King Rehoboam by Abihail (2 Chron. 11:18-19).

ZAHAR Source of wool traded with Tyre (Ezek. 27:18 NIV; "Sahar," TEV; "Suhar," REB). KJV, NASB, and RSV translate the Hebrew as "white wool."

ZAIR Place-name that means "small." Place where Joram, king of Judah (853–841 BC), fought with Edom (2 Kings 8:20-21). The location of Zair is still in dispute. Some place it south of the Dead Sea near Edom. Others equate it with Zoar (Gen. 13:10) or Zior (Josh. 15:54; cp. 2 Chron. 21:9).

ZALAPH A personal name meaning "caper plant." Father of Hanun, who helped Nehemiah repair the walls of Jerusalem (3:30).

ZALMON Personal name and place-name meaning "little dark one" or "small image." **1.** Mountain near Shechem where Abimelech and his men cut brush with which to burn the tower of Shechem (Judg. 9:48-49). **2.** One of David's 30 mighty men (2 Sam. 23:28). He is also known as Ilai (1 Chron. 11:29). **3.** Psalm 68:14 mentions a "hill of Bashan" named Zalmon (KJV, "Salmon"). This may refer to the Golan Heights.

ZALMONAH Place-name meaning "dark" or "shady." Israel's first stop after leaving Mount Hor (Num. 33:41-42). The place cannot be identified.

ZALMUNNA Personal name meaning "Protection is withdrawn" or "Zelem (god) rules." King of Midian captured and killed by Gideon (Judg. 8:1-21; Ps. 83:11).

ZAMZUMMIM or **ZAMZUMMITES** (NIV) Name the Ammonites gave to the Rephaim. They lived east of the Jordan River until the Ammonites drove them out (Deut. 2:20).

ZANOAH Place-name meaning "broken district" or "stinking." **1.** Village in Judah identified with Khirbet Zanu about three miles south-southeast of Beth-shemesh (Josh. 15:34). **2.** City in the highlands of Judah (Josh. 15:56), whose identification with Khirbet Zanuta, 10 miles southwest of Hebron or Khirbet Beit Amra, is disputed.

ZAPHENATH-PANEAH or **ZAPHNATH-PAANEAH (KJV)** Personal name meaning "The god has said, he will live." Pharaoh's name for Joseph when he made Joseph second only to himself in Egypt (Gen. 41:45). See *Joseph.*

ZAPHON Place-name meaning "north." **1.** City east of the Jordan River in Gad's territory (Josh. 13:27). **2.** Mountain viewed as home of the gods in Canaanite thought, perhaps referred to in Ps. 48:2 (NIV), Isa. 14:13 (NRSV), and Job 26:7 (NRSV), showing Yahweh controls what Canaan thought their gods possessed.

ZAREPHATH Place-name possibly meaning "smelting, refining." A town on the Mediterranean seacoast just south of Sidon. At God's command Elijah fled there after prophesying a drought in Israel (1 Kings 17:2-9). While in Zarephath he was hosted by a widow and her son. Although the drought affected the widow's income, too, her supply of meal and oil were miraculously sustained (17:12-16). Elijah also restored her son to life and health (17:17-23).

ZARETAN (KJV, Josh. 3:16) See *Zarethan.*

ZARETH-SHAHAR (KJV) See *Zereth-shahar.*

ZARETHAN Place-name, perhaps meaning "cooling." The Jordan River backed up and Israel passed over into Canaan on dry ground near there (Josh. 3:16).

ZARHITE KJV form of Zerahite, descendants of Zerah, one of the twins born to Judah by Tamar (Num. 26:20; cp. 1 Chron. 9:6; Neh. 11:24).

ZATTHU (KJV) or **ZATTU** Head of family who returned to Jerusalem after the exile (Ezra 2:8; Neh. 7:13). Some of the sons of Zattu put away their foreign wives (Ezra 10:27). He seems to be the same as the "Zatthu" who signed the covenant in Nehemiah's time (10:14).

ZAYIN Seventh letter of the Hebrew alphabet. Title of Ps. 119:49-56, where each verse begins with this letter.

ZAZA Son of Jonathan and descendant of Jerahmeel (1 Chron. 2:33).

ZEALOT One who had a "zeal" for a particular cause. The term came to refer to a Jewish segment that sought to overthrow foreign control over Palestine, particularly Roman control. See *Jewish Parties in the New Testament.*

ZEBADIAH Personal name meaning "Yahweh has given." **1.** Son of Beriah (1 Chron. 8:15). **2.** Son of Elpaal (1 Chron. 8:17). **3.** Son of Jehoram of Gedor (1 Chron. 12:7). **4.** A gatekeeper (1 Chron. 26:2). **5.** Fourth captain in David's army (1 Chron. 27:7). **6.** One of nine Levites sent by Jehoshaphat to teach the law in the towns of Judah (2 Chron. 17:8). **7.** Son of Ishmael who ruled civil cases in a court system Jehoshaphat set up (2 Chron. 19:11). **8.** Son of Shephatiah who returned to Jerusalem from Babylon (Ezra 8:8). **9.** Priest who put away his foreign wife in Ezra's time (10:20).

ZEBAH Personal name meaning "slaughter" or "sacrifice." He and Zalmunna were Midianite kings whom Gideon captured and killed because they had killed Gideon's brothers (Judg. 8:4-21; Ps. 83:11; Isa. 9:4; 10:26). This account shows the act of blood revenge that often prevailed in that day and marks a turning point in Israel's struggles against Midian.

ZEBAIM Home of the children of Pochereth (Ezra 2:57) who returned to Jerusalem from Babylonian captivity (KJV).

ZEBEDEE Greek form of Hebrew personal name meaning "gift." A fisherman on the Sea of Galilee and father of James and John, two of Jesus' first disciples (Mark 1:19-20). Based at Capernaum on the north shore of the sea, Zebedee ran a fishing business that included several hired servants, Simon Peter, and Andrew (Luke 5:10). His wife also followed Jesus and ministered to Him (Matt. 27:56). The Bible does not say if Zebedee ever became a believer, but he did not stand in the way of his son or wife becoming Jesus' disciple.

ZEBIDAH Personal name meaning "gift." Daughter of Pedaiah of Rumah and the mother of King Jehoiakim (2 Kings 23:36; KJV "Zebudah").

ZEBINA Personal name meaning "purchased." One who had a foreign wife during Ezra's time (Ezra 10:43).

ZEBOIIM Place-name, possibly meaning "hyenas." One of the cities in the Valley of Siddim (Gen. 14:2-3) at the southern end of the Dead Sea. The site probably is under water now. Although the text is not clear, it appears the city was delivered when Abram defeated Chedorlaomer (14:16-17). Zeboiim was destroyed when God sent fire and brimstone on Sodom and Gomorrah (Deut. 29:23 cp. Hos. 11:8). Recent attempts to identify Zeboiim in the Ebla tablets have been hotly debated.

ZEBOIM Place-name meaning "hyenas" or "a wild place." Not to be confused with Zeboiim. **1.** One of the towns the Benjamites occupied upon returning to Palestine from exile (Neh. 11:34). It may be Khirbet Sabije. **2.** Valley in Benjamin between Michmash and the wilderness overlooking the Jordan River (1 Sam. 13:17-18). It may be Wadi el-Oelt or Wadi Fara.

ZEBUL Personal name meaning "prince" or "captain." Resident of Shechem who was a follower of Abimelech, son of Gideon. When Gaal plotted against Abimelech in Shechem, Zebul sent word to Abimelech who came to Shechem and defeated Gaal (Judg. 9:30-41).

ZEBULUN Personal and tribal name, probably meaning "elevated dwelling." Jacob's tenth son and sixth by Leah (Gen. 30:20). The tribe named for him settled in the area between the Sea of Galilee and Mount Carmel (Josh. 19:10-16). The tribe hosted the other tribes with religious festivals at Mount Tabor (Deut. 33:18-19). Their menu included the delicacies fished from the Sea of Galilee. Militarily the tribe distinguished itself in the struggles to possess the land, fighting faithfully in the armies of Deborah and Barak, and Gideon (Judg. 4:6; 6:35).

A tomb in Jerusalem which is said by local tradition to be Zechariah's tomb.

ZECHARIAH Personal name meaning "Yah (in long form Yahweh) remembered." **1.** Son of Jeroboam II, who reigned over Israel for six months in the year 746 BC until he was assassinated by Shallum (2 Kings 15:8-12). See *Israel.* **2.** The Prophet Zechariah, who flourished immediately after the exile in 520–518 BC and urged the people of Judah to rebuild the temple. **3.** Grandfather of Hezekiah (2 Kings 18:2). **4.** Priest and prophet whom the people stoned and Joash the king, killed (2 Chron. 24:20-22). **5.** Postexilic gatekeeper of temple (1 Chron. 9:21). **6.** Member of family who lived in Gibeon (1 Chron. 9:37). **7.** Temple musician (1 Chron. 15:20). **8.** Community leader Jehoshaphat the king sent to teach in the cities of Judah (2 Chron. 17:7). **9.** One of Josiah's overseers in repairing the temple (2 Chron. 34:12). **10.–11.** Men who accompanied Ezra on return from Babylon (Ezra 8:3,11). **12.** Man whom Ezra sent to get Levites to return from Babylon (Ezra 8:16). **13.** Israelite with foreign wife (Ezra 10:26). **14.** Man who helped Ezra as he taught the law (Neh. 8:4), perhaps identical with 12. or other one above. **15.** Ancestor of postexilic resident of Jerusalem (Neh. 11:4). **16.** Ancestor of postexilic resident of Jerusalem (Neh. 11:5). **17.** Ancestor of priest in Nehemiah's day (Neh. 11:12). **18.** Leading priest in time of Joiakim's high priesthood, possibly the same as the prophet (Neh. 12:16). **19.–20.** Priestly musicians who helped Nehemiah celebrate (Neh. 12:35,41). **21.** High official Isaiah used as witness, perhaps the same as 3. above. **22.** Son of Jehoshaphat the king whom his brother Jehoram killed upon becoming king (2 Chron. 21:2-4). **23.** Godly advisor of King Uzziah (2 Chron. 26:5). **24.** Descendant of tribe of Reuben (1 Chron. 5:7). **25.** Father of leader of eastern half of tribe of Manasseh (1 Chron. 27:21). **26.–34.** Levites (1 Chron. 15:18,24; 24:25; 26:2,14; 26:11; Chron. 20:14; 29:13; 35:8). **35.** A priest in Jerusalem and the father of John the Baptist (Luke 1:5-64).

ZECHARIAH, BOOK OF Eleventh of the so-called Minor Prophets. In 538 Cyrus the Great, emperor of the Persian Empire, issued an edict (Ezra 1:2-4; 6:3-5) allowing the Jews in exile in Babylon to return to Jerusalem. Over the next two decades, many exiles took advantage of Persia's leniency, returned home, and began to reestablish life in Jerusalem or Judah. Apparently an effort was made to begin rebuilding the temple under an official named Sheshbazzar (Ezra 5:14-16) and perhaps Zerubbabel (Ezra 3:1-13; Zech. 4:9), but the work stopped due to opposition from persons who had not been in exile and from the local officials. Cyrus was succeeded by his son Cambysees, who died in 521 BC with no heir, so the empire was thrown into disarray as two men, Darius I and Gautama, fought for the crown. In the midst of that turmoil, God raised up two prophets, Haggai and Zechariah, to urge the people to finish the temple.

The message of Zechariah may be summarized under two headings: prosperity and purification. Simply put, God promised the people of Judah and Jerusalem prosperity if they purified themselves from sin. This message is found in the first six chapters of the book of Zechariah. Those chapters are written in the form of eight visions, with two messages of exhortation. The structure of the book anticipates the structure of later books called apocalypses, books like Revelation; the book of Zechariah itself is not, however, an apocalypse.

ZECHER Form of Zechariah (1 Chron. 9:37) used in 1 Chron. 8:31. See *Zechariah.*

ZEDAD Place-name meaning "a sloping place" or "mountainous." It is Sadad, 62 miles north of Damascus, the northern border of Canaan (Num. 34:8; Ezek. 47:15).

ZEDEKIAH Personal name meaning "Yahweh is my righteousness" or "Yahweh is my salvation." **1.** False prophet who advised King Ahab to fight against Ramoth-gilead, assuring the king of victory (1 Kings 22). His prophecy conflicted with that of Micaiah, who predicted defeat. **2.** Last king of Judah (596–586 BC). Zedekiah was made king in Jerusalem by Nebuchadnezzar of Babylon (2 Kings 24:17). When he rebelled, the Babylonian army besieged Jerusalem and destroyed it. Zedekiah was taken to Riblah along with his family. At Riblah he witnessed the executions of his sons before his own eyes were blinded (25:7). Then Zedekiah was taken to Babylon. He apparently died in captivity. **3.** Son either of Jehoiakim or Jeconiah (1 Chron. 3:16), the Hebrew text being unclear at this point. **4.** Signer of Nehemiah's covenant (10:1; spelled Zidkijah by KJV). **5.** Prophet who promised quick hope to exiles in Babylon (Jer. 29:21). Jeremiah pronounced God's judgment on him. **6.** Royal official in Jeremiah's day (36:12).

ZELA (NRSV, REB, RSV, TEV) or **ZELAH** Place-name meaning "rib, side, slope." Town allotted to Benjamin (Josh. 18:28) in which the bones of Saul and Jonathan were buried (2 Sam. 21:14). The site is probably Khirbet Salah between Jerusalem and Gibeon or else another site in the hills north and west of Jerusalem.

ZELEK Personal name meaning "cleft, fissure." One of David's 30 elite warriors (2 Sam. 23:37; 1 Chron. 11:39).

ZELOPHEHAD Personal name meaning "protection from terror" or "the kinsman is my protector." A Hebrew who wandered in the wilderness with Moses. He had no sons to receive his property and carry on his name, so his daughters pled with Moses to receive a share of inheritance following his death (Num. 26:33; 27:1-4). Despite the inheritance customs which allowed only men to own property, God led Moses to declare the daughters eligible (27:6-7). The only stipulation was that the women had to marry within their own tribe (36:5-9).

ZELOTES KJV transliteration of name for Simon, Jesus' disciple. Modern translations translate as "Zealot."

ZELZAH Unidentified site near Rachel's tomb in the territory of Benjamin, site of the first of three signs that Samuel promised Saul as confirmation of his kingship (1 Sam. 10:1-2).

ZEMARAIM Place-name meaning "twin peaks." **1.** Town allotted to the tribe of Benjamin (Josh. 18:22), likely Ras ex-Zeimara about five miles northeast of Bethel. **2.** Mountain in the territory of Ephraim where Abijah rebuked Jeroboam (2 Chron. 13:4).

ZEMARITES Canaanites inhabiting the area north of Lebanon between Arvad and Tripolis (Gen. 10:18; 1 Chron. 1:16). The Zemarites possibly gave their name to the town Sumra in this region. The town figures in the Tell Amarna letters and in Assyrian records. NRSV emended the text of Ezek. 27:8 to read "men of Zemer" (KJV, "thy wise men, O Tyrus").

ZEMER Place-name meaning "wool." See *Zemarites.*

ZEMIRA(H) Personal name meaning "song." Descendant of Benjamin (1 Chron. 7:8).

ZENAN Place-name meaning "flocks." Village in the Shephelah (wilderness) district of Judah (Josh. 15:37), likely identified with 'Araq el-Kharba. Zenan is perhaps identical to Zaanan (Mic. 1:11).

ZENAS Abbreviated form of the personal name Zenodoros meaning "gift of Zeus." Christian lawyer whom Paul asked Titus to send, together with Apollos, on his way, lacking nothing (Titus 3:13). Paul had in mind, no doubt, material provisions for itinerant evangelistic work. Zenas and Apollos perhaps delivered Paul's letter to Titus.

ZEPHANIAH Personal name meaning "Yahweh sheltered or stored up" or "Zaphon (god) is Yahweh." **1.** Prophet whose preaching produced the 36th book of the OT. **2.** Priest whom King Zedekiah sent asking Jeremiah to pray for the nation threatened by Nebuchadnezzar of Babylon (Jer. 21:1-7; 37:3). He reported false prophecy from Babylon to Jeremiah (29:24-32). When Jerusalem fell, the priest was executed (52:24-27). **3.** Father of Josiah and Hen (Zech. 6:10,14), possibly identical with 2. above. **4.** A Levite (1 Chron. 6:36), perhaps the same as Uriel (1 Chron. 6:24).

ZEPHANIAH, BOOK OF Only three chapters in length, this book looks toward the punishment of all sinful nations, including Judah, followed by the restoration of Judah and the nations as well.

The Prophet Zephaniah The first verse tells all we really know about the prophet. His ancestry is traced back four generations to a man named Hezekiah. Some scholars think Hezekiah was the king of Judah by that name who reigned in the late eighth century during the ministry of Isaiah (2 Kings 18–20). If so, Zephaniah would have belonged to the royal line. According to 1:1, Zephaniah's ministry occurred during the reign of Josiah (640–609 BC). Most scholars date the book in 630 or between 630 and 621.

Contents of the Book Zephaniah looked toward a future punishment. In 1:2-6 he predicted punishment upon the whole world, including Jerusalem. The second chapter contains a series of threats against the Philistines (vv. 4-7), the Moabites and Ammonites (vv. 8-11), the Ethiopians (v. 12), and the Assyrians (vv. 13-15). Zephaniah called all nations to repent and become righteous and meek. The third chapter is marked by a change in perspective between verses 7 and 8. God's purpose is expressed in vv. 9–13 to purify from the nations a people united to worship Him. Their speech will be cleansed of sinful pride and idolatry (Isa. 2:17–18; 6:5; Hos. 2:17). Terms used of the remnant in v. 13 are used of the Lord in v. 5. It will be a time of right, of truth, and of security (cf. Jer. 50:19, Ezek. 34:14; Mic. 4:4; 7:14).

ZEPHATH Place-name meaning "watchtower." City in southwestern Judah in the vicinity of Arvad. Following their destruction of the city, the tribes of Judah and Simeon renamed the site Hormah (Judg. 1:17).

ZEPHATHAH Place-name meaning "watchtower." Asa met Zerah, the Ethiopian king, in battle "in the valley of Zephathah at Mareshah" (2 Chron. 14:10). The earliest Greek translation translated *Zaphon* "north" instead of Zephathah. If Zephathah is identified with Safiyah, less than two miles northeast of Beit Jibrin, the "valley of Zephathah" is the Wadi Safiyah.

ZEPHI or **ZEPHO** Short form of personal name meaning "purity" or "good fortune." Descendant of Esau (1 Chron. 1:36) called Zepho in the parallel passage (Gen. 36:11,15).

ZEPHON Personal name, perhaps meaning "north." Eldest son of Gad and ancestor of the Zephonites (Num. 26:15). The Samaritan Pentateuch and the earliest Greek translation support the identification with Ziphion (Gen. 46:16).

ZEPHONITE Member of clan of Zephon.

ZER Place-name meaning "narrow" or "enemy." Fortified town in the territory of Naphtali (Josh. 19:35), possibly identified with Madon, which is conspicuously absent from this list. Commentators often take "Zer" as a copyist's modification, repeating the Hebrew for "fenced cities."

ZERAH Personal name meaning "sunrise." **1.** A twin born to Tamar and her father-in-law, Judah (Gen. 38:30; Zarah, KJV). One of his descendants was Achan, who was executed for taking forbidden booty (Josh. 7:1,25). Zerah is included in Matthew's genealogy of Christ, although Perez was the direct ancestor (1:3). **2.** Descendant of Esau and thus clan leader of Edomites (Gen. 36:13,17). **3.** Ancestor of Edomite ruler (Gen. 36:33). **4.** Clan leader in tribe of Simeon (Num. 26:13), apparently same as Zohar (Gen. 46:10). **5.** Levite (1 Chron. 6:21,41). **6.** Cushite general God defeated in answer to Asa's prayer about 900 BC (2 Chron. 14:8-13).

ZERAHIAH Personal name meaning "Yahweh has dawned." **1.** Priest descended from Phineha (1 Chron. 6:6,51; Ezra 7:4). **2.** Descendant of Pahath-Moab ("governor of Moab") and father of Eliehoenai (Ezra 8:4).

ZERAHITES Name of two families, one from the tribe of Simeon (Num. 26:13), the other from the tribe of Judah (Num. 26:20; Josh. 7:17), descended from men named Zerah. Two of David's 3 elite warriors, Sibbecai and Maharai, were Zerahites (1 Chron. 27:11,13).

ZERED River name, perhaps meaning "white thorn." A stream that empties into the southern end of the Dead Sea. Its entire length is only about 38 miles, but it drains a large area of land. Israel crossed the Zered after wandering in the wilderness for 38 years (Deut. 2:13-14).

ZEREDA or **ZEREDAH** Place-name of uncertain meaning. **1.** Site in Ephraim of the home of Jeroboam (1 Kings 11:26), possibly identified as Ain Seridah in the Wadi Deir Ballut in western Samaria. **2.** City in the Jordan Valley (2 Chron. 4:17). The parallel text in 1 Kings 7:46 reads Zerethan.

ZEREDATHAH (KJV, 2 Chron. 4:17) See *Zereda.*

ZERERAH or **ZERERATH** (KJV) Site on the route by which the defeated Midianites fled from Gideon (Judg. 7:22; KJV, Zererath); possibly a variant rendering of Zarethan (Josh. 3:16; 1 Kings 4:12; 7:46) or Zeredah (2 Chron. 4:17). See *Zarethan.*

ZERESH Personal name meaning "shaggy head, disheveled." Haman's wife and counselor (Esther 5:10,14; 6:13).

ZERETH Personal name, perhaps meaning "splendor." Descendant of Judah (1 Chron. 4:7).

ZERETH-SHAHAR Place-name meaning "splendor of the dawn." The city located "on the hill of the [Dead Sea] valley" was allotted to Reuben (Josh. 13:19).

ZERI Personal name meaning "balsam." Levitical harpist (1 Chron. 25:3). Zeri is possibly a copying variant of Izri (25:11).

ZEROR Personal name meaning "bundle, pouch" or "particle of stone." Ancestor of Saul (1 Sam. 9:1).

ZERUAH Personal name meaning "stricken" or "leprous." Mother of King Jeroboam (1 Kings 11:26).

ZERUBBABEL Personal name meaning "descendant of Babel." The grandson of King Jehoiachin (taken to Babylon in the first exile in 597 BC by Nebuchadnezzar; 2 Kings 24:10-17) and the son of Shealtiel (Ezra 3:2), second son of Jehoiachin (1 Chron. 3:16-17). He is named in Ezra 2:2 among the leaders of those who returned from exile. The list in Ezra 2:1-67 (cp. Neh. 7:6-73a) probably names people who returned in 539, the first year of the reign of Cyrus the Great, ruler of the Persian Empire (Ezra 1:1), or between 539 and 529, despite the contention of many American scholars that the list belongs to an unmentioned second return led by Zerubbabel in 521/520.

According to Ezra 3, Zerubbabel and Jeshua (or Joshua, the high priest) rebuilt the altar and in their second year (538?) laid the foundation of the temple, but their work was halted by opposition from persons who had remained in Palestine during the exile (4:1-6,24). Darius (Persian emperor, 522–486 BC) granted the Jews permission to continue rebuilding the temple (6:1-12). Under the urging of Haggai (1:1,12-15; 2:1,20) and Zechariah (4:6-10a), Zerubbabel, now governor (Hag. 1:1) in place of Sheshbazzar (Ezra 5:14), resumed the task (Ezra 5:1-2), completed in 515 BC.

Zerubbabel himself, however, disappeared from view. He was a Davidic prince, so it is possible that the Jews tried to crown him king during the civil war surrounding the rise of Darius as emperor (522/521). Zechariah 6:9-14 may reflect the wish to crown Zerubbabel, but his fate remains unknown.

ZERUIAH Personal name meaning "perfumed with mastix" or "bleed." Mother of three of David's generals: Joab, Abishai, and Asahel (2 Sam. 2:18).

ZETHAM Personal name meaning "olive tree." Levite who served as a temple treasurer (1 Chron. 23:8; 26:22).

ZETHAN Personal name meaning "olive tree" or "olive merchant." Member of the tribe of Benjamin (1 Chron. 7:10).

ZETHAR Personal name, perhaps meaning "slayer," "kingdom," or "victor." One of seven eunuchs who served King Ahasuerus of Persia (Esther 1:10).

ZEUS Greek god of the sky and chief of the pantheon; ruler over all the gods. His devotees believed all the elements of weather were under his control. The worship of Zeus was very prevalent throughout the Roman Empire during the first century. Barnabas was mistaken for Zeus (equivalent of the Roman god, Jupiter) by the people of Lystra after Paul healed a cripple (Acts 14:8-12).

ZIA Personal name meaning "trembling." Head of a family of the tribe of Gad (1 Chron. 5:13).

ZIBA Personal name, perhaps Aramaic for "branch." Servant of Saul. When David desired to show kindness to surviving members of Jonathan's family, Ziba directed David to Mephibosheth (2 Sam. 9:1-8). David placed Ziba in charge of Mephibosheth's restored property (9:9-13). During Absalom's rebellion, Ziba assisted David with supplies and (falsely) accused Mephibosheth of treason (2 Sam. 16:1-4).

ZIBEON Personal name meaning "little hyena." Horite chieftain (Gen. 36:29) and ancestor of one of Esau's wives (Gen. 36:2). Zibeon established kinship between the Horites and Edomites (Gen. 36:20,24,29; 1 Chron. 1:38,40).

ZIBIA Personal name meaning "gazelle." Head of a family of Benjaminites (1 Chron. 8:9).

ZIBIAH Personal name meaning "female gazelle." Mother of King Jehoash (Joash) of Judah (2 Kings 12:1; 2 Chron. 24:1).

ZICHRI or **ZICRI** (NIV) Personal name meaning "remembrance, mindful." **1.** Levite in Moses' time (Exod. 6:21). **2.** Heads of three families of Benjaminites (1 Chron. 8:19,23,27). **3.** Levite (1 Chron. 9:15), perhaps identical to Zaccur (1 Chron. 25:2,10; Neh. 12:35) and Zabdi (Neh. 11:17). **4.** Descendant of Moses assisting with David's treasury (1 Chron. 26:25). **5.** Reubenite (1 Chron. 27:16). **6.** Father of one of Jehoshaphat's army commanders (2 Chron. 17:16). **7.** Father of one of Jehoiada's generals (2 Chron. 23:1). **8.** Ephraimite warrior assisting Pekah in the elimination of Ahaz's family and advisors (2 Chron. 28:7). **9.** Father of the leading Benjaminite in postexilic Jerusalem (Neh. 11:9). **10.** Postexilic priest (Neh. 12:17).

ZIDDIM Place-name meaning "sides." Fortified town in Naphtali (Josh. 19:35), perhaps identical with Hattin el-Qadim about eight miles west-northwest of Tiberias. Some commentators see it as copyist's repetition of "fenced cities."

ZIDKIJAH (KJV, Neh. 10:1) See *Zedekiah*.

ZIDON, ZIDONIANS KJV alternate forms of Sidon and Sidonians.

ZIGGURAT Stepped building, usually capped by a temple. The architecture was made popular by the Babylonians. The design consisted of placing smaller levels of brick on top of larger layers. Those so far excavated reveal advanced building techniques used by ancient civilizations. Most biblical scholars believe the tower of Babel was a ziggurat (Gen. 11:3-9).

(Above)The ziggurat, or temple tower, located at Ur in ancient Mesopotamia (modern Iraq). (Below) A reconstruction of a ziggurat dating to the Babylonian period (605–550 BC).

ZIHA Egyptian personal name meaning "the face of Horus (god) has spoken." **1.** Family of temple servants (*nethinim*) (Ezra 2:43; Neh. 7:46). **2.** Overseer of postexilic temple servants (Neh. 11:21).

ZIKLAG City in tribal inheritance of Judah given to Simeon (Josh. 15:31; 19:5). Ziklag appears to have belonged to the Philistines and was taken by Israel during the time of Israel's judges (1 Sam. 27:6). The town was given to David by Achish, king of

Gath, during David's "outlaw" period. The gift may have been a means of shortening Philistia's over-extended borders. Ziklag appears never to have been a part of Philistia proper.

ZILLAH Personal name meaning "shadow." Second wife of Lamech and mother of Tubal-Cain and Naamah (Gen. 4:19,22-23).

ZILLETHAI Personal name; an abbreviated form of "Yahweh is a shadow," that is, a protector. **1.** Family of Benjaminites (1 Chron. 8:20). **2.** Manassite supporter of David at Ziklag (1 Chron. 12:20).

ZILPAH Personal name, perhaps meaning "short-nosed." Leah's maid (Gen. 29:24; 46:18), given to Jacob as a concubine (30:9; 37:2); mother of Gad and Asher, who were regarded as Leah's sons (30:10,12; 35:26).

ZILTHAI (KJV) See *Zillethai.*

ZIMMAH, ZIMNAH (TEV) Personal name; perhaps an abbreviation of "Yahweh has considered or resolved." A Levite (1 Chron. 6:20,42; 2 Chron. 29:12).

ZIMRAN Personal name meaning "celebrated in song, famous" or "mountain goat." Son of Abraham and Keturah and ancestor of an Arabian tribe (Gen. 25:2; 1 Chron. 1:32), possibly identified with Zabram, located somewhere west of Mecca on the Red Sea, and with Zimri (Jer. 25:25).

ZIMRI Short form of personal name meaning "Yah helped," "Yah is my protection," or "Yah is my praise." **1.** Son of Zerah and grandson of Judah (1 Chron. 2:6). **2.** Chariot captain in Israel who usurped the throne by killing Elah (1 Kings 16:9-10). **3.** Leader of tribe of Simeon slain by Phinehas for bringing Midianite woman into the wilderness camp (Num. 25). **4.** Descendant of Saul (1 Chron. 8:36). **5.** A difficult name of a nation God judged (Jer. 25:25), often taken as a copying change from the Hebrew for Cimmerians or a coded designation for Elam clarified by the immediate mention of Elam. Nothing is known of a nation of Zimri.

ZIN, WILDERNESS OF Rocky desert area through which Israel passed en route from Egypt to Canaan (Num. 20:1; 27:14; 33:36). The Wilderness of Zin, stretching from Kadesh-barnea to the Dead Sea, formed part of the southern border of Canaan and later Judah (Num. 34:3-4; Josh. 15:1,3). The Wilderness of Zin should be distinguished from the Wilderness of Sin, which embraces the western Sinai plateau.

ZION Transliteration of the Hebrew and Greek words that originally referred to the fortified hill of pre-Israelite Jerusalem between the Kedron and Tyropean Valleys. Scholars disagree as to the root meaning of the term. Some authorities have suggested that the word was related to the Hebrew word that meant "dry place" or "parched ground." Others relate the word to an Arabic term that is interpreted as "hillcrest" or "mountainous ridge."

An overview of the Canaanite/Jebusite Jerusalem. Notice the "stepped-stone structure" in the center of the photograph. One view is that this is "the stronghold of Zion."

The name "Zion" was mentioned first in the account of David's conquest of Jerusalem (2 Sam. 5:6-10; 1 Chron. 11:4-9). The most common usage of Zion was to refer to the city of God in the new age (Isa. 1:27; 28:16; 33:5).

Zion was understood, also, to refer to the heavenly Jerusalem (Isa. 60:14; Heb. 12:22; Rev. 14:1), the place where the Messiah would appear at the end of time. The glorification of the messianic community will take place on the holy mountain of "Zion."

ZIOR Place-name meaning "smallness." Village allotted to Judah, located in the hill country near Hebron (Josh. 15:54). Archaeological research indicates that the frequently suggested site Si'ir about five miles north-northeast of Hebron was uninhabited before AD 400.

ZIPH Personal name and place-name, perhaps meaning "flowing." **1.** Son of Mareshah and grandson of Caleb (1 Chron. 2:42). The text perhaps means Mareshah was the founder of Ziph near Hebron. **2.** Family of the tribe of Judah (1 Chron. 4:16). **3.** Town in the Judean hill country (Josh. 15:24), likely Tell Zif about three miles southeast of Hebron. **4.** Town in the Negev (Josh. 15:24), likely Khirbet ez-Zeifeh, southwest of Kurnub.

ZIPHAH Clan name, perhaps meaning "flowing." Family of the tribe of Judah (1 Chron. 4:16).

ZIPHIMS KJV alternate form of Ziphites (superscription of Ps. 54). See *Ziph*.

ZIPHRON Place-name, perhaps meaning "fragrance." Site on the northern border of Canaan, near Hazar-enan (Num. 34:9). It may be modern Zapherani, southeast of Restan between Hamath and Homs.

ZIPPOR Personal name meaning "(little) bird." Father of King Balak of Moab (Num. 22:2,4,10).

ZIPPORAH Personal name meaning "small bird" or "sparrow." Moses' first wife (some believe the woman named in Num. 12:1 may be a reference to Zipporah, too) and mother of his children Gershom and Eliezer (Exod. 2:21-22; 18:4). She was one of the daughters of Reuel, a priest of Midian. She saved Moses' life when the Lord sought to kill him by circumcising Gershom (4:24-25). It appears that Zipporah stayed with her father until Moses had led the people out of Egypt (18:2-6).

ZITHER Stringed instrument composed of 30 to 40 strings placed over a shallow soundboard and played with a pick and fingers (Dan. 3:5,7,10,15 NASB margin).

ZIV Second month of calendar (1 Kings 6:1).

ZIZ Place-name meaning "blossom." Site involved in Judah's battle plans with Ammon and Moab (2 Chron. 20:16). A pass through a steep place where the people of Ammon, Moab, and Mount Seir were going to enter Judah to attack King Jehoshaphat. It is often located at Wadi Hasasa, southeast of Tekoa near the Dead Sea. The Lord won this battle for His people without their fighting (vv. 22-30), causing surrounding nations to fear God.

ZIZA or **ZIZAH** Personal name meaning "shining" or "brightness." **1.** Son of Shiphi who was a part of the expansion of the tribe of Simeon into Gedor (1 Chron. 4:37). **2.** Son of Shimei, a Levite from Gershon, following some manuscript and early translation evidence (1 Chron. 23:10). "Zina" is the reading of KJV, NASB, REB following Hebrew text. **3.** One of Rehoboam's sons by Maachah (2 Chron. 11:20).

ZOAN Hebrew name for Egyptian city of Tanis located at San el-Hagar on the Tanitic arm of the Nile. Zoan became capital of Egypt about 1070 BC under Smendes I and remained so until 655 BC. Numbers 13:22 notes that Hebron was seven years older than Zoan, but the exact date when either was built is not known. The prophets used Zoan to refer to the Egyptian government and its activities (Isa. 19:11,13; 30:4; Ezek. 30:14). The psalmist praised God for exodus miracles near there (Ps. 78:12,43).

ZOAR Place-name meaning "small." One of the cities in the Valley of Siddim, also known as Bela (Gen. 14:2). It was attacked by Chedolaomer but apparently delivered by Abraham (14:17). Lot fled to Zoar with his family just before God destroyed Sodom and Gomorrah (19:23-24).

ZOBA(H) City-state name, perhaps meaning "battle." First Saul (1 Sam. 14:47), then David (2 Sam. 8:3) fought the kings of Zobah (cp. title of Ps. 60). Zobah seems to be roughly where Syria later became a nation, northeast of Damascus.

ZOBEBAH Personal name of uncertain meaning. Descendant of Judah (1 Chron. 4:8; NIV "Hazzobebah").

ZOHAR Personal name, perhaps meaning "witness." **1.** Hittite (Gen. 23:8; 25:9). **2.** Son of Simeon (Gen. 46:10; Exod. 6:15), also called Zerah (Num. 26:13; 1 Chron. 4:24). **3.** Descendant of Judah according to the traditional marginal correction (*Qere*) at 1 Chron. 4:24. The Hebrew text reads *Izhar*.

ZOHELETH Place-name meaning "creeping one," "sliding," or "serpent stone." Stone of sacrifice where Adonijah offered sacrifices in light of his coming coronation as king (1 Kings 1:9). This place was near En-rogel, a spring or well near Jerusalem where the Kidron Valley and the Valley of Hinnom meet. Adonijah's bid for the throne was short lived. David named Solomon to follow him on the throne (vv. 29-30).

ZOHETH Personal name of uncertain meaning. Son of Ishi (1 Chron. 4:20) and the head of one of the families in Judah.

ZOPHAH Personal name, perhaps meaning "jug." Family in the tribe of Asher (1 Chron. 7:35-36).

ZOPHAI Personal name, perhaps meaning "honeycomb." Son of Elkanah (1 Chron. 6:26).

ZOPHAR Personal name of uncertain meaning. One of Job's three friends who came to sit with him in his misery (2:11). Zophar probably was the youngest of the three since he is mentioned last. He was the sharpest critic of the three men and was more philosophical in his criticism of Job. His words were more coarse and his dogmatism more emphatic. Although there was a place called Naamah in Judah (Josh. 15:41), doubt remains that it was Zophar's home.

ZOPHIM Place-name meaning "watchers" or common noun meaning "the Field of the Watchers" (REB) or lookout post. It was a high place at "the top of Pisgah," near the northeastern end of the Dead Sea. Balak took Balaam there to curse the Israelites (Num. 23:14).

ZORAH Place-name meaning "wasps" or "hornets." City of Dan (Josh. 19:41) about 13 miles west of Jerusalem on the border with Judah (Josh. 15:33; KJV, "Zoreah"). It was the home of Manoah, Samson's father (Judg. 13:2). Rehoboam, king of Judah, strengthened Zorah in case of war (2 Chron. 11:5-12). It is modern Sarah.

ZORATHITES Descendants of Shobal who lived in Zorah (1 Chron. 2:52-53).

ZOROASTER Ancient Iranian prophet after whom a religion called Zoroastrianism was named. See *Persia*.

ZOROBABEL (KJV, Matt. 1:12-13; Luke 3:27) See *Zerubbabel*.

ZUAR Personal name meaning "young" or "small." Member of the tribe of Issachar (Num. 1:8; 2:5; 7:18,23; 10:15).

ZUPH Personal name and place-name meaning "honeycomb." **1.** Levitic ancestor of Elkanah and Samuel (1 Sam. 1:1; 1 Chron. 6:16,26,35) from Ephraim. He is called a Levite in another passage (1 Chron. 6:16,26,35). **2.** "Land of Zuph" where Saul was looking for some donkeys (1 Sam. 9:5). Its exact location is not known.

ZUR Personal name meaning "rock." **1.** Midianite tribal chief (Num. 25:15 NIV) whose daughter, Cozbi, was killed along with an Israelite man by Phinehas. Zur was later killed in a battle Moses led (Num. 31:7-8). **2.** King Saul's uncle (1 Chron. 8:30; 9:36).

ZURIEL Personal name that may mean "God is a rock." Son of Abihail and head of the Merari family of Levites (Num. 3:35).

ZURISHADDAI Personal name meaning "shaddai is a rock." The father of Shelumiel, a leader of the tribe of Simeon, in the wilderness wanderings (Num. 1:6).

ZUZIM or **ZUZITE** (NIV) National name of uncertain meaning. People who lived in Ham and were defeated by Chedorlaomer (Gen. 14:5). They are apparently called the Zamzummin in Deut. 2:20.

ART CREDITS

Holman Bible Publishers expresses deep gratitude to the following persons and institutions for use of the graphics in this book.

PHOTOGRAPHS

Museum Abbreviations
JAC = Joseph A. Calloway Archaeological Museum, The Southern Baptist Theological Seminary, Louisville, Kentucky
MGV = Museum of Giula Villa, Rome Italy
NMN = Naples Museum, Naples, Italy
TLP = The Louvre, Paris, France

Photographers
Arnold, Nancy, Freelance Photographer, Nashville, Tennessee: pages 187, 230, 245 middle, 283 right, 368 middle right.

Biblical Illustrator: page 281.

Biblical Illustrator **(James McLemore, photographer), Nashville, Tennessee**: pages 41, 47, 78, 109, 153, 219, 272, 290 middle left, 332 lower, 359.

Biblical Illustrator **(David Rogers, photographer), Nashville, Tennessee**: pages 15, 18, 33, 52, 157 right, 159 left, 159 right, 168 (TLP), 198 right, 210, 211 lower, 224, 239, 244 middle, 270 lower right, 280 middle right, 284 lower right, 288, 315, 323 (JAC), 326, 327, 330, 346, 375.

Biblical Illustrator **(Bob Schatz, photographer), Nashville, Tennessee**: pages 4, 8, 22 middle right, 29, 71, 104, 121 right, 133 right, 138 right, 139, 147, 148, 155, 158, 169, 197, 202, 231, 246 middle, 253 upper left, 258, 285, 292, 321, 322, 324, 339, 347, 369.

Biblical Illustrator **(Ken Touchton, photographer), Nashville, Tennessee**: pages 22 lower left, 55, 58, 76, 77, 80, 97, 114, 121 left, 122, 126 left, 127, 128, 137, 141, 151, 157 left, 160, 188 lower, 193, 221, 227, 248, 253 lower right, 264, 282, 287 upper right, 287 lower left, 310, 311, 318, 319 upper right, 335, 349, 352, 365 upper right.

Brisco, Thomas V., Dean and Professor of Biblical Backgrounds and Archaeology, Logsdon School of Theology, Hardin-Simmons University, Abilene, Texas: pages 20, 40, 89, 99, 100, 103, 204, 228 upper, 246 lower, 254, 312, 317, 336, 337, 338 upper, 338 lower, 354 middle left, 357, 358, 391.

Corel Images: page 192.

Couch, Ernie, Graphics Consultant, Nashville, Tennessee: page 271.

Ellis, C. Randolph, M.D., General Practice, Surgery, and Anesthesiology, Malvern, Arkansas: pages 273, 307.

Illustrated World of the Bible: page 242.

Langston, Scott, Associate Professor of Biblical Studies, Southwest Baptist University, Bolivar, Missouri: pages 54, 199, 229, 280 lower left, 330 middle right, 354 upper right, 372 upper right, 376 upper left.

Scofield Collection, E.C. Dargan Research Library, LifeWay Christian Resources, Nashville, Tennessee: pages 3, 35, 44, 53, 59, 75, 77 upper, 79, 85, 86, 87, 116, 118, 119 left, 119 right, 125, 130, 133 left, 138 left, 173, 175, 183, 214 upper, 232 upper, 244 upper left, 245 upper, 283 lower left, 284 upper left, 290 lower right, 301, 315, 328 upper, 328 lower, 340 upper right, 369, 370 upper, 371, 372 lower left, 377, 383 upper, 383 lower, 386.

Southwestern Baptist Theological Seminary, A. Webb Roberts Library, Fort Worth, Texas: page 1.

Stephens, Bill, Retired Senior Curriculum Coordinator, LifeWay Christian Resources, Nashville, Tennessee: pages 195, 205, 209, 211 upper, 212, 214 lower, 228 middle left, 232 lower, 237, 240, 250 (MGV), 261 (MGV), 267, 268, 270 middle left, 291, 297 upper left, 299, 317 (NMN—The Farnese Collection), 320, 329 upper right, 341 upper, 349, 362 middle right, 362 lower left, 370 lower, 375 middle, 377 upper.

Tolar, William B., Retired Distinguished Professor of Biblical Backgrounds, Southwestern Baptist Theological Seminary, Fort Worth, Texas: pages 67, 101, 123, 154, 198 left, 208, 235, 259, 279, 297 lower left, 331, 332 middle, 344, 353 upper, 353 middle, 364, 365 middle left, 353 lower, 375 lower, 390 upper.

ILLUSTRATIONS AND RECONSTRUCTIONS

Biblical Illustrator, **Linden Artist, London, England:** page 10.

Latta, Bill, Latta Art Services, Mt. Juliet, Tennessee: pages 24, 188 upper, 189, 236, 277, 341 lower, 342, 348, 373, 374, 377, 390 lower.